COMPANY LAW

COMPANY LAW

Second Edition

BRENDA HANNIGAN, MA, LLM,

Solicitor (Ireland)
Professor of Corporate Law
University of Southampton

OXFORD
UNIVERSITY PRESS

OXFORD
UNIVERSITY PRESS

Great Clarendon Street, Oxford OX2 6DP

Oxford University Press is a department of the University of Oxford.
It furthers the University's objective of excellence in research, scholarship,
and education by publishing worldwide in

Oxford New York

Auckland Cape Town Dar es Salaam Hong Kong Karachi
Kuala Lumpur Madrid Melbourne Mexico City Nairobi
New Delhi Shanghai Taipei Toronto

With offices in

Argentina Austria Brazil Chile Czech Republic France Greece
Guatemala Hungary Italy Japan Poland Portugal Singapore
South Korea Switzerland Thailand Turkey Ukraine Vietnam

Oxford is a registered trade mark of Oxford University Press
in the UK and in certain other countries

Published in the United States
by Oxford University Press Inc., New York

British Library Cataloguing in Publication Data

Data available

Library of Congress Cataloging in Publication Data

Hannigan, Brenda.
Company law / Brenda Hannigan. — 2nd ed.
p. cm.
ISBN 978–0–19–928638–6
1. Corporation law—Great Britain. I. Title.
KD2079.H35 2009
346.41'066—dc22   2009012764

Typeset by Newgen Imaging Systems (P) Ltd, Chennai, India
Printed in Great Britain
on acid-free paper by
Ashford Colour Press Ltd., Gosport, Hampshire

ISBN 978–0–19–928638–6

1 3 5 7 9 10 8 6 4 2

Preface

This second edition comes 6 years after the first, a gap caused in part by the (seemingly) interminable wait for Parliament to enact and then commence the Companies Act 2006 which finally comes fully into force on 1 October 2009.

The origins of the Act lie in the Company Law Review initiated in March 1998 which reported in 2001. Eventually, after further White Papers, this process culminated in a statute of 1300 sections and 16 Schedules which at the time of Royal Assent was the largest statute ever enacted (though it is soon to be overtaken, it seems, by the Corporate Tax Bill 2009). Of course, while awaiting the enactment of the Companies Act 2006, the courts addressed many significant issues and European developments continued apace, including the implementation of the Takeovers Directive, putting the Takeover Panel on a statutory footing for the first time. The result is a company law landscape completely changed from that of 2003, the year of the first edition of this book, thus requiring a complete re-write for this second edition. As before, the aim is to explain and analyse the law in a way which engages the student reader at whom the book is aimed, though hopefully a wider audience will also find much of interest within.

The major reform in the CA 2006 was the inclusion for the first time of a statutory statement of directors' duties (which is set out in Appendix 1 for ease of reference). This statutory statement necessitated the complete re-writing of Chapters 7–12 and while the statement brings a degree of clarity and accessibility to this area, it has also generated its own complexities which are explored in depth. The duty to obey the constitution in CA 2006, s 171 brings together the discrete but related issues of want and abuse of authority. A full discussion of the duty and the key decisions in *Criterion Properties plc v Stratford UK Properties LLC* [2006] 1 BCLC 729, HL and *Wrexham AFC Ltd v Crucialmove Ltd* [2008] 1 BCLC 508, CA, together with an analysis of the subtly redrafted CA 2006, s 40 can be found in Chapter 8. The uncertain scope of s 172 (duty to promote the success of the company) and the overlapping and extensive provision for conflicts of interest in ss 175–177 are discussed in Chapters 9 and 11. A major innovation here is the provision for directors to authorise conflicts—uncharted waters, as Lord Wedderburn commented—the impact of this change is discussed in Chapter 11. Despite its length, the CA 2006 stopped short of a statutory statement of remedies for breach of duty by directors and a new Chapter 13 brings together the issues surrounding remedies, an often neglected topic on undergraduate courses.

Another major change is the introduction for the first time of a statutory derivative claim which consigns to history the common law derivative action. The new remedy is considered in detail in Chapter 18. Another theme in the CA 2006 is that of shareholder engagement—now a very topical concern. Chapter 15 reviews the much changed provision on company meetings and shareholders' rights in CA 2006, Part 15, while Chapter 5 also addresses the role of institutional shareholders and the introduction of provision for the enfranchisement of indirect holders, another new development addressed by CA 2006, Part 9. Chapter 3 has been rewritten to address more comprehensively the recent case law on rules of attribution in relation to companies and what is sometimes called dis-attribution, i.e. a director's potential personal liability in tort. Chapter 21 too has been recast to focus on the key decisions on company charges, *Re Spectrum Plus* [2005] 2 BCLC 269, HL and *Re Brumark Investments Ltd* [2001] 2 BCLC 188, PC. The changed status of the memorandum of association and the long awaited demise of the ultra vires rule with consequential changes to the role of the articles and the new provisions for entrenchment are discussed in Chapter 4.

On the insolvency side, the material has been restructured so as to reduce the coverage of administrative receiverships, given that they are of decreasing importance, while extending the coverage of administration which is rapidly becoming the insolvency regime of choice, especially the pre-pack administration. The changes to liquidation expenses following the reversal of *Re Leyland Daf* [2004] 1 BCLC 281, HL by the CA 2006 is considered in Chapter 24 on liquidation.

Every effort has been made to place the material in context. For example, the discussion of rights issues in Chapter 19 reflects the current difficulties faced by companies in trying to raise share capital. The discussion of the directors' remuneration report in Chapter 5 notes the potential for shareholders to use their advisory votes on this report to signal their dissatisfaction with directors' pay packages. The analysis of the capital maintenance doctrine in Chapter 20 concentrates on the fundamental role which the distribution rules play in protecting creditor interests, especially in the light of the relaxation of the capital rules by the CA 2006 in other areas, such as permitting reduction of capital via a solvency statement.

As ever, the pace of change in company law is relentless and changes which came too late to be addressed in the text include the Financial Reporting Council review of the effectiveness of the Combined Code on Corporate Governance and the related Walker review of bank governance. The implementation of the Shareholder Rights Directive is imminent, but unfortunately the final version of the implementing regulations is still awaited, as is the implementation of changes to listing status as proposed by the Financial Services Authority. The European Commission meanwhile is reviewing the content and application of the Accounting Directives. On occasion, reference is made to draft statutory instruments as the final measures for implementing the CA 2006 are still being put in place.

References in the text to BERR are to the Department for Business, Enterprise and Regulatory Reform, formerly know as the Department of Trade and Industry. References to the Company Law Review are to the review of company law mentioned in the second paragraph above (and discussed in detail in Chapter 2) which was the catalyst for the introduction of the Companies Act 2006.

I am most grateful to the OUP editorial and production team for their assistance at every stage of this work.

The law is stated as of 1 February 2009.

Brenda Hannigan
17 March 2009

Outline Contents

Contents

PART III CORPORATE GOVERNANCE—SHAREHOLDERS' RIGHTS AND REMEDIES

Table of Statutes

Table of Statutory Instruments

Table of Cases

Table of European Legislation

PART I

THE CORPORATE STRUCTURE

1

Formation, classification and registration of companies

A Introduction

Registered companies

Companies registered under the Companies Act 2006 (CA 2006) and its predecessors **1-1** are the focus of this book. In this initial chapter we consider the mechanics of formation and registration and the various types of companies which may be formed, as well as looking briefly at alternative vehicles for business. Before looking at these matters in detail, an overview of the process of formation and the key players in a registered company may be helpful for the student reader at whom this book is aimed.

An overview of the formation of a registered company

To form a registered company under the CA 2006, all that is required is one person **1-2** and a lawful purpose (s 7). Some brief documentation must be submitted (either electronically or on paper) to the registrar of companies (located at Companies House, Cardiff) together with a registration fee of £15 (if electronic) and £20 (if paper). Once the formalities are completed correctly, the registrar of companies issues a certificate of incorporation whereupon the company comes into existence. This process need take no more than seven days (if paper-based), and probably less, and it can be completed in a single day if speed is important. The process is simple, quick and inexpensive.

Imagine that A and B wish to form a registered company to run a printing business. A **1-3** alone could form a company since, as noted above, only one person is required, but for these purposes we will assume A and B wish to form a company together. There are a few initial decisions which A and B have to make. First, they have to decide how they are going to split the ownership of the company. Assume they agree that they will split the ownership of the business 70% and 30% to reflect the contributions that they are going to make to it. The division of ownership is entirely a matter of choice for them, obviously, as is the number of shares to issue. They may decide to issue:

- 1,000 £1 shares with A taking 700 of the shares, putting £700 into the company's finances in the form of share capital, and B taking 300 shares, putting £300 into the share capital; or

- 100 £1 shares with A taking 70 (£70) and B taking 30 (£30); or
- 100 1p shares with A taking 70 (70p) and B 30 (30p); or
- 10 1p shares with A taking seven shares (7p) and B taking three shares (3p).

1-4   Share capital is considered in detail later; for the moment it suffices to appreciate that A and B have complete flexibility as to the amount of money which they wish to put into the company in the form of share capital and the value, called the nominal value, they wish to assign to the shares. They have complete flexibility as to the number of shares they wish to issue and the same ownership division can be achieved by issuing 10 or 100 or 1,000 shares. Shares typically carry one vote per share so, on any of the examples given above, A has 70% of the votes and B has 30% of the votes. Most matters within a company can be decided on a simple majority vote so A has effective control of the company with B as a minority shareholder, a role which may prove to be an uncomfortable one, as we shall see. Depending on the circumstances, A and B might look at a 60/40 split, or a 90/10 split, or even a 50/50 split, but a 50/50 split has an in-built deadlock problem if the two shareholders disagree, so it is not advisable. As can be seen, it is possible to form a company with very little capital, though in the case of a public company wishing to carry on business, there is a minimum share capital requirement of £50,000 (CA 2006, s 763, see **1–53**). For the moment, though, we will concentrate on private companies. The distinction between public and private status is discussed later in the chapter.

1-5   As the shareholders of the company, A and B appoint the directors who will manage the business. Given his voting control, A could impose his choice of directors, but frequently it will have been agreed that A and B will be the directors. The result is that A and B are the shareholders and A and B are also the directors of the company, a form of structure which is very common.

1-6   Equally, A and B may decide to bring other family members into the business and issue further shares to them and/or appoint them to the board. With additional shares issued, the shareholders might be A, B, C and D with only A and B being directors; or A and B might be the only shareholders with the board made up of A, B, C and D; or A and B may be the only shareholders while C and D are the directors. In other words, while uniformity of identify between the shareholders and the directors is very common in small companies, that need not be the case. Indeed one of the advantages of incorporation is that it allows the ownership of the company to be separated from the management of the business. It is possible to be a shareholder without being a director and vice versa and, of course, in the largest companies with hundreds of thousands of shareholders, there can be no question of the shareholders being the directors and the directors usually have only minuscule shareholdings compared to the total number of shares in issue.

1-7   Now we have the key players as far as company law is concerned, the directors and the members or shareholders (for the most part, the terms 'members' and 'shareholders' are synonymous). Basically, the members or shareholders are the owners of the company with ultimate control of the company through their shareholdings while the directors provide the management of the company. Of course, many other constituencies, or stakeholders as they are often called, have an important role to play in the company, employees and creditors come instantly to mind, but their relationships with the company are primarily a matter of employment law, contract law and insolvency law whereas the focus of company law is the company and its shareholders and directors.

Returning to A and B, they must also decide on the type of company that they want to form. The CA 2006 provides for various types of company, but the most commonly adopted form is the private company limited by shares (the distinction between private and public companies is discussed below). By limited by shares is meant that the liability of the members is limited to the amount, if any, unpaid on the shares held by them (CA 2006, s 3(2)).   **1-8**

Let us imagine that A has taken 70 £1 shares and B has taken 30 £1 shares, the £100 company being a very common structure.[1] With only £100 of share capital, the company will initially seek to finance its activities through bank financing and so it must arrange loans and overdrafts with the bank. The company, the separate entity formed on incorporation, will acquire employees and premises, the company will enter into contracts and the company will incur debts. If the company incurs, say, debts of £25,000 and collapses into insolvency, it is the company that owes the creditors £25,000. The members' liability is limited to the amount unpaid, if any, on the shares held by them. The liability of A is limited to the £70 due on his shares and B's liability is limited to the £30 due on his shares. Assuming that A and B paid for their shares at the time the company issued the shares to them, as would be typical, A and B have already paid the sums due and no further payments can be required from them to meet the company's liabilities to its creditors. The only caveat being that, in some cases, A and B may have been prevailed upon by one or more creditors (typically, the company's bank) to give personal guarantees and security over personal assets which the bank can call upon in the event that, on insolvency, the company's assets are insufficient to meet the debts due to the bank.   **1-9**

For the purposes of the discussion above, it was assumed that the parties wishing to register a company will put together the documentation and submit it to the registrar of companies. In fact, it is common to purchase a company from a company formation agent. Company formation agents provide ready-made companies, literally companies incorporated earlier and available for immediate use, because the formalities have already been completed and the certificate of incorporation issued. Such companies are ready to be purchased 'off-the-shelf' by persons wishing to set up a company. There are various reasons for preferring or needing an off-the-shelf company, such as a concern not to incur any personal liabilities. As a company does not exist prior to the issue of the certificate of incorporation, any debts incurred by A and B in obtaining premises, hiring equipment, etc prior to that point are incurred personally.   **1-10**

For similar reasons, A and B may opt for same-day incorporation where the registrar processes all the documentation and issues the certificate of incorporation on the   **1-11**

---

[1] Of the 2,547,400 companies on the register with an issued share capital at March 2007, 1,921,700 had an issued share capital of up to £100: see Companies House, *Statistical Tables on Companies Registration Activities 2006–07* (hereinafter Companies House *Statistical Tables*), Table A7. These statistical tables are available on the Companies House website: www.companieshouse.gov.uk. Unfortunately, Table A7 which gave a breakdown of the register by issued share capital has been omitted from the Tables for 2007–08.

same day as the application for registration is made.[2] Same-day incorporation may also make sense where there is a need to secure a particular name for the company since, once registered, no other company can have the same name, or even a name considered 'too like' that name (CA 2006, s 67).

1-12   Having incorporated, A and B, as the directors and shareholders, have taken on new legal roles and responsibilities, the discharge of which is the subject of the remainder of this book. Sometimes, the ease and speed of incorporation can obscure these legal realities and it is often the case that the parties themselves have only a minimal understanding of their changed legal status and potential liabilities. In part, this lack of understanding is due to the fact that incorporation, either directly or by the purchase of a company off-the-shelf, can be achieved without any professional advice being sought or required. The result can be a failure on the part of the incorporators to appreciate the duties and responsibilities of directors including their obligations to the company's creditors, the need for the company's affairs to be run in a manner which takes account of minority shareholder interests and does not unfairly prejudice them, and the ongoing obligations which companies have with respect to filing information with the registrar of companies so as to ensure that the public register is up to date and accurate. This is not to say that access to limited liability should be restricted, but rather that all concerned need to appreciate the legal responsibilities attached to acquiring corporate status.[3]

1-13   Of course, A and B are not compelled to incorporate and there are some other options open to them which are worth considering before we look at the formation of registered companies.

Alternative structures to the registered company

1-14   As noted above, conducting a business through the mechanism of a registered company has the particular advantages of the separate legal status of the company, the limited liability of the members and the possible separation of ownership and management of the company, but where these attributes are either not important or not attainable (for example, because of the small scale of the business), then a registered limited company may not be the most appropriate legal structure. Incorporation brings with it a changed set of legal roles and responsibilities which the parties may not wish to bear. It may be that for some parties, therefore, another structure may be more appropriate than a registered company.

A sole trader

1-15   One option is for an individual to act as a sole trader and with very large numbers of companies having no more than two members and an issued share capital of (at most)

---

[2] The same-day incorporation fee is £50 (if paper) or £30 (if electronic).
[3] To assist in this regard, Companies House provides guidance on directors' duties and company formation.

£100, it is debatable whether some of those businesses might not be conducted more appropriately as sole traders. A sole trader is simply that—an individual carrying on business as an individual. The disadvantage is that the sole trader has unlimited liability, but many shareholders in small companies obtain only partial limited liability in any event, as they may have given personal guarantees to major creditors of the company, such as banks. The main advantage in being a sole trader is privacy as there is no obligation to register any information as to the business or its financial position with a public registry.[4]

Partnership

Partnership is the relation which subsists between persons carrying on a business in common with a view of profit.[5] Partnerships are governed by the Partnership Act 1890 but most partnerships draw up their own partnership agreements which override the Act. Partnerships are not separate legal entities and partners do not have limited liability. The advantage of this structure is that the business affairs of a partnership are entirely private and there is no obligation to register financial or partnership information at a public registry.[6] **1-16**

Limited partnership

For the moment, limited partnerships are governed by the Limited Partnership Act 1907 but the Government has signalled that it intends to modernise and simplify the law on limited partnerships in line with recommendations previously made by the Law Commissions.[7] The Limited Partnerships Act 1907 is to be repealed and new provisions about limited partnerships inserted into the Partnership Act 1890. **1-17**

Limited partnerships must be registered at Companies House, but there is no disclosure of their accounts. A limited partnership allows for limited partners alongside general partners with unlimited liability. The liability of a limited partner for the debts of the partnership is limited to the amount of their contribution to the partnership, but a possible disadvantage of this structure is that a limited partner must be excluded from all management functions. On the other hand, a limited partnership is a useful business vehicle for investors who are content to allow the general partners to manage the assets, particularly again as financial privacy is ensured. This structure is used throughout the venture capital investment industry and so the limited partnership has evolved into a somewhat specialised business vehicle.[8] **1-18**

---

[4] BERR Statistics show that there were 2,984,755 sole proprietorships in the UK in 2007 while noting that it is difficult to get an accurate figure: see BERR, *Small and Medium Enterprise Statistics for the UK and Regions* (2007).   [5] Partnership Act 1890, s 1.

[6] BERR Statistics show that there were 506,805 partnerships in the UK in 2007 though BERR acknowledges it is difficult to get an accurate figure: see BERR, *Small and Medium Enterprise Statistics for the UK and Regions* (2007).

[7] See BERR Consultation Document, 'Reform of Limited Partnership Law, Legislative Reform Order to repeal and replace the Limited Partnerships Act 1907' (August 2008) URN 08/1153. See Law Commission Report, *Partnership Law* (Law Comm No 283), November 2003.

[8] There were 15,589 on the register as of March 2008, see statistical tables: Companies House *Statistical Tables 2007–08*, Table E2.

Limited liability partnership

1-19   Limited liability partnerships (LLPs) are something of a hybrid between a company and a partnership. A limited liability partnership is a body corporate with legal personality separate from that of its members which is formed by being registered at Companies House. LLPs are governed by the Limited Liability Partnerships Act 2000 and the Limited Liability Partnership Regulations 2001 which apply many parts of the CA 1985 to LLPs including for example, the rules governing accounts and audits, with appropriate modifications.[9] The intention is to update the Regulations to apply the CA 2006 to LLPs in the same way as the CA 1985.

1-20   To register an LLP, there must be two or more persons associated for carrying on a lawful business with a view to profit.[10] Details of the registered office and of the members (an LLP does not have a share capital, so there are no shareholders) must be provided. There must be at least two designated members who are named members with particular responsibilities such as with respect to signing and delivering accounts to the registrar of companies. The constitution of the LLP, the members' internal agreement dealing with such matters as the division of management powers and profits, is not registered. To that extent, members of an LLP retain some of the essential privacy of a partnership. An LLP is required to file annual accounts and an annual return so a considerable level of financial disclosure is required. In return the liability of the members is limited, in this case to such amount as they have agreed internally to contribute to the debts of the LLP. On insolvency, all the corporate insolvency regimes are available and applicable to an LLP which remains liable to its creditors to the full amount of its assets. As of March 2008, 32,066 LLPs were registered with Companies House.[11]

1-21   As can be seen from this brief discussion, the key attributes of separate legal personality and limited liability are what differentiate between the available mechanisms with the LLP being a relatively recent hybrid creation straddling the line between partnerships and companies and one which appears to be gaining in popularity. One other option to note is the possibility of forming an unlimited company, i.e. a company without any limit on the liability of its members (CA 2006, s 3(4)). This status might appear an unattractive option, given the open-ended commitment by the members to meet the company's liabilities, yet there were 5,400 on the register at 31 March 2008.[12] The advantage which an unlimited company has over other forms of registered company is that generally there is no obligation to file accounts with the registrar of companies (s 448). Where privacy is a major consideration, therefore, and the risk of insolvency is remote (for example, because the company is not trading but holding investments), unlimited liability may be attractive. On the other hand, the accounting disclosure

---

[9] See generally *Palmers' Limited Liability Partnership Law* (2001). LLPs were introduced following intense pressure over a long period of time by accountancy firms which were concerned that ever increasing liabilities with respect to negligent audits made partnership (with its unlimited personal liability for the debts of the partnership) an unattractive business vehicle for the profession. But when the legislation was enacted, it was decided to make it available to all rather than restrict it to the professions.

[10] LLPA 2000, s 2(1)(a).   [11] See Companies House *Statistical Tables 2007–08*, Table E4.

[12] Companies House *Statistical Tables 2007–08*, Table A2.

requirements have been significantly reduced in recent years for small limited companies[13] so this advantage may not be as attractive as it once was. There may be taxation reasons, however, why an unlimited company may be advantageous.

Even so, the popularity of these other mechanisms such as the LLP (32,066 on the register), the limited partnership (15,589 on the register) or the unlimited company (5,400) has to be put in the context of a register of 2.4m companies,[14] the vast majority of which are companies limited by shares combining a separate legal entity with limited liability.   **1-22**

B Company formation—companies limited by shares

The most common type of registered company is the company limited by shares so, assuming that A and B wish to register a company limited by shares, they must draw up certain documents and submit them to the registrar of companies together with the registration fee (£15 if electronic incorporation; £20 if paper-based).[15]   **1-23**

Memorandum of association

An application for registration must be accompanied by a memorandum of association (CA 2006, s 9(1)). The memorandum is a short prescribed document[16] stating that the subscribers wish to form a company under the CA 2006 and agree to become members of the company and, in the case of a company with a share capital, they agree to take at least one share each (s 8(1)). This form of memorandum is new and the intention is that it is to be of merely historical significance indicating the initial founding of the company. Previously, the memorandum of association was an important external-facing document telling the outside world the key facts about the company: its name, its status as a public company (if that was the case), the jurisdiction in which it was registered, the company's objects, that the members' liability was limited, and setting out the amount and division of the company's authorised share capital. Now the memorandum simply records the identity of the original founders of the company and indicates how many shares they took on formation. In many cases, the original founders will be formation agents (see **1-10**) and so the document will have no continuing relevance.   **1-24**

---

[13] See CA 2006, s 444 and the thresholds for this category are quite high, see s 382.

[14] Companies House *Statistical Tables 2007–08*, Table A2.

[15] See Drury, 'The "Delaware Syndrome": European Fears and Reactions' [2005] JBL 709 at 726–7 on why the fee is so low (otherwise indirect tax on raising of capital).

[16] The memorandum of a company with a share capital must be in the form set out in the Companies (Registration) Regulations 2008, SI 2008/3014, reg 2(a), Sch 1.

Application for registration

1-25 The company's application for registration must state:

- the company's proposed name;
- whether the registered office is to be situated in England and Wales, Wales, Scotland or Northern Ireland;
- whether the members' liability is to be limited and, if so, whether by shares or by guarantee;
- whether the company is to be a public or a private company (CA 2006, s 9(2)).

The application must contain:

- a statement of capital and initial shareholdings (if a company limited by shares) or a statement of guarantee (if a company limited by guarantee);
- a statement of the company's proposed officers, including the proposed company secretary if the company is a public company or where a private company chooses to have a company secretary;
- a statement of the intended address of the company's registered office;
- a copy of any proposed articles of association unless the intention is to rely on the model default articles, discussed below (CA 2006, s 9(4), (5)).

Statement of capital and initial shareholdings

1-26 The statement of capital and initial shareholdings must state:[17]

- the total number of shares and the aggregate nominal value of the shares to be taken on formation by the subscribers to the memorandum,
- for each class of shares, prescribed particulars of the rights attached to them, the total number of shares of that class and the aggregate nominal value of those shares,
- the amount to be paid up, and the amount, if any, unpaid on each share (CA 2006, s 10(2)).

1-27 The statement of capital is a useful innovation in the CA 2006 which provides important information as to the share structure of the company. The share structure is important in terms of (1) establishing how much share capital has been raised and how much is paid and unpaid and (2) identifying the rights attached to the shares where there are classes of shares. Most companies have only one type of share, an ordinary share, such as the £1 share noted above held by A and B, and class rights are irrelevant in such a company. Class of shares are discussed at **14-16**. As from the date of incorporation, the subscribers to the memorandum become holders of the shares specified in the statement of capital and initial holdings (CA 2006, s 16(5)).

---

[17] The statement of capital and initial shareholdings must contain the name and address of each subscriber to the memorandum of association: The Companies (Registration) Regulations 2008, SI 2008/3014, reg 3.

Statement of the proposed officers

Particulars of the initial director(s) of the company[18] must be delivered with the appli-   **1-28**
cation for registration and the directors must indicate their consent to act (CA 2006,
s 12(1),(3)). If the company is a public company (or where a private company chooses
to appoint a secretary) particulars of the proposed secretary of the company must also
be given and their consent so to act. From the date of incorporation, those persons
so named as directors and company secretary are deemed to have been appointed to
office (s 16(6)).

Statement of the address of the company's registered office

Every company must have a registered office (CA 2006, s 86) which essentially is the   **1-29**
administrative office of the company, and all business letters, order forms and websites
of the company must give the address of the registered office[19] which may be a service
address. The registered office is the location at which members and others may consult
the various registers which the company is obliged to maintain,[20] such as the register
of members and the register of company charges. The registered office is also the place
where documents must be deposited, such as the statement by the company's auditor
on ceasing to hold office (s 519), and where legal documents may be served on a company. It is also the address with which the registrar of companies corresponds so it is
important that any change of address of the registered office is notified promptly to
the registrar.

Copy of articles of association

The application for registration must contain a copy of the proposed articles of asso-   **1-30**
ciation (CA 2006, s 9(5)) and if, on formation, articles are not registered or, if articles
are registered, in so far as they do not exclude or modify the relevant model articles,
the relevant model articles form part of the company's articles automatically (s 20(1)).
Model forms of articles are provided for public and private companies limited by
shares and for companies limited by guarantee and any company may adopt all or
any of the provisions of the relevant model articles for that type of company.[21] The
articles of association are a key element of the company's constitution and set out the
rules governing the internal running of the company. The matters typically covered
in the articles include the conduct of meetings and voting procedures; capital matters
including share transfer and transmission; the appointment and removal of directors

---

[18] A private company must have at least one director, a public company must have at least two: CA
2006, s 154.

[19] The Companies (Trading Disclosures) Regulations 2008, SI 2008/495, reg 7.

[20] Companies may choose a single alternative inspection location as well as the registered office, see CA
2006, s 1136 and The Companies (Company Records) Regulations 2008, SI 2008/3006, reg 3.

[21] CA 2006, s 19(3). See The Companies (Model Articles) Regulations 2008, SI 2008/3229. It is the model
table in force at the time of the company's registration which applies: CA 2006, s 20(2); and subsequent
amendments of the model articles do not affect a company registered before the amendment: s 19(4). Many
companies on the register of companies remain subject to the 1985 Table A and some are still governed by
the 1948 Table A.

and their powers; and the declaration of dividends. A detailed account of the articles can be found in Chapter 4.

Statement of compliance

1-31   In order to minimise the amount of checking which needs to be done by the registrar of companies, a statement of compliance (i.e. a statement that the requirements as to registration have been complied with) must be delivered to the registrar of companies with the registration application (CA 2006, s 13(1)). The statement must be in the form prescribed (by rules to be made by the registrar of companies) and be authenticated by the prescribed persons, but it need not be witnessed. It is an offence to make a false statement of compliance (s 1112).

The company name

1-32   Care must be taken as to the choice of company name for various reasons but essentially because a name may be rejected by the registrar on a variety of grounds and there may be problems with other persons and businesses who may claim goodwill in the same or a similar name. With respect to the latter issue, the CA 2006 makes provision in ss 69–74 for a procedure whereby a person may object to a registered name on the ground that it is the same as a name associated with the applicant in which he has goodwill or that it is sufficiently similar to such a name that its use in the UK would be likely to mislead by suggesting a connection between the company and the person objecting. Objections are considered by a company names adjudicator[22] and, if an objection is upheld, the company will be required to change its name (s 73). Detailed rules as to company names are set out in CA 2006, Part 5, ss 54–85 and related statutory instruments.[23] In addition to complying with those requirements, a company needs to consider any risk of being sued for passing off by other businesses and any possibility of an infringement of an existing trade mark.[24] A company may trade under a business name and, in that case, it must also comply with the business name regulations (CA 2006, s 82).

1-33   Essentially, the scheme governing company names is as follows:

- Certain designations or their alternatives are required unless the company meets the criteria for exemption.[25] The required designations are 'ltd' or 'limited' for a

---

[22] See CA 2006, ss 70–74 and The Company Names Adjudicator Rules 2008, SI 2008/1738. The names adjudicator is a new role created by the CA 2006. The adjudicators are based at UK Intellectual Property Office rather than at Companies House.

[23] See in particular the draft Company and Business Names (Miscellaneous Provisions) Regulations 2009; final version not available at time of writing.

[24] An important innovation is that it is now possible, via the Business Link advice service, to search against the companies names index and the trade-mark index so it is easy to establish whether a possible name will be a problem in either respect: see www.businesslink.gov.uk.

[25] CA 2006, ss 60–63.

private company and 'plc' or 'public limited company' for a public company (or their Welsh equivalents).[26]

- A company must not be registered with a name if, in the opinion of the Secretary of State (i.e. the registrar of companies), its use by the company would constitute an offence or it is offensive.[27]

- The use of certain other 'sensitive' names requires the consent of the Secretary of State or some other designated body.[28]

- A company must not be registered with a name which is the same as another name appearing in the registrar's index of company names.[29]

A company must display its registered name at its registered office and any other loca-   **1-34**
tion at which the company's records are available for inspection and at any other location at which it carries on business.[30] A company must also disclose its registered name on a wide range of business documentation and correspondence and on its websites.[31] The company name must be engraved on the company's seal, if it has one.[32] In addition to its name, a company on registration is allotted a registered number[33] which is important in distinguishing between companies.

A company may alter its name by special resolution or by any other means (such as an   **1-35**
ordinary resolution or resolution of the directors) allowed by the company's articles.[34] It may be directed to change its name in certain circumstances, as where it is 'too like' an existing name.[35] There are also restrictions on the use of certain names by former directors of a company which has gone into insolvent liquidation.[36]

The certificate of incorporation

Once all the required documents are submitted together with the registration fee, and   **1-36**
assuming there has been proper compliance with the formalities and no problems

---

[26] CA 2006, ss 58–59.   [27] CA 2006, s 53.

[28] CA 2006, ss 54–56. 'Sensitive' words include words such as 'Royal', 'University', 'Chartered' which suggest some status or association and which could be used improperly to mislead people.

[29] CA 2006, s 66(1).

[30] CA 20006, s 82; Companies (Trading Disclosures) Regulations 2008, SI 2008/495, regs 3 and 4. There is an exemption for a location which is primarily used for living accommodation designed to assist small companies which carry on business from the directors' homes.

[31] CA 20006, s 82; Companies (Trading Disclosures) Regulations 2008, SI 2008/495, reg 6. The categories of document which must disclose the registered name are set out in reg 6 and include business letters; bills of exchange, promissory notes, endorsements and order forms; cheques purporting to be signed by or on behalf of the company; orders for money, goods or services purporting to be signed by or on behalf of the company; and, crucially, a catch-all category of 'all other forms of its business correspondence and documentation', see reg 6(g).

[32] CA 2006, s 45(2). A company is not required to have a company seal, s 45(1), but may choose to do so.

[33] CA 2006, s 1066.

[34] CA 2006, s 77(1) and see s 77(2). A special resolution requires a 75% majority while an ordinary resolution requires a simple majority: see ss 282, 283.

[35] CA 2006, s 67; see also ss 75, 76.

[36] See IA 1986, s 216; IR 1986, rr 4.228–4.230; see the discussion at **25-34**.

about the company name, the registrar issues a certificate of incorporation of the company which is conclusive evidence that there has been compliance with the requirements of the CA 2006 in respect of registration (CA 2006, s 15). From the date of incorporation mentioned in the certificate, the subscribers to the memorandum, together with such other persons as may from time to time become members of the company, are a body corporate (s 16(2)).

1-37   Once incorporated, the company is a separate legal entity from the shareholders which means that it is the company which conducts the business, owns property, hires employees, incurs debts, makes profits, etc. The separate existence of the company means that the membership may be constantly changing, as shareholders transfer or sell their shares, but the business of the company is unaffected. The members, as noted, enjoy limited liability and are not required to participate in the management of the company which is a matter for the directors. These many advantages, in particular the separate legal status of the company, the limited liability of the members, and the separation of ownership and management of the company ensure that the registered company limited by shares, is an immensely popular and successful vehicle for the conduct of business in this jurisdiction.

C Company formation—companies limited by guarantee

1-38   A company limited by guarantee is a company having the liability of its members limited by its constitution to such amount (usually very small, £1 or £5) as the members undertake to contribute to the assets of the company in the event of its being wound up.[37] Such a company does not have a share capital (no contribution is required until winding up) and so these companies have members and not shareholders. Given the absence of share capital, such companies must necessarily be private and not public companies[38] (the distinction between private and public companies is discussed below).

1-39   While there is no prohibition on trading by companies limited by guarantee, such companies are predominantly found in the not-for-profit sector and are widely used for community and sporting groups, local associations, flat management companies, and for educational and charitable purposes.[39] The advantages of incorporation for such organisations lie in legal personality and limited liability so facilitating the

---

[37] CA 2006, s 3(1), (3).

[38] See CA 2006, s 4(2). The formation of companies limited by guarantee with a share capital has been prohibited since 22 December 1980.

[39] See Companies House, *Statistical Tables on Companies Register Activities 2006–07* (hereinafter Companies House *Statistical Tables 2006–07*), Table A7 which shows 88,800 companies on the register with no issued share capital (for some reason this Table is omitted from the 2007–08 Tables). Not all of these would be companies limited by guarantee, but it could be assumed that the majority are companies limited

ownership of property and the contracting of obligations despite a fluctuating membership and without exposing the members to personal liabilities.

The incorporation process for these companies is identical in most respects to a **1-40** company limited by shares, save for necessary modifications; for example, a statement of guarantee is required instead of a statement of capital and initial shareholdings (see **1-26**).

Membership of a company limited by guarantee is governed by the articles of associ- **1-41** ation. The model form of articles, if adopted, provides that new members may not be admitted unless approved by the directors, membership is not transferable and ceases on death and a member can withdraw on giving seven days' notice.[40] The duration of membership and the events or matters which terminate it will also be set out in the articles. For example, if the company is a flat management company, it is common to provide that membership ceases when ownership of one of the flats ceases.

A common misconception is that companies limited by guarantee are prevented from **1-42** distributing their profits. The prohibition on distribution of profits is a condition for exemption (CA 2006, s 62) from the use of the word 'Ltd' in the company name (CA 2006, s 60)[41] and has nothing to do with a company's status as a company limited by guarantee. Of course, the nature of the activities commonly undertaken by companies limited by guarantee does mean that such companies are rarely in a position to distribute profits,[42] but there is no prohibition on such distribution unless the company has sought exemption under s 61.

Companies limited by guarantee are often seen as very democratic organisations as **1-43** it is a case of one member one vote whereas in a company limited by shares, it is usually one share one vote so voting power is dependent on the number of shares held. However, there is no reason why a company limited by guarantee cannot adopt different voting rights if it wishes.[43]

Companies limited by guarantee must file accounts with the registrar of companies **1-44** but they may qualify for a variety of accounting exemptions[44] in the same manner as a small company limited by shares. An annual return must be delivered to the registrar of companies, but details of the members are not required.[45]

A company limited by guarantee may re-register as an unlimited company (CA 2006, **1-45** s 102), but it cannot re-register as a company limited by shares. There is no mechanism

by guarantee. Given the active register is approximately 2.4m companies, it can be appreciated that only a very small number of companies opt to be a company limited by guarantee.

[40] See The Companies (Model Articles) Regulations 2008, SI 2008/3229, reg 3, Sch 2, arts 21 and 22.

[41] See CA 2006, s 60 and associated regulations.

[42] If the company wishes to prohibit the distribution of income as dividend, the structure of the community interest company may be more appropriate, see the C(AICE) Act 2004.

[43] See *Re NFU Development Ltd* [1973] 1 All ER 135.

[44] For example, a company limited by guarantee, if a small company, may qualify for exemption from the requirement to have the accounts audited (CA 2006, s 477) and may file abbreviated accounts (s 444).

[45] See CA 2006, ss 854, 855.

for transfer between those two forms of companies and, if that is required, it is necessary to wind up the company limited by guarantee and form a new company limited by shares.

1-46   In practice, it is difficult to see much meaningful distinction between a private company limited by shares with a small number of members and minimal capital and a company limited by guarantee or at least a distinction meaningful enough to require the continued provision of a different structure for companies limited by guarantee. Of course, guarantee companies have a not-for-profit ethos which is often seen as desirable, but the same can be achieved with a company limited with shares through a suitably drafted constitution. The rather obscure law on companies limited by guarantee, as reflected in a dearth of modern case law on such companies, would suggest that it is a rather uncertain vehicle for modern business ventures. Certainly it would not appear to be the most obvious corporate structure for a body with responsibility for running the national rail network, but that is indeed the structure chosen for Network Rail, surely one of the most unusual examples of the use of a company limited by guarantee.[46]

D Private and public companies

Introduction

1-47   For those forming a company, a further choice is whether to register as a private or a public company. In practice, the vast majority of companies are formed as private companies limited by shares. As of March 2008, there were 2,423,200 companies on the register for Great Britain of which 2,412,700 (99.6%) were private companies and 10,500 (0.4%) were public companies.[47] Even those companies which are public companies are usually formed initially as private companies and subsequently re-register as public companies (re-registration is discussed below at **1-64**) As of March 2008, out of 372,400 new incorporations that year, only 600 were public companies.[48]

1-48   As to the definition of a public and private company, CA 2006, s 4 states that a 'private company' is a company which is not a public company'; and 'a public company is a company limited by shares or by guarantee and having a share capital,[49] whose

---

[46] In July 2008 the members of Network Rail voted to establish a governance 'Review Group' to consider the effectiveness of the company's corporate governance practices, with particular reference to the accountability of the board to its members and of its members to the company's wider stakeholders: see Network Rail Press Release, 16 July 2008. The House of Commons Select Committee on Transport, HC 219, 10th Report Session 2007–08, HC 219, paras 58–66 also called for a review of the company's structure.

[47] See Companies House *Statistical Tables 2007–08*, Table A1, A2.

[48] See Companies House *Statistical Tables 2007–08*, Table A2.

[49] As of 22 December 1980, such companies cannot be formed: CA 2006, s 5(1), so the vast majority of public companies are companies limited by shares.

certificate of incorporation states that it is a public company, and which has complied with the requirements of the Companies Acts in relation to public companies.'

Differences between public and private companies

On many issues, the CA 2006 imposes quite different requirements on public and pri- **1-49**
vate companies and the general regulatory approach is that the statutory requirements with respect to public companies are more onerous than those imposed on private companies. For example, public companies do not qualify for the many accounting and audit exemptions available to private companies.

CA 2006, s 4(4) draws attention to what it describes as 'the two major differences' **1-50**
between public and private companies, namely the prohibition on private companies offering their securities (essentially shares) to the public (s 755); and the requirement for a trading certificate (s 761) but, arguably, it is the former which is the key distinction. Other distinctions which might be noted would relate to the company name, accounting and audit requirements, officer requirements, and corporate formalities.

Public offers by private companies

The key distinction between public and private companies is that a public company **1-51**
may offer its securities to the public (although it is not obliged to do so) while a private company is prohibited from offering its securities to the public. While there is no longer a criminal sanction attached to a breach, a private company may be subject to an order restraining a contravention, a requirement to re-register as a public company or even an order for the compulsory winding up of the company (CA 2006, ss 755–760).

As noted above, the general approach is that the regulation of public companies is **1-52**
stricter than that for private companies. The reason why stricter regulation is imposed is because of the possibility that a public company may offer its shares to the public. All of the other requirements (minimum capital, fuller accounts, more formal corporate governance structures, etc) could be imposed on a private company, but Parliament chooses not to do so, because a private company does not cross the threshold which would justify and require additional regulation. The threshold that does justify additional regulation is the possibility that the company may offer its shares to the public. This is not an arbitrary threshold, rather it is the precise point at which the public interest intrudes into the classification debate. Corporate self-interest in raising capital meets the public interest in the protection of investors. Investor protection requirements form a package which consists of more than mere prospectus requirements (a prospectus is the formal public document offering shares for sale) and includes the accounting requirements, the corporate governance requirements, more formal decision making, etc which are characteristic of a public company.

Trading certificate and share capital

A public company formed as such cannot commence trading without a trading cer- **1-53**
tificate issued by the registrar of companies which he may only do if satisfied that the

nominal value of the company's allotted share capital is not less than the authorised minimum (CA 2006, s 761). The nominal value of a public company's allotted share capital must be not less than the authorised minimum which is £50,000 or the pre-scribed euro equivalent which is €65,600 (s 763).[50] There is no minimum share capital for a private limited company, hence the ability of A and B in the example given at the beginning of this chapter to set up a private company with very small amounts of cap-ital; and a private company can trade immediately on incorporation without any need for a trading certificate. In general, the rules governing payment for share capital and dealings in share capital are stricter for public companies, as is discussed in Chapters 19 and 20.

Company name

1-54   The most visible distinction between a public and a private company lies in the name which, in the case of a public company, must end in 'public limited company' or its abbreviation 'plc' (or Welsh equivalent) while the name of a private company must end in 'limited' or its abbreviation 'Ltd' (or Welsh equivalent).[51] In certain circumstances, a private company (but not a public company) may be exempted from ending its name with the word 'limited'.[52]

Accounting and audit requirements

1-55   A public company cannot qualify for the accounting exemptions (discussed in Chapter 16) available to small or medium-sized companies[53] or the audit exemp-tion available to small companies.[54] Public companies also have a shorter period (six months rather than nine months) within which to deliver their accounts to the registrar of companies (CA 2006, s 442(2)) and the penalties for late filing are more substantial for a public company.[55]

Officers and members

1-56   A public company must have at least two directors while a private company requires only one (CA 2006, s 154). A public company must have a company secretary.[56]

Corporate formalities

1-57   A public company must hold an annual general meeting (CA 2006, s 336) and may not use written resolutions (s 281(2)). In recognition of the informal manner in which many private companies conduct their business, private companies are not required to hold annual general meetings and are expected to use written resolutions rather than hold meetings of any sort.[57]

---

[50] See The Companies (Authorised Minimum) Regulations 2008, SI 2008/729, reg 2.
[51] CA 2006, ss 58, 59.   [52] See CA 2006, ss 60, 61.   [53] See CA 2006, ss 384(1)(a), 467(1)(a).
[54] See CA 2006, s 478(1)(a).
[55] CA 2006, s 453(2) and The Companies (Late Filing Penalties) and Limited Liability Partnerships (Filing Periods and Late Filing Penalties) Regulations 2008, SI 2008/497, reg 2.
[56] CA 2006, ss 270, 271.   [57] See CA 2006, s 281(1).

Publicly traded companies

Public companies can be further classified depending on whether they are traded **1-58** though it has to be borne in mind that only a small percentage of public companies (remember there are 10,500 public companies on the register) market and trade their shares on an organised exchange. For those that do, there are a number of further classifications to note, namely listed, quoted and publicly traded companies. The growing number of classifications reflect the myriad ways in which shares can now be traded as technology renders obsolete the idea of a single stock exchange market floor.

A listed public company is one whose securities are included in the Official List main- **1-59** tained by the UK Listing Authority (UKLA)—the Financial Services Authority (FSA) when acting as the competent authority for listing is referred to as the UKLA.[58] To be accepted for listing, the securities must be admitted to trading on a recognised investment exchange (RIE) market for listed securities[59] and the FSA has recognised a number of RIEs, the most well known being the London Stock Exchange.[60] There are 10,500 public companies on the register of companies, as noted above, but only 1,200 approximately are listed on the London Stock Exchange.[61] In essence, these listed public companies have sought to maximise the ability to offer their shares to the public by seeking to use the organised markets (and the most highly regulated markets) for dealings in their shares. In addition to complying with the companies legislation, listed companies must comply with the Listing Rules drawn up by the FSA which cover a wide range of matters including the need for shareholder approval for major transactions, continuing disclosure obligations and provisions regulating directors and their conduct. In the event of a contravention of the Listing Rules, the FSA can impose penalties on the company and on individual directors and may issue statements of censure.[62]

'Quoted company' is a term used in the CA 2006 in the context of certain disclosure **1-60** requirements, for example with regard to website publication of poll results (CA 2006, s 341); the directors' remuneration report (s 420); website publication of accounts (s 430); and the right of members to require publication of audit concerns on the website (s 527). This category is broader than that of listed company and is defined in s 385 as encompassing a company (incorporated in the UK) whose equity share capital is officially listed in the UK or in an EEA State or is admitted to dealing either on the NYSE or Nasdaq (i.e. the main American stock exchanges).

Another term used frequently in the context of the application of European Directives **1-61** is 'publicly traded companies'. Recognised investment exchanges operate a variety of markets including 'regulated markets' (which meet EU requirements) and exchange regulated markets. Companies trading on 'regulated markets' are subject, as a general

---

[58] See Financial Services and Markets Act 2000, s 74; the FSA when acting as the competent authority for listing is referred to as the UK Listing Authority (UKLA).

[59] LR 2.2.3R.

[60] Another RIE to note is Plus Markets plc: the full list is available on the FSA website: see www.fsa.gov.uk/register/home.do.

[61] See the monthly Primary Fact Sheets published by the London Stock Exchange which give statistical information on the markets, available at www.londonstockexchange.com.   [62] See FSMA 2000, s 91.

rule, to the full application of EU Directives (if EU companies) while companies trading on exchange regulated markets are subject to the (usually lighter) regulation of the relevant exchange. There is some evidence of regulatory flight, in the sense of companies trying to maintain the advantages of being publicly traded without being subject to the regulation imposed on regulated markets, as increasingly the regulatory focus at the European level has been on this broader category of publicly traded companies.[63]

1-62   Exchanges for their part wish to attract the greatest number of companies to their markets and so increasingly they offer a variety of different markets with differing regulatory requirements. For example, the London Stock Exchange offers a Main Market which is for listed securities and is a regulated market, a Professional Securities Market which is for listed (debt) securities but is an exchange regulated market, and the Alternative Investment Market (AIM) which is for unlisted securities and is an exchange regulated market. The complexity has increased with the rise of multilateral trading facilities (MTFs) as permitted by Mifid, the Markets in Financial Instruments Directive, so alternative Pan-European trading platforms (secondary trading) such as Chi-X Europe (see www.chi-x.com) and Turquoise (see www.tradeturquoise.com) have emerged to challenge existing stock markets.[64]

1-63   Such is the complexity now, driven by the technological ease of creating an infinite number of electronic markets, that the FSA is considering the structure and labelling of the market segments as part of a wider review of the overall structure of the Listing Regime in the UK.[65]

E Re-registration of companies

1-64   It is possible for a company to alter its status by re-registration in accordance with CA 2006, Pt 7. The most common alterations of status are when a private company decides to re-register as a public company[66] and when a public company decides to re-register as a private company.[67]

1-65   As noted at **1-47**, a private company re-registering as a public company is the most common way in which public companies are formed. A detailed re-registration procedure is laid down in the statute, but in essence the company must secure the consent of its shareholders,[68] alter its name and its articles to reflect its new status, and comply with the share capital requirements for public companies.[69] Assuming that

---

[63] For example, see the Transparency Directive which applies to companies whose securities are admitted to trading on a regulated market, Directive 2004/109/EC OJ L 390, 31.12.2004, p 38.

[64] See Directive 2004/39/EC on markets in financial instruments, OJ L 145, 30.04.2004, p 1.

[65] See FSA, 'A Review of the Structure of the Listing Regime', DP08/01 (January 2008) and response in CP 08/21 (December 2008). See also Alcock, [2007] JBL 733.   [66] See CA 2006, ss 90–96.

[67] See CA 2006, ss 97–101. It is also possible for a private company to re-register as unlimited (ss 102–104) and for a public company to re-register as an unlimited company (ss 108–110), but for obvious reasons of liability, those options are rarely exercised.

[68] See CA 2006, s 90(1)(a), a special resolution is required (a 75% majority, see s 283).

[69] See CA 2006, s 90(2), (3).

the documentation is correct, the registrar of companies then issues a certificate of incorporation as a public company (CA 2006, s 96). There are a number of reasons why a company might seek a change of status. The change may be driven by economic growth which the directors and shareholders feel should be reflected in the more closely regulated legal structure of a public company. It may be that the company needs to raise share capital and wants to offer its shares to the public and the original owners may wish to realise some of the value of their holding in the company by selling out to the public. It may be that the owners have no interest in raising capital, but wish simply to secure the more prestigious status of being a public company.

Just as companies may decide to move 'up' to the status of a public company, others may wish to 'retreat' from being a public company to being a private company. This change may be because the need for capital (and therefore the facility of offering their shares to the public) is no longer a priority for the company. In that situation, the company is incurring the burden of the additional regulation which is imposed as a consequence of public company status for no purpose and it makes sense to re-register. In many cases, this move backwards is achieved by the original founders of the company buying back the shares of the company in the hands of the public and returning the company to the private status and ownership which it once had. Unless there are tangible benefits from being a public company, many directors and shareholders prefer the lighter regulation and the more limited media focus on private companies. The detailed procedure is laid down in CA 2006, ss 97–101, but in essence the company must secure the consent of its shareholders[70] and alter its name and articles of association to reflect its new status. Assuming that the documentation is correct, the registrar of companies then issues a certificate of incorporation as a private company (s 101). **1-66**

F Groups of companies

Of course, businesses are not confined to operating through one company and it is common for larger enterprises to organise their affairs through a group of companies made up of a holding company and subsidiaries and myriad combinations thereof. **1-67**

The CA 2006, s 1159(1) defines a company as a 'subsidiary' of another company, its 'holding company', if that other company: **1-68**

'(a) holds a majority of the voting rights in it, or

(b) is a member of it and has the right to appoint or remove a majority of its board of directors, or

(c) is a member of it and controls alone, pursuant to an agreement with other shareholders or members, a majority of the voting rights in it,

or if it is a subsidiary of a company which is itself a subsidiary of that other company.'[71]

---

[70] See CA 2006, s 97(1)(a): a special resolution is required (a 75% majority, see s 283).

[71] The meaning of each of the categories is expanded upon in CA 2006, Sch 6.

1-69   This provision identifies three mechanisms by which a company may be a subsidiary of another company so where Company A meets these criteria with respect to its control of Company B, Company B is a subsidiary of Company A. Equally, if Company B meets these criteria in respect of Company C, Company C is a subsidiary of Company B. The effect of the definition is that, on this example, Company A is a holding company and its subsidiaries are B and C, while B is also a holding company with a subsidiary, C. Each company is a separate legal entity and is formed under the CA 2006 in accordance with the formalities discussed earlier in this chapter with the only difference being the presence of corporate shareholders rather than individuals.

1-70   The requirement in CA 2006, s 1159(1)(a) is that the holding company holds a majority of the voting rights in the subsidiary company for, as noted above, it is voting power which gives control of a company. Equally, the person who controls the board in practice has control of the company so s 1159(1)(b) recognises that situation. Section 1159(1)(c) expands the definition further to ensure that the situation where a member does not have control of a company on paper but does have control as the result of some agreement with other shareholders or members is also encompassed by the definition. In all of these situations, the level of the holding company's control is such that the other company is a subsidiary company. A company is a 'wholly-owned subsidiary' (see s 1159(2)) where, for example, Company A above is the only shareholder in Company B—B is a wholly owned subsidiary. This is an advantageous structure for Company A for it avoids any difficulties arising from any minority interests within Company B which might otherwise affect the way in which Company A may run Company B.

1-71   There are many good business reasons (and often tax reasons) why a company chooses to expand and/or divide its activities through subsidiary companies. It may be administratively convenient and economically efficient to divide activities between subsidiaries. It may make geographic sense depending on the nature of the company's business. It may be financially appropriate allowing assets and liabilities to be allocated efficiently and it may facilitate external borrowings. The business and practical reasons for proceeding through a variety of subsidiary companies within a group structure in this way are clear but the relationship between the individual companies within the group can give rise to some interesting legal issues. These are considered in Chapter 3.

G The Registrar of Companies and the public registry

The role of disclosure

1-72   Disclosure has always been seen as the price to be paid by incorporators in return for the conferring of limited liability which, as we noted above, insulates the shareholders' personal fortunes from the reach of the company's creditors, unless the shareholders have been persuaded to give personal guarantees. To redress the balance, Parliament has required the disclosure of information by companies in a variety of ways, of which the most important is to the registrar of companies at Companies House. In addition, disclosure is required at the company's registered office and, for public companies, at annual general meetings. Traded companies are obliged by listing and exchange rules to keep the markets informed. Increasingly, companies make extensive use of their websites to maintain ongoing disclosure with their shareholders and, in the case of quoted companies, they are obliged to use their websites for this purpose, as noted above at **1-60.**

The merits of disclosure are frequently debated in terms of economic value but the **1-73** justifications for imposing wide-ranging disclosure requirements centre particularly on the provision of information to assist creditors in assessing the risks of dealing with a limited company.[72] The company puts forward information about its business and the creditor decides in the light of that information whether to deal with the company and on what terms (for example, as to price, interest, and security required). In addition, it is generally thought that disclosure promotes efficient management as directors appreciate that their actions are subject to disclosure and scrutiny. Informed shareholders are in a better position to monitor the quality and conduct of the company's management and the economic performance of the company. More broadly, accountability and transparency are thought to be desirable in the conduct of corporate affairs and are a valuable means of ensuring high standards of conduct from those businesses which value their reputations.

An unforeseen burden of disclosure is the possibility that it exposes directors and others **1-74** connected with a company to risks of harassment and even violence from activists opposed to the company's activities. The most high profile case involved Huntingdon Life Sciences, a company which was targeted for many years by animal rights protestors. The protestors were able to target the directors' home addresses because of the disclosure of this information on the public register at Companies House.

Initially the Government response was to allow directors (and others, including the **1-75** company secretary) at serious risk of violence or intimidation to apply to the registrar of companies for a confidentiality order.[73] The issue continued to dominate political debate, however, and following further actions by animal rights protestors (including grave robbing)[74] and threatening letters to shareholders in GlaxoSmithKline,[75] the Government decided that all directors would be exempt in future from any need to provide a residential address and the Companies Act 2006 now so provides. Instead directors may provide the registrar with a service address (which may be the address of the registered office) as well as their residential address. Only the service address is accessible generally to the public. The residential address is available to a wide range of

---

[72] On disclosure generally, see Villiers, *Corporate Reporting and Company Law* (2006).

[73] See CA 1985, ss 723B–723F; Companies (Particulars of Usual Residential Address) (Confidentiality Orders) Regulations 2002, SI 2002/912.

[74] See 'Animal rights militants admit grave robbing', *The Guardian*, 11 April 2006.

[75] See 'Animal rights extremists send threatening letter to individual GSK investors', *Financial Times*, 9 May 2006.

public authorities, and liquidators, creditors and others may seek a court order requiring disclosure of the residential address.[76] The information on members contained in the annual return made by companies to the registrar of companies[77] has also been curtailed and while names and details of shareholdings will be required in all cases, names, details and addresses are only required of members who hold 5% or more of the issued shares of any class of a company whose shares are traded on a regulated market.[78] The register of members has always required the names and addresses of members (s 113) and it has always been permissible to use a service address for that purpose but access to the register is also now subject to restrictions (see s 116 and **14-94**). While the threat posed by animal rights protestors and others is real, it is relevant to only a tiny percentage of the 2.4m companies on the register, so removing from the register details relating to all 2.4m companies seems a disproportionate response to the problem, as those with business reasons for attempting to contact directors and shareholders will no doubt discover. Disclosure issues are considered in more detail in Chapter 16.

The public registry

1-76   Registration under the Companies Act 2006 is the responsibility of the Registrar of Companies based at Companies House in Cardiff. Companies House is a public registry with three main functions:[79]

- the incorporation, re-registration and striking off of companies;
- the registration of information relating to companies which is required to be delivered under companies, insolvency and related legislation; and
- the provision of company information to the public; together with compliance functions relating to these matters.

1-77   The scale of the operation can be seen from some of the statistics relating to the workload of Companies House for 2007–08. The effective register of companies was 2,423,200; new incorporations amounted to 372,400; 7.8m documents were filed throughout the year; and 3,971,000 searches were made of the register, practically all of them electronically.[80] Companies House is a highly advanced electronic registry which it needs to be to cope with a register of this scale. It must facilitate over two million companies needing to file information and it must then make that information publicly available. Previous research by Companies House identified that searchers using the register fall into the following discrete groups: roughly 40% of those accessing the register fall into the category of users of the information, such as banks, lawyers, other commercial

---

[76] See CA 2006, ss 243, 244, 1088; The Companies (Disclosure of Address) Regulations 2009, SI 2009/214.

[77] See CA 2006, ss 855, 856.

[78] CA 2006, s 857; The Companies Act 2006 (Annual Return and Service Addresses) Regulations 2008, SI 2008/3000.

[79] A great deal of information on the functions and role of Companies House can be found on its website at www.companieshouse.gov.uk.

[80] Companies House *Statistical Tables 2007–08*, Tables A1, F1, F5.

parties with individuals accounting for 10% of this figure; 60% of users are essentially information providers who access the information on the public register and add value to it by packaging it in various ways, for example grouping together information on particular sectors, or providing financial analysis or credit rating services using the available information.[81]

Reflecting the different types of companies on the register and the different users of the information available, Companies House provides a variety of services, some aimed at the infrequent user, i.e. the smaller companies and the occasional searcher (these services are designated as web filing or web searching, using the Companies House website). Other services are aimed at the frequent user, i.e. the large companies which file information on a very frequent basis and the professional searchers who are bulk users of the available information for their own information businesses.   **1-78**

The functions of Companies House

The focus of operations of Companies House is on getting in information from companies and providing the means whereby the public can then access that information. Turning first to the matters which must be notified to Companies House, the broad categories into which this information falls are: **1-79**

- *Disclosure on incorporation* As noted at **1-25** above, incorporation requires the submission of various documents to the registrar of companies who then issues a certificate of incorporation signalling the commencement of the company's existence.

- *Continuing disclosure* Once incorporated and on the register of companies, companies are subject to continuing disclosure obligations to ensure that the company's public record remains up to date. There are two aspects to these ongoing obligations:

  - *Occasional disclosure*—companies must notify the registrar of what can be described as occasional changes, such as changes of directors or changes to the articles of association or the creation of company charges, etc. These changes occur on a random basis with some companies having to report very frequently and others only occasionally, depending on the size and the nature of their activities.

  - *Annual disclosure*—the most significant disclosure requirements imposed on companies are the annual requirements with respect to (1) the filing of accounts (financial information), possibly supplemented by a directors' and/or an auditors' report (the accounting requirements are discussed in Chapter 16) and (2) the filing of an annual return which essentially provides information on the company's share capital and people behind the company and includes details of the directors, the company secretary, if any, and the members (CA 2006, ss

---

[81] Companies House, *Development Plan 2001–04*, para 1.13.

855, 856). The annual return must be accompanied by a fee of £15 which is the only annual fee required of a registered company although other fees may arise on occasion.[82]

- *Disclosure on dissolution* There are a variety of mechanisms, such as receivership, administration and liquidation, all of which are discussed in later chapters, which may end with the dissolution of the company and its removal from the register. Disclosure is required of these processes, therefore, so that those searching the public record are aware of the termination, or the imminent termination, of the company's existence.

An electronic registry

1-80   Companies House is working towards the provision of an all-electronic registry. Its electronic services are grouped into two main categories dealing with filing and searching.

Filing services

1-81   A web-filing service enables occasional presenters (i.e. smaller companies where there are minimal changes to their information from year to year) to submit information via the Companies House website. A wide variety of documents can be filed in this way including, crucially, the two annual documents, the accounts (where the accounts being filed are abbreviated audit exempt accounts or dormant accounts, categories which make up 90% of the accounts filed[83]) and the annual return. Companies can also use this service for notifications regarding changes to the registered office, the directors or the company secretary. The advantage for the company is that it can summon up its public record at any time and make changes directly on the website and receive an immediate response from Companies House in the case of any errors etc.

1-82   A software filing service is available for those presenters filing on a daily or weekly basis (i.e. with respect to the larger companies) and this facility enables presenters to submit notifications regarding the registered office, the directors and the company secretary, and to file the annual return. The major challenge for Companies House is to provide electronic filing of full company accounts.

1-83   Since 2001 Companies House has provided an electronic incorporation service designed for high-volume users such as company formation agents and more than 90% of companies are now incorporated electronically in this way. In due course, it is expected that (in keeping with Government policy and the requirements of the First Company Law Directive),[84] this service will be extended to individual users who will be able to incorporate companies via the Companies House website.

---

[82] For example, there is a fee of £30 (if paper) or £15 (if electronic) to register a company charge.
[83] Companies House *Statistical Tables 2007–08*, Table F2.
[84] First Council Directive 68/151/EEC, OJ L 65, 14.3.1968, p 8.

Searching the register

One of the key functions of Companies House is to facilitate access by the public to the   **1-84**
wealth of information filed by companies. Some basic information about each company is provided free on the Companies House website, for example the date of incorporation; the registered office address; the due dates for the last accounts and annual
returns; the status of the company (i.e. whether it is a 'live' company or dissolved), all
of which helps the searcher decide whether to proceed with a search.

For someone who wishes to search the register, there are essentially two main packages   **1-85**
to choose from. The WebCHeck service is a web-sales facility which allows customers to buy and receive a range of detailed company information from the Companies
House website using a credit card for payment. A wide range of information is available in this way including the most recently filed set of accounts, annual return, and
information about the directors.[85] The Companies House Direct service is a subscrip-
tion-based internet service which provides online access for frequent searchers who
may want to access all the available information about a company.

---

[85] The fees involved depend on the information required, but a basic package of information can be
obtained for as little as £1 or £2. Since 2008 a searcher can view the entire filing history for the company and
then select which of the documents filed he wishes to view.

2

The framework of company law

A The statutory framework

Background

The subject of this work is the law governing registered companies, that is companies **2-1**
registered under the Companies Act 2006 and its predecessors.

Incorporation by registration was first made possible by the Joint Stock Companies **2-2**
Act 1844. At that time, limited liability was unknown and it was not introduced until
the Limited Liability Act 1855. The pattern of company law, thereafter, was of major
consolidating legislation at regular intervals, such as the Companies Act 1908, the
Companies Act 1929, the Companies Act 1948. The most recent consolidation was the
Companies Act 1985, subsequently amended, in particular, by the Companies Act 1989
and by the Companies (Audit, Investigations and Community Enterprise) Act 2004.
More discrete material was to be found in the Company Directors Disqualification
Act 1986 and the Business Names Act 1985.

Insolvency matters were hived off initially to the Insolvency Act 1985, a major piece **2-3**
of reforming legislation introduced in response to the Cork Committee Report on
Insolvency Law and Practice (1982).[1] The Insolvency Act 1985 was then consolidated
with elements of the Companies Act 1985 in the Insolvency Act 1986. Limited technical
amendments to insolvency law followed in the Insolvency Act 1994 and the Insolvency
(No 2) Act 1994. More significant reforms were effected by the Insolvency Act 2000
and the Enterprise Act 2002. Meanwhile, the increasing importance of cross-border
insolvency issues is recognised by the EC Regulation on Insolvency Proceedings No
1346/2000[2] and The Cross Border Insolvency Regulations 2006.[3]

In addition to these company and insolvency statutes which are of central importance **2-4**
to this book, there are other substantial statutes which intrude from time to time on
company law matters, such as the Financial Services and Markets Act 2000, though
securities regulation is very much a specialist area in its own right.

The three legislative pillars until recently then were the Companies Act 1985, the **2-5**
Insolvency Act 1986 and the Financial Services and Markets Act 2000. The IA 1986 and

---

[1] *Report of the Review Committee on Insolvency Law and Practice* (Cmnd 8558, 1982).
[2] OJ L 160, 30.6.2000, p 1.   [3] SI 2006/1030.

FSMA 2000 were the product of major reviews in those subject areas which left the CA 1985 as most in need of reform, especially as it was subject to much piecemeal amendment over the years. In March 1998, the Department of Trade and Industry (DTI), now the Department for Business, Enterprise and Regulatory Reform (known as BERR), decided that the time was right for a comprehensive three-year review of company law.[4]

The Company Law Review

2-6   Launching the initial consultation document,[5] the DTI acknowledged the numerous problems with the CA 1985. The legislation was drafted in excessive detail, it used over-formal language, it over-regulated some issues (such as capital maintenance) while other matters were inadequately provided for or needed legal underpinning (such as the duties of directors and the conduct of meetings).[6] The Government's intention was stated as being that new arrangements should be devised to provide a more effective, including cost-effective, framework based on principles of consistency, predictability and transparency.[7] The task of reviewing the existing arrangements and suggesting the way forward fell to the Company Law Review made up of a Steering Group, comprised essentially of businessmen and lawyers, and numerous working groups from which emerged a stream of consultation documents.[8] The Company Law Review (hereinafter CLR) produced its Final Report in 2001 which concentrated on the following issues:[9]

- For small and private companies,[10] the recommendations centred on simplified decision-making and streamlining internal administration. There should be no need for such companies to hold general meetings or to appoint a company secretary. They should have a simplified constitution; shareholders should be encouraged to use mediation and arbitration to resolve their disputes instead of litigation; the rules on share capital should be relaxed and the financial reporting and audit requirements of these companies should be reduced.[11]

---

[4] See DTI, *Modern Company Law for a Competitive Economy* (1998). For a comprehensive account of the Review process, see Rickford, 'A History of the Company Law Review' in De Lacy (ed), *The Reform of United Kingdom Company Law* (2002).   [5] DTI, *Modern Company Law for a Competitive Economy* (1998).

[6] See DTI, *Modern Company Law for a Competitive Economy* (1998), paras 3.2, 3.4, 3.7.

[7] See DTI, *Modern Company Law for a Competitive Economy* (1998), para 3.1.

[8] For the account of the workings of the review, see Rickford, above n 4. The most important documents, all of which go under the heading Modern Company Law for a Competitive Economy, were *The Strategic Framework* (February 1999) URN 99/654; *Developing the Framework* (March 2000) URN 00/656; *Completing the Structure* (November 2000) URN 00/1335. Some topics were the subject of specific consultations, see *Company General Meetings and Shareholder Communication* (October 1999); *Company Formation and Capital Maintenance* (October 1999); *Reforming the Law Concerning Oversea Companies* (October 1999); *Capital Maintenance: Other Issues* (June 2000); *Registration of Company Charges* (October 2000).

[9] See CLR, *Modern Company Law for a Competitive Economy, Final Report*, vols I and II (2001) URN 01/942.

[10] Research carried out for the CLR showed that 70% of companies have only one or two shareholders and 90% have fewer than five shareholders: CLR, *Developing the Framework* (2000), URN 00/656, para 6.9.

[11] See CLR, *Modern Company Law for a Competitive Economy, Final Report*, vol I (2001) URN 01/942, Chs 2 and 4; *Completing the Structure* (2000) URN 00/1335, Ch 2; *Developing the Framework* (2000) URN 00/656, Chs 6 and 7.

- On directors, the key recommendation was for the inclusion in the statute of a statement of directors' duties.[12]
- On shareholders' rights and remedies, there were recommendations for the creation of a statutory derivative action and measures to enhance the exercise of shareholders' rights at meetings.[13]
- On accounting and audit requirements, a significant recommendation was for larger companies to publish an operating and financial report. No changes were proposed to auditors' duties of care.[14]

The CLR considered briefly whether it would be preferable to opt for a separate free-standing limited liability vehicle for small companies with separate legislation, but it rapidly concluded that the main obstacles to that approach would be definition problems and transition difficulties as companies grow.[15] An integrated Companies Act, but one focused on small rather than larger companies, was its preferred approach.[16] On reflection, it also considered that the focus of the legislation should be on private companies, as it is the private/public distinction which is crucial,[17] as noted at **1-52**, and it was appropriate to deregulate private companies across the board rather than attempting to define some new category of small company.[18] In other words, the CLR thought that the legislation should reflect reality which is that the register of companies is made up predominantly of small private companies, though the CA 1985 envisaged a register dominated by large public companies. This 'think small first' approach has now become something of a tenet of regulation, both domestically and at the European level.

2-7

The Government responded to the CLR Report with a White Paper entitled *Modernising Company Law*[19] published in July 2002 which broadly adopted the Review's recommendations. Further progress was deferred, however, while the Government addressed what was perceived to be a more urgent matter, namely the strengthening of audit regulation in the wake of the collapse of the American energy group, Enron, with billion dollar losses. The resulting legislation, the Companies (Audit, Investigations and Community Enterprise) Act 2004, concentrated therefore on audit matters. The main reform agenda was revived by a further White Paper, *Company Law Reform*[20] in March 2005 before, at last, a Company Law Reform Bill was introduced in November 2005.

2-8

---

[12] CLR, *Modern Company Law for a Competitive Economy, Final Report*, vol I (2001), Ch 3; *Completing the Structure* (2000), Ch 3; *Developing the Framework* (2000), paras 3.12–3.85.

[13] *Developing the Framework* (2000), Ch 4.

[14] CLR, *Modern Company Law for a Competitive Economy, Final Report*, vol I (2001), Ch 8.

[15] See CLR, *Developing the Framework* (2000) URN 00/656, para 6.19; *The Strategic Framework* (1999) URN 99/654, para 5.2.

[16] See CLR, *The Strategic Framework* (1999) URN 99/654, para 5.2.

[17] See CLR, *Final Report*, vol I (2001) URN 01/942, para 2.7.

[18] See CLR, *Completing the Structure* (2000) URN 00/1335, Ch 2; *Developing the Framework* (2000) URN 00/656, Chs 6 and 7.

[19] CM 5553-I, 5553-II (July 2002). See Goddard, 'Modernising Company Law: The Government's White Paper' (2003) 66 MLR 402.

[20] Cm 6456 (2005).

2-9   At that stage the intention was to retain substantial elements of the Companies Act 1985 alongside the CLR Bill, but eventually the Government was persuaded that the most sensible way forward was to bring those parts of the CA 1985 which were not being repealed up into the CLR Bill. As there was no time for further review, those provisions of the CA 1985 which were brought up into the Bill were merely restated so as to ensure that their drafting is consistent with the plain English of the Bill provisions, but no substantive changes were made to the CA 1985 provisions. The result is a statute which is a mixture of new and old, though the old has been restated in plain English so that, at least, it looks new![21] As a result of the addition of the CA 1985 provisions to the Bill, its title was changed to the Companies Bill which received Royal Assent on 8 November 2006 as the Companies Act 2006, some eight and a half years after the launch of the Company Law Review.

The Companies Act 2006

2-10   The Companies Act 2006 is the largest statute ever passed by Parliament. It has 1,300 sections and 16 Schedules. The transition from the CA 1985 to the CA 2006 was slow and laborious with commencement of the legislation taking place piecemeal between 6 April 2007 and 1 October 2009. It is now, finally, fully in force (with a few very minor exceptions).

2-11   Despite its length, many Parts of the Act rely on secondary legislation to supplement the statutory framework. This scheme is part of a deliberate strategy to create some flexibility to accommodate future developments since it is unlikely that Parliamentary time for further primary legislation will be available in the foreseeable future. In any event, after taking more than a decade to progress from the launch of the Company Law Review to the final commencement of the CA 2006, it is fair to say that there is no appetite for further change, though there may still be some European developments to accommodate, as we shall see.

B The European framework

Overview of the European agenda and approach

2-12   As the limited liability company is the main vehicle for private industry across Europe, it was understood from the earliest days of the European Community that at least some measure of harmonisation of national laws would be required to ensure a common or

---

[21] There is always the risk when restating a provision that the result is a change in the law which may create an interpretation conundrum for the courts when faced with wording which alters the meaning of a provision but a declared legislative intent merely to restate. For example CA 2006, s 40(1) restates CA 1985, s 35A(1) but the wording is altered and the consequence is that the law has been altered, see discussion at **8-20** et seq.

single market, given that the legal structures of companies vary significantly across the Member States. The Treaty establishing the European Community recognised this need and imposes on the European Commission and Council an obligation to:[22]

'...co-ordinate to the necessary extent the safeguards which, for the protection of the interests of members and others, are required by Member States of companies or firms...with a view to making such safeguards equivalent throughout the Community.'

Harmonisation

The European Commission (hereinafter the Commission) proceeded initially by way of a Company Law harmonisation programme which resulted in the adoption of a series of numbered directives[23] (The First Company Law Directive, The Second Company Law Directive and so on). Some of the Directives concern relatively discrete (and highly technical) matters, such as the Eleventh Directive on disclosures by branches of overseas companies.[24] Others are of broader significance, such as the Second Company Law Directive which lays down many of the share capital rules for public limited companies.[25] The Fourth and Seventh Directives—the Accounting Directives—prescribe the content and format of company accounts and have formed the framework for accounting disclosure for the past 30 years.[26]

This harmonisation stage lasted roughly from 1968 to 1989 but it then more or less **2-14** stalled, in part because other areas, such as financial services, took centre stage, in part because it was difficult to garner support for this type of highly technical harmonisation. The result was that from the mid-1990s until early 2000 there was little activity on the company law front.[27]

Modernisation

In September 2001 company law issues moved up the Commission's agenda again, **2-15** however, and a High Level Group of Company Law Experts (HLG) was formed to review the need for the modernisation of company law in Europe. The impetus for this change in attitude came in part from the need to implement the Financial Services Action Plan which aimed to ensure an integrated capital market by 2005. There were concerns that corporate scandals and collapses (including Enron in the US, but also the collapse of the Italian company, Parmalat) had damaged investor confidence which is central to the successful and efficient operation of capital markets. The collapse of Enron with billion dollar losses brought a speedy (and severe)

---

[22] Treaty Establishing the European Community (Consolidated version) OJ C 325, 24.12.2002, p 33, art 44(2)(g).

[23] Some of the Directives have fallen by the wayside (for example, nos 5 and 9 and, it seems, no 14) leaving Company Law Directives numbered 1–4, 6–8, 10–13.

[24] Eleventh Council Directive (EEC) 89/666, OJ L 395, 30.12.1989, p 36.

[25] Second Council Directive (EEC) 77/91, OJ L 26, 31.1.1977, p 1.

[26] Fourth Council Directive (EEC) 78/660, OJ L 222, 14.8.1978, p 11; Seventh Council Directive (EEC) 83/349, OJ L 193, 18.7.1983, p 1.

[27] See generally Wouters, 'European Company Law: Quo Vadis?' (2000) 37 CMLR 257.

legislative response by the American authorities, notably through the Sarbanes-Oxley Act.[28] The European authorities were anxious to show an equally positive and identifiable European response which, with an emphasis on transparency and accountability, would ensure high standards of corporate governance and restore investor confidence. Added urgency was given to the situation by the imminent accession (in May 2004) of new Member States, many of them Eastern European countries with a limited history of open corporate markets, given the post-war Soviet occupation of their countries. A further impetus for change was the general globalisation of trade and increase in cross-border economic activity and a concern that the EU had to be proactive in facilitating that trade. The HLG published a consultation document and a report in 2002[29] and the Commission responded in May 2003 with an Action Plan for Company Law which set out a number of priorities for reform divided into short (03–06), medium (06–08) and long-term actions (09 onwards).[30] The guiding criteria in drawing up the Plan were the need to respect subsidiarity and proportionality; the requirement for flexible application based on firm principles; and the need to shape international regulatory developments.[31]

2-16   The short-term priorities of the Action Plan focused on securing a shareholders' rights Directive, a Recommendation on directors' remuneration and on the role of non-executive directors, the creation of a European Corporate Governance Forum and amendments to the Accounting Directives to ensure greater transparency and accountability. This phase ran (roughly) from 2001 to 2006 and was driven by a need to modernise company law across the Member States. There was less of an emphasis on harmonisation and a greater emphasis on framework Directives, so leaving Member States more leeway in addressing their particular circumstances. Such Directives may be easier to negotiate (an important consideration now that there are 27 Member States), but may encourage divergence between Member States rather than harmonisation. The Commission also turned to greater use of Recommendations and Communications which are not legally binding (so-called 'soft-law') with committees of experts, such as the European Corporate Governance Forum, being used by the Commission to encourage co-ordination and convergence on corporate governance measures.[32] The advantage in proceeding in this way is that measures can be agreed swiftly by the Commission and, by identifying and setting standards of best practice, market forces can compel Member States practice to converge, in effect, on

[28] For an interesting overview of the Sarbanes-Oxley Act 2002, see Canada, Kuhn, and Sutton, 'Accidentally in the public interest: The perfect storm that yielded the Sarbanes-Oxley Act' (2008) Critical Perspectives in Accounting 987.

[29] See Report of the High Level Group of Company Law Experts, 'A Modern Regulatory Framework for Company Law in Europe' (November 2002) which was preceded by a consultation paper of the same name in April 2002.

[30] See European Commission Communication, Modernising Company Law and Enhancing Corporate Governance in the European Union—A Plan to Move Forward, COM (2003) 284, 21.5.2003. For an overview, see Baums, 'European Company Law after the 2003 Action Plan' (2007) 8 EBOR 143.

[31] See Commission Action Plan, COM (2003) 284, pp 4–5.

[32] The Commission also set up an Advisory Committee on Corporate Governance and Company Law to provide detailed technical advice to the Commission.

such standards.[33] This sudden spurt of activity from 2001 to 2005 came to a somewhat abrupt end in 2006 when, at the broader political level, it became apparent that there was some resistance to further EU integration generally (as seen in the resistance to the adoption of a European Constitution). There was more than an element of regulatory fatigue for all concerned and a backlash against what was seen as burdensome EU-derived regulation (a flame fuelled by opportunist Eurosceptics who chose to ignore the extent to which domestic Governments generate bureaucratic regulation and gold-plate European requirements).

Simplification

Though good progress was made on the short-term priorities identified in the Action Plan, the Commission decided in December 2005 to hold a further consultation to determine whether to proceed with the remaining elements of the Plan.[34] The outcome was a shift in focus from generating initiatives (other than those seen as 'enabling' measures such as with regard to the European Private Company Statute) to simplification and a reduction of regulatory burdens.[35] This move was in keeping with a broader simplification exercise which the Commission had commenced in 2005 across a range of areas as part of a drive to 'Better Regulation'. Company law was identified as one of the priority areas within that programme for simplification.[36] As part of the 'Better Regulation' project, the Commission announced in January 2007 an Action Programme to reduce administrative burdens on business which specifically identified the Third and Sixth Company Law Directives on mergers and divisions of public companies, the First and Eleventh Company Law Directives with regard to disclosure requirements and the Fourth and Seventh Company Law Directives (the Accounting Directives) as candidates for simplification.

2-17

Against this backdrop of emerging priorities, the Commission consulted in July 2007 on possible simplification (including repeal) of a broad sweep of company law, accounting and audit requirements including the Second Company Law Directive.[37] The response, slightly surprisingly, was not in favour of outright repeal (which it was thought would

2-18

---

[33] Others criticise this approach as contributing to divergence which is inconsistent with a single market and a level playing field for all. See the collection of essays on these issues in Gordon & Roe (eds), *Convergence and Persistence in Corporate Governance* (2004); also McCahery et al (eds), *Corporate Governance Regimes, Convergence and Diversity* (2002).

[34] See 'Consultation on Future Priorities for the Action Plan on Modernising Company Law and enhancing Corporate Governance in the European Union' (December 2005) text available at http://ec.europa.eu/internal_market/company/docs/consultation/consultation_en.pdf.

[35] In fact there is now so much emphasis on simplification that it is difficult to keep track of the various EU initiatives and the picture is complicated further by the involvement of two Directorates, Enterprise and the Internal Market, in driving forward these programmes.

[36] See Commission Communication, *Implementing the Community Lisbon programme: A strategy for the simplification of the regulatory environment*, COM (2005) 535, OJ C 309, 16.12.2006, pp 18–21; also Commission Communication, *Better Regulation for Growth and Jobs in the European Union*, COM (2005) 97, 16.3.2005.

[37] See Commission, *Communication on a simplified business environment for companies in the areas of company law, accounting and auditing*, COM (2007) 394, 10.7.2007.

only generate further costs and uncertainties) but greater simplification.[38] The goal now is to create a 'simplified business environment' starting from a 'think small first' position. The result is that the two programmes (reduction of administrative burdens and Company Law Action Plan) are now closely linked with fast-track amendments being made to a number of the Company Law Directives under the simplification programme[39] while the priorities under the Company Law Action Plan are now focused on simplification. The most recent manifestation of this shift is a proposal to remove the smallest businesses from the scope of the Accounting Directives entirely so leaving it to Member States to determine the level of accounting disclosure required of them and a proposal that there should be a fundamental review of the application and scope of the Accounting Directives.[40]

2-19   Much of this shift in focus is intended to recognise the central role that SMEs (small and medium-sized enterprises) play in the EU economy.[41] To reflect this focus, the Commission adopted a Small Business Act in 2008,[42] which is not a piece of legislation but a package of 10 principles[43] and a number of proposed actions, intended to guide the Commission and Member States in dealing with SMEs. One of the proposals within that package is for the creation of a new legal structure, the European Private Company, discussed below at **2-57**, to facilitate cross-border activities by SMEs.

2-20   As by their very nature, European measures are integral to and form part of substantive domestic law, the content of a particular measure is discussed in the chapter dealing with the substantive law on that issue, hence the capital requirements for public companies are discussed in Chapter 19; the substantive accounting and audit requirements are discussed in Chapter 16; and so on. The rest of this chapter focuses on an overview of the measures taken or planned in order to give the reader a sense

---

[38] For a summary of the responses, see http://ec.europa.eu/internal_market/company/docs/simplification/consultation_report_20071219_en.pdf.

[39] See Press Release 'Commission cuts unnecessary administrative burdens in EU company law', IP/08/598, 17.04.2008, announcing fast-track amendments to the First and Eleventh Directives (see COM (2008) 194, 17.04.2008) and the Accounting Directives. This was followed by the announcement of fast track amendments to the Third and Sixth Directives, see Press Release 'Commission proposes further simplification of EU rules on mergers and divisions,' IP/08/1407, 25.09.2008.

[40] See announcement by Commission McCreevy, Memo 08/589, 29.09.2008.

[41] Commission research shows that there are around 23m SMEs in the EU, representing 99.8% of all enterprises. They account for almost 70% of total employment and are responsible for most of the net job creation in the EU: see Commission Impact Assessment accompanying Commission Communication 'Think Small First—a Small Business Act for Europe', COM (2008) 394, para 2.1. The position is the same in the UK where small and medium-sized enterprises (SMEs) together account for 99.9% of all enterprises and 59.2% of private sector employment: see BERR, *Small and Medium Enterprise Statistics for the UK and Regions* (2007).

[42] The 'Small Business Act' for Europe (SBA) was adopted by the European Commission on 25 June 2008. See COM (2008) 394.

[43] The 10 guiding principles relate to matters such as granting a second chance for business failures, facilitating access to finance and enabling SMEs to turn environmental challenges into opportunities. Member States are urged to ensure that the time needed to start a new company should be no more than one week, the maximum time to obtain business licences and permits should not surpass one month and that one-stop-shops should be available to assist start-ups.

of the level of EU involvement in the development of company law.[44] Three major (overlapping) themes emerge:

(1) an emphasis on disclosure and transparency—these are the standard regulatory tools of any jurisdiction dealing with limited entities—the aim is primarily but not exclusively creditor protection;

(2) a focus on corporate governance in publicly traded companies aimed primarily at shareholder protection and investor confidence; and

(3) a focus on structures/restructuring and corporate mobility which is consistent with the underlying rationale of the development of an integrated internal market across the European Union.

Disclosure/creditor protection

Transparency and disclosure are key themes in the domestic Member State regula-   **2-21** tion of limited liability companies and it is not surprising therefore that many of the European company law measures have focused on these issues.[45] Indeed, transparency was one of the themes of the First Company Law Directive[46] which, amongst other things, requires companies to publish certain documents (for example, the constitution and accounts) and particulars (for example, of directors) on a public register. That information must be accessible to the public and copies must be available at a price not exceeding the administrative cost of providing the information—the public register meeting these requirements is maintained here by Companies House, as discussed at **1-76**. The Eleventh Company Law Directive[47] augments these requirements by imposing disclosure requirements in respect of branches opened in a Member State by companies from another Member State. The intention is to ensure that companies cannot avoid disclosure requirements in another Member State by opening branches rather than subsidiary companies.

Of course, the most important disclosure required of limited entities is disclosure of   **2-22** their financial position as evidenced by their accounts and it is with respect to accounting disclosures that the EU influence has been greatest. The accounting disclosure requirements are dominated by the Fourth and Seventh Company Law Directives. The

---

[44] It is also worth noting that a private initiative is underway with a view to developing a European Model Company Law Act, along the lines of the American Model Acts. The intention is to provide a draft model law which legislatures would be free to adopt in whole or in part. The hope is that it is possible to build a structure based on broadly acceptable uniform rules, building on the common legal traditions of the Member States and the existing *acquis* and developing practice: see Baums and Andersen, 'The European Model Company Law Act Project', Working Paper 097/2008, European Corporate Governance Institute (March 2008).

[45] Other Directives such as the Prospectus Directive also provide for extensive financial disclosures for current and prospective shareholders, creditors and the wider securities markets: see Directive 2003/71/EC on the prospectus to be published when securities are offered to the public or admitted to trading, OJ L 345, 31.12.2003, pp 64–89.

[46] First Council Directive 68/151/EEC, OJ L 65, 14.3.1968, p 8. See Edwards, *EC Company Law* (1999), Ch II.

[47] Eleventh Council Directive (EEC) 89/666, OJ L 395, 30.12.1989, p 36. See Edwards, *EC Company Law* (1999), Ch VIII.

Fourth Directive deals with the presentation and content of a company's individual accounts[48] and the Seventh Directive deals with the presentation and content of consolidated or group accounts:[49] together they are known as the Accounting Directives.

2-23   The Accounting Directives have been amended on numerous occasion, for example especially to allow for derogations in favour of small and medium-sized enterprises[50] and significantly to allow for fair value accounting for financial instruments.[51] Most importantly, the Directives were amended by the Modernisation Directive,[52] adopted in May 2003, which updated the accounting disclosure requirements to reflect modern accountancy standards. This move followed the adoption in June 2002 of a Regulation on the application of International Accounting Standards (IAS)[53] which, from 1 January 2005, requires listed companies to draw up their consolidated accounts in accordance with IAS (now IFRS—International Financial Reporting Standards).[54] This Regulation was a transformational measure which necessitated a general overhaul of the accounting framework in the EU for companies falling within the scope of the Regulation.

2-24   The Accounting Directives were further amended by Directive 2006/46/EC.[55] The focus of the amendments was:

(1) to further increase the thresholds for small and medium companies so ensuring that they are exempt from the more onerous disclosure requirements of the Accounting Directives (in fact, very little is now required of small companies in particular);

(2) to provide for additional disclosure of certain off balance sheet items and transactions with related parties—these matters are of particular concern to regulators and investors; and

(3) to require publicly traded companies to include a corporate governance statement in their annual reports and to ensure the collective responsibility of board members for the annual accounts and reports.[56]

---

[48] Fourth Council Directive (EEC) 78/660, OJ L 222, 14.8.1978, p 11.

[49] Seventh Council Directive (EEC) 83/349, OJ L 193, 18.7.1983, p 1.

[50] Directive 90/604, OJ L 317, 16.11.1990, p 57. Also amended, for example, to extend their application to cover general and limited partnerships where the responsible partners are themselves companies or limited companies, see Directive 90/605, OJ L 317, 16.11.1990, p 60.

[51] Directive 2001/65, OJ L 283, 27.10.2001, p 28.

[52] See Directive 2003/51/EC amending and updating Council Directives 78/660/EEC, 83/349/EEC, 86/635/EEC and 91/674/EEC on the annual and consolidated accounts of certain types of companies, banks and other financial institutions and insurance undertakings, OJ L 178, 17.7.2003, p 16.

[53] Regulation (EC) No 1606/2002 of 19 July 2002 on the application of international accounting standards, OJ L 243, 11.09.2002, p 1; and see the European Commission Press Release, IP/02/827, 7 June 2002.

[54] International Accounting Standards were issued by the International Accounting Standards Committee which has since been replaced by the International Accounting Standards Board (IASB) which issues International Financial Reporting Standards (IFRS).   [55] OJ L 224, 16.08.2006, p 1.

[56] These requirements are reflected in the CA 2006, Part 15 on accounts with the exception of the requirement for a corporate governance statement which is addressed by the Disclosure and Transparency Rules of the FSA: see DTR 7.2.

The latter two elements, in particular, were part of the European response to the prob-   **2-25**
lems identified in the collapse of Enron, noted at **2-8** above. Further amendments to
the Accounting Directives were brought forward in April 2008 as part of the ongoing
simplification programme noted above at **2-17** and these will reduce the information
provided by SMEs in the notes to their accounts and provide some relaxation of the
requirements for group accounts.[57]

All of these measures together are designed to ensure the highest standards of trans-   **2-26**
parency (compatible with the economic size of the company) and comparability for
accounts of companies formed in the Member States. For larger companies, the key
development is the move to international accounting standards rather than standards
derived from accounting practice in individual Member States.

It is clear from the preceding paragraphs that the Accounting Directives have been   **2-27**
central to the development of accounting requirements over the past 30 years and that
they have been significantly amended over that time. In September 2008, a proposal
was put forward for a comprehensive review of the accounting requirements starting
from a 'think small first' perspective.[58] The outcome, especially given the widespread
collapse of banking companies in autumn 2008, is likely to be further de-regulation
of small and medium-sized enterprises coupled with more intensive regulation of
the largest enterprises, especially in the banking and insurance sectors, given their
importance to the overall stability of markets and economies.

Of course, disclosure of accounting information alone is insufficient without   **2-28**
assurance as to the quality of that information which comes from the requirement
that the accounts be audited. Audit issues are governed by the Eighth Company Law
Directive,[59] adopted in 2006, which replaces an earlier version from 1984[60] which
laid down minimum requirements and qualifications for auditors. The 'new' Eighth
Directive makes comprehensive provision for all matters pertaining to the statutory
auditor, his qualifications, role and independence, as well as providing for disciplinary
processes, quality assurance and public oversight of the audit profession. Adoption
of the Directive means that the Commission can now focus on more specific issues,
especially the ownership and independence of audit firms, auditors' liabilities (a matter which was the subject of a Recommendation in 2008)[61] and independent public
oversight and external quality assurance (also the subject of a Recommendation
in 2008).[62]

---

[57] See Proposal for a Directive of the European Parliament and of the Council amending Council
Directives 78/660/EEC and 83/349/EEC as regards certain disclosure requirements for medium-sized companies and obligation to draw up consolidated accounts, COM (2008) 195, 17.04.2008.

[58] See announcement by Commissioner McCreevy, Memo 08/589, 29.09.2008.

[59] Directive 2006/43/EC on statutory audits of annual accounts and consolidated accounts, OJ L 157,
9.6.2006, p 87.

[60] Eighth Council Directive (EEC) 84/253, OJ L 126, 12.5.1984, p 20.

[61] See Commission Recommendation of 5 June 2008 concerning the limitation of the civil liability of
statutory auditors and audit firms: OJ L 162, 21.06.2008, p 39.

[62] See Commission Recommendation of 6 May 2008 on external quality assurance for statutory auditors
and audit firms auditing public interest entities, OJ L 120, 07.05.2008, p 20.

2-29   The Accounting Directives and the Audit Directive have a major role to play in terms of creditor protection, of course, since they are intended to ensure the provision of comparable accounts backed up by high quality audits which give creditors the information they need to asses the risk of dealing with limited companies. The other traditional protective device is the use of capital maintenance rules to ensure that companies cannot return capital to their shareholders ahead of a winding up other than in accordance with statutory procedures designed to protect creditors. Capital maintenance revolves around two types of provisions, payment rules and return of capital rules and these are found in the Second Company Law Directive which provides for the formation of public limited companies and the maintenance and alteration of their share capital.[63] Adopted in 1976, the focus was on public companies because of their economic significance and the fact that their activities could be expected to extend beyond national boundaries. Given those features, the preamble to the Directive notes the importance of ensuring minimum equivalent protection throughout the EC for both creditors and shareholders of such companies.

2-30   The Second Directive is one of the most significant European company law measures for it prescribes in detail the capital rules applicable to public companies, especially with respect to capital maintenance and the rules governing distributions to members. The drawback with the Second Directive has always been the level of prescription imposed by it and there has been pressure on the Commission, a lot of it emanating from the UK, for radical reform, if not outright repeal, of the Directive.[64] This pressure increased as a result of a view that the Directive sits uneasily beside implementation of IFRS (noted above at **2-23**) and as a result makes it difficult for companies to make distributions, i.e. declare a dividend to their shareholders. In response to these broader concerns, the Commission initiated a feasibility study on an alternative to the capital maintenance regime.[65] The study (published in February 2008) concluded, to the surprise of its critics, that in fact the Second Directive is flexible in many ways and its requirements do not cause significant operational problems for companies nor does it (nor the application of IFRS) pose a major obstacle to dividend distribution. The Commission therefore concluded that 'no follow-up measures or changes in the Second Company Law Directive are foreseeable in the immediate future'.[66] Limited changes were made to the Directive, however, as part of the simplification programme.[67] These capital matters are discussed in detail in Chapters 19 and 20.

---

[63] Second Council Directive (EEC) 77/91, OJ L 26, 31.1.1977, p 1; see generally, Edwards, *EC Company Law* (1999), Ch III.

[64] BERR, Note and Consultation on European Commission Consultation on Simplification of EU Company Law etc, August 2007, available at www.berr.gov.uk/files/file41189.doc.

[65] The full text of this lengthy study which was led by KPMG is available at http://ec.europa.eu/internal_market/company/docs/capital/feasbility/study_en.pdf.

[66] See Response of the Commission to the results of the external study on the feasibility of an alternative to the Capital Maintenance regime of the Second Company Law Directive and the impact of the adoption of IFRS on profit distribution: http://ec.europa.eu/internal_market/company/docs/capital/feasbility/markt-position_en.pdf.

[67] See Directive 2006/68/EC amending Directive 77/91/EEC, OJ L 264, 25.9.2006, p 32. See Government Response to consultation on implementation of amendments to the Second Company Law Directive: URN 07/1300; also DTI, 'Implementation of the Companies Act 2006' (Feb 2007) URN 07/666, Ch 6.

Corporate governance

Corporate governance is a term much in use in the past decade and it can mean dif-   **2-31**
ferent things depending on the context[68] but essentially the focus is on how boards of
companies operate and the relationship between the directors and the shareholders.
The Commission has acted relatively cautiously on these matters with non-binding
Recommendations on directors' remuneration and on the role of independent directors (board structures) and only recently securing a Directive on shareholder rights
(enhancing shareholder engagement). The backseat role of the Commission on these
issues reflects the fact that domestically many Member States have taken broadly similar measures on corporate governance over the past 20 years and so little action is
needed at European level. The Commission initiated a review of corporate governance
codes across the EU in 2002 and that review found that at that time practically every
Member State had at least one code and all the codes had very similar characteristics so the Commission saw and sees no need for a European corporate governance
code.[69] On the other hand, the variety of codes available can be somewhat confusing
and so publicly traded companies are required by the Accounting Directives to provide an annual corporate governance statement (either in the directors' report or by
cross-reference to the directors' report) so as to highlight the corporate governance
structures in their company.

Leaving aside a European code, the Commission has been content to use   **2-32**
Recommendations to highlight best practice. The Commission Recommendation
on directors' remuneration, issued in 2004 and aimed at publicly traded companies,
stressed the importance of disclosure of remuneration policies and the remuneration
packages of individual directors and the need for shareholder approval of remuneration
policy.[70] A Commission Recommendation on the role of non-executive or supervisory
directors and on board committees was also issued in 2004. The purpose was to identify
minimum standards, for example on the creation, composition and role of nomination,
remuneration and audit committees; the criteria for independence required of non-
executive directors; and the minimum disclosure of directors' remuneration.[71]

---

[68] See the definition in FSMA 2000, s 890(2) which provides that corporate governance in relation to an
issuer (a company) includes: (1) the nature, constitution or functions of the organs of the issuer; (2) the manner in which organs of the issuer conduct themselves; (3) the requirements imposed on organs of the issuer;
(4) the relationship between the different organs of the issuer; (5) the relationship between the organs of the
issuer and the members of the issuer or holders of the issuer's securities.

[69] See Commission *Communication on Modernising Company Law*, COM (2003) 284, 21.05.2003, para 3.1;
Weil, Gotshal & Manges, *Comparative Study of Corporate Governance Codes Relevant to the European Union
and its Member States* (January 2002). The Commission is considering carrying out a further study in 2009
to get a comprehensive picture of all the available codes and their practical application.

[70] See *Recommendation on fostering an appropriate regime for the remuneration of directors of listed companies*, OJ L 385, 29.12.2004, p 55. A Commission review of the effectiveness of the Recommendation in 2007
concluded that there was greater disclosure of individual packages, but less so in respect of remuneration
policies, and with a few exceptions there was little involvement by shareholders in deciding on or approving
remuneration policy. The Commission intends to continue to monitor the position before deciding on any
further action. See Commission Report, SEC (2007) 1022, 13.07.2007.

[71] See *Recommendation on the role of non-executive or supervisory directors of listed companies and on the
committees of the (supervisory) board*, OJ L 52, 25.02.2005, p 51. A Commission review of the effectiveness

2-33   The most substantial achievement has been the adoption of a Directive on shareholder rights (Directive 2007/36).[72] The Directive sets out detailed minimum requirements with respect to the notice to be given of general meetings, the information to be provided to shareholders, the right to ask questions and receive answers at meetings, the right to add items to the meeting agenda, voting procedures including electronic participation, proxy rights etc. In other words, the focus is on the process of shareholder engagement. Much is talked about the need for greater engagement by shareholders and for a dialogue between shareholders and their boards, but it cannot happen without procedures to facilitate that dialogue. Domestically, many of these issues are addressed by the CA 2006, Part 13 which has been thoroughly revised to facilitate shareholder participation in meetings of public companies and the Shareholder Rights Directive is in a similar mould.

2-34   A more controversial initiative involved a wide-ranging debate on voting rights in publicly traded companies, the one share, one vote (ISIV), or proportionality between capital and control, issue. One share, one vote is the standard structure in this jurisdiction, but most other Member States are accustomed to much more opaque structures with voting control commonly retained by small numbers of shareholders, often reflecting long-standing family holdings. Basically, the argument is that if a company wants to accept shareholders' capital, it should be prepared to give them voting rights proportionate to the capital contributed and allow them a say in the conduct of the company's affairs through the mechanism of the general meeting. This ensures a powerful shareholder voice as a brake on the board of directors which might otherwise enjoy a cosy relationship with the key shareholders leading to a sharing between them of private benefits not available to the other shareholders. The countervailing argument runs along the lines that these are pure contractual matters and that shareholders purchasing shares in these companies contract on the basis that they will have limited voting rights and that limitation is (a) accepted by them voluntarily and (b) reflected in the price that they pay for their shares. It is also suggested that these structures are embedded in different corporate cultures which accept and respect long-standing family control and there is no demand for change. If there was a concern, the market would reflect that concern by marking down the share value of companies with restricted voting rights, but no such write-downs occur which suggests it is not a matter of concern to investors. The discussion of these matters came to a slightly abrupt end when in October 2007 Commissioner McCreevy announced that, following a review of a study on proportionality in the EU[73] and an impact assessment of the issue of proportionality, no further action would be taken on the matter. In part, the decision came about because

of the Recommendation in 2007 revealed a substantial measure of compliance by Member States but the Commission also found some areas of concern, mainly with respect to the independent element of audit and remuneration committees. The Commission intends to continue to monitor the position before deciding on any further action. See Commission Report, SEC (2007) 1021, 13.07.2007.

[72] Directive 2007/36/EC on the exercise of certain rights of shareholders in listed companies, OJ L 184, 14.7.2007, p 17. Adopted in July 2007, it must be implemented by 3 August 2009.

[73] *Report on the Proportionality Principle in the European Union* carried out by ISS Europe, ECGI, Shearman & Sterling for the European Commission (May 2007).

the empirical evidence available to the Commission did not provide sufficient evidence of the existence and extent of private benefit extraction resulting from a lack of proportionality.[74] There was also significant political opposition to any change, especially from the Nordic countries where such concentrated shareholdings are commonplace. If there is to be movement on the matter, it will have to come from pressure by market participants on individual companies.[75] Having said that, the issue has evolved into a wider discussion, especially in the European Parliament, of the actual nature and role of shareholders, especially institutional shareholders and hedge funds. The collapse of leading financial institutions in 2008-09 means that that debate as to the role of shareholders is likely to gather momentum, but in a different context.

Corporate restructuring/mobility

A variety of measures have been adopted to facilitate mergers and takeovers as companies seek to expand through acquisitions and also to provide a range of corporate structures so as to facilitate operations across the internal market.[76]   **2-35**

The most significant European contribution in terms of mergers and takeovers is the Thirteenth Company Law Directive, now more commonly called The Takeover Directive, which applies to takeover bids for securities of a company governed by the law of a Member State where all or some of the securities are admitted to trading on a regulated market.[77] Seventeen years elapsed from the initial proposal to the Directive coming into force on 20 May 2006.[78] The Directive lays down a framework of principles which govern takeovers and requires offers to be made to all shareholders. There are detailed rules as to the conduct of the bid and the documentation which must be provided to shareholders, but the requirements are somewhat watered down by a variety of Member State opt outs. Nevertheless, given the history of the Directive, it was an achievement merely to have secured at least a framework for the conduct of takeovers throughout the EU. The Directive was implemented by CA 2006, Part 28 and has had minimal impact here given that the position under the Directive to a large extent   **2-36**

---

[74] See Commission Impact Assessment on the Proportionality between Capital and Control in Listed Companies, SEC (2007) 1705, 12.12.2007.

[75] See the interesting paper by Khachaturyan, 'Trapped in Delusions: Democracy, Fairness and the One-Share-One-Vote Rule in the European Union' (2007) 8 EBOR 335 who argues that the case for ISIV being made mandatory has not been made out and that ISIV is not as valuable as is assumed and that it is neither a sufficient nor a necessary condition for shareholder democracy in general or shareholder empowerment in the EU in particular. See also OECD Report on the issue, 'Lack of Proportionality Between Ownership And Control: Overview And Issues For Discussion' issued by the OECD Steering Group On Corporate Governance, December 2007.

[76] We can note in passing the Twelfth Company Law Directive, Directive 89/667 EEC, OJ L 395, 30.12.1989, p 40 which allows for the formation of private companies having one member. It is of little significance as this is now commonplace and the CA 2006 permits public and private companies to have a single member (CA 2006, s 7).

[77] Directive 2004/25/EC on takeover bids, OJ L 142, 30.4.2004, p 12.

[78] The first proposal for a Directive on Takeovers was put forward by the European Commission in 1989: see OJ C 64/8 14.3.1989. It was revised in 1990: see OJ C 240/7, 6.9.1990; in 1996: see COM (95) 655, 07.02.1996; in 1997, see OJ C 378, 13.12.97; followed by a new proposal in 2002, see OJ C 45 E, 25.02.2003, p 1.

reflects the UK position on takeovers as set out in the Takeover Code. The Directive is considered in detail in Chapter 26.

2-37 The Third and Sixth Company Law Directives are concerned with mergers and divisions of public companies within a single Member State.[79] They are of limited significance in this jurisdiction since they apply to mergers by way of the transfer of assets and liabilities from one company to another whereas acquisitions by purchase of the shares in the entity rather than the underlying assets is the mechanism commonly used here. The Commission did suggest the repeal of the Third and Sixth Directives,[80] something the UK supported, but the consensus favoured their simplification (now in hand)[81] rather than outright repeal. The package is completed by the Tenth Company Law Directive[82] which facilitates mergers of companies from different Member States and was implemented by the Cross-Border Mergers Regulations,[83] though for the same reasons it is unlikely that much use will be made by UK companies of these mechanisms. For many years, there have been discussions about a proposed Fourteenth Company Law Directive on the transfer of a company's registered office from one Member State to another. In the light of the European jurisprudence on the mobility of companies, discussed below, the Commission has decided, however, that there is no need to take forward that proposal: see **2-47** below.

Freedom of establishment

2-38 As can be seen above, there has been a measure of Commission activity in the area of corporate restructuring etc, but the greatest impetus to corporate mobility has come, not from the Commission, but from the European Court of Justice. A practice had developed of businesses from other Member States incorporating in the UK, driven by the absence of minimum capital requirements for private companies and the speed, ease and low cost of incorporation (see discussion in Chapter 1). This practice was not welcomed by the 'home' Member States of those businesses which sought to challenge or hinder such business from operating in the original home Member State. This raised issues as to freedom of establishment under arts 43 and 48 of the EC Treaty[84]

---

[79] Third Company Law Directive 78/855/EEC concerning mergers of public limited liability companies, OJ L 295, 20.10.1978, p 36; Sixth Company Law Directive 82/891/EEC concerning the division of public limited liability companies, OJ L 378, 31.12.1982, p 47.

[80] See Commission Communication on a simplified business environment for companies, COM (2007) 394, 10.7.2007, para 3.1.

[81] See Directive 2007/63/EC amending Council Directives 78/855/EEC and 82/891/EEC as regards the requirement of an independent expert's report on the occasion of merger or division of public limited liability companies, OJ L 300, 17.11.2007, p 47. Shareholders are given the option to dispense with the required expert reports which are costly and time-consuming to prepare and publish. There is a further proposal for simplification by reducing the reporting obligations imposed by the Directives and allowing documentation to be provided to shareholders via websites and email, see above n 39 and Press Release, IP/08/1407, 25.09.2008.

[82] Directive 2005/56/EC on cross-border mergers of limited liability companies, OJ L 310, 25.11.2005, p 1.

[83] See The Companies (Cross-Border Mergers) Regulations 2007, SI 2007/2974.

[84] Treaty establishing the European Community (Consolidated version) OJ C 325, 24.12.2002, p 33, art 43 provides for freedom of establishment and art 48 requires companies formed in a Member State to be treated in the same way as natural persons who are nationals of Member States.

which were addressed by the European Court of Justice in a series of notable cases, namely the *Centros, Uberseering, Inspire Art* and *Sevic* cases.

In *Centros Ltd v Erhvervs-og Selskabsstyrelsen*, Case C-212/97,[85] a Danish couple set   **2-39**
up and registered a private company in England (which never carried on any activities in England) and then applied to the Danish authorities for permission to operate a branch in Denmark, so circumventing the stricter minimum capital requirements imposed on Danish private companies.[86] The Danish authorities refused to register the branch on the basis that the couple were carrying on their principal establishment in Denmark in breach of national law. The issue was referred to the ECJ which concluded that it is contrary to the right of freedom of establishment for a Member State to refuse to register a branch of a company in these circumstances.

The Treaty provisions on freedom of establishment are intended, the court said, spe-   **2-40**
cifically to enable companies formed in accordance with the law of a Member State and having their registered office, central administration or principal place of business within the Community, to pursue activities in other Member States through an agency, branch or subsidiary. Member States are entitled to take measures to prevent their nationals from attempting, under cover of Treaty rights, improperly to circumvent their national legislation or from improperly or fraudulently taking advantage of Community provisions. The fact that a national of a Member State chooses to form a company in the Member State whose company law rules seem the least restrictive and to set up branches in other Member States does not, in itself, however, constitute an abuse of the right of establishment.

This position was strengthened by the ruling in the *Uberseering*[87] case where the   **2-41**
ECJ confirmed that Member States must recognise companies incorporated in other Member States without further formality and without any need for the Member States to enter into conventions concerning the mutual recognition of companies. In *Uberseering* the company had been incorporated in the Netherlands but came to conduct all of its activities in Germany and all its shareholders were German. When the company tried to sue on a civil matter in Germany, it was denied locus standi on the basis that it had no legal capacity in Germany, not having been incorporated there. The ECJ held that the failure to recognise the company's standing and effectively to require its reincorporation in Germany was an infringement of the freedom of establishment and incompatible with arts 43 and 48 of the EC Treaty.

A strategy which some Member States adopted to maintain some control over these   **2-42**
companies (sometimes described as pseudo-foreign or formally foreign companies) was not to deny recognition to the entity validly incorporated under the law of another Member State, but to impose additional constraints on them when the formally

---

[85] [1999] ECR I-1459, [2000] 2 BCLC 68, ECJ.

[86] The minimum capital requirement at the time was D Kr 200,000 since reduced to D Kr 125,000 (€17,000).

[87] *Uberseering BV v Nordic Construction Co Baumanagement Gmbh (NCC)* Case C-208/00 [2002] ECR I-9919, [2005] 1 WLR 315, ECJ.

foreign company carried on all or most of their activities in their Member State (as in *Centros*). In *Inspire Art Ltd*[88] the ECJ concluded that such measures also infringe the right of freedom of establishment.

2-43   In *Inspire Art* the company was incorporated in England but its sole director was based in, and all its activities were conducted in, the Netherlands. The Dutch authorities tried to subject this formally foreign company to disclosure and minimum capital requirements which would put it on a footing similar to companies incorporated in the Netherlands. A failure to comply would result in personal liability for the directors so denying them the protection of limited liability despite the business having been incorporated as a limited liability company. The court considered this attempt to impose capital requirements to be a breach of freedom of establishment in that it made it restrictive and therefore less attractive. In so far as disclosure requirements could be imposed, the ECJ held, they were limited to the requirements of the Eleventh Company Law Directive on disclosure by branches which adequately protected the interests of creditors in the Netherlands by ensuring that they were aware of the status and nature of the foreign company.

2-44   The ECJ accepted, as it had in *Überseering*,[89] that in certain circumstances and under certain conditions the protection of creditors, minority shareholders and employees[90] and the preservation of the effectiveness of fiscal supervision and the fairness of commercial transactions may justify measures restricting the freedom of establishment.[91] But measures restricting the fundamental freedoms must fulfil four conditions: they must be applied in a non-discriminatory manner; they must be justified by imperative requirements in the general interest; they must be suitable for securing the attainment of the objective which they pursue; and they must not go beyond what is necessary in order to attain it.[92] In *Überseering*, however, creditor protection did not demand measures beyond disclosure.

2-45   The latest stage in this emerging jurisprudence is the decision in *Re Sevic Systems AG*[93] where the German authorities refused to register a merger between a Luxembourg company and a Germany company on the basis that the German registration provisions applied only to mergers between two German companies. The ECJ held that a difference in treatment of mergers according to whether they were internal within a Member State or of a cross-border nature between a company formed in one Member State and a company formed in another was a measure likely

---

[88] *Kamer van Koophandel en Fabrieken voor Amsterdam v Inspire Art Ltd* Case C-167/01, [2003] ECR I-10155, [2005] 3 CMLR 34.

[89] See [2005] 1 WLR 315 at 348.

[90] As to whether measures to protect employee rights of co-determination, as in Germany, might be acceptable, see Johnston, 'EC Freedom of Establishment: Employee Participation in Corporate Governance and the limits of Regulatory Competition' (2006) 6 JCLS 71.

[91] [2006] 2 BCLC 510 at 529, para 28.

[92] *Gebhard v Consiglio dell'Ordine degli Avvocati e Procuratori di Milano* Case C-55/94 [1996] All ER (EC) 189, [1995] ECR I-4165 (para 37).

[93] Case C-411/03 [2006] 2 BCLC 510, ECJ; and see Siems, 'Sevic: Beyond Cross-Border Mergers' (2007) 8 EBOR 307.

to hinder cross-border mergers and to deter the exercise of the freedom of establishment. The result in *Sevic* has been overtaken by the adoption of the Tenth Company Law Directive on cross-border mergers[94] which requires Member States to recognise such mergers and determines how such mergers are to be conducted.

Side by side with these decisions upholding the right of freedom of establishment has been extensive tax litigation before the ECJ (beyond the scope of this work) where Member States have sought to restrict, in particular, the ability of large groups to structure their activities through subsidiaries etc in a way that attracts the lowest rates of corporation and other taxes. The ECJ has identified national tax measures discriminating between resident and non-resident activities and structures also as a restriction and inhibition on the freedom of establishment.[95] The effect of these measures is to constrain the location of a company's activities and so inhibit corporate mobility. In addition therefore to the need for 'incoming' Member States to recognise the legal entity seeking to exercise its rights of freedom of establishment within that Member State, Member States must also ensure that they do not impose barriers, whether through taxation or other exit obligations, which restrict the ability of their own companies to exit the jurisdiction in exercise of their rights of freedom of establishment.[96]   **2-46**

The net result of this activist jurisprudence from the ECJ is that there is now a considerable measure of corporate mobility within the EU, so much so that the European Commission has decided that it is no longer necessary to proceed with a proposed Fourteenth Company Law Directive allowing for the cross-border transfer of the registered office of limited companies.[97] The same result can be achieved by the mechanisms outlined above, especially by the use of a cross-border merger whereby the company which wishes to move to another jurisdiction can now set up a company in that other jurisdiction, merge the existing company into that new company, and dissolve the first company, so effecting a transfer of the business and the registered office to the new jurisdiction.[98] It is also possible for a European Company, subject to detailed formalities, to transfer its registered office.[99] Critics would argue that companies should not need   **2-47**

---

[94] Directive 2005/56, OJ L 310, 25.11.2005, pp 1–9. See The Companies (Cross-Border Mergers) Regulations 2007, SI 2007/2974.

[95] See, for example, *Cadbury Schweppes plc v Inland Revenue Commissioners* (C-196/04) [2007] 1 CMLR 2; *Marks & Spencer plc v Halsey (Inspector of Taxes)* (C-446/03) [2005] ECR I-10837, [2006] 1 CMLR 18, ECJ. For a comprehensive review of the activist role of the ECJ in taxation, see Kingston, 'A Light In The Darkness: Recent Developments in the ECJ's Direct Tax Jurisprudence' (2007) 44 CML Rev 1321.

[96] See Vossestein, 'Exit restrictions on Freedom of Establishment after Marks & Spencer' (2006) 7 EBOR 863.

[97] Following consideration of an impact assessment of the proposed Directive published in December 2007, Commissioner McCreevy decided there was no need to proceed with EU action on this matter, see at http://ec.europa.eu/internal_market/company/seat-transfer/index_en.htm.

[98] See Siems, 'Sevic: Beyond Cross-Border Mergers' (2007) 8 EBOR 307.

[99] See Council Regulation 2157/2001 on the Statute for the European Company, OJ L 294, 10.11.2001, pp 1–21, art 8. A major limitation on the process is that the SE's registered office and head office must be in the same Member State (see art 7); also Ringe, 'The European Company Statute in the Context of Freedom of Establishment' (2007) 7 JCLS 185. The ECJ has ruled that the freedoms established by art 43 EC and art 48 EC (see n 84 above) do not prevent a Member State from precluding a company incorporated under the law of that Member State from transferring its seat to another Member State while retaining its status as a company

to use such 'detour' mechanisms but should be offered a straightforward mechanism for the transfer of the registered offices and so a Directive is still needed,[100] but the Commission is not persuaded.

2-48   To sum up, businesses may choose where to incorporate and that choice may be dictated, especially for smaller companies, by considerations such as whether (and, if so, the level at which) a minimum share capital is required. Once incorporated in Member State A: (1) that company must be recognised as such in all other Member States, even if it conducts no business in the state of incorporation (*Uberseering*); (2) that company can choose to operate in another Member State either through a subsidiary, branch or agency (*Centros*); (3) where the choice is to act through a branch, the Member State cannot impose obligations on the branch equivalent to those imposed on businesses incorporated in that Member State (*Inspire Art*).

2-49   One consequence of the *Centros* line of authorities has been that some Member States have moved to liberalise their domestic requirements and speed up their formation processes in order to compete with this jurisdiction which is seen as having the lowest entry requirements with minimum formalities (as discussed in Chapter 1) and, of course, no minimum share capital requirement for private companies. In France, for example, the minimum capital requirement for SARLs (a type of company equivalent to a private company here) was removed while Germany brought forward legislation to modernise the law governing private limited companies (GmbH).[101]

2-50   While there have been concerns that the *Centros* jurisprudence will lead to a degree of forum shopping by businesses (most matters are determined by the law of the place of incorporation), in practice, different languages, business cultures and legal systems constrain the choice of place of incorporation which is also much influenced by tax considerations.[102] Indeed it may be that true mobility, at least in terms of legal requirements, does require a European Private Company Statute as is now proposed and is discussed below at **2-57**. Equally, concerns that the outcome will be a 'race to laxity' or a 'race to the bottom' (i.e. that Member States in their anxiety to appear attractive

governed by the law of the Member State of incorporation: *Cartesio Oktato* (Case C-210/06), 16 December 2008, ECJ, OJC 44, 21.02.2009, p 31.

[100] See Wymeersch, 'Is a Directive on Corporate Mobility needed?' (2007) 8 EBOR 161; also Mucciarelli, 'Company "Emigration" and EC Freedom of Establishment: Daily Mail Revisited' (2008) 9 EBOR 267; and see *Cartesio Oktato*, N 99.

[101] For an interesting account of the German changes, see Noack and Beurskens, 'Modernising the German GmbH—Mere Window Dressing or Fundamental Redesign' (2008) 9 EBOR 97; also Seibert, 'Close Corporations—Reforming Private Company Law: European and International Perspectives' (2007) EBOR 83. The reformed GmbH Act also provides for a new category of GmbH (an UG in German), but popularly known as the 'mini-GmbH', which can be started with a capital of just €1. The UG must put aside one quarter of annual profits to allow its share capital to grow to the GmbH level. Once this level has been reached, the accumulated capital can be converted into share capital and the UG can then change its name to a GmbH.

[102] See generally Lowry, 'Eliminating Obstacles to Freedom of establishment: The Competitive Edge of UK Company Law' (2004) CLJ 331.

to business will cease to impose protections necessary for shareholders and creditors) have failed to materialise.[103]

C European structures

In addition to facilitating movement between Member States and takeovers across   **2-51** jurisdictions, the Commission has also looked to create new European structures. An example is the European Economic Interest Grouping (EEIG) which can be established between two or more trading entities based in different Member States.[104] It is of limited appeal as is clear from the fact that, as of 31 March 2008, there were just 205 on the register.[105] The reason for its limited appeal is that its activities have to be ancillary to the activities of its members (so it is confined to areas such as research, marketing or training) and it cannot be profit-making in its own right.

The European Company (SE)

After decades of discussion,[106] agreement was reached in 2001 on the European   **2-52** Company, the Societas Europaea (SE), with a Council Regulation providing for the European Company Statute[107] while a Council Directive supplements the statute and makes provision for the involvement of employees.[108]

An SE may be formed in one of four ways: **2-53**

- by the merger of two or more existing public limited companies from at least two different EU Member States;

---

[103] For an interesting account of this issue, often contrasted with the Delaware syndrome (Delaware being the US State which attracts the greatest number of incorporations as a result of ensuring that its corporate law is seen as the most attractive to business), see Drury, 'The "Delaware Syndrome": European Fears and Reactions' [2005] JBL 709; also Gelter, 'The Structure of Regulatory Competition in European Corporate Law' (2005) 5 JCLS 247; Lowry, above n 102.

[104] See Council Regulation EEC/2137/85, OJ L 199, 31.7.1985, p 1; and the European Economic Interest Grouping Regulations 1989, SI 1989/638. See generally Keegan, 'The European Economic Interest Grouping' [1991] JBL 457.

[105] See *Statistical Tables on Companies Registration Activities 2007–08*, Table E3, available on Companies House website at www.companieshouse.gov.uk/about/companiesRegActivities.shtml.

[106] For the history of the proposal, see Edwards, *EC Company Law* (1999) pp 399–404. First proposed by the Commission in 1970, discussions over the years were dogged by controversy over issues such as the interface between national and European law, the appropriate taxation regime and, most particularly, by an inability to reach agreement on the appropriate provisions for employee involvement.

[107] Council Regulation (EC) No 2157/2001 on the Statute for a European Company (SE), OJ L 294, 10.11.2001, p 1. Implemented by The European Public Limited-Liability Company Regulations 2004, SI 2004/2326.

[108] Council Directive 2001/86/EC supplementing the Statute for a European Company with regard to the involvement of employees, OJ L 294, 10.11.2001, p 22.

- by the formation of a holding company promoted by public or private limited companies from at least two different Member States;
- by the formation of a subsidiary of companies from at least two different Member States;
- by the transformation of a public limited company which has, for at least two years, had a subsidiary in another Member State.

2-54   An SE must have a minimum share capital of €120,000. The board of directors can be organised either on the basis of a supervisory and a management board or as a unitary board. The registered office of an SE must be in the same Member State as its head office and the registered office can be transferred to another Member State without the need to wind up the company. The provisions contained in the accompanying Directive on worker involvement are complex, given that they are the result of decades of negotiations designed to accommodate the very differing views on this issue across the Member States. Essentially, levels of worker participation in the pre-existing entities must be replicated in the SE but, if there were none, the SE need not make provision for any such participation, though there are default rules as to the provision of information to and consultation with employees.

2-55   The laws applicable to the SE are those laid down in the Regulation and Directive and where no provision is made (and no provision is made on matters such as capital maintenance, directors' duties, shareholders rights and insolvency), the matter is governed by the laws applicable to public companies of the Member State in which the SE has its registered office. The result is an element of uncertainty as to the applicable law, but given the significance of the matters governed by the law of the Member State of the registered office, these entities begin to look like national public companies, which is a long way from the concept of a European company as originally envisaged.

2-56   It is also the case that the SE has been somewhat overtaken by other developments, such as the breadth of the freedom of establishment articulated by the European Court of Justice, discussed above at **2-38** et seq, and the ease of transfer between Member States as a result of the Tenth Company Law Directive on Cross-Border Mergers, noted above at **2-37**. The Commission has made considerable strides also in devising a package of uniform obligations with respect to publicly traded companies, not just in terms of disclosure and corporate governance as discussed above, but with regard to other matters, such as public offers of shares.[109] The result is that the existing structures may facilitate operations across the EU without the need for a specific European Company. Certainly, the SE has not proved attractive in this jurisdiction[110] although it has been used to some extent in other Member States.[111]

---

[109] See Directive 2003/71/EC on the prospectus to be published when securities are offered to the public or admitted to trading, OJ L 345, 31.12.2003, p 64.

[110] At 31 March 2008, there were five SEs on the register at Companies House: see n 105 above.

[111] The European Trade Union Institute which monitors SEs reports that, as of July 2008, almost 200 SEs have been established in a total of 18 EU member states (including the EEA), but that only a small fraction of these (45) can be considered 'normal SEs' in the sense that they have business activities and employees

The European Private Company (SPE)

The complexity of the European Company means that it is unlikely to prove attract-   **2-57**
ive to small and medium-sized enterprises and it was never envisaged that it might be
appropriate for such entities. Instead the idea has been mooted for many years that
the Commission should consider a European Private Company Statute. As part of the
Company Law Action Plan, therefore, the Commission did initiate a feasibility study
on the issue in 2005.[112] The results were divided but the idea gathered momentum with
support from the European Parliament[113] and the Small Business Act announced by
the Commission in June 2008 (see **2-19**) included a proposal for a Regulation on the
Statute for a European Private Company.[114]

The key aspects of a Societas Privata Europaea (SPE), as currently proposed, include   **2-58**
the following:

- It is to be a private company limited by shares, with a minimum share capital of
  €1 and a name ending in 'SPE'.

- It may be formed from scratch or created from another form and it may be formed
  by one or more persons.

- It may be registered in any Member State and its registered office and centre of
  activities may be in different Member States. It may transfer its registered office
  without winding up.

- It need not initially have any cross-border activities or connections.

- The legal framework for the SPE is provided by the Statute so ensuring uniform
  rules across the EU, but the detailed regulation of the internal working arrangements within the SPE is a matter for the articles, though the content of the articles
  is prescribed to some extent by the Statute and the Commission is likely to provide model articles to assist small companies in using this structure.

- For matters not governed by the Statute or the articles, the law of the Member
  State in which the SPE is registered will apply.

The Commission envisages that the proposed Regulation will come into force on 1 July   **2-59**
2010. As with the SE, it is not clear that there is demand for this structure given, as the

---

(of these 19 are headquartered in Germany). See at www.worker-participation.eu/european_company/
se_companies.

[112] See Feasibility Study of a European Statute for SMEs (2005) available at http://ec.europa.eu/
internal_market/company/epc/index_en.htm.

[113] See Report of the European Parliament, Committee for Legal Affairs, with recommendations to the
Commission on the European private company statute, A6–0434/2006, 29.11.2006.

[114] See the *Proposal For A Council Regulation On The Statute For A European Private Company*, COM
(2008) 396, 25.06.2008. See Drury 'The European Private Company' (2008) 9 EBOR 125. A leading proponent of the idea, Drury comments (at 130) that, amongst its attractions, the SPE would provide a uniform
structure for a Europe-wide group of companies, would facilitate inward investment by providing a vehicle
that can operate in and move to any part of the Union under a single set of rules, and would give a European
identity to businesses for marketing purposes.

Commission itself conceded and is acknowledged by the proposal, most small businesses have no interest in cross-border trading and are reasonably content with the range of business vehicles offered by their domestic jurisdiction. It might be attractive to businesses from jurisdictions with high minimum share capital requirements, especially since it need not actually engage in any cross-border activities (at least under the current proposal), but as noted above many jurisdictions have already reformed their laws to abolish or significantly reduce the minimum share capital required. After initial enthusiasm, interest in the proposal for an SPE seems to have diminished and its future is uncertain.

3

Corporate personality

A A separate legal entity

The *Salomon* principle

On incorporation, a company becomes a separate legal entity distinct and separate **3-1** from its shareholders and it is not the agent of those shareholders, not even if it is a one-man company with one shareholder controlling all its activities. This fundamental principle of company law was established by the House of Lords in *Salomon v Salomon & Co Ltd*.[1]

In this case, Mr Salomon sold his shoe business to a company which he had set up **3-2** for the purpose under the Companies Act 1862. The formalities under the Act (very similar to those still required today) were completed and the members of the company were Salomon, Mrs S and their five children (a minimum of seven members being required at that time).[2] As part of the consideration for the sale of the business, Mr Salomon received fully paid-up shares and debentures to the value of £10,000 which he subsequently assigned to another party. In effect, the debentures meant that initially Mr Salomon, and subsequently the assignee, were creditors of the business with first claim on the remaining assets should the company go into liquidation, as indeed happened. The company became insolvent and was unable to meet the full claim of the assignee or to meet at all the claims of the other (unsecured) creditors. The liquidator attempted to hold Mr Salomon liable for the debts of the company on a variety of grounds including that the whole transaction was a fraud on the company's creditors from which Salomon should not be allowed to benefit and that the company was simply his agent and he should therefore indemnify the company (and its creditors) with respect to the debts incurred by the company.

At first instance, the court agreed that the company was merely an agent of Salomon **3-3** and therefore, as principal, he was liable for its debts.[3] The Court of Appeal rejected Salomon's appeal and concluded that the formation of the company and the issue of the debentures was a mere scheme to enable Salomon to carry on business in the name

---

[1] [1897] AC 22, HL. See generally Grantham & Rickett (eds), *Corporate Personality in the 20th Century* (1998) which is an interesting collection of essays assessing the modern significance of the decision in *Salomon*.

[2] The CA 2006 permits single member private and public companies: see s 7.

[3] See *Broderip v Salomon* [1895] 2 Ch 323.

of a company with limited liability contrary to the true intent and meaning of the Companies Act 1862. In essence he was a sole trader screening himself from liabilities and as such it was a device to defraud creditors.[4] Lopes LJ noted that 'it would be lamentable if a scheme such as this could not be defeated'.[5]

3-4   On a further appeal by Salomon, the House of Lords concluded that there was nothing untoward with this transaction and it reversed the decision of the lower courts. The company had been duly formed and registered and was not the mere alias or agent of or trustee for Mr Salomon. There was no sham or fraud, the transactions were not contrary to the true intent and meaning of the Companies Act 1862 and Mr Salomon was not liable to indemnify the company against the creditors' claims.

3-5   Lord Macnaghten noted that when the memorandum[6] is duly signed and registered, a body corporate is formed and it cannot lose that status by issuing the bulk of its shares to one person. He went on:[7]

> 'The company is at law a different person altogether from the subscribers to the memorandum; and, though it may be that after incorporation the business is precisely the same as it was before, and the same persons are managers, and the same hands receive the profits, the company is not in law the agent of the subscribers or trustee for them. Nor are the subscribers as members liable, in any shape or form, except to the extent and in the manner provided by the Act.'

3-6   As for the description of these companies as 'one-man companies', Lord Macnaghten said that if that was intended to convey that a company under the absolute control of one person was not a legally incorporated company, it was inaccurate and misleading.[8] Likewise, Lord Halsbury emphasised that the sole guide to matters was the statute which did not enact requirements as to the extent or degree of interests which may be held by the subscribers to the memorandum of association.[9] The House of Lords had little sympathy for the unsecured creditors who had only themselves to blame, having had full notice that they were no longer dealing with an individual.[10]

3-7   The result was that the House of Lords affirmed that a company is not, per se, the agent of its shareholders, even if control is concentrated in only one shareholder. The mere fact that a person owns all the shares in a company does not make the business carried on by that company his business. Once the company is legally incorporated, the company must be treated like any other independent person with rights and liabilities of its own.[11] The effect of the decision was to legitimate the one-man company and to reject the lower courts' views that such a structure was contrary to the legislation.

---

[4] See [1895] 2 Ch 323 at 338–9, per Lindley LJ.   [5] [1895] 2 Ch 323 at 340–1.
[6] See CA 2006, s 8 and **1-24** as to the memorandum of association.   [7] [1897] AC 22 at 51, HL.
[8] [1897] AC 22 at 53.   [9] [1897] AC 22 at 29–30.
[10] See [1897] AC 22 at 53, per Lord Macnaghten; at 45, per Lord Herschell.
[11] [1897] AC 22 at 31, per Lord Halsbury.

A further illustration of this point can be found in *Gramophone & Typewriter Co Ltd* **3-8**
v Stanley.[12] The shares in a German company were owned by an English company. At
issue was whether the business of the German company was really the business of its
English shareholder since, if it was, that exposed the shareholder to a greater tax liability. Given that there was factual evidence that the German company was a real company with a real business, Buckley LJ said that the question became one of whether the
German company was really the agent of the English shareholder. But, he said, it was
well established that the holding of all of the shares does not establish the relationship
of principal and agent between a shareholder and the company. There was no agency
relationship and the business was the business of the German company.

In legitimating the one-man company, the decision in *Salomon* also legitimates the **3-9**
group concept with each subsidiary company being a separate and distinct entity and
not the agent of its controlling or sole shareholder, its parent company.[13] The relationship between a parent and a subsidiary company is the same as between Mr Salomon
and his company. The parent company (i.e. the corporate shareholder in the subsidiary) and the subsidiary company are separate legal entities and each company is entitled to expect that the court will apply the principles of *Salomon v A Salomon & Co
Ltd*[14] in the ordinary way and respect the separate identity of each company in the
group.[15] This is so even if the subsidiary company has a small paid-up capital and a
board of directors all or most of whom are also directors or executives of the parent
company.[16]

Consequences of *Salomon*

As a separate legal entity, separate and distinct from its shareholders, the company **3-10**
must be treated like any other independent person with rights and liabilities appropriate to itself.[17] It is the company which conducts business, it is the company which
enters into contracts and incurs debts. The company can own property and its property is not the property of its main shareholder who cannot insure it,[18] but who can
be charged with stealing from the company.[19] The company can employ people and

---

[12] [1908] 2 KB 89; see also *Tunstall v Steigmann* [1962] 2 QB 593; *Ebbw Vale UDC v South Wales Traffic Area
Licensing Authority* [1951] 2 KB 366.

[13] *Salomon v Salomon & Co Ltd* [1897] AC 22; *The Albazero* [1977] AC 774 at 807, HL, per Roskill LJ; *Bank
of Tokyo Ltd v Karoon* [1987] AC 45 at 64, CA; *Adams v Cape Industries plc* [1990] BCLC 479 at 519–20. The
definition of holding (parent) and subsidiary company is set out in CA 2006, s 1159, and see the discussion
of corporate groups at **1-67** et seq.

[14] [1897] AC 22, HL.

[15] *Adams v Cape Industries plc* [1990] BCLC 479 at 520, CA; *Ord v Belhaven Pubs Ltd* [1998] 2 BCLC 447
at 458, CA.

[16] See *Re Polly Peck International plc (No 3)* [1996] BCLC 428 at 441, per Robert Walker J (despite a subsidiary company having negligible capital, no separate management, and the most minimal role in certain
bond issues, the court did not accept that it was an agent of its parent company).

[17] *Salomon v Salomon & Co Ltd* [1897] AC 22, HL; see also *Maclaine Watson & Co Ltd v International Tin
Council* [1989] 3 All ER 523 at 531.

[18] *Macaura v Northern Assurance Co* [1925] AC 619, HL.

[19] *A-G's Reference (No 2 of 1982)* [1984] QB 624, CA.

can even employ its controlling shareholder.[20] The company has perpetual existence and succession and this continuity is important and convenient. The membership may be constantly changing but the entity continues until steps are taken to bring it to an end through winding up. Equally, the company can sue and be sued in its own name and this is advantageous to third parties who do not have to concern themselves with identifying who are the shareholders at any given moment. Most important of all, the debts are the debts of the company and not of the shareholders whose only obligation is to contribute to the company's assets such amount, if any, unpaid on the shares held by them (CA 2006, s 3(2)). Ultimately, it is the company which may go into insolvency.

3-11   Sometimes the fact that the company is a distinct legal entity works to the shareholder's disadvantage and the courts are unwilling to allow a shareholder to elect to have the benefits without the disadvantages of incorporation.[21] This is particularly true with regard to attempts by shareholders to claim for what is termed reflective loss, i.e. losses suffered by shareholders which are only reflective of loss suffered by the company and in respect of which the company should sue. In keeping with the separate legal personality of the company, the rule in *Foss v Harbottle*[22] establishes that where a wrong is done to the company, the company is the proper plaintiff in respect of it. It follows that a personal claim by a shareholder in respect of the diminution in value of his shareholding as a result of a wrong done to the company (for example, where the company has a claim in negligence against a third party) is misconceived and will be struck out. The shareholder's loss is merely reflective of the loss suffered by the company and that loss will be fully remedied if the company enforces its full rights against the wrongdoer.[23] This principle respects company autonomy and ensures that a party (the shareholder) does not recover compensation for a loss suffered by another (the

---

[20] See *Lee v Lee's Air Farming Ltd* [1961] AC 12 where a controlling shareholder was a 'worker' for workers' compensation purposes when he was killed in the course of his work. See also *Secretary of State for Trade and Industry v Bottrill* [2000] 2 BCLC 448, CA: a controlling shareholder of a company can be an employee of the company for the purposes of redundancy payments from the National Insurance Fund under the Employment Rights Act 1996, s 166, but whether such an employer/employee relationship exists depends on the facts of the particular case; see also *Venables v Hornby (Inspector of Taxes)* [2004] 1 All ER 627; *Gladwell v Secretary of State for Trade and Industry* [2007] ICR 264, EAT.

[21] See, for example, *Diamantides v JP Morgan Chase Bank* [2005] All ER (D) 404 (Feb), where the claimant began an action alleging essentially that the defendant bank owed him a duty of care. Through P Ltd, he had purchased high risk investments from the bank which had proved disastrous. He was the sole shareholder and controller of P Ltd and he provided it with the funds for investment. The court struck out the claim commenting that it regarded the case as an unprincipled attempt by an individual, who chose to invest through a corporate vehicle, to pierce the veil of his own company. The purpose of doing so was to secure (under the statutory scheme as it then was) the additional protection afforded to private investors when in reality P Ltd was the customer. But in a deserving case the courts may be willing to lift the corporate veil to impose fiduciary obligations on an adviser owed not just to the company but to the people behind it: see *Conway v Ratiu* [2006] 1 All ER 571 at 573, para [78], CA; vice versa, where a company owes fiduciary obligations to a client, it is possible for the directors also to owe such duties: see *Satnam Investments Ltd v Dunlop Heywood & Co Ltd* [1999] 1 BCLC 385, CA; *JD Wetherspoon plc v Van de Berg & Co Ltd* [2007] PNLR 28, Ch D.

[22] (1843) 2 Hare 461.

[23] *Prudential Assurance Co Ltd v Newman Industries Ltd (No 2)* [1982] 1 All ER 354 at 366–7; *Johnson v Gore Wood & Co* [2001] 1 BCLC 313, HL; see **18–61**.

company).[24] This issue of reflective loss is discussed in detail in Chapter 18, as is the rule in *Foss v Harbottle*.

B Exceptions to the separate entity principle

While the fundamental principle is that a company is an entity distinct from, and not the agent of, its shareholders, there are exceptions to the principle, namely: **3-12**

(1) where, on the facts, an agency relationship does exist between a company and its shareholders; and

(2) where the corporate structure is a mere façade concealing the true facts. In this case, the court will disregard the separate legal entity and reach to the shareholders behind, a process described as piercing the corporate veil.

Each is discussed in detail below.

There are also various statutory provisions where, typically for reasons of taxation and financial transparency, the separate legal entity is disregarded. For example, the companies legislation requires parent companies to prepare consolidated group accounts showing the affairs of the parent and subsidiary undertakings.[25] Other provisions, such as IA 1986, s 214 (liability for wrongful trading), are often described as examples of statutory piercing of the corporate veil, but they are not true piercing provisions in the sense that the corporate entity is discarded and liability attached to the members of the company. Rather, they are provisions which impose liabilities on directors as a consequence of their involvement in the running of a company.   **3-13**

An agency relationship

Although *Salomon v Salomon & Co Ltd*[26] establishes that a company is not, per se, the agent of its shareholders, it may be that, on the particular facts, an agency relationship can be established between a company and its shareholders.[27] This may be the case as between a company and individual shareholders but it more commonly arises in the group context where sometimes it can be advantageous for a parent company to plead that a subsidiary company is a mere agent of the parent. Of course, as a general rule, a parent company would wish to reject any agency relationship to ensure that no liability attaches to it for the subsidiary's debts.   **3-14**

A classic agency example is *Smith, Stone & Knight Ltd v Birmingham Corp*[28] where at issue was the compensation for compulsory purchase payable by a local authority when the property of a subsidiary company was acquired. To maximise the compensation   **3-15**

---

[24] *Johnson v Gore Wood & Co* [2001] 1 BCLC 313 at 338, per Lord Bingham, HL.
[25] See CA 2006, ss 399, 403–406.   [26] [1897] AC 22, HL.
[27] See *Gramophone & Typewriter Ltd v Stanley* [1908] 2 KB 89 at 96, 100.   [28] [1939] 4 All ER 116.

payable, the parent company on this occasion was happy to argue that the subsidiary carried on business as agent for the parent.

3-16   Atkinson J said that whether there is an agency relationship is a question of fact in each case. The question is whether the subsidiary is carrying on the business as the parent company's business or as its own.[29] Atkinson J identified a variety of factors which he thought relevant to the determination of that issue, namely who was really carrying on the business, who received the profits, who was actually conducting the business, who appointed those persons, who was the head and brains of the venture and who was in effective and constant control of the business.

3-17   Having reviewed the facts,[30] the court agreed that the arrangement here between the parent and subsidiary was such that the business and profits belonged as a matter of law to the parent company. Atkinson J thought the subsidiary in this instance was a legal entity and nothing more, so comprehensive was the parent company's control and conduct of the business. As the subsidiary was not operating on its own behalf, but on behalf of the parent company, the parent company was the party entitled to claim compensation. While the facts were exceptional, the case confirms that it is possible for an agency relationship to exist between a company (the agent) and its shareholders (the principal).

3-18   In *Re FG (Films) Ltd*,[31] a film was made by an English company which claimed the film was a British film in order to attract certain tax advantages. The company had a capital of £100, no premises other than its registered office and no staff. The financing of the film (some £80,000) was provided by an American company which through a nominee held 90% of the company's shares. The court concluded that the film did not qualify as a British film as the company acted at all times as the agent and nominee of the American company and the English company's existence was purely colourable.

3-19   In *Adams v Cape Industries plc*[32] it was argued that certain US subsidiaries were agents of an English parent company such that the English parent company was conducting business in the US. The presence of the English company in the US was necessary if a US court judgment was to be enforced against it. As is clear from the authorities above, it is necessary for the court to look in detail at the relationship between the English parent company and the US subsidiaries to see whether the subsidiaries are carrying on their own businesses or the business of the English parent company.

3-20   With respect to one particular subsidiary,[33] the evidence was that it leased premises, employed people and carried on activities on its own account as principal. It earned

---

[29] [1939] 4 All ER 116 at 121.

[30] The parent company held all (except five) of the shares in the subsidiary company and the profits of the subsidiary were treated as the profits of the parent company. The parent company appointed the persons who conducted the business and it was in effective and constant control of the business.

[31] [1953] 1 All ER 615. See also *Firestone Tyre and Rubber Co Ltd v LLewellin* [1957] 1 All ER 561 (an assessment of tax upheld where business of parent and subsidiary carried on by the subsidiary as agent for the parent).   [32] [1990] BCLC 479.

[33] The subsidiary in this case was NAAC: see the discussion at [1990] BCLC 479 at 520–2.

profits, paid its taxes and had its own debtors and creditors. For all the closeness of the relationship with the English parent company whose products it marketed, it had no power to bind the parent company to any contractual obligation and it never did effect a transaction in a manner such that the parent company became subject to any contractual obligations to any person. The Court of Appeal concluded that it was indisputable that a substantial part of the business carried on by the subsidiary was in every sense its own business.[34] There was no agency relationship with the parent company.

To sum up, applying *Salomon*, a registered company is not, per se, the agent of its shareholders. The mere fact that a person owns all the shares in a company does not make the business carried on by that company his business. It is possible that an agency relationship may arise from the facts, but it must do so from circumstances other than mere control of the company or ownership of its shares. Whether such circumstances exist involves the court in a detailed factual examination in order to determine whether the company is carrying on business on its own account or on the account of a controlling (individual or corporate) shareholder.   **3-21**

Piercing the corporate veil—the mere façade test

The courts will pierce the corporate veil where special circumstances exist indicating that it is a mere façade concealing the true facts, as the House of Lords confirmed in *Woolfson v Strathclyde Regional Council.*[35]   **3-22**

The facts in this case concerned the amount of compensation payable on the compulsory acquisition of certain land by a local authority. The land was owned by W and by S Ltd (W held 20 of the 30 issued shares in S Ltd and his wife held the remaining 10 shares). The land was occupied by C Ltd which carried on its business from there (the shares in C Ltd were held 999 by W and 1 by his wife). W argued that he, C Ltd and S Ltd should all be treated as a single entity embodied by himself who should be regarded as the owner and occupier of the land for compensation purposes.   **3-23**

On appeal, the House of Lords confirmed the rejection of this argument by the lower courts. It is appropriate to pierce the corporate veil only where special circumstances exist indicating that the company is a mere façade concealing the true facts. In this case, there were no grounds for treating the company structure as a mere façade so that W might claim to be treated as the owner and occupier of the land. The company which carried on business from these premises which were to be compulsorily acquired, C Ltd, had no control over the owners of the land who were S Ltd and W. W held only two-thirds of the shares in S Ltd while S Ltd had no interest in C Ltd. W could not be treated as the sole owner of C Ltd since it had not been found that the   **3-24**

---

[34] With regard to another subsidiary (CPC), see the discussion at [1990] BCLC 479 at 523–4, the court thought the facts were even weaker in that it was not a wholly-owned subsidiary but was an independently owned company. While the English company had provided funding for it, it carried on business on its own account and not as agent for the English company.

[35] (1979) 38 P & CR 521, HL. See generally Rixon, 'Lifting the Veil between Holding and Subsidiary Companies' [1986] 102 LQR 415.

one share held by his wife was held by her as his nominee. Accordingly, their Lordships held that there was no basis consonant with principle on which the corporate veil could be pierced to the effect of holding W to have been the true owner of the business of C Ltd or of the assets of S Ltd.[36] As the occupier of the land and the owner of the business carried on there, any direct loss as a result of the compulsory purchase fell on C Ltd and not on W whose claim for compensation was dismissed.

3-25   The mere façade test has been endorsed in numerous cases subsequently including by the Court of Appeal in *Adams v Cape Industries plc*[37] and by Sir Andrew Morritt V-C in *Trustor AB v Smallbone*.[38] In *Trustor* almost £39m had gone missing from the claimant company with £20m ending up in a company, I Ltd, which was essentially a front for S, the former managing director of the claimant company. In order to pursue a claim against S for the £20m, the claimant company needed to pierce the corporate veil to establish that receipt by I Ltd was receipt by S. Applying the test laid down in *Woolfson*, the court found that I Ltd was a device or façade used for the receipt of the claimant company's money which had been misapplied by S in what the court described as inexcusable breaches of his duties as a director of the claimant company. As the veil would be pierced in this case, S had no defence to the claim that he had received the £20m.

3-26   It is somewhat pointless now to argue, though counsel continue to do so, that the corporate veil may be pierced where it is necessary to do so in the interests of justice. The Court of Appeal indicated its reservations about any such principle in *Adams v Cape Industries plc*,[39] a view endorsed by Sir Andrew Morritt V-C in *Trustor AB v Smallbone*.[40] The English courts will pierce the veil only where the company structure is a mere façade concealing the true facts.

Identifying a mere façade

3-27   Over the years, there have been plenty of examples of the courts applying this 'façade' test and of course, sometimes the company literally is a façade, in the sense that it is nothing more than a name. In *Gencor ACP Ltd v Dalby*[41] a director in breach of his fiduciary duty had profited personally by diverting to himself business opportunities which came to him as a director of the company. The company sought to recover the proceeds which had been paid direct to an offshore company wholly owned and controlled by the director who tried to argue that he had not profited personally. Rimer J found that the company had no staff or business and its only function was to receive these profits. In essence, the court said, it was no more than the director's offshore bank account. Rimer J considered that such a company was quite insufficient, in his words, to prevent equity identifying it with the director and he ordered that the company and the director were both accountable for the profits.[42]

---

36 (1979) 38 P & CR 521 at 526.   37 [1990] BCLC 479 at 515.   38 [2001] 2 BCLC 436, Ch D.
39 [1990] BCLC 479 at 512–13.
40 [2001] 2 BCLC 436 at 444–5. See also *Ord v Belhaven Pubs Ltd* [1998] 2 BCLC 447 at 457.
41 [2000] 2 BCLC 734.   42 [2000] 2 BCLC 734 at 744.

More broadly, the authorities have generally provided, as the Court of Appeal acknow-   **3-28**
ledged in *Adams v Cape Industries plc*,[43] 'sparse guidance' as to the principles which
should guide the courts in determining whether particular arrangements amount to
a façade for these purposes.

Without providing a comprehensive definition of these principles, the Court of Appeal   **3-29**
took the opportunity in *Adams v Cape Industries plc*[44] to engage in a lengthy review
of the circumstances in which it is appropriate to pierce the veil. As noted at **3-19**,
this case concerned jurisdictional issues relating to the enforcement of a US judgment
against an English parent company and central to that issue was whether the English
company had been present in the US. Subsidiary companies of the English company
had been active in the US and the issue was whether their presence and activities there
sufficed to render the parent company also present in the US.

The starting point, of course, is *Salomon v Salomon & Co Ltd*:[45] each company is a   **3-30**
separate legal entity from its shareholders, whoever they are, however many there
are, or how few. The presence of the US subsidiaries did not automatically amount to
the presence of the English parent company. At issue was whether the court should
pierce the corporate veil, i.e. whether it should conclude that the company structure
was a mere façade concealing the true facts, applying *Woolfson v Strathclyde Regional
Council*.[46] Following an extensive review of the authorities, the Court of Appeal was
prepared to accept that the essence of those cases where piercing does occur (i.e. where
the structure is a façade) is that they involve situations where a corporate structure has
been used by a defendant to evade:

(1) limitations imposed on his conduct by law;

(2) such rights of relief as third parties already possess against him.[47]

Company structure used to evade limitations imposed on conduct by law   The classic   **3-31**
examples of cases where the veil is pierced because the corporate structure is being used
to evade limitations imposed on the defendant's conduct by law are *Jones v Lipman*[48]
and *Gilford Motor Co Ltd v Horne*.[49]

In *Jones v Lipman*[50] the defendant, in an attempt to evade an order for specific per-   **3-32**
formance, transferred a property to a company which he set up and of which he and
a clerk of his solicitors were the only shareholders and directors. The court ordered

---

[43] [1990] BCLC 479 at 519.

[44] [1990] BCLC 479. The agency arguments in this case were discussed above at **3-19–3-20** where it was
noted that the court concluded that the facts showed that the American subsidiaries carried on business on
their own account.

[45] [1897] AC 22, HL.   [46] (1979) 38 P & CR 521, HL.   [47] [1990] BCLC 479 at 519.

[48] [1962] 1 All ER 442.   [49] [1933] Ch 935, CA.

[50] [1962] 1 All ER 442. See also *Re Bugle Press Ltd* [1961] Ch 270 where a company was formed solely to
facilitate the expropriation of minority shareholders in another company by use of CA 1985, s 429, now
CA 2006, s 979, which allows an offeror who has acquired 90% of the shares to compulsorily acquire the
remaining 10% in certain circumstances. It was held that the incorporation was an abuse of the statutory
provisions.

specific performance against the company since it was merely a mask used by the defendant to try to evade his obligations. In *Gilford Motor Co Ltd v Horne*[51] a director of a company was subject to a restraint of trade provision on leaving the company. Subsequently, he wished to carry on a competing business in breach of that contractual provision and he did so through a company set up with his wife and an employee as directors and shareholders. The court held that the company was formed as a device to mask the carrying on of business by the defendant in breach of his pre-existing legal duty and an injunction was granted against the company and the defendant.

3-33   A further illustration is *Re H*[52] where Customs and Excise were able to get restraining orders preventing various individuals and companies owned by them from dealing with their realisable property. Customs and Excise considered that the parties had been engaged in excise fraud in a sum estimated to be in excess of £100m. The defendants argued that the receiver appointed by Customs and Excise could not treat the assets of the companies as the realisable property of the individual shareholders. The Court of Appeal held that where the defendant uses the corporate structure as a device or façade to conceal his criminal activities, the court may lift the corporate veil and treat the assets of the company as the realisable property of the defendants. Stock held in the company's warehouses and the companies' motor vehicles could therefore be treated as the property of the defendants.

3-34   As the Court of Appeal emphasised in *Adams v Cape Industries plc*,[53] and as is obvious from the facts above, the motive of the defendant is a significant element for the court to consider. In each of the cases above, the motive behind the use of the corporate structure was patently improper.

3-35   *Company structure used to evade rights of relief which third parties already possess*   In some instances, the corporate structure is simply interposed belatedly as an attempt by the defendant to evade rights of relief which third parties already possess against him. For example, in *Re a Company*[54] a chain of companies was used by the defendant to put assets out of the reach of the plaintiffs after proceedings against the defendant had been commenced. It was held that the veil would be pierced to enable the plaintiffs to pursue the assets.[55] In *Trustor AB v Smallbone*,[56] discussed at **3-25**, the court pierced the veil where a company was used by a director to conceal his receipt of money extracted improperly by him from the claimant company. In *Kensington International Ltd v Republic of Congo*[57] the court pierced the corporate veil with respect to a variety of companies used to disguise the sale of oil by the Republic of the Congo. Sales were

---

[51] [1933] Ch 935, CA.   [52] [1996] 2 BCLC 500, CA.   [53] [1990] BCLC 479 at 516, 518, CA.

[54] [1985] BCLC 333, CA. Although the court reached the correct conclusion in this case, it did so on the now discredited ground that the court had a jurisdiction to pierce the veil in the interests of justice (see at 338).

[55] See also *BCCI SA v BRS Kumar Bros Ltd* [1994] 1 BCLC 211 where a company shifted assets to another company to avoid the reach of charges granted to creditors of the first company. Held: a receiver would be appointed over the assets of the second company which was arguably nothing more than the first company in a new guise.

[56] [2001] 2 BCLC 436.   [57] [2006] 2 BCLC 296.

conducted through a series of companies which were set up to conceal the identity of the Congo as seller and the fact that it was the recipient of the proceeds of sale. These structures were adopted so as to avoid, so far as possible, attachment of the oil or of the proceeds of sale by existing creditors of the Congo in circumstances where it was known that the creditors were taking aggressive action with a view to enforcing the Congo's debts.

On the other hand, the court declined to lift the veil on this basis in *Ord v Belhaven Pubs Ltd*.[58] The plaintiffs brought an action in 1991 against the defendants alleging that the defendants had misrepresented the turnover and profitability of a public house which the plaintiffs had leased from them. Subsequently, the plaintiffs sought leave to substitute the parent company for the original defendant (subsidiary) company since, following a restructuring of the group assets in 1992, the original defendant no longer had substantial assets.   **3-36**

The Court of Appeal held that, while the court has jurisdiction to pierce the corporate veil where a company is a mere façade concealing the true facts, no evidence existed of any such façade here. There was no impropriety alleged in the group restructuring, no transfer away of assets of the defendant company at an undervalue, and no improper motive. The restructuring was a normal attempt to rationalise the group's operating structure in the light of recessionary market circumstances and had not been undertaken in order to evade any liability towards the plaintiffs. In the absence of any impropriety, sham or concealment in the restructuring of the group, the court said it would be wrong to lift the corporate veil in order to make the shareholders of the company (i.e. the parent company) liable instead of the subsidiary company.   **3-37**

Rights of relief which third parties may in future acquire   Having identified the basis on which it is appropriate to pierce the corporate veil, the Court of Appeal in *Adams v Cape Industries plc*[59] was emphatic that the veil should not be pierced where the corporate structure is used to evade such rights of relief as third parties may in the future acquire. Slade LJ noted:[60]   **3-38**

> '...we do not accept as a matter of law that the court is entitled to lift the corporate veil as against a defendant company which is the member of a corporate group merely because the corporate structure has been used so as to ensure that the legal liability (if any) in respect of particular future activities of the group (and correspondingly the risk of enforcement of that liability) will fall on another member of the group rather than the defendant company. Whether or not this is desirable, the right to use a corporate structure in this way is inherent in our corporate law.'

Counsel had argued that the veil should be pierced because the purpose of the group structure in *Adams* was that the English parent company could trade in the US through the subsidiaries without running the risk of tortious liability with respect to its asbestos trade. Slade LJ acknowledged that this might indeed be the purpose of the   **3-39**

---

[58] [1998] 2 BCLC 447, CA.   [59] [1990] BCLC 479 at 516, 518.   [60] [1990] BCLC 479 at 520.

structure adopted, but he went on:[61]

> '...in our judgment, Cape [the English company] was in law entitled to organise the group's affairs in that manner and...to expect that the court would apply the principle in *Salomon v Salomon & Co Ltd* [1897] AC 22 in the ordinary way.'

C The corporate group—separate entities or single unit

Separate legal entities

3-40   As noted, the decision in *Salomon v Salomon & Co Ltd*[62] legitimated the one-man company and from that evolved the modern phenomenon of the corporate group with subsidiary companies owned by corporate shareholders, each also a separate legal entity from its shareholders.

3-41   Shareholding alone does not make an entity the agent of the shareholder, whether that shareholder be an individual or another company and, as discussed, the English courts have been robust in their application of the *Salomon* principle in the group context. As the Court of Appeal commented in *Adams v Cape Industries plc*:[63]

> '...save in cases which turn on the wording of particular statutes or contracts, the court is not free to disregard the principle of *Salomon v Salomon & Co Ltd* merely because it considers that justice so requires. Our law, for better or worse, recognises the creation of subsidiary companies, which though in one sense the creatures of their parent companies, will nevertheless under the general law fall to be treated as separate legal entities with all the rights and liabilities which would normally attach to separate legal entities....'

3-42   The clear position in this jurisdiction is that companies in a group of companies are separate legal entities and are not the agents of their controlling shareholder. Equally, as noted, there are exceptions to the general principle, namely agency and piercing the corporate veil. It is possible that there is an agency relationship between a subsidiary and a parent company such that the subsidiary is acting as an agent for the parent company, as we saw in *Smith, Stone & Knight Ltd v Birmingham Corp*,[64] at **3-15**. Equally, the corporate veil may be pierced where the subsidiary company is a mere façade concealing the true facts.[65] Applying *Salomon*, however, the fact that the shares are wholly within the control of one shareholder does not make the company a façade nor, as discussed at **3-38**, is a group structure a façade where it is set up with a view to minimising liabilities which might arise in the future.[66]

---

[61] [1990] BCLC 479 at 520.   [62] [1897] AC 22, HL.   [63] [1990] BCLC 479 at 513.
[64] [1939] 4 All ER 116.   [65] *Woolfson v Strathclyde Regional Council* (1979) 38 P & CR 521, HL.
[66] See *Adams v Cape Industries plc* [1990] BCLC 479 at 520.

It is sometimes suggested that this adherence to a strict *Salomon* approach, affording **3-43** separate legal status to each entity, is inappropriate in the modern business world where much commercial activity is carried on in corporate groups in a way which could not have been envisaged in 1897. Various alternative approaches have been proposed from time to time such as, for example, that the courts should allow the corporate veil to be pierced more freely in the group context. More fundamentally, it is argued that the law should develop a mechanism whereby obligations and responsibilities could attach to the group and not to individual companies. In this way, the law would reflect the economic reality which is that these companies trade as a group, raise capital as a group, and are considered by those dealing with them to be a group.

While some support for the development of a group enterprise law was offered by Lord **3-44** Denning MR in *DHN Food Distributors Ltd v Tower Hamlets LBC*,[67] it was robustly rejected by the House of Lords in *Woolfson v Strathclyde Regional Council*[68] which doubted whether the Court of Appeal had applied the correct principle in *DHN*. Generally, the English courts have shown a strong determination not to embark on any such development. In *Adams v Cape Industries plc*[69] Slade LJ noted:

> 'There is no general principle that all companies in a group of companies are to be regarded as one. On the contrary, the fundamental principle is that "each company in a group of companies (a relatively modern concept) is a separate legal entity possessed of separate legal rights and liabilities": see *The Albazero* [1975] 3 All ER 21 at 28, [1977] AC 774 at 807 per Roskill LJ.'

Slade LJ went on:[70] **3-45**

> 'We agree…that the observations of Robert Goff LJ in *Bank of Tokyo Ltd v Karoon* [1986] 3 All ER 468 at 485, [1987] AC 45 at 64 are apposite:
>
> > "Counsel suggested beguilingly that it would be technical for us to distinguish between parent and subsidiary company in this context; economically, he said, they were one. But we are concerned not with economics but with law. The distinction between the two is, in law, fundamental and cannot here be bridged."'

Pressed to regard a group of companies as a separate economic unit in *Re Polly Peck* **3-46** *International plc (No 3)*,[71] Robert Walker J concluded that he could not accede to that submission for it would create a new exception to the *Salomon* principle unrecognised by the Court of Appeal in *Adams v Cape Industries plc*,[72] something which was not open to the court.[73] A further rebuttal of the idea that a group of companies might be regarded as a single unit can be found in *Ord v Belhaven Pubs Ltd*,[74] discussed at **3-36**. It will be recalled that the case involved an attempt by the plaintiffs to substitute the original defendant subsidiary company with either its parent company or another wholly-owned subsidiary in the group as, following a restructuring of the group, the original defendant no longer had substantial assets. The Court of Appeal noted that

---

[67] [1976] 3 All ER 462 at 467, CA. The other judges decided the case on a narrower basis.
[68] (1979) 38 P & CR 521.   [69] [1990] BCLC 479 at 508.   [70] [1990] BCLC 479 at 514.
[71] [1996] 1 BCLC 428.   [72] [1990] BCLC 479.   [73] [1996] 1 BCLC 428 at 444.
[74] [1998] 2 BCLC 447, CA.

the trial judge (who had permitted the substitution of the defendants) appeared to have viewed the whole group as an economic entity and therefore thought substitution was appropriate. Hobhouse LJ emphatically rejected this approach, noting:[75]

> 'The approach of the judge in the present case was simply to look at the economic unit, to disregard the distinction between the legal entities which were involved and to say: since the company cannot pay, the shareholders who are the people financially interested should be made to pay instead. That of course is radically at odds with the whole concept of corporate personality and limited liability and the decision of the House of Lords in *Salomon v Salomon & Co Ltd* [1897] AC 22.'

3-47   The true position, Hobhouse LJ said, is that companies are entitled to organise their affairs in group structures and to expect the courts to apply the principles of *Salomon v A Salomon & Co Ltd* in the ordinary way.[76]

3-48   While the legal position in this jurisdiction is therefore well established and clearly not open to change by the courts, the regulation of groups of companies continues to raise issues of concern[77] as to the position of the creditors of a subsidiary company (especially tort creditors), the duties of directors of a subsidiary, and the protection of minority interests in a subsidiary, each of which is considered briefly below.

Creditor issues

3-49   The primary legal reason for the use of a group structure is to further limit liabilities[78] since ultimately, as Templeman J memorably put it in *Re Southard Ltd*,[79] a parent company can discard the runt of the litter. He noted:[80]

> 'A parent company may spawn a number of subsidiary companies, all controlled directly or indirectly by the shareholders of the parent company. If one of the subsidiary companies, to change the metaphor, turns out to be the runt of the litter and declines into insolvency to the dismay of the creditors, the parent company and other subsidiary companies may prosper to the joy of the shareholders without any liability for the debts of the insolvent subsidiary.'

3-50   Of course, as a matter of good business practice, many parent companies will not insist on their strict legal right to walk away from the liabilities of their subsidiaries, but will meet a subsidiary's obligations, particularly if the subsidiary's creditors are also creditors and suppliers of the parent company and other companies in the group. A concern for its business reputation may also make a parent company meet a liability which legally it could otherwise disown. Once the scale of liabilities is significant, however, a

---

[75] [1998] 2 BCLC 447 at 457.   [76] [1998] 2 BCLC 447 at 458.

[77] See generally, Blumberg, *The Multinational Challenge to Corporation Law* (1993) and Dine, *The Governance of Corporate Groups* (2000). Much of the literature on groups focuses on the problem of group insolvency, see Mevorach, 'Centralising insolvencies of pan-European corporate groups: a creditor's dream or nightmare?' [2006] JBL 468; Shandro and Montgomery, 'COMI and Groups' (2005) Insolv Int 158.

[78] There are numerous business reasons why businesses want to use a group structure, such as diversification, geography, and administrative convenience.

[79] [1979] 3 All ER 556.   [80] [1979] 3 All ER 556 at 565.

parent company is unlikely voluntarily to accept the liabilities of the subsidiary since its own shareholders and creditors will be endangered by such action.

It is important therefore that creditors of a group company identify the precise subsid-   **3-51** iary with which they are dealing and appreciate that *Salomon* will prevent their having a claim against assets elsewhere in the group. It may be the case that the subsidiary has a share capital of £100 and no assets of its own. Of course, this could equally be the position where a creditor deals with a company with individual rather than corporate shareholders, so the position is not peculiar to corporate groups.

If the creditors are to protect their position and extend their reach to the assets of   **3-52** the parent company and/or other companies in the group, they must use contractual devices to do so, recognising that the superior negotiating power of financial insti- tutions may mean that the ordinary contract creditor has little bargaining power. Creditors such as banks, on the other hand, will be in a position to ensure that they have cross-guarantees and security from all the companies in the group. Typically, a bank will require each subsidiary company to provide security and guarantees that it will meet its own liabilities to the bank and the liabilities of any other company in the group to the bank. These contractual devices ensure that the bank is able to ignore the separate legal entities and in effect to lend to the group and to recover from the group. The consequence for the creditors of an individual subsidiary company may be that difficulties elsewhere in the group will force the bank to call in the cross-guarantees resulting in all probability in the collapse of the entire group.[81]

For creditors without the bargaining power to secure cross-guarantees, the most that   **3-53** they may be able to extract is a letter of comfort from the parent company. An illus- tration of this situation can be found in *Kleinwort Benson v Malaysia Mining Corp.*[82] Here a bank intended to lend several million pounds to a subsidiary company and sought some protection against the risk of default by the subsidiary from the parent company. The most the parent company was willing to give was a letter of comfort which stated: 'it is our policy to ensure that the business of the subsidiary is at all times in a position to meet its liabilities to you'. When the subsidiary collapsed, the parent company denied any liability to the creditor under the letter of comfort. The Court of Appeal agreed that this letter had no contractual effect. The court concluded that the concept of a comfort letter to which the parties had resort when the parent company refused to accept liability was known by both sides to amount to the parent assuming, not a legal liability to ensure repayment of the liabilities of the subsidiary, but a moral responsibility only.

Nevertheless, in the absence of a guarantee, creditors still seek letters of comfort in the   **3-54** hope that the parent company will, for business reasons, decide to honour that moral responsibility. Of course, a letter of comfort given dishonestly to induce another party to provide funding would be actionable, as would a letter of comfort which on closer

---

[81] For an example of these arrangements, see *Facia Footwear Ltd v Hinchcliffe* [1998] 1 BCLC 218.
[82] [1989] 1 All ER 785; a subordination agreement is another possibility for creditors to consider, see **24-97**.

analysis proves to be a binding contractual obligation, so care must be exercised in the giving and drafting of such letters.

3-55   It is also possible that, on insolvency, a liquidator may be able to establish that the parent company has exercised such control over the subsidiary as to constitute itself a shadow director of the subsidiary. This would open up the possibility of potential civil liability by the parent company as a shadow director for matters such as wrongful trading by the subsidiary company.[83] In practice, such potential liability is a remote prospect. Shadow directors are discussed at **6-20**; wrongful trading is considered at **25-17**.

3-56   As for tort creditors of a subsidiary company, it is often argued that the application of the *Salomon* principle is particularly unfair in their case since they are involuntary creditors.[84] It is clear from *Adams v Cape Industries plc*,[85] however, that the English courts see no need to regard such creditors as deserving of any particular flexibility in terms of applying the *Salomon* principle. The claimants in that case were tort creditors. They were employees of the US subsidiaries who had suffered asbestos-related illness as a result of their employment, but, as discussed at **3-41**, *Adams* is a strong reaffirmation by the Court of Appeal of the *Salomon* principle. Far from showing a willingness to pierce the veil because the claimants were tort creditors, the Court of Appeal emphasised that the use of a group structure in this way to insulate the rest of the group from future liabilities of a particular subsidiary is inherent in English company law.

Directors' duties

3-57   As far as the duties of a director are concerned, the position where the company is one of a group of companies is that the directors must continue to act to promote the success of that company (given that it is a separate legal entity with its own separate creditors)[86] and not look solely to the overall interests of the group. The proper test is whether an intelligent and honest man in the position of a director of the company concerned could, in the whole of the existing circumstances, reasonably believe the transaction to be for the benefit of the company.[87] Of course, at a practical level, the two issues are likely to be quite intertwined since what promotes the success of the group may be relevant to promoting the success of the company.[88]

3-58   This approach may mean that it is appropriate for a solvent subsidiary to provide financial support for the rest of a group, though the group is in financial difficulty, when the continued prosperity and the very existence of the subsidiary may depend on

---

[83] See *Re Hydrodam Ltd* [1994] 2 BCLC 180.

[84] See Muchlinski, 'Holding Multinationals to account: Recent Developments in English Litigation and the Company Law Review' (2002) 23 Company Lawyer 168.

[85] [1990] BCLC 479, CA.   [86] See *Re Polly Peck International plc (No 3)* [1996] 1 BCLC 428 at 440.

[87] *Charterbridge Corpn Ltd v Lloyds Bank Ltd* [1969] 2 All ER 1185 at 1194.

[88] In *Nicholas v Soundcraft Electronics Ltd* [1993] BCLC 360, for example, the directors of a subsidiary company were not in breach of their duties to the company when they failed to take action to recover debts owed to it by the parent company. The parent company was the sole distributor of the subsidiary's products and was in serious financial trouble and it was in the interests of the subsidiary company that the parent should not go into liquidation.

the group remaining in business, as is commonly the case. The problem arises because modern banking arrangements, as noted at **3-52**, typically require each subsidiary to guarantee the indebtedness of all the other companies in the group with the result that the insolvency of one company in the group can trigger the collapse of the remaining companies as well. These arrangements commonly are in the interests of the subsidiary company as much as the interests of the group, because the subsidiary gets access to a level of borrowing and on more favourable terms than would otherwise be possible on its own account.

The difficulty in separating group interests and the company's interests is illustrated by *Facia Footwear Ltd v Hinchcliffe*[89] where a cash-rich subsidiary had entered into cross-guarantees whereby the subsidiary guaranteed the indebtedness of the group.[90] At issue were million pound payments made to other group companies by the directors of the subsidiary two months prior to the subsidiary going into administration. The administrators sought summary judgment against the directors on the grounds that making these payments in disregard of the creditors' interests (i.e. the creditors of the subsidiary company) at that time was a breach of the directors' duties to the subsidiary company (see now CA 2006, s 172(3), discussed at **9-42**).   **3-59**

The application for summary judgment was refused.[91] The directors in their defence had maintained that the payments were in the normal course of implementation of group treasury arrangements and there was no suggestion that the payments were for private purposes or in breach of any statutory obligation or were otherwise than for the trading purposes of the recipient companies. Most importantly, if the group of companies collapsed, the subsidiary would collapse also under the weight of the cross-guarantees. Moreover, the court found that the directors were intent on keeping the group afloat as they believed a refinancing scheme was a serious possibility.   **3-60**

Sir Richard Scott acknowledged the difficulties facing the directors of the subsidiary. It was clear, he said, that in continuing trading in those final months, the directors were taking a risk; clear too that, given the parlous financial state of the group, the directors had to have regard to the interests of creditors. But, he noted, the creditors of the group, and of the subsidiary in particular, would clearly have been best served by a refinancing that could support a continuation of profitable trading. The cessation of trading followed by the disposal of the assets of the companies on a forced sale basis would, it was always realised, lead to heavy losses for the creditors. The creditors' only chance of being paid in full lay in a continuation of trading. In his opinion, it was, therefore, not in the least obvious that in continuing to trade in those final two months the directors were ignoring the interests of the creditors of the subsidiary.[92]   **3-61**

---

[89] [1998] 1 BCLC 218.

[90] No challenge was made to the propriety of the decision as to the subsidiary's participation in the security arrangements: see [1998] 1 BCLC 218 at 224.

[91] This outcome does not mean that the court would not have found against the directors in a full hearing, but simply that the case against them was not so convincing that the court would grant a summary judgment. In the event, the administrators did not pursue the case.

[92] [1998] 1 BCLC 218 at 228.

3-62   An interesting case in the other direction is *Re Genosyis Technology Management Ltd, Wallach v Secretary of State for Trade and Industry*.[93] In this instance, the directors of a subsidiary company entered into a settlement agreement with a defaulting creditor which involved the creditor making a significant payment to the parent company rather than to the subsidiary. The subsidiary had stood to gain €1.25m from earlier drafts of the settlement but, under the version actually signed, payment was direct to the parent company which undertook to make payments to the subsidiary amounting to £166,000. In disqualification proceedings against the two directors of the subsidiary, the court noted that the company was insolvent at the time of the agreement, therefore the interests of the creditors intruded and the directors owed a fiduciary duty to act in their interests. Instead the court found there was no evidence that the directors, who were also directors of the parent company, at any time considered the separate interests of the subsidiary and of its creditors. The directors were culpable in not doing so and were disqualified for five years. Likewise in *Re Mea Corporation Ltd, Secretary of State for Trade and Industry v Aviss*,[94] directors of three related companies were disqualified for periods ranging from 7 to 11 years. At a time when each of the companies was insolvent and under pressure from creditors, the directors allowed such cash as was available to be paid out to other related companies in disregard of the interests of the creditors of the individual companies.

Minority shareholders

3-63   As for the position of minority shareholders in the case of a subsidiary other than a wholly-owned subsidiary, the difficulties that they can encounter can be illustrated by *Scottish Co-operative Wholesale Society Ltd v Meyer*.[95] In this case the majority shareholder had no longer any need for the subsidiary so ran down its business to the point where it had no business. The minority shareholders petitioned for relief under CA 1948, s 210 (the precursor to CA 2006, s 994, the unfairly prejudicial remedy, discussed in detail in Chapter 17). The House of Lords concluded that the affairs of the subsidiary had been conducted by the controlling shareholder in an oppressive manner and ordered the majority to buy out the minority shareholders on a valuation basis which presupposed that no oppressive conduct had occurred. This option of seeking judicial relief with respect to the conduct of the company's affairs by the majority shareholders is still available to minority shareholders under CA 2006, s 994 which in fact is a more generous provision than that relied on in *Scottish Co-operative*, see **17-31**.

Concluding points

3-64   It is clear from the authorities that there will be no significant judicial development of the law away from the *Salomon* principle and so only legislative development can alter the picture as it currently stands. It might be thought that this area would have been ripe for consideration by the Company Law Review (CLR) but in fact there was

---

[93] [2007] 1 BCLC 208.   [94] [2007] 1 BCLC 618 at 635, 643.   [95] [1959] AC 324, HL.

a reluctance to engage with this issue. Pointing out that contract creditors can protect themselves by contract terms and pricing mechanisms from the risks of trading with an insolvent subsidiary,[96] the CLR commented that it saw no merit in imposing a more integrated regime on groups which would take away flexibility and strike at the limited liability basis of company law.[97] Furthermore, there was no evidence before it of abuse of corporate status by parent companies to avoid tort liabilities.[98] The CLR did put forward a very modest proposal for an elective regime allowing parent companies to avoid some disclosure requirements in return for accepting liability for a subsidiary's acts,[99] but the proposal was roundly criticised[100] and rejected by the Government before being dropped from the CLR's Final Report.[101]

At one time, the European Commission had ambitions for a Directive on Groups,[102] **3-65** but discussion never progressed very far and the Commission accepted the recommendation of the High Level Group of Experts on Company Law that any plans in that direction should be abandoned.[103] The Commission is content to proceed instead by emphasising the need for greater transparency from groups,[104] especially when they include listed companies, so ensuring that creditors are well informed as to the risks they run in contracting with such structures.

D Corporate liabilities

Though it is an artificial legal entity, a company can enter into and enforce contracts   **3-66** and can commit and be the victim of torts and criminal offences. Corporate liability, whether as a matter of civil or criminal law, may be established either:

(1) by the application of specific rules of attribution whereby the acts of someone else, typically but not necessarily directors, are attributed to the company, a process which involves 'the identification of the natural person or persons who are to be regarded as representing the juridical person for the purposes of the

---

[96] See Company Law Review, *Modern Company Law for a Competitive Economy, Completing the Structure* (2000) (hereinafter *Completing the Structure*), para 10.58. For a more comprehensive review, see the Report by the Australian Companies & Securities Advisory Committee, *Corporate Groups* (May 2000) which contains much of relevance to this jurisdiction.   [97] See *Completing the Structure* (2000), para 10.20.

[98] See *Completing the Structure* (2000), paras 10.58–10.59.

[99] See *Completing the Structure* (2000), paras 10.19–10.57.

[100] For a scathing commentary, see Boyle (2002) 23 Co Law 35.

[101] Company Law Review, *Final Report*, vol 1 (2001), para 8.26.

[102] There had been some discussions in the 1970s and 1980s with respect to draft proposals for a Ninth Company Law Directive on Groups based on complex German provisions, but no progress was made, see Edwards, *EC Company Law* (1999), pp 390–1.

[103] See the Report of the High Level Group of Company Law Experts entitled *A Modern Regulatory Framework for Company Law in Europe*, 4 November 2002, Brussels, Ch V of which is devoted to Groups.

[104] See Communication from the Commission to the Council and the European Parliament, *Modernising Company Law and Enhancing Corporate Governance in the European Union—A Plan to Move Forward*, Brussels, 21.5.2003, COM (2003) 284.

substantive rule in question' (historically known as the directing mind and will doctrine);[105] or

(2) on the basis of wider rules of attribution, namely agency and vicarious liability, where the company accepts responsibility for the wrongful acts of its agents or employees, as is the case with any principal or employer.

3-67   As Nourse LJ noted in *El Ajou v Dollar Land Holdings plc*,[106] given that a company has no mind or will of its own, the need for attribution arises because the criminal law often requires mens rea as a constituent of the crime, and the civil law may require intention or knowledge as an ingredient of the cause of action or defence. Nourse LJ also made the point that there is no divergence of approach between the criminal and civil jurisdictions with the authorities on attribution in each being cited indifferently in the other. The need to rely on specific rules of attribution, as we shall see, is greatest in the context of criminal liability (where vicarious liability has only a limited role to play) so the discussion on those rules of attribution is set out at **3-98** et seq dealing with criminal liability.

3-68   In the civil context, the rules of agency and vicarious liability suffice, for the most part, to establish liability and no further rules of attribution are required. A company is liable for the wrongful acts of an agent or employee acting within the scope of his authority or in the course of his employment.[107] On occasion, however, the answer to a civil issue will require use of the identification rule of attribution, as can be illustrated by the following cases. In *Stone & Rolls Ltd v Moore Stephens*[108] a firm of accountants was able to defeat a claim in negligence brought against it by a corporate client by relying on the defence of ex turpi causa non oritur actio (which precludes claims based on illegality). The claim was essentially based on an argument that the defendants as the company's auditors should have detected that the company was being run in a fraudulent manner by S, its sole shareholder and director. The Court of Appeal found S to be the sole directing mind and will of the company such that his dishonest acts should be attributed to the company with the result that the company was not the victim of the fraudster, but was the fraudster itself.[109] Any claim by the company based on the fraudulent conduct of the business was therefore barred by the ex turpi causa principle. In *KR v Royal & Sun Alliance plc*[110] a company could not rely on an insurance policy which excluded liability for deliberate acts of the company. The acts in question had been carried out by the company's managing director and majority shareholder. The court found that he was the directing mind and will of the company; indeed, the court said, he was the company and his acts were attributed to it with the result that it was unable to claim on the policy.

---

[105] *Man Nutzfahrzeuge AG v Freightliner Ltd* [2005] EWHC 2347 (Comm), [2005] All ER (D) 357(Oct), QBD, para 154, per Moore Bick LJ.

[106] [1994] 1 BCLC 464.

[107] The ordinary 'course of employment' has an extended scope for these purposes to include acts so closely connected with the acts that the employee was authorised to do that for the purpose of liability they can fairly and properly be said to be done by the employee while acting in the ordinary course of his employment: *Lister v Hesley Hall Ltd* [2001] 2 All ER 769, HL; *Dubai Aluminium Co Ltd v Salaam* [2003] 1 BCLC 32, HL.

[108] [2008] 2 BCLC 461, CA.   [109] [2008] 2 BCLC 461 at 493, per Rimer LJ.   [110] [2007] BCC 522.

Corporate liability in contract

Parties wishing to enforce contractual obligations entered into by companies must ensure that: **3-69**

(1) the commitments made are within the capacity of the company and the authority of the executing officer or employee as agent, although much statutory protection is provided to ensure that this is the case; and

(2) any due formalities of execution have been observed (see CA 2006, ss 44 and 46). A company may enter into a contract in writing under its seal (if it has one)[111] or, more commonly, a contract may be made on behalf of the company by a person (such as a director or manager) acting under its authority, express or implied (s 43).

Issues of capacity are of ever-decreasing significance (see discussion at **4-12**) so the essential contractual issues revolve around the authority of the contracting agent and whether it suffices to bind the company. Those issues of authority involve the application of the rules of agency as to the actual or apparent authority of the agent acting for the company. These agency rules are bolstered by statutory provisions (CA 2006, ss 39 and 40) designed to minimise the risk to third parties of any lack of authority. A further complication may be that the agent has authority to enter into the transaction but is acting for an improper purpose. All of these matters are discussed in Chapter 8. A key point to note is that contractual liabilities attach to the company as the contracting party and not to the agent who negotiates on behalf of the company, though exceptionally an agent may be sued for breach of a warranty of authority.   **3-70**

Corporate liability in tort

A company is entitled to sue in respect of torts committed against it and it can be sued for a tort committed by it. As the company is an artificial legal entity, all torts of a company (even torts of omission) are committed through human agents. As noted, a company is vicariously liable for the acts of an agent or employee acting within the scope of his authority or in the course of his employment.[112] The agent or employee is liable personally and the company vicariously and they are joint tortfeasors (each joint tortfeasor being liable for the entire loss caused). The position was explained in *Lloyd v Grace, Smith & Co*[113] as follows: **3-71**

> '... the general rule [is] that the principal is liable to third persons in a civil suit 'for the frauds, deceits, concealments, misrepresentations, torts, negligences, and other malfeasances or misfeasances, and omissions of duty of his agent in the course of his employment, although the principal did not authorise, or justify, or participate in, or indeed know of such misconduct, or even if he forbade the acts, or disapproved of them.'

---

[111] Companies are not required to have a company seal and documents executed by signature in accordance with CA 2006, s 44 have the same effect as if executed under seal.

[112] As to the extended meaning of the ordinary 'course of employment' in this context, see above n 107.

[113] [1912] AC 716 at 737, HL.

3-72   Corporate liability is straightforward and it is obviously possible for a director who commits a wrongful act to be personally liable on this basis, as an agent acting within the scope of his authority and, as we shall see, the House of Lords now favours that straightforward approach. But there has been some debate as to whether it is more appropriate, given the company is a separate legal entity, that wrongful acts by a director should be attributed to the company so only the company is liable. This approach is sometimes referred to as the 'disattribution' theory whereby if an act is attributed to the company on this basis, it is 'disattributed' to the director personally.[114]

3-73   This question of the personal liability of a director is particularly important where the company is a one-man company or the company is insolvent and the only person able to meet any liability in damages is the director personally (or his insurers), but there are conflicting policy issues here.[115] On the one hand, a willingness to hold a director liable personally for torts committed by the company runs the risk of disregarding the corporate entity contrary to the principle in *Salomon v Salomon & Co Ltd*[116] and, where the director is the controlling shareholder, denying the protection of limited liability conferred by incorporation.[117] The general approach is that a director is not automatically to be identified with his company for the purpose of the law of tort, for enterprise must not be discouraged by subjecting directors to such onerous personal obligations without due regard to the part the director plays personally in respect of the acts complained of.[118] On the other hand, the courts are concerned that an individual should not be able to avoid liability for tortious acts committed by him by sheltering behind the corporate veil.[119] For that reason, where a director commits a tort personally, his status as a director should not (and does not) confer any immunity from personal liability.[120] Of course, deciding whether the director has committed the tort personally is the difficulty, given that his argument is that he is not acting personally but acting on behalf of the company. As we shall see, the courts are working towards a

---

[114] A leading advocate of this approach is Grantham, see, in particular, Grantham & Rickett, 'Directors' Tortious' Liability: Contract, Tort or Company Law?' (1999) 62 MLR 133, and Grantham, 'Company Director's Personal Liability in Tort' (2003) CLJ 15, but the disattribution idea is robustly rejected by Campbell & Armour, 'Demystifying The Civil Liability of Corporate Agents' (2003) CLJ 290. For a response, see Grantham, 'The Limited Liability Of Company Directors' [2007] LMCLQ 362.

[115] See generally Noonan & Watson, 'Directors' Tortious Liability—Standard Chartered Bank and the Restoration of Sanity' [2004] JBL 539; Grantham (2007), above n 114.

[116] [1897] AC 22, HL.

[117] See *Williams v Natural Life Health Foods Ltd* [1998] 1 BCLC 689 at 698, HL; also the dissenting judgment of Sir Patrick Russell in *Williams v Natural Life Health Foods Ltd* [1997] 1 BCLC 133, CA. But see Shapira, 'Liability of Corporate Agents: *Williams v Natural Life*' (1999) 20 Co Law 130 at 135 who makes the point that imposing liability on directors does not nullify the many other benefits of limited liability and incorporation.

[118] *C Evans and Sons Ltd v Spritebrand Ltd* [1985] BCLC 105 at 115, per Slade LJ; see also *Rainham Chemical Works Ltd (in liq) v Belvedere Fish Guano Co Ltd* [1921] 2 AC 465 at 488; also *Trevor Ivory Ltd v Anderson* [1992] 2 NZLR 517 at 524–8.

[119] See Chadwick LJ in *MCA Records Inc v Charly Records Ltd* [2003] 1 BCLC 93 at 116.

[120] *Standard Chartered Bank v Pakistan National Shipping Corp* [2003] 1 BCLC 244 at 258, per Lord Rodger.

pragmatic compromise between the twin policy concerns of eroding the protection of incorporation and enforcing the personal liability of those who commit a tort.

Personal liability for torts committed by a director

The debate as to whether a director should be personally liable where he commits a   **3-74** tort has been clearly answered in the affirmative by the House of Lords in *Standard Chartered Bank v Pakistan National Shipping Corpn (No 2)*.[121] The facts essentially were that the managing director of a shipping company presented false shipping documents that resulted in the company obtaining payment of $1.1m from a bank. The bank subsequently sued the company and the director in deceit. The company was held liable, but the Court of Appeal allowed an appeal by the director against a finding of personal liability concluding that he had made the fraudulent representation on behalf of the company and not personally.[122] The bank appealed successfully to the House of Lords.

Lord Hoffmann noted that the director made a fraudulent misrepresentation intend-   **3-75** ing the bank to rely upon it and the bank did rely on it. The fact that, by virtue of the law of agency, his representation and the knowledge with which he made it would also be attributed to the company would be of interest, Lord Hoffmann said, in an action against the company.[123] However, this did not detract from the fact that they were his representations and his knowledge.[124] Lord Hoffmann noted that the director was not being sued for the company's tort. He was being sued for his own tort and all the elements of that tort were proved against him. He was liable, not because he was a director, but because he committed a fraud.[125]

Lord Rodger, concurring, noted that someone who commits a tortious act is liable for   **3-76** their consequences; whether others (such as a company) are also liable depends on the circumstances.[126] All the ingredients of the tort of deceit (false statement made knowingly or recklessly intending other party to rely on it to his detriment) were made out against the director. That being so, there was no conceivable basis on which the director should not be held liable for the loss suffered by the bank.[127] His status as a director when he executed the fraud could not invest him with immunity[128] and he was liable in deceit.[129]

The position of the House of Lords in *Standard Chartered* is that the starting point   **3-77** when considering possible liability for the commission of the wrongful acts. The wrongful acts are the acts of the individual for which he is liable, even if they can

---

[121] [2003] 1 BCLC 244, HL. See Noonan & Watson, above n 115; Todd, 'Assuming Responsibility for Tort' [2003] 119 LQR 199; Grantham (2003) CLJ 15.

[122] See [2000] 1 All ER (Comm) 1, CA.   [123] [2003] 1 BCLC 244 at 251.

[124] [2003] 1 BCLC 244 at 251.   [125] [2003] 1 BCLC 244 at 252.

[126] [2003] 1 BCLC 244 at 257.   [127] [2003] 1 BCLC 244 at 257.

[128] [2003] 1 BCLC 244 at 258.

[129] See also *Daido Asia Japan Co Ltd v Rothen* [2002] BCC 589; *Noel v Poland* [2001] 2 BCLC 645; *Edginton v Fitzmaurice* (1885) 29 Ch D 459.

also be attributed to the company for the purposes of corporate liability. In effect, the decision shows a shift in emphasis or indeed a return to first principles.[130] Instead of approaching the issue by attributing acts to the entity so establishing a corporate liability and then looking at the possibility of some basis for a personal liability, the first consideration is to establish whether the director committed the tort. If he did, a personal liability ensues which brings with it a vicarious liability on the part of the company for the acts of its agent.

3-78   For whatever reason, perhaps because of the welcome clarity brought to these issues by the decision in *Standard Chartered*, perhaps because of the increasing availability of directors' and officers' liability insurance, perhaps because, in hard times, every avenue is worth pursuing if it increases the claimant's chances of actual recovery, there appears to be something of an increase in claims in deceit against individual directors.

3-79   In *GE Commercial Finance Ltd v Gee*[131] the executive chairman of a group of companies (who was also the 80% shareholder) and the group's finance director were liable in deceit and in conspiracy to the sum of £16m following an orchestrated and substantial fraud on the claimant involving the raising of false debts under a debt financing arrangement. The finance director knew that the figures communicated to the claimant were false, and the court found that his intention in making the false representations was to induce the claimant to make and to continue making the payments they did make. The court found that the executive chairman knew and encouraged what the finance director was doing.

3-80   In *Contex Drouzhba Ltd v Wiseman*[132] an action in deceit lay against a director who signed on behalf of the company a document containing a fraudulent misrepresentation. The Court of Appeal found that his signature was not only that of the company but also his personal signature making him a person who made a fraudulent misrepresentation. The facts were that the company entered into an agreement with a supplier that payments would be made to the supplier within 30 days of the shipment of the goods. The agreement was signed by the defendant as managing director of the company. The court found that, at the time he signed the agreement, the defendant knew that the company would be unable to make payment for the goods at all, let alone within 30 days of invoice or a reasonable period thereafter. The court found that the director had made that representation knowingly and with no reasonable belief in its truth. In these circumstances, the director was personally liable.

3-81   The Court of Appeal noted that it is clear, following the decision in *Standard Chartered Bank v Pakistan National Shipping Co*,[133] that, even if a company is liable for a deceit carried out by its director, the director also has a personal liability for his own fraud. Where a document contains a fraudulent representation made by a director, there is

---

[130] See Campbell & Armour, above n 114; also Shapira, above n 117.   [131] [2006] 1 Lloyd's Rep 337.
[132] [2008] 1 BCLC 631, CA, aff'g [2007] 1 BCLC 758. See also *UBAF Ltd v European American Banking Corp* [1984] 2 All ER 226.
[133] [2003] 1 BCLC 244.

no reason, the court said, why his signature on the document should not render him personally liable. The court agreed that not every contract signed by a director would contain implied representations by the director. Each case would depend on its own facts. But a director signing a document which contains a promise of payment on certain terms may be making an implied representation about the ability of the company to pay since there is, by implication, a representation that the company has the capacity to meet the payment terms. Here the defendant had made a fraudulent representation in writing as to the credit or ability of the company and he was liable.[134]

In cases where the claim is based on deceit, it is clear that the relevant policy considerations favour personal liability given the deliberate nature of the wrongdoing and the courts are anxious to prevent directors from avoiding this liability by hiding behind their companies.[135] On the other hand, there is possibly a greater reluctance to hold a director liable personally for negligent misrepresentations made by his company.   **3-82**

This issue was addressed by the House of Lords in *Williams v Natural Life Health Foods Ltd*[136] which concerned negligent advice given by what was essentially a one-man company. M was the managing director and principal shareholder of a company which held itself out as having the expertise to provide advice on running health food shops, expertise derived from M's experience in running his own shop. The plaintiffs had relied on financial projections negligently produced by the company in opening their health shop which had collapsed leaving them with significant losses. The company was liable for the negligently produced figures, but it had been dissolved. The question was whether M could be personally liable.[137] The lower courts thought so,[138] but the House of Lords disagreed.   **3-83**

Their Lordships agreed with the dissenting judge in the Court of Appeal that the fact that, in a one-man company, the functions of the company must necessarily be centred on this individual does not make him personally liable.[139] A director could only be personally liable to third parties for loss which they suffer as a result of negligent   **3-84**

---

[134] The Court of Appeal noted counsel's point that this route of suing in deceit offers creditors a possible direct remedy against directors which is more advantageous to them than liquidators bringing claims against directors for fraudulent or wrongful trading where any recovery is a collective one for the benefit of all the creditors: see [2008] 1 BCLC 631 at 633.

[135] See Noonan & Watson, above n 115, also Grantham (2007), above n 114.

[136] [1998] 1 BCLC 689, HL. There are numerous commentaries on this case, see Payne, 'Negligent Misstatement—A Healthier Decision for Company Directors' (1998) CLJ 456; Griffin, 'Company Director's Personal Liability in Tort' [1999] 115 LQR 36; Grantham & Rickett, above n 114; Shapira, above n 117; Todd, above n 121; Reynolds, 'Personal Liability of Company Directors in Tort' (2003) 33 Hong Kong LJ 51.

[137] It had not been pleaded that the director was a joint tortfeasor with the company, see **3-89**, but even if it had been pleaded, it would have failed since, as Lord Steyn pointed out, the basis for a claim for negligent misstatement is a special relationship between the parties giving rise to an assumption of responsibility. Joint tortfeasor liability is based on procuring etc others to act so there cannot be any special relationship between the parties and therefore joint tortfeasor liability could not be relevant to liability for negligent misstatement: see [1998] 1 BCLC 689 at 698.

[138] The Court of Appeal decision is reported at [1997] 1 BCLC 131; the first instance judgment at [1996] 1 BCLC 288.

[139] [1998] 1 BCLC 689 at 697. See also *Trevor Ivory Ltd v Anderson* [1992] 2 NZLR 517.

advice given to them by the company if he assumes personal responsibility for that advice and the plaintiffs rely on that assumption of responsibility.[140] It is not sufficient that there be a special relationship between the injured party and the company. There must be an assumption of responsibility such as to create a special relationship with the director himself and that will depend on things said and done by or on behalf of the director.[141] Moreover, the test of reliance is not simply reliance in fact but whether the plaintiffs can reasonably rely on the assumption of responsibility.[142] On the facts in *Williams*, their Lordships found that there were no personal dealings between M and the claimants, he never crossed the line to assume a personal responsibility towards them and he was not personally liable.[143]

3-85   The decision in *Standard Chartered Bank v Pakistan National Shipping Corp*[144] has clarified that where all of the elements of a tort claim can be established against an individual director, such as where fraudulent misrepresentations are made by a director, the fact that he is a director does not and should not act to bar his personal liability. There is no inconsistency between that decision and the decision in *Williams*. If the elements of negligent misstatement had been established in *Williams*, the individual director would have been liable, but they were not, and so the director was not personally liable. On the other hand, what *Williams*[145] does show is that only in exceptional cases would a claim for negligent misstatement succeed against an individual director. If in a one-man company, such as *Williams*, there was no assumption of responsibility and therefore no liability, it is difficult to imagine an assumption of responsibility by directors in other contexts.[146]

3-86   This outcome in respect of economic loss caused by negligence, reached through an application of tort law, in effect reinforces *Salomon v Salomon & Co Ltd*[147] by leaving liability to fall on the entity, if at all. Liability for economic loss from negligent misstatements is precisely the type of business risk which incorporation is used to manage. This outcome ensures the effectiveness of incorporation in those circumstances and is especially important in the context of small or one-man companies which provide advice and services.[148] On the other hand, there is no justification for allowing

---

[140] [1998] 1 BCLC 689 at 695, but see Todd, above n 121.

[141] [1998] 1 BCLC 689 at 695. See also *Noel v Poland* [2001] 2 BCLC 645.

[142] [1998] 1 BCLC 689 at 696.

[143] See criticisms of this finding of fact by Shapira, above n 117, p 133. For an exceptional case where the line was crossed, see *Fairline Shipping Corp v Adamson* [1974] 2 All ER 967 where a director involved himself personally with a customer of the company to such an extent that it was clear that he regarded himself, and not the company, as concerned with the storage of the customer's goods. The director had therefore assumed a duty of care to the customer.

[144] [2003] 1 BCLC 244, HL.   [145] [1998] 1 BCLC 689, HL.

[146] See Campbell & Armour, above n 114, p 301 who make the point that this difficulty in establishing an assumption of responsibility will make it difficult to bring a successful claim against any agent acting on behalf of a principal, not just company directors.

[147] [1897] AC 22, HL.

[148] See Payne, above n 136. Noonan & Watson, above n 115, p 548 make the point that the very act of incorporation will often be an effective disclaimer of personal liability by a director giving advice on behalf of the company.

individuals to use corporate structures to avoid liability in tort for deliberate wrong-doing by them individually.[149]

The balance struck in *Williams* and in *Standard Chartered* can be seen as a display of   **3-87**
judicial dexterity to resolve the uncertainties which were beginning to gain ground in this area. The decisions are welcome at every level: doctrinally it is important that tort law should apply to directors in the same way as anyone else; pragmatically because the policy issues have been resolved in a practical way which does not allow directors to evade their personal responsibilities while equally ensuring that a director is not always personally liable for all torts arising in the course of a business. The courts are essentially determining whether, as a matter of policy, in the particular context it is appropriate for the entity (negligence) or the entity and the individual (deceit) to bear the liability.

In bringing much needed clarity to this difficult area, their Lordships have taken the   **3-88**
opportunity to assert or reassert the primacy of vicarious liability (and so reduce the importance of other specific rules of attribution) in this context with their Lordships asserting in *Williams v Natural Life Health Foods Ltd*[150] and in *Standard Chartered Bank v Pakistan National Shipping Corp*[151] that the matter is an agency matter, one of the personal liability of the agent and corporate vicarious liability for the wrongs of that agent.[152]

Director's liability for procuring wrongdoing

The discussion above centred on the situation where a director personally commits   **3-89**
a tort. Another way of imposing liability on a director is to hold a director liable as a joint tortfeasor with the company where the director has authorised, directed or pro-cured the wrongful act though he has not committed the tort himself.[153] For example, if an employee of the company makes a fraudulent misrepresentation on behalf of the company, a director could be personally liable if he procured the making of the false statement.[154]

The difficulty is defining the nature and extent of the participation of the director in   **3-90**
the tortious act which renders him personally liable on this basis. This is an elusive question, as Slade LJ described it in *C Evans and Sons Ltd v Spritebrand Ltd*,[155] but important guidance has been provided by the Court of Appeal which considered the

---

[149] See Grantham (2007), above n 114, who makes the point that, when expressing concerns about allow-ing those engaged in business to shift the risk of their endeavours to others, we must not forget that that is actually the purpose of the legislation allowing for the incorporation of limited liability entities.

[150] [1998] 1 BCLC 689, HL.   [151] [2003] 1 BCLC 244, HL.

[152] See Lord Hoffmann in *Standard Chartered Bank v Pakistan National Shipping Corp* [2003] 1 BCLC 244 at 251–2; Lord Steyn in *Williams v Natural Life Health Foods Ltd* [1998] 1 BCLC 689 at 694.

[153] *Rainham Chemical Works Ltd (in liq) v Belvedere Fish Guano Co Ltd* [1921] 2 AC 465 at 488, HL; *Performing Right Society Ltd v Ciryl Theatrical Syndicate Ltd* [1924] 1 KB 1; *C Evans and Sons Ltd v Spritebrand Ltd* [1985] BCLC 105.

[154] See *Daido Asia Japan Co Ltd v Rothen* [2002] BCC 589 at 597.

[155] See [1985] BCLC 105 at 117.

matter at length in *MCA Records Inc v Charly Records Ltd*.[156] The facts in the case were relatively straightforward. At issue was the liability of Y who did not hold the office of director but who was described as the controller of C Ltd which had infringed the copyright vested in the claimants with respect to certain recordings. Y appealed against a finding that he was personally liable as a joint tortfeasor in respect of the infringement by the company.

3-91 The Court of Appeal emphasised that a director is not liable as a joint tortfeasor with the company if he does no more than carry out his constitutional role in the governance of the company, i.e. by voting at board meetings (likewise a controlling shareholder is not liable merely if he exercises control through use of his voting powers).[157] But, if a director or controlling shareholder chooses to exercise control otherwise than through the constitutional organs of the company, and the circumstances are such that he would be liable if he were not a director or controlling shareholder, the court thought that there was no reason why he should not be liable with the company as a joint tortfeasor.[158] The issue is whether A would be liable as a joint tortfeasor with the primary infringer B, whether or not the relationship between A and B is that A is a director of B.[159]

3-92 Chadwick LJ emphasised that the relevant enquiry is whether the individual has been personally involved in the commission of the tort to the extent sufficient to attract liability as a joint tortfeasor. The director must be concerned with the company in a joint act done in pursuance of a common purpose so as to attract liability.[160] But, Chadwick LJ went on:[161] 'if all that a director is doing is carrying out the duties entrusted to him as such by the company under its constitution, the circumstances in which it would be right to hold him liable as a joint tortfeasor with the company would be rare indeed'.

3-93 Returning to the facts of the dispute in *MCA Records Inc v Charly Records Ltd*,[162] the court noted that, in the context of intellectual property, liability as a joint tortfeasor might arise where the individual intends and procures and shares a common design that the infringement take place. On the facts, Y induced the company to copy the recordings and to issue them to the public, he planned the exploitation of the recordings, and intended that the company should continue to do so for as long as possible. He was rightly liable, the court held, as a joint tortfeasor.

3-94 In *Koninklijke Philips Electronics NV v Prico Digital Disc GmbH*[163] the defendant director was in charge of the day-to-day running of the defendant company. It was admitted that the company imported into the UK and kept and disposed of recordable CDs of a kind that the court previously had held infringed the claimant's patent. The

---

[156] [2003] 1 BCLC 93, CA. See also *SEI Spa v Ordnance Technologies (UK) Ltd (No 2)* [2008] 2 All ER 622 (managing director and sole shareholder of a company liable as joint tortfeasor with the company having shared a common design that the acts complained of, the infringement of design rights, should take place. The director encouraged or procured the breach by the company's engineers).

[157] [2003] 1 BCLC 93 at 116–17.   [158] [2003] 1 BCLC 93 at 116–17.   [159] [2003] 1 BCLC 93 at 113.

[160] [2003] 1 BCLC 93 at 111, applying *The Koursk* [1924] P 140.   [161] [2003] 1 BCLC 93 at 117.

[162] [2003] 1 BCLC 93, CA.   [163] [2004] 2 BCLC 50.

director had been responsible for the decision to import the infringing CDs into the UK and for the cultivation of A as a customer for those products. The director also made a decision to indemnify A against liability for royalties when the claimant sued A for infringement. The court concluded that the director's close involvement with the day-to-day actions of the company, and his independent authority in respect of those actions, were sufficient to render him liable as a joint tortfeasor with the company.

Clearly a factual analysis of the director's conduct is needed in each instance and, in essence, where the director acts appropriately and seeks to ensure that the company's agents and employees conduct themselves in accordance with the law, personal liability is unlikely. The importance of potential liability as a joint tortfeasor, however, is that it ensures that a director cannot easily evade liability by the device of ensuring that another agent or employee carries out wrongful acts at his direction.   **3-95**

Criminal liability of the company

A company is subject to the criminal law in the same manner as any other person although, as an artificial legal entity, there are some offences which a company is deemed unable to commit such as bigamy or offences of assault and some offences for which it cannot be convicted as the only penalty is imprisonment, such as murder.[164] Otherwise, the requisite actus reus and mens rea can be sought in the relevant agent and the fact that there is a mens rea requirement is no obstacle to corporate liability. Thus, a company can be held liable for offences involving an intent to deceive;[165] for conspiracy to defraud,[166] and for filing false tax returns.[167]   **3-96**

Generally, a company may be liable because: **3-97**

(1) the offence is committed by persons who are the embodiment of the company itself such that their acts are the acts of the company[168]—this involves the application of specific rules of attribution to determine whose acts are the acts of the company for this purpose; or

(2) the offence is one for which the company may be liable vicariously as an employer or principal for the wrongful acts or omissions of its servants and agents in the course of their employment and exercise of their authority.[169] Vicarious liability has only a limited role to play in criminal law, mainly arising from statutory requirements, and so in this context the key issues revolve around the specific rules of attribution.

[164] See generally Wells, *Corporations and Criminal Responsibility* (2nd edn, 2001).
[165] *DPP v Kent and Sussex Contractors Ltd* [1944] 1 All ER 119.
[166] *R v ICR Haulage Ltd* [1944] 1 All ER 691.   [167] *Moore v I Bresler Ltd* [1944] 2 All ER 515.
[168] *Lennard's Carrying Co Ltd v Asiatic Petroleum Co Ltd* [1915] AC 705 at 713, HL; and see Lord Denning in *H L Bolton (Engineering) Co Ltd v TJ Graham & Sons Ltd* [1957] 1 QB 159 at 172, CA.
[169] *Mousell Bros v London and North-Western Rly Co* [1917] 2 KB 836. See *R v British Steel plc* [1995] 1 WLR 1356; *National Rivers Authority v Alfred McAlpine Homes East Ltd* [1994] 4 All ER 286; *Re Supply of Ready Mixed Concrete (No 2), Director General of Fair Trading v Pioneer Concrete (UK) Ltd* [1995] 1 BCLC 613, HL.

Rules of attribution

3-98 A company may be criminally liable because the offence is committed by those persons who are the embodiment of the company such that their wrongful acts are the acts of the company. In deciding whose acts are the acts of the company, various rules of attribution apply. As Lord Hoffmann noted in *Meridian Global Funds Management Asia Ltd v Securities Commission*,[170] a Privy Council decision much cited on this issue, the primary rule of attribution is that acts of the board, of the shareholders in general meeting, or the unanimous informal assent of the shareholders are acts of the company.[171] But it is unlikely that the criminal act will have been committed through any of those mechanisms and so further rules of attribution are required, the most established being that the court will look to identify who is 'the directing mind and will of the company' (the identification doctrine). This doctrine derives from *Lennard's Carrying Co Ltd v Asiatic Petroleum Co Ltd*[172] where Viscount Haldane famously noted:

> 'My Lords, a corporation is an abstraction. It has no mind of its own any more than it has a body of its own; its active and directing will must consequently be sought in the person of somebody who for some purposes may be called an agent, but who is really the directing mind and will of the corporation, the very ego and centre of the personality of the corporation.'

3-99 To identify the directing mind and will of the company, it is necessary to consult the company's constitution which typically vests all powers of management in the board and there is no doubt that the board collectively represents the directing mind and will of the company. Equally, at the other end of the spectrum, it is clear that not all acts of all employees can be attributed to the company, for not all will have the status and authority which in law makes their acts in the matter under consideration the acts of the company.[173] As Lord Denning explained in *HL Bolton (Engineering) Co Ltd v TJ Graham & Sons Ltd*:[174]

> 'Some of the people in the company are mere servants and agents who are nothing more than hands to do the work and cannot be said to represent the mind or will. Others are directors and managers who represent the directing mind and will of the company and control what it does. The state of mind of those managers is the state of mind of the company and is treated by the law as such.'

3-100 That 'the directing mind and will' does not encompass more junior management was confirmed by the House of Lords in *Tesco Supermarkets Ltd v Nattrass*.[175] In this case, Tesco was prosecuted under the Trade Descriptions Act 1968 for the failure of one of its shop managers to ensure that goods advertised for sale at a particular price were in fact being offered for sale at that price. It was found as a fact that the company had

---

[170] [1995] 2 BCLC 116, PC.   [171] [1995] 2 BCLC 116 at 121, PC.
[172] [1915] AC 705 at 713, HL; See also Lord Denning in *HL Bolton (Engineering) Co Ltd v TJ Graham & Sons Ltd* [1957] 1 QB 159 at 172, CA.
[173] *R v Andrews Weatherfoil Ltd* [1972] 1 All ER 65 at 70, per Eveleigh J.
[174] [1957] 1 QB 159 at 172, CA.   [175] [1972] AC 153, HL.

exercised reasonable care in devising a proper system for the operation of the store. It was a defence under the 1968 Act to show that the act was due to the default of some other person. The company pleaded on appeal that the manager did not amount to the directing mind and will of the company and therefore the company could assert that the act was due to the default of some other person. The House of Lords agreed and held that the shop manager, one of several hundred, could not be treated as the embodiment of the company and his acts and defaults could not be attributed to the company. The offence, consequently, was indeed due to the act or default of 'another person', and not of the company itself. As Lord Reid noted:[176]

> 'Normally the board of directors, the managing director and perhaps other superior officers carry out the functions of management and speak and act as the company. Their subordinates do not.'

There the law rested until relatively recently when Lord Hoffmann, initially in *El Ajou v Dollar Land Holdings plc*,[177] and then authoritatively in *Meridian Global Funds Management Asia Ltd v Securities Commission*,[178] set out a broader approach which considers the issue of attribution not from the position in the corporate hierarchy of the defaulting agent or employee, but rather with a view to the purpose of the penal (or other) provision and to furthering that purpose. The necessity for taking this broader approach arises from the situation where the acts in question have been carried out by, or the knowledge at issue lies with, individuals who cannot be identified as the directing mind and will of the company in circumstances where vicarious liability is not relevant. In those circumstances, unless another rule of attribution can be applied, the acts and knowledge of those individuals cannot be attributed to the company and the relevant rule cannot be applied to the company (given the absence of vicarious liability). **3-101**

In *Meridian Global Funds Management Asia Ltd v Securities Commission*,[179] two employees of a Hong Kong investment management company (Meridian), one of them the company's chief investment officer, used company funds to purchase a 49% stake in a listed New Zealand company. The purchase was not disclosed by Meridian as required under the New Zealand Securities Amendment Act 1988 which essentially required the disclosure of significant shareholdings 'knowingly' acquired in public companies. The question was whether the knowledge of the employees should be attributed to Meridian so that it was in breach of the statutory requirement. The company argued that in the absence of knowledge by the directing mind and will (i.e. the board) of the acquisition of the shares, there was no breach. **3-102**

---

[176] [1972] AC 152 at 171.

[177] [1994] 1 BCLC 464, (a civil case, but the authorities on 'directing mind and will' tend to be applied without distinction). In this case, the Court of Appeal accepted that the fraudulent intent of the non-executive chairman of a company should be imputed to the company in a 'knowing receipt' case. He was the 'directing mind and will of the company' with respect to the particular transaction at issue—the company's receipt of investment funds which the chairman knew to be the proceeds of fraud—and his knowledge was the company's knowledge.

[178] [1995] 2 BCLC 116, PC.   [179] [1995] 2 BCLC 116, PC.

3-103   The Privy Council found that, on a true construction of the relevant statute and in view of the policy of the legislation, it was appropriate to attribute the knowledge of a senior employee (the chief investment officer) to the company, since otherwise the policy of the Act would be defeated and there would be a premium on the board paying as little attention as possible to what its investment managers were doing. Accordingly, Meridian knew that it was a substantial shareholder in another company when that was known to the employee who had authority to acquire the shares. Meridian was therefore in breach of the disclosure requirement.

3-104   In a now much cited speech, Lord Hoffmann reviewed the whole question of the application of the criminal law to companies. He noted that if the court decided that a substantive rule of law was intended to apply to a company, it then had to decide how the rule was intended to apply and whose act or knowledge or state of mind was for that purpose intended to count as the act, knowledge or state of mind of the company. Although in some cases that could be determined by applying the test of whose was the 'directing mind and will' of the company so that his fault or knowledge became the company's fault or knowledge, that test was not appropriate in all cases.

3-105   Instead, Lord Hoffmann said, it was a question of construction in each case as to whether the particular rule requires that the knowledge that an act has been done, or the state of mind with which it was done, should be attributed to the company. For example, in *Tesco Supermarkets Ltd v Nattrass*[180] discussed above at **3-100**, the acts or defaults of the store manager were not attributed to the company, Lord Hoffmann explained, because the purpose of the statutory provision in that case, the protection of consumers, did not require that the offence be an absolute one.[181] On the other hand, in *Re Supply of Ready Mixed Concrete (No 2), Director General of Fair Trading v Pioneer Concrete (UK) Ltd*,[182] it was necessary to attribute the acts of the employees to the company. In this case, a company was liable in contempt when its employees, while acting in the course of their employment but contrary to instructions issued by the board, carried out a deliberate act contrary to a restrictive practices order imposed on the company. The restrictive practices legislation would otherwise be worth little, Lord Hoffmann noted, if the company could avoid liability for what its employees did on the basis that the board did not know about it.[183]

3-106   In other words, to ensure the effective application of a statutory provision to a company, it may be necessary to consider different approaches to attribution. But, Lord Hoffmann ended with a note of caution, pointing out that their Lordships:[184]

> '...would wish to guard themselves against being understood to mean that whenever a servant of a company has authority to do an act on its behalf, knowledge of that act will for all purposes be attributed to the company. It is a question of construction in each case as to whether the particular rule requires that the knowledge that an act has

---

180 [1972] AC 153, HL.   181 [1995] 2 BCLC 116 at 122.   182 [1995] 1 BCLC 613, HL.
183 [1995] 2 BCLC 116 at 123.   184 [1995] 2 BCLC 116 at 126.

been done, or the state of mind with which it was done, should be attributed to the company.'

Following the decision in *Meridian*, there was some uncertainty as to the continuing   **3-107**
role of the orthodox attribution rule requiring intent to be found in the 'directing mind
and will' of the company at board or 'superior officer' level. The point was addressed by
the Court of Appeal in *A-G's Reference (No 2 of 1999)*[185] which noted that:

> '...Lord Hoffmann's speech in the *Meridian* case, in fashioning an additional special
> rule of attribution geared to *the purpose of the statute* [emphasis added], proceeded on
> the basis that the primary 'directing mind and will' rule still applies although it is not
> determinative in all cases. In other words, he was not departing from the identification
> theory but re-affirming its existence.'

The starting point remains therefore the application of the directing mind and will   **3-108**
theory. The question is whether it is possible to identify someone whose acts can
be equated with the directing mind and will of the company such that his acts and
knowledge, being the acts and knowledge which constitute the offence, are the acts
and knowledge of the company. If, on the other hand, the 'guilty' party cannot be
identified as the directing mind and will of the company so that route of attribution is
not open, the issue is whether the purpose and policy of the rule under consideration
(such as the statutory provision in *Meridian*) requires the application of a special rule
of attribution in order to ensure that the particular prohibition/requirement can be
applied to companies.

An illustration of the use of a special rule of attribution in this way arising from the   **3-109**
need to apply a particular statutory provision to a company can be seen in *Re Bank
of Credit and Commerce International SA (in liquidation) (No 15); Morris v Bank of
India*.[186] The liquidators of BCCI alleged that the defendant bank, by entering into various transactions, knowingly participated in the fraudulent trading of BCCI. Under
the Insolvency Act 1986, s 213, civil liability can be imposed on those 'knowingly'
party to fraudulent trading. The key issue was whether those at the bank responsible
for entering into the transactions at issue knew that they were thereby assisting BCCI
to perpetrate a fraud on its creditors and whether their knowledge should be attributed to the bank. The various transactions had been assisted and provided by a bank
official (S) who was the general manager of the London branch of the bank.

Applying *Meridian*, the Court of Appeal looked to the construction and purpose of   **3-110**
IA 1986, s 213 and concluded that the wording and policy behind the section indicated that it would be inappropriate to limit attribution for its purposes to the board
or those specifically authorised by a resolution of the board. The crucial question was
whose knowledge counted, for the purposes of IA 1986, s 213, as corporate knowledge
of the bank. Given that transactions of this nature would be dealt with at a level below
that of the board, it would in practice defeat the effectiveness of the section, the court

[185] [2000] 2 BCLC 257 at 268.   [186] [2005] 2 BCLC 328.

said, if liability was limited to those cases in which the board of directors was directly privy to the fraud. Turning to the facts of the case, the court thought this was plainly an appropriate case for attribution. S had a senior position in the bank, he brought the transactions to the bank, the board relied on him in relation to them, he was given a free hand to negotiate them and they were plainly suspicious.[187] His knowledge was more relevant than that of any member of the board or of anyone else in the bank and it was necessary, given the purpose of the provision, to attribute his knowledge to the bank which was therefore liable.

3-111   On the other hand, the Court of Appeal was careful to emphasise (as their Lordships had done in *Meridian*) that it would be wrong to attribute to a company the knowledge of any agent irrespective of the particular facts. It is necessary in each case to look at the purpose of the statutory provision and consider whether, in those particular circumstances, the statutory purpose will be defeated unless a special rule of attribution (which may include attributing the acts of employees lower down the corporate hierarchy) is applied.[188]

3-112   To sum up, in looking to attribute acts to a company, the starting point is the primary rules of attribution (a decision of the board etc). If that does not resolve the matter, the rules of agency and vicarious liability may do so. If none of those avenues is appropriate, the identification theory applies and the question is whether the acts are the acts of the directing mind and will of the company, but if that approach would defeat the legislative intent, it may be appropriate to use a special rule of attribution which involves asking 'whose act (or knowledge or state of mind) was *for this purpose* intended to count as the act etc of the company'.[189]

3-113   *Corporate manslaughter*   In the context of criminal liability, a particularly difficult issue has been liability for corporate manslaughter.[190] It was the case at common law that a company could be prosecuted for manslaughter but only if gross negligence on the part of those identified as the directing mind and will could be found, something which proved very difficult to establish in large organisations, such as rail and ferry companies. When fatalities occur in those industries, it is likely to be the result of gross negligence much lower down in the company, for example at the level of signalman or seaman, rather than at a level which could be equated with the directing mind and will of the company.

3-114   The common law position was considered in detail in *R v P & O European Ferries (Dover) Ltd*[191] where individual defendants and the company were charged with counts of manslaughter as a result of the sinking of the car ferry, *The Herald of Free Enterprise*, in March 1987, which resulted in almost 200 deaths. On the facts, it was not possible

---

[187] [2005] 2 BCLC 328 at 360–1.   [188] [2005] 2 BCLC 328 at 360–1.

[189] *Meridian Global Funds Management Asia Ltd v Securities Commission* [1995] 2 BCLC 166 at 122.

[190] See generally Wells, *Corporations and Criminal Responsibility* (2nd edn, 2001); Clarkson, 'Kicking Corporate Bodies and Damning their Souls' (1996) 59 MLR 557.

[191] (1990) 93 Cr App Rep 72.

to identify the appropriate mens rea for the offence in any officers who were the directing mind and will of the ferry company for these purposes and the prosecution failed. Other disasters such as rail crashes at Clapham, Southall, Paddington and Hatfield, all of which involved substantial loss of life, focused public attention on the issue of the criminal liability of the companies involved, as did a fire at King's Cross tube station and the sinking on the Thames of the pleasure craft, *The Marchioness*. The common law position was confirmed, however, in *A-G's Reference (No 2 of 1999)*[192] where the Court of Appeal held that the directing mind and will rule of attribution was the only basis in common law for corporate liability for gross negligence manslaughter. Unless an identified individual's conduct, characterised as gross criminal negligence, could be attributed to the company, the company was not liable for manslaughter at common law.[193] This reference was brought to clarify the law following a failed prosecution of a train company for manslaughter arising out of the Southall accident in which seven people died.

A conviction for manslaughter was secured in *R v Kite and OLL Ltd*,[194] in respect of a **3-115** water sports company and its managing director (it was essentially a one-man business) following the deaths of four teenagers while they were attending a course of instruction provided by the company. The company was fined £60,000 and the director was jailed. The case merely served to highlight that, while a conviction could be secured in a one-man company, it could not easily be secured in larger companies (where arguably the public interest in high standards of behaviour is greater) because of the need to identify the required mens rea at the level of the directing mind and will of the company.

This unsatisfactory state of the common law prompted calls for reform and in 1996 **3-116** the Law Commission recommended the introduction of a new offence of corporate killing which would essentially comprise killing by gross carelessness.[195] A similar proposal followed from the Home Office in 2000.[196] After much delay, the Corporate Manslaughter and Corporate Homicide Act 2007 received Royal Assent on 26 July 2007 and came into force, for the most part, on 6 April 2008. The Act replaces the common law on corporate manslaughter for England and Wales. The offence of corporate manslaughter may be committed by organisations including companies formed under the Companies Act, but not by individuals, and an organisation is guilty of the offence if the way in which any of its activities are managed or organised by its senior management[197] causes a person's death and amounts to a gross breach of a relevant duty of care

---

[192] [2000] 2 BCLC 257.   [193] [2000] 2 BCLC 257 at 267.   [194] (1994) *Times*, 9 December.

[195] See Law Commission, *Legislating the Criminal Code: Involuntary Manslaughter* (Law Comm No 237), 1996.

[196] See Home Office, *Reforming the Law on Involuntary Manslaughter: The Government's Proposals* (May 2000); and see Gobert, 'Corporate Killing at Home and Abroad—Reflections on the Government's Proposals' [2002] 118 LQR 72.

[197] See Gobert, 'The Corporate Manslaughter and Corporate Homicide Act 2007—Thirteen years in the making but was it worth the wait?' (2008) 71 MLR 413 at 427–8 who queries whether the focus on 'senior management' will actually bring the discussion back to identification issues.

(i.e. an existing civil law duty of care) to the deceased. Readers are referred to works on criminal law for a detailed assessment of this legislation.[198]

3-117   Though the Act is now in force, it is not expected that there will be many prosecutions of this offence in any given year for it is intended to be used only in the most serious cases. For most companies, the risk of prosecution under health and safety legislation remains a greater concern.

[198] See Gobert, above n 197, for an interesting assessment of the legislation which he considers to be lacking in vision and flawed in various respects but which may be important for its symbolic value.

4

The company constitution

A Defining the constitution

The company's constitution is defined in CA 2006, s 17 in the following terms: **4-1**

'Unless the context otherwise requires, references in the Companies Acts to a company's constitution include—

(a) the company's articles, and

(b) any resolutions and agreements to which Chapter 3 applies (see section 29).'

Every company must have articles of association contained in a single document   **4-2**
divided into paragraphs numbered consecutively.[1] Model forms of articles are provided for public and private companies limited by shares and for companies limited by guarantee and any company may adopt all or any of the provisions of the relevant model articles for that type of company.[2] Model articles are not intended to be a strait-jacket and the draftsman is free to add, subtract or vary, as the needs of the case suggest.[3]

Every company must register their articles (CA 2006, s 18(2)) and if, on formation of   **4-3**
a limited company, articles are not registered or, if articles are registered, in so far as they do not exclude or modify the relevant model articles, the relevant model articles form part of the company's articles automatically (s 20(1)). Larger companies usually exclude all of the model articles and draw up an entire set of articles appropriate to their circumstances, while drawing on the model articles in many respects. Even with smaller companies, the shareholders on formation may have matters of particular concern to them, such as issues concerning share transfers or the appointment of directors, and it is preferable for these matters to be the subject of provisions specifically drawn up to cover their individual circumstances. These provisions can then be combined with the remainder of the model articles by stating that the model articles apply except to the extent that they are excluded (s 20(1)(b)).

---

[1] CA 2006, s 18(1), (3).

[2] CA 2006, s 19(3). See The Companies (Model Articles) Regulations 2008, SI 2008/3229. It is the model articles in force at the time of the company's registration which apply: s 20(2); and subsequent amendments of the model articles do not affect a company registered before the amendment: s 19(4). Many companies on the register of companies remain subject to the 1985 Table A and some are still governed by the 1948 Table A.

[3] *Gaiman v National Association for Mental Health* [1971] Ch 317; CA 2006, s 18(3).

4-4   While it is possible to include the model provisions by reference,[4] it is preferable and more consistent with the requirement that the articles be in a single document that the company draws up articles which include the customised matters and the matters relied on from the model articles. This approach avoids the inconsistencies which can arise from having two documents and prevents uncertainty as to the extent to which specific model provisions have been excluded or modified. At common law persons dealing with a company are deemed under the doctrine of constructive notice to have notice of the company's articles of association,[5] but the impact of this doctrine is much reduced by CA 2006, ss 39–40 (s 39 is discussed below; s 40 is discussed in Chapter 8).

4-5   The resolutions and agreements referred to in CA 2006, s 17(b) (i.e. those to which Chapter 3 applies) are resolutions and agreements listed in s 29 which must be registered with the registrar of companies under s 30. Basically there are two types of resolutions,[6] ordinary and special resolutions. An ordinary resolution is a resolution passed by a simple majority (s 282(1)) and a special resolution is a resolution passed by a majority of not less than 75% (s 283(1)). Resolutions are considered at **15-16**.

4-6   The categories of resolutions which must be registered are:

- any special resolution (CA 2006, s 29(1)(a));
- any resolution or agreement whether of the company or of a class of shareholders which is effective because of the *Duomatic* principle[7] that informal unanimous assent is tantamount to a resolution (s 29(1)(b) and (c));
- any resolution varying class rights which is not a special resolution (s 29(1)(d));
- other resolutions (i.e. ordinary resolutions) which are required by statute to be registered (s 29(1)(e)). This ensures that ordinary resolutions of importance must also be registered. For example, a resolution granting authority for an allotment of shares by the directors, though an ordinary resolution, must be registered,[8] as must an ordinary resolution granting a company authority for market purchases of its own shares,[9] and an ordinary resolution of members of a private company incorporated before 1 October 2008 allowing the directors to authorise conflicts of interest.[10] An example of a resolution which must be registered by virtue of another enactment would be a resolution for voluntary winding up under IA 1986, s 84(1)(a) to which CA 2006, ss 29 and 30 apply.[11]

4-7   There has always been some uncertainty as to whether the requirement for registration extends to shareholders' agreements (s 29 and its predecessors refer to resolutions

---

[4] See *Explanatory Notes to the Companies Act 2006*, para 76.

[5] *Ernest v Nicholls* (1857) 6 HL Cas 401; *Mahony v East Holyford Mining Co* (1875) LR 7 HL 869; *Irvine v Union Bank of Australia* (1877) 2 App Cas 366, PC; *Wilson v Kelland* [1910] 2 Ch 306.

[6] The CA 2006 has abolished the category of extraordinary resolutions (essentially required 75% majority of those voting, but differed from a special resolution in that only 14 rather than 21 days' notice was required) though it remains effective where a company's articles or a contract require an extraordinary resolution.

[7] *Re Duomatic Ltd* [1969] 1 All ER 161, discussed at **15-73**, though it was noted in the Parliamentary debates that the requirement to register resolutions based on informal unanimous assent is rarely observed.

[8] CA 2006, s 551(8), (9).   [9] CA 2006, s 701(1), (8).

[10] The Companies Act 2006 (Commencement No 5, Transitional Provisions and Savings) Order 2007, SI 2007/3495, art 9, Sch 4, Part 3, para 47.   [11] IA 1986, s 84(3).

or agreements) and this matter is not clarified by the Companies Act 2006. In practice, shareholders' agreements are not registered and are regarded as purely private contractual documents. Anyone consulting the company's articles needs to bear in mind, therefore, the possibility (which they should enquire about) that there is a private shareholders' agreement behind the public constitution. Shareholder agreements are discussed at **4-76**.

The definition of the constitution in CA 2006, s 17 is not exhaustive ('include') and is subject to context. Beyond the articles and resolutions, the memorandum of association would also be considered to be a constitutional document. Its importance is limited by s 8 to signalling the intention of the subscribers to form a company, and their agreement to become members of the company and to take at least one share each. An indication of other documents which make up the company's constitution can be found in s 32 which identifies the constitutional documents which must be provided to members on request as including the company's articles, any resolutions and agreements that have been recorded by the registrar under s 29; a copy of the company's current certificate of incorporation, and a current statement of capital (which will give the total number of shares in the company, their aggregate nominal value, any class rights and the amount paid or unpaid, on the shares). The definition of the constitution is also subject to context. For example, for the purposes of Part 10 (directors' duties), an expanded definition is provided in s 257 to include (a) any resolution or other decision come to in accordance with the constitution (for example, where the articles require an ordinary resolution on some matter[12]) and (b) any decision by the members which is treated as equivalent to a decision by the company, a reference to decisions reached on the basis of the informal unanimous assent of the shareholders which, applying *Re Duomatic Ltd*,[13] discussed at **15.73**, is equivalent to a decision of the company. The expanded definition means therefore that the directors must act in accordance with the articles (s 17(a)), any special (or other) resolution registrable with the registrar of companies (s 17(b)), any resolution or other decision reached under the articles (s 257(1)), and any informal unanimous assent of the shareholders (s 257(2)). **4-8**

While all of these elements, articles, resolutions, agreements, and other documents make up the constitution, for most purposes, the key document, and the focus of this chapter, is the articles of association. **4-9**

B Content of the articles

Internal rules

The articles set out the internal rules and regulations which govern the relationship between the members and the company. The matters typically covered in the articles **4-10**

---

[12] Generally, ordinary resolutions are not registered with the registrar of companies: see CA 2006, ss 29 and 30.

[13] [1969] 1 All ER 161.

include the conduct of meetings and voting procedures; capital matters including share transfer and transmission; the appointment and removal of directors and their powers; and the declaration of dividends.

Provisions previously contained in a company's memorandum

4-11   As noted, prior to the reforms effected by the CA 2006, a company's memorandum of association was an important constitutional document whereas under s 8 it serves to record the agreement of the members to form an association. For companies formed under the CA 1985 and its predecessors, provisions that were contained in the memorandum are treated now as provisions of the company's articles and as such may be altered by a special resolution under CA 2006, s 21. Provisions previously entrenched in the memorandum are treated as entrenched provisions of the articles[14] and governed by s 22. Entrenchment is discussed below at **4-17**.

Objects clauses

4-12   Prior to the CA 2006, companies were required to state their objects in the memorandum and the objects determined the company's capacity. Acts outside of the objects were ultra vires and void,[15] though the impact of that doctrine was reduced almost to obsolescence by a combination of drafting techniques, judicial interpretation and statutory reform.[16] The position has been further affected by a significant change effected by the CA 2006.

4-13   Companies are no longer required to state their objects and, unless a company's articles specifically restrict the objects of the company, a company's objects are unrestricted (CA 2006, s 31(1)). It is not expected that companies formed under the CA 2006 will restrict their objects (though some businesses such as charitable companies may still find it useful to do so) and therefore most companies have unrestricted capacity and no issue of ultra vires can arise. For companies formed under the CA 1985 and its predecessors, as mentioned above, the objects clauses previously set out in the memorandum now become part of their articles and are open to alteration and deletion by way of special resolution under CA 2006, s 21. For such companies, deleting their objects puts them in the same position as companies formed under the CA 2006. Their capacity will be unrestricted and no issue of ultra vires can arise.

4-14   Alternatively, companies formed under the CA 1985 and its predecessors may choose to retain their objects clauses in their articles and, as mentioned, some companies formed under the CA 2006 may find it useful to restrict their objects as permitted by s 31. Strictly speaking, such companies may still enter into ultra vires transactions, i.e. acts beyond the restricted capacity limited by their objects clauses, but this is irrelevant

---

[14] CA 2006, s 28(2), (3); see also s 22(1).

[15] *Ashbury Railway Carriage and Iron Co Ltd v Riche* (1875) LR 7 HL 653.

[16] Legislative intervention to protect third parties arose out of the need to implement the First Company Law Directive, Directive 68/151/EEC 1968 OJ Spec Ed (1) 41, art 9.

since s 39 provides that the validity of an act done by a company cannot be called into question on the ground of a lack of capacity by reason of anything in the company's constitution.[17] The ultra vires point cannot be raised and the doctrine is irrelevant. What remains is a failure by the directors to act in accordance with the constitution, a matter governed by s 171 and addressed in Chapter 8: see **8-7**.

C Amending the articles

The statutory power to amend the articles

A company may amend its articles of association by special resolution[18] (CA 2006,   **4-15**
s 21(1)) and any agreement or article purporting to deprive a company of the power to amend its articles is invalid on the ground that it is contrary to the statute.[19] A member joins a company on the understanding that the articles may be changed.[20] Therefore, if a member has concerns and wishes to protect himself from particular alterations, he will need to consider various protective devices which are available, mechanisms which in effect erode the principle that a company cannot be denied power to alter its articles.

One possibility is weighted voting rights granted to a shareholder or group of share-   **4-16**
holders to ensure that the other shareholders cannot muster the necessary votes to achieve a special resolution.[21] Another possibility is that shareholders reach an agreement outside of the articles as to how they will exercise their voting rights on any resolution to alter the articles,[22] so ensuring a special resolution altering the articles cannot be passed. Another possibility is to rely for protection not on the articles but on a shareholders' agreement governing the parties' relationships. A shareholders'

---

[17] Note that the application of CA 2006, s 39 is modified for charitable companies, see s 42.

[18] A special resolution requires a 75% majority, see CA 2006, s 283(1). The special resolution amending the articles must be forwarded to the registrar of companies within 15 days: ss 29(1)(a), 30(1); and a copy of the articles as altered must be sent to the registrar not later than 15 days after the amendment takes effect: s 26. As to penalties for non-compliance, see s 27.

[19] *Walker v London Tramways Co* (1879) 12 Ch D 705; *Malleson v National Insurance & Guarantee Corpn* [1894] 1 Ch 200; *Punt v Symons & Co Ltd* [1903] 2 Ch 506. See also *Russell v Northern Bank Development Corp Ltd* [1992] 3 All ER 161, HL. While a company cannot be precluded from altering its articles, to act on the altered articles may nevertheless be a breach of contract (giving rise to liability in damages) if it is contrary to a stipulation in a contract validly made before the alteration: *Southern Foundries (1926) Ltd v Shirlaw* [1940] AC 701 at 740–1; *Cumbrian Newspapers Group Ltd v Cumberland and Westmorland Herald Newspaper and Printing Co Ltd* [1986] 2 All ER 816 at 831.

[20] *Allen v Gold Reefs of West Africa Ltd* [1900] 1 Ch 656 at 672–3, per Lindley MR; *Greenhalgh v Arderne Cinemas Ltd* [1950] 2 All ER 1120 at 1127, per Evershed MR; *Malleson v National Insurance & Guarantee Corp* [1894] 1 Ch 200 at 205, 206. See also *Peters' American Delicacy Co Ltd v Heath* (1939) 61 CLR 457 at 507, per Dixon J.

[21] See *Bushell v Faith* [1969] 1 All ER 1002.

[22] This type of arrangement is not caught by the prohibition on the company restricting its power to alter its articles, see *Russell v Northern Bank Development Corp Ltd* [1992] 3 All ER 161, HL.

agreement is a separate contract between the shareholders which cannot be altered without consent. Shareholder agreements are discussed below at **4-76**.

4-17   Another possibility is to entrench certain provisions in the articles, a mechanism provided for the first time by the CA 2006, s 22. An entrenched provision is one which can be amended or repealed only if conditions are met, or procedures are complied with, that are more restrictive than those applicable to a special resolution.

4-18   In part, this innovation was necessary as a result of the changes made to the memorandum of association demoting it from its previous role as an important constitutional document. Previously, when shareholders wished to entrench provisions of the constitution, they could do so by including them in the memorandum and precluding their alteration. With the memorandum reduced to the status of a declaration of association (CA 2006, s 8), a new method of entrenchment is required and s 22(1) provides that:

> 'A company's articles may contain provision ("provision for entrenchment") to the effect that specified provisions of the articles may be amended or repealed only if conditions are met, or procedures are complied with, that are more restrictive than those applicable in the case of a special resolution.'[23]

4-19   A provision for entrenchment may be included in the articles on formation or it can be added subsequently to the articles if agreed to by all the members of the company.[24] In either case (i.e. whether entrenched on formation or added by way of an alteration of the articles) the registrar must be informed (CA 2006, s 23) so as to ensure that anyone searching the register appreciates that the articles contain such provisions.[25]

4-20   Initially, it was intended that an entrenched provision could not be altered or repealed, but the Government was subsequently persuaded that rendering a provision unalterable would create problems. An entrenched provision can be altered therefore in the following ways:

(1) in accordance with the method indicated in the provision;

(2) by agreement of all the members of the company (s 22(3)(a)) (so even a provision which is stated to be irrevocable can be overridden);

(3) by order of the court or other authority having power to alter the company's articles (s 22(3)(b)).

4-21   When a company alters its articles, having previously notified the registrar of the existence of an entrenched provision, it must also provide a statement of compliance, certifying that any alteration has been made in accordance with the articles (CA 2006, s 24(2)).[26]

---

[23] A condition might be that a 90% majority is required for alteration. The procedures to be complied with may be more restrictive than for a special resolution, for example, with regard to giving notice of the resolution.

[24] CA 2006, s 22(2). The Government considers that, in practice, few companies will wish to entrench provisions in this way.   [25] See *Explanatory Notes to the Companies Act 2006*, para 84.

[26] In the Parliamentary debates, it was explained that the purpose of this requirement is to force the directors to pause and take stock and ensure that they have satisfied themselves that any necessary restrictions

Even in the absence of entrenchment or other protective measures, the power to alter **4-22** the articles is not entirely unrestricted with limits imposed by statute and, more importantly, at common law. For example, an alteration cannot require a member to take more shares or in any way increase his liability to contribute to the company without his consent (CA 2006, s 25) and an alteration cannot vary or abrogate class rights without compliance with s 630(2) which governs such matters (class rights are discussed at **14-23**).[27] Crucially, at common law, the power to alter the articles must be exercised bona fide for the benefit of the company as a whole.

Common law limits to the power to amend the articles

The important common law limitation on the power to alter the articles was famously **4-23** articulated by Lindley MR in *Allen v Gold Reefs of West Africa Ltd*[28] as follows:

'Wide, however, as the language of s 50 [CA 2006, s 21(1)] is, the power conferred by it must, like all other powers, be exercised subject to those general principles of law and equity which are applicable to all powers conferred on majorities and enabling them to bind minorities. It must be exercised, not only in the manner required by law, but also bona fide for the benefit of the company as a whole, and it must not be exceeded.'

In this case the court permitted an alteration which extended a company's lien (and **4-24** powers of sale) on partly paid shares to fully paid up shares, despite the fact that the change impacted on only one shareholder holding fully paid shares (or rather on his estate, as he was deceased at the time of the alteration). It was because the member had died owing arrears on partly paid shares that the company wanted to extend the lien to fully paid shares which formed part of his estate. The court agreed that it was bona fide for the benefit of the company as a whole that the company should have a lien to secure debts due to it.[29] An alteration applicable to all members and for the benefit of the company cannot be impeached on the grounds of bad faith merely because its practical impact is felt by only one member.[30] As Warrington LJ put it later in *Sidebottom v Kershaw, Leese & Co Ltd*,[31] it is commonly the case that the circumstance of an individual member may awake the directors to the problem which the alteration is designed to resolve, but the fact that it impacts on one shareholder of itself does not call into question the bona fides of the shareholders.[32]

in the constitution have been observed; it also ensures that the public record is accurate; and if the company has overlooked any special requirements in altering the articles, the registrar of companies is able to ask the company as to the position: see 678 HL Debs GC19, 30 January 2006.

[27] In the context of takeovers, where a company has passed an opt in resolution under CA 2006, s 966, an alteration of its articles inconsistent with the requirements of s 966(2) (which imposes conditions as to the content of the articles for the purposes of an opt in resolution) has no effect until the company has passed a special resolution opting out of s 966: s 967(7). As to opting in and opting out resolutions, see **26-75**.

[28] [1900] 1 Ch 656 at 671, CA.

[29] Vaughan Williams LJ dissented as he thought that the resolution was not passed in good faith, being really passed merely to defeat the existing rights of an individual shareholder: see [1900] 1 Ch 656 at 677.

[30] [1900] 1 Ch 656 at 675. See also *Sidebottom v Kershaw, Leese & Co Ltd* [1920] 1 Ch 154; *Greenhalgh v Arderne Cinemas Ltd* [1950] 2 All ER 1120; *Shuttleworth v Cox Bros & Co (Maidenhead) Ltd* [1927] KB 9.

[31] [1920] 1 Ch 154, CA.   [32] [1920] 1 Ch 154 at 171–2; and see at 166–7, per Lord Sterndale MR.

4-25   Beyond this famous dictum of Lindley MR, the judgments in *Allen v Gold Reefs of West Africa Ltd*[33] offer little guidance as to the scope and substance of this 'bona fide for the benefit of the company as a whole' test (hereinafter the *Allen* test) and to some extent the courts ever since have been exercised by its meaning. Indeed, the test has been criticised as 'almost meaningless', particularly in the context of an alteration adjusting the conflicting interests of the shareholders,[34] a view which gains judicial support from the Privy Council in *Citco Banking Corp NV v Pusser's Ltd*,[35] which is discussed at **4-35** below.

4-26   Some elaboration of the *Allen* test can be found in two subsequent Court of Appeal judgments: *Shuttleworth v Cox Bros & Co (Maidenhead) Ltd*[36] and *Greenhalgh v Arderne Cinemas Ltd*[37] of which *Shuttleworth* is the more illuminating.[38]

4-27   In *Shuttleworth v Cox Bros & Co (Maidenhead) Ltd*[39] a provision in the company's articles conferred life tenure on the directors unless disqualified on one of six grounds. One of the directors failed to account for company money and property and the articles were altered to add a further ground for disqualification, namely that any director should resign on being asked by all his co-directors to resign. Once the articles had been altered, the defaulting director was asked to resign. He unsuccessfully challenged the validity of the alteration.

4-28   The Court of Appeal started by criticising the view that had been expressed in the lower court in the earlier case of *Dafen Tinplate Co Ltd v Llanelly Steel Co Ltd*[40] that the *Allen* test had two distinct components: (1) bona fides; and (2) the benefit of the company.[41] The Court of Appeal stressed that there is only one test and the proper approach was summed up by Scrutton LJ as follows:[42]

> '...when persons, honestly endeavouring to decide what will be for the benefit of the company and to act accordingly, decide upon a particular course, then, *provided* [emphasis added] there are grounds on which reasonable men could come to the same decision, it does not matter whether the Court would or would not come to the same decision or a different decision. It is not the business of the Court to manage the affairs of the company. That is for the shareholders and directors.'

4-29   The central question is whether the shareholders honestly believe the alteration to be for the benefit of the company as a whole; but in order that the test should not be wholly subjective, there is the proviso that, even if the shareholders' honesty is unchallenged,

---

[33] [1900] 1 Ch 656 at 671, CA.

[34] See *Peters' American Delicacy Co Ltd v Heath* (1939) 61 CLR 457 at 512, per Dixon J; also Rixon, 'Competing Interests and Conflicting Principles: An Examination of the Power of Alteration of Articles of Association' (1986) 49 MLR 446.

[35] See [2007] 2 BCLC 483 at 491.   [36] [1927] 2 KB 9, CA.   [37] [1950] 2 All ER 1120, CA.

[38] The difficulties with Evershed MR's judgment in *Greenhalgh* are such (see Hannigan, n 95 below at 479–80) that it is probably best relegated to the sidelines but, of course, until overruled it stands as an authority. See also Davies, *Gower and Davies' Principles of Modern Company Law* (8th edn, 2008), p 661 who comments that the guidance to be gained from *Greenhalgh* is limited.

[39] [1927] 2 KB 9.   [40] [1920] 2 Ch 124, Ch D.   [41] [1927] 2 KB 9 at 19, 22.

[42] [1927] KB 9 at 23.

an alteration will not stand if it is such that 'no reasonable men could consider it for the benefit of the company'.[43]

The first requirement, that the shareholders exercise their power to alter the articles **4-30** in good faith, is simply a reflection of the traditional equitable constraints on the ability of a majority to bind a minority, as Lindley MR said in *Allen v Gold Reefs of West Africa Ltd*.[44] It protects the minority by ensuring that alterations motivated by malice, fraud and personal benefit cannot stand while respecting the commercial judgment of shareholders acting genuinely for the benefit of the company.[45]

The proviso, that an alteration will not stand if it is such that 'no reasonable men could **4-31** consider it for the benefit of the company' simply confirms that there are some alterations that 'cannot be regarded as being for the benefit of the company, no matter how honestly the majority believe them to be'.[46] Subjective good faith cannot be allowed to prevail where a reasonable shareholder can see no benefit to the company and the absence of such benefit would in any event cast doubt on the assertions of bona fides by the shareholders.[47]

The core element to the test (and the proviso) is the requirement that the alteration be for **4-32** the benefit of the company as a whole. That is the limit to the power which 'must not be exceeded', to use Lord Lindley's words,[48] otherwise the exercise is a fraud on a power and void.[49] In this context, Evershed MR in *Greenhalgh v Arderne Cinemas Ltd*[50] had no doubt that the phrase 'the company as a whole' meant the shareholders as a body, though dicta elsewhere can be read as interpreting the phrase as meaning the corporate entity.[51]

[43] [1927] 2 KB 9 at 18, per Bankes LJ: '[an alteration must not be]...so oppressive as to cast suspicion on the honesty of the persons responsible for it, or so extravagant that no reasonable men could really consider it for the benefit of the company.'; at 24, per Scrutton LJ: '[an alteration will not stand if]...the decision of the shareholders, though honest, is such that no reasonable men could have come to it upon proper materials...'); qualifications endorsed by Atkin LJ at p 26. See Sealy, '"Bona Fides" and "Proper Purposes" in Corporate Decisions' [1989] 15 Monash U L Rev 265 at 277–8.   [44] [1900] 1 Ch 656 at 671.

[45] See *Rights & Issues Investment Trust Ltd v Stylo Shoes Ltd* [1964] 3 All ER 628 at 631; *Sidebottom v Kershaw, Leese & Co Ltd* [1927] 2 KB 9 at 23, 26, per Atkins LJ: 'It is not a matter of law for the Court whether or not a particular alteration is for the benefit of the company; nor is it the business of the judge to review the decision of every company in the country on these questions.'

[46] *Constable v Executive Connections Ltd* [2005] 2 BCLC 638 at 649–50; and see Sealy, above n 43; *Hutton v West Cork Rly Co* (1993) 23 Ch D 654 at 671, per Bowen LJ: 'Bona fides cannot be the sole test, otherwise you might have a lunatic conducting the affairs of the company, and paying away its money with both hands in a manner perfectly bona fide yet perfectly irrational'.

[47] See *Shuttleworth v Cox Bros & Co (Maidenhead) Ltd* [1927] 2 KB 9 at 23.

[48] *Allen v Gold Reefs of West Africa Ltd* [1900] 1 Ch 656 at 671.

[49] See Worthington, 'Corporate Governance: Remedying and Ratifying Directors' Breaches' (2000) 116 LQR 638 at 646–50—majority shareholders are not allowed to use their powers for purposes outside the contemplation of the grant; *Vatcher v Paul* [1915] AC 372 at 378; *British Equitable Assurance Co Ltd v Bailey* [1906] AC 35 at 42, per Lord Lindley; *Re Halt Garage (1964) Ltd* [1982] 3 All ER 1016 at 1037, per Oliver J; *Peters' American Delicacy Co Ltd v Heath* (1939) 61 CLR 457 at 511–12, per Dixon J. Also note Rimer J in *Redwood Master Fund Ltd v TD Bank Europe Ltd* [2006] 1 BCLC 149 at 182 though this is not a case involving an alteration of articles but the variation of the terms of a loan facility.

[50] [1950] 2 All ER 1120 at 1126.

[51] See Rixon, above n 34, p 449 who notes that Lindley MR in *Allen v Gold Reefs of West Africa Ltd* [1900] 1 Ch 656 clearly meant the corporate entity.

4-33   In *Greenhalgh*, the company's articles contained restrictive provisions governing the transfer of shares. Anyone wishing to sell their shares in the company were required to offer them first to existing members. If no member wished to purchase the shares, the shares could then be sold to an outside purchaser, but only with the consent of the board of directors. The articles were altered to allow for the direct sale of shares to an outsider without having to offer them first to the existing shareholders, provided the sale was approved by an ordinary resolution of the company in general meeting. A minority shareholder challenged the validity of this alteration. The court concluded that the alteration was merely a relaxation of the very stringent restrictions on transfer in the existing articles and as such was bona fide for the benefit of the company as a whole.[52]

4-34   Regarding 'the company as a whole' as the corporators as a whole makes sense in the context of the power which is being exercised. It is a power to alter the contractual relationship between the members inter se[53] and between them and the company and as such should be governed by considerations as to what is in the best interests of the members as a whole. In any event, it is perhaps unwise to waste too much time on this issue of entity versus corporators in this context for it is not clear that interpreting 'the company as a whole' as the entity rather than the corporators would actually produce a different result. For example, it was in the interests of the corporators and the company in *Allen*[54] that the company obtained security with respect to debts owed to it; it was in the interests of the corporators and the company in *Greenhalgh*[55] that the company's strict pre-emption provisions on transfer were relaxed;[56] it was in the interests of the corporators and the company in *Shuttleworth*[57] that the articles were amended to facilitate the removal of unsatisfactory directors. In fact, when the cases are considered in detail, there is evidence of considerable judicial wavering (even within a case) between viewing the company as an entity and the company as the corporators.[58]

4-35   Given the general approach of the courts to the *Allen* test, it is unsurprising that it is rare for a challenge to an alteration to succeed (and the onus of proof is on the person challenging the alteration).[59] This judicial reluctance to interfere in this area was confirmed recently by the Privy Council in *Citco Banking Corp NV v Pusser's Ltd*.[60] In this case the alteration to the articles had the effect of giving the company chairman voting

---

[52] [1950] 2 All ER 1120 at 1127.

[53] *Peters' American Delicacy Co Ltd v Heath* (1939) 61 CLR 457 at 506, per Dixon J.

[54] *Allen v Gold Reefs of West Africa Ltd* [1900] 1 Ch 656.

[55] *Greenhalgh v Arderne Cinemas Ltd* [1950] 2 All ER 1120.

[56] The company's interest would lie in the ability to raise capital by issuing shares as a result of their increased marketability following the relaxation of the pre-emption provisions.

[57] *Shuttleworth v Cox Bros & Co (Maidenhead) Ltd* [1927] KB 9.

[58] See, for example, *Sidebottom v Kershaw, Leese & Co Ltd* [1920] 1 Ch 154 at 166, 169; Rixon, above n 34, p 454 who concluded: 'In short, "the company as a whole" is a Delphic term employed by different judges in different circumstances to signify different things…'; Sealy, above n 43, at pp 269–70.

[59] *Peters' American Delicacy Co Ltd v Heath* (1939) 61 CLR 457; *Citco Banking Corp NV v Pusser's Ltd* [2007] 2 BCLC 483, PC.   [60] [2007] 2 BCLC 483, PC. See Williams (2007) CLJ 500.

control of the company. The Privy Council dismissed a challenge to the validity of the alteration, applying *Shuttleworth*, and accepted that the test can be stated succinctly by asking whether reasonable shareholders could consider the amendment to be for the benefit of the company.[61]

Stated like this, the test looks more objective than subjective, but this is the traditional test, i.e. could the shareholders genuinely have believed the alteration to be for the benefit of the company and was that belief one which a reasonable shareholder could have held? The authorities in any event make it difficult to determine whether the subjective or objective element is pre-eminent[62] which, of course, may be the result of a quite deliberate conflating of the issues by the courts so as to avoid criticism that the court is substituting its judgment for that of the shareholders.[63]   **4-36**

Their Lordships in *Citco* did accept that the 'bona fides for the benefit of the company as a whole' test is not appropriate in the context of an alteration adjusting the conflicting interests of the shareholders,[64] and that 'some other test of validity is required',[65] but it was not necessary to determine that other test since the case could be resolved by the application of the traditional test.   **4-37**

On the facts in *Citco*, the shareholders could have concluded in good faith that they accepted the arguments as to why the amendment would be in the interests of the company (the company needed capital and potential investors wished the chairman to have control of the company). Just as an alteration may be for the benefit of the company though it is to the detriment of one member (as in *Allen*) so an alteration may be for the benefit of the company as a whole notwithstanding that it operates to the particular advantage of some or one shareholder.[66] In the absence of any attack on his bona fides, the Privy Council also confirmed that there is no reason why a member who benefits from an alteration (in this case, the chairman) should not vote, as a shareholder, in favour of that alteration.[67]   **4-38**

The Privy Council focus on *Shuttleworth v Cox Bros & Co (Maidenhead) Ltd*[68] suggests that their Lordships are content that the position now reached on the 'bona fides' test maintains a proper balance between the freedom necessary for the majority to make constitutional changes and the need to protect the minority against unfair alterations. The resolutely minimalist judgment in *Citco* indicates a preference for the established   **4-39**

---

[61] [2007] 2 BCLC 483 at 491, PC, per Lord Hoffmann.

[62] See *Sidebottom v Kershaw, Leese & Co Ltd* [1920] 1 Ch 154 at 165–6, 171–2 where the court appears to give almost equal weight to the requirement of subjective good faith and an objective benefit to the company in ridding itself of a competing shareholder.

[63] See Davies, above n 38, p 654: 'The courts have hovered uncomfortably between an unwillingness to determine how businesses should be run and an equally deeply felt unease that simple majoritarianism would leave the minority exposed to opportunistic treatment.'

[64] See *Peters' American Delicacy Co Ltd v Heath* (1939) 61 CLR 457 at 512, per Dixon J; also Rixon, above n 34.

[65] [2007] 2 BCLC 483 at 491.

[66] [2007] 2 BCLC 483 at 490. See *Rights & Issues Investment Trust Ltd v Stylo Shoes Ltd* [1964] 3 All ER 628 at 631.

[67] [2007] 2 BCLC 483 at 493, citing the established principle that shareholders are free to exercise their votes in their own interests, see *Burland v Earle* [1902] AC 83 at 94.   [68] [1927] 2 KB 9, CA.

approach.[69] While there was support, as noted at **4-37**, for the view that the 'bona fides for the benefit of the company as a whole' test is not appropriate in the context of an alteration adjusting the conflicting interests of the shareholders and that 'some other test of validity is required',[70] no guidance was given as to what that test might be. But as the concerns lie in whether it is appropriate to define 'the company as a whole' as the entity or the corporators and, as discussed above at **4-34**, the courts already show considerable flexibility as to which category of interests they are considering, and as many of the cases can be viewed either as a case concerning the entity and/or the corporators, it is not entirely clear that some 'new' test is required.[71] In *Citco* itself, it could be argued that the alteration impacted on both the entity and the members. It affected the company's ability to raise capital and it adjusted the conflicting interests of the members because it altered their respective voting rights, but still their Lordships were content to apply the traditional test.

4-40   More broadly, their Lordships may have been content to rely on the existing settled law because an aggrieved shareholder always has the option of seeking redress by way of a petition under CA 2006, s 994, the unfairly prejudicial remedy (discussed in detail in Chapter 17). This provision, as we shall see, allows the court considerable latitude in terms of assessing whether conduct is unfairly prejudicial and so provides a basis for challenging an unfair alteration in an appropriate case.

4-41   Having said that, the one area which remains of some interest, and where the courts have been more responsive to complaints and have rejected alterations, is where majority shareholders seek an unrestricted power, in their own interests, to compulsorily acquire the shares of the minority. The courts are alert to the fact that such alterations frequently confuse the interests of the majority with the benefit of the company as a whole, but even here there are limits to the court's willingness to interfere.

Compulsory transfer provisions

4-42   The application of the *Allen* test in the context of compulsory transfer provisions is dominated by three decisions: *Sidebottom v Kershaw, Leese & Co Ltd*;[72] *Brown v British Abrasive Wheel Co Ltd*;[73] and *Dafen Tinplate Co Ltd v Llanelly Steel Co Ltd*.[74]

4-43   In *Sidebottom v Kershaw, Leese & Co Ltd*[75] the alteration allowed the directors to require any shareholder who competed with the company's business to transfer his

---

[69] Their Lordships declined the opportunity to consider further the meaning of Evershed MR's judgment in *Greenhalgh v Arderne Cinemas Ltd* [1950] 2 All ER 1120 or to explore the controversial Australian decision in *Gambotto v WCP Ltd* (1995) 182 CLR 432, discussed below at **4-50**.

[70] [2007] 2 BCLC 483 at 491.

[71] A new test might lie along the lines of 'proper purpose' or oppression as suggested by Dixon J in *Peters' American Delicacy Co Ltd v Heath* (1939) 61 CLR 457 at 512, but the adoption of a proper purpose test in *Gambotto v WCP Ltd* (1995) 182 CLR 432, see **4-50**, attracted considerable criticism precisely on the ground that a proper purpose test is no more certain in application in this context than the 'bona fides' test, while an oppression test (also favoured in *Gambotto*) is unnecessary in the light of CA 2006, s 994 (unfairly prejudicial conduct). See Hollington, *Shareholders' Rights* (5th edn, 2007), para 5–33: '…does not appear to be a significant improvement on the traditional test'.

[72] [1920] 1 Ch 154, CA.   [73] [1919] 1 Ch 290.   [74] [1920] 2 Ch 124.

[75] [1920] 1 Ch 154, CA.

shares at their full value to nominees of the directors. The plaintiffs (who held 711 out of 7,620 issued shares) sought a declaration that the alteration was invalid.[76]

The court accepted that such a power could be included in the articles from incorp-   **4-44**
oration[77] and could be included subsequently by way of alteration of the articles, provided the exercise of the power of alteration is beyond challenge, being done bona fide
for the benefit of the company as a whole.[78] It had already been established that an
alteration applicable to all is not open to impeachment solely on the basis of its impact
on a particular shareholder.[79] Looking at the facts in *Sidebottom*, the Court of Appeal
had no hesitation in finding that the resolution had been passed bona fide for the benefit of the company as a whole. The court accepted that it was clearly for the company's
benefit 'that they should not be obliged to have amongst them as members persons
who are competing with them in business, and who may get knowledge from their
membership which would enable them to compete better'.[80]

In *Brown v British Abrasive Wheel Co Ltd*[81] the majority shareholders held 98% of   **4-45**
the shares and wished to alter the articles so as to permit them to acquire at fair value
the shares of the remaining 2% shareholders. The majority anticipated that further
capital would be required for the development of the company and they were willing
to provide it only if they could acquire the 2% minority.[82] The plaintiff shareholders
(who held 50 shares out of an issued share capital of 50,000) successfully sought an
injunction preventing the company from altering the articles in this way. Astbury J
held that the proposed alteration was merely for the benefit of the majority, enabling
them to do forcibly what they were unable to effect by agreement with the minority.[83] This judgment is unsound on the law for, as the Court of Appeal pointed out
in *Sidebottom*,[84] Astbury J did not apply the *Allen* test.[85] Notwithstanding that clear
error, Astbury J did expressly find that the shareholders had acted for their own benefit
in approving the alteration rather than honestly endeavouring to act for the benefit of
the company.[86] On that basis, even the Court of Appeal was agreed that the decision
in the case was right.[87]

---

[76] [1920] 1 Ch 154 at 163–5.   [77] *Phillips v Manufacturers' Securities Ltd* (1917) 116 LT 290.

[78] [1920] 1 Ch 154 at 164, per Lord Sterndale MR.

[79] *Allen v Gold Reefs of West Africa Ltd* [1900] 1 Ch 656; see also *Greenhalgh v Arderne Cinemas Ltd* [1950]
2 All ER 1120; *Shuttleworth v Cox Bros & Co (Maidenhead) Ltd* [1927] KB 9.

[80] [1920] 1 Ch 154 at 166, per Lord Sterndale MR.   [81] [1919] 1 Ch 290.

[82] Without further capital, the majority said the company might have to go into liquidation, see [1919] 1
Ch 290 at 295–6.   [83] [1919] 1 Ch 290 at 294.

[84] See *Sidebottom v Kershaw, Leese & Co Ltd* [1920] 1 Ch 154 at 163, 170 and 173, per Lord Sterndale MR,
Warrington LJ and Eve J, respectively.

[85] Astbury J took a broad approach and asked whether the enforcement of the proposed alteration against
the minority was within the ordinary principles of justice and whether it was for the benefit of the company
as a whole: [1919] 1 Ch 290 at 295–6.

[86] [1919] 1 Ch 290 at 298. There is some evidence in the case that the majority had an eye to personal
profit in seeking to buy out the minority. The company's position had improved, bank funding was accessible, opportunities were anticipated and the court seemed to find that there was an element of the majority
seeking to ensure that the spoils of future prosperity went to them and were not shared with any minority
shareholders.

[87] See *Sidebottom v Kershaw, Leese & Co Ltd* [1920] 1 Ch 154 at 167, per Lord Sterndale MR; at 172, per
Warrington LJ.

4-46   The final authority is *Dafen Tinplate Co Ltd v Llanelly Steel Co Ltd*.[88] The background was that the company had been formed on the basis of an expectation (though no legal obligation) that the shareholders would purchase supplies from the company. One shareholder who had an interest in a competing business began purchasing his supplies from that other company. Being unable to acquire his shares by agreement, the company altered the articles to provide that the majority of shareholders could determine that the shares of any member (other than one principal shareholder) should be offered for sale by the directors to anyone of their choice at a fair value to be fixed by the directors.

4-47   The court refused to permit the alteration saying that it would have enabled the majority shareholder compulsorily to acquire the shares of any other member '…although there may be no complaint of any kind against his conduct and it cannot be suggested that he has done, or contemplates doing, anything to the detriment of the company'.[89] To say that such an unrestricted and unlimited power of expropriation was for the benefit of the company, Peterson J said, was to confuse the interests of the majority with the benefit of the company as a whole.[90]

4-48   The approach taken by Peterson J[91] was criticised by the Court of Appeal in *Shuttleworth v Cox Bros (Maidenhead) Ltd*[92] without casting doubt, however, on the outcome of the case which was clearly correct, given the finding that the majority in supporting the alteration were not honestly endeavouring to act for the benefit of the company.

4-49   On the basis of these authorities, it might be thought that the law is clear. The difficulty is that the authorities are of limited value, being two first instance decisions which have been criticised by the Court of Appeal on a point of law, and a Court of Appeal decision which is of limited value since the facts were so clear-cut. Interestingly, when a court was asked to consider the position in the more modern setting of altering the articles to include a 'drag-along' clause,[93] as in *Constable v Executive Connections Ltd*,[94] the court indicated some uncertainty as to the boundaries of permissible alterations to allow for compulsory transfer.[95]

4-50   It is worth digressing, therefore, to consider the controversial decision of the Australian High Court, *Gambotto v WCP Ltd*[96] on this issue. The court specifically rejected the 'bona fide for the benefit of the company' test as the appropriate test governing

---

[88] [1920] 2 Ch 124.   [89] [1920] 2 Ch 124 at 138.   [90] [1920] 2 Ch 124 at 141.

[91] See [1920] 2 Ch 124 at 140.

[92] [1927] 2 KB 9 at 19, 22. The court criticised the suggestion by Peterson J that where there was a conflict between the view of the shareholders and of the court as to the merits of the alteration, the court's view should prevail.

[93] The essence of a drag-along provision is that, on an offer for shares in a company being accepted by the majority of shareholders, the majority may require the minority to transfer their shares to the offeror on the same terms.

[94] [2005] 2 BCLC 638.

[95] For a detailed discussion of the issues surrounding alterations to allow for compulsory transfer provisions, see Hannigan, 'Altering the Articles to Allow for Compulsory Transfer—Dragging Minority Shareholders to a Reluctant Exit' [2007] JBL 471.

[96] (1995) 182 CLR 432, noted Prentice (1996) 112 LQR 194. See generally Boros, 'Altering the Articles of Association to Acquire Minority Shareholdings' in Rider (ed), *The Realm of Company Law* (1998); and

alterations and favoured a more objective consideration of the proper purpose for the exercise of the power of alteration.[97] More specifically, the court considered that the proper purpose for the expropriation of shares is if it could reasonably be apprehended that the continued shareholding is detrimental to the company and expropriation is a reasonable means of eliminating or mitigating that detriment.[98] The court went on to note that the majority cannot expropriate the minority merely to secure for themselves some commercial advantage to be derived from a new corporate structure.[99] The court further considered that the burden in expropriation cases is on the majority to prove that the alteration is for a proper purpose and is fair in all the circumstances.[100]

In this case, the alteration (approved without the majority shareholder voting) would   **4-51**
have enabled the majority (99.7%) shareholder to acquire the minority's shares (50,590 shares, 0.3%) at full value which would have generated tax advantages of approximately A$4m for the company.[101] The minority shareholders who objected held 15,898 shares, 0.1% of the issued share capital. The Australian High Court found the alteration to be invalid.

On the facts, there was no suggestion that the continued presence of the minority was   **4-52**
harmful to the company's business activities or that they had acted in any way to the company's detriment. All that was suggested was that there were tax and administrative advantages for the company in expropriating the minority shareholders.[102] The court did not accept that such commercial advantages of themselves could constitute a proper purpose for an alteration of the articles allowing for expropriation and so the alteration was invalid.

The decision attracted considerable criticism on a variety of grounds[103] including, so   **4-53**
far as compulsory transfer was concerned, that the result was economically inefficient and gave too much weight to proprietary interests and too much power to the minority shareholders.[104]

In fact, the approach taken by the Australian High Court on the compulsory transfer   **4-54**
point has much to commend it[105] and is compatible with the outcome of the English

---

the very useful collection of essays on the case in Ramsay (ed), *Gambotto v WCP Ltd: Its Implications for Corporate Regulation* (1996), hereinafter Ramsay (ed).

[97] (1995) 182 CLR 432 at 444.

[98] (1995) 182 CLR 432 at 445–6; the examples given by the court were expropriation of a competitor or if necessary to ensure that the company could continue to comply with a regulatory regime governing the principal business of the company, for example regarding foreign ownership of shares in a regulated industry.

[99] (1995) 182 CLR 432 at 446.   [100] (1995) 182 CLR 432 at 447.

[101] The alteration would have enabled any member entitled to 90% or more of the issued shares to acquire compulsorily the remaining shares at $1.80 per share.

[102] The court noted that it was difficult to conceive of circumstances in which financial and administrative benefits would not be a consequence of the expropriation of minority holdings: (1995) 182 CLR 432 at 448.

[103] See generally the commentaries on the case noted in n 96 above.

[104] See Hannigan, above n 95, at 488 and the commentaries cited there.

[105] See generally Hannigan, above n 95, and esp at 490–2. Essentially any alteration to add a compulsory transfer provision fundamentally alters the implicit basis of the bargain made between the shareholders on coming together in the company. The essence of the association is that the investment made by each

compulsory transfer cases, even if the legal basis is different. *Sidebottom v Kershaw, Leese & Co Ltd*[106] was a case where the continued presence of the minority share-holder (a competitor) was detrimental to the conduct of the company's business so the alteration was rightly allowed. In *Brown v British Abrasive Wheel Co Ltd*[107] and *Dafen Tinplate Co Ltd v Llanelly Steel Co Ltd*[108] the alterations provided for the inclusion of naked compulsory transfer provisions for the benefit and advantage of the majority shareholders and rightly were not allowed. The difference is that *Gambotto* contains a clearly articulated position on the issue of what is a permissible compulsory transfer provision whereas, as *Constable v Executive Connections Ltd*[109] makes clear, the position here is more uncertain.

4-55   The Company Law Review declined to embrace *Gambotto*, preferring to leave the matter to the courts to develop.[110] As noted above, their Lordships in the Privy Council in *Citco Banking Corp NV v Pusser's Ltd*[111] also considered it unnecessary to consider *Gambotto* (*Citco* did not concern compulsory transfer) but they did note that *Gambotto* has no support in English authorities.[112] It also looks unlikely to attract any support for it is possible to see in *Citco* a judicial unwillingness to move from reliance on the open-ended discretion of *Allen* to determine what is an acceptable alteration, even if it leaves first instance judges unsure as to the permissible limits of compulsory purchase.

D Interpreting the articles

A contract with distinctive features

4-56   As noted above, the articles form a contract, but it is a contract with its own distinctive features, as the Court of Appeal explained in *Bratton Seymour Service Co Ltd v Oxborough*.[113] First, the contract derives its binding force not from a bargain struck between parties but from the terms of the statute. Secondly, unlike an ordinary contract, it is not defeasible on the grounds of misrepresentation, common law mistake, mistake in equity, undue influence or duress. Also, as noted, the articles can be altered by a special resolution (i.e. without the consent of all the contracting parties) under CA 2006, s 21(1). Moreover, the articles cannot be rectified by the court even if the

---

shareholder is permanent and the relationship between the shareholders inter se is ongoing until such time as a shareholder chooses to exercise his right of voluntary exit. The bargain can be altered by agreement of the parties or by statute, but not by the exercise of majority power to alter the articles, save where the continued presence of the minority is detrimental to the conduct of the company's business.

[106] [1920] 1 Ch 154, CA.   [107] [1919] 1 Ch 290.   [108] [1920] 2 Ch 124.
[109] [2005] 2 BCLC 638.
[110] See Company Law Review, *Modern Company Law for a Competitive Economy: Completing the Structure* (2000) paras 5.94–5.99.
[111] [2007] 2 BCLC 483.   [112] [2007] 2 BCLC 483 at 492.   [113] [1992] BCLC 693 at 698, CA.

articles do not accord with what is proved to have been the intention of the parties.[114] In that situation, the parties must use s 21 to alter the articles.

The articles are a commercial document and, in the event of any ambiguity, the courts **4-57** will construe them so as to give them reasonable business efficacy where a construction tending to that result is admissible on the language of the articles.[115] In *Tett v Phoenix Property and Investment Co Ltd*,[116] for example, the court was able as a matter of construction to resolve difficulties surrounding the operation of a badly drafted pre-emption clause in the articles.

Terms cannot be implied from extrinsic circumstances, however, to give business effi- **4-58** cacy to the contract. In *Bratton Seymour Service Co Ltd v Oxborough*[117] the court was unable to imply a term in the articles of association of a company set up to manage a block of flats that the shareholders should make a financial contribution to the upkeep of the amenity areas of the development. Such a term could not be derived from the language of the articles, but purely from extrinsic circumstances and was, the court said, a type of implication which, as a matter of law, can never succeed in the case of articles of association.[118]

There can be a fine line between refusing to imply terms from extrinsic circumstances **4-59** and a generous construction of a provision in the articles to give effect to the obvious intention of the parties. In *Folkes Group plc v Alexander*[119] Rimer J was faced with an alteration of the articles which (as a result of the misplacing of an inserted provision) gave rise to an absurd result. The company's share capital was divided into voting and non-voting shares and contained a provision which enfranchised the non-voting shares in the event that the Folkes family shareholders fell below 40% of the voting shares for a consecutive period of 14 days. The amendment to the articles should have had the effect of increasing the qualifying shares which would be classified as Folkes family holdings for these purposes. Due to the manner in which the amendment was worded and inserted, however, it had the effect of narrowing the class with the result that the Folkes family holding would fall to less than 24% so triggering the enfranchisement of the non-voting shares.

As a matter of construction, Rimer J concluded that the result of the face value of the **4-60** words inserted was so absurd that something had to have gone seriously wrong with the drafting. The court was therefore entitled to construe the article by supplying five words (which had obviously been mistakenly omitted) such that the articles assumed a common sense meaning reflecting a true sense of what was intended. Rimer J acknowledged that his approach to the interpretation of the amended article might be regarded

---

[114] *Scott v Frank F Scott* [1940] 1 Ch 794 (articles should have included a provision on pre-emption on the death of a shareholder; the court could not rectify the articles to include such a provision).

[115] *Holmes v Keyes* [1958] 2 All ER 129 at 138; also *BWE International Ltd v Jones* [2004] 1 BCLC 406, CA.

[116] [1986] BCLC 149. See also *Pennington v Crampton* [2004] BCC 611.

[117] [1992] BCLC 693, CA. See also *Mutual Life Insurance Co of New York v The Rank Organisation Ltd* [1985] BCLC 11.

[118] [1992] BCLC 693 at 698, per Steyn LJ.   [119] [2002] 2 BCLC 254.

as close to the limits of what is permissible as a pure exercise of construction, but he had no doubt that this construction, with the additional words, reflected the true sense of the intended amendment.

E Enforcing the articles

4-61   Generally, the courts have been reluctant to hold that an individual member has a right to have all of the articles observed, despite the wording of CA 2006, s 33(1) which provides that:

> 'The provisions of a company's constitution bind the company and its members to the same extent as if there were covenants on the part of the company and of each member to observe those provisions.'

4-62   The wording in CA 2006, s 33 is a clarification of the wording in CA 1985, s 14 ('…articles, when registered, bind the company and the members to the same extent as if they had been signed and sealed by each member…'). But, as was emphasised in the Parliamentary debates,[120] the only purpose of the amended wording is to state the law explicitly, i.e. that the company, as well as the members, is a party to the constitution, as established by *Hickman v Kent or Romney Marsh Sheep-Breeders Association*[121] which is discussed below. The new wording does not extend a member's right to enforce the articles. Likewise, the existence now of a specific statutory duty on directors to act in accordance with the constitution (CA 2006, s 171) does not alter the position and does not confer on members a right to enforce every provision of the constitution.

4-63   The reason for imposing limits to the enforcement of the articles is linked to the rule in *Foss v Harbottle*[122] (discussed at **18-1**) which has two elements: first, the proper plaintiff in respect of a wrong allegedly done to a company is prima facie the company; secondly, where the alleged wrong is a transaction which might be made binding on the company by a simple majority of the members, no individual member of the company is allowed to bring a claim in respect of it.[123] The rule is based on two fundamental principles of company law, namely respect for the separate legal personality of the company and the principle of majority rule. In addition to reflecting those fundamental principles, the rule has certain practical advantages. It prevents multiplicity of shareholder suits and eliminates wasteful and vexatious actions by shareholders trying to harass the company.

---

[120] See 450 HC Debs, col 1087, 19 October 2006; 686 HL Debs, col 435, 2 November 2006.

[121] [1915] 1 Ch 881.   [122] (1843) 2 Hare 461.

[123] *Prudential Assurance Co Ltd v Newman Industries Ltd (No 2)* [1982] 1 All ER 354 at 357, CA; and see *Edwards v Halliwell* [1950] 2 All ER 1064 at 1066, per Jenkins LJ. As Mellish LJ explained in *MacDougall v Gardiner* (1875) 1 Ch D 13 at 25 '…if the thing complained of is a thing which in substance the majority of the company are entitled to do…there can be no use in having litigation about it, the ultimate end of which is only that a meeting has to be called, and then ultimately the majority gets its wishes.'

If a member can classify his grievance with the company as being an infringement   **4-64**
of his personal rights, a wrong done to him personally rather than a wrong done to
the company, then he is untroubled by the rule in *Foss v Harbottle* and may proceed
with his personal claim. It can be appreciated, therefore, that an expansive view of
his personal rights under the articles might enable him to sidestep the rule entirely,
something which the courts would regard as unacceptable, given the policies underlying the rule.

The courts have reconciled their desire to uphold the rule in *Foss v Harbottle*[124] and the   **4-65**
fact that the statute creates a contract between the company and the members under
CA 2006, s 33 by drawing a difficult distinction between: (1) provisions in the articles
which do create enforceable personal rights conferred on a member qua member (not
subject to the rule in *Foss v Harbottle*); and (2) provisions which relate to matters of
internal management of the company. The latter breaches of the articles amount only
to internal irregularities and as such are open to ratification by the majority and not
actionable by individual shareholders.

Company may enforce the articles against a member

The first matter, which has been clarified by the rewording of CA 2006, s 33 (noted above   **4-66**
at **4-61**) is that the company and the members are parties to the contract established
by the articles, a point established in *Hickman v Kent or Romney Marsh Sheepbreeders'
Association*.[125] In this case, the articles provided that disputes between the company
and a member should be referred to arbitration. A member in dispute with the company commenced legal proceedings and the company brought proceedings to stop his
action and require him to go to arbitration. The court held that a company is entitled as
against its own members to enforce and restrain breaches of the articles. On the facts,
the member was bound and the dispute was referred to arbitration.

A member may enforce the articles against a member

It is also the case, as was accepted in *Rayfield v Hands*,[126] that a member may enforce   **4-67**
the articles directly against the other members. In that case, as a matter of construction of the articles, a member wishing to transfer his shares was able to require the
other members to take the shares and the court allowed a member to enforce that provision against the other members. Such actions are unusual and, more generally, the
expectation would be that the contract would be enforced through the company.[127]

A member cannot always enforce the articles against the company

As noted above, a shareholder's entitlement to enforce what he perceives to be his   **4-68**
rights under the articles is problematic with the courts taking a restrictive approach to
the issue in order not to undermine the rule in *Foss v Harbottle*.[128]

---

[124] (1843) 2 Hare 461.   [125] [1915] 1 Ch 881.   [126] [1960] Ch 1.
[127] See *Welton v Saffery* [1897] AC 299 at 315.   [128] (1843) 2 Hare 461.

4-69   The many conflicting authorities on this issue were reviewed in *Hickman v Kent or Romney Marsh Sheepbreeders' Association*[129] and Astbury J concluded that the effect of the authorities is that rights purporting to be given by the articles in a capacity other than that of a member cannot be enforced against the company. Only membership rights which have been conferred on the member qua member can be enforced and so, when considering whether a provision can be enforced, it has to be asked whether it is intended to confer rights on a member in that capacity. Provisions identified by the courts as conferring rights on the members qua members include the right of a member to have his vote recorded,[130] to have a dividend paid in cash if the articles so specify,[131] and to enforce a declared dividend as a legal debt.[132] For example, in *Pender v Lushington*[133] the chairman of a general meeting of shareholders improperly refused to record some of the votes cast. This refusal was an infringement of a member's right qua member and the shareholders were able to get an injunction restraining the company from acting on the resolutions passed. In *Wood v Odessa Waterworks Co*[134] a member was entitled to require the company to pay a dividend in cash when the articles so provided. Rights with respect to share transfer, for example to enforce compliance with a pre-emption provision on transfer, may also be enforced.[135] Members qua members may also insist on the proper conduct of meetings.[136]

4-70   Given that a special resolution (a 75% majority) is required to amend the articles (CA 2006, s 21), it might be expected that a shareholder may prevent the company acting in disregard of a requirement in the articles without seeking to amend them by a special resolution. Certainly examples can be found where the court was prepared to restrain the company in such circumstances. In *Edwards v Halliwell*,[137] for example, two members of a trade union (similar to a company for these purposes) successfully restrained an attempt by a delegate meeting to increase the members' contribution without obtaining the two-thirds majority required under their rules. In *Quin & Axtens Ltd v Salmon*[138] the articles of association provided that certain transactions could not be entered into without the consent of both managing directors. In this instance one of the directors dissented, but the company in general meeting nevertheless tried to

---

[129] [1915] 1 Ch 881 at 900.   [130] See *Pender v Lushington* (1877) 6 Ch D 70.

[131] See *Wood v Odessa Waterworks Co* (1889) 42 Ch D 636.

[132] See *Mosely v Koffyfontein Mines Ltd* [1904] 2 Ch 108, CA.

[133] (1877) 6 Ch D 70. Cf *McDougall v Gardiner* (1875) 1 Ch D 13 (a member was denied relief when a chairman refused to call a poll in circumstances prescribed by the articles, the court regarding the matter as one of internal management: this case has been much criticised and is best confined to its facts).

[134] (1889) 42 Ch D 636.

[135] *Hurst v Crampton Bros (Coopers) Ltd* [2003] 1 BCLC 304 (when a member purported to transfer shares in breach of the pre-emption requirements in the articles, that transfer was defeasible at the suit of a member). See also *Re a company (No 005136 of 1986)* [1987] BCLC 82 where Hoffmann J took the view that a member had a right to prevent the dilution of his shareholding by improper allotments of shares, but it is difficult to find any support for this view, see Joffee, *Minority Shareholders* (3rd edn, 2008), para 2.61 who notes that the decision should be treated with caution.

[136] See *Kaye v Croydon Tramways Co* [1899] 1 Ch 861; *Tiessen v Henderson* [1898] 1 Ch 358; and *Baillie v Oriental Telephone and Electric Co Ltd* [1915] 1 Ch 503 (shareholders can prevent the company acting on resolutions improperly passed because of inadequate notice of the resolution to the shareholders).

[137] [1950] 2 All ER 1064.   [138] [1909] AC 442.

authorise the transaction without that director's consent. The court rejected the purported authorisation, finding that this was an attempt to alter the terms of the contract between the parties by an ordinary rather than a special resolution.

However, there is considerable inconsistency in the case law on these matters and in *Grant v United Kingdom Switchback Railways Co*[139] and *Irvine v Union Bank of Australia*[140] the courts permitted the majority in general meeting to ratify conduct by the directors in breach of the articles. In *Grant* the directors had entered into a particular contract with a third party although, under the terms of the articles, all of the directors bar one were prevented from voting on that contract because of a conflict of interest. The majority in general meeting passed a resolution approving and adopting the agreement, and authorising the directors to carry it into effect. The court rejected an application by a shareholder for an injunction to restrain the company from proceeding with the contract. In *Irvine* the directors borrowed money in excess of a credit limit imposed by the articles and the court accepted that such an internal irregularity was ratifiable by a simple majority of shareholders. Ratification of an unauthorised act, the court said, is not the same as conferring a general power to do similar acts in the future. The shareholders' action is not so much approval of a breach of the articles, but rather the adoption or affirmation of an unauthorised act and, as such, it has no implications for the future. The directors meanwhile have acted in breach of the constitution and therefore their duty under CA 2006, s 171: see **8-63–8-66.** **4-71**

These cases are supposedly distinguishable from the general principle that the majority cannot prevail where a special resolution is required on the basis that they involved only internal irregularities and were not attempts to alter for all time the terms of the contract between the members as embodied in the articles. Drawing the line between conduct which is an attempt by a simple majority to ignore the requirement for a special majority and conduct which is merely the ratification of an internal management irregularity is difficult, but it is clear that the scope for ratifying internal irregularities undermines the protection afforded to the minority by the need for a special resolution to amend the articles. **4-72**

In practice, a shareholder aggrieved at difficulties in enforcing his rights under the articles of association, or at non-compliance by the majority with the terms of the articles, is likely to petition for relief under CA 2006, s 994, alleging that the affairs of the company are being conducted in a manner which is unfairly prejudicial to his interests. This route is preferable to attempting to overcome the difficulties inherent in trying to enforce the contract established by CA 2006, s 33. **4-73**

The articles are not enforceable by outsiders

The articles are a statutory contract between the company and the members and do not constitute a contract between a company and an outsider (i.e. a non-member) **4-74**

---

[139] (1888) 40 Ch D 135.   [140] (1877) 2 App Cas 366.

or members claiming in a capacity other than as a member.[141] In *Eley v Positive Life Assurance Co*[142] a person named in the articles as a solicitor was unable to enforce that provision when the company employed someone else; the articles conferred no rights as between him and the company.

4-75   Any right claimed by an outsider must be conferred by a separate agreement outside the articles.[143] On occasion, that extrinsic contract may be made by the company with an outsider on the basis of the articles and such a contract may even be inferred from the conduct of the parties.[144] In *Re New British Iron Co, ex p Beckwith*[145] the articles provided for the annual remuneration of the directors. As such, of course, the articles did not constitute a contract to pay that amount of remuneration to the directors. But, the court said, where on the footing of that article, the directors were employed by the company and accepted office, the terms of that article as to remuneration were embodied in and formed part of the contract between the company and the directors.[146] An extrinsic contract derived from the articles in this way suffers from the disadvantage that the articles can be unilaterally changed by the company by special resolution under CA 2006, s 21 so altering the implied contract.[147]

F Supplementing the constitution— shareholders' agreements

4-76   In addition to the articles of association, shareholders may enter into a shareholders' agreement which is a separate contractual agreement between shareholders (or some of them) dealing with various aspects of their relationship. Matters commonly dealt with in a shareholders' agreement include voting matters, the provision of capital, the transfer of shares, and the appointment of directors.

4-77   A shareholders' agreement has a number of advantages over the standard articles of association:

- the agreement is a contract and binding as such and subject to all the usual contractual remedies. It does not involve the parties in discussions as to whether

---

[141] *Pritchard's Case* (1873) LR 8 Ch 956; *Melhado v Porto Alegre Rly Co* (1874) LR 9 CP 503; *Eley v Positive Life Assurance Co* (1876) 1 Ex D 20, 88; *Browne v La Trinidad* (1887) 37 Ch D 1; *Hickman v Kent or Romney Marsh Sheepbreeders' Association* [1915] 1 Ch 881; *Beattie v E & F Beattie Ltd* [1938] Ch 708.

[142] (1876) 1 Ex D 20, 88.

[143] This point is confirmed by the Contracts (Rights of Third Parties) Act 1999, s 6(2) which provides that the 1999 Act does not confer any rights on a third party in the case of any contract binding on a company and its members under CA 1985, s 14 (now CA 2006, s 33).

[144] *Swabey v Port Darwin Gold Mining Co* (1889) 1 Meg 385.

[145] [1898] 1 Ch 324.   [146] [1898] 1 Ch 324 at 326.

[147] See *Swabey v Port Darwin Gold Mining Co* (1889) 1 Meg 385 (where the terms as to the directors' remuneration were changed subsequently); but such alteration must not be retrospective.

a right is conferred qua member or whether the rule in *Foss v Harbottle*[148] applies. Likewise, enforcement of outsider rights conferred by the agreement is not a problem. A disadvantage is that the agreement can only bind those party to it, of course, and so a new agreement is required where there is a change in the composition of the shareholders;

- the agreement is drawn up to address the particular position of the shareholders whereas the standard articles operate without regard to individual circumstances;

- the process of drawing up an agreement can be useful in getting the members to focus on issues of concern to them and identifying ways in which disputes should be resolved, were they to arise;

- the agreement cannot be altered by a majority of the parties, as the articles can, so a shareholder party to the agreement is assured that changes cannot occur without his consent;

- the agreement is a private contract whereas the articles, as we saw, must be registered with the registrar of companies.

These various advantages mean that a shareholders' agreement is particularly useful **4-78** in certain circumstances, such as small family companies where it may help them address more fully the nature of their relationships inter se and with the company and, crucially, the manner of exiting from the business (given that a shareholder cannot simply demand back his capital). A shareholders' agreement is also useful in the quite different context of joint venture companies where commercially astute parties do not want their relationship to be governed by the vagaries of CA 2006, s 33.

[148] (1843) 2 Hare 461.

PART II

CORPORATE GOVERNANCE— DIRECTORS' ROLES AND RESPONSIBILITIES

5

Corporate governance—board structure and shareholder engagement

A Introduction

As the number of shareholders in a company increases, it is obviously impossible for all **5-1** to be involved in the management and control of the company's affairs so a separation commonly develops between those who collectively own the company (the shareholders) and those who manage it (the directors).[1] Problems can arise from this separation of ownership and control as distance from the day-to-day running of the business makes it difficult for shareholders to restrain any managerial excesses, whether such excesses are the result of incompetence, self-dealing, or outright fraud.

The relationship between management and shareholders is at the heart of the corpo- **5-2** rate governance debate[2] which over the past two decades has moved up the political agenda as large corporate collapses, such as Enron in the US and Parmalat in Italy, led to multi-billion dollar/euro losses.[3] The problems are most acute in and most attention has focused on listed public companies with widely dispersed shareholdings, but corporate governance is an issue for all public companies and even large private companies.

It is clear that no single mechanism can provide an answer to the problems presented **5-3** by the separation of ownership and control and a variety of responses are required. Much of the focus is on internal mechanisms (such as shareholders' rights and board structures) though external mechanisms too have a role to play. For underperforming

---

[1] The theory of the separation of ownership and control originates in the famous work by Berle & Means, *The Modern Corporation and Private Property* (1932). For a modern study of the position in Europe where, unlike the UK and the US, shareholding is much more concentrated and dominant blockholders are common: see Barca & Becht, *The Control of Corporate Europe* (2001).

[2] There is a vast literature now on corporate governance, but as a starting point, see Armour and McCahery (eds), *After Enron* (2006); Coffee, *Gatekeepers: The Professions and Corporate Governance* (2006); Hopt, Wymeersch et al (eds), *Corporate Governance in Context* (2005); Charkham, *Keeping Better Company: Corporate Governance Ten Years On* (2005).

[3] See Coffee, 'What Caused Enron: A Capsule Social and Economic History of the 1990s' (2004) 89 Cornell L R 269.

management, the markets may operate as a constraining force with takeovers provid-ing a means by which to displace an existing board. That threat of displacement, it is argued, provides an incentive for efficient management. For dishonest and fraudulent management, external mechanisms lie in the hands of various regulatory authorities. The maintenance of confidence in the proper conduct of business and the protection of investors and markets may require intervention and, possibly, an investigation of the company's affairs. The exercise of investigation powers is primarily a matter for BERR acting through the Companies Investigation Branch. Listed companies can expect scrutiny by the Financial Services Authority (FSA). Beyond the regulatory powers lie the police and the Serious Fraud Office.

5-4   Good corporate governance primarily stems from internal structures, however, and the substantive corporate governance debate has centred on:

(1) the structure and role of the board of directors and, in particular, the role of non-executive directors;

(2) shareholder engagement with an emphasis on enhancing the role of institu-tional investors, revitalising the general meeting as a shareholders' forum, and facilitating the engagement of the indirect investor in recognition of the fact that shareholdings are now commonly held by nominees through a chain of intermediaries, possibly even a cross-border chain.

The role of the board and issues of shareholder engagement are the focus of this chapter. A further important governance mechanism is the imposition of disclosure requirements to ensure that business is conducted in an open and transparent way. The assumption is that the full glare of publicity makes directors more circumspect in their activities, and this assists shareholders in monitoring those activities and allows shareholders and creditors to assess the risks involved. Much effort has been expended to this end on improving the content of the annual accounts and reports and, crucially, ensuring the quality of the external audit of those accounts. Accounting and audit issues are considered in Chapter 16.

B The structure of the board—the Combined Code

Introduction

5-5   In large public companies, it is customary to find a board made up of executive and non-executive directors, typically presided over by a non-executive chairman. Executive directors are those directors concerned with the actual management of the company. They will have extensive management powers delegated to them by the art-icles and they typically have service contracts with the company which together with the articles delimit their powers and responsibilities.[4] Non-executive directors are

---

[4] *Harold Holdsworth & Co (Wakefield) Ltd v Caddies* [1955] 1 All ER 725.

directors without executive management responsibilities but who are concerned with general management policy and strategy and the monitoring of the executive directors[5] although their precise role (particularly with respect to their monitoring responsibilities) is the subject of debate.[6] They commonly have letters of appointment setting out their role and responsibilities.

It might be fair to say that the executive directors see the non-executive directors as **5-6** fulfilling managerial and strategic responsibilities while shareholders and the broader investing public and, to some extent, the Government tend to focus on their monitoring responsibilities. The Companies Act 2006 makes no reference to executive and non-executive directors for these are essentially business terms. In either case, the legal position is the same and all directors are subject to the general duties laid down in CA 2006, Part 10 though, when considering the duty of care and skill, the different functions of the non-executive directors will be relevant.

The focus on the role of non-executive directors received its impetus initially from a **5-7** series of corporate collapses in the late 1980s which raised concerns as to the effectiveness of the traditional board structure when dominated by powerful executive directors. These concerns prompted the setting up of the Cadbury Committee[7] and later the Hampel Committee[8] to address issues surrounding the composition, structure and effectiveness of boards of directors. At around the same time, the Greenbury Committee[9] was asked to consider issues surrounding directors' remuneration.

The Cadbury Committee reported in December 1992 and its central recommenda- **5-8** tion was that the boards of all listed companies registered in the UK should comply with a Code of Best Practice governing the structure and responsibilities of boards of directors.[10] This pioneering work by the Cadbury Committee encouraged other bodies (and indeed other jurisdictions) to devise their own codes of corporate governance. For example, the Association of British Insurers, the National Association of Pension Funds, the Association of Investment Companies, the Quoted Companies Alliance, all now issue their own guidance on corporate governance matters. Other groups such as PIRC (Pensions Investment Research Consultants, a high profile independent corporate governance advisor) and Hermes (an independent institutional fund manager)

[5] See, for example, the comments of Rimer J in *Re Kaytech International plc, Secretary of State for Trade and Industry v Kaczer* [1999] 2 BCLC 351 at 407; Park J in *Re Continental Assurance Co of London plc* [2007] BCLC 287 at 443.

[6] On non-executive directors generally, see Sweeney-Baird, 'The role of the Non-executive Director in Modern Corporate Governance' (2006) 27 Co Law 67; Parkinson, 'Evolution and Policy in Company Law: The Non-executive Director' in Parkinson, Gamble and Kelly (eds), *The Political Economy of the Company* (2000).

[7] The Committee on the Financial Aspects of Corporate Governance, chaired by Sir Adrian Cadbury, set up in 1991 by the Financial Reporting Council, the London Stock Exchange and the accountancy profession.

[8] The Committee on Corporate Governance, chaired by Sir Ronald Hampel, set up in November 1995 on the initiative of the Financial Reporting Council.

[9] The Study Group on Directors' Remuneration, chaired by Sir Richard Greenbury, set up in January 1995 on the initiative of the CBI.

[10] *Report of the Committee on the Financial Aspects of Corporate Governance* (1992).

also publish influential guidance.[11] In the light of developing practice and drawing particularly on the work of the Cadbury Committee, the Hampel Committee in 1998 drew up the Combined Code on Corporate Governance[12] consisting of a statement of best practice set out in the form of Main Principles (and supporting principles) and Code Provisions. References hereinafter to the Code are to the Combined Code.

5-9   The Combined Code was the subject of a major overhaul in 2003 following the publication of the Higgs Report on the role and effectiveness of non-executive directors[13] and the Smith Report on audit committees.[14] Further amendments were made in 2006 and 2008 on the initiative of the Financial Reporting Council (FRC) which has overall responsibility for the content of the Code and which monitors its operation. The current version therefore is that of June 2008 and the next review is scheduled for 2010.

5-10   At the European level, in 2002 the European Commission initiated a review of corporate governance codes throughout the EU which concluded that practically every Member State had at least one code, that all the codes were remarkably similar and that they served as a converging force for governance practices across the EU.[15] In the light of these findings the Commission rapidly concluded that there is no need for a European code,[16] though it has tried to guide on best practice by the use of Recommendations on directors' remuneration in 2004[17] and on the role of non-executive directors in 2005 (see discussion at **2-32**).[18] More substantively, the Commission secured the adoption of a Directive on Shareholders' Rights in 2007,[19] see **15-4**.

The Combined Code: application and status

5-11   The Combined Code is a voluntary code so to an extent it applies to any company that chooses to adhere to it. In practice, its core application is to listed companies since the Listing Rules require listed companies to indicate in their annual reports whether they have complied with it and to explain any areas of non-compliance ('comply or explain'). The Cadbury Committee pioneered this 'comply or explain' approach which

---

[11] See *PIRC Shareholder Voting Guidelines* 2008; *The Hermes Corporate Governances Principles* (2008).

[12] See the *Final Report of the Committee on Corporate Governance* (1998).

[13] Higgs, *Review of the role and effectiveness of Non-executive Directors* (January 2003) preceded by a consultation paper of the same name (June 2002).

[14] Audit Committees, Combined Code Guidance, Report to the FRC by group chaired by Sir Robert Smith (January 2003) now FRC, Guidance on Audit Committees (2008).

[15] See Weil, Gotshal & Manges, *Comparative Study of Corporate Governance Codes Relevant to the European Union and its Member States* (January 2002).

[16] See European Commission, *Modernising Company Law and Enhancing Corporate Governance in the EU—A Plan to Move Forward*, COM (2003) 284 final, 21.5.2003, para 3.1. The Commission is considering carrying out a further study in 2009 to get a comprehensive picture of all the available codes and their practical application.

[17] *Recommendation on fostering an appropriate regime for the remuneration of directors of listed companies*, OJ L 385, 29.12.2004, p 55.

[18] *Recommendation on the role of non-executive or supervisory directors of listed companies and on the committees of the (supervisory) board*, OJ L 52, 25.02.2005, p 51.

[19] Directive 2007/36/EC on the exercise of certain rights of shareholders in listed companies, OJ L 184, 14.7.2007, p 17.

has now gained widespread acceptance and is a near universal feature of corporate governance codes.[20] As far as compliance is concerned, the FRC stresses that companies must not approach the exercise as a box-ticking process; rather, they should look to use the Code to help them develop better corporate governance. When an explanation is required, the FRC has stressed that there should be:

'…a careful and clear explanation which shareholders should evaluate on its merits. In providing an explanation, the company should aim to illustrate how its actual practices are consistent with the principle to which the particular provision relates and contribute to good corporate governance.'[21]

Likewise, the FRC emphasises that shareholders should consider such explanations carefully on an individual basis rather than routinely condemn any non-compliance with the Code and shareholders must be prepared to engage in a dialogue if they do not accept the company's position.[22]

The Listing Rules require that a listed company[23] includes in its annual financial report:[24]   **5-12**

(1) a statement of how the company has applied the Main Principles of the Code in a manner that would enable shareholders to evaluate how the principles have been applied: LR 9.8.6(5)R; and

(2) a statement as to whether or not the company has complied with all relevant Code provisions; and, if necessary, identifying those provisions it has not complied with, and the period of non-compliance, and the company's reasons for non-compliance: LR 9.8.6.(6)R.

The Listing Rules further require the auditors to review the company's statement of compliance[25] so far as the statement relates to: **5-13**

(1) the directors' explanation in the annual report of their responsibility for preparing the company's accounts;[26]

---

[20] It is also now enshrined in the Fourth Company Law Directive, 78/660/EEC on the annual accounts of certain types of companies, OJ L 222, 14.08.1978, p 11, as amended by Directive 2006/46, OJ L 224, 16.08.06, p 1. See art 46a(1) of the Fourth Directive which requires companies to state which corporate governance code they comply with, any non-compliance and the reasons for that non-compliance.

[21] See Code Preamble, para 5. The FRC also notes that companies need to raise the general standard of their explanations for non-compliance and shareholders for their part need to satisfy companies that they devote sufficient resources and scrutiny to engagement with the company, para 9.

[22] See Code Preamble, para 7 and Code E.2.

[23] The Combined Code does not apply to AIM companies but the Quoted Companies Alliance (which represents traded companies outside the FTSE 350) has published *Corporate Governance Guidelines for AIM Companies* (2007) which are generally accepted as setting the appropriate standards for AIM companies. The NAPF has also issued guidelines for AIM Companies (see *Corporate Governance Policy and Voting Guidelines for AIM Companies* (March 2007)), while stressing that AIM companies too should be familiar with and seek to apply the Main Principles of the Combined Code.

[24] An overseas company with a primary listing in the UK must disclose in its annual report and accounts: (1) whether or not it complies with the corporate governance regime of its country of incorporation; (2) the significant ways in which its actual corporate governance practices differ from those set out in the Combined Code: LR 9.8.7. Given this requirement, many such companies choose to comply with the Combined Code.

[25] Listing Rules r 9.8.10R(2).   [26] As required by the Combined Code, C1.1.

(2) the directors' annual review of the effectiveness of the internal control systems (discussed further below);[27] and

(3) the company's practice as to the establishment, role and responsibilities of the audit committee (also discussed below).[28]

5-14   As a voluntary code, no legal sanction attaches to non-compliance with the Combined Code, but failure to include in the annual report the statement required by the Listing Rules is a breach of the Listing Rules and punishable as such.[29] Otherwise, the sanction is expected to come from the market reaction to non-compliance.[30] Depending on the nature of the default, that reaction might range from indifference to a significant fall in share price. More particularly, non-compliance with the Code elicits a response from institutional shareholders who would expect a dialogue with the board as to the reasons for non-compliance, as noted at **5-11**. Having said that, the consensus is that there is a high level of compliance amongst FTSE 100 companies, but perhaps less so amongst the smaller companies beyond the FTSE 350.[31]

5-15   The position with respect to the status of the Combined Code alters slightly now that the Fourth Company Law Directive (as amended by Directive 2006/46)[32] requires all companies admitted to trading on a regulated market to include a corporate governance statement either in the directors' report, or as a separate stand alone report, or on the company's website. In part this is driven by the point, noted above at **5-10**, that there are so many corporate governance codes across Europe, that it is thought useful to require traded companies to: (1) indicate which code the company is complying with (in the UK, obviously, this will be the Combined Code), and explain any non-compliance; (2) describe the features of the company's internal control and risk management systems in relation to the financial reporting process; and (3) include a description of the composition of the board and its committees. The Government decided to implement this Directive requirement through FSA rules[33] and the relevant requirements are in the FSA, Disclosure and Transparency Rules, DTR 7.2 et seq.

---

[27] As required by the Combined Code, C2.1. The Turnbull Guidance on internal controls, paras 33–38, offers guidance as to what the company needs to disclose for the purposes of making a statement on internal controls, see **5-19** below on the Turnbull Guidance.

[28] As required by the Combined Code, C3.1–3.7.

[29] Listed companies must comply with the Listing Rules: Financial Services and Markets Act 2000, s 96(1); and penalties may be imposed for non-compliance: s 91(1).

[30] The Company Law Review found no support for putting the Combined Code on a statutory basis: Company Law Review, *Final Report*, vol 1 (2001), para 3.49; *Completing the Structure* (2000), para 12.50. The Government agreed that the Combined Code should remain as a non-statutory document: see *Modernising Company Law* (Cmnd 5553-I, 2002), paras 5.7–5.16.

[31] The Company Law Review considered that there had been a high level of compliance with the Combined Code and while it admitted that the benefits are hard to quantify, it considered that the Combined Code heightens awareness of the importance of effective board structures and creates a climate of openness and accountability: Company Law Review, *Completing the Structure* (2000), para 4.44; *Developing the Framework* (2000), para 3.125.

[32] See Fourth Company Law Directive 78/660/EEC on the annual accounts of certain types of companies, OJ L 222, 14.08.1978, p 11, as amended by Directive 2006/46, OJ L 224, 16.08.06, p 1, art 46a(1).

[33] See FSMA 2000, s 89O (inserted by CA 2006, s 1269) allowing the FSA to draw up corporate governance rules.

There is a considerable degree of overlap between what is required under the DTR rules and the Combined Code,[34] but the requirements are not identical.[35] The DTR rules are mandatory, unlike the Combined Code, so companies must ensure that they meet the requirements of the DTR even if they choose not to comply with elements of the Combined Code. For example, under the Combined Code a company could elect to give minimal information as to internal controls and explain that decision, but the DTR require a description of internal control systems so the ability to explain rather than comply is now constrained by the requirements of DTR 7.2.

The Combined Code: content

The board of directors

Every company should be headed by an effective board collectively responsible for the success of the company with all directors taking decisions objectively in the interests of the company (Code A.1: all references in this section are to the Combined Code unless otherwise indicated). The emphasis is on an informed board, acting on detailed timely information, meeting regularly under the guidance of an effective chairman, with a formal schedule of matters specifically reserved to the board (A.1.1).   **5-16**

The board should include a balance of executive and non-executive directors (including independent non-executive directors) such that no individual or small group of individuals can dominate the board's decision taking (A.3). There is no prescribed size, but the board should not be so large as to be unwieldy and, while it should be balanced to prevent a small number of people dominating the board, there should be a strong presence of both executive and non-executive directors.   **5-17**

There should be a formal, rigorous and transparent procedure for the appointment of new directors to the board (A.4) and all directors should be required to submit themselves for re-election at regular intervals and at least every three years (A.7.1). The board should undertake a formal and rigorous annual evaluation of its own performance and that of its committees and its individual directors (A.6).   **5-18**

A core obligation in the Combined Code is that the board must maintain a sound system of internal control to safeguard shareholders' investment and the company's assets (C.2). The directors should conduct a review, at least annually, of the effectiveness of the group's system of internal controls and should report to shareholders that they have done so (C.2.1). That review should cover all material controls, including financial, operational and compliance controls and risk management systems (C.2.1). The implementation of this element of the Combined Code is the subject of further   **5-19**

---

[34] Compliance with the specified equivalent provisions of the Combined Code will satisfy the requirements of the DTR, see DTR 7.2.8G.

[35] For example, DTR 7.2.5R requires a description of the main features of the company's internal control and risk management systems in relation to the financial reporting process whereas the Combined Code requires the board to report that the annual review of the effectiveness of the internal control system has been carried out.

guidance, known as the Turnbull Guidance[36] (first issued in 1999 and revised in 2005). Additionally, DTR 7.2.5R, noted above at **5-15**, requires listed companies to describe the main features of the internal control and risk management systems in relation to the financial reporting process.

5-20   The emphasis throughout the Turnbull Guidance and the Combined Code is that responsibility for the company's system of internal control rests with the board of directors. It is for the board to set appropriate policies on internal control and to seek regular assurance that enables it to satisfy itself that the system is functioning effectively. The board must further ensure that the system of internal control is effective in managing risks in the manner which it has approved.[37] An essential component of a sound system of internal control, the Turnbull Guidance emphasises, is effective monitoring on a continuous basis.[38] This statement on internal control in the annual report is subject to auditor review (LR 9.8.10R), as noted at **5-13** above.

The chairman of the board

5-21   Considerable importance is attached to separating the posts of chairman and chief executive. The Code states that there should be a chairman responsible for leading the board and a chief executive with executive responsibility for the running of the company's business. The Code is quite clear that no one individual should hold these posts and when, from time to time, companies choose not to comply with this element, it has generally been a contentious issue with their shareholders, even in well-respected companies.[39] The position adopted in the Code is that there should be two posts and a division of responsibility between the chairman and the chief executive should be clearly established, set out in writing and agreed by the board (A2.1).[40]

5-22   The chairman should be independent on appointment and the chief executive of a company should not move up to become chairman (A2.2), another bone of contention from time to time. The chairman should hold meetings with the non-executive directors without executive directors being present (A.1.3).

5-23   The chairman's role as envisaged by the Combined Code (A.2) is:

(1) leadership of the board;

---

[36] See FRC, *Internal Control, Revised Guidance for Directors on the Combined Code* (2005), hereinafter the Turnbull Guidance. The Guidance derived from a report under the auspices of the Institute of Chartered Accountants in England and Wales and the chairmanship of Andrew Turnbull, see ICAEW, *Internal Control: Guidance for Directors on the Combined Code* (September 1999).

[37] See the Turnbull Guidance, n 36 above, para 15.

[38] See the Turnbull Guidance, n 36 above, para 26.

[39] A recent example of a high profile dispute over this issue involved Marks and Spencer's decision to move its chief executive, Sir Stuart Rose, to the post of executive chairman which provoked fury from institutional investors. Ultimately 22% of shareholders either voted against or abstained on his appointment (a very high percentage in this type of company). See 'Sir Stuart Rose and the thorny issue of corporate governance' *Financial Times*, 10 March 2008; 'M & S shareholders give Sir Stuart dressing down in promotion vote' *Financial Times*, 10 July 2008.

[40] On the evolving and increasingly important role of the chairman, see Owen & Kirchmaier, 'The Changing Role of the Chairman: Impact of Corporate Governance Reform in the UK 1995–2005' (2008) 9 EBOR 187.

(2) ensuring that the board is effective and all of the directors are properly informed;

(3) ensuring effective communication with shareholders;

(4) facilitating the contribution of the non-executive directors and ensuring a constructive relationship between executive and non-executive directors.

A public company must have a company secretary (CA 2006, s 271). In listed com-   **5-24**
panies, in particular, the company secretary has important corporate governance responsibilities which are recognised by the Combined Code and which makes the appointment of and removal of the company secretary a matter for the board as a whole (A.5.3). The company secretary is responsible for advising the board through the chairman on all governance matters and for ensuring compliance with board procedures (A.5.3).[41]

The board and the shareholders

The board as a whole has responsibility for ensuring satisfactory dialogue takes place   **5-25**
with the company's shareholders (D.1). It is accepted that this dialogue is mainly a matter for the chief executive and the finance director, but the company chairman (and the senior independent director, discussed below, and other appropriate directors) are expected also to maintain sufficient contact with major shareholders to understand their issues and concerns (D.1). Non-executive directors should also be offered the opportunity to attend meetings with the company's major shareholders (D.1.1).

The Code emphasises the importance of the board using the annual general meet-   **5-26**
ing to communicate with investors and includes various recommendations as to best practice with regard to the conduct of the meeting. For example, there should be separate resolutions for each substantive matter; appropriate proxy arrangements should be in place allowing for votes to be cast for and against resolutions and for votes to be withheld; and voting outcomes should be announced as soon as practical and should be posted on the company's website. The chairmen of the audit, remuneration and nomination committees should be at the general meeting and available to answer questions from shareholders and all directors should attend the annual general meeting, of which at least 20 days' notice should be given. Most of these matters are now the subject of specific statutory requirements in any event under CA 2006, Part 13 which is discussed in Chapter 15.

The non-executive directors

Number and independence   At least half the board, excluding the chairman, should   **5-27**
be independent non-executive directors (A.3.2). Smaller companies[42] should have at least two independent non-executive directors (A.3.3). The board should appoint one of the independent non-executive directors to be the company's senior independent

---

[41] See generally ICSA Guidance, *The Corporate Governance role of the Company Secretary* (October 2008).
[42] Defined as below the FTSE 350.

director. This senior director should meet with the non-executive directors without the chairman being present at least annually to appraise the chairman and on other occasions as deemed appropriate (A.1.3). The senior independent director is also available to shareholders if they have concerns that are not addressed elsewhere (A.3.3). When these powers were introduced, this role assigned to the senior independent director was criticised as potentially dangerous and divisive to a unitary board. There is little evidence, however, that the post of senior director has evolved into a significant role, probably because company chairmen have been anxious to prevent any dilution of their position.

5-28   *Appointment and remuneration*   Non-executive directors should be selected (as should all the directors) through a formal process. They should be appointed for specific terms subject to re-election but any proposal that someone be re-elected for a term beyond six years should be rigorously reviewed (A.7.2). A non-executive can serve for more than nine years, but should then be subject to annual re-election and the Code cautions that such a period of service 'could' be relevant to determining whether the director is independent (A.7.2). It has to be remembered that the Code is a reflection of market consensus to a large extent and it cannot be more prescriptive without risking a loss of support, but on some of these issues it is noticeably lax. It is difficult to believe that someone who has served for nine years could or should be regarded as independent.

5-29   The annual report must identify each non-executive director considered by the board to be independent,[43] and it is for the board to determine whether the director is independent in character and judgement and whether there are relationships or circumstances which are likely to affect, or could appear to affect, the director's judgement (A.3.1). The board should state its reasons if it determines that a director is independent notwithstanding the existence of relationships or circumstances which may appear relevant to its determination, including if the director:

- has been an employee of the company or group within the last five years;
- has, or has had within the last three years, a material business relationship with the company either directly, or as a partner, shareholder, director or senior employee of a body that has such a relationship with the company;
- has received or receives additional remuneration from the company apart from a director's fee, participates in the company's share option or a performance-related pay scheme, or is a member of the company's pension scheme;
- has close family ties with any of the company's advisers, directors or senior employees;
- holds cross-directorships or has significant links with other directors through involvement in other companies or bodies;

---

[43] The Company Law Review noted that independence cannot be legislated for since 'the quality required is a state of mind and character and relevant experience, rather than some formal indication of independence', see Company Law Review, *Developing the Framework* (2000), para 3.148.

- represents a significant shareholder; or
- has served on the board for more than nine years from the date of their first election (A.3.1).

Role   The Combined Code clearly identifies the non-executive director's role as being   **5-30**
centred on the areas of strategy, performance, risk and directors' remuneration. The
Code states that, while part of a unitary board, the non-executive directors:

- should constructively challenge and help develop proposals on strategy;
- should scrutinise the performance of management in meeting agreed goals and objectives and monitor the reporting of performance;
- should satisfy themselves on the integrity of financial information and that financial controls and systems of risk management are robust and defensible; and
- are responsible for determining appropriate levels of remuneration of executive directors and have a prime role in appointing, and where necessary removing, senior management and in succession planning (Code A.1).

The Combined Code goes on to spell out key roles for non-executive directors on   **5-31**
certain committees of the board, namely the nomination, audit and remuneration
committees.

Board committees

The nomination committee   By definition this committee has a limited role. It is   **5-32**
restricted to leading the process for board appointments and making recommendations to the board, though it brings a certain level of arm's length positioning to the
process given that a majority of the committee's members must be independent non-
executive directors (A.4.1). The Code also states that the committee should explain
if neither an external search consultancy nor open advertising has been used in the
appointment of the chairman or a non-executive director (A.4.6).

The audit committee   The audit committee has become the key corporate governance   **5-33**
committee and the Combined Code has extensive guidance on its composition and role.
This part of the Code is much influenced by the recommendations of the Smith Report
(the Smith Guidance) published originally in January 2003 but updated and reissued
by the FRC in October 2008.[44] The Guidance emphasises that the audit committee has
'a particular role, acting independently of the executive, to ensure that the interests
of shareholders are properly protected in relation to financial reporting and internal
control'.[45] Details of the work of the committee must be set out in the company's annual
report (C.3.3), a requirement, the Guidance notes, which 'deliberately puts the spotlight
on the committee and gives it an authority that it might otherwise lack'.[46]

---

[44] See FRC, *Guidance on Audit Committees* (2008), previously Audit Committee Combined Code
Guidance, Report to the FRC by group chaired by Sir Robert Smith (January 2003).

[45] See FRC, *Guidance on Audit Committees* (2008), para 1.4.

[46] See FRC, *Guidance on Audit Committees* (2008), para 1.6.

5-34   The Combined Code recommends that the board should establish an audit committee consisting of at least three, or in the case of smaller companies (i.e. below FTSE 350) two, independent non-executive directors, at least one of whom has 'recent and relevant financial experience' (C.3.1).[47] In the case of smaller companies, the chairman may be a member of the committee in addition to the two independent members provided the chairman was considered independent on appointment as chairman (C.3.1). This concession was introduced in 2008 and is unwelcome as the potential exists for the chairman to exert disproportionate influence over what is the most important of the committees required by the Combined Code, especially so if there are only two other members. Circumstances may arise where the audit committee is at odds with the rest of the board and the presence of the chairman on the committee may result either in the committee being stifled in its endeavours or the chairman having already taken sides by the time a matter is progressed to the board. Either is unsatisfactory. The requirement that the chairman must have been considered independent on appointment offers little reassurance as to his actual independence, given he may have been on the board for some time.

5-35   The main roles and responsibilities of the committee (C.3.2) are:

- to monitor the integrity of the financial statements of the company;
- to review the company's internal financial controls and, unless otherwise reviewed, to review the internal control and risk management systems;[48]
- to monitor and review the effectiveness of the company's internal audit function (and if there is none, the committee should draw attention to that fact in their report);
- to make recommendations in relation to the appointment of the external auditor;
- to review and monitor the external auditor's independence, objectivity, terms of engagement and the effectiveness of the audit process; and
- to develop and implement policy on the engagement of the auditor for non-audit services.

5-36   In carrying out its functions, the FRC Guidance emphasises the need for a robust committee which is well informed, well resourced, and well remunerated for the wide-ranging responsibilities which it must undertake.[49] Above all, the Guidance stresses the importance of a frank, open working relationship and a high level of mutual respect between the audit committee chairman, the board chairman, the chief executive and the finance director.[50]

---

[47] The FRC *Guidance on Audit Committees* (2008) notes that it is desirable that the person considered to have 'recent and relevant financial experience' should have a professional qualification from one of the professional accountancy bodies: see para 2.16.

[48] The FRC *Guidance on Audit Committees* (2008), para 4.5 defines internal financial controls as systems established to identify, assess, manage and monitor financial risks.

[49] See FRC *Guidance on Audit Committees* (2008), paras 1.8–1.11.

[50] See FRC *Guidance on Audit Committees* (2008), para 1.7.

The voluntary aspect of the requirements to have an audit committee has been over-   **5-37**
taken by the Eighth Company Law Directive on audit which requires companies
admitted to trading on a regulated market to have an audit committee.[51] This requirement is implemented by the FSA Disclosure and Transparency Rules, DTR 7.1, but
compliance with the provisions of the Code noted above also suffices for compliance
with DTR 7.1.1R—7.1.5R (DTR 7.1.7G).

The remuneration committee   As noted at **5-7** above, matters relating to directors'   **5-38**
remuneration were first addressed by the Greenbury Committee in 1995 which drew
up a Code of Best Practice on Directors' Remuneration.[52] The Greenbury Code focused
on the establishment of remuneration committees of non-executive directors to determine a company's policy on executive remuneration and the specific remuneration
packages for each of the executive directors.

Despite this move, there continued to be widespread dissatisfaction concerning this   **5-39**
issue, especially over the levels of compensation payments payable when directors are
dismissed (often termed 'rewards for failure') see **12-17**. The Government decided as
a consequence that voluntary disclosure was no longer adequate or appropriate and
mandatory disclosure was required.[53] Quoted companies are required therefore to
publish a report on directors' remuneration as part of the company's annual reports
and to disclose within that report comprehensive details (prescribed by regulation) of
each individual director's remuneration package as well as the company's remuneration policy, the role of the board and the membership and role of the remuneration
committee.[54]

This remuneration report must be submitted for shareholder approval by way of an   **5-40**
ordinary resolution at the general meeting at which the company's accounts are laid.[55]
The shareholders are not entitled to vote on an individual director's package but vote
only on the report as a whole. Nevertheless, this advisory vote has proved surprisingly effective.[56] It has galvanised shareholders into positively considering directors'

---

[51] Directive 2006/43/EC on statutory audits of annual accounts and consolidated accounts, OJ L 157,
9.6.2006, p 87, art 41.

[52] *Directors' Remuneration, Report of a Study Group chaired by Sir Richard Greenbury* (1995). The committee was set up on the initiative of the Confederation of British Industry after a period of sustained public
criticism of the levels of directors' remuneration, particularly in the context of the directors of the (then)
recently privatised utilities.

[53] See DTI, *Directors' Remuneration, A Consultative Document* (1999), following by another consultative
document of the same name in 2001.

[54] CA 2006, s 420. The details of the required disclosure are set out in The Large and Medium-sized
Companies and Groups (Accounts and Reports) Regulations 2008, SI 2008/410, Sch 8. A quoted company
is a company listed in the UK, or officially listed in an EEA State, or admitted to dealing on either the New
York Stock Exchange or Nasdaq (an American stock exchange): CA 2006, s 385.

[55] CA 2006, ss 420–422.

[56] A review for the DTI concluded that there was much greater clarity in the information being provided
by directors and that the advisory vote had had a significant impact on directors' attitudes and behaviour:
see Deloitte's *Report on the Implementation of the Directors' Remuneration Report Regulations for the DTI*
(2004), Ch 7. The review focused on the FTSE 350 (i.e. the largest 350 companies by market capitalisation)
in August 2004. It is interesting to note that the shareholders consulted said that they did not want any

remuneration packages rather than passively accepting them as a fait accompli, as was often the case in the past. The small number of companies which have had their reports voted down have suffered considerable adverse publicity with the result that boards go to some lengths to prevent rejection. This concern forces them into extensive discussions beforehand with the institutional shareholders to ensure their approval and so there is a measure of shareholder control over the remuneration packages available. There remains considerable concerns but the advisory vote at least allows the shareholders to express their displeasure in a very public way. Following the focus on the remuneration report, the Government consulted further on whether additional measures were required,[57] but found no appetite for further legislation and, in the light of the apparent effectiveness of the advisory vote on remuneration, has been content to leave these issues to guidance from institutional investors and best practice as dictated by the Combined Code.[58]

5-41   The approach of the Combined Code remains as envisaged by the Greenbury Committee, i.e. the emphasis is on the use of a remuneration committee and extensive disclosure. The Code provides that the remuneration committee should comprise at least three, or in the case of smaller companies two, independent non-executive directors and, in addition, the chairman may be a member of the committee if he was considered independent on appointment as chairman (B.2.1). The Combined Code stresses that levels of remuneration should be sufficient to attract, retain and motivate directors, but companies should avoid paying more than is necessary for this purpose (B.1). A company should have a formal and transparent procedure for developing policy on executive remuneration and for fixing the remuneration packages of individual directors with no director being involved in deciding on his or her own remuneration (B.2).

5-42   The Code considers that performance-related elements of remuneration should form a significant proportion of the total remuneration package of executive directors, and should be designed to align their interests with those of shareholders and should give directors keen incentives to perform at the highest level (B.1.1). The Code requires notice or contract periods to be set at one year or less (B.1.6) which is important in minimising the amount of compensation payable on dismissal. This aspect of the Code has been very successful with practically all listed companies now setting one-year periods or less.[59] That change in practice is reflected in the CA 2006 also which

---

additional information, but better communication by companies of their plans, since shareholders are already spending considerable sums in evaluating and analysing these very detailed remuneration reports.

[57] See DTI, 'Rewards for Failure', Directors' Remuneration—Contracts, Performance and Severance (2003), URN 03/652; also HC Trade and Industry Select Committee Report, Rewards for Failure, 16th Report, Session 2002–03, HC 914.

[58] See Written Statement to Parliament by Secretary of State for Trade and Industry, Patricia Hewitt, 430 HC Debs 10–11WS, 25 January 2005.

[59] See the Joint Statement on Executive Contracts and Severance by the Association of British Insurers (ABI) and the National Association of Pension Funds (NAPF), February 2008, which stresses (at para 3.5) that a one-year notice period should not be seen as a floor. The Statement strongly encourages boards to

requires shareholder approval for directors' service contracts longer than two years (reduced from five years in the CA 1985) (CA 2006, s 188) see **12-12**.

Notwithstanding the requirement for an advisory vote and the level of disclosure required under the Combined Code and by the remuneration report,[60] concerns about remuneration continue to dominate corporate governance discussions. The high profile accorded to the issue is driven to some extent by media interest in the topic but it is also driven by legitimate shareholder concerns that disclosure has done little to curb the following practices: (1) excessive compensation payments to departing executives (who are often departing because of under-performance); (2) excessive remuneration payments to executives in post paid notwithstanding the fact that the company is under-performing the market to a considerable extent; and (3) the recent practice of paying retention sums, i.e. lump sum payments to directors entirely unrelated to performance but solely to ensure they remain with the company when they have been passed over for the top job in the company.[61] For the moment, the focus is firmly on ending the bonus culture in financial institutions and that may have some knock-on effect in the broader corporate sector. In any event, in recessionary times, shareholders are unlikely to look kindly on executive bonuses unless linked to clearly identifiable shareholder value. Market sentiment may therefore resolve this issue, at least in the short term.

5-43

C Shareholder engagement

As well as an effective board, good corporate governance depends on effective shareholder control of the board. The main forum for shareholders is the general meeting, but it has long been accepted that the general meeting can be a weak and ineffectual method of control, mainly because the meetings are poorly attended and the shareholders ill-informed. The emphasis in recent years has been on trying to ensure that the general meeting does act as an effective counterbalance to the all-powerful board and considerable attention is now paid to this issue in the interests of good corporate governance.

5-44

consider shorter periods since compensation for risks run by senior executives is already implicit in the absolute level of remuneration which they receive.

[60] The Large and Medium-sized Companies and Groups (Accounts and Reports) Regulations 2008, SI 2008/410, Sch 8.

[61] In early 2008, as the economy worsened, there was evidence of considerable shareholder resistance to excessive remuneration packages. GlaxoSmithKline, Royal Dutch Shell and HSBC all attracted substantial votes against their remuneration reports though none were actually voted down: see 'HSBC draws fire over executive remuneration' *Financial Times*, 30 May 2008; 'GSK faces revolt over retention bonus'; 'Paying for Staying'; and 'Pay back as investors flex some financial muscle' *Financial Times*, 21 May 2008. GSK had the dubious distinction in 2003 of being the first company to have its remuneration report voted down by shareholders, see 'Investors Reject GSK executive pay policy' *Financial Times*, 20 May 2003, when shareholders refused to endorse arrangements which included a two year notice period and munificent exit package for the company's chief executive.

5-45   One way of enhancing the importance of the general meeting is to return specific powers to the shareholders, by statute if necessary. As noted at **5-40**, giving the shareholders an advisory vote on the directors' remuneration report has proved surprisingly effective, even if only in generating adverse media attention which has forced a re-think on some remuneration packages. It might be possible to identify other issues which could be the subject of specific approval, such as the directors' report on the effectiveness of internal controls (discussed at **5-19**). The CA 2006 already requires shareholder approval of various actions (such as a purchase of the company's own shares[62]) or transactions (such as substantial property transactions) where directors have an acute conflict of interest.[63] The result is a greater level of transparency and accountability and, in cases where shareholder authorisation is required, control over these matters by the shareholders. But there is a balance to be struck between requiring shareholder approval of matters and being unduly restrictive of ordinary management power. Calling general meetings in public companies with large numbers of shareholders is a time-consuming and expensive business. Probably, the current range of matters which require shareholder approval is an appropriate balance and the issue is not so much that the general meeting's jurisdiction is too limited, but rather that procedures need to be fine-tuned to ensure effective shareholder participation at the general meeting.

5-46   Attention has turned therefore to matters such as the conduct of meetings in an electronic age, attendance at general meetings, and the voting record and practices of shareholders.

Effective meetings

5-47   As for the actual conduct of meetings, the rules in this regard were comprehensively overhauled by the CA 2006 and they are discussed in Chapter 15. It suffices to highlight a few key issues here.

(1) There is a greater emphasis on electronic means of communication which offer low cost and timely disclosure to all shareholders equally: see at **15-5**. The largest companies with widely dispersed shareholdings now make increasing use of their websites for instant communication with all shareholders. For example, it is common to have simultaneous webcasts of analyst and other meetings so that all shareholders, rather than just the largest, can be part of the process. Documentation can be made available to all shareholders quickly and at very low cost.

(2) Voting, attendance and participation rights at meetings have been reviewed, modified and extended so that mechanisms are available which allow shareholders flexibility as to how they engage with the company. For example, the CA 2006 confers enhanced rights on proxies to attend, speak and vote at general meetings: see **15-10**. Members crossing certain thresholds (typically 10% of the

---

[62] CA 2006, ss 694, 701.   [63] See CA 2006, s 190.

total voting rights, though in some cases it is 5%) are able to require the circulation of statements concerning resolutions to be moved at a meeting or any other
business of the meeting (s 314: see **15-38**). Members can require the circulation
of a written resolution in the case of a private company (s 292: see **15-28**), or the
circulation of a proposed resolution at an annual general meeting of a public
company (s 338: see **15-31**), and they can requisition a general meeting (s 303:
see **15-46**). The costs issue (which in the past has been a deterrent to the use
of such powers) has also been addressed with the company required to carry
the costs of circulation in some instances. Members of a quoted company can
demand an independent assessment of the outcome of a poll (s 342: see **15-15**)
and can raise audit concerns on the company's website (s 527) see **16-50**. The
result should be that shareholders are able to influence the agenda of the meeting rather than being dictated to by the board, though it has to be acknowledged
that some of these powers have always been available and shareholders have
shown little interest in exercising them.

(3) The CA 2006 has moved to enfranchise the indirect investor or at least to
acknowledge that the shareholder on the register is frequently the nominee
holder for an ultimate beneficial owner who may be several steps removed. The
standard position pre-2006 was that the nominee on the register was able to vote
or not as he chose (depending on any contractual arrangement to the contrary
with the ultimate beneficial owner) and did not need to pass on documentation
from the company (for example, as to rights issues or annual reports etc). Often
the result was that the person with the voting rights was uninterested in exercising them (being concerned only with overall shareholder returns) whereas the
ultimate owner of the shares might have been interested but did not have the
legal right to exert any direct influence over the company in which his money
was invested. The classic example is the pension fund investment where sums
are passed through the hands of trustees and managers in an ever-lengthening
chain to the company raising capital. The position of the indirect investor is
discussed further below.

Activist institutional shareholders

If there is to be meaningful shareholder engagement with companies, in effect it means   **5-48**
there must be engagement between the institutional shareholders and the board of
directors as institutions are the largest block of shareholders in listed UK companies.
The latest ONS (Office of National Statistics) report on share ownership found that, as
at 31 December 2006, institutional shareholders held 41.1% of UK ordinary shares in
listed companies with insurance companies holding 14.7% and pension funds 12.7% of
that total.[64] The issue is the role that such well-informed, well-financed and influential

---

[64] ONS, *Share Ownership Report for 2006*. See also ABI, *Insurance Key Facts* (September 2008). See
generally Cheffins, *Corporate Ownership and Control: British Business Transformed* (2008); also Dignam &
Galanis, 'Corporate Governance and the Importance of the Macroeconomic Context' (2008) 28 Ox JLS 201.

institutional shareholders can play and the contribution that they can make to high standards of corporate governance.[65] Their role might be seen as focused on improved corporate performance which would be reflected in shareholder value. Some would see institutional investors as having a broader role and in a position to protect the stakeholder interests not otherwise directly addressed by company law mechanisms, so institutional shareholders might police corporate environmental practices, social responsibility and compliance with human rights.[66] Indeed, some would see institutional investors as effectively policing large companies for the benefit of all, adopting an almost regulatory-like role.

5-49   For the past decade and more, institutional investors have come increasingly to the fore in corporate governance matters, intervening especially on issues such as board composition, directors' remuneration, company strategy and corporate social responsibility. Usually this intervention occurs behind the scenes[67] but increasingly institutional investors are willing to be seen to be taking a more public stance.[68] It is still exceptional, however, for an institutional shareholder to put resolutions to the annual general meeting or to vote against the reappointment of incumbent management, though increasingly they are willing to withhold their votes on an issue. This tactic allows them to avoid a positive vote against the board while still expressing their disquiet about a particular matter.

5-50   Some of the more prominent investors have issued statements as to the standards that they expect in companies in which they invest; for example, the National Association of Pension Funds issues its own influential guidance on corporate governance and voting matters,[69] as does Hermes (a leading institutional investor).[70] Particularly influential in this area is the Institutional Shareholders Committee (ISC) 'Statement

---

[65] See Garrido & Rojo, 'Institutional Investors and Corporate Governance: Solution or Problem ?' in Hopt & Wymeersch, *Capital Markets and Company Law* (2003).

[66] These responsibilities are more explicitly integrated into directors' duties now by CA 2006, s 172 which is discussed in Chapter 9.

[67] See the interesting paper by Becht et al, 'Returns to Shareholder Activism, Evidence from a Clinical Study of the Hermes UK Focus Fund' ECGI Finance Working Paper, No 138 (2008) which found that practically all of the engagement of this fund with investee companies took place privately and without resort to mechanisms such as resolutions. This study also concluded that there were substantial effects and benefits associated with shareholder activism in the form of private engagements by an activist fund. See also Goergen et al, 'Do UK Institutional Shareholders Monitor their Investee Firms?' (2008) JCLS 39.

[68] The ABI has developed an Institutional Voting Information System which provides reports on companies and which colour codes those reports on the basis of issues of corporate governance concern with the key categories being red (strong concerns) and amber (concern). This mechanism has become quite effective with companies anxious to avoid being 'red topped' on any particular issue such as board composition or remuneration: see 'Barclays practises appeasement' *Financial Times*, 18 November 2008 (in dispute over capital raising by the bank which attracted a 'red top' alert by the ABI); but see also 'Mideast fracas puts investors' power in doubt' *Financial Times*, 21 November 2008. Some examples of shareholder activism are noted by Roach, 'CEOs, Chairmen and Fat Cats' (2006) 27 Co Law 297.

[69] See NAPF, *Corporate Governance Policy and Voting Guidelines* (November 2007); AIC, *Code of Corporate Governance: a framework of best practice for member companies* (May 2007).

[70] See *The Hermes Corporate Governance Principles* (2008).

of Principles on the Responsibilities of Institutional Investors'.[71] The Statement was first issued in 2002 and the latest version in June 2007.

In the Statement of Principles, the ISC attempts to draw some boundaries to the role **5-51** which institutional shareholders might undertake and the ISC is particularly concerned to point out that the primary role of the institutions is as investors and not as micro-managers. Institutional investors owe fiduciary duties to their own end-beneficiaries, the people who invest in their insurance and savings products, and their legal obligation is to act in the interests of those beneficiaries. To the extent that monitoring and dialogue with company management assists in ensuring the value of, or minimising the chance of loss to, their investments, the institutional shareholders are willing to play their part in corporate governance, but they should not be regarded as fulfilling some wider role in the public interest.

The purpose of the ISC Statement of Principles is to set out best practice for institu- **5-52** tional shareholders in relation to their responsibilities in companies in which they invest. The Statement requires the institutions to set out publicly their policy on how they will discharge their responsibilities, clarifying the priorities attached to particular issues and when they will take action. They must monitor the performance of, and establish, where necessary, a regular dialogue with investee companies. They must intervene where necessary, evaluate the impact of their engagement and report back to clients/beneficial owners. Institutions should also set out publicly their policy on voting and voting disclosure.

The importance of this Statement of Principles is reinforced by the Combined Code **5-53** which states that institutional investors should apply the principles and that the principles should be reflected in contracts with fund managers (Code E.1).[72] The newly revised Myners Principles for pension fund investment also state that pension fund trustees should adopt, or ensure their investment managers adopt, the Institutional Shareholders' Committee Statement of Principles.[73]

One of the most difficult issues is whether institutional shareholders should be made **5-54** to vote at general meetings, given the significant blocks of shares which they hold. The Combined Code merely points out the responsibility of institutional shareholders to make considered use of their votes (Code E.3). It also states that institutional shareholders should on request make available to their clients information about their voting practices,[74] but it does not go further than that. The ISC too remains of the

---

[71] The ISC is composed of the ABI and NAPF together with the Association of Investment Companies (AIC) and the Investment Management Association (IMA).

[72] Successive surveys by NAPF have suggested high levels of support for the Statement of Principles: see NAPF Research Report, *Pension Funds' Engagement with Companies* (September 2008) which showed that 79% of pension funds' statements of investment principles refer to the ISC Principles.

[73] See HM Treasury, *Updating the Myners Principles: A Response to Consultation*, Appendix A (October 2008).

[74] The NAPF Research Report, above n 72, reports that 54% of pension funds covered by the survey (i.e. funds with more than £1bn in assets) disclose their general policy on voting to scheme members with 24% making more specific disclosures. 66% of the funds responding to the survey had their own policies on

view that disclosure of voting decisions should be a voluntary matter, while noting that an increasing number of institutional investors do now put details of their voting records on their websites.[75] The Government has threatened from time to time that it will consider introducing a legal requirement to vote if institutions do not exercise their voting rights and that threat has had a salutary effect. It is reinforced by the fact that the Government has power in CA 2006, ss 1277–1280 to bring in regulations to require institutions to provide information as to the exercise of their voting rights.[76] The Government has made clear that it has no immediate plans to exercise that power, but, clearly, that option is available to it.

Enfranchising the indirect investor

5-55   In keeping with the general theme of shareholder engagement, especially in larger companies, the CA 2006, Part 9 introduces some innovative provisions with respect to the enfranchisement of indirect holders. The modern practice is that most individual investors hold shares through an intermediary and have no direct relationship with the company in which they have invested. For its part, the company looks solely to the legal owner as reflected in the register of members and does not have regard to beneficial interests (CA 2006, s 126). It is often argued that shareholder engagement demands some mechanism whereby the indirect investor, the actual provider of the capital, can engage with and be recognised by the company.[77] These enfranchisement provisions were the subject of intense debate in Parliament with various permutations being considered before agreement was finally reached on what is now CA 2006, Part 9. The idea of enfranchising or involving the indirect investor seems attractive, but in practice it is difficult to devise a workable, cost-effective, mechanism. Traded companies with large numbers of registered shareholders and unquantifiable numbers of beneficial interests behind them are concerned that a liberal approach to enfranchising those beneficial interests could lead to administrative chaos and dramatically increase the costs of maintaining and operating their share registers. The CA 2006, Part 9 is therefore a modest step forward, reflecting the numerous compromises necessary to gain Parliamentary approval, rather than a radical departure from the general rule that the company looks to the registered shareholder.

---

corporate governance. The pensions funds were forced to greater engagement because it was one of the Myners Principles on Institutional Investment which they were expected to comply with on a comply or explain basis: see Myners, *Institutional Investment in the UK: A Review*, March 2001 and text to n 73 above.

[75] See ISC, *Framework on Voting Disclosures* (June 2007). The ISC noted that 16 major fund managers now make disclosures via their websites and others plan to do so.

[76] See generally Schmolke, 'Institutional Investors Mandatory Voting Disclosure' (2006) 7 EBOR 767.

[77] The Company Law Review noted the growing separation between the legal ownership and beneficial ownership and considered the grant of at least some 'control rights' to the beneficial owners, such as rights to information and to attend at meetings and to vote, while envisaging that market solutions will emerge as electronic communications make it easier for companies, intermediaries and ultimate beneficial owners to exercise these control rights: see Company Law Review, *Final Report*, vol 1 (2001), para 3.51, para 7.1; also *Completing the Structure* (2000), paras 5.2–5.12; *Developing the Framework* (2000), paras 4.7–4.18.

Part 9 allows for the recognition of indirect investors in two ways: (1) any company **5-56** can choose to permit the registered member to nominate another person to enjoy or exercise all or any specified rights of the member in relation to the company (CA 2006, s 145); and (2) traded companies can allow a member to nominate another person to enjoy 'information rights' so that the company must communicate with that other person directly (s 146).[78]

Nominating another to exercise rights of a member

Any company may provide in its articles that a member can nominate another person **5-57** to enjoy or exercise all or any specified rights of that member in relation to the company (CA 2006, s 145). Anything which can be done by the member can then be done by the nominated person, in particular the nominated person can exercise the rights to circulate resolutions and statements (ss 292, 314, 338), to require the directors to call a meeting (s 303), to appoint a proxy (s 324) and to receive written resolutions, notice of meetings and annual accounts and reports (ss 291, 310, 423). To date, few companies, if any, appear to have chosen to alter their articles to allow for nomination in this way.

Information rights

A member in a traded company can nominate a person on whose behalf he holds **5-58** shares to enjoy 'information rights' by which is meant that the nominee has the right to receive all shareholder communications and the right to receive the annual accounts and reports (CA 2006, s 146). The rights of the nominee are in addition to the rights of the registered member (s 150(5)). A registered member is not required to nominate another person for information rights and, even if nominated, the registered member can terminate the nomination at any time (s 148(2)).[79] The documents or information which the nominee is entitled to are provided by a website, unless the nominee requests the registered member to notify the company that the nominee wishes to receive hard copies and the nominee provides a postal address for that purpose (s 147(2), (5)).

Where a notice of a meeting is sent to a nominated indirect shareholder, the notice **5-59** must state that, depending on the agreement between the registered shareholder and the indirect investor, the nominated person *may* have the right to be appointed as a proxy or to appoint someone else as a proxy and *may* be able to give his voting instructions directly to the registered shareholder (s 149). A failure by the company to recognise information rights is actionable (as a breach of the articles) only by the registered shareholder and not by the nominated person (s 150(2)).

After all the Parliamentary discussion, once enacted the provisions appear to have **5-60** attracted little interest. In so far as the provisions require companies to facilitate the changes by choosing to alter their articles (to allow for nomination of another), they

---

[78] For detailed guidance on Part 9, see ICSA *Guidance on Part 9, Companies Act 2006, Indirect Investors— Information Rights and Voting* (2007).

[79] Furthermore, CA 2006, s 148(7) provides that a nomination can be terminated where no response is received within 28 days to a query from the company as to whether the indirect investor wishes to retain his information rights (only one such enquiry may be made per annum).

have shown no inclination to do so, not least because there is no pressure from share-holders for the articles to be changed. In so far as nominee shareholders may nominate the beneficial owners to enjoy information rights, it would appear they have not done so, perhaps out of inertia or a concern about the administrative burden of altering existing arrangements. In so far as the whole process depends on the indirect invest-ors showing some interest in exercising these rights, they have not done so, proba-bly because the rights mainly amount to a right to receive information via a website (a compromise based on the need to limit the costs involved). As much of the informa-tion on websites is anyway on open access in the public domain, shareholders have no particular reason to exercise these rights. The provisions are then on the statute book but they have had little impact to date.

6

Board composition—qualification and disqualification

A Appointment of directors

The directors are responsible for the management of the company's business, for **6-1** which purpose they may exercise all the powers of the company.[1] The expectation is that the directors act collectively as a board but the articles invariably provide that any of the powers conferred on the directors by the articles can in turn be delegated by them to smaller committees or individual directors or other persons.[2] The proceedings of the board are regulated by the articles of association which will contain detailed rules covering such matters as voting,[3] the required quorum[4] and the calling of meetings.[5] Minutes must be kept of all board meetings.[6]

'Director' as such is not defined in the Companies Act 2006 which provides simply **6-2** that 'director' includes any person occupying the position of director, by whatever name called,[7] so making it clear that title is not the determining factor in deciding whether someone is a director. It is possible therefore for someone to be a director

---

[1] See The Companies (Model Articles) Regulations 2008, SI 2008/3229, reg 2, Sch 1, art 3 (Ltd); reg 4, Sch 3, art 3 (Plc).

[2] See The Companies (Model Articles) Regulations 2008, SI 2008/3229, reg 2, Sch 1, art 5 (Ltd); reg 4, Sch 3, art 5 (Plc).

[3] The general rule about decision making by the directors of a private company is that any decision must be either a majority decision of the directors at a meeting or a unanimous decision (of those eligible to vote on the matter) by written resolution: see The Companies (Model Articles) Regulations 2008, SI 2008/3229, reg 2, Sch 1, arts 7–8 (Ltd), and see also art 16 ('subject to the articles, the directors may make any rule which they think fit about how they take decisions…'). Likewise in the case of a public company, though the equivalent art 7 is expressed in terms of 'may' rather than must: see arts 7, 13, 18–19 (Plc).

[4] See The Companies (Model Articles) Regulations 2008, SI 2008/3229, reg 2, Sch 1, art 11(2) (Ltd); reg 4, Sch 3, art 10(2) (Plc).

[5] See The Companies (Model Articles) Regulations 2008, SI 2008/3229, reg 2, Sch 1, art 9 (Ltd); reg 4, Sch 3, art 8 (Plc).

[6] CA 2006, s 248. There is no provision for inspection of such minutes by the members unlike the minutes of any general meeting which are available for inspection by any member: s 358.

[7] CA 2006, s 250. See Browne-Wilkinson V-C in *Re Lo-Line Electric Motors Ltd* [1988] 2 All ER 692 at 699: 'In my judgment the words "by whatever name called" show that the subsection is dealing with nomenclature; for example where the company's articles provide that the conduct of the company is committed to "governors" or "managers".'

though described as a manager or governor. Equally, companies may describe employees as marketing or personnel directors, for example, without their occupying the position of director in law. Legally, there are three classes of director which concern us, the de jure director, the de facto director and the shadow director, each of which is considered in detail below.

De jure directors

6-3   A de jure director is someone formally and validly appointed to the board. The application for registration of a company which is submitted to the registrar of companies must contain the names of the proposed first directors (first directors and company secretary, if the company is a public company, or is a private company which has chosen to have a company secretary)[8] and they must give their consent so to act (CA 2006, s 12(3)). On the certificate of incorporation being issued by the registrar, those so named are deemed to have been appointed to office (s 16(6)). Thereafter the manner of appointment is a matter for the articles which typically provide that appointments may be made by ordinary resolution or by a decision of the directors.[9]

6-4   A private company need have only one director whereas a public company must have at least two (CA 2006, s 154). For the first time, the CA 2006 sets a minimum age for a director which is 16 years and an appointment in breach of this requirement is void.[10] Under-age directors in office on 1 October 2008 automatically ceased to be directors (s 159(2)).

6-5   At least one director must be a natural person, otherwise corporate directors are permissible.[11] The Government had wanted to prohibit corporate directors, but had to settle on this compromise following objections on behalf of the 64,000 corporate directors on the register.[12] The Government had concerns that corporate directors make it difficult to determine who controls a company and to apply sanctions against corporate directors. Certainly the investigation and prosecution of corporate frauds can be impeded when it is possible to have corporate shareholders and directors, often

---

[8] CA 2006, s 9(4)(c).

[9] See The Companies (Model Articles) Regulations 2008, SI 2008/3229, reg 2, Sch 1, art 17 (Ltd); reg 4, Sch 3, art 20 (Plc). In the case of a public company, such an appointment is held only until the next following annual general meeting when the appointee can be re-elected: art 20(2)(a). Usefully, the model articles for private companies provide that where, as a result of death, a private company is left with no shareholders and no directors (as where the company is a sole member company and the sole member is also the sole director) the personal representative of the last shareholder to die has the right to appoint a director: see art 17(2) (Ltd).

[10] CA 2006, s 157(1), (4), though such 'directors' remain liable for their acts: see s 157(5). Regulations may allow for exceptional cases: s 158 (it might be appropriate for younger directors of, say, a company operating as a youth charity). A previous restriction (CA 1985, s 293) on persons aged 70 or more acting as a director of a public company has been repealed.

[11] CA 2006, s 155; *Re Bulawayo Market and Offices Co Ltd* [1907] 2 Ch 458. The register of directors must include the corporate name and registered office of any company holding the office of director as well as other details: CA 2006, s 164.

[12] See *Modernising Company Law* (Cmnd 5553-I, 2002), paras 3.32–3.34.

based on further layers of corporate entities, some of which may be registered in other jurisdictions. The Secretary of State has a new power to direct a company to appoint the right number of directors or to ensure that at least one director is a natural person.[13]

In the case of a public company, each proposed director must be voted on individu- **6-6** ally unless there is unanimous consent of those voting to a block resolution (CA 2006, s 160(1)). This is to ensure that shareholders can express their disapproval of any particular director without having to reject the entire board. Failure to comply with this requirement means that the resolution is void (s 160(2)).

The model articles for public companies (see **4-2**) provide for the appointment of alter- **6-7** nate directors. Such a director is appointed by a director to exercise that director's powers and carry out that director's responsibilities in relation to the taking of decisions by the directors.[14] Except as otherwise provided, alternate directors are deemed for all purposes to be directors and are liable for their own acts and omissions and are not agents of or for their appointors.[15]

The acts of a director are valid notwithstanding any defect which may afterwards be **6-8** discovered in his appointment or qualification.[16] This covers the situation where there has been a breach of the requirements regarding appointment with the result that the appointment is defective, but it does not validate the acts of someone who has never been appointed at all but who simply purports to fill the office of director;[17] nor can it assist a party having knowledge of the facts giving rise to the defect or a party who is put on inquiry but does not inquire.[18]

Every company must keep a register of its directors, giving the following details for **6-9** an individual director: name, a service address (there is no longer any requirement for residential addresses to be given), the country or state (or part of the UK) in which he is usually resident, nationality, business occupation (if any), and date of birth.[19] This register must be open to inspection at the registered office or other specified place by members of the company, free of charge, and by the public for such fee as may be prescribed.[20] Details of directors' service contracts must also be available for inspection at the registered office or other specified place.[21] A major change in the CA 2006 is that there is no longer a requirement for a director's usual residential address to be

---

[13] CA 2006, s 156; criminal sanctions attach to a failure to comply with this requirement: s 156(6).

[14] See The Companies (Model Articles) Regulations 2008, SI 2008/3229, reg 4, Sch 3, arts 25–27 (Plc). As an alternate is deemed for all purposes to be a director (art 26(2)(a)), his appointment must be notified to the registrar of companies as required by CA 2006, s 167.

[15] See The Companies (Model Articles) Regulations 2008, SI 2008/3229, reg 4, Sch 3, art 26(2) (Plc).

[16] CA 2006, s 161, even in the case of an appointment which is void under s 160 (appointment of directors of a public company to be voted on individually).

[17] *Morris v Kanssen* [1946] AC 459; *British Asbestos Co Ltd v Boyd* [1903] 2 Ch 439; *Dawson v African Consolidated Land and Travel Co* [1898] 1 Ch 6.

[18] See *Re New Cedos Engineering Co Ltd* [1994] 1 BCLC 797 at 812; *British Asbestos Co Ltd v Boyd* [1903] 2 Ch 439.

[19] CA 2006, s 162(1), (2). There is no longer any requirement to give details of other directorships held by that director.

[20] CA 2006, s 162(3), (5); SI 2008/3006.   [21] See CA 2006, s 228(1), (2); SI 2008/3006.

given in the register of directors. Instead a service address may be given and that service address may be stated as the company's registered office (s 163(5)). This change was introduced in order to provide additional protection for directors from harassment and threats by persons such as animal rights extremists. As with the decision to limit unrestricted access to the register of members (see **14-94**), this reduction in transparency across a register of 2.4m companies is a disproportionate response to the criminal activities of a small number of extremists. The company is required to maintain a register of directors' residential addresses (s 165), but this register is not open to inspection. The details contained on the company's register of residential addresses are notified to the registrar of companies on the appointment of a director (s 167). This information is classified as 'protected information' which cannot be disclosed by the company or by the registrar of companies save to the extent permitted by the Act,[22] for example disclosure on the order of a court.

6-10   Appointments (and resignations) of directors must be notified within 14 days to the registrar of companies (CA 2006, s 167) and any such notification is then publicised by the registrar in the *London Gazette*.[23]

De facto directors

6-11   A de facto director is someone who assumes the status and functions of a company director so as to make himself responsible as if he were a de jure director.[24] As Millett LJ explained in *Re Hydrodam (Corby) Ltd*:[25]

> 'To establish that a person was a de facto director of a company it is necessary to plead and prove that he undertook functions in relation to the company which could probably be discharged only by a director. It is not sufficient to show that he was concerned in the management of a company's affairs or undertook tasks in relation to the business which can probably be performed by a manager below board level.'

6-12   The difficulty lies in trying to distinguish someone who assumes the status of a director from someone who acts for, or otherwise in the interests of, a company but is never more than, for example, a mere agent, employee or adviser.[26]

---

[22] CA 2006, ss 240–246; and s 1087(1)(b); see also The Companies (Disclosure of Address) Regulations 2009, SI 2009/214.

[23] CA 2006, ss 1077, 1078. A company cannot rely against other persons on any change among the company's directors if that change has not been officially notified in the *Gazette* at the material time unless the other person was aware of it; and it cannot rely on any change within 15 days of the notice in the *Gazette* if the other party was unavoidably prevented from knowing of the change at that time: s 1079(1)–(3). However, the effect of s 1079 is purely negative and it does not entitle the company to treat the gazetting of an event as notice to all the world: *Official Custodian for Charities v Parway Estates Developments Ltd* [1984] 3 All ER 679.

[24] See *Re Kaytech International plc, Secretary of State for Trade and Industry v Kaczer* [1999] 2 BCLC 351, CA; also *Secretary of State for Trade and Industry v Tjolle* [1998] 1 BCLC 333 at 343–4; *Re Hydrodam (Corby) Ltd* [1994] 2 BCLC 180 at 183. See generally Noonan & Watson, 'Examining Company Directors through the Lens of De Facto Directorship' [2008] JBL 587.

[25] [1994] 2 BCLC 180 at 183.

[26] See *Secretary of State for Trade and Industry v Hollier* [2007] BCC 11.

The question whether someone is a de facto director is likely to arise where a stat-   **6-13**
ute imposes an obligation or a liability on a director and the individual in question
attempts to evade the obligation or liability by relying on the fact that he is not a de jure
director (i.e. a formally and properly appointed director). The issue may arise in the
context of disqualification proceedings under the Company Directors Disqualification
Act 1986 which may be brought against a 'director' including a de facto director.[27] The
issue may arise also in the context of civil proceedings by liquidators where they seek
to make recoveries from a person identified as a de facto director.[28]

In determining whether a person has assumed the status and function of a company   **6-14**
director (and it is very much a question of degree) the court takes into account all the
relevant factors including at least: whether or not there was a holding out by the company of the individual as a director, whether the individual used the title, whether
the individual had proper information (e.g. management accounts) on which to base
decisions, and whether the individual had to make major decisions.[29] This list of factors to be considered is not exhaustive and there is no requirement for all of these
elements to be present.[30] As was noted in one instance, what is important is not what
the person calls himself, but what he does.[31] The crucial question is whether the individual is part of the corporate governing structure, able to participate in the notional
boardroom.[32]

In *Secretary of State for Trade and Industry v Hollier*[33] the directors concerned   **6-15**
were members of one family and the issue was the extent to which a wife and sons
were also de facto directors together with the father.[34] Etherton J drew together what
he thought were the principles to be applied in determining whether someone is a de

---

[27] *Re Lo-Line Electric Motors Ltd* [1988] BCLC 698 at 706.

[28] See, for example, *Primlake Ltd v Matthews Associates* [2007] 1 BCLC 666.

[29] *Secretary of State for Trade and Industry v Tjolle* [1998] 1 BCLC 333 at 343–4. In *Re Neath Rugby Ltd, Hawkes v Cuddy* [2008] 1 BCLC 527 the court described a wife who was a de jure director as a mere cipher for her husband such that all of her acts and omissions were his acts and omissions and he was a de facto director. An individual may through his control of a corporate director constitute himself a de facto director of a subject company but whether or not he does so depends on what the individual procures the corporate director to do: *Secretary of State for Trade and Industry v Hall* [2006] All ER (D) 432 (Jul), Ch D.

[30] *Re Kaytech International plc, Secretary of State for Trade and Industry v Kaczer* [1999] 2 BCLC 351 at 423–4, CA.

[31] See Lewison J in *Re Mea Corporation Ltd, Secretary of State for Trade and Industry v Aviss* [2007] 1 BCLC 618 at 637.

[32] *Secretary of State for Trade and Industry v Elms*, unreported 16 January 1997 approved in *Secretary of State for Trade and Industry v Tjolle* [1998] 1 BCLC 333 at 343–4; and in *Re Mea Corporation Ltd, Secretary of State for Trade and Industry v Aviss* [2007] 1 BCLC 618 at 637; *Secretary of State for Trade and Industry v Hollier* [2007] BCC 11 at 24. See also *Re Kaytech International plc, Secretary of State for Trade and Industry v Kaczer* [1999] 2 BCLC 351 at 423. A shareholder, even if acting to protect their investment, may act in a way which makes them a de facto director: see *Secretary of State for Trade and Industry v Becker* [2003] 1 BCLC 555 at 573; *Secretary of State for Trade and Industry v Hollier* [2007] BCC 11 at 27.

[33] [2007] BCC 11.

[34] The court found the wife and one of the sons were de facto directors and they were disqualified. On the facts, and the court emphasised that these cases all turn on their own special facts, the other son was not a de facto director: see [2007] BCC 11 at 27, 44.

facto director, as follows:[35]

> '(1) The touchstone is whether the defendant is part of the corporate governing structure.
>
> (2) Inherent in that touchstone is the distinction between someone who participates, or has the right to participate, in collective decision making on corporate policy and strategy and its implementation, on the one hand, and others who may advise or act on behalf of, or otherwise for the benefit of, the company, but do not participate in decision making as part of the corporate governance of the company. Accordingly, the test is not satisfied by someone who was at all times and in all material decisions subordinate to the de jure directors.
>
> (3) The defendant may have been a de facto director even though he or she did not have day to day control of the company's affairs, and even though he or she was only involved in part of the company's activities.
>
> (4) The issue is to be determined objectively on the basis of all relevant facts. Whether the defendant was held out by the company, or claimed or purported, to be a director, and whether the defendant had access or the ability to obtain access to relevant company information is likely to be highly relevant and may be decisive. Factors such as a family relationship with other admitted directors and the defendant's financial interest in the company may also be relevant, sometimes supporting and sometimes negating the allegation that the defendant was a de facto director.'

6-16   In *Secretary of State for Trade and Industry v Hollier*[36] a son was not a de facto director when the court found that he acted in a particular company motivated by a wish to assist his father in his business, but the son did not wish or intend or act so as to participate in strategic or policy decisions on a par with any other directors of the company. The court found that another son was a de facto director for he did exercise real control and gave instructions over a wide range of the company's activities, even though equally motivated to help his father. In *Re Kaytech International plc, Secretary of State for Trade and Industry v Kaczer*,[37] the Court of Appeal concluded that a person who was deeply and openly involved in the company's affairs, who devoted himself to the company's financial and property interests and who dealt with creditors, suppliers and the company's professional advisers, was not merely a consultant or company secretary but a de facto director. In *IRC v McEntaggart*[38] an undischarged bankrupt (and therefore someone automatically disqualified from being a director) who was described as the moving spirit within a construction company and whose role extended to matters such as negotiating and signing contracts, and who was involved in nearly all aspects of the management of the company's affairs, was a de facto director.

6-17   In *Secretary of State for Trade and Industry v Tjolle*,[39] however, the court concluded that a manager employed by a holiday company who had a variety of titles including

---

[35] [2007] BCC 11 at 27.

[36] [2007] BCC 11. See also *Gemma Ltd v Davies* [2008] 2 BCLC 281 (wife with purely clerical functions who was not involved in decision-making and who had no real influence in the governance of the company was not a de facto director).

[37] [1999] 2 BCLC 351, CA.

[38] [2006] 1 BCLC 476. See also *Re Moorgate Metals Ltd* [1995] 1 BCLC 503.

[39] [1998] 1 BCLC 333. See also *Re Red Label Fashions Ltd* [1999] BCC 308.

'sales and marketing director' and even, for a period, 'deputy managing director', who sometimes attended board meetings, but who was never involved in any financial matters and who had no access to the company accounts, was not a de facto director.

In *Secretary of State for Trade and Industry v Hollier*[40] Etherton J considered that de facto directorships and shadow directorships are alternatives although he accepted that there may be cases, particularly where the defendant's influence in the corporate governance is partly concealed and partly open, where it may not be entirely straightforward which of the two descriptions is most apposite. Millett J in *Re Hydrodam (Corby) Ltd*[41] had thought that the categories did not overlap and were for the most part mutually exclusive, but that view has been criticised and it is accepted that there can be element of overlap between the categories, though by and large they will not both be relevant.[42] Lewison J in *Re Mea Corporation Ltd, Secretary of State for Trade and Industry v Aviss*[43] thought they may even co-exist as where a person assumes the functions of a director as regards one part of the company's activities (say, marketing) and gives directions to the board as regards another (say, manufacturing and finance) so constituting him a de facto and a shadow director at the same time. The distinction may matter with regard to the application of fiduciary duties which do apply to de facto directors, but the position is unclear with respect to shadow directors: see **7-4**. **6-18**

Whether a particular statutory provision which applies to a 'director' applies to a de facto director is a question of construction of the provision.[44] There is a consensus that a de facto director, having assumed the position of a director, is subject to the fiduciary and other duties of a director.[45] After all, as noted above, he is someone participating in the notional boardroom and part of the corporate governing structure.[46] In *Primlake Ltd v Matthews Associates*[47] a company had sold land with significant development potential and much of the purchase money found its way into the hands of an architect involved in the sale. On the company going into liquidation, the liquidators alleged that the architect was actually a de facto director of the company who had received the money (£800,000 approx) in breach of his duties to the company. The defendant argued that he was merely a consultant to the company assisting it in finding a purchaser for the land and that the sums received had been professional fees due for his services. The court found that the individual controlled the company and ran **6-19**

---

[40] [2007] BCC 11 at 27.　　[41] [1994] 2 BCLC 180 at 183.

[42] See, for example, *Secretary of State for Trade and Industry v Becker* [2003] 1 BCLC 555 at 564–5; *Re Kaytech International plc* [1999] 2 BCLC 351 at 424. See Noonan & Watson, 'The Nature of Shadow Directorship: Ad Hoc Statutory Intervention or Core Company Law Principle' [2006] JBL 763 who are critical of the failure to maintain clear distinctions between the categories which perform different functions.

[43] [2007] 1 BCLC 618 at 639.

[44] See *Re Lo-Line Electric Motors Ltd* [1988] BCLC 698; *Dean v Hiesler* [1942] 2 All ER 340.

[45] See *Statek Corp v Alford* [2008] BCC 266 at 290 (de facto director owed fiduciary duties in respect of company assets within his control); *Shepherds Investment Ltd v Walters* [2007] 2 BCLC 207 at 214–16 (de facto director in breach of the no conflict duty in developing a competing business and exploiting and diverting business opportunities of the company for his own benefit).

[46] See *Secretary of State for Trade and Industry v Elms* (16 January 1997, unreported) approved in *Secretary of State for Trade and Industry v Tjolle* [1998] 1 BCLC 333 at 343–4.

[47] [2007] 1 BCLC 666.

its entire business. He negotiated the crucial contracts and made all decisions, both tactical and strategic.[48] It was only for tax reasons, the court found, that he had not actually been appointed as a director. He was a de facto director and, the court held, in breach of duty by enriching himself at the expense of the company.

Shadow directors

6-20   A number of provisions in the Companies Act 2006 and the Insolvency Act 1986, particularly those requiring disclosure and regulating certain types of transactions by directors, apply to a shadow director.[49] This category is used to extend the reach of these statutory provisions to include individuals who are influential in the running of the company but who do not take up a position on the board.[50]

6-21   A shadow director is defined in CA 2006, s 251(1) as a person in accordance with whose directions or instructions the directors of a company are accustomed to act.[51] A person is not deemed to be a shadow director, however, by reason only that the directors act on advice given by him in a professional capacity (s 251(2)).[52]

6-22   In practice, the issue as to whether someone is a shadow director is most likely to arise in the context of disqualification proceedings under the Company Directors Disqualification Act 1986 brought against persons who, because they are bankrupts[53] or are already the subject of a disqualification order or undertaking, have not sought (and cannot seek) formal appointment to the board as a de jure director. The issue may also arise in the context of liability for wrongful trading under IA 1986, s 214 (discussed at **25-17**) which applies to directors and shadow directors.

6-23   The statutory definition of a 'shadow director' was considered in detail by the Court of Appeal in *Secretary of State for Trade and Industry v Deverell*[54] where Morritt LJ set out the following propositions:[55]

> '(1) The definition of a shadow director is to be construed in the normal way to give effect to the parliamentary intention ascertainable from the mischief to be dealt with and the words used.

---

[48] [2007] 1 BCLC 666 at 731.

[49] See CA 2006, s 223; IA 1986, ss 206(3), 214(7). In theory, the appointment of shadow directors must be notified to the registrar of companies under CA 2006, ss 162, 167, but unsurprisingly this rarely happens.

[50] See generally Noonan & Watson, above n 42.

[51] A one-off instruction or involvement is not sufficient and it is necessary to show a pattern of conduct in which the de jure director or directors are accustomed to act on the instructions of the alleged shadow director: *Secretary of State for Trade and Industry v Becker* [2003] 1 BCLC 555; see also *Ultraframe (UK) Ltd v Fielding* [2005] All ER (D) 397(Jul) Ch, [2005] EWHC 1638.

[52] There is a further exemption for holding companies in CA 2006, s 251(3).

[53] An undischarged bankrupt is automatically disqualified from acting as a company director save with the leave of the court: CDDA 1986, s 11.

[54] [2000] 2 BCLC 133. See Noonan & Watson, above n 42, who are critical of the approach taken in this case.

[55] [2000] 2 BCLC 133 at 144–5.

(2) The purpose of the legislation is to identify those, other than professional advisers, with real influence in the corporate affairs of the company. But it is not necessary that such influence should be exercised over the whole field of its corporate activities....

(3) Whether any particular communication from the alleged shadow director, whether by words or conduct, is to be classified as a direction or instruction must be objectively ascertained by the court in the light of all the evidence. In that connection I do not accept that it is necessary to prove the understanding or expectation of either giver or receiver. In many, if not most, cases it will suffice to prove the communication and its consequence.... Certainly the label attached by either or both parties then or thereafter cannot be more than a factor in considering whether the communication came within the statutory description of direction or instruction.

(4) Non-professional advice may come within that statutory description. The proviso excepting advice given in a professional capacity appears to assume that advice generally is or may be included. Moreover the concepts of "direction" and "instruction" do not exclude the concept of "advice" for all three share the common feature of "guidance".

(5) It will, no doubt, be sufficient to show that in the face of "directions or instructions" from the alleged shadow director the properly appointed directors or some of them[56] cast themselves in a subservient role or surrendered their respective discretions. But I do not consider that it is necessary to do so in all cases.... Such a requirement would be to put a gloss on the statutory requirement that the board are 'accustomed to act in accordance with' such directions or instructions....'

Morritt LJ also observed that 'lurking in the shadows may occur but it is not an essential ingredient to the recognition of a shadow director'.[57]   **6-24**

In *Deverell*, the proceedings were disqualification proceedings against two individuals who claimed that they were consultants to the insolvent company and were not therefore directors or shadow directors in respect of whom disqualification proceedings could be brought. The court found that one was concerned at the most senior level and with most aspects of the direction of the company's affairs[58] while the other's involvement went far beyond that of a consultant on matters directly affecting the company's financial affairs.[59] The court concluded that both individuals were shadow directors.[60]   **6-25**

In *Re Mea Corporation, Secretary of State for Trade and Industry v Aviss*[61] the evidence was that the two individuals in question (one of whom was the owner of the businesses) decided matters with regard to the recruitment of employees and the payments of creditors, they handled funding negotiations with the banks and tax matters   **6-26**

---

[56] See also *Ultraframe (UK) Ltd v Fielding* [2005] All ER (D) 397(Jul) Ch, [2005] EWHC 1638—it is sufficient if the governing majority of the board is accustomed to act on the directions of the shadow director.

[57] [2000] 2 BCLC 133 at 146.   [58] [2000] 2 BCLC 133 at 150.   [59] [2000] 2 BCLC 133 at 153.

[60] Arguably, one of the defendants, given his level of involvement with the actual conduct of the company's affairs, should more accurately have been classified as a de facto director rather than a shadow director. See Noonan & Watson, above n 42 at p 773, who make the point that this reasoning might have been a result of a desire on the court's part to ensure that these individuals were disqualified—the Secretary of State had not claimed they were de facto directors.

[61] [2007] 1 BCLC 618.

with the Inland Revenue. The key allegation, as far as the court was concerned, was that they decided on the application within a group of companies of a group treasury policy which resulted in all companies remitting funds to the parent company which then determined how those funds were used and which creditors got paid. In particular, funds were paid to companies outside of the group in which one of the directors had a personal interest. Despite the protestations of the boards of companies in the group, this policy persisted which, the court said, showed the level of control exercised by these individuals. The court had no hesitation in finding that this ability to dictate policy in an area of corporate affairs as critical as the application of trading income and the payment of trade creditors made them shadow directors.[62]

6-27   There is a possibility that a parent company may find itself a shadow director of a subsidiary when the level of control which it exercises is such that the directors of the subsidiary are accustomed to act in accordance with its directions or instructions and it will be a question of fact in each case as to whether this level of control exists.[63] Any controlling shareholder is potentially at risk of being classified as a shadow director and it is a question of asking whether that person has exercised real influence in the conduct of the company's affairs.[64] The fact that the shareholder is so acting in order to protect his investment does not prevent him being classified as a de facto director. The courts have heard argument as to secured creditors[65] and bankers[66] being so classified, but the courts have yet to be persuaded.

6-28   As noted above, whether a statutory provision applies to a shadow director is determined by the express wording of the section. Whether shadow directors are subject to the fiduciary duties of directors is unclear. The matter was not resolved by the Delphic wording of CA 2006, s 170(5) which merely provides that the general duties apply to shadow directors where, and to the extent that, the corresponding common law rules or equitable principles so apply.[67] At common law, the authorities are unclear and all are first instance. In *Ultraframe (UK) Ltd v Fielding*[68] Lewison J did not think that it necessarily followed from the fact that someone fell within the statutory definition of shadow director that it would be right to impose on him the same fiduciary duties as

---

[62] [2007] 1 BCLC 618 at 643.

[63] See *Re Hydrodam (Corby) Ltd* [1994] 2 BCLC 180 at 184. A limited exemption for parent companies is contained in CA 2006, s 251(3).

[64] See *Re Mea Corporation, Secretary of State for Trade and Industry v Aviss* [2007] 1 BCLC 618; also *Secretary of State for Trade and Industry v Jones* [1999] BCC 336 at 349.

[65] See *Re PFTZM Ltd, Jourdain v Paul* [1995] 2 BCLC 354, but the mere exercise of rights as a secured creditor is insufficient: see at 367.

[66] See *Re a Company No 005009 of 1987, ex p Copp* [1989] BCLC 13 at 21, a claim later abandoned: see [1990] BCLC 324 at 326.

[67] See Prentice and Payne (2006) 122 LQR 558 at 564. The Explanatory Notes, *Companies Act 2006*, para 310 states that this provision means that '…where a common law rule or equitable principle applies to a shadow director, the statutory duty replacing that common law rule or equitable principle will apply to the shadow director in place of the common law rule or principle. Where the rule or principle does not apply to a shadow director, the statutory duty replacing the rule will not apply either.' In the Parliamentary debates, Lord Goldsmith commented that it is for the courts to decide if shadow directors are subject to fiduciary duties and if so which apply: HL Deb, vol 681, col 828, 9 May 2006.

[68] [2005] All ER (D) 397(Jul) Ch, [2005] EWHC 1638.

are owed by a de jure or de facto director. In his view, the indirect influence exerted by a paradigm shadow director who did not directly deal with, or claim the right to deal directly with, the company's assets would not usually be sufficient to impose fiduciary duties upon him.[69] It does seem strained and artificial to suggest that a shadow director owes duties of honesty and loyalty to the company. If the issue is the need to impose liabilities on shadow directors, that liability can be imposed on the standard basis of dishonest receipt and knowing assistance rather than any need to categorise them artificially as fiduciaries. Having said that, in *Re Mea Corporation Ltd, Secretary of State for Trade and Industry v Aviss*[70] Lewison J seems to have assumed that a shadow director owed a duty to act in the company's interests, but on the facts there may have been more of an element of de facto director about the conduct of the directors in that case. As noted at **6-18**, there is an element of overlap between the two categories.

Remuneration of directors

Executive directors, at least in public companies and larger private companies, typic-   **6-29**
ally have a service contract with the company covering such matters as their remuneration, the duration of the appointment, and the amount of compensation payable in
the event of dismissal. In public listed companies, controversy over such contracts and,
in particular, over the remuneration and compensation packages contained within
them, has been a central issue in the corporate governance debate. In smaller private
companies, the directors may not have express service contracts, relying instead on
more informal arrangements, but this practice should be avoided as it can be a source
of subsequent disputes.[71] Non-executive directors are typically appointed on the basis
of a formal letter of appointment, especially in larger companies, and this too is a formal contractual document.

In the absence of a contract, a director cannot rely on the articles as constituting a   **6-30**
contract between himself and the company,[72] although it may be possible for a director
to pursue a claim to recover payment on the basis of an implied extrinsic contract.[73]
Exceptionally, a director may attempt to claim on a quantum meruit basis for services
rendered and accepted by the company,[74] or on the basis of an equitable allowance,[75]
but the courts are reluctant to allow such claims by directors.[76]

---

[69] [2005] All ER (D) 397(Jul) Ch; [2005] EWHC 1638, para 1289. Noonan & Watson, above n 42, argue that shadow directors should be liable to the same extent as the directors they instruct, so if the instruction makes the director liable for breach of duty, then the shadow director should have a secondary liability in respect of that breach.

[70] [2007] 1 BCLC 618 at 643. See also Toulson J in *Yukong Line of Korea Ltd v Rendsburg Corp Investment* [1998] 2 BCLC 485 at 502.   [71] See, for example, *Lloyd v Casey* [2002] 1 BCLC 454.

[72] *Hickman v Kent or Romney Marsh Sheep-Breeders Association* [1915] 1 Ch 881: see discussion at **4-74**.

[73] See *Re New British Iron Co, ex p Beckwick* [1898] 1 Ch 234.

[74] *Currencies Direct Ltd v Ellis* [2002] 2 BCLC 482, CA; *Craven-Ellis v Canons Ltd* [1936] 2 KB 403; but there is no scope for a quantum meruit claim by a director when the articles have already made express provision for special remuneration for a director: *Guinness plc v Saunders* [1990] 1 All ER 652, HL.

[75] See *Boardman v Phipps* [1967] 2 AC 46.

[76] The position on quantum meruit and equitable allowance claims was restrictively stated in *Guinness plc v Saunders* [1990] 1 All ER 652, HL. Directors are precluded from contracting with their companies for their

6-31   The mere holding of office by itself does not entitle a director to remuneration,[77] but the articles invariably provide, as the model articles do, that the directors are entitled to such remuneration as the directors determine both for their services as directors (i.e. for holding the office) and for any other services (i.e. as executive or non-executive directors) which they undertake.[78] Allowing the directors to determine their own remuneration gives rise to an obvious conflict of interest which in larger public companies is managed by delegating matters to a remuneration committee composed exclusively of non-executive directors, as is recommended by the Combined Code on Corporate Governance (see discussion at **5-38**), together with increased disclosure for quoted companies via a directors' remuneration report (see CA 2006, s 420 and **5-39**).

6-32   Where remuneration is paid, the court does not concern itself with the quantum of that remuneration and does not attempt to compare the market value of the services rendered with the amount of remuneration actually paid.[79] The court must be satisfied that the payment is genuinely remuneration, however, and not a sham transaction masking an improper return of capital to the shareholders.[80] Equally, however, as the Court of Appeal noted in *Currencies Direct Ltd v Ellis*,[81] there is no requirement that there is a specific agreement fixing the level or rate of remuneration or defining a formula for ascertaining a definite amount to be paid. Remuneration is consideration for work done or to be done and it may be paid in an infinite variety of ways and not necessarily to the person providing the consideration.[82] Excessive payments at a time when the company is in financial difficulties may be challenged by a liquidator[83] and such payments are often relied on as evidence of unfitness in disqualification proceedings: see **6-87**.

6-33   Long-term service contracts (essentially longer than two years) require shareholder approval, subject to certain exceptions (see s 188 and **12-12**), as do payments for loss of office in certain circumstances: see **12-17**.

services except in the circumstances authorised by the articles of association; likewise there should be no remuneration for their services except as provided by the articles of association. To allow otherwise might encourage fiduciaries to put themselves in a position where there is a conflict between their personal interest and their duties as fiduciaries.

[77] *Hutton v West Cork Rly Co Ltd* (1883) 23 Ch D 654.

[78] See The Companies (Model Articles) Regulations 2008, SI 2008/3229, reg 2, Sch 1, art 19 (Ltd); reg 4, Sch 3, art 23 (Plc). Equally the general meeting may resolve to pay a director for the mere holding of office, even if he undertakes no specific duties: *Re Halt Garage (1964) Ltd* [1982] 3 All ER 1016. If the articles require a specific body to determine the remuneration and the correct body has not done so, the director has no claim for payment under the articles: *Guinness plc v Saunders* [1990] 1 All ER 652, HL.

[79] See *Re Halt Garage (1964) Ltd* [1982] 3 All ER 1016 at 1039, per Dillon J: '…assuming that the sum is bona fide voted to be paid as remuneration, it seems to me that the amount…must be a matter of management for the company to determine in accordance with its constitution which expressly authorises payment for directors' services.'

[80] *Re Halt Garage (1964) Ltd* [1982] 3 All ER 1016.

[81] [2002] 2 BCLC 482.

[82] [2002] 2 BCLC 482 at 487.

[83] For example, under IA 1986, s 212 (misfeasance); see also *Re Halt Garage (1964) Ltd* [1982] 3 All ER 1016.

B Termination of appointment

Removal from office

A company may by ordinary resolution at a meeting remove a director before the **6-34** expiration of his period of office, notwithstanding anything in any agreement between him and the company (CA 2006, s 168(1)).[84] There are a number of practical consider- ations which the company must bear in mind, however, before exercising this power of removal.

A particular issue is the amount of damages which may be payable to a dismissed dir- **6-35** ector as the statutory power to remove a director does not deprive a person removed under it of compensation or damages payable in respect of the termination of his appointment as director or of any appointment terminating with that as director (CA 2006, s 168(5)). Compensation for loss of office is discussed at **12-17**.

In smaller private companies, exercise of the power of removal may trigger a petition **6-36** by the sacked director/shareholder under CA 2006, s 994 alleging that his removal from the board amounts to unfairly prejudicial conduct for the purposes of that pro- vision: see **17-66**. A shareholder/director in this type of company can protect himself to some extent against the possibility of removal by the inclusion of a provision in the articles entitling the director to weighted votes on any resolution to remove him from the board, a practice permitted by the House of Lords in *Bushell v Faith*.[85] In that case, the articles of the company provided that on a resolution to remove a particular direc- tor, his shares would carry three times the number of votes they normally carried. As a consequence, it was impossible for the other shareholders to pass the required ordi- nary resolution to remove him. Ungoed-Thomas J at first instance refused to permit the practice saying that it made a mockery of the Act, but the Court of Appeal and the House of Lords approved it[86] and it remains a valid method of entrenchment for directors.

Retirement

The model articles for public companies provide for the retirement of all the direct- **6-37** ors at the first annual general meeting and for the rotation of directors thereafter

---

[84] A written resolution may not be used: CA 2006, s 288(2)(a). At least 28 days' notice of the resolution must be given and the director concerned is entitled to be heard at the meeting where it is proposed to remove him and to have representations circulated to the shareholders, subject to certain constraints: s 169. The power to remove a director under this provision does not derogate from any power to do so by any other method: s 168(5)(b), such as a provision in the articles allowing for the removal of a director by resolution of the board.

[85] [1970] 1 All ER 53, HL.

[86] See [1970] 1 All ER 53 at 57, per Upjohn LJ: 'Parliament has never sought to fetter the right of a company to issue shares with such rights or restrictions as it thinks fit.'

with a selected number retiring each year, although they remain eligible for re-election.[87]

Resignation

6-38   A director may resign at any time by notice to the company and he will cease to be a director in accordance with the terms of that notice.[88]

Vacating office

6-39   A person ceases to be a director in the event of the occurrence of various events specified in the articles including, for example, on being prohibited by law from being a director or a bankruptcy order being made.[89] It is common to include a provision that a person ceases to be a director if he is requested in writing to resign by all his co-directors.[90]

Disqualification from office

6-40   The Company Directors Disqualification Act 1986 provides for a variety of grounds on which a person may be disqualified from being a director of a company and these are discussed in detail below.

C Disqualification of directors

Legislative framework and purpose

6-41   A particular concern in the early 1980s related to the ability of a person trading through the medium of one or more companies with limited liability to allow such a company to become insolvent, form a new company, and then carry on trading much as before, leaving behind a trail of unpaid creditors and often repeating the process

---

[87] See The Companies (Model Articles) Regulations 2008, SI 2008/3229, reg 4, Sch 3, art 21 (Plc). Private companies commonly dispense with rotation hence there is no provision for rotation in the model articles for private companies.

[88] See The Companies (Model Articles) Regulations 2008, SI 2008/3229, reg 2, Sch 1, art 18(f) (Ltd); reg 4, Sch 3, art 22(f) (Plc).

[89] See The Companies (Model Articles) Regulations 2008, SI 2008/3229, reg 2, Sch 1, art 18(a), (b) (Ltd); reg 4, Sch 3, art 22(a), (b) (Plc).

[90] Such a provision is effective and the office is vacated on the service of the notice even if the directors making the request act for an ulterior motive: *Lee v Chou Wen Hsien* [1985] BCLC 45.

several times.[91] The Companies Act 1985 already provided for the disqualification of directors on certain grounds, but it was decided to strengthen and extend those provisions and, in particular, to provide for the disqualification of unfit directors of insolvent companies. These reforms were implemented by the Insolvency Act 1985 and the provisions were subsequently consolidated and re-enacted as the Company Directors Disqualification Act 1986 (CDDA 1986).[92]

Further amendments were effected by the Insolvency Act 2000 (IA 2000) and the **6-42** Enterprise Act 2002. Prior to the reforms implemented by the IA 2000, an application for a disqualification order had to be made to the court in all cases (save for undischarged bankrupts who are automatically disqualified: CDDA 1986, s 11), a requirement which created considerable pressure on court resources. That pressure was relieved initially by the development of a procedure whereby disqualification proceedings might be dealt with by the court in a summary fashion,[93] but even such proceedings required court time. In order to expedite matters further, the IA 2000 made provision for disqualification undertakings which are agreed between a director and the Disqualification Unit of the Insolvency Service without the need to involve the courts.[94]

The ability to offer disqualification undertakings applies only to cases of unfitness **6-43** on insolvency and to unfitness identified after an investigation of a company (CDDA 1986, s 1A). The use of undertakings enables non-contentious cases to advance speedily so hastening the commencement of the disqualification period (to the advantage both of the public and the disqualified director) and reducing the burden of costs on the disqualified director. Of course, there is no obligation on a director to offer an undertaking nor on the Secretary of State to accept it and disputed cases are still a matter for the courts, but most disqualifications now are the subject of undertakings rather than court orders.[95]

Undischarged bankrupts are automatically disqualified from acting as directors or in **6-44** the promotion, formation or management of a company without the leave of the court (CDDA 1986, s 11). The Enterprise Act 2002 (EA 2002) made significant changes to the bankruptcy regime, however, with provision for the automatic discharge of nearly all

---

[91] See the *Report of the Review Committee on Insolvency Law and Practice* (the Cork Committee) (Cmnd 8558), para 1813, and generally Chs 43, 45.

[92] On disqualification, see generally Walters and Davis-White, *Directors' Disqualification and Bankruptcy Restrictions* (2nd edn, 2005); Finch, *Corporate Insolvency Law: Perspectives and Principles* (2002), pp 521–40; Hicks, 'Director Disqualification: Can it Deliver' [2001] JBL 433.

[93] Known as the Carecraft procedure after the case where it was initially adopted: *Re Carecraft Construction Co Ltd* [1993] BCLC 1259 which was endorsed by the Court of Appeal in *Secretary of State for Trade and Industry v Rogers* [1996] 2 BCLC 513.

[94] The background and purpose of the changes is described in *Re Blackspur Group plc (No 3), Secretary of State for Trade and Industry v Davies (No 2)* [2002] 2 BCLC 263 at 283–90; and see also *Re INS Realisations Ltd, Secretary of State for Trade and Industry v Jonkler* [2006] 2 BCLC 239 at 247.

[95] The latest statistics in the Insolvency Service Annual Report and Accounts 2006–07, p 15 show 80% of disqualifications that year were by undertakings, the same percentage as the previous year.

bankrupts after a maximum period of 12 months. Given that the period during which a person will be an undischarged bankrupt is significantly reduced by the EA 2002, it was considered necessary to introduce provisions to ensure that unfit bankrupts, despite the discharge of their bankruptcy, do not become directors. Provision is made therefore for bankruptcy restriction orders (BROs) which are very similar to disqualification orders. BROs may be made by the court on the application of the Secretary of State or the Official Receiver in respect of those bankrupts whose conduct the court finds to be culpable. Provision is made for the acceptance of bankruptcy restriction undertakings (BRUs) in the same manner as for disqualification undertakings. It remains an offence for a person to act as a director of a company, or directly or indirectly to take part in or be concerned in the promotion, formation or management of a company, without the leave of the court, at a time when (1) he is an undischarged bankrupt or (2) a BRO (or undertaking) is in force in respect of him (CDDA 1986, s 11). An undischarged bankrupt so acting is also civilly liable for the debts of the company incurred when so acting (CDDA 1986, s 15): see discussion at **6-89.**

The purpose of the CDDA 1986

6-45   The purpose of the CDDA 1986 was stated succinctly by Lord Woolf MR in *Re Blackspur Group plc, Secretary of State for Trade and Industry v Davies*[96] as follows:

> 'The purpose of the 1986 Act is the protection of the public, by means of prohibitory remedial action, by anticipated deterrent effect on further misconduct and by encouragement of higher standards of honesty and diligence in corporate management, from those who are unfit to be concerned in the management of a company.'

6-46   The protective purpose is to protect the public (broadly defined to include all relevant interest groups, such as shareholders, employees, lenders, customers and other creditors)[97] against the future conduct of companies by persons whose past records as directors of insolvent companies have shown them to be a danger to creditors and others.[98] That the protection of the public is the key consideration is evident from the wording of the statute itself which authorises an application for disqualification (and the acceptance of a disqualification undertaking) where it appears that it is expedient in the public interest for the director to be disqualified (CDDA 1986, s 7).

6-47   The deterrent element is evident, obviously, in the exclusion of the director affected from the management of a company and it is intended to deter future misconduct by him and also by other directors.[99] The role which disqualification plays in raising the standards expected of directors was emphasised by the Court of Appeal in *Secretary of*

---

[96] [1998] 1 BCLC 676 at 680.

[97] See *Re Tech Textiles Ltd, Secretary of State for Trade and Industry v Vane* [1998] 1 BCLC 259 at 268; also *Hill v Secretary of State for the Environment, Food and Rural Affairs* [2006] 1 BCLC 601 at 608 (the 'public' consists of, or at least includes as a primary class, those who might extend credit to the company).

[98] See *Re Lo-Line Electric Motors Ltd* [1988] 2 All ER 692 at 696; also *Re Sevenoaks Stationers (Retail) Ltd* [1991] 1 BCLC 325 at 329; *Re Westmid Packing Services Ltd, Secretary of State for Trade and Industry v Griffiths* [1998] 2 BCLC 646 at 654–5; *Re Barings plc (No 5)* [1999] 1 BCLC 433 at 482.

[99] *Re Westmid Packing Services Ltd, Secretary of State for Trade and Industry v Griffiths* [1998] 2 BCLC 646 at 655.

State for Trade and Industry v Gray:[100]

'The concept of limited liability and the sophistication of our corporate law offers great privileges and great opportunities for those who wish to trade under that regime. But the corporate environment carries with it the discipline that those who avail themselves of those privileges must accept the standards laid down and abide by the regulatory rules and disciplines in place to protect creditors and shareholders...The Parliamentary intention to improve managerial safeguards and standards for the long term good of employees, creditors and investors is clear.'

In practice the enforcement of directors' duties through actions by the company or   **6-48** derivative claims by shareholders is unusual and so, in effect, disqualification proceedings provide an enforcement mechanism. Its importance must not be overstated, however, for this is enforcement without any personal liability on the part of the director to account for any gains or make good any losses arising from any breach of his duties.[101] Disqualification is not a criminal matter, but a civil proceeding and disqualification is not intended as a punitive measure, though there is a punitive element to the proceedings. Removing the privilege of trading through a limited liability company does involve a substantial interference with the freedom of the individual[102] and carries a degree of stigma for anyone who is disqualified.[103] On the other hand, it has to be recalled that there are approximately 2.4 million companies on the register, each of which must have at least one director, so the numbers actually being disqualified (approximately 2,000 per annum) are very small and likely to remain so.[104]

The disqualification order or undertaking

A disqualification order is an order made against a person that for a period specified   **6-49** in the order, he shall not be a director of a company, act as receiver of a company's property or in any way, whether directly or indirectly, be concerned or take part in the promotion, formation or management of a company unless (in each case) he has the leave of the court, and he shall not act as an insolvency practitioner (CDDA 1986, s 1).[105] The courts take a broad approach to the prohibition on being concerned in the

---

[100] [1995] 1 BCLC 276 at 288, per Henry LJ, CA; see also *Re Landhurst Leasing plc, Secretary of State for Trade and Industry v Ball* [1999] 1 BCLC 286 at 344; *Secretary of State for Trade and Industry v Collins* [2000] 2 BCLC 223 at 231.

[101] Exceptionally, in *Official Receiver v Doshi* [2001] 2 BCLC 235, disqualification proceedings and a wrongful trading action by a liquidator under IA 1986, s 214 to recover a contribution from the director were combined so ensuring both disqualification and civil recovery.

[102] See *Re Lo-Line Electric Motors Ltd* [1988] 2 All ER 692 at 696, per Browne-Wilkinson V-C; also *Re Crestjoy Products Ltd* [1990] BCLC 677 at 681.

[103] *Re Westminster Property Management Ltd, Official Receiver v Stern* [2000] 2 BCLC 396 at 423, per Henry LJ.

[104] The latest statistics in the Insolvency Service Annual Report and Accounts 2006–07, p 15 show 1,200 disqualifications in 2006–07, up from 1,173 in 2005–06. In fact, there has been a year-on-year decrease in disqualifications from 2001–02 when the figure was 1,761 disqualification orders. See Finch, *Corporate Insolvency Law: Perspectives and Principles* (2002), pp 531–40.

[105] See also The Companies (Model Articles) Regulations 2008, SI 2008/3229, reg 2, Sch 1, art 18 (Ltd), reg 4, Sch 3, art 22 (Plc) which provide that a director ceases to be a director as soon as he is prohibited

management of a company given it is widely cast in order to make it impossible for a disqualified person to be part of the management and central direction of a company's affairs.[106] In *Re Market Wizard Systems (UK) Ltd*,[107] having reviewed the authorities, Carnwath J agreed that it is difficult to define a succinct test which covers being 'concerned in the management of a company' which must turn on the facts of the particular case, but he accepted that there must be an element of policy and decision-making affecting the enterprise as a whole. In *Hill v Secretary of State for the Environment, Food and Rural Affairs*[108] Hart J accepted that an undischarged bankrupt (and therefore someone prohibited from being concerned in the management of a company: CDDA 1986, s 11) who was the effective manager running a company and who made two important contracts on its behalf affecting its future activities was a person concerned in the management of a company for these purposes.

6-50   The court cannot pick and choose elements of the prohibitions in CDDA 1986, s 1 to apply in a particular case but must order that the person be disqualified from any of these activities for the set period.[109] The purpose of an order is not to prohibit a person from earning his living, but to preclude him from doing so under the protection of limited liability, save with the leave of the court.

6-51   A disqualification undertaking is an undertaking to identical effect to a disqualification order and undertakings are possible only in cases of disqualification on the grounds of unfitness on insolvency and unfitness identified after an investigation of a company (CDDA 1986, s 1A(1)).

6-52   Once made or given, the order or undertaking is notified to the registrar of companies for entry on the register of disqualified directors which is open to inspection by the public (CDDA 1986, s 18).[110]

The period of disqualification

6-53   The period of disqualification varies depending on the grounds for disqualification. Where a person is disqualified for persistent default, or on conviction of an indictable offence by a court of summary jurisdiction, or on conviction of summary offences in relation to returns to the registrar of companies, the maximum period of disqualification is five years.[111] In any other case, the maximum period is 15 years.[112] Where

---

from being a director by law. A person who is disqualified is also prohibited from being a member of a limited liability partnership without the leave of the court: Limited Liability Partnerships Regulations 2001, SI 2001/1090, reg 4(2).

[106] *R v Campbell* [1984] BCLC 83.   [107] [1998] 2 BCLC 282 at 298–301.
[108] [2006] 1 BCLC 601.
[109] *R v Cole* [1998] 2 BCLC 234, CA; *Re Gower Enterprises Ltd (No 2)* [1995] 2 BCLC 201.
[110] The disqualified directors register can be accessed directly and without charge from the Companies House web site: see www.companies-house.gov.uk. The Insolvency Service also maintains a database of directors disqualified under the IA 1986, s 6 (unfit directors of insolvent companies) which is available at www.insolvency.gov.uk/doitonline/ddbase.htm.
[111] CDDA 1986, ss 3(5), 2(3)(a), 5(5).   [112] CDDA 1986, ss 2(3)(b), 4(3), 6(4), 8, 10.

the court makes a disqualification order on the grounds of unfitness in the case of insolvency, there is a minimum period of disqualification of two years.[113]

In *Re Sevenoaks Stationers (Retail) Ltd*[114] the Court of Appeal identified three brackets of periods of disqualification as follows: **6-54**

(1) the top bracket of disqualification for periods over 10 years should be reserved for particularly serious cases. These may include cases where a director who has already had one period of disqualification imposed on him falls to be disqualified yet again;[115]

(2) the minimum bracket of two to five years' disqualification should be applied where, though disqualification is mandatory, the case is, relatively, not very serious;

(3) the middle bracket of disqualification for from six to 10 years should apply for serious cases which do not merit the top bracket.[116]

Reference by the courts to these brackets is standard practice and the majority of disqualifications fall into the minimum bracket.[117] Where a director agrees to an undertaking, there is likely to be an element of discount to the usual tariff, with lesser periods being negotiated.   **6-55**

In *Re Westmid Packing Services Ltd, Secretary of State for Trade and Industry v Griffiths*[118] Lord Woolf MR noted that in truth the fixing of the period of disqualification is little different from any sentencing exercise. The period of disqualification should be fixed, he said, by starting with an assessment of the correct period to reflect the gravity of the offence and then allowing for any mitigating factors.[119] The court may take into account the former director's age and state of health, the length of time he has been in jeopardy, whether he has admitted the offence, his general conduct before and after the offence, and the periods of disqualification of his co-directors that   **6-56**

---

[113] CDDA 1986, s 6(4).   [114] [1991] BCLC 325 at 328.

[115] See *Official Receiver v Stern* [2002] 1 BCLC 119 (12 years—cumulative effect of serious charges increased the seriousness of the case as a whole justifying the top bracket); *Secretary of State for Trade and Industry v McTighe* [1996] 2 BCLC 477 (12 years—successive insolvencies and misappropriation of assets); (*Re Mea Corporation Ltd, Secretary of State for Trade and Industry v Aviss* [2007] 1 BCLC 618 (11 years—a serious case was aggravated by the fact that the director was subject to an existing disqualification order); *Re Vintage Hallmark plc, Secretary of State for Trade and Industry v Grove* [2007] 1 BCLC 788 (15 years—directors had been recklessly indifferent and grossly negligent in the conduct of the company's affairs).

[116] See, for example, *Re J A Chapman & Co Ltd, Secretary of State for Trade and Industry v Amiss* [2003] 2 BCLC 206 (nine years appropriate given dishonesty of director and scale of sums involved which had been obtained from clients of the business); also *Re Bunting Electric Manufacturing Co Ltd, Secretary of State for Trade and Industry v Golby* [2006] 1 BCLC 550 (six years for finance director who dishonestly disregarded the statutory protections for creditors contained in the 'whitewash' procedure in the CA 1985 which enabled private companies to give financial assistance for the purchase of their own shares).

[117] The Annual Report of the Insolvency Service 2006–07 gives some information, but not an actual breakdown of the numbers, but it seems as if, on average, approximately 60% fall into the 2–5 year bracket with 30–35% in the 5–10 year bracket and 5–10% in the 10–15 bracket.

[118] [1998] 2 BCLC 646.   [119] [1998] 2 BCLC 646 at 655.

might have been ordered.[120] A period of de facto disqualification (while awaiting the outcome of proceedings) may be relevant.[121]

6-57   A director may appeal against his disqualification and the Secretary of State may (and does) appeal against the length of disqualification imposed by the court.[122] A person subject to a disqualification undertaking[123] may apply to the court to reduce the period for which the undertaking is in force or to reduce it such that it ceases to be in force (CDDA 1986, s 8A), but this jurisdiction does not extend to annulling or rescinding the undertaking from the start.[124] Given that undertakings are voluntary, the court does not see the CDDA 1986, s 8A as an open-ended invitation to directors to try subsequently to renegotiate their disqualification; rather, it is a jurisdiction which the court will exercise sparingly and only where there are special circumstances.[125] Those special circumstance require either some ground sufficient to discharge a private law contract (for example, mistake or misrepresentation) or some ground of public interest which outweighs the importance of holding the director to his agreement.[126] Having established those parameters in *Re INS Realisations Ltd, Secretary of State for Trade and Industry v Jonkler*[127] the court went on to discharge a disqualification undertaking given by a director which had been based essentially on her inactivity in relation to the conduct of a company carried on by her former husband. Subsequently, disqualification proceedings against him had been discontinued by the DTI. The court thought this unusual combination of events meant that the only director of the company who ended up being disqualified was the one director who had nothing to do with the insolvency of the company. If she merited disqualification on the basis of inactivity, it was implicit that the active director who ran the company also merited disqualification so, once the DTI considered there was no public interest in pursuing proceedings against him, the court thought no public interest would be served by maintaining the undertaking against her which therefore ceased to be in force.

---

[120] [1998] 2 BCLC 646 at 657; see also *Re Bradcrown Ltd, Official Receiver v Ireland* [2001] 1 BCLC 547 at 551.

[121] [1998] 2 BCLC 646 at 657 ; and see also *Re Sykes (Butchers) Ltd, Secretary of State for Trade and Industry v Richardson* [1998] 1 BCLC 110 at 131.

[122] See *Secretary of State for Trade and Industry v McTighe (No 2)* [1996] 2 BCLC 477 (eight and four-year periods increased to 12 and six years respectively); *Secretary of State for Trade and Industry v Ettinger, Re Swift 736 Ltd* [1993] BCLC 896, CA (three-year period increased to five years).

[123] The undertaking must not have expired: see *Re Blackspur Group plc (No 4), Eastaway v Secretary of State for Trade and Industry* [2006] 2 BCLC 489.

[124] *Re Blackspur Group plc (No 4), Eastaway v Secretary of State for Trade and Industry* [2006] 2 BCLC 489 at 508 (undertaking had expired but director wanted it annulled so that his professional body (he was a chartered accountant) would not use it as a basis for disciplinary proceedings against him—court refused application); see also *Re INS Realisations Ltd, Secretary of State for Trade and Industry v Jonkler* [2006] 2 BCLC 239 at 251.

[125] *Re INS Realisations Ltd, Secretary of State for Trade and Industry v Jonkler* [2006] 2 BCLC 239 at 253–4.

[126] *Re INS Realisations Ltd, Secretary of State for Trade and Industry v Jonkler* [2006] 2 BCLC 239 at 250.

[127] [2006] 2 BCLC 239.

Leave to act despite being disqualified

The statute expressly provides that a disqualified person (whether disqualified by order or by undertaking) may apply for leave to act (other than to act as an insolvency practitioner).[128] The court's discretion to grant leave is unfettered by any statutory condition or criterion.[129] On an application for leave, the court has to balance the protection of the public and the need that the applicant should be able to act as a director of a particular company.[130] The court must also bear in mind the legislative policy of disqualifying unfit directors to minimise the risk of harm to the public and that objective must not be undermined by the approach of the court to the issue of leave.[131]   **6-58**

In carrying out this balancing task, the court must pay attention in particular to the nature of the defects in company management which led to the disqualification and ask itself whether, if leave were granted, a situation might arise in which there would be a risk of recurrence of those defects.[132] The court may be particularly concerned if the conduct of a director has been tainted by any dishonesty and if there has been trading to the detriment of the creditors coupled with excessive remuneration for the director.[133]   **6-59**

As regards the need to act, essentially this is a question of practical need, there must be some sufficient reason why the company in question has a business need for the applicant to act in that particular capacity or the applicant has some legitimate interest in so acting,[134] which interest may be a personal interest.[135] The court is very unlikely to contemplate making an order that a disqualified director should be, in effect, a sole proprietor of another company, however, for then the disqualification order would be robbed of any effect.[136]   **6-60**

---

[128] CDDA ss 1(1), 17. An application for leave should: (1) be made at the same time as the disqualification proceedings so as to enable the same judge to determine both issues; and (2) be supported by clear evidence as to the precise role which the director would play in the company in question and up-to-date and adequate information about that company: *Secretary of State for Trade and Industry v Collins* [2000] 2 BCLC 223, CA. See Clench, 'Applications for permission to act under section 17 of the Company Directors Disqualification Act 1986' (2008) 21 Insolv Intel 113.

[129] *Re Dawes & Henderson (Agencies) Ltd (No 2)* [1999] 2 BCLC 317.

[130] *Re Barings plc (No 4), Secretary of State for Trade and Industry v Baker* [1999] 1 BCLC 262 at 269; *Re Dawes & Henderson (Agencies) Ltd* [1999] 2 BCLC 317.

[131] See *Re Tech Textiles Ltd, Secretary of State for Trade and Industry v Vane* [1998] 1 BCLC 259 at 267; *Re Barings plc (No 4), Secretary of State for Trade and Industry v Baker* [1999] 1 BCLC 262 at 269.

[132] *Re Barings (No 4), Secretary of State for Trade and Industry v Baker* [1999] 1 BCLC 262 at 269; *Re Dawes & Henderson (Agencies) Ltd (No 2)* [1999] 2 BCLC 317 at 325.

[133] See *Re Barings plc (No 4), Secretary of State for Trade and Industry v Baker* [1999] 1 BCLC 262 at 265.

[134] See *Re Tech Textiles Ltd, Secretary of State for Trade and Industry v Vane* [1998] 1 BCLC 259 at 269; see also *Secretary of State for Trade and Industry v Barnett* [1998] 2 BCLC 64 at 72; *Re Dawes & Henderson (Agencies) Ltd (No 2)* [1999] 2 BCLC 317 at 326. In *Re Servaccomm Redhall Ltd* [2006] 1 BCLC 1 a director sought leave on the basis that his disqualification related to two companies to which he had really merely lent his name because they were involved with his hobbies (horse racing) whereas the two companies for which he needed leave to act were his active businesses and source of his employment. His application was granted.

[135] See *Re Dawes & Henderson (Agencies) Ltd* [1999] 2 BCLC 317 at 328; in this case, the director's interest (need) lay in securing a tax advantage and the court granted him leave.

[136] See *Re Britannia Homes Centres Ltd, Official Receiver v Cahill* [2001] 2 BCLC 63.

6-61 The court may grant leave subject to certain conditions,[137] typically restricting the director to acting in a named company or companies, limiting the roles which the individual may undertake and imposing conditions as to the composition of the board in the company in question.[138] In *Secretary of State for Trade and Industry v Collins*,[139] however, Ferris J noted that very great caution should be exercised in granting conditional leave for the conditions may be too easily disregarded and may be impossible to police. A failure to observe the conditions of leave means that the director is acting without leave and in breach of his disqualification order[140] which is a criminal offence and leaves him open to potential personal liability (see discussion at **6-89**).[141]

Grounds for disqualification

6-62 While the CDDA 1986 provides for a wide variety of grounds on which disqualification orders may be made (and, as noted, undischarged bankrupts are automatically disqualified: see **6-44**), in practice practically all disqualification orders or undertakings are made under CDDA 1986, s 6 (duty of court to disqualify unfit directors of insolvent companies).[142] For that reason, we concentrate on that category below while merely noting here the other grounds on which an order may be made.

6-63 The court may make a disqualification order:

- where a person has been convicted of an indictable offence in connection with the promotion, formation, management, liquidation or striking off of a company[143] (CDDA 1986, s 2);

- where it appears to the court that a person has been persistently in default in relation to filing documents with the registrar of companies[144] (CDDA 1986, s 3);

- where, in the course of the winding up of a company, it appears (1) that a person has been guilty of an offence for which he is liable (whether he has been convicted or not) under CA 1985, s 458 (fraudulent trading), or (2) that he has otherwise

---

[137] See *Secretary of State for Trade and Industry v Collins* [2000] 2 BCLC 223 at 235; *Re Tech Textiles Ltd, Secretary of State for Trade and Industry v Vane* [1998] 1 BCLC 259.

[138] See, for example, *Re Dawes & Henderson Ltd* [1999] 2 BCLC 317 at 328; *Re Gibson Davies Ltd* [1995] BCC 11; *Re Godwin Warren Control Systems Ltd* [1993] BCLC 80.

[139] [2000] 2 BCLC 223 at 239.

[140] *Re Brian Sheridan Cars Ltd, Official Receiver v Sheridan* [1996] 1 BCLC 327.

[141] I.e. under CDDA 1986, ss 13, 15. Other persons involved with the management of the company may also face potential personal liability, see s 15(1)(b).

[142] BERR and the Insolvency Service no longer provide a detailed breakdown of disqualification statistics, but the pattern prior to 2005–06, the last year there was a breakdown, was that 90% of disqualifications were under CDDA 1986, s 6 (unfit directors of insolvent companies).

[143] In determining whether an offence is 'in connection with the management of a company', the test is whether the offence has some relevant factual connection with the management of the company, not whether the offence relates to the management of a company, such as keeping accounts or filing returns, or has been committed in the course of managing a company: *R v Creggy* [2008] 1 BCLC 625, CA; *R v Goodman* [1993] 2 All ER 789.

[144] CDDA 1986, s 3; see also s 5. 'Persistent' means nothing more than that there should be some degree of continuance or repetition: *Re Arctic Engineering Ltd (No 2)* [1986] 2 All ER 346.

been guilty, while an officer, of any fraud or of any breach of his duty in relation to the company (CDDA 1986, s 4);

- where the court is satisfied on an application from the Secretary of State following an investigation[145] that a person's conduct makes him unfit to be concerned in the management of a company.[146] The company need not be insolvent in this case and a disqualification undertaking may be accepted (CDDA 1986, ss 1A, 8);

- where in certain circumstances a director has been involved in an infringement of competition law[147] (CDDA 1986, ss 9A–9E);

- where a person has been found liable to make a contribution to a company's assets under IA 1986, s 213 (fraudulent trading) or s 214 (wrongful trading) and whether or not an application for a disqualification order is made (CDDA 1986, s 10);

- where a court revokes an administration granted under the County Courts Act 1984 (concerning an agreement between an individual debtor and his creditors) (CDDA 1986, s 12).

Unfit directors of insolvent companies

The procedure

If it appears to an official receiver, liquidator, administrator or administrative receiver (collectively referred to as the office-holder) that in the case of a person who is or has been a director[148] or shadow director[149] of a company which has become insolvent, that his conduct as a director of that company (either taken alone or taken together with his conduct as a director of any other company or companies)[150] makes him unfit to be concerned in the management of a company, he must forthwith report the matter to the Secretary of State for Trade and Industry.[151] In practice, the report is made to the Disqualification Unit which is part of the Insolvency Service which in turn is an

6-64

---

[145] I.e. following an investigation under a wide range of investigation powers such as CA 1985, ss 437, 447, 448; FSMA 2000, ss 165, 167–169, 171–173, 175, 286; Criminal Justice Act 1987, s 2.

[146] See *Re Looe Fish Ltd* [1993] BCLC 1160; *Re Samuel Sherman plc* [1991] BCC 699; *Re Aldermanbury Trust Ltd* [1993] BCC 598.

[147] This power to make competition disqualification orders was added by the Enterprise Act 2002 but there appears to have been few, if any, applications for such orders to date.

[148] The word 'director' in this context includes a de facto director: *Re Lo-Line Electric Motors Ltd* [1988] 2 All ER 692; *Re Kaytech International plc, Secretary of State for Trade and Industry v Kaczer* [1999] 2 BCLC 351. A corporate director may be disqualified: see *Official Receiver v Brady* [1999] BCC 847.

[149] CDDA 1986, s 6(3C). As to shadow directors, see discussion at **6-20**.

[150] The provision envisages a single 'lead company', as it is called, and one or more collateral companies, but the provision is not limited to that permutation and there may be more than one lead company: *Re Surrey Leisure Ltd, Official Receiver v Keam* [1999] 2 BCLC 457, CA. There has to be evidence of unfitness in connection with the director's management of the lead company which must have gone into insolvency and evidence of his conduct in connection with the collateral companies should assist the court in reaching a conclusion of unfitness in connection with the lead company: *Secretary of State for Trade and Industry v Ivens* [1997] 2 BCLC 334; *Secretary of State for Trade and Industry v Goldberg* [2004] 1 BCLC 597.

[151] CDDA 1986, s 7(3); and see The Insolvent Companies (Reports on Conduct of Directors) Rules 1996, SI 1996/1909.

executive agency of the Department of Business, Enterprise and Regulatory Reform (BERR), formerly known as the Department of Trade and Industry.

6-65   A company 'becomes insolvent' for these purposes if:

(1)   the company goes into liquidation[152] at a time when its assets are insufficient for the payment of its debts and other liabilities and the expenses of the winding up;

(2)   the company enters administration; or

(3)   an administrative receiver of the company is appointed (CDDA 1986, s 6(2)).[153]

6-66   Reports by the office-holder (known as D reports because that is the designation of the prescribed forms) are required on every person who is or was a director or shadow director of the company and the report must be made within six months of the relevant date (for example, the passing of the resolution for voluntary winding up).[154] A report is required, however, only when a company is subject to one of the specified insolvency regimes, and each year a large number of companies are struck off the register of companies without going through any of these regimes; there may or may not be unfit directors within such companies but there is no mechanism for reviewing their conduct.[155]

6-67   Having considered the report, if it appears to the Secretary of State (i.e. the Disqualification Unit) that it is expedient in the public interest[156] that a disqualification order under CDDA 1986, s 6 should be made against any person, an application may be made by the Secretary of State to the court for a disqualification order (and, where the company is being wound up by the court in England and Wales, by the Official Receiver).[157] Before this occurs, the Disqualification Unit will give notice to the director of the intention to proceed under CDDA 1986, s 6 and this notice

---

[152] Defined by IA 1986, s 247, incorporated by CDDA 1986, s 22(3), as the time when the company passes a resolution for voluntary winding up or the time of the court order in the case of a compulsory winding up.

[153] See *Secretary of State for Trade and Industry v Jabble* [1998] 1 BCLC 598 (directors challenged whether company fell into these categories).

[154] See the Insolvent Companies (Reports on Conduct of Directors) Rules 1996, SI 1996/1909, r 4. Statutory reports under CDDA 1986, s 7(3) are not privileged and their disclosure may be sought by the respondent in disqualification proceedings: *Re Barings plc, Secretary of State for Trade and Industry v Baker* [1998] 1 BCLC 16.

[155] See Hicks, 'Director Disqualification: Can it Deliver' [2001] JBL 433. The Companies House, *Statistical Tables on Companies Registration Activities 2007–2008* available on the Companies House website at www.companieshouse.gov.uk. show that, for Great Britain, in that year, 216,000 companies were struck off while 15,281 companies went into insolvent liquidation: see Tables C1 and C2.

[156] The question whether it is expedient in the public interest to commence and thereafter to pursue applications for disqualification is a matter for the Secretary of State and not for the court: *Re Blackspur Group plc, Secretary of State for Trade and Industry v Davies* [1998] 1 BCLC 676 at 680; *Re Barings plc (No 3), Secretary of State for Trade and Industry v Baker* [1999] 1 BCLC 226 at 252; and see *Re Blackspur Group plc (No 3), Secretary of State for Trade and Industry v Davies (No 2)* [2002] 2 BCLC 263 at 287, per Chadwick LJ. This discretion is subject to the court's inherent power in exceptional circumstances to stay proceedings on the ground of abuse of process: see *Secretary of State for Trade and Industry v Reyna* [2001] 2 BCLC 48 at 59.

[157] CDDA 1986, s 7(1).

will draw his attention to the possibility of his offering a disqualification undertaking rather than having the matter determined by the court.[158]

Except with the leave of the court, an application for a disqualification order under CDDA 1986, s 6 must not be made after the end of two years beginning with the day on which the company became insolvent, as defined at **6-65**.[159] In deciding whether to grant leave for a late application, the court takes into account all relevant factors including but not limited to (1) the length of the delay, (2) the reasons for the delay, (3) the strength of the case against the director (i.e. the gravity of the charges) and (4) the degree of prejudice caused to the director by the delay.[160] **6-68**

Once commenced, disqualification proceedings must be pursued with appropriate diligence and undue delay may amount to an infringement of the European Convention on Human Rights, art 6(1), which entitles a person to a hearing within a reasonable time in the determination of his civil rights. In the light of this article, special diligence in bringing disqualification proceedings to an expeditious end is called for, given the impact which the proceedings have on a director's reputation and ability to practise his profession.[161] Hence delays of four years and five months (*EDC v UK*)[162] and five years and six months (*Davies v UK*[163] and *Eastaway v UK*)[164] have been held to be an infringement of art 6(1). **6-69**

Following the application by the Secretary of State or Official Receiver, the court must make a disqualification order for a minimum period of two years and a maximum of 15 years if it is satisfied that the conduct of that person as a director of that company makes him unfit to be concerned in the management of a company.[165] **6-70**

Approach to the issue of unfitness

A review of reported cases where disqualification proceedings have been brought under CDDA 1986, s 6 (unfitness in cases of insolvency) reveal a very similar fact scenario in each case.[166] Often the director has been associated with a number of companies which have gone into insolvent liquidation over a relatively short period of time. In *Re Swift 736 Ltd*,[167] for example, the court noted that two of the directors had **6-71**

---

[158] As to the content of this notice, see *Re Surrey Leisure Ltd, Official Receiver v Keam* [1999] 1 BCLC 731.

[159] CDDA 1986, s 7(2). The two-year time period runs from the happening of the first of the events specified (going into liquidation, administration etc) in CDDA 1986, s 6(2): *Re Tasbian (No 1) Ltd* [1991] BCLC 56, CA. Where a company has gone into compulsory winding up, the two-year period runs from the date of the court order and not from the date of presentation of the winding-up petition: *Re Walter L Jacob & Co Ltd* [1993] BCC 512.

[160] *Secretary of State for Trade and Industry v Davies* [1997] 2 BCLC 317, CA; *Secretary of State v McTighe, Re Copecrest Ltd* [1994] 2 BCLC 284, CA; *Re Probe Data Systems Ltd (No 3), Secretary of State for Trade and Industry v Desai* [1992] BCLC 405, CA.

[161] *Davies v UK* [2006] 2 BCLC 351, ECtHR.   [162] [1998] BCC 370, EComHR.

[163] [2006] 2 BCLC 351, ECtHR.   [164] [2006] 2 BCLC 361, ECtHR.   [165] CDDA 1986, s 6(1), (4).

[166] See, for example, *Re Amaron Ltd, Secretary of State for Trade and Industry v Lubrani* [2001] 1 BCLC 562, affg [1997] 2 BCLC 115; *Re Galeforce Pleating Co Ltd* [1999] 2 BCLC 704; *Re Landhurst Leasing plc, Secretary of State for Trade and Industry v Ball* [1999] 1 BCLC 286; *Secretary of State for Trade and Industry v McTighe (No 2)* [1996] 2 BCLC 477.

[167] [1993] BCLC 1. The case was subsequently appealed on a different point, see [1993] BCLC 896, CA.

set up six companies which carried on the business of making shirts. Each company in succession became insolvent and immediately upon its insolvency the next company took over the same business and at the same premises. Hoffmann J noted:[168]

> 'That form of trading, where one has a succession of companies which no doubt pay a salary to their principal directors and are then allowed to sink, having lived on involuntary credit provided by the Crown, is the very thing which the provisions for disqualification of directors is intended to prevent....'

6-72   The allegations of unfitness typically include that the director caused or permitted the company to trade to the detriment of its creditors; that the company continued trading while insolvent, usually by means of pursuing a policy of paying only those creditors who pressed; and that Crown debts were retained to finance continued trading.[169] Despite the financial difficulties, the directors continue throughout the period to obtain significant personal benefits in terms of actual remuneration and frequently by misappropriating corporate assets and opportunities. Invariably, in this type of situation, the directors will not have maintained adequate accounting records, as they are required to do by CA 2006, s 386, which in turn means that they will have failed to prepare and file annual accounts and returns with the registrar of companies.

6-73   It is clear that the factual scenarios outlined above (which merit disqualification) contain many breaches of a director's duties, though in this context the conduct is usually described in terms of a failure to meet the required standards of competence and probity.[170] For example, trading in disregard of creditors' interests is a failure to act as required by CA 2006, s 172(3), while managerial incompetence and inertia is a failure to exercise care and skill as required by s 174, and the continued receipt of excessive personal benefits and the misappropriation of corporate assets involves breaches of the no conflict rule set out in s 175. Other matters, such as a failure to maintain accounting records and to prepare accounts,[171] are breaches of statutory duties.

6-74   A finding of breach of duty is neither necessary (had it been so, the section would not be defined in terms of 'unfitness') nor of itself sufficient for a finding of unfitness, however, as was explained by Jonathan Parker J in *Re Barings plc (No 5), Secretary of State for Trade and Industry v Baker (No 5)*,[172] a point specifically endorsed by

---

[168] [1993] BCLC 1 at 3; see also Browne-Wilkinson V-C in *Re Travel Mondial (UK) Ltd* [1991] BCLC 120 at 123. For an example of this phoenix syndrome, see *Re Brittanic Home Centres Ltd* [2001] 2 BCLC 63 at 74–5.

[169] See *Re Sevenoaks Stationers (Retail) Ltd* [1991] BCLC 325, CA; *Secretary of State for Trade and Industry v McTighe* [1996] 2 BCLC 477; *Re Amaron Ltd, Secretary of State for Trade and Industry v Lubrani* [2001] 1 BCLC 562. Crown debts essentially are sums due to HM Revenue and Customs in respect of PAYE, National Insurance and VAT receipts.

[170] See *Re Landhurst Leasing plc* [1999] 1 BCLC 286 at 344; *Secretary of State for Trade and Industry v Gray* [1995] 1 BCLC 276 at 286.

[171] See CA 2006, ss 386, 394. See also *Re Bunting Electric Manufacturing Co Ltd, Secretary of State for Trade and Industry v Golby* [2006] 1 BCLC 550 (director disregarded the statutory requirements surrounding the 'whitewash' procedure when a private company gave financial assistance for the purchase of its own shares under the CA 1985). See also *Re Bath Glass* [1988] BCLC 329 at 333.

[172] [1999] 1 BCLC 433 at 486.

the Court of Appeal.[173] In particular, unfitness by reason of incompetence may be established without proof of a breach of duty,[174] as Jonathan Parker J indicated, as where a respondent shows himself so completely lacking in judgement as to justify a finding of unfitness, notwithstanding that he has not been guilty of misfeasance or breach of duty.[175] Lewison J agreed on this point in *Secretary of State for Trade and Industry v Goldberg*[176] while acknowledging that the court must be very careful before holding that a director was unfit because of conduct that did not amount to a breach of any duty (whether contractual, tortious, statutory or equitable). It is easier to appreciate Jonathan Parker J's converse proposition that the fact that a director may have been guilty of misfeasance or breach of duty does not necessarily mean that he is unfit and should be disqualified.[177]

Just as it is not necessary to show a breach of duty (though there commonly is a breach),   **6-75** it is not necessary to show dishonesty,[178] though often that too is present,[179] and unfitness may be shown by conduct which is merely incompetent. Where there is no dishonesty of any kind, however, because of the serious nature of a disqualification order, the burden is on the Secretary of State to satisfy the court that the conduct complained of demonstrates incompetence of a high degree.[180]

The burden of proof is to the civil standard of the balance of probabilities though, as   **6-76** Laddie J made clear in *Re Living Images Ltd*,[181] given the nature of the serious allegations of unfitness which may be made in these proceedings, the court looks for cogent evidence of such misconduct.[182] It is for the Secretary of State to establish, to the requisite standard of proof, the matters on which the allegations of unfitness are based and for the court to be satisfied that the conduct alleged is sufficiently serious to warrant disqualification.[183]

---

[173] See [2000] 1 BCLC 523 at 535.

[174] *Secretary of State for Trade and Industry v Goldberg* [2004] 1 BCLC 597 at 607, per Lewison J.

[175] Another example, Jonathan Parker J thought, might be trading at the risk of creditors even if it does not amount to wrongful trading under IA 1986, s 214.

[176] [2004] 1 BCLC 597.

[177] See, for example, *Re Deaduck Ltd, Baker v Secretary of State for Trade and Industry* [2000] 1 BCLC 148.

[178] See *Secretary of State for Trade and Industry v Goldberg* [2004] 1 BCLC 597 at 611.

[179] See, for example, *Re Bunting Electric Manufacturing Co Ltd, Secretary of State for Trade and Industry v Golby* [2006] 1 BCLC 550 (finance director dishonestly acting in his personal interests in breach of duty to the company).

[180] *Re Barings plc (No 5), Secretary of State for Trade and Industry v Baker (No 5)* [1999] 1 BCLC 433 at 483–6; endorsed on appeal, [2000] 1 BCLC 523 at 535, CA, but the degree of incompetence required should not be exaggerated. See also *Re Sevenoaks Stationers (Retail) Ltd* [1991] 1 BCLC 325 at 337: incompetence or negligence 'in a very marked degree' is enough to render a director unfit, but it need not be 'total' incompetence.

[181] [1996] 1 BCLC 348; see also *Re Verby Print for Advertising Ltd, Secretary of State for Trade and Industry v Fine* [1998] 2 BCLC 23.

[182] [1996] 1 BCLC 348 at 355–6; and see *Re Bunting Electric Manufacturing Co Ltd, Secretary of State for Trade and Industry v Golby* [2006] 1 BCLC 550 at 561–2; *Secretary of State for Trade and Industry v Swan* [2005] BCC 597 at 605; *Secretary of State for Trade and Industry v Goldberg* [2004] 1 BCLC 597 at 612.

[183] *Secretary of State for Trade and Industry v Swan* [2005] BCC 597 at 606, per Etherton J.

6-77   Overall, the question for the court to decide, taking a broad brush approach,[184] is whether the conduct complained of, viewed cumulatively and taking into account any extenuating circumstances accompanying the conduct in question, has fallen below the standards of probity and competence appropriate for persons fit to be directors of companies trading with the privilege of limited liability.[185] In considering the director's conduct, the court must have regard to CDDA 1986, Sch 1,[186] but the Schedule is not exhaustive,[187] and the court is entitled to take into account any misconduct that shows unfitness.[188] Part 1 of the Schedule is applicable in all cases, Part II is applicable only if the company has become insolvent.[189]

6-78   Part 1 requires the court to have regard to:

- any misfeasance or breach of any fiduciary or other duty by the director in relation to the company;

- any misapplication or retention by a director of, or any conduct by the director giving rise to an obligation to account for, any money or other property of the company;

- the extent of the director's responsibility for the company entering into any transaction liable to be set aside under the Insolvency Act 1986;[190]

- the extent of the director's responsibility for the company's failure to comply with various disclosure requirements;[191]

- the extent of the director's responsibility for any failure by the directors of the company to comply with the provisions relating to the keeping of accounting records or preparation of annual accounts or the approval and signature of the accounts.[192]

6-79   Part II requires the court to have regard to:

- the extent of the director's responsibility for the causes of the company becoming insolvent;[193]

---

[184] See *Secretary of State for Trade and Industry v Goldberg* [2004] 1 BCLC 597 at 611; *Re Westmid Packing Services Ltd, Secretary of State for Trade and Industry v Griffiths* [1998] 2 BCLC 646 at 658; also *Re Bath Glass* [1988] BCLC 329 at 333.

[185] *Secretary of State for Trade and Industry v Gray* [1995] 1 BCLC 276 at 284; see also *Re Barings plc (No 5), Secretary of State for Trade and Industry v Baker (No 5)* [1999] 1 BCLC 433 at 483; endorsed on appeal, [2000] 1 BCLC 523 at 535, CA.   [186] CDDA 1986, s 9.

[187] *Re Barings plc (No 5), Secretary of State for Trade and Industry v Baker (No 5)* [1999] 1 BCLC 433; *Re Migration Services International Ltd, Official Receiver v Webster* [2000] 1 BCLC 666 (breach of IA 1986, s 216—misuse of company name—may be taken into account even though not mentioned in the Schedule).

[188] *Re Amaron Ltd, Secretary of State for Trade and Industry v Lubrani* [2001] 1 BCLC 562, aff'g [1997] 2 BCLC 115.

[189] CDDA 1986, s 9(1). Part I alone would be relevant, for example, where a disqualification order is sought under s 8 following an investigation where the company involved might not be insolvent.

[190] I.e. under IA 1986, Pt XVI.

[191] I.e. provisions relating to matters such as the maintenance of the registers of directors and secretaries, the register of members and the register of charges.

[192] I.e. under CA 2006, ss 386, 388, 394, 414, 433.

[193] The courts take a broad approach to this issue, eschewing nice legal concepts of causation: *Re Barings plc (No 5), Secretary of State for Trade and Industry v Baker (No 5)* [1999] 1 BCLC 433 at 483, endorsed on appeal, see [2000] 1 BCLC 523 at 535.

- the extent of the director's responsibility for any failure by the company to supply any goods or services which have been paid for, in whole or in part;
- the extent of the director's responsibility for the company entering into any transaction at an undervalue or giving any preference which is liable to be set aside;[194]
- the extent of the director's responsibility for any failure by the directors to comply with the requirements of the IA 1986 in relation to creditors' meetings;[195]
- any failure by the director to comply with certain provisions of the IA 1986, such as to supply any statement of affairs or attend meetings, or to co-operate with any office-holder under the Insolvency Act 1986.[196]

As noted at **6-74**, it is not necessary to establish a breach of duty on the part of the director to establish unfitness, but in practice in most cases a lack of probity and competence is established by showing breaches of directors' duties and that framework is used below to illustrate how disqualification is used to enforce directors' duties.   **6-80**

Lack of probity—failure to have regard to creditors' interests

As discussed in Chapter 9, the duty of directors to act to promote the success of the company includes an obligation to have regard to the interests of the company's creditors in cases of insolvency or doubtful solvency: see CA 2006, s 172(3) and the discussion at **9-42**. Breaches of that obligation, often described in disqualification proceedings as trading while insolvent to the detriment of the creditors, are central to the allegations of unfitness in most disqualification proceedings brought under CDDA 1986, s 6, given that it is a pre-condition that the company must have become insolvent (as defined in CDDA 1986, s 6(2)), set out at **6-65**.   **6-81**

A common problem in these cases is that the directors continue to trade after a point in time when the company's financial position is hopeless instead of putting the company into insolvent liquidation and so the continued trading is unwarranted and at the creditors' risk. Merely trading while the company is insolvent is insufficient; it must be established that, in addition to causing the company to trade while insolvent, the director knew or ought to have known that there was no reasonable prospect of meeting creditors' claims. Both elements of the test must be satisfied, as was made clear by the Court of Appeal in *Secretary of State v Creggan*.[197] As Chadwick J explained in *Secretary of State for Trade and Industry v Gash*:[198]   **6-82**

> 'The companies legislation does not impose on directors a statutory duty to ensure that their company does not trade while insolvent; nor does that legislation impose an obligation to ensure that the company does not trade at a loss. Those propositions need only to be stated to be recognised as self-evident. Directors may properly take the view that it is in the interests of the company and of its creditors that, although insolvent,

---

[194] I.e. under IA 1986, ss 127, 238–40; and see *Re Sykes (Butchers) Ltd, Secretary of State for Trade and Industry v Richardson* [1998] 1 BCLC 110.

[195] I.e. under IA 1986, s 98.

[196] I.e. under IA 1986, Sch B1, para 47; IA 1986, ss 66, 47, 99, 131, 234, 235. See, for example, *Secretary of State for Trade and Industry v Blunt* [2005] 2 BCLC 463.

[197] [2002] 1 BCLC 99 at 101, CA.   [198] [1997] 1 BCLC 341 at 348–9.

the company should continue to trade out of its difficulties. They may properly take the view that it is in the interests of the company and its creditors that some loss-making trade should be accepted in anticipation of future profitability. They are not to be criticised if they give effect to such view. But the legislation imposes on directors the risk that trading while insolvent may lead to personal liability.'

6-83   The courts are alert to and very critical of such trading without a reasonable prospect of meeting creditors' claims. In *Secretary of State for Trade and Industry v Collins*[199] the directors (who were disqualified for periods of 7–9 years) caused the company to continue to trade to September 1994 when they knew by November 1993 that there was no reasonable prospect of avoiding insolvent liquidation. The company was eventually compulsorily wound up with a deficiency of £11.3m. In *Re Amaron Ltd, Secretary of State for Trade and Industry v Lubrani*[200] the directors (who were disqualified for three years) continued to trade for 21 months after the time when they knew the company was making losses on an increasingly large scale.[201] In *Re Living Images Ltd*[202] the court found that the three directors were aware by late 1989 at the latest that the company was extremely unlikely to avoid liquidation yet they kept the company going until the end of April 1990, during which period the company continued to incur further substantial losses. The company was ultimately wound up with a deficiency in excess of £1.5m. The court concluded that the directors in effect 'used the cover of limited liability to suck in more creditors to prop up an obviously moribund company'.[203] They were disqualified for periods ranging from two and a half years to six years. On the other hand, in *Secretary of State for Trade and Industry v Gill*[204] the court rejected any suggestion of unfitness where directors continued to accept customer deposits to facilitate continued trading while they searched for a commercial solution to the company's difficulties. The key difference was that, while the company did subsequently go into liquidation, the court accepted that at all material times there was a reasonable prospect of avoiding insolvency.

6-84   A common scenario is that in a group situation, or where there are related businesses, the directors disregard the interests of the creditors of an individual company in the interests of the overall business in clear breach of their duty to promote the success of that individual company. For example, in *Re Mea Corporation Ltd, Secretary of State for Trade and Industry v Aviss*[205] directors were disqualified for periods ranging from 7 to 11 years in essence for causing or allowing each of three companies to trade to the detriment of creditors. At a time when those companies were under increasing pressure from creditors and were each insolvent, the directors allowed such cash as was available to be paid out to other companies in which one of the directors had a substantial personal interest in disregard of the interests of the creditors of the individual companies. In *Re Genosyis Technology Management Ltd, Wallach v Secretary of State for*

---

[199] [2000] 2 BCLC 223. See also *Secretary of State for Trade and Industry v McTighe (No 2)* [1996] 2 BCLC 477; *Official Receiver v Stern (No 2)* [2002] 1 BCLC 119, CA; *Secretary of State for Trade and Industry v Hollier* [2007] BCC 11.

[200] [2001] 1 BCLC 562, aff'g [1997] 2 BCLC 115.   [201] See [2001] 1 BCLC 562 at 566.

[202] [1996] 1 BCLC 348.   [203] [1996] 1 BCLC 348 at 367–8.   [204] [2006] BCC 725.

[205] [2007] 1 BCLC 618 at 635, 643.

Trade and Industry[206] two directors were disqualified for entering, on behalf of the company, into a settlement agreement with a customer under which the company gave up a claim for €1.25m (which was instead paid to its parent company) and gained a maximum of £166,000. Given the company was insolvent at the time of the settlement, the court found the directors in breach of their duty to have regard to the creditors' interests.

Another common scenario is that as the company's financial position worsens, the   **6-85** directors adopt a policy of paying only those creditors who press for payment or those who are essential to the continued operation of the company. In effect, they operate a policy of unfair discrimination between creditors.[207] In *Re Sevenoaks Stationers (Retail) Ltd*[208] the Court of Appeal held that the adoption of such a policy, of itself, merits a finding of unfitness and disqualification.[209] The directors are taking unfair advantage of the forbearance on the part of the creditors not pressing for payment and are trading at those creditors' expense while the company is in financial difficulty. A related issue is the non-payment of Crown debts which often account for a significant proportion of the deficiency on liquidation.[210] Initially the courts regarded the non-payment of Crown debts as particularly culpable,[211] but in *Re Sevenoaks Stationers (Retail) Ltd*[212] the Court of Appeal rejected this approach. The issue is the significance of that non-payment and whether it is part of a deliberate decision by the directors only to pay those creditors who press for payment and to retain sums which should have been paid to creditors (be they the Crown or otherwise) to fund the company's continued trading.[213] As noted above, that in itself is evidence which justifies a finding of unfitness.

Of course, while the directors are running the company in this fashion, with mount   **6-86** ing debts, pressing creditors and increasing liabilities for Crown debts, they either deliberately or inadvertently fail to maintain adequate accounting records as they are required to do by CA 2006, s 386. Consequently, they also fail to comply with their

---

[206] [2007] 1 BCLC 208. See also *Secretary of State for Trade and Industry v Goldberg* [2004] 1 BCLC 597 (director disqualified for, inter alia, allowing company monies to be used for the purpose of other businesses connected with the controller of the company in disregard of the corporate personalities and interests of the companies involved).

[207] See *Re Verby Print for Advertising Ltd, Fine v Secretary of State for Trade and Industry* [1998] 2 BCLC 23; *Official Receiver v Dhaliwall* [2006] 1 BCLC 285.

[208] [1991] 3 All ER 578.

[209] [1991] BCLC 325 at 337. See *Re Hopes (Heathrow) Ltd, Secretary of State for Trade and Industry v Dyer* [2001] 1 BCLC 575; *Re Structural Concrete Ltd, Official Receiver v Barnes* [2001] BCC 578; *Secretary of State for Trade and Industry v McTighe (No 2)* [1996] 2 BCLC 477 at 486–7; *Secretary of State for Trade and Industry v Laing* [1996] 2 BCLC 324 at 343; *Re GSAR Realisations Ltd* [1993] BCLC 409 at 412.

[210] Crown debts are sums sue to HM Revenue and Customs in respect of PAYE, National Insurance and VAT receipts, see *Re Sevenoaks Stationers (Retail) Ltd* [1991] BCLC 325 at 319, CA.

[211] See *Re Lo-Line Electric Motors Ltd* [1988] Ch 477 at 488; [1988] 2 All ER 692 at 698, per Browne-Wilkinson V-C; agreeing with Vinelott J in *Re Stanford Services Ltd* [1987] BCLC 607.

[212] [1991] BCLC 325.

[213] [1991] BCLC 325 at 337. See also *Re GSAR Realisations Ltd* [1993] BCLC 409 at 412, per Ferris J; *Re Verby Print for Advertising Ltd, Fine v Secretary of State for Trade and Industry* [1998] 2 BCLC 23; *Secretary of State for Trade and Industry v Paulin* [2005] 2 BCLC 667.

statutory obligations regarding the filing of annual accounts with the registrar of companies, as required to do by s 441. Such failures are viewed seriously by the courts for disclosure is part of the price to be paid for the privilege of trading through a limited liability company.[214] A failure to maintain adequate accounting records means that the directors do not know the company's financial position with accuracy and so cannot appreciate the need to take steps to protect their creditors[215] while a failure to file information with the registrar deprives creditors of information which would influence their behaviour.[216]

Lack of probity—breach of the no-conflict rule

6-87   In many cases and despite looming insolvency, the directors continue to receive remuneration and to obtain other personal benefits from their positions. While directors are entitled to continue to receive remuneration even as the company's financial position worsens, in a number of cases the courts have been critical of directors continuing to award themselves sums variously described as 'unreasonable'[217] or 'excessive' remuneration.[218] Examples of the type of misconduct commonly featured in the cases include the granting of preferences to themselves and personal friends,[219] the transfer or use of the company's assets for inadequate consideration or without security for the sale price,[220] and undisclosed conflicts of interest resulting in personal gain.[221] For example, in *Secretary of State for Trade and Industry v McTighe*,[222] the director disposed of the proceeds of sale of an asset of the company without accounting for them to the company; in *Secretary of State for Trade and Industry v Paulin*,[223] a director caused the company to dispose of its business and assets to companies under his control without obtaining payment for the company; and in *Secretary of State for Trade and Industry v Blunt*[224] a director removed the company's remaining stock of carpets and tried to conceal their existence from the company's liquidator. In each case, the director was found unfit and disqualified.

---

[214] See *Secretary of State for Trade and Industry v Ettinger, Re Swift 736 Ltd* [1993] BCLC 896, CA.

[215] See *Re Firedart Ltd, Official Receiver v Fairall* [1994] 2 BCLC 340 at 352; also *Re Hitco 2000 Ltd* [1995] 2 BCLC 63 at 70; *Re New Generation Engineers Ltd* [1993] BCLC 435.

[216] See *Re Pamstock Ltd* [1994] 1 BCLC 716; also *Re Tansoft Ltd* [1991] BCLC 339. A persistent failure to file is also an independent ground for disqualification, see CDDA 1986, s 3.

[217] *Re Amaron Ltd, Secretary of State for Trade and Industry v Lubrani* [2001] 1 BCLC 562, aff'g [1997] 2 BCLC 115 (directors continued with previous salary levels despite a sharp deterioration in the company's position).

[218] *Secretary of State for Trade and Industry v Van Hengel* [1995] 1 BCLC 545 (remuneration substantially more than the company could afford); see also *Official Receiver v Stern* [2002] 1 BCLC 119, CA (drawings in excess of remuneration to which they were entitled).

[219] See *Secretary of State for Trade and Industry v Gray* [1995] 1 BCLC 276; *Re Living Images Ltd* [1996] 1 BCLC 348; *Re Sykes (Butchers) Ltd, Secretary of State for Trade and Industry v Richardson* [1998] 1 BCLC 110; *Re Funtime Ltd* [2000] 1 BCLC 247.

[220] *Secretary of State for Trade and Industry v McTighe (No 2)* [1996] 2 BCLC 477; *Re Keypak Homecare Ltd* [1990] BCLC 440.

[221] *Re Dominion International Group plc (No 2)* [1996] 1 BCLC 572; *Re Godwin Warren Control Systems plc* [1993] BCLC 80.

[222] [1996] 2 BCLC 477.   [223] [2005] 2 BCLC 667.   [224] [2005] 2 BCLC 463.

Lack of competence—breach of the duty of care and skill

As noted at **6-75**, where there is no dishonesty of any kind, the burden is on the   **6-88**
Secretary of State to satisfy the court that the conduct complained of demonstrates
incompetence of a high degree[225] and an ordinary commercial misjudgement is in
itself not sufficient to justify disqualification.[226] Obviously a finding of unfitness on
the basis of incompetence requires that the director's conduct be assessed against the
component elements of the duty of care and skill in order to determine whether there
has been a breach. That duty (and the many disqualification cases where it is addressed)
is discussed in detail in Chapter 10.

Consequences of acting while disqualified

It is a criminal offence punishable by imprisonment or a fine or both for a person   **6-89**
to act in breach of a disqualification order or undertaking or while an undischarged
bankrupt or subject to a bankruptcy restriction order or undertaking (CDDA 1986, ss
11 and 13). Even more effective than the criminal penalty, probably, is the civil liability
which applies under CDDA 1986, s 15 whereby any disqualified person who, in contravention of a disqualification order or undertaking, is involved in the management of a
company may incur personal liability for the debts of the company contracted at that
time. The liability also applies to any person who is involved in the management of the
company and who acts or is willing to act on instructions given without leave of the
court by a person whom he knows at that time to be disqualified.[227] This liability has a
significant deterrent effect by making it risky for a co-director to act with a disqualified person in the management of a company.

The effect of CDDA 1986, s 15 was considered in *Re Prestige Grindings Ltd, Sharma v*   **6-90**
Yardley[228] where the court held that it confers on each creditor a direct statutory right
of action against the disqualified director in respect of the debt owed to him by the
company, but the right must be exercised by individual creditors and it is not open to
a liquidator to use the section as a representative of all the creditors. On the facts here,
the Inland Revenue and Customs as an individual creditor was able to claim the debt
due to it by the company from the two directors, on the grounds of one of them acting
while disqualified and the other acting on the instructions of someone whom he knew
to be disqualified. Likewise in *Inland Revenue Commissioners v McEntaggart*,[229] an
undischarged bankrupt who acted as a director was liable for the company's debts due
to the Revenue in respect of PAYE. The court noted that, in effect, CDDA 1986, s 15
imposes a collateral liability on the part of the disqualified directors for the debts of
the company. Moreover, in the absence of an express statutory provision to that effect,
the fact that the bankruptcy had subsequently been annulled did not take away the

---

[225] *Re Barings plc (No 5)* [1999] 1 BCLC 433 at 483–6; endorsed on appeal, [2000] 1 BCLC 523 at 535, CA.
[226] *Re Lo-Line Electric Motors Ltd* [1988] 2 All ER 692 at 696, per Browne-Wilkinson V-C; also *Re McNulty's Interchange Ltd* [1989] BCLC 709; *Re Douglas Construction Services Ltd* [1988] BCLC 397.
[227] As to whether they are willing so to act, note the presumption in CDDA 1986, s 15(5).
[228] [2006] 1 BCLC 440.   [229] [2006] 1 BCLC 476.

criminal liability under s 11 nor the civil liability under s 15. Furthermore, as liability is in respect of recovery of a debt by a third party, it is not open to the director to seek relief under CA 2006, s 1157 which allows the court to grant relief where a director has been held liable to the company for negligence, default, breach of duty or breach of trust (see **13-55**). This ability of an individual creditor to bring a direct claim in this way is very valuable and is clearly one which the Revenue at least seem intent on utilising. Quite apart from such (occasional) civil liability (and to date there is little evidence of many creditors being in a position to take advantage of this direct liability), in practice, there is little policing of disqualification orders and undertakings once they have been put in place. Such enforcement action as occurs is likely to arise only when the conduct of the disqualified director has been brought to the attention of the Secretary of State in some way, such as where a further venture collapses or a member of the public complains.

6-91   Finally, contracts entered into by a disqualified person on behalf of the company are not illegal and void for it cannot have been the Parliamentary intention to prevent the company suing on contracts entered into in the course of being unlawfully managed since that would prejudice the creditors who are the very persons the CDDA 1986 is designed to protect.[230]

[230] *Hill v Secretary of State for the Environment, Food and Rural Affairs* [2006] 1 BCLC 601.

7

A statutory statement of directors' duties

A Introduction

One of the most important changes implemented by the CA 2006 is the inclusion for **7-1** the first time of a statutory statement of directors' general duties in Part 10, Ch 2 (full text of which is set out at Appendix 1). The background to this change was a recommendation in 1996 from the Law Commission, following a review of directors' duties that there should be a statement of the principal duties, but without any alteration to them.[1] From the outset, the Company Law Review (CLR) indicated that it regarded the case for a legislative statement of the general duties of directors as clearly made out.[2] It brushed aside concerns from the legal profession that such a statement would restrict the development of the law; would create uncertainty while the 'new' duties are interpreted by the courts; would encourage the courts to second-guess business decisions; and would be of little assistance to the lay director who would still need advice as to the nature of the obligations imposed.[3]

The CLR considered that a legislative statement was important for three main reasons:[4] **7-2** on grounds of clarity and accessibility; to enable the law to be updated to reflect modern business practices, especially on conflicts of interest; and to address what the CLR called the 'scope' issue, i.e. in whose interests companies should be run. The CLR's clear intention was to modernise and alter the law and not merely to replicate the current position in a statutory statement. Accordingly, it recommended a full codification of directors' duties replacing the corresponding equitable and common law rules.[5]

---

[1] See Law Commission, *Company Directors: Regulating Conflicts of Interests and Formulating a Statement of Duties* (Law Comm No 261), (Cm 4436, 1999), para 4.36 and the draft statement of principles set out in Appendix A (hereinafter Law Commission Report); preceded by a consultation paper of the same name, Consultation Paper No 153 (1998), Pt 13 of which surveys previous proposals for a statutory statement of directors' duties.

[2] See Company Law Review, *Developing the Framework* (2000), paras 3.14–3.19; also *Completing the Structure* (2000), paras 3.6, 3.11–3.31; *Final Report*, vol 1 (2001), paras 3.5–3.11.

[3] See Law Society Company Law Committee, *Company Law Review—Developing the Framework* Memorandum No 401 (August 2000), pp 1–22; also Memorandum No 412 (February 2001); Company Law Review, *Completing the Structure* (2000), para 3.6 (the Review noted 'we do not find these objections convincing').   [4] Company Law Review, *Final Report*, vol 1 (2001), para 3.7.

[5] See Company Law Review, *Final Report*, vol 1 (2001), paras 3.9–3.10.

B The statutory statement

7-3   The statutory statement of the general duties is set out in CA 2006, Part 10, Ch 2 which provides for the following duties of directors:

- duty to act within their powers (s 171);
- duty to promote the success of the company (s 172);
- duty to exercise independent judgment (s 173);
- duty to exercise reasonable care, skill and diligence (s 174);
- duty to avoid conflicts of interest (s 175);
- duty not to accept benefits from third parties (s 176);
- duty to declare interest in proposed transactions with the company (s 177).

7-4   All the duties are fiduciary duties (which has implications for remedies) other than the duty of care, skill and diligence in CA 2006, s 174 which reflects the common law of negligence (see s 178(2)). The general duties are owed by a director which means a de jure director (i.e. one formally appointed to the office) and it also includes a de facto director (see **6-11**). As discussed at **6-19** it is clear that fiduciary duties are owed by a de facto director, i.e. someone not formally appointed but who has assumed the status and functions of a director. For the avoidance of doubt, s 170(2) ensures that former directors remain subject to ss 175 and 176 as to the exploitation of property, information or opportunity (see **11-36**) and the receipt of benefits from third parties (see **11-76**) after they resign. The purpose is to prevent what would otherwise be an easy avoidance of fiduciary duty. As for shadow directors, s 170(5) provides that the general duties of directors apply to shadow directors where, and to the extent that, the corresponding common law rules or equitable principles so apply, but as it is not clear at common law that shadow directors do owe fiduciary duties to the company, this somewhat obscure provision is rather unhelpful: see **6-28**.

7-5   The duties are cumulative as CA 2006, s 179 makes clear. It provides that 'except as otherwise provided, more than one of the general duties may apply in any given case'. For example, while directors might be able and willing to authorise a conflict of interest under s 175(4)(b), they also have to bear in mind their duty under s 172 to promote the success of the company. An exercise of the duty of care, skill and diligence (s 174) will often overlap with the need to exercise independent judgment (s 173). The duty to exercise powers for the purposes for which they are conferred (s 171(b)) will overlap with the duty to promote the success of the company (s 172) and the need to act in accordance with the constitution (s 171(a)).

7-6   Often, the overlap is quite complicated and the precise inter-relationship of the statutory duties is something which will occupy judicial time in the future. For example, CA 2006, s 175 does not apply to a conflict of interest arising in relation to a proposed transaction or arrangement with the company which is governed by s 177 while the obligation to disclose an interest in an existing transaction or arrangement with the company is governed by s 182 (which is not part of the general duties at all). It is also possible for a transaction to be governed initially by one of these provisions, for example s 182, and then to develop in ways which might subsequently attract the application of s 177 or s 175 (see the discussion at **11-105**). Furthermore, the relationship between s 176 and s 175 is unclear, in particular as to whether it is possible for directors to authorise (under s 175(4)(b)) the acceptance of benefits from third parties which are otherwise prohibited under s 176 (see discussion at **11-77**). Also, a director is not required to comply with s 175 or s 176 if the conflicted transaction is approved by the shareholders or is exempt from approval under CA 2006, Part 10, Ch 4, but the other duties do continue to apply (s 180(2)). So there are numerous permutations here and the interplay between the various elements is quite complex. The relationship with other provisions must also be taken into account such as, as already mentioned, ss 182–187 (interest in existing transactions with the company), but also s 232(4) (provisions in articles dealing with conflicts of interest), s 239 (ratification of acts of directors) and Part 10, Ch 4, ss 188–226 which deal with specific conflicts of interests. The statement of duties in CA 2006, Part 10, Ch 2 may contain only 12 sections, but they are complex statements of the law far removed from the type of accessible statement of duties which the Law Commission originally envisaged[6] and which the CLR had asserted would be one of the main advantages of a statutory statement.[7]

The statement of duties in CA 2006, Part 10, Ch 2 is not exhaustive. It merely sets out the general duties, but directors are subject to various other duties including duties with respect to specific conflicts of interest governed by CA 2006, Part10, Ch 4; statutory duties under the CA 2006 itself (such as the duty to maintain accounting records and prepare accounts, ss 386, 394), duties under the IA 1986, and duties under the general law such as employment law or health and safety legislation. **7-7**

The statement does not set out the remedies for breach of duty. The Government was unable to draft a satisfactory statutory codification of the myriad remedies available for breach of fiduciary duty and so limited itself to stating in CA 2006, s 178 that breach of the statutory duties attracts the same remedies as breach of the corresponding common law or equitable rules. In most instances, this is unlikely to cause a problem since the standard remedies for breach of fiduciary duty are well established, typically a liability to account to the company for profits made and/or to indemnify the company for loss caused by the breach of duty. But even here the introduction of the statutory statement may be of some consequence. For example, the remedy to account for profits made has been applied strictly by the court in order to strip the disloyal fiduciary of all possible gains, an approach based on long-standing judicial opposition to any dilution of the fundamental no conflict principle (see discussion at **11-3**). Now that duty can be avoided with the authorisation of independent directors: see s 175(4)(b). In the event of **7-8**

---

[6] See Law Commission Report, above n 1, Appendix A.

[7] Eventually, in the course of the Parliamentary debates, the Government was forced to acknowledge that it will be necessary to provide plain language guidance for directors (probably via the registrar of companies) summarising the main legal requirements placed on directors by company and insolvency legislation. See *Modernising Company Law* (Cm 5553-I, 2002), para 3.17.

a procedural failure with respect to authorisation (for example, it is subsequently discovered that in error an interested director participated in the granting of authorisation and the meeting would have been inquorate without him), the director is in breach
of the no conflict duty. The question is whether the courts will look to apply the full
rigour of the common law in stripping the fiduciary of all his profits in those circumstances. Parliament has signalled that the duty not to profit, far from being necessary
to the upholding of the highest standards of fiduciary conduct, is in fact an impediment to entrepreneurial activity, so the courts may take their cue from that legislative
stance and adopt a more relaxed approach to devising an appropriate remedy.[8]

7-9   A final concern is the uncertain relationship between the statutory statement and the
pre-existing law on directors' duties, a matter addressed in CA 2006, s 170(3) and (4)
which state:

> '(3) The general duties are based on certain common law rules and equitable principles
> as they apply in relation to directors and have effect in place of those rules and prin-
> ciples as regards the duties owed to a company by a director.
>
> (4) The general duties shall be interpreted and applied in the same way as common
> law rules or equitable principles, and regard shall be had to the corresponding common
> law rules and equitable principles in interpreting and applying the general duties.'

7-10   The difficulty is clear on the face of the provisions. Given the express statement in CA
2006, s 170(3) that these provisions apply 'in place of' the old rules, applying the usual
rules of statutory interpretation, existing case law on the 'old' law should no longer
be relevant and the starting point should be to interpret the language of the statute.[9]
Section 170(4) states, however, that the general duties are to be interpreted and applied
in the same way as common law or equitable principles and regard is to be had to the
corresponding common law rules and equitable principles in interpreting and applying the general duties.

7-11   To the extent that the duties have a basis in corresponding common law or equitable
principles, the existing authorities can be invoked to explain the nature of the now
statutory duty, but it is not entirely clear that it is possible to identify a corresponding common law or equitable principle in all cases. Some of the provisions clearly do
state the existing law or at least something quite close to it; for example, the director's
duty to exercise his powers for the purposes for which they are conferred (CA 2006,
s 171) is a positive statement of the common law prohibition on exercising powers for
a collateral purpose. The duty to exercise care, skill and diligence in s 174 is identical
to all intents and purposes to the common law duty of care and skill. Equally, some of
the provisions are modified versions of the common law and equitable principles. For
example, the duty to act bona fide in the interests of the company has been restated in
s 172 as a duty to promote the success of the company. Other duties have been comprehensively altered, most notably, the no conflict duty which now allows independent

---

[8] See, for example, *Murad v Al-Saraj* [2005] All ER (D) 503 (Jul), CA paras 82–3, per Arden LJ; paras 121–2,
per Jonathan Parker LJ.

[9] See *Bank of England v Vagliano Brothers* [1891] AC 107 at 144–5, per Lord Herschell.

directors to authorise profit making by directors in a situation of a conflict of interest (s 175(4)(b)). Identifying precisely which authorities are retained by s 170(4), therefore, is not easy.

The issue of the relationship between CA 2006, s 170(3) and (4) was considered at length in the Parliamentary debates before the Solicitor General was moved to comment as follows:[10]   **7-12**

> '...the courts should continue to refer to existing case law on the corresponding common law rules and equitable principles, *except where it is obviously irreconcilable with the statutory statement* [emphasis added]. The rich body of case law on and wisdom about the general duties may continue to be used—no one would benefit from abandoning the wisdom accumulated over several centuries—we do not propose to lose that.'

In practice, there may be a pragmatic judicial response to these difficulties. As the Solicitor General noted, no one is anxious to lose the accumulated wisdom of the common law and the courts will be anxious not to create unnecessary uncertainty in an area as commercially important as directors' duties. In all probability, the development of directors' duties will continue in much the same way as in the past 150 years with the main difference being that that development is now based on a statutory framework—which rather raises the question as to whether it was worthwhile devoting so much time (and generating so much controversy) to the inclusion of a statutory statement.   **7-13**

C Duties owed to the company

Directors owe their general duties to the company and not to the shareholders, individually or collectively;[11] nor do they owe any duties directly to the company's creditors, individually or collectively.[12] This common law principle[13] is expressed in CA 2006, s 170(1). It follows that enforcement of the general duties is a matter for the company, a point which the Government was keen to emphasise in the Parliamentary debates whenever concerns were expressed that the inclusion of a statutory statement exposes directors to a greater risk of being sued, particularly in the light of the introduction of the statutory derivative claim in CA 2006, Part 11 (see Chapter 18).   **7-14**

An application of the principle can be seen in *Peskin v Anderson*.[14] A dispute arose out of the sale by the Royal Automobile Club Ltd (RACL) of its motoring services business   **7-15**

---

[10] HC Debs, Session 2005–06, Standing Committee D, column 536 (6 July 2006).

[11] Not even if appointed as the nominee of a particular shareholder or class of shareholders: *Scottish Co-operative Wholesale Society Ltd v Meyer* [1958] 3 All ER 66, HL; *Boulting v ACTT* [1963] 1 All ER 716, CA.

[12] *Multinational Gas and Petrochemical Co v Multinational Gas and Petrochemical Services Ltd* [1983] 2 All ER 563; *Yukong Line Ltd of Korea v Rendsburg Investments Corp of Liberia* [1998] 2 BCLC 485.

[13] See *Percival v Wright* [1902] 2 Ch 421.   [14] [2001] 1 BCLC 372.

which essentially resulted in the shareholders in RACL receiving £34,000 each in respect of the sale. The claimants were all former shareholders whose membership had ceased before the sale and so they did not receive any part of the benefits flowing from the sale. They brought an action against the directors of RACL claiming damages for breach of fiduciary duty by the directors in failing to disclose to the shareholders the proposals relating to the sale of the business. The Court of Appeal dismissed the claim for directors do not, solely by virtue of the office of director, owe fiduciary duties to the shareholders, collectively or individually.

7-16   The shareholders may specifically appoint the directors as their agents in any matter, of course, in which case the directors will owe them the fiduciary duties arising from that agency relationship.[15] Directors may also find themselves liable to shareholders under ordinary legal principles, for example in misrepresentation, if they give misleading advice or abuse their position.[16] Liability issues under this heading may be an issue in the context of takeovers where shareholders rely on the advice of the directors as to the merits of any bid before them. Where a takeover bid has been made, the directors must give sufficient information to the shareholders and refrain from misleading them.[17] In the case of competing bids, the directors must do nothing to prevent the sharehold-ers from choosing to take the best price,[18] but the courts do not accept that the board must inevitably be under a positive duty to recommend and take all steps within its power to facilitate whichever is the highest offer.[19] If directors take it on themselves to give advice to current shareholders, they have a duty to advise in good faith and not fraudulently and not to mislead, whether deliberately or carelessly.[20] If a director misrepresents the financial position of the company so as to induce the shareholders to transfer their shares to him for a nominal consideration, he is liable in damages for negligent misrepresentation in the usual way.[21]

7-17   Exceptionally the courts may consider that the relationships within the company do give rise to fiduciary duties as between the directors and their shareholders. The lead-ing authority is *Coleman v Myers*,[22] a decision of the New Zealand Court of Appeal which has been cited with approval by the English courts. In this case, the court held that the directors did owe fiduciary duties to the shareholders including a duty not to mislead them on the sale of their shares. The court thought the fiduciary obliga-tion arose from the nature of the relationships within this family company where the minority shareholders habitually looked to the directors for guidance on matters affecting their interests.[23]

---

[15] *Allen v Hyatt* (1914) 30 TLR 444; *Briess v Woolley* [1954] 1 All ER 909.

[16] *Gething v Kilner* [1972] 1 All ER 1166; *Dawson International plc v Coats Paton plc* [1989] BCLC 233, CS (OH); *Platt v Platt* [2001] 1 BCLC 698.

[17] *Re a Company* [1986] BCLC 382; *Gething v Kilner* [1972] 1 All ER 1166.

[18] *Heron International Ltd v Lord Grade* [1983] BCLC 244.   [19] *Re a Company* [1986] BCLC 382.

[20] *Dawson International plc v Coats Paton plc* [1989] BCLC 233, CS (OH).

[21] See *Platt v Platt* [2001] 1 BCLC 698, CA.   [22] [1977] 2 NZLR 225.

[23] See also the interesting decision of the New South Wales Court of Appeal in *Brunninghausen v Glavanics* (1999) 46 NSWLR 538, noted Goddard (2000) 116 LQR 197.

The approach in *Coleman v Myers* was endorsed in *Re Chez Nico (Restaurants) Ltd*[24] by   **7-18**
Browne-Wilkinson V-C who agreed that fiduciary duties can arise between the directors and the shareholders which might include a duty of disclosure where directors are
purchasing shares in the company from shareholders.

In *Peskin v Anderson*,[25] noted at **7-15** above, the claimants failed to establish that the   **7-19**
directors owed duties to the shareholders so the claimants attempted to argue in the
alternative that their circumstances brought them within the *Coleman v Myers* qualification, i.e. that special circumstances existed which brought the directors into a fiduciary relationship with the shareholders. The Court of Appeal agreed that a fiduciary
duty may be owed by a director to a shareholder personally where a special factual
relationship exists between the parties in the particular case. As Mummery LJ noted,
events may take place which bring a director into direct and close contact with the
shareholders in a manner capable of generating fiduciary obligations.[26] On the facts
in *Peskin*, however, the court found that there were no relevant dealings, negotiations,
communications or other contact directly between the directors and the shareholders. The actions of the directors had not caused the shareholders to leave the company
when they did. Most important of all, prior to being approached by a bidder for the
business, there was nothing sufficiently concrete and specific, either in existence or in
contemplation, for the directors to disclose to the shareholders.[27] The court concluded
that there was nothing special in the factual relationship between the directors and the
shareholders to give rise to a fiduciary duty of disclosure.[28]

[24] [1992] BCLC 192 at 208.   [25] [2001] 1 BCLC 372.   [26] [2001] 1 BCLC 372 at 379.
[27] [2001] 1 BCLC 372 at 384.
[28] [2001] 1 BCLC 372 at 384. See also *Platt v Platt* [1999] 2 BCLC 745 where, at first instance, the court
was prepared to find that a fiduciary relationship had arisen between a director and two shareholders (his
brothers). The director had acquired their shareholdings on the basis of a misrepresentation and, the court
found, in breach of a fiduciary duty owed to them. The Court of Appeal confirmed the finding as to a liability
in misrepresentation, but expressly declined to comment on the correctness of the finding of a breach of a
fiduciary duty: see [2001] 1 BCLC 698.

8

Duty to act within constitution and powers

A Introduction

'A director of a company must—

(a) act in accordance with the company's constitution, and

(b) only exercise powers for the purposes for which they are conferred.' (CA 2006, s 171)

At common law the equivalent obligation was stated in terms of a duty to act bona **8-1** fide in the interests of the company and a requirement for directors to exercise their powers for a proper purpose and not for any collateral (i.e. personal or sectional) purpose. The CA 2006 splits that duty into distinct obligations: to act in accordance with the constitution (defined s 257) and to exercise powers for the purposes for which they are conferred in s 171 and to act to promote the success of the company in s 172. This demarcation clarifies the elements of these obligations, in particular that it is not sufficient to justify the actions of a board of directors by invoking the incantation 'a decision taken bona fide in the interests of the company',[1] but there remains a degree of overlap between them. This chapter concentrates on s 171 while s 172 is discussed in Chapter 9.

Turning to the distinct components of CA 2006, s 171. First, s 171(a) is concerned with **8-2** ensuring that the directors respect the division of power agreed within the company as between the shareholders and the directors. As we shall see, the typical division of power is that, subject to the articles and any directions given by the shareholders by special resolution,[2] the directors are 'responsible for the management of the company's business for which purpose they may exercise all the powers of the company'.[3] The issues under s 171(a) are the scope of the authority given to the directors by the constitution, see **4-8** and the implications, internally and externally, when they ignore or breach the terms of that mandate, whether collectively or individually.

---

[1] *Re a company, ex p Glossop* [1988] BCLC 570 at 577, per Harman J.

[2] See The Companies (Model Articles) Regulations 2008, SI 2008/3229, reg 2, Sch 1, art 4 (Ltd); reg 4, Sch 3, art 4 (Plc).

[3] See The Companies (Model Articles) Regulations 2008, SI 2008/3229, reg 2, Sch 1, art 3 (Ltd); reg 4, Sch 3, art 3 (Plc).

8-3   Secondly, CA 2006, s 171(b) sets out the duty to exercise powers for the purposes for which they are conferred, i.e. to promote the success of the company and not, say, to advance the personal interests of a director or directors. In the past it was considered that the issue of an abuse of authority by the exercise of a power for an improper purpose is distinct from the agency issue presented by an absence of authority,[4] but it is now clear, as is discussed below and as s 171 implicitly acknowledges, that the two issues are more directly intertwined.[5] The issues under s 171(b) include determining whether a power has been exercised for an improper purpose and the implications, internally and externally, of such an abuse of power.

8-4   The overall picture is complex but progress is being made to a more coherent framework based solidly on agency law.[6] Unfortunately, the opportunity was not taken in the CA 2006 to expressly state that framework nor indeed to address some of the recognised uncertainties with regard to the scope of CA 2006, s 40 which, as we shall see below, has an important role to play in terms of protecting third parties against any want of authority on the part of the directors.

B The constitutional division of power within a company

Authority conferred

8-5   Before considering problems of a want of authority, it is useful to consider the authority normally conferred by the constitution (as defined in s 257). As determined by the Court of Appeal in *Automatic Self-Cleansing Filter Syndicate Co Ltd v Cuninghame*,[7] the relationship between a board and the shareholders is a contractual relationship based on the articles which determine the extent of the management powers conferred on the board. The model articles provide (and this provision is common to practically

---

[4] See Millett J in *Macmillan Inc v Bishopsgate Investment Trust plc (No 3)* [1995] 3 All ER 747 at 753, relying on *Bowstead on Agency* but the *Bowstead* position on this has changed, see *Bowstead and Reynolds on Agency* (18th edn, 2006), para 3–008.

[5] See *Criterion Properties plc v Stratford UK Properties LLC* [2006] 1 BCLC 729, HL; also the valuable analysis of these issues in Payne & Prentice, 'Company Contracts and Vitiating Factors: Developments in the Law on Directors' Authority' [2005] LMCLQ 447. Payne and Prentice go on to comment (at 455) that 'the distinction between an act being an abuse of authority and one being in excess of authority is wafer thin, but nevertheless they are conceptually distinct and explicit in s 35A (now CA 2006 s 40).' That provision addresses a want of authority, not an abuse of power, but as an abuse of power gives rise to a want of authority, the overlap is clear: see **8.17**.

[6] See *Criterion Properties plc v Stratford UK Properties LLC* [2006] 1 BCLC 729, HL; and Payne & Prentice, above n 5.

[7] [1906] 2 Ch 34, CA; *Gramophone and Typewriter Ltd v Stanley* [1908] 2 KB 89 at 98, CA; *Salmon v Quin & Axtens Ltd* [1909] 1 Ch 311, CA; aff'd sub nom *Quin & Axtens Ltd v Salmon* [1909] AC 442, HL; *Howard Smith Ltd v Ampol Petroleum Ltd* [1974] AC 821 at 837, PC; see also *Breckland Group Holdings Ltd v London & Suffolk Properties Ltd* [1989] BCLC 100.

all companies) that 'subject to the articles, the directors are responsible for the management of the company's business for which purpose they may exercise all the powers of the company',[8] but the shareholders may by special resolution direct the directors to take, or refrain from taking, specified action.[9] The shareholders do have a residual power of management, but this exceptional power only arises if the board is unable to act,[10] or is deadlocked or for all practical purposes has ceased to exist.[11] The shareholders may resolve the situation by appointing another director and, once a functioning board is in operation, the powers of management revert to it.

The division of power is predominantly in favour of the board then at the expense **8-6** of the shareholders and the CA 2006 has shifted the balance further in favour of the board. The CA 1985 permitted certain corporate actions when authorised by the shareholders by resolution or by the articles (such as an allotment of shares (CA 1985, s 80), or purchase of the company's own shares (CA 1985, s 162)), but the position regarding these matters under the CA 2006 is that the company (and therefore the directors in the exercise of their management powers) has the particular power unless prohibited by the articles. In other words, now there must be a positive decision via the articles to subject a power to shareholder control, otherwise the power vests in the directors. For example, the company has power to purchase its own shares unless restricted by the articles (CA 2006, s 690) and the directors of a private company with one class of shares (which is almost invariably the case) have the power to allot shares unless prohibited by the articles (s 550).

The division of power is not entirely one-sided, however, and some matters are reserved **8-7** for the shareholders by statute, such as the right to amend the articles (CA 2006, s 21), to reduce the share capital (s 641), and to petition for a voluntary winding up (IA 1986, s 84(1)(b)). As noted at **8-5**, the delegation of power to the directors is subject to the articles and to any directions given, on an ad hoc basis, by way of a special resolution.[12] Constraints which might be imposed via the articles might include monetary limits on powers to borrow, or a requirement for the consent of named directors to the exercise of a particular power,[13] or constraints in the form of procedural requirements, for example with respect to the calling of meetings, quorum requirements or procedures for the execution of documents. As discussed in Chapter 4, companies may restrict

---

[8] See The Companies (Model Articles) Regulations 2008, SI 2008/3229, reg 2, Sch 1, art 3 (Ltd); reg 4, Sch 3, art 3 (Plc). In turn the directors may delegate any of the powers conferred on them to any committee or any director or any other person, as they think fit: art 5 (Ltd); art 5 (Plc). There must be an actual delegation if a director is to claim internally that he has powers of management separate from the collective board: *Mitchell & Hobbs (UK) Ltd v Mill* [1996] 2 BCLC 102; externally, a third party may be able to rely on the appearance of authority: see discussion at **8-14**.

[9] See The Companies (Model Articles) Regulations 2008, SI 2008/3229, reg 2, Sch 1, art 4 (Ltd); reg 4, Sch 3, art 4 (Plc). See also the discussion at **4–8**.

[10] *Foster v Foster* [1916] 1 Ch 532.   [11] *Barron v Potter* [1914] 1 Ch 895.

[12] See The Companies (Model Articles) Regulations 2008, SI 2008/3229, reg 2, Sch 1, art 4 (Ltd); reg 4, Sch 3, art 4 (Plc). Giving directions on an ad hoc basis tends to be difficult because shareholders lack the necessary information to intervene at an early stage and typically only find out about events after they have happened.

[13] See *Quin & Axtens Ltd v Salmon* [1909] 1 Ch 311, CA, aff'd [1909] AC 442. HL.

their objects under the CA 2006, s 31 and companies formed under previous legislation may choose to retain their objects clauses in the articles. In either case, the objects act as a constraint on directors' authority (third parties are protected against issues of lack of capacity by s 39). The articles also normally confer on the shareholders a power to appoint directors though the directors usually also have a power to appoint.[14] If the company is a listed company, the Listing Rules require shareholder approval of certain transactions,[15] and shareholders in quoted companies have an advisory vote on the directors' remuneration report (s 439). Most crucially, the shareholders have power to remove a director (s 168) and the shareholders retain ultimate control of the company through their ability to sell their shares to new owners.[16]

8-8   Notwithstanding the existence of these powers vested in shareholders, and assuming that the company has articles in the form of the model articles, the practical position is that all the powers of the company are vested in the directors. Having said that, it is worth noting that there is a considerable variation in practices within companies, especially as between the largest public companies and the small private company.

8-9   In a small private company, a formal division of power between the directors and the shareholders is often meaningless as they are frequently the same individuals acting as shareholders and as directors without differentiating particularly between those capacities. This reality is recognised by the CA 2006 which dispenses with much of the formal decision-making mechanisms which otherwise operate. For example, private companies need not hold an annual general meeting (agm) of shareholders unless they want to while public companies must hold an agm (CA 2006, s 336). The expectation is that, in a private company, many if not all decisions will be taken by written resolution rather than through formal meetings (see s 281). To that end, the procedures for written resolutions have been modified and, in particular, the requirement for unanimity dropped (ss 282(2), 283(2)). In their day-to-day activities then it can be said that these companies are untroubled by any formal division of responsibilities between the directors and the shareholders. Nevertheless, even in such companies, it is important for the persons involved to appreciate their respective roles as directors and as shareholders because of the consequences which may attach to failing to act in the way required by the appropriate capacity. For example, directors are subject to fiduciary duties which do not apply to shareholders. Equally, on occasion a decision may need to be taken or a transaction authorised by the shareholders rather than the directors, for example on a reduction of capital (s 641).

8-10   In large private and public companies, on the other hand, there is a distinct division of power and responsibility between the board of directors and the shareholders with all powers of management firmly vested in the board and very little power retained by the shareholders. The board's role in practice is supervisory rather than managerial

---

[14] See The Companies (Model Articles) Regulations 2008, SI 2008/3229, reg 2, Sch 1, art 17 (Ltd); reg 4, Sch 3, art 20 (Plc). In the case of a public company a director appointed by the directors must retire at the next annual general meeting, though he may be reappointed: art 21(2)(a) (Plc).

[15] See UKLA, *Listing Rules,* LR10 Significant transactions.

[16] See *Howard Smith Ltd v Ampol Petroleum Ltd* [1974] AC 821 at 837–8.

with extensive powers delegated to individual directors and to professional executive managers, a group largely ignored by the legal structure.[17] The issue in these companies is trying to ensure shareholder engagement so that the shareholders act as an effective counterbalance to all powerful directors. These corporate governance issues are discussed in Chapter 5.

C Types of authority

Actual authority

Actual authority may be express or implied actual authority. As noted, the directors collectively have extensive actual authority. For an individual director, express actual authority arises from an explicit conferring of authority on a director which would typically be recorded in the board minutes. Implied actual authority arises from the position which the individual holds. For example, if an individual is appointed as a managing director, implied authority authorises him to do all such things as fall within the usual scope of that office.[18] In *Hely-Hutchinson v Brayhead Ltd*[19] the chairman of the company also acted as its de facto managing director.[20] He entered into contracts on the company's behalf on his own initiative and subsequently reported them to the board which acquiesced in this practice. Later the board refused to honour certain undertakings which the director had given. The Court of Appeal found that the director lacked express actual authority and he had no implied actual authority as the office of chairman did not carry authority to enter into contracts without the sanction of the board. As de facto managing director, however, he did have implied actual authority. This authority would be implied from the circumstance that the board by its conduct over many months had acquiesced in his acting as managing director and committing the company to contracts without the necessity of sanction from the board.[21]

8-11

It is clear that a managing director (or in modern terminology a chief executive officer or CEO) by virtue of his position has actual or apparent authority co-extensive with the power of the board to manage the business. It is likely that the courts would also consider a finance director, or chief financial officer (CFO), certainly in a large company, to have extensive authority, actual and apparent, with respect to matters within the usual scope of the office of a finance director.[22] These individual directors by virtue of their positions are seen, therefore, as having extensive authority to bind the

8-12

---

[17] See Berle and Means, *The Modern Corporation and Private Property* (1932); Eisenberg, *The Structure of the Corporation* (1976); Parkinson, *Corporate Power and Responsibility* (1993), Ch 2.

[18] *Hely-Hutchinson v Brayhead Ltd* [1967] 3 All ER 98, CA; *Hopkins v TL Dallas Group Ltd* [2005] 1 BCLC 543.   [19] [1967] 3 All ER 98, CA.

[20] A de facto director is someone who assumes the office of director without being formally appointed to the position: see the discussion of de facto directors at **6-11**.

[21] [1967] 3 All ER 98 at 103, CA.   [22] See *Harold Holdsworth & Co v Caddies* [1955] 1 All ER 725.

company. The position is different with respect to the company chairman, for his main function is to manage the conduct of the board, not to manage the business of the company, so his actual authority to bind the company is limited, likewise his apparent authority. Beyond these CEO and CFO offices, individual directors will have such actual authority as is delegated to them expressly and such implied authority as arises from any position they hold as an executive director, i.e. they are impliedly authorised to do such things as fall within the usual scope of that office.[23] They may have considerable apparent authority also: see the discussion below.

8-13 Bearing these points in mind, it is clear that there is a hierarchy of authority where the board has the greatest actual and apparent authority to manage the business, with CEOs and CFOs having extensive authority in respect of matters within the usual scope of their offices. Individual directors as such may have the least express actual authority to bind the company, though they have implied actual authority consistent with the scope of their office and possible apparent authority.

Apparent authority

8-14 Apparent (or ostensible) authority is the authority of an agent as it appears to others[24] and it can operate to enlarge actual authority[52] or to create authority where no actual authority exists,[25] but it cannot be relied on if the third party knows that the agent has no actual authority or is put on inquiry as to an absence of authority.[26] Its use in the company context is primarily to provide authorisation for the individual director who does not hold one of the executive posts (such as CEO or CFO) which the law recognises as conferring considerable actual authority, as discussed above, and so has no or limited actual authority to bind the company on the basis of the position which he holds. The leading authority is *Freeman and Lockyer v Buckhurst Park Properties (Mangal) Ltd*[27] where the director in question managed the company's property and acted on its behalf. In that role he employed the plaintiff architects to draw up plans for the development of land held by the company. The development ultimately collapsed and the plaintiffs sued the company for their fees. The company denied that the director had any authority to employ the architects. The court found that, while he had never been appointed managing director (and therefore had no actual authority, express or implied), the actions of the director were within his apparent authority and the board had been aware of his conduct and had acquiesced in it.[28]

---

[23] *Hely-Hutchinson v Brayhead Ltd* [1967] 3 All ER 98.

[24] *Hely-Hutchinson v Brayhead Ltd* [1967] 3 All ER 98 at 102, CA, per Lord Denning.

[25] See *First Energy (UK) Ltd v Hungarian International Bank Ltd* [1993] BCLC 1409.

[26] *A L Underwood Ltd v Bank of Liverpool* [1924] 1 KB 775, CA; *B Liggett (Liverpool) Ltd v Barclays Bank Ltd* [1928] 1 KB 48; *Morris v Kanssen* [1946] 1 All ER 586, HL; *Rolled Steel Products (Holdings) Ltd v British Steel Corpn* [1985] 3 All ER 52, CA; and see *Criterion Properties plc v Stratford UK Properties LLC* [2006] 1 BCLC 729 at 741, per Lord Scott.   [27] [1964] 1 All ER 630, CA.

[28] It is difficult to distinguish this case from *Hely-Hutchinson* (see above **8-11**), where the court found the director had implied actual authority. Indeed Diplock LJ thought the trial judge in *Freeman & Lockyer* might have concluded that there was actual authority there also: see [1964] 1 All ER 630 at 643, CA. See *Bowstead & Reynolds on Agency* (18th edn, 2006), paras 3-001–3-005: the distinction essentially is between

The architects were entitled to rely on that apparent authority and the company was liable for the fees.

For apparent authority to arise, the agent must have been held out by someone with actual **8-15** authority[29] to carry out the transaction and an agent cannot hold himself out as having authority.[30] The acts of the principal must constitute a representation that the agent has a particular authority and must be reasonably so understood by the other party who deals with the agent on the faith of the representation. In determining whether a principal has represented his agent as having authority to enter into the particular transaction, the court has to consider the totality of the principal's conduct.[31] The commonest form of holding out is permitting the agent to act in the conduct of the principal's business[32] and in many cases the holding out consists solely of the fact that the company has invested the agent with a particular office, e.g. 'managing director' or 'secretary'.[33] The very act of appointing someone as a director is a representation that they have the usual authority of someone in that position. The holding out may also come from a course of conduct where the agent has a course of dealing with a particular contractor and the principal acquiesces in the practice and honours transactions arising out of it.[34] For these reasons, an individual director may acquire considerable apparent authority.

The problem with apparent authority is that it cannot be relied upon if the other **8-16** party knows or is put on inquiry as to some limitation which prevents the authority arising.[35] This may be knowledge, including constructive notice,[36] of the company's

actual authority arising from the consensual relationship between the principal and agent and authority as it appears to third parties. 'The link is that the authority which the third party is entitled to assume the agent has is in most situations the authority which would normally be implied between principal and agent in the circumstances. The actual and apparent authority will therefore normally coincide' (para 3-005).

[29] Although the courts have also accepted the following principle set out in *Bowstead and Reynolds on Agency* (18th edn, 2006), para 8-021: 'It seems correct in principle to say that an agent can have apparent authority to make representations as to the authority of other agents, provided that his own authority can finally be traced back to a representation by the principal or to a person with actual authority from the principal to make it.' See *Re Ing (UK) Ltd v Verischerung* [2007] 1 BCLC 108, esp at 127.

[30] *Freeman and Lockyer v Buckhurst Park Properties (Mangal) Ltd* [1964] 1 All ER 630, CA; *British Bank of the Middle East v Sun Life Assurance Co of Canada (UK) Ltd* [1983] BCLC 78, HL; *Armagas Ltd v Mundogas SA* [1986] 2 All ER 385, HL.

[31] *Egyptian International Foreign Trade Co v Soplex Wholesale Supplies Ltd, The Raffaella* [1985] BCLC 404 at 411, CA, per Browne-Wilkinson V-C.

[32] *Freeman and Lockyer v Buckhurst Park Properties (Mangal) Ltd* [1964] 1 All ER 630 at 645, per Diplock LJ.

[33] *Egyptian International Foreign Trade Co v Soplex Wholesale Supplies Ltd, The Raffaella* [1985] BCLC 404 at 411, CA, per Browne-Wilkinson V-C. As Toulson J commented in *Re Ing (UK) Ltd v Verischerung* [2007] 1 BCLC 108 at 128: '… many instances of ostensible authority arise by implication from acts of a quite general nature, typically putting an agent in a position which may normally be expected to carry a certain level of authority': see also at 132–3.

[34] See *Armagas Ltd v Mundogas SA* [1986] 2 All ER 385 at 389–90, HL, per Lord Keith.

[35] *A L Underwood Ltd v Bank of Liverpool* [1924] 1 KB 775, CA; *B Liggett (Liverpool) Ltd v Barclays Bank Ltd* [1928] 1 KB 48; *Morris v Kanssen* [1946] 1 All ER 586, HL; *Rolled Steel Products (Holdings) Ltd v British Steel Corpn* [1985] 3 All ER 52, CA; *Criterion Properties plc v Stratford UK Properties LLC* [2006] 1 BCLC 729, HL.

[36] Constructive notice is abolished for anyone seeking to rely on CA 2006, s 40, but it has not been abolished otherwise. CA 1985, s 711A which would have done so was never brought into force and is repealed by CA 2006, s 1295, Sch 16.

articles which might clearly indicate a lack of authority, for example, where the articles state that no individual director may enter into a transaction in excess of £1m. A third party is deemed (by the doctrine of constructive notice) to be aware of that limitation even if the third party has not actually read the articles, though if he can rely on CA 2006, s 40, discussed below, the third party is unaffected even by actual knowledge of such a limitation.

8-17   It may be that the third party is put on inquiry as to the authority of the agent by the very nature of the proposed transaction which may indicate that a director is acting for an improper purpose. As Lord Scott commented in *Criterion Properties plc v Stratford UK Properties LLC*[37] (see **8-59**):

> '...if a person dealing with an agent knows or has reason to believe that the contract or transaction is contrary to the commercial interests of the agent's principal, it is likely to be very difficult for the person to assert with any credibility that he believed the agent did have actual authority. Lack of such a belief would be fatal to a claim that the agent had apparent authority.'

8-18   In *A L Underwood Ltd v Bank of Liverpool*[38] a bank was put on inquiry when a director paid cheques drawn in favour of the company into his personal bank account. If put on inquiry by the circumstances, the third party should make such inquiries as ought reasonably to be made to ensure the agent's authority is sufficient to bind the principal.[39] In *Hopkins v TL Dallas Group Ltd*[40] a third party was unable to hold a company to undertakings given by a deputy managing director (who had subsequently been dismissed for dishonesty) when the recipient of the undertakings had been on the clearest notice that the transactions were abnormal and suspicious. In those circumstances, the court said, the recipient should have sought confirmation of the propriety and regularity of the transaction from the managing director of the company. The director had no actual authority to execute the undertakings[41] and the recipient could not rely on any apparent authority on the director's part in the light of his failure to inquire. Accordingly, the undertakings were not binding on the defendant company and could not be enforced against it.

8-19   In *Wrexham AFC Ltd v Crucialmove Ltd*[42] the third party knew that the director executing a particular agreement on behalf of the company (which was a football club) had a conflict of interest between his interests and his duty to the company. The director executed a declaration that the freehold of the club's ground (purchased with funding provided by the third party) was held on trust for the third party. What had not been disclosed was that the director and the third party had entered into a joint

---

[37] [2006] 1 BCLC 729 at 741, HL.   [38] [1924] 1 KB 775, CA.

[39] *Hopkins v TL Dallas Group Ltd* [2005] 1 BCLC 543.   [40] [2005] 1 BCLC 543.

[41] Obviously he had no express actual authority. Equally, despite the title of deputy managing director, he had no implied actual authority because the giving of undertakings of this nature did not fall within the usual scope of the office of deputy managing director. He was subordinate to an executive chairman and to an executive managing director and had no responsibility in relation to these types of undertakings.

[42] [2008] 1 BCLC 508, CA. See too *Rolled Steel Products (Holdings) Ltd v British Steel Corpn* [1984] BCLC 466 at 507–8, 517–18, CA.

venture agreement for the redevelopment of the ground to their personal advantage. The ownership of the freehold was subsequently challenged. The court found that this was a highly unusual case where the third party was not dealing with company officers of whom he knew nothing. Because of the joint venture agreement, the third party knew of all the circumstances that meant that the director had a conflict of interest in securing the freehold of the land and in making the declaration of trust. The third party was bound to inquire whether the transaction had been authorised or approved by the company or its board. Given he was on notice and had failed to inquire, the Court of Appeal held that the third party could not rely on any apparent authority of the director as a matter of agency law nor, as we shall see, on the statutory protection provided for third parties by CA 2006, s 40.[43] The Court of Appeal upheld a declaration by the lower court that the freehold of the land was held on trust for the club, the company, subject to a charge in favour of the third party in respect of the purchase price.

D Statutory protection for third parties

As discussed above, the directors' mandate to manage the business, their authority to act on the company's behalf, is derived from the constitutional division of power within the particular company set out primarily (but not exclusively) in the articles[44] as well as the authority conferred on them by agency law. A failure to act within the scope of their authority is a breach by the directors of CA 2006, s 171(a) and leaves persons dealing with the company through them as parties to an unauthorised transaction. The problem here is a want of authority. This risk of being party to an unauthorised transaction would seem to require third parties to scrutinise carefully the company's constitution and the limits to the directors' authority, collectively and individually. But that type of scrutiny is time-consuming and expensive in the context of commercial operations and, therefore, both domestically and as a result of EU requirements, the policy balance here favours commercial certainty and the protection of the third party over any need externally to uphold constitutional constraints on the authority of the directors. That policy is reflected in CA 2006, s 40 and, at common law, by the rule in *Turquand's* case, discussed at **8-41**.

8-20

As far as third parties are concerned, the practical context in which a problem is likely to arise is where a company wishes to disown a transaction (usually as a result of a fall in the market which has made the transaction disadvantageous) by alleging that the director or directors responsible had no authority to enter into it. A third party may have an action for damages for breach of an implied warranty of authority against a

8-21

---

[43] [2008] 1 BCLC 508 at 523–4.

[44] The constitution is defined more broadly than the articles, see CA 2006, s 17. It is also possible that the directors' powers may be limited by directions given by the shareholders by special resolution: see The Companies (Model Articles) Regulations 2008, SI 2008/3229, reg 2, Sch 1, art 4 (Ltd); reg 4, Sch 3, art 4 (Plc).

director in such circumstances,[45] but he is usually more concerned with holding the company to the transaction. The answer to this problem of a want of authority lies in a combination of agency law and company law, common law and statute.

Companies Act 2006, s 40

8-22   Statutory protection for third parties dealing with the company is provided by CA 2006, s 40 which implements the requirements of the First EC Company Law Directive in this regard.[46] Section 40(1) states:

> 'In favour of a person dealing with a company in good faith, the power of the directors to bind the company, or authorise others to do so, is deemed to be free of any limitation under the company's constitution.'

The statutory provision operates only 'in favour of' a person dealing with a company in good faith so the company needs to authorise the transaction if it wants to hold the other party to it.

8-23   Note in particular that the section has effect subject to CA 2006, s 41 where the parties to the transaction include a director of the company or of its holding company or a person connected (as defined in s 252) with such a director.[47] In that situation, the transaction is voidable at the instance of the company subject to the possibility that the right to avoid may be lost in the usual ways (restitutio impossible, rights of bona fide third parties for value intervene, etc: see s 41(4)). Further, the director and connected person and any director who authorised the transaction (subject to the defence in s 41(5)) may be civilly liable under s 41(3) and/or under any other rule of law such as for breach of duty (s 41(1)). The application of s 41 may give rise to the situation where a transaction is valid with respect to one party under s 40(1), because they are unaffected by the application of s 41 (see s 41(6)), and voidable with respect to another party to the same transaction if they are a director or connected person under s 41(2). In that situation, the court has wide powers to affirm, sever or set aside the transaction on such terms as appears to be just (s 41(6)).

---

[45] *Hely-Hutchinson v Brayhead Ltd* [1967] 3 All ER 98, CA.

[46] The relevant provision is art 9 of the First Council Directive on Company Law, 68/151/EEC, OJ Spec Edn 1968, p 41 which provides as follows: '(1) Acts done by the organs of the company shall be binding upon it even if those acts are not within the objects of the company, unless such acts exceed the powers that the law confers or allows to be conferred on those organs. However, Member States may provide that the company shall not be bound where such acts are outside the objects of the company, if it proves that the third party knew that the act was outside those objects or could not in view of the circumstances have been unaware of it; disclosure of the statutes shall not of itself be sufficient proof thereof. (2) The limits on the powers of the organs of the company, arising under the statutes or from a decision of the competent organs, may never be relied on as against third parties, even if they have been disclosed'. See detailed account of art 9 by Edwards, *EC Company Law* (1999), Ch 1, pp 33–45, though some of the difficulties in implementation identified there (see pp 42–4) appear to have been addressed by subtle changes in the drafting of CA 2006, s 40: see discussion in text.

[47] CA 2006, ss 40(6), 41(2). Section 40 also has effect subject to s 42 where the company is a charity: s 40(6).

A person dealing in good faith

An issue which has arisen is whether a director can be a 'person' for these purposes so **8-24** as to rely on the protection of CA 2006, s 40. In *Smith v Henniker-Major & Co*,[48] while agreed that, as a matter of ordinary language, 'person' may include a director, the majority in the Court of Appeal did not accept that a director could rely on the statutory provision with respect to an error as to authority when he was the author of his own mistake.[49] The judicial reluctance to accept that a director (where he is the author of and hopes to be the beneficiary of the lack of authority) can rely on the protection of the statutory provision is understandable. As Schiemann LJ commented, there should be no difficulty in excluding from 'person' the very directors who overstepped the limitations in the company's constitution. But the case is not a very useful authority for the facts were exceptional,[50] as the court stressed, and there are three difficult judgments agreeing and conflicting with one another in almost equal measure.[51] There may be no need to consider it further for the position seems to have been clarified by a slight rewording in CA 2006, s 40(6) which now states expressly that s 40 has effect subject to s 41.[52] In other words, when a director is a party (or one of the parties) to the transaction, his position is governed by s 41, not s 40. The starting point is not that the director can rely on s 40, but that, as regards a director, the transaction is voidable under s 41.[53]

In *EIC Services Ltd v Phipps*,[54] the Court of Appeal was also robust in rejecting, obiter, **8-25** a first instance finding that a shareholder could rely on CA 2006, s 40 as a 'person' dealing in good faith. The case concerned an unauthorised bonus issue to shareholders in breach of the articles and the question was whether the shareholders could rely on s 40 so as to be able to hold on to the shares which had been erroneously allocated (and which had increased in value significantly). As discussed below, the court held in any event that a bonus issue does not amount to a 'dealing' with the company, but had there been a dealing, the court did not accept that a shareholder could be a 'person' for these purposes. Peter Gibson LJ, with whom Sedley LJ and Newman J agreed, thought the answer lay in the First Company Law Directive, art 9, which is implemented by CA 2006, s 40 and which is intended to protect 'third parties'. While noting that the

---

[48] [2002] 2 BCLC 655, CA.

[49] See [2002] 2 BCLC 655 at 684, per Carnwath LJ who stressed that the director here was also the chairman and the person entrusted with ensuring that the constitution was observed; also at 687, per Schiemann LJ. Robert Walker LJ dissented on the basis of the relationship between what is now CA 2006, s 40 and s 41, but the basis of his dissent has been eroded by the fact that s 40(6) now states expressly that s 40 has effect subject to s 41.

[50] The facts were that a 30% shareholder and director, Smith, at an inquorate board meeting (attended only by himself) had the company assign to him what was in effect its sole asset, namely a claim against a firm of solicitors for damages in respect of a sale of land. The validity of the assignment was challenged by the solicitors. Mr Smith claimed that, as he was a person dealing with the company in good faith, he could rely on the statutory protection and was unaffected by any (quorum) limitation on the powers of the board.

[51] See Walters, 'Section 35A and Quorum Requirements: Confusion Reigns' (2002) 23 Co Law 325.

[52] The previous wording was that CA 1985, s 322A (now CA 2006, s 41) had effect notwithstanding CA 1985, s 35A (now CA 2006, s 40): CA 1985, s 35A(6).

[53] See CA 2006, s 41(2), (6).   [54] [2004] 2 BCLC 589, CA.

Directive does not define 'third parties', Peter Gibson LJ thought it tolerably clear from the Directive itself that the term 'third parties' does not include the company or its members and there was no reason to think that a provision intended to implement the Directive had gone further than the Directive in the absence of any other known mischief which the section was intended to counteract.[55]

8-26   For the purpose of CA 2006, s 40, a person 'deals with' a company if he is a party to any transaction or other act to which the company is a party.[56] In *EIC Services Ltd v Phipps*,[57] as noted, the Court of Appeal did not accept that an issue of bonus shares by a company to its shareholders (an internal arrangement involving no change in proportionate shareholdings and no action by the shareholders, merely passive receipt of the shares) could amount to a 'dealing'.[58] Peter Gibson LJ noted that, as a matter of ordinary language, the section contemplates a bilateral transaction between the company and the person dealing with the company or an act to which both are parties.[59]

8-27   As to the good faith requirement, the statute goes to great lengths to ensure that it is difficult for a person dealing with a company to be in bad faith, especially by imposing a presumption of good faith. CA 2006, s 40(2)(b) provides as follows:

> '(2) For this purpose—...
>
> (b) a person dealing with a company—
>
>   (i)   is not bound to enquire as to any limitation on the powers of the directors to bind the company or authorise others to do so,
>
>   (ii) is presumed to have acted in good faith unless the contrary is proved, and
>
>   (iii) is not to be regarded as acting in bad faith by reason only of his knowing that an act is beyond the powers of the directors under the company's constitution.'

8-28   A person cannot be regarded then as acting in bad faith by reason *only* of his knowing that an act is beyond the powers of the directors under the company's constitution (i.e. beyond their authority). At common law, persons dealing with a company are deemed under the doctrine of constructive notice to have notice of the company's articles of association and various public documents (and this doctrine has never been formally repealed)[60] but this deemed knowledge is irrelevant now in the context of CA

---

[55] [2004] 2 BCLC 589 at 660–1. Nor did he think that any inference as to the application of CA 2006, s 40 to shareholders could be drawn from the fact that the legislature dealt specifically with transactions with directors in s 41.

[56] CA 2006, s 40(2)(a). This wording ensures that the provision applies to gratuitous as well as commercial transactions.

[57] [2004] 2 BCLC 589, CA.

[58] See Payne and Prentice, above n 5, p 463, who cogently criticise this finding and point out that at the very least a bonus issue amounts to an act to which the company is a party: see CA 2006, s 40(2)(a). See also *Cottrell v King* [2004] 2 BCLC 413 at 420 where it was doubted, obiter, whether the operation of transfer provisions in the articles could be said to be 'dealing with the company' for these purposes.

[59] [2004] 2 BCLC 589 at 660.

[60] See *Ernest v Nicholls* (1857) 6 HL Cas 401; *Mahony v East Holyford Mining Co* (1875) LR 7 HL 869; *Irvine v Union Bank of Australia* (1877) 2 App Cas 366, PC. The doctrine of constructive notice was to have been abolished by CA 1985, s 711A but that provision was never brought into force and it was repealed by CA 2006, s 1295, Sch 16. That deemed notice can prevent apparent authority arising at common law: see **8-16** above.

2006, s 40 since even actual knowledge of a constitutional limitation does not establish bad faith.

To establish bad faith, it is necessary to show something additional such as knowledge of or being put on inquiry as to an improper purpose or collusion by the third party in a breach by the directors of their duties.[61] Knowledge or being put on inquiry as to an improper purpose negates belief in actual authority and would rebut the presumption of good faith: see below. Of course there is an element of linkage here as to how a person is put on inquiry as to an improper purpose. While knowledge of a constitutional limitation (i.e. of a lack of authority) does not affect a person dealing in good faith with the company (CA 2006, s 40(2)(b)(iii)), that knowledge might put the third party on inquiry as to an exercise of a power for an improper purpose. A failure then to inquire will negate this presumption of good faith.[62]   **8-29**

The circumstances needed to rebut the presumption of good faith is considered in *Wrexham AFC Ltd v Crucialmove Ltd*,[63] discussed at **8-19**, where the third party knew that the director executing a particular agreement on behalf of the company had a conflict of interest. As discussed, the Court of Appeal held that the third party who knows of, or is on inquiry as to, an improper purpose and who fails to inquire cannot rely on apparent authority and cannot hold the company to the transaction.[64] The Court of Appeal also held that CA 2006, s 40 was of no assistance to the third party as the statutory provision does not absolve a person dealing with the company from any duty to inquire when the circumstances are such as to put that person on inquiry.[65] This case provides important clarification of the limits to the good faith presumption in s 40(2)(b)(ii). The section operates to negate any knowledge (actual or constructive) of constitutional limitations on the powers of the directors to bind the company and to relieve the third party from the obligation to enquire as to such limitations. But if a third party is put on inquiry by the circumstances of the transaction and fails to inquire, then he cannot rely on s 40 (but he must be put on inquiry by something other than knowing of a lack of authority). The policy objectives of securing commercial certainty and the protection of the third party do not extend to protecting a third party with notice of a problem.   **8-30**

To sum up, if the problem is merely a want of authority, CA 2006, s 40 offers full protection to a third party assuming the elements of the statutory requirements are met. But where the third party is put on inquiry (by something other than merely knowing of a lack of authority such as knowledge, actual or constructive, of an improper purpose) and fails to inquire, the statutory presumption of good faith in CA 2006, s 40(2)(b)(ii) is rebutted and the protection of the section is not available to him.   **8-31**

If for some reason (for example, no 'dealing' for these purposes) a third party cannot bring himself within CA 2006, s 40, he must rely on the rules of agency to bind the   **8-32**

---

[61] See *Barclays Bank Ltd v TOSG Trust Fund Ltd* [1984] BCLC 1 (on the earlier but similarly worded provision, European Communities Act 1972, s 9).

[62] See *Wrexham AFC Ltd v Crucialmove Ltd* [2008] 1 BCLC 508; Payne and Prentice, above n 5, at p 455.

[63] [2008] 1 BCLC 508, CA.   [64] [2008] 1 BCLC 508 at 523.   [65] [2008] 1 BCLC 508 at 523.

company but even constructive notice of a want of authority puts him on inquiry and a failure to inquire means that he cannot rely on any apparent authority. Likewise, as a matter of agency law, being put on inquiry as to an improper purpose means a lack of a credible belief in the agent's actual authority which, as Lord Scott commented in *Criterion Properties plc v Stratford UK Properties LLC*[66] (see at **8-17**) is fatal to any claim that the agent had apparent authority: see discussion at **8-59**.

Constitutional limitations may be disregarded

8-33   Assuming these thresholds in terms of 'a person' 'dealing' and 'good faith' can be met, limitations imposed by the company's constitution on the directors' powers to bind the company or their powers to delegate to others may be disregarded. For example, if the articles limit the power of the directors to borrow to £5m, a bank which lends in excess of that amount to the company is unaffected by the limitation, assuming the bank deals in good faith. Constitutional limitations are found primarily in the company's articles (CA 2006, s 17) but s 40(3) broadens the application of the section to include limitations deriving from a resolution of the company or any class of shareholders, or from any agreement between the members of the company or of any class of shareholders.[67] Such limitations on the powers of the directors do not affect a person dealing with the company in good faith.

8-34   The wording of CA 2006, s 40(1) (see at **8-22**), *the power of the directors*, differs slightly but significantly from its predecessor, CA 1985, s 35A. The 1985 wording referred to constitutional limitations on the power of *the board of directors* which led to debate as to whether requirements such as quorum requirements for a valid board meeting were limitations on the power of the board (and so within the section) or addressed the logically prior question of what constitutes a board of directors (and so were not within the section). A majority in the Court of Appeal in *Smith v Henniker-Major & Co*,[68] obiter, favoured the former view, though the latter view had been favoured at first instance.[69] By removing the reference to 'the board', the wording expands the scope of the section and eliminates, it would seem, any scope for further debate as to whether procedural limitations are included. The section applies to any constitutional limitations on the powers of the directors to bind the company which must include quorum or other procedural requirements as these are matters that limit the powers of the directors to act.[70] The alternative interpretation leaves us with the sort of contorted categorisation of provisions in the articles evident in the judgments in *Smith v*

---

[66] [2006] 1 BCLC 729 at 741, HL.

[67] Resolutions of the company would include either resolutions of the board or the shareholders which addresses a concern raised by Edwards, above n 46, pp 43–4, as to the improper implementation of the First Directive, art 9.

[68] [2002] 2 BCLC 655 at 668, 687.

[69] See [2002] BCC 544 where Rimer J had concluded that, as the board was inquorate, there was no act of the board to which CA 1985, s 35A might apply.

[70] See *TCB Ltd v Gray* [1986] 1 All ER 587 at 597 where Browne-Wilkinson V-C thought that any provision in the articles as to the manner in which the directors can act as agents of the company (such as rules governing the affixing of the company seal) is a limitation on their power to bind the company.

Henniker-Major & Co[71] ('constitutional limitations', 'procedural requirements' and 'nullities'). Rather than indulge in such debate, it is preferable to adopt a generous approach to the section and the protection of third parties in line with the purpose of the First Directive.[72]

The wording of CA 2006, s 40 (see **8-22**) also raises a question which had arisen under **8-35** a previous version of the provision,[73] namely as to the meaning of 'directors' in this context. Having changed the wording from the 'board of directors' to 'directors', it is clear that the section covers acts of the board and of any director authorised (in the sense of having actual authority to bind the company) to represent the company.[74] Support for interpreting 'directors' in accordance with that approach can be found in *Criterion Properties plc v Stratford UK Properties LLC*[75] which concerned the authority of two of the directors and the court accepted that CA 1985, s 35A (now CA 2006, s 40) might be relevant and in *Wrexham AFC Ltd v Crucialmove Ltd*[76] which concerned a company chairman and a managing director and where again the court considered s 35A to be relevant. In *International Sales & Agencies Ltd v Marcus*[77] too the court was content to apply the protection to someone who dealt with a sole effective director to whom all actual authority to act for the company had been delegated.

The result is a statutory provision which increases significantly the security of third **8-36** parties dealing with the company though, as noted at **8-23**, CA 2006, s 41 operates to prevent directors and connected persons relying on the protection of s 40. The other side of the coin is that it diminishes what little control is retained by the shareholders who are denied the option of disowning unauthorised transactions. But the shareholders are not entirely powerless and, as noted, a third party on inquiry as to an improper purpose is not protected so a balance is struck between commercial certainty and shareholder protection.

Possible redress for shareholders

A member may obtain an injunction to restrain 'the doing of an act which is beyond **8-37** the powers of the directors although no such proceeding may lie in respect of an act to be done in fulfilment of a legal obligation arising from a previous act of the company' (CA 2006, s 40(4)). An injunction cannot be obtained, therefore, to restrain the execution of an executory contract. Given that s 40 prevents the shareholders from disowning an unauthorised transaction, it might be thought that shareholders have an incentive to monitor the conduct of the directors in order to prevent such transactions by injunctive relief. The practical difficulties of doing this, and the natural inertia

---

[71] [2002] 2 BCLC 655 at 668, 687.   [72] See Payne & Prentice, and above n 5, pp 457–8.

[73] I.e. under s 9 of the European Communities Act 1972 which referred to decisions of the directors: see Farrar & Powles (1973) MLR 270; Collier & Sealy (1973) CLJ 1.

[74] To be within the section, the directors must have actual (express or implied) authority to bind the company since the purpose of the provision is to prevent limits imposed on an existing authority from affecting a third party. See Edwards, *EC Company Law* (1999), pp 43–4.

[75] [2006] 1 BCLC 729 at 740, HL.   [76] [2008] 1 BCLC 508 at 523.

[77] [1982] 3 All ER 551 at 560.

of many shareholders, mean that this is unlikely to occur. In practice the members simply never find out about transactions in time to seek injunctive relief.

8-38   A director who acts without authority is in breach of the fiduciary duty imposed by CA 2006, s 171(a) to act in accordance with the constitution and he is liable to account for any profit made and to indemnify the company for any loss suffered. An unauthorised transaction is void so, for example, in *EIC Services Ltd v Phipps*[78] the board's failure to observe the requirements of the articles governing the issue of bonus shares meant that the issue was void. In *Guinness plc v Saunders*[79] a committee of the board purported to award remuneration to an individual director when it had no power to do so under the articles. The contract in question was void for want of authority. A third party (where not protected by the statute or agency law) is required to account for benefits received under a void contract and so the company was entitled to recover £5.2m received by the director on the ground of a total failure of consideration.

8-39   It is open to the board or the shareholders, as appropriate, subsequently to affirm or adopt an unauthorised transaction entered into in circumstances in which there is a want of authority.[80] Whether the shareholders wish to exempt a director from any liability for breach of fiduciary duty is a separate matter and the limits to the shareholders' powers to ratify breaches of duty are discussed in Chapter 18.

8-40   That the director is liable for breach of duty is confirmed by CA 2006, s 40(5) which provides that the protection afforded by s 40(1) does not affect any liability incurred by the directors, or any other person, by reason of the directors exceeding their powers. Likewise, a third party may be liable to account for any benefits received on the basis of involvement in a breach of duty by the director. In *International Sales and Agencies Ltd v Marcus*[81] Lawson J considered the European Communities Act 1972 (ECA 1972), s 9 (an earlier version of CA 2006, s 40) and decided that liability as a constructive trustee can arise separately from and distinct from the statute. In that case, company money had been paid by a director to third parties to repay personal debts of a deceased shareholder in breach of the director's fiduciary duty as a trustee of the company's money. The recipients knew that the money received came from the company's accounts and not from the estate of the deceased. On an action being brought by the company against the recipients to recover the money, Lawson J dismissed an argument that the recipients were within ECA 1972, s 9(1) and were not liable. The statutory provision, he said, did not affect the principles of constructive trust in relation to the recipients of company money knowingly paid in breach of trust.[82] The statutory purpose, he said, was to protect innocent parties who entered into transactions which the companies might otherwise seek to avoid but the statute did not affect the operation of a constructive trust if

---

[78] [2004] 2 BCLC 589.

[79] [1990] BCLC 402, HL. See also *Clark v Cutland* [2003] 2 BCLC 393, CA.

[80] An act in excess of the board's authority can be affirmed or adopted by an ordinary resolution even though an alteration to the board's powers for all time would require a special resolution: *Irvine v Union Bank of Australia* (1877) 2 App Cas 366, PC; *Grant v United Kingdom Switchback Railways Co* (1888) 40 Ch D 135, CA.

[81] [1982] 3 All ER 551.   [82] [1982] 3 All ER 551 at 559–60.

the facts gave rise to such a trust.[83] In any event, as already noted, a third party who knows or is put on inquiry as to an improper purpose and who fails to inquire cannot rely on the statutory protection. The improper purpose renders the transaction void and the third party is liable to account for any benefits obtained under the void transaction (see **8-38**), so there is no need to look for constructive trust liability.

The indoor management rule

In addition to the protection afforded by apparent authority and the CA 2006, s 40, a third party may look to the common law rule in *Royal British Bank v Turquand*[84] which provides that persons dealing with a company are not obliged to inquire into the internal proceedings of a company but can assume that all acts of internal management had been properly carried out, save where an outsider knows or is put on inquiry as to the failure to adhere to procedures.[85] Insiders, i.e. persons holding positions within the company, are prevented from relying on the rule as they are in a position to know whether there has been compliance with the internal requirements.[86]   **8-41**

In *Royal British Bank v Turquand*[87] the board of directors had borrowed money without having the transaction authorised by a resolution of the company in general meeting as required by the deed of settlement (i.e. their articles). The court held that the company was bound by the borrowing as the resolution was a matter of internal management which the third party could assume had been correctly carried out.[88] In *Mahony v East Holyford Mining Co*[89] a bank was entitled to accept cheques drawn and signed by the directors in the manner authorised by the articles and was not obliged to query whether the individuals signing the cheques were validly appointed as directors.   **8-42**

The question is whether any role remains for the rule in *Turquand's* case in the light of CA 2006, s 40 and other sections, such as s 161 precluding challenges to the acts of a   **8-43**

---

[83] A position reinforced by *Cooperatieve Rabobank 'Vecht en Plassengebied' BA v Minderhoud* [1998] 2 BCLC 507, ECJ where the court agreed that the provisions of the First Company Law Directive (which are reflected in CA 2006, s 40) are intended to protect innocent parties dealing with the company but they do not prevent the application of national laws on matters such as conflicts of interests to any agreement purportedly entered into by a company. See also Edwards, *EC Company Law* (1999), Ch 1 at pp 38–9.

[84] (1856) 6 E & B 327.

[85] *B Liggett (Liverpool) Ltd v Barclays Bank Ltd* [1928] 1 KB 48; *Morris v Kanssen* [1946] 1 All ER 586, HL; *Rolled Steel Products (Holdings) Ltd v British Steel Corpn* [1985] 3 All ER 52, CA; *Wrexham AFC Ltd v Crucialmove Ltd* [2008] 1 BCLC 508 at 523, CA.

[86] *Morris v Kanssen* [1946] 1 All ER 586, HL; *Howard v Patent Ivory Manufacturing Co* (1888) 38 Ch D 156; cf *Hely-Hutchinson v Brayhead Ltd* [1967] 3 All ER 98. A further refinement to the rule is that it does not apply if the document which the outsider seeks to rely on is a forgery although this limitation is criticised: see *Ruben v Great Fingall Consolidated* [1906] AC 439, HL; also *Kreditbank Cassel GmbH v Schenkers Ltd* [1927] 1 KB 826, CA.

[87] (1856) 6 E & B 327.

[88] The court noted that the party here, on reading the deed of settlement, would find not a prohibition from borrowing but a permission to do so on certain conditions. Finding that the authority might be made complete by a resolution, he would have a right to infer the fact of a resolution authorising that which on the face of the document appeared to be legitimately done.

[89] (1875) LR 7 HL 869.

director on the basis of a defect in his appointment. For example, the situation in *Royal British Bank v Turquand*[90] itself would now be within s 40 as it involved a limitation on the board's authority to act. The scope of CA 2006, s 40 is broader in that it applies to any constitutional limitation on the powers of the directors whereas the rule in *Turquand* is limited to internal procedural irregularities. The circumstances in which the protection of the section and of the rule are lost are similar (party is put on inquiry and fails to inquire) but it may be possible to resort to the rule where a third party cannot bring themselves within the thresholds set by CA 2006, s 40 (for example, as to 'dealing with the company') though insiders are precluded from relying on the rule. All of which makes it difficult to envisage circumstances in which it would still be necessary to have recourse to the rule. It might conceivably be of some assistance with respect to reliance on the apparent authority of an individual director, but it does not enable a party to hold the company to an unauthorised transaction entered into by a director. It allows a third party to assume that a transaction within the authority of the directors has been properly carried out, but it requires the third party to establish the fact of authority, actual or apparent, in the first place.

E Exercise of a power for an improper purpose

8-44 The duty to exercise a power for the purposes for which it is conferred, set out in CA 2006, s 171(b) (see **8-1**), applies to the exercise by the directors of any of their powers, be it the power to make allotments of shares;[91] to make calls on shares;[92] to refuse to register share transfers;[93] to order the forfeiture of shares;[94] to alienate the property of the company;[95] to expel a member;[96] to enter into agreements with third parties.[97] The wider the power conferred, the more difficult it may be to restrain the directors,[98] but the duty brings an objective measure of control to the exercise of a power in contrast to s 172 which, as discussed in Chapter 9, is primarily subjective (a director must act in the way he considers, in good faith, is most likely to promote the success of the company for the benefit of the members as a whole).

---

[90] (1856) 6 E & B 327.

[91] See *Punt v Symons & Co Ltd* [1903] 2 Ch 506; *Piercy v S Mills & Co Ltd* [1920] 1 Ch 77; *Hogg v Cramphorn Ltd* [1966] 3 All ER 420; *Bamford v Bamford* [1969] 1 All ER 969; *Howard Smith Ltd v Ampol Petroleum Ltd* [1974] 1 All ER 1126.

[92] *Galloway v Halle Concerts Society* [1915] 2 Ch 233; *Alexander v Automatic Telegraph Co* [1900] 2 Ch 56.

[93] *Re Smith & Fawcett Ltd* [1942] 1 All ER 542; *Re Bede Steam Shipping Co Ltd* [1917] 1 Ch 123.

[94] *Re Agriculturalist Cattle Insurance Co, Stanhope's Case* (1866) 1 Ch App 161.

[95] See *Bishopsgate Investment Management Ltd v Maxwell* [1993] BCLC 1282.

[96] See *Gaiman v National Association for Mental Health* [1970] 2 All ER 362; noted Prentice (1970) 33 MLR 700.

[97] See *Lee Panavision Ltd v Lee Lighting Ltd* [1992] BCLC 22, CA.

[98] See *Re Smith & Fawcett Ltd* [1942] 1 All ER 542; *Gaiman v National Association for Mental Health* [1970] 2 All ER 362, noted Prentice (1970) 33 MLR 700.

The substantial purpose for exercise

The leading authority on the proper purpose duty is the Privy Council decision in   **8-45**
Howard Smith Ltd v Ampol Petroleum Ltd.[99] The leading speech was given by Lord
Wilberforce who explained that the proper approach to an exercise of a power is:[100]

> '... to start with a consideration of the power whose exercise is in question.... Having
> ascertained, on a fair view, the nature of this power, and having defined as can best
> be done in the light of modern conditions the, or some, limits within which it may be
> exercised, it is then necessary for the court, if a particular exercise of it is challenged, to
> examine the substantial purpose for which it was exercised, and to reach a conclusion
> whether that purpose was proper or not.'

The first step is to construe the article conferring the power in order to ascertain the   **8-46**
nature of the power and the limits within which it may be exercised. In theory, the
article could be limitless, permitting the exercise of the power in question for any
purpose,[101] but even an apparently limitless power is inherently limited by a need to
exercise it in order to promote the success of the company.

Having established the limits, if any, to the power, the second step is to determine the   **8-47**
substantial purpose or purposes for which it was exercised. This is not always easy to
decide and may involve a detailed examination of the facts. Here Lord Wilberforce
noted that:[102]

> '... the court ... is entitled to look at the situation objectively in order to estimate how
> critical or pressing, or substantial or, per contra, insubstantial an alleged requirement
> may have been. If it finds that a particular requirement, though real, was not urgent, or
> critical, at the relevant time, it may have reason to doubt, or discount, the assertions of
> individuals that they acted solely in order to deal with it, particularly when the action
> they took was unusual or even extreme.'

In keeping with the reluctance of the judiciary to review the business decisions of dir-   **8-48**
ectors, Lord Wilberforce accepted that there are difficulties of proof here which will
require crediting the bona fide opinion of the directors, if such is found to exist, and
respecting their judgement as to matters of management.[103] Having done so, he went
on, the ultimate conclusion must be as to the side of a fairly broad line on which the
case falls.[104]

Having carried out this exercise and identified the actual purpose for which the   **8-49**
power was exercised, that actual purpose then has to be measured against the range
of permissible purposes for the exercise of that power, as indicated by the articles or
ascertained by the court, in order to decide whether that actual exercise was proper.
Provided that the substantial purpose for which the power was exercised is a proper

---

[99] [1974] AC 821, PC.   [100] [1974] AC 821 at 835.

[101] See *Re Smith & Fawcett Ltd* [1942] 1 All ER 542 at 545, per Lord Greene; also Prentice (1970) 33
MLR 700.

[102] *Howard Smith Ltd v Ampol Petroleum Ltd* [1974] AC 821 at 832.

[103] [1974] AC 821 at 832.   [104] [1974] AC 821 at 835.

purpose, the exercise of the power is not invalidated by the presence of some other improper, but insubstantial, purpose. For example, some incidental benefit obtained by a director does not invalidate the exercise of the power unless his self-interest was the substantial purpose for the exercise of the power.[105] Equally, if the substantial purpose was improper, a director's honest belief that he was acting in the interests of the company is insufficient to validate the exercise of the power.[106]

8-50   Returning to the facts in *Howard Smith Ltd v Ampol Petroleum Ltd*,[107] the case concerned a takeover battle for a company where the directors favoured a particular bidder and made an allotment of shares to that bidder with a view to diluting the holdings of the potential rival bidders (who were the existing majority shareholders) for the company. The Privy Council agreed with the trial judge that, although the directors had acted honestly, it was unconstitutional for the directors to use their fiduciary powers over the shares in the company for the purpose of destroying an existing majority or creating a new majority. As the directors' primary objective was to alter the majority shareholding, the directors had improperly exercised their powers and the allotment was invalid.

8-51   The Privy Council did accept in *Howard Smith Ltd v Ampol Petroleum Ltd*[108] that, as far as a power to allot shares is concerned, that power is not restricted to cases where the company requires additional capital. Such a power may be used (unless the articles otherwise provide) to foster business connections,[109] to ensure that the company has the requisite number of shareholders to exercise its statutory functions[110] and to reach the best commercial agreement for the company, even if this has the effect of defeating a takeover bid.[111]

8-52   As is clear from *Howard Smith Ltd v Ampol Petroleum Ltd*[112] the courts are alert to attempts by the directors to manipulate the control of the company by the improper exercise of the power to allot shares and this case is but one of a long line of authorities on this issue. In *Punt v Symons & Co Ltd*[113] an injunction was granted to prevent the company from holding a meeting when an improper allotment had been made for the purpose of securing the passing of a resolution at that meeting; in *Piercy v S Mills & Co Ltd*[114] an allotment made for the purpose of destroying the voting control of the

---

[105] *Ngurli v McCann* (1954) 90 CLR 425 at 440; *Mills v Mills* (1938) 60 CLR 150 at 164–5; *Hirsche v Sims* [1894] AC 654 at 660–1. See also *Whitehouse v Carlton Hotel Pty Ltd* (1987) 5 ACLC 421 at 427 where the Australian High Court added the refinement that where there are competing permissible and impermissible purposes, the preferable view is that regardless of whether the impermissible purpose was the dominant one or but one of a number of significant contributing causes, an allotment will be invalidated if the impermissible purpose was causative in the sense that but for its presence the power would not have been exercised (citing Dixon J in *Mills v Mills* (1938) 60 CLR 150).

[106] *Howard Smith Ltd v Ampol Petroleum Ltd* [1974] AC 821; *Re a company, ex p Glossop* [1988] BCLC 570 at 577; *Lee Panavision Ltd v Lee Lighting Ltd* [1992] BCLC 22 at 31; *Extrasure Travel Insurances Ltd v Scattergood* [2003] 1 BCLC 598 at 619.

[107] [1974] AC 821.   [108] [1974] AC 821 at 835.

[109] See *Harlowe's Nominees Pty Ltd v Woodside Oil Co* (1968) 121 CLR 483, H Ct Aust.

[110] See *Punt v Symons & Co Ltd* [1903] 2 Ch 506.

[111] See *Teck Corpn Ltd v Millar* (1972) 33 DLR (3d) 288, S Ct BC; noted Ziegel [1974] JBL 85.

[112] [1974] AC 821.   [113] [1903] 2 Ch 506.   [114] [1920] 1 Ch 77.

existing majority shareholders was held to be invalid; in *Hogg v Cramphorn Ltd*[115] an allotment was invalid where its primary purpose was to ensure control of the company by the directors and their supporters; likewise in *Bamford v Bamford*[116] an allotment was invalid when made with an eye primarily on the exigencies of a takeover and not with a single eye to the benefit of the company.[117]

It should be noted that, in addition to the constraints imposed by CA 2006, s 171, **8-53** improper allotments of shares to manipulate the control position within a company are constrained by statutory requirements (see **19-30** et seq). Directors must have authority to allot either via the articles or by resolution (s 551) and generally allotments must be on a rights basis subject to certain exceptions, exclusions and disapplications.[118] The CA 2006 does allow directors of a private company with one class of shares to allot shares without shareholder approval (s 550), a power which is potentially open to abuse as the cases above illustrate, but the requirement for a rights issue remains, subject to the statutory exceptions. Further, shareholders can challenge allotments as being unfairly prejudicial conduct under CA 2006, s 994[119] (the unfairly prejudicial jurisdiction is discussed in Chapter 17). In larger public companies, the directors' ability to manipulate control in takeover situations is subject also to the constraints imposed on defensive actions by incumbent management by the Takeover Code (see discussion in Chapter 26).

As noted above, the duty to exercise a power for the purposes for which it is conferred **8-54** applies to all the powers which directors possess and is not limited to the exercise of the power to allot shares. In *Extrasure Travel Insurances Ltd v Scattergood*,[120] for example, two directors transferred funds from the company to another company in the group in order to meet the demands of a pressing creditor of that other company. Applying *Howard Smith v Ampol*, the court concluded that:[121]

- the power in question was the directors' ability to deal with the assets of the company in the course of trading;
- the purpose for which that power was conferred on the directors was broadly to protect the company's survival and to promote its commercial interests in accordance with its objects;
- the substantial purpose for which the power was actually exercised was to enable the recipient company to meet its liabilities and not to preserve the transferor company;
- it followed that the purpose for which the transfer was made was plainly improper.

---

[115] [1966] 3 All ER 420.   [116] [1970] Ch 212.

[117] See *Dalby v Bodilly* [2005] BCC 627 where an allotment made by the company's sole director and 50% shareholder which had the effect of diluting the other 50% shareholder to a 5% shareholder was held to be the plainest possible breach by the director of his fiduciary duty.

[118] A rights issue requires that shares are offered to existing shareholders in proportion to their existing holdings; the mechanics of rights issues are discussed at **19-36**.

[119] See, for example, *Dalby v Bodilly* [2005] BCC 627, above n 117.

[120] [2003] 1 BCLC 598.   [121] [2003] 1 BCLC 598 at 633.

8-55   In *Lee Panavision Ltd v Lee Lighting Ltd*[122] the court found that it was unconstitutional and beyond the powers of outgoing directors, however much they thought it in the company's interests, to commit the company to a management agreement with a third party (with whom the outgoing directors were closely associated) which would have deprived the incoming directors of all management powers. In *Bishopsgate Investment Ltd v Maxwell (No 2)*[123] the court found a director in breach of his fiduciary duty when he gave away the company's assets for no consideration to a private family company of which he was a director. This was an exercise of the power to alienate property of the company for an improper purpose and the director was liable to indemnify the company for its loss.[124]

8-56   The criticism levied at these authorities is that the courts are imposing limits on powers which have not been so limited, either expressly or impliedly, by the shareholders (see **8-5**: the articles commonly grant all powers to the directors without limit) and that the courts are using this doctrine to do what they consistently say they do not do, namely review business decisions reached by the directors. Of course, there is an element of the courts reviewing business decisions according to their perception of the standards expected of a fiduciary office holder,[125] reflecting in essence objective judgements as to the conduct expected of directors,[126] but the approach is not unduly interventionist[127] and it has to be set against the more subjective test in CA 2006, s 172. It is useful to contrast the approach in *Extrasure Travel Insurances Ltd v Scattergood*,[128] and in *CAS (Nominees) Ltd v Nottingham Forest FC plc*.[129] In *Extrasure*, see **8-54**, the directors allowed company funds to be transferred away to assist companies with which the directors were connected and which were in financial difficulty. The directors had no regard to the company's interests (or its creditors) in so acting and they were held liable.

8-57   In *CAS (Nominees) Ltd v Nottingham Forest FC plc*[130] the directors had a choice as to whether to sell shares in a subsidiary direct to an outsider in order to raise much needed funds for the subsidiary or to raise funds via the parent company shareholders. This was not a case where there was an issue as to diluting the existing shareholders' interests, as was the scenario in the cases discussed at **8-52**. Instead a good faith business decision was taken to sell shares directly to an outsider and bypass the shareholders in the parent company. The shareholders argued that the board had exercised its powers for an improper purpose. The court dismissed the shareholders' petition finding that the directors were exercising their powers of management of the business (in this case managing an asset, the investment in the subsidiary) and, given a genuine

---

[122] [1992] BCLC 22 at 30.   [123] [1993] BCLC 1282.   [124] [1993] BCLC 1282 at 1286.

[125] See Nolan, 'The Proper Purpose Doctrine and Company Directors' in Rider (ed), *The Realm of Company Law* (1998), pp 20–2.

[126] See Sealy, '"Bona Fides" and "Proper Purposes" in Corporate Decisions' (1989) 15 Mon ULR 265 at 276: 'the courts are in truth making naked value judgments'; and see Sealy, 'Directors' Duties Revisited' (2001) Co Law 79 at 82.

[127] See Lord Wilberforce in *Howard Smith Ltd v Ampol Petroleum Ltd* [1974] AC 821 at 832 cautioning against second-guessing the business judgment of directors.

[128] [2003] 1 BCLC 598.   [129] [2002] 1 BCLC 613.   [130] [2002] 1 BCLC 613.

desire to raise capital, they had not exercised their powers to manage for a purpose foreign to their proper ambit. At issue ultimately was a business choice as to how to solve a funding problem in a subsidiary. In the absence of a breach of any statutory requirements or bad faith on the part of the directors, the court was content to let their business judgment stand.

Consequences of exercise for improper purpose

As a matter of agency law, it is clear that 'subject to a contrary agreement, an agent only **8-58** has authority to act for the benefit of the principal'.[131] A failure so to act negates any actual authority and the transaction is void as regards the principal.[132] The exercise by a director (the agent) of a power for an improper purpose is clearly not for the benefit of the company (the principal) and so negates the director's actual authority to act. A third party can still rely on the agent's apparent authority, but the ability to do so is lost if the third party knows or is put on inquiry as to the exercise of the power for an improper purpose.[133]

These issues were central to the House of Lords decision in *Criterion Properties plc v* **8-59** *Stratford UK Properties LLC*.[134] The question was whether a managing director of a company and another director could commit the company to an arrangement known as a poison pill (which has the effect of warding off takeover bidders and deterring them from making a bid to shareholders) which in this case was drafted in extremely wide and onerous terms but which was beneficial to the directors concerned. There had been considerable confusion in the lower courts as to the proper approach to this issue,[135] but their Lordships were resolutely clear that the matter is one of agency law.[136] The issue which needed to be resolved was whether the directors had actual or apparent authority to enter into such an arrangement, a factual matter which was remitted to trial. Lord Scott explained the position succinctly:

> '... if a person dealing with an agent knows or has reason to believe that the contract or transaction is contrary to the commercial interests of the agent's principal, it is likely to be very difficult for the person to assert with any credibility that he believed the agent did have actual authority. Lack of such belief would be fatal to a claim that the agent had apparent authority.'

---

[131] See *Bowstead and Reynolds on Agency* (18th edn, 2006), para 3-008; *Hopkins v TL Dallas Group Ltd* [2005] 1 BCLC 543 at 572; see *Criterion Properties plc v Stratford UK Properties LLC* [2006] 1 BCLC 729 at 741.

[132] See *Bowstead and Reynolds on Agency* (18th edn, 2006), para 3-008; *Hopkins v TL Dallas Group Ltd* [2005] 1 BCLC 543 at 573; see *Criterion Properties plc v Stratford UK Properties LLC* [2006] 1 BCLC 729 at 741.

[133] *Rolled Steel Products (Holdings) Ltd v British Steel Corpn* [1985] 3 All ER 52, CA.

[134] [2006] 1 BCLC 729, HL.

[135] See [2003] 2 BCLC 129, CA, [2002] 2 BCLC 151, Ch D. In error, the lower courts had approached the matter essentially on the basis of the unconscionability of the conduct of the third party and issues of 'knowing receipt', see [2006] 1 BCLC 729 at 739, HL, a 'faulty elision of the issues' as Lord Nicholls commented (at 732).

[136] [2006] 1 BCLC 729 at 740.

8-60   Further, as *Wrexham AFC Ltd v Crucialmove Ltd*[137] makes clear, the third party in this situation is equally unable to rely on CA 2006, s 40 because the section imposes the same duty to inquire as agency law.[138] In this case (the facts are given at **8-19**), the third party knew that the director executing a particular agreement was in breach of his fiduciary duties to the company. In those circumstances, the third party was bound to inquire whether the transaction had been authorised or approved by the company or its board. Given he was on notice and had failed to inquire, the Court of Appeal held that the third party could not rely as a matter of agency law on any apparent authority of the director and nor could he rely on CA 2006, s 40 for the statutory provision, the court said, does not absolve a person dealing with the company from any duty to inquire when the circumstances are such as to put that person on inquiry.[139] Where the third party knows or is put on inquiry as to the improper purpose and fails to inquire, the outcome is the same under agency law or the Companies Act. The third party is not protected and if in receipt of assets/benefits under the contract must account for them,[140] for the transaction is void and the company is not bound.[141] A third party who is not aware and is not put on inquiry as to an improper purpose is able to hold the company to the transaction relying on the apparent authority of the directors to act in the way they have (assuming there are no other problems with the transaction).

8-61   It is open to the shareholders to affirm a transaction though entered into for an improper purpose, provided the transaction is not open to challenge on other grounds. Here it is necessary to consider *Bamford v Bamford*[142] where the Court of Appeal decided that an exercise of powers for an improper purpose (in that case an allotment of shares made to manipulate control within the company) was voidable and open to ratification by the shareholders by ordinary resolution. That decision looks to be wrong now, given that an improper purpose negates any authority to act so there is nothing for the shareholders to ratify (as indeed Plowman J considered at first instance in *Bamford* before being overruled by the Court of Appeal).[143] Actually, *Bamford* is still correct, even if the language of voidability is wrong. As discussed above, the exercise of a power

---

[137] [2008] 1 BCLC 508, CA.

[138] It is arguable that CA 2006, s 40 has no application here as it deals only with constitutional limitations on an authority which the director otherwise possesses (as discussed at **8-34** et seq) and does not apply to an exercise of power for an improper purpose. But, even if the exercise of a power for an improper purpose can be classed as a constitutional limitation (and s 171 might support that argument) the position is the same whether or not s 40 applies. A third party put on inquiry with respect to the exercise of a power for an improper purpose and who fails to inquire cannot rely on either apparent authority or the statute for protection.   [139] [2008] 1 BCLC 508 at 523–4.

[140] See *Guinness v Saunders* [1990] BCLC 402, HL; and see *Criterion Properties plc v Stratford UK Properties LLC* [2006] 1 BCLC 729 at 732, HL; *Rolled Steel Products (Holdings) Ltd v British Steel Corpn* [1985] 3 All ER 52, CA.

[141] *Rolled Steel Products (Holdings) Ltd v British Steel Corpn* [1985] 3 All ER 52, CA.

[142] [1969] 1 All ER 969, CA.

[143] See also *Hogg v Cramphorn* [1967] Ch 254. See Nolan, 'The Proper Purpose Doctrine and Company Directors' in Rider (ed), *The Realm of Company Law* (1998), p 32 who comments that there is no good reason why a majority of shareholders should be able to ratify a colourable allotment of shares, while also noting that *Hogg* and *Bamford* are out of line with earlier authorities that an exercise of a power for an improper purpose is void: see *Punt v Symons & Co Ltd* [1903] 2 Ch 506; *Piercy v S Mills & Co Ltd* [1920] 1 Ch 77.

for an improper purpose renders the transaction void in the sense that the directors have no authority to enter into it. A transaction void for want of authority can be subsequently authorised or affirmed by the shareholders as a matter of ordinary agency law. This is an affirmation of an exercise of a power not a ratification of the director's breach of duty which remains a separate matter (though shareholders can ratify a good faith exercise of power for an improper purpose as in *Bamford*). The limits to ratification are considered in Chapter 18.

As a breach of a director's duty under CA 2006, s 171(b), a director is liable to account **8-62** for any gain and to indemnify the company for any loss caused by the exercise of the power for an improper purpose (where the shareholders choose not to ratify the breach of duty)[144] and, in an appropriate case, the exercise of powers for an improper purpose is evidence of unfitness justifying disqualification.[145]

F Summary

Where a director acts in breach of a constitutional limitation on his authority (i.e. a want **8-63** of authority to act), the director is in breach of the fiduciary duty laid down in CA 2006, s 171(a) and liable to account for any gain and to indemnify the company for loss suffered. The transaction is void, but a third party can hold the company to the transaction on the basis of apparent authority (as a matter of agency law) provided the third party is not aware and is not put on inquiry as to the lack of authority to act and his protection in this regard is greatly enhanced by s 40 which he can rely on even when knowing of a lack of authority. This problem of lack of authority is resolved therefore either by agency law or the statutory protection. But in either case, the third party loses protection if he knows or is put on inquiry and fails to inquire (remembering that knowledge of a lack of authority is not sufficient to put him on inquiry for the purposes of s 40).

Where a director has authority to act in respect of a particular matter, but exercises the **8-64** power to act for an improper purpose, the director is in breach of the fiduciary duty laid down in CA 2006, s 171(b) and liable to account for any gain and to indemnify the company for loss suffered. The transaction is void (the director has no actual authority to act for an improper purpose), but a third party can rely on apparent authority and hold the company to the transaction provided he is not aware of the improper purpose and is not put on inquiry by the circumstances of the transaction as to the actual authority of the director to so act. This problem of improper purpose is primarily a matter for agency law. But a third party who knows or is put on inquiry as to an improper purpose and who fails to inquire cannot rely on actual or apparent authority, nor on s 40 (for the fact that he has been put on inquiry will also operate to rebut the presumption of good faith).

---

[144] See *Bishopsgate Investment Ltd v Maxwell (No 2)* [1993] BCLC 1282; also *Extrasure Travel Insurances Ltd v Scattergood* [2003] 1 BCLC 598 at 619.
[145] See, for example, *Re Looe Fish Ltd* [1993] BCLC 1160.

8-65   In either case, given the issue is one of agency law, it is open to the shareholders by ordinary resolution to authorise or adopt the transaction or exercise of the power in question.[146] The question whether the shareholders can and wish to ratify the director's breach of fiduciary duty is a separate matter and the limits to the powers of shareholders to ratify breaches of duty are discussed in Chapter 18, see **18-33**.

8-66   A lack of authority and the exercise of authority for an improper purpose are therefore distinct issues as CA 2006, s 171 makes clear, but there is considerable overlap between them, as explained at **8-29**. Each problem is now resolved in much the same way (subject to some lingering uncertainties as to the application and scope of s 40), bringing much needed coherence to this important aspect of directors' duties.

[146] *Grant v United Kingdom Switchback Railways Co* (1888) 40 Ch D 135; *Irvine v Union Bank of Australia* (1877) 2 App Cas 366.

9

Duty to promote the success of the company

A Introduction

At common law, directors were under a fiduciary duty to act bona fide in what they **9-1** considered to be in the interests of the company, interpreted as meaning in the interests of the shareholders as a general body, balancing the short-term interests of the present members against the long-term interests of future members with shareholders' interests defined primarily in terms of enhancing shareholder value.[1] The courts further developed the duty to include within it a requirement for directors to have regard to the interests of creditors where the company was insolvent or of doubtful solvency.[2] There was also a statutory obligation on directors to 'have regard in the performance of their functions to the interests of the company's employees in general as well as the interests of its members' (CA 1985, s 309). The duty to act bona fide was essentially a subjective test but further control over the directors was imposed at common law by the obligation to exercise their powers for a proper purpose.

The proper purpose doctrine is retained by CA 2006, s 171 which is discussed in **9-2** Chapter 8. The duty to act bona fide has been modified and restated in s 172(1) as a duty to act to promote the success of the company,[3] as follows:

> '(1) A director of a company must act in the way he considers, in good faith, would be most likely to promote the success of the company for the benefit of its members as a whole, and in doing so have regard (amongst other matters) to—
>
> (a) the likely consequences of any decision in the long term,
>
> (b) the interests of the company's employees,
>
> (c) the need to foster the company's business relationships with suppliers, customers and others,
>
> (d) the impact of the company's operations on the community and the environment,

---

[1] *Re Smith & Fawcett Ltd* [1942] Ch 304 at 306; Second Savoy Hotel Investigation, Report of the Inspector (1954) HMSO; *Gaiman v National Association for Mental Health* [1971] Ch 317.

[2] *West Mercia Safetywear Ltd v Dodd* [1988] BCLC 250, CA.

[3] It is qualified by CA 2006, s 247 which permits the directors to act in the interests of employees on the cessation of business, even though such acts are not to promote the success of the company (restating CA 1985, s 719).

(e) the desirability of the company maintaining a reputation for high standards of business conduct, and

(f) the need to act fairly as between members of the company.'

This duty has effect 'subject to any enactment or rule of law requiring directors, in certain circumstances, to consider or act in the interests of creditors of the company' (s 172(3)).

B Duty to act in good faith

9-3   The first point about the duty in CA 2006, s 172(1) is that it is a subjective test. A director must act in the way he considers (not what a court may consider), in good faith, would be most likely to promote the success of the company[4] for the benefit of its members and the duty applies to all acts of a director. The issue here was explained by Jonathan Parker J in *Regentcrest plc v Cohen*[5] as follows:

> 'The question is not whether, viewed objectively by the court, the particular act or omission which is challenged was in fact in the interests of the company; still less is the question whether the court, had it been in the position of the director at the relevant time, might have acted differently. Rather, the question is whether the director honestly believed that his act or omission was in the interests of the company. The issue is as to the director's state of mind.'

9-4   In *Regentcrest plc v Cohen*[6] the directors of a property development company waived a clawback claim (valued at £1.5m) which the company had under an agreement with the vendors of certain property to it. The vendors (S and F) were members of the board of the company and the clawback payment was waived at a meeting which took place 12 days before a petition for winding up the company was presented by a creditor. In return for waiving the claim, S and F undertook to work for the company for no remuneration for a period of years. The interested directors declared their interest and took no part in the proceedings nor did they vote in respect of the resolution to waive the clawback.

9-5   On winding up, the liquidators claimed that the directors who waived the clawback claim had acted in breach of their duty to the company and were liable to make good the loss to the company. It was alleged that the directors did not honestly believe that the waiver was in the interests of the company and that the sole reason for agreeing to it was to protect the vendors (their fellow directors) from liability.

9-6   Applying the subjective approach noted above, the court found that the board had acted bona fide. The decisive consideration in the minds of the directors in agreeing to waive the clawback claim had been the need to maintain a united board, and not to

---

[4] *Re Smith & Fawcett Ltd* [1942] Ch 304 at 306.   [5] [2001] 2 BCLC 80 at 105.
[6] [2001] 2 BCLC 80. See also *Re Welfab Engineers Ltd* [1990] BCLC 833.

create a situation in which two of the directors were being sued by the company and were contesting the claim. The company was in difficult negotiations with its creditors at that time and suing two of its directors would have given rise to the gravest misgivings on the part of anyone concerned in trying to save the company. In voting in favour of the waiver, the court concluded that the directors honestly believed that they were acting in the best interests of the company. Accordingly, the claim for breach of fiduciary duty failed.

This test does give a director considerable leeway—his duty is to act in the way he   **9-7**
considers most likely to promote the success of the company. As the court noted in *Extrasure Travel Insurances Ltd v Scattergood*[7] (discussed at **9-12**):

> 'The fact that his alleged belief was unreasonable may provide evidence that it was not in fact honestly held at the time but, if having considered all the evidence, it appears that the director did honestly believe that he was acting in the best interests of the company, then he is not in breach of his fiduciary duty merely because that belief appears to the trial judge to be unreasonable, or because his actions happen, in the event to cause injury to the company.'

It is important to appreciate that underlying this approach of the courts is the trad-   **9-8**
itional concern that the courts must not get involved in reviewing the exercise of business judgement by the directors and, in particular, must avoid reviewing a situation with the benefit of hindsight.[8] That approach has long been summed up by the famous dictum of Lord Eldon LC in *Carlen v Drury*[9] to the effect that the court is not to be required 'to take the management of every playhouse and brewhouse in the kingdom'. As Lord Wilberforce put it:[10]

> 'There is no appeal on merits from management decisions to courts of law: nor will courts of law assume to act as a kind of supervisory board over decisions within the powers of management honestly arrived at'.

On the other hand, while the test is essentially subjective, there are clearly some limits   **9-9**
to it, and the court will not accept in an unquestioning way a director's assertion that he acted bona fide when the facts might appear to suggest otherwise, bearing in mind Bowen LJ's comments in *Hutton v West Cork Rly Co*[11] to the effect that bona fides cannot be the sole test, for a lunatic may act perfectly bona fide yet perfectly irrationally.

The limits to the subjective test lie along the boundaries of unreasonableness and detri-   **9-10**
ment to the company. The question is whether an intelligent and honest director could in the whole of the circumstances reasonably believe the transaction to be for the benefit of the company.[12] As Jonathan Parker J noted in *Regentcrest plc v Cohen*,[13] where it

---

[7] [2003] 1 BCLC 598 at 619.

[8] See *Regentcrest plc v Cohen* [2001] 2 BCLC 80 at 106–7; also *Facia Footwear Ltd v Hinchcliffe* [1998] 1 BCLC 218 at 228.   [9] (1812) 1 Ves & B 154 at 158.

[10] *Howard Smith Ltd v Ampol Petroleum Ltd* [1974] 1 All ER 1126 at 1131; see also *Burland v Earle* [1902] AC 83 at 93, per Lord Davey.   [11] (1993) 23 Ch D 654 at 671.

[12] *Charterbridge Corp Ltd v Lloyds Bank Ltd* [1969] 2 All ER 1185 at 1194.

[13] [2001] 2 BCLC 80 at 105.

is clear that the act or omission under challenge resulted in substantial detriment to the company, the director will have difficulty in persuading the court that he honestly believed it to be in the company's interest. For example, in *Re Genosyis Technology Management Ltd, Wallach v Secretary of State for Trade and Industry*[14] two directors were disqualified for entering, on behalf of the company, into a settlement agreement with a customer under which the company gave up a claim for €1.25m (which was instead paid to its parent company) and gained a maximum of £166,000. Even if it was accepted that the directors honestly believed this settlement to be in the interests of the company, the court said they had no reasonable grounds for that belief and were in breach of their duties.[15]

9-11   Often the bad faith of the director is relatively evident. In *Neptune (Vehicle Washing Equipment) Ltd v Fitzgerald (No 2)*[16] the court had little difficulty in concluding that a sole director was not acting in the interests of the company, but was acting exclusively to further his own personal interests, when he procured an ex gratia payment to him by the company of £100,000 on termination of his service contract with the company.[17] Likewise, a director who pays away significant sums of the company's money either knowing that the recipient is not entitled to it, or at the very least, without regard to the entitlement of the recipient, cannot be said to have an honest belief that payment was in the interests of the company.[18] Similarly, a director who releases a significant quantity of stock to a customer (who already owes the company money in circumstances where there is no real prospect of recouping it) without prepayment cannot reasonably believe the transaction to be in the interests of the company.[19]

9-12   In *Extrasure Travel Insurances Ltd v Scattergood*[20] the defendant directors caused the company to transfer moneys to another company in the group to enable that company to pay a pressing creditor without any honest belief that the transfer was in the interests of the transferor company. The court found that the directors made the transfer simply because the other company needed the money, the transferor company had the money and the creditor of the other company was pressing. The court dismissed the suggestion that the directors believed the transfer was in the group's interests and therefore beneficial to the company, for the court did not believe that they had actually formed any opinion on that issue at all.[21]

---

[14] [2007] 1 BCLC 208.   [15] [2007] 1 BCLC 208 at 213.

[16] [1995] BCC 1000. Cf *Runciman v Walter Runciman plc* [1992] BCLC 1084 where the court accepted that the directors had acted bona fide and in the interests of the company in extending a director's service contract for five years.

[17] See [1995] BCC 1000 at 1017 for a discussion of the evidence which showed a lack of bona fides on the part of the director which included, for example, the furtive and secretive manner in which he acted and the fact that he knew the shareholders would not have approved the payment.

[18] See *Primlake v Matthews Associates* [2007] 1 BCLC 666 at 731 (de jure director paid out in excess of £800,000 from the company's funds to a de facto director when neither director had an honest belief that the de facto director was entitled to payment).

[19] See *Simtel Communications Ltd v Rebak* [2006] 2 BCLC 571 at 596: 'An intelligent and honest man in the position of the director could not in all the circumstances have reasonably believed that the transaction was for the benefit of the company.'

[20] [2003] 1 BCLC 598.   [21] [2003] 1 BCLC 598 at 632–3.

C The success of the company for the benefit of the members as a whole

The duty in CA 2006, s 172 is expressed in terms of promoting the success of the com-   **9-13**
pany rather than acting in the interests of the company. The success of the company is
a matter for the members to determine; they define the objectives of the company and
then it is for the directors to promote the success of the company in those terms.[22] The
directors will be guided by their business judgment and their knowledge of the nature
and purpose of the company, helped by anything in the company's constitution.[23] In
practice, directors will probably prefer not to have anything specific on this issue in
the articles so as to give them maximum flexibility to determine the direction of the
company's business, safe in the knowledge that the courts will not second-guess their
business judgment.

For most companies, as was acknowledged in the Parliamentary debates, success is   **9-14**
usually defined in terms of a long-term increase in shareholder value reflecting the
economic success of the company,[24] but success may be measured in more limited
terms. For example, where the company is formed to acquire a business or carry out
a joint venture, success is measured against those objectives. Some companies exist
clearly for purposes other than the benefit of the members and s 172(2) envisages that
companies may have a combination of purposes, commercial and altruistic.[25] In those
cases it may be more difficult for the directors to determine the extent to which they
are entitled to promote the success of the company for the benefit of the members, but
that is a matter for them in the exercise of their honest business judgment.[26] Those
wishing to form companies with objectives other than or in addition to increasing
shareholder value, such as charitable ventures, may decide to include objects clauses
in their articles to ensure that the constitution reflects the company's priorities and
so guide the directors as to their duties. A failure to observe those objects will put the
directors in breach of s 171.

Where the company is one of a group, the requirement remains that the directors must   **9-15**
act to promote the success of the company (given that it is a separate legal entity) and
not look solely to the overall interests of the group.[27] It may be, of course, that the most

---

[22] See HL Deb, vol 678, GC258 (6 February 2006).

[23] CA 2006, s 171(a) requires a director to act in accordance with the constitution and the constitution is
broadly defined for the purposes of directors' general duties as including the articles and all binding decisions of the members, whether formal or informal (ss 17, 257), so the directors may have to take into account
ordinary resolutions of the shareholders in determining what can be regarded as 'success' in a particular
company: see HL Deb, vol 678, GC 255–8 (6 February 2006).

[24] See HL Deb, vol 678, GC 258 (6 February 2006).

[25] CA 2006, s 172(2) provides that where or to the extent that the purposes of the company consist of or
include purposes other than the benefit of its members, sub-s (1) has effect as if the reference to promoting
the success of the company for the benefit of its members were to achieving those purposes.

[26] See *Explanatory Notes to the Companies Act 2006*, para 330.

[27] A failure to have regard to the interests of the separate legal entity may be grounds for disqualification: see *Secretary of State for Trade and Industry v Goldberg* [2004] 1 BCLC 597 at 650, 673; *Re Genosyis*

210 DUTY TO PROMOTE THE SUCCESS OF THE COMPANY

effective way to promote the success of the company is to promote the success of the group. For example, it may be appropriate for a subsidiary to provide financial support for the rest of a group, though the group is in financial difficulty, when the continued prosperity and the very existence of the subsidiary may depend on the group remaining in business, as is commonly the case.[28] These group issues are considered in Chapter 3.

9-16   As discussed at **9-1**, at common law the duty was to act bona fide in the interests of the company and it was clear that, for most purposes, this meant the interests of the commercial entity which prevailed over the interests of the then members. It is also long established that where there are different classes of shareholders so decisions may adversely affect the interests of one class and benefit another, the question is not so much one of the interests of the company as one of what is fair as between different classes of shareholders.[29] Indeed, regardless of whether there are different classes as such, directors must act fairly as between different shareholders.[30] The leading authority is *Mutual Life Insurance Co of New York v Rank Organisation Ltd*[31] where the company decided to make an issue of shares to its existing ordinary shareholders excluding any ordinary shareholders from the United States and Canada. The exclusion was imposed in order to avoid the onerous regulatory requirements of those jurisdictions. The excluded shareholders objected but the court concluded that the directors had exercised their powers in good faith in the interests of the company and they had exercised their powers fairly as between the different shareholders. The exclusion of the North American shareholders did not affect their shares nor the rights attached to them and was because of a difficulty resulting only from their own personal situation. The directors honestly believed that raising capital in this way was advantageous to the company and gave a prospect of continuing benefit to all the shareholders. In *Re BSB Holdings Ltd (No 2)*[32] the requirement to act fairly meant that the directors (when undertaking a complex financing agreement) should have considered the effect of the proposals on the different groups of shareholders within the company, but the law does not require the interests of the company to be sacrificed to the particular interests of a group of shareholders.[33]

9-17   The position on these matters has not been altered by CA 2006, s 172. The phrase 'to promote the success of the company for the benefit of the members as a whole' would

---

Technology Management Ltd [2007] 1 BCLC 208; Re Mea Corporation Ltd, Secretary of State for Trade and Industry v Aviss [2007] 1 BCLC 618.

[28] See *Facia Footwear Ltd v Hinchcliffe* [1998] 1 BCLC 218; also *Nicholas v Soundcraft Electronics Ltd* [1993] BCLC 360.

[29] *Mills v Mills* (1938) 60 CLR 150 at 164, per Latham CJ; *Howard Smith Ltd v Ampol Petroleum Ltd* [1974] 1 All ER 1126 at 1134.

[30] *Mutual Life Insurance Co of New York v Rank Organisation Ltd* [1985] BCLC 11; *Re BSB Holdings Ltd (No 2)* [1996] 1 BCLC 155.

[31] [1985] BCLC 11; see also *Re BSB Holdings Ltd (No 2)* [1996] 1 BCLC 155 at 249.

[32] [1996] 1 BCLC 155.

[33] See [1996] 1 BCLC 155 at 251. On the facts, the court concluded that while the directors had failed to act fairly by considering the impact of the proposed scheme on different groups of shareholders, that failure did not amount to unfairly prejudicial conduct for the purposes of CA 1985, s 459 (now CA 2006, s 994).

appear to give greater weight to the interests of the current shareholders than to the commercial entity, but directors must also have regard to the consequences of any decision in the long term which suggests the interests of the commercial entity are as relevant now as they have always been.[34] The need to act fairly between the members is also a specific factor to which the directors must have regard (s 172(1)(f)). Overall, there is nothing to suggest that s 172 is intended to alter the balance between the competing 'entity' and 'membership' interests which has already been established at common law.

D Having regard to various factors

One of the most controversial elements of CA 2006, s 172 is the list of factors in s 172(1)   **9-18** (a)–(f) to which a director must have regard (amongst other matters) when acting in the way he considers, in good faith, would be most likely to promote the success of the company for the benefit of the members as a whole.

Background—the pluralist debate

The issue for the Company Law Review (CLR) was whether directors should be   **9-19** required to adopt a more inclusive approach and consider the interests not just of the company's shareholders, employees and creditors, but broader constituencies such as its suppliers, customers, and the community at large.[35] The CLR defined the issue as one of the scope of the company law, meaning for what purposes and in whose interests should companies be run, which for the CLR essentially involved a choice between the enlightened shareholder value and the pluralist approaches.[36]

The enlightened shareholder value approach is based on the idea that maximising   **9-20** shareholder value is in principle the best means of securing overall prosperity.[37] The pluralist approach is based on the idea that a company should serve a wider range of interests not subordinate to, or as a means of achieving, shareholder value, but as valid in their own right, i.e. the interests of a number of groups should be advanced without the interests of a single group (shareholders) prevailing.[38] This approach would enable, and indeed require, the directors to override shareholders' interests in circumstances where this would be in the interests of the company as widely defined by these stakeholders.

---

[34] See generally, Keay, 'Ascertaining the Corporate Objective: An Entity Maximisation and Sustainability Model' (2008) 71 MLR 663.

[35] See Goldenberg, 'Shareholders v Stakeholders: The Bogus Argument' (1998) 19 Co Law 34; Plender, *A Stake in the Future: the Stakeholding Solution* (1997); RSA Inquiry, *Tomorrow's Company* (1995); Parkinson, *Corporate Power and Responsibility* (1993) Ch 9.

[36] Company Law Review, *Completing the Structure* (2000), para 3.1; also *Strategic Framework* (1999), Ch 5; *Developing the Framework* (2000), Chs 2 and 3; *Completing the Structure* (2000), Ch 3.

[37] Company Law Review, *Strategic Framework* (1999), para 5.1.11.

[38] Company Law Review, *Strategic Framework* (1999), paras 5.1.12–5.1.13.

9-21   As the enlightened shareholder value approach is essentially the status quo, the argument for the CLR centred on whether the pluralist approach should be adopted. Following consultation, the CLR found that there were strong philosophical arguments against such an approach on the grounds that:

- it would not necessarily achieve its objective and would have the effect of leaving the directors with a broad (and largely unpoliced) managerial discretion;

- it was unnecessary since broader interests such as employees and creditors are included within the range of interests to which directors have to have regard at common law and it would suffice simply to clarify the legal position;

- the pluralist approach would achieve external benefits through company law which are better served by specific legislation applicable to all businesses (and not just registered companies) on planning, environmental and competition law, etc;

- there was a risk that the pluralist approach (by diluting the obligation owed to shareholders) would enable directors to frustrate takeovers against the wishes of the shareholders and so distort the operation of the market for corporate control which is an important mechanism in holding directors to account.[39]

9-22   More generally, there were concerns that any alteration to a pluralist approach would turn directors away from business decision makers into moral, political and economic arbiters.[40]

9-23   A number of technical difficulties with the pluralist approach were also identified including:[41]

- the need to decide which interest should prevail if there was a conflict;

- the need to frame directors' duties differently to take account of the shift in approach;

- the need to alter board composition to reflect the differing interests;

- the need to rethink the division of power between the board and the general meeting as well as the ability of one interest group (the shareholders) to appoint and remove the board; and

- the proper approach to the enforcement of such a duty (a key objection as far as the CLR was concerned).[42]

9-24   Following consultation, the CLR found support for and duly recommended retaining the existing common law duty on directors to operate companies for the benefit of their shareholders,[43] but that the duty should be framed in an inclusive way which would give due recognition to the importance of considering the long-term implications of

---

[39] Company Law Review, *Developing the Framework* (2000), para 3.24; see also *Strategic Framework* (1999), paras 5.1.25–5.1.29; also HL Deb, vol 678, GC273 (6 February 2006).

[40] See Company Law Review, *Developing the Framework* (2000), paras 2.21.

[41] Company Law Review, *Developing the Framework* (2000), paras 3.26–3.31; and see Ch 2.

[42] See Company Law Review, *Completing the Structure* (2000), para 3.5.

[43] Company Law Review, *Developing the Framework* (2000), para 2.11.

decisions and of fostering effective relationships over time with employees, customers and suppliers and in the community more widely.[44] The CLR rejected the pluralist approach as neither workable nor desirable[45] and it considered that a more inclusive statement, while it would make little difference to the common law position, would have a major influence on changing behaviour and the climate of decision making.[46] The Government was in favour of this type of approach which it considered would also make the law clearer to directors than any duty defined in terms of acting bona fide in the interests of the company.[47]

The inclusive statement

The directors are required by CA 2006, s 172(1) to have regard to all of the factors on   **9-25**
the list, but they are not precluded from considering other matters ('amongst other matters').[48] For example, the list makes no reference to short-term considerations, only long-term consequences, but this does not preclude directors considering short-term matters. Likewise, there is no mention of pension matters, but this issue would fall within the requirement to have regard to the interests of the employees. Some of the factors merely reflect the pre-existing position—for example, the directors' obligation to have regard to the likely consequences of any decision in the long term (s 172(1)(a));[49] to have regard to employees' interests (s 172)(1)(b));[50] and the need to act fairly as between members of the company (s 172(1)(f)).[51] The remaining factors: the need to foster business relationships, (s 172(1)(c)); the impact of operations on the community and the environment (s 172(1)(d)); and the desirability of maintaining a reputation for high standards of business conduct (s 172(1)(f)) are new in the sense that they have not been explicitly articulated in this way and, as noted at **9-24**, they are intended to give effect to the desire for a more inclusive definition of this duty. On the other hand, as was pointed out in the Parliamentary debates, these factors are matters which any well-informed and conscientious director would have regard to in any event.[52] The difference now is that there is a legal duty on directors to have regard to each of these factors when acting on behalf of the company. The provision is not limited to reaching decisions, formal or informal, nor to business conducted at board meetings.

[44] Company Law Review, *Developing the Framework* (2000), para 2.11, Ch 2, paras 3.17–3.31; *Completing the Structure* (2000), paras 3.1–3.24; *Final Report*, vol 1 (2001), paras 3.5–3.10.

[45] Company Law Review, *Completing the Structure* (2000), para 3.5.

[46] See Company Law Review, *Developing the Framework* (2000), para 3.58, but see Worthington, 'Reforming Directors' Duties' (2001) 64 MLR 439 at 445–8.

[47] The White Paper *Modernising Company Law* (Cm 5553-I, 2002), paras 3.3–3.5.

[48] See HL Deb, vol 678, GC271 (6 February 2006).

[49] Second Savoy Hotel Investigation, Report of the Inspector (1954) HMSO; *Gaiman v National Association for Mental Health* [1971] Ch 317 at 330, per Megarry J.

[50] Previously CA 1985, s 309.

[51] *Mutual Life Insurance Co of New York v Rank Organisation Ltd* [1985] BCLC 11.

[52] See DTI, *CA 2006, Duties of Company Directors, Ministerial Statements* (June 2007), p 2 (available on BERR website at www.berr.gov.uk/files/file40139.pdf): '…pursuing the interests of shareholders and embracing wider responsibilities are complementary purposes, not contradictory ones' (Minister Margaret Hodge).

9-26   There is the possibility, even a probability, that in any given scenario there will be a conflict between two or more of the factors. An example would be where there is a possible takeover bid for the company which will give the shareholders a significant financial return but which will result in job losses, or a decision to continue with opencast mining might be to the advantage of the shareholders and the employees, but to the detriment of the environment, and so on. The resolution of such conflicts is a matter for the business judgment of the directors, acting in good faith and exercising appropriate care and skill.

Having regard to the factors

9-27   There was some criticism in the Parliamentary debates as to the nature of the requirement 'have regard' and the Government was careful to emphasise that that standard must be measured against the overall requirements for directors to act in good faith and with care and skill which means that directors cannot pay mere lip service to the statutory requirements.[53]

9-28   The fact that more than lip service is required raises the question of how directors will be able to prove that they have complied with the section, should the matter become contentious. A particular concern while the Companies Bill was being debated was whether the effect is to require directors to document on every occasion that they have indeed had regard to the factors set out in CA 2006, s 172. This is particularly problematic, given that not every decision is taken at a board meeting; indeed the converse is the position: relatively few matters are decided formally by the board compared to the large variety of matters decided upon every day by the directors.

9-29   The Government's position on this was that, as there is nothing new in CA 2006, s 172, merely an articulation of the factors which a reasonable director exercising care and skill in the carrying out of his functions would do anyway, nothing new or additional is required in terms of documentation,[54] merely the normal documentation which would accompany any decision of the directors.[55]

9-30   Notwithstanding these assurances, concerns remain and clearly the approach taken to CA 2006, s 172 will vary from private to public companies and from transaction to transaction. Many decisions of an everyday nature will require no additional documentation in the light of s 172 and of course many ordinary decisions of directors generate no documentation. In a public company, and a fortiori in a listed public company, however, directors may want to make sure that formal board decisions are

[53] What is required is a 'proper consideration' of the issues, that the directors think about them rather than merely tick boxes, according to Minister Margaret Hodge: see HC Deb, vol 450, col 789, (17 October 2006). See also *Explanatory Notes to the Companies Act 2006*, para 328; HL Deb, vol 681, GC 846 (9 May 2006).

[54] See HL Deb, vol 681, GC 841 (9 May 2006) where Lord Goldsmith speaking for the Government refused to accept that anything about CA 2006, s 172 makes it is necessary to have some particular form of paper trail.

[55] HC Official Report, SCD (Company Law Reform Bill), cols 591–2.

challenge-proof so board procedures may alter to reflect the new requirements. For example, it may be tempting to litter the board minutes with formal references to s 172. For more controversial decisions, directors may want to bolster those decisions with references to internal papers, perhaps even consultants' reports and advice from outside experts, so as to show, not only that they had regard to the factors, but that they exercised appropriate care and skill in considering them. To the extent that such practices develop within larger companies, decision making will be slower and costlier and minutes lengthier.[56]

Precisely in order to stop such practices from taking hold, the GC100 group has advised companies not to adopt the practice of referring to CA 2006, s 172 in the minutes.[57] The GC100 advice makes the point that, prior to the CA 2006, board minutes did not record that the directors, in reaching decisions, had complied with their duties. Nothing about the CA 2006 requires a change to that practice. It is possible now that the media interest, which to some extent led debate about the scope of s 172, has died down, and given the determination of bodies such as GC100 not to be forced into expensive, time-consuming, bureaucratic processes, that decision-making by directors will continue much as before. As discussed at **9-35**, the duty set out in s 172 is not enforceable by any of the stakeholder groups, only by the company or shareholders bringing a derivative claim on behalf of the company, so litigation is likely to be rare and that too will reinforce the status quo. Honest decision-making based on reasonable grounds is what is required. Assuming the directors reach that standard, they are at no greater risk of liability under s 172 than they were under their previous obligation to act bona fide in the interests of the company.   **9-31**

The link to the business review

The proper place to refer to the CA 2006, s 172 factors is in the business review part of the directors' report and a business review is required of all companies other than small companies (s 417(1)): see **16-26**.[58] The purpose of the review is expressly stated to be 'to inform members of the company and help them assess how the directors have performed their duty under section 172' (see s 417(2)).   **9-32**

---

[56] For an interesting consideration of whether lawyers' advice to corporate clients on the scope and implementation of CA 2006, s 172 will change boardroom practice in this way, see Loughrey, Keay, Cerioni, 'Legal Practitioners, Enlightened Shareholder Value and the Shaping of Corporate Governance' (2008) 8 JCLS 79.

[57] The GC100 group essentially represents general counsel and company secretaries of the FTSE 100 companies; its publications are available at www.practicallaw.com/6-78-7923.

[58] The CLR was keen to require large public and private companies to report widely on the business and its affairs as part of their annual reporting requirements. See Company Law Review, *Final Report,* vol 1 (2001), paras 3.28–3.45; *Completing the Structure* (2000), paras 3.7–3.10; 3.32–3.42; *Developing the Framework* (2000), paras 2.19–2.26, 3.85, 5.74–5.100; *Strategic Framework* (1999), paras 5.1.44–5.1.47. Initially the largest companies were to prepare an Operating and Financial Review (OFR) but that proposal was discarded by the Government in favour of the business review required in any event by the Modernisation Directive amending the Accounts Directives: see Directive 2003/51, OJ 2003 L178/16, 17.7.2003. See Johnston, 'After the OFR: Can UK Shareholder Value Still be Enlightened' (2006) 7 EBOR 819 for an explanation and criticism of the decision to drop the requirement for the OFR.

9-33   The business review must contain a fair review of the company's business, and a description of the principal risks and uncertainties facing the company. It must provide a balanced and comprehensive analysis of the development, performance and position of the company's business during and at the end of the financial year, consistent with the size and complexity of the business. More detailed requirements are imposed on quoted companies which must include in the business review, to the extent necessary for an understanding of the development, performance or position of the company's business, information on, inter alia, environmental matters (including the impact of the company's business on the environment), the company's employees, and social and community issues, all of which are reflected in s 172 as factors to which the directors must have regard.

9-34   The role assigned to the business review by CA 2006, s 417 reflects the Government's intention that the restated duty in s 172 should bring about a cultural change in how companies perceive their responsibilities,[59] rather than generate pointless bureaucratic procedures restricting decision-making. The focus on disclosure of the company's conduct in the business review is designed to force companies to acknowledge and respond to the interests of the stakeholders affected by their activities. Of course, corporate social responsibility (CSR) is now an important industry in its own right to which large companies, in particular, pay considerable regard. To some extent, this aspect of s 172 has been overtaken by events. Ideas which seemed radical 10 years ago (disclosure of CSR-type activities) when the Company Law Review was set up (in March 1998) are commonplace by the time of the final commencement of the CA 2006 in October 2009.

Litigation risk

9-35   Some of the concerns surrounding the impact of CA 2006, s 172 relate to the introduction by the CA 2006, Part 11 of a statutory derivative claim. Part 11 provides for claims by any member against any director for a breach of any duty owed by a director to the company including, for the first time, in respect of alleged negligence by a director (s 260(3)). Recovery is solely for the benefit of the company and not for the individual claimant. Derivative claims and Part 11 are discussed in Chapter 18.

9-36   The concern is that shareholder activists may use the combination of the new derivative procedure and s 172 to challenge business decisions of directors on the basis of an alleged failure to have regard to the factors set out in that section. A derivative claim could be used to seek judicial review, in effect, of a commercial decision of management.

9-37   Throughout the Parliamentary debates, the Government emphasised that CA 2006, Part 11 does not introduce any major change of principle (derivative claims were possible at common law) and there is no reason to expect any significant increase in the

---

[59] See Minister Margaret Hodge, '...s 172 is a "radical departure" from the previous law which catches a cultural change...': see Introduction to Ministerial Statements, above n 52.

number of derivative actions.[60] The intention behind Part 11 is to strike a balance between protecting directors from vexatious and frivolous claims[61] so allowing them to take business decisions in good faith while protecting the rights of shareholders to bring meritorious claims.[62] Of course, even if shareholders brought a derivative claim and could establish a failure to consider a particular factor or factors, it is not clear what an appropriate remedy might be or how any loss might be quantified. For example, if it was established that the directors failed to take into account the interests of the employees in a particular matter and 50 of them had lost their jobs, there would be a breach of duty on the part of the directors but no loss suffered by the company to which the duty is owed.

Even so, the Government felt the need to respond to the concerns expressed by busi-   **9-38**
ness and practitioners and it brought forward amendments to Part 11 designed to enhance the protection for directors by (1) strengthening the judicial controls of derivative claims (discussed in Chapter 18); and (2) by restating s 172 (initially it was two clauses with the factors listed in a separate subsection) to emphasise that the over-riding obligation of directors remains to promote the success of the company for the benefit of its members as a whole.[63] In this way, it is hoped to curb the scope for allegations of a breach of duty arising from a supposed failure to have regard to one or more of the factors set out in s 172(1).

In the Parliamentary debates, the Government stressed that there are not two duties   **9-39**
in s 172—a duty to act in good faith and to have regard to the factors listed[64]—there is only one duty: it is for directors to decide what would be most likely to promote the success of the company for the benefit of its members as a whole.[65] It is a matter of business judgment for the directors and the Government wished to make clear that the factors are 'subordinate to the overriding duty to act in the way the director considers in good faith would be most likely to promote the success of the company for the benefit of its members as a whole'.[66]

As discussed at **18-56–18-60**, it is unlikely in practice that there will be a significant   **9-40**
increase in the use of the derivative claim and these concerns about the combined effect of s 172 and Part 11 will prove unfounded.

---

[60] For the Government's position, see 679 HL Official Report (5th series), cols GC 4–5, 27 February 2006; 681 HL Official Report (5th series), col 883, 9 May 2006; HC Official Report, SC D (Company Law Reform Bill), 13 July 2006, cols 664–6.

[61] 679 HL Official Report (5th series), col GC6, 27 February 2006.

[62] See 681 HL Official Report (5th series), col 883, 9 May 2006.

[63] See 681 HL Official Report (5th series), cols 883–4, 9 May 2006.

[64] See comments by Minister Margaret Hodge, HC Official Report, SC D (Company Law Reform Bill), 13 July 2006, cols 591–2. Originally, the drafting required that the directors 'must' have regard to these factors, but the Bill was amended to remove the second 'must', as it was suggested that using 'must' twice might have implied a separate duty: see also HL Deb, vol 681, col 845 (9 May 2006).

[65] See comments by Minister Margaret Hodge, HC Official Report, SC D (Company Law Reform Bill), 13 July 2006, col 591—the duty is not a pluralist duty: directors are required to have regard to the factors laid out when promoting the success of the company for the benefit of its members but a director who puts one of those factors ahead of his overarching duty to promote the success of the company acts in a breach of that duty to the company.   [66] HL Report, col 845.

9-41   It is difficult to assess the significance of the changes effected by CA 2006, s 172. At one level, it may be said that the law is playing catch-up with a developing business culture which does look to a much wider agenda and broader constituencies than merely a company's own shareholders. A decade has passed since the Company Law Review focused on these issues and in that time companies, especially multinational companies, have attached ever-increasing importance to the value of their reputations and their brands. Whether the CA 2006 is the appropriate vehicle for advancing a corporate social responsibility agenda is another matter. A review of the debates on s 172 in the House of Commons show a focus on matters of genuine concern—the use of child labour, gas flaring in the Niger Delta, environmental damage in Siberia and fair trade issues. But the solution to such issues is unlikely to be found in legislation devoted to constructing the legislative skeleton for the corporate vehicle. These matters must remain, in some cases, for market solutions; in others, for regulation through domestic law on matters such as planning, environmental and competition law and, in others, to the work of international organisations and treaties. A respect for human rights is not likely to depend on or be influenced by finely crafted sections of the Companies Act.

E Creditors' interests

9-42   A director's duty to act in the way he considers, in good faith, would be most likely to promote the success of the company for the benefit of its members as a whole has effect 'subject to any enactment or rule of law requiring directors, in certain circumstances, to consider or act in the interests of creditors of the company' (CA 2006, s 172(3)). The outright obligation in s 172(1) is qualified therefore ('subject to'), but only 'in certain circumstances' and it may only require consideration of the creditors' interests as opposed to an obligation to act in their interests ('to consider or act').[67]

9-43   Relevant enactments requiring a focus on creditors' interests are the Company Directors Disqualification Act 1986 and the Insolvency Act 1986. Trading to the detriment of creditors' interests warrants a finding of unfitness and disqualification under the CDDA 1986, s 6 (disqualification is discussed at **6-41**) and potential liability for wrongful trading under IA 1986, s 214 (i.e. continuing to trade after a point in time when a director knew or ought to have known that there was no reasonable prospect of avoiding insolvent liquidation: see **25-17**).[68] The IA 1986 also regulates transactions which adversely affect creditors' interests such as transactions at an undervalue (IA 1986, s 238, see **25-53**) and preferences (IA 1986, s 239, see **25-68**).

---

[67] For a detailed analysis of this issue, see Keay, *Company Directors' Responsibilities to Creditors* (2007) which draws on numerous articles by the author on this topic.

[68] It is a defence for a director to show that he took every step with a view to minimising the potential losses to the company's creditors as he ought to have taken: IA 1986, s 214(3).

At common law, the requirement to consider or act in creditors' interests had its ori-   **9-44**
gins in influential Australian and New Zealand decisions to this effect.[69] This approach
was endorsed by the Court of Appeal in *West Mercia Safetywear Ltd v Dodd*[70] where
Dillon LJ approved the following statement by the New South Wales Court of Appeal
in *Kinsela v Russell Kinsela Pty Ltd*:[71]

'In a solvent company the proprietary interests of the shareholders entitle them as a
general body to be regarded as the company when questions of the duty of directors
arise.... But where a company is insolvent the interests of the creditors intrude. They
become prospectively entitled, through the mechanism of liquidation, to displace the
power of the shareholders and directors to deal with the company's assets. It is in a
practical sense their assets and not the shareholders' assets that, through the medium
of the company, are under the management of the directors pending either liquidation,
return to solvency, or the imposition of some alternative administration.'[72]

In the *West Mercia* case, a director had arranged for his company to partially repay a   **9-45**
debt due from the company to its parent company. The reason he had organised the
payment of £4,000 was that he had personally guaranteed the debts of the parent company and the part-payment of the debt reduced his personal liabilities in that respect.
The court found that the director in causing the company, which he knew to be insolvent, to make this payment at that time had acted in disregard of the interests of the
general creditors of the company and in breach therefore of his duty to the company.
He was ordered to repay £4,000 with interest.

This obligation to have regard to the interests of creditors in this way, though initially   **9-46**
the subject of some criticism,[73] over time became an established element of the fiduciary duty to act bona fide in the interests of the company.[74] It was to be expected therefore that the obligation would be fully reflected in the statutory statement of directors'
duties, but this turned out to be a matter on which, surprisingly, the Company Law
Review had little of substance to say.[75] For its part, the Government is content to leave
the matter to develop at common law[76] so CA 2006, s 172(3) merely indicates that

---

[69] Especially *Walker v Wimborne* (1976) 50 ALJR 446 and *Nicholson v Permakraft (NZ) Ltd* [1985] 1 NZLR
242. See Dawson, 'Acting in the Best Interests of the Company—For whom are Directors "Trustees"?' (1984)
11 NZULR 68.

[70] [1988] BCLC 250. See also *Brady v Brady* [1988] 2 All ER 617, HL; *Re Horsley & Weight Ltd* [1982] 3 All
ER 1045 at 1055–6.

[71] (1986) 4 ACLC 215 at 223, per Street CJ.   [72] [1988] BCLC 250 at 252.

[73] See Sealy, 'Directors' Duties—An Unnecessary Gloss' (1988) CLJ 175 at 177.

[74] For example, see *Yukong Line Ltd of Korea v Rendsburg Investments Corp of Liberia* [1998] 2 BCLC 485
at 502: removal of funds by a director from insolvent company's bank account with a view to putting those
funds beyond the reach of the company's sole creditor was a clear breach of the director's fiduciary duties.

[75] Initially the CLR was not inclined to include any specific obligation to creditors though there was
concern that, without some reference to creditors, the statutory statement of directors' duties would not be
exhaustive. Some limited proposals were included belatedly in the Final Report, but rejected in any event
by the Government which preferred to proceed as set out in CA 2006, s 172(3). See Company Law Review,
Developing the Framework (2000), paras 3.72–3.73; also the draft statutory statement of directors' duties in
Company Law Review, *Final Report*, vol 1 (2001), Annex C, paras 8 and 9; and, *Final Report*, vol 1 (2001),
paras 3.12–3.20.

[76] See *Modernising Company Law* (Cm 5553-I, 2002), paras 3.8–3.14.

in certain circumstances directors may be required to consider or act in the creditors' interests rather in than the interests of the members.

9-47   The main issue of concern to directors is the point in time at which this obligation to consider or act in the interests of the creditors supplements or displaces the duty to act for the benefit of the members as a whole. Clearly where the company is solvent, there is no need for directors to consider or act in the interests of the creditors who will get paid in the usual way or who can otherwise enforce their contractual rights to payment. Clearly where the company is insolvent, the interests of the creditors should be the focus of the directors' decisions and conduct. The difficult area is when the company is under financial pressure so it may weave in and out of 'doubtful solvency' or 'near insolvency'. For example, a company may lose a major customer and endure a difficult period before subsequently gaining a new order when its finances improve. In some sectors, such as the airline industry, companies may flirt with insolvency because of extraneous circumstances such as soaring oil prices. Depending on the duration of the problem, companies may survive or may collapse. Yet the imposition of an obligation to have regard to creditors' interests in precisely that 'zone of insolvency' or in the 'vicinity of insolvency', to use the American terminology, is essential to curb the incentives for directors at that stage to take on excessive risks (basically because all is lost and a further throw of the dice is all that remains).[77]

9-48   In one of the influential New Zealand decisions, *Nicholson v Permakraft (NZ) Ltd*,[78] Cooke J thought creditors were entitled to consideration if the company was insolvent, or near-insolvent, or of doubtful solvency, or if a contemplated payment or other course of action would jeopardise its solvency. In *Re MDA Investment Management Ltd, Whalley v Doney*,[79] the court thought the obligation to have regard to creditors' interests arose where the company was in 'a dangerous financial position' or the company was 'in financial difficulties to the extent that its creditors are at risk'. In *Facia Footwear v Hinchcliffe*,[80] Sir Richard Scott thought that, given 'the parlous financial state of the company', the directors had to have regard to the interests of the creditors when paying out company's funds (at a time when it was hopelessly insolvent) to support the continued trading of other companies in the group.[81]

9-49   Much discussion has centred on trying to refine these thresholds into a defined point in time when this duty arises, but it is difficult to identify a precise legal test when directors must turn from the members' interests to considering or acting in the creditors' interests. The practical position is that the duty in CA 2006, s 172(3) only has an impact if the company actually becomes insolvent and goes into either liquidation or administration. Only then will the issue of the directors' duties to consider creditors' interests

---

[77] See generally Davies, 'Directors' Creditor—Regarding Duties in Respect of Trading Decisions in the Vicinity of Insolvency' (2006) 7 EBOR 301. Also Milman, 'Strategies for Regulating Managerial Performance in the Twilight Zone: Familiar Dilemmas, New Considerations' [2004] JBL 493.

[78] [1985] 1 NZLR 242 at 249, 250.   [79] [2004] 1 BCLC 217 at 247–8.   [80] [1998] 1 BCLC 218

[81] [1998] 1 BCLC 218 at 228. See discussion at **3-59** and court's comments on the importance of not applying hindsight in judging the directors' conduct and recognition of the commercial reality that the interests of the creditors sometimes lie in conduct which ensures a continuation of trading.

come to the forefront as a liquidator or administrator tries to establish a liability on the directors' part (which may be valuable to the creditors, especially if the directors have liability insurance).

The reason why it is a matter for a liquidator or administrator is that directors' duties **9-50** are owed to the company (CA 2006, s 170(1): see **7-14**) and so this duty is not owed directly to the creditors.[82] An individual creditor is not entitled, therefore, to sue for breach.[83] Enforcement occurs indirectly (if at all) through misfeasance proceedings (for breach of duty) by liquidators under IA 1986, s 212 (see **25-4**), or wrongful trading proceedings under IA 1986, s 214 (see **25-17**) or challenges to transactions on the basis of their being a preference (see **25-68**) or at an undervalue (see **25-53**). Disqualification proceedings under the CDDA 1986 may also ensue (see **6-41**). For example, in *Re Mea Corporation Ltd, Secretary of State for Trade and Industry v Aviss*[84] directors were disqualified in essence for causing or allowing each of three companies to trade to the detriment of creditors. At a time when those companies were under increasing pressure from creditors and were each unable to pay their debts as they fell due (i.e. were insolvent), the directors allowed such cash as was available to be paid out to other companies in which one of the directors had a substantial personal interest. In *Re Genosyis Technology Management Ltd, Wallach v Secretary of State for Trade and Industry*[85] two directors were disqualified for entering, on behalf of the company, into a settlement agreement with a customer under which the company gave up a claim for €1.25m (which was instead paid to its parent company) and gained a maximum of £166,000. Given the company was insolvent at the time of the settlement, the court found the directors in breach of their duty to have regard to the creditors' interests, see also **3-62**.

A director must focus on whether the company is insolvent[86] or, as Cooke J put it **9-51** *Nicholson v Permakraft (NZ) Ltd*,[87] whether a contemplated payment or other course of action would jeopardise its solvency so administration or liquidation (and therefore actions against the directors by administrators or liquidators) is likely. In either scenario (insolvent or transaction would jeopardise solvency), if the directors are to diminish the risk of subsequent personal liability, they must be aware of the obligation under CA 2006, s 172(3) to consider or act in the creditors' interests rather than the interests of the members as a whole. To determine whether the company is insolvent or whether a contemplated payment or course of action would jeopardise its solvency, the directors need to know or be aware of the company's financial position. This is not a problem since a variety of obligations ensure that the directors do indeed know and appreciate the company's financial position.

[82] *Multinational Gas and Petrochemical Co v Multinational Gas and Petrochemical Services Ltd* [1983] 2 All ER 563 at 585; *Yukong Line Ltd of Korea v Rendsburg Investments Corp of Liberia* [1998] 2 BCLC 485. See also *Kuwait Asia Bank EC v National Mutual Life Nominees Ltd* [1990] 3 All ER 404, PC.
[83] *Yukong Line Ltd of Korea v Rendsburg Investments Corp of Liberia* [1998] 2 BCLC 485.
[84] [2007] 1 BCLC 618 at 635, 643.   [85] [2007] 1 BCLC 208.
[86] See IA 1986, s 123: a company may be insolvent on a cash flow basis of being unable to pay its debts as they fall due or on a balance sheet basis (liabilities exceed assets).
[87] [1985] 1 NZLR 242 at 249, 250.

9-52   First, every company must keep adequate accounting records sufficient to disclose, with reasonable accuracy, at any time, the financial position of the company at that time (CA 2006, s 386(1), (2)(b)). Directors must prepare annual accounts and large and medium-sized companies must have those accounts audited which should ensure an appreciation of the company's position.[88] Secondly, the directors are obliged under s 174 to exercise care, skill and diligence which requires an appropriate level of knowledge of the company's affairs and its financial position at any time (see **10-27**).[89] Thirdly, it is implicit in many of the factors to which directors must have regard under s 172(1) that the directors need to be aware of the company's financial position. In considering any matter and in order to have proper regard to the interests of the employees, or to the need to foster business relationships with suppliers, or to the impact of the company's operations on the community, a director needs to know the company's financial position. Indeed, more broadly, it is difficult to see how any director could honestly fulfil his duty to promote the success of the company if he is unaware of the company's financial position (at least in general terms).

9-53   Against the backdrop of these various obligations, a reasonable director acting in accordance with the requirements of CA 2006, s 174 as to care and skill should be able to form a view as to whether the company is insolvent or whether a contemplated payment or other course of action would jeopardise its solvency. That consideration determines whether the director should continue to look to his obligations under s 172(1) or whether s 172(3) comes into play.

---

[88] Small companies are exempt from an audit (CA 2006, s 477, see discussion at **16-38** et seq) unless they choose to have one and the downside to the exemption may be that the directors do not have outside accounting/audit advice which would draw their attention to the company's financial position. The risk of directors breaching the obligation to have regard to creditors' interests may therefore be greater in an audit exempt company, but whether a liquidator or administrator would pursue a remedy is another matter. Disqualification is the most likely sanction.

[89] See *Re Westmid Packing Services Ltd, Secretary of State for Trade and Industry v Griffiths* [1999] 2 BCLC 704; *Re Galeforce Pleating Co Ltd* [1999] 2 BCLC 704; *Re Landhurst Leasing plc, Secretary of State for Trade and Industry v Ball* [1999] 1 BCLC 286; *Re Park House Properties Ltd* [1997] 2 BCLC 530.

10

Duty of care, skill and independent judgment

A Introduction

It is important that, in addition to their fiduciary obligations, directors should be **10-1** subject to duties of care and skill appropriate to the modern commercial world, bearing in mind the increased emphasis on higher standards of corporate governance. The duty of care, skill and diligence is not a fiduciary duty, as CA 2006, s 178(2) makes clear. It is a statutory statement of a common law duty of care imposed on those who assume responsibility for the property and affairs of others, governed therefore by the normal common law rules as to liability for negligence. The most often cited explanation of the distinction between fiduciary and other duties is that given by Millett LJ in *Bristol & West Building Society v Mothew*[1] where he emphasised that fiduciary duties are duties peculiar to fiduciaries, breach of which attract legal consequences different from those consequent upon the breach of other duties. Breach of fiduciary duties attracts equitable remedies which are primarily restitutionary or restorative rather than compensatory, as would be the case on a breach of a duty of care. Millett LJ went on to make the point that the core of fiduciary duties is loyalty and a breach of fiduciary duty is primarily about disloyalty, so mere incompetence is not enough.[2] The duty of care and skill is therefore a common law duty and liability for breach may lie in tort or additionally in contract where a director has a contract of employment as it is an implied term that an employee will exercise reasonable care and skill in the performance of his duties.[3]

Prior to the CA 2006, the courts had looked to IA 1986, s 214(4) as an accurate state- **10-2** ment of the general standard of care and skill expected of directors,[4] applying it

---

[1] [1996] 4 All ER 698 at 711–12.

[2] [1996] 4 All ER 698 at 711–12. See also *Extrasure Travel Insurances Ltd v Scattergood* [2003] 1 BCLC 598 at 618: 'Fiduciary duties are concerned with concepts of honesty and loyalty, not with competence' (Deputy Judge Jonathan Crow).

[3] *Lister v Romford Ice & Cold Storage Ltd* [1957] 1 All ER 125.

[4] See *Re D'Jan of London Ltd, Copp v D'Jan* [1994] 1 BCLC 561; *Norman v Theodore Goddard* [1991] BCLC 1028; *Re Landhurst Leasing plc, Secretary of State for Trade and Industry v Ball* [1999] 1 BCLC 286 at 344; *Cohen v Selby* [2001] 1 BCLC 176 at 183.

beyond the confines of that section (which concerns wrongful trading).[5] Section 214(4) requires the conduct of a director to be measured against the standard of a reasonably diligent person having both the general knowledge, skill and experience that may reasonably be expected of a person carrying out the same functions as are carried out by that director in relation to the company, and the general knowledge, skill and experience that that director has.

10-3   That approach was endorsed by the Law Commission,[6] the Company Law Review[7] and the Government[8] and is reflected in CA 2006, s 174 which, with minimal changes,[9] reproduces the wording of IA 1986, s 214(4). The standard of care, skill and diligence therefore remains as previously established and the existing case law remains relevant (CA 2006, s 170(4)).

10-4   Though the standard expected is now clearly identified, the content of this duty is still under development by the courts and it is not always easy to draw from the cases a comprehensive and coherent statement of what is required of directors. To some extent there is a dearth of authority. For a period, much valuable guidance on the duty of care and skill was found in the large number of reported cases on disqualification proceedings brought against a director of an insolvent company on the ground that his conduct has shown him to have fallen below the standards of probity and competence (i.e. care and skill) expected of a director.[10] But disqualification is now mainly dealt with by administrative undertakings (see **6-42**) with the result that this source of authorities on care and skill has largely dried up.

10-5   The importance of the disqualification authorities reflects the fact that, in practice, directors are rarely sued for negligence in the management of a company's affairs. As with other duties of directors, enforcement of the duty of care and skill takes place, if at all, when the company goes into insolvent liquidation or administration where a liquidator or administrator may consider it worthwhile to pursue a director for misfeasance (see **25-4**) or wrongful trading under IA 1986, s 214 (see **25-17**). As noted above, disqualification proceedings may also be brought on the grounds of unfitness, though here the relevant standard is more frequently described as a standard of 'probity and competence', rather than stated in the traditional terms of care and skill,[11] but

---

[5] Liability for wrongful trading arises where a director is found to have continued trading after a point in time when he knew or ought to have concluded that there was no reasonable prospect of the company avoiding insolvent liquidation: see **25-17**.

[6] Law Commission, *Company Directors: Regulating Conflicts of Interests and Formulating a Statement of Duties* (Law Comm No 261), 1999, Ch 5.

[7] Company Law Review, *Final Report*, vol 1 (2001), p 346 and Annex C; and see *Developing the Framework* (2000), pp 40–3.

[8] See *Modernising Company Law* (Cm 5553-I, 2002), paras 3.2–3.7.

[9] 'Diligence' is expressly included in the section but the case law had already established the need for a director to exert and apply himself in the conduct of the company's affairs and the courts had penalised those found to be inattentive to their duties: see, for example, *Re Park House Properties Ltd* [1997] 2 BCLC 530.

[10] CDDA 1986, s 6.

[11] See *Re Landhurst Leasing plc, Secretary of State for Trade and Industry v Ball* [1999] 1 BCLC 286 at 344; *Secretary of State for Trade and Industry v Gray* [1995] 1 BCLC 276 at 286.

if the allegation is incompetence without dishonesty, it must be incompetence to a high degree[12] (see **6-75**).

Of course, for many small companies, family ties are usually stronger than concerns   **10-6**
about standards of care and skill. For solvent private companies, in so far as allegations of negligence arise, they tend to do so in the context of unfairly prejudicial petitions under CA 2006, s 994 and with limited success (see **17-57**). In part there is a judicial view that directors are elected by the shareholders and if the shareholders choose to appoint poor managers then, short of insolvency, that is a matter for them (and of course in many small companies the directors and the shareholders are the same people). Another constraint on judicial enthusiasm for negligence claims against directors is their long-held view that the courts should not interfere or second-guess directors on matters of business judgment (see **9-8**) and frequently what is presented as a claim in negligence is merely a disagreement on business strategy or decisions. Furthermore, as the courts frequently point out, directors are not trustees and they are appointed precisely in order to take risks in an environment of risk; after all, that is the purpose of the limited company.

Issues of competence are more central to corporate governance concerns in respect to   **10-7**
public companies. The Combined Code, with which listed public companies are expected to comply or to explain any non-compliance (see **5-11**), emphasises the need for an effective board with an appropriate balance of the skills and experience needed for the business and for directors regularly to update their skills and knowledge.[13] Moreover, the board is expected to undertake an annual evaluation of its own performance and that of its committees and to review the effective contribution and commitment to the company of each director.[14] Often issues of competence are the subject of media comment or criticism by individual shareholders at a general meeting and a public airing of the issue and, occasionally, a timely resignation may be the most which can be achieved.

Occasionally and exceptionally, a public company with a new board in place may   **10-8**
sue the company's former directors for negligence and such litigation has a powerful impact, even when unsuccessful, as in the *Equitable Life* case (where the claims were dropped).[15] There are some concerns that the statutory derivative claim under CA 2006, Part 11 (which for the first time allows derivative claims to be brought on the basis of negligence) will encourage litigation but, as discussed at **18-56**, this is unlikely. Any attempt to pursue a claim in negligence faces the difficulty of establishing that a duty of care was owed in respect of the kind of loss which has occurred.[16] Where the

---

[12] *Re Sevenoaks Stationers (Retail) Ltd* [1991] 1 BCLC 325 at 337; *Re Barings plc (No 5)* [1999] 1 BCLC 433, Ch D, [2000] 1 BCLC 523, CA.

[13] FRC, The Combined Code on Corporate Governance (2008) Principles A.3, A.5.

[14] FRC, The Combined Code on Corporate Governance (2008) Principle A.6.

[15] For the story of this litigation which was ultimately dropped, see *Equitable Life Assurance Society v Bowley* [2004] 1 BCLC 180; also Reed (2006) 27 Co Law 170.

[16] See *Re Continental Assurance Co of London plc* [2007] 2 BCLC 287 at 437, 445; see also *Bishopsgate Investment Management Ltd v Maxwell (No 2)* [1993] BCLC 814 at 829–30. Generally see *Customs and Excise Commissioners v Barclays Bank* [2006] 4 All ER 256; *MAN Nutzfahrzeuge AG v Freightliner Ltd* [2008] 2 BCLC 22, CA; also Arden LJ in *Johnson v Gore Wood & Co* [2003] EWCA Civ 1728 at [91]; [2003] All ER (D) 58 (Dec).

breach of duty is constituted by inactivity (which is frequently the allegation made against directors), the court must construct, as Briggs J put it in *Lexi Holdings plc v Luqman*[17] 'a necessarily hypothetical edifice so as to ascertain what would probably have happened if the relevant duties had been performed, so as to ascertain whether in that event the losses actually suffered by [the company] would, probably, not have been suffered'.[18] In *Lexi* the court found two directors of a company in breach of their duties in not informing the board of the criminal convictions for fraud of another director (their brother) who went on to misappropriate large sums of the company's money. However, the court also held that, had the directors disclosed the convictions, the result would have been that other directors would have resigned and the company's bank might have not increased its loans to the business, but the misappropriations by their brother would have continued. The claim against the two directors failed therefore as a matter of causation. There are considerable obstacles then in the way of a successful claim based on the duty of care and skill. Nevertheless, in public companies, the threat to reputations of even a failed claim in negligence has raised concerns as to whether able people are deterred from accepting directorships. In part, the fears are overblown and usually additional reassurance can be found in the form of increased salaries and in the extensive indemnities and insurance cover commonly provided by larger companies for their directors, see **13-42**.

10-9   Finally, it must be borne in mind that the general duties imposed on directors under CA 2006, Part 10, Ch 2, are cumulative (s 179) and conduct which is in breach of care and skill may be equally open to challenge on the grounds that the director has acted for an improper purpose in breach of s 171 or has failed to promote the success of the company in breach of s 172 or failed to exercise independent judgment as required by s 173. In *Re Bradcrown Ltd, Official Receiver v Ireland*,[19] for example, a finance director was in breach of his duty of care in abdicating all responsibility for a complex transaction whereby the company transferred away its assets valued at £3.7m for no consideration. In so acting the director also failed to act bona fide in the interests of the company and he used his powers for an improper purpose in divesting the company of its assets for no consideration. In many cases therefore where liability is established in respect of a breach of fiduciary duty, it would also have been possible to have brought a claim for breach of care and skill. As noted at **10-1**, there are certain practical advantages in pursuing a breach of fiduciary duty rather than a claim in negligence.

B The statutory standard of care, skill and diligence

Collective and individual responsibilities

10-10   The starting point is the collective responsibility of the board for the management of the company's affairs, but equally directors' duties are 'personal and inescapable'

---

[17] [2008] 2 BCLC 725.   [18] [2008] 2 BCLC 725 at 735.   [19] [2001] 1 BCLC 547 at 561.

duties,[20] and so within that collective responsibility, each director must meet the appropriate standard of care, skill and diligence. Much cited on this is the statement of Lord Woolf MR in *Re Westmid Packing Services Ltd, Secretary of State for Trade and Industry v Griffiths* as follows:[21]

> '...the collegiate or collective responsibility of the board of directors of a company is of fundamental importance to corporate governance under English company law. That collegiate or collective responsibility must however be based on individual responsibility. Each individual director owes duties to the company to inform himself about its affairs and to join with his co-directors in supervising and controlling them.'

The standard expected is laid down in CA 2006, s 174:   **10-11**

> '(1) A director of a company must exercise reasonable care, skill and diligence.
>
> (2) This means the care, skill and diligence that would be exercised by a reasonably diligent person with—
>
>   (a) the general knowledge, skill and experience that may reasonably be expected of a person carrying out the functions carried out by the director in relation to the company, and
>
>   (b) the general knowledge, skill and experience that the director has.'

The standard set by CA 2006, s 174 is an objective minimum standard, that of a rea-   **10-12**
sonably diligent person who has taken on the office of director, set in the context of the functions undertaken, with that objective minimum standard capable of being raised (but not lowered) in the light of the particular attributes of the director in question.[22] For example, if a director is a professional person, such as a chartered accountant, s 174(2) requires him to meet the standard to be expected of a reasonably diligent director carrying out the functions carried out by him in that company and having that personal attribute. The personal attributes of the director cannot lower the standard set in s 174(2)(a) for that would mean that a subjective standard would always apply, determined by those personal attributes. On the other hand, the standard set is of the reasonably competent director in the position undertaken and with those personal attributes and the courts will not allow the test to be used to impose unrealistically high levels of skill. For example, non-executive directors of an insurance company can be expected to appreciate the general accounting requirements applicable to insurance companies, but cannot be required to be specialists in sophisticated accounting issues pertaining to insurance companies, even if they possess accounting qualifications.[23]

---

[20] See *Secretary of State for Trade and Industry v Goldberg* [2004] 1 BCLC 557 at 608, per Lewison J, relying on *Re Westmid Packing Services Ltd, Secretary of State for Trade and Industry v Griffiths* [1998] 2 BCLC 646 at 654.

[21] [1998] 2 BCLC 646 at 653, a view endorsed by the courts on many subsequent occasions: see, for example, *Re Kaytech International plc, Secretary of State for Trade and Industry v Kaczer* [1999] 2 BCLC 351 at 425, CA; *Re Landhurst Leasing plc* [1999] 1 BCLC 286 at 346; *Re Barings plc (No 5)* [1999] 1 BCLC 433 at 486.

[22] See *Re Brian D Pierson (Contractors) Ltd* [2001] 1 BCLC 275 at 302.

[23] See *Re Continental Assurance Co of London plc* [2007] 2 BCLC 287 at 401–2.

Functions undertaken

10-13   Flexibility in the application of the statutory standard is maintained by the obligation to have regard to the functions carried out by the director in relation to the company in question. This point was emphasised by Jonathan Parker J in *Re Barings plc (No 5), Secretary of State for Trade and Industry v Baker (No 5)*[24] where he stressed that the competence of the director must be assessed in the context of and by reference to the role in the management of the company which was in fact assigned to him or which he in fact assumed and by reference to his duties and responsibilities in that role.[25] He went on:[26]

> 'Thus the existence and extent of any particular duty will depend upon how the particular business is organised and upon what part in the management of that business the respondent could reasonably be expected to play (see *Bishopsgate Investment Management Ltd (in liq) v Maxwell (No 2)* [1993] BCLC 1282 at 1285 per Hoffmann LJ). For example, where the respondent was an executive director the court will assess his conduct by reference to his duties and responsibilities in that capacity. Thus, while the requisite standard of competence does not vary according to the nature of the company's business or to the respondent's role in the management of that business—and in that sense it may be said that there is a 'universal' standard—that standard must be applied to the facts of each particular case.'

10-14   By focusing on the functions which an individual undertakes or which are entrusted to him, the court is able to calibrate the content of the duty in the light of the size and complexity of the business and the position of the individual director.[27] In this way, it is possible to accommodate within the same legal standard the managing director of a multi-million pound banking company, the non-executive director of an insurance company, and a teenage director of a family company carrying on business in a limited way. It is clear that there are certain minimum functions expected of any director who takes on the office of director which include compliance with the statutory requirements with regard to the maintenance of proper accounting records and the preparation of accounts.[28] The relevant functions beyond the minimum will depend on the post held, the tasks assigned and how the company organises its affairs.

The functions of an executive director

10-15   If a director is an executive director, his conduct must be considered against what could be expected of a reasonably diligent person carrying out his duties and responsibilities as an executive director in that company. A managing director, for example, would have

---

[24] [1999] 1 BCLC 433, endorsed on appeal [2000] 1 BCLC 523, CA.

[25] [1999] 1 BCLC 433 at 484, endorsed on appeal [2000] 1 BCLC 523 at 535, CA. See also *Re Continental Assurance Co of London plc, Secretary of State for Trade and Industry v Burrows* [1997] 1 BCLC 48 at 57–8; *Re Produce Marketing Consortium Ltd (No 2)* [1989] BCLC 520 at 550; *Re Vintage Hallmark Ltd, Secretary of State for Trade & Industry v Grove* [2007] 1 BCLC 788 at 793.

[26] [1999] 1 BCLC 433 at 484.

[27] See *Re Produce Marketing Consortium Ltd (No 2)* [1989] BCLC 520 at 550.

[28] See *Re Produce Marketing Consortium Ltd (No 2)* [1989] BCLC 520 at 550; *Re Queens Moat Houses plc, Secretary of State for Trade and Industry v Bairstow (No 2)* [2005] 1 BCLC 136.

general responsibility to oversee the activities of the company.[29] An executive director would normally have responsibility (subject to any appropriate delegation, discussed below) for common management tasks such as signing cheques. A reasonably diligent director in that position would not sign blank cheques,[30] nor cheques of such a large amount in the context of the company's business as would put him on enquiry, without first seeking a full explanation as to their purpose,[31] nor sign a simple insurance proposal form without checking the accuracy of its contents.[32] If the director performs a special function, such as a 'finance director', the special skills expected of a person in that capacity are to be expected of him[33] and a failure to meet those standards will be a breach of his individual responsibilities. In *Re AG (Manchester) Ltd, Official Receiver v Watson*[34] the court was particularly critical of a finance director who allowed an inner group of directors to take key decisions on dividends and other financial matters without reference to the board as a whole. Such conduct fell below the standard expected of a finance director who, in a private company, is often an essential brake, the court said, on the financial ambitions of the shareholders. It was the finance director's duty, whatever the conduct of the other directors, the court said, to ensure that the company was run in accordance with the articles and the Companies Act.[35]

The functions of a non-executive director

Much of the interest in this area concerns the standards expected of non-executive directors in public companies. The concerns arise as a result of a number of factors: the greater prominence given to the role of non-executives and the wide-ranging functions required of them by the Combined Code (see **5-27**); the *Equitable Life* litigation (though it was unsuccessful and the claims were ultimately dropped);[36] the potential for speculative derivative claims by activist shareholders under CA 2006, Pt 11, given that derivative claims are now possible for negligence (see s 260(3) and **18-56**) though this threat is probably exaggerated. In determining what is expected of such directors the courts must balance the need to promote higher standards of corporate governance against a concern not to deter able people from accepting directorships.   **10-16**

The standard set by CA 2006, s 174 accommodates non-executive directors by emphasising the need to link the expectations as to care, skill and diligence to the functions carried out by the non-executive director. The difficulty to some extent lies in reaching   **10-17**

---

[29] See *Re Continental Assurance Co of London plc* [2007] 2 BCLC 287 at 443.

[30] *Dorchester Finance Co Ltd v Stebbing* [1989] BCLC 498. When signing cheques, a director is only required to satisfy himself that the cheque has been authorised by the board. He need not verify that the money is in fact required for the particular purpose specified or is indeed expended on that purpose, assuming that the cheque comes before him for signature in the regular way having regard to the usual practice of that company: *Re City Equitable Fire Insurance Co Ltd* [1925] Ch 407 at 452.

[31] *Secretary of State for Trade and Industry v Swan* [2005] BCC 596 at 617–18.

[32] *D'Jan of London Ltd, Copp v D'Jan* [1994] 1 BCLC 561: the effect of the lack of care in this instance was to deprive the company of insurance cover when the policy was invalidated because of inaccuracies in the proposal form.

[33] *Re Brian D Pierson (Contractors) Ltd* [2001] 1 BCLC 275 at 310.

[34] [2008] 1 BCLC 321.   [35] [2008] 1 BCLC 321 at 373–4.

[36] See *Equitable Life Assurance Society v Bowley* [2004] 1 BCLC 180; also Reed (2006) 27 Co Law 170.

agreement as to those functions with a reluctance to overemphasise any monitoring or supervising function of non-executives (though there is judicial support for that view of their role)[37] for fear of undermining the unitary board. The position is clearest with respect to listed public companies where the Combined Code[38] provides considerable guidance as to the role of a non-executive, summing up the essential elements as follows:

> 'As part of their role as members of a unitary board, non-executive directors should constructively challenge and help develop proposals on strategy. Non-executive directors should scrutinise the performance of management in meeting agreed goals and objectives and monitor the reporting of performance. They should satisfy themselves on the integrity of financial information and that financial controls and systems of risk management are robust and defensible. They are responsible for determining appropriate levels of remuneration of executive directors and have a prime role in appointing, and where necessary removing, executive directors, and in succession planning.' (Code A.1)

10-18   As discussed in Chapter 5, the non-executive directors play particularly important roles on the key audit and remuneration committees (see at **5-30**). Given those roles, a non-executive director of a listed company approached by senior executives about possible financial wrongdoing within the company is not acting as a reasonably careful and diligent director if he merely discussed the concerns with the chief executive and the finance director and took no further steps in the matter, as happened in *Secretary of State for Trade and Industry v Swan*,[39] a disqualification case. In this case, the non-executive director was also the deputy chairman of the company and a member of the company's audit committee, the company was a listed company, and the matter concerned financial impropriety involving significant sums of money. The allegations were serious, the sources reliable and merely consulting the finance director was an inadequate response, the court thought, in a situation where 'decisive, courageous and independent action (including consulting his fellow non-executives and the auditors) was required of a non-executive director. The director's want of competence, the court said, related to a failure to pursue an enquiry with sufficient vigour.[40] Given his conduct fell below that expected of someone in his position and with his experience, he was disqualified.

Functions in a family business

10-19   As to the extent of a director's functions, of course, it is not the case that all directors must be involved in all of the company's affairs. A director is not under any obligation

---

[37] In *Re Continental Assurance Co of London plc* [2007] 2 BCLC 287 at 443, Park J accepted that one of the duties of non-executive directors is to monitor the performance of the executive directors. See also Rimer J in *Re Kaytech International plc, Secretary of State for Trade and Industry v Kaczer* [1999] 2 BCLC 351 at 407: 'The functions of a non-executive lie in the monitoring of the manner in which the executives are conducting the affairs of the company'; also Langley J in *Equitable Life Assurance Society v Bowley* [2004] 1 BCLC 180 at 189 '... plainly arguable that a company may reasonably at least look to non-executive directors for independence of judgment and supervision of executive management'.

[38] FRC, *The Combined Code on Corporate Governance* (2008).   [39] [2005] BCC 596.

[40] [2005] BCC 596 at 625.

to undertake a definitive part in the conduct of the company's business and roles vary according to the size and business of the particular company.[41] Equally, a director cannot reduce his role to such an extent that he is in effect making no or only the most minimal contribution to the collective responsibility of the directors to supervise and control the company's business,[42] not even if it is a family company.

In such businesses, there is a tendency for a spouse or offspring to take on a director-   **10-20**
ship without ever playing any role (or indeed intending to play any role) in the management of the company's affairs. Typically such individuals regard themselves as simply having a nominal or honorific title. The courts do not accept that a director may have such a role. As was noted in *Re Brian D Pierson (Contractors) Ltd*:[43]

> 'The office of director has certain minimum responsibilities and functions, which are not simply discharged by leaving all management functions, and consideration of the company's affairs to another director without question, even in the case of a family company.... One cannot be a "sleeping" director; the function of "directing" on its own requires some consideration of the company's affairs to be exercised.'

In *Re Park House Properties Ltd*[44] the directors of a company were a husband, his wife   **10-21**
and his two teenage children. The husband was responsible for the conduct of the affairs of the company and he was disqualified as unfit on the grounds of continuing to trade in disregard of creditors' interests, non-filing of company accounts and allowing the company to expend £173,000 on an extension to a property, the benefit of which be to the director personally rather than the company. His wife played no part whatever in the affairs of the company and his son and daughter played only very marginal roles in its affairs. None of them received any remuneration as directors. Nevertheless, all three were disqualified. The court held that each of them, by virtue of sheer inactivity over the period of their respective directorships, had been guilty of conduct which made him or her unfit. Neuberger J emphasised that:[45]

> 'The law imposes statutory and fiduciary duties on directors of companies and even where, as here, the respondents received no payment, and any advice given to [the

---

[41] See *Re Barings plc (No 5), Secretary of State for Trade and Industry v Baker (No 5)* [1999] 1 BCLC 433 at 436.

[42] See *Re Westmid Packing Services Ltd, Secretary of State for Trade and Industry v Griffiths* [1998] 2 BCLC 646 at 653. An incentive to act may be found in the many provisions of the CA 2006 which impose criminal sanctions on the company and on any 'officer in default'. An officer is in default if he authorises or permits, participates in *or fails to take all reasonable steps* to prevent the contravention: s 1121(3). On this basis (the definition is different from that which previously applied, CA 1985, s 730(5), which was limited to officers who knowingly and wilfully authorised or permitted the contravention), the inactive, ill-informed, director may find it difficult to escape liability for contraventions by others.

[43] [2001] 1 BCLC 275 at 309–10. The case concerned a director's wife who though also a director and drawing remuneration as such had only a very limited clerical role in the company. The court found that Mrs Pierson, in ignoring the signals of financial difficulties and failing to appreciate even the questions that ought to have been asked about the company's affairs, was instrumental in the company continuing to trade and therefore was liable for wrongful trading under IA 1986, s 214.

[44] [1997] 2 BCLC 530. See also *Re Westminster Property Management Ltd (No 2), Official Receiver v Stern (No 2)* [2001] BCC 305 at 352–5.

[45] [1997] 2 BCLC 530 at 555–6.

husband] would have been unlikely to have been acted on, they cannot escape from those duties. [Their] complete inactivity in relation to, and complete uninvolvement with, the running of the company, the financial problems of the company, the preparation and filing of the accounts, and the decision to spend a substantial sum on the construction of the extension...lead to the conclusion that, in the absence of special circumstances, they are unfit.'

10-22   In *Re Galeforce Pleating Co Ltd*[46] a textile company collapsed with losses of approximately £438,000. The directors of the company included a husband and wife and one other. In the disqualification proceedings brought against the wife, she pleaded that she had 'a most negligible actual involvement in the running of the company'.[47] Disqualifying her for a period of five years, the court emphasised that it was not a sufficient discharge of a director's responsibilities to maintain 'a negligible actual involvement' in the affairs of the company. So long as an individual continues to hold office as a director, and in particular to receive remuneration from it, it is incumbent upon that person, the court said, to inform himself as to the financial affairs of the company and to play an appropriate role in the management of its business. If a director is not prepared to discharge his responsibilities properly, the appropriate course is to resign. Furthermore, the court stressed that it is not an excuse for a director to say that the running of a company is left to his or her spouse.[48]

10-23   For the same reasons, the courts are unwilling to accept that someone can be a professional nominee director acting for hundreds, if not thousands, of companies in return for an annual fee.[49] Such a person cannot realistically be carrying out any functions with regard to these companies.

C The content of the duty

10-24   While the statute now identifies the standard of care, skill and diligence required, it provides little by way of guidance as to the content of the duty in terms of what is expected of a reasonably diligent director as to matters such as his participation in the conduct of the company's affairs. It is for the courts to develop the content of the duty as they have been doing under IA 1986, s 124(4) and in the disqualification cases. Unfortunately most of the authorities to date are first instance decisions and there has been little opportunity for the higher courts to explore these issues. A leading authority is the decision of Jonathan Parker J in *Re Barings plc (No 5) Secretary of State for Trade and Industry v Baker (No 5)*[50] where he identified certain propositions,

---

[46] [1999] 2 BCLC 704.   [47] [1999] 2 BCLC 704 at 716.   [48] [1999] 2 BCLC 704 at 716.

[49] See *Official Receiver v Vass* [1999] BCC 516. See also *Re Kaytech International plc, Secretary of State for Trade and Industry v Kaczer* [1999] 2 BCLC 351 (director claimed to be a director of 1,000 Isle of Man companies, see at 414). The court noted in *Kaytech* that the law should give no encouragement to the notion that if a man takes on so many directorships that he cannot remember them, he is thereby released from the heavy responsibilities which he has undertaken: [1999] 2 BCLC 351 at 426, per Robert Walker LJ.

[50] [1999] 1 BCLC 433, endorsed on appeal, [2000] 1 BCLC 523 at 535, CA.

now widely cited, with which the Court of Appeal subsequently agreed without further elaboration.

In the *Barings* case a number of senior directors of an investment bank were found   **10-25**
to be unfit (though there was no question as to their honesty and integrity) and disqualified as a result of their failure to supervise a 'rogue trader' within the bank whose unauthorised trading resulted in losses of £827m and the collapse of the bank. Jonathan Parker J summarised the duties of directors as follows:[51]

(1) Directors have, both collectively and individually, a continuing duty to acquire and maintain a sufficient knowledge and understanding of the company's business to enable them properly to discharge their duties as directors.

(2) Whilst directors are entitled (subject to the articles of association of the company) to delegate particular functions to those below them in the management chain, and to trust their competence and integrity to a reasonable extent, the exercise of the power of delegation does not absolve a director from the duty to supervise the discharge of the delegated functions.

(3) No rule of universal application can be formulated as to the duty referred to in (2) above. The extent of the duty, and the question whether it has been discharged, must depend on the facts of each particular case, including the director's role in the management of the company.

We look in more detail at each of these elements below, but in practice they overlap   **10-26**
and cannot be regarded as discrete elements of a director's duty of care and skill. All the elements are often present: a lack of understanding of the business, a failure to participate and supervise, an absence of knowledge which prevents a director from exercising independent judgment, all of which make it difficult for a director to assert that he is acting in a way likely to promote the success of the company. It is a cumulative picture of incompetence and breach of other duties which typically emerges.

Knowledge of the company's affairs

The importance of sufficient knowledge and understanding of the company's busi-   **10-27**
ness, both collectively and individually, in order to supervise and control the conduct of the company's affairs, is highlighted by the *Barings* case itself. As noted at **10-25**, the Barings group of companies collapsed in 1995 with losses of £827m following the unauthorised trading activities of a single 'rogue trader' in Singapore. The disqualification proceedings reported in *Re Barings plc (No 5), Secretary of State for Trade and Industry v Baker (No 5)*[52] concerned three of the directors, all of whom were found to be unfit and they were disqualified for periods ranging from four to six years. In essence, the court concluded that the directors had little understanding of the nature of the rogue trader's activities and were not therefore in a position to exercise the

51 [1999] 1 BCLC 433 at 489; [2000] 1 BCLC 523 at 535, CA.
52 [1999] 1 BCLC 433, endorsed on appeal, [2000] 1 BCLC 523 at 535.

requisite level of supervision.[53] The court noted with respect to the most senior director that his failures in this regard amounted 'not so much to bad management but non-management'. Jonathan Parker J commented that 'it is a truism that if a manager does not properly understand the business which he is seeking to manage, he will be unable to take informed management decisions in relation to it'.[54]

10-28   As noted at **10-20**, in a family business, it is not uncommon for family members to be directors without having anything to do with the running of the business and so they have no knowledge of the company's affairs. The courts have consistently found such directors to be unfit: see *Re Brian D Pierson (Contractors) Ltd;*[55] *Re Park House Properties Ltd;*[56] and *Re Galeforce Pleating Co Ltd*[57] (see **10-21–10-22**). For similar reasons, as noted at **10-23**, the courts do not accept that someone can be a professional nominee director of hundreds of companies for it is impossible for the nominee to have a sufficient knowledge of the companies to discharge his duties as a director of them.[58]

10-29   This is not to say that each director must have detailed knowledge of the day-to-day conduct of a company's affairs, for their role depends on the way in which the company's business is organised. The question is whether they have knowledge sufficient to exercise their collective and individual responsibility to supervise and monitor the conduct of the company's affairs.[59]

10-30   The court assesses a director's level of knowledge against the standard set in CA 2006, s 174, set out at **10-11**. In *Re Queens Moat Houses plc, Secretary of State for Trade and Industry v Bairstow (No 2)*[60] dividends had been declared improperly on the strength of accounts which were misleading and did not give a true and fair view of the company's affairs. In disqualification proceedings, the court assessed the defendant director's knowledge on the basis of objectively considering (as required by CA 2006, s 174(2)(a)) what could be expected of a reasonably diligent person who was the chairman and senior executive director of the company and subjectively considering (as required by s 174(2)(b)) what could be expected of the director, given his wide business experience and knowledge of the company's affairs (he had been a director for 20 years) while also acknowledging that he had no formal accountancy qualifications. The court accepted that, given the preparation of the accounts had been properly delegated to the finance director, the director was not in breach of his duty in failing to appreciate that the accounting treatment of certain items in the accounts (i.e. technical specialist information beyond his competence) was misleading. Because of his business experience and knowledge of the company's affairs, he ought to have been aware, however, that the accounts showed inflated turnover and profits (i.e. business information within

---

[53] See [1999] 1 BCLC 433 at 528–9, 574–5, 600.   [54] See [1999] 1 BCLC 433 at 528.
[55] [2001] 1 BCLC 275.   [56] [1997] 2 BCLC 530.   [57] [1999] 2 BCLC 704.
[58] See *Official Receiver v Vass* [1999] BCC 516. See also *Re Kaytech International plc, Secretary of State for Trade and Industry v Kaczer* [1999] 2 BCLC 351 at 414.
[59] See *Re Vintage Hallmark, plc, Secretary of State for Trade & Industry v Grove* [2007] 1 BCLC 788 at 810—what is required is a good general knowledge of the business.
[60] [2005] 1 BCLC 136.

his comprehension) and were therefore misleading. He was in breach of duty and disqualified for six years.

In *Re Westmid Packing Services Ltd, Secretary of State for Trade and Industry v Griffiths,*[61] **10-31**
also disqualification proceedings, the court found that the directors did not know that the dominant director had used company assets to support other businesses of his own and did not know that he had the company cross-guarantee the borrowings of those businesses. This failure to keep themselves properly informed about the company's financial position was sufficient to justify their disqualification though it was the sole allegation of unfitness established against them. In *Re Kaytech International plc, Secretary of State for Trade and Industry v Rimer,*[62] Rimer J thought that a non-executive director has to ensure that he is informed about the company's constitution, its board membership, the nature and course of its business and its financial position from time to time so that he is in a position to monitor the manner in which the executives are conducting the company's affairs. In *Lexi Holdings plc v Luqman*[63] the court did not accept that non-executive directors of a company engaged in the business of making loans secured on real property had a duty to appraise themselves of the detailed provisions of the loan facility agreement which the company had with Barclays Bank (that task could properly be delegated to one of the executive directors with banking experience), but they did have a duty to have made some study of the company's loan book since that lay at the heart of understanding the company's business.

On the other hand, the law does not require an unreasonable level of knowledge, as **10-32**
was made clear in *Re Continental Assurance Co of London plc.*[64] This case concerned the collapse of a small insurance company in 1992. Large and unexpected losses had arisen which came to the board's attention in June 1991. In this litigation the liquidators sought contributions to the company's assets from the directors on the grounds of wrongful trading and/or misfeasance, see **25-17**. A particular issue was an allegation that the company applied inappropriate accounting policies which showed the company to be solvent in July 1991 when, had an appropriate accounting policy been adopted by the company, the directors would and should have appreciated that the company was insolvent and they should have taken steps to stop trading. The court found that for the directors to have reached that conclusion would have required of them knowledge of accounting concepts of a particularly sophisticated nature. Declining to hold the directors liable, Park J rejected any idea that the law imposes such an unrealistically high standard of skill. He noted:[65]

'...In my view, [the directors] would have been expected to be intelligent laymen. They would need to have a knowledge of what the basic accounting principles for an insurance company were.... They would be expected to be able to look at the company's accounts and, with the guidance which they could reasonably expect to be available from the finance director and the auditors, to understand them. They would be expected to be able to participate in a discussion of the accounts, and to ask intelligent questions of

---

[61] [1998] 2 BCLC 646 at 652.   [62] [1999] 2 BCLC 351 at 407.   [63] [2008] 2 BCLC 725.
[64] [2007] 2 BCLC 287.   [65] [2007] 2 BCLC 287 at 402–3.

the finance director and the auditors. What I do not accept is that they could have been expected to show the sort of intricate appreciation of recondite accounting details possessed by a specialist in the field ....'

10-33 On the facts, Park J found that the directors took a wholly responsible and conscientious attitude both to the company's position and to their own responsibilities as directors at all times from and after the first crisis board meeting in 1991 when the unexpected losses were reported to them. The directors did not ignore the question of whether the company could properly continue to trade; on the contrary, the court found that they considered it directly, closely and frequently.[66] The case against them was dismissed.

Delegation and the residual duty of supervision

10-34 It has long been accepted that an intelligent devolution of labour must be possible[67] and a company could not hope to run its business in an efficient manner if the directors were required to do everything themselves and were not permitted to delegate on a wide scale, though the extent to which they can do so depends on the provisions of the company's articles.[68] At the same time, some matters must remain the collective responsibility of the board of directors, such as the responsibility of the board to approve the company's annual accounts.[69] With respect to listed companies, the Combined Code identifies maintaining a sound system of internal control as a matter for the collective responsibility of the board.[70]

10-35 Having permitted delegation, and in the absence of grounds for suspicion, the law does not require that the directors should distrust and constantly supervise those to whom tasks have been delegated for this would defeat the whole purpose. Directors do retain a residual duty of supervision, however, as was made clear by Jonathan Parker J in *Re Barings plc (No 5), Secretary of State for Trade and Industry v Baker (No 5)*,[71] as set out in (2) and (3) at **10-25**. The key point is that it is delegation, not abdication, which is permissible. A number of common scenarios emerge from the authorities.

10-36 First, there is the dominant member syndrome, where directors defer to a particular individual on the board such that in effect they delegate all power to him, abdicate their own responsibilities and exercise no residual supervision. The dominant director(s) may be someone on whom the other directors are unduly reliant and therefore they are reluctant to challenge or question him. They may owe him their

---

[66] [2007] 2 BCLC 287 at 360.

[67] *Dovey v Cory* [1901] AC 477 at 485; also *Huckerby v Elliott* [1970] 1 All ER 189.

[68] The model articles provide that, subject to the articles, the directors are responsible for the management of the company's business, for which purpose they may exercise all the powers of the company and they may delegate any of the powers conferred on them under the articles. See The Companies (Model Articles) Regulations 2008, SI 2008/3229, reg 2, Sch 1, arts 3, 5 (Ltd); reg 4, Sch 3, arts 3, 5 (Plc).

[69] CA 2006, s 414. See *Re Landhurst Leasing plc, Secretary of State for Trade and Industry v Ball* [1999] 1 BCLC 286 at 346, relying on *Re City Equitable Fire Insurance Co Ltd* [1925] Ch 407.

[70] FRC, *The Combined Code on Corporate Governance* (2008), Principle C.2.

[71] [1999] 1 BCLC 433, endorsed on appeal, [2000] 1 BCLC 523, CA.

positions on the board, particularly if they are former employees promoted by him to the board. The courts are clear, however, that a board must not permit one individual to dominate and use the other directors in this way. In *Re Westmid Packing Services Ltd, Secretary of State for Trade and Industry v Griffiths*,[72] for example, the court disqualified two of the executive directors for breach of their inescapable personal responsibilities by allowing themselves to be manipulated and deceived by another member of the board who was the dominant and controlling influence in the business. Their failure to act allowed the dominant director to use the company's assets to fund his other businesses by way of interest-free unsecured loans which ultimately proved irrecoverable and brought the company to ruin.[73]

In *Re Landhurst Leasing plc, Secretary of State for Trade and Industry v Ball*[74] the court **10-37** disqualified two executive directors who had taken a relatively subordinate role (reflecting the fact that they had been promoted to the board from the ranks of the employees) vis-à-vis the conduct of the affairs of the company by two forceful joint managing directors who were convicted of criminal offences in respect to their management of the company. The disqualified directors had failed to draw the board's attention to sham transactions of which they were aware and to ensure that the accounts made adequate provision for bad debts and credit risks.[75] As to the boundaries of delegation, Hart J concluded that a director might rely on his co-directors to the extent that (1) the matter in question lay within their sphere of responsibility given the way in which the particular business was organised, and (2) that there existed no grounds for suspicion that that reliance might be misplaced.[76] However, Hart J continued, even where there were no reasons to think the reliance was misplaced, a director might still be in breach of duty if he left to others matters for which the board as a whole had to take responsibility, for example the responsibilities of the board to approve the company's annual accounts.[77]

Sometimes the dominant element is not an individual but an inner group of direc- **10-38** tors, as in *Re AG (Manchester) Ltd, Official Receiver v Watson*.[78] In this case, the court disqualified for six years a finance director and subsequent chief executive who acquiesced in a system under which members of an inner group of directors took all the key decisions without reference to the board as a whole with the result that the other directors were effectively reduced to the role of departmental managers with no serious input at board meetings on issues affecting the running of the company.[79]

---

[72] [1998] 2 BCLC 646.   [73] [1998] 2 BCLC 646 at 653.

[74] [1999] 1 BCLC 286. See also *Re Bradcrown, Official Receiver v Ireland* [2001] 1 BCLC 547 where a finance director (who had been promoted from being an employee) was found to have exercised no independent judgement and to have deferred in all matters to the managing director. The court noted that this was the clearest case of accepting office as a director but intending from the outset to act as a loyal employee.

[75] See [1999] 1 BCLC 286 at 349 and 353.

[76] [1999] 1 BCLC 286 at 346; see also *Cohen v Selby* [2001] 1 BCLC 176 at 185.

[77] [1999] 1 BCLC 286 at 346, relying on *Re City Equitable Fire Insurance Co Ltd* [1925] Ch 407.

[78] [2008] 1 BCLC 321.

[79] See [2008] 1 BCLC 321 at 373–4. The other directors had given disqualification undertakings, presumably on the basis of their abdication of their responsibilities. See also *Secretary of State for Trade and Industry v Goldberg* [2004] 1 BCLC 597.

10-39   A second scenario is the abdication of responsibility to other directors without exercising any residual supervision by an inactive director of a family business: see the examples in *Re Brian D Pierson (Contractors) Ltd*,[80] *Re Galeforce Pleating Co Ltd*[81] and *Re Park House Properties Ltd*,[82] discussed at **10-21**, **10-22**. In *Re Westminster Property Management Ltd, Official Receiver v Stern (No 2)*[83] a property development company had collapsed with multi-million pound losses and the two directors before the court in disqualification proceedings were a father and son. With respect to the son, the court considered that 'he was not conscious of his position or duties as a director, that he never undertook those duties except as dictated by his father (for example, to sign cheques or accounts) and that he applied his mind barely, if at all, to the consequences of his position as a director'. He was disqualified for four years for this abrogation of his duties as a director.[84] As well as disqualification, inactivity on the part of a director can lead to a personal liability. For example, the courts have held that a director who knowingly allows a practice of improper loans to directors to continue is to be treated as having authorised the payments, even though he does not have actual knowledge of each individual payment at the time when it is made, and is jointly and severally liable therefore for their repayment.[85] In such circumstances, the Court of Appeal considers also that it is the duty of a director aware of the improper payments, not merely to ensure that a stop is put to the practice, but that steps are taken to recover the indebtedness outstanding to the company.[86]

10-40   A third scenario is where financial and accounting matters are delegated to a finance director. When a problem subsequently emerges, the other directors tend to claim that they had no responsibility in the matter, given that it was properly delegated to another. Again the issue is their failure to exercise any residual supervision.

10-41   The situation can be illustrated by *Re Queens Moat Houses plc, Secretary of State for Trade and Industry v Bairstow (No 2)*,[87] the facts of which are at **10-30**. In this case the court agreed that, with regard to the preparation and content of the financial statements, the chief executive was entitled to delegate those matters to the finance director. Such matters were properly within the finance director's area of responsibility and competence and the chief executive had no reason to doubt that the functions

---

[80] [2001] 1 BCLC 275.   [81] [1999] 2 BCLC 704.   [82] [1997] 2 BCLC 530.
[83] [2001] BCC 305 at 354–5.

[84] See also *Re AG (Manchester) Ltd, Official Receiver v Watson* [2008] 1 BCLC 321 where a director who was the wife of the controlling shareholder was disqualified. Though a director, she left all financial and strategic decisions to an inner group of directors (including her husband) and was content to take substantial dividends from the company regardless of how and whether they could be paid. The court found her conduct in failing to act independently and in the interests of the company amounted to an abdication of responsibility and justified her disqualification for four years (see at 374–5).

[85] *Queensway Systems Ltd v Walker* [2007] 2 BCLC 677; *Neville v Krikorian* [2007] 1 BCLC 1, CA. This liability would not extend, however, to transactions preceding those actually authorised by the director concerned: see *Lexi Holdings plc v Luqman* [2008] 2 BCLC 725 at 771.

[86] *Neville v Krikorian* [2007] 1 BCLC 1, CA. The director's liability on this basis is for the difference between the amount which the company could have recovered at the date when the director became aware of the improper loans and the amount recoverable at the time of the claim.

[87] [2005] 1 BCLC 136.

properly delegated had been properly performed. But many of the matters in the accounts were matters that it should have been apparent to the chief executive, given his business experience and knowledge of the company, were of doubtful accuracy and propriety. He was in breach of his duties, not for having improperly delegated the task of preparing the financial statements, but for failing to exercise his residual duty of supervision when those financial statements came to the board for approval.[88] The position can be contrasted with that in *Re Continental Assurance Co of London plc*,[89] the facts of which are at **10-32**. Park J there concluded that the board of an insurance company was entitled to rely on the advice of the finance director and the company's auditors as to whether the company was solvent and the appropriateness of the company's accounting policies and systems. The directors did not blindly accept what was put before them, but engaged in detailed and critical consideration of the company's accounts,[90] while looking for detailed guidance on technical matters to the finance director and the auditors as they were perfectly entitled to do.[91]

Another example of a failure to supervise can be found in *Secretary of State for Trade and Industry v Swan*[92] where a chief executive of a listed company was disqualified for signing large cheques (two for £1m each, two for £4m each) without enquiring what they were for, though the court considered that (because of their size in the context of the company's business) they called out for comment and enquiry.[93] His defence (that he relied on his finance director and finance department to verify the cheques) was rejected as an abdication of his responsibilities. His duty of supervision should have been trigged by the size of the cheques and the unusual nature of the transactions.[94] His unfitness in this case lay, the court said, in an absence of vigilance.[95]   **10-42**

Clearly, the extent of the residual duty to supervise depends on a variety of factors including the nature of the business; the nature and extent of the delegation; the standing and status of the person to whom the matter is delegated; the remuneration of the director;[96] the nature of the transaction and the potential risk/losses involved.[97] In larger companies with complex businesses, whether a director has discharged his   **10-43**

---

[88] See [2005] 1 BCLC 136 at 158.   [89] [2007] 2 BCLC 287.   [90] [2007] 2 BCLC 287 at 444.

[91] [2007] 2 BCLC 287 at 410–11, 444. See also *Secretary of State for Trade and Industry v Gill* [2006] BCC 725.

[92] [2005] BCC 596.   [93] [2005] BCC 596 at 612.

[94] [2005] BCC 596 at 618, 621–2. There was no supporting documentation with the cheques which were matching cheques of equal and extraordinary amounts related to the company's practice of cheque-kiting, a practice which generates brief false balances in bank accounts and which the court described as, at the very least, commercially improper and unacceptable. On the other hand, it was not unreasonable for the chief executive to delegate and rely on the finance director and other accounting personnel to deal with and confirm details in a circular to shareholders in the absence of anything to alert him to some discrepancy.

[95] [2005] BCC 596 at 622.

[96] On this, see *Re Barings plc (No 5)* [1999] 1 BCLC 433 at 488. Even an unpaid director has obligations which they accept when they become director: see *Re Park House Properties Ltd* [1997] 2 BCLC 530 at 555–6.

[97] The more critical the risk or the more extensive the potential losses (for example, from unauthorised derivatives trading where the losses can run out of control very quickly), the greater the duty of residual supervision.

individual role involves an examination of the systems for which he personally has responsibility while, at board level, the collective responsibility of the directors is to satisfy themselves that the task delegated and the system instituted is appropriate to the level of risk involved—hence the emphasis in the Combined Code on the collective responsibility of the board for maintaining a sound system of internal control.[98]

10-44   The final variation on the delegation/abdication point comes with reliance on professional advisers. Of course, there are many circumstances in which reliance on professional advisers, such as auditors, is perfectly proper, as was noted in *Re Continental Assurance Co of London plc*.[99] Similarly in *Re Stephenson Cobbold Ltd, Secretary of State for Trade and Industry v Stephenson*[100] where it was alleged that a non-executive director (who was a cheque signatory) should be disqualified as unfit on the grounds, inter alia, that he had allowed an executive director to use company funds for personal expenditure. The court found that the non-executive director had queried the transactions at issue with the company's auditors and, in those circumstances, he was entitled to rely on the explanations given by the auditors (that the payments were part of the director's usual remuneration arrangements) as reassurance that the financial side of the company was being run properly.

10-45   On the other hand, excessive reliance amounting to a total abrogation of responsibility can be seen in *Re Bradcrown Ltd, Official Receiver v Ireland*[101] where a finance director relied entirely on professional advisers in respect of a complex transaction, the net effect of which was that the company transferred away its main assets for no consideration. In terms of reliance on professional advisers, the court noted that the issue is essentially one of degree. In the instant case, although the director was entitled to rely on professional advice, he had asked no questions and simply did what he was told, abdicating all responsibility. In those circumstances, the court held that he could not seek refuge in the fact that professional advisers were involved in the transactions and he was disqualified for two years.

10-46   There is a risk that if too great a reliance on professional advisers is permitted then, in larger companies especially, directors will expend the shareholders' money in having professional advisers approve their every move in order to reduce the individual risk to themselves. A line needs to be drawn therefore between justified reliance and abrogation of responsibility and these lines depend on the nature of the company and its business and the position of the director. Essentially, the issue is whether it is reasonable in all the circumstances for the director to rely on the professional adviser. A director of a small family company may be entitled to put greater reliance on professional

---

[98] FRC, The Combined Code on Corporate Governance (2008) Principle C.2.

[99] [2007] 2 BCLC 287.

[100] [2000] 2 BCLC 614. See also *Norman v Theodore Goddard* [1991] BCLC 1028 where it was reasonable for a director to rely on information regarding the company's investments supplied to him by a solicitor who was a partner in an eminent firm of City solicitors. It turned out that the solicitor had misappropriated the company's money. Looked at in the light of how standards have developed since this decision, the case seems close to the borderline with the director almost abrogating his responsibilities to the company.

[101] [2000] 1 BCLC 547.

advisers than a highly paid and qualified finance director at an international bank; conversely, the complexity of transactions in the latter situation may justify greater reliance on advisers in certain circumstances.

D Duty to exercise independent judgment

The CA 2006, s 173 states, as a fiduciary duty, that a director must exercise independent judgment.   **10-47**

'(1) A director of a company must exercise independent judgment.

(2) This duty is not infringed by his acting—

(a) in accordance with an agreement duly entered into by the company that restricts the future exercise of discretion by its directors, or

(b) in a way authorised by the company's constitution.'

As was explained in the Parliamentary debates, this obligation in s 173(1) to exercise independent judgment does not restrict a director's ability to take advice or to rely on advice (to the extent permissible under the duty of care and skill, as discussed above) nor does it require the director himself to be independent.[102]   **10-48**

Section 173(2)(a) reflects long-standing common law authorities on the directors' obligation not to fetter their discretion. An important authority on this issue is *Thorby v Goldberg*[103] where the directors of a company agreed as part of a broader restructuring transaction to allot shares in a particular manner at a later date. They then failed to do as they had promised. In an action to force them to make the allotment of the shares, they pleaded that the undertaking was an invalid fettering of their discretion on their part. The court rejected this argument, holding that the time for exercising their discretion was at the time of entering into the agreement. Provided they had considered the interests of the company at that time, the agreement was valid. It was not the case that the directors had wrongly fettered their discretion, rather that they had already exercised it.[104]   **10-49**

In *Fulham Football Club Ltd v Cabra Estates plc*[105] the Court of Appeal emphatically endorsed the approach taken in *Thorby v Goldberg.*[106] In this case, the directors of a company had entered into undertakings to support, and to refrain from opposing, planning applications by another party for the development of certain land in return for the receipt by the company of large sums of money. The directors subsequently wanted to give evidence to a planning inquiry opposing the development and sought a declaration that they were not bound by the undertakings and were entitled to give such evidence to the inquiry as they considered to be in the interests of the company.   **10-50**

---

[102] HC Official Report, SC D (Company Law Reform Bill), 11 July 2006, col 598.

[103] (1964) 112 CLR 597, H Ct of Australia. See Prentice (1977) 89 LQR 107 at 111–13.

[104] (1964) 112 CLR 597 at 618, per Owen J.   [105] [1994] 1 BCLC 363; noted Griffiths [1993] JBL 576.

[106] (1964) 112 CLR 597.

10-51   The Court of Appeal held that they were bound by the undertakings. As the undertakings given by the directors were part of contractual arrangements which conferred substantial benefits on the company, the directors had not improperly fettered the future exercise of their discretion by giving those undertakings. Nor was there any scope for the implication of a term into those undertakings that the directors would not be required to do anything that would be inconsistent with their fiduciary duties to the company.[107]

10-52   The distinction which must be drawn, the court said, is between directors fettering their discretion (which is prohibited) and directors exercising their discretion in a way which restricts their future conduct (which is permissible). The directors had exercised their independent judgment at the time when they gave the undertakings not to oppose the planning application and therefore it was not a case of fettering their discretion, but rather a case that they had already exercised it. Certainly there will be many transactions where the proper time for the exercise of the directors' judgment is the time of the negotiation of the contract rather than the time when the contract is to be performed.[108]

10-53   The duty to exercise independent judgment is not infringed by a director acting in a way authorised by the company's constitution: CA 2006, s 173(2)(b). As already noted (see **10-34**), it is accepted that directors may delegate their powers to the extent permitted by the company's articles. The model articles for public and private companies provide that, subject to the articles, the directors may delegate any of the powers conferred on them under the articles.[109] As discussed above, this right to delegate is subject to the obligation to maintain a residual duty of supervision: see **10-35**.

10-54   One possibility raised in the Parliamentary debates is that this provision makes it possible for the status of the nominee director to be enshrined in the constitution.[110] It has always been the position that a nominee once appointed owes his duty to the company, as is the case with any director (CA 2006, s 170(1): see **7-14**), and the nominee is not able to, nor required to, follow the instructions of the person nominating him, though in practice the legal position is no doubt often ignored.[111] Section 173(2)(b), set out at **10-47** above, allows the position to be regularised in that the articles may relieve

---

[107] To the extent that earlier authorities (*John Crowther Group plc v Carpets International plc* [1990] BCLC 460 and *Rackham v Peek Foods Ltd* [1990] BCLC 895—directors' undertakings to use best endeavours to secure shareholder consent to transactions were subject to directors' duties to act in interests of the company) could be read as laying down a general proposition that directors can never bind themselves as to the future exercise of their fiduciary powers, the Court of Appeal considered they were wrong and the decisions should be limited to the particular facts: [1994] 1 BCLC 363 at 393.

[108] See *Thorby v Goldberg* (1964) 112 CLR 597 at 605–6.

[109] See The Companies (Model Articles) Regulations 2008, SI 2008/3229, reg 2, Sch 1, arts 3, 5 (Ltd); reg 4, Sch 3, arts 3, 5 (Plc).

[110] HC Official Report, SC D (Company Law Reform Bill), 11 July 2006, col 601.

[111] See *Re Neath Rugby Ltd, Hawkes v Cuddy* [2008] 1 BCLC 527 at 539 where the court noted that the appropriate compromise is that the director is entitled (and possibly obliged, depending on the terms of the agreement by which he was appointed) to have regard to the interests or requirements of his appointor to the extent that those interests or requirements are not incompatible with his duty to act in the interests of the company.

a nominee director from this fiduciary obligation to exercise independent judgment. Section 173(2)(b) applies only to the duty to exercise independent judgment, however, and the nominee director remains subject to all the other general duties, in particular his duty under s 172 to act in the way he considers, in good faith, would be most likely to promote the success of the company. A nominee director continues therefore to have a somewhat uncomfortable role in terms of managing the conflicting demands of duties to the company (s 170(1)) and the expectations of his nominating shareholder.

11

Duty to avoid a conflict of interest

A Introduction

For all fiduciaries, not just directors, the core of their obligations is a duty of loyalty[1] which includes two key components: a duty to avoid conflicts of interest[2] (no conflict) and not to make secret profits from their fiduciary position[3] (no profit). These long-established principles are stated in CA 2006, s 175 as follows:

> '(1) A director of a company must avoid a situation in which he has, or can have, a direct or indirect interest that conflicts, or possibly may conflict, with the interests of the company.
> (2) This applies in particular to the exploitation of any property, information or opportunity (and it is immaterial whether the company could take advantage of the property, information or opportunity).'

The courts will interpret and apply these duties in the light of the corresponding common law rules and equitable principles (s 170(4)) so the existing case law on these matters remains relevant.

The no-conflict and no-profit rules exist independently of each other and so either or both may apply in a given situation. The usual scenario is that a conflict of interest is exploited by a director for personal advantage so both will apply, but the no-conflict duty can apply on its own, as where someone is in a situation of conflict or possible conflict, but does not seek to exploit it. The no-profit duty too can apply on its own, for example if a director has resigned (in which case the no-conflict rule no longer applies) but he is still prohibited (see CA 2006, s 170(2)(a)) from exploiting information etc of which he became aware at a time when he was a director.[4] The exact relationship between the

11-1

11-2

---

[1] See generally Conaglen, 'The Nature and Function of Fiduciary Loyalty' (2005) 121 LQR 452.

[2] See *Aberdeen Railway Co v Blaikie Bros* (1854) 1 Macq 461 at 471–2, per Lord Cranworth; also *Cook v Deeks* [1916] 1 AC 554, PC; *Industrial Development Consultants Ltd v Cooley* [1972] All ER 162; *Bhullar v Bhullar* [2003] 2 BCLC 241.

[3] See *Keech v Sandford* (1726) Sel Cas Ch 61; *Ex p James* (1803) 8 Ves 337; *Parker v McKenna* (1874) 10 Ch App 96; *Boston Deep Sea Fishing and Ice Co Ltd v Ansell* (1888) 39 Ch D 339, CA; *Regal (Hastings) Ltd v Gulliver* [1942] 1 All ER 378, HL; *Boardman v Phipps* [1966] 3 All ER 721 at 756, HL; *Guinness plc v Saunders* [1990] 1 All ER 652, HL.

[4] See *Quarter Master UK Ltd v Pyke* [2005] 1 BCLC 245 at 264; *CMS Dolphin Ltd v Simonet* [2001] 2 BCLC 704 at 733; *A-G v Blake* [1998] 1 All ER 833 at 841. Also *Ultraframe (UK) Ltd v Fielding* [2005] EWHC 1638, paras 1329–30, where Lewison J considered, likewise, on the appointment of an administrative receiver, the

two elements has been the subject of much comment over the years,[5] but the statutory scheme clearly adopts the no-conflict rule, set out in s 175(1), as the broader obligation with s 175(2) reflecting the no-profit obligation as a sub-set of that broader obligation.[6]

11-3   Traditionally the courts have applied the no-conflict, no-profit, duties with unyielding strictness, regarding it as of fundamental importance that a company is entitled to the undivided loyalty of its directors.[7] As Rix LJ noted in *Foster Bryant Surveying Ltd v Bryant*,[8] these duties are 'exacting requirements, exactingly enforced'. Two main justifications are put forward for such a strict approach. First, the deterrent argument, i.e. the duties must be rigorously applied so as not to offer any encouragement to fiduciaries (in this context, directors) to pursue their own interests at the expense of their beneficiaries (in this context, the shareholders).[9] Secondly, a strict approach is an efficient way of addressing the agency problem within companies, by which is meant the difficulty which shareholders have in monitoring the conduct of their directors.[10] Holding fiduciaries to exacting obligations reduces the need for such monitoring.

11-4   Notwithstanding that starting point, the position is not one of unremitting severity for the emphasis on the fact-specific nature of these fiduciary obligations has always allowed a certain amount of judicial flexibility in the application of the duties[11] and, as Arden LJ noted, 'equity has been able skilfully to adapt remedies against defaulting fiduciaries to meet the justice of the case'.[12] Also, a fiduciary who wants relief from

no-conflict duty does not apply to a director in respect of assets within the control of the receiver, but the no-profit rule would still apply, to preclude the director profiting from any exploitation of the company's assets.

[5] See, for example, *Chan v Zacharia* (1984) 154 CLR 178 at 198; *Ultraframe (UK) Ltd v Fielding* [2005] EWHC 1638, paras 1305–6; *Don King Productions Inc v Warren* [2000] 1 BCLC 607 at 629–30, CA; *Gencor ACP Ltd v Dalby* [2000] 2 BCLC 734 at 741.

[6] See *Boardman v Phipps* [1966] 3 All ER 721 at 756, per Lord Upjohn; *New Zealand Netherlands Society 'Oranje' Inc v Kuys* [1973] 2 All ER 1222. See *Quarter Master UK Ltd v Pyke* [2005] 1 BCLC 245 at 263–4 for a useful discussion of the overlap between these obligations; also generally Conaglen, 'The Nature and Function of Fiduciary Loyalty' (2005) 121 LQR 452. The distinguished Australian judge and author, PD Finn, described the no-profit rule as a 'loose end' to the general no-conflict rule: see Finn, *Fiduciary Obligations* (1977), p 246.

[7] See *Parker v McKenna* (1874) 10 Ch App 96 at 124, per James LJ; *New Zealand Netherlands Society 'Oranje' Inc v Kuys* [1973] 2 All ER 1222 at 1225, per Lord Wilberforce; *Industrial Development Consultants Ltd v Cooley* [1972] 2 All ER 162 at 173–4, per Roskill J.

[8] [2007] 2 BCLC 239 at 266.

[9] See, for example, *Lindsley v Woodfull* [2004] 2 BCLC 131 at 140; *Murad v Al-Saraj* [2005] All ER (D) 503 (Jul), CA, para 74; also generally Conaglen, 'The Nature and Function of Fiduciary Loyalty' (2005) 121 LQR 452. See too Grantham, 'Can Directors Compete with the Company?' (2003) 66 MLR 109 who comments (at 112) that equity imposes such rigorous obligations because of the beneficiary's vulnerability to the fiduciary, the need to maintain the sanctity of relationships of trust and confidence and the difficulty of actually proving breach of duty.

[10] See *Item Software (UK) Ltd v Fassihi* [2005] 2 BCLC 91 at 110.

[11] See Rix LJ in *Foster Bryant Surveying Ltd v Bryant* [2007] 2 BCLC 239 at 266: '… there has been some flexibility, both in the reach and extent of the duties imposed and in the findings of liability or non-liability'; see also *Wilkinson v West Coast Capital* [2007] BCC 717 at 767, [2005] All ER (D) 346 (Dec), Ch D, para 245; *In Plus Group Ltd v Pyke* [2002] 2 BCLC 201 at 222, per Sedley LJ; *Henderson v Merrett Syndicates* [1995] AC 145 at 206, per Lord Browne-Wilkinson; *Boardman v Phipps* [1966] 3 All ER 721 at 756–7, per Lord Upjohn.

[12] See *Murad v Al-Saraj* [2005] All ER (D) 503 (Jul), para 81.

the strict application of the law always has the option of seeking the informed consent of the shareholders after full and frank disclosure of all relevant matters,[13] an option retained by CA 2006, s 180(4)(a): see **11-66**.

From time to time, there have been judicial suggestions (and academic comment) that   **11-5** the unrelenting application of the no-profit duty, in particular, might be relaxed, out of concerns that the unyielding application of the duty might operate harshly and unduly restrict entrepreneurial freedom to compete with companies.[14] Those concerns have been addressed by the Companies Act 2006 which modifies the strict application of the no-conflict and no-profit duty to permit disinterested directors to authorise conduct which would otherwise be a breach of duty (see s 175(4)(b)). It remains to be seen whether this change in position might encourage the courts to take a more relaxed view of whether there is a conflict of interest in a particular case on the basis that Parliament no longer supports the idea of 'exacting obligations, exactingly applied'. Equally, given the availability of authorisation, the courts may take the view that the director who chooses not to seek authorisation should continue to be subject to the full rigour of the law.

B Scope of the duty to avoid conflicts of interest

Situations of conflict, or possible conflict, of interest

Liability under CA 2006, s 175(1) arises from a situation of conflict, or of possible   **11-6** conflict, with 'possible' being limited, in the words of Lord Upjohn in *Boardman v Phipps*,[15] to 'whether a reasonable man looking at the relevant facts and circumstances would think that there is a real sensible possibility of conflict' with the interests of those whom the fiduciary is bound to protect.[16] For example, if the company's activities are predominantly in one sector of the economy, there is no real sensible possibility of a conflict where a director sets up a company to pursue activities in an entirely different

[13] *New Zealand Netherlands Society 'Oranje' Inc v Kuys* [1973] 2 All ER 1222; *Gwembe Valley Development Co Ltd v Koshy* [2004] 1 BCLC 131 at 151; *Crown Dilmun v Sutton* [2004] 1 BCLC 468 at 511; *Murad v Al-Saraj* [2005] All ER (D) 503 (Jul), CA, para 71; *Quarter Master (UK) Ltd v Pyke* [2005] 1 BCLC 245 at 269. There must be actual disclosure and consent; what the beneficiaries might have done, if there had been disclosure is irrelevant: *Murad v Al-Saraj*, above, paras 71–2; and the disclosure must be of all material facts: see Mummery LJ in *Gwembe Valley Development*, above, at 151; *Newgate Stud Co v Penfold* [2008] 1 BCLC 46 at 102.

[14] See, for example, *Murad v Al-Saraj* [2005] All ER (D) 503 (Jul), CA, paras 82–3, per Arden LJ; paras 121–2, per Jonathan Parker LJ, but see criticisms by Conaglen (2006) CLJ 278. For academic commentary, see Lowry & Edmunds, 'The No Conflict-No Profit Rules and the Corporate Fiduciary: Challenging the Orthodoxy of Absolutism' [2000] JBL 122, and criticisms by Kershaw, 'Lost in Translation: Corporate Opportunities in Comparative Perspective' (2005) 25 Ox JLS 603.

[15] [1966] 3 All ER 721 at 756.

[16] See also *Aberdeen Railway Co v Blaikie Bros* (1854) 1 Macq 461 at 471–2, per Lord Cranworth; *Transvaal Lands Company v New Belgium (Transvaal) Land and Development Company* [1914] 2 Ch 488. See also *Cowan de Groot Properties Ltd v Eagle Trust plc* [1991] BCLC 1045 at 1116; *Re Dominion International Group plc (No 2)* [1996] 1 BCLC 572 at 597.

sector.[17] This limitation is reflected by s 175(4)(a) which provides that the no-conflict duty does not apply if the situation cannot reasonably be regarded as likely to give rise to a conflict of interest.[18] The rule exists, after all, to protect the company from abuse of position, not to stifle entrepreneurial activity. As was stated in *Boulting v ACTAT* :[19]

> '...a broad rule like this must be applied with common sense and with an appreciation of the sort of circumstances in which over the last 200 years and more it has been applied and thrived. It must be applied realistically to a state of affairs which discloses a real conflict of duty and interest and not to some theoretical or rhetorical conflict.' (Upjohn LJ)

11-7   The initial question for a director in any given situation is simply whether that situation attracts the application of the no-conflict duty.[20] This 'bright line' approach, epitomised by *Bhullar v Bhullar*,[21] means that the question is simple. The difficulty lies in identifying whether the situation is one in which the director has, or can have, a conflict or possible conflict of interest.

Conflict between interest and duty and between duties

11-8   The no-conflict rule applies (see CA 2006, s 175(7)) whether the conflict is between 'interest' and 'duty' (i.e. between the personal interests of a director and his duty to advance the interests of the company) and also where there is a conflict or possible conflict between 'duties' (for example, where a director is a director of two or more companies and has a separate duty to advance the interests of each company).[22]

Multiple directorships

11-9   There is no rule that a director cannot be a director of another company, even a company which is wholly or partly engaged competitively in the same trade.[23] Of course,

---

[17] See *Wilkinson v West Coast Capital* [2007] BCC 717 at 768; [2005] All ER (D) 346 (Dec), Ch D, paras 252–3.

[18] The Government considered that CA 2006, s 175(4)(a) introduces a requirement of reasonableness, see HL Deb, vol 678, GC293 (6 February 2006), but it is not clear that this does much other than reflect the limitation already identified by Lord Upjohn.

[19] [1963] 2 QB 606 at 637–8.

[20] There seems to be some perception that CA 2006, s 175 is broader than the common law which preceded it, that the no-conflict rule did not apply to 'situations' but only when the director entered into a conflicted transaction, but this is more an issue of perception (or non-compliance) than anything else, see, for example, Sedley LJ in *In Plus Group Ltd v Pyke* [2002] 2 BCLC 201 at 225, '...the law will take notice of a situation of impending or potential breach, as well as of an actual breach and without the need of any proven breach, will set aside a transaction entered into in the shadow of a conflict of interest'; also *Bhullar v Bhullar* [2003] 2 BCLC 241; *Industrial Development Consultants Ltd v Cooley* [1972] 2 All ER 162 at 173–4.

[21] [2003] 2 BCLC 441, noted Prentice & Payne (2004) 120 LQR 198 at 202.

[22] See *Transvaal Lands Company v New Belgium (Transvaal) Land and Development Company* [1914] 2 Ch 488 where a director of the plaintiff company voted in favour of a resolution for the purchase of shares from the defendant company. It turned out that, as a trustee, he held 0.5% of the shares in the defendant company. This conflicting interest was held sufficient to found a claim to avoid the transaction.

[23] *London and Mashonaland Exploration Co Ltd v New Mashonaland Exploration Co Ltd* [1891] WN 165, approved in *Bell v Lever Bros* [1932] AC 161, HL. See the discussion of the *Mashonaland* principle in *In Plus*

there is a significant potential for a conflict of interest in that case, for example, where a director of company A is also a director of Company B which is a customer or supplier of Company A. Disclosure and consent is the key to this situation and the director who holds two directorships in situations of potentially conflicting interests is in breach of the obligation of undivided loyalty unless he secures the informed consent of both companies.[24] Even then, the director will find it difficult to serve two masters without being in breach of his obligation to one or the other.[25] As Millett LJ commented in *Bristol and West BS v Mothew*:[26]

'Even if a fiduciary is properly acting for two principals with potentially conflicting interests he must act in good faith in the interests of each and must not act with the intention of furthering the interests of one principal to the prejudice of those of the other...He must not allow the performance of his obligations to one principal to be influenced by his relationship with the other. He must serve each as faithfully and loyally as if he were his only principal.'

The difficulty in walking such a tightrope is obvious and once the director finds himself in a position of actual (as opposed to possible) conflict, he may have no alternative but to resign from one of his positions.[27] **11-10**

This issue of multiple competing directorships is important in practice and it has given rise to concerns as to how the statutory duty in CA 2006, s 175(1) can be met. As already noted, the first stage is to disclose the potential conflict and seek consent or authorisation to hold the posts, as discussed below. Even with consent to occupy the various posts, practical difficulties persist, for example as to how conflicts as they arise will be dealt with and the fact that, in some circumstances, a director's duty of confidentiality to one company will prevent him even revealing the conflict of interest to the other company. On that scenario, resignation is the only possible course and, in practice, multiple competing posts are difficult if not impossible to maintain. **11-11**

Illustrations of conflicts of interest

As Jonathan Parker LJ noted in *Bhullar v Bhullar*,[28] the no-conflict rule is essentially a simple rule, 'albeit it may in some cases be difficult to apply'.[29] The problem lies in **11-12**

Group Ltd v Pyke [2002] 2 BCLC 201, CA, noted Grantham (2003) 66 MLR 109; also Christie, 'The Director's Fiduciary Duty not to Compete' (1992) 55 MLR 506.

[24] See *Bristol and West BS v Mothew* [1996] 4 All ER 698 at 712, per Millett LJ.

[25] See *In Plus Group Ltd v Pyke* [2002] 2 BCLC 201 at 222, CA, where Sedley LJ made clear that he thought the position of a competing director is almost unsustainable. While Brooke and Jonathan Parker LJJ declined in this case to explore the precise scope of the *Mashonaland* principle, it seems clear that all three judges believed it to be of very limited application, as where in effect the position of the director in one company is purely nominal to such an extent that the director attracts no fiduciary obligations from that position. See Grantham on *In Plus Group Ltd* at (2003) 66 MLR 109. See *Scottish Co-operative Wholesale Society Ltd v Meyer* [1959] AC 324 at 367–8, HL.   [26] [1996] 4 All ER 698 at 713.

[27] See *Bristol and West BS v Mothew* [1996] 4 All ER 698 at 713, per Millett LJ.

[28] [2003] 2 BCLC 241.

[29] [2003] 2 BCLC 241 at 253. See *Wilkinson v West Coast Capital* [2007] BCC 717 at 768; [2005] All ER (D) 346 (Dec), Ch D, paras 252–3 on the difficulty in identifying in any given situation whether the relevant element of conflict is present.

identifying that a conflict exists and directors are poor at realising when they are in a position of conflict (or perhaps they recognise the conflict but choose to ignore it), as the cases illustrate.

11-13   A leading modern authority on conflict of interest is *Bhullar v Bhullar*[30] where two directors of a family company were held to be in breach of the no-conflict rule when they acquired property adjacent to the company without telling the company that the property was available for purchase. They had come across the information that the property was for sale quite by chance and in circumstances which had nothing to do with their directorships. Their personal interest in acquiring the land was in conflict with their duty to promote the company's interests which required them to communicate the existence of the opportunity to the company which could then have considered whether to acquire it. There was a real sensible possibility of conflict and they were in breach of their duty when they acquired the property for themselves.

11-14   An older authority is *Cook v Deeks*[31] where two of the three directors of a Canadian railway company diverted a contract in which the company was interested to another company which they had formed. The Privy Council found that the opportunity to obtain this contract had come to the directors in their capacity and by virtue of their position as directors of the company. While still retaining that position, while still acting as managers, and with their duties to the company entirely unchanged, they had proceeded to negotiate in reality on their own behalf.[32] There was a clear conflict between their personal interests in securing the contract and their duty to secure it for the company. The court held that the contract was one which in equity belonged to the company and the directors were bound to hold it on behalf of the company.[33]

11-15   In *Industrial Development Consultants Ltd v Cooley*,[34] Cooley had been employed as managing director by the company (IDC) and was actively involved in negotiations with the Eastern Gas Board to secure certain construction contracts for IDC.[35] It became clear that the Gas Board was not prepared to contract with IDC. A year later, the Gas Board approached Cooley and indicated a willingness for him personally to take on the management of these construction projects. He promptly resigned from IDC (giving the company the misleading impression that he was ill) and took the contracts offered by the Gas Board which were in substance the work that the company had unsuccessfully attempted to obtain the previous year.

11-16   Roskill J held that Cooley was liable to account as he had one capacity and one capacity only at the time when the Gas Board approached him and that was as managing

---

[30] [2003] 2 BCLC 441, CA; noted Prentice & Payne (2004) 120 LQR 198; Armour (2004) CLJ 33.
[31] [1916] 1 AC 554, PC. See *Ultraframe (UK) Ltd v Fielding* [2005] EWHC 1638, para 1334, per Lewison J; *Wilkinson v West Coast Capital* [2007] BCC 717 at 771; [2005] All ER (D) 346 (Dec) Ch D, para 264, per Warren J; both are agreed that *Cook v Deeks* is a classic no-conflict case rather than a no-profit case, as it is usually described.
[32] [1916] 1 AC 554 at 559–60.   [33] [1916] 1 AC 554 at 564.   [34] [1972] 2 All ER 162.
[35] It is also important that it was Cooley who was conducting the negotiations: see *Furs Ltd v Tomkies* (1936) 54 CLR 583; *Framlington Group plc v Anderson* [1995] 1 BCLC 475.

director of the plaintiff company,[36] a fiduciary position which subjected him to an obligation to avoid possible conflicts between his personal interests and his fiduciary duty. Information which came to him while he was managing director (i.e. the knowledge that the Gas Board was back in the market and looking to place these construction contracts) and which was of concern to the company and was relevant to the company to know was information which it was his duty, because of his fiduciary position, to pass on to the company.[37] Instead he embarked upon what was, the court found,

'. . . a deliberate policy and course of conduct which put his personal interest . . . in direct conflict with his pre-existing and continuing duty as managing director of [the company]'.[38]

In each of these cases, it is clear that the directors found themselves in a situation where their personal interests and their duties to the company conflicted such that now there would be a breach of CA 2006, s 175(1).   **11-17**

Disclosure of the conflict

These cases further highlight, as Sedley LJ explained in *In Plus Group Ltd v Pyke*,[39] that not only must the fiduciary not place himself in a position of conflict or possible conflict: if, even accidentally, he finds himself in such a position, he must regularise or abandon it. In practice, this means he must disclose the conflict of interest and seek authorisation or resign his position, though resignation will not allow him to exploit property, information or opportunity of which he became aware as a director (CA 2006, s 170(2)(a)). The no-conflict duty ceases to apply once a director resigns[40] since that duty is intended to prevent a director, in the exercise of his powers, from being swayed by his self-interest. If he is no longer a director, he has no powers to exercise and there is no risk that he will be swayed by self-interest.[41]   **11-18**

As far as disclosure is concerned, as part of a director's duty to promote the success of the company (CA 2006, s 172), he must disclose information of relevance or concern to the company.[42] The fact that that information may relate to his own conduct (in the form of a conflict of interest or the exploitation of company assets) or that of his fellow directors does not alter that obligation of disclosure.[43] Given the duty is to avoid situations of conflict, the non-disclosure of the conflict (even if it is not exploited by the director) is itself a breach of duty.   **11-19**

---

[36] [1972] 2 All ER 162 at 173.   [37] [1972] 2 All ER 162 at 173–4.

[38] [1972] 2 All ER 162 at 173–4.   [39] [2002] 2 BCLC 201 at 225.

[40] See *Quarter Master UK Ltd v Pyke* [2005] 1 BCLC 245 at 264; *CMS Dolphin Ltd v Simonet* [2001] 2 BCLC 704 at 733; *A-G v Blake* [1998] 1 All ER 833 at 841.

[41] See *Ultraframe (UK) Ltd v Fielding* [2005] EWHC 1638, paras 1309–10, per Lewison J; also *Wilkinson v West Coast Capital* [2007] BCC 717 at 768; [2005] All ER (D) 346 (Dec), Ch D, para 251.

[42] *Industrial Development Consultants Ltd v Cooley* [1972] All ER 162; *Bhullar v Bhullar* [2003] 2 BCLC 241; *Item Software (UK) Ltd v Fassihi* [2005] 2 BCLC 91; see also *Crown Dilmun v Sutton* [2004] 1 BCLC 468 at 511; *Shepherds Investments v Walters* [2007] 2 BCLC 202 at 229–30; *Secretary of State for Trade and Industry v Goldberg* [2004] 1 BCLC 597 at 647–8; and Watts (2007) 123 LQR 21.

[43] See also *British Midland Tool Ltd v Midland International Tooling Ltd* [2003] 2 BCLC 523; *Coleman Taymar Ltd v Oakes* [2001] 2 BCLC 749.

11-20   This disclosure issue was addressed by the Court of Appeal in *Item Software (UK) Ltd v Fassihi*[44] where a director should have disclosed that, while the company was negotiating for the renewal of an important distribution contract, the director was also negotiating to secure the contract for his personal benefit. The court held that the director could not have fulfilled his duty of loyalty to the company except by disclosing his plans including that he had set up his own company and planned to acquire the distribution contract for himself.[45] In effect, given that the director will be unwilling to disclose his plans, the requirement of disclosure forces him to resign. Arden LJ gave three reasons for imposing this duty of disclosure.[46] It is efficient in economic terms as the company does not have to expend resources in investigating the conduct of its directors; a failure to disclose means that the company may reach erroneous business decisions on incomplete information so to condone non-disclosure is to condone inefficient outcomes; and the requirement of disclosure addresses the agency problem (how shareholders monitor their directors) and supports the board in managing its oversight of the conduct of executive directors. The fact that directors will not comply with this obligation to disclose is not, Arden LJ said,[47] a reason for not imposing the obligation. Imposing the obligation makes it easier to establish a breach of duty and forces a director to disclose his own or other directors' plans at an early stage so limiting the potential damage to the company from their remaining in post while in a position of conflict of interest.

Exploiting property, information or opportunity

11-21   In addition to avoiding a situation of conflict as required by CA 2006, s 175(1), the no-profit rule in s 175(2) particularly prohibits the exploitation of any property, information or opportunity in circumstances where there is a conflict, or possible conflict, of interest. This prohibition is not limited to the exploitation of the director's position or of property, etc of the company ('any property')[48] as was explained in *Quarter Master UK Ltd v Pyke*:[49]

> 'It is not because he made a profit from trust property or a profit from his fiduciary position that the director is liable under the conflict rule. Rather, it is because, being in a fiduciary position, he has entered into a transaction, inconsistent with his fiduciary duty of loyalty to the company, which has yielded the profit and he has thereby misused his position.... *his liability in respect of the profit arises because of the conflict of interest* [emphasis added]. In many cases where the conflict rule applies, the director will also have taken advantage of the property of the company or of his fiduciary position, but this will not always be so.'

---

[44] [2005] 2 BCLC 91, noted Berg (2005) 121 LQR 213 who is critical of the imposition of a duty to disclose misconduct; see also Ho and Lee, 'A Director's Duty to Confess: A Matter of Good Faith' (2007) CLJ 348.

[45] [2005] 2 BCLC 91 at 104.   [46] [2005] 2 BCLC 91 at 109–10.   [47] [2005] 2 BCLC 91 at 110.

[48] This wording was deliberately chosen as it is for the courts to determine whether the exploitation of the property, information or opportunity has given rise to a conflict of interest, see HL Deb, vol 681, GC864 (9 May 2006).

[49] [2005] 1 BCLC 245 at 263, per Paul Morgan QC, sitting as a Deputy Judge.

In *Bhullar v Bhullar*[50] Jonathan Parker LJ also emphasised that it is not a pre-requisite   **11-22**
of accountability that there should be some improper dealing with property 'belonging' to the party to whom the fiduciary duty is owed. The issue is the exploiting of
property, information or opportunity in circumstances where there is a conflict, or
possible conflict, of interest between the director and the company.

This 'bright line' approach, epitomised by *Bhullar v Bhullar*,[51] avoids any need for   **11-23**
a corporate opportunities doctrine in the sense of asking whether the director has
appropriated a 'maturing business opportunity'. This approach, involving typically
a consideration of the factors identified by Laskin J in *Canadian Aero Service Ltd v
O'Malley*[52] such as 'the position or office held, the nature of the corporate opportunity,
its ripeness, its specificness and the director's relation to it, the amount of knowledge
possessed, the circumstances in which it was obtained, etc' is not necessary.[53] All that
is required is to look to the simple approach endorsed by Jonathan Parker LJ in *Bhullar
v Bhullar*[54] and to ask the question whether the director was in a position of conflict.
Of course, there is an element of overlap in the sense that the nature of the opportunity etc is relevant to whether the director has a conflict of interest. But once it is established that the director has a conflict, then the obligation not to exploit the situation
applies (CA 2006, s 175(2)).

At common law, the no-profit duty has its origins in the leading trust case of *Keech*   **11-24**
v Sandford[55] but the most famous application of the rule in company law is *Regal
(Hastings) Ltd v Gulliver*.[56] In this case a company could not finance the acquisition of
additional cinemas which it wished to acquire. It was unable to put up sufficient share
capital for the acquiring subsidiary and instead that capital was put up by the directors
who then profited personally on the sale of the shares in the subsidiary. The new controllers of the company successfully sued the former directors to recover those profits.

The House of Lords found that the directors had obtained their profits by reason of   **11-25**
and in the course of the execution of their office as directors of Regal.[57] They had
entered into the transaction in the course of their management and in utilisation of
their opportunities and special knowledge as directors.[58] They were thus liable to
account, notwithstanding the fact that they had acted bona fide throughout. As directors, they were in a situation of conflict between their personal interests and their
duty to the company and they exploited the conflict to their own advantage. In such
circumstances, the court said, 'the profiteer, however honest and well-intentioned,
cannot escape the risk of being called upon to account'.[59]

---

[50] [2003] 2 BCLC 241 at 252. See also Lewison J in *Ultraframe (UK) Ltd v Fielding* [2005] EWHC 1638,
para 1355: 'The application of the no-conflict rule does not depend on establishing that the company has a
proprietary interest in the business opportunity that has been diverted'.
[51] [2003] 2 BCLC 241.   [52] (1973) 40 DLR (3d) 371 at 391.
[53] See also *Island Export Finance Ltd v Umunna* [1986] BCLC 460 at 481–2.
[54] [2003] 2 BCLC 241 at 252.   [55] (1726) Sel Cas Ch 61.   [56] [1942] 1 All ER 378, HL.
[57] [1942] 1 All ER 378 at 389, per Lord Russell.   [58] [1942] 1 All ER 378 at 392, per Lord Macmillan.
[59] [1942] 1 All ER 378 at 386, per Lord Russell. The actual decision in *Regal* has been criticised: see Gower
and Davies, *Principles of Modern Company Law* (7th edn, 2003), p 418: '...carrying equitable principles to an
inequitable conclusion'; also Jones (1968) 84 LQR 472 at 497. But see Sullivan (1979) 42 MLR 711, who points

11-26   In *Gencor ACP Ltd v Dalby*[60] a director had in effect been running a parallel competing business for many years, diverting contracts for the company's products to companies which he controlled in breach of the no-conflict and no-profit duties. In *Crown Dilmun v Sutton*[61] the director of a property development company took for himself a development opportunity despite the clear conflict of interest between him and the company. As a director, he had a duty to disclose the existence of the opportunity to the company yet he secured it for himself and concealed his involvement in the contract from the company. In *Quarter Master UK Ltd v Pyke*[62] the directors, at a time when the company was in significant financial difficulties, engaged in a strategy to salvage for themselves a major ongoing contract with a customer. They also exploited the company's database of customers and its goodwill in securing the contract for themselves. There was a conflict of interest between their seeking to obtain the contract for themselves and their duty to the company to seek ways to maximise the value of the contract for the company and its creditors (even if the company was no longer in a position to continue the contract itself). The court held that they acted in breach of the no-conflict and the no-profit rule.

11-27   In all these cases, the directors, while still in post, have allowed a clear conflict to arise between their personal interests and their duties of loyalty to their companies and they have sought to exploit the conflict for their personal advantage. In such circumstances, the courts have no hesitation in finding the directors in breach of the no-conflict and no-profit duties and now they would be liable for breach of CA 2006, s 175(1) and (2).

Liability regardless of the company's position

11-28   This strict liability to account applies regardless of whether the company could take advantage of the property, opportunity or information (CA 2006, s 175(2)). It suffices that the director has profited from a situation of conflict and it is better to apply a strict rule than to attempt to investigate whether, in fact, the company could or would have exploited the opportunity.[63] That is a particularly difficult matter to investigate given that many of the factors relevant to it may lie within the director's control (such as the company's ability to borrow money) which the director may have manipulated precisely in order to show that the company could not or would not have exploited the opportunity. For these reasons, the courts prefer the strict approach (reflected in s 175(2)) that the company's position is not a relevant issue when considering the liability of a director who has exploited a conflict of interest. In *Regal (Hastings) Ltd v Gulliver*,[64] for example, Lord Russell commented that the question of liability does not

---

out that the directors had a would-be purchaser in mind throughout and that there were other shareholders in Regal who could have put up some of the money required but who were not invited to do so. See also *Boardman v Phipps* [1966] 3 All ER 721, HL.

[60] [2000] 2 BCLC 734.   [61] [2004] 1 BCLC 468.   [62] [2005] 1 BCLC 245.

[63] See *Regal (Hastings) Ltd v Gulliver* [1942] 1 All ER 378 at 392; also *Furs Ltd v Tomkies* (1936) 54 CLR 583 at 592, approved in *Gwembe Valley Development Co v Koshy* [2004] 1 BCLC 131 at 146; and *Wilkinson v West Coast Capital* [2007] BCC 717 at 769; [2005] All ER (D) 346 (Dec) Ch D para 255. But for criticism of the view that investigation of these matters is too difficult, see *Murad v Al-Saraj* [2005] All ER (D) 503 (Jul), CA, paras 82, 155.   [64] [1942] 1 All ER 378, HL.

depend on 'fraud, or absence of bona fides; or upon such questions or considerations as whether the profit would or should otherwise have gone to the plaintiff [company]'.[65] Likewise in *Industrial Development Consultants Ltd v Cooley,*[66] discussed at **11-15**, the fact that the company only had a 10% chance of securing the construction contracts at issue was irrelevant to the liability of the director.[67] In *Crown Dilmun v Sutton,*[68] noted at **11-26**, it was irrelevant whether the company would/could have taken the major contract which the director diverted to a company that he had formed.[69] There were suggestions that the company could not have taken the opportunity for financial reasons or that the third party might not have been willing to deal with the company, but each was irrelevant to the liability of the director. In *Quarter Master UK Ltd v Pyke,*[70] noted at **11-26**, the fact that a key client had indicated that it was not likely to renew a contract with the company (which was in significant financial difficulties) was irrelevant to the directors' liability to account when they took the contract on their own behalf.

This point was emphasised by the Court of Appeal in *Bhullar v Bhullar.*[71] As noted at **11-13**, two of the directors of a family company acquired property adjacent to the company's premises without disclosing to the company that the property was on the market. They accepted that the property would have been commercially attractive to the company, but they argued that, as negotiations were underway for the company's business to be sold, the company would not have had an interest in pursuing the matter. Jonathan Parker LJ noted: **11-29**

'Whether the Company could or would have taken that opportunity, had it been made aware of it, is not to the point: the existence of the opportunity was information which it was relevant for the Company to know, and it follows that the appellants were under a duty to communicate it to the Company.'[72]

Having acquired the property in circumstances where there was a real sensible possibility of conflict between their personal interests and their duties to the company, the court had no doubt that the directors were liable to account.

The inability of a company to exploit an opportunity (because of a lack of resources etc) is not the same as a structural restriction that prevents the company from exploiting the opportunity—in that case, the no-conflict rule would not apply.[73] If the   **11-30**

---

[65] [1942] 1 All ER 378 at 386.   [66] [1972] 2 All ER 162, CA.
[67] [1972] 2 All ER 162 at 176.   [68] [2004] 1 BCLC 468.
[69] [2004] 1 BCLC 468 at 511. See also *Gencor ACP Ltd v Dalby* [2000] 2 BCLC 734 where a director was held liable for diverting contracts in which the company had an interest to his own business. The court dismissed a defence that the director had dealt mainly in second-hand equipment which was a market which the company was not interested in pursuing.
[70] [2005] 1 BCLC 245.   [71] [2003] 2 BCLC 241, CA.   [72] [2003] 2 BCLC 241 at 256.
[73] See *Wilkinson v West Coast Capital* [2007] BCC 717 where two directors personally acquired another business when, it was argued, the company should have been given the opportunity to do so. The distinguishing feature here was a shareholders' agreement which effectively prevented the company from making any further acquisitions. In these circumstances, the court held that the no-conflict duty did not apply as the company was structurally incapable of pursuing the opportunity.

opportunity is something which, in that sense, the company cannot pursue, then there is no conflict of interest.

The no-conflict rule and the departing director

11-31　A director may resign at any time even though such resignation may damage or harm the company.[74] Equally, there is nothing to stop a person forming the intention, while a director, to set up in competition with his company after his directorship ceases (subject to any contractual constraints) for the no-profit rule is not intended to hinder directors in the exploitation of the general fund of knowledge and expertise acquired while a director.[75] A director is also able to take preliminary steps to investigate or forward that intention to compete, provided he does not engage in any actual competitive activity[76] and so does not reach the situation where there is a conflict or possible conflict between his interests and his duty to the company.[77]

11-32　The problem is that it is difficult to identify the point in time when the mere intention to compete turns into a conflict of interest[78] and, by and large, the case law shows that directors in that situation commonly overstep the mark.

11-33　The discussion below is limited to liability for breach of fiduciary duty but many directors will have service agreements with express provisions governing the solicitation of customers and use of confidential information post-resignation. In many cases, therefore, the director may also face claims based on a breach of contract or common law obligations of confidence.

Intending to resign

11-34　In *Colman Taymar Ltd v Oakes*[79] the director failed to disclose his intention to compete with the company and, while still a director, used confidential information and the company's staff to assist him in securing leases and hiring equipment for his new business. In *Shepherds Investments Ltd v Walters*[80] the defendant directors, while still directors, took very active steps to promote a competing business to be carried on by them in the future. They drew up business plans and financial projections, contacted advisers, sought backers and devised complicated documentation relating to the new company's financial products. In *Simtel Communications Ltd v Rebak*,[81] while still a director and employee of the company, the defendant director set up a competing

---

[74] See *CMS Dolphin Ltd v Simonet* [2001] 2 BCLC 704 at 729.

[75] See *Island Export Finance Ltd v Umunna* [1986] BCLC 460 at 482–3; *Balston Ltd v Headline Filters Ltd* [1990] FSR 385 at 412.

[76] See *Balston Ltd v Headline Filters Ltd* [1990] FSR 385 at 412, per Falconer J; also *Framlington Group plc v Anderson* [1995] 1 BCLC 475 at 495–6, 498.

[77] The director must also be mindful of any express contractual restrictions on his conduct: see *Kingsley IT Consulting Ltd v McIntosh* [2006] BCC 875.

[78] See *Shepherds Investments Ltd v Walters* [2007] 2 BCLC 202 at 223–4; *Balston Ltd v Headline Filters Ltd* [1990] FSR 385 at 412, per Falconer J; also Watts, 'The Transition from Director to Competitor' (2007) 123 LQR 21.

[79] [2001] 2 BCLC 749.　　[80] [2007] 2 BCLC 202.　　[81] [2006] 2 BCLC 571.

company, diverted contracts to that company, solicited the company's customers, removed information and destroyed computer files, all to the advantage of his new business.

Given that practically any preparatory steps to form a competing business will give   **11-35**
rise to a possible conflict of interest[82] and given the obligation, discussed at **11-21**, to convey to the company information which it is relevant for it to know[83] (such as a director's intention to resign and compete with the company), it is clear that the effect of these decisions is to impel the director towards resignation at the earliest possible moment.[84] This approach provides maximum protection for the company by ensuring, in effect, that a director cannot remain in post without disclosing his intention to resign and to compete. This forced early disclosure allows a company to manage the process, for example by requiring that the director leaves immediately or, where a period of notice is enforced, ensuring that the departing director no longer has access to customer data or commercially valuable information.

Resignation

By resigning, as Hart J noted in *British Midland Tool Ltd v Midland International*   **11-36**
Tooling Ltd,[85] a director 'puts an end to his fiduciary obligations to the company so far as concerns any future activity by himself, provided it does not involve any exploitation of confidential information or business opportunities available to him by virtue of his directorship'. As noted at **11-2**, the no-conflict duty falls away on resignation,[86] but the no-profit obligation continues and prohibits the exploitation by the director of any property, information or opportunity of which he became aware when he was a director (CA 2006, s 170(2)). This duty obviously comes with a built-in expiry date in the sense that the longer the period post-resignation, the less likely it is that it can be established that the former director is exploiting property etc of which he became aware when he was a director. This prohibition cannot extend to *any* property, information, or opportunity of which he became aware during that period for such a restriction would be contrary to public policy.[87] There must be some link between the exploitation of the property, information or opportunity and the fiduciary position which the director held (as s 170(2) indicates). The link is to the exploitation of property, information or opportunity acquired in circumstances where the director had a

---

[82] See *British Midland Tool Ltd v Midland International Tooling Ltd* [2003] 2 BCLC 523 and *Shepherds Investments Ltd v Walters* [2007] 2 BCLC 202 as to what may be permissible, but the courts are reluctant to give precise guidance as the circumstances vary so much from case to case.

[83] *Industrial Development Consultants Ltd v Cooley* [1972] All ER 162; *Bhullar v Bhullar* [2003] 2 BCLC 241; *Item Software (UK) Ltd v Fassihi* [2005] 2 BCLC 91; see also *Crown Dilmun v Sutton* [2004] 1 BCLC 468 at 511; *Shepherds Investments Ltd v Walters* [2007] 2 BCLC 202 at 229–30; and Watts (2007) 123 LQR 21.

[84] See *British Midland Tool Ltd v Midland International Tooling Ltd* [2003] 2 BCLC 523; *Coleman Taymar Ltd v Oakes* [2001] 2 BCLC 749.

[85] [2003] 2 BCLC 523.

[86] See *Ultraframe (UK) Ltd v Fielding* [2005] EWHC 1638, para 1310, per Lewison J; also *Wilkinson v West Coast Capital* [2007] BCC 717 at 768; [2005] All ER (D) 346 (Dec) Ch D para 251, per Warren J.

[87] See *Island Export Finance Ltd v Umunna* [1986] BCLC 460 at 482–3; *Murad v Al-Saraj* [2005] All ER (D) 503 (Jul), para 62, CA.

conflict, or possible conflict, of interest. As noted at **11-2**, the no-profit duty in s 175(2) is an element of the broader no-conflict duty in s 175(1) and the authorities show that there can be no liability under the no-profit rule in the absence of an exploitation of a conflict of interest. The intention is to prevent the easy evasion of the no-conflict rule by resignation rather than to inhibit unduly the entrepreneurial activities of individuals merely because they once held a directorship.

11-37   For example, in *CMS Dolphin Ltd v Simonet*[88] a director of the claimant company, an advertising agency, left the company and set up a new business. All the staff of the company subsequently joined him as did the principal clients of the company. The company brought an action against him claiming breach of fiduciary duty and seeking an account of profits made by him. The court found that the director took away from the company the benefit of contracts with existing clients and the business opportunities it had with those clients.

11-38   Lawrence Collins J concluded as follows:[89]

'In my judgment the underlying basis of the liability of the director who exploits after his resignation a maturing business opportunity of the company is that the opportunity is to be treated as if it were property of the company in relation to which the director had fiduciary duties. By seeking to exploit the opportunity after resignation he is appropriating for himself that property. He is just as accountable as a trustee who retires without properly accounted for trust property. In the case of the director he becomes a constructive trustee of the fruits of his abuse of the company's property which he has acquired *in circumstances where he knowingly had a conflict of interest, and exploited it by resigning from the company*'. [emphasis added]

11-39   Further examples can be seen in *Industrial Development Consultants Ltd v Cooley*,[90] discussed at **11-15**, where the director resigned in order to take a contract with the Gas Board which the company was anxious to secure for itself. In *Simtel Communications Ltd v Rebak*[91] (see **11-34**) the director diverted contracts which the company was pursuing to a competing company set up by the director and a former employee. In *Kingsley IT Consulting Ltd v McIntosh*[92] a company had secured two contracts from a client and had just signed a third contract when the director resigned. The client then terminated the third contract with the company and awarded it to a company set up by the director prior to his resignation.[93] The court found that the director had acquired the third contract in circumstances where he was bound to carry it out for the benefit of the company if he was to carry it out at all. In all these cases, the directors are liable for exploiting an opportunity of which they became aware when they were directors and in respect of which they had a conflict of interest at that time.

11-40   The circumstances of resignation can vary greatly, however, as Rix LJ noted in *Foster Bryant Surveying Ltd v Bryant*,[94] and while the cases discussed above are clear

---

[88] [2001] 2 BCLC 704.   [89] [2001] 2 BCLC 704 at 733.   [90] [1972] 2 All ER 162.
[91] [2006] 2 BCLC 571.   [92] [2006] BCC 875.
[93] No explanation was given as to why the client terminated the contract, but the court concluded that it happened because the director asked the client to transfer the contract to his new company.
[94] [2007] 2 BCLC 239, CA.

examples of directors resigning precisely in order to exploit property, information or opportunity in a situation of a conflict of interest, other cases are less clear cut and require careful consideration by the courts. Often resignation is as a result of a break-down in relations within a company rather than an intention, as above, to exploit a conflict of interest. In that scenario, when the defendant does resign and secures a contract with the company's main customer, the courts have been content (in the absence of use of actual company property, such as customer data or technical draw-ings) to find there is no liability to account.[95] This scenario can be seen in *Island Export Finance Ltd v Umunna*,[96] *In Plus Group Ltd v Pyke*,[97] and in *Foster Bryant Surveying Ltd v Bryant*,[98] but it must be noted that the facts of these cases are quite exceptional.[99]

In *Island Export Finance Ltd v Umunna*[100] following a breakdown in relations within   **11-41**
the company, a director (whom the court considered to be the managing director only in name)[101] resigned and within a few months obtained orders from the Cameroon postal authorities for his new company (this was business which previously the com-pany had secured). At the time of his resignation, the court found the company was not actively pursuing further business with the Cameroon authorities. The court rejected a claim for breach of duty finding that there was no conflict of interest at the time he resigned (given the company had moved on to new activities) and, even if there was, the director did not resign in order to exploit it, hence there was no liability to account.[102] *In Plus Group Ltd v Pyke*[103] the director in question had been excluded from all aspects of running the company for almost 15 months before his resigna-tion which he had delayed to protect his interests as a shareholder in the company. In the absence of a fiduciary relationship (as a result of his exclusion) and any mis-use of company property, he was not liable to account on contracts which he subse-quently obtained from the company's main customer. In *Foster Bryant Surveying Ltd v Bryant*[104] the period was shorter. The director had ceased to act in any role as a director three months before his formal resignation, but the scenario was the same. Personal relations within the company had broken down and after a period effectively of iso-lation the director resigned and subsequently secured contracts from the company's main customer.[105] The Court of Appeal upheld the trial judge's finding that there was no breach of fiduciary duty by the director. His resignation had been innocent of any disloyalty or conflict of interest, i.e. he had not resigned to exploit a conflict of interest, and he was not liable.

---

[95] See Rix LJ in *Foster Bryant Surveying Ltd v Bryant* [2007] 2 BCLC 239 at 271: 'As for the innocence of [the director's] resignation, although the matter may not be free of doubt, it seems well arguable on the authorities that it is critically opposed to liability to account [in the case of a retiring director] where there is no active competition or exploitation of company property while the defendant remains a director.'

[96] [1986] BCLC 460.   [97] [2002] 2 BCLC 201, CA.   [98] [2007] 2 BCLC 239, CA.

[99] See Lowry and Sloszar, 'Judicial Pragmatism: Directors' Duties and Post-resignation Conflict of Duty' [2008] JBL 83.

[100] [1986] BCLC 460; see Grantham (2003) 66 MLR 109.   [101] [1986] BCLC 460 at 468.

[102] [1986] BCLC 460 at 482.   [103] [2002] 2 BCLC 201, CA.

[104] [2007] 2 BCLC 239, see Lowry and Sloszar [2008] JBL 83.

[105] A feature of this case was that the company's major client was willing to continue to use the company for as much work as it could handle but wished also to continue to work with the departing director and to that end offered to (and did) set him up in business following his departure from the company.

Limits to scope of the duty

11-42   The strictness of the duty imposed by CA 2006, s 175(1) and (2) is tempered by the disapplications set out in s 175(3)–(4) and by the possibility of authorisation in accordance with s 180, all of which are discussed below.

Transactions with the company

11-43   Section 175 does not apply to a conflict of interest arising in relation to a transaction or arrangement *with the company* (CA 2006, s 175(3)). Where a director is interested directly or indirectly in a proposed transaction or arrangement with the company, the matter is governed by a separate duty of disclosure under s 177: see **11-83**. The obligation to disclose an interest in an existing transaction or arrangement with the company is governed by s 182, see **11-104**.

Situation cannot reasonably be regarded as a conflict

11-44   The no-conflict duty does not apply to a situation which cannot reasonably be regarded as likely to give rise to a conflict of interest (CA 2006, s 175(4)(a)).[106] As noted at **11-6**, this provision is intended to restrict the scope of what is a 'possible' conflict so as to place some limit to the breadth of the no-conflict duty in s 175(1).

Authorisation by independent directors

11-45   Prior to the CA 2006, the position was that a fiduciary who wanted relief from the strict application of the no-conflict duty had to seek the informed consent of the shareholders after full and frank disclosure of all relevant matters,[107] although the articles typically allowed for certain conflicts (essentially interests in transactions with the company and related companies) to be dealt with by disclosure to the board (see Table A, art 85).[108] The ability of the shareholders to authorise or ratify conflicts was and is subject to ill-defined common law limits on authorisation and ratification: see discussion at **18-35** et seq, while the directors' ability to deal with conflicts was in essence

---

[106] The problem with relying on this exemption is that the need to do so will arise necessarily where the director subsequently is accused of a breach of CA 2006, s 175(1) and he may then face a difficulty in establishing how he came to the view that the conflict fell within s 175(4)(a). To some extent, this evidential difficulty almost requires disclosure of the conflict anyway in order that the other directors can confirm that the situation is within s 175(4)(a).

[107] *New Zealand Netherlands Society 'Oranje' Inc v Kuys* [1973] 2 All ER 1222; *Gwembe Valley Development Co Ltd v Koshy* [2004] 1 BCLC 131 at 151; *Crown Dilmun v Sutton* [2004] 1 BCLC 468 at 511; *Murad v Al-Saraj* [2005] All ER (D) 503 (Jul), para 71; *Quarter Master (UK) Ltd v Pyke* [2005] 1 BCLC 245 at 269.

[108] The Companies (Tables A to F) Regulations 1985, SI 1985/805, Table A, art 85 provided as follows: 'Subject to the provisions of the Act, and provided that he has disclosed to the directors the nature and extent of any material interest of his, a director notwithstanding his office—(a) may be a party to, or otherwise interested in, any transaction or arrangement with the company or in which the company is otherwise interested; (b) may be a director or other officer of, or employed by, or a party to any transaction or arrangement with, or otherwise interested in, any body corporate promoted by the company or in which the company is otherwise interested; and (c) shall not, by reason of his office, be accountable to the company for any benefit which he derives from any such office or employment or from any such transaction or arrangement or from any interest in any such body corporate and no such transaction or arrangement shall be liable to be avoided on the ground of any such interest or benefit.'

limited to the type of provision found in Table A, art 85, and the articles could not be used to modify further the no-conflict duty.[109]

The major change in the CA 2006 is that independent directors may authorise a con-   **11-46**
flict of interest and profiting therefrom (CA 2006, s 175(4)(b)). This might mean no more, of course, than authorising multiple directorships, but the section is not so limited and so a conflicted director may be authorised to act, whatever the nature of the conflict, including presumably authorised to start a competing business.[110] Authorisation overrides any common law requirement for shareholder approval *unless* (and this is an important qualification in terms of shareholder protection) an enactment[111] or the company's constitution imposes a requirement for shareholder approval (see s 180(1)). But broad though s 175(4)(b) is, there are some constraints on this power to authorise. It must be exercised by independent directors acting in accordance with their duties, such as the duty to act in a way most likely to promote the success of the company (s 172). The conflicted director seeking authorisation remains subject to his duties (other than s 175) and he needs also to consider whether he is acting in accordance with s 172.[112] The example, given above, of authorising a director to start a competing business is unlikely to meet these requirements. Of course, whether anyone would subsequently be in a position to challenge either the authorised director or the authorising directors as to their compliance with their duties is another matter, so these constraints may be more theoretical than real.

As Lord Wedderburn, the distinguished company lawyer, commented in the House of   **11-47**
Lords, to alter from a position of shareholder approval to a point where only the authorisation of the board is required is to enter uncharted territory[113] and the Government accepted in the Parliamentary debates that this is a significant change to the law.[114]

The change originates from a recommendation of the Company Law Review (CLR)   **11-48**
that 'the statute should (subject to any stricter rule in the company's constitution, or adopted by agreement) allow the company's rights to be waived by the board, acting independently of any conflicted director'.[115] The justifications suggested by the CLR

---

[109] *Movitex Ltd v Bulfield* [1988] BCLC 104.   [110] See HL Deb, vol 678, GC288 (6 February 2006).

[111] For example, CA 2006, Part 10, Ch 4 requires shareholder approval in many instances, but the overlap between that Chapter and s 175 is addressed by s 180(2)—approval by the shareholders means that s 175 need not be complied with: see **11-69**.

[112] See GC100 Guidance, para 2.10. The GC100 group essentially represents general counsel and company secretaries of the FTSE 100 companies and it has issued guidance on conflicts: GC100: *Companies Act 2006—Directors' Conflicts of Interest*, 18 January 2008 (hereinafter the GC100 Guidance), available at www. practicallaw.com/6-378-7923.

[113] HL Deb, vol 678, GC321–322, and 324 (9 February 2006). See generally De Mott, 'The Figure in the Landscape: A Comparative Study of Directors' Self-interested Transactions' (1999) CfiLR 190.

[114] See HL Deb, vol 678, GC337 (9 February 2006): 'This is an area where the statutory statement of the general duties of directors will have made changes—I do not shrink from saying that they are significant changes—to the common law rules and equitable principles concerning conflicts of interest' (Lord Goldsmith for the Government). It is because of the significance of the change that companies formed under the CA 1985 are only able to take advantage of the new provisions if they alter their articles to authorise independent authorisation: see **11-56**.

[115] Company Law Review, *Final Report,* vol 1 (2001), para 3.24.

for such a change (while acknowledging the possibility of board collusion) included that requiring shareholder approval is impractical and onerous; it is inconsistent with the principle that it is for the board to make business assessments; and it stifles entrepreneurial activity.[116] The CLR concluded that allowing independent board approval would 'strike the right balance between...encouraging efficient business operations and the take-up of new business opportunities...and providing effective protection against abuse'.[117] The Government agreed that it was important that the no-conflict duty did not 'impose impractical and onerous requirements which stifle entrepreneurial activity'.[118]

11-49   The argument that the no-conflict duty stifles entrepreneurial activity ignores the fact that the duty merely prevents a director in a situation of a conflict of interest from exploiting that situation. It does not mean that an economic opportunity is discarded. The opportunity will be exploited instead by someone other than a fiduciary with a conflict of interest. The central concern of the CLR and the Government initially seems to have been the narrow issue of liability in circumstances where the company could not or would not have taken the opportunity (a matter which, as discussed at **11-28**, is irrelevant to the application of the duty). The question was whether that element of the duty might be relaxed. The final broader change to the law arose because the CLR concluded, as the courts have done, that requiring a director to prove that the company could not have exploited the opportunity would raise major factual uncertainties. The solution, as far as the Review and the Government was concerned, was to provide for independent board authorisation.[119]

11-50   It is difficult to justify this change in the law even if it is accepted, as is sometimes argued, that the application of the no-conflict duty can be somewhat harsh (though in fact it is difficult to identify cases where the outcome could be so described).[120] In any event, the harshness of the application of fiduciary duties has always been an integral element of their deterrent effect and the harshness can be mitigated in terms of the remedies which the court is prepared to grant.[121] Far from 'encouraging efficient business operations' as the Company Law Review envisaged,[122] this shift to board authorisation will encourage the type of conduct which was criticised in earlier times. Instead of directors avoiding situations of possible conflict, they have the option of considering situations with a view to exploiting them personally, assuming they can get authorisation. They will be tempted to consider opportunities with half an eye to the personal exploitation of the opportunity rather than looking at it solely in terms of their duty to promote the success of the company in the interest of the members as a whole.

[116] Company Law Review, *Final Report*, vol 1 (2001), para 3.23.
[117] Company Law Review, *Final Report*, vol 1 (2001), para 3.27.
[118] DTI, *Company Law Reform* (Cm 6456, 2005), para 3.3.
[119] Company Law Review, *Final Report*, vol 1 (2001), para 3.24.
[120] *Regal (Hastings) Ltd v Gulliver* [1942] 1 All ER 378, is commonly cited as an example, but see n 59 above; in fact it is difficult to identify cases where the outcome could be described as harsh.
[121] See *Murad v Al-Saraj* [2005] All ER (D) 503 (Jul), para 81, per Arden LJ.
[122] See Company Law Review, *Final Report*, vol 1 (2001), para 3.27.

Public companies   With regard to public companies, it is difficult to see why inde-   **11-51**
pendent directors in such companies should ever authorise private profit making by
a director in a situation of possible conflict between his personal interest and his duty
to the company, especially in the light of the remuneration arrangements commonly
available to directors of such companies. The shareholders in these companies rightly
demand and expect single-minded loyalty of their highly paid directors.[123] It might be
argued that shareholders in public companies have a choice on this matter, given that
they need to agree to the inclusion of an authorisation provision in the articles (see
CA 2006, s 175(5)(b)).[124] In practice, the widely dispersed nature of shareholdings in
public companies means that shareholders exercise little influence over the content of
the constitution. Here, as on other matters, it is for institutional shareholders to take
the lead, but it appears that they do not intend to oppose the adoption of authorisation
provisions in the articles.[125] Presumably they take the view that their presence and
influence ensures that most boards of public companies will be circumspect in their
use of this new power.

Also, in public companies, the independent directors will be wary of granting authori-   **11-52**
sation as they remain bound by their general duties including the duty to exercise care
and skill, the duty to act within their powers and, in particular, the duty to act in the
way most likely to promote the success of the company.[126] They will also have an eye
to protecting their own reputations. The net result may be that in public companies,
certainly large public companies, the power may be used for little other than authorising multiple directorships.[127]

Private companies   The greatest concern about this change must lie with regard to the   **11-53**
private company with a small number of shareholder/directors. In such companies,
the exclusion of the interested director from the board for the purposes of authorisation will do little to turn the board into an independent arbiter of this issue. In
all probability the remainder of the board will be family members or close business

---

[123] See *Bristol & West BS v Mothew* [1996] 4 All ER 698 at 712, per Millett LJ.

[124] Public companies formed under the CA 1985 needed to change their articles to allow for authorisation
so their shareholders can be said to have chosen to allow authorisation. Public companies formed under the
CA 2006 may choose to have an authorisation provision in their articles from formation in which case it is
more difficult to say that the shareholders 'choose' to allow authorisation since shareholders notoriously are
ill-informed as to the content of their articles. The Model Articles do not make any provision for authorisation so it cannot arise by default: see The Companies (Model Articles) Regulations 2008, SI 2008/3229, art 14
(Ltd); art 16 (Plc).

[125] The GC100 Guidance, see above n 112, para 1.8 notes that the expectation is that shareholders (i.e.
institutional shareholders) are unlikely to raise objections to the exercise of these authorisation powers
provided the company has a sound governance structure, effective procedures for exercising the powers and
confirms compliance with such procedures.

[126] See HL Deb, vol 678, GC326 (9 February 2006).

[127] As the independent directors will need to consider how allowing the conflict would promote the success of the company, (the GC100 Guidance (above n 112) suggests, for example, that allowing other directorships could be seen as gaining access to industry or sector expertise which could be valuable to the company),
there is some difficulty in seeing the benefit to the company the case where a director seeks authorisation to
pursue and profit from an opportunity in circumstances where there is a conflict of interest.

colleagues who are likely to be incapable of exercising any independence on the issue of a director personally exploiting an opportunity in circumstances where he has a conflict between his personal interests and the interests of the company. It will be difficult to assess the motives of the independent directors in such small companies and in any event the courts have always been sceptical (or realistic) about their ability to determine directors' motives in the face of an assertion that the directors honestly considered the interests of the company.[128]

11-54   The diversion and exploitation of corporate opportunities, information etc is central to the many disputes in these companies[129] which end up in court as petitions alleging unfairly prejudicial conduct under CA 2006, s 994 (see Chapter 17). Prior to the CA 2006, the courts regarded the exploitation of property, information or opportunity in circumstances of a conflict of interest as conduct clearly in breach of fiduciary duty and conduct of the company's affairs in an unfairly prejudicial manner (see **17-51**). With this change in the law, the position alters significantly. It is now possible (with a little ingenuity and bearing in mind that the courts will not second-guess the business judgment of directors) for directors to approve at a board meeting the diversion of assets and opportunities to one of their number, assuming a quorate board of independent directors can be assembled. Of course, theoretically, as mentioned at **11-46,** all the directors concerned are subject to their individual fiduciary duties, including the duty to promote the success of the company (s 172). But, as noted above, enforcing those duties is problematic, not least for the difficulties which the court would face in determining the motives behind authorisation, especially given their well-known reluctance to second-guess business decisions. The result may be that the minority shareholder finds himself in a company with dwindling assets and business. The difference is that, following the change in the law, the diversion of contracts, exploitation of information and opportunities etc becomes approved profit making by a director and there is no breach of duty constituting unfairly prejudicial conduct. A petitioner would need to show that the exercise of the power to authorise (or possibly even seeking authorisation) was contrary to understandings between the shareholders such that it amounted to conduct of the company's affairs in an unfairly prejudicial manner.[130] That may be difficult in the absence of a provision in the articles to that effect, given that an exclusion of the power to authorise must be contained in the articles (CA 2006, s 175(5)(a)).

11-55   It is also possible to envisage situations where the risk is to the company's creditors as where the directors (in a mutually beneficial way) divert business away from the company, as part of authorised conflicts, until eventually the company is left with insufficient assets to meet the claims of creditors. Again, theoretically, a claim for misfeasance

---

[128] See *Regal (Hastings) Ltd v Gulliver* [1942] 1 All ER 378 at 392, HL, per Lord Wright; *Ex p James* (1803) 8 Ves 337 at 345: 'no court is equal to the examination and ascertainment of the truth in these cases'.

[129] See for example, *Re Little Olympian Each-Ways Ltd (No 3)* [1995] 1 BCLC 636; *Re Full Cup International Trading Ltd* [1995] 1 BCLC 636; *Lloyd v Casey* [1995] 1 BCLC 636; *Allmark v Burnham* [1995] 1 BCLC 636; *Re Baumler (UK) Ltd, Gerrard v Koby* [2005] 1 BCLC 92.

[130] See **17-60**; also *O'Neill v Phillips* [1999] 2 BCLC 1, HL.

under IA 1986, s 212 could lie against the interested director (not for breach of CA 2006, s 175, but possibly for breach of s 172) or against the independent directors who authorised the transaction (again, possibly for breach of s 172 or even s 171), but whether it would be brought is problematic, not least given the costs issues involved in funding litigation by a liquidator.

For private companies, there must not be anything in the constitution which invali- **11-56** dates authorisation by the directors (CA 2006, s 175(5)(a)). Private companies formed under the CA 2006 are able automatically to rely on s 175(5)(a). Private companies incorporated under the CA 1985 must pass an ordinary resolution permitting author- isation to be given by the directors in accordance with s 175(5)(a).[131]

Obtaining authorisation   Authorisation by independent directors is required. It is not **11-57** clear whether authorisation by committee is possible, but it seems unlikely. Of course, it may be very practical to use a committee (especially for large companies with a number of directors needing authorisation at any time) and it is common for many management matters to be delegated to committees rather than being dealt with by the full board. It is difficult to accept, however, that Parliament, having effected such a radical change in the law and conferred a statutory power on 'the directors', intended that these matters would and could be dealt with by a committee.[132] The trust of the provision is consideration of 'the matter' by the directors as a board.

Authorisation may be unconditional or subject to any restrictions which the inde- **11-58** pendent directors choose to impose. For example, they may choose to limit the author- isation to the circumstances before them so that, if the circumstances change and with it the nature of the conflict changes, a further authorisation is required. Authorisation is required with regard to specific transactions ('the matter') and it is not possible for a director to give a general notice of matters giving rise to a conflict of interest in contrast with the position under CA 2006, s 177(2): see **11-98**. The explanation given in the Parliamentary debates for the difference in approach was that s 177 deals with transactions where the company is a party to the transaction and will know the mat- ters surrounding it, but the type of conflict of interest governed by s 175 will neces- sarily relate to things of which the company knows nothing and in respect of which a general notice would not suffice.[133]

---

[131] See The Companies Act 2006 (Commencement No 5, Transitional Provisions and Savings) Order 2007, SI 2007/3495, art 9, Sch 4, para 47. In theory, existing companies could simply rely on the new statutory pro- vision, but the requirement for an ordinary resolution was imposed as a transitional measure. The intention presumably is to ensure that shareholders in such companies are at least alerted to the change in the law since, as discussed above, there is some potential for it to be used to the disadvantage of the minority in these companies. The resolution is not a special resolution since private companies do not need authorisation in their articles so the resolution is not a resolution amending the articles which would require a special reso- lution (CA 2006, s 21).

[132] Interestingly, the GC100 Guidance, see above n 112, envisages companies using a reviewing committee to review annually the exercise of the power, but the power should be exercised by the board (see para 4.10).

[133] See HL Deb, vol 678, GC328 (9 February 2006) where Lord Goldsmith noted that a general notice in this context would leave the company too much in the dark.

11-59 There is no prescribed level of disclosure by a director and the court will be guided, no doubt, by the common law requirement of full and frank disclosure as to the nature of the opportunity so that the other directors can see what the director's interest is and how far it extends.[134] A director will have every incentive to make maximum disclosure, for the consequence of inadequate disclosure is that authorisation is not validly obtained and the director would be in breach of the no-conflict duty.

11-60 Authorisation is only effective if the director in question and any other 'interested directors' are excluded from the quorum[135] (but they are not excluded from participation in the discussion)[136] and their votes are excluded or the matter would have been agreed even if their votes had not been counted (CA 2006, s 175(6)). There is no definition of who counts as an 'interested' director for these purposes and so is excluded. Many family companies have husbands and wives as directors and the question is whether a husband (as an independent director for the purpose of s 175(4)) could authorise another director, his wife, to exploit a situation on her own account.[137] The CA 2006 does not expressly address this point[138] but if it is possible for a spouse to be treated as an independent director for these purposes, the risk of board collusion is significantly increased.

11-61 The answer lies not in definitions of family relationships for there is always a risk that the exercise of fiduciary duty may be influenced by any personal relationship.[139] The proper approach is to focus on the substance of the transaction (which in this context is the granting of authorisation) and ask whether the director, though not having a personal interest in the transaction, has a conflict of interest with regard to the granting of the authorisation (i.e. a conflict between a personal interest in facilitating the other director by granting authorisation and the interests of the company). If so, that director has to step aside and cannot count towards the quorum or vote by virtue of his obligations under CA 2006, s 175(1).

11-62 This same approach would apply to business associates on the board who may be close personal friends of the director seeking authorisation, though not related by family connection. As discussed at **11-54**, there is a risk of mutually supportive collusion between the interested director and such associates who may divide up opportunities

---

[134] *Movitex Ltd v Bulfield* [1988] BCLC 104 at 121; *Imperial Mercantile Credit Association v Coleman* (1873) LR 6 HL 189 at 205.

[135] The Government emphasised that compliance with the requirements of CA 2006, s 175(6) (quorum and voting position) does not of itself guarantee that it is a valid authorisation, but non-compliance with these elements renders it automatically invalid and the constitution may impose additional requirements: see HL Deb, vol 678, GC326 (9 February 2006).

[136] See Clark, 'UK Company Law Reform and Directors' Exploitation of "Corporate Opportunities" (2006) ICCLR 231 at 239 who notes that, given the degree of influence that directors may exert on fellow directors, the interested directors should have been excluded from participation.

[137] See Prentice & Payne (2004) 120 LQR 198 at 201.

[138] Many provisions of CA 2006, Part 10, Ch 4 (see for example, s 190) extend the application of various provisions to directors and connected persons (as defined in s 252) but this categorisation is not used for the purposes of s 175(5).

[139] See David Richards J on this issue in *Newgate Stud Co v Penfold* [2008] 1 BCLC 46 at 105–6.

between themselves and the company on a basis which favours their personal interests rather than the interests of the company as a whole. The risk from such collusion lies on the minority shareholders and the creditors. As appropriate, such directors too should be treated as having a conflict of interest and excluded from the quorum and voting.

In small private companies, these exclusions may mean that there are no independ-   **11-63**
ent directors capable of forming a quorum or voting and so authorisation may not be possible,[140] which solves the problems identified at **11-54**. Of course, in any type of company, there may be occasions when all the directors are conflicted.[141] In these situations, the common law option of seeking the informed consent of the sharehold-ers (to the director's personal exploitation of the relevant opportunity, etc) following full disclosure of all relevant information,[142] which is retained by CA 2006, s 180(4) (a), would then come into play, though there are ill-defined common law limits to the power to authorise breaches of duty: see **18-35** et seq.

Given the significance of the change in the law, it is curious that there is no provi-   **11-64**
sion for shareholders to be notified of any authorisation granted under CA 2006, s 175(4)(b), whether in a public or in a private company (bearing in mind that share-holders do not have access to board minutes) though the CLR indicated that disclo-sure of the transaction in the annual accounts and reports would be an important safeguard.[143] Companies were required under the CA 1985 to include details of direc-tors' interests in material transactions with the company in the notes to the company's accounts.[144] This provision was not carried forward by the CA 2006 and when it was suggested to the Government that this matter needed to be addressed in the directors' report, the Government responded by saying such safeguards were unnecessary.[145] The absence of disclosure in the publicly disclosed accounts also means that the busi-ness media are not able to draw attention to these matters. Given that position, share-holders should consider imposing a disclosure requirement via the articles and larger companies, in the interests of transparency, may want to find a disclosure mechanism which is appropriate in their context.[146]

[140] In more dubious cases, we can expect to see people appointed to the board for short time periods pre-cisely to provide a quorum of independent directors who can authorise the matter and the courts will need to be alert to this possibility, as they were in a different context in *Re In a Flap Envelope Ltd* [2004] 1 BCLC 64.

[141] See, for example, *Lee Panavision Ltd v Lee Lighting Ltd* [1992] BCLC 22.

[142] *New Zealand Netherlands Society 'Oranje' Inc v Kuys* [1973] 2 All ER 1222; *Gwembe Valley Development Co Ltd v Koshy* [2004] 1 BCLC 131 at 151; *Crown Dilmun v Sutton* [2004] 1 BCLC 468 at 511; *Murad v Al-Saraj* [2005] All ER (D) 503 (Jul), CA, para 71; *Quarter Master (UK) Ltd v Pyke* [2005] 1 BCLC 245 at 269.

[143] Company Law Review, *Final Report*, vol 1 (2001), para 3.24.

[144] CA 1985, s 232(2), Sch 6, Part 11.

[145] See HL Deb, vol 678, GC325–6 (9 February 2006); also DTI, *Company Law Reform* (Cm 6456, 2005) para 3.3 where concern was expressed that disclosure must be proportionate and not unnecessarily complex. The Department clearly had in mind concerns about the excessive disclosure of directors' loans etc required under CA 1985, Sch 6, Pts 2 and 3, and did not wish to repeat that experience with the unfortunate conse-quence that no provision has been made for disclosure of authorisations granted under CA 2006, s 175.

[146] See GC100 Guidance, above n 112, which suggests including information in the annual corporate governance element of the director's report.

11-65   There are also issues as to recording internally any authorisations granted as it will be important for the conflicted director that there is no ambiguity about the authorisation, its date, terms and any restrictions. Likewise, it is in the company's interests to maintain a detailed record. No doubt, in larger companies, practice will evolve over time into a requirement along the lines of a register of authorisations.[147]

Authorisation/ratification by the company

11-66   All the general duties imposed on directors, including CA 2006, s 175, are subject to any rule of law enabling the company to give authority, for anything to be done or omitted by the directors, or any of them, that would otherwise be a breach of duty (s 180(4)(a)). The common law on ratification of breaches of duty is likewise retained by s 239(7).

11-67   The ill-defined common law limits to these powers of the shareholders to authorise or ratify, preserved by s 180(4)(a) and s 239(7), lie along the lines of fraud on creditors and fraud on the minority and are discussed at **18-35**. The fraud on the minority category prevents shareholders from authorising or ratifying acts which amount to the misappropriation of 'money, property or advantages which belong to the company or in which the other shareholders are entitled to participate'.[148] On the other hand, the non-disclosure of a conflict of interest, as in *Aberdeen Rly Co v Blaikie Bros*[149] is ratifiable and *Regal (Hastings) Ltd v Gulliver*[150] suggests that bona fide incidental profit making is ratifiable.[151] Of course, drawing the line between misappropriation amounting to a fraud on a minority and the incidental self-serving conduct of *Regal* is not easy so there is some blurring of the boundaries to ratification of conflicts of interest.

11-68   A conflict may only be ratified, therefore, if it does not fall into the fraud on the minority category and only if ratification can be secured while observing the voting restrictions imposed on ratification by interested directors and others by CA 2006, s 239.[152] If a director fails to obtain authorisation under s 175(4)(b), this option of shareholder approval is possible within the constraints outlined above, the application of which will depend on the circumstances of the conflict.

11-69   A director is not required to comply with CA 2006, s 175 if the conflicted transaction is approved or is exempt from approval under CA 2006, Part 10, Ch 4 which requires shareholder approval of specific transactions with directors (see Chapter 12). If the transaction is exempt under Part 10, Ch 4, it is because Parliament considered that the particular conflict of interest is not a matter of concern, and if the shareholders have approved the conflict of interest under Part 10, Ch 4, there is no need to impose a further requirement of compliance with s 175.

---

[147] See GC100 Guidance, above n 112, para 4.7.

[148] *Burland v Earle* [1902] AC 83 at 93, per Lord Davey; *Cook v Deeks* [1916] 1 AC 554; *Daniels v Daniels* [1978] 2 All ER 89.

[149] (1854) 1 Macq (HL) 461.   [150] [1942] 1 All ER 378.

[151] See [1942] 1 All ER 378 at 389, per Lord Russell; also at 394, per Lord Wright.

[152] On ratification, the CA 2006 makes a significant change by providing that on any resolution to ratify a breach of duty, the votes of the interested director (if a member of the company) and any member connected with him (as defined in ss 252–255) must be disregarded, see s 239(3), (4).

Authorisation via the articles

It is possible for a company to make provision in its articles to deal with conflicts of **11-70** interest, and the general duties owed by a director are not infringed by anything done or omitted to be done in accordance with those provisions (CA 2006, s 180(4)(b)). The extent to which such provision may be made is limited, however, by s 232 which pro- hibits provisions exempting directors from liability for breach of duty, save such provi- sions in the articles 'as has previously been lawful for dealing with conflicts of interest' (s 232(4)). There is uncertainty as to how much leeway this gives with respect to modi- fying the application of s 175 via provisions in the articles. When it is considered that Parliament has already significantly modified the no-conflict duty[153] via s 175(4)(b), it seems unlikely that the courts will see much scope for further dilution of the duty by provisions in the articles, a point surely confirmed by the wording of s 232(4) ('such provision as has previously been lawful').

Measures 'previously lawful' include those such as Table A, art 85[154] (now reflected to **11-71** a certain extent in CA 2006, s 177) and provisions dealing with quorum and voting requirements for board meetings dealing with conflicts as in Table A, arts 94 and 95 (dealt with by CA 2006, s 175(6) when authorisation by directors is sought). Possible inclusions might be:

- Provisions dealing with multiple directorships: in the Parliamentary debates it was envisaged that once a director had secured authorisation for multiple pos- itions, a company might want to make provision in its articles for 'managing' the conflict, for example to deal with the practicalities where the director found himself with confidential information arising from one or other post which he is not able to disclose to the other board.

- Provisions identifying certain transactions as not being transactions which can reasonably be regarded as likely to give rise to a conflict of interest for the pur- poses of CA 2006, s 175(4)(a) (and therefore exempt from the application of s 175): use of the articles to identify some de minimis category might be acceptable, pro- vided the court did not think the provision went too far and infringed s 232(1) outlawing provisions that exempt a director from liability for breach of any duty.

- It probably is possible to use the articles to regulate transactions between the dir- ector and a subsidiary or a holding company (apart from transactions etc requir- ing shareholder approval under CA 2006, Part 10, Ch 4). Table A, art 85 dealt with

---

[153] The Government emphasised in the debates that it did not want a return to the days of widely drafted exemption clauses: see HL Deb, vol 682, cols 721–2 (23 May 2006), see Lord Sainsbury for the Government: 'Two major principles have guided our approach. The first is that we cannot agree to return to the pre-1928 position, under which companies were able to include widely drafted exemption clauses in their articles. The current law sets the balance. It is acceptable for the articles to exempt directors from liability for certain con- flicts. But for the necessary protection of the company, it is not acceptable for articles to exempt the directors from others. The second principle is that we do not want to prevent the articles doing what they can now do in relation to these matters…the articles may contain provisions for dealing with conflicts of interest, and the directors will not be in breach of duty if they act in accordance with those provisions.'

[154] The text of art 85 is set out at n 108 above.

transactions with subsidiary companies and the model articles also suggest that provisions governing transactions with subsidiaries (at least) are permissible.[155]

- It is unlikely, in the context of CA 2006, s 175, that the courts would accept a 'blanket' authorisation via the articles, for example with regard to conflicts arising from a particular class of transactions.[156] The Parliamentary intention is clear, that 'the matter', i.e. the nature and extent of the specific conflict, must be considered by the independent directors, followed by authorisation, if appropriate, in the due exercise of their duties to the company.

11-72   Another possible use of the articles is to use them to tighten, not to loosen, the requirements of CA 2006, s 175 by requiring shareholder approval in addition to authorisation by the directors (see s 180(1)). In some companies shareholders may be more comfortable with the protection of shareholder approval rather than director approval, however independent.

C Benefits from third parties

Introduction

11-73   The CA 2006, s 176 makes provision for a distinct aspect of the no-conflict duty, namely the acceptance of benefits from third parties including the acceptance of bribes.

11-74   The relationship between s 176 and s 175 is unclear, in particular as to whether it is possible for directors to authorise (under s 175(4)(b)) the acceptance of benefits from third parties. On the one hand, there seems no reason why they cannot so authorise since, as s 179 makes clear, the fiduciary obligations of directors are cumulative. The obligation to comply with s 176 does not negate the application of s 175, as the Explanatory Notes make clear.[157] Clearly a situation where a director benefits from his position can fall into both sections, as a conflict and exploitation of a conflict within s 175 (there must be a conflict for s 176 to apply) and an acceptance of a benefit under s 176. If s 175 also applies, then s 175(4)(b) must apply in the absence of any provision excluding its particular application in the context of s 176. It would also be strange that under s 175 a director could be authorised by independent directors to exploit an opportunity for his personal benefit while his acceptance of a benefit arising from his position (which while generating a conflict may be quite modest in impact) cannot be so authorised. Further support for the view that s 175 does apply is that s 180 deals with specific

---

[155] See The Companies (Model Articles) Regulations 2008, SI 2008/3229, art 14 (Ltd); art 16 (Plc). Transactions with subsidiary or holding companies are not within s 177 which is limited to proposed transactions with *the company*.

[156] Take, for example, where the articles purport to allow the directors individually to compete with the company in respect of online sales so allowing each director to run a personal website in competition with the company's website. That type of blanket authorisation in the articles is not permissible.

[157] See Explanatory Notes to the Companies Act 2006, para 344.

overlaps and exclusions between ss 175, 176, 177 and Part 10, Ch 4. It would have been easy for Parliament to have added a clause excluding the application of s 175 in cases where s 176 applies, but it did not do so.

The contrary arguments would include that the Explanatory Notes rule out the pos-   **11-75**
sibility of board authorisation for the purposes of CA 2006, s 176.[158] It could also be argued that the reason why benefits and bribes were singled out in CA 2006, s 176 is to ensure that they cannot be so authorised. Equally, it could be argued that the reason for singling them out was to deal with the consequences of acceptance of an improper benefit or bribe, an issue which at common law was the subject of some conflict.[159] By imposing a distinct fiduciary duty in this way, the statute highlights a director's obligations with respect to benefits received from third parties and makes clear the consequences of accepting such benefits which are that any benefit or bribe received without approval or authorisation is a breach of fiduciary duty such that the benefit or bribe is held on constructive trust for the company:[160] see **13-10**. The need to resolve these issues may justify dealing with benefits and bribes from third parties as a separate duty without the need to deny the possibility of authorisation under s 175(4)(b). On balance, there seems no reason why independent directors cannot authorise the acceptance of benefits, though of course they cannot authorise bribes.

The scope of the duty

Section 176 imposes a duty on directors not to accept benefits from a third party con-   **11-76**
ferred by reason of his being a director, *or* by reason of his doing or not doing anything as a director. The prohibition applies to former directors who may not accept benefits from third parties conferred by reason of things done or omitted by the director before he ceased to be a director (s 170(2)(b)).

'Benefit' for these purposes is to be given its ordinary dictionary meaning, of 'a favour-   **11-77**
able or helpful factor, circumstance, advantage or profit' and, in particular, 'benefit' is not limited to a tangible corporeal advantage.[161] All benefits whether in cash or kind are included, such as appointing the director to another position.[162]

---

[158] See Explanatory Notes to the Companies Act 2006, para 344, though it is not entirely free from ambiguity also, stating first that the acceptance of a benefit giving rise to an actual or potential conflict of interest will fall within s 175 as well as this duty before then stating that s 176 is not subject to any provision for board authorisation. Of course, if s 175 applies, then s 175(4)(b) applies.

[159] There was an unresolved conflict between the Privy Council decision in *Attorney General for Hong Kong v Reid* [1994] 1 All ER 1, PC and the decision of the Court of Appeal in *Lister v Stubbs* (1890) Ch D 1 which, though discredited, was technically binding on the English courts. In *Daraydan Holdings Ltd v Solland International Ltd* [2005] 4 All ER 73 at 93, Lawrence Collins J had indicated that, if necessary, he would have followed *AGHK v Reid* and would not have felt constrained by the doctrine of binding precedent to follow *Lister v Stubbs*.

[160] The result is to give statutory effect to the decision in *Attorney General for Hong Kong v Reid* [1994] 1 All ER 1, PC.

[161] See HC Official Report, SC D (Company Law Reform Bill) 11 July 2006, col 622 (Solicitor General).

[162] See HL Deb, vol 678, GC330 (9 February 2006).

11-78   The provision is limited to benefits accepted by the director, leaving some apparent scope for evasion by way of benefits conferred on persons connected with the director. For example, a third party might pay the university fees of the director's children in return for the director's support in ensuring that the company awards a contract to that third party. Leaving aside the difficulty in discovering such arrangements, the director would be in a position of conflict and CA 2006, s 175(1) would apply so such arrangements would be caught.

Limits to the duty

Benefits from related companies or service agreements

11-79   There are exemptions for benefits received from the company or associate companies or from persons acting on their behalf or from companies which provide services to the company via the director (CA 2006, s 176(2)). These exemptions are designed to ensure that directors' remuneration and service contract agreements, especially the common arrangement for the provision of a director's services via a management company, are not within the prohibition (see s 176(3)).

Acceptance not likely to give rise to conflict

11-80   There is no de minimis financial threshold with the Government choosing instead to limit the scope of the provision by reference to the risk of a conflict of interest[163] and so the duty is not infringed if the acceptance of the benefit cannot reasonably be regarded as likely to give rise to a conflict of interest: CA 2006, s 176(4). This limitation means that 'ordinary' commercial hospitality (meals, gifts, tickets for entertainment or sporting events) is not caught. Guidance as to benefits which 'cannot reasonably be regarded as likely to give rise to a conflict of interest' may be provided in the articles: see **11-82**.

Benefits approved or exempt under Part 10, Ch 4

11-81   A director is not required to comply with CA 2006, s 176 if the transaction in respect of which the benefit arises is approved or is exempt from approval in accordance with CA 2006, Part 10, Ch 4: s 180(2). Part 10, Ch 4 requires shareholder approval of specific transactions with directors and those provisions are discussed in detail in Chapter 12.

Authorised by the company or via the articles

11-82   Whether independent directors can authorise the acceptance of benefits is discussed at **11-74**. The position is uncertain, but it is arguable that they can. The shareholders may authorise the acceptance of benefits from third parties (CA 2006, s 180(4)(a)) and may ratify a breach of s 176 (subject to s 239), subject to the common law limits

---

[163] See HC Official Report, SC D (Company Law Reform Bill) 11 July 2006, cols 622–4 (Solicitor General). The Government considered that any financial thresholds would be purely arbitrary.

on authorisation and ratification discussed at **18-35**. Acceptance of a bribe would be a breach of s 172 and s 176 and cannot be authorised or ratified by the shareholders, not even unanimously;[164] a fortiori, acceptance cannot be authorised by the directors under s 175(4)(b). The articles may make provision for the acceptance of benefits from third parties (s 180(4)(b)), subject to s 232(4)) and it was clear in the Parliamentary debates[165] that the expectation is that the articles might be used, for example, to set financial thresholds; to identify procedures internally for notification and authorisation of benefits, to set limits to 'hospitality' etc.[166]

D Proposed transactions with the company

Introduction

The distinct situation where a director is interested in a proposed transaction or   **11-83** arrangement *with the company* is governed by CA 2006, s 177, not by s 175.[167] The director must disclose the conflict to the board before the transaction is entered into so enabling the board to decide how to proceed in the light of this information.[168]

The provision is limited to proposed transactions with the company and does not   **11-84** extend to proposed transactions with a subsidiary or holding company of the company which will fall within CA 2006, s 175 and which must therefore be authorised by the directors under s 175(4)(b) or possibly dealt with under the articles: see **11-71**. Though not required to comply with s 175, a director subject to the disclosure obligations of s 177 remains subject to all the other general duties (s 179). Particularly relevant in this context is his duty (under s 171) to act within his powers and (under s 172) to promote the success of the company. Disclosure under s 177 does not obviate the need for compliance with Part 10, Ch 4 where the transaction or arrangement falls within one of the categories regulated by that Chapter and which may require disclosure and approval by the shareholders in addition to disclosure to the directors under s 177 (s 180(3)).

---

[164] Bribery is an evil practice which threatens the foundations of any civilised society: *Attorney General for Hong Kong v Reid* [1994] 1 All ER 1 at 4, per Lord Templeman. See too *Fyffes Group Ltd v Templeman* [2000] 2 Lloyd's Reports 643.

[165] See Solicitor General, HC Official Report, SC D (Company Law Reform Bill) 11 July 2006, col 624.

[166] The 'value' of some of these benefits, such as tickets to prestigious events) may be much greater than their financial value and hospitality over a long period of time may be cumulatively valuable so it may be difficult to determine what is an appropriate threshold for inclusion in the articles—there must come a point at which 'hospitality' crosses over into a conflict of interest prohibited by s 176.

[167] Of course, a situation under CA 2006, s 175 of potential conflict may evolve into a situation which then is governed by s 177 when that conflict gives rise to an actual transaction or arrangement with the company, for example, the director who is a potential supplier to the company (so within s 175) and who then secures a supply contract with the company for his business (and so is within s 177): see the GC100 Guidance, above n 112.

[168] The company can consider whether to enter into the transaction, on what terms and with what safeguards, see HL Deb, vol 678, GC334 (9 February 2006).

11-85   Compliance with s 177 overrides any common law requirement for shareholder approval, unless the company's constitution imposes a requirement for shareholder approval (see s 180(1)).

11-86   The leading authority on conflicts of interest is *Aberdeen Rly Co v Blaikie Bros*[169] where a company was entitled to set aside a contract for the purchase of railway equipment entered into between it and a partnership when it transpired that the chairman of its board of directors was also the managing partner of the partnership. The conflict of interest is obvious: the director is obliged to act in the interests of the company, in this case, to purchase goods on behalf of the company at the lowest possible price while, as a member of the partnership, he wishes to sell the goods at the highest price. Where such a conflict exists, the law recognises that the director, despite his best intentions, may be swayed by his own self-interest.[170] The fact that the director is only one member of the partnership which is contracting with the company does not affect the application of the no-conflict rule nor does the fact that the transaction is fair.[171] All that is relevant is the existence of a possible conflict of interest and duty.

11-87   A director's conflict of interest in a transaction with the company may arise in all sorts of direct and indirect ways. In *Aberdeen Rly Co v Blaikie Bros*,[172] as noted, the director was effectively both the purchaser and the seller of goods. In *Movitext Ltd v Bulfield*[173] the directors leased property which they owned to the company and took security from the company with respect to its obligations under the lease. As the owners of the property, the directors were the lessors while, as directors of the company, they were acting for the tenant. In *Gwembe Valley Development Co Ltd v Koshy*[174] the company purchased foreign currency from another business controlled by the company's managing director. In these transactions, the director is on both sides of the relationship, acting on behalf of the company and acting on his own behalf and so in a position of conflict between his personal interest and the interests of the company.

11-88   Of course, the mere existence of a conflict of interest is not necessarily to the company's disadvantage and the application of a strict no-conflict duty with regard to transactions with the company can be commercially inconvenient. The director may be willing to give the company a favourable deal and the prohibition of dealings between a director and his company may force a company to incur costs in contracting with an outsider when an insider is the sole or most favourable source of the goods or services which the company requires.[175] The director may have been appointed to the board precisely in order to foster certain business relationships and so possible conflicts may exist from the outset. Prohibiting all conflicts might simply drive these matters underground with directors going to some lengths to hide their involvement in particular transactions. At common law, the commercial inconvenience typically was overcome by a provision in the articles (usually in the form of Table A, art 85)

---

[169] (1854) 1 Macq 461.   [170] (1854) 1 Macq 461 at 471–2.   [171] (1854) 1 Macq 461 at 471–2.
[172] (1854) 1 Macq 461.   [173] [1988] BCLC 104.   [174] [2004] 1 BCLC 131.
[175] See *Boulting v Association of Cinematograph, Television and Allied Technicians* [1963] 2 QB 606 at 637.

permitting directors to be interested in contracts with the company or in which the company was otherwise interested, provided the nature and extent of that interest was disclosed to the board of directors.[176]

Scope of the duty under s 177

The significant change effected by the CA 2006 is that the disclosure regime commonly imposed by the Table A articles has become the statutory regime,[177] expressed in terms of a fiduciary duty[178] imposed on a director who is in any way, directly or indirectly, interested in a proposed transaction or arrangement with the company to declare the nature and extent of that interest to the other directors,[179] before the company enters into the transaction or arrangement (s 177(1), (4)). Disclosure of the conflict of interest is required, not approval. As the disclosure is before the company enters into the transaction, the board has the choice whether or not to proceed. If not, that ends the matter. If, following compliance with s 177, the company does proceed, the transaction is not voidable at the option of the shareholders, unless an enactment[180] or the articles require shareholder approval (s 180(1)).

11-89

In the event of a failure to disclose as required, the director is in breach of duty and the extent to which the shareholders can authorise or ratify the breach is discussed below. The common law consequences of an undisclosed conflict of interest apply—any resulting contract with the company is voidable and may be set aside at the instance of the company without any enquiry as to the fairness or otherwise of the transaction.[181] The company has a choice whether to affirm or avoid the contract.[182] The right to avoid the contract is lost if: (1) the company delays unduly before rescinding; or (2) restitutio in integrum becomes impossible; or (3) the rights of bona fide third parties intervene.[183] If the company wishes to rescind the contract, the decision to rescind must be communicated clearly and promptly and until then the contract is valid and

11-90

---

[176] See above n 108 which sets out the text of art 85.

[177] The Company Law Review took the view that if, in practice, all companies opted out of the rule in *Aberdeen Rly Co v Blaikie Bros* (1854) 1 Macq 461 and substituted disclosure requirements instead, the law should reflect that practice and the rule should be disclosure.

[178] This ends the debate as to whether the no-conflict rule merely subjects fiduciaries to certain disabilities, as suggested by *Movitex Ltd v Bulfield* [1988] BCLC 104, though in any event the Court of Appeal had doubted the usefulness of that approach in *Gwembe Valley Development Co v Koshy* [2004] 1 BCLC 131 at 161.

[179] This provision does not apply to shadow directors unlike CA 2006, s 182 which is specifically applied to shadow directors by s 187.

[180] For example, CA 2006, Part 10, Ch 4 requires shareholder approval in many instances, but the overlap between that Chapter and s 175 is addressed by s 180(2)—approval by the shareholders means that s 177 need not be complied with: see **11-69.**

[181] CA 2006, s 178(1); *Aberdeen Rly Co v Blaikie Bros* (1854) 1 Macq 461 at 471–2, per Lord Cranworth; and see *Movitex Ltd v Bulfield* [1988] BCLC 104 at 123.

[182] A contract can be affirmed even if the company is in liquidation: *Ultraframe (UK) Ltd v Fielding* [2005] EWHC 1638, para 1441. An unqualified demand for payment of sums due under a voidable contract amounts to an election to affirm the contract: *Ultraframe (UK) Ltd v Fielding* [2005] EWHC 1638, para 1449.

[183] *Hely-Hutchinson v Brayhead Ltd* [1967] 3 All ER 98.

binding and continues in existence.[184] The contract cannot be rescinded if has been fully performed.[185]

11-91   Regardless of whether the contract is set aside, the company may hold the director to account for any profit which he has made from the transaction or require him to indemnify the company against any loss incurred. This position reflects the fact that the obligation to disclose imposed by s 177 is a fiduciary duty. The normal remedy for breach of fiduciary duty is a liability to account for any gain or make good any loss and it is not dependent on the company rescinding the contract.[186] A liability regardless of rescission is also consistent with the statutory remedies in CA 2006, ss 195(3) and 213(3). The director is not liable, however, for losses which the company would probably have suffered even if the director had complied with the rules on disclosure of interests.[187]

11-92   The fiduciary duty of disclosure in s 177 applies only to proposed transactions with the company whereas s 182 imposes a statutory duty of disclosure where the director has an interest in an existing transaction. As was explained in the Parliamentary debates, the reason for the distinction is that where it is a proposed transaction, the company is still in a position to decide whether it wishes to proceed with the transaction in the light of the conflict of interest, whereas if the conflict has arisen in respect of an existing transaction, the company has limited options in terms of responding to the conflict.[188] In the latter case, it is still important for disclosure to be made so that the company is aware of the director's conflict of interest, but it will probably be too late for the company to avoid the transaction. Section 182 is discussed below. The distinction initially appears helpful, but the position in practice may be more complex than this neat division may suggest: see discussion at **11-105**.

Interests which must be disclosed

11-93   The disclosure obligation applies to any interest, direct or indirect, of the director so a disclosure obligation may arise even though the director is not actually a party to the transaction. It is not clear whether there is a duty on a director to disclose an

---

[184] See *Re Marini Ltd* [2004] BCC 172 at 196.   [185] See *Re Marini Ltd* [2004] BCC 172.

[186] See *Gwembe Valley Development Co Ltd v Koshy* [2004] 1 BCLC 131 at 150–1 (director liable to account for profit made on undisclosed conflict of interest in transaction with the company despite the contract having long been performed and therefore incapable of being set aside); also *Re MDA Investment Management Ltd, Whalley v Doney* [2004] 1 BCLC 217 at 260 where likewise the conflicted transaction could no longer be set aside but the director was liable to account for profit gained by him personally on the transaction; also dissenting judgment of Bowen LJ in *Re Cape Breton* (1885) 29 Ch D 795. This position clarifies the confusion which arose from the majority decision in that case which was that the company could not affirm the contract *and* hold the director to account: *Re Cape Breton Co* (1885) 29 Ch D 795; *Burland v Earle* [1902] AC 83;

[187] *Gwembe Valley Development Co Ltd v Koshy* [2004] 1 BCLC 131 at 174–5. See also *Bishopsgate Investment Management Ltd v Maxwell (No 2)* [1993] BCLC 1282 at 1285, per Hoffmann J who noted that, in cases where the alleged breach of duty is an omission, the plaintiff must prove that compliance with the duty would have prevented the damage; also *Galoo v Bright Grahame Murray* [1995] 1 All ER 16; *Re Continental Assurance Co of London plc* [2007] 2 BCLC 287 at 445–6; *Cohen v Selby* [2001] 1 BCLC 176 at 183, 186.

[188] See HL Deb, vol 678, GC334 (9 February 2006).

interest in transactions or arrangements between the company and a connected person (as defined in CA 2006, s 252), but it seems implicit in the statutory scheme that such disclosure is required. Section 177(2)(b)(ii) allows for the giving of a general notice of interests for the purposes of s 177 and s 185(2)(b) provides that a general notice may indicate that the director is to be regarded as interested in any transactions between the company and a specified connected person which rather supposes that such interests are within the indirect interests of a director.[189] This seems the most practical interpretation of the provision which would otherwise be open to easy invasion, but it would have been helpful had the legislation spelt out that this is the position.

The disclosure requirement extends to any transaction within CA 2006, Part 10, Ch 4   **11-94** so that transaction still requires formal disclosure to the directors[190] in accordance with s 177. Of course, given that Part 10, Ch 4 requires shareholder approval (unless the transaction is exempt under that Part), it may be possible to establish that the directors 'knew or ought to have been aware' of the transaction and so disclosure is not required (s 177(6)(b)), but rather than rely on that provision, it is preferable, and easy, to make a formal declaration under s 177.

Interests excluded from disclosure

The expansive scope of CA 2006, s 177(1) is modified by certain exclusions in s 177(5)   **11-95** and (6). Disclosure is not required of the following interests:

- an interest of which the director is not aware or where the director is not aware of the transaction or arrangement in question, which might be the case in respect of indirect interests (the director is treated, however, as being aware of matters of which he ought reasonably to be aware)[191] (s 177(5));

- an interest that cannot reasonably be regarded as likely to give rise to a conflict of interest (s 177(6)(a)). The company may use the articles to identify 'de minimis' transactions which fall within this category and do not require disclosure under s 177. In a case of doubt, of course, it is preferable (given it is a fiduciary duty) to make a declaration;

---

[189] This interpretation is supported by the Explanatory Notes which state: 'An interest of another person in a contract with the company may require the director to make a disclosure under this duty, if that other person's interest amounts to a direct or indirect interest on the part of the director.': see Explanatory Notes to the Companies Act 2006, para 347.

[190] The exemption in CA 2006, s 180(4)(b) for transactions approved or exempt under Part 10, Ch 4 applies only to ss 175 and 176 and not to s 177.

[191] Although this issue as to what the director ought reasonably to be aware of was the subject of some debate in Parliament, the Government's view was that the requirement reflected the current law. On the equivalent wording in CA 2006, s 182, the Solicitor General commented that 'this is an objective test so that it will take into account any relevant circumstances relating to that director; it will focus on the individual director. This is the question that will be asked: what is it reasonable to expect a director in those circumstances to have been aware of? For example, a non-executive director might be expected generally to be less aware of the individual transactions or arrangements entered into by a company': see HC Official Report, SC D (Company Law Reform Bill) 11 July 2006, col 628.

- an interest if and to the extent that the other directors are already aware of it (for these purposes, the other directors are treated as aware of anything of which they ought reasonably to be aware)[192] (s 177(6)(b)). The problem with this exemption is that, given that the consequence of non-disclosure is a breach of duty, few directors will want to rely on this exclusion and the safest course of action is to make a formal declaration;

- an interest in the terms of a director's service contract which terms have been or are to be considered by a meeting of the directors or a committee of the directors appointed for the purpose under the company's constitution,[193] an exclusion which addresses an issue which had arisen in the case law (s 177(6)(c)).[194]

Manner and timing of disclosure

11-96   The courts will require strict compliance with the requirements of CA 2006, s 177 as it is a fiduciary duty and, as at common law,[195] the burden of proof is on a director to show that he made full disclosure before the company entered into the transaction or arrangement (s 177(3)). The disclosure required is full and frank disclosure of the nature and extent of the director's interest so that the other directors can see what the director's interest is and how far it extends.[196] Once made, further disclosure may be needed where a declaration proves to be, or becomes, inaccurate or incomplete (s 177(3)), but there is no need to update the original disclosure unless the transaction is still a 'proposed transaction' for these purposes, but s 182 would then apply.

11-97   Disclosure must be to the other directors and it would seem that disclosure to a committee of directors is insufficient[197] other than where the committee is merely the mechanism by which information is conveyed to all the directors. As disclosure has to be made to the other directors, there is no requirement of disclosure in the case of a private company with a sole director, but the director in such a case must have regard

---

[192] For a situation where the directors were aware or ought reasonably to have been aware of the nature and extent of a conflict, see *Re Marini Ltd* [2004] BCC 172. Previously, there were conflicting views as to whether formal disclosure was required even though all of the directors were aware informally of the conflict of interest: see *Lee Panavision Ltd v Lee Lighting Ltd* [1992] BCLC 22 at 33.

[193] The requirement that the committee be 'appointed for the purpose under the company's constitution', suggest that it must be a formal appointments/remuneration committee rather than an ad hoc management committee.

[194] See *Runciman v Walter Runciman plc* [1992] BCLC 1084.

[195] See *Movitex Ltd v Bulfield* [1988] BCLC 104 at 126.

[196] *Movitex Ltd v Bulfield* [1988] BCLC 104 at 121; *Imperial Mercantile Credit Association v Coleman* (1873) LR 6 HL 189 at 205; CA 2006, s 170(4). See also *Ultraframe (UK) Ltd v Fielding* [2005] EWHC 1638, para 1432.

[197] See *Guinness plc v Saunders* [1988] BCLC 607 at 611; also *Gwembe Valley Development Co Ltd v Koshy* [2004] 1 BCLC 131 at 150; *Re MDA Investment Management Ltd, Whalley v Doney* [2004] 1 BCLC 217 at 255. For the same reasons, disclosure to the company secretary is insufficient unless, again, the secretary is the mechanism by which information is relayed to all the directors: see comments by Solicitor General, HC Official Report, SC D (Company Law Reform Bill) 11 July 2006, col 630.

to his obligations under CA 2006, s 171 (to act in accordance with the constitution), and s 172 (to promote the success of the company).[198]

The declaration may (but need not) be made at a meeting of the directors[199] or it can **11-98** be by notice to the directors in writing[200] or by way of a general notice.[201] There are detailed requirements in ss 184 and 185 as to what is a notice in writing or a general notice for these purposes. In either case, the matter must be dealt with at a meeting for s 184(5) provides that a specific notice is deemed to form part of the proceedings of the next meeting. In effect a specific notice puts the item on the agenda for that next meeting and s 185(4) provides that a general notice must be brought up and read at the next meeting. It is not entirely clear whether the notice must be discussed as opposed to merely read into the board proceedings, but the former would seem to be required if the other directors are to exercise their duties, for example, to act in a way most likely to promote the success of the company under s 172.

A further issue is whether a director, having made a declaration of a conflict of inter- **11-99** est, is able to participate in the meeting which considers the transaction. The model articles provide that the director is not to be counted for quorum or voting purposes, subject to (1) a decision of the company by ordinary resolution to allow him to be counted, or (2) where the director's interest cannot reasonably give rise to a conflict (which is somewhat pointless since the section does not apply when the interest cannot reasonably give rise to a conflict s 177(6)(a)) or (3) where the director's conflict of interest arises from a permitted cause as defined in the model articles (which includes transactions of benefit to the company such as guarantees, indemnities and subscriptions for securities).[202]

It is noticeable that there is no mechanism for shareholders to discover whether any **11-100** disclosure has been made under CA 2006, s 177. Companies were required under the CA 1985 to include details of directors' interests in material transactions with the company in the notes to the company's accounts,[203] but this provision was not carried

---

[198] To require a sole director to make disclosure to himself is a nonsense, see HL Deb, vol 678, GC343 (6 February 2006).

[199] There are merits in a formal declaration at a board meeting, see Lightman J in *Neptune (Vehicle Washing Equipment) Ltd v Fitzgerald* [1995] 1 BCLC 352 at 359: all the directors are reminded of the interest, it is an occasion for a statutory pause for thought about the existence of the conflict of interest and the duty to prefer the interests of the company; and the disclosure should be a distinct happening at a meeting and be recorded in the minutes.

[200] A notice in writing under CA 2006, s 184 is deemed to form part of the proceedings of a meeting of directors and therefore must be formally recorded in the minutes (applying s 248): see s 184(5).

[201] CA 2006, s 177(2). A general notice must be given at a meeting or it must be brought up and read at the next board meeting after it is given, to ensure that it forms part of the minutes of the meeting: ss 185(4), 248. A general notice may be to the effect that the director is a member of a specified company or firm and is to be regarded as interested in any contract which may, after the date of the notice, be made with that company or firm; or that the director is connected with a specified person and is to be regarded as interested in any contract which may, after the date of the notice, be made with that person: s 185(2).

[202] See The Companies (Model Articles) Regulations 2008, SI 2008/3229, art 14 (Ltd); art 16 (Plc).

[203] CA 1985, s 232(2), Sch 6, Part 11.

forward by the CA 2006.[204] The absence of disclosure in the publicly disclosed accounts also means that the business media are not able to draw attention to these matters. Given this position, shareholders should consider imposing a disclosure requirement via the articles and larger companies may want to consider how this information should be made available to their shareholders.

Authorisation by the shareholders or articles

11-101   All the general duties imposed on directors, including CA 2006, s 177, are subject to any rule of law enabling the company to give authority, for anything to be done or omitted by the directors, or any of them, that would otherwise be a breach of duty (s 180(4)(a)).

11-102   As discussed at **11-67**, there are ill-defined common law limits (along the boundaries of fraud on the minority and fraud on creditors) to the powers of the shareholders to authorise or ratify what would otherwise be a breach of duty but transactions with the company may be authorised by the shareholders (where they do not fall foul of the limitations above) on the basis of full disclosure as to the nature and extent of the conflict[205] and likewise may be ratified, subject now to the voting restrictions imposed on ratification by interested directors and others by CA 2006, s 239.[206]

11-103   As noted, it is possible for a company to make provision in its articles to deal with conflicts of interest, and the general duties owed by a director are not infringed by anything done or omitted to be done in accordance with those provisions (s 180(4)(b)). The potential breadth of any provision in the articles is limited by CA 2006, s 232(4) to such provision in the articles 'as has previously been lawful for dealing with conflicts of interest'. As noted at **11-89**, the previous standard provision in the articles on conflicts, Table A, art 85 is now reflected in CA 2006, s 177 so obviously there is no point in including that provision in the articles. Table A also included provisions on quorum and voting requirements for board meetings and provisions on these matters are in the model articles which companies may choose to adopt.[207] Other possible inclusions would be provisions identifying certain transactions as not being transactions which can reasonably be regarded as likely to give rise to a conflict of interest for the purposes of s 177(6)(a) and therefore exempt from the application of s 177. Finally, the articles can require shareholder approval in addition to compliance with s 177 (see s 180(1)).

---

[204] When it was suggested to the Government that this matter needed to be addressed in the directors' report, the Government responded by saying such safeguards were unnecessary, see HL Deb, vol 678, GC 325–6 (9 February 2006).

[205] *New Zealand Netherlands Society 'Oranje' Inc v Kuys* [1973] 2 All ER 1222; *Gwembe Valley Development Co Ltd v Koshy* [2004] 1 BCLC 131 at 151; *Crown Dilmun v Sutton* [2004] 1 BCLC 468 at 511; *Murad v Al-Saraj* [2005] All ER (D) 503 (Jul), CA, para 71; *Quarter Master (UK) Ltd v Pyke* [2005] 1 BCLC 245 at 269.

[206] On ratification, the CA 2006 makes a significant change by providing that on any resolution to ratify a breach of duty, the votes of the interested director (if a member of the company) and any member connected with him (as defined in ss 252–255) must be disregarded, see s 239(3), (4).

[207] See The Companies (Model Articles) Regulations 2008, SI 2008/3229, art 14 (Ltd); art 16 (Plc).

E Existing transactions with the company

Section 182 provides that a director (and a shadow director)[208] who is in any way, dir-   **11-104**
ectly or indirectly, interested in a transaction or arrangement that has been entered
into by the company, must declare the nature and extent of the interest to the other
directors[209] as soon as is reasonably practicable.[210] This provision does not impose a
fiduciary duty, merely a statutory obligation of disclosure.

A number of possible scenarios will attract the application of CA 2006, s 182. One pos-   **11-105**
sibility is that the director had an interest in a proposed transaction with the company
which he neglected to disclose under s 177, in which case he is in breach of s 177 and
also in breach of s 182, assuming that the transaction has been entered into and he has
not disclosed his interest. Another possibility is that the director had no interest in the
transaction for the purpose of s 177 at the time it was entered into, but subsequently
becomes interested, directly or indirectly, in the transaction or becomes aware of an
interest in the transaction (assuming it was not one which he ought reasonably to have
been aware of, s 177(5)). On this basis, he need comply only with s 182. A third scenario is where he becomes interested in a transaction after it has been entered into (for
example, he becomes a shareholder in a company which has secured a supply contract
from the company) and so must disclose his interest under s 182. Time passes and
the renegotiation of the contract arises, in which case it is arguable that the contract
becomes a proposed transaction again and he now comes under a duty to disclose his
interest under s 177, unless he chooses to rely on the defence in s 177(6)(b) that the
other directors are aware or ought reasonably to be aware of his interest. Section 175
does not apply in this scenario (see s 175(3)), but there is potential here for the application of that provision as where the company in which the director now has an interest
competes with his company in respect of some transaction, for example both look to
win a contract from the same customer. In that case, the director now falls within s 175
again. It is important therefore in every scenario to remember that more than one
duty may apply and the various duties may apply in different ways at different stages of
what in business terms might be seen as all one transaction (such as an ongoing supply
relationship).

The wording of s 182 reflects that of CA 1985, s 317 and the nature of that section was   **11-106**
considered by the Court of Appeal in *Hely-Hutchinson v Brayhead Ltd*[211] which concluded that s 317, now CA 2006, s 182, merely created a statutory duty of disclosure.[212]
The only sanction for non-compliance with s 182 is that a director is liable to a fine
and a breach of s 182, or indeed compliance with it, has no effect on the validity of any

---

[208] CA 2006, s 187: in this case notice in writing is required in accordance with s 184: s 187(4).

[209] As to the required disclosure where there is only one director though there should be more, see s 186.

[210] CA 2006, s 182(1), (4). Failure to make a declaration as soon as is reasonably practicable does not affect
the underlying duty to make the declaration.

[211] [1967] 3 All ER 98; endorsed by Lord Goff in *Guinness plc v Saunders* [1990] 1 All ER 652 at 665.

[212] See [1967] 3 All ER 98 at 109, per Lord Pearson.

contract entered into by the company. Likewise, non-compliance with s 182 does not give a company a separate right of action for damages against a director; any right of action must arise from a breach of fiduciary obligation by a director and not from a contravention of the section.[213]

11-107   The disclosure requirements under CA 2006, s 182 are identical to those outlined at **11-98** with respect to s 177. Disclosure may be at a meeting or by notice in writing or a general notice (s 182(2)). If the declaration proves to be or becomes inaccurate or incomplete, a further declaration must be made (s 182(3)). A declaration is not required if the interest has already been declared under s 177 (i.e. when it was merely a proposed transaction); or if the interest cannot reasonably be regarded as likely to give rise to a conflict of interest; or is an interest that the other directors are already aware of or ought reasonably to be aware; or the interest concerns the director's service contract which has been or is to be considered by a meeting or committee of directors appointed for that purpose (s 182(1), (6)).

---

[213] *Coleman Taymar Ltd v Oakes* [2001] 2 BCLC 749; *Movitex Ltd v Bulfield* [1988] BCLC 104 at 125.

12

Specific conflicts—CA 2006, Pt 10, Ch 4

A Introduction

Following the discussion in Chapter 11 of the general duties governing conflict of interests, we turn in this chapter to consider CA 2006, Part 10, Ch 4, which regulates specific transactions with directors where the conflict of interest between the director's personal interests and his duty to the company is particularly acute. **12-1**

To a large extent, the provisions of Ch 4 reflect the long-established position on these transactions previously set out in CA 1985, Part X. Such changes as have been made are a result, primarily, of a Law Commission review of CA 1985, Part X.[1] The approach recommended by the Law Commission was generally adopted by the Company Law Review[2] and by the Government[3] and is reflected in CA 2006, Part 10, Ch 4. The result is a number of mainly technical changes to the provisions and a closer alignment of their requirements so as to give greater consistency of approach. The criminal penalties imposed by CA 1985, Part X were also removed on the basis that the civil consequences of breach provide sufficient deterrence.[4] **12-2**

Overlap with general duties

In entering into any transaction, a director must comply with the general duties set out in CA 2006, Part 10, Ch 2. In particular, a director is required to act in accordance with the constitution and in a way he considers most likely to promote the success of the company and he must exercise reasonable care, skill and diligence. In addition to **12-3**

---

[1] See Law Commission, *Company Directors: Regulating Conflicts of Interests and Formulating a Statement of Duties* (Law Comm No 261), 1999, esp Part 8 (hereinafter Law Commission Report); also Law Commission, *Company Directors: Regulating Conflicts of Interests and Formulating a Statement of Duties, A Joint Consultation Paper* (Law Comm No 261), 1998, 153.

[2] See Company Law Review, *Developing the Framework* (2000), paras 3.86–3.89 and Annex C where these provisions are considered in detail; also *Completing the Structure* (2000) paras 4.8–4.21; and the *Final Report* (2001), paras 6.8–6.14.

[3] See *Modernising Company Law* (2002) Cm 5553-I, paras 3.19–3.20; *Company Law Reform* (2005) Cm 6456, para 3.3.

[4] See 678 HL Official Report (5th Series) GC359 (9 February 2006).

complying with those obligations (s 180(3)) and because of the acute conflict of interest, CA 2006, Part 10, Ch 4 provides that shareholder approval is required for the following transactions, namely:

- directors' service contracts;
- payments for loss of office;
- substantial property transactions; and
- loans and similar financial transactions.

12-4   For these transactions, directors must adhere to their duties under CA 2006, Part 10, Ch 2 *and* seek shareholder approval, so compliance with s 175 or s 177 alone is not sufficient if the transaction requires shareholder approval under Part 10, Ch 4 (s 180(3)).

12-5   If the transaction is approved by the shareholders, however, or is exempt from approval under CA 2006, Part 10, Ch 4, then it is not necessary for the directors also to comply with s 175 (duty to avoid conflicts of interest) or s 176 (duty not to accept benefits from third parties): s 180(2).

12-6   Directors remain under an obligation to comply with CA 2006, s 177 (duty to declare an interest in a proposed transaction or arrangement) and s 182 (declaration of interest in existing transaction or arrangement). Of course, it is possible that disclosure under s 177 (or s 182) will not be required because the other directors are aware or ought reasonably to be aware of the transaction, but that might not always be the case. If the company is a private company and the matter is dealt with by written resolution, it is possible to envisage circumstances in which some of the directors might not be aware that shareholder approval has been given, so there is a case for requiring disclosure to the other directors under s 177 or s 182 even though shareholder approval is obtained. The case for retaining disclosure is even stronger where the transaction is exempt because there is no reason to expect the other directors necessarily to be aware of the transaction in that case.[5]

12-7   As we shall see below, the amendments effected by the CA 2006 to the CA 1985, Part 10 mean that the provisions of CA 2006, Part 10, Ch 4 generally relax the constraints on these particular transactions. Given that approach, it is important that directors, whether recipients under these arrangements or merely instrumental in setting them up, remember their need to adhere to their general duties in ss 171–177. Minority shareholders and creditors may have to rely on those general duties for protection against abuse of the now more permissive provisions of Part 10, Ch 4.

Overview of the general scheme of Part 10, Ch 4

12-8   The provisions apply to directors including shadow directors (CA 2006, s 223(1)). In many instances, the provisions extend also to transactions with connected persons,

---

[5] Of course, if the transaction is exempt, it may be because it is minimal and so it may be that it cannot reasonably be regarded as likely to give rise to a conflict of interest in any event so disclosure would not be required under CA 2006, s 177 or s 182: see s 177(6)(a) and s 182(6)(a).

a category defined at length in ss 252–256. Essentially, the key categories of persons connected with a director are:

- members of his family;[6]
- a body corporate with which he is connected;[7]
- trustees of a trust the beneficiaries of which are the director or members of his family or companies with which he is connected;
- any partner of the director or a partner of any person who by virtue of any of the other categories is connected with that director; and
- certain firms with which the director is connected (s 252(2)).

The overall scheme adopted in CA 2006, Part 10, Ch 4 is that, for each class of con- **12-9**
flicted transaction, shareholder approval is required by an ordinary resolution unless the articles specify a higher majority.[8] Where the director is a director of the company's holding company, the transaction must also be approved by the members of the holding company.[9] Shareholder approval is not required in respect of these transactions where the company is not a UK-registered company[10] or where the company is a wholly-owned subsidiary of another body corporate.[11]

Where approval in a private company is by way of the written resolution, a memo- **12-10**
randum setting out particulars of the proposed transaction/payments etc[12] must be circulated to the members eligible to vote on the resolution at or before the time at which the proposed resolution is sent to the members.[13] An accidental failure to send a memorandum to one or more members is disregarded for the purposes of determining whether this requirement has been met, subject to any provision to the contrary effect

---

[6] Defined in CA 2006, s 253: includes a director's spouse, parents, his children or step-children of whatever age (previously, the category was limited to minor children); any cohabiting partner and minor children of the cohabitant if they live with the director.

[7] Defined in CA 2006, s 254. Essentially, a director is connected with a body corporate if the director and persons connected with him together are interested in at least 20% of the equity share capital of that company or are entitled to exercise or control the exercise of more than 20% of the voting power at any general meeting. See also s 255.

[8] References to a resolution (as in CA 2006, s 188, payments for loss of office) are to an ordinary resolution: s 281(3). Informal unanimous consent also suffices, even in the absence of compliance with the statutory requirements: *Wright v Atlas Wright (Europe) Ltd* [1999] 2 BCLC 301, CA, provided the provisions are imposed for the protection of shareholders alone (and therefore they are able to waive them). If the statutory scheme is also intended to protect creditors' interests, unanimous shareholder approval cannot remedy a failure to adhere to the statutory scheme: *Re R W Peak (Kings Lynn) Ltd* [1998] 1 BCLC 193; and see *Kinlan v Crimmin* [2007] 2 BCLC 67.

[9] CA 2006, ss 188(2), 190(2), 197(2), 198(3), 200(3), 210(3), 203(2), 217(2), 218(2).

[10] Defined CA 2006, s 1158; the effect is to exclude companies not formed and registered under the CA 2006 or its predecessors.

[11] CA 2006, ss 188(6), 190(4), 197(5), 200(6), 201(6), 217(4), 218(4), 219(6).

[12] Other than in the case of a substantial property transaction within CA 2006, s 190 where there is no requirement of a memorandum, but the company still needs to ensure that the shareholders have sufficient information if they are to pass a resolution approving the transaction.

[13] CA 2006, ss 188(5), 197(3), 198(4), 200(4) 203(3), 217(3), 218(3), 219(3).

in the company's articles.[14] Where approval is by way of a resolution at a meeting, a like memorandum must be made available for inspection by the members for not less than 15 days before the meeting and at the meeting itself.[15]

12-11   A transaction which falls within more than one provision (for example a director may obtain a loan from the company and enter into a substantial property transaction at the same time) requires approval under each applicable provision (which should not prove a problem in practice since they are relatively uniform in approach) but it is not necessary to pass a separate resolution for the purposes of each provision.[16]

B Directors' long-term service contracts: CA 2006, ss 188–189

12-12   The length of directors' service contracts, particularly in public companies, has been controversial because of the level of compensation payable in the event of termination of the contract.

12-13   CA 2006, s 188 requires shareholder approval of any provision under which the guaranteed term of a director's employment[17] with the company (or where he is the director of a holding company, within the group consisting of that company and its subsidiaries) is, or may be, longer than two years.[18]

12-14   The guaranteed term of employment,[19] for these purposes, is the period during which the director is employed and the contract cannot be determined by the company by

---

[14] CA 2006, s 224; this provision on accidental failures was added for the avoidance of doubt on this matter, but it does seem generously drafted. See 681 HL Official Report (5th Series), col 872 (9 May 2006). In small private companies, it may be opportune on occasion to have an 'accidental' failure to circulate the required memorandum if the resolution can be effective without it. It may be difficult to prove that the omission was anything other than accidental. When coupled with the ability to pass a written resolution by a majority (see CA 2006, s 282) rather than unanimity, as was previously the case, minority shareholders may find themselves ill-informed and unable to prevent approval being given.

[15] CA 2006, ss 188(5)(b), 197(3)(b), 198(4)(b), 200(4)(b) 203(3)(b), 217(3)(b), 218(3)(b), 219(3)(b).

[16] CA 2006, s 225. See 678 HL Official Report (5th Series) GC360 (9 February 2006).

[17] 'Employment' is defined as including any employment under a director's service contract which is then broadly defined in CA 2006, s 227.

[18] CA 2006, s 188(1); the period was reduced from 5 years under the CA 1985. As before, rolling contracts, where the contract is novated daily so that on any day there is always a two-year period of notice to run, remain an option. The Law Commission was critical of the use of such devices to circumvent the statutory policy (see Law Commission Report, above n 1, paras 9.31–9.33) but the Company Law Review took the position that such rolling contracts are consistent with the policy objective of limiting the maximum period of notice in respect of which the director can receive compensation on termination: see Company Law Review, *Developing the Framework* (2000), paras 3.86–3.89 and Annex C.

[19] For listed companies, the Combined Code on Corporate Governance recommends that notice or contract periods should be set at one year or less, see Combined Code, para B.1.6. There is some anecdotal evidence that, if anything, this limitation has had an upward effect on compensation agreements with directors requiring even larger sums to compensate for the insecurity, as they perceive it, of one-year contracts.

notice or it can be so terminated only in specified circumstances (CA 2006, s 188(3)). A provision included in contravention of s 188 and without the approval of the members is void and the contract is deemed to contain a term entitling the company to terminate the contract at any time by the giving of reasonable notice (s 189).

Directors' service contracts are defined in CA 2006, s 227 (set out below) as including **12-15** contracts of service, contracts for services *and,* for the first time, letters of appointment as directors (commonly used for non-executive appointments)[20] and details of these service contracts must be available for inspection by any member at the company's registered office or other specified place.[21]

'Directors' service contracts

(1) For the purposes of this Part a director's "service contract", in relation to a company, means a contract under which—

   (a) a director of the company undertakes personally to perform services (as director or otherwise) for the company, or for a subsidiary of the company, or

   (b) services (as director or otherwise) that a director of the company undertakes personally to perform are made available by a third party to the company, or to a subsidiary of the company.

(2) The provisions of this Part relating to directors' service contracts apply to the terms of a person's appointment as a director of a company.

They are not restricted to contracts for the performance of services outside the scope of the ordinary duties of a director (CA 2006, s 227).'

The scope of CA 2006, s 227 was explained by Lord Sainsbury in the Parliamentary **12-16** debates in the following terms:[22]

'Subsection (1)(a) covers contracts of service such as any employment contract that the director may hold with a company or a subsidiary of the company of which he is director, for example, as executive director, or any contract for services that he personally undertakes to perform as such.

   Subsection (1)(b) covers the case where those services are made available to the company through a third party such as a personal services company. In either case, the contract must require the director personally to perform the service or services in question.

   Subsection (2) brings within the definition of a service contract letters of appointment to the office of director. Many directors will have no contract of service or for services with the company. The second sentence of subsection (2) ensures that the definition of "service contracts" includes arrangements under which the director

---

[20] See 678 HL Official Report (5th Series) GC 361–2 (9 February 2006); and Law Commission Report, above n 1, paras 9.9–9.11.

[21] CA 2006, s 228; the 'specified place' is a single alternative location situated in the same part of the UK as the company's registered office: s 1136, The Companies (Company Records) Regulations 2008, SI 2008/3006, reg 3. Members have rights to inspect and to take copies of any service contract: CA 2006, s 229, SI 2008/3006, Part 3. These disclosure requirements extend to shadow directors (s 230) but they are unlikely to have service contracts.

[22] 678 HL Official Report (5th Series) GC361–2 (9 February 2006).

performs duties within the scope of the ordinary duties of the director, as well as contracts to perform duties outside the scope of the ordinary duties of the director. Without that, the term "service contract" might be interpreted as applying only to the latter type of contract.'

C Payments for loss of office: CA 2006, ss 215–221

12-17   Directors' remuneration arrangements typically make provision for payments to the director as compensation for the loss of office or on retirement from office. Problems most commonly arise when the company attempts to dismiss an executive director with a service contract. If, say, the finance director, is appointed by contract for a fixed term and the company exercises its power to remove him as a director before that term expires, the company will be liable in damages as the courts will imply a term that the company undertakes to do nothing of its own accord (for example, by terminating his post as a director) to bring to an end the circumstances necessary to enable a person to act as finance director.[23]

12-18   Compensation payments (sometimes dubbed 'rewards for failure') are often controversial, particularly in listed public companies where the size of such payments has attracted media attention and investor anger, especially as resignations or retirements may arise as a result of poor performance. As discussed at **12-13**, in certain circumstances, directors' service contracts in excess of two years must be approved by the shareholders (CA 2006, s 188), a measure designed at least to draw the shareholders' attention to the compensation which may be payable should the director be dismissed. The Combined Code on Corporate Governance (see **5-8**) states that notice or contract periods should be set at one year or less,[24] the purpose being to reduce the compensation payments which would otherwise be payable: see **5-42**. The Code also states that remuneration committees should consider the compensation commitments which would arise if a director's contract is terminated and that the remuneration committee should take a robust line on reducing compensation to reflect the obligation on a departing director to mitigate his or her loss,[25] an obligation which in practice seems frequently to be overlooked. To address these concerns, the statutory controls on payments for loss of office have been tightened in the CA 2006 (when compared with CA 1985, ss 313–316) with an emphasis now on anti-avoidance provisions.

---

[23] *Shindler v Northern Raincoat Co Ltd* [1960] 2 All ER 239; *Southern Foundries (1926) Ltd v Shirlaw* [1940] 2 All ER 445, HL. Where a director does not have a separate service contract and has simply been appointed under the articles, his position can be terminated at any time and he cannot recover any damages: *Read v Astoria Garage (Streatham) Ltd* [1952] 2 All ER 292. Indeed the company may specifically alter its articles to facilitate the removal of such a director and he will not be entitled to any relief: *Shuttleworth v Cox Bros & Co (Maidenhead) Ltd* [1927] 2 KB 9. It would be unusual now for a director, certainly in larger companies, not to have a service contract.

[24] FRC, Combined Code, B.1.6.   [25] FRC, Combined Code, B.1.5.

Payments requiring approval

The basic scheme is that a company may not make a payment for loss of office (or on **12-19** retirement) to a director of the company or to a director of its holding company unless the payment has been approved by a resolution of the members of the company and, if necessary, the members of the holding company (CA 2006, s 217). Similar provisions apply: (1) where a payment for loss of office is made in connection with the transfer of the whole or any part of the undertaking or property of the company (s 218); and (2) where a payment for loss of office is in connection with a transfer of shares in the company, or in a subsidiary of the company, resulting from a takeover bid[26] (s 219).

The key to the statutory scheme is the expanded definition of 'payment for loss of office' **12-20** in CA 2006, s 215 which includes payments for loss of office or on retirement as a director but also for loss of or in connection with retirement from any other office or employment in connection with the management of the company's affairs or the affairs of a subsidiary. The Law Commission had recommended this change in order to address a gap in the protection afforded to shareholders which had been revealed by the decision of the Privy Council in *Taupo Totara Timber Co Ltd v Rowe*[27] (interpreting the equivalent New Zealand section). The Privy Council had concluded that the then statutory disclosure requirement did not apply to any payment made to a director in respect of his executive position with the company. That loophole is now closed by CA 2006, s 215(1).

The definition extends to payments in cash and in kind (CA 2006, s 215(2)); payments **12-21** by other persons at the direction of the company (s 215(4)); payments to connected persons and to other persons at the direction or for the benefit of the director or connected person (s 215(3));[28] and payments to directors of holding companies.[29] All these payments need shareholder approval, unless they fall within the exempt categories, discussed below.

Payments not requiring approval

Approval is not required for a payment made in good faith: **12-22**

(1) in discharge of an existing legal obligation,[30]

---

[26] The purpose of the provision is to avoid the risk that directors may obtain advantageous payments from persons launching a takeover bid which should in fact go to the members in return for their shares, see comments by Lord Sainsbury, 678 HL Official Report (5th Series) GC358 (9 February 2006).

[27] [1978] AC 537, [1977] 3 All ER 123. See Law Commission Report, above n 1, paras 7.38–7.48.

[28] The Law Commission considered that the provision should not be extended to connected persons, but the Company Law Review disagreed on the basis that other provisions of this Part apply to connected persons and therefore this loophole should also be closed: see the Company Law Review, *Developing the Framework* (2000), Annex C, para 5.

[29] CA 2006, ss 217(2), 218(2). The Law Commission had recommended this change to reflect the reality that many companies are today organised in groups and to prevent avoidance: see the Law Commission Report, above n 1, paras 7.68–7.71.

[30] The 'existing legal obligation' must arise independently (for example, from a contract of employment) of the event giving rise to the payment for loss of office. It will not suffice if, as part of the event giving rise to the loss of office, a legal obligation is entered into to pay compensation: CA 2006, s 220(2), (3). The exemption

(2) by way of damages for breach of such an obligation,

(3) by way of settlement or compromise of any claim arising in connection with the termination of a person's office or employment, or

(4) by way of pension in respect of past services.[31]

12-23 The exemption for payments in discharge of existing legal obligations gives statutory effect to the interpretation of the previous provision adopted by the Privy Council in *Taupo Totara Timber Co Ltd v Rowe*[32] and so merely states what was considered to be the law in any event.

12-24 The civil consequences of breach of these provisions is clarified so that if a payment is made in contravention of the requirement for member approval, the payment is held by the recipient on trust for the company making the payment and any director who authorised the payment is jointly and severally liable to indemnify the company that made the payment for any loss resulting from it.[33]

12-25 The exceptions noted above are wide enough (especially the exemption for payments in discharge of existing legal obligations and pension payments) to ensure that few payments need the approval of the general meeting hence the significant level of shareholder dissatisfaction in listed public companies with these payments.

12-26 Details of directors' remuneration and payments for loss of office must be included in notes to the accounts.[34] Quoted companies[35] must draw up a detailed directors' remuneration report containing a full explanation of the company's policy on service contracts and on notice periods and termination as well as comprehensive details of the remuneration and compensation packages of each individual director.[36] This remuneration report (though not individual remuneration packages) must be put to an advisory vote of the shareholders (CA 2006, s 439) which has had the effect of

allows payments to be made by associated companies (see s 220(2)) so a subsidiary may make a payment to a director in respect of a legal obligation of its holding company: see 678 HL Debs, GC350 (9 February 2006).

[31] A further (and it would seem pointless) exception is provided for small payments which do not exceed £200: CA 2006, s 221.

[32] [1977] 3 All ER 123 (interpreting the equivalent New Zealand provision). The Law Commission had recommended that, as that decision was likely to be followed, the statutory provision should be amended to make the position clear: Law Commission Report, see above n 1, paras 7.6–7.16.

[33] CA 2006, s 222(1); s 222(2)–(5) set out the permutations where more than one requirement is breached. In particular, the claims of the offeree shareholders under s 219 have priority over those of the company under s 217; see Explanatory Notes to the Companies Act 2006, para 413.

[34] CA 2006, s 412; The Small Companies and Groups (Accounts and Directors' Report) Regulations 2008, SI 2008/409, reg 5, Sch 3; The Large and Medium-sized Companies and Groups (Accounts and Reports) Regulations 2008, SI 2008/410, reg 8, Sch 5.

[35] Defined CA 2006, s 385 as a company whose equity share capital '(a) has been included in the official list in accordance with the provisions of the Financial Services and Markets Act 2000, Pt 6; or (b) is officially listed in an EEA State (EU with Norway, Iceland and Liechtenstein); or (c) is admitted to dealing on either the New York Stock Exchange or Nasdaq.'

[36] See CA 2006, ss 420–422; the content is prescribed by The Large and Medium-sized Companies and Groups (Accounts and Reports) Regulations 2008, SI 2008/410, reg 11, Sch 8.

focusing attention on the levels of remuneration and the type of compensation agreements which are in place. The result has been considerable shareholder criticism and media attention which has had some effect in creating a culture which is more critical and questioning of these packages. The directors' remuneration report is discussed at **5-39**.

D Substantial property transactions: CA 2006, ss 190–196

A particular conflict of interest which may give rise to problems is where directors purchase assets from, or sell assets to, their companies or companies in which they have an interest.   **12-27**

Substantial property transactions are governed by CA 2006, s 190 (previously CA 1985, ss 320–322) which provides that, subject to certain exceptions, a company may not enter into an arrangement under which: **12-28**

'(a) a director of the company or its holding company, or a person connected with such a director,[37] acquires or is to acquire from the company (directly or indirectly) a substantial non-cash asset; or

(b) the company acquires or is to acquire a substantial non-cash asset (directly or indirectly) from such a director or a person so connected;

unless the arrangement has been approved by a resolution of the members of the company or is conditional on such approval being obtained.'[38]

If the arrangement is with a director of the company's holding company or a person connected with such a director, the arrangement must also be approved by a resolution of the members of the holding company.[39]   **12-29**

The purpose of requiring prior shareholder approval is to provide the members of a company with an opportunity to check on any potential abuse of position by directors   **12-30**

---

[37] Defined CA 2006, s 252.

[38] Previously, the transaction would have had to be disclosed in the notes to the company's accounts, see CA 1985, s 232, Sch 6, Pt II, para 15(c), but this is no longer a requirement. A substantial property transaction might in some circumstances have to be recorded in the notes to the accounts as a related party transaction, see The Large and Medium-sized Companies and Groups (Accounts and Reports) Regulations 2008, SI 2008/410, Sch 1, para 72. Disclosure to the directors is required under CA 2006, s 177 so the item will be recorded in the board minutes (s 248(1)) and companies must keep records of shareholder resolutions and minutes of general meetings (s 355), but such records of resolutions and meetings are open to inspection only by the members (s 358(3)) and so neither creditors nor would-be investors, nor the business media (unless they become members) can have any sense of the extent to which the directors are interested in transactions with the company (save where the matter is reported as a related party transaction).

[39] CA 2006, s 190(2). For an example of the importance of securing the approval of the holding company (where necessary), see *British Racing Drivers' Club Ltd v Hextall Erskine & Co* [1997] 1 BCLC 182.

and it allows a matter to be more widely considered and a more objective decision reached.[40] The section does not prohibit the interested director from voting as a shareholder in favour of the arrangement at the general meeting,[41] but the shareholders as a body are limited by common law restrictions along the boundaries of fraud on the minority and fraud on creditors which are discussed at **18-35**.

12-31   Allowing a company to enter into a conditional arrangement is a new provision which follows a Law Commission recommendation that companies should have the commercial freedom and flexibility to enter into such arrangements.[42] If the transaction is conditional on approval which is not secured, the company is not subject to any liability by reason of the failure to obtain the required approval (s 190(3)). If approval is not obtained, the transaction is voidable (s 195(2)) but it is possible for the members (and, if necessary, the members of the holding company) to affirm the arrangement within a reasonable period (s 196).

12-32   Approval is required only if the value of the non-cash asset,[43] at the time the arrangement is entered into, exceeds 10% of the company's asset value and is more than £5,000 (previously £2,000: CA 1985), or exceeds £100,000 (s 191); and the onus is on the person alleging the contravention of the statutory provision to prove that the value of the non-cash asset exceeds the requisite value.[44]

12-33   The application of the statutory provision can be illustrated by *Re Duckwari plc (No 1)*,[45] a case under the CA 1985, but still relevant under the CA 2006. In this case, a company (Offerventure) entered into a contract to purchase a property for £495,000. Having paid the deposit, Offerventure agreed to pass the property on to Duckwari in return for Duckwari repaying the deposit to Offerventure and undertaking to pay the remaining purchase price. The shareholders in Offerventure were C and his wife and C was a director of Duckwari. The transaction was an agreement therefore by a company (Duckwari) to acquire a non-cash asset[46] from a person (Offerventure) connected with one of its (Duckwari's) directors. The acquisition was of a non-cash asset

---

[40] See *British Racing Drivers' Club Ltd v Hextall Erskine & Co* [1997] 1 BCLC 182 at 198. Informal unanimous assent suffices: see *NBH Ltd v Hoare* [2006] 2 BCLC 649.

[41] The limitations on a director voting in CA 2006, s 239(4) apply only to voting to ratify a breach of duty.

[42] See the Law Commission Report, above n 1, paras 10.8–10.10.

[43] 'Non-cash asset' is defined in CA 2006, s 1163. A new anti-avoidance provision requires a series of arrangements or transactions to be aggregated: see s 190(5). A company's 'asset value' means the value of the company's net assets determined by reference to its most recent statutory accounts, or if no such accounts have been so prepared, the amount of the company's called-up share capital: s 191(3).

[44] *Niltan Carson Ltd v Hawthorne* [1988] BCLC 298. See also the Scottish case *Micro Leisure Ltd v County Properties and Developments Ltd* [2000] BCC 872 where the court concluded that the value should be determined in the context of the particular transaction which might include taking into account the value of the property to the director which may be different from the market value.

[45] [1997] 2 BCLC 713.

[46] Millett LJ noted that the asset acquired could be described either as the benefit of the purchase contract (i.e. the right of Offerventure to call for completion of the contract and conveyance of the property on the payment of the purchase price) or as Offerventure's beneficial interest in the property which was subject to an unpaid vendor's lien for the balance of the purchase money: see [1997] 2 BCLC 713 at 724–5.

within the statutory threshold[47] and the approval of the shareholders of Duckwari was required under CA 1985, s 320 (now CA 2006, s 190). Given such approval had not been obtained, the transaction was in contravention of the statutory requirements. The liabilities arising from this contravention are discussed below.

Approval is not required for a transaction between a company and a person in his char-   **12-34**
acter as a member of the company whether the acquisition is by a member from the company,[48] or, and this is a new element, by the company from a member (s 192(a)). It is not clear why the provision was extended to cover acquisitions by the company from a member qua member and there may be some potential for abuse in that situation.

Approval is not required in the case of a transaction between a holding company and   **12-35**
its wholly-owned subsidiary, or between two wholly-owned subsidiaries of the same holding company (CA 2006, s 192(b)). This exemption is designed to facilitate intra-group activities which might otherwise be affected because one of the companies is a connected person of a director[49] and so the transaction would be within the general provision.

Approval is not required (either of the members of the company or of the holding com-   **12-36**
pany) for an arrangement entered into by a company which is being wound up (unless it is a members' voluntary winding up[50]) or is in administration (CA 2006, s 193).[51] The purpose is to ensure that a liquidator or administrator is not hampered in the execu-tion of his duties when the directors may be the only possible purchasers of the assets of the company in liquidation or administration.

For the avoidance of doubt, CA 2006, s 190(6) makes clear that approval is not required   **12-37**
in respect of a transaction so far as it relates to anything to which a director of the com-pany is entitled under his service contract (as defined in s 227) or to payments for loss of office (as defined in s 215).[52]

As the consequences of contravention of the substantial property provisions (see CA   **12-38**
2006, s 195) and the consequence of contravention of loan, quasi-loan, etc provisions (see s 213) are essentially identical, the matter is discussed below in the context of contravention of the loan provisions.

---

[47] Millett LJ noted that on whatever view was taken of the nature of the non-cash asset, see above n 46, the asset was worth at least £49,500, see [1997] 2 BCLC 713 at 725. The trial judge had established that 10% of the company's asset value in this case was £44,399 and therefore the case fell within the relevant financial thresholds: see [1997] 2 BCLC 713 at 715, 721.

[48] Lord Sainsbury noted that the intention in providing an exemption for members is to ensure that trans-actions such as a dividend in specie, the distribution of assets to a member on a winding up in satisfaction of his rights qua member, a duly sanctioned return of capital other than in cash, and issues of shares are clearly within the exemption and do not require shareholder approval: see 678 HL Debs, GC347 (9 February 2006). All these examples are of acquisitions by the members from the company, not vice versa.

[49] See CA 2006, s 252.

[50] In that case, the members retain an interest in the disposal of the company's assets.

[51] See 681 HL Official Report (5th Series), col 870 (9 May 2006). The exemption was not extended to receivers or administrative receivers apparently for fear of abuse of the provision, see HC Official Report, SC D (Company Law Reform Bill) (11 July 2006), col 632; also *Demite Ltd v Protech Health Ltd* [1998] BCC 638.

[52] See the Law Commission Report, above n 1, paras 10.11–10.13.

E Loans, quasi-loans and credit transactions: CA 2006, ss 197–214

12-39   The CA 2006 significantly alters the position on loans from that which applied under the CA 1985. That Act prohibited (on pain of criminal sanctions) loans to directors and to connected persons and further prohibited quasi-loans and credit transactions in the case of relevant companies (essentially public companies or companies part of a group which contained a public company).

Shareholder approval required

12-40   Now, in the case of private companies (other than private companies associated with public companies, see below), loans[53] to directors[54] and directors of the holding company are permissible with the approval of the members and, if necessary, the members of the holding company and there are no criminal sanctions. Shareholder approval is also required if the company is to give guarantees or provide security in connection with a loan made by any person to a director of the company or of its holding company. There are no restrictions on loans to connected persons (other than the need for the directors to adhere to their general duties when entering into such arrangements) nor on loans to directors of subsidiary companies provided that the director is not also a director of the holding company.

12-41   Public companies and companies associated with a public company[55] require shareholder approval for loans, as above, but also for quasi-loans;[56] credit transactions;[57] and for the giving of guarantees and the provision of security, in this case whether the arrangement is for a director of the company or a director of its holding company or a person connected with such a director.

---

[53] 'Loan' is not defined by the statute but the essence of a loan is a requirement for repayment: see *Champagne Perrier-Jouet SA v HH Finch Ltd* [1982] 3 All ER 713 at 717; *First Global Media Group Ltd v Larkin* [2003] EWCA Civ 1765, para 41. Frequently, there is a dispute as to whether the sum paid has been paid as a loan (subject to repayment) or as an advance on remuneration (not subject to repayment): see, for example, *Currencies Direct Ltd v Ellis* [2002] 2 BCLC 482, CA.

[54] 'Director' includes shadow directors: CA 2006, s 223(1)(c).

[55] 'Associated company' is defined in CA 2006, s 256 which replaces a more complex definition of a relevant company in CA 1985, s 331. A holding company is associated with all its subsidiaries and a subsidiary is associated with its holding company and all the other subsidiary companies of its holding company: see Explanatory Notes to the Companies Act 2006, para 406.

[56] CA 2006, s 199(1): a quasi-loan is a transaction whereby payments are made by a creditor (the company) on behalf of the borrower (the director), or the company reimburses expenditure incurred by another party for the director, on terms that the director or a person on his behalf will reimburse the company or in circumstances giving rise to a liability on the part of the director to reimburse the company.

[57] CA 2006, s 202(1): a credit transaction is a transaction under which one party (the creditor): supplies any goods or sells any land under a hire-purchase agreement or a conditional sale agreement leases or hires any land or goods in return for periodical payments; or otherwise disposes of land or supplies goods or services on the understanding that payment, in whatever form, is to be deferred.

If prior approval is not obtained, the arrangement is voidable, but it is possible for **12-42** the members (and, if necessary, the members of the holding company) to affirm the arrangement within a reasonable period (CA 2006, s 214).

In addition to shareholder approval, details of advances, credits and guarantees must **12-43** be included in the notes to the company's accounts.[58]

This change from prohibition to shareholder approval may have a significant impact **12-44** (and some potential for abuse[59]) in private companies where the members and the directors are mostly the same people. In small private companies, shareholder approval would be easy to secure, though shareholders are constrained by common law limits to voting power drawn along the lines of fraud on the minority and fraud on creditors which are discussed at **18-35**. Directors remain subject to their general duties in CA 2006, ss 171–177, as noted above.

As before, in order to reduce the possibility of transactions being constructed in a way **12-45** which circumvents the requirements for approval, arrangements such as back-to-back transactions (whereby another person enters into a transaction which, if it had been entered into by the company, would have required approval) and the assignment and assumption by the company of rights and obligations which if entered into directly by the company would require shareholder approval, also require shareholder approval (CA 2006, s 203(1)).

Shareholder approval not required

There are a variety of exemptions when approval by the members is not required. **12-46** Generally the CA 2006 relaxed the exemptions and, in some cases, modified their application, for example to extend them to directors of holding companies and connected persons. Exemptions under more than one heading may apply.

Expenditure incurred on company business

This generous exemption, being the most general in application, is important in prac **12-47** tice for directors. Approval is not required for anything done by a company to provide a director of the company, or of its holding company, or a person connected with any such director with funds to meet expenditure incurred or to be incurred by him for the purposes of the company or for the purpose of enabling him properly to perform his duties as an officer of the company, or to enable any such person to avoid incurring

[58] CA 2006, s 413 is a modified version of the disclosure requirements previously contained in CA 1985, s 232, Sch 6, Pt II; and see The Small Companies and Groups (Accounts and Directors' Report) Regulations 2008, SI 2008/409, reg 3, Sch 1, para 57; The Large and Medium-sized Companies and Groups (Accounts and Reports) Regulations 2008, SI 2008/410, reg 3, Sch 1, para 63. The simplified disclosure requirements reflect the limited requirements of the Fourth and Seventh Company Law Directives (see Explanatory Notes to the Companies Act 2006, para 663).

[59] Liquidators commonly find significant sums outstanding from directors to the company which, under the CA 1985, could be challenged and recovery sought, but in future they are likely to find that the loans have shareholder approval and it may be difficult, save in egregious cases, to challenge that approval.

such expenditure (CA 2006, s 204). In this case, the aggregate value of the transactions must not exceed £50,000 (previously £20,000).

Expenditure on defending proceedings or in connection with regulatory action or investigation

12-48   Approval is not required for anything done by a company to provide a director of the company, or of its holding company, with funds to meet expenditure incurred or to be incurred by him in defending any criminal or civil proceedings in connection with[60] any negligence, default, breach of duty or breach of trust by him in relation to the company or an associated company or in connection with an application for relief[61] or to enable any director to avoid incurring such expenditure (CA 2006, s 205), see **13-43**. The terms of the loan must provide for the loan to be repaid, or any liability of the company incurred in connection with any such loan to be discharged, in the event that the director is convicted in the proceedings or judgment is given against him (s 205(2)).

12-49   A new provision, added for the avoidance of doubt,[62] is an exception from the need for shareholder approval for anything done by the company to provide a director of the company or of its holding company with funds to meet expenditure incurred or to be incurred by him in defending himself in an investigation by a regulatory authority or against action proposed to be taken by a regulatory authority in connection with any alleged negligence, default, breach of duty or breach of trust by him in relation to the company or an associated company or to enable any such director to avoid incurring such expenditure (CA 2006, s 206), see **13-44**. In this instance, notably, there is no requirement that the funds be repaid.

Small amounts

12-50   A company may make a loan or quasi-loan or give a guarantee or provide security (whether to or for a director of the company or of a holding company or even to a connected person) provided the aggregate of the relevant amounts does not exceed £10,000 (previously £5,000) (CA 2006, s 207(1)). Approval is not required for credit transactions where the aggregate value does not exceed £15,000 (previously £10,000) (s 207(2)). There is also an exemption for credit transactions if the company enters into the transaction in the ordinary course of its business and the value of the transaction is not greater and the terms are not more favourable than those which it is reasonable to expect the company to have offered to a person of the same financial standing but unconnected with the company (s 207(3)).

---

[60] This exemption was narrowed from the equivalent provision in CA 1985, s 337A which applied to expenditure incurred in defending 'any criminal or civil proceedings'.

[61] I.e. an application under CA 2006, s 661 (acquisition of shares by innocent nominee) or, more commonly, an application under s 1157 (general power of court to grant relief).

[62] In the Government's opinion such expenditure is already included within the exemption for defence expenditure: see 678 HL Official Report (5th Series) GC351–2 (9 February 2006); 681 HL Official Report (5th Series), col 871 (9 May 2006).

Loans to associated companies

Approval is not required for loans or quasi-loans to, or credit transactions for, an asso- **12-51** ciated body corporate or the giving of a guarantee or provision of security in connection with a loan or quasi-loan to an associated body corporate (CA 2006, s 208). The definition of associated body corporate in s 256 means that this exemption has been extended in scope to allow in essence for any transactions within a group.

Money-lending companies

A company which is a money-lending company (defined CA 2006, s 209(2)) may make **12-52** a loan or quasi-loan to any person provided the loan is made in the ordinary course of the company's business and the amount of the loan is not greater, and the terms are not more favourable, than that or those which it is reasonable to expect the company to have offered to a person of the same financial standing but unconnected with the company (s 209). There is no monetary limit (previously £100,000).

A money-lending company may also make a loan to a director or a director of its hold- **12-53** ing company or one of its employees to enable such a person to purchase their only or main residence, to improve their dwelling house, or in substitution for a loan provided by a third party for any of those purposes, provided that loans of that type are ordinarily made by the company to its employees on terms no less favourable (s 209(3),(4)).

Consequences of contravention of loan or substantial property provisions

One of the aims of the restatement of these provisions in CA 2006, Part 10, Ch 4, **12-54** was to align the remedies more closely so the consequence of breach are practically identical[63] in s 195 (consequence of contravention of substantial property provisions) and s 213 (consequence of contravention of loan, quasi-loan, etc, provisions). The abolition of the criminal sanctions attached to improper loans further clarifies the position regarding remedies since there is no longer any issue of recovery on an illegal contract.[64]

Any arrangement or any transaction entered into in pursuance of the arrangement **12-55** (and in the case of a substantial property transaction, whether by the company or by any other person) without members' approval in contravention of the relevant statutory requirement is voidable at the instance of the company unless:

(1) restitution of any money or other asset that was the subject matter of the arrangement or transaction is no longer possible, or

(2) the company has been indemnified for the loss or damage suffered by it; or

---

[63] There is a slight difference in the wording as between CA 2006, s 195(2)(b) and s 213(2)(b) but it is difficult to see that it makes any practical difference.

[64] See *Currencies Direct Ltd v Ellis* [2002] 1 BCLC 193, appealed on other grounds, see [2002] 2 BCLC 482, CA; *Tait Consibee (Oxford) Ltd v Tait* [1997] 2 BCLC 349.

(3) rights acquired in good faith, for value and without actual notice of the contravention by a person who is not a party to the arrangement or transaction would be affected by its avoidance (CA 2006, ss 195(2), 213(2)).

12-56   Regardless of whether the arrangement has been avoided, and without prejudice to any liability which might otherwise arise,[65] any director with whom the company entered into the arrangement; any connected person who entered into the arrangement with the company; the director with whom any such person is connected; and any other director who authorised the transaction or arrangement is liable as follows (CA 2006, ss 195(4), 213(4)), subject to certain defences:[66]

(1) to account to the company for any gain that he has made directly or indirectly by the arrangement or transaction; and

(2) (jointly and severally with any other person so liable) to indemnify the company[67] for any loss or damage resulting from the arrangement or transaction (ss 195(3)(a) and (b), 213(3)(a) and (b)).[68]

12-57   The scope of the obligation to indemnify the company was considered in *Re Duckwari plc (No 2)*,[69] the facts of which are discussed at **12-33**. The company, Duckwari, acquired a non-cash asset (a property) from a person connected with one of its directors in 1989 for £495,000. There was no evidence that the property had been under- or over-valued at the time of purchase. By May 1993, however, when the property was valued for the purposes of the proceedings, and following the collapse of the property market, it was valued at £90,000. As it was no longer possible to avoid the transaction, the company sought an indemnity for the loss suffered by it. This hearing revolved around the point in time at which the loss or damage caused by the transaction should be measured.

12-58   The Court of Appeal held that the loss recoverable is the difference between the cost of the unauthorised acquisition and the amount realised on the sale of the asset and not the difference between the cost of the acquisition and the market value of the acquisition at that date. In other words, the full risk of the depreciation in value of the

---

[65] CA 2006, ss 195(8), 213(8).

[66] If the arrangement is between a company and a connected person, the director to whom he is connected is not liable if he shows that he took all reasonable steps to secure the company's compliance with the statutory requirements: CA 2006, ss 195(6), 213(6). In any case, a person so connected and any director who authorised the transaction are not liable if he can show that, at the time the arrangement was entered into, he did not know the relevant circumstances constituting the contravention: ss 195(7), 213(7). See *Lexi Holdings plc v Luqman* [2008] 2 BCLC 725 at 771.

[67] See, for example, *Re Duckwari plc (No 3)* [1998] 2 BCLC 315 where the liability fell on the director and the connected person.

[68] In the case of a substantial property transaction in contravention of CA 2006, s 190(1)(a) (purchase at an undervalue), the liability is to account under s 195(3)(a) and, in the case of a contravention of s 190(1)(b) (sale at an overvalue), the liability is to indemnify against loss under s 195(3)(b): see *Re Duckwari plc (No 2), Duckwari plc v Offerventure Ltd* [1998] 2 BCLC 315 at 320; *NBH Ltd v Hoare* [2006] 2 BCLC 649 at 667; CA 2006, s 190 is set out at **12-28**. In either case, it must be a gain made *by* or loss resulting *from* the arrangement or transaction.

[69] [1998] 2 BCLC 315, CA.

asset (which in fact occurred here) falls on the director or connected person who are treated as trustees liable to make good the misapplication of the company's money.[70] Such liability to account for the amount of the company's loss is strict and no question of foreseeability or remoteness, in particular, the foreseeability of a depreciation in value, arises.[71]

There was some difficulty prior to the CA 2006 in reconciling this approach taken in *Re Duckwari plc* with the problematic first instance decision in *Re Ciro Citterio Menswear plc*[72] to the effect that, in the absence of rescission of the voidable contract, the company's claim in respect of an improper loan under the CA 1985 gave rise only to a liability in personam and did not give the company any proprietary claim to the assets acquired by the improper loan.   **12-59**

The situation is clear now under the CA 2006. As noted at the beginning of this Chapter, a director's obligations to comply with Part 10, Ch 4 is in addition to his obligation to comply with Part 10, Ch 2 (general duties of directors) including his duties under s 171 (obey the constitution) and s 172 (to promote the success of the company). A breach of fiduciary duty in respect of an improper loan would make the recipient director a recipient of trust moneys for which he must account as a constructive trustee so giving the company a proprietary claim in respect of assets obtained with those trust moneys.[73] The potential for liability under the general duties is emphasised by express provisions in ss 195(8), 213(8) that the liability under those provisions is without prejudice to any liability which might otherwise arise.   **12-60**

---

[70] See [1998] 2 BCLC 315 at 322, and *Re Duckwari plc (No 3)* [1999] 1 BCLC 168 at 171.

[71] *Re Duckwari plc (No 3)* [1999] 1 BCLC 168 at 172. At this subsequent hearing, the Court of Appeal clarified that the indemnity extends only to the loss resulting from the acquisition and does not extend to the means by which the acquisition was brought about. Duckwari could not recover, therefore, for costs incurred when it borrowed to fund the acquisition.

[72] [2002] 1 BCLC 672.   [73] *Re Lands Allotment Co* [1894] 1 Ch 616 at 631.

13

Directors' liabilities for breach of duty

A Introduction

Having reviewed the nature and extent of directors' duties to the company in Chapters 8 to 12, we turn in this chapter to consider the extent of the potential liabilities of directors for breach of those duties.

13-1

As the duties of directors are owed to the company (CA 2006, s 170(1)), it is for the company to sue, though in limited circumstances a shareholder may sue derivatively on behalf of the company under CA 2006, Part 11 (derivative claims are discussed in Chapter 18). While it is for the company to sue, a claim may not be brought, despite an apparent breach of duty, for a number of reasons. The decision to litigate is a management matter for the board which must weigh up the time, costs, adverse publicity involved and the likelihood of success and of recovery from the defaulting director. All things considered, the board may legitimately decide that it is not in the company's interests to sue.[1] Of course, in reaching that decision, the directors have to bear in mind their own duties, especially under s 172 to promote the success of the company and under s 174 to exercise care and skill. Frequently, a quiet resignation and possibly some agreement as to the repayment of sums to the company is preferable and justifiable. Litigation may be resorted to on a change of control following a takeover when an incoming board may consider it has grounds for complaint against the former directors, or on a liquidation where a liquidator may consider pursuing misfeasance (breach of duty) claims against the directors in the hope of recovering some funds for creditors.

13-2

As far as the shareholders collectively are concerned, they too may choose to settle or waive or compromise a claim against a director for breach of duty[2] and they may also choose to ratify the breach of duty (subject to certain limits to ratification, discussed at **18-33**). Individual shareholders may bring a derivative claim under CA 2006, Part 11, but for the reasons discussed at **18-56** such claims are likely to be a relatively unusual

13-3

---

[1] See CA 2006, s 239(6)(b) which confirms that the directors have the power to agree not to sue or to settle or release a claim made by them on behalf of the company.

[2] *Smith v Croft* [1986] BCLC 207.

event. Shareholders are more likely to make use of the broad unfairly prejudicial jurisdiction under CA 2006, s 994 (see Chapter 17) but the purpose there usually is to force the majority shareholders to buy out the minority rather than to seek recovery for the company in respect of breach of directors' duties.

13-4   In addition or as an alternative to a claim for breach of fiduciary duty a claim may be made in negligence for breach of s 174 (the duty of care and skill) which, as noted, is not a fiduciary duty. Another possibility is a claim for breach of the director's contract of employment, if he has one,[3] but a company cannot claim for an account of profits for breach of duty and for damages for breach of contract arising out of the same actions, but must elect as to which remedy to pursue.[4] It may also be that the acts complained of (especially where business is diverted to another company set up by a director) amount to the tort of conspiracy to injure the company's business by unlawful means.[5]

13-5   In addition to civil claims, there is a possibility of criminal prosecution, for example for fraud under the Fraud Act 2006 and a dishonest agreement by directors to impede a company in the exercise of its right to recover secret profits made by them may constitute a conspiracy to defraud.[6] Disqualification proceedings post-insolvency are also a possibility, essentially on the basis that breaches of duty establish that a person is unfit to be involved in the management of a company (disqualification is discussed in Chapter 6). There are then a variety of possible consequences where directors act improperly.

13-6   The focus of this chapter is the extent of a director's potential liability for breach of fiduciary duty and that of third parties involved in some way in the breach of duty. The ability to mitigate liability through indemnity provisions, insurance and by application to the court for relief is also considered.

B Claim for breach of fiduciary duty

Introduction

13-7   As noted at 7-8, it was hoped that it would be possible to complement the statutory statement of directors' duties with a statement of remedies for breach of duty, but it

---

[3] *Hivac Ltd v Park Royal Scientific Instruments Ltd* [1946] 1 All ER 350 at 353; and see *Simtel Communications Ltd v Rebak* [2006] 2 BCLC 571; *Shepherds Investments Ltd v Walters* [2007] 2 BCLC 202 (breach of express term forbidding involvement in other business activities). As to whether a third party who engages with the defaulting fiduciaries in a new venture is liable on the basis of having induced a breach of contract on their part, see *Mainstream Properties Ltd v Young* [2007] 4 All ER 545, HL.

[4] *Coleman Taymar Ltd v Oakes* [2001] 2 BCLC 749; and see *Dranez Anstalt v Hayek* [2002] 1 BCLC 693, reversed in part [2003] 1 BCLC 278, CA; *CMS Dolphin Ltd v Simonet* [2001] 2 BCLC 704.

[5] See *OBG Ltd v Allan* [2007] 4 All ER 545, HL. See also *Simtel Communications Ltd v Rebak* [2006] 2 BCLC 571; also *British Midland Tool Ltd v Midland International Tooling Ltd* [2003] 2 BCLC 523.

[6] *Adams v R* [1995] 2 BCLC 17, PC.

proved impossible to devise a coherent and comprehensive statement of the multiple options available and so CA 2006, s 178 merely preserves the existing law and allows for its continued development in the normal way. Section 178 provides that:

'(1) The consequences of breach (or threatened breach) of sections 171 to 177 are the same as would apply if the corresponding common law rule or equitable principle applied.

(2) The duties in those sections (with the exception of section 174 (duty to exercise reasonable care, skill and diligence)) are, accordingly, enforceable in the same way as any other fiduciary duty owed to a company by its directors.'

A fiduciary was defined by Millett LJ in *Bristol & West BS v Mothew*[7] as someone who has undertaken to act for or on behalf of another in a particular matter in circumstances which give rise to a relationship of trust and confidence. Given that typically directors have all powers of management over the company and its assets, directors are indisputably fiduciaries[8] and the general duties owed by directors (other than the duty of care and skill) are fiduciary duties, as CA 2006, s 178(2) makes clear. There are advantages in obligations being categorised as fiduciary obligations, primarily with respect to the availability of what have been described as 'more elastic' remedies.[9] For example, claims for breach of fiduciary duty may be subject to more generous limitation periods than if the claim was for breach of a common law obligation,[10] and claims to make good losses arising from a breach are not equated to common law claims for damages for breach of contract so issues of foreseeability and remoteness are not relevant.

13-8

As directors are fiduciaries and as the most common class of fiduciaries are trustees, it is common to describe directors as trustees, to describe breaches of duty by them as breaches of trust or fiduciary duty, and so to equate directors with trustees for the purpose of measuring their liability to make good losses caused by breaches of fiduciary duty.[11] The classic statement of their position is that of Lindley LJ in *Re Lands Allotment Co*:[12]

13-9

'Although directors are not properly speaking trustees, yet they have always been considered and treated as trustees of money which comes to their hands or which is

---

[7] [1996] 4 All ER 698 at 711. See generally Millett, 'Equity's Place in the Law of Commerce' (1998) 114 LQR 214.

[8] See Finn, *Fiduciary Obligations* (1977), Ch 1; Finn, 'The Fiduciary Principle' in Youdan (ed), *Equity, Fiduciaries and Trusts* (1989), Ch 1; *Regal (Hastings) Ltd v Gulliver* (1942) 1 All ER 378 at 395.

[9] See *Swindle v Harrison* [1997] 4 All ER 705 at 732, per Mummery LJ.

[10] See the Limitation Act 1980, s 21: no period of limitation prescribed by this Act applies to an action by a beneficiary under a trust in respect of any fraud or fraudulent breach of trust to which the trustee was a party or privy; or to recover from the trustee trust property or the proceeds of trust property in the possession of the trustee, or previously received by the trustee and converted to his use. See also *JJ Harrison (Properties) Ltd v Harrison* [2002] 1 BCLC 162; *Gwembe Valley Development Co Ltd v Koshy* [2004] 1 BCLC 131. But the limitation issues here are complex, see Mather, 'Fiduciaries and the Law of Limitation' [2008] JBL 344; Mitchell, 'Dishonest Assistance, Knowing Receipt and the Law of Limitation' [2008] Conv 226.

[11] The analogy is not entirely accurate, of course, as directors, unlike trustees, are risk takers and appointed as such.

[12] [1894] 1 Ch 616 at 631. See also *Great Eastern Railway Co v Turner* (1872) LR 8 Ch App 149.

actually under their control; and ever since joint stock companies were invented directors have been liable to make good moneys which they have misapplied upon the same
footing as if they were trustees.'

13-10   The various obligations on the director are an obligation to reinstate the trust (company) assets (either directly if still in their possession or by payment of a monetary
sum), to account for any profit made and to make good any losses suffered by the
company; and claims may be on multiple grounds, subject to the court being alert to
attempts at double recovery.[13] The obligation to make good losses suffered by the company (equitable compensation) applies on a stricter basis than a common law obligation to pay damages (issues of foreseeability and remoteness are, in general irrelevant)
though the loss must still be shown to have been caused by the breach of fiduciary
duty.[14] Liability is an individual liability and, as between defaulting directors, liability
is joint and several.[15] An innocent director is not liable unless he is in breach of his
duty of care and skill in allowing the wrongdoing to occur.

13-11   Where the claim arises from a misuse of company property, the company has a personal claim against the director to account for the asset and any gain derived therefrom and may seek proprietary relief if it can be shown that the company's property
or its traceable proceeds are in the ownership of the defendant[16] in which case the
court will order the director to transfer it in specie to the company.[17] The advantage of
proprietary relief is that the company's claim prevails over all who hold the property
or its traceable proceeds other than a bona fide purchaser for value without notice of
the breach.[18] A personal liability may be enforced against the director's estate in the
manner of a claim by any unsecured creditor while a proprietary claim ensures priority over the claims of the director's other creditors. The position is explained by Lord

---

[13] See the valuable analysis of the remedies awarded against defaulting fiduciaries by Elliott & Mitchell,
'Remedies for Dishonest Assistance' (2004) 67 MLR 16, esp at 23–36.

[14] *Swindle v Harrison* [1997] 4 All ER 705 at 732–3, per Mummery LJ, noted (1998) 114 LQR 181; also *Target
Holdings Ltd v Redferns* [1995] 3 All ER 785; *Nocton v Lord Ashburton* [1914] AC 932. See *United Pan-Europe
Communications NV v Deutsche Bank AG* [2000] 2 BCLC 461 at 484, CA, per Morritt LJ, 'comparison with
the remedy in damages is unhelpful'. See Elliott & Mitchell, above n 13, at 28–30. See *Shepherds Investments
Ltd v Walters* [2007] 2 BCLC 202 for an example of where there was a breach of the no-conflict rule but the
claimant was unable to show any loss as a consequence, though the directors remained liable to account for
the profits made in breach of duty.

[15] See *Re Lands Allotment Co* [1894] 1 Ch 616; also *Bishopsgate Investment Management Ltd v Maxwell
(No 2)* [1993] BCLC 1282.

[16] See *Foskett v McKeown* [2000] 2 All ER 97 at 120, per Lord Millett; also *Boscawen v Bajwa* [1995] 4 All
ER 769.

[17] See *Foskett v McKeown* [2000] 3 All ER 97 at 120. As Lord Millett emphasised in *Boscawen v Bajwa*
[1995] 4 All ER 769 at 777, this is only one of the proprietary remedies which is available to a court of equity. If
the plaintiff's money has been applied by the defendant, for example not in the acquisition of a landed property but in its improvement, then the court may treat the land as charged with the payment to the plaintiff of
a sum representing the amount by which the value of the defendant's land has been enhanced by the use of
the plaintiff's money. And if the plaintiff's money has been used to discharge a mortgage on the defendant's
land, then the court may achieve a similar result by treating the land as subject to a charge by way of subroga-
tion in favour of the plaintiff: see, for example, *Primlake Ltd v Matthews Associates* [2007] 1 BCLC 666.

[18] *Foskett v McKeown* [2000] 3 All ER 97 at 120.

Millett in *Foskett v McKeown*[19] as follows:

> 'A beneficiary's claim against a trustee for breach of trust is a personal claim. It does not entitle him to priority over the trustee's general creditors unless he can trace the trust property into its product and establish a proprietary interest in the proceeds. If the beneficiary is unable to trace the trust property into its proceeds, he still has a personal claim against the trustee, but his claim will be unsecured. The beneficiary's proprietary claims to the trust property or its traceable proceeds can be maintained against the wrongdoer and anyone who derives title from him except a bona fide purchaser for value without notice of the breach of trust. The same rules apply even where there have been numerous successive transactions,[20] so long as the tracing exercise is successful and no bona fide purchaser for value without notice has intervened.'[21]

An innocent volunteer in possession must yield to the proprietary claim, but no personal claim arises against the volunteer in the absence of participation in some way in the breach of duty,[22] so in *Clark v Cutland*[23] where misappropriated company funds were diverted to the director's pension fund, the trustees of the pension fund, though no personal claim lay against them, held the property on behalf of the company.[24] Third party participation may give rise to claims either on the basis of dishonest assistance or knowing receipt, discussed below.   **13-12**

The director as trustee

Sometimes a director in breach of duty is said to be a constructive trustee of the   **13-13** company's assets. As Millett LJ explained in *Paragon Finance plc v D B Thakerar & Co*,[25] the term 'constructive trustee' is used in two ways, first, in the sense of someone who is really a trustee and, secondly, where a constructive trust is imposed as a remedy consequent to some unlawful transaction. The latter category is primarily of importance in respect of third party liability while a director who has obtained the company's property for himself in breach of duty falls into the first category and is frequently described as a constructive trustee which really means as a trustee.[26] In such

---

[19] [2000] 3 All ER 97.

[20] If the claim is against a mixed fund, the company can still claim a proprietary interest in the proportionate part of the assets: [2000] 3 All ER 97 at 120. See also *Bracken Partners v Gutteridge* [2004] 1 BCLC 377, CA.   [21] [2000] 3 All ER 97 at 122.

[22] See *Foskett v McKeown* [2000] 3 All ER 97 at 120; also *Clark v Cutland* [2003] 2 BCLC 393, CA. The company is able to assert its title to the property against any third party in whose hands it is, even if the recipient is not aware that it is trust property, but the recipient is not personally liable to account as trustee. If the recipient has the requisite knowledge, he can be liable on the basis of knowing receipt: see *Re Diplock's Estate* [1948] 2 All ER 318; *Re Montagu's Settlement Trusts* [1992] 4 All ER 308; *Westdeutsche Landesbank Girozentrale v Islington LBC* [1996] 2 All ER 961 at 990, per Lord Browne-Wilkinson.

[23] [2003] 2 BCLC 393, CA. See also *Primlake Ltd v Matthews Associates* [2007] 1 BCLC 666 at 736.

[24] The company is entitled to trace the asset (the payments made into the pension fund) and to seek proprietary relief in the form of a charge over the pension fund assets to secure the sum due to the company: see [2003] 2 BCLC 393 at 404.

[25] [1999] 1 All ER 400; also *Halton International v Guernroy* [2006] 1 BCLC 78, upheld on appeal see [2006] EWCA Civ 801. See generally Smith, 'Constructive Trusts and Constructive Trustees' (1999) CLJ 294.

[26] *JJ Harrison (Properties) Ltd v Harrison* [2002] 1 BCLC 162 at 175; *Re Lands Allotment Co* [1894] 1 Ch 616 at 631, 638, 657; *Cook v Deeks* [1916] AC 554 at 564; *Keech v Sandford* (1726) Sel Cas Ch 61. See

circumstances, to revert to the language of Millett LJ in *Paragon*:[27]

> '... [the director] does not receive the trust property in his own right but by a trans-action by which both parties intend to create a trust from the outset and which is not impugned by the [company]. His possession of the property is coloured from the first by the trust and confidence by means of which he obtained it, and his subsequent appro-priation of the property to his own use is a breach of that trust.'

13-14   This position was adopted by the Court of Appeal in *JJ Harrison (Properties) Ltd v Harrison*[28] where Chadwick LJ agreed that if a director, in breach of his fiduciary duties to the company, comes into possession of the company's property, his obliga-tions as a trustee in relation to the property do not arise from the transaction by which he obtained it but predate it and arise out of his pre-existing duties as a director.[29] As liability is imposed on a director as a trustee for the misapplication of the trust prop-erty, the issue of loss to the company is irrelevant to the issue of liability although it may have a bearing on the relief which the court will order.[30]

13-15   If neither the property nor its proceeds can any longer be identified, a personal claim against the defaulting director remains, but in the event of insolvency, the claim is an unsecured claim against the director's estate. As noted, the advantage of a proprietary claim is that a third party in possession of the trust property or its traceable proceeds will be defeated by the company's proprietary claim, other than a bona fide purchaser for value without notice.[31]

13-16   The obligation to reinstate the trust (company) asset can be seen in cases such as *Bairstow v Queens Moat Houses plc*[32] where the former directors of a company were liable to repay the entire amount of unlawful dividends which they had declared, regard-less of whether the company might through other mechanisms have lawfully declared such dividends with the result that there was no loss to the company. The issue is not whether there has been a loss, but the liability of directors/trustees to make good any misapplication by them of the company's assets.[33] Another straightforward example of a director's liability to account can be seen in *Primlake Ltd v Matthews Associates*[34] where

---

generally Goode, 'The Recovery of a Director's Improper Gains: Proprietary Gains for Infringement of Non-Proprietary Rights' in McKendrick (ed), *Commercial Aspects of Trusts and Fiduciary Obligations* (1992).

[27] *Paragon Finance plc v D B Thakerar & Co* [1999] 1 All ER 400 at 409.

[28] [2002] 1 BCLC 162.

[29] [2002] 1 BCLC 162 at 175. See, for example, *Belmont Finance Corp Ltd v Williams Furniture Ltd (No 2)* [1980] 1 All ER 393 at 405 (improper financial assistance); *Bishopsgate Investment Management Ltd v Maxwell (No 2)* [1993] BCLC 1282 (director gave away the company's assets for no consideration to a private family company of which he was a director); *Bairstow v Queens Moat Houses plc* [2001] 2 BCLC 531 (unlaw-ful distributions by directors in breach of the common law prohibition of distributions out of capital and the statutory prohibition on distributions in contravention of the requirements of CA 1985, Pt VIII); see also *Rolled Steel Products v British Steel* [1985] 3 All ER 52 at 88.

[30] See *Bairstow v Queens Moat Houses plc* [2001] 2 BCLC 531, CA.

[31] *Foskett v McKeown* [2002] 3 All ER 97 at 120, per Lord Millett.   [32] [2001] 2 BCLC 531, CA.

[33] In this context of reinstatement, the issue of loss suffered is irrelevant, see Elliott & Mitchell, above n 13, at 24–5.

[34] [2007] 1 BCLC 666.

a de facto director paid himself £836,500 out of company funds in breach of duty. He was liable to account for the money or its traceable proceeds.[35] This is a personal claim against him and a proprietary claim for the company's funds or their traceable proceeds. The director's wife, as a volunteer with no knowledge of the circumstances, was liable to the extent that she still had control of funds which were identifiable as the property or the substitute for the property of the company, but she was not liable with respect to funds which had passed through their joint account and no personal claim lay against her.[36]

Not only must the director make good the trust property, but where the misuse of the company's assets has given rise to a gain to the director/trustee, the gain belongs to the company. In *JJ Harrison (Properties) Ltd v Harrison*[37] a director acquired land at an undervalue from his company in circumstances which amounted to a breach of his fiduciary duty to act in the interests of the company (now CA 2006, s 172). The director subsequently sold that land for a substantial gain. The court held that his possession of the land was coloured from the first by the trust and confidence by means of which he obtained it, relying on Millett LJ in *Paragon Finance plc v D B Thakerar & Co*,[38] discussed at **13-13**. The Court of Appeal concluded that his possession of the land was subject to his pre-existing obligations as a trustee of that land, derived not from the transaction by which he came to possess the property, but from his appointment as a director. He was in breach of his fiduciary duty to the company in allowing the land to be sold to him without insisting that the company receive up-to-date information on the planning position and the development potential of the site. In effect, the director sought personally to exploit the commercial opportunities relating to the land of which he, but not the company, was aware. He therefore held the land as trust property. The land having been sold, the company was entitled to the proceeds of sale, subject to an allowance to the director limited to any expenditure incurred by him for the preservation or enhancement of the value of the land.[39]   **13-17**

The corporate opportunity cases too are classified as (*Paragon*) class one constructive trusts (see at **13-13**). The court treats the opportunity as if it were property of the company so that the director who exploits an opportunity on his own behalf holds the opportunity, the contract diverted from the company, as a trustee on behalf of the company. The position was explained by Lawrence Collins J in *CMS Dolphin Ltd v Simonet*:[40] (see facts at **13-23**):   **13-18**

> 'In my judgment the underlying basis of the liability of the director who exploits after his resignation a maturing business opportunity of the company is that *the*

---

[35] [2007] 1 BCLC 666 at 736–7. The couple also used some of the money to repay the mortgage on their home and release it from a bank security. The court held that the company was entitled to be subrogated to the bank's position to the extent that the company's money had been used to discharge the debt and redeem the charge. See also *Boscawen v Bajwa* [1995] 4 All ER 769.

[36] [2007] 1 BCLC 666 at 736.   [37] [2002] 1 BCLC 162.

[38] [1999] 1 All ER 400 at 409.   [39] See [2002] 1 BCLC 162 at 182–3.

[40] [2001] 2 BCLC 704 at 733; the analysis was endorsed in general terms by the Court of Appeal in *In Plus Group Ltd v Pyke* [2002] 2 BCLC 201 at 220; and in *Foster Bryant Surveying Ltd v Bryant* [2007] 2 BCLC 239 at 245–6; see also *Shepherds Investments Ltd v Walters* [2007] 2 BCLC 202 at 231.

opportunity is to be treated as if it were property of the company [emphasis added] in relation to which the director had fiduciary duties. By seeking to exploit the opportunity after resignation he is appropriating for himself that property. He is just as accountable as a trustee who retires without properly accounted for trust property. In the case of the director he becomes a constructive trustee of the fruits of his abuse of the company's property which he has acquired in circumstances where he knowingly had a conflict of interest, and exploited it by resigning from the company.'

13-19   A bribe too is treated as property of the company for these purposes, giving rise to a proprietary claim by the company for the bribe and its traceable proceeds. Where a director receives a secret profit in the form of a bribe or commission with respect to a particular transaction, it is appropriate to allow proprietary relief rather than a mere personal liability to account to ensure that the company recovers both the bribe and any assets representing the bribe, which is particularly valuable where those assets have increased in value.[41] This matter has been problematic as there was an issue as to whether the courts should follow *Lister v Stubbs*[42] (Court of Appeal decision that there was only a personal liability to account for a bribe and there was no scope for proprietary remedies) or *Attorney General for Hong Kong v Reid*[43] (persuasive Privy Council decision that *Lister v Stubbs* was wrongly decided and a proprietary remedy is entirely appropriate to ensure that the fiduciary cannot benefit from his breach of duty[44]) where Lord Templeman commented:[45]

'The decision in *Lister & Co v Stubbs* is not consistent with the principles that a fiduciary must not be allowed to benefit from his own breach of duty, that the fiduciary should account for the bribe as soon as he receives it and that equity regards as done that which ought to be done. From these principles it would appear to follow that the bribe and the property from time to time representing the bribe are held on a constructive trust for the person injured.'

13-20   In *Daraydan Holdings Ltd v Solland International Ltd*[46] Lawrence Collins J indicated that, if necessary, he would have followed *AGHK v Reid* and would not have felt constrained by the doctrine of binding precedent to follow *Lister v Stubbs*.[47] On the facts in *Daraydan*, it was possible to distinguish *Lister v Stubbs* as the price paid by the company for the services obtained had been increased by the suppliers to cover the bribes which the suppliers had had to pay to secure the contract. The bribes were derived directly from the claimants' property, therefore, and the claimants were entitled to proprietary relief.[48]

---

[41] *Attorney General for Hong Kong v Reid* [1994] 1 All ER 1, PC.

[42] (1890) 45 Ch D 1, CA.   [43] [1994] 1 All ER 1, PC.

[44] See [1994] 1 All ER 1 at 9, per Lord Templeman. In *Reid*, the bribes had been invested in a number of properties which had increased in value substantially. The fiduciary had to account not just for the bribe but for the increased value of the property representing the bribe since otherwise he would receive a benefit from his breach of duty.

[45] [1994] 1 All ER 1 at 9.   [46] [2005] 4 All ER 73, noted Halliwell [2005] Conv 88.

[47] [2005] 4 All ER 73 at 92–3. Support can be found in *Ultraframe (UK) Ltd v Fielding* [2005] EWHC 1638, para 1490, per Lewison J.

[48] [2005] 4 All ER 73 at 93.

A benefit received by a director in breach of CA 2006, s 176(1), i.e. a benefit from a third **13-21** party conferred by reason of (1) his being a director, or (2) his doing (or not doing) anything as director, would be subject to the same analysis. The fiduciary must not be allowed to benefit, he should account and the benefit should be treated as if the director had received it for the company. A proprietary claim is therefore available if the benefit and its traceable proceeds can be identified. On the other hand, as the Court of Appeal held in *Gwembe Valley Development Co Ltd v Koshy*,[49] a director is not a trustee of profits made out of a transaction involving an undisclosed conflict of interest in breach of what is now CA 2006, s177. The company was aware that the director had an interest in currency transactions entered into by the company, but he failed to disclose that he stood to make almost \$5m from the transactions. The Court of Appeal concluded that he had no pre-existing trust-like responsibilities in relation to the sums and so did not fall within category 1 in *Paragon*, discussed at **13-13**, and therefore merely had a personal liability to account.[50]

The liability to account

As to the extent of a fiduciary's duty to account for a profit made, the court is inclined **13-22** to order the widest possible accounting limited only by the need for a reasonable connection between the breach of duty and the profit for which the fiduciary is accountable.[51] The purpose of a liability to account for secret profits is to strip the defaulting fiduciary of his profit[52] and the burden of proof is on the defaulting fiduciary to show that the profit is not one for which he should account.[53]

In *CMS Dolphin Ltd v Simonet*[54] a director of the claimant company, an advertising **13-23** agency, left the company and set up a new business. All the staff of the company subsequently joined him as did the principal clients of the company. The court found that the director took away from the company the benefit of contracts with existing clients and the business opportunities the company had with those clients. The director was held liable to account for the profits derived from those contracts/opportunities which he had diverted from the company to his new business, together with a sum to take account of other benefits derived from those contracts.[55] For example, other contracts

---

[49] [2004] 1 BCLC 131.

[50] See [2004] 1 BCLC 131 at 165, per Mummery LJ: '...it is clear in our view that any trust imposed on [the director] is a class 2 trust within Millett LJ's classification.' (for Millett LJ's classification, see **13-13**). See criticism of the decision by Elliott & Mitchell, above n 13, at 32.

[51] *CMS Dolphin Ltd v Simonet* [2001] 2 BCLC 704 at 733–4; *Ultraframe (UK) Ltd v Fielding* [2005] EWHC 1638, para 1588. But see *Murad v Al-Saraj* [2005] EWCA Civ 959, [2005] All ER (D) 503 (Jul), where Clarke LJ (dissenting) was disposed to be more flexible on the accounting.

[52] See *Murad v Al-Saraj* [2005] EWCA Civ 959; [2005] All ER (D) 503 (Jul), at para 56, per Arden LJ; at para 108, per Jonathan Parker LJ; *United Pan-Europe Communications NV v Deutsche Bank AG* [2000] 2 BCLC 461 at 484, CA.

[53] See *Murad v Al-Saraj* [2005] EWCA Civ 959; [2005] All ER (D) 503 (Jul), para 77.

[54] [2001] 2 BCLC 704.

[55] [2001] 2 BCLC 704 at 733–4, subject to taking into account the expenses connected with those profits and a reasonable allowance for overheads.

might not have been won, or profits made on them, without the opportunity or cash-flow benefit which flowed from the contracts unlawfully obtained.[56]

13-24   In *Lindsley v Woodfull*[57] (the case concerned a partnership but the same principles apply) a partner who diverted to his own business a contract which the partnership had been pursuing had to account for the profits from the contract *and* the profits from its subsequent renewal[58] as those profits are consequent upon the breach of duty. Likewise in *Kingsley IT Consulting Ltd v McIntosh*[59] the director's liability to account extended from the profit derived from the contract which he had diverted from his company to the profit derived from two subsequent extensions of that contract.

13-25   If the improper profit is made through a company used by the director as a device to mask his breach of fiduciary duty, the courts have no hesitation in piercing the corporate veil and treating the company's gain as the director's gain.[60] In *Gencor ACP Ltd v Dalby*,[61] see **3-27**, a director had for some time diverted business opportunities away from the company to another company which he owned and controlled. The court found that the other company had no staff or activities and its only function was to make and receive payments. The court concluded that it was little other than the director's offshore bank account in a nominee name and it had no hesitation in piercing the veil in such circumstances. In *Trustor AB v Smallbone*[62] two directors had misappropriated significant sums of money from their company with some of the money ending up in the hands of a company controlled by one of the directors, see **3-25**. The court held that receipt by the company was receipt by the director where the company was merely a device or façade to conceal the true facts and was being used to avoid or conceal any liability of an individual. Piercing the corporate veil in this way to treat the receipt by the company as receipt by the director is limited, however, to circumstances where the company is a mere façade concealing the true facts, see **3-22**.[63]

13-26   Save for the situation where the company is a mere façade in this way, the fact that the fiduciary has a substantial or even a controlling interest in a company[64] which knowingly receives trust property does not make the fiduciary personally accountable for the receipt,[65] though the director remains liable for his own breach of duty and the

---

[56] [2001] 2 BCLC 704 at 733–4.   [57] [2004] 2 BCLC 131.

[58] There will come a point, of course, as Jonathan Parker LJ noted in *Murad v Al-Saraj* [2005] EWCA Civ 959; [2005] All ER (D) 503 (Jul), para 115 when it can safely be said that profits of a business are not attributable to the opportunity taken from the original company and are not tainted by the conflict in which the defaulting directors had placed themselves.

[59] [2006] BCC 875.   [60] See *Ultraframe (UK) Ltd v Fielding* [2005] EWHC 1638, para 1576.

[61] [2000] 2 BCLC 734.

[62] [2001] 2 BCLC 436; and see *Lindsley v Woodfull* [2004] 2 BCLC 131 at 140.

[63] *Woolfson v Strathclyde Regional Council* [1978] SC (HL) 90.

[64] See *Crown Dilmun v Sutton* [2004] 1 BCLC 468 where the defaulting director held 49% of the company which secured the contract diverted by the director from his own company. The recipient company was liable on the basis of knowing receipt because the director's knowledge of his breach of duty was attributed to the company with serious consequences for the majority shareholder who had no knowledge of the breach of fiduciary duty (see at p 515).

[65] *Ultraframe (UK) Ltd v Fielding* [2005] EWHC 1638, para 1576. See *Quarter Master UK Ltd v Pyke* [2005] 1 BCLC 245 at 172.

company (as a recipient) may be liable on the basis of dishonest assistance or knowing receipt.[66] An example can be seen in *Quarter Master UK v Pyke*[67] where directors who obtained a contract for themselves, in breach of the no-conflict rule, when the contract should have been obtained for their company were liable to account for the personal profits made by them (see **11-26**). The company to which they diverted the contract was also liable to account for the profits derived by it from the arrangements on the basis of knowing receipt. The director's liability is to account for all of *his* gain and where his gain is indirect through, for example, an increase in value of his shareholding in a company which exploited the opportunity etc, he must still account for that gain, but as part of his personal liability to account for all of his profits.[68] Where there is an overlap between the recipient company's liability and the director's liability to account, the court is careful to prevent double recovery and, where the claimant company does not or cannot pursue the claim against the recipient, the director remains liable to indemnify the company for the full loss.

Likewise, if a director diverts contracts, opportunities, etc to a partnership where he is only one of the number of partners, he is liable to account to the full extent of his gain, even if his partners are entitled to a share of those profits and are ignorant of his breach of duty.[69] To the extent that a number of the partners are implicated in the breach of duty, they are jointly and severally liable.[70]   **13-27**

This extensive liability to account applies even though it can result in a windfall to the company and can appear unduly harsh to the faithless fiduciary, as in *Regal (Hastings) Ltd v Gulliver*[71] (where the company could not put up the funding required: see **11-24**) or, as in *Industrial Development Consultants Ltd v Cooley*[72] (see **11-15**) where the court thought that the company only had a 10% chance of getting the contract secured by the   **13-28**

---

[66] In *CMS Dolphin Ltd v Simonet* [2001] 2 BCLC 704 Lawrence Collins J seemed to favour holding the director and the company jointly and severally liable though the director personally had not received the profit; see too *Simtel Communications Ltd v Rebak* [2006] 2 BCLC 571 at 591. The correctness of that approach was doubted by Lewison J in *Ultraframe (UK) Ltd v Fielding* [2005] EWHC 1638 paras 1565–76 who concluded that each party should be liable for his own gain—the director for breach of fiduciary duty, third parties on the basis of dishonest assistance or knowing receipt.

[67] [2005] 1 BCLC 245.

[68] *Gwembe Valley Development Co Ltd v Koshy* [2004] 1 BCLC 131 at 172. See also *Shepherds Investments Ltd v Walters* [2007] 2 BCLC 202 at 239—the claimant company chose only to pursue the gain by the defaulting directors rather than a claim against the company set up by them which had shareholders other than the defaulting directors. The claim against the former directors was for an account of the profits made by them in consequence of their unlawful conduct in promoting the establishment of the competing business. A claim for the loss suffered by the company failed for on the facts no loss attributable to the breach of duty could be established.

[69] See *CMS Dolphin Ltd v Simonet* [2001] 2 BCLC 704.

[70] *Imperial Mercantile Credit Association v Coleman* (1873) LR 6 HL 189.

[71] [1942] 1 All ER 378. Many of the cases have a windfall element to them, for example, see *Crown Dilmun v Sutton* [2004] 1 BCLC 468 (not clear company could or would have pursued the opportunity diverted by the director to himself); *Quarter Master UK v Pyke* [2005] 1 BCLC 245 (company could not have obtained the contract diverted by the directors as the third party was not willing to deal with the company due to its financial position).

[72] [1972] 2 All ER 162.

director for himself yet the director had to account for all the gain made by him from carrying it out. This response is justified on the basis of the need to deter fiduciaries from breach of fiduciary duty,[73] though concern has been expressed that 'the liability of the fiduciary should not be transformed into a vehicle for the unjust enrichment of the plaintiff'.[74]

13-29   In keeping with this strict approach, the courts are reluctant to exercise their discretion to grant any equitable allowance to the fiduciary for his efforts in generating the profits,[75] so as to ensure that fiduciaries are denied any incentive to act in breach of fiduciary duty. An allowance will only be granted if it can be given without undermining the fiduciary obligation to avoid conflicts of interest, and doubts were expressed in *Guinness plc v Saunders*[76] as to whether such an allowance could ever be permitted in the case of company directors acting in breach of their fiduciary obligations. In *Quarter Master UK Ltd v Pyke*,[77] applying *Guinness plc v Saunders*, the court refused any allowance for the directors who diverted a contract away from the company to themselves. There was no evidence that they had exercised any special skills or taken unusual risks and the fact that the company could not have obtained the contract (it was in severe financial difficulties) did not make the facts sufficiently special to persuade the court to exercise its discretion.

13-30   Many of the cases concern a liability to account for a profit made by the director in breach of duty but the claim may equally be one to indemnify the company in respect of losses incurred. Where an asset has been misapplied and there has been a subsequent loss in value of the asset, that loss must be made good by the director/trustee, not in the sense of a liability for loss at common law, but as part of the process of reinstating that trust asset.[78]

13-31   In *Re Duckwari plc (No 2), Duckwari plc v Offerventure Ltd (No 2)*[79] the company had acquired an asset which had subsequently fallen in value in part due to the collapse

---

[73] See *Guinness plc v Saunders* [1990] BCLC 402; *Lindsley v Woodfull* [2004] 2 BCLC 131 at 140; *Murad v Al-Saraj* [2005] EWCA Civ 959; [2005] All ER (D) 503 (Jul), paras 74–5; also *Quarter Master UK v Pyke* [2005] 1 BCLC 245 at 269 where the court made the point that a director can always free himself from the obligation to account by obtaining the informed consent of the company (and now by obtaining the authorisation of independent directors under CA 2006, s 175(4)(b)).

[74] *Warman International Ltd v Dwyer* (1995) 182 CLR 544 at 561, Aust HC; a point taken on board by Lewison J in *Ultraframe (UK) Ltd v Fielding* [2005] EWHC 1638, para 1588. See also *Fyffes Group Ltd v Templeman* [2000] 2 Lloyd's Rep 643 at 672; *Crown Dilmun v Sutton* [2004] 1 BCLC 468 at 517.

[75] The court has a discretion to grant an allowance for the skills and efforts of the defaulting trustee: see *Phipps v Boardman* [1966] 3 All ER 721.

[76] [1990] 1 All ER 652. See also *JJ Harrison (Properties) Ltd v Harrison* [2002] 1 BCLC 162 at 183: the director was only permitted an allowance for expenditure on costs which enhanced the value of the land which he had acquired in breach of his duties to the company and sold at a considerable profit; in *CMS Dolphin Ltd v Simonet* [2001] 2 BCLC 704 at 733 an allowance was possible for overheads and expenses connected with exploiting the corporate opportunity which the wrongdoer had diverted to his own business, but not a salary for the wrongdoer.

[77] [2005] 1 BCLC 245 at 271–2.

[78] See Millett, 'Equity's Place in the Law of Commerce' (1998) 114 LQR 214 at 227.

[79] [1998] 2 BCLC 315, see **12-33**.

of the property market. The transaction by which the company had acquired the asset was in contravention of the statutory provisions governing substantial property transactions between a company and a director or person connected with a director, see **12-27**.[80] The court held the director was liable to make good the full amount of the misapplication of the company's funds so the loss arising from the acquisition (including the loss as a result of the fall in the property market) fell on the director/trustee, see **12-58**. Imposing liability, Nourse LJ noted: 'it is well recognised that the basis on which a trustee is liable to make good a misapplication of trust moneys is strict and sometimes harsh, especially where, as here, there has been a huge depreciation in the value of the asset acquired'.[81] He also noted that, given the failure to obtain shareholder approval, as requested, it was not unfair for the loss to fall on the director.

Liability of third parties

Third party liability may arise on one of two grounds (in some cases, both):[82] (1) on the   **13-32** basis of 'dishonest assistance' where the third party has participated or assisted in the breach by the director of his duties; or (2) on the basis of 'knowing receipt' of company funds. In each case the third party is often described as liable as a constructive trustee. In this case, the term 'constructive trust' is being used in the second sense identified by Millett LJ in *Paragon Finance plc v D B Thakerar & Co*[83] (see **13-13**), in the sense of a constructive trust imposed as a remedy consequent to some unlawful transaction:

> 'The second class of case is different. It arises when the defendant is implicated in a fraud. Equity has always given relief against fraud by making any person sufficiently implicated in the fraud accountable in equity. In such a case he is traditionally though I think unfortunately described as a constructive trustee and said to be "liable to account as constructive trustee". *Such a person is not in fact a trustee at all* [emphasis added], even though he may be liable to account as if he were. He never assumes the position of a trustee, and if he receives the trust property at all it is adversely to the plaintiff by an unlawful transaction which is impugned by the plaintiff. In such a case the expressions "constructive trust" and "constructive trustee" are misleading, for there is no trust and usually no possibility of a proprietary remedy; they are "nothing more than a formula for equitable relief": *Selangor United Rubber Estates Ltd v Cradock (No 3)* [1968] 2 All ER 1073 at 1097, per Ungoed-Thomas J.'

This constructive trust is the response of equity in supplying a remedy for dealing with   **13-33** the consequences of a breach of duty.[84] This liability is fault-based and the remedy is compensatory. It is a personal claim for a sum intended to compensate the beneficiary for the wrongful interference with the due performance of the fiduciary duties.[85] As

---

[80] See now CA 2006, ss 190–196.   [81] [1998] 2 BCLC 315 at 324.

[82] See, for example, *Crown Dilmun v Sutton* [2004] 1 BCLC 468.

[83] [1999] 1 All ER 400 at 409. See also *Halton International v Guernroy* [2006] 1 BCLC 78 at 141, upheld on appeal, see [2006] EWCA Civ 801, para 16.

[84] *Gwembe Valley Development Co Ltd v Koshy* [2004] 1 BCLC 131 at 156, per Mummery LJ.

[85] *Royal Brunei Airlines v Tan* [1995] 3 All ER 97 at 104, PC, per Lord Nicholls; *Twinsectra Ltd v Yardley* [2002] 2 All ER 377 at 405, per Lord Millett.

Lord Millett noted in *Twinsectra Ltd v Yardley*:[86]

> 'The cause of action is concerned with attributing liability for misdirected funds. Liability is not restricted to the person whose breach of trust or fiduciary duty caused their original diversion. His liability is strict. Nor is it limited to those who assist him in the original breach. It extends to everyone who consciously assists in the continuing diversion of the money. Most of the cases have been concerned, not with assisting in the original breach, but in covering it up afterwards by helping to launder the money.'

Dishonest assistance

13-34   A liability in equity to make good to the company any resulting losses attaches to any third party who dishonestly procures or assists a director in a breach of fiduciary duty to the company.[87] The Privy Council in *Royal Brunei Airlines v Tan*[88] established that, in this context, acting dishonestly means simply not acting as an honest person would in the circumstances; and for the most part dishonesty is to be equated with conscious impropriety.[89] The court, when deciding whether a person is acting honestly, looks at all the circumstances known to the third party at the time and has regard to the personal attributes of the third party such as his experience and intelligence and the reason why he acted as he did.[90] It is not necessary for the third party to know every element of the breach of duty, but he must know that the fiduciary is doing something which he is not entitled to do.[91]

13-35   The House of Lords in *Twinsectra Ltd v Yardley*[92] muddied the waters somewhat by supporting what was interpreted as a two-prong test for dishonesty—whether what is done is dishonest by the standards of ordinary people[93] and whether the defendant knows that his conduct is dishonest by the ordinary standards of honest and reasonable men.[94] The second element of this test proved problematic and their Lordships, in the guise of the Privy Council, sought to clarify the position in *Barlow Clowes*

---

[86] [2002] 2 All ER 377 at 404.

[87] *Royal Brunei Airlines v Tan* [1995] 3 All ER 97, PC; *Barnes v Addy* (1874) LR 9 Ch App 244. As to the nature of the liability for dishonest assistance, see the valuable analysis of Elliott and Mitchell, 'Remedies for Dishonest Assistance' (2004) 67 MLR 16. For a critical account of the case-law and the debates as to the scope of the jurisdiction, see *Attorney General of Zambia v Meer Care & Desai* [2007] EWHC 952, paras 332–71, per Peter Smith J. In *Ultraframe (UK) Ltd v Fielding* [2005] EWHC 1638, para 1594, Lewison J considered that, in addition to making good any loss, the dishonest assistant must also account for any profit made, see Prentice & Payne (2006) 122 LQR 558 at 563 who note that this is 'a 'substantial extension' of the available remedies.

[88] [1995] 3 All ER 97, PC.   [89] [1995] 3 All ER 97 at 106, PC.   [90] [1995] 3 All ER 97 at 107, PC.

[91] *Ultraframe (UK) Ltd v Fielding* [2005] EWHC 1638, paras 1505–6. For examples of dishonest assistance, see *Simtel Communications Ltd v Rebak* [2006] 2 BCLC 571 (former employee dishonestly assisted in director's breach of duty as contracts diverted from the company to a new business set up by the director and former employee); *Statek Corpn v Alford* [2008] BCC 266 (individual dishonestly assisted two directors misappropriate $19.8m from a company by passing company money from its accounts through his bank accounts and on to the two directors).

[92] [2002] 2 All ER 377.

[93] [2002] 2 All ER 377 at 382–3, 'a consciousness that one is transgressing ordinary standards of honest behaviour', per Lord Hoffmann.

[94] [2002] 2 All ER 377 at 387, per Lord Hutton.

International Ltd v Eurotrust International Ltd[95] where Lord Hoffmann (regretting the ambiguity which was generated by *Twinsectra*) commented:[96]

'Although a dishonest state of mind is a subjective mental state, the standard by which the law determines whether it is dishonest is objective. If by ordinary standards a defendant's mental state would be characterised as dishonest, it is irrelevant that the defendant judges by different standards.'

While this is a helpful persuasive steer by the Privy Council,[97] it has not quelled the debate, as can be seen in the Court of Appeal in *Abou-Ramah v Abacha*[98] where Arden LJ was prepared to accept that the test of honesty is 'predominantly' objective while Rix LJ seemed to suggest there is some element of subjectivity to it and Pill LJ thought it unnecessary to enter the debate.[99] The 'mix' of subjectivity and objectivity required is probably best encapsulated by Lord Hoffmann in *Barlow Clowes*, as quoted above, which statement the Privy Council accepted as a correct statement of the law[100] and which in the view of Arden LJ in *Abacha* can be accepted also as a statement of the law of England and Wales.[101]   **13-36**

Knowing receipt

The claim in the case of knowing receipt is receipt-based and restitutionary.[102] The claim is a personal claim against the knowing recipient for any benefit which he has received or acquired as a result of the knowing receipt.[103] A much cited statement of the position on knowing receipt by a third party is that of Buckley LJ in *Belmont Finance Corp v Williams Furniture Ltd (No 2)*:[104]   **13-37**

'...if the directors of a company in breach of their fiduciary duties misapply the funds of their company so that they come into the hands of some stranger to the trust who receives them with knowledge (actual or constructive) of the breach, he cannot conscientiously retain those funds against the company unless he has some better equity. He becomes a constructive trustee for the company of the misapplied funds.'

The nature of 'knowing receipt' liability was comprehensively reviewed and the current state of the law is as stated by the Court of Appeal in *Bank of Credit and Commerce*   **13-38**

---

[95] [2006] 1 All ER 333, PC, see comments by Conaglen & Gaymour (2006) CLJ 18; Yeo (2006) 122 LQR 171.   [96] [2006] 1 All ER 333 at 337.

[97] The position is confused, of course, by precedent issues as to whether the Court of Appeal can depart from a House of Lords ruling in favour of a decision of the Privy Council. Arden LJ was able to resolve the difficulty by deciding that the statement of the Privy Council in *Barlow Clowes* represented a statement of the law of England and Wales as set down in *Twinsectra*, so that it was possible to follow the guidance given by the Privy Council without departing from the House of Lords ruling: see [2007] 1 Lloyd's Rep 115 at 129–30.

[98] [2007] 1 Lloyd's Rep 115; see comments by Ryan [2007] Conv 168, Lee [2007] JBL 209.

[99] See [2007] 1 Lloyd's Rep 115 at 129 (Arden LJ), at 119, 120 (Rix LJ) and at 133 (Pill LJ).

[100] See [2006] 1 All ER 333 at 337.   [101] See [2007] 1 Lloyd's Rep 115 at 129–30.

[102] See *Twinsectra Ltd v Yardley* [2002] 2 All ER 377 at 404, per Lord Millett.

[103] See *Ultraframe (UK) Ltd v Fielding* [2005] EWHC 1638, para 1577.

[104] [1980] 1 All ER 393 at 405, CA. See also *JJ Harrison (Properties) Ltd v Harrison* [2002] 1 BCLC 162; *Bairstow v Queens Moat Houses plc* [2001] 2 BCLC 531; *Re Duckwari plc (No 2), Duckwari plc v Offerventure Ltd (No 2)* [1998] 2 BCLC 315 at 321, per Nourse LJ. See Sealy, 'The Director as Trustee' (1967) CLJ 83.

International (Overseas) Ltd v Akindele[105] which adopted a markedly different approach to the basis of liability than the earlier authorities which had focused on liability arising from (increasingly convoluted) degrees of knowledge.

13-39   The Court of Appeal held that dishonesty is not an essential ingredient of a claim for knowing receipt, and the test for knowledge in such a claim is simply whether the defendant's knowledge makes it unconscionable for him to retain the benefit of the receipt. Although such a test cannot avoid difficulties of application, the court thought it preferable to the complexity of the previous categorisations of knowledge for these purposes.[106] Moreover, Nourse LJ thought, this approach should better enable the courts to give common-sense decisions in the commercial context in which claims in knowing receipt are now frequently made, paying equal regard, on the one hand, to the need to avoid the mischief of paralysing trade and, on the other hand, to the realisation that there are cases in which a commercial man should not be allowed to shelter behind the exigencies of commercial life.[107]

13-40   The pragmatic response to the commercial realities evident in *BCCI v Akindele*[108] is also evident in the robust approach taken by the courts as to what is to be regarded as property or funds of the company for these purposes. Clearly, property vested in the company prior to the breach of fiduciary duty is included,[109] but it also extends to property in the form of maturing business opportunities so the recipient of a contract diverted away from a company by a director in breach of duty may be liable on the basis of knowing receipt of company property.[110] In *Crown Dilmun v Sutton*[111] the court found that the defendant company had received the claimant company's property (in the form of a contract which was a maturing business opportunity of the claimant: see **11-26**) and the defendant company had knowledge of the director's breach of duty.[112] Accordingly, it was unconscionable for the defendant company to retain the benefits of the contract and it was liable to account for the profits it had received (even though

---

[105] [2000] 4 All ER 221, applying *Belmont Finance Corporation Ltd v Williams Furniture Ltd (No 2)* [1980] 1 All ER 393; *Charter plc v City Index Ltd* [2008] 3 All ER 126 at 130. See also *El Ajou v Dollar Land Holdings plc* [1994] 2 All ER 685 at 700.

[106] The older authorities had established that a third party who received company funds might be liable to the company if he received the funds with *knowledge* of the directors' breach of duty, whether it be actual knowledge, or knowledge in the sense that he wilfully shut his eyes to the obvious, or wilfully and recklessly failed to make the type of inquiries which an honest and reasonable man would have made: see *Selangor United Rubber Estates Ltd v Cradock (No 3)* [1968] 2 All ER 1073; *Eagle Trust plc v SBC Securities Ltd* [1992] 4 All ER 488; *Re Montagu's Settlement Trusts* [1992] 4 All ER 308; *Polly Peck International plc v Nadir (No 2)* [1992] 4 All ER 769; *Cowan de Groot Properties Ltd v Eagle Trust plc* [1992] 4 All ER 700.

[107] [2000] 4 All ER 221 at 236.   [108] [2000] 4 All ER 221.

[109] See, for example, *JJ Harrison (Properties) Ltd v Harrison* [2002] 1 BCLC 162.

[110] See *Ultraframe (UK) Ltd v Fielding* [2005] EWHC 1638, paras 1487–93; *CMS Dolphin Ltd v Simonet* [2001] 2 BCLC 704 at 733; the line is drawn at rights under merely executory contracts, see *Criterion Properties plc v Stratford UK Properties LLC* [2006] 1 BCLC 729 at 739–40, per Lord Scott.

[111] [2004] 1 BCLC 468.

[112] The sole director of the company knew of the defaulting director's breach of fiduciary duty and that knowledge was attributed to the company with the result that the company was liable on the basis of knowing receipt of the benefit of the contract diverted from the claimant company by the faithless fiduciary: see [2004] 1 BCLC 468 at 515.

this was disadvantageous to the majority shareholder in the company who was an innocent party to the breach of fiduciary duty).

C Claims for negligence

A director's duty of care and skill (CA 2006, s 174) is not a fiduciary duty, as s 178   **13-41** makes clear, and a breach of this duty gives rise to the standard common law liability in damages for negligence. Claims against directors in negligence are rare for the reasons discussed at **10-5**, to which the reader is referred.

D Managing potential liabilities

Given that a director is potentially liable on the various grounds discussed above,   **13-42** the next issue is the extent to which it is possible for directors to manage those potential liabilities through mechanisms such as contractual clauses excluding or limiting liability or through insurance cover. Another option is to seek authorisation or ratification from the shareholders, as discussed at **18-33**. Liability is also reduced in some contexts by the provision of 'safe harbours,' for example in the context of misleading statements in the directors' report: see the discussion at **16-28**. Another possibility is that the amount of the liability might be reduced or waived where the director successfully applies for relief under CA 2006, s 1157 which requires the director to satisfy the court that he has acted honestly and reasonably and ought fairly to be excused.

Quite apart from any potential liability for breach of duty, a major concern for any   **13-43** director is the potential litigation costs involved if he is sued whether by the company or by a third party such as a shareholder or creditor. Commercial litigation tends to be lengthy and directors are concerned that funding an expensive and lengthy defence may exhaust their personal resources so that by the time they win (if they do) and the case is dismissed, they are personally bankrupt. This particular issue is addressed by CA 2006, s 205 whereby companies are permitted (but not required) to provide a director of the company or of a holding company with funds to meet expenditure incurred or to be incurred by a director in defending any criminal or civil proceedings in connection with any alleged negligence, default, breach of duty or breach of trust by him in relation to the company (which would include any derivative claim) or in connection with any application by him to the court for relief under s 1157. Of course, the decision to grant such funding must be taken by the other directors in accordance with their fiduciary duties, in particular the duty to exercise their powers for a proper purpose and the duty to promote the success of the company (ss 171 and 172). If funding is provided, it must be repaid if the director is convicted in criminal proceedings, or judgment is given against him in any civil proceedings, or the court refuses him relief on an application under s 1157 (s 205(2)), save to the extent that the director has a qualifying third party indemnity, discussed below, which indemnifies the director in respect of liabilities incurred in civil proceedings brought by third parties.

13-44   Directors of larger companies are almost equally concerned about becoming embroiled in a regulatory investigation or disciplinary proceeding which can also be a lengthy process requiring legal representation. To address such concerns, a company may provide a director or a director of its holding company with funds on a similar basis as above to meet expenditure incurred in defending himself in an investigation by a regulatory authority, or against action proposed to be taken by a regulatory authority, such as the Financial Services Authority, in connection with any alleged negligence, default, breach of duty or breach of trust by the director in relation to the company or an associated company (CA 2006, s 206). In this case, strangely, there is no express requirement for the funding to be repaid in the way provided by s 205(2)), noted at **13-43**. Interestingly, in neither case is shareholder approval required for the provision of this funding.

Exemption provisions

13-45   Historically, companies included in their articles widely drafted exemption clauses relieving their officers from liability arising from breaches of their duties save in the case of wilful negligence or default,[113] but the Greene Committee on Company Law recommended that the practice be prohibited.[114] The current prohibition is set out in CA 2006, s 232(1) which provides that any provision, whether contained in the articles or in any contract with the company or otherwise,[115] that purports to exempt a director of a company (to any extent) from any liability that would otherwise attach to him in connection with any negligence, default, breach of duty or breach of trust in relation to the company is void.[116]

13-46   An important qualification to the prohibition is that it does not prevent the company from including in its articles 'such provision as has previously been lawful for dealing with conflicts of interest' (s 232(4)). Unfortunately the extent to which companies can

---

[113] See *Re Brazilian Rubber Plantations and Estates Ltd* [1911] 1 Ch 425; *Re City Equitable Fire Insurance Co Ltd* [1925] Ch 407.

[114] The Greene Committee on Company Law (Cmnd 2657, 1929), paras 46–7. The prohibition was introduced by CA 1929, s 152.

[115] CA 2006, s 232(3). The words 'or otherwise' are to be construed eiusdem generis with the preceding words 'whether contained in the company's articles or in any contract with the company', the genus being any arrangement between the company and its officers: *Burgoine v London Borough of Waltham Forest* [1997] 2 BCLC 612.

[116] CA 2006, s 232(2): see generally *Burgoine v London Borough of Waltham Forest* [1997] 2 BCLC 612. The equivalent provision with respect to the liability of auditors is CA 2006, s 532. As to 'default', see *Customs & Excise Commissioners v Hedon Alpha Ltd* [1981] 2 All ER 697; and n 125 below.

lawfully include provisions in their articles in respect of conflicts is unclear: see the discussion at **11-70**.

Indemnity provisions

As with exemption provisions, likewise CA 2006, s 232(2) provides that any provision **13-47** by which a company directly or indirectly provides an indemnity (to any extent) for a director of the company, or of an associate company,[117] against any liability in connection of any such negligence or breach of duty etc in relation to the company of which he is a director, is also void though this prohibition does not rule out the provision of insurance cover for a director nor the provision of qualifying indemnities under CA 2006, ss 234 and 235.

The background to the introduction of indemnities (by the Companies (Audit, **13-48** Investigations and Community Enterprise) Act 2004) was that there had been several high-profile cases including in particular litigation involving the non-executive directors of Equitable Life,[118] which generated a sense that directors are subject to significant litigation risks which may deter able people from accepting posts unless they are protected against that risk. Domestically, there were concerns about the length of possible proceedings; the difficulty of funding legal representation (which of course is a general problem, not particular to company directors); and the enormous sums being claimed which are likely to far outstrip any available insurance. For larger companies with operations in the US, there were concerns that their directors were exposed to even greater litigation risks because of features of the US legal system such as the common use of shareholder class actions and, possibly, more activist regulators. There was also a sense of more activist shareholders with some, such as aggressive hedge funds, perhaps more attuned to using litigation than had previously been the case. It was also argued that the availability of a statutory derivative action, now enacted in CA 2006, Part 11, coupled with the statutory statement of directors' duties, would encourage and facilitate litigation (though for reasons discussed at **18-56**, this is unlikely).

There is no doubt an element of truth in these concerns, but no doubt too that they **13-49** were exaggerated in order to extract the maximum possible concessions from the Government. The result is that, despite the initial impression given by CA 2006, s 232(2) prohibiting indemnities (see **13-47**), companies may provide extensive indemnities protecting their directors against personal liability in a wide range of circumstances,

---

[117] A parent company cannot indemnify the directors of its subsidiary and the subsidiary cannot indemnify the directors of its parent company. It used to be the practice in some groups that one group company would indemnify the director of another group company and so circumvent the rule that a company could not indemnify its own directors. This loophole was closed by the CAICE Act 2004.

[118] For the story of this litigation, see *Equitable Life Assurance Society v Bowley* [2004] 1 BCLC 180; also Reed (2006) 27 Co Law 170. In a nutshell, the new owners of Equitable Life sued the previous board essentially alleging that the company's acute financial difficulties arose as a result of incompetence on the part of the directors—the claim was ultimately dropped.

though not where the liability is to the company itself. There, Parliament did draw the line.

Qualifying third party indemnity provisions

13-50   In essence, a company may indemnify a director against liability incurred (including costs) by the director to a third party (i.e. someone other than the company or an associated company, defined CA 2006, s 256), such as a shareholder or regulator provided certain conditions are met: s 234.[119] These indemnities are known as qualifying third party indemnity provisions (QTPIPs).

13-51   A company (likewise an associated company) cannot provide an indemnity in respect of:

- any liability of a director to the company or to an associated company;
- any criminal penalties;
- any regulatory penalties;
- any liability incurred by the director in defending criminal proceedings in which he is convicted, or civil proceedings brought by the company or associated company in which judgment is given against him, or in respect of an unsuccessful application for relief[120] (CA 2006, s 234(2)).

13-52   The existence of any QTPIP must be disclosed in the directors' report (s 236) and copies of the qualifying indemnity provision must be available for inspection by any member (s 237), but shareholder approval of the QTPIP is not required.

13-53   As with decisions on defence costs funding (see **13-43**), the decision to grant indemnities to directors must be taken by the other directors in accordance with their fiduciary duties, in particular the duty to exercise their powers for a proper purpose and the duty to promote the success of the company (ss 171 and 172). In practice, for large companies, the granting of indemnities has become routine with annual reports commonly recording that the company has provided indemnities to their directors to the extent permitted by law.[121]

Insurance provision

13-54   A company is not prevented from purchasing and maintaining for a director of the company, or of an associate company, insurance against any liability attaching to a director in connection with any negligence, default, breach of duty or breach of trust in relation to the company of which he is a director: CA 2006, 233. It is commonplace

---

[119] A failure to meet the conditions means that the indemnity is void since it then falls back within the prohibition in CA 2006, s 232(2): see **13-47**. Equivalent indemnity provision is available for directors of corporate trustees of occupational pension schemes: see s 235.

[120] I.e. under CA 2006, s 1157.

[121] See The Companies (Model Articles) Regulations 2008, SI 2008/3229, reg 2, Sch 1, art 52 (Ltd); reg 4, Sch 3, art 85 (Plc) (note the width of the drafting).

for public companies to purchase directors and officers' liability insurance,[122] though concerns remain as to its cost and coverage.

Application to court for relief

The court has power under CA 2006, s 1157 to relieve an officer[123] of the company **13-55** from liability[124] where the officer is or may be liable in respect of negligence, default,[125] breach of duty or breach of trust, if the court is satisfied that he has acted honestly and reasonably and that, having regard to all the circumstances of the case, he ought fairly to be excused.[126] The scope of the provision is limited to relief in cases where the company or someone on its behalf (such as a liquidator) is seeking to enforce the personal duties that directors owe to the company.[127] The provision does not apply to proceedings by a third party (i.e. a creditor) to recover a debt owed by the director.[128]

It is an absolute precondition to the grant of relief that the director has acted honestly **13-56** and reasonably and the burden of proving honesty and reasonableness is on those who ask for relief.[129] Whether the directors have acted honestly and reasonably is

---

[122] For an overview of the insurance issues, see Deane, 'D & O Insurance' (2008) PLC 23. See also The Companies (Model Articles) Regulations 2008, SI 2008/3229, reg 2, Sch 1, art 53 (Ltd); reg 4, Sch 3, art 86 (Plc).

[123] Defined CA 2006, s 1173 as including a director, manager or secretary. It does not extend to shadow directors in the absence of an express provision to that effect: see *Ultraframe (UK) Ltd v Fielding* [2005] EWHC 1638, para 1452.

[124] Including a liability to account for profits, see *Coleman Taymar Ltd v Oakes* [2001] 2 BCLC 749; but not a liability to repay sums paid to a director under a void contract: *Guinness plc v Saunders* [1990] 2 AC 663 at 695, 702; or, it seems, a liability to make a contribution for wrongful trading under IA 1986, s 214: *Re Produce Marketing Consortium Ltd* [1989] 3 All ER 1.

[125] By 'default' is meant some fault or misconduct by a director or officer in their capacity as such in the discharge of their obligations under the companies legislation, see *Customs & Excise Commissioners v Hedon Alpha Ltd* [1981] 2 All ER 697. It was accepted, obiter, in *Re Duckwari plc (No 2)* [1998] 2 BCLC 315 at 325 that 'default' includes the personal liability of directors to indemnify the company under the statutory provisions governing conflicts of interest, now set out in CA 2006, Part 10, Ch 4 (specific conflicts); and see *Queensway Systems Ltd v Walker* [2007] 2 BCLC 577 at 595.

[126] The CA 2006, s 1157 restates CA 1985, s 727 without substantive amendment. The CLR proposed, but the Government rejected, that the 'reasonableness' requirement be dropped. For a valuable analysis of the provision and the CLR proposals, see Edmunds & Lowry (2003) 66 MLR 195 which notes, inter alia, its importance in the context of directors of small family companies where directors' liability insurance is not feasible.

[127] *Customs & Excise Commissioners v Hedon Alpha Ltd* [1981] 2 All ER 697; *IRC v McEntaggart* [2006] 1 BCLC 476.

[128] For that reason, relief is not available with respect to liability incurred under the 'phoenix' name prohibition in IA 1986, ss 216, 217: *First Independent Factors & Finance Ltd v Mountford* [2008] 2 BCLC 297; or in proceedings under CDDA 1986, s 15 (liability of disqualified person for debts incurred when acting though disqualified): *IRC v McEntaggart* [2006] 1 BCLC 476; or in proceedings to recover taxes: *Customs & Excise Commissioners v Hedon Alpha Ltd* [1981] 2 All ER 697 (no relief in respect of liability for unpaid betting and gaming tax).

[129] *Bairstow v Queens Moat Houses plc* [2001] 2 BCLC 531, CA; and see *Re in a Flap Envelope Ltd* [2004] 1 BCLC 64. It is not reasonable for directors to fail to make provision in the accounts for the possibility that tax relief might not be forthcoming on a particular scheme with the result that improper dividends are paid: *Re Loquitur Ltd* [2003] 2 BCLC 442.

essentially an objective test.[130] In applications under this section, the court tends to take a broad look at all the circumstances of the case[131] in order to determine whether the director ought fairly to be excused, rather than seek for these purposes to impose discrete thresholds as to 'honesty' and 'reasonableness',[132] and conduct may be reasonable for this purpose despite amounting to a lack of reasonable care at common law. In *Re D'Jan of London Ltd*[133] a director in breach of his duty of care had signed an insurance form without reading it. Had he done so, he would have discovered the inaccurate information which subsequently caused the insurance company to repudiate liability under the policy. Although he was careless, the court granted him partial relief, finding that he had acted honestly and reasonably and Hoffmann LJ thought that what had happened could have happened to any busy man.[134]

13-57 Ultimately, the court has considerable discretion under this provision for, once a director establishes that he has acted honestly and reasonably, the court must still be satisfied that the director 'ought fairly to be excused'. The court is very unlikely to exercise its discretion to relieve a director from liability if the director has obtained a material personal benefit through a breach of duty,[135] or if the director gains at the expense of the creditors, as where he seeks to be relieved of a liability to repay money to the company which would be available to meet the creditors' claims.[136]

[130] See *Bairstow v Queens Moat Houses plc* [2001] 2 BCLC 531 at 550 (criticising *Coleman Taymar v Oakes* [2001] 2 BCLC 749 which seemed to suggest to the contrary); see the discussion at **13-34** as to the standard of 'honesty' in the context of dishonest assistance, though the complexities revealed in that context should not be imported into this provision.

[131] See *Ultraframe (UK) Ltd v Fielding* [2005] EWHC 1638, para 1451: 'the expression "the circumstances of the case" does not mean the litigation, it primarily means the circumstances in which the breach took place but it may include a review of the director's stewardship of the company, but not a more wide ranging inquiry into the director's character and behaviour'.

[132] Sometimes the court finds that the director has acted honestly but not reasonably and sometimes that he has acted honestly and reasonably but in the circumstances ought not to be excused, though the section envisages that 'honesty' and 'reasonableness' are threshold requirements which trigger the court's discretion to look at the fairness of the situation: see Edmunds & Lowry, above n 126, on the mingling of these elements by the courts.

[133] [1994] 1 BCLC 561. See also *Inn Spirit Ltd v Burns* [2002] 2 BCLC 780 at 787–8.

[134] [1994] 1 BCLC 561 at 564; see Edmunds & Lowry, above n 126, 207–10, on the appropriateness of the approach adopted by Hoffmann LJ in this instance.

[135] *Re in a Flap Envelope Co Ltd* [2004] 1 BCLC 64 (director as a shareholder was a beneficiary of improper financial assistance given by the company in breach of CA 1985, s 151); *Re Marini Ltd* [2004] BCC 172 (receipt of improper dividends—it would not be fair if the director benefited and the creditors suffered).

[136] See *Inn Spirit Ltd v Burns* [2002] 2 BCLC 780 at 788: '... I cannot see that the court could or should excuse [the directors] from liability at the expense of the creditors of the company...' (Rimer J) (improper dividend paid to directors/shareholders which amounted to an improper misapplication of almost the entire assets of the company); also *First Global Media Group Ltd v Larkin* [2003] EWCA 1765 (improper drawings by directors... out of the question, the Court of Appeal said, that the directors could be fairly excused from repaying the money when the people out of the money were the creditors of the company); *Queensway Systems Ltd v Walker* [2007] 2 BCLC 577 at 596.

PART III

CORPORATE GOVERNANCE— SHAREHOLDERS' RIGHTS AND REMEDIES

14

Membership and the incidents of membership

A Becoming a member

Membership of a company is governed by CA 2006, s 112 which provides: (1) that **14-1** the subscribers of a company's memorandum of association (discussed at **1-24**) are deemed to have agreed to become members of the company and on its registration become members and must be entered as such in its register of members; and (2) that every other person who agrees[1] to become a member of a company, and whose name is entered in its register of members,[2] is a member of the company.[3] Entry on the register is a matter for the directors and routine entries are dealt with by the company secretary (where there is a company secretary). Listed public companies use the services of professional registrars to maintain their share registers. The nature of the register of members and its rectification is discussed in detail below. For the most part, entry on the register of members happens without any difficulty and so, having acquired some shares, the shareholder becomes a member of the company. In general, the shareholders are the members of the company and the terms 'shareholders' and 'members' may be used interchangeably.[4]

---

[1] This requirement of agreement is satisfied when a person assents to become a member and it does not require that there should be a binding contract between the person and the company: *Re Nuneaton Borough Association Football Club Ltd* [1989] BCLC 454, CA.

[2] Some companies have uncertificated shares which may be transferred electronically and, for such companies, the company's register of members means the company's issuer register of members and the Operator register of members: The Uncertificated Securities Regulations 2001, SI 2001/3755, reg 20(4). The 'Operator' is the electronic settlement platform for shares and other securities known as CREST. CREST became operational in 1996 and merged in 2002 with Euroclear, the European securities settlement system. CREST is now operated by Euroclear UK and Ireland. See https://www.euroclear.com/site/public. The legal underpinning of electronic settlement is provided by CA 2006, Part 21, Ch 2 and regulations made thereunder (see s 784), i.e. by virtue of s 1297 (continuity of the law) The Uncertificated Securities Regulations 2001, noted above.

[3] CA 2006, s 112(2); and see *Re Florence Land and Public Works Co, Nicol's Case, Tufnell and Ponsonby's Case* (1885) 29 Ch D 421, CA.

[4] Exceptional cases are (1) where the company is a company limited by guarantee without a share capital, in which case the company has members but no shareholders; and (2) where a company limited by shares has issued bearer share warrants, in which case the holders of the bearer share warrants are shareholders, but not members, because their names have not been entered on the register of members; subject to any provision in the articles deeming the bearer to be a member: see CA 2006, s 122(1), (3).

14-2   As practically all the companies on the register of companies are companies limited by shares, the initial stage in the process of becoming a member of a company involves becoming a shareholder and there are four methods of becoming a shareholder:

(1) by subscribing to the memorandum;

(2) by taking up an allotment of shares by the company;

(3) by a transfer of shares from an existing member;

(4) by a transmission of shares on the death or bankruptcy of a member.

14-3   As noted above, the subscribers to the company's memorandum are deemed to have agreed to become members and on registration of the memorandum they must be entered as such in the company's register of members (CA 2006, s 112(1)). The memorandum states that each subscriber agrees to become a member and undertakes, in the case of a company having a share capital, to take at least one share (s 8(1)). It is unusual for any problems to arise with regard to subscribers.

14-4   The allotment of shares by the company to existing or new investors is a matter for the directors, subject to certain statutory constraints. The duties of directors in this regard (to exercise their powers for a proper purpose) are discussed in Chapter 8 while the statutory constraints and mechanics of allotment are discussed in Chapter 19. Following an allotment, the company issues share certificates to the shareholders (unless the shares are being held in uncertificated form: discussed below) and the shareholders' names are entered on the register of members. Few problems with entry on the register of members occur in these cases since, obviously, the company has decided to allot more shares and is willing to accept new members.

14-5   Problems are most likely to arise on the transfer and transmission of shares. Here the company is a bystander to transactions (in the case of transfers) and dispositions (in the case of transmission) which alter the membership of the company. On occasion, particularly in private companies, the directors may be unhappy at a change in the membership and this can give rise to problems for the transferees with respect to securing the entry of their names on the register of members.

14-6   In terms of the process of transfer, for most companies, the process involves a proper instrument of transfer (i.e. a paper form) and a (paper) share certificate. The company gives effect to the transfer or transmission by removing the transferor from the register of members and inserting the name of the transferee. The company cancels the share certificate in the name of the transferor and issues a new certificate in the name of the transferee. Larger publicly traded companies have uncertificated shares which are transferred electronically and in this case there is no requirement for a proper instrument of transfer and share certificates are not issued; instead the member's shareholding is recorded electronically. The majority of private investors hold their shareholdings in certificated form while institutional and professional investors hold their shareholdings in uncertificated form.

14-7   Little progress has been made in recent years on dematerialisation, as the process of moving from share certificates to electronic shareholding is known. In 2001 working groups from various bodies attempted to move matters forward but the momentum appeared to stall.[5] An ad hoc group of interested parties (companies, brokers, registrars, Euroclear and APCIMS[6]) was set up in 2005 under the auspices of the Institute of Chartered Secretaries and Administrators (ICSA) to continue working on the issue. The CA 2006, ss 783–790 makes provision for regulations to allow dematerialisation (as was the case under the CA 1985) but also for regulations requiring companies to adopt electronic holdings (s 786(1)(b)). The ad hoc market group via ICSA asked the Treasury in September 2008 to confirm that the Government remains committed to the dematerialisation of shares and will bring forward the necessary regulations.[7] It may be that the financial crisis of late 2008 will have the effect of driving significant numbers of individual holders permanently out of the market so making it easier for the Government to move to compulsory dematerialisation.

Share certificates

Unless the conditions of issue of the shares otherwise provides, within two months after the allotment of any shares, or within two months after a transfer of any shares being lodged with a company, the company must complete and have ready for delivery the relevant share certificates.[8] This requirement to issue a share certificate does not apply where the shares are in uncertificated form.[9]   **14-8**

The certificate is prima facie (not conclusive) evidence of title (CA 2006, s 768(1)) and the presumption arising from it can be rebutted, but the company may be estopped from denying the facts stated in the certificate. In *Re Bahia and San Francisco Rly Co*[10] the court noted: **14-9**

> 'The power of giving certificates is . . . for the benefit of the company in general; and it is a declaration by the company to all the world that the person in whose name the certificate is made out, and to whom it is given, is a shareholder in the company, and it is given by the company with the intention that it shall be so used by the person to whom it is given, and acted upon in the sale and transfer of shares.'

For example, if the company issues certificates which describe shares as fully paid up when they are not and a third party relies on the certificate, the company is estopped from denying that they are fully paid.[11] In *Bloomenthal v Ford*[12] a lender to a company took shares in the company as collateral security. The certificate stated that he was the   **14-10**

---

[5] See CREST, *Moving towards a Dematerialised Securities Market, a Consultation Document* (July 2001); APCIMS, *Report of the APCIMS Electronic Shareholding Working Party, A Consultation Document* (May 2001).   [6] The Association of Private Client Investment Managers and Stockbrokers.

[7] See ICSA Statement on Dematerialisation, 21 October 2008, and letter to HM Treasury of 16 September 2008, available at www.icsa.org.uk/knowledge/policy/2016.

[8] CA 2006, ss 769(1), 776(1), subject to the exemptions in ss 769(2), 776(3).

[9] See The Uncertificated Securities Regulations 2001, SI 2001/3755, reg 38(2).

[10] (1868) LR 3 QB 584 at 595. See also *Cadbury Schweppes plc v Halifax Share Dealing Ltd* [2007] 1 BCLC 497 where the company was estopped from denying the validity of share certificates issued to fraudsters (and subsequently sold by them) who had stolen the identities of genuine shareholders.

[11] See *Burkinshaw v Nicolls* (1878) 3 App Cas 1004. Where there is a subsequent transfer and the transferor had acquired a good title by estoppel, the transferee acquires a good title even if he had actual notice that the shares were only partly paid: *Re Stapleford Colliery Co, Barrow's Case* (1880) 14 Ch D 432, CA. Cf *Re London Celluloid Co* (1888) 39 Ch D 190 at 197, CA.   [12] [1897] AC 156, HL.

holder of 10,000 fully-paid ordinary shares when the shares were not in fact fully paid. It was held by the House of Lords that the company was estopped from denying the certificate. The lender could have found out the true position by enquiry but there was no actual notice and he had acted in good faith.

14-11   If a share certificate is issued following the presentation of a forged transfer, the company is not estopped from denying its validity. This is because the person presenting the transfer impliedly warrants the authenticity of the transfer.[13] A purchaser from such a person is in a better position and can claim compensation from the company if he is displaced by the true owner since the purchaser relies not on the forged transfer but on the certificate issued by the company.[14] A forged share certificate is a nullity and does not bind the company.[15]

Restrictions on membership

14-12   As a general rule, anyone may be a member but there are restrictions imposed on some classes of persons.

Minors

14-13   There is no prohibition on minors[16] being shareholders although the company may refuse to accept a minor as a shareholder.[17] Applying ordinary contract law rules, a contract to purchase shares is voidable by a minor before or within a reasonable time of attaining his majority. If the minor repudiates the contract, he is not liable for future calls but he cannot recover the purchase price unless there has been a total failure of consideration,[18] which is unlikely to be the case. Given that shares are normally issued as fully paid, there is little reason now for repudiation and it is rare for problems with minors to arise, unlike in the late nineteenth century when there were many cases of heirs and heiresses seeking to repudiate contracts for shares. Until the minor repudiates, he has full rights of membership.

Subsidiary companies

14-14   A company cannot be a member of itself, a point originally established in *Trevor v Whitworth*[19] and now stated in CA 2006, s 658 which provides that any purported

---

[13] The presentor of the improper transfer must also indemnify the company against liability arising from the company's acting on the invalid transfer: *Sheffield Corporation v Barclay* [1905] AC 392; *Yeung Kai Yung v Hong Kong & Shangai Banking* [1980] 2 All ER 599.

[14] *Re Bahia and San Francisco Railway Co* (1868) LR 3 QB 584; *Balkis Consolidated Co v Tomkinson* [1893] AC 396; *Dixon v Kennaway & Co* [1900] 1 Ch 833.

[15] *Ruben v Great Fingall Consolidated* [1906] AC 439; see Sealy & Worthington, *Cases and Materials in Company Law* (8th edn, 2008), p 447.

[16] That is anyone under 18 years of age in England and Wales: Family Law Reform Act 1969, s 1; anyone under 16 in Scotland.

[17] *Re Asiatic Banking Corpn, Symon's Case* (1870) Ch App 298. For companies with uncertificated shares, the power to refuse to register a transfer to a minor is retained: see The Uncertificated Securities Regulations 2001, SI 2001/3755, regs 27(4)(b), 28(4)(b).

[18] *Steinberg v Scala (Leeds) Ltd* [1923] 2 Ch 452, CA.   [19] (1887) 12 App Cas 409, HL.

acquisition by a company of its own shares other than in accordance with the provisions of the Act is void (see **20-17**) and an offence by the company and any officer in default. The Act further provides that, subject to certain exceptions, a body corporate cannot be a member of its holding company and any allotment or transfer of shares in a company to its subsidiary is void (s 136).[20] The policy behind this prohibition is to reinforce the rule in *Trevor v Whitworth*[21] and prevent any reduction of capital whereby capital provided by a parent company to a subsidiary is returned by the subsidiary to the parent company. The prohibition cannot be avoided by using a nominee for the prohibition applies to a nominee acting on behalf of a subsidiary as to the subsidiary itself (s 144).

There are a number of exceptions, however, when a subsidiary may hold shares in its holding company, for example where the subsidiary holds the shares only as a personal representative or trustee (CA 2006, s 138),[22] or in the ordinary course of its business as an authorised dealer in shares (s 141). Equally, where a company acquired shares in circumstances where it would not have been within the prohibition on a subsidiary being a member of its holding company, but would now fall within the prohibition, the company may remain as a member of the holding company (and receive bonus issues in respect of its holding) but it has no right to vote those shares on a written resolution or in general or class meetings (s 137). Likewise, where a company becomes a holder of shares in another company on or after 1 October 2009 and subsequently becomes a subsidiary of that other company, it may continue to hold those shares (and receive bonus issues in respect of them) but may not vote those shares on a written resolution or at general or class meetings (s 137).   **14-15**

B Classes of shares

It is common for the articles of association to give a company complete freedom to issue shares with such rights and restrictions as the company may by ordinary resolution determine[23] although most companies (public and private) limit their structures to ordinary shares. Where a more sophisticated share structure is required (for example, to facilitate a division of control in a joint venture company), the company may have more classes of shares, typically ordinary and preference shares, and possibly several forms of each. The London Stock Exchange encourages public listed companies to restrict themselves to one class of shares, favouring the equality of treatment and the transparency of rights which such a capital structure ensures. The nature of ordinary   **14-16**

---

[20] 'Holding company' and 'subsidiary' are defined in CA 2006, s 1159 and Sch 6.

[21] (1887) 12 App Cas 409, HL.

[22] Unless the holding company or a subsidiary of it is beneficially interested under the trust, see CA 2006, s 138(1).

[23] See The Companies (Model Articles) Regulations 2008, SI 2008/3229, reg 2, Sch 1; art 22 (Ltd), reg 4, Sch 3, art 43 (Plc).

and preference shares is outlined below, but it must be stressed that the particular rights in any given company depend on the terms of issue.

Ordinary shares

14-17   Ordinary shares (often loosely described as equities) carry the residual rights of participation in the income and capital of the company which have not been granted to other classes. Ordinary shareholders have no right to any fixed dividend (i.e. a return on their investment usually expressed as so many pence per share) on their shares, but after the payment of any dividends to preference shareholders, the ordinary shareholders enjoy the remainder of the surplus profits actually distributed as dividend by the directors. Distributions are considered in detail in Chapter 20.

14-18   In difficult times, the ordinary shareholders run the risk that the profits available for distribution will be inadequate and will not extend beyond (or indeed to) the payment of the dividend due on the preference shares. In prosperous times, however, the preference shareholders are restricted to their fixed dividend and the ordinary shareholders enjoy all of the surplus distributable profits. For example, if the company has distributable profits of £30,000 but the fixed dividend payable to preference shareholders costs £20,000, then the ordinary shareholders share a fund of £10,000. On the other hand, if the company has distributable profits of £300,000, the preference shareholders remain entitled as before to their dividend of £20,000 and the ordinary shareholders share the remaining £280,000. The ordinary shareholders run the risk of no dividend or a small dividend, as we can see, but they also stand to scoop the pool in the event that the company makes significant profits. Preference shareholders take less risk and so are entitled to less return.

14-19   Ordinary shareholders have a right to a return of capital ranking after the preference shares but, as with dividends, ordinary shares claim the pool of surplus assets in a solvent winding up after the return of capital to all other shareholders.

14-20   Ordinary shares usually carry one vote per share although companies may attach such voting rights as they choose. For example, a company may provide that ordinary shares carry 10 votes per share or it may divide its ordinary shares into two classes of ordinary shares, one voting and one non-voting class. Non-voting ordinary shares are not common and are disapproved of by the Stock Exchange. Preference shareholders generally have limited voting rights so it is the ordinary shareholders who have voting control in general meetings.

Preference shares

14-21   Typically, a preference share has a fixed preferential cumulative dividend[24] and a priority as to a return of capital on a winding up which ensures that the preference

---

[24] The payment of dividends is still dependent on the company having distributable profits as required by CA 2006, Part 23, but if there are such profits then the terms of issue of preference shares usually require the payment of a dividend on fixed dates.

shareholders get their capital back ahead of the ordinary shareholders although, as shareholders, the preference shareholders rank after secured and unsecured creditors. Preference shareholders are non-participating as to surplus both while the company is a going concern (i.e. with respect to any further distributions of profits) and on a winding up (i.e. with respect to any surplus assets remaining after the creditors have been paid and capital has been returned to the shareholders). To ensure participation in any such surpluses, preference shares may be issued as participating preference shares, i.e. participating as to dividend and/or capital which means that the shares carry additional rights to participate in profits or assets. Preference shares usually have restricted voting rights limited to matters which affect their rights such as when their dividends are in arrears.

In some ways, the position of preference shareholders is akin to that of creditors and **14-22** preference shares are often regarded as a hybrid category of investment between equity or share capital and loan capital. The fixed dividend payable to preference shareholders resembles the fixed interest payable on loan capital and the priority to a return of capital in a winding up resembles a creditor's right to a return of the capital sum. Equally, preference shares can carry rights quite similar to ordinary shares and the company may issue preference shares which are convertible into ordinary shares either on a set date or at the option of the shareholders or, in some circumstances, at the option of the company. As with all shares, the precise nature of a preference share depends on the terms of issue.

C Class rights

Identifying a class right

As noted at **14-16**, it is common for the articles of association to provide that a com- **14-23** pany may issue shares with such rights and restrictions as the company may by ordinary resolution determine. Class rights may be set out in the articles or in the resolution creating them. In practice, they are usually set out in the articles.[25] If all the shares fall within one class, there are no class rights, only shareholder rights.[26] Where particular rights (such as the right to a dividend or to a return of capital on a winding up) are attached to certain shares, these are described as class rights.

In *Cumbrian Newspapers Group Ltd v Cumberland and Westmorland Herald Co Ltd*,[27] **14-24** Scott J broadened the classification of class rights to include rights conferred on a

---

[25] The statement of capital which accompanies a return of allotment of the shares must give, for each class, the prescribed particulars of the rights attached to the shares, and the total number of shares of that class: CA 2006, s 555(3),(4). The registrar must also be notified of the assignment of a new name or designation to any class of members and of variations of class rights: ss 636, 637.

[26] See *Union Music Ltd v Watson* [2003] 1 BCLC 453 at 464, where there are no rights conferred on one shareholder which have not also been conferred on the other shareholder(s), there are no classes of shares.

[27] [1986] 2 All ER 816.

member of a company in his capacity as a member which rights are not attached to any particular class of shares. The member in that case had been given by name certain rights of pre-emption, the right to appoint a director and rights to transfer shares, the purpose being to enable the member to obstruct an attempted takeover. Scott J concluded that the shares for the time being held by that member constituted a class for the purposes of the statutory procedure for variation of class rights.[28] He said:[29]

> 'In my judgment, a company which, by its articles, confers special rights on one or more of its members in the capacity of member or shareholder thereby constitutes the shares for the time being held by that member or members a class of shares for the purposes of s 125 [variation of class rights, now CA 2006, s 630]. The rights are class rights.'

14-25   The value of a right being classified as a class right is that the variation of rights attached to a class of shares is subject to CA 2006, s 630 which essentially provides that such rights cannot be varied or abrogated other than in accordance with a variation provision in the articles or, if the articles make no provision for variation, with the consent of the class in accordance with s 630. The situation in *Cumbrian* is within s 630(1) for the three requirements of the section are met: (1) there is a class of shares, as Scott J determined, (2) there are rights attached *to the class*, and (3) there is a proposed variation of those rights. Provisions which are classified as class rights therefore confer greater security on the beneficiary than rights conferred merely by the articles which are open to the risk of alteration by a special resolution under s 21(1), although it is now possible to offer protection through entrenched provisions in the articles, as noted at **4-17**. Class rights can therefore form a valuable element in the protection of minority shareholders[30] or any other special interests.[31] It is for this reason that the broad approach taken in *Cumbrian* is important, though not everyone agrees with it.[32]

14-26   The application of CA 2006, s 630(1) must not be confused by reference to s 629 which addresses a quite distinct issue. Section 629 provides that 'for the purposes of the CA 2006, shares are of one class if the rights attached to them are in all respects

---

[28] [1986] 2 All ER 816 at 830.

[29] [1986] 2 All ER 816 at 830. See also *Re Blue Arrow plc* [1987] BCLC 585 at 590 (a right conferred on an individual unrelated to any shareholding in any way cannot be described as a class right).

[30] For example, the courts will not exercise their discretion under CA 2006, s 306 to call a general meeting if to do so would override a class right with respect to the calling of meetings: see *Harman v BML Group Ltd* [1994] 2 BCLC 674, see **15–53**.

[31] Sometimes Governments use class rights to retain control of privatised companies by way of a so-called 'golden share', typically nothing more elaborate than a single £1 special preference share. The extent to which the use of golden shares to retain control in this way is permissible under Community Law has been addressed by the European Court of Justice which essentially concluded that such measures are contrary to the free movement of capital, but may in some circumstances be permissible in the protection of the public interest, provided the measures adopted are proportionate, objective and non-discriminatory. See *Commission v Portugal* (Case C-367/98), *Commission v France* (Case C-483/99), *Commission v Belgium* (Case C-503/99) [2003] QB 233.

[32] See Polack [1986] CLJ 399; Morse [2008] JBL 96 at 98 who variously describes it as an unwise and an unfortunate decision.

uniform.[33] In other words, this section defines when 'shares are of one class' rather than what is a class of shares (the heading to the section is misleading in this regard).[34] The definition in s 629 is needed for the application of various provisions such as s 550 (directors' power to allot when private company has only one class of shares) and s 569 (disapplication of pre-emption rights when private company has only one class of shares).[35]

Rules of construction

Certain rules of construction have been developed by the courts to assist them in identifying the rights attaching to each class of shares, given that they vary from company to company. It must be stressed, however, that each case ultimately turns on the particular terms of issue.   **14-27**

A presumption of equality

There is a presumption of equality as between shareholders with all shareholders being deemed to be entitled to the same proportionate part in the capital of the company.[36] This presumption is easily rebutted by an issue of shares on terms which gives special rights with respect to matters such as dividends, the return of capital, or to voting at meetings of the company. As noted above, preference shareholders typically have a preferential right to a dividend and to a return of capital on a winding up.   **14-28**

Rights granted are deemed to be exhaustive

There is a presumption that any rights attached to a share are deemed to be exhaustive.[37] The position was clearly expressed by Sargant J in *Re National Telephone Co*[38] as follows: **14-29**

> '...the weight of authority is in favour of the view that, either with regard to dividend or with regard to the rights in a winding up, the express gift or attachment of preferential rights to preference shares, on their creation, is, prima facie, a definition of the whole of their rights in that respect, and negatives any further or other right to which, but for the specified rights, they would have been entitled.'

In *Will v United Lankat Plantations Co*[39] the attachment of preferential dividend rights to preference shares was presumed to be exhaustive as to their dividend rights. This had the effect of negating any right to further participation in any surplus profits   **14-30**

---

[33] For these purposes, the rights attached to shares are not regarded as different from those attached to other shares by reason only that they do not carry the same rights to dividends in the 12 months immediately following their allotment: CA 2006, s 629(2).

[34] A point confirmed by the Explanatory Notes to the Companies Act 2006, para 934 which points out that the statute does not define what amounts to a class which remains a matter for the common law.

[35] Other provisions to note are CA 2006, s 725(1) (Treasury shares: maximum holding); s 974(2)(b) (Meaning of 'takeover offer').

[36] *Birch v Cropper, Re Bridgewater Navigation Co Ltd* (1889) 14 App Cas 525 at 543, per Lord Macnaghten, HL.

[37] *Re National Telephone Co* [1914] 1 Ch 755.   [38] [1914] 1 Ch 755 at 774.   [39] [1914] AC 11.

of the company. This presumption of exhaustive rights can be rebutted by expressly declaring the shares to be participating preference shares with a right of participation in surplus profits after a certain percentage of dividend has been paid to the ordinary shareholders.[40]

14-31   Likewise where preference shares are given an express priority to a return of capital on a winding up, this negates any right to participate in surplus assets in a winding up.[41] Again, the terms of issue may enable preference shareholders to share in surplus assets with the other shareholders after their capital had been repaid, but it is for preference shareholders to show that they are entitled to participate further in this way.[42]

A cumulative dividend

14-32   Prima facie, preference shares are entitled to a cumulative dividend, even in the absence of any such provision in the terms of issue.[43] This means that the preference shareholders are entitled to have any deficiencies in a given year made up from the profits of subsequent years before anything is distributed to other shareholders. Alternatively, preference shares may be issued as non-cumulative, but this must be clearly stated to ensure that the presumption does not apply.[44]

14-33   On a winding up, if the company is solvent, a question concerning the payment of arrears of dividend may arise. There is a prima facie presumption that dividends and arrears thereof are only payable while the company is a going concern and are no longer payable once winding up has begun.[45] That inference is rebuttable where there are express words in the terms of issue to the contrary or a definition in the right to dividend which is inconsistent with it.[46]

14-34   The net effect of these rules of construction is that class rights are usually spelt out in great detail in the terms of issue to avoid falling foul of one or other presumption.

Variation or abrogation of class rights

14-35   The statutory scheme for variation of class rights was simplified on the recommendation of the Company Law Review and it is intended to provide a comprehensive code setting out the manner in which rights attached to a class of shares can be varied.[47]

---

[40] See *Re Isle of Thanet Electric Supply Co Ltd* [1950] Ch 161.

[41] *Scottish Insurance Corpn Ltd v Wilsons and Clyde Coal Co Ltd* [1949] 1 All ER 1068; *Prudential Assurance Co Ltd v Chatterley-Whitfield Collieries Ltd* [1949] 1 All ER 1094, HL.

[42] *Re Isle of Thanet Electric Supply Co Ltd* [1950] Ch 161, CA; *Scottish Insurance Corpn Ltd v Wilsons and Clyde Coal Co Ltd* [1949] 1 All ER 1068, HL.

[43] *Webb v Earle* (1875) LR 20 Eq 556.

[44] *Staples v Eastman Photographic Materials Co* [1896] 2 Ch 303, CA (the terms of issue referred specifically to dividends paid out of the profits of each year).   [45] *Re Crichton's Oil Co* [1902] 2 Ch 86.

[46] *Re E W Savory Ltd* [1951] 2 All ER 1036 (reference to the ranking of the preference shares must have been a reference to what would happen on winding up); *Re Walter Symons Ltd* [1934] Ch 308.

[47] See Company Law Review, *Final Report,* vol 1 (2001), URN 01/942, para 7.28; *Completing the Structure* (2000), URN 00/1335, paras 5.42–5.44; *Developing the Framework* (2000), URN 00/656, paras 4.147–4.151. The major change effected by the CA 2006 is to extend the statutory provisions on variation of class rights to companies without a share capital, see s 631.

A variation or abrogation[48] must be carried out in accordance with a variation provi-   **14-36**
sion in the articles or, if no provision is made in the articles, in accordance with the
scheme in CA 2006, s 630. That scheme requires the consent in writing of the holders
of not less than three-quarters in nominal value of the issued shares of that class or
a special resolution of the class approving the variation at a separate class meeting
(s 630(4)).[49] At a class meeting so held, the shareholders must have regard to what is in
the interests of the class.[50] In practice provisions in the articles are generally drafted in
broadly similar terms to the statutory scheme, but it is possible for the articles either
to impose a stricter scheme or a less onerous one (for example, requiring an ordinary
resolution). In either case, the articles must be obeyed for the statutory scheme only
applies in the absence of provision in the articles.[51]

An important point to note is CA 2006, s 630(3) which provides that the section is   **14-37**
without prejudice to other restrictions on variation, so where a class right is entrenched
in accordance with s 22, see **4-17**, that provision governs and those rights cannot be
altered by using s 630.[52]

Where a class has consented to a variation, the holders of not less in total than 15%   **14-38**
of the issued shares of that class, provided that they did not consent to or vote for
the variation, may apply to the court within 21 days to have the variation cancelled,
in which case the variation does not take effect until it has been confirmed by the
court (CA 2006, s 633(2)–(4)). If the court is satisfied that the variation would unfairly
prejudice the shareholders of the class represented by the applicant, it may disallow the
variation; otherwise, it must confirm it and the court's decision is final (s 633(5)). In
practice, this provision is rarely used, not least because it is unlikely that a court will
overturn a variation which has been agreed to by three-quarters of the class. A member of a class who feels aggrieved may try to bring a more broadly based case under
the unfairly prejudicial remedy under CA 2006, s 994 which is discussed in detail in
Chapter 17.

Judicial interpretation of 'variation or abrogation'

The statutory protection outlined above (and that provided by equivalent provisions   **14-39**
in the articles) only applies if what has occurred amounts to a variation or abrogation
of the rights attached to a class (CA 2006, s 630(1), (6)) and the courts have restricted

---

[48] References to variation include reference to abrogation: CA 2006, s 630(6). An alteration of an existing variation provision or the insertion of a variation procedure is itself a variation of class rights: s 630(5).
The Court of Session in *Re House of Fraser plc* [1987] BCLC 293 at 301 noted that 'variation' presupposes
the continuance of rights in a varied state while 'abrogation' presupposes the termination of rights without
satisfaction or fulfilment.

[49] As to the application of CA 2006, Part 13, Ch 3 (meetings) to class meetings, see s 334. Note in particular
that the quorum requirement for a variation of class rights is two persons present holding at least one-third
in nominal value of the issued shares of the class in question: s 334(4)(a). This provision overrides any provision in the company's articles.

[50] *British America Nickel Corpn Ltd v O'Brien* [1927] AC 369; *Re Holders Investment Trust Ltd* [1971] 2 All
ER 289.

[51] See Explanatory Notes to the CA 2006, paras 936, 937.

[52] See Explanatory Notes to the CA 2006, para 937.

the application of the section (and articles) by interpreting 'variation' and 'abrogation' restrictively.

14-40   In approaching the question of whether a variation or abrogation has occurred, the courts have drawn a distinction between matters affecting the rights attached to each share and matters affecting the enjoyment of those rights. Only variations or abrogations affecting the rights attached to a class of shares attract the protection of CA 2006, s 630. Where only the enjoyment of the right is affected, the shares may be commercially less valuable but their rights remain what they always were and the shareholders cannot demand the protection of the section.[53]

14-41   A typical case is *White v Bristol Aeroplane Co Ltd*[54] where an issue of preference shares which would dilute the control of the existing preference shareholders was held not to be a variation. The new shares were to be issued to the existing ordinary shareholders and paid for out of the company's reserves. The company's articles provided that all or any of the rights or privileges attached to any class of shares might be affected, modified, varied, dealt with or abrogated in any manner with the sanction of an extraordinary resolution passed at a separate meeting of the members of that class. It was argued by the plaintiff preference shareholder that the word 'affect' was wide and must be taken to cover a transaction which, though not necessarily modifying or varying rights, would in some way otherwise affect them. On this basis, it was argued, the proposed allotment was a variation requiring the consent of the existing preference shareholders.

14-42   The Court of Appeal disagreed. Evershed MR concluded that the new issue did not affect the rights or privileges of the existing preference shareholders which remained exactly as they were before. The preference shareholders might be affected as a matter of business by reason of the new preference shares which would be in the possession of the ordinary shareholders and which would have a majority over the existing preference shares. This outcome would only affect the enjoyment of the rights, however, and not the rights themselves and so the consent of the existing preference shareholders was not required. Romer LJ drew a distinction between rights on the one hand and the result of exercising the rights on the other hand. He noted:[55]

> 'The rights, as such, are conferred by resolution or by the articles, and they cannot be affected except with the sanction of the members on whom those rights are conferred; but the results of exercising those rights are not the subject of any assurance or guarantee under the constitution of the company, and are not protected in any way.'

14-43   Similarly, in *Greenhalgh v Arderne Cinemas Ltd*[56] a subdivision of a class of 10 shilling ordinary shares into two shilling shares was held not to vary the rights of

---

[53] The Company Law Review considered the provision of a specific remedy for shareholders in this situation but concluded that if shareholders in a class wish protection for their broader economic interests (as well as their rights) then they should contract for that protection: Company Law Review, *Completing the Structure* (2000), URN 00/1335, para 5.81, and see discussion at **14-51** of contractual protection for class interests.

[54] [1953] Ch 65, CA. See also *Re John Smith's Tadcaster Brewery Co Ltd* [1953] 1 All ER 518.

[55] [1953] Ch 65 at 82, CA.   [56] [1946] 1 All ER 512, CA.

Mr Greenhalgh, a holder of the existing two shilling ordinary shares, although the result of the sub-division was to alter control of the company. The court accepted that the effect was to alter his position as a matter of business but, as a matter of law, his rights were quite unaltered.[57]

Reduction of capital and variation of class rights

Schemes for the reduction of capital (see **20-56** et seq) may involve paying off prefer- **14-44** ence shareholders who are often reluctant to be 'expelled' from the company in this way, particularly when it means an end to high dividend returns which are no longer available in the market. The issue for the court is whether such a reduction of capital amounts to a variation or abrogation of the class rights of the preference shareholder so requiring the consent of the class.

The approach of the courts is to look at what the class rights would be in a winding up **14-45** and to compare that with the position which would arise under the proposed reduction. If what is proposed on reduction is in accordance with the class rights on a winding up, there is no variation requiring the consent of the class.[58]

For example, if the reduction is because capital has been lost or is unrepresented by **14-46** available assets and the classes rank pari passu (equally), then prima facie the loss should be borne equally;[59] but if there are preference shares which have priority as to a return of capital on a winding up, the ordinary shares must bear the loss as they would do if the company was being wound up.[60] Alternatively, if the reduction of capital involves the return of surplus capital, that return will normally be to the preference shareholders who will usually have priority as to repayment of capital in a winding up.[61]

These issues were considered in *House of Fraser plc v ACGE Investments Ltd*[62] where **14-47** the ordinary shareholders passed a special resolution approving the paying off of the whole of the preference share capital of the company as being in excess of the wants of the company. No class meeting of the preference shareholders was held to approve the reduction. The company's articles provided that the special rights attached to any class of shares could only be modified, commuted, affected or dealt with, with the consent of the holders of the class of shares. The preference shareholders argued that the failure to obtain their consent meant that the court could not confirm the reduction of capital.

---

[57] [1946] 1 All ER 512 at 518, CA.

[58] *Re Saltdean Estate Co Ltd* [1968] 3 All ER 829; *House of Fraser v ACGE Investments Ltd* [1987] AC 387, HL.

[59] See *Bannatyne v Direct Spanish Telegraph Co* (1886) 34 Ch D 287, CA where the preference shareholders had no preference as to capital, but only as to dividend.

[60] *Re Floating Dock Company of St Thomas Ltd* [1895] 1 Ch 691.

[61] *Re Chatterley-Whitfield Collieries Ltd* [1948] 2 All ER 593, aff'd sub nom *Prudential Assurance Co Ltd v Chatterley-Whitfield Collieries Ltd* [1949] 1 All ER 1094, HL; *Scottish Insurance Co Ltd v Wilsons & Clyde Coal Co Ltd* 1948 SC 360, aff'd [1949] 1 All ER 1068, HL; *Re Fowlers Vacola Manufacturing Co Ltd* [1966] VR 97; *Re Saltdean Estate Co Ltd* [1968] 3 All ER 829; *House of Fraser v ACGE Investments Ltd* [1987] AC 387, HL.   [62] [1987] AC 387, HL.

14-48   The House of Lords accepted that this issue was definitively addressed by Buckley J in *Re Saltdean Estate Co Ltd*,[63] a case on almost identical facts. In a much cited judgment Buckley J confirmed the long-established position that, where capital is to be repaid, that class of capital should first be repaid which would be returned first in a winding up of the company.[64] If the preference shareholders are entitled to prior repayment of capital in a winding up, the first class of capital to be repaid should prima facie be the preferred shares. Such a proposed cancellation is not an abrogation of the rights attached to those shares when it is in accordance with the right and liability to prior repayment of capital attached to their shares. The liability to prior repayment on a reduction of capital, corresponding to their right to prior return of capital in a winding up, forms an integral part of the definition or delimitation of the bundle of rights which make up the preferred share. Giving effect to it does not involve the variation or abrogation of any rights attached to such shares. Buckley J concluded that this vulnerability to prior repayment in this way is, and has always been, a characteristic of preferred share.[65]

14-49   Applying that approach in *House of Fraser plc v ACGE Investments Ltd*,[66] the House of Lords found that the proposed reduction of capital involved the extinction of the preference shares in strict accordance with the contract embodied in the articles of association to which the preference shareholders were party. The preference shareholders had a right to a return of capital in priority to other shareholders and that right was not affected, modified, dealt with or abrogated, but was given effect to by the proposed reduction with the result that the consent of the preference shareholders was not required.[67]

14-50   This is the position in any instance where the preference shareholders have priority as to a return of capital, even if they also have further rights of participation as regards dividend.[68] It is not clear whether preference shares which are participating as to surplus on a winding up could be dealt with in this way although *Re William Jones & Sons Ltd*[69] suggests that they can.

Deemed variations or abrogations—a contractual solution

14-51   The decisions noted above in cases such as *White v Bristol Aeroplane Co Ltd*,[70] *Greenhalgh v Arderne Cinemas Ltd*[71] and *House of Fraser plc v ACGE Investments Ltd*[72] highlight the limits to the degree of protection which can be conferred by class

---

[63] [1968] 3 All ER 829.   [64] See especially [1968] 3 All ER 829 at 831–2.

[65] [1968] 3 All ER 829 at 833–4. See also *Bannatyne v Direct Spanish Telegraph Co* (1886) 34 Ch D 287, CA; *Scottish Insurance Co Ltd v Wilsons & Clyde Coal Co Ltd* 1948 SC 360, aff'd [1949] 1 All ER 1068 at 1077–8, per Lord Simonds, HL.

[66] [1987] AC 387, HL.   [67] [1987] AC 387 at 393.

[68] *Re Saltdean Estate Co Ltd* [1968] 3 All ER 829.

[69] [1969] 1 All ER 913. In that instance, however, the preference shareholders raised no objection to being paid off, probably because they were to be paid off in full although the shares stood at less than par. Moreover, there was no present prospect of the company being wound up so the enjoyment of any surplus on a winding up would not occur for many years.

[70] [1953] Ch 65, CA.   [71] [1946] 1 All ER 512, CA.   [72] [1987] AC 387, HL.

rights when it is left to the courts to determine whether a variation or abrogation has occurred.

A class of shareholders can avoid the risk of a restrictive interpretation by the courts **14-52** of what constitutes a variation of their class rights by identifying in the terms of issue matters (such as a reduction of capital or an increase in capital) which are deemed to be a variation or abrogation of the rights attached to that class and so will require the consent of the class. In that way, the scope for judicial determination of whether a variation or abrogation has occurred is reduced.

The courts will give effect to such provisions and will interpret them in the light of **14-53** their protective purpose. In *Re Northern Engineering Industries plc*[73] the articles stated that the rights of any class were to be deemed to be varied by the reduction of the capital paid up on those shares. The company proposed to reduce its capital by paying off its preference shares and cancelling them without obtaining the consent of the class. The company argued that the provision in the articles only applied to a 'reduction', i.e. something which involved a diminution or lessening from one number to a smaller number. It did not apply to a reduction to zero.

The Court of Appeal rejected this argument finding that the provision in the articles **14-54** must be construed in the light of its purpose, namely the protection of the shareholders of the class affected. It applied both where there was a piecemeal reduction of capital and where there was complete repayment of their investment. A reduction of capital without the consent of the class affected could not be confirmed.

Given that the expectation in future is that reductions of capital by private compa- **14-55** nies will not require court confirmation (the directors will proceed instead by way of a solvency statement: see CA 2006, s 641(1) and discussion at **20-66**) it becomes all the more important that those acquiring a class of shares should take care to: (1) specify the rights attached to the class, (2) provide a mechanism for the variation of those rights in the articles, and (3) identify matters of concern which are to be deemed to be variations so triggering that variation mechanism. Alternatively, depending on the circumstances, it may be advisable to look to entrench the rights in the articles (s 22).

D Share transfer and transmission

Introduction

Shares are personal property (CA 2006, s 541) and are transferable in the manner pro- **14-56** vided by the company's articles (s 544(1)), subject to the Stock Transfer Act 1963 which overrides any requirements in the articles to allow fully paid shares to be transferred

---

[73] [1994] 2 BCLC 704.

by a simplified process and to regulations[74] which allow for the electronic transfer of shares (CA 2006, s 544(2)).

14-57 A company may not register a transfer of shares unless a proper instrument of transfer has been delivered to the company (s 770(1)). A proper instrument of transfer for these purposes is an instrument appropriate or suitable for stamp duty purposes[75] and this restriction is imposed to facilitate the raising of taxation. The requirement as to a proper instrument of transfer is subject to exceptions where the transfer is an exempt transfer within the Stock Transfer Act 1982, or is in accordance with regulations dealing with uncertificated securities (CA 2006, s 770(1)).

A prima facie right to transfer shares

14-58 A shareholder has a prima facie right to transfer his shares and directors have no discretionary powers, independent of any powers given to them by the articles, to refuse to register a transfer.[76] Any restriction of this right to transfer must be clearly stated in the articles and the right to transfer is not to be cut down by uncertain language or doubtful implications.[77] If restrictions on transfer are laid down by the articles, they must be complied with. The directors have no power to authorise registration in circumstances where there has been a breach of the articles and any purported transfer in breach of the articles is defeasible at the suit of a member.[78]

Restrictions on the transfer of shares

14-59 In practice, it is customary for the articles of a private company (and private companies make up 99.6% of the register of companies) to impose restrictions on the transfer of shares.[79] These restrictions are usually justified on the basis that many such companies are small family concerns or quasi-partnership-type ventures where it is important to the existing members to retain control over the membership of the company. But it is not just a case of controlling the membership; as Arden LJ explained in *BWE International Ltd v Jones*,[80] there are two conflicting economic interests in this situation, that of the shareholder who wishes to transfer his shares and realise his investment and that of the other shareholders who may wish to prevent a transfer or take the shares themselves. It is unusual for public companies to impose any restrictions on transfer, while shares in listed public companies must be freely transferable.[81]

---

[74] See The Uncertificated Securities Regulations 2001, SI 2001/3755, as amended.

[75] *Nisbet v Shepherd* [1994] 1 BCLC 300.

[76] *Re Smith, Knight & Co, Weston's Case* (1868) 4 Ch App 20.

[77] *Re Smith & Fawcett Ltd* [1942] 1 All ER 542; *Stothers v William Steward (Holdings) Ltd* [1994] 2 BCLC 266, CA. See also *BWE International Ltd v Jones* [2004] 1 BCLC 406 at 413.

[78] *Hurst v Crampton Bros* [2003] 1 BCLC 304; *Tett v Phoenix Property and Investment Co Ltd* [1986] BCLC 149, CA. See also *Curtis v J J Curtis & Co* [1986] BCLC 86, NZCA.

[79] Until 1980 it was mandatory for private companies to include a restriction on the transfer of their shares in the articles: see CA 1948, s 28 repealed by CA 1980, Sch 4.

[80] [2004] 1 BCLC 406 at 413–14, CA.

[81] See Listing Rules LR 2.2.4R, subject to very limited exceptions which are irrelevant for our purposes.

A provision commonly included in the articles is one to the effect that the directors may, in their absolute discretion and without assigning any reason therefor, decline to register any transfer of any share, whether or not it is a fully paid share.[82] The CA 2006 modified that type of provision by requiring the company to give reasons for a refusal to register a transfer (s 771(1)) though this does not affect the right to refuse.

In addition to a discretion conferred on directors to refuse to register transfers, pre-emption provisions are commonly included to ensure that existing members have the opportunity to buy any shares that may be for sale before they are offered outside the company. For example, a member wishing to sell is often permitted to transfer his shares to an existing member without restriction, but where he seeks to transfer to an outsider, a pre-emption provision comes into effect. This provision normally requires the intending transferor to give notice to the company secretary or other nominated person who must notify the other members that there are shares available for purchase.[83] If the other members make an offer for the shares, the transferor may accept or reject their offer but, if he rejects it, he is precluded normally from proceeding with the transfer of the shares to an outsider. If the shares are not taken up by the other shareholders, the transferor is usually entitled at that stage to offer his shares to an outside purchaser, subject to the proviso that the directors may refuse to register a transfer in such circumstances.[84]   **14-60**

Triggering a pre-emption provision

The first step in the pre-emption process normally involves establishing that a shareholder wishes/desires/intends (depending on the wording of the relevant provision in the company's articles) to transfer his shares. An issue is whether such a pre-emption provision is triggered by dealings in the beneficial interests in the shares or whether it applies only when there is an attempt to transfer the legal title to the shares. The issue is important in practice for shareholders who do not wish to be obliged to offer their shares to the other shareholders must be careful not to deal with their shares in a way which inadvertently triggers the pre-emption mechanism.   **14-61**

This issue as to whether dealing in the beneficial interests suffices to trigger the pre-emption mechanism was considered in *Safeguard Industrial Investments Ltd v National Westminster Bank Ltd*[85] where the defendant bank, as the executor of a deceased shareholder, had been registered in respect of the deceased's holding. The bank held the shares as trustee for two beneficiaries to whom, for the moment at least,   **14-62**

---

[82] This provision was contained in the 1948 Table A, see CA 1948, Sch 1, Table A Part II, reg 3.

[83] Notice to the members of a pre-emption right having been triggered amounts to an option conferred on the other members to purchase the shares at the price determined by the articles—that option creates an equitable interest which prevails over the interest of a donee of the shares incorrectly registered as the holder of the shares: *Cottrell v King* [2004] 2 BCLC 413; *Tett v Phoenix Property and Investment Co Ltd* [1984] BCLC 599 at 619 revd on other grounds [1986] BCLC 149.

[84] These pre-emption provisions tend to be lengthy and complex and the courts sometimes have to interpret them purposefully to give them business efficacy: see *Pennington v Crampton* [2004] BCC 611; *Tett v Phoenix Property and Investment Co Ltd* [1986] BCLC 149, CA.

[85] [1982] 1 All ER 449, CA.

it did not propose to transfer the shares. The articles provided that any member who desired to transfer his shares (the proposing transferor) had to give notice to the company which would notify the existing members who could then purchase the shares.

14-63   One of the existing members who wished to acquire some of these shares argued that the bank's position (it could at any moment be required to transfer the shares to the beneficiaries) was such that it did fall within the pre-emption requirement and was under a duty to serve a transfer notice on the company so enabling the other shareholders to purchase the holding.

14-64   The Court of Appeal disagreed. 'Transfer' in the articles only embraces the transfer of the legal title and is inapt to apply to the transfer of beneficial interests. The mere fact that there was someone who could make an immediate demand for the transfer of the shares did not make the existing member (the bank in this case) a proposing transferor for these purposes.

14-65   The court distinguished the position in *Safeguard* from that which had arisen in an earlier case, *Lyle & Scott Ltd v Scott's Trustees*.[86] In that case, a number of shareholders entered into an agreement with a third party under which they received £3 per share and bound themselves, inter alia, to vote as he desired so putting him as fully in control of the company as they could without actually presenting transfers for registration. It was alleged that they were 'desirous of transferring' (which was the trigger in this case on the wording of the particular articles) and so the pre-emption provision in the articles came into effect.

14-66   In this instance, the House of Lords agreed. Having agreed to sell their shares and having received the purchase price, the vendors held the shares as trustees for the purchasers. They were bound to do everything to perfect the title of the purchaser. It was impossible that they could have done as they did unless they desired to transfer their shares, so triggering the mechanism in the articles.[87]

14-67   Oliver LJ in *Safeguard* thought the two cases were clearly distinguishable. In *Lyle & Scott Ltd* the parties had entered into an unconditional agreement to sell which obliged the shareholders to transfer when requested on payment of the price, which price had been paid and which agreement remained uncancelled and unrepudiated at the time of the hearing. This position, in his opinion, was a thousand miles away from the position in *Safeguard*.[88] The fact that the bank in *Safeguard* was under a duty to transfer the shares on request did not mean that it had the necessary desire to transfer for the purpose of the articles.[89]

---

[86] [1959] 2 All ER 661.

[87] [1959] 2 All ER 661 at 665, HL. See also *Re Macro (Ipswich) Ltd* [1994] 2 BCLC 354 where two shareholders had entered into a sale agreement in favour of a third and had executed declarations of trusts of the shares. They had delivered the share certificates and forms of transfer duly executed in blank and had agreed as to the receipt of dividends and the exercise of voting rights. The court found they had done more than deal in the beneficial interests and nothing remained to be done by them with the result that they did desire to sell their shares and had triggered the pre-emption provision in the articles requiring them to offer the shares to all the existing members.

[88] [1982] 1 All ER 449 at 454, CA.   [89] See also *Pennington v Crampton* [2004] BCC 611.

Another example of dealing with beneficial interests in a way which does not trigger **14-68** the pre-emption mechanism can be found in *Theakston v London Trust plc*.[90] In theory the transfer under scrutiny was from one member of the company (London Trust) to another (Paul) so avoiding the pre-emption provision contained in the articles. However, the transfer was being financed by an outsider, Matthew Brown (MB). MB also paid the stamp duty due and gave Paul certain tax indemnities. The agreement provided that Paul would: (1) endeavour to have the shares registered in MB's name; (2) charge the shares in favour of MB; (3) vote the shares as directed by MB; (4) account to MB with respect to any distributions received in connection with the shares; (5) accept any offer for the shares as and when made by MB and endeavour to have MB registered as the owner of the shares; and (6) not accept any other offer for any shares in the company.

The question was whether the effect of this agreement was such that the transfer from **14-69** London Trust to Paul was really a transfer to MB (an outsider) so triggering the pre-emption provisions.

Harman J accepted as a fact that London Trust had sold its shares to Paul. He in turn **14-70** had charged the shares to MB. In other words, in keeping with the *Safeguard* position, the court looked to see what had happened to the legal title to the shares. Moving on from that conclusion, the next suggestion was that, given the relationship between Paul and MB, Paul should be regarded as proposing to transfer his shares to MB so triggering the mechanism at this second stage. Having reviewed *Lyle* and *Safeguard*, Harman J thought the agreement did not make Paul a person who proposed to transfer the shares. Some further steps would need to be taken under the agreement before the question of triggering the mechanism could arise and any steps taken would have to be examined to see whether they were sufficiently unequivocal to indicate that he was then proposing to transfer.[91]

The effect of these decisions, as Lord Sorn anticipated in *Lyle & Scott Ltd v Scott's* **14-71** *Trustees*,[92] is to leave open the obvious manoeuvre of dealing in the beneficial interest thus defeating the draftsman's attempt to ensure that control of the company is retained by the existing shareholders.[93]

A recent illustration of these manoeuvrings can be seen in *Re Sedgefield Steeplechase* **14-72** *Co (1927) Ltd, Scotto v Petch*.[94] The company's articles contained rights of pre-emption

---

[90] [1984] BCLC 390.

[91] [1984] BCLC 390 at 401. See also *Re a company (No 005685 of 1988), ex p Schwarcz (No 2)* [1989] BCLC 427 where a conditional agreement to sell subject to several events occurring (which were not within the control of either party to the agreement) did not constitute a present and unequivocal desire to transfer or dispose of shares.

[92] See 1958 SC 230 at 250.

[93] As Vinelott J stressed at first instance in *Safeguard*, this gap in the articles cannot be filled by construction and if the parties wish to preclude dealing in the beneficial interests in this way then they must do so expressly: see [1980] 3 All ER 849 at 860. Equally, the court could conclude that the parties' dealings, as in *Lyle*, went further than dealings in the beneficial interests and are within the restriction on transfer.

[94] [2000] 2 BCLC 211, Ch D, aff'd [2001] BCC 889, CA. See also *Re Claygreen Ltd, Romer-Ormiston v Claygreen Ltd* [2006] 1 BCLC 715.

which required any member who 'intends to transfer shares' to give notice of his intention in writing to the board which could then offer the shares to the other members.

14-73   A bidder for the company entered into agreements with shareholders holding approximately 80% of the shares which effected the sale of the beneficial ownership of their shares to the bidder. A shareholder holding the remaining shares alleged that the effect of the agreements was that those shareholders had indicated an intention to transfer their shares and therefore they were obliged to give notice to the company so that their shares might be offered to the other shareholder. The agreements with the bidder required the shareholders to act in accordance with any directions given by the bidder (but expressly stated that this was subject to an obligation not to act so as to contravene any subsisting pre-emption rights) and to use their best endeavours to requisition a meeting to pass a resolution to delete the pre-emption provision in the articles.

14-74   Lord Hoffmann, sitting as an additional judge in the Chancery Division, held that the obligation to serve a transfer notice under the articles did not attach until the shareholder had entered into arrangements such as a sale or grant of an option which placed him under a contractual obligation to execute and deliver a transfer in violation of the rights of pre-emption. The agreements with the bidder were not of this nature and it followed that the shareholders did not intend to transfer their shares within the meaning of the pre-emption provision and were not bound to give notice to the board.

14-75   The Court of Appeal reached the same conclusion as Lord Hoffmann but on a narrower point of interpretation of the documentation in the case. Here Nourse LJ stressed that in his view these issues are very much matters of interpretation of particular articles and documentation and on which, he considered, the authorities were of little guidance.[95] He was particularly dismissive of the value of the decision in *Lyle & Scott Ltd v Scott's Trustees*[96] which Lord Hoffmann had thought provided important guidance in drawing attention to 'the danger that incautious arrangements between a proposed bidder and the holders of shares subject to rights of pre-emption could trigger an enforceable obligation to give a notice under the articles before the parties wished to do so'.[97] This was the position in *Hurst v Crampton*[98] which involved a gift rather than a sale, but the result was the same. A gift by a member to another person triggered a pre-emption provision which applied on any 'transfer' since 'transfer' must be construed as any parting with the shares whether by sale or by gift. As the donor had completed the gift, there was a transfer for these purposes, even though the donee made no attempt to have his name entered on the register of members. The result was to require the shares to be offered to the existing members.

14-76   Certainly, Nourse LJ is correct that these decisions depend very much on the construction and effect of the particular articles of association which vary significantly from company to company. Nevertheless, the authorities from *Lyle & Scott Ltd* onwards do establish that, in the absence of express provision to the contrary, pre-emption

---

[95] See [2001] BCC 889 at 901. See the comments of Hale LJ as to the obvious artificiality of the arrangements in this case (at 904).

[96] [1959] 2 All ER 661.   [97] See [2000] 2 BCLC 211 at 218.   [98] [2003] 1 BCLC 304.

provisions are triggered only by dealings in the legal interests in the shares. Obviously, whether the transferor has taken unequivocal steps to transfer or dispose of that legal interest in his shares is a matter which can only be determined on the facts of the particular case.

Where a shareholder triggers a pre-emption mechanism, the next requirement is to notify the company (typically through the company secretary where the company has a secretary) indicating the number of shares which the member wishes to transfer and sometimes the price at which he wishes to sell.[99] The company secretary in turn notifies those members who are entitled under the pre-emption provision to make an offer to purchase the shares in question. The articles may also determine the price to be paid for the shares and frequently the price is stated to be the fair value as certified by the company's auditor acting as an expert whose opinion is binding and conclusive.   **14-77**

The valuation issue is one which frequently gives rise to problems as the transferor may be dissatisfied with the figure determined by the valuer. The courts will not permit challenges to such valuations (for the parties have agreed to be bound by the expert opinion) save in the exceptional circumstance where the valuer has departed from his instructions in a material respect.[100] Where the appointment of the valuer is in breach of the terms of the articles (for example, because he lacks the independence required by the articles), however, there may be scope for a petition alleging unfairly prejudicial conduct under CA 2006, s 994.[101] Additionally, where an error has occurred, it may be possible for a disaffected party to bring a claim for negligence against a valuer.[102]   **14-78**

Refusal to register a transfer of shares

It is frequently the case that, having gone through the various stages outlined above (i.e. an existing shareholder has found an internal or external transferee whether for value or as a gift), the transfer of the shares is then blocked by a refusal by the directors to register the transfer and enter the name of the transferee on the company's register of members. The significance of entry on the register of members has been noted above, at **14-1**, as has the fact that it is common practice for private companies to give the directors discretionary powers to refuse to register any transfer, either in terms of an absolute discretion or on more limited grounds, see **14-59**.   **14-79**

---

[99] Notification operates as an invitation to treat (subject to any provision in the articles) and it is for would-be purchasers to make an offer to purchase, leaving the transferor to decide whether to accept: *Tett v Phoenix Property and Investment Co Ltd* [1986] BCLC 149, CA. If the transferor is required to specify the price of the shares, it is not sufficient to put forward a formula to determine the price, the price must be stated in detail, wholly and completely: *BWE International Ltd v Jones* [2004] 1 BCLC 406.

[100] *Jones v Sherwood Computer Services plc* [1992] 2 All ER 170; see also *Macro v Thompson* [1997] 1 BCLC 626; any departure from instructions is material unless it can truly be characterised as trivial or de minimis in the sense of it being obvious that it could make no possible difference to either party: *Veba Oil Supply & Trading Gmbh v Petrotrade Inc* [2002] 1 All ER 703, CA.

[101] See *Re Benfield Greig Group plc, Nugent v Benfield Greig Group plc* [2002] 1 BCLC 65, CA.

[102] See *Killick v PricewaterhouseCoopers* [2001] 1 BCLC 65.

14-80   The Companies Act 2006, Part 10 with its statutory statement of directors' duties brings into starker relief, however, that a director must exercise his powers (including his power to refuse to register a transfer) for the purposes for which they are conferred (s 171) and must act in the way he considers, in good faith, would be most likely to promote the success of the company for the benefit of the members as a whole, having regard, inter alia, to the need to act fairly as between the members (s 172(1)). These duties, coupled with the requirement now to give reasons for any refusal to register a transfer (s 771(1)), and bearing in mind that a shareholder may petition for relief under s 994 when the company's affairs are being conducted in an unfairly prejudicial manner, mean that these powers are not as absolute as they may appear in the articles. In determining the purpose for which the power to refuse a transfer is conferred, it is worth bearing in mind the conflicting economic interests identified by Arden LJ in *BWE International Ltd v Jones*.[103] On the one hand, there is the interest of a shareholder in realising his investment and, on the other hand, the interest of the remaining shareholders in preventing a transfer or taking the shares themselves. A power granted to the directors to refuse to register a transfer has to be considered in the context of those sorts of commercial considerations and bearing in mind, as Arden LJ noted, that a restriction on transfer is one of the indicia of a quasi-partnership (as to which, see **17-62**).

Absolute discretion to refuse registration

14-81   With regard to an absolute discretion, a common provision is one which states that the directors may, in their absolute discretion, decline to register any transfer of any share. The leading authority is *Re Smith & Fawcett Ltd*[104] where the Court of Appeal accepted that where the articles contain a provision such as this, drafted in the widest possible terms, there is no limitation on the exercise by directors of that power other than the standard requirement that, as a fiduciary power, it must be exercised bona fide in what the directors consider—and not what a court may consider—to be in the interests of the company, and not for any collateral purpose.[105] In other words, the power to refuse to register may be exercised subject to the directors' fiduciary duties as now expressed in CA 2006, ss 171 and 172. An article in this form[106] gives the directors considerable discretion to take into account any matter which they consider (not what the court considers) most likely to promote the success of the company for the benefit of the members as a whole, but arguably the distinct obligation in s 171 to exercise powers for the purposes for which they are conferred gives a more objective element to their obligations in this regard. Given the judicial acknowledgement of the importance of these provisions in private companies, as exemplified by the Court of Appeal in *Re Smith & Fawcett*,[107] the courts are likely to be still quite generous in the amount

---

[103] [2004] 1 BCLC 406 at 413–14, CA.   [104] [1942] 1 All ER 542.

[105] [1942] 1 All ER 542 at 543. See *Re Bell Brothers, ex p Hodgson* (1891) 7 TLR 689; *Re Coalport China Co* [1895] 2 Ch 404; also *Popely v Planarrive Ltd* [1997] 1 BCLC 8.

[106] The Companies (Model Articles) Regulations 2008, SI 2008/3229, reg 2, Sch 1, art 26(5), (Ltd) provides simply that 'the directors may refuse to register a transfer of a share…'.

[107] [1942] 1 All ER 542.

of leeway which they give directors exercising an absolute power of this nature, in the absence of evidence of bad faith.

It may be easier to find evidence of bad faith (or at least material which might be relevant to a petition alleging unfairly prejudicial conduct) because of the obligation now for the company to give reasons for a refusal to register a transfer (CA 2006, s 771(1)).[108] It remains to be seen whether this will be a significant change or whether a standard formula of words emerges which is less than illuminating. The transferee can ask for further information as to the reasons for the refusal though the company is not required to hand over board minutes (s 772(1)(b)). On the other hand, even some evidence as to the reasons for the refusal may help the minority, perhaps in the context of an unfairly prejudicial petition under s 994. Directors are presumed to have acted in good faith[109] and the onus of proof is on those challenging their decision.[110]   **14-82**

A limited power to refuse registration

The directors' power to refuse to register may be a more limited power and such provisions vary greatly from company to company. For example, the articles may provide that the directors may refuse to register any transfer: (1) where the company has a lien on the shares; (2) where it is not proved to their satisfaction that the proposed transferee is a responsible person; (3) where the directors are of the opinion that the proposed transferee is not a desirable person to admit to membership.[111]   **14-83**

In *Re Bede Steam Shipping Co*[112] the articles provided that the directors might decline to register a transfer of any shares if, in their opinion, it was contrary to the interests of the company that the proposed transferee should be a member thereof. The directors admitted that no inquiry had been made as to the fitness of the transferees. The transfers in question had been rejected because a majority of the board objected to the transferor disposing of single shares or small lots of shares to individuals with a view to increasing the number of shareholders who would support him. The Court of Appeal found that the articles required the directors to focus on the qualities of the transferee and identify reasons why he was unsuitable. The particular objections which the directors had focused on were more concerned with the motives and attitudes of the transferor. These were not grounds provided for by the articles and so the transferees were entitled to be registered.   **14-84**

---

[108] Reversing the long standing common law position that the directors could not be required to give reasons: *Re Gresham Life Assurance Society, ex p Penney* (1872) 8 Ch App 446.

[109] See *Tett v Phoenix Property and Investment Co Ltd* [1984] BCLC 599 at 621.

[110] See *Charles Forte Investments Ltd v Amanda* [1963] 2 All ER 940; *Re Coalport China Co* [1895] 2 Ch 404; *Popely v Planarrive Ltd* [1997] 1 BCLC 8 at 16; *Village Cay Marina Ltd v Acland* [1998] 2 BCLC 327, PC.

[111] See *Re Coalport China Co* [1895] 2 Ch 404. Other examples can be found in *Re Gresham Life Assurance Society, ex p Penney* (1872) 8 Ch App 446; *Berry and Stewart v Tottenham Hotspur Football & Athletic Co* [1935] Ch 718.

[112] [1917] 1 Ch 123. See also *Re Bell Brothers, ex p Hodgson* (1891) 7 TLR 689; *Re The Ceylon Land & Produce Co, ex p Anderson* (1891) 7 TLR 692.

Time-limits

14-85 Registration may be secured as a result of the failure of the directors to exercise their discretion to refuse registration within the requisite time period. The directors must register the transfer, or decide to refuse (and notify the transferee of the refusal and give reasons for the refusal): in either case they must act as soon as practicable and, in any event, within two months of the transfer being lodged with the company (CA 2006, s 771(1)). Once the two-month period has elapsed, the directors are no longer able to exercise their discretion[113] and an application can be made under s 125 to have the register rectified by the inclusion of the name of the transferee.

Position as between the vendor and purchaser when registration refused

14-86 Where the directors have correctly exercised their discretion so making the decision to refuse registration unimpeachable, the vendor and the purchaser of the shares are left in the position that they cannot now complete the transaction by having the purchaser registered. The position on a sale of shares is that the equitable title to the shares passes to the purchaser once the contract is made and the legal title passes on completion and registration by the company.[114] The vendor provides the purchaser with a duly signed transfer form and the share certificates for submission to the company for registration.[115] Unless the contract so provides, the vendor does not promise to secure registration and, if the directors do refuse to register the transfer, the vendor is not liable in damages for breach although he will hold the shares as bare trustee for the purchaser.[116] Where the parties are agreeable to such an outcome, they can negate the effect of the directors' refusal to register.

Transmission of shares

14-87 Transmission arises by operation of law on the death or bankruptcy of a member. On the death of a shareholder, the shares are transmitted to his personal representative and the production of the grant of probate of the will or letters of administration of the estate or confirmation as executor of a deceased person must be accepted by the company as sufficient evidence of the grant (CA 2006, s 774). In the case of bankruptcy,

---

[113] This outcome is not required by CA 2006, s 771 which simply imposes a fine for default (s 771(3)) but it was accepted in *Re Swaledale Cleaners Ltd* [1968] 3 All ER 619 that this can be the only consequence of requiring the power to be exercised within two months; also *Re Inverdeck Ltd* [1998] 2 BCLC 242. Where the directors take a decision to refuse to register a transfer, but fail to notify the transferee of the refusal, the failure to notify (while it attracts a fine) does not nullify the decision: *Popely v Planarrive Ltd* [1997] 1 BCLC 8.

[114] *Societe Generale de Paris v Walker* (1885) 11 App Cas 20; see also *Roots v Williamson* (1888) 38 Ch D 485; *Ireland v Hart* [1902] 1 Ch 522.

[115] In the case of a gift of shares which is typically perfected by the delivery of the share transfer form and the relevant certificates, an equitable assignment may take place though there is no delivery of a stock transfer form: see *Pennington v Waine* [2002] 2 BCLC 448; *Re Rose* [1949] Ch 78; *Re Rose, Rose v IRC* [1952] 1 All ER 1217.

[116] *Re Rose, Rose v IRC* [1952] 1 All ER 1217. As to the position of the vendor under an uncompleted contract for the sale of shares, see *Musselwhite v Musselwhite & Son Ltd* [1962] 1 All ER 201; *JRRT (Investments) Ltd v Haycraft* [1993] BCLC 401; *Michaels v Harley House (Marylebone) Ltd* [1999] 1 BCLC 670, CA.

the beneficial interest in the shares vests in the trustee in bankruptcy whose position is similar to that of the personal representative.

The position on transmission is generally governed by the articles and the model art-   **14-88**
icles provide that a person becoming entitled to a share in consequence of death or bankruptcy (a transmittee) may choose either to become a holder of the share or to have someone else registered as the transferee.[117] Usually, the election by the personal representative or trustee in bankruptcy to be registered or to have someone else registered has the effect of triggering any pre-emption provisions which may exist and will be subject to any discretion vested in the directors to refuse to register any transfer.

Often the articles make detailed provision for the procedures which are to apply on the   **14-89**
death of a shareholder. For example, the articles may allow for an executor, a widow, widower or children of a deceased shareholder or other defined category of relative to be registered automatically without triggering a pre-emption requirement.[118] Equally, the articles may provide not just that the death of a member triggers a pre-emption requirement in the articles but that the person becoming entitled to the shares of the deceased member is deemed to have given a notice to the other shareholders offering the shares for sale so setting in motion the machinery for sale.[119]

E The register of members

Status and contents of the register of members

Every company must maintain a register of members (CA 2006, s 113) and entry on the   **14-90**
register is essential to membership in all cases save that of subscribers to the memorandum (s 112).[120] A company registered in England and Wales is not concerned with trusts over its shares and no notice of any trust, expressed, implied or constructive, is to be entered on the register or be receivable by the registrar.[121] The register is prima facie but not conclusive[122] evidence of any matters directed or authorised by the Companies Act to be inserted in it (s 127).

[117] See The Companies (Model Articles) Regulations 2008, SI 2008/3229, reg 2, Sch 1, art 27(2) (Ltd), reg 4, Sch 3, art 66(2) (Plc). An instrument of transfer of a share of a deceased member may be made by his personal representative (though not himself a member) and it is as effective as if he had been a member at the time of execution of the instrument: CA 2006, s 773. See also *Scott v Frank F Scott (London) Ltd* [1940] Ch 794.

[118] See, for example, the provisions at issue in *Stothers v William Steward (Holdings) Ltd* [1994] 2 BCLC 266. If an executor can be registered without triggering a pre-emption requirement arising on a transfer, the executor and successors in title can continue to hold the shares after completion of the administration also without triggering the pre-emption provision: see *Pennington v Crampton* [2004] BCC 611.

[119] See, for example, the provisions at issue in *Re Benfield Greig Group plc, Nugent v Benfield Greig Group plc* [2000] 2 BCLC 488 at 497.

[120] If the company holds shares as treasury shares (see **20-38**), the company must be entered in the register as the member holding those shares: CA 2006, s 124(2).

[121] CA 2006, s 126; *Societe Generale de Paris v Walker* (1885) 11 App Cas 20.

[122] See *Reese River Silver Mining Co v Smith* (1869) LR 4 HL 64 at 80, per Lord Cairns; also *Re Briton Medical and General Life Association* (1888) 39 Ch D 61 at 72, per Stirling J.

14-91   The register must include details of the names and addresses (which need not be residential addresses) of the members of the company (s 113(2)). The register of members must disclose the date of entry on the register as a member and the date of ceasing to be a member (s 113(2)), dates which affect voting and dividend rights and the right to participate in corporate actions such as a rights issue. If the number of members of a limited company falls to one or increases from one to two or more members, the register of members must include a statement that the company has only one member, or has ceased to have only one member, as the case may be, and must give the dates of these occurrences (s 123).

14-92   The register of members must be available for inspection at the registered office or other place specified by the regulations[123] and the registrar of companies must be notified of that place (s 114). Larger public companies do not maintain their own registers, but use professional registrar services instead, hence the need to permit the register to be inspected other than at the registered office. In an age of computerised records, the physical location of the register becomes less important, provided it is not outside the country of registration.

14-93   The register of members helps creditors and investors identify those behind the company which may affect any decision to invest or provide credit. The register of members is also constantly monitored by public companies in order to detect bidders building up a stake with which to launch a takeover bid.

Inspection of the register

14-94   Traditionally, the register of members has been open to inspection. This general principle of access is maintained by CA 2006, s 116 but it is subject now to a 'proper purpose' requirement[124] which is one of the more controversial changes effected by the CA 2006.

14-95   The background lies in concerns raised by the Company Law Review about improper use of the statutory rights to access and copy the register by commercial organisations which then use the register for mail shots to the annoyance of the company and its members.[125] Subsequently concerns emerged as to access to the register by animal rights protesters who use the information to harass shareholders, most notably in the case of Huntingdon Life Sciences which has been the subject of a prolonged campaign, much of it involving acts of criminal assault and damage.[126] As the Companies Bill progressed through Parliament, an example of this harassment arose when shareholders in the listed pharmaceutical company, GlaxoSmithKline, received letters from animal

---

[123] See CA 2006, s 1136 and see SI 2008/3006.

[124] As is the register of debentures, see CA 2006, ss 743–747.

[125] Company Law Review, *Final Report*, vol I (2001), para 11.44; *Completing the Structure* (2000), paras 8.11–8.12; *Developing the Framework* (2000), paras 10.15–10.22.

[126] For an account of the campaign waged against the company which has now resulted in seven animal rights activists being convicted of conspiracy to blackmail, see 'Activists in live testing trial deny blackmail' *Financial Times*, 6 October 2008; 'Tough sentences for animal rights extemists' *Financial Times*, 22 January 2009.

rights activists threatening them unless they sold their shares in the company.[127] The Government therefore decided to amend the provisions regarding access to the register of members.

The position now is that any person seeking to exercise the right either to inspect the register or to obtain a copy thereof or a copy of any part of the register must make a request to the company to that effect (CA 2006, s 116(3)). The request must: **14-96**

(1) identify the name and address of the individual making the request or the name and address of the individual responsible for making a request on behalf of an organisation;

(2) specify the purpose for which the information is to be used;

(3) indicate whether the information is to be disclosed to any other person; if so, full details must be given of that other person and the purpose for which the information is to be used by that person (s 116(4)).

It is an offence for a person knowingly or recklessly in making a request to include a statement which is misleading, false or deceptive in a material particular (s 119(1)). It is also an offence for a person in possession of information following a request to inspect the register to disclose the information obtained to another person knowing or having reason to suspect that that person may use the information for a purpose which is not a proper purpose (s 119(2)).   **14-97**

The company has five working days either to comply with the request or to apply to the court for an order that the company need not comply with the request. If following an application the court does not so order, the company must immediately comply with the request to inspect the register (s 117(5)). It is an offence for the company to fail to do so in the absence of a court order allowing it to refuse and the court can compel disclosure if need be (s 118(3)).[128] If the court is satisfied that the inspection is not for a proper purpose, it can direct the company not to comply with the request and can extend the order to preclude compliance with similar requests (s 117(4)) so ensuring that a company cannot be bombarded with like requests and forced to go to court every time to get an order justifying non-compliance. In addition, where the court concludes that the purpose is not a proper purpose, the court can order that the company's costs of the application be paid in whole or in part by the person who made the inspection request, even if he is not party to the application to the court (s 117(3)(b)).   **14-98**

Until some case-law develops as to what the courts consider to be a proper purpose for these purposes (there being no statutory guidance),[129] this potential liability in costs may deter those seeking to inspect the register. The Institute of Chartered Secretaries   **14-99**

---

[127] See 'Animal rights extremists send threatening letter to individual GSK investors' *Financial Times*, 9 May 2006.

[128] The court's power to compel inspection is discretionary, see *Pelling v Families Need Fathers Ltd* [2002] 1 BCLC 645.

[129] In the Parliamentary debates, the Government indicated that it was content for this matter to be developed by the courts on a case-by-case basis.

and Administrators (ICSA) has produced guidance on 'proper purpose' which essentially tries to draw a line at communications with shareholders in their capacity as such for purposes linked to the management of the company, their shareholdings or the exercise of related rights. It would consider communications which are unlawful, which threaten or harass, cold-calling share offers and commercial mailings to be for an 'improper purpose'. But it is arguable that commercial mailings linked to the company's activities are not 'improper' even if, as the Company Law Review noted, they are irritating to many of the recipients. Equally, it is not clear that animal rights extremists will be prevented from reaching shareholders by these restrictions. An animal rights activist may still buy a small number of shares in company X involved in the pharmaceutical industry and then seek access to the register in order to write to all the shareholders urging them to persuade the management to change strategy/direction/operating methods or to abandon certain products. This would seem a perfectly proper purpose for access, being linked to the operations of the company and its management, even if it would probably still unnerve the shareholders.

14-100   It is regrettable that the actions of a small number of animal rights protesters have resulted in legislation which so restricts access to the register of members. While the actions of such protesters undoubtedly require a legal response, the appropriate response (and one which the authorities are now pursuing) is the criminal prosecution of those threatening and harassing shareholders and directors.[130] The problem had been addressed also by allowing directors and others at risk to obtain confidentiality orders removing their personal information from the public register. Instead the Government has chosen to step back from the general transparency which has hitherto characterised English company law, encouraged by the small business lobby which saw an opportunity to use the debate on access generated by the animal rights issue affecting a small number of companies to reduce the information disclosed by all companies.

14-101   It is worth noting here that, in addition to the information on the members contained in the company's register of members, all companies are required to deliver an annual return to the registrar of companies (CA 2006, s 854) giving the address of the company's registered office, the prescribed particulars of the directors and the company secretary (if there is one), identifying the type of company and its business activities (s 855), providing information about its share capital (s 856) and including a list of the members. A full list of members is required in the first annual return following incorporation and then every third year,[131] but addresses are not required other than in respect of traded companies and then only service addresses in respect of members holding more than 5% of the issued share capital (which is a very high threshold in a traded company).[132] The Company Law Review had considered reducing this

---

[130] As is now happening: see above n 126.

[131] In the intervening years the company need only provide information on those who become members, or cease to be members, or any share transfers: CA 2006, s 856(3), (5). Larger companies prefer to provide a full list of members every year rather than attempt to track changes in the intervening two years.

[132] See CA 2006, ss 856A, 856B and The Companies Act 2006 (Annual Return and Service Addresses) Regulations 2008, SI 2008/3000, regs 4, 12.

requirement for an annual return, particularly with respect to small private companies, but after consideration concluded that it is in the public interest to retain this requirement, thus ensuring that a public record is available as well as the company's register of members.[133] In many instances, existing and potential investors and creditors may prefer to inspect the public record discreetly rather than approach the company to inspect the register of members, but the public record may not be as up to date as it should be which is why access to the company register may well be desirable.

Rectification of the register of members

The details in the register of members can be challenged, for instance, on the grounds **14-102** of mistake, but any shareholder wishing to challenge an entry must act promptly.[134] Rectification of the register is governed by CA 2006, s 125 which provides that if:[135]

'(a) the name of any person is, without sufficient cause, entered in or omitted from the company's register of members; or

(b) default is made, or unnecessary delay takes place in entering on the register the fact of any person having ceased to be a member;

the person aggrieved, or any member of the company, or the company may apply to the court for rectification of the register.'

The court has a discretion to refuse the application or to order rectification and the **14-103** payment by the company of any damages sustained by any party aggrieved (s 125(2)). There is no necessity to show any wrongdoing by the company and any question of omission by error or entry by error can be raised.

The power to rectify has been exercised where there was no valid allotment of shares;[136] **14-104** or the allotment was irregular;[137] or where a transfer of shares was improperly registered or registration was refused.[138]

---

[133] See Company Law Review, *Final Report*, vol 1 (2001), para 11.45; *Completing the Structure* (2000), para 8.15; *Developing the Framework* (2000), paras 10.45–10.52.

[134] *Re Scottish Petroleum Co* (1883) 23 Ch D 413 at 434, CA.

[135] The directors of a company may rectify the register of members without any application to the court if there is no dispute about the matter and the circumstances are such that the court would order rectification: *Reese River Silver Mining Co v Smith* (1869) LR 4 HL 64 at 74; *Hartley's Case* (1875) 10 Ch App 157; *First National Reinsurance Co Ltd v Greenfield* [1921] 2 KB 260 at 279; but ordinarily the protection of the court's order is essential to any rectification by the removal of the name of a registered holder of shares: *Re Derham and Allen Ltd* [1946] Ch 31 at 36.

[136] See *Re Homer District Consolidated Gold Mines, ex p Smith* (1888) 39 Ch D 546 at 551; *Re Portuguese Consolidated Copper Mines Ltd* (1889) 42 Ch D 160, CA.

[137] See *Re Homer District Consolidated Gold Mines, ex p Smith* (1888) 39 Ch D 546; *Re Cleveland Trust plc* [1991] BCLC 424 (register rectified by deletion of bonus shares after bonus issue mistakenly made); *Re Thundercrest Ltd* [1995] 1 BCLC 117 (register rectified by cancellation of improper allotment to two members).

[138] See *Re Copal Varnish Co Ltd* [1917] 2 Ch 349; *Welch v Bank of England* [1955] 1 All ER 811 (restoration of status quo after forged transfers); *International Credit and Investment Co (Overseas) Ltd v Adham* [1994] 1 BCLC 66 (restoration of status quo: no proper share transfers were executed merely entries made in share register purporting to deprive the true owner of his entire holding); *Re New Cedos Engineering Co Ltd* [1994] 1 BCLC 797 (on their true construction, a right to be registered existed under the articles); *Stothers v William*

14-105   The nature of the jurisdiction to rectify the register was considered in *Re Piccadilly Radio plc*.[139] In this instance, shares in a radio company were transferred without obtaining the consent of the Independent Broadcasting Authority (IBA) as required by the articles of association. Other shareholders in the company, with a view to preventing certain proposals being agreed to at a general meeting, sought rectification of the share register by deleting the names of the transferees and restoring the name of the original transferor. Millett J, despite finding that there had been a breach of the articles, refused rectification. In his opinion, the statutory procedure provided a discretionary remedy and the court must consider the circumstances in which and the purpose for which the relief was sought. The circumstances here did not warrant rectification for a number of reasons. The applicants had no interest in the shares and were not seeking to have their own names restored to the register. They were seeking to disenfranchise opposition to certain proposals to be put to the general meeting and had seized on a breach of an article of which the IBA itself did not complain. Moreover, the transferor did not seek rectification and the company itself did not support the application.

Steward (Holdings) Ltd [1994] 2 BCLC 266 (directors purported to exercise discretion to refuse registration which power, on the true construction of the articles, they did not possess).

[139] [1989] BCLC 683.

15

Decision-making and company meetings

A Introduction

As discussed in Chapter 8, the typical division of power within a company is that **15-1** the power to manage the company is vested in the board of directors with very limited powers retained by the shareholders: see **8-5**. Those powers include statutory rights, such as the right to alter the articles (CA 2006, s 21), or to increase or reduce the share capital,[1] and other powers, such as the power to appoint the directors, customarily given to the general meeting by the articles.[2] In some instances, the statute requires shareholder approval of various transactions, such as any purchase of the company's own shares[3] or transactions where directors have an acute conflict of interest.[4] Previously, the forum for the shareholders to exercise such powers as they possess was the general meeting of the company and the mechanism was by resolutions of the shareholders passed at such meetings. The Companies Act 1985 therefore provided a basic framework for meetings while allowing matters of detail to be determined by the company's articles.

For private companies, given the small numbers of shareholders involved, it is accepted **15-2** now that a formal general meeting is not a significant or appropriate forum for most decision-making. Instead, it should be possible for shareholders in such companies to reach decisions in any manner which is appropriate to their circumstances. In keeping with the 'think small first' philosophy (see **2-7**), the CA 2006 therefore provides that a resolution of the members of a private company may be passed as a written resolution or at a meeting (s 281(1)) and the underlying expectation is that the members will act through written resolutions and meetings will be the exception.[5]

---

[1] See CA 2006, ss 617–619 (increasing share capital) and s 641 (reduction of share capital).

[2] The Companies (Model Articles) Regulations 2008, SI 2008/3229, reg 2, Sch 1, arts 17–18 (Ltd); reg 4, Sch 3, arts 20–22 (Plc).

[3] CA 2006, ss 690–701.

[4] For example, substantial property transactions governed by CA 2006, s 190.

[5] For single member companies, details of decisions which have effect as if agreed to by the company in general meeting (for example, where the statute requires a shareholder resolution on some matter, such as a reduction of capital: CA 2006, s 641) must be provided to the company so as to ensure there is a record of the decision and it can be seen that there is compliance with the statutory requirements: CA 2006, s 357.

15-3   For public companies, the scheme is quite different. In a public company, decisions must be made at a meeting of the members (CA 2006, s 281(2)) and the CA 2006 precludes public companies from using written resolutions.[6] Moreover public companies must hold an annual general meeting within six months of the financial year end (s 336(1)). For publicly traded companies, this annual general meeting of shareholders is intended to provide an opportunity for the shareholders not only to take decisions but to hold the directors to account for their stewardship of the company. Too often, the reality is that the shareholders are a remote dispersed group with individually little influence and collectively lacking a unified voice on matters of substance. The emphasis in recent years therefore has been on trying to ensure that the general meeting does act as an effective counterbalance to the board and considerable attention is now paid to this issue in the interests of good corporate governance, see **5-44**.

15-4   As discussed previously, shareholders in traded companies range from individual shareholders with a few hundred shares to institutional shareholders with millions of shares and it is not unusual to find that 80% of the company's shareholders are individuals but they hold only 20% of the shares (and the votes attached) while 20% of the shareholders are institutions holding 80% of the shares and the votes. The effectiveness of shareholder control through the general meeting to a large extent will be determined therefore by the willingness of the institutional investors (typically insurance companies and pension funds) to exercise their voting power: see the discussion of these corporate governance issues at **5-48**. In this chapter, we look at the mechanisms for meetings. If the general meeting is to assume its intended role as an important component of our corporate governance structures, the legal requirements must be designed to enhance its effectiveness, to ensure that shareholders are heard and to facilitate all shareholders, whether individual or institutional, in the exercise of their voting power. Many of these issues were addressed in detail by the Company Law Review which essentially concluded in favour of incremental reform of company meeting procedures rather than wholesale changes.[7] The Shareholder Rights Directive (which must be implemented by 3 August 2009) also focuses on improving the mechanisms of participation, especially cross-border participation, so as to facilitate and encourage shareholder engagement in traded companies.[8] The Directive looks to ensure that shareholders in such companies have sufficient advance notice of the annual general meeting and have details as to the agenda. Shareholders must

---

[6] There is some debate as to whether the prohibition applies only to resolutions required by the Companies Act 2006 as opposed to resolutions required by the company's articles.

[7] See Company Law Review, *Modern Company Law for a Competitive Economy, Final Report*, vol 1 (2001) URN 01/942, paras 7.5–7.16; *Completing the Structure* (2000) URN 00/1335, paras 5.18–5.40; *Developing the Framework* (2000) URN 00/656, paras 4.24–4.64; *Company General Meetings and Shareholder Communication* (1999) URN 99/1144.

[8] Directive 2007/36/EC on the exercise of certain rights of shareholders in listed companies, OJ L 184, 14.7.2007, p 17. The Directive comes into force on 3 August 2009 and is to be implemented by regulations to be made under the European Communities Act 1972, s 2(2). See BERR, 'Implementation of the Directive on the Exercise of Certain Rights of Shareholders in Listed Companies', A consultation document (October 2008) URN 08/1362, Annex A of which contains a draft of the proposed regulations, The Companies (Shareholders' Rights) Regulations 2009.

also have the possibility of adding items to that agenda and have the right to ask questions and have them answered. The Directive prohibits obstacles to electronic participation which is important if shareholders in Member States other than the state of incorporation are to be able to participate to the fullest extent and, for the same reason, it must be possible for shareholders to appoint proxies and to vote directly by correspondence ahead of a meeting. Many of these matters are already addressed by the CA 2006, but some amendments (to be made by regulations) are necessary to give full effect to the Directive. In keeping with that general theme of shareholder engagement, the CA 2006 Part 9 introduces some measures aimed at engaging with indirect shareholders and that aspect is considered at **5-55**.

Another change effected by the CA 2006 is a significant shift in emphasis in terms of the use of electronic communications. Large companies have always been concerned about the costs involved in communicating with a widely dispersed shareholder base and electronic communication offers low cost and speedy methods of overcoming those problems. Likewise in small companies, the ease of electronic communication can and should be used to facilitate and expedite decision-making. The use of electronic communication had been endorsed by the Companies Act 1985 (Electronic Communications) Order 2000, SI 2000/3373, but only to a limited extent and effect. The intention in the CA 2006 is to move more purposefully to greater use by companies (and greater uptake by shareholders) of electronic processes, for example by giving companies power to opt for website communication (if so authorised by the shareholders) with shareholders being deemed to assent unless they positively opt to have hard copies (see below). Companies may be deemed also to have accepted electronic communications from shareholders. For example, if a company in a notice calling a meeting, or in an instrument of proxy sent out by the company, or an invitation to appoint a proxy issued by the company, gives an electronic address, it is deemed to have agreed that any document or information relating to the meeting may be sent by electronic means to that address (s 333) and the largest companies are using this method to deal, for example, with proxy appointments. **15-5**

The overall communications scheme (CA 2006, ss 1143–1148 and Schs 4 and 5) is somewhat complex, but essentially the Act allows companies to communicate with shareholders by hard copy, electronically or via a website or any other mechanism agreed with the recipient.[9] Hard copy documents may be handed to the shareholder or posted and hard copies are always available to shareholders free of charge even if they opt for other methods of communication.[10] Electronic communications such as email may be used if the shareholder opts in to such use and provides an email address.[11] Websites can be used to communicate with shareholders if the company's articles or a shareholder resolution allow for such use.[12] Where a company has that power, it must ask the shareholder individually whether he consents to website communication, but crucially if the shareholder declines to answer, he is deemed to have assented **15-6**

---

[9] CA 2006, Sch 5, paras 2, 5, 8, 15.   [10] CA 2006, s 1145(1), (3), also Sch 5, para 3.
[11] CA 2006, Sch 5, paras 6, 7.   [12] CA 2006, Sch 5, para 10(2).

to website use.[13] In this way, shareholder inertia is turned into assent to website communication though any shareholder, at any time, can require communications in hard copy. Where shareholders have assented or have been deemed to have assented, the company must still send them a notification, either by letter or email, alerting them to the fact that information has been posted on the website.[14]

15-7   The largest companies already make extensive use of their websites as a means of communicating with their investors and this is both facilitated (as noted above) and required by the legislation. The CA 2006 requires quoted companies[15] to use their website to publish their annual accounts and reports (s 430); to report the results of polls taken at a general meeting and any independent assessor's report on such polls (ss 341, 351); and members of the company holding a certain percentage of the shares can require a statement to be put on the website setting out any audit concerns which they may have (s 527). The Shareholders' Rights Directive (see **15-5**) requires a traded company to publish on a website a wide variety of information in advance of a meeting and that information must be available for a period of at least 21 days before the meeting.[16]

B Voting entitlement

Voting in person

15-8   Subject to any provision in the company's articles, on a vote on a show of hands each member present in person has one vote (as has every proxy present who is duly appointed by one member) and on a poll (where the actual votes cast by each member are counted) every member has one vote for every share of which he is the holder (CA 2006, ss 284, 324). In practice, voting rights are spelt out expressly in the articles. The CA 2006 recognises that a member may hold shares on behalf of a number of beneficial owners and s 152 provides that a member holding shares in a company on behalf of more than one person is not required to exercise all the rights attached to the shares (which would include voting rights) in the same way. A member is able therefore to cast votes for and against a resolution in accordance with the instructions of the beneficial owners.

---

[13] CA 2006, Sch 5, para 10(3).

[14] CA 2006, Sch 5, para 13. There are still some costs to the company though these will be minimal if the notification can be sent by email. Even if sent by letter, this scheme allows for a significant reduction in the costs of printing and posting what are often very substantial documents (annual reports and accounts of publicly traded companies, for example, commonly exceed 100 pages).

[15] Defined CA 2006, ss 361, 385 as a company whose equity share capital: (a) has been included in the official list in accordance with the provisions of FSMA 2000, Pt VI; or (b) is officially listed in an EEA State (i.e. EU with Norway, Iceland and Liechtenstein); or (c) is admitted to dealing on either the New York Stock Exchange or Nasdaq (an American stock exchange).

[16] The information to be published includes the notice of the meeting, details of the share capital and voting rights, as well as members' statements, resolutions and matters of business received by the company: Directive 2007/36/EC, see above n 8, art 5(4).

Certain classes of shares may carry restricted voting rights; for example it is com-   **15-9** monly the case that preference shareholders may only vote on matters of direct concern to them, see **14-21**. Equally, the articles may confer enhanced rights; for example, a shareholder may be given three times the number of votes on a particular matter than is otherwise the case.[17]

Voting by proxy

Proxies are instruments executed by voting members of a company in favour of   **15-10** another person, enabling that person to exercise the member's voting rights and a person may appoint multiple proxies. The position with respect to proxy rights was clarified and improved by the Companies Act 2006 and the company's articles can confer even more extensive rights (s 331). Any member of a company who is entitled to attend and vote at meetings (including class meetings) of the company may appoint another person, whether a member or not, as his proxy to exercise all or any of his rights to attend and to speak and vote at a meeting of the company (s 324). A proxy is entitled to vote on a show of hands and on a poll and a proxy can demand a poll and his demand is the same as a demand by a member (s 329(1)). It is common to appoint the company chairman as the proxy, but given the new rights for a proxy to speak at a meeting, that may not be entirely appropriate since it could result in the chairman having to speak against a resolution. Furthermore, in the case of a company having a share capital, a member may appoint more than one proxy in relation to a meeting (s 324(2)). This flexibility is particularly important in larger companies where the registered shareholder is frequently a nominee for a number of beneficial owners and the ability to appoint multiple proxies allows their differing interests to be individually represented at the meeting.

The instrument appointing a proxy may be in writing or contained in an electronic   **15-11** communication.[18] The proxy must be lodged with the company ahead of the meeting and the company's articles may not contain any requirement that it be received by the company more than 48 hours before a meeting in order that the appointment be effective.[19] This is to ensure that the shareholders have flexibility and are not forced at an early date to decide whether they will attend or appoint a proxy. At the same time, the 48-hour window allows the company enough time to determine who is to attend and in what capacity. The notice of the meeting must draw attention to the rights to appoint a proxy (CA 2006, s 325).

---

[17] See *Bushell v Faith* [1969] 1 All ER 1002 (shareholder had three times the number of votes he usually had where the resolution was for his removal from the board, so giving him an effective veto on his own removal).

[18] Notice of the appointment of a proxy may be by electronic communication where the company is agreeable to appointments being made in this way and has provided an address for this purpose: CA 2006, s 333. As to the content and form of a proxy, see The Companies (Model Articles) Regulations 2008, SI 2008/3229, reg 2, Sch 1, art 45 (Ltd); reg 4, Sch 3, art 38 (Plc). The Listing Rules require a proxy to be a three way (for, against, withheld) in keeping with the requirements of the Combined Code, D.2.1, see LR9.3.6R.

[19] CA 2006, s 327. Non-working days are excluded when calculating the earliest deadline that can be specified in the articles.

Voting by corporate representatives

15-12 Companies may hold shares in other companies and such corporate shareholders attend meetings through corporate representatives. The position on corporate representatives was inadvertently complicated by the CA 2006. A problem arose because s 323 (which cannot be overridden by a company's articles) allows for both single and multiple corporate representatives to be appointed. It also goes on to provide that where there are multiple corporate representatives and they exercise a power of the corporate member in different ways, the power is treated as not having been exercised at all (s 323(4)). On one interpretation, this meant that where multiple corporate representatives vote in differing ways, as is very likely since the use of multiple corporate members is likely to be in order to reflect different voting intentions, the votes are treated as not exercised. Another interpretation was that this provision is subject to and governed by s 152 which allows a member holding shares on behalf of more than one person to exercise the rights attached to the shares in different ways. Given the uncertainties, the situation caused practical difficulties which were initially resolved by reliance on a solution devised by the Institute of Chartered Secretaries with support from the legal profession.[20] The solution was for one of the corporate representatives to be the designated corporate representative (DCR). The DCR might take instructions from the other representatives as to how to vote and then cast some votes one way and some another so achieving the desired outcome. This solution is administratively cumbersome and the preferred route is to use multiple proxies and avoid the problems of multiple corporate representatives altogether.[21] The problem with using proxies is that notice of the appointment must be given to the company not later than a clear 48 hours before the meeting which in some circumstances may be equally impractical. The need to implement the Shareholder Rights Directive (see **15-4**) presented the opportunity to resolve the issue and a proposed amendment will allow corporate representatives representing the same holder to vote in different ways from one another in respect of different blocks of shares.[22] Voting is only a nullity if corporate representatives vote the same shares in different ways.

Polls

15-13 Resolutions at meetings can be and in smaller companies are normally passed on a show of hands but a poll (where the votes cast are counted) may be demanded to obtain a more accurate picture reflecting the members' shareholdings.[23] Increasingly larger

---

[20] See ICSA Guidance on Proxies and Corporate Representatives at General Meetings (January 2008).

[21] That solution is suggested by the Explanatory Notes to the Companies Act 2006 which state 'If a corporation wishes to appoint people with different voting intentions or with authority to vote different blocks of shares, they should appoint proxies' (para 569).

[22] See the proposed Shareholders' Rights Regulations, above n 8, and BERR, 'Implementation of the Directive on the Exercise of Certain Rights of Shareholders in Listed Companies', A Consultation Document (October 2008), paras 3.8–3.10.

[23] The model articles provide that a resolution put to a vote at a general meeting must be decided on a show of hands unless a poll is duly demanded: see The Companies (Model Articles) Regulations 2008, SI 2008/3229, reg 2, Sch 1, art 43 (Ltd), reg 4, Sch 3, art 34 (Plc).

companies vote only on a poll so as to avoid complexities in counting votes on a show of hands where multiple proxies or corporate representatives are present.

The company's articles cannot exclude the right to demand a poll at a general meeting, save in respect of the election of the chairman and the adjournment of the meeting.[24] Furthermore, the articles cannot make ineffective a demand for a poll which is made either by not less than five voting members, or by a member or members representing not less than 10% of the total voting rights of all members having the right to vote on the resolution, or by a member or members holding shares conferring a right to vote on the resolution, being shares on which an aggregate sum has been paid up equal to not less than 10% of the total sum paid up on all the shares conferring that right (CA 2006, s 321(2)). On a poll taken at a general meeting of the company, a member entitled to more than one vote need not, if he votes, use all his votes or cast all the votes he uses in the same way (s 322). Where a poll is taken at a general meeting of a quoted company,[25] the company must ensure that information on the outcome of the poll is made available on a website (s 341). In particular, the number of votes cast in favour and the number of votes cast against the resolution must be set out.

15-14

Further provision is made for the proper scrutiny of polls of quoted companies in the light of concerns expressed as to the accuracy of polls. Members of a quoted company representing not less than 5% of the total voting rights of all the members who have the right to vote on the matter, or not less than 100 members having the right to vote on the matter and holding shares paid up on average per member of not less than £100,[26] may require the directors to obtain an independent report on any poll taken or to be taken at a general meeting of the company (CA 2006, s 342). Despite concerns about the expense of an independent poll, the Government considered this new procedure to be an important mechanism for ensuring the accuracy of polls.[27] Any report made by the independent assessor on a poll must be made available on the company's website (s 351). This mechanism may prove valuable to companies where the resolution is controversial or the margin of victory, or defeat, narrow. For example, there is already considerable interest in the precise voting pattern on the advisory vote on the directors' remuneration report in the case of quoted companies (see **5-40**).

15-15

---

[24] CA 2006, s 321(1)(a) and (b). The Companies (Model Articles) Regulations 2008, SI 2008/3229, reg 2, Sch 1, art 45(2) (Ltd), reg 4, Sch 3, art 36(2) (Plc) allow a poll to be demanded by the chairman, the directors, two or more persons having the right to vote on the resolution or a person or persons representing not less than one-tenth of the total voting rights of all shareholders.   [25] See definition in n 15 above.

[26] Indirect investors, subject to the requirements of CA 2006, s 153 being met, may count towards the 100 figure.

[27] There has been concern for some time about 'lost' votes, i.e. that the chain of intermediaries is now so long from beneficial owner through to the registered shareholder that voting instructions and/or votes get lost along the way so that either votes are not cast in accordance with instructions, or votes are not counted because of a confusion of instructions, or that agents are not acting on instructions. The matter has been the subject of much work by the Shareholder Voting Working Group made up of interested parties such as the ABI, NAPF, Euroclear and Lloyds TSB Registrars which has commissioned a series of reports by Paul Myners on the issue. See Myners, *Review of Impediments to Voting UK Shares* (2004) with follow-up reports in 2005 (twice) and in 2007. A further report is expected in 2009. Overall, the picture is of increased voting levels with about 63% of votes being cast in general meetings of FT100 companies, but continuing failures in the voting process so that votes continue to be 'lost'.

C Resolutions

15-16   Resolutions fall into two categories, ordinary and special[28] and, in the case of a private company, may be passed either in writing or at a meeting (CA 2006, s 281(1)). A public company may not use written resolutions (a change effected by the CA 2006) but must pass resolutions (including resolutions of a class of members) at a meeting (s 281(2)). A resolution at a meeting is validly passed if notice of the meeting and of the resolution is given, and the meeting is held and conducted in accordance with the provisions of the CA 2006 governing the conduct of meetings and annual general meetings (i.e. Part 13, Chs 3 and 4) and the company's articles (s 301).

Ordinary resolutions

15-17   If the Companies Acts require 'a resolution', this means an ordinary resolution unless the articles require a higher majority or unanimity (CA 2006, s 281(3)). If the statute requires an ordinary resolution (or a special resolution), the articles cannot impose a different majority requirement than that specified in the Act. An ordinary resolution is a resolution passed by a simple majority of the members or a class of members (s 282(1)). A written resolution is passed by a simple majority if it is passed by members representing a simple majority of the total voting rights of eligible members (s 282(2)).[29] A resolution passed at a meeting on a show of hands is passed by a simple majority of those entitled (i.e. as members or proxies) to vote (s 282(3)). A resolution passed on a poll is passed by a simple majority if it is passed by members representing a simple majority of the total voting rights of members who being entitled to do so vote in person or by proxy on the resolution (s 282(4)).

15-18   There are no specific notice requirements for a resolution and the company will give notice of the resolution to the shareholders at the same time as it gives notice of the meeting (discussed at **15-57**). In a few instances, the statute requires that special notice is given *to* the company of an ordinary resolution, for example on any resolution to remove a director[30] or an auditor.[31] A company's articles may also make provision for special notice. Special notice, for the purpose of provisions of the CA 2006, requires that notice of the intention to move the resolution is given to the company at least 28 days before the meeting (s 312(1)).

---

[28] Previously, there were also extraordinary and elective resolutions. Elective resolutions were used by private companies to elect to opt out of certain provisions of the companies legislation: CA 1985, s 379A; extraordinary resolutions required a 75% majority and 14 days' notice—they remain effective where a company's articles or a contract made provision for them: see the Companies Act 2006 (Commencement No 3, Consequential Amendments, Transitional Provisions and Savings) Order 2007, SI 2007/2194, art 9, Sch 3, para 23.

[29] 'Eligible members' in relation to a written resolution of a private company is defined by CA 2006, s 289 as the members who would have been entitled to vote on the resolution on the circulation date (defined s 290 as the date on which the written resolution is sent to the members).

[30] CA 2006, s 168(2), or to appoint someone in his stead at the meeting at which he is removed.

[31] CA 2006, s 511(1). Special notice is also required of a resolution to appoint as auditor a person other than the retiring auditor: s 515(2).

Special resolutions

A special resolution means a resolution passed by a majority of not less than 75% (CA 2006, s 283(1)) and it is required by the legislation on a number of occasions typically involving a matter of some significance, such as constitutional changes,[32] changes to the capital structure of the company,[33] or where the company resolves to go into winding up.[34] Anything that can be done by an ordinary resolution may equally be done by a special resolution (s 282(5)). **15-19**

A special resolution which is passed as a written resolution must be passed by a majority of not less than 75% of the total voting rights of eligible members (s 283(2)).[35] Where a resolution of a private company is passed as a written resolution, the resolution is not a special resolution unless it is stated that it was proposed as a special resolution and, if the resolution so states, it may only be passed as a special resolution (s 283(3)). **15-20**

A resolution passed at a meeting on a show of hands must be passed by a majority of not less than 75% of those entitled (i.e. as members or proxies) to vote (s 283(4)). A resolution passed on a poll is passed by a 75% majority if it is passed by members representing a 75% majority of the total voting rights of members who being entitled to do so vote in person or by proxy on the resolution (s 283(5)). **15-21**

A resolution passed at a meeting is not a special resolution unless the notice of the meeting includes the text of the resolution and specifies the intention to propose the resolution as a special resolution and if the notice of the meeting so states, the resolution may only be passed as a special resolution (s 283(6)). If the resolution is to be validly passed, it must be the same resolution as that identified in the notice of the meeting.[36] **15-22**

Written resolutions

As noted at the beginning of this chapter, the emphasis in the CA 2006 is on the use of written resolutions by private companies which is intended to expedite decision-making in such companies and to enable them to avoid the formalities involved in calling a meeting. The key advantages are speed (no notice of a meeting is required) and costs (likely to be minimal). Subject to two exceptions, any resolution may be passed as a written resolution (CA 2006, s 281(1)) and any provision in the company's articles precluding the use of written resolutions is void (s 300). The exceptions are that written **15-23**

---

[32] For example, a special resolution is required on an alteration of the articles of association: CA 2006, s 21(1); on a change of name: s 77(1); on the re-registration of a public company as a private company: s 97(1).

[33] For example, a special resolution is required on disapplying the statutory pre-emption rights: CA 2006, s 570; on a reduction of share capital: s 641; on the occasion of an off-market purchase of a company's own shares: s 694.

[34] For example, a special resolution is required where a company resolves that it be wound up voluntarily: IA 1986, s 84(1)(b); and where a company resolves that the company be wound up by the court: s 122(1)(a).

[35] As to the definition of 'eligible members' see above n 29.

[36] *Re Moorgate Mercantile Holdings Ltd* [1980] 1 All ER 40.

resolutions may not be used (s 288(2)): (1) to remove a director under s 168; and (2) to remove an auditor from office under s 510 since, in these instances, the directors and auditors have the right to make representations at, or to, a general meeting.[37]

15-24   A major change effected by the CA 2006 is that written resolutions need no longer be unanimous. The CA 1985 requirement for unanimity limited their usefulness and it was removed by the CA 2006. A written resolution requires the same majority (simple or 75%) as required for an ordinary or special resolution passed at a meeting, as discussed above. The change means that in many private companies the resolution will effectively be passed before it is even circulated since minority shareholders by definition cannot block an ordinary resolution and may not (depending on their percentage holding) be in a position to block a special resolution. Of course, the same would be true of a resolution proposed at a meeting, but at least a meeting requires the majority to put forward some case for the action being undertaken and to hear opposing views. The minority may find it doubly frustrating to be outvoted and not heard. Some balance is restored, however, as shareholders representing a 10% or possibly 5% holding can require a meeting to be held (see CA 2006, s 303 and **15-46**) and can require a written resolution of their own to be circulated (see s 292 and **15-31**).

15-25   The statutory scheme for written resolutions for private companies is mandatory with CA 2006, s 288(1) stating that a written resolution is a resolution proposed and passed in accordance with Part 13, Ch 2 which means that companies must follow the statutory scheme rather than any written resolution provisions which companies may have in their articles. The CA 2006 no longer permits public companies to use written resolutions, at least for resolutions required by an enactment. This is a change to the previous law which permitted public companies to include provisions for written resolutions in their articles though their practical use was limited by the requirement that such resolutions had to be passed unanimously. Nevertheless in some circumstances they were of use to public companies. There seems no reason why public companies cannot use written resolutions for matters other than statutory requirements, if their articles so provide. In so far as it is permissible and practicable, public companies can rely also on informal unanimous assent (the *Duomatic*[38] principle which is discussed at **15-73**).

15-26   Given the obligation to follow the statutory scheme on written resolutions, the key points to note are:

- A copy must be sent to every eligible member (i.e. every member entitled to vote on the resolution, CA 2006, s 289);[39] accompanied by a statement as to how the member may signify agreement and a date by which the resolution must be passed otherwise it lapses under s 297 (s 291(4)). If the resolution is to be a special resolution, it must so state (s 283(3)).

---

[37] See CA 2006, ss 169, 511(3), (5).   [38] *Re Duomatic Ltd* [1969] 1 All ER 161, CA.

[39] A copy of the proposed resolution must be sent to the company's auditors: CA 2006, s 502, but merely for information. The auditor cannot delay the process and is not required to assent in any way to it so a failure to provide a copy has no consequence.

- The resolution may be circulated in hard copy or electronically or by way of a website, subject to compliance with the rules on electronic communications noted at **15-6**, and it must be sent at the same time (so far as reasonably practical) to all members.[40]

- Certain statutory schemes, such as those relating to a purchase by a company of its own shares (see **20-5**), require documents to be available for inspection by shareholders at the general meeting. Where a written resolution is used, copies of such documents as would otherwise be available at a general meeting must be circulated to the members at or before the time when the resolution is supplied for signature.[41]

- A written resolution lapses if the time-limit imposed by the articles elapses or, if there is no such limit, within 28 days of the circulation date (i.e. the date when the resolution is first sent to any member: s 290): s 297.

A written resolution of a private company is passed when the required majority of   **15-27**
eligible members signify their agreement to it (CA 2006, s 296(4)) and they do so when the company receives an authenticated document,[42] whether in hard copy or electronic form, identifying the resolution and indicating agreement to it (s 296(1), (2)).[43] Once a member has signified his agreement to a written resolution, he may not revoke his agreement (s 296(3)). A written resolution of a private company has effect as if passed by the company in general meeting or by a meeting of a class of members (s 288(5)). The company must keep a copy of all written resolutions for at least 10 years (s 355(1), (2)).

Circulation of members' written resolutions

Directors may circulate a written resolution at any time (s 291) but an important   **15-28**
innovation is that members holding 5% of the total voting rights of members entitled to vote on the resolution (or such lesser figure as specified in the articles) may require the company to circulate a proposed written resolution and with it a statement of not more than 1,000 words on the subject matter of the resolution (s 292). Such matter is to be circulated at the members' expense, however, unless the company otherwise resolves (s 294(1)). If the company has not so resolved, it need not circulate the resolution and statement until the members deposit or tender a sum reasonably sufficient to meet the company's expenses in circulating it (s 294(2)).

---

[40] If the resolution is sent via a website, it is not validly sent unless it is available on the website throughout the period from the circulation date (defined CA 2006, s 290) to the date on which the resolution lapses under s 297: s 299.

[41] For examples, see disapplication of pre-emption rights (CA 2006, 571(7)); off-market purchases of own shares (s 696(2)); redemption or purchase of own shares out of capital (s 718(2)); approval of directors' long-term service contracts (s 188(5)).

[42] If the company gives an electronic address in the document containing or accompanying the written resolution, it is deemed to have agreed to a response being made to that address: see CA 2006, s 298.

[43] There is no requirement for a signature, merely that agreement is signified, so could be by email or even a text message, for example, where electronic communications are permitted.

However, the costs may be modest if the shareholders have agreed to electronic or website communications and non-existent if the company has few members.

15-29   The company, or any person aggrieved, may apply to the court for an order that the company is not bound to circulate any statement on the ground that the right to have a resolution circulated is being abused (s 295(1)) and there is potential for the members concerned to be penalised in costs (s 295(2)), a possibility that should prevent vexatious use of these provisions.

15-30   If the company fails to comply with the requirement to circulate the resolution when otherwise required to do so, every officer of the company who is in default is liable to a fine (s 293(1), (5)).

Circulation of resolutions for public company annual general meeting

15-31   Members of a public company representing not less than 5% of the total voting rights of all the members entitled to vote on the resolution or not less than 100 members having the right to vote on the resolution holding shares paid up to the sum, per member, of at least £100 (CA 2006, s 338(3)),[44] may require the company to give notice of a resolution to be moved at the next annual general meeting. It must be a resolution that may properly be moved and is intended to be moved at the annual general meeting so excluding resolutions which would be ineffective (because inconsistent with an enactment, the company's constitution or otherwise), defamatory, frivolous or vexatious (s 338(1), (2)).[45]

15-32   A request may be in hard copy or electronic form, must identify the resolution of which notice is to be given and it must be authenticated by the persons making it (CA 2006, s 338(4)). The request must be received by the company not later than six weeks before the annual general meeting to which it relates or, if later, the time at which notice is given of that meeting (s 338(4)).

15-33   The company must carry the costs of circulation if the resolution is received before the end of the financial year preceding the annual general meeting (CA 2006, s 340(1)), otherwise the members must bear the costs of circulation, unless the company otherwise resolves. If the company has not so resolved, it need not circulate the resolution until the members deposit or tender a sum reasonably sufficient to meet the company's expenses in circulating the resolution (s 340(2)), which may be an inhibiting factor, depending on the size of the company. Of course, if the company is using electronic or website communication, the costs may be modest, being limited in effect to circulating hard copies to those who have opted for that mode of delivery.

---

[44] Indirect investors, subject to the requirements of CA 2006, s 153 being met, may count towards the 100 figure.

[45] The Shareholders' Rights Directive, see above n 8, extends this provision to a traded company: see the proposed Shareholders' Rights Regulations, also above n 8. This right to require the circulation of a resolution is extended in the case of a traded company to a right to include other items in the business to be dealt with at an annual general meeting.

If the company fails to comply with the requirement to circulate the resolution when **15-34** otherwise required to do so, every officer of the company who is in default is liable to a fine (s 339(4)).

Registering resolutions

The resolutions and agreements listed in CA 2006, s 29 must be registered with the **15-35** registrar of companies under s 30. The categories of resolutions which must be registered are:

- any special resolution (s 29(1)(a));
- any resolution or agreement whether of the company or of a class of shareholders which is effective because of the *Duomatic* principle,[46] discussed at **15-73**, that informal unanimous assent is tantamount to a resolution (s 29(1)(b) and (c));
- any resolution varying class rights which is not a special resolution (s 29(1)(d));
- other resolutions (i.e. ordinary resolutions) which are required by statute to be registered (s 29(1)(e)). This ensures that an ordinary resolution of importance must also be registered. For example, a resolution granting authority for an allotment of shares by the directors, though an ordinary resolution, must be registered,[47] as must an ordinary resolution granting a company authority for market purchases of its own shares,[48] and an ordinary resolution of members of a private company incorporated before 1 October 2008 allowing the directors to authorise conflicts of interest.[49] An example of a resolution which must be registered by virtue of another enactment would be a resolution for voluntary winding up under IA 1986, s 84(1)(a) to which CA 2006, ss 29 and 30 apply.[50]

A copy of the resolution (or, if not in writing, a memorandum setting out its terms) **15-36** must be registered with the registrar of companies within 15 days after it is passed. A failure to comply with the registration requirement is an offence (CA 2006, s 30(2)).

D General meetings

Meeting convened by the directors

The directors may at any time convene a meeting of the company (CA 2006, s 302) on **15-37** 14 clear days' notice[51] (unless the articles require a longer period of notice). In the case of a public company, the directors must call an annual general meeting on 21 clear

---

[46] *Re Duomatic Ltd* [1969] 1 All ER 161.   [47] CA 2006, s 551(8), (9).   [48] CA 2006, s 701(1), (8).
[49] The Companies Act 2006 (Commencement No. 5, Transitional Provisions and Savings) Order 2007, SI 2007/3495, art 9, Sch 4, Part 3, para 47.
[50] IA 1986, s 84(3).   [51] CA 2006, s 307(2); the clear day rule is in s 360.

days' notice,[52] and they must also call a general meeting when a public company suffers a serious loss of capital (s 656). Under the CA 1985 and the 1985 Table A, all general meetings other than the annual general meeting were called extraordinary general meetings,[53] but that terminology is not carried forward to the CA 2006. All meetings are general meetings and a public company must call an annual general meeting.

15-38   Subject to certain thresholds being met, members have a right under CA 2006, s 314 to circulate a statement of not more than 1,000 words to any general meeting of any company, public or private. This statement may be in addition to a resolution which the members (or other members) wish to circulate, it may be in respect of a resolution which the directors have given notice of, or it may be in respect of any other business to be conducted at the meeting. The same requirements are imposed, as discussed at **15-31** et seq, with regard to the percentage of members required to trigger the right (s 314(2)), the restrictions on statements which are defamatory, vexatious etc (s 317), the position on costs so far as they apply to a public company (s 316) and that it is an offence by each officer in default if the company fails to circulate a statement when otherwise required to do so (s 315(3)).

15-39   Notice of a general meeting must be given to the company's auditor who is entitled to attend and to be heard on any part of the business which concerns him as auditor, a potentially very wide category (s 502).

Annual general meeting of a public company

15-40   A public company must hold an annual general meeting within six months of its accounting reference date, i.e. the financial year end (CA 2006, s 336(1)). Non-compliance is an offence.[54] Private companies are not required to hold an annual general meeting, but may do so if they choose or if their articles require.

15-41   Convening a general meeting is a matter for the directors (s 302) and the notice calling the meeting must specify that it is the annual general meeting (s 337(1)). At least 21 clear days' notice is required (s 307(2))[55] and consent to shorter notice must be unanimous (s 337).

15-42   The statute does not dictate the business to be conducted at an annual general meeting but the typical business of such a meeting includes:

- laying the annual accounts, the directors' report, the auditors' report and, if the company is a quoted company, the directors' remuneration report, before the meeting;[56]

---

[52] CA 2006, s 307(2)(a); the clear day rule is in s 360.

[53] See, for example, CA 1985, s 368; Table A, reg 36.

[54] CA 2006, s 336(4). Repeated failures to hold annual general meetings may amount to unfairly prejudicial conduct under CA 2006, s 994: see *Re a company (No 00789 of 1987), ex p Shooter* [1990] BCLC 384.

[55] For companies subject to the Combined Code (see **5-11**), notice must be sent at least 20 working days before the meeting: see D.2.4.   [56] CA 2006, ss 437(1), 471(2).

- re-electing retiring directors and electing new directors;[57]
- appointing an auditor, if required to do so,[58] and setting the auditor's remuneration[59] although in practice that issue is often delegated to the board; and
- declaring a dividend.[60]

15-43 Any other matter may be included in the business of a general meeting provided proper notice of the matter (see below) has been given. Public companies typically include resolutions relating to the allotment of shares and disapplying the statutory pre-emption rights[61] and quoted companies[62] must submit the directors' remuneration report for shareholder approval by way of an ordinary resolution (s 439).

15-44 Notice of the meeting must state the intention to propose any special resolution and must set out the text of any special resolution to be considered at the meeting. For other matters, a difficult issue is the degree of detail which must be given with respect to matters other than the standard matters of business, for if the notice given is misleading, the court can restrain the holding of the meeting[63] and resolutions incorrectly notified are invalid and not binding on the company.[64] The key requirement is that the notice must disclose all relevant facts so that a member can exercise an informed business judgement as to whether he ought to attend the meeting[65] and this requires a fair, candid and reasonable explanation of the purpose or purposes for which the meeting is summoned.[66] Particular attention must be given to full and frank notice of any resolution involving a personal advantage to a director.[67] For example, a notice to the shareholders of an agreement to sell the business which failed to disclose the substantial payments which would be made to the directors personally as part of the agreement was invalid.[68]

15-45 As noted, members meeting certain threshold requirements may require a proposed resolution to be circulated (CA 2006, s 338 and see **15-31**) and also have a power to require the circulation of a statement concerning a proposed resolution or any other business to be conducted at the meeting (s 314 and see **15-38**).

Meeting requisitioned by the members

15-46 The directors are required to call a general meeting once requested to do so by members representing at least 10% (this threshold will be reduced to 5% once the Shareholders'

---

[57] CA 2006, s 160. See The Companies (Model Articles) Regulations 2008, SI 2008/3229, reg 2, Sch 1, art 17 (Ltd); reg 4, Sch 3, arts 20–22 (Plc).

[58] See CA 2006, ss 485(1), 489(1).   [59] CA 2006, s 492(1).

[60] See The Companies (Model Articles) Regulations 2008, SI 2008/3229, reg 2, Sch 1, art 30 (Ltd); reg 4, Sch 3, art 70 (Plc).

[61] Under CA 2006, ss 551, 571.   [62] For the definition of 'quoted company', see above n 15.

[63] *Jackson v Munster Bank* (1884) 13 LR IR 118.

[64] *Baillie v Oriental Telephone and Electric Co Ltd* [1915] 1 Ch 503.

[65] *Tiessen v Henderson* [1899] 1 Ch 861.

[66] *Kaye v Croydon Tramways Company* [1898] 1 Ch 358 at 373, per Rigby LJ.

[67] *Baillie v Oriental Telephone and Electric Co Ltd* [1915] 1 Ch 503; *Tiessen v Henderson* [1899] 1 Ch 861; *Kaye v Croydon Tramways Company* [1898] 1 Ch 358.

[68] *Kaye v Croydon Tramways Company* [1898] 1 Ch 358.

Rights Directive is implemented[69]) of the paid-up capital of the company as carries the right to vote in general meetings (CA 2006, s 303(2)). The obligation to convene the meeting can only arise if the request is valid and where it is ineffective because of a defect in its form then, despite the threshold requirements being met, the directors are not obliged to call a meeting.[70]

15-47   A request must state the general nature of the business to be dealt with at the meeting and must be authenticated by the persons making it.[71] It may include the text of a resolution that may properly be moved and is intended to be moved at the meeting (CA 2006, s 303(4)) excluding resolutions which would be ineffective (because inconsistent with an enactment, the company's constitution or otherwise), defamatory, frivolous or vexatious (s 303(5)). If the resolution is a special resolution, the notice of the meeting must so state (s 283(5)). Notice of any resolution included in the request must be included in the notice of the meeting.[72]

15-48   If within 21 days of becoming required to do so the directors do not call a meeting, to be held on a date not more than 28 days after the date of the notice convening the meeting, the members may themselves call a meeting (CA 2006, s 305(1)).

Meeting convened by the court

15-49   The court has a discretionary power under CA 2006, s 306 to order a general meeting to be held in such manner as it thinks fit if it is impracticable to call a meeting in the normal way or to conduct the meeting in the manner prescribed by the company's articles or the CA 2006. The court may exercise this power either of its own motion, or on the application of any director, or on the application of any member of the company who would be entitled to vote at the meeting.[73] The court may direct, in particular, that one member of the company present be deemed to constitute a meeting (s 306(4)).

15-50   The intention behind the power is to allow a company 'to get on with managing its affairs without being frustrated by the impracticability of calling or conducting a general meeting in the manner prescribed by the articles and the Act'.[74] This power may be

---

[69] See above n 8.

[70] *Rose v McGivern* [1998] 2 BCLC 593; *Isle of Wight Railway Co v Tahourdin* (1883) 25 Ch D 320; see also *PNC Telecom plc v Thomas* [2003] BCC 202.

[71] CA 2006, s 303(4) and (6). A meeting convened on requisition cannot transact any business other than that covered by the terms of the requisition: *Ball v Metal Industries Ltd* 1957 SC 315, together with any resolutions which the directors might put forward and of which due notice has been given, see *Rose v McGivern* [1998] 2 BCLC 593.

[72] CA 2006, ss 303(4)(b), 304(2), (3).

[73] CA 2006, s 306(2). The mere fact that a petition alleging unfairly prejudicial conduct has been presented under s 994 does not automatically oust the court's jurisdiction, but it may be a relevant factor in determining whether the court should exercise its discretion to call a meeting: *Harman v BML Group Ltd* [1994] 2 BCLC 674, CA; *Re Whitchurch Insurance Consultants Ltd* [1993] BCLC 1359; cf. *Re Sticky Fingers Restaurant Ltd* [1992] BCLC 84.

[74] *Vectone Entertainment Holding Ltd v South Entertainment Ltd* [2004] 2 BCLC 224 at 231.

invoked, for example, where a company finds itself without directors able to convene a meeting, or there is uncertainty as to who are the members, or the members are overseas and the company is unable to serve notice on them.[75] Occasionally, the power of the court is invoked because of the potential for violence. In *Re British Union for the Abolition of Vivisection*,[76] for example, it was impractical to call a general meeting of all 9,000 members of the BUAV when a previous meeting had degenerated into near riot and had been stopped by the police.

This power of the court to convene a meeting is often used to resolve cases where shareholders have refused to attend meetings so rendering them inquorate. By absenting themselves, the shareholders hope to prevent the majority shareholders from exercising their voting powers on a particular issue, typically the removal of the absent shareholders from office as directors.[77] The courts have generally refused to allow absent shareholders to gain an effective veto over company business in this way and so will order a meeting to be held which is quorate despite the absence of those shareholders.[78]   **15-51**

In *Re Opera Photographic Ltd*,[79] for example, the company had an issued share capital of 100 hundred shares, divided 51/49 between the two parties who were also the directors. The articles provided that the quorum for a meeting of the directors or the shareholders was two. The parties fell out and the 51% shareholder wanted to hold a general meeting in order to remove the 49% shareholder from office as a director, but no meeting could be held because of the lack of a quorum. The court granted an application to convene a meeting of the company, taking the view that the quorum requirements in the articles of association could not be treated as conferring on the 49% shareholder a form of veto to prevent the holding of a meeting to consider removing him from office as a director. Likewise in *Re Whitchurch Insurance Consultants Ltd*[80] where a husband and wife were the only directors of the company and held 666 and 334 of the 1,000 issued shares of the company respectively: the personal and business relationship between them broke down and the husband wanted to hold a general meeting to pass a resolution removing his wife as a director. The quorum requirement was set at two members so no meeting could be held. The court agreed that an order convening a meeting should be made to allow a board of directors to be appointed.   **15-52**

There are limits to the discretion of the court under CA 2006, s 306, however, and there are two clear categories of cases where the discretion will not be exercised. In *Harman v BML Group Ltd*[81] the company's capital was divided into A and B shares and   **15-53**

---

[75] See *Harman v BML Group Ltd* [1994] 2 BCLC 674 at 677. It is not sufficient that the meeting is to be chaired by a director whom some of the shareholders wish to remove from office—this does not render it 'impracticable' to call a meeting: *Might SA v Redbus Interhouse plc* [2004] 2 BCLC 449; see also *Monnington v Easier plc* [2006] 2 BCLC 283.

[76] [1995] 2 BCLC 1.

[77] See *Re El Sombrero Ltd* [1958] Ch 900; also *Re HR Paul & Son* (1973) 118 Sol Jo 166.

[78] See, for example, *Vectone Entertainment Holding Ltd v South Entertainment Ltd* [2004] 2 BCLC 224.

[79] [1989] BCLC 763.   [80] [1993] BCLC 1359.   [81] [1994] 2 BCLC 674.

no shareholders' meeting was quorate without a B shareholder or proxy being present. The parties fell out and the other shareholders applied for an order under CA 1985, s 371 (CA 2006, s 306) allowing them to hold meetings without B. The Court of Appeal refused the application as the effect of ordering meetings without B would be to override a quorum requirement which, the court found, constituted a class right conferred on B so as to protect him from removal from office as a director. In *Ross v Telford*[82] a husband and wife were the directors of two companies and they were also equal shareholders of one of the companies. The quorum for board and general meetings of both companies was two with the result that both companies were potentially deadlocked at board and general meeting levels. The Court of Appeal refused an application by the husband for a court order convening a meeting with the view to appointing an additional director. It concluded that CA 1985, s 371 (CA 2006, s 306) is not an appropriate vehicle for resolving deadlock between two equal shareholders. It is a procedural section and is not designed to affect substantive voting rights or to shift the balance of power between shareholders by permitting a 50% shareholder to override the wishes of the other 50% shareholder. The shareholders had agreed that power would be shared equally and potential deadlock was a matter which they must be taken to have been agreed on with the consent and for the protection of each of them.

15-54   The limits to the court's discretion therefore are that the court will not order a meeting under CA 2006, s 306 where to order a meeting would negate a class right conferred on a shareholder[83] or where it would shift the balance of power in a company which is deadlocked 50/50 by virtue of the parties' agreement. The Court of Appeal confirmed these limitations to the court's discretion in *Union Music Ltd v Watson*.[84] The case concerned a dispute between a company, A Ltd, and the opera singer, Russell Watson. Watson was a 49% shareholder in the company and Union (representing his management) held 51% of the shares. Watson and Union were also the only directors of the company. There were numerous disputes between the parties as to the provision of services by Watson to the company with the company alleging breach of contract by Watson and Watson alleging unreasonable restraint of trade by the company. A shareholders' agreement provided that the consent of both shareholders was required for any meeting of the shareholders and the quorum for board meetings was set by the articles at two.

15-55   The net result of the disputes was that the company was deadlocked at general meeting level and also at board level, with the majority shareholder unable to call a general meeting to appoint a further director without the consent of Watson, which consent was not forthcoming. In these circumstances, Union applied to the court for an order directing a general meeting be held. The trial judge rejected the request, taking the

---

[82] [1998] 1 BCLC 82.

[83] See also *Alvona Developments Ltd v The Manhattan Loft Corporation (AC) Ltd* [2006] BCC 119 where, although there was no class right as such, the court did not think it would be appropriate to make an order (for a meeting to appoint further directors) when it would override an agreement between the parties that there would be one jointly appointed director.

[84] [2003] 1 BCLC 453, CA.

view that it was not for him 'to intervene to try to cut a Gordian knot of the parties' own making'.[85]

On appeal, the Court of Appeal disagreed with the approach taken by the trial judge   **15-56** and ordered that a general meeting be held for the sole purpose of appointing another director which meeting was to be attended by Union only. The court considered that this case was distinguishable from *Harman v BML Group Ltd*[86] and *Ross v Telford*.[87] Outside of the circumstances in those cases, the court said, a provision as to the consent of the shareholders to a meeting could be overridden by a court order so as to enable a company to have an effective board in a position to manage its affairs properly. One side or other has to prevail and Peter Gibson LJ could not see that the contractual provisions in the shareholders' agreement provided a sufficient reason why the power to order a meeting should not be exercised given that, on the facts in *Union Music*, neither of the exceptional circumstances limiting the court's discretion was applicable.

E Meeting procedures

Notice of meetings

Minimum periods of notice

In the case of a general meeting, at least 14 days' (clear days) notice must be given,[88]   **15-57** and, in the case of the annual general meeting of a public company, the minimum notice period is 21 clear days (CA 2006, s 307(1), (2)).[89] Failure to give timely notice invalidates the meeting and nullifies the proceedings.[90] It is possible for meetings to be called at shorter notice than that noted above (s 307(4)) with the consent of a majority in number of the members having the right to attend and vote at the meeting and holding at least 95% in nominal value of the shares carrying voting rights in public companies and 90% in private companies.[91] Once there is agreement to short notice,

---

[85] See [2003] 1 BCLC 453 at 460, CA.

[86] [1994] 2 BCLC 674.   [87] [1998] 1 BCLC 82.

[88] This period is reduced from the 21 days' notice required by the CA 1985 where a special resolution was proposed and this is a valuable speeding up of the process, especially for public companies for whom time is often of the essence. The position for traded companies is complicated by the Shareholders' Rights Directive, see above n 8, which requires 21 days' notice but gives Member States the option (which the UK intends to take up) to call meetings on 14 days' notice, provided that shareholders pass a resolution approving the calling of meetings on 14 days' notice and that the company 'offers the facility for shareholders to vote by electronic means accessible to all shareholders': see BERR, Consultation Document on Implementation of the Directive, above n 8, paras 3.15–3.17.

[89] The periods of notice prescribed must be clear both of the day of notice and of the day of the meeting: CA 2006, s 360.

[90] *Smyth v Darley* (1849) 2 HLC 789.

[91] Private companies can increase that 90% threshold to 95% by their articles: CA 2006, s 307(6).

there is no minimum period of notice which is required and it can be as brief as the members choose.

Manner of notice

15-58   Notice of a general meeting must be given in hard copy form, electronically or by means of a website or partly by one such means and partly by another (CA 2006, s 308).

Persons entitled to notice

15-59   Subject to any provision of the company's articles, and any enactment, notice of a general meeting must be given to every member (including any person entitled to a share in consequence of the death or bankruptcy of a member, if the company has been notified of their entitlement) and every director (CA 2006, s 310) and to the company's auditor (s 502).

15-60   An omission (other than an accidental omission within CA 2006, s 313) to give notice to any person entitled to it invalidates the meeting and nullifies the proceedings.[92] Failure to give notice because of an error on the part of directors, for example where they were under the erroneous impression that someone had ceased to be a member of the company, is not an accidental omission for these purposes.[93]

Contents of notice

15-61   The notice must specify the time and date and place of the meeting and, subject to the company's articles, must state the general nature of the business to be dealt with at the meeting (CA 2006, s 311(2)).[94] Every notice calling a meeting of a company (or of any class of the members) must contain a reasonably prominent statement that the member is entitled to appoint a proxy or proxies (see **15-10**) to attend and vote instead of him and that a proxy need not be a member (s 325). Where the meeting is the annual general meeting of a public company, the notice calling the meeting must so state (s 337). A quoted company, when giving notice of an accounts meeting, must draw attention to the right of the members to use the company website to draw attention to audit concerns.[95]

Location of meetings

15-62   In order for a meeting of members to be validly constituted, it is not necessary for all the members to be physically present in the same room. A valid meeting can be held using overflow rooms provided that all due steps are taken to direct those unable

---

[92] CA 2006, s 301; *Smyth v Darley* (1849) 2 HLC 789.

[93] *Musselwhite v C H Musselwhite & Son Ltd* [1962] Ch 964.

[94] A company whose shares are admitted to trading on a regulated market must provide information to holders on: (1) the place, time and agenda of meetings; (2) the total number of shares and voting rights; and (3) the rights of holders to participate in meetings: DTR 6.1.1.12R.

[95] See CA 2006, s 529; for the definition of 'quoted company,' see above n 15; and for the 'accounts meeting' see CA 2006, s 437(3), essentially the general meeting of a public company at which the company's accounts are laid.

to get into the main meeting into the overflow room, and that there are adequate audio-visual links to enable those in all the rooms to see and hear what is going on in the other rooms and that there is appropriate opportunity to participate in the debate.[96]

Chairman of meetings

Subject to any provision in the articles stating who may or may not be chairman, any   **15-63** member may be elected to be chairman by a resolution passed at the meeting (CA 2006, s 319).[97] The articles commonly provide that the chairman of the board of directors or, in his absence, some other director nominated by the directors, is to act as the chairman of the meeting.[98] It is the chairman's duty to preserve order, to conduct proceedings regularly, to deal with the business of the meeting and to take care that the sense of the meeting is properly ascertained with regard to any question before it.[99] In the case of a vote on a resolution by show of hands, a declaration by the chairman that the resolution has/has not passed or passed with a particular majority is conclusive evidence of that fact without proof of the number or proportion of the votes in favour of or against the resolution (s 320(1)).[100] In the event of a dispute, the solution is to demand a poll[101] (see **15-13**).

Adjournment of meetings

The chairman must adjourn if directed to do so by the meeting or if, within half an   **15-64** hour before the start, a quorum is not present, or if at any time during the meeting a quorum ceases to be present.[102]

The chairman may adjourn a meeting if the meeting consents to the adjournment or if   **15-65** it appears necessary to do so to protect the safety of any person attending the meeting or to ensure that the business of the meeting is conducted in an orderly manner.[103]

---

[96] *Byng v London Life Association Ltd* [1989] BCLC 400, CA.

[97] See The Companies (Model Articles) Regulations 2008, SI 2008/3229, reg 2, Sch 1, art 40 (Ltd); reg 4, Sch 3, art 31 (Plc).

[98] There is no requirement that the chairman be 'neutral' and he may occupy the chair even though the matter for discussion is the removal of all of the directors including himself and the appointment of a new board: *Might SA v Redbus Interhouse plc* [2004] 2 BCLC 449.

[99] *National Dwelling Society v Sykes* [1894] 3 Ch 159. An (unintended) result of the definitions in CA 2006, ss 281(3) and 282 is that a chairman cannot use a casting vote to secure the passage of an ordinary resolution at a general meeting (though this was permissible under the 1985 Table A, reg 50). A saving provision in the Companies Act 2006 (Commencement No 5, Transitional Provisions and Savings) Order 2007, SI 2007/3495, art 11, Sch 5, para 2(5) allows companies which previously had such a provision in their articles to retain it, but no such saving is available for companies formed since 1 October 2007 when CA 2006, ss 281(3) and 282 came into force. For those companies, the chairman's casting vote at general meetings is abolished.

[100] See The Companies (Model Articles) Regulations 2008, SI 2008/3229, reg 2, Sch 1, art 45(2) (Ltd); reg 4, Sch 3, arts 35 and 36(2)(Plc).

[101] A chairman may call a poll: see The Companies (Model Articles) Regulations 2008, SI 2008/3229, reg 2, Sch 1, art 42 (Ltd); reg 4, Sch 3, art 33 (Plc).

[102] See The Companies (Model Articles) Regulations 2008, SI 2008/3229, reg 2, Sch 1, art 42 (Ltd), reg 4, Sch 3, art 33 (Plc); *Salisbury Gold Mining Co Ltd v Hathorn* [1897] AC 268, PC.

[103] See The Companies (Model Articles) Regulations 2008, SI 2008/3229, reg 2, Sch 1, art 42 (Ltd), reg 4, Sch 3, art 33 (Plc).

15-66   A chairman's decision to adjourn is invalid not only if it is taken in bad faith but also if he fails to take into account relevant factors, or takes into account irrelevant factors, or reaches a conclusion which no reasonable chairman could have reached, having regard to the purpose of his power to adjourn which is to ensure that the members have a proper opportunity to debate and vote on resolutions.[104]

15-67   In *Byng v London Life Association Ltd*[105] the Court of Appeal found that in deciding to adjourn an overcrowded general meeting from the morning to the afternoon, the chairman had failed to take into account relevant factors. The court thought that there must be very special circumstances to justify a decision to adjourn the meeting to a time and place where, to the knowledge of the chairman, it could not be attended by a number of the members who had taken the trouble to attend the original meeting and who could not even lodge a proxy vote because it was too late to do so.[106]

15-68   No business is to be transacted at an adjourned meeting other than business which might properly have been transacted at the meeting from which the adjourned meeting took place. Resolutions passed at an adjourned meeting take effect from the date on which they are in fact passed and are not deemed passed on any earlier date (CA 2006, s 332).

Quorum for meetings

15-69   Subject to the articles, two qualifying persons present at a meeting are a quorum,[107] but not if the two persons present are corporate representatives or proxies for the same member.[108] In other words, the requirement is that two separate members are represented. Any resolution passed at a meeting which is inquorate is void.[109]

15-70   One shareholder cannot form a meeting,[110] except:

- if there is only one shareholder in a class of shareholders, the assent of that shareholder is the equivalent of a meeting of the class;[111]

---

[104] *Byng v London Life Association Ltd* [1989] BCLC 400.

[105] [1989] BCLC 400.

[106] As to when a proxy must be lodged, see CA 2006, s 327 and **15-10**.

[107] See The Companies (Model Articles) Regulations 2008, SI 2008/3229, reg 2, Sch 1, art 39 (Ltd); reg 4, Sch 3, art 30 (Plc).

[108] CA 2006, s 318(2). The wording is unclear because it appears to provide that neither of the two representatives or proxies can count towards the quorum (neither being a qualifying person), as opposed to allowing them to count as one member personally present.

[109] *Re Cambrian Peat, Fuel and Charcoal Ltd, De La Mott's Case and Turner's Case* (1875) 31 LT 773; *Re Romford Canal Co, Pocock's Claims* (1883) 24 Ch D 85.

[110] *Sharpe v Dawes* (1876) 2 QBD 25; *Re London Flats Ltd* [1969] 2 All ER 744.

[111] *East v Bennett Bros* [1911] 1 Ch 163; *Re RMCA Reinsurance Ltd* [1994] BCC 378. The case of a single member of a class is exceptional and limited to cases where there is only one person in the particular class. Otherwise the ordinary meaning of the word 'meeting' is the coming together of two or more persons: *Re Altitude Scaffolding Ltd, Re T & N Ltd* [2007] 1 BCLC 199 (court refused to sanction a scheme of arrangement (under what is now CA 2006, s 899) which provided for class meetings requiring the attendance in person or by proxy of one member of a class only).

- if the company is a single member company (whether public or private, limited by shares or by guarantee), one qualifying person present is a quorum (CA 2006, s 318(1)); and

- where the court convenes a meeting under s 306 (discussed at **15-49**), a direction may be given that one member present may constitute a quorum (s 306(4)).

Minutes of meetings

Every company is required to keep minutes of general meetings (CA 2006, s 355(1)(b))   **15-71**
and of directors' meetings (s 248). Any minute purporting to be signed by the chairman of the meeting at which such proceedings took place or by the chairman of the next succeeding meeting is evidence of those proceedings.[112] Where a sole member takes any decision which has effect as if agreed by the company in general meeting, he must provide the company with details of the decision (s 357(2)).

The minutes of general meetings are open to inspection by any member without   **15-72**
charge, and a member is entitled, on payment of a small fee, to copies (s 358(3),(4)). Where inspection is refused, the court may by order compel inspection (s 358(7)).

F The *Duomatic* principle—informal unanimous agreement

Recognising that shareholders do not always observe all of the formalities of meetings   **15-73**
and resolutions as envisaged by the legislation, the courts also accept that the informal unanimous assent of all shareholders who have a right to attend and vote at a general meeting of the company is as binding as a resolution of the company in general meeting provided the persons assenting are competent to effect the act to which they have assented.[113]

This principle that unanimous assent is tantamount to a resolution of a properly con-   **15-74**
vened general meeting is known as the *Duomatic* principle and companies often have to resort to it if they are to validate actions which are otherwise not in conformity with the requirements of the statute or of the articles. For example, in *Wright v Atlas Wright (Europe) Ltd,*[114] informal unanimous assent was needed to validate a director's contract of employment which had not been put before the shareholders for approval at a meeting as required by CA 1985, s 319, now CA 2006, s 188.[115]

---

[112] CA 2006, s 356(4).

[113] *Re Duomatic Ltd* [1969] 1 All ER 161 at 168, per Buckley J; *Parker & Cooper v Reading* [1926] Ch 975; *Re Oxted Motor Co Ltd* [1921] 3 KB 32; *Re Express Engineering Works Ltd* [1920] 1 Ch 466; *Re New Cedos Engineering Co Ltd* [1994] 1 BCLC 797.   [114] [1999] 2 BCLC 301, CA.

[115] Likewise, informal unanimous assent can override the need for shareholder approval imposed by CA 1985, s 320, now CA 2006, s 190, for substantial property transactions between directors (and others) and the company: see *NBH Ltd v Hoare* [2006] 2 BCLC 649.

15-75   The *Duomatic* principle may override requirements of the articles,[116] or the statute,[117] or a shareholders' agreement[118] and it applies also where the consent required is of a class of shareholders rather than all the shareholders of the company.[119]

15-76   Assent by the shareholders for these purposes may be given formally or informally (i.e. without any meeting at all); it need not be in writing; and it need not be given simultaneously but at different times.[120] The assent may be tacit, in the form of acquiescence by the shareholders with knowledge of the matter, rather than express,[121] but the principle cannot apply where the assent of the shareholders has never been sought[122] or where there is no evidence of any discussion or knowledge of the facts to enable them to assent.[123] Also, the persons assenting must be competent to effect the act to which they have assented.[124]

15-77   An issue has been the extent to which statutory requirements as to how a transaction or scheme might be carried out can be overridden by informal consent in this way. The answer lies in a consideration of the purpose and underlying rationale of the particular statutory formality in question.[125] The limit to the *Duomatic* principle, as established by the Court of Appeal in *Wright v Atlas Wright (Europe) Ltd*,[126] is that it cannot be used to override statutory provisions whose purpose and rationale extends beyond the protection of the class which has purported to waive the provision.

15-78   The issue in *Wright* was whether unanimous informal consent met the requirement for shareholder approval of a director's service contract in excess of five years, as required by CA 1985, s 319. The Court of Appeal concluded that the purpose of s 319 did not extend beyond the benefit and protection of the shareholders of the company. It was therefore amenable to waiver by the class for whose protection it was designed in circumstances where it was clear that they were fully informed.

---

[116] See *Re Duomatic Ltd* [1969] 1 All ER 161.

[117] See *Wright v Atlas Wright (Europe) Ltd* [1999] 2 BCLC 301, CA.

[118] *Re Euro Brokers Holdings Ltd v Monecor (London) Ltd* [2003] 1 BCLC 506, CA (shareholders had accepted as valid and therefore were bound by a call for more capital made by email though the shareholders' agreement provided for capital calls to be made by formal notice from the board).

[119] *Re Torvale Group Ltd* [1999] 2 BCLC 605.

[120] *Parker & Cooper Ltd v Reading* [1926] Ch 975.

[121] See *Re Torvale Group Ltd* [1999] 2 BCLC 605; *Re Bailey Hay & Co Ltd* [1971] 3 All ER 693.

[122] *EIC Services Ltd v Phipps* [2004] 2 BCLC 689 at 623-4, Ch D, per Neuberger J (appealed on other grounds unrelated to the *Duomatic* principle). Shareholder authorisation was required for the capitalisation of reserves and an allotment of bonus shares and, while the shareholders were informed in advance of the bonus issue, their authorisation was not sought. The court concluded that no formal or informal assent had been obtained and there could be no reliance on *Duomatic*. The court noted that it is not enough for *Duomatic* purposes to show that assent would probably have been given if asked: there had to be an actual assent.

[123] *Queensway Systems Ltd v Walker* [2007] 2 BCLC 577.

[124] *Re New Cedos Engineering Co Ltd* [1994] 1 BCLC 797; and see *Wright v Atlas Wright (Europe) Ltd* [1999] 2 BCLC 301 at 314-15, CA.

[125] *Wright v Atlas Wright (Europe) Ltd* [1999] 2 BCLC 301, CA.   [126] [1999] 2 BCLC 301.

The Company Law Review concluded that the *Duomatic* principle should be   **15-79**
codified,[127] but the Government rejected that recommendation on the grounds that
the common law position is very flexible (as can be seen from the discussion above)
and codification would lead to rigidity and restrictions on the operation of this very
beneficial principle.[128] Hence the Companies Act 2006 confirms that nothing in the
provisions governing resolutions and meetings affects any enactment or rule of law as
to things done otherwise than by passing a resolution (CA 2006, s 281(4)(a)).[129]

[127] Company Law Review, *Modern Company Law for a Competitive Economy, Final Report*, vol 1 (2001)
URN 01/942, paras 7.17–7.26; also *Completing the Structure* (2000) URN 00/1335, paras 5.13–5.17; *Developing
the Framework* (2000) URN 00/656, paras 4.21–4.23.
[128] See *Modernising Company Law* (Cm 5553-I, 2002), paras 2.31–2.35.
[129] See also CA 2006, s 239(6)(a).

16

Informed shareholders and stakeholders—disclosure and the limited company

A Introduction

The role of disclosure

16-1 Disclosure has always been seen as the price to be paid by those forming a company in return for the conferring of limited liability which insulates shareholders' personal wealth from the reach of the company's creditors (unless the shareholders have been persuaded to give personal guarantees).[1] Disclosure is required in a variety of ways including to the registrar of companies for inclusion on the public register (the role of the registrar is discussed in Chapter 1). In addition, disclosure is required at the company's registered office and, for public companies, at annual general meetings and, for traded companies, to the markets. The media too plays a role in bringing corporate information to the attention of the public. Increasingly, companies make extensive use of their websites to maintain ongoing disclosure with their shareholders and quoted companies are obliged to post information on their websites in certain circumstances.[2] Most disclosure is addressed to shareholders and/or creditors, present and future, but there are a wide variety of stakeholders who have an interest in corporate disclosure including employees and customers, the wider public, the media and local and national authorities.[3]

---

[1] Given that disclosure is designed primarily to protect creditors and others dealing with a limited liability company, an unlimited company (subject to certain exceptions) need not deliver accounts to the registrar of companies: CA 2006, s 448, though unlimited companies must prepare accounts for their shareholders: s 394.

[2] See CA 2006, s 341 (obligation to post poll results on website); s 430 (obligation to publish annual accounts and reports on website); s 527 (ability of members to post audit concerns on the website); also n 44 below (quoted company).

[3] See Company Law Review, *Modern Company Law for a Competitive Economy, Developing the Framework* (2000), para 5.4; also *Modern Company Law for a Competitive Economy, The Strategic Framework* (1999), paras 5.144–5.147.

16-2   In devising an appropriate disclosure strategy, the Company Law Review identified the following key considerations:[4]

- timely information for all concerned;
- equal access to information so far as reasonably possible;
- recognition of the differing needs of users, including simpler information for most private shareholders;
- the best use of information technology to facilitate access to information; and
- the need for rules to be flexible to respond to changing business needs and practices.

16-3   In keeping with the general thrust of the Review which was to put small companies first, the Review identified separate basic principles underpinning their approach to financial disclosure requirements with respect to small companies. For such companies, the Review considered the important considerations to be:[5]

(1) there must be sufficient information to support the management process and to enable monitoring and review of management on behalf of those with a legitimate interest;

(2) legal requirements should not be imposed where self-interest or the market can be relied on to achieve the necessary effect;

(3) legal requirements must be proportionate to the benefits. The Review noted that the benefits of disclosure in public interest terms in these companies can be comparatively small.

It is clear that the Review regarded disclosure merely as an internal tool to assist management rather than an external device to allow others to observe the workings of the company. Talk of market pressure in the context of small companies is particularly irrelevant.

16-4   While there are many reasons for requiring disclosure, three of the fundamental objectives would be:[6]

(1) to assist creditors to assess risk. Historically, disclosure requirements have been seen as a mechanism to assist creditors in assessing the risks of dealing with a limited company. The company puts forward information about itself and the creditor decides in the light of that information whether to deal with the company and on what terms (for example, as to price, interest, and security required). In that context, financial information in the form of timely, independently

---

[4] See Company Law Review, *Modern Company Law for a Competitive Economy, Completing the Structure* (2000), para 6.6; also *Developing the Framework* (2000), para 5.20.

[5] *Developing the Framework* (2000), para 8.3.

[6] On disclosure generally, see Villiers, *Corporate Reporting and Company Law* (2006); Ebke, 'The Impact of Transparency Regulation on Company Law' in Hopt and Wymeersch, *Capital Markets and Company Law* (2003).

audited, annual accounts is particularly crucial and those requirements are the focus of this chapter.

(2) to assist shareholders and others to hold management to account. The establishment of high standards of corporate governance requires quality financial and non-financial disclosure to enable shareholders and future investors to assess the company's management and profitability. Disclosure promotes efficient management as directors appreciate that their actions are subject to disclosure and scrutiny. That transparency linked to concerns for their own business reputations can be effective in maintaining appropriate standards of conduct. In Chapter 5, we discussed the importance of shareholders, large and small, exercising an active voice in the governance of their companies. To do this effectively shareholders require detailed accessible information, detailed enough for the sophisticated investor to appreciate what is going on and accessible enough so that even the less sophisticated investor has an understanding of the state of the company's affairs.

(3) to facilitate the operation of the capital markets. Investors need appropriate information to facilitate informed investment choice and the efficient allocation of capital by them. The role of disclosure in the capital markets is beyond the scope of this book, but an example of its importance can be seen in the context of capital raising where the Prospectus Directive[7] imposes significant disclosure requirements on companies seeking to raise capital and/or be admitted to trading on a regulated market: see **19-108**.

The merits of disclosure are frequently debated in terms of cost-benefit analysis though **16-5** it is difficult to put a monetary value on the benefits of an open transparent system.[8] For the past 30 years, there has been significant pressure from business to lessen disclosure requirements, especially financial disclosures, particularly for small companies (the definition of which includes companies meeting two of the following criteria: a turnover of not more than £6.5m; a balance sheet total of not more than £3.26m and not more than 50 employees (CA 2006, s 382) which may not meet everyone's idea of a small business).[9] The result is that little public disclosure is now required of such companies. It is debatable whether such an extensive reduction in disclosure is compatible with the policy goal of sufficient disclosure to enable an informed assessment of the risks of dealing with limited companies. The ability of small business organisations to lobby for the removal of the burdens of incorporation while retaining the benefits should not be underestimated.

---

[7] Directive 2003/71/EC on the prospectus to be published when securities are offered to the public or admitted to trading and amending Directive 2001/34/EC, OJ L 345, 31.12.2003, p 64.

[8] For example, it is impossible to quantify and value wrongdoing which has been deterred by disclosure requirements.

[9] More recently, the pressure has shifted to the removal of directors' residential addresses from the register, restricting rights of access to the register of members and removing the addresses of shareholders from the annual return. The justification in these cases being that shareholders and directors are being targeted by animal rights activists: see discussion at **1-74** and **14-94**.

The regulatory framework on accounting requirements

16-6   The statutory framework on accounts is laid down in CA 2006, Part 15 (Accounts)[10] augmented by a number of statutory instruments as a result of the decision to remove much of the accounting detail from the CA 2006 in the interests of clarity and to allow for ease of amendment in future. The key instruments which need to be read together with Part 15 include the Small Companies and Groups (Accounts and Directors' Report) Regulations 2008, SI 2008/409 and the Large and Medium-sized Companies and Groups (Accounts and Directors' Report) Regulations 2008, SI 2008/410 which, respectively, set out the detailed requirements as to the content and form of the accounts and the directors' report for small companies and for all other companies.

16-7   The statutory framework on accounts is dominated by the requirements of the Fourth and Seventh Company Law Directives. The Fourth Directive deals with the presentation and content of a company's individual accounts[11] and the Seventh Directive deals with the presentation and content of consolidated or group accounts:[12] together they are known as the Accounting Directives.

16-8   The Accounting Directives have been amended on numerous occasions, most importantly by the Modernisation Directive,[13] adopted in May 2003, which updated the accounting disclosure requirements to reflect modern accountancy standards. This move followed the adoption in June 2002 of a Regulation on the application of International Accounting Standards (IAS)[14] which, from 1 January 2005, requires listed companies to draw up their consolidated accounts (in terms of form and content) in accordance with IAS now referred to as IFRS.[15] The idea behind this change is that the accounts of listed companies across the EU are more transparent and comparable when drawn up in accordance with international accounting standards rather than national requirements.[16]

16-9   The IAS requirements apply to publicly traded companies governed by the law of a Member State. If such a company is required to prepare consolidated accounts,[17] the

---

[10] As amended by Companies Act 2006 (Amendment) (Accounts and Reports) Regulations 2008, SI 2008/393.

[11] Fourth Council Directive (EEC) 78/660, OJ L 222, 14.8.1978, p 11.

[12] Seventh Council Directive (EEC) 83/349, OJ L 193, 18.7.1983, p 1.

[13] See Directive 2003/51/EC amending and updating Council Directives 78/660/EEC, 83/349/EEC, 86/635/EEC and 91/674/EEC on the annual and consolidated accounts of certain types of companies, banks and other financial institutions and insurance undertakings, OJ L 178, 17.7.2003, p 16.

[14] Regulation (EC) No 1606/2002 of 19 July 2002 on the application of international accounting standards, OJ L 243, 11.09.2002, p 1; and see the European Commission Press Release, IP/02/827, 7 June 2002.

[15] International accounting standards are now known as IFRS—International Financial Reporting Standards. International Accounting Standards were issued by the International Accounting Standards Committee which has since been replaced by the International Accounting Standards Board (IASB), an independent standard-setting body which issues IFRS.

[16] The requirement to use IAS is intended to end, what the then European Commissioner Bolkestein described as, 'the current Tower of Babel' in financial reporting. See Commission Press Release, IP/02/827, 7 June 2002.

[17] I.e. if it is a parent company (other than a small company) and is not within the exemptions in CA 2006, ss 400–402: s 399; 'parent company' is defined in s 1173.

directors must state in the notes to the accounts that the accounts have been prepared in accordance with IAS (CA 2006, s 406). A company has the option of preparing its individual accounts either in accordance with IAS or the CA 2006 (i.e. applying UK GAAP[18]) but in general a company required to apply IAS to its consolidated accounts would do likewise in respect of its individual accounts. A parent company must ensure that its individual accounts and the individual accounts of its undertakings are prepared using the same framework, whether that is IAS or CA 2006, except to the extent that in the directors' opinion there are good reasons for not doing so (CA 2006, s 407). If a company prepares either its consolidated or individual accounts according to IAS for a financial year, it cannot switch back to the CA 2006 requirements in subsequent years (s 395(3)) subject to a limited number of exceptions (ss 395(4), 403(5)). The intention is to prevent a company confusing users of the accounts by constantly changing between accounting frameworks.

The Accounting Directives were further amended by Directive 2006/46/EC.[19] The focus of the amendments was:[20]   **16-10**

(1) to further increase the thresholds for small and medium companies so ensuring that they are exempt from the more onerous disclosure requirements of the Accounting Directives;

(2) to provide for additional disclosure of certain off-balance sheet items and transactions with related parties—these matters are of particular concern to regulators and investors; and

(3) to require publicly traded companies to include a corporate governance statement in their annual reports and to ensure the collective responsibility of board members for the annual accounts and reports (see **5-15**).

The latter two elements were part of the European response to the problems identified in the collapse of the American energy group, Enron, with billion-dollar losses. Further proposed amendments to the Accounting Directives were brought forward in April 2008 as part of the ongoing European Commission simplification programme (see discussion at **2-17**). These proposals are focused particularly on simplifying reporting requirements for medium-sized companies and on providing some clarification of the requirements for group accounts.[21]   **16-11**

All of these measures together are designed to ensure the highest standards of transparency (compatible with the economic size of the company) and comparability for accounts of companies formed in the Member States. For larger companies, the key   **16-12**

---

[18] Generally Accepted Accounting Standards (GAAP).   [19] OJ L 224, 16.08.2006, p 1.

[20] These requirements are reflected in the CA 2006, Part 15 on accounts with the exception of the requirement for a corporate governance statement which is addressed by the Disclosure and Transparency Rules of the FSA: see DTR 7.2, discussed at **5-15** with consequential amendments to the CA 2006 by the Companies Act 2006 (Accounts, Reports and Audit) Regulations 2009 (SI number not available at time of writing).

[21] See Proposal for a Directive of the European Parliament and of the Council amending Council Directives 78/660/EEC and 83/349/EEC as regards certain disclosure requirements for medium-sized companies and obligation to draw up consolidated accounts, COM (2008) 195, 17.04.2008.

development is the move to international accounting standards rather than standards derived from accounting practice in individual Member States.

16-13 The Accounting Directives clearly have been central to the development of accounting requirements over the past 30 years and the last 10 years has seen a relatively continuous process of updating and amending. In September 2008, a proposal was put forward by European Commissioner McCreevy for a comprehensive review of the accounting requirements starting from a 'think small first' perspective.[22] The outcome is likely to be further de-regulation of small and medium-sized enterprises coupled with more intensive regulation of the largest enterprises. This will be the case particularly in the banking and insurance sectors given the widespread collapse of banking companies and related problems for insurance companies in late 2008 and their importance to the overall stability of markets and economies.

B The statutory scheme

16-14 The statutory provisions governing company accounts are lengthy and complex and it is not intended to provide a detailed accounting treatment in this chapter, but rather an overview of the requirements so as to appreciate the obligations on directors and the level and type of disclosure which is available to shareholders and stakeholders.

Accounting records

16-15 Every company must keep adequate accounting records sufficient to show and explain the company's transactions and to disclose with reasonable accuracy at any time its financial position at that time and to enable the directors to ensure that any accounts required to be prepared comply with the CA 2006 and, where applicable, IAS requirements.[23] A failure to maintain records is an offence by every officer in default[24] and prosecutions for breach of this requirement are (relatively) common. Non-compliance with this requirement is also a common basis for a finding of unfitness warranting the disqualification of a director[25] (disqualification is considered in Chapter 6, see **6-86**).

---

[22] See announcement by Commissioner McCreevy, Memo 08/589, 29.09.2008.

[23] CA 2006, s 386. Records must be maintained for three years in the case of a private company and six years if a public company: s 388(4). The records may be maintained at the company's registered office or such other place as the directors think fit and must be available for inspection by the officers of the company: s 388(1). Inspection of company records is governed by The Companies (Company Records) Regulations 2008, SI 2008/3006.

[24] CA 2006, s 387(1); unless the officer can show that he acted honestly and that in the circumstances the default was excusable: s 387(2).

[25] For example, see *Re Galeforce Pleating Co Ltd* [1999] 2 BCLC 704; *Secretary of State for Trade and Industry v Arif* [1997] 1 BCLC 34.

Prepare accounts

Having maintained the required accounting records, the directors must prepare for the shareholders: **16-16**

(1) individual accounts for each financial year (CA 2006, s 394);

(2) a directors' report reviewing the company's activities (s 415);

(3) if the company is a quoted company,[26] a directors' remuneration report (s 420); and

(4) an auditors' report (ss 475, 495), though many companies are audit exempt (see **16-38** below).

The directors must prepare individual accounts for the company for each financial   **16-17**
year.[27] A company's individual accounts consist of a balance sheet and a profit and loss account and notes thereto (CA 2006, s 396(1), (3)). The format is determined by whether the company is a small or other company and is dictated by the relevant regulations, noted above at **16-6**.

If a company's individual accounts are prepared as IAS individual accounts, the   **16-18**
directors must state in a note to the accounts that the accounts have been prepared in accordance with international accounting standards (CA 2006, s 397). If the individual accounts have been prepared in accordance with the CA 2006, the accounts must give a true and fair view of the state of the affairs of the company and its profit or loss for the financial year (s 396(2)). The significance of the 'true and fair view' is reinforced by s 393 which states that directors must not approve accounts unless they are satisfied that they give a true and fair view of the assets, liabilities, financial position and profit or loss of the company and this requirement applies to all accounts whether prepared in accordance with the CA 2006 or IAS requirements. The statute does not define what is meant by a 'true and fair view', but compliance with the appropriate accounting standards is normally necessary if the accounts are to give a true and fair view.

The Accounting Standards Board (ASB) is the prescribed body with responsibility   **16-19**
for determining accounting standards (see **16-34**)[28] and it regards accounting standards as definitive statements of how particular types of transactions and other events should be reflected in financial statements. It also envisages that only in exceptional circumstances would departure from an accounting standard be necessary in order for accounts to give a true and fair view. Ultimately, however, the question whether the accounts do give a true and fair view is a matter of law for the courts to decide.[29]

---

[26] Defined CA 2006, s 385 and see n 44 below.

[27] CA 2006, s 394: a company's financial year is determined in accordance with s 390.

[28] Prescribed under CA 2006, s 464; see The Accounting Standards (Prescribed Body) Regulations 2008, SI 2008/651.

[29] See Accounting Standards Board, *Foreword to Accounting Standards* (June 1993) and counsel's opinion annexed thereto; see also Evans, ' "True and fair" Revisited' [1990] LMCLQ 255; McGee, 'The True and Fair View Debate: A Study in the Legal Regulation of Accounting' (1991) 54 MLR 874.

16-20   Given the importance of the issue, and the changes involved as a result of the application of IAS requirements which require financial statements to present fairly the
financial position of the company[30] (rather than a 'true and fair view'), the FRC (see
16-34) took counsel's opinion in 2008 as to the 'true and fair' requirement.[31] A key
conclusion of counsel was that the requirement set out in international accounting
standards that the accounts present fairly the position of the company is not a different requirement to that of showing a true and fair view but is a different articulation of
the same concept. Further, the preparation of financial accounts is not a mechanical
process where compliance with the accounting standards automatically ensures that
the accounts give a true and fair view, or a fair presentation; while highly likely to have
that outcome, it does not guarantee it. Directors must consider whether, taken in the
round, the financial statements that they approve are appropriate. Similarly, auditors
are required to exercise professional judgment before expressing an audit opinion. As
a result, the Opinion confirms that it is not sufficient for either directors or auditors to
reach such conclusions solely because the financial statements are prepared in accordance with applicable accounting standards.[32]

Small companies

16-21   Exemptions are available as to the accounts to be prepared and delivered by small or
medium-sized companies which meet certain statutory criteria relating to turnover,
balance sheet total and number of employees and which are not otherwise ineligible.
To qualify as a small company, a company must satisfy two or more of the following criteria in relation to the relevant year: the company's turnover must not exceed
£6.5m; the balance sheet total must not exceed £3.26m; and the number of employees
must not exceed 50 (CA 2006, s 382); and the company must not be excluded under
s 384 from the small companies regime (i.e. must not be a public company, certain
financial services companies or a member of an ineligible group).

16-22   The accounts (i.e. balance sheet, profit and loss accounts and accompanying notes) prepared for the members of a small company must comply with the required form and
content and information to be provided in the notes as prescribed (CA 2006, s 396(3)).[33]
The directors of a company subject to the small companies regime are only required to
deliver the balance sheet to the registrar of companies (s 444(1)). A further refinement
is that the directors of a small company can choose to deliver a modified balance sheet
in which case the accounts are referred to as abbreviated accounts (s 444(3)).[34] Small

---

[30] See IAS 1, para 13.

[31] The Opinion of Martin Moore QC is posted on the FRC website at www.frc.org.uk/about/trueandfair.
cfm. Previous legal opinions on this issue were written by Lord Hoffmann and Dame Mary Arden in 1983
and 1984 and by Dame Mary Arden in 1993 (commissioned by the ASB: see above n 29) are also available
on the website. Martin Moore refers to the 'almost iconic status' achieved by these Opinions (see para 7 of
his Opinion).

[32] See Martin Moore Opinion, above n 31, paras 41–6.

[33] I.e. as laid down in The Small Companies and Groups (Accounts and Directors' Report) Regulations
2008, SI 2008/409, Sch 1.

[34] The content in this case is as laid down in The Small Companies and Groups (Accounts and Directors'
Report) Regulations 2008, SI 2008/409, Sch 4.

companies which wish to take advantage of this exemption therefore need to prepare two sets of accounts, one for their members and one for the registrar of companies. As the main benefit is the provision of minimal information to the public registry, some companies are happy to bear the additional cost. While the company may be happy to incur the cost in preparing a separate abbreviated balance sheet for the registrar of companies, those searching the public registry may find this an unsatisfactory level of disclosure. The Company Law Review was scathing about abbreviated accounts, noting their cost, their limited usefulness, the fact that the information conveyed is not meaningful, and that their sole benefit seemed to be to deny information to competitors.[35] In its Final Report, the Review recommended that this facility for filing abbreviated accounts be abolished and that small companies be required to prepare one set of accounts for circulation to their members and for filing with the registrar of companies.[36] The Government in the White Paper, *Modernising Company Law*,[37] accepted this recommendation but later changed its position and abbreviated accounts are retained by CA 2006, s 444(3). If a company delivers abbreviated accounts and it is not exempt from the requirement to have an audit (see at **16-38**) or it has chosen not to take advantage of audit exemption, it must deliver a special auditors' report (s 449(1)). This report does not state that the accounts give a true and fair view (the auditors would not be willing so to state with regard to abbreviated accounts) but states that, in the auditor's opinion, the company is entitled to deliver abbreviated accounts and that the abbreviated accounts are properly prepared (s 449(2)).

Medium-sized companies

To qualify as a medium-sized company, a company must satisfy two or more of the following criteria in relation to the relevant year: the company's turnover must not exceed £25.9m; the balance sheet total must not exceed £12.9m; and number of employees must not exceed 250 (CA 2006, s 465); and the company must not be excluded under s 467 from the medium-sized companies regime (i.e. must not be a public company, certain financial services companies or a member of an ineligible group). For medium-sized companies, the exemptions available are modest, allowing for the delivery to the registrar of companies of an abbreviated profit and loss account which aggregates gross profits and omits details as to turnover, but a balance sheet and a directors' report must be delivered in the usual way.[38]   **16-23**

Group accounts

A parent company (other than a small parent company within CA 2006, s 383[39] and provided it is not within the exceptions in ss 400–402) must prepare its own   **16-24**

---

[35] See *Developing the Framework* (2000), paras 8.32–8.34.

[36] Company Law Review, *Modern Company Law for a Competitive Economy, Final Report*, vol 1 (2001), para 4.38.

[37] Cmnd 5553-I, (2002), para 4.26.

[38] CA 2006, s 445, see The Large and Medium-sized Companies and Groups (Accounts and Directors' Report) Regulations 2008, SI 2008/410, para 4.

[39] A parent company is not required to prepare and deliver group accounts if it heads a group which qualifies as a small group and it is not an ineligible group: CA 2006, ss 399(1), 383, 384(2). A group qualifies as

individual accounts *and* group accounts (s 399(2)), namely, a consolidated balance sheet and consolidated profit and loss account for the whole group (s 404). In some cases consolidated accounts must be prepared in accordance with IAS (s 403(1)), as noted at **16-8**; otherwise group accounts may be prepared in accordance with IAS or CA 2006 requirements (s 403(2)). The content and format are as prescribed by regulations.[40] Companies Act group accounts must give a true and fair view of the state of affairs of the group and the profit or loss of the group.[41] If the group accounts are prepared as IAS group accounts, the directors must state in a note to the accounts that the accounts have been prepared in accordance with international accounting standards (s 406).

The directors' report

16-25   Every company must prepare and (save in the case of a small company) deliver a directors' report for each financial year (CA 2006, s 415).[42] If the company is a small company, there is no requirement to deliver a directors' report though the company may choose to deliver it (s 444(1)). The content of the directors' report is as prescribed by regulations[43] but must include the directors' names, the principal activities of the company and, save in the case of small companies, the amount recommended for a dividend payment (s 416). In the case of companies admitted to trading on a regulated market, it must include information as to voting and control structures as required by the Takeovers Directive (see **26-76**) and a corporate governance statement, see **5-15**.

16-26   The directors' report must include a business review (CA 2006, s 417) which is a review of the development of the company's business and information on matters such as dividend payments, transfers to reserves, political and charitable donations, employment policies and details of the directors' shareholdings. The importance of the business review was considered in Chapter 9 as it is specifically linked to the directors' duty to act to promote the success of the company imposed by CA 2006, s 172: see **9-32**.

16-27   The directors' report must also contain a statement by the directors that there is no relevant audit information (i.e. information needed by the auditor in connection with the preparation of his report) of which the auditor is unaware and there are criminal sanctions for false statements to this effect (CA 2006, s 418). A director exercising care

a small group if it meets two of the following criteria in the relevant year: turnover must not exceed £6.5m net; the balance sheet total must not exceed £3.26m net; and the number of employees must not exceed 50: s 383(4).

[40] See The Large and Medium-sized Companies and Groups (Accounts and Reports) Regulations 2008, SI 2008/410, reg 9, Sch 6, Part 1.

[41] CA 2006, s 404(2); there is provision for the exclusion of some subsidiary undertakings from the group accounts: see s 405; and a parent company is allowed to prepare a modified individual profit and loss account: s 408.

[42] For delivery requirements, see CA 2006, ss 445–447.

[43] See The Small Companies and Groups (Accounts and Directors' Report) Regulations 2008, SI 2008/409, reg 7, Sch 5; The Large and Medium-sized Companies and Groups (Accounts and Reports) Regulations 2008, SI 2008/410, reg 10, Sch 7.

and skill needs to make such necessary enquiries of his fellow directors and otherwise as to enable him to meet his obligations under this provision (s 418(4)).

Given the level of disclosure now required in the directors' report, directors have **16-28** become increasingly concerned about potential liabilities arising from erroneous statements, especially in the context of the business review requirements which for the largest companies requires the inclusion of forward-looking statements. The Government decided to provide a safe-harbour provision (CA 2006, s 463) to alleviate these fears. This provision imposes liability on directors to compensate the company (only) for loss suffered by it as a result of any untrue or misleading statement in the directors' report (or in the directors' remuneration report, see below) but a director can only be liable if he knew the statement was untrue or misleading or was reckless as to whether it was untrue or misleading. In other words, liability can only arise in deceit (which is quite unlikely) and not in negligence and liability can only be to the company (which is quite unlikely to sue) and only for loss suffered as a result of the statement (which it would be difficult to identify). Hence the safe harbour.

The directors' remuneration report

Quoted companies are required to draw up a detailed directors' remuneration report **16-29** containing a full explanation of the company's policy on directors' service contracts and on notice periods and termination as well as comprehensive details of the remuneration (and compensation) packages of each individual director and the membership and role of the remuneration committee (CA 2006, s 420).[44] Part of the report is subject to review by the auditors who must state whether that part of the report has been properly prepared in accordance with the requirements of the CA 2006.[45] This remuneration report must be submitted to the annual general meeting for shareholder approval of the report by way of an ordinary resolution (s 439). See discussion of this report and its impact at **5-40**. The safe harbour discussed at **16-28** applies also to untrue or misleading statements in the directors' remuneration report.

Approving accounts

The accounts must be approved by the board and signed on the balance sheet on behalf **16-30** of the board by a director (CA 2006, s 414); likewise, the directors' report (s 419) and the directors' remuneration report (s 422). The directors must not approve the accounts unless they are satisfied that the accounts give a true and fair view of the company's assets, liabilities, financial position and profit or loss (s 393(1)). Provision is made for the revision of defective accounts or reports, either voluntarily by the directors

---

[44] The details of the required disclosure are set out in The Large and Medium-sized Companies and Groups (Accounts and Reports) Regulations 2008, SI 2008/410, para 11, Sch 8. 'Quoted company' means a company whose equity share capital—(a) has been included in the official list in accordance with the provisions of Part 6 of the Financial Services and Markets Act 2000; or (b) is officially listed in an EEA State (EU with Norway, Iceland and Liechtenstein); or (c) is admitted to dealing on either the New York Stock Exchange or Nasdaq: CA 2006, s 385.   [45] CA 2006, s 421(1); SI 2008/410, reg 11, Sch 8, Part 3.

(s 454)[46] or, in the case of accounts, on the intervention of the Secretary of State (s 455) whose powers in this respect with regard to public and large private companies are exercised by the Financial Reporting Review Panel:[47] see **16-34** below.

Circulating, laying and filing accounts

16-31   A copy of the accounts and reports must be sent to each member[48] and, if the company is a public company, laid by the directors before a general meeting (CA 2006, s 437(1)); this meeting is known as the 'accounts meeting': s 437(3). The accounts may be sent to the members in hard copy or electronic form, subject to the rules governing electronic communications: see **15-5**. A copy of the accounts and reports must be delivered by the directors to the registrar of companies.[49] A quoted company must publish its accounts and reports on its website as soon as reasonably practicable (s 430) and is required to publish its financial statements within four months of the end of the financial year.[50] Companies may provide summary financial statements (derived from the annual accounts and the directors' report) to their shareholders instead of the full annual accounts and reports (s 426).[51] This option (originally limited to listed companies, but now available to all companies) enables companies to save costs and provides shareholders with information in a more accessible format.

16-32   The obligation to deliver the accounts to the registrar of companies falls on the directors (CA 2006, s 441). In the case of a private company, a copy of the accounts must be sent to the members not later than nine months from the end of the financial year or, if earlier, the date on which the company actually delivers its accounts to the registrar (s 424(2)(a), s 444(2)). Nine months is a lengthy period which means that the accounts are of limited value when they finally appear on the public record. Public companies must send the accounts to the members at least 21 days before the relevant accounts meeting (s 424(3)), see **16-31**, and must deliver the accounts to the registrar of companies within six months from the end of the financial year (s 442(2)(b)). The effect of these long lead-in times for delivery to the registrar of companies means that, even with respect to compliant companies, the information provided to the public registry is quite dated. Despite these generous timescales, there are significant levels of non-compliance by companies, even though a failure to deliver accounts to the registrar of companies is a criminal offence by the directors (s 451(1)) and late filing penalties apply (s 453).[52]

---

[46] See also The Companies (Revision of Defective Accounts and Reports) Regulations 2008, SI 2008/373.

[47] See Companies (Defective Accounts and Directors' Reports) (Authorised Person) and Supervision of Accounts and Reports (Prescribed Body) Order 2008, SI 2008/623.

[48] CA 2006, s 423(1)(a); and also to the holders of the company's debentures and to every person entitled to receive notice of the company's meetings: s 423(1)(b), (c).

[49] CA 2006, s 441 subject to small company exemptions, see **16-22**. Unlimited companies are exempt: see s 448.

[50] FSA, Disclosure and Transparency Rules, DTR 4.1.3.

[51] The form and content is governed by The Companies (Summary Financial Statements) Regulations 2008, SI 2008/374. The auditors must state that the summary financial statement is consistent with the annual accounts and directors' report: CA 2006, s 427(4)(d); s 428(4)(d).

[52] See Companies (Late Filing Penalties) and Limited Liability Partnerships (Filing Periods and Late Filing Penalties) Regulations 2008, SI 2008/497. The penalty imposed varies in amount depending on the

C The auditors' role

The regulatory framework for audit

Disclosure of accounting information alone is insufficient without assurance as to the **16-33** quality of that information which comes from the requirement that the accounts be audited. The regulatory framework for company audits and auditors is provided by CA 2006, Part 16 (Audits) and Part 42 (Statutory Auditors); the latter Part concentrates on the regulation of the audit profession and public oversight issues. The origin of many of the provisions lies in domestic reforms enacted post-Enron (see **16-11**) initially in the Companies (Audit, Investigations and Community Enterprise) Act 2004 (CAICE) and in European requirements set out in the 'new' Eighth Company Law Directive.[53]

A major element of the CAICE reforms was the restructuring of the regulatory bodies **16-34** with responsibility for accounting standards and auditing away from a self-regulatory environment to one which ensures public oversight.[54] The key independent regulator now is the Financial Reporting Council (FRC) with responsibility for promoting high standards of corporate reporting and corporate governance. The FRC operates through a variety of important operating bodies which issue accounting standards (the Accounting Standards Board, ASB); seek to establish high auditing standards (the Auditing Practices Board, APB); have independent oversight of the regulation of the accounting and auditing professions (the Professional Oversight Board, POB); operate an independent investigation and disciplinary body for accountants and actuaries (the Accountancy and Actuarial Discipline Board, AADB); and seek to ensure that the annual accounts of public companies and large private companies comply with the requirements of the Companies Act 2006 and applicable accounting standards (the Financial Reporting Review Panel, FRRP). All of these bodies have now established standing as important regulators in their respective areas and are actively involved in the maintaining and raising of standards in corporate reporting, accounting and auditing.

type of company and the period of the delay and the levels were increased by these Regulations. Fines run from £150 for a private company which is not more than one month late filing up to £1,500 if more than six months late; equivalent figures for public companies are £750 and £7,500; penalties double if the offence is repeated in two consecutive years. See *R (on the application of Pow Trust) v Chief Executive and Registrar of Companies* [2003] 2 BCLC 295 where the court rejected a claim that such penalties infringe the European Convention on Human Rights.

[53] Directive 2006/43/EC on statutory audits of annual accounts and consolidated accounts: OJ L 157, 9.6.2006, p 87.

[54] The background to the reforms can be found in the reports of the Co-ordinating Group on Audit and Accounting Issues, *Interim Report*, July 2002, URN 02/1092; *Final Report*, 29 January 2003, URN 03/567; also the HC Treasury Committee Report, *The Financial Regulation of Public Limited Companies*, 6th Report, Session 2001–02, HC 758-I (2002); and the Government's Response, 13th Special Report, Session 2001–02, HC 1219 (2002).

16-35   The Eighth Company Law Directive,[55] adopted in 2006, replaces an earlier version
from 1984 which laid down minimum requirements and qualifications for auditors.
The 'new' Eighth Directive makes comprehensive provision for all matters pertaining
to the statutory auditor, his qualifications, role and independence, as well as providing
for disciplinary processes, quality assurance and public oversight of the audit profession. Adoption of the Directive means that the European Commission can now focus
on more specific issues, specifically the ownership and independence of audit firms,
auditors' liabilities (a matter which was the subject of a Recommendation in 2008)[56]
and independent public oversight and external quality assurance (also the subject of a
Recommendation in 2008).[57]

Appointment of auditors

16-36   Every company must appoint an auditor or auditors unless for each financial year
the directors reasonably resolve otherwise on the ground that audited accounts are
unlikely to be required (CA 2006, ss 485(1), 489(1)).[58] In the case of public companies, where an auditor is to be appointed (which will be in all cases other than where
the company qualifies as dormant) the appointment must be made at the accounts
meeting: see **16-31** (s 489(2)). Auditors may be individuals or firms and they must
be appropriately qualified (s 1219). They must be members of recognised supervisory
bodies (s 1212)[59] and meet independence requirements (s 1214). The CA 2006 gives
the Secretary of State power by regulations to make provision for the disclosure of the
terms on which a company's auditor is appointed, remunerated or performs his duties
(s 493). This power has not been exercised to date.

16-37   In addition to their role as the company auditor, auditors frequently provide the
company (especially larger companies) with additional services, such as advice
on taxation matters, on corporate restructuring, information technology and on
human resources. For companies other than small and medium-sized companies,
the amount of any remuneration received by the auditor in respect of such non-audit
services must be included in a note to the company's accounts.[60] The concern about

---

[55] Directive 2006/43/EC on statutory audits of annual accounts and consolidated accounts: OJ L 157,
9.6.2006, p 87.

[56] See Commission Recommendation of 5 June 2008 concerning the limitation of the civil liability of
statutory auditors and audit firms: OJ L 162, 21.06.2008, p 39.

[57] See Commission Recommendation of 6 May 2008 on external quality assurance for statutory auditors
and audit firms auditing public interest entities: OJ L 120, 07.05.2008, p 20.

[58] Auditors appointed as such are officers of the company for the periods for which they are appointed:
Mutual Reinsurance Co Ltd v Peat Marwick Mitchell & Co [1997] 1 BCLC 1; *Re London and General Bank*
[1895] 2 Ch 166; *Re Kingston Cotton Mill Co* [1896] 1 Ch 6.

[59] For example, they may be members of the Institute of Chartered Accountants of England and Wales
(ICAEW) or the Institute of Chartered Accountants of Scotland (ICAS) or the Association of Chartered
Certified Accountants (ACCA).

[60] CA 2006, s 494; and see The Companies (Disclosure of Auditor Remuneration and Liability Limitation
Agreements) Regulations 2008, SI 2008/489. Small and medium-sized companies must disclose the audit fee
paid to their auditors: reg 4. All other companies must make extensive disclosure of both the audit fee and
all other fees receivable by the auditors for services supplied by them and their associates to the company, its

the provision of non-audit services, which are typically much more lucrative than the statutory audit, is that the value of the services may compromise the independence of the auditor.

Exemption from obligation to appoint auditors

Generally, the expectation would be that all companies' accounts should be audited, but one of the de-regulatory measures designed to reduce the costs and burdens of regulation on smaller businesses (see above at **16-5**) was an exemption from the statutory requirement for an audit.[61]   **16-38**

The argument against the statutory audit for these companies is essentially one of the costs involved particularly when, it is argued, it is difficult to identify a real need for, or benefit from, the statutory audit. In many small companies, the shareholders typically are also the directors and often all concerned are members of one family so there is no shareholder need for an audit. Equally, the company's creditors in many cases consist of the company's bank (which would have its own picture of the company's finances) and a small number of trade creditors providing limited amounts of credit on short timescales. Hence, it is argued, there is no identifiable creditor need for an audit either.   **16-39**

The arguments in favour of retaining the audit centre on the value to these small companies of obtaining professional assistance with their accounts at least once a year. Many of these companies are woefully unaware of their obligations with respect to a variety of accounting and taxation matters and the annual audit offers an opportunity for some professional advice. It also means that the auditors are in a position to draw the directors' attention to matters such as a drift towards insolvency (and their corresponding duties to creditors: see **9-42**) and the risk of possible liability for wrongful trading (see **25-17**) and disqualification (see **6-64**). Filing unaudited accounts with the registrar reduces the value of the public registry as searchers are unable to assess the reliability of the information being presented by the company. Finally, given that not all small companies are wholly owned by the directors or families, minority shareholders who are not directors and who do not have access to the company's records need the reassurance of an annual independent review of the accounts.   **16-40**

The case for exemption prevailed, however, and the requirement for an audit was abolished in 1994, initially for companies with a turnover below £90,000.[62] That threshold has been raised on a number of occasions and now stands at £6.5m.[63] In 2007–08, 69.1% of the companies on the register (1.25m companies) filed audit-exempt   **16-41**

---

subsidiaries and associated pension schemes: reg 5(1). This level of disclosure was part of the quid pro quo for the introduction of liability limitation agreements: see **16-73**.

[61] See generally, Freedman and Godwin, 'The Statutory Audit and the Micro Company—An Empirical Investigation' [1993] JBL 105; also ICAEW, 'The Statutory Audit For Small Companies: The Case For Reform', FRAG/1992, April 1992.

[62] See The Companies Act 1985 (Audit Exemption) Regulations 1994, SI 1994/1935.

[63] CA 2006, s 477(1) as amended by Companies Act 2006 (Amendment) (Accounts and Reports) Regulations 2008, SI 2008/393, reg 5(1)(a).

accounts; the figure for 2003–04 was 56.9% of the register.[64] Shareholders representing more than 10% in nominal value of the issued share capital may require the company to have an audit (CA 2006, s 476).

16-42   There are two main ways in which companies may be exempt from the audit requirement:[65]

(1) where the company is a small company which qualifies as a small company in relation to that year under s 382: see **16-21** above, and its turnover in that year is not more than £6.5 million, and its balance sheet total for that year is not more than £3.26 million (s 477); and it is not an excluded company within s 478;[66]

(2) where the company is a dormant company within s 480. A company is a dormant company if it has no significant accounting transaction during the period in question, i.e. no transaction that requires to be entered in the company's accounting records (s 1169). A dormant company may be either a public or a private company, provided it is not otherwise ineligible (ss 480, 481). A company may be dormant for a variety of reasons. For example, it may have been incorporated to protect a company name; or it may be part of a group of companies where activities have been transferred to other parts of the group; or it may have been incorporated to carry out a venture which never got off the ground.

16-43   In either case (small or dormant), a company is not entitled to the audit exemption unless the balance sheet contains a statement by the directors to the effect that:

(1) the company is entitled to the exemption (CA 2006, s 475(2));

(2) shareholders holding 10% of the shares have not sought an audit under s 476 (s 475(3)(a));

(3) the directors acknowledge their responsibility for keeping accounting records and the preparation of the accounts (s 475(3)(b)).

If that statement is false, criminal penalties may arise for approving accounts which do not comply with the statutory requirements (s 414(4), (5)).

Removal and resignation of auditors

16-44   A company may by ordinary resolution at any time remove an auditor from office (CA 2006, s 510). An auditor who is not re-appointed after expiry of his term of office may require the company to allow him to make representations to the members (s 514). An auditor may resign his office at any time by depositing a notice in writing to that effect

---

[64] See BERR, *Companies Register Activities 2007—2008*, Table F2, available on the Companies House website at www.companieshouse.gov.uk/about/companiesRegActivities.shtml.

[65] There is also a limited exemption in respect of non-profit-making companies subject to public sector audit: see CA 2006, s 482.

[66] Excluded categories essentially are public companies or certain financial services or special register companies; CA 2006, s 478; special rules apply to small companies which are part of a group, see s 479.

at the company's registered office (s 516) and the company must send a copy of that notice to the registrar of companies (s 517). In the case of an unquoted company, where an auditor ceases for any reason to hold office (i.e. removal or failure to re-appoint or resignation), he must deposit at the company's registered office a statement of any circumstances connected with his ceasing to hold office which he considers should be brought to the attention of the members or creditors of the company or, if he considers that there are no such circumstances, a statement that there are none (s 519).[67] An auditor who deposits a statement about the circumstances of his departure can require the directors to call a meeting to discuss those circumstances (s 518) and he must send notice of his resignation to the registrar of companies (s 521). An auditor of a major audit[68] who ceases to hold office for any reason must notify the appropriate audit authority,[69] as must an auditor in any other case who leaves office before the expiry of his term of office (s 522). The appropriate audit authority must in turn notify the Secretary of State and the appropriate accounting authorities (s 524).[70] As is obvious, there is now quite an elaborate degree of notification required which is designed to eliminate practices which may have existed in the past whereby disagreements between management and auditors were resolved by timely resignations or failures to re-appoint which left the shareholders (and the regulators) unaware of any audit concerns or tensions at the root of the departures.

The auditor's report

An auditor's primary task is to make a report to the company's members on the annual accounts of the company (CA 2006, s 495(1)). As Lord Oliver commented in *Caparo Industries plc v Dickman*:[71]   **16-45**

> '…the primary purpose of the statutory requirement that a company's accounts shall be audited annually is almost self-evident. The structure of the corporate trading entity, at least in the case of public companies whose shares are dealt with on an authorised stock exchange, involves the concept of a more or less widely distributed holding of shares rendering the personal involvement of each individual shareholder in the day to day management of the enterprise impracticable, with the result that management is necessarily separated from ownership. The management is confided to a board of directors which operates in a fiduciary capacity and is answerable to and removable by the shareholders who can act, if they act at all, only collectively and only through the

[67] The auditor must make up his own mind as to whether there are circumstances which need to be brought to the attention of the mentioned parties; and the court will presume that the auditors are acting in faithful discharge of their duty and not in pursuit of any private or collateral interest, unless the contrary is shown: *Jarvis plc v PricewaterhouseCoopers* [2000] 2 BCLC 368.

[68] Defined as an audit of a listed company or another entity where there is a major public interest: CA 2006, s 525(2).

[69] The 'appropriate audit authority' means, in the case of a major audit, the Public Oversight Board, see **16-34** CA 2006, s 525(1)(a); the Statutory Auditors (Delegation of Functions etc) Order 2008, SI 2008/496, art 5; and for audits other than major audits, the relevant supervisory body: CA 2006, s 525(1)(b).

[70] The appropriate accounting authorities are the Secretary of State and the FRRP: CA 2006, s 524(2).

[71] [1990] 1 All ER 568 at 583.

medium of the general meeting. Hence the legislative provisions requiring the board annually to give an account of its stewardship to a general meeting of shareholders.'

16-46   The auditor's report must identify the accounts and the financial reporting framework that has been applied (CA 2006, s 495(2)) and it must describe the scope of the audit. The report must state whether in the auditor's opinion the accounts give a true and fair view:

(1) in the case of an individual balance sheet, of the state of affairs of the company as at the end of the financial year;

(2) in the case of an individual profit and loss account, of the profit or loss of the company for the financial year;

(3) in the case of group accounts, of the state of affairs as at the end of the financial year, and the profit or loss for the financial year, of the undertakings included in the consolidation as a whole, so far as concerns members of the company (s 495(3)(a)).

The report must also state whether the annual accounts have been properly prepared in accordance with the relevant financial reporting framework and the requirements of the CA 2006 and, where applicable, IAS (s 495(3)(b), (c)).

16-47   The auditor's report must state whether the directors' report is consistent with the accounts (s 496) and, if the company is a quoted company, whether that part of the directors' remuneration report which is subject to review by the auditors has been properly prepared (s 497). If the auditor is of the opinion that adequate accounting records have not been kept; or the accounts are not in agreement with the accounting records; or the auditable part of the directors' remuneration report is not in agreement with the accounting records, he must so state in the audit report (s 498(2)). If an auditor fails to obtain the information necessary for the purposes of the audit, he must so state in the audit report (s 498(3)); if the directors have claimed to be entitled to use the small companies regime and in the auditor's opinion, they are not so entitled, he must so state in the audit report (s 498(5)). If certain information is not disclosed as to directors' benefits and remuneration when it is required to be disclosed, the auditor must include the particulars in his report (s 498(4)). Clearly, the statute now dictates much of the content of the report. The report must state the auditors' names and be signed and dated by them (s 503). The report can be qualified or unqualified and the auditor may draw attention to matters by way of emphasis without qualifying the report (s 495(4)).

16-48   The form and content of the auditors' report is also the subject of extensive professional guidance[72] which imposes additional requirements such as a requirement that the auditor's report states that the preparation of the financial statements are the responsibility of the directors while the auditor's responsibility is to audit those statements.[73]

---

[72] Standards are determined by the Auditing Practices Board in the form of ISAs (International Standards on Auditing), see **16-34**. The current ISA on the auditor's report is ISA (UK and Ireland) 700 *The Auditor's Report on Financial Statements* (December 2004).

[73] See ISA 700, above n 72, paras 5, 9.

There must also be a statement that the audit has been planned and performed so as to obtain reasonable reassurance that the financial statements are free from material misstatement, whether caused by fraud, or other irregularity, or error.[74]

Such is the level of detail now required that the thrust of the auditor's report and the key elements of it are in danger of being swamped by the surrounding information. Unsurprisingly, the point has been reached where the content of the report is under review by the APB (see **16-34** above).[75] The consensus emerging is for a shorter, more focused report which concentrates on the three discrete items which are central to the report, namely whether the accounts have been properly prepared in accordance with the applicable financial reporting framework, whether they have been prepared in accordance with the applicable law and whether they give a true and fair view. **16-49**

The significance of the audit report is enhanced by a requirement that the senior statutory auditor sign the report (ss 503, 504). In other words, the audit engagement partner must sign his own name as well as the name of the firm, which does not increase his personal liability in any way (s 504(3)) but is designed to reinforce his appreciation of his personal professional responsibilities with regard to the audit. There is also a new criminal offence in CA 2006, s 507 of knowingly or recklessly causing an auditor's report on the annual accounts to include any matter that is misleading, false or deceptive in a material particular or to omit statements otherwise required by s 498.[76] It is also important to note the valuable right conferred on members of a quoted company[77] holding a certain percentage of the shares to require a company to put a statement on the company's website setting out any audit concerns which they may have (s 527). The company when giving notice of an accounts meeting (see **16-31**) must draw attention to the right of the members to use the company website in this way (s 529). **16-50**

Many corporate collapses in the past have revealed significant fraudulent activity by the directors and/or other employees, often long-running wrongdoing and usually on a massive scale. In most cases, these activities have gone undetected by the company's auditors which raises issues as to (1) the manner in which the auditors conduct an audit and (2) their liabilities in the event that the audit fails to detect wrongdoing or significant poor performance by the company such that the accounts give an erroneous picture of the company's business. **16-51**

The conduct of the audit

An auditor's task is to conduct the audit in a manner which provides reasonable reassurance that material misstatements in financial documents will be detected.[78] The **16-52**

---

[74] See ISA 700, above n 72, para 13.

[75] See APB, Exposure Draft of proposed revisions to ISA (UK and Ireland) 700 *The Auditor's Report on Financial Statements*; also APB Press Notice 94, 1 September 2008; the Exposure Draft was preceded by a Discussion Document entitled *The Auditor's Report: A time for change?* (2007).

[76] I.e. a failure to include a statement that the accounts do not agree with accounting records, or that necessary information has not been included; or that the directors are wrongly using the small companies exemption: see CA 2006, s 507(2).   [77] Defined CA 2006, s 385: see above n 44.

[78] See *Barings plc v Coopers & Lybrand* [1997] 1 BCLC 427; see ISA 700, above n 72, para 13.

audit includes an examination, on a test basis, of evidence relevant to the amounts and disclosures in the financial statements.[79] There are a number of older authorities which establish that an auditor is not an insurer[80] nor is he required to approach his work with suspicion or with a foregone conclusion that something is wrong; and he is justified, in the absence of suspicion, in believing employees in whom confidence is placed by the company.[81] An auditor should approach his work with an inquiring mind,[82] however, and once put on inquiry, he is under a duty to get to the bottom of the matter in question.[83] These older authorities must be treated with some caution for the courts are likely to expect higher standards from today's highly paid, professional auditors but they do provide some basic pointers as to what is expected of auditors.

16-53   In *Sasea Finance Ltd v KPMG*[84] the Court of Appeal concluded that where a company's auditors discover that a senior employee is defrauding the company on a massive scale, and that employee is in a position to continue doing so, the auditors would normally have a duty to report the discovery to the management immediately, not merely when rendering their report; and if the management are implicated in the wrongdoing, the auditors would have to report directly to a third party without the management's knowledge or consent.

16-54   To assist the auditors in their task, they have a right of access at all times to the company's books and accounts and they are entitled to require a wide range of persons, in particular the company's officers and employees, to provide them with such information and explanations as they think necessary for the performance of their duties (CA 2006, s 499). Criminal sanctions apply where the information or explanation is misleading, false or deceptive in a material particular (s 501).[85] Auditors of a parent company with overseas subsidiaries can require the parent company to obtain from the subsidiary, its officers etc such information or explanations as the auditor reasonably requires for the purposes of his duties as auditor and the parent company must take all such steps as are reasonably open to it to obtain that information etc (s 500). An auditor is entitled to receive all communications relating to a proposed written resolution of a private company and also has the right to be notified of and to attend any general meeting and to speak on any part of the business of the meeting which concerns him as auditor (s 502(2)). In practice, auditors rarely need to rely on their statutory rights in this regard since an auditor who is dissatisfied with his access to information or to the shareholders has other mechanisms at his disposal, most notably the ability to qualify his report (s 495(4)(a)), to add statements short of qualification (s 495(4)(b)) or to resign (s 516): see **16-47**.

---

[79] See ISA 700, above n 72, para 14.
[80] See *Re London and General Bank Ltd (No 2)* [1895] 2 Ch 673.
[81] *Re Kingston Cotton Mill Co (No 2)* [1896] 2 Ch 279.
[82] See Lord Denning in *Fomento (Sterling Area) Ltd v Selsdon Fountain Pen Co Ltd* [1958] 1 WLR 45 at 61.
[83] *Re Thomas Gerrard & Son Ltd* [1967] 2 All ER 525.
[84] [2000] 1 BCLC 236.
[85] There is a right against self-incrimination: see CA 2006, s 499(3).

D Auditors' liability and limitation of liability

Duty of care of auditors

One of the most contentious issues is the extent of any duty of care owed by the com-   **16-55**
pany's auditors to the company, the shareholders and others who read and rely on the
audited accounts. While there is much case-law on the matter involving auditors (and
other professionals), the general trend is a reluctance to find that a professional adviser
owes a common law duty of care to a non-client.[86]

There are two possible types of claims: **16-56**

(1) claims by clients against their auditors which would be straightforward claims
in contract (since the auditors owe the company appointing them a duty to exercise reasonable care and skill in performing their contractual obligations) and
in tort;[87] and

(2) claims in tort by third parties who are not in any direct relationship with the
auditors but who claim damages for losses arising from reliance on negligently
audited accounts. The extent of any duty of care in tort to such users of the
company's accounts is problematic. A duty of care may arise between an auditor and another under two different but interrelated approaches:[88] because of
an assumption of responsibility for the task/advice in question; or because of
meeting the three-fold test (foreseeability, proximity and fairness) established
in *Caparo Industries plc v Dickman*.[89] In practice the courts apply one or other
or both approaches depending on the circumstances. The House of Lords in

---

[86] See *Bank of Credit and Commerce International (Overseas) Ltd v Price Waterhouse* [1998] BCC 617 at
636, per Sir Brian Neill; *BDG Roof-Bond v Douglas* [2000] 1 BCLC 401 at 420, per Park J. The Company Law
Review made no recommendation for any statutory extension of auditors' duties of care, preferring to leave
the issue to the development of the law of negligence through the cases in the normal way: see *Final Report*
(2001), paras 8.134–8.135.

[87] One of the most common consequences of a negligent audit is that the company will continue to pay
dividends and bonuses on the basis of the false picture painted by the accounts. Such payment of improper
dividends or bonuses is the natural and probable result of the false picture which the auditors have allowed
the accounts to present and therefore the auditors would be liable for the amount of the dividends: *Re Thomas
Gerrard & Son Ltd* [1967] 2 All ER 525 (auditors aware of discrepancies but failed to investigate further); *Re
London and General Bank (No 2)* [1895] 2 Ch 673 (auditors omitted information from report to shareholders); and see *Barings plc v Coopers & Lybrand (No 1)* [2002] 2 BCLC 364; *Equitable Life Assurance Society v
Ernst & Young* [2003] 2 BCLC 603.

[88] There is possibly a third approach—the incremental approach suggested by Lord Bridge in *Caparo
Industries plc v Dickman* [1990] 1All ER 568 at 576 where he stated that it is preferable that 'the law should
develop novel categories of negligence incrementally and by analogy with established categories, rather than
by a massive extension of a prima facie duty of care restrained only by indefinable "considerations which
ought to negative, or to reduce or limit the scope of the duty or the class of person to whom it is owed".'
But this approach is of limited help in identifying when a duty of care will arise: see Mitchell and Mitchell,
'Negligence Liability for Pure Economic Loss' (2005) 121 LQR 194; also *Customs and Excise Commissioners
v Barclays Bank* [2006] 4 All ER 256 at 263, per Lord Bingham.

[89] [1990] 1 All ER 568.

Customs and Excise Commissioners v Barclays Bank[90] made it clear that it is not possible to force the law into a single test.[91]

An assumption of responsibility for the task/advice in question

16-57   Where the parties have a contractual or 'almost contractual' relationship (for example, a client relationship or a relationship between an auditor and a regulatory authority[92]) and so fall clearly within the *Hedley Byrne & Co Ltd v Heller & Partners Ltd*[93] principle, the matter is relatively straightforward. This assumption of responsibility rests upon a relationship between the parties, which may be general or specific to the particular transaction, and which may or may not be contractual in nature.[94] Whether there is such an assumption of responsibility is a matter to be considered objectively.[95] Accountants who carry out specific reporting obligations under a statutory requirement to do so owe a duty of care to the regulatory authority to whom they report;[96] likewise, auditors may assume a duty of care to a regulatory authority.[97]

Meeting the three-fold test established in *Caparo*

16-58   Most disputes arise where there is no relationship between the auditor and the claimant but the claimant alleges that the parties are sufficiently proximate to give rise to a duty of care on the part of the auditor. The leading authority on auditors' liability is *Caparo Industries plc v Dickman*[98] where, having reviewed the authorities, the House of Lords concluded that in order for a duty of care to arise, there must be:[99]

(1) a reasonable foreseeability of damage;

(2) a relationship of sufficient 'proximity' between the party owing the duty and the party to whom it is owed; and

(3) the imposition of the duty of care contended for should be just and reasonable in all the circumstances.

16-59   It is relatively easy to establish the first element, a foreseeability of damage if accounts are negligently audited, but that is not sufficient of itself. The third element, the 'just and reasonable' consideration was imposed by the court in order to prevent foreseeability alone giving rise, in the famous words of Cardozo CJ in *Ultramares Corpn v Touche*,[100] to 'liability in an indeterminate amount for an indeterminate time to an indeterminate class'.

---

[90] [2006] 4 All ER 256, HL.

[91] See *Customs and Excise Commissioners v Barclays Bank* [2006] 4 All ER 256, HL.

[92] See *Andrew v Kounnis Freeman* [1999] 2 BCLC 641.   [93] [1963] 2 All ER 575.

[94] *Henderson v Merrett Syndicates Ltd* [1994] 3 All ER 506 at 520, HL, per Lord Goff.

[95] *Electra Private Equity Partners v KPMG Peat Marwick* [2001] 1 BCLC 589; and on the issue of assumption of responsibility, see *Henderson v Merrett Syndicates Ltd* [1994] 3 All ER 506 at 518–21; *Spring v Guardian Assurance plc* [1994] 3 All ER 129; *Williams v Natural Life Health Foods Ltd* [1998] 1 BCLC 689; *Peach Publishing Ltd v Slater & Co* [1998] BCC 139.

[96] See *Law Society v KPMG Peat Marwick* [2000] 4 All ER 540.

[97] See *Andrew v Kounnis Freeman* [1999] 2 BCLC 641.

[98] [1990] 1 All ER 568; noted [1990] LQR 349; [1990] MLR 824.

[99] [1990] 1 All ER 568 at 573–4, per Lord Bridge.   [100] (1931) 255 NY 170 at 179.

Most discussion has focused on the second element as to whether, on a particular set **16-60** of facts, there is a relationship of sufficient proximity for the duty to arise. In *Caparo*, Lord Oliver identified the circumstances which should exist in order to establish the necessary relationship of proximity between the person claiming to be owed the duty (the advisee) and the adviser:[101]

(1) the advice is required for a purpose, whether particularly specified or generally described, which is made known, either actually or inferentially, to the adviser at the time the advice is given;

(2) the adviser knows, either actually or inferentially, that his advice will be communicated to the advisee, either specifically or as a member of an ascertainable class, in order that it should be used by the advisee for that purpose;

(3) it is known, either actually or inferentially, that the advice so communicated is likely to be acted upon by the advisee for that purpose without independent inquiry; and

(4) it is so acted upon by the advisee to his detriment.

The key elements then are that the auditor knows (whether actually or inferen- **16-61** tially) that his report will be communicated to a person (whether individually or as a member of a class) specifically for a particular purpose and that there would be reliance on it.

In *Caparo*, as already noted at **16-45**, the House of Lords concluded that the purpose **16-62** of the audit is to enable the shareholders as a body to exercise informed control of the company.[102] It follows that auditors do not owe a duty of care to members of the public at large who rely on the audited accounts to buy shares; nor to an individual shareholder in the company who wishes to buy more shares in the company since an individual shareholder is in no better position than a member of the public at large;[103] nor do they owe a duty of care to existing or future creditors who extend credit on the strength of the audited accounts.[104] Likewise, auditors owe no duty of care to possible takeover bidders[105] though the position may be different where representations are made after an identified bidder has emerged[106] where it may be possible, on the facts, to establish that a duty of care has been assumed.[107] In none of these cases is the relationship proximate enough, without more, to give rise to a duty of care. Returning to the facts in *Caparo*, the House of Lords found the auditors owed no duty of care to an existing shareholder in the company who purchased additional shares and took over

---

[101] [1990] 1 All ER 568 at 589.   [102] See [1990] 1 All ER 568 at 583–4, 606–7.

[103] [1990] 1 All ER 568 at 581, 601, 607.

[104] *Al Saudi Banque v Clark Pixley* [1989] 3 All ER 361; *Berg Sons & Co Ltd v Mervyn Hampton Adams* [1993] BCLC 1045.

[105] *Caparo Industries plc v Dickman* [1990] 1 All ER 568; see also *James McNaughton Papers Group Ltd v Hicks Anderson & Co* [1991] BCLC 163.

[106] See *Morgan Crucible Co plc v Hill Samuel Bank Ltd* [1991] BCLC 18; *Galoo Ltd v Bright Grahame Murray* [1994] 2 BCLC 492.

[107] See *ADT v BDO Binder Hamlyn* [1996] BCC 808; also *Electra Private Equity Partners v KPMG Peat Marwick* [2001] 1 BCLC 589.

the company in reliance on the audited accounts only to discover that the accounts were inaccurate. The auditors owed their duty to the shareholders as a body and not to an individual investor.

16-63   These issues can be illustrated by considering *Barings plc v Coopers & Lybrand (No 1)*.[108] This case arose out of the collapse of the Barings Bank group of companies as a result of the unauthorised activities of a rogue trader in the Far East who accumulated losses of about £800m. The parent company (P1) had a subsidiary (S1) which had a subsidiary (S2) and the rogue trader was an employee of S2. Following the collapse of the group, an action in contract and tort was brought by S2 against its auditors (D&T) in respect of their allegedly negligent audits of the company. An action in tort was also commenced against the auditors by P1 and S1. Essentially, these companies argued that had the audit been conducted properly, the wrongdoing would have been uncovered, these companies would not have continued to advance funding to S2, and the group would not have collapsed. The court struck out most of these claims.

16-64   Turning to the criteria established by *Caparo*, Evans-Lombe J pointed out that, in the case of a claim in tort against an auditor, it is necessary to plead and prove that at the time the auditor undertook his services, he must have had in contemplation that they would be relied on by the claimant for the purpose of a particular transaction or class of transactions. That reliance then must have resulted in the loss for which compensation was claimed. Evans-Lombe J noted that these limitations (reliance on the audit for a contemplated purpose) were necessary to control the scope of claims in this area of the law. He went on:[109]

> 'To the outsider it would seem far-fetched that the negligence of a subsidiary auditor of one of the minor subsidiary companies of a complex and substantial banking group should expose that auditor to liability for massive damages flowing from the collapse of the entire group, notwithstanding that it can be said that but for his negligence that collapse would not have taken place.'

16-65   In acting as the auditors of S2, however, the auditors never had it in contemplation that their report would be used by the other companies in the group in deciding to meet the trader's funding requests through S2. Equally, no transactions made by P1 which resulted in it losing the value of the entire group could be identified as having been embarked upon in reliance on the audit and which the auditors had in contemplation when they undertook that audit. The claims were struck out.

16-66   This case highlights another issue, causation (but see below). Even if a duty of care can be established, the alleged breach of duty must be the effective or dominant cause of the claimants' loss as opposed to merely the occasion for the loss. In determining that issue, the court applies its common sense to the issue. In *Galoo Ltd v Bright Grahame Murray*[110]

---

[108] [2002] 2 BCLC 364, Ch D.   [109] [2002] 2 BCLC 364 at 394–5.

[110] [1994] 2 BCLC 492. On the other hand, in *Sasea Finance Ltd v KPMG* [2000] 1 BCLC 236 the court accepted that where the auditors failed in breach of duty to 'blow the whistle' on fraudulent and dishonest activities of senior staff, it was arguable that that failure caused continued losses brought about by such frauds.

the court struck out a claim for losses arising from continued trading after a negligent audit. It was argued that, had the audit been conducted properly, the companies involved would not have continued to trade and therefore the claim was for the losses arising from the continued trading. The court rejected the claim. The breach of duty gave the companies the opportunity to continue and to incur losses, but it did not 'cause' the loss in the sense that 'cause' is used in law.

More recently the authorities have moved away from a focus on causation and *Galoo* is better analysed now in terms of the scope of the duty of care. The overall situation was summed up by Arden LJ in *Johnson v Gore Wood & Co*[111] in the following way: **16-67**

> 'Starting with *Caparo v Dickman*, the courts have moved away from characterising questions as to the measure of damages for the tort of negligence as questions of causation and remoteness. The path that once led in that direction now leads in a new direction. The courts now analyse such questions by enquiring whether the duty which the tortfeasor owed was a duty in respect of the kind of loss of which the victim complains. Duty is no longer determined in abstraction from the consequences or vice-versa. The same test applies whether the duty of care is contractual or tortious. To determine the scope of the duty the court must examine carefully the purpose for which advice was being given and generally the surrounding circumstances. The determination of the scope of the duty thus involves an intensely fact-sensitive exercise. The final result turns on the facts, and it is likely to be only the general principles rather than the solution in any individual case that are of assistance in later cases.'

Two key points emerge: first the focus is on the scope of the duty in terms of whether there was a duty in respect of the kind of loss of which the victim complains; and, secondly, these issues are intensely fact-sensitive. An illustration of this approach can be seen in *MAN Nutzfahrzeuge AG v Freightliner Ltd*[112] where the Court of Appeal dismissed a claim by a parent company for breach of duty by an auditor of a subsidiary company.   **16-68**

Essentially, the facts were that a subsidiary company (S1) was sold by its parent company (P1) to M by way of a share purchase agreement. It later transpired that for some time previously the accounts of S1 had been persistently manipulated by its financial controller, E, who was responsible for a systematic VAT fraud. E had played a prominent role in the negotiations for the sale and made dishonest representations to the purchaser as to the accuracy of the accounts. P1 settled a claim in deceit against it by M and the issue before the Court of Appeal was whether P1 could look for a contribution from S1's auditors who accepted that, if the audit had been conducted with due care and skill, the defects in the accounts would have been identified. The auditors were aware of the importance of the accounts in the negotiations with M.   **16-69**

The Court of Appeal accepted that it was within the scope of the auditors' duty of care to protect S1 from the consequences of decisions taken by S1 or by its shareholders in relation to the affairs of S1 on the basis that the accounts were free from material misstatement. Though it was not necessary to decide the point, the court considered   **16-70**

---

[111] [2003] EWCA Civ 1728 at [91]; [2003] All ER (D) 58 (Dec).   [112] [2008] 2 BCLC 22, CA.

that it would also have been within the scope of a special duty of care owed by the auditors to protect P1 from the consequences of representations and warranties made in the share purchase agreement with M. But the auditors could not be held to have assumed responsibility for the fraudulent use which the dishonest employee made of the subsidiary's accounts in the negotiations for the sale of S1 since that would impose on the auditors a liability greater than they could reasonably have thought they were undertaking. P1's losses were the direct result of the dishonesty of S1's employee rather than the inaccuracy of the accounts themselves and the auditors did not undertake a special audit duty to P1 in respect of representations made by E as to the accuracy of the accounts. For all those reasons the auditors were not liable for the loss which P1 had suffered.

16-71   Auditors will also take heart from the decision of the Court of Appeal in *Moore Stephens v Stone & Rolls Ltd*.[113] Essentially a claim was brought against the defendant auditors in respect of allegedly negligent audits of the claimant company (now in liquidation). The company was a one-man company under the control of S who used the company to perpetrate a substantial letter of credit fraud against various banks. The banks had sued the company which was now in liquidation and the liquidator sought to recover damages from the company's auditors for negligence. The allegation centred on whether the auditors were negligent in not discovering the fraud and bringing it to an end so limiting the company's losses. The auditors argued that the claim (which was funded by a third party) should be struck out on the basis that, applying the usual rules of attribution as between S and the company, the company was itself guilty of fraud, see **3-66**. Accordingly, the claimant was seeking to rely upon and recover a loss caused by its own fraud which would infringe the maxim ex turpi causa non oritur actio. The auditors lost at first instance where the judge was persuaded that the ex turpi causa rule did not necessarily rule out the claim so long as care was taken to preclude any recovery which would inure to the benefit of the individual perpetrator or perpetrators of the impugned conduct. The Court of Appeal emphatically reversed that ruling holding that the *Hampshire Land* principle (knowledge of a fraud would not be attributed to a company when the fraud was practised on the company itself) was limited to when that fraud was being practised *on* the company.[114] But this was not such a case, the court said; rather, the claimant was itself the fraudster. As such, the ex turpi causa maxim applied and the claim was barred by that principle. This is not a discretionary principle but one based on public policy and it must be applied, the court said. The court also dismissed out of hand the proposition that the ex turpi causa maxim was overruled when the illegality which gave rise to its application (i.e. the fraudulent conduct of the company's business) was 'the very thing' in respect of which the defendant had been retained and paid for (to take reasonable care to detect fraud in the affairs of the company). There was no duty of care, the court said, to the fraudster company which was a party to the fraud to take reasonable care to detect its fraud. The judgment is also interesting for the critical comments by Mummery LJ

---

[113] [2008] 2 BCLC 461, CA.   [114] *Re Hampshire Land Co* [1896] 2 Ch 743.

about what he described as 'this astounding claim'. Having dismissed all legal basis for the claim, Mummery LJ concluded that, quite apart from the law, it was 'contrary to all common sense to uphold a claim that would confer direct or indirect benefit on the corporate vehicle, which was used to commit the fraud and was not the victim of it and the fraudulent driver of the fraudulent vehicle'.[115] As many cases where the auditor fails to discover a fraud will fall within the scenario in *Stone & Rolls*, auditors have another defence in the maxim ex turpi causa to any liability.

Limiting auditors' liabilities

Faced with concerns as to the extent of their possible liability for negligent audits **16-72** (though, as noted above, there are considerable limitations to that liability and it is not as open-ended as auditors would have us believe), the auditing profession has been anxious to secure some legal haven against liability. The starting point is CA 2006, s 532(2) which provides that any provision, whether contained in a company's articles or in any contract with the company or otherwise, for exempting an auditor of a company (to any extent) from any liability that would otherwise attach to him in connection with any negligence, default, breach of duty or breach of trust in relation to the company occurring in the course of the audit of accounts, is void. Despite this restriction, there are a number of ways in which auditors successfully limit or manage their potential liabilities for negligent audits, not least by indemnities and liability limitation agreements which are expressly permitted by s 532(2).

(1) Audit firms may incorporate as companies with limited liability or they may register as limited liability partnerships (LLPs) under the Limited Liability Partnerships Act 2000: see **1-19**. Indeed LLPs were originally conceived as a mechanism to protect auditors from limitless personal liability, though they are now available to all.[116]

(2) Insurance—auditors may purchase insurance to protect themselves, but insurance is expensive and adequate cover may not be available, at any price. If a claim is for hundreds of millions of pounds, there is likely to be a significant shortfall between the cover (which might be for, say, £50m) and the amount claimed.

(3) Indemnities—a company may indemnify its auditor against any liability incurred by him in defending proceedings (whether civil or criminal) in which judgment is given in his favour or he is acquitted, or in connection with an application under CA 2006, s 1157 in which relief is granted to him by the court (s 533).

---

[115] [2008] 2 BCLC 461 at 504, CA.

[116] For a critical review of this response to auditors' concerns, see Freedman & Finch, 'Limited Liability Partnerships: Have Accountants Sewn up the "Deep Pockets" Debate?' [1997] JBL 387.

(4) Court relief—auditors are amongst those entitled to apply to the court for relief under CA 2006, s 1157 (power of court to grant relief in case of honest and reasonable conduct): see the discussion of s 1157 at **13-55**.

(5) It is now possible for companies and their auditors to enter into liability limitation agreements (LLAs).

Liability limitation agreements

Background

16-73   The background to LLAs is the long-running concern of auditors, noted above, that they risk catastrophic losses in the event of liability in negligence, a concern fuelled by the implosion in 2002 of Arthur Andersen (then one of the world's largest audit firms), following the collapse of the American energy company, Enron, which had been audited by Andersen. The particular concern of auditors is that joint and several liability in English law means that, following a corporate collapse, there is no one left to sue who is worth suing other than the auditors who are treated as the deep pockets to meet the entire losses though the directors and others may also be culpable. As is clear from the case-law, the legal position is somewhat more complex with the law limiting the auditor's liability to the company rather than to third parties and with liability in turn limited by the scope of the duty of care imposed. Nevertheless, the auditing profession has been relentless in its pursuit of legal protection against claims.

16-74   The collapse of Arthur Andersen also increased concerns amongst regulators and national authorities that with the 'Big Five' auditing firms now reduced to the 'Big Four' (PricewaterhouseCoopers, Deloitte, Ernst & Young, KPMG), a further collapse would mean very limited audit choice for the largest companies and indeed a risk that the largest companies would find it very difficult to appoint an auditor at all.

16-75   This last aspect sufficiently concerned the European Commission that it concluded that unlimited liability for auditors combined with insufficient insurance cover poses significant problems for the development of a competitive audit market.[117] In 2008, therefore it issued a Recommendation to Member States that Member States should take national measures to limit audit firms' liabilities, save in cases of intentional breach of duty by an auditor.[118] The Recommendation suggests three possible limitation methods: a financial cap, a mechanism for proportionate liability, or a contractual

---

[117] The European Commission has launched a consultation exercise on control structures in audit firms to examine possible ways to stimulate the emergence of new players in the international audit market: see Directorate General For Internal Market And Services Working Paper: *Consultation On Control Structures In Audit Firms And Their Consequences On The Audit Market* (November 2008). This initiative follows a report commissioned by DG Internal Market on audit firm ownership: see Oxera, *Ownership Rules Of Audit Firms And Their Consequences For Audit Market Concentration* (October 2007).

[118] Commission Recommendation of 5 June 2008 concerning the limitation of the civil liability of statutory auditors and audit firms, OJ L 162, 21.06.2008, p 39.

limitation approved by the shareholders, but it is for the Member States to decide on the appropriate method for limiting liability. The Recommendation also sets out the key principles to be followed by Member States when they select a limitation method, including that a limitation of liability should not apply in the case of an intentional breach of duty by an auditor; and it should not prevent injured parties from being fairly compensated (in other words, only a limitation and not an exemption from liability should be provided), but a limitation should apply to limit claims by the company and by any third party entitled under national law to bring a claim for compensation.[119] The Commission will review the position in 2010 in the light of the actions taken by the Member States in the wake of this Recommendation. Anticipating or leading these developments, the UK made provision for auditor LLAs in the CA 2006, ss 532–538 which came into force on 6 April 2008.

Given the novelty of allowing auditors to limit their liability, the FRC (see **16-34**)   **16-76** thought it would be helpful to issue guidance on the content of LLAs and the issues which the directors should bear in mind when considering an LLA. This FRC Guidance includes specimen clauses and explains the process to be followed to obtain shareholder approval together with specimen shareholder resolutions.[120] While there are concerns (also expressed about the EU Recommendation) that there is an insufficient balance between the protection of auditor interests and shareholder interests, the FRC comments that these concerns must be assessed in the light of the efforts being made to improve audit quality, the need for LLAs to be approved by shareholders and that, under CA 2006, s 537, the court has the power to disapply the LLA unless it is satisfied that the agreement is fair and reasonable. At the same time the Institutional Shareholders Committee issued a statement indicating that institutional investors will expect companies to employ the specimen principal terms for agreements laid out in the FRC's Guidance.[121] This position suggests that the FRC Guidance will become in effect a code to be followed by the largest companies when considering entering into an LLA.

Agreeing a liability limitation agreement

A 'liability limitation agreement' is an agreement that purports to limit the amount of   **16-77** a liability owed to a company by its auditor in respect of any negligence, default, breach of duty or breach of trust, occurring in the course of the audit of accounts, of which the auditor may be guilty in relation to the company (CA 2006, s 534(1)). Each company

---

[119] The Recommendation follows an earlier consultation on liability, see DG Internal Market Commission Staff Working Paper: *Consultation on Auditors' Liability and its Impact on the European Capital Markets* (January 2007); also London Economics, *Report on Economic Impact of Auditors' Liability Regimes* for EC-DG Internal Market and Services (September 2006). See also the earlier study commissioned by the European Commission: *A study on systems of civil liability of statutory auditors in the context of a Single Market for auditing services in the European Union* (2001).

[120] See FRC, *Guidance on Auditor Liability Limitation Agreements* (June 2008).

[121] See Institutional Shareholders' Committee Statement on Auditor Liability Limitation Agreements (June 08). Membership includes the Association of British Insurers and National Association of Pension funds, the two most influential institutional shareholder groups.

must negotiate its own LLA and there cannot be group-wide agreements. A liability limitation agreement cannot apply to more than one financial year and it must specify the financial year in relation to which it applies (s 535(1)); so, for example, auditors cannot negotiate five-year deals. Shareholder authorisation is required by an ordinary resolution unless the articles require a higher majority.[122] A private company can pass a resolution waiving the need for approval, or pass a resolution before entering into the agreement, approving its principal terms,[123] or it can pass a resolution approving the (entire) agreement after the company has entered into it (s 536(2)); likewise for a public company, but a public company cannot waive the need for approval (s 536(3)). Authorisation may be withdrawn by the company passing an ordinary resolution to that effect at any time before the company enters into the agreement, or if the company has already entered into the agreement, before the beginning of the financial year to which the agreement relates (s 536(5)). A company which has made a liability limitation agreement must disclose in a note to the accounts its principal terms and the date of the approval resolution (or resolution waiving the need for approval, in the case of a private company) passed by the company's members.[124]

16-78   A significant safeguard imposed is that a liability limitation agreement is not effective to limit the auditor's liability to less than such amount as is fair and reasonable in all the circumstances of the case having regard (in particular) to the auditor's responsibilities under CA 2006, Part 16, the nature and purpose of the auditor's contractual obligations to the company, and the professional standards expected of him (s 537(1)).[125]

16-79   There are limits to what can be agreed and an auditor cannot limit its liability in an unreasonable way. A liability limitation agreement that purports to limit the auditor's liability to less than an amount that is fair and reasonable in all the circumstances takes effect as if so limited so the court will simply adjust the limitation downwards when it is set too high (s 537(2)).[126] In determining what is fair and reasonable in all the circumstances of the case no account is to be taken of matters arising after the loss or damage in question has been incurred, or matters (whenever arising) affecting the possibility of recovering compensation from other persons liable in respect of the same loss or damage (s 537(3)). For example, the fact that the liability is shared with an employee who is not worth suing is ignored.[127]

---

[122] CA 2006, ss 534(2)(b); 281(3).

[123] The 'principal terms' of an agreement are terms specifying, or relevant to the determination of the kind (or kinds) of acts or omissions covered by the LLA, the financial year to which the LLA relates, or the limit of the auditor's liability: CA 2006, s 535(4).

[124] CA 2006, s 538; The Companies (Disclosure of Auditor Remuneration and Liability Limitation Agreements) Regulations 2008, SI 2008/489, reg 8.

[125] The Government has a power by regulations to prescribe specific provisions or to prohibit certain provisions: CA 2006, s 535(2); but it does not intend to exercise the power at the moment.

[126] In other words, auditors risk nothing by overreaching in an LLA for the LLA does not become void, but is merely rewritten by the court. This may seem favourable to the auditors but it reflects the fact that all concerned will have made arrangements, such as insurance cover, on the basis of a liability limitation being in place. Note the UCTA 1977, ss 2(2), 3(2) do not apply to LLAs: CA 2006, s 534(2)(b).

[127] See *Explanatory Notes to the Companies Act 2006*, para 828.

The legislation does not impose a limitation mechanism and in particular, the limit on the amount of the auditor's liability need not be a sum of money, or a formula, specified in the agreement (s 535(4)). It is clear from the Institutional Shareholders Committee's statement on LLAs (**16-76**) that institutional shareholders will only accept agreements providing for proportionate liability ((liability based on the auditor's share of the responsibility for the company's loss) or a liability expressed in terms of what is fair and reasonable, but they will not support fixed caps.[128] Proportionate liability is likely therefore to become the norm for large companies.[129] For smaller companies, in time, other options will emerge possibly based on a multiple of the audit fee or other variations.   **16-80**

Despite these provisions on LLAs coming into force in April 2008, to date there has been little movement on the issue. Something of a stand-off seems to have developed between the companies (where the directors do not want to take the initiative in agreeing something that restricts the ability of the company to recover losses) and the audit firms who do not wish to appear to be pressing to limit their liability. Given how long auditors have sought this protection, the stand-off is unlikely to last and it is likely that the annual general meeting round in 2009 will see LLAs appearing on the agenda. Certainly many involved will have wished to have the FRC Guidance before acting, but with it now in place, and a European Recommendation providing encouragement for limitations, it is unlikely that audit firms will ignore the opportunity to put in place a binding LLA.   **16-81**

The issue for the directors is whether they should yield to pressure from the auditors to sign up to an LLA, given their duty to promote the success of the company (s 172), see **9-2**. On the one hand, the company may need to enter into an LLA if auditors refuse to act without one (though there is no evidence to date of this) and use of LLAs may help the company secure a high quality audit. The Government also considers that the introduction of LLAs will enhance the pool of audit quality (new entrants will enter the market if they can manage their potential liabilities effectively) which should lead to a more competitive market and a reduction in costs. These public interest arguments are likely to have little sway over individual directors. An alternative point of view is that these changes are too favourable to auditors (who after all are able now to operate through LLPs) and too unfavourable to shareholders who pay large fees to auditors in the expectation that they will do a careful and skilful job. The pressure on auditors to raise standards of audit quality may reduce if they are protected by an LLA. Given that an LLA limits the company's ability to recover losses against the only deep pocket, the effect may be to render auditors less accountable, and less careful, and may increase rather than reduce costs. The FRC Guidance and the Institutional Shareholders Committee Statement, while reiterating the importance of the directors observing their fiduciary duties, do accept that it may be in the interests of the company to enter into these agreements. The FRC Guidance notes, for example, that it   **16-82**

---

[128] See above n 121.

[129] The ABI and NAPF have indicated that their members should vote against any LLA drawn up on any other basis.

may enable the company to obtain audit services from an audit firm of the company's choice at an acceptable price.[130] The ISC Statement stresses, however, that the directors must look to see what the company will get out of the arrangement in terms of assurances that audit quality will be preserved and enhanced by the auditors and that 'other benefits' (not defined) might be secured for the company.[131]

[130] See FRC Guidance, above n 120, Section 3 'What Issues should the Directors consider?', para 3.6.
[131] See ISC Statement, above n 121, p 2.

17

The unfairly prejudicial remedy and the minority shareholder

A Introduction

The most important shareholder remedy in practice is the ability of a member to petition for relief on the ground that the affairs of the company are being or have been conducted in a manner which is unfairly prejudicial to the interests of members generally or of some part of its members under CA 2006, s 994, previously CA 1985, s 459. **17-1**

Before examining the unfairly prejudicial remedy in detail, it may be useful to draw attention to some background considerations which should be borne in mind. **17-2**

Disputes in private companies

The vast majority of companies registered under the CA 2006 and its predecessor, the CA 1985, are private companies. These companies typically have only a small number of shareholders,[1] most if not all of whom are also the directors, and many of whom are also employees of the company. Often the shareholders will be members of the same family and, even if they are not, the relationships involved tend to be personal as well as commercial. Disputes too tend to be personal and bitter and settling such cases can be difficult. **17-3**

A typical scenario would involve the initial enthusiastic participation of all the shareholders in the company as directors and employees rapidly followed by disagreements among the participants, perhaps about the direction of the company, or the respective merits of the contributions made by each participant, or the extent to which the parties are benefiting financially from the business, and culminating in the majority shareholder or shareholders voting to remove the minority shareholder from his position as a director and dismissing him as an employee. Voluntary exit by the **17-4**

---

[1] Research carried out for the Company Law Review showed that 70% of the companies on the register had only one or two shareholders and 90% had fewer than five shareholders: Company Law Review, *Developing the Framework* (2000), para 6.9. The position is unlikely to have changed significantly since then.

minority shareholder from the company at this point is the desirable option but it may be difficult to achieve.

17-5   Finding a purchaser for a minority stake in a private company is not easy and, even if a purchaser is found, the minority shareholder may find that the company's articles of association constrain him as to whom he can sell. For example, the articles may require him to offer the shares initially to the existing members and may require the price to be determined by the company's auditor and not by the vendor. It is commonly the case that the board of directors has a power in any event to refuse to register any transfer of any shares (see discussion at **14-59**). Voluntary exit can be difficult to achieve, therefore, and legal action, or at least the threat of legal action, may be necessary.

17-6   The position of minority shareholders once they are in disagreement with the majority is exacerbated by difficulties in obtaining accurate information about the company's affairs, especially where the shareholder has been removed from the board and no longer has access to management accounts and minutes of board meetings[2] although shareholders are entitled to the annual accounts.[3]

Disputes in public companies

17-7   Disputes in public companies do not have the focus on personal participation and remuneration which characterises disputes in private companies. Instead there may be complaints about the standard of management and the level of their remuneration. A variety of mechanisms can be deployed to address these issues with litigation and legal redress generally low on the shareholders' range of options, though there are concerns that legal redress may feature more prominently in future given the availability of the statutory derivative action (see CA 2006, Part 11). How realistic those fears are is considered in Chapter 18.

17-8   Management under-performance may be addressed by setting contractual targets and linking remuneration to performance. Many of the shareholders in these companies will be institutional shareholders who are able to exercise influence by voicing their concerns directly to the board. In the worst cases of mismanagement, a declining share price may mean that the company becomes a target of a takeover and so underperforming management may be replaced through the market for corporate control. Takeovers are discussed in Chapter 26.

17-9   Shareholders who have a grievance in these companies typically will resolve the problem by simply selling their shares, something which is generally easier in public

---

[2] Shareholders have no right of access to board minutes, only to minutes of general meetings: see CA 2006, s 358; but they can obtain details of directors' service contracts: s 228; and inspect statutory registers such as the register of members, s 116, subject to the company's ability to refuse permission under s 117. As to a petitioner's entitlement to disclosure of company documents, see *CAS (Nominees) Ltd v Nottingham Forest FC plc* [2002] 1 BCLC 613; *Arrow Trading & Investment Est 1920 v Edwardian Group Ltd* [2005] 1 BCLC 696.

[3] The accounts may be quite dated, however, since a private company has nine months from the end of the financial year in which to send the accounts to each member: see CA 2006, ss 423–424, 442.

companies and particularly easy in the case of a public company with shares admitted to trading on a market.

Majority and minority shareholders

Most disputes necessarily involve minority shareholders seeking redress as the majority can secure redress for themselves through the exercise of their voting power.[4] It should be borne in mind, however, that minority shareholders too can behave in an obstructive and damaging way with a view to forcing the majority to buy them out at an inflated value simply to rid themselves of the nuisance.[5]

17-10

Anticipating and preventing disputes

As Professor Prentice has commented, a feature of shareholder disputes particularly in smaller private companies is the parties' chronic failure to anticipate the nature, extent and consequences of a breakdown in their relationship.[6] He identified a variety of reasons for this stance including an unwillingness to contemplate breakdown of the relationship at the beginning of the venture; an inability in any event to anticipate all future contingencies; and the fact that the costs of trying to so anticipate may simply not be justified.[7]

17-11

These difficulties are compounded by the practice in this jurisdiction whereby a substantial percentage of companies incorporated annually are shelf companies (i.e. purchased from a formation agent as a ready-made company, see **1-10**), with the result that those incorporating in this way are likely to have had minimal, if any, advice and the company's articles of association will simply be a standard version which do not address future breakdown.[8]

17-12

Governing principles

Shareholder remedies were the subject of a detailed review[9] by the Law Commission in 1996–97 and that work was considered and generally adopted by the Company

17-13

---

[4] See *Re Legal Costs Negotiators Ltd* [1999] 2 BCLC 171; *Re Baltic Real Estate Ltd (No 2)* [1993] BCLC 503.

[5] The courts are alert to this possibility, see *Re a Company (No 007623 of 1984)* [1986] BCLC 362 at 367, per Hoffmann J: '... the very width of [the unfairly prejudicial] jurisdiction mean that unless carefully controlled, it can become a means of oppression'.

[6] Prentice, 'Protecting Minority Shareholders' Interests' in Feldman & Meisel (eds), *Corporate and Commercial Law: Modern Developments* (1996) at p 80.

[7] Prentice, 'Protecting Minority Shareholders' Interests' in Feldman & Meisel (eds), *Corporate and Commercial Law: Modern Developments* (1996) at pp 89–93.

[8] See Prentice, 'Protecting Minority Shareholders' Interests' in Feldman & Meisel (eds), *Corporate and Commercial Law: Modern Developments* (1996) at p 90.

[9] See Law Commission, *Shareholder Remedies* (Law Comm No 246) (Cm 3769, 1997) (hereinafter referred to as the Law Commission Report).

Law Review[10] which did not devote much time to this issue. The Law Commission in its report identified what it considered to be the governing principles appropriate to this area, principles which we encounter throughout our consideration of company law, namely the proper plaintiff rule, the principle of majority rule in matters of internal management, non-interference by the courts in commercial decisions, recognition of the sanctity of contract and freedom from unnecessary shareholder interference.[11]

17-14 The proper plaintiff rule means that normally the company should be the only party entitled to enforce a cause of action belonging to it, reflecting the fact that the company is a separate legal entity. Accordingly, a member should be able to maintain proceedings about wrongs done to the company only in exceptional circumstances. The majority rule reflects the basic mechanism for decision-making in companies which has its corollary that an individual member should not be able to pursue proceedings on behalf of the company about matters of internal management, that is, matters which the majority are entitled to regulate by ordinary resolution. These two principles are central to the derivative claim which is discussed in Chapter 18.

17-15 The importance of the courts having proper regard for the decisions of directors on commercial matters, provided the decision is made in good faith, on proper information and in the light of the relevant considerations, and appears to be a reasonable decision for the directors to have taken, is a central theme in judgments for a century or more.[12]

17-16 The principle of freedom from unnecessary shareholder interference is reflected in the tight judicial control of the derivative claim, discussed in Chapter 18. The intention is that, in keeping with the right of directors to manage the company's affairs, shareholders should not be able to involve the company in litigation without good cause, or where they intend to cause the company or the other shareholders embarrassment or harm rather than genuinely pursue the relief claimed.

17-17 The principle of sanctity of contract means that a member is taken to have agreed to the terms of the constitution when he became a member, whether or not he appreciated what it contained at the time. In the interests of commercial certainty, the law should continue to treat him as so bound unless he shows that the parties have come to some other agreement or understanding which is not reflected in the constitution. The basis of the parties' relationship, whether it be restricted to the articles or the subject of wider agreements or understandings, is central to the judicial approach to the unfairly prejudicial remedy which is the subject of this chapter.

---

[10] Company Law Review, *Developing the Framework* (2000), paras 4.70–4.71; Company Law Review, *Completing the Structure* (2000), para 5.106.

[11] See Law Commission Report, para 1.9.

[12] The courts' reluctance to interfere in commercial decisions is long standing: see *Carlen v Drury* (1812) 1 Ves & B 154: 'the court could not undertake the management of every brewhouse and playhouse in the kingdom' (per Lord Eldon); also *Burland v Earle* [1902] AC 83 at 93, per Lord Davey; *Hogg v Cramphorn Ltd* [1966] 3 All ER 420 at 428, per Buckley J; and *Shuttleworth v Cox* [1927] 2 KB 9 at 23: 'It is not the business of the court to manage the affairs of the company.'

B Petitioning on the grounds of unfair prejudice

The most valuable shareholder remedy is that contained in the Companies Act 2006, **17-18**
s 994(1), (previously CA 1985, s 459) which provides that:

'A member of a company may apply to the court by petition for an order on the
ground

(a) that the company's affairs are being or have been conducted in a manner which
is unfairly prejudicial to the interests of members generally or of some part of its
members (including at least himself), or

(b) that an actual or proposed act or omission of the company (including an act or
omission on its behalf) is or would be so prejudicial.'[13]

Where the court is satisfied that a petition under s 994 is well founded, it may make **17-19**
such order as it thinks fit for giving relief in respect of the matters complained of
(s 996(2)). In practice, the relief most commonly sought is a purchase order requiring
the respondents to purchase the shares of the petitioner (s 996(2)(e)).

This statutory remedy is not restricted to private companies, but it has proved invalu- **17-20**
able in that context, given the nature of disputes within such companies, as outlined
at **17-3**. The only possible resolution to most of these disputes is that the minority
shareholder must leave the company and a purchase order under CA 2006, s 996 will
ensure that he exits at a fair value.

In the past, it was a feature of litigation under the unfairly prejudicial remedy that **17-21**
much of it was unduly lengthy and therefore expensive.[14] Even when the parties are
agreed as to the exit of the minority shareholder, disputes over the valuation of the
minority shareholding can be protracted. The courts have frequently expressed dis-
may at the level of costs involved and are often critical of parties (and their lawyers)
who unduly prolong these proceedings. The case management powers under the Civil
Procedure Rules (CPR) now help to reduce the length and cost of the proceedings and
ensure that these matters are dealt with expeditiously and fairly and in a manner proportionate to the issues and the money involved.[15]

It is also the case that a petition will be struck out if the respondents have made the **17-22**
petitioner a fair offer[16] (typically to buy him out) which gives him everything he would
be entitled to under CA 2006, s 994. This sanction offers a further incentive for members to resolve their differences without resort to the court and reflects the fact that

---

[13] See generally Joffe, *Minority Shareholders* (3rd edn, 2008), Chs 5, 6; Hollington, *Shareholders' Rights*
(5th edn, 2007), Chs 7–9; Payne, 'Sections 459–461 Companies Act 1985 in flux: the future of shareholder
protection' (2005) CLJ 647; Boyle, *Minority Shareholders' Remedies* (2002). The right of a shareholder to petition under CA 2006, s 994 is an inalienable statutory right which cannot be limited or removed by agreement
or contract or otherwise: *Exeter City AFC Ltd v The Football Conference Ltd* [2005] 1 BCLC 238.

[14] See comments in *Profinance Trust SA v Gladstone* [2002] 1 BCLC 141 at 144; also *Re a Company
(No 004415 of 1996)* [1997] 1 BCLC 479 at 494.

[15] SI 1998/3132, rr 1.2–1.4.   [16] See *O'Neill v Phillips* [1999] 2 BCLC 1.

the outcome in successful petitions is entirely predictable, that the minority must be bought out.

The petitioner

17-23   Only members[17] have a right to petition, including persons to whom shares have been transferred or transmitted by law (CA 2006, s 994(2)), i.e. personal representatives and trustees in bankruptcy.[18] A petition may be brought by a nominee shareholder. In *Atlasview Ltd v Brightview Ltd*[19] the court refused to strike out a petition holding that it was arguable that the 'interests' of a nominee shareholder were capable of including the economic and contractual interests of the beneficial owners of the shares. To hold otherwise would produce the arbitrary result that the registered shareholder would have standing to petition as a member but no 'interests' for these purposes, while the beneficial owner would have an interest but no standing to present a petition, not being a member.

17-24   There is nothing to preclude a majority shareholder from petitioning, but the court would normally expect a majority shareholder to exercise his control of the company to being to an end of the conduct complained of.[20]

17-25   While there is no requirement that a petitioner should come to the court with clean hands, the conduct of the petitioner may, depending on the seriousness of the matter and the degree of its relevance, lead the court to refuse relief, even if the conditions for the exercise of the discretion in his favour are otherwise satisfied.[21]

Conduct of the company's affairs

17-26   The conduct complained of must relate to the conduct of the affairs of the company and it can relate to a course of conduct or a specific act. It must be concerned with acts done or left undone by the company or those authorised to act as its organs and

---

[17] In certain circumstances, the Secretary of State may petition on the same grounds under CA 2006, s 995, but this power is never used.

[18] For example, in *Re McCarthy Surfacing Ltd, Hecquet v McCarthy* [2006] EWHC 832, [2006] All ER (D) 193 (Apr), Ch D, the court allowed a petition by two shareholders (who had executed a transfer of their shares) and the transferee (whose request for registration had been refused by the directors), noting that the transferee has to have standing to petition for a period of time after the transfer and before registration, otherwise CA 2006, s 994(2) would have no effect. The court also considered that there was nothing to prevent the three petitioners having concurrent standing, though care would need to be exercised on any relief being ordered to prevent double recovery.

[19] [2004] 2 BCLC 191. The court noted with some surprise that this precise point as to the standing of a nominee shareholder had not previously been determined, but it also noted that numerous successful proceedings have been brought by nominee shareholders.

[20] See *Re Legal Costs Negotiators Ltd* [1999] 2 BCLC 171 at 199, 201.

[21] *Richardson v Blackmore* [2006] BCC 276; *Re London School of Electronics Ltd* [1985] BCLC 273; *Re R A Noble & Sons (Clothing) Ltd* [1983] BCLC 273. If the conduct of the petitioner is neither sufficiently serious, nor sufficiently closely related to the respondents' unfairly prejudicial conduct, however, it is not appropriate for the court to refuse its discretion to grant relief: *Richardson v Blackmore*.

not simply with the conduct of an individual shareholder acting in a personal capacity.[22] As Harman J noted in *Re Unisoft Group Ltd (No 3)*,[23] shareholders' disputes
between themselves are not the same as unfair conduct of the company's business. He
went on:

> '...the vital distinction between acts or conduct of the company and the acts or con-
> duct of the shareholder in his private capacity must be kept clear. The first type of act
> will found a petition under s 459 [s 994]; the second type of act will not.'

For example, in *Re Legal Costs Negotiators Ltd*[24] the complaint was about the failure of   **17-27**
a shareholder to sell his shares. The company had been set up by four individuals with
equal shareholdings. All the shareholders were directors and employees of the company. Three of the directors fell out with the fourth who was dismissed as an employee
and resigned from the board just prior to being removed as a director. Having failed
to persuade the fourth member to sell his shareholding to them, the majority shareholders petitioned for an order that he should transfer or sell his shares to them. In
essence, they were unhappy with his continued presence as a shareholder in the prosperous business that they were creating. The Court of Appeal rejected the petition for
complaints about the respondent's retention of his shares is not a complaint about the
conduct of the company's affairs or an act or omission of the company.

Likewise, in *Re Leeds United Holdings plc*[25] the court dismissed a petition arising from   **17-28**
a disagreement between shareholders as to the manner of the disposal of their shares.
Again, the matter does not relate to the conduct of the company's affairs.

In *Arrow Nominees Inc v Blackledge*[26] the Court of Appeal dismissed a petition based   **17-29**
on allegations against the majority shareholders who were significant lenders and suppliers to the company. The court noted that the complaints against the majority related
to the terms of the loan and supply contracts which, even if established, related to the
majority's conduct as a lender and supplier to the company and did not relate to the
conduct of the company's affairs by the majority. The decision to lend to the company
at a certain rate of interest or supply goods at a particular price could not amount to
unfairly prejudicial conduct of the company's affairs. That would only arise if the majority used their position to compel the company to accept the funds/supplies at that rate
of interest/price by preventing it securing other, more favourable, funding/suppliers.

Generally, the petitioner's complaints will be of the past conduct of the company's   **17-30**
affairs,[27] but proposed acts of the company (such as resolutions of the general

---

[22] See *Re Legal Costs Negotiators Ltd* [1999] 2 BCLC 171; *Re Unisoft Group Ltd (No 3)* [1994] 1 BCLC 609.

[23] [1994] 1 BCLC 609 at 623.

[24] [1999] 2 BCLC 171. See also *Re Astec (BSR) plc* [1998] 2 BCLC 556 where the court dismissed a petition
based in part on pessimistic statements by the majority shareholder about the company's finances which
allegedly depressed the share price. The statements could not amount to conduct of the company's affairs
since the statements were made on behalf of the shareholder and not on behalf of the company.

[25] [1996] 2 BCLC 545.   [26] [2000] 2 BCLC 167.

[27] Past acts of the company which have been remedied may be the basis of a petition if they are likely to
recur, but if they are unlikely to recur, the court would have no scope to give relief. See *Re Kenyon Swansea
Ltd* [1987] BCLC 514 at 521; *Re Legal Costs Negotiators Ltd* [1999] 2 BCLC 171 at 198.

meeting) which, if carried out or completed, would be prejudicial to the interests of the petitioner may be the subject of a petition.[28] The petitioner must not be too hasty, however, in seeking relief. In *Re Astec (BSR) plc*[29] the petition was premature when it was brought at a time when the majority had only made statements as to steps which they would or might take in the future, but they had not taken any of those steps at the time of the petition.

17-31   In keeping with the judicial view that the wide ambit of CA 2006, s 994 should not be artificially constrained,[30] the Court of Appeal accepted in *Re Citybranch Group Ltd, Gross v Rackind*[31] that conduct of a company's affairs can extend to the conduct of the affairs of a subsidiary of that company and, vice versa, the conduct of the affairs of a subsidiary can include the affairs of its holding company, especially where the subsidiary is wholly owned and the directors of the holding company also represent a majority of the directors of the subsidiary. This ruling enables a shareholder in a parent company to petition for relief in respect of the conduct of the subsidiary's affairs.[32]

Conduct unfairly prejudicial to the interests of the members

17-32   The conduct complained of must be conduct which is unfairly prejudicial to the interests of the member as a member as opposed to any other interests which the member might possess.[33] For example, in *Re J E Cade & Son Ltd*[34] the petition was struck out when the petitioner was protecting his interests as a freeholder of a farm rather than his interests as a member of the company running the farm. As this decision illustrates, the courts are unsympathetic to claims which have nothing to do with the member's interests as a member. On the other hand, the courts have also been careful to emphasise that the requirement that the prejudice must be suffered as a member

---

[28] See *Re Kenyon Swansea Ltd* [1987] BCLC 514; *Re a Company (No 00314 of 1989), ex p Estate Acquisition and Development Ltd* [1991] BCLC 154.

[29] [1998] 2 BCLC 556; see also *Re a Company (No 005685 of 1988), ex p Schwarcz (No 2)* [1989] BCLC 427 at 451 (concerns about what might happen if the company was re-registered as a private company were premature).

[30] See *Re Macro (Ipswich) Ltd* [1994] 2 BCLC 354 at 404: 'the jurisdiction under s 459 [CA 2006, s 994] has an elastic quality which enables the courts to mould the concepts of unfair prejudice according to the circumstances of the case', per Arden J; *Re Little Olympian Each-Ways Ltd* [1994] 2 BCLC 420 at 429; *O'Neill v Phillips* [1999] 2 BCLC 1 at 15; *Gamlestaden Fastigheter AB v Baltic Partners Ltd* [2007] 4 All ER 164 at 175–6, PC.

[31] [2004] 4 All ER 735 at 743–4. See also agreement on this point in *Re Ravenhart Service (Holdings) Ltd, Reiner v Gershinson* [2004] 2 BCLC 376 and in *Irvine v Irvine (No 1)* [2007] 1 BCLC 349 at 418. Note that, in each case, the subsidiaries were wholly owned and had boards substantially similar to the parent company.

[32] See Goddard & Hirt, 'Section 459 and Corporate Groups' [2005] JBL 247 which criticises the court's failure to respect the separate legal entities involved and also considers that this approach gives an unnecessarily wide interpretation to the statutory provision.

[33] *Re a Company (No 004475 of 1982)* [1983] 2 All ER 36 at 44; *Re a Company (No 00314 of 1989), ex p Estate Acquisition & Development Ltd* [1991] BCLC 154 at 160.

[34] See [1992] BCLC 213; see also *Re Unisoft Group Ltd (No 3)* [1994] 1 BCLC 609 at 626 where the allegations concerned the relationship of the parties as landlord and tenant rather than as members of the company.

must not be too narrowly construed and that the courts should take a broad view of what may properly be regarded as a petitioner's interests as a member.[35]

In particular, the courts have consistently held that, if the terms on which a person **17-33**
became or continues as a member include his participation in the management of the company, his removal *as a director* is a prejudice suffered in his capacity as a member[36] entitling him to petition for relief under CA 2006, s 994. This point is very important in practice, for removal as a director is the most common basis for petitions.

A broad approach to what constitutes the interests of a member as a member may **17-34**
also allow the court to take account of the members' interests as creditors in certain circumstances. In *R & H Electrical Ltd v Haden Bill Electrical Ltd*[37] there were four equal shareholders and directors. The petitioner was one of the shareholders and he provided the company with its working capital through loans from another company wholly owned by him. These loans formed an essential part of the arrangements between him and his fellow shareholders who regarded it as immaterial whether the funding came from the petitioner or through his other company. The relationship between the parties broke down and the others attempted to remove the petitioner from office as a director. He petitioned for relief and the respondents argued that, in so far as he had concerns, they related to his role as a creditor of the company rather than matters affecting his interests as a member. In the circumstances, however, Robert Walker LJ considered the loan arrangements were sufficiently closely associated with his membership of the company[38] to be within the scope of CA 2006, s 994. It was unfairly prejudicial to his interests as a member, therefore, to remove him from management of the company while he was a significant creditor of the company and he was entitled to relief.

That broad interpretation was endorsed by the Privy Council in *Gamlestaden* **17-35**
Fastigheter AB v Baltic Partners Ltd[39] where similarly a joint venture company was funded primarily by loans by the petitioner (again via a company associated with the petitioner) and the court considered it would be appropriate to take into account the member's interest as a creditor of the company when considering whether to grant relief under the statutory provisions. Lord Scott, giving the ruling of the Privy Council, emphasised the importance of the funding arrangements being part of, or in pursuance of, the joint venture arrangements between the parties (as was the case in *Haden Bill* above).

Finally, it should be noted that the removal of the company's auditor from office on **17-36**
grounds of divergence of opinions on accounting treatments or audit procedures, or

---

[35] See *Re Macro (Ipswich) Ltd* [1994] 2 BCLC 354 at 404: 'the jurisdiction under s 459 [CA 2006, s 994] has an elastic quality which enables the courts to mould the concepts of unfair prejudice according to the circumstances of the case', per Arden J; *O'Neill v Phillips* [1999] 2 BCLC 1 at 15: 'the requirement that prejudice must be suffered as a member should not be too narrowly or technically construed', per Lord Hoffmann.

[36] See *O'Neill v Phillips* [1999] 2 BCLC 1 at 14–15; and see also *R & H Electric Ltd v Haden Bill Electrical Ltd* [1995] 2 BCLC 280 at 292–3.

[37] [1995] 2 BCLC 280.   [38] [1995] 2 BCLC 280 at 293–4.

[39] [2007] 4 All ER 164, PC; noted Walters (2007) 28 Co Law 289; Singla [2007] 123 LQR 542.

on any other improper grounds, is treated as being unfairly prejudicial to the interests of some part of the company's members so as to enable a member to petition for relief in those circumstances (CA 2006, s 994(1A)).[40] This provision gives effect to the Directive on statutory audit[41] which requires Member States to ensure that statutory auditors may only be dismissed on proper grounds and is intended to safeguard the independence of auditors from undue pressure by the company's directors.

Unfairly prejudicial conduct

17-37 Whether the company's affairs are being or have been conducted in a manner which is unfairly prejudicial to the petitioner's interests is an objective, and not a subjective, matter.[42] The prejudice must be real, rather than merely technical or trivial[43] and the petitioner does not have to show that the persons controlling the company have acted deliberately in bad faith, or with a conscious intent to treat him unfairly.[44] The conduct complained of must be prejudicial in the sense of causing prejudice or harm to the relevant interest of the member and also unfairly so and it is not sufficient if the conduct satisfies only one of these tests.[45]

17-38 For example, it might be prejudicial to remove a member from office as a director, but not unfairly so, if his conduct merited removal, as in *Grace v Biagioli*.[46] It can be prejudicial not to consult a minority shareholder, but not unfair, if the petitioner has chosen to withdraw from active involvement in the business, as in *Re Metropolis Motorcycles Ltd, Hale v Waldock*.[47] Conduct may be unfair but not prejudicial, as in *Irvine v Irvine (No 1)*[48] where the court found that there had been a failure to meet the statutory requirements as to approving the accounts and holding of annual general meetings, but the failures could not be said to have caused the petitioner any material prejudice.

17-39 The leading authority on the scope of the unfairly prejudicial jurisdiction is *O'Neill v Phillips*[49] which is the sole House of Lords authority on the provision.

17-40 The petitioner, O, joined the company as a manual worker in 1983. In 1985, the respondent, P, impressed by O's abilities, gave him 25% of the issued shares and appointed him a director. Between 1985 and 1990, P retired from the board, leaving O as sole

---

[40] Added by Companies Act 2006 (Commencement No 5, Transitional Provisions and Savings) Order 2007, SI 2007/3494, reg 42(1).

[41] Directive 2006/43/EC of 17 May 2006 on statutory audits of annual accounts and consolidated accounts, OJ L 157, 9.06.2006, p 87, art 38.

[42] *Re Saul D Harrison & Sons plc* [1995] 1 BCLC 14, CA; *Re Guidezone Ltd* [2000] 2 BCLC 321.

[43] *Re Saul D Harrison & Sons plc* [1995] 1 BCLC 14, CA.

[44] See *Re R A Noble & Sons (Clothing) Ltd* [1983] BCLC 273 at 290–1.

[45] *Re Saul D Harrison & Sons plc* [1995] 1 BCLC 14 at 31, CA; also *Re R A Noble (Clothing) Ltd* [1983] BCLC 273.

[46] [2006] 2 BCLC 70.   [47] [2006] 1 BCLC 520.   [48] [2007] 1 BCLC 349.

[49] [1999] 2 BCLC 1; noted Prentice and Payne, 'Section 459 of the Companies Act 1985—The House of Lords View' [1999] 115 LQR 587; Goddard, 'Taming the Unfair Prejudice Remedy: Sections 459–461 of the Companies Act 1985 in the House of Lords' (1999) CLJ 487; Boyle (2000) 21 Co Law 253.

director. The company prospered and O was credited with half of the profits. There were discussions with a view to O obtaining a 50% shareholding, but no agreement was concluded.

In 1991 P, being alarmed about the company's financial position and concerned about **17-41** O's management, resumed personal command and gave O the option of managing, under him, the UK or the German branches of the business. O chose to go to Germany and remained on the board as a director. Later that year P determined that O would no longer receive 50% of the profits but would be paid only his salary and any dividends payable upon his 25% shareholding. O decided to sever his links with the company and petitioned the court claiming that the company's affairs were being conducted in a manner 'unfairly prejudicial' to his interests.

Following a difference of opinion in the lower courts, the matter reached the House **17-42** of Lords where Lord Hoffmann (who gave the sole opinion in the case) concluded that a member will not ordinarily be entitled to complain of unfairness unless there has been:

(1) some breach of the terms on which the member agreed that the affairs of the company should be conducted; or

(2) some use of the rules in a manner which equity would regard as contrary to good faith—i.e. cases in which equitable considerations make it unfair for those conducting the affairs of the company to rely upon their strict legal powers.[50]

As P had not acted in breach of the terms upon which it was agreed that the affairs **17-43** of the company should be conducted and there was no ground, consistent with the principles of equity, for any belief that O was entitled to half the profits and half the shareholding, O could not bring his claim within either basis for relief and his petition was dismissed.

If the company is purely a commercial relationship, as would usually be the case **17-44** where the company is a public company, and is often the case in private companies, a petitioner will be confined to allegations, under (1) above, of breaches of the articles (or other contractual arrangements governing the shareholders' relationship), or of the statute including directors' duties. In the case of a public company, the expectation generally would be that the entire relationship of the parties is exhaustively determined by the constitution[51] and there is no scope for equitable considerations to arise and therefore no basis for relying on heading (2) above. This is particularly so if the company is a listed public company, a point made forcibly in *Re Astec (BSR) plc*[52] by Jonathan Parker J:

'If the market in a company's shares is to have any credibility members of the public dealing in that market must, it seems to me, be entitled to proceed on the footing that

---

[50] [1999] 2 BCLC 1 at 8.   [51] See *Re Saul D Harrison & Sons plc* [1995] 1 BCLC 14.

[52] [1998] 2 BCLC 556 at 588. See also *CAS (Nominees) Ltd v Nottingham Forest FC* [2002] 1 BCLC 613 at 627; *Re Tottenham Hotspur plc* [1994] 1 BCLC 655 (the shareholders are entitled to expect that the entire relationship between the company and the chief executive is set out in his service agreement and the constitution).

the constitution of the company is as it appears in the company's public documents, unaffected by any extraneous equitable considerations and constraints.'

17-45   Likewise, where the relationship of the parties is spelt out in detailed agreements, especially agreements drafted and advised upon by professional advisers, there is little scope for arguing that the relationship is other than a purely commercial one.[53] It is possible therefore to use carefully drafted agreements as a method of limiting the availability of the unfairly prejudicial remedy.

17-46   On the other hand, if the company has the characteristics of a quasi-partnership (discussed below) such that equitable considerations arise, the petitioner may bring his claim under heading (1) and/or (2), so the section applies more broadly in that context.

17-47   In considering the nature of the company, it is important to appreciate that the parties' relationship may change over time. A company may start out on a purely commercial footing, but become one where equitable considerations come into play, as was the case in *O'Neill v Phillips*.[54] The petitioner initially was an employee of the company but the relationships within the company changed over the years as he became a shareholder and a director such that the company became a quasi-partnership. Equally, a relationship which begins on a quasi-partnership footing may become a more commercial venture, as in *Re a Company (No 005134 of 1986), ex p Harries*.[55] In that case, the parties did operate initially as a quasi-partnership, but as the business developed, the petitioner withdrew into the role of a passive shareholder with the result that the relationship moved on to a purely commercial footing.

17-48   Finally, note that in *O'Neill v Phillips*[56] Lord Hoffmann expressly rejected reliance on 'legitimate expectations' as a basis for a petition. This reliance had become a prominent element of the case-law prior to this decision with petitions being brought effectively on the basis that a petitioner was aggrieved that (what he perceived to be) his legitimate expectations as to the conduct of the company's affairs had not been met. For example, in *O'Neill* the petitioner (who held 25% of the shares) felt that he had 'legitimate expectations' to 50% of the shares in the company and 50% of the profits, although he could establish no entitlement in law or equity to such equality. Lord Hoffmann in *O'Neill* noted that he himself had used the phrase 'legitimate expectations' in *Re Saul D Harrison & Sons plc*[57] but he conceded that this use was a mistake.[58]

Breach of the terms on which the affairs of the company should be conducted

17-49   In considering the scope of the unfairly prejudicial jurisdiction, Lord Hoffmann emphasised in *O'Neill v Phillips*[59] the need to appreciate the business context in which it operates. Companies are associations of persons for economic purposes where the

---

[53] See *Re a Company (No 005685 of 1988), ex p Schwarz (No 2)* [1989] BCLC 427.
[54] [1999] 2 BCLC 1.   [55] [1989] BCLC 383.   [56] [1999] 2 BCLC 1.   [57] [1995] 1 BCLC 14.
[58] [1999] 2 BCLC 1 at 11.   [59] [1999] 2 BCLC 1.

terms of association are contained in the articles and perhaps in shareholder agreements.[60] It follows that a member will not ordinarily be able to complain of unfairness unless there has been some breach of these terms on which he has agreed that the affairs of the company should be conducted.[61]

Typical allegations under this heading will be of breaches of directors' duties (usually involving misappropriation of corporate assets, improper allotments of shares and allegations of mismanagement); breaches of the articles and breaches of the Companies Act (often involving allegations regarding meetings, accounts and disclosure). Each is considered in more detail below.   **17-50**

Misappropriation of assets   It is a common feature of many of these disputes that when the majority and minority shareholders fall out, the majority look to run down the business of the company (so reducing the value of the minority's holding) and transfer their activities to another entity wholly owned by them. In the process, the majority appropriate to the new company opportunities and contracts which properly belong to the first company. Such clear breaches of directors' duties (the duty to promote the success of the company under CA 2006, s 172 and the no-conflict duty under CA 2006, s 175, in particular[62]) have consistently been found to be unfairly prejudicial conduct.   **17-51**

Illustrations of such breaches of duty amounting to unfairly prejudicial conduct can be found in the following cases: **17-52**

- In *Re Little Olympian Each-Ways Ltd (No 3)*[63] the assets of the company were transferred at an undervalue as part of a 'hiving up' operation to another company wholly owned by the majority shareholders. The assets were then sold on at their market value to a third party.

- In *Re Full Cup International Trading Ltd*[64] the respondents were found to have stifled the business of the company. They deprived it of its stock and business which was transferred to another entity in which they, but not the petitioner, had an interest.

- In *Re Brenfield Squash Racquets Club Ltd*[65] the majority shareholders and directors caused the company's assets to be used as security for debts of their businesses and transferred to those businesses assets that rightfully belonged to the company.

- In *Lloyd v Casey*[66] a director arranged a variety of transactions for his own ultimate benefit including payments to a company controlled by him and additional contributions to his own pension fund.

---

[60] See [1999] 2 BCLC 1 at 7; *Re Saul D Harrison & Sons plc* [1995] 1 BCLC 14 at 17–18.

[61] A shareholder who has agreed or acquiesced for a period of years in the company being run quite informally is entitled subsequently, on giving reasonable notice, to revive reliance on her strict entitlements under the articles: see *Fisher v Cadman* [2006] 1 BCLC 499.

[62] In future, the issues may not be so clear-cut, given the ability of independent directors to authorise directors to exploit conflicts of interests on their own account: see s 175(4)(b) and **11-45**.

[63] [1995] 1 BCLC 636.

[64] [1995] BCC 682.   [65] [1996] 2 BCLC 184.   [66] [2002] 1 BCLC 454.

- In *Allmark v Burnham*[67] the majority shareholder and director opened a competing business in the same street as the company's main retail outlet, failed to consult the minority shareholder and director on management matters and doubled his own salary once he had removed the minority shareholder from the board.
- In *Re Baumler (UK) Ltd, Gerrard v Koby*[68] the company was split 49% and 51% between two shareholders who were also the two directors. An opportunity to acquire the company's premises and adjoining land from their landlord was taken up by a third party acting on information provided to him by the 51% respondent with the expectation of a secret profit. The court found that the underhand conduct of the respondent in procuring the acquisition of the properties was a breach of duty by him and conduct unfairly prejudicial to the petitioner.
- In *Irvine v Irvine (No 1)*[69] the respondent in breach of the articles awarded himself excessive and unauthorised remuneration without reference to the board or the shareholders. A consequence of this conduct was that the petitioner received less by way of dividend than should have been received consistent with the company's historic policy of maximum profit distribution.
- In *Grace v Biagioli*[70] the respondents consciously and deliberately failed to pay a dividend which had been declared. Instead the available profits were distributed in the guise of management fees to the respondents.

17-53   *Improper allotments*   A common ploy in these disputes is for the directors to make an allotment of shares in order to dilute the petitioner's interest in the company, something which is in breach of the directors' duty to act in accordance with the constitution and to exercise their powers for the purposes for which they are conferred (CA 2006, s 171). The court has little difficulty in finding such conduct to be unfairly prejudicial.

17-54   The ability of directors to manipulate allotments is limited to some extent by the statutory requirement for a rights issue under CA 2006, s 561, i.e. the requirement to allot shares to existing shareholders in proportion to existing holdings, though there are exceptions to that requirement as is discussed at **19-41**. A failure to allot on a rights basis when required to do so is clearly unfairly prejudicial conduct as can be seen in *Re a Company (No 005134 of 1986), ex p Harries*.[71] In this case, the majority shareholder and director made an allotment of shares on a non-rights basis (in breach of the statutory requirements for a rights issue) for the purpose of increasing the respondent's holding and decreasing the petitioner's holding (from 40% to 4%) in the company.

17-55   In *Re Coloursource Ltd, Dalby v Bodilly*[72] an allotment made by the company's sole director and 50% shareholder without regard to the statutory obligation to have a rights

---

[67] [2006] 2 BCLC 437.   [68] [2005] 1 BCLC 92.   [69] [2007] 1 BCLC 349.
[70] [2006] 2 BCLC 70.
[71] [1989] BCLC 383. However, where there was a genuine desire to raise capital, a scheme proposed by the directors, although devised so as to avoid the need for a rights issue, was not conduct which was unfairly prejudicial to those shareholders who were thereby denied the possibility of taking up additional shares: see *CAS (Nominees) Ltd v Nottingham Forest FC plc* [2002] 1 BCLC 613 at 627–32.
[72] [2005] BCC 627.

issue had the effect of diluting the other 50% shareholder to a 5% shareholder. There were allegations of other misconduct, but Blackburne J thought it was sufficient to look at the allotment of shares which was the plainest possible breach by the director of his fiduciary duty and unfairly prejudicial conduct.[73]

In some circumstances, even a rights issue can be unfairly prejudicial, as in *Re Regional Airports Ltd*[74] where a proposed rights issue was intended to enhance the majority's position and to increase pressure on the (now to be diluted) minority to sell their shares.[75] A rights issue can also be unfairly prejudicial if it is known that a particular shareholder does not have sufficient funds to take up the offer and it is made for that reason, or where a shareholder is engaged in litigation with the majority and the offer is designed to deplete the resources available to him to finance that litigation.[76] **17-56**

Mismanagement   The courts are reluctant to accept that disagreements over man- **17-57** agerial decisions can amount to unfairly prejudicial conduct.[77] Essentially, the judicial view is that complaints of mismanagement often involve differences as to commercial judgment which are not for the courts to resolve.[78] Furthermore, the directors are appointed by the shareholders and, if they are disappointed with the quality of the management provided, the remedy lies in the shareholders' power to dismiss the directors. If the mismanagement causes actual financial loss to the company, however, the petition is more likely to succeed.

In *Re Macro (Ipswich) Ltd*[79] it was possible to point to specific acts of mismanagement **17-58** repeated over many years causing financial loss to the company. The company had a substantial portfolio of properties which had been mismanaged by the sole director who was 83 years of age and the father of the petitioners in this case. He had failed to institute a proper maintenance system for the properties or to ensure that they were properly let and rents duly paid with the result that the value of these assets had been depleted. Such conduct was unfairly prejudicial conduct. In *Re Elgindata Ltd*,[80] on the

---

[73] [2005] BCC 627 at 631. In the circumstances, it was irrelevant that no dividend had been declared on any of the additional shares or that no use had been made of the additional shareholding.

[74] [1999] 2 BCLC 30.

[75] It was obvious to the majority shareholder that the minority shareholders either could not or would not take up the rights issue, therefore their holdings were bound to be diluted as a consequence of the issue: see [1999] 2 BCLC 30 at 73.

[76] See *Re a Company (No 002612 of 1984)* [1985] BCLC 80. In this case, Harman J granted an injunction to restrain a proposed rights issue which had followed immediately on the presentation by the minority shareholder of a petition. Had it gone ahead, it would have reduced the petitioner's shareholding from 33% of the company to 0.33%.

[77] See *Re Elgindata Ltd* [1991] BCLC 959 at 993–4; *Re Saul D Harrison & Sons plc* [1995] 1 BCLC 14 at 31, CA.

[78] In *Fisher v Cadman* [2006] 1 BCLC 499 the court rejected complaints from a shareholder about the inactive management of a property company's assets by its directors. It was the practice for the company to hold properties in the hope of realising capital gains without expending large sums of money on repairing and letting the properties. The court thought that the decision to manage the assets in that way was within the range of reasonable business decisions available to the directors as managers and did not amount to mismanagement.

[79] [1994] 2 BCLC 354.   [80] [1991] BCLC 959.

other hand, the complaint was a broad complaint where the shareholder was simply disappointed as to the poor quality of the management.[81] That was insufficient, the court said, as a basis for an allegation of unfairly prejudicial conduct.

17-59   *Breach of statutory rights*   A breach of the members' statutory rights, for example repeated failures to hold annual general meetings and to lay accounts before the members (when required to do so[82]) so depriving members of their right to know and consider the state of the company's affairs[83] may merit a petition, subject to the general qualification that trivial infringements will not found a petition.[84]

Use of the rules in an inequitable manner

17-60   The second basis for a petition under CA 2006, s 994 identified by the House of Lords in *O'Neill v Phillips*[85] is that there has been some use of the rules in a manner which equity would regard as contrary to good faith.

17-61   As noted at **17-48**, care must be taken in relying on this ground and vague assertions that some legitimate expectations of the petitioner have not been met will be rejected by the court. The correct approach is to start by establishing whether equitable considerations have arisen to affect or constrain the exercise of legal powers.

17-62   The type of company which will typically give rise to such equitable constraints on the exercise of legal powers is a company which has one or probably more of the characteristics identified by Lord Wilberforce in *Ebrahimi v Westbourne Galleries Ltd*,[86] namely:

(1)   an association formed or continued on the basis of a personal relationship involving mutual confidence;

(2)   an agreement, or understanding, that all or some (for there may be 'sleeping' members) of the shareholders shall participate in the conduct of the business; and

(3)   restrictions on the transfers of shares so that a member cannot take his stake and go elsewhere.

17-63   These companies are commonly described as 'quasi-partnerships' though 'it is clear that Lord Wilberforce was not intending to set out an exhaustive list of factors, and that the term quasi-partnership is only intended as a useful shorthand label'.[87]

17-64   Where these elements or some of them are present, the company is something more than the usual commercial association and there is a common understanding on all

---

[81] [1991] BCLC 959 at 993–4.

[82] Only public companies are required to hold annual general meetings or to lay accounts before such meetings: see CA 2006, ss 336, 437.

[83] See *Re a Company (No 00789 of 1987), ex p Shooter* [1990] BCLC 384; *Fisher v Cadman* [2006] 1 BCLC 499.

[84] See *Re Saul D Harrison & Sons plc* [1995] 1 BCLC 14 at 18, CA; also *Irvine v Irvine (No 1)* [2007] 1 BCLC 349.

[85] [1999] 2 BCLC 1.   [86] [1972] 2 All ER 492 at 500.

[87] *Fisher v Cadman* [2006] 1 BCLC 499 at 526.

sides that the articles of association do not represent the complete and exhaustive statement of the parties relationships.[88] In addition to the articles, there are understandings and promises (though not contractually binding) between the parties, typically about matters such as participation in the management of the company, financial returns, and, more broadly, the nature of the venture on which the parties have embarked. While these understandings etc will usually be found at the time of entering into the association, there may be later promises, by words or conduct, which it may be unfair to ignore,[89] given that relationships are not static but evolve over time. As Arden LJ explained in *Strahan v Wilcock*:[90] 'In determining what equitable obligations arise between the parties, the court must look at all the circumstances, including the company's constitution, any written agreement between the shareholders and the conduct of the parties.'

If the company is of this nature, i.e. something broader than a commercial association, equity will hold the majority shareholders to the mutual agreements, promises or understandings which form the basis of the relationship, assuming the minority has acted in reliance on them.[91] Complaints on this ground therefore have to show that the conduct of the company's affairs, while not necessarily a breach of directors' duties or of the constitution or of the statute, is a breach of the understandings which form the basis of the association. A useful test, as Patten J explained in *Grace v Biagioli*,[92] is to 'ask whether the exercise of the power or rights in question would involve a breach of an agreement or understanding between the parties which it would be unfair to allow a member to ignore'.   **17-65**

Understandings as to participation in management   Complaints about removal from office are central to most unfairly prejudicial petitions. If the parties have come together on the basis that all or some of them shall participate in the management of the company, the exclusion of a shareholder from management by removing him as a director (a power open to the majority by ordinary resolution under CA 2006, s 168) will amount to unfairly prejudicial conduct in the absence of a fair offer by the majority to buy the petitioner's shares or to make some other fair arrangement.[93]   **17-66**

A typical example is *Brownlow v G H Marshall Ltd*[94] where the company was a family business built up over a long period of time and with the shares now held equally by a brother and two sisters, all of whom were directors. Following various disagreements and the breakdown of the personal relationships involved, an attempt was made to   **17-67**

---

[88] *Fisher v Cadman* [2006] 1 BCLC 499 at 528.

[89] See *O'Neill v Phillips* [1999] 2 BCLC 1 at 10–11. See also *Fisher v Cadman* [2006] 1 BCLC 499 where the court noted that the family relationship between the parties (two brothers and a sister) was as important as the relationship defined by the articles of association. In this instance, the company was a quasi-partnership though the petitioner had never taken any role in the management of the company and had contributed no capital, having been given or inherited her shares from her parents.

[90] [2006] 2 BCLC 555 at 565.

[91] See *Re Guidezone Ltd* [2000] 2 BCLC 321 at 356; and see *Re a Company (No 005685 of 1988), ex p Schwarz (No 2)* [1989] BCLC 423 at 440.

[92] [2006] 2 BCLC 70 at 92.   [93] *O'Neill v Phillips* [1999] 2 BCLC 1 at 16.

[94] [2000] 2 BCLC 655.

exclude one of the sisters from the board. The court held that attempting to exclude her without a fair offer for her shares was unfairly prejudicial conduct entitling her to relief.

17-68   An issue which has arisen is whether the fact that the director complaining of removal has a service agreement undermines his case, i.e. by suggesting that the relationship is a commercial one rather than a broader association based on mutual understandings. The courts have been reluctant so to conclude if when viewed overall the relationship is broader than a mere commercial association. In *Brownlow v G H Marshall Ltd*,[95] for example, the directors did have service agreements with the company but the court found that there was nothing in the arrangements reached which altered the basis on which the company operated, i.e. that it was a quasi-partnership. The service agreements were not designed, the court thought, to affect the shareholders' position as shareholders or to preclude any potential remedy which a shareholder might have under CA 2006, s 994, but were designed to ensure fair arrangements for the working directors.[96] A similar approach can be found in *Quinlan v Essex Hinge Co Ltd*[97] where the court agreed that the existence of a service agreement between the director and the company did not prevent the company having the characteristics of a quasi-partnership.

17-69   The position would be different if, as in *Re a Company (No 005685 of 1988), ex p Schwarz (No 2)*[98] the entire relationship between the parties is spelt out in detailed agreements, drafted and advised upon by professional advisers. The more detailed the agreements, the more likely it is that the company is being operated on a purely commercial basis and does not have the characteristics of a quasi-partnership.

17-70   In the absence of these personal, quasi-partnership elements, every director is subject to the possibility of removal and has no right to remain in office.[99] Of course, removal of a director for cause will not merit a petition for while such removal is prejudicial to the petitioner, it is not unfair.[100] If, as in *O'Neill v Phillips*,[101] and despite a changing relationship between the parties, the respondent chooses to continue to work with the petitioner without attempting to remove him from office, no grounds for complaint exist.

17-71   *Understandings as to participation in financial returns*   Dividend issues can loom large in disputes in small companies. In *Grace v Biagioli*[102] a dividend had actually been declared but the respondents (aggrieved by the conduct of the petitioner) then

---

[95] [2000] 2 BCLC 655.   [96] [2000] 2 BCLC 655 at 669.   [97] [1996] 2 BCLC 417.

[98] [1989] BCLC 427, esp at 440–1.

[99] *Re Estate Acquisition and Development Ltd* [1995] BCC 338; *Re Tottenham Hotspur plc* [1994] 1 BCLC 655; *Re a Company (No 005134 of 1986), ex p Harries* [1989] BCLC 383; *Re a Company (No 005685 of 1988), ex p Schwarcz (No 2)* [1989] BCLC 427; *Re Blue Arrow plc* [1987] BCLC 585.

[100] See *Grace v Biagioli* [2006] 2 BCLC 70 where the court held it was not unfairly prejudicial conduct to remove the petitioner as a director when he had been secretly negotiating to acquire a company dealing in the same line of business as the company, and had put himself in a position of actual or potential conflict with his duties as a director.

[101] [1999] 2 BCLC 1.   [102] [2006] 2 BCLC 70.

deliberately chose not to pay it and instead distributed the available profits as management fees to themselves. This non-payment, the court held, was unfair prejudice. More commonly, the problem is that the company does not declare any dividends while continuing to amass reserves. The majority shareholders meanwhile are rewarded via directors' remuneration. The courts are open to the argument that such conduct may be unfairly prejudicial conduct if it can be shown to be contrary to the understandings of the parties as to how the financial rewards are to be shared.[103] Generally the courts have not had to rule on this issue of non-payment for it has been possible to establish unfairly prejudicial conduct on other grounds, such as removal from office as a director, or unauthorised remuneration for the respondent, but the courts are clearly willing, given appropriate circumstances, to find the non-payment of dividends in such circumstances to be unfairly prejudicial conduct.

In *Quinlan v Essex Hinge Co Ltd*[104] the company did not declare dividends and profits   **17-72** were distributed by bonus payments to working directors or retained in the company. The result was that the company built up substantial reserves of £500,000. Having been removed from his position as a director and excluded from the management of the company, the petitioner received no dividends on his 15% shareholding. The court found that the petitioner had been unfairly prejudiced by his removal and so did not need to decide on the issue of non-payment of dividends, but it did indicate that it believed that the petitioner also had a legitimate complaint on that ground.

In *Irvine v Irvine (No 1)*,[105] though the company was not a quasi-partnership, the court   **17-73** concluded that payment of excessive and unauthorised remuneration by a majority shareholder to himself as executive director of the company was unfairly prejudicial conduct. The consequence of the excessive payments was that the minority shareholders were prevented from receiving as much by way of dividend as they would have received consistent with the historic policy of maximum profit distribution in the company.

On the other hand, if, as in *Re Metropolis Motorcycles Ltd, Hale v Waldock*,[106] the   **17-74** company's financial situation prevents the company declaring dividends, the minority shareholder has no grounds for complaint, even if the majority shareholder as a director is able to continue drawing a salary. It would not necessarily be fair for this position to go on forever, however, the court said, and the majority would have to recognise that the minority could be said to have a legitimate claim to some form of return.

---

[103] See *Irvine v Irvine (No 1)* [2007] 1 BCLC 349; *Quinlan v Essex Hinge Co Ltd* [1996] 2 BCLC 417; *Re a Company (No 004415 of 1996)* [1997] 1 BCLC 479; *Re Sam Weller & Sons Ltd* [1990] BCLC 80. In *Re a Company (No 004415 of 1996)* Sir Richard Scott noted that, if it is established at trial that dividends have been kept at an unreasonably low level, that fact would be reflected in the price which would be set for the petitioner's shares if a purchase order is made under CA 2006, s 996.

[104] [1996] 2 BCLC 417.   [105] [2007] 1 BCLC 349.

[106] [2007] 1 BCLC 520. In this case, the court found that the situation which had occurred—the inability of the company to make payments to the minority shareholder—had not been contemplated by the parties when they had set up the company so, in the absence of anything in the nature of a promise of payments to the minority shareholder, there was no basis for an order that he be bought out.

17-75   It is unfairly prejudicial conduct for the majority shareholder and directors to pay themselves remuneration when the understanding of the parties is that remuneration will not be paid.[107]

17-76   *Understandings as to the basis of the relationship*   In *O'Neill v Phillips*[108] Lord Hoffmann also considered that relief will be available under CA 2006, s 994 where some event has occurred which puts an end to the basis on which the parties entered into association with each other, so making it unfair that one shareholder should insist on the continuance of the association (a frustration-type situation[109]). As Jonathan Parker LJ explained in *Re Guidezone Ltd*,[110] the unfairness in these cases lies not in the changed circumstances, but in the conduct of the majority in insisting upon the continuance of the association in those changed circumstances.

17-77   Clearly something more is needed than merely an assertion by the petitioner that the association should be brought to an end. Returning to the facts in *O'Neill v Phillips*,[111] it will be recalled that the House of Lords found that there was no unfairly prejudicial conduct. The minority shareholder had not been removed from office and there was no basis for his complaints that he should have received 50% of the shares and of the profits of the company. It was argued further by counsel that, even if nothing unfair had occurred, the trust and confidence between the parties had broken down to such an extent that there had to be a parting of the ways, and it would be unfair to leave the petitioner locked into the company as a minority shareholder. Lord Hoffmann noted that the argument essentially was that, in a quasi-partnership company, one partner ought to be entitled at will to require the other partner to buy his shares at a fair value where he considered that trust and confidence between the partners had broken down. Lord Hoffmann rejected the argument, noting that he could find no support in the authorities for such a stark right of unilateral withdrawal where the member has not been dismissed or excluded from the company.[112] The purpose of the statutory provision (CA 2006, s 994) is 'to provide relief for shareholders who have been unfairly prejudiced, not to enable a locked-in minority shareholder to require the company to buy him out'.[113] In *Re Phoenix Office Supplies Ltd*[114] the Court of Appeal likewise rejected a claim by a shareholder that his co-shareholders and directors were obliged to purchase his shares when he decided (for purely personal reasons) to leave the company. The Court of Appeal noted that a quasi-partnership company relationship does not give rise to an entitlement to a 'no-fault divorce' enabling one partner at will to require the other partners to buy his shares at fair value.

---

[107] See *Fisher v Cadman* [2006] 1 BCLC 499: the directors provided only limited services to the company which merely held properties for investment purposes and it was the understanding of all concerned that they would not be paid. It was unfairly prejudicial conduct, therefore, for them to award themselves remuneration in excess of £50,000.

[108] [1999] 2 BCLC 1.

[109] [1999] 2 BCLC 1 at 11 where Lord Hoffmann noted that the analogy of contractual frustration suggested itself.

[110] [2000] 2 BCLC 321 at 357.   [111] [1999] 2 BCLC 1.   [112] [1999] 2 BCLC 1 at 13.

[113] *Re a Company* [1983] Ch 178 at 191.

[114] [2003] 1 BCLC 76. See also *Re Jayflex Construction Ltd, McKee v O'Reilly* [2004] 2 BCLC 145.

The circumstances which would fall within Lord Hoffmann's quasi-frustration cat-   **17-78**
egory were considered in *Re Metropolis Motorcycles Ltd, Hale v Waldock*.[115] In this
case, Mann J noted that:

> '. . . Lord Hoffmann was demonstrating that unfairness does not arise only out of a fail-
> ure to comply with prior agreements or to fulfil prior expectations. The relationships
> between shareholders are more subtle than that, and Lord Hoffmann was recognis-
> ing that unfairness can come out of a situation where the game has moved on so as to
> involve a situation not covered by the previous arrangements and understanding. In
> those circumstances the conduct of the affairs of the company can be unfairly preju-
> dicial within the section notwithstanding the absence of the prior arrangements, and
> the court can thus intervene. However, for the court to intervene the change in circum-
> stances must be such that it is not reasonable or fair to require the former association
> to remain as it was, and such that the court's intervention is required to adjust matters.
> Lord Hoffmann's words have to be borne in mind: "[circumstances] making it unfair
> that one shareholder should insist upon the continuance of the association".'[116]

On the facts in *Re Metropolis Motorcycles Ltd*[117] the court did not feel that the case fell   **17-79**
into this 'quasi-frustration' category. The parties had an understanding that only the
majority shareholder would be a director. The minority expected to be able to make
monthly drawings from the company on account of profits, but the parties failed to
anticipate that circumstances might arise which would prevent the minority having
any return on his substantial investment in the company. The company fell into financial difficulties and, while the majority shareholder continued to get a financial return
as a director, the company was not in a position to declare a dividend to the minority. The court concluded that that was a failure by the parties to anticipate what had
occurred rather than a change in the circumstances requiring court intervention to
bring the association to an end.

Mann J indicated, however, that it might be appropriate for the minority to return to   **17-80**
the court at a later date if the majority did not respond to the changed circumstances
and make some provision for a return to the minority shareholder.[118] In those circumstances, it would then be open to the minority to rely on the frustration analogy and
to argue that circumstances were such that it would be unfair for the majority shareholder to insist upon the continuation of the association on a basis that gave a return
to him but none to the minority shareholder. Alternatively, if the situation persisted,
the minority could simply argue that the company's affairs were being conducted in a
manner unfairly prejudicial to his interests.

A fair offer—striking out the petition

As noted above, a petition may be brought either on the basis of a breach of the terms   **17-81**
on which the affairs of the company should be conducted or use of the rules in an
inequitable manner, as per *O'Neill v Phillips*.[119] However, while those are the grounds
on which a petition may be based, it is not necessarily the case that the petition can

---

[115] [2007] 1 BCLC 520.   [116] [2007] 1 BCLC 520 at 560.   [117] [2007] 1 BCLC 520.
[118] See [2007] 1 BCLC 520 at 561.   [119] [1999] 2 BCLC 1.

proceed for, in some circumstances, the petition may be struck out by the court. Generally, the court will strike out a petition if an offer has been made to the petitioner (whether as required by the articles or otherwise) that gives the petitioner all the relief that he could realistically expect to obtain on the petition and it would therefore be an abuse to continue with the litigation.[120]

17-82   Tactically it is important for the respondent to consider answering a legitimate complaint by a minority shareholder with a fair offer which will mean that the petition is struck out. A failure to make an offer where the petitioner has legitimate grievances means that ultimately the court will force the respondent to make a fair offer (through a purchase order under CA 2006, s 996) and all that has been achieved is that time and resources have been expended in litigation and the respondent will be liable in costs. Likewise, a petitioner must be careful not to reject a fair offer for the court will not allow a petition to proceed in those circumstances. In effect, the fair offer/strike out rule is used to force the parties to the negotiating table.

17-83   In a quasi-partnership, to be a fair offer, the offer typically has to be an offer to purchase the minority shares on a pro rata basis on a valuation made by an independent valuer.[121] The offer should be on a pro rata basis because, as Lord Millett explained in *CVC/Opportunity Equity Partners Ltd v Demarco Almeida*,[122] the matter should be approached as a sale of the whole business to an outside purchaser. Lord Millett considered that, in order to be free to manage the business without regard to the relationship of trust and confidence which formerly existed, the majority must buy the whole business, 'part from themselves and part from the minority, thereby achieving the same freedom to manage the business as an outside purchaser would enjoy'.[123]

17-84   The valuer must be independent and, while this does not automatically rule out the company's auditors, the nature of the auditors' relationship with the majority shareholders and their past involvement in matters which will affect the valuation means that in many instances the court will agree that the petitioner need not accept such a valuation and the petition can continue.[124]

17-85   Valuable guidance on what is a fair offer, such that a petition should be struck out, was given by Lord Hoffmann in *O'Neill v Phillips*[125] as follows, and this now provides the basic benchmark for a fair offer:

'i)   the offer must be to purchase the shares at a fair value.

---

[120] *O'Neill v Phillips* [1999] 2 BCLC 1. See also *Re a Company (No 007623 of 1984)* [1986] BCLC 362; *Re a Company (No 004377 of 1986)* [1987] BCLC 94; *Re a Company (No 003843 of 1986)* [1987] BCLC 562; *Re a Company (No 006834 of 1988), ex p Kremer* [1989] BCLC 365; *Re Castleburn Ltd* [1991] BCLC 89; *Re a Company (No 00836 of 1995)* [1996] 2 BCLC 192. Typically the offer will be to buy out the petitioner, but it need not be, see *Music Sales Ltd v Shapiro Bornstein & Co Inc* [2006] 1 BCLC 311.

[121] See *Re a Company (No 00836 of 1995)* [1996] 2 BCLC 192.

[122] [2002] 2 BCLC 108.   [123] [2002] 2 BCLC 108 at 119.

[124] See *North Holdings Ltd v Southern Tropics Ltd* [1999] 2 BCLC 625 at 639; *Re Rotadata Ltd* [2000] 1 BCLC 122 at 132–3; *Re Benfield Greig Group plc* [2002] 1 BCLC 65, CA; also *Re Belfield Furnishings Ltd, Isaacs v Belfield Furnishings Ltd* [2006] 2 BCLC 705 at 722.

[125] [1999] 2 BCLC 1 at 16.

ii) the value, if not agreed, should be determined by a competent expert;

iii) the offer should be to have the value determined by the expert as an expert. It is not required that the offer should provide for the full machinery of arbitration or the half-way house of an expert who gives reasons. The objective should be economy and expedition, even if this carries the possibility of a rough edge for one side or the other (and both parties in this respect take the same risk) compared with a more elaborate procedure;

iv) the offer should provide for equality of arms between the parties. Both should have the same right of access to information about the company which bears upon the value of the shares and both should have the right to make submissions to the expert; and

v) when the offer is made after a lengthy period of litigation, it cannot serve as an independent ground for dismissing the petition, on the assumption that it was otherwise well founded, without an offer of costs. But this does not mean that payment of costs need always be offered. If there is a breakdown in relations between the parties, the majority shareholder should be given a reasonable opportunity to make an offer (which may include time to explore the question of how to raise finance) before he becomes obliged to pay costs.'

An example of an offer which did not amount to a fair offer (and so it was possible **17-86** to continue with the petition) can be seen in *North Holdings Ltd v Southern Tropics Ltd*[126] where the allegations related to alleged misuse by the respondents of the company's assets and goodwill to develop the business of another company in which they were interested. The court thought that valuation of the petitioner's shares in this case raised serious questions of law (as to the extent of the first company's interest in the second company, given the alleged misuse of the first company's assets) which it was not appropriate to leave to a valuer, and the petition should not be struck out. Another example is *Allmark v Burnham*[127] where the court found that the purported 'offers' did not offer the petitioner a satisfactory alternative remedy which he ought reasonably to have accepted. There were a variety of defects in the 'offers' including an absence of equality of arms between the parties with the respondent, but not the petitioner, being allowed to influence the valuation; an absence of detail on matters such as the fair value to be paid (i.e. whether a minority discount would apply) and the date of valuation; and the absence of proper accounts in relation to the company.

Court's power to grant relief

Where the court is satisfied that a petition under CA 2006, s 994 is well founded, it may **17-87** make such order as it thinks fit for giving relief in respect of the matters complained of (CA 2006, s 996(1)). Without prejudice to the generality of the court's powers, CA

---

[126] [1999] 2 BCLC 625.

[127] [2006] 2 BCLC 437. See also *Rahman v Malik* [2008] 2 BCLC 403 (petitioner had not acted unreasonably in refusing offers which did not make provision for the under-declaration of profits by the company and unpaid dividends).

2006, s 996(2) indicates certain types of orders which the court may make,[128] such as regulating the conduct of the company's affairs in the future, or requiring the company to refrain from doing or continuing an act complained of by the petitioner, or to do an act which the petitioner has complained it has omitted to do. The remedy most commonly sought and obtained, however, is a purchase order requiring the respondents to purchase the petitioner's shares at a fair value which normally requires the shares to be valued as if the wrongdoing had not occurred so ensuring that the shareholder recovers any diminution in the value of his shares caused by the wrongdoing.[129]

17-88   The courts have consistently taken the view that the wording of CA 2006, s 996 ('such order as the court thinks fit') offers the widest possible discretion to grant relief, even relief for the company.[130] In making an order under CA 2006, s 996, the court must consider the whole range of possible remedies and it is not limited merely to reversing or putting right the immediate conduct which justifies the order, but it must also look to cure for the future the unfair prejudice suffered by the petitioner[131] so any likelihood of the conduct recurring is a relevant consideration. In determining what is the appropriate remedy, as Patten J noted in *Grace v Biagioli*,[132] the court is 'entitled to look at the realities and practicalities of the overall situation, past, present and future'.

17-89   Interim remedies are available[133] and the court may make an order against third parties[134] and for the benefit of the company.[135] In *Gamlestaden Fastigheter AB v Baltic Partners Ltd*[136] the Privy Council (considering the Jersey statutory equivalent[137] of CA 2006, s 996) accepted that the court could order that damages be paid by the wrongdoers to the company. Indeed the Privy Council was prepared in that case to accept that, given the width of the jurisdiction to give relief, exceptionally, the court may grant relief though the company is insolvent and will remain insolvent (meaning that

---

[128] In the exceptional case where a member petitions with respect to the improper removal of an auditor under CA 2006, s 994(1A) (which gives effect to Directive 2006/43/EC on statutory audit, OJ L 157, 9.06.2006, p 87, art 38.1 of which requires Member States to ensure that statutory auditors may only be dismissed on proper grounds) the court could order the re-appointment of the original auditors, the appointment of new auditors, or any other remedy which the court deems appropriate. In practice, it is unlikely that much use will be made of this provision.

[129] See, for example, *Re Little Olympian Each-Ways Ltd (No 3)* [1995] 1 BCLC 636.

[130] See *Re a Company (No 005287)* [1986] BCLC 68 at 71, per Hoffmann J; *Atlasview Ltd v Brightview Ltd* [2004] 2 BCLC 191 at 206; *Lowe v Fahey* [1996] 1 BCLC 262 at 268; *Re Little Olympian Each-Ways Ltd (No 3)* [1994] 2 BCLC 420 at 429.

[131] *Re Bird Precision Bellows Ltd* [1985] BCLC 493 at 499–500; *Grace v Biagioli* [2006] 2 BCLC 70.

[132] [2006] 2 BCLC 70 at 90.

[133] See *Pringle v Callard* [2008] 2 BCLC 505, where Arden LJ gives useful guidance on the role of interim remedies in this context; also *Re Ravenhart Service (Holdings) Ltd, Reiner v Gershinson* [2004] 2 BCLC 376; *Hawkes v Cuddy* [2008] BCC 125.

[134] In *Clark v Cutland* [2003] 2 BCLC 393 the petition was based on unauthorised payments of company money (£145,000) by a director to his pension fund. The court made a declaration that the company was entitled to a charge over the pension fund cash reserves to secure the sum of £145,000 (set off by £100,000 owed by the company to the pension fund).

[135] See *Clark v Cutland* [2003] 2 BCLC 393; *Bhullar v Bhullar* [2003] 2 BCLC 241; *Anderson v Hogg* [2002] BCC 923, SC. See also n 171 below.

[136] [2008] 1 BCLC 468, PC, noted Walters (2007) 28 Co Law 289; Singla (2007) 123 LQR 542.

[137] See Companies (Jersey) Law 1991, art 141.

the petitioner cannot benefit in his capacity as a shareholder) so long as the petitioner derives some real financial benefit from the petition.[138]

The petitioners in *Gamlestaden* were minority shareholders in a joint venture and the   **17-90**
essence of their allegation was that the directors had negligently allowed the bulk of the company's assets to have been lost rendering it insolvent (in effect the assets were withdrawn from the business for no consideration by the majority shareholders). The minority shareholder had lent the company DM165.5m and an award of damages to the company, while it would not restore the company to solvency, would at least offer some prospect for the minority as creditors to recover some of these loans.[139]

The respondent directors unsuccessfully applied to have the petition struck out on the   **17-91**
basis that relief had to be of benefit to the petitioner in his capacity as a member rather than for the benefit of the creditors. The Privy Council concluded that, given the width of the jurisdiction to give relief under what is CA 2006, s 996, exceptionally the court may grant relief though the company is insolvent and will remain insolvent so long as the petitioner derives some real financial benefit from the petition. The exceptional element in *Gamlestaden* was that the company was a joint venture formed on the basis of an agreement between the joint venturers that the company be funded through share and loan capital. These funding arrangements were so closely connected to the petitioner's membership of the joint venture that if the relief sought was of real value to the joint venturer in recovering some part of his investment, then, in their Lordships' opinion, he ought not to be precluded from relief on the ground that it would benefit him as a loan creditor and not as a member.[140]

Purchase orders

As noted, in practice, a petitioner typically requests an order under CA 2006, s 996(2)(e),   **17-92**
requiring the respondents to purchase the shares held by the petitioner and, as the Court of Appeal commented in *Grace v Biagioli*[141] in most cases of unfairly prejudicial conduct, nothing less than a clean break between the parties is likely to be required. In this case the respondents consciously and deliberately failed to pay a dividend which had been declared and the available profits were distributed instead as management

---

[138] Their Lordships rejected the argument that, as on a winding-up petition, the petitioner under CA 2006, s 994 needs to show a tangible interest in the winding up (essentially that surplus funds would be available), on the basis that the public interest considerations which underlie that requirement in winding up do not apply to unfairly prejudicial petitions: see [2008] 1 BCLC 468 at 478. It is difficult to see much difference between a 'real financial benefit' and a tangible interest, but the tangible interest must accrue to the shareholder as such whereas a real financial benefit can arise, as *Gamlestaden* demonstrates, in any capacity.

[139] The loans had been provided in fact by the petitioner's parent company, though procured by the petitioner pursuant to its obligations to do so under the joint venture agreement. Their Lordships agreed with Robert Walker J in *R & H Electric Ltd v Haden Bill Electrical Ltd* [1995] 2 BCLC 280 at 294, where there was a similar arrangement, that this feature should not bar the petitioner from relief, see [2008] 1 BCLC 468 at 480 and discussion at **17-34**.

[140] [2008] 1 BCLC 468 at 479. In reaching this conclusion, their Lordships endorsed the approach to this effect of Robert Walker J in *Re R & H Electric Ltd v Haden Bill Electrical Ltd* [1995] 2 BCLC 280, although in that case the company was solvent.

[141] [2006] 2 BCLC 70.

fees to the respondents. At first instance, the trial judge declined to make an order requiring the respondents to purchase the petitioner's shares, holding that the appropriate relief was to order the company to pay the petitioner the missing dividend plus interest.

17-93   On appeal, the Court of Appeal concluded that the judge had erred as to the scope of the discretion to order relief, in particular as to the need to cure the problem for the future. In this case, there was some evidence of changes in trading arrangements which would reduce the profits available to be distributed as dividends, a change which the court noted 'does not bode well for future relations between the parties'.[142] Taking everything into account, the Court of Appeal thought that nothing short of a purchase order would provide appropriate protection for the petitioner.[143] A purchase order, the court said, frees the petitioner from the company and enables him to extract his share of the value of the business and assets in return for forgoing any future right to dividends.[144] It also preserves the company and its business for the benefit of the respondents, free from the petitioner's claims and removes the possibility of future difficulties between the shareholders.[145]

17-94   In *Re Coloursource Ltd, Dalby v Bodilly*[146] the unfairly prejudicial conduct was an improper allotment of shares which had the effect of diluting a 50% shareholder to a 5% shareholder. The respondent argued that the appropriate relief was a reversal of the allotment, rectification of the register of members and an undertaking by him not to make further allotments of shares. The court refused to limit the relief in that way and granted the purchase order sought by the petitioner. A buy-out order was an entirely appropriate order, the court said, when the respondent had conducted himself in such a way as to forfeit the other shareholder's confidence in the respondent's ability to conduct the company's affairs in a proper way.

17-95   In *Irvine v Irvine (No 1)*[147] the unfairly prejudicial conduct was the payment of excessive and unauthorised remuneration, but the court considered that the breakdown in trust between the parties had gone too far to be rectified by an order requiring the respondent to repay the excessive amount and fixing the level of his remuneration as to the future. A purchase order requiring him to purchase the minority's shares was the only appropriate remedy.

17-96   *Valuation issues*   The basic approach to the valuation of the shares to be acquired was established in *Re Bird Precision Bellows Ltd*[148] which has been followed in numerous

---

[142] [2006] 2 BCLC 70 at 100.

[143] [2006] 2 BCLC 70 at 96–7, 100. The court also noted, see [2006] 2 BCLC 70 at 101, that it would not have been appropriate in any event to order the company, as opposed to the respondents, to pay the missing dividend.   [144] [2006] 2 BCLC 70 at 96–7.

[145] Typically, the order will require the respondents to purchase the shares of the petitioner, but exceptionally, the court may order the respondents to sell to the petitioner: see *Re Brenfield Squash Racquets Club Ltd* [1996] 2 BCLC 184; *Clark v Cutland* [2003] 2 BCLC 393. Where there is an equality of shareholdings, the court may order the persons responsible for the unfairly prejudicial conduct to sell their shares to the petitioner: see *Re Planet Organic Ltd* [2000] 1 BCLC 366.

[146] [2005] BCC 627.   [147] [2007] 1 BCLC 349.

[148] [1984] BCLC 195, aff'd [1985] BCLC 493.

cases. The key considerations are:

(1) The price fixed by the court must be fair so if assets have been misappropriated by the respondents, the company must be valued as if the misappropriation had not occurred.[149]

(2) There is no rule that the shares have to be bought on a pro rata basis, but nor is there a general rule that they have to be bought on a discounted basis to reflect the fact that they are a minority holding. It all depends on the circumstances of the case.

(3) In general, however, the court would distinguish between two types of share-holding in small private companies (a) where the holding is in what is essentially a quasi-partnership and the sale is being forced on the holder because of the unfairly prejudicial manner in which the majority have conducted the affairs of the company and (b) where the company is not a quasi-partnership.

(4) Where the sale is of a holding acquired in what is essentially a quasi-partnership and the sale is being forced on the holder because of the unfairly prejudicial manner in which the majority have conducted the affairs of the company then, as a general rule, the correct course would be to fix the price pro rata according to the value of the shares as a whole and without any discount.

As already explained, the majority of petitions do relate to quasi-partnerships and therefore the general approach is to require a pro rata valuation. The offer should be on a pro rata basis because, as Lord Millett explained in *CVC/Opportunity Equity Partners Ltd v Demarco Almeida*[150] the matter should be approached as a sale of the whole business to an outside purchaser. He commented that, in order to be free to manage the business without regard to the relationship of trust and confidence which formerly existed between the parties, the majority must buy the whole business, 'part from themselves and part from the minority, thereby achieving the same freedom to manage the business as an outside purchaser would enjoy'.[151]   **17-97**

In *Strahan v Wilcock*[152] it was argued that this general rule (pro rata valuation in a quasi-partnership) should be set aside. In that case the parties' relationship had developed from one of employer/employee into a quasi-partnership, but the acquisition of shares in the business by the petitioner had also been the subject of commercial option agreements. The question was whether such commercial aspects to the relationship meant that a pro rata basis should be set aside in favour of a discounted value.   **17-98**

The Court of Appeal concluded that the relationship overall was correctly classified as a quasi-partnership involving aspects arising from the petitioner's employment, his rights under the option agreements (the terms of which did not suggest a purely commercial relationship) and his participation in the management of the business. Given all the circumstances of the relationship, on the petitioner's exclusion from the management of the company, fairness required that his shares be purchased on a non-discounted basis.   **17-99**

---

[149] See, for example, *Re Little Olympian Each-Ways Ltd (No 3)* [1995] 1 BCLC 636.
[150] [2002] 2 BCLC 108.   [151] [2002] 2 BCLC 108 at 119.   [152] [2006] 2 BCLC 555, CA.

17-100   Where the company is not a quasi-partnership, different considerations apply and the price fixed will normally be discounted to reflect the fact that it is a minority holding. Indeed, in *Strahan v Wilcock*,[153] Arden LJ commented that it is difficult to conceive of circumstances in which a pro rata valuation would be appropriate where there is no quasi-partnership relationship. In *Re Elgindata Ltd*[154] a discounted value was appropriate for the shares had been acquired by the petitioners for investment purposes. In *Re a Company (No 005134 of 1986), ex p Harries*[155] the company had started out as a quasi-partnership but it had ceased to be so after a period of years and had reverted to a more commercial footing, therefore a discounted value for the petitioner's shareholding was appropriate. In *Re Planet Organic Ltd*[156] the purchase order related to preference shareholders and the court concluded that, as they were investors rather than active participants in the running of the company, they should be bought out at a discount. A discounted valuation applies, even if the minority holding is substantial, as in *Irvine v Irvine (No 2)*.[157] In this case, the petitioners tried to persuade the court that their 49.96% shareholding was so substantial that the holding should be valued on a pro rata, non-discounted basis, though the company was not a quasi-partnership. The court rejected their claim and ruled that a minority shareholding, even where the extent of the minority is slight, is to be valued as a minority shareholding unless a good reason exists (i.e. that the company is a quasi-partnership or some other exceptional circumstance) to attribute to it a pro rata share of the overall value of the company. In the instant case, the company was not a quasi-partnership and there were no exceptional circumstances. Accordingly, the court held that the shares should be valued on a discounted basis.

17-101   In addition to disputes as to the basis of valuation, it is common for there also to be disagreements as to the appropriate date for valuation, for this may have a significant bearing on the outcome. Commonly, the shares will be valued at the date of the order for purchase, as that is the time when the unfairly prejudicial conduct is brought to an end, and an interest in a going concern should be valued at the date when it is ordered to be sold.[158] As the overriding criterion is fairness, however, fairness may require, in the circumstances of a particular case, that the valuation be directed to take place at an earlier date, such as the date of the petition.[159]

Relationship with other shareholder remedies

17-102   The range of conduct covered and the flexibility of the relief offered means that petitioning for relief under CA 2006, s 994 is almost invariably the most attractive solution

---

[153] [2006] 2 BCLC 555 at 561, CA.   [154] [1991] BCLC 959.   [155] [1989] BCLC 383.
[156] [2000] 1 BCLC 366.   [157] [2007] 1 BCLC 445.
[158] See *Profinance Trust SA v Gladstone* [2002] 1 BCLC 141.
[159] Guidance as to the circumstances in which an earlier valuation might be called for was given by the Court of Appeal in *Profinance Trust SA v Gladstone* [2002] 1 BCLC 141. In determining the date, the Court of Appeal emphasised that the date of valuation may be heavily influenced by the parties' conduct in making and accepting or rejecting offers either before or during the course of the proceedings, in keeping with the emphasis in *O'Neill v Phillips* [1999] 2 BCLC 1 on the importance of a fair offer.

for an aggrieved shareholder but there are other options available which may be relevant in some circumstances including various statutory rights under the CA 2006, see **18-88**.

Winding up on the just and equitable ground

In addition to petitioning for relief under CA 2006, s 994, a petitioner may petition in   **17-103** the alternative for a winding-up order on the just and equitable ground under IA 1986, s 122(1)(g) (there being no power to make a winding-up order under CA 2006, s 996). The effect of petitioning under the winding up jurisdiction is to oblige the company to seek a validation order[160] under IA 1986, s 127 which otherwise avoids dispositions of company property made after the commencement of the winding up (i.e. after the presentation of the petition), see **24-41**. The requirement of a validation order under IA 1986, s 127 means that presenting a winding-up petition alongside the unfairly prejudicial petition maximises the pressure that the petitioner can bring to bear on the respondents. The courts have been alert to the oppressive possibilities of this tactic and a Practice Direction makes clear that a petitioner should not seek relief under CA 2006, s 994 and winding up unless winding up is the relief which the petitioner prefers or it is thought that it may be the only relief to which he is entitled;[161] but this latter point has been overtaken by the decision in *Re Guidezone Ltd*,[162] discussed below.

In practice, it is very unlikely that a petitioner does want a winding-up order. As dis-   **17-104** cussed, the successful petitioner is able under CA 2006, s 996 to obtain a purchase order and exit the company and has no reason to pursue a winding-up order. Moreover, the very availability of relief under s 994 means that the court may refuse to exercise its discretion to make a winding-up order: see IA 1986, s 125(2), discussed at **18-75**.

The ability to obtain an order under IA 1986, s 122(1)(g) remains of importance only   **17-105** if that jurisdiction is broader than under CA 2006, s 994 so that there might conceivably be cases where the petitioner would not succeed on a petition but might get a winding-up order under the Insolvency Act. This point was considered by Jonathan Parker J in *Re Guidezone Ltd*[163] who concluded that conduct which is not unfair within CA 2006, s 994 cannot found a petition for winding up for that jurisdiction is, at the very least, no wider than CA 2006, s 994.[164] While this approach has been criticised as a conflation of the two jurisdictions,[165] the practical position is that shareholders no

---

[160] A validation order permits the company to make dispositions of its property after the commencement of the winding up.

[161] See CPR, PD 49b which contains a standard IA 1986, s 127 validation order.

[162] [2000] 2 BCLC 321.   [163] [2000] 2 BCLC 321.

[164] In so far as *Re R A Noble & Sons (Clothing) Ltd* [1983] BCLC 273 suggested to the contrary, the court considered that it was inconsistent with *O'Neill v Phillips* [1999] 2 BCLC 1: see [2000] 2 BCLC 321 at 357.

[165] See Boyle, *Minority Shareholders' Remedies* (2002) pp 96–100; Acton, 'Just and Equitable Winding up: the Strange Case of the Disappearing Jurisdiction' (2001) 22 Co Lawyer 134 where it is argued that the winding-up jurisdiction is wider than the unfairly prejudicial jurisdiction in that it will apply to deadlock cases involving a breakdown in mutual trust where winding up is warranted but where there is no objective unfairness as will support a petition under CA 2006, s 994. Jonathan Parker J made clear in *Re Guidezone Ltd* [2000] 2 BCLC 321 at 356 that such breakdown cases are cases of unfairness, the unfairness arising from the majority using its legal powers to maintain the association in circumstances to which the minority can reasonably say it did not agree, see **17-76**, and therefore such cases are within CA 2006, s 994.

longer look to the winding-up remedy. For a fuller discussion of the overlap between the remedies, see **18-86**.

A derivative claim

17-106   As is evident from the authorities discussed above in this chapter, breaches of directors' duties are classic examples of conduct which is unfairly prejudicial to the interests of members 'generally'[166] and therefore within the unfairly prejudicial jurisdiction. But such breaches are also wrongs done to the company, of course, and in respect of which the company may sue or a derivative claim may lie under CA 2006, Part 11. The clear overlap between the jurisdictions does not concern the courts and the mere fact that the conduct would merit a derivative claim is not a reason to strike out the petition.[167] If the only substantive relief sought on the petition is a claim on behalf of the company against a third party, however, the court will not necessarily allow the claimant to proceed by petition instead of by derivative claim;[168] and where the derivative action and the petition raise substantially the same issues, the court may require that the proceedings be consolidated, typically in the petition.[169]

17-107   A petition under CA 2006, s 994 has the merit of avoiding the procedural obstacles surrounding the derivative claim where the claimant must obtain the permission of the court to continue the claim, a potentially lengthy and difficult process (see the discussion in Chapter 18). A petition secures a personal remedy for the petitioner rather than a remedy for the company, as would be the case with a derivative action. On the other hand, a derivative action may be attractive where the shareholder does not wish to have his shares purchased (that being the typical remedy under CA 2006, s 994), but wants a remedy for misconduct and the recovery of assets belonging to the company and he wishes to take advantage of the indemnity for costs which is available with respect to a derivative action.[170] The availability now of a derivative claim under CA 2006, Part 11, should result in clearer lines now being drawn between these distinct remedies.[171] Derivative claims are discussed in Chapter 18.

---

[166] See *Atlasview Ltd v Brightview Ltd* [2004] 2 BCLC 191 at 207–8.

[167] See *Re a Company (No 005287)* [1986] BCLC 68; *Lowe v Fahey* [1996] 1 BCLC 262; *Re Little Olympian Each-Ways Ltd (No 3)* [1995] 1 BCLC 636 at 665.

[168] *Lowe v Fahey* [1996] 1 BCLC 262.

[169] See *Cooke v Cooke* [1997] 2 BCLC 28; see also *Clark v Cutland* [2003] 2 BCLC 393 at 396.

[170] There has been some blurring of the lines on this issue with the court in *Clark v Cutland* [2003] 2 BCLC 393 at 405 accepting that where, exceptionally, corporate relief is ordered on a petition, the petitioner is entitled to an indemnity for costs.

[171] See Hannigan, 'Drawing boundaries between derivative claims and unfairly prejudicial petitions' [2009] JBL, forthcoming.

18

The derivative claim and the rule in *Foss v Harbottle*

A Corporate claims for wrongs done to the company

The rule in *Foss v Harbottle*

At common law shareholders' remedies are dominated by the rule in *Foss v Harbottle*[1]   **18-1**
which has two elements: first, the proper plaintiff in respect of a wrong allegedly done
to a company is prima facie the company; secondly, where the alleged wrong is a transaction which might be made binding on the company by a simple majority of the
members, no individual member of the company is allowed to bring a claim in respect
of it.[2] As Mellish LJ explained in *MacDougall v Gardiner*: '…if the thing complained
of is a thing which in substance the majority of the company are entitled to do…there
can be no use in having litigation about it, the ultimate end of which is only that a
meeting has to be called, and then ultimately the majority gets its wishes'.[3] In *Foss v
Harbottle*[4] the court refused to permit two shareholders to bring an action on behalf of
the company against the directors and promoters who had sold property to the company at an inflated value. The court found that it was not open to individual members
to assume to themselves the right of suing in the name of the company. The company
was the proper person to sue and, while that was a rule that could be departed from,
it should not be, save for very urgent reasons. The rule is based on two fundamental
principles of company law, namely respect for the separate legal personality of the
company and the principle of majority rule. In addition to reflecting those fundamental principles, the rule has certain practical advantages. It is convenient and efficient
that the company should sue in respect of a wrong done to it rather than have a multiplicity of shareholder suits. It eliminates wasteful litigation where the only outcome
can be that the majority pass a resolution approving the 'wrongdoing'. It prevents vexatious actions started by troublesome shareholders trying to harass the company: the

---

[1] (1843) 2 Hare 461.
[2] *Prudential Assurance Co Ltd v Newman Industries Ltd (No 2)* [1982] 1 All ER 354 at 357, CA; and see
Edwards v Halliwell [1950] 2 All ER 1064 at 1066, per Jenkins LJ.
[3] (1875) 1 Ch D 13 at 25.   [4] (1843) 2 Hare 461.

process is for the collective benefit of the shareholders and, where there is any issue as to the solvency of the company, the creditors.

The common law derivative claim

18-2   Where the wrong done to the company has been committed by a third party, the directors in the exercise of their management powers will decide whether the company should sue.[5] This is not a matter which is within the remit of the shareholders, at least where the company's articles include the standard delegation of all powers of management to the board.[6]

18-3   Where the wrong is committed by those in control of the company, however, it is inappropriate that the first element of the rule (that the company is the proper plaintiff) should prevent an action in respect of that wrongdoing (because the wrongdoer in control will ensure that the company does not claim)—hence the development of an exception to the rule whereby, in limited circumstances (consistent with respect for the second element of the rule), a shareholder may sue derivatively, i.e. on behalf on the company to obtain a remedy for the company. The circumstances meriting a derivative claim were explained as follows in *Burland v Earle*:[7]

> 'The cases in which the minority can maintain such an action are, therefore, confined to those in which the acts complained of are of a fraudulent character or beyond the powers of the company. A familiar example is where the majority are endeavouring directly or indirectly to appropriate to themselves money, property, or advantages which belong to the company, or in which the other shareholders are entitled to participate, as was alleged in the case of *Menier v. Hooper's Telegraph Works*[8]. It should be added that no mere informality or irregularity which can be remedied by the majority will entitle the minority to sue, if the act when done regularly would be within the powers of the company and the intention of the majority of the shareholders is clear.'

18-4   As a preliminary matter, then, the court required the claimant in a derivative claim to establish a prima facie case that the company was entitled to the relief claimed and that the action fell within the proper boundaries of the exception to the rule in *Foss v Harbottle* as identified above, namely: (1) that the wrong was a fraud on the minority, in the sense of an unratifiable wrong not capable of 'cure' by the majority; and (2) that wrongdoer control of the company prevented the company itself bringing an action in its own name.[9] Further, even when a prima facie case existed, the court would not permit a derivative action to proceed where the majority of the shareholders who were independent of the wrongdoers, for disinterested reasons, did not wish the proceedings to continue.[10]

---

[5] See *Breckland Group Holdings Ltd v London and Suffolk Properties Ltd* [1989] BCLC 100.

[6] See The Companies (Model Articles) Regulations 2008, SI 2008/3229, hereinafter 'Model Articles', art 3 (Ltd); art 3 (Plc), previously SI 1985/805, Table A, reg 70; see *Automatic Self-Cleansing Filter Syndicate Ltd v Cunninghame* [1906] 2 Ch 34.

[7] [1902] AC 83 at 93–4, per Lord Davey.   [8] (1874) LR 9 Ch App 350.

[9] *Prudential Assurance Co Ltd v Newman Industries Ltd (No 2)* [1982] 1 All ER 354 at 366; *Smith v Croft (No 2)* [1987] 3 All ER 909 at 945.   [10] *Smith v Croft (No 2)* [1987] 3 All ER 909.

In practice, derivative actions were rare which was unsurprising, given the restrictive   **18-5**
effect of the rule in *Foss v Harbottle*, the difficulty in establishing standing to bring a
derivative claim and the absence of personal relief. The derivative jurisdiction was also
less attractive given the development of a broad unfairly prejudicial jurisdiction under
what is now CA 2006, s 994 under which a petitioner can secure personal relief without having to overcome these types of obstacles as to locus standi.

Statutory reform

A report on shareholders' remedies by the Law Commission in 1997 concluded that: **18-6**
(1) the rule in *Foss v Harbottle* was complicated and unwieldy; (2) the scope of the
exception to the rule (i.e. the circumstances when a derivative claim could be brought)
was uncertain; and (3) the procedural difficulties were such that simply establishing
standing to sue could amount to a mini-trial.[11] The Law Commission recommended,
therefore, that the common law action be replaced with a statutory derivative procedure with more modern, flexible and accessible criteria for determining whether
a shareholder may bring a claim.[12] The intention was to put a derivative claim on a
clearer and more rational basis, which would give the courts flexibility to allow cases
to proceed in appropriate circumstances, while giving guidance to advisers as to the
matters which the court would take into account in deciding whether to grant leave to
bring a claim.[13] The Law Commission thought that a statutory procedure would give
greater transparency to the requirements for a claim; it would alert interested parties
to the availability of a derivative claim; and it would ensure that the Companies Act
constituted a more complete code (with the unfairly prejudicial remedy) with regard
to shareholders' remedies.[14] The Law Commission also thought that, in an age of international business, it is important to set out the rules in the statute in keeping with
other jurisdictions.[15]

The Law Commission's recommendations were endorsed by the Company Law Review   **18-7**
without much further deliberation[16] and the statutory derivative claim, now found in

---

[11] Law Commission, *Shareholder Remedies* (Law Com No 246) (Cm 3769, 1997) (hereinafter Law
Commission Report), para 6.4. The Report was preceded by a Consultation Paper of the same name: Con
Paper No 142 (1996). For comments on the Law Commission's proposals, see Boyle, *Minority Shareholders'
Remedies* (2002), Ch 3; Poole & Roberts, 'Shareholder Remedies—Corporate Wrongs and the Derivative
Action' [1999] JBL 99.

[12] Law Commission Report, para 6.15.   [13] Law Commission Report, para 6.14.

[14] Law Commission Report, paras 6.16–6.18.

[15] Law Commission Report, para 6.9. See the Canadian Business Corporations Act 1975, s 239, and
Cheffins, 'Reforming the Derivative Action: The Canadian Experience and British Prospects' [1997]
Company, Financial and Insolvency Law Review 227; the New Zealand Companies Act 1993, ss 165–168,
and Watson, 'A Matter of Balance: The Statutory Derivative Action in New Zealand' (1998) 19 Co Law 236;
the Australian Corporations Act 2001, ss 236–242, and Ramsay and Saunders, 'Litigation by Shareholders
and Directors: An Empirical Study of the Australian Statutory Derivative Action' [2006] 6 JCLS 397.

[16] See Company Law Review, *Developing the Framework* (2000), paras 4.112–4.139 for the main discussion of the issues; also *Completing the Structure* (2000), paras 5.82–5.89; and *Final Report* (2001), paras
7.46–7.51.

CA 2006, Part 11, is modelled largely on the Law Commission's proposals. It replaces the common law derivative action.[17]

18-8   Not everyone welcomed the introduction of a statutory derivative claim. There were particular concerns about introducing it alongside the statutory statement of directors' duties (specifically, the obligation in CA 2006, s 172 requiring directors to promote the success of the company having regard to the factors set out in that section). The concern was that shareholder activists might use the combination of the new derivative procedure and s 172 to challenge business decisions of directors on the basis of an alleged failure to have regard to the factors set out in that section, see **9-35**. A derivative claim, it was argued, could be used to seek judicial review, in effect, of a commercial decision of management. For example, shareholders with an interest in environmental issues might try to challenge a board decision to open a new mine on the grounds that the directors did not have regard to 'the impact of the company's operations on the community and the environment' as required by s 172(1)(d). Equally, if a company incurs a regulatory fine, say for breaches of competition law or health and safety requirements, the concern is that shareholders may try to bring a derivative claim to recover the amount of the fine from the directors on the basis that the breach and fine shows that the directors have not conducted the company's affairs in accordance with s 172 or have failed to exercise appropriate care and skill as required by s 174.

18-9   A further concern was that the restrictive common law thresholds of fraud on the minority and wrongdoer control have been replaced and derivative claims are possible in respect of a breach of any duty owed by a director to the company including, for the first time, in respect of alleged negligence by a director (s 260(3)). In addition, the rules on ratification have been altered to preclude directors, as shareholders, voting to ratify their own wrongdoing (s 239). As the critics see it, the result is that there are more grounds for a derivative claim, but less possibility of ratification.

18-10   At a practical level, there are concerns that there is more scope for speculative or vexatious litigation now for a variety of reasons: the availability of conditional fee agreements;[18] the rise of activist shareholders ranging from those representing a particular 'lobby' (such as environmentalists) to hedge funds with deep pockets; and the increased presence of US shareholders and lawyers in London who may be more attuned to vindicating investor rights through the courts rather than a discreet market exit and for whom derivative actions are merely another mechanism for holding underperforming directors to account.

---

[17] The Law Commission recommended that the statutory derivative claim supersede the common law derivative action in order to allow for the development of a coherent body of law based on Part 11 alone: see Law Commission Report, paras 6.51–6.55.

[18] There is some debate as to whether conditional fee agreements are possible with respect to derivative claims: see the differing views of Payne, 'Sections 459–461 Companies Act 1985 in Flux: The Future of Shareholder Protection' (2005) CLJ 647 at 665; Reisberg, 'Funding Derivative Actions: A re-examination of costs and fees as incentives to commence litigation' (2004) 4 JCLS 345 at 380.

This combination of factors (expanded duties; the availability of a statutory derivative   **18-11**
claim; and activist shareholders) creates, it is argued, a threat of litigation which will
deter people from taking up directorships of public companies.

Throughout the Parliamentary debates, the Government emphasised that CA 2006,   **18-12**
Part 11 does not introduce any major change of principle and there is no reason to
expect any significant increase in the number of derivative actions.[19] The intention
behind Part 11 is to strike a balance between protecting directors from vexatious and
frivolous claims[20] so allowing them to take business decisions in good faith while protecting the rights of shareholders to bring meritorious claims.[21] The derivative claim,
the Government noted, is a well-established mechanism which has certain inherent
characteristics which limit the potential for speculative litigation, including that a
claim can only be brought on behalf of the company with any sums recovered going
to the company and not to the claimant who runs the risk of incurring substantial
costs.[22] Even so, the Government felt the need to respond to the concerns expressed
by business and practitioners and it brought forward amendments to Part 11 designed
to enhance the protection for directors[23] by (1) strengthening the judicial controls of
derivative claims (discussed below), and (2) by restating the duty of directors to act
to promote the interests of the company (in CA 2006, s 172(1)) to emphasise that the
overriding obligation of directors remains to promote the success of the company for
the benefit of its members as a whole, see **9-38**. In this way, it is hoped to curb the scope
for allegations of a breach of duty arising from a supposed failure to have regard to one
or more of the factors set out in that section.

Impact on the rule in *Foss v Harbottle*

Before discussing CA 2006, Part 11 in detail,[24] it is worth emphasising that the rule in   **18-13**
Foss v Harbottle[25] has not been swept aside. As noted above, there are two elements to
the rule: the proper plaintiff element and the majority rule element.

As regards the proper plaintiff aspect, the position remains that the proper plaintiff in   **18-14**
respect of a wrong allegedly done to a company is prima facie the company.

---

[19] For the Government's position, see 679 HL Official Report (5th series), cols GC4–5, 27 February 2006;
681 HL Official Report (5th series), col 883, 9 May 2006; HC Official Report, SC D (Company Law Reform
Bill), 13 July 2006, cols 664–6.

[20] 679 HL Official Report (5th series), col GC6, 27 February 2006.

[21] See 681 HL Official Report (5th series), col 883, 9 May 2006.

[22] See 679 HL Official Report (5th series), cols GC4–5, 27 February 2006; HC Official Report, SC D
(Company Law Reform Bill), 13 July 2006, col 665.

[23] See 681 HL Official Report (5th series), cols 883–4, 9 May 2006.

[24] See generally Hannigan, 'The Derivative Claim—An Invitation to Litigate?' in Hannigan & Prentice,
The Companies Act 2006—A Commentary (2009); also Nessen, Goo and Low, 'The Statutory Derivative
Action: Now Showing Near You' [2008] JBL 627; Keay & Loughrey, 'Something Old, Something New,
Something Borrowed: an Analysis of the New Derivative Action under the Companies Act 2006' (2008) 124
LQR 469.

[25] (1843) 2 Hare 461.

18-15   The majority rule element meant that, at common law, a shareholder could not bring a derivative claim in respect of an act which was capable of being confirmed by the majority.[26] Under Part 11, actual authorisation or ratification is required to bar a claim (s 263(2)(b), (c)). Otherwise, the possibility of authorisation or ratification is a matter to be taken into account by the court when deciding whether to give permission for a claim to proceed (s 263(3)(c) and (d)). The position is therefore clearer under the statute in that actual authorisation or ratification is required to bar a claim, but it makes no substantive change to the general principle of majority rule in that if the majority chooses to authorise or ratify the conduct in question, assuming it is ratifiable, then that ends the matter. Derivative claims, though facilitated by the new procedural mechanism of Part 11, remain subject to the general principle of majority rule.[27]

18-16   What has altered is that the derivative claim (i.e. the procedural mechanism) invented by the courts as an exception to the rule in *Foss v Harbottle* (based on wrongdoer control and unratifiable wrongs) is replaced by the statutory mechanism and thresholds laid down in CA 2006, Part 11.

B The derivative claim—CA 2006, Part 11

Bringing a derivative claim

18-17   A derivative claim may be initiated by a member who then requires the permission of the court to continue with it: CA 2006, s 261(1).[28] The claimant must be a member[29] at the time of the proceedings,[30] but no minimum shareholding is required.[31] In theory, this means that litigious parties could purchase one share with a view to bringing a case against the directors, but whether the court would permit such a claimant to proceed (see below) is another matter. In any event, there is little advantage to a person

---

[26] *MacDougall v Gardiner* (1875) 1 Ch D 13 at 25, CA; *Burland v Earle* [1902] AC 83 at 93–4.

[27] *Burland v Earle* [1902] AC 83 at 93–4.

[28] See CPR 19.9(4), 19.9A(4) and Practice Direction on Derivative Claims; also *Portfolios of Distinction Ltd v Laird* [2004] 2 BCLC 741. It is also possible for a member to apply for permission to continue as a derivative claim a claim commenced by the company or by another member: CA 2006, ss 262(1), (2), 264, but these scenarios are rather unlikely. A derivative claim may also be brought by a group of members with respect to unauthorised political donations (see CA 2006, s 370) but such claims are also unlikely.

[29] References to a 'member' include a person who is not a member but to whom shares in the company have been transferred or transmitted by operation of law: CA 2006, s 260(5)(c).

[30] It is immaterial whether the cause of action arose before or after the would-be claimant became a member of the company: CA 2006, s 260(4). See Law Commission Report, para 6.98; 679 HL Official Report (5th series), col GC15, 27 February 2006; *Seaton v Grant* (1867) LR 2 Ch App 459.

[31] Concerns were raised that vulture funds, environmentalists, animal rights activists and US lawyers, amongst others, would seek to take advantage of the absence of any minimum shareholding: see 679 HL Official Report (5th series), cols GC11–13, 27 February 2006. But, as Lord Cairns explained in *Seaton v Grant* (1867) LR 2 Ch App 459 at 465, the quantum of the claimant's interest is irrelevant, if the claim is one which should otherwise be brought, for the aggregate interest of all the shareholders is amply sufficient to sustain the claim.

acquiring a single share with a view to bringing a derivative claim since any recovery is for the benefit of the company and the claimant runs the risk that he will be penalised in costs.

A derivative claim may be brought against a director (including a shadow director) or another person or both: s 260(3). Former directors are included[32] (s 260(5)(a)) and claims against such directors might arise, for example, where directors have resigned in order to exploit an opportunity which came to their attention while they were directors and where there is a conflict of interest between their interests and the interests of the company: see **11-2**.   **18-18**

The intention behind permitting derivative claims against 'another person' is to allow a claim to be made against a person who has assisted a director in a breach of duty or who is a recipient of corporate assets in circumstances where he knows the director is acting in breach of his duties,[33] but the basis for suing them derivatively must be their involvement in the director's breach of duty. A derivative claim cannot be brought where the breach of duty etc is solely that of the third party, such as a negligent auditor. As the Law Commission noted, the decision whether to sue a third party (i.e. someone who is not a director and where the claim is not closely connected with a breach of duty by a director) is one for the board.[34]   **18-19**

A derivative claim may be brought in respect of a cause of action arising from an actual or proposed[35] act or omission involving negligence, default,[36] breach of duty or breach of trust by a director of the company (s 260). The significant change here is that a claim may be brought in respect of any breach of duty by a director. At common law the conduct complained of had to amount to an unratifiable wrong not capable of 'cure' by the majority i.e. acts of an ultra vires, illegal or fraudulent character which typically involved the misappropriation of money, property, or advantages belonging to the company, and which are generally described as a fraud on the minority.[37] All   **18-20**

---

[32] Their inclusion avoids the problem that they would otherwise be classed as third parties whom the current board would be expected to sue (or not) on behalf of the company, see Ford's *Principles of Corporations Law* (11th edn, 2003), para 11.250.

[33] See Law Commission Report, paras 6.35, 6.36; 679 HL Official Report (5th series), cols GC9–10, 27 February 2006; HC Official Report, SC D (Company Law Reform Bill), 13 July 2006, col 666.

[34] See Law Commission Report, paras 6.34, 6.35. A derivative claim may lie, however, where the board's decision not to pursue a claim against a third party is itself a breach of duty by the directors, subject to difficulties of causation and quantification in such circumstances: see Law Commission Report, para 6.32.

[35] The ability to bring claims with respect to proposed acts may offer some scope for shareholders to take pre-emptive action, as where the directors make known their intention, say, to make certain acquisitions or look to expansion overseas. Shareholders might look to bring a claim alleging that such actions would be in breach of s 172 (promote the success of the company) or s 174 (exercise care and skill) and seeking an injunction to prevent the directors proceeding. It is difficult to envisage the court encouraging that type of behaviour, but the possibility is there because the section covers 'proposed' acts.

[36] 'Default' enables claims to be brought in respect of breaches of statutory obligations imposed by the companies legislation: *Customs and Excise Commissioners v Hedon Alpha Ltd* [1981] 2 All ER 697.

[37] *Burland v Earle* [1902] AC 83 at 93–4, per Lord Davey, see **18-3** above; and see *Menier v Hooper's Telegraph Works* (1874) LR 9 Ch App 350; *Cook v Deeks* [1916] 1 AC 554; *Daniels v Daniels* [1978] 2 All ER 89.

other breaches of duty, being ratifiable, could not be the subject of a derivative action at common law, even if the breaches had not actually been ratified.[38] Now the restrictive concept of 'fraud on the minority' no longer applies and breach of any duty is potentially actionable (subject to the ability of the majority to ratify breaches of duty: see below at **18-33**).

18-21   The extension of the derivative claim to negligence[39] was recommended by the Law Commission which noted that, while investors take the risk that those who manage companies may make mistakes, they do not have to accept that directors will fail to comply with their duties,[40] a view endorsed by the Company Law Review.[41] Of course, while negligence will found a derivative claim, the courts will continue to distinguish between commercial misjudgements and negligent conduct (and negligence is ratifiable).

18-22   To sum up, a derivative claim may be brought:

- by any member (however few shares he holds and however recently acquired);
- against any director (including former and shadow directors) and other persons implicated in the breach;
- in respect of negligence, default, breach of duty and breach of trust by a director of the company.

18-23   While it is possible to commence a derivative claim on this basis and therefore Part 11 looks to be a much broader jurisdiction than the common law derivative claim, as we shall see the statutory claim may not proceed very far for the claimant must obtain the permission of the court to continue the claim.

Judicial control of a derivative claim

18-24   There are two stages involved once a derivative claim has been commenced. At the first stage, a prima facie case must be made, otherwise the court must dismiss the claim. At the second stage, a variety of factors must be considered, some of which oblige the court to dismiss the claim. Otherwise, the court has a broad discretion to give or refuse permission or adjourn the proceedings and give such directions as it thinks fit.

18-25   The first stage requires the court to dismiss the claim if the application and the evidence filed by the applicant in support of it do not disclose a prima facie case for giving permission: CA 2006, s 261(2).

18-26   The Government was initially reluctant to set any particular threshold requirements, preferring to let the matter progress to a hearing when the court would consider the

---

[38] *MacDougall v Gardiner* (1875) 1 Ch 13 at 25; *Burland v Earle* [1902] AC 83 at 93–4.

[39] At common law, mere negligence from which the director did not benefit personally could not found a derivative claim: *Pavlides v Jensen* [1956] 2 All ER 518, and it was necessary to show that the negligence was of the self-serving variety seen in *Daniels v Daniels* [1978] 2 All ER 89 where the board sold an asset at a gross undervalue to one of the directors.

[40] See Law Commission Report, para 6.41.

[41] Company Law Review, *Developing the Framework* (2000), para 4.127.

factors set out in s 263(3). The concern was to avoid turning the preliminary stages of a claim into an expensive and time-consuming mini-trial and to allow the court over a period of time to develop appropriate thresholds for these claims.[42] Following criticisms that there were inadequate filters to prevent vexatious litigation, however, the Government was persuaded that the court should have a specific power to dismiss unmeritorious cases at an early stage without involving the company and this prima facie threshold was included for that purpose.[43]

18-27 It remains to be seen whether this prima facie requirement presents much of a challenge to the would-be claimant. Faced with a new procedure designed to make derivative actions more accessible to shareholders, the courts may be reluctant to throw out a remotely plausible case at the first threshold.[44] There may be some judicial willingness to allow shareholder claimants the opportunity at least for a second-stage consideration of their concerns, bearing in mind that it is still possible for the court to stop the proceedings at that stage.[45]

18-28 If the case is not dismissed at this prima facie threshold, the court may think an adjournment appropriate to allow the company to seek authorisation or ratification of the conduct in question which will then act as a complete bar to the claim proceeding (see CA 2006, s 261(4)).

18-29 In effect, therefore, the claim will only proceed if the wrong is not capable of authorisation (as was the case with claims at common law) or, where the wrong may be authorised or ratified, the majority chooses not to do so. The latter scenario is unlikely since, in such a case, it might be expected that the majority would deal with the wrongdoing director without the need for the minority to bring a derivative claim. Authorisation and ratification are discussed further below.

Absolute bars to a derivative claim proceeding

18-30 Permission to continue a claim must be refused if the court is satisfied that:

(1) a director acting in accordance with CA 2006, s 172 (duty to promote the success of the company) would not seek to continue the claim; or

(2) the act or omission has been authorised by the company or ratified by the company (CA 2006, s 263(2)).

---

[42] See 679 HL Official Report (5th series), col GC22, 27 February 2006; Law Commission Report, paras 6.4, 6.71.

[43] The provision was added at Report Stage in the House of Lords, see 681 HL Official Report (5th series), cols 883–4, 9 May 2006. The court's power to dismiss the application at this stage is reinforced by CA 2006, s 261(2)(b) which enables the court to penalise an applicant with costs orders or deter a nuisance applicant with a civil restraint order (restraining a person from making any application to a civil court without the consent of a judge).

[44] See 679 HL Official Report (5th series), col GC14, 27 February 2006.

[45] See Cheffins, above n 15, at 244 who noted that the Canadian courts, while not granting leave as a matter of course, were unwilling to impose particularly onerous thresholds at the equivalent stage in a statutory derivative claim. Instead they were content to restrict their enquiry to whether the complainant had raised fair questions which should properly be considered in an action.

18-31   The issue under (1) is not what conclusion the court would come to nor what a reasonable director would conclude. The question is whether a director acting subjectively to promote the success of the company would not seek to continue the claim.[46]

18-32   As a director's obligations under s 172 have been written in quite expansive (and novel) terms, the court may be reluctant to conclude under s 236(2)(a) that a director, faced with a prima facie case justifying a derivative claim (which there must be for the application to have reached the second stage), and given his obligation to have regard to the factors listed, would not seek to continue the claim. In that case, the focus of attention will shift to s 263(2)(b) and (c) which require evidence of actual authorisation or ratification. Looking at evidence of such tangible matters may be more palatable to the court than attempting to decide what a hypothetical director might have concluded in the circumstances.

18-33   *Authorisation and ratification by the company*   Actual authorisation or ratification provides a complete defence to a derivative claim.[47] Authorisation ensures that there is no breach of duty while ratification cures any breach that previously existed. Authorisation or ratification by the company may mean by the shareholders or by the directors. For most purposes it will be by the shareholders, though by virtue of CA 2006, s 175(4)(b) the directors may authorise what would otherwise be a conflict of interest and, by virtue of s 173(2)(b), the articles may authorise what would otherwise be a breach of a duty to exercise independent judgment. Concentrating on shareholders' powers for the moment, the scope for a derivative claim will be determined by the ability (and willingness) of the shareholders to authorise the conduct at issue or to ratify breaches of duty. There are two issues to be considered: (1) whether the wrong is capable of authorisation or ratification; and (2) whether there is sufficient support amongst the shareholders for authorisation or ratification.

18-34   The ability of shareholders to authorise or ratify acts of the directors is limited by common law restrictions which are preserved by s 180(4)(a) (authorisation) and s 239(7) (ratification).[48]

18-35   Shareholders cannot authorise or ratify acts which are illegal or acts which are ultra vires[49] in the sense of transactions which constitute a return of capital to shareholders

---

[46] See *Regentcrest plc v Cohen* [2001] 2 BCLC 80; HC Official Report, SC D (Company Law Reform Bill), 13 July 2006, col 678. As the Law Commission noted, 'this does not mean that the court is bound to accept the views of the director—the existence of a conflict of interest may affect the weight to be given to those views and the court would give no weight to views which no reasonable director could hold': see Law Commission Report, para 6.79, n 110.

[47] This is a change from the common law where a derivative action did not lie in respect of an act which was capable of being confirmed by the majority: *Burland v Earle* [1902] AC 83 at 93–4, PC; *MacDougall v Gardiner* (1875) 1 Ch D 13, CA.

[48] See generally Hannigan, 'Limitations on a Shareholder's Right to Vote—Effective Ratification Revisited' [2000] JBL 493.

[49] Ultra vires transactions in the sense of transactions beyond the company's objects were capable of ratification by a special resolution under CA 1985, s 35(3). Companies formed under the CA 2006 have unrestricted objects (see s 31) unless they choose to restrict them, but a restriction will operate only to limit the authority of the directors and so a breach of a restriction will be capable of ratification (or, more accurately,

other than with the sanction of the court or in accordance with a statutory scheme. Such transactions can be described as a fraud on the creditors and are incapable of ratification.[50] Equally, shareholders cannot authorise or ratify acts which amount to the misappropriation of 'money, property or advantages which belong to the company or in which the other shareholders are entitled to participate', a category usually described as a fraud on the minority[51] though, as Sealy notes,[52] a fraud on the company would be a more accurate description.

Subject to these constraints, many breaches of duty by directors are ratifiable, such as the non-disclosure of a conflict of interest, as in *Aberdeen Rly Co v Blaikie Bros*;[53] or mere negligence, as in *Pavlides v Jensen*;[54] or the exercise of powers bona fide but for a collateral purpose, as in *Bamford v Bamford*,[55] while *Regal (Hastings) Ltd v Gulliver*[56] suggest that bona fide incidental profit-making is ratifiable.[57] Of course, drawing the line between misappropriation amounting to a fraud on a minority and the incidental self-serving conduct of *Regal* is not easy but it is a type of exercise undertaken by judges every day[58] with an inexact line being drawn depending on the degree of damage to the company and the degree of benefit to the wrongdoer.[59] As Professor Boyle has noted: 'It is ultimately an ethical judgment (as to the degree of directorial misbehaviour for which ratification is permissible) in the guise of legal principle'[60] so some blurring of the boundaries to ratification is inevitable.   **18-36**

As noted, the CA 2006, s 175(4)(b) allows independent directors to authorise a director to exploit property, information or opportunity though there is a conflict between the directors' interests and the interests of the company. Such exploitation of property, information, opportunity, etc, by a director where he has a conflict of interest was not ratifiable at common law by the shareholders, being a 'fraud on the minority',[61] and still cannot be ratified by the shareholders (the common law on ratification having   **18-37**

authorisation by the shareholders); *Bamford v Bamford* [1969] 1 All ER 969; *Hogg v Cramphorn* [1966] 3 All ER 420.

[50] *Trevor v Whitworth* (1887) 12 App Cas 409; *Ridge Securities Ltd v IRC* [1964] 1 All ER 275; *Re Halt Garage (1964) Ltd* [1982] 3 All ER 1016; *Aveling Barford Ltd v Perion Ltd* [1989] BCLC 626; also *Barclays Bank plc v British and Commonwealth Holdings plc* [1996] 1 BCLC 1 at 7. See *Rolled Steel Products (Holdings) Ltd v British Steel Corp* [1985] 3 All ER 52 at 86, per Slade LJ.

[51] *Burland v Earle* [1902] AC 83 at 93, per Lord Davey; *Atwool v Merryweather* (1867) LR 5 Eq 464n; *Menier v Hooper's Telegraph Works* (1874) 9 Ch App 350; *Cook v Deeks* [1916] 1 AC 554; *Daniels v Daniels* [1978] 2 All ER 89. 'belonging' in the sense that the opportunities etc are treated as if they were property of the company, see Lawrence Collins J in *CMS Dolphin v Simonet* [2001] 2 BCLC 704 at 733.

[52] Sealy, *Cases and Materials in Company Law* (8th edn, 2008), p 524.   [53] (1854) 1 Macq (HL) 461.

[54] [1956] 2 All ER 518.   [55] [1969] 1 All ER 969, see also *Hogg v Cramphorn* [1966] 3 All ER 420.

[56] [1942] 1 All ER 378.

[57] See [1942] 1 All ER 378 at 389, per Lord Russell; also at 394, per Lord Wright.

[58] See Sealy (1981) CLJ 29 at 32; Baxter, 'The True Spirit of *Foss v Harbottle*' [1987] 38 NILQ 6 at 42–5.

[59] See Hannigan, 'Limitations on a Shareholder's Right to Vote—Effective Ratification Revisited' [2000] JBL 493 at 504–7.

[60] See Boyle, 'The Private Law Enforcement of Directors' Duties' in Hopt and Teubner (eds), *Corporate Governance and Directors' Liabilities* (1984), p 265; also Sealy (1981) CLJ 29.

[61] See *Cook v Deeks* [1916] 1 AC 554; *Atwool v Merryweather* (1867) LR 5 Eq 464n; *Menier v Hooper's Telegraph Works* (1874) 9 Ch App 350.

been preserved by s 239(7)), but it can be authorised in advance by independent directors under s 175.[62]

18-38   Shareholders cannot authorise or ratify acts in breach of the company's constitution where the matter is a breach of a shareholder's substantive rights.[63] Shareholder rights are derived essentially from the articles and, since the articles can only be amended by a special resolution (CA 2006, s 21), there should be no question of the majority being able to ratify breaches of the articles. The position is not that clear-cut, however, for the extent to which the articles confer substantive rights on the shareholders is problematic, as was discussed at **4-65**. The preservation of the common law on authorisation and ratification by s 180(4)(a) and s 239(7) means that the distinction drawn in the case-law (discussed at **4-69**) between matters of internal management[64] (within the control of the majority: *MacDougall v Gardiner*[65]) and rights conferred by the constitution qua member (and not within the control of the majority: *Pender v Lushington*[66]) remains. The net result is that some breaches of the articles are ratifiable, others are not, with the dividing line being drawn between matters of internal management and matters affecting rights conferred qua member.

18-39   Assuming the wrongdoing is capable of authorisation or ratification, the second issue is whether there is sufficient shareholder support for it. Here the CA 2006 makes a significant change by providing that on any resolution to ratify a breach of duty, the votes of the interested director (if a member of the company) and any member connected with him (as defined in ss 252–255) must be disregarded (see s 239(3), (4)),[67] so securing the necessary majority to ratify may not be possible in any given case. Further, in a widely held company, authorisation or ratification may not be a realistic option, either in terms of the time and costs involved in holding shareholder meetings, or indeed in terms of the wider dissemination of information on the matter which would then occur.

18-40   Looking at the absolute bars to a derivative claim proceeding in s 263(2), it is clear that there is the potential for this to be a lengthier and costlier stage than is desirable. Equally, practice may evolve such that little use is made of this power to dismiss a claim. For the reasons discussed above, the courts may be reluctant to decide that a director would not continue the case and to dismiss the claim on that basis. It is also quite likely that there is no evidence of authorisation or ratification for, had there been, the shareholder would not have considered bringing a derivative claim (unless

---

[62] It is somewhat anomalous, given CA 2006, s 175(4)(b), that it cannot be ratified, but that is the effect of CA 2006, s 239(7). Possibly it was a legislative oversight, especially since ratification would have to be by disinterested shareholders: s 239(4).

[63] See *Pender v Lushington* (1877) 6 Ch D 70; *MacDougall v Gardiner* (1875) 1 Ch D 13 at 25, CA.

[64] See *Grant v United Kingdom Switchback Railways Co* (1888) 40 Ch D 135; *Irvine v Union Bank of Australia* (1877) 2 App Cas 366.

[65] (1875) 1 Ch D 13.   [66] (1877) 6 Ch D 70.

[67] Determining whose votes must be disregarded will not be straightforward, given the breadth of the definition of a connected person, and the issue of whether or not there has been effective ratification may quickly evolve into a costly mini-trial. As before, other shareholders are entitled to exercise their votes as they please: *North-West Transportation Co Ltd v Beatty* (1887) 12 App Cas 589.

he wishes to dispute whether the matter was capable of authorisation or validly ratified). The result may be that, in most instances, there will be no basis on which to dismiss the claim under s 263(2) and the court will proceed to consider the matter under
s 263(3) for, had there been evidence to support dismissal under s 263(2), the claim
would not have progressed to this stage.[68] In practice, successful reliance on s 263(2)
will probably only arise where the court adjourns the proceedings and the company
uses the adjournment to authorise or ratify the breach of duty which means the court
must dismiss the case.

Finally, even if a director cannot muster sufficient votes for authorisation or ratifica-   **18-41**
tion, or if the wrong cannot be authorised or ratified, it does not necessarily follow
that a derivative claim can be brought. Effective authorisation or ratification is an
absolute bar to a claim, but its absence merely means that the court has a discretion as
to whether the claim can proceed which it must exercise in the light of the factors set
out in CA 2006, s 263(3).

Discretion to allow a claim to proceed

In considering whether to give permission for a claim to proceed, the court must take   **18-42**
into account, in particular, a number of factors which are set out in CA 2006, s 263(3)
as follows:

(a) whether the member is acting in good faith in seeking to continue the claim;

(b) the importance that a director acting to promote the success of the company
would attach to continuing it;

(c) whether the act or omission (still to occur) would be likely to be authorised or
ratified by the company or,

(d) where the cause of action arises from an act or omission that has already
occurred, whether the act or omission could be, and in the circumstances would
be likely to be, ratified by the company;

(e) whether the company has decided not to pursue the claim;

(f) whether the act or omission in respect of which the claim is brought gives rise
to a cause of action that the member could pursue in his own right rather than
on behalf of the company.

The factors listed in s 263(3) are not exhaustive and so, while the court must take them   **18-43**
into account 'in particular', it can also consider any other matter which it considers
to be relevant. The court is expected to take into account all of the factors together
(which could turn this into quite a lengthy process) and in no particular order and how

---

[68] There is evidence of this approach in the very small number of reported cases to date where permission
to bring a derivative claim has been sought: see *Mission Capital plc v Sinclair* [2008] All ER (D) 225 (March);
Franbar Holdings Ltd v Patel [2009] 1 BCLC 1. In each of these cases, the court quickly concluded that there
were no grounds for dismissing the application under the mandatory requirements of CA 2006, s 263(2), but
equally quickly dismissed the application under the discretionary jurisdiction in s 263(3) instead.

important each is in any case will be for the court to determine having regard to all the circumstances.[69] In weighing up the overall merits, the court is likely to be guided by the purpose of a derivative claim, namely to give a remedy for a wrong which would otherwise escape redress.[70]

18-44   *Member acting in good faith—s 263(3)(a)*   The motives of the claimant will be an important filter used by the courts to deal particularly with the type of speculative litigation which it is alleged Part 11 will attract. It is for the shareholder seeking permission to establish to the satisfaction of the court that he is a person acting in good faith and should be allowed to sue on behalf of the company.[71] An interest in the commercial benefits to be gained from the litigation would not necessarily rule out a claim if the court otherwise thinks it is in the company's interests.[72] A claimant will not be in good faith, however, if motivated to litigate by personal considerations rather than in the interests of the company.[73]

18-45   *Importance a director would attach to continuing the claim—s 263(3)(b)*   Accepting that a director would seek to continue the claim for the purpose of s 263(2)(a) (otherwise the case would not have reached this stage), the court moves on to assessing the importance which a director would attach to continuing it. The court may be as reluctant to reach a firm view on this issue as under s 263(2)(a). The same type of task is required—the court has to look at the matter from the subjective perspective of the hypothetical director acting to promote the success of the company. The court must assess the commercial considerations (time and costs involved, the distraction of management, damage to reputation, likelihood of success and recovery, size of the loss) which the director would regard as relevant in assessing the importance of continuing the claim. Clearly, it would be influential if independent non-executive directors, whose conduct is not the subject of the claim, were opposed to the claim proceeding.[74]

18-46   *Authorisation/ratification—s 263(3)(c) and (d)*   Two issues arise under these provisions. First, whether the breach of duty can be authorised or ratified—the position on authorisation and ratification was discussed above at **18-33**—and this will involve an assessment not just as to whether the breach is capable of authorisation or ratification, but also whether ratification is possible given the voting constraints set out in s 239(3), (4). Secondly, the question whether an act or omission is likely to be authorised

---

[69] See 679 HL Official Report (5th series), col GC26, 27 February 2006. Boyle, above n 11, suggests that the factors are ill-suited to the circumstances likely to arise in public listed companies.

[70] See *Burland v Earle* [1902] AC 83 at 93–4; *Prudential Assurance Co Ltd v Newman Industries Ltd* [1982] 1 All ER 354 at 357–8; *Smith v Croft (No 2)* [1987] 3 All ER 909 at 945.

[71] *Barrett v Duckett* [1995] 1 BCLC 243 at 250.

[72] See Law Commission Report, para 6.76. See *Franbar Holdings Ltd v Patel* [2009] 1 BCLC 1.

[73] *Barrett v Duckett* [1995] 1 BCLC 243 (claimant not pursuing claim bona fide in the interests of the company, but for personal reasons associated with the divorce of the company's sole director and the claimant's daughter); and see Payne, '"Clean Hands" in Derivative Actions' (2002) CLJ 76 at 81.

[74] CA 2006, s 263(4) requires the court to have regard to the views of disinterested members; s 263(3)(e) requires the court to have regard to the views of the company; and this provision, s 263(3)(b), provides a mechanism by which the court may have regard to the views of the independent directors. The cumulative effect is to require the court to consider all possible constituencies within the board and the shareholders.

or ratified requires the court to consider the factual position within the individual company, bearing in mind that it is always open to the court to adjourn the proceedings (under s 261(4)(c)) to allow a meeting to be called for the purposes of authorisation or ratification.[75]

Company has decided not to pursue the claim—s 263(3)(e)   The decision of the com-   **18-47**
pany not to pursue the claim (as opposed to authorising or ratifying the breach) may be taken by the directors or the shareholders.[76] If the company has not actually considered the matter, the court may use its powers to adjourn proceedings to allow for that consideration.[77] As Knox J explained in *Smith v Croft (No 2)*,[78] the purpose of the adjournment is to obtain for the court a realistic assessment of the practical desirability of the claim going forward made by the organ that has the power and ability to take decisions on behalf of the company.

A cause of action that a member could pursue in his own right—s 263(3)(f)   The   **18-48**
focus of this provision is on whether there is a cause of action that a member could pursue as a personal claim. It is not entirely clear how this differs from a consideration of whether there is an alternative remedy available[79] to the claimant, though the Government considered there to be a difference.[80] As noted above, in practice derivative claims are unusual and unattractive for petitioners given the development of a broad unfairly prejudicial jurisdiction under what is now CA 2006, s 994 which gives the petitioner personal relief. As breaches of directors' duties will found a derivative claim and an unfairly prejudicial petition, in many instances, there may indeed be a cause of action that a member could pursue in his own right.[81] In *Jafari-Fini v Skillglass*

---

[75] See 679 HL Official Report (5th series), cols GC27–8, 27 February 2006; HC Official Report, SC D (Company Law Reform Bill), 13 July 2006, col 679. If it is clear that the breach will be ratified, it is pointless to call a meeting, and the court can simply refuse permission to continue the claim: *Smith v Croft (No 2)* [1987] 3 All ER 909 at 957; see also Law Commission Report, para 6.84.

[76] 679 HL Official Report (5th series), cols GC8, 29–30, 27 February 2006. As was noted in *Prudential Assurance Co Ltd v Newman Industries Ltd (No 2)* [1982] 1 All ER 354 at 365, a board might conclude that to pursue the claim would not be to the company's advantage and to allow someone to do so might result in the company being 'killed by kindness'.

[77] See HC Official Report, SC D (Company Law Reform Bill), 13 July 2006, col 679.

[78] [1987] 3 All ER 909 at 956.

[79] At common law, the position concerning the availability of an alternative remedy was not entirely clear, with *Barrett v Duckett* [1995] 1 BCLC 243 supporting that it was a bar to a derivative claim, but Lawrence Collins J in *Konamaneni v Rolls Royce Industrial Power (India) Ltd* [2002] 1 BCLC 336 at 346 suggested that that was an incorrect reading of the position. In *Jafari-Fini v Skillglass Ltd* [2005] BCC 842 the Court of Appeal, while citing *Barrett v Duckett*, based the decision on the fact that it was in the company's interests in that case for the alternative remedy to be pursued, rather than that an alternative remedy is an actual bar; see also *Mumbray v Lapper* [2005] BCC 990 (alternative remedy is a factor but not an absolute bar).

[80] During the Parliamentary debates, the Government declined on two grounds to adopt an Opposition amendment which would have required the court to consider specifically the availability of an alternative remedy, namely (1) that an alternative remedy in the form of an offer to buy the claimant's shares is not an appropriate remedy in the circumstances of a derivative claim, and (2) that this approach might encourage vulture funds to tell companies that they must either buy them out or face a possible derivative claim: see 682 HL Official Report (5th series), cols 726–728 (23 May 2006).

[81] In *Mission Capital plc v Sinclair* [2008] All ER (D) 225 (March) one of the reasons for refusing permission to continue a derivative claim was that the court did not consider that the claimants were seeking

Ltd[82] permission to bring a derivative claim at common law was refused when, on the same grounds, the claimant could and was bringing a claim for breach of contract. The court concluded that it was better for that contractual claim to be determined first than for the company to be put to the cost of funding a derivative claim in respect of the same issues. Of course, a shareholder may be able to show the court that he wishes to remain a member of the company and so would prefer a corporate remedy rather than a personal remedy under s 994 which would typically see him exit from the company with his shares being purchased by the respondents to the petition.[83] The other advantage to pursing a derivative claim, assuming personal relief is not required, is the possibility of obtaining an indemnity for costs (see discussion below at **18-53**). There may be reasons therefore why, despite the possibility of pursuing relief in his own right, a shareholder wishes to bring a derivative claim. There is also the possibility that it will not be possible to meet the requirement under s 994 that the company's affairs are being or have been conducted in a manner which is unfairly prejudicial where the complaint relates to an issue of misconduct by a director.[84] Essentially s 263(3)(f) requires the court to focus on the essence of the complaint and the most appropriate redress rather than merely the existence of an alternative remedy.

18-49   *Views of disinterested shareholders—s 263(4)*   Distinct from the factors listed in s 263(3), there is a mandatory requirement in s 263(4) for the court to have particular regard to any evidence before it as to the views of members of the company who have no personal interest, direct or indirect, in the matter. This requirement is intended to reflect the position adopted by Knox J in *Smith v Croft (No 2)*[85] as to the weight to be given to the influential views of those shareholders who are independent of the wrong-doers.[86] Knox J was unconvinced that a just result is achieved by a single minority shareholder having the right to involve a company in an action for recovery of compensation for the company if all the other minority shareholders are, for disinterested reasons, satisfied that the proceedings will be productive of more harm than good.[87]

18-50   It was also suggested in the Parliamentary debates that this provision allows the opinions of shareholders in a major quoted company to be taken into account while acknowledging that it is not practicable or desirable in such companies to ask shareholders

---

anything which could not be recovered by means of an unfair prejudice petition under CA 2006, s 994; likewise in *Franbar Holdings Ltd v Patel* [2009] 1 BCLC 1, permission was refused when the acts complained of gave rise to claims by the member in his own right for breach of a shareholders' agreement and under CA 2006, s 994 which the court considered should give him all the relief sought.

[82] [2005] BCC 842, CA.

[83] See Law Commission Report, paras 6.10–6.12. See, for example, *Airey v Cordell* [2007] BCC 785, where the claimant wished to use a derivative claim (essentially founded on a diversion of corporate assets to another entity) to recover those assets for the company (so that he could participate in the long-term gains to be expected from their exploitation) rather than be bought out of the company.

[84] See *Re Charnley Davies Ltd (No 2)* [1990] BCLC 760.   [85] [1987] 3 All ER 909 at 957.

[86] See 681 HL Official Report (5th series), cols 883–4, 888, 9 May 2006. This provision was part of the package of amendments introduced to meet concerns that there were inadequate filters to deter vexatious claims: see para **18-12** above.

[87] [1987] 3 All ER 909 at 956.

formally to approve directors' commercial decisions.[88] Ratification or authorisation may not have taken place, nor be likely to; likewise, there may not be an actual decision of the company not to continue the claim, but it may nevertheless be possible to show that the shareholders are content to support the directors in respect of what has occurred.[89]

A practical concern, particularly in widely held companies, is how to identify 'persons who have no personal interest, direct or indirect', in the matter[90] and how to obtain evidence as to their views on the claim. There must also be a question mark over whether such persons, assuming they can be identified, would be willing to become involved in a claim, even at this level.[91] A scenario may be envisaged where institutional shareholders make known to the court their view that a claim should not continue and the court refuses permission for the claim to continue. If it later emerged that the claim was well founded, the institutions would face criticism for the role they played in preventing the claim proceeding. Independent shareholders may prefer to remain on the sidelines rather than risk being put in such a position. Where the institutions positively favour a claim being pursued, a derivative claim will probably be unnecessary for the institutions will be able to effect board changes which ensure that the company pursues the matter.

18-51

Having reviewed all the factors in s 263(3) and considered the views of the disinterested shareholders under s 263(4), the court may grant permission for the claim to proceed, refuse permission, or adjourn the proceedings and give such directions as it thinks fit; but even if permission is given, it is merely permission to continue the claim,[92] and costs will be an important consideration at this stage.

18-52

Costs of bringing a derivative claim

The CA 2006, Part 11 makes no specific provision for costs and the Law Commission's position was that the court's power to make costs indemnity orders in derivative actions should remain unchanged. The position is governed by the Court of Appeal decision in *Wallersteiner v Moir (No 2)*[93] which held that where a shareholder has, in good faith and on reasonable grounds, sued as plaintiff in a minority shareholder's action, the benefit of which if successful will accrue to the company and only indirectly to the

18-53

---

[88] See 681 HL Official Report (5th series), col 884, 9 May 2006.

[89] See 681 HL Official Report (5th series), col 884, 9 May 2006.

[90] The Law Commission had considered this issue in terms of seeking the opinion of an independent organ (see Law Commission Report, paras 6.88–6.89), a term derived from *Smith v Croft (No 2)* [1987] 3 All ER 909 at 957–60, but it was criticised as being unclear. The formulation in the statute has avoided that problem, but may be difficult to apply in a widely held company.

[91] Institutional shareholders dominate in widely held companies, but nothing in the 'Statement of Principles of Institutional Shareholders and their Agents' drawn up the Institutional Shareholders Committee (June 2007) would suggest any appetite on their part for this type of role.

[92] Note that once permission to continue the claim has been given, the court may order that the claim cannot be discontinued, or settled, or compromised without the court's permission, see CPR 19.9F; Practice Direction 19C—Derivative Claims.

[93] [1975] 1 All ER 849.

plaintiff as a member of the company, and which action it would be reasonable for an independent board of directors to bring in the company name, the court may order the company to pay the plaintiff's costs.[94]

18-54   The ability to secure an indemnity from the company is an important consideration for a shareholder contemplating a derivative action,[95] but concerns that the very possibility of obtaining an indemnity order will encourage vexations claims are misplaced.[96] Claimants cannot be sure that the court will exercise its discretion and make an indemnity order, so a claimant does have a potential exposure to significant costs and the indemnity does not act as an actual incentive to bring a claim.[97] Of course, for a limited number of claimants, such as hedge funds, the issue of costs may not be a deterrent.

18-55   Companies may fund expenditure incurred by a defendant director in derivative proceedings, but those costs must be refunded if the director loses the case: CA 2006, s 205(1), (2). In larger companies, directors will also have insurance cover against personal liability (paid for by the company) and they will want to ensure derivative claims and associated legal costs are covered. It is possible that companies may end up funding the claimant (under a *Wallersteiner* order) and the defendant directors (through insurance and by way of loans to meet defence costs) and so a derivative claim may be expensive for the company.

Potential for derivative claims

18-56   Initially Part 11 looks as if it dramatically alters the landscape of shareholders' remedies, allowing any member (regardless of size of shareholding or length of membership) to bring a derivative claim in respect of any breach of duty (including negligence) or default by any director, but many caveats must be added to that picture of openended liability.

---

[94] [1975] 1 All ER 849 at 868–9, per Buckley LJ; see also CPR 19.9E (the indemnity may cover the costs incurred in obtaining permission to continue and in the claim itself). In *Smith v Croft* [1986] 2 All ER 551, Walton J took a restrictive view of the jurisdiction to make an indemnity order, but this restrictive approach was not followed in *Jaybird v Greenwood Ltd* [1986] BCLC 318. For examples of situations where an indemnity order was refused, see *Halle v Trax BM Ltd* [2000] BCC 1020 (in effect asking company to fund dispute between two partners in a joint venture); *Mumbray v Lapper* [2005] BCC 990 (essentially a partnership break-up); also *Watts v Midland Bank plc* [1986] BCLC 15 (no indemnity order where company hopelessly insolvent). See generally Reisberg, 'Funding Derivative Actions: A Re-Examination of Costs and Fees as Incentives To Commence Litigation' [2004] 4 JCLS 345; Quigxiu Bu, 'The Indemnity Order in a Derivative Action' (2006) 27 Co Law 2.

[95] See Reisberg, 'Derivative Actions and the Funding Problem: The Way Forward' [2006] JBL 445 who argues that, until US-type contingency fee agreements are introduced in this jurisdiction, financing the litigation will remain a major obstacle to use of the derivative claim.

[96] See 679 HL Official Report (5th series), col GC13, 27 February 2006.

[97] Reisberg, above n 94, argues that the only real incentive for shareholders to bring derivative actions would be if the courts could order some element of personal recovery for them when the claim is successful; see also Cheffins, above n 15, 256–60.

First, derivative claims, though facilitated by the new mechanism of Part 11, remain **18-57** subject to the general principle of majority rule, as discussed above. Moreover, the newly available power of directors to authorise conflicts and profit-making to the extent permitted by CA 2006, s 175 significantly reduces the potential for 'fraud on the minority'-type conduct which in the past formed the basis of typical derivative actions.

Secondly, the threshold tests are sufficient, cumulatively, to deter many would-be **18-58** claimants, especially when costs issues are factored in, not to mention the informational disadvantages facing a claimant.[98] The judiciary will be anxious not to open the doors here to the sort of speculative litigation sometimes seen in the US and tight judicial control will be imposed. In particular, the courts will want to make use of the power at all stages to adjourn the proceedings to allow for authorisation or ratification. Considerable efforts will be expended also on settling claims before the mini-trial seeking permission gets out of hand. In the Parliamentary debates, there was much emphasis on the expectation that the courts will maintain the long tradition of not second-guessing directors' business judgment and that message may well curb judicial enthusiasm for a liberal approach to the jurisdiction. Overall, few cases are likely to proceed to full-blown trials of the issue, and this has been the experience of other jurisdictions which have introduced statutory derivative actions.[99] At the moment, derivative claims are uncommon and that position is unlikely to change under Part 11.

Thirdly, the position remains that recovery is for the benefit of the company, not the **18-59** individual claimant who can only benefit to the extent that benefit to the company is reflected in the value of his shares, so there is no incentive to litigate via a derivative claim. Save where a claimant is determined to remain as a member of the company, it will be preferable to petition for relief under CA 2006, s 994 (unfairly prejudicial conduct) without the need for any permission of the court and with the prospect of personal recovery.

When all these factors are considered, it is difficult to conclude that the mere intro- **18-60** duction of the statutory derivative claim dramatically increases the litigation risk to directors, at least to the level that it would deter people from acting as a director of a public company. Occasionally, there may be a high profile case pursued as much for the publicity as recovery and settled long before trial, but there is unlikely to be any significant increase in the number of claims being brought.

---

[98] See Kosmin, 'Minority Shareholders' Remedies: A Practitioner's Perspective' [1997] Company, Financial and Insolvency Law Review 211.

[99] The evidence from Canada, New Zealand and Australia is that the statutory derivative procedures in those jurisdictions have been used to an insignificant degree and mainly in respect of private companies (not public companies as might have been anticipated): see Ramsay and Saunders, above n 15, 420; Cheffins, above n 15, 241. There is nothing about CA 2006, Part 11 which suggests that the experience here will be any different. See also Hannigan, 'Drawing boundaries between derivative claims and unfairly prejudicial petitions' [2009] JBL, forthcoming.

C Corporate loss and reflective loss

18-61   The decision of the Court of Appeal in *Prudential Assurance Co Ltd v Newman Industries Ltd (No 2)*,[100] hereinafter *Prudential*, establishes that a personal claim by a member in respect of the diminution in value of his shareholding as a result of a wrong done to the company is misconceived and should be struck out, for the shareholder's loss is merely reflective of the loss suffered by the company, and that loss will be fully remedied if the company enforces its full rights against the wrongdoer.[101] The wrongdoer may be a director[102] or a third party, such as a solicitor or other adviser to the company.[103] The no reflective loss principle was affirmed by the House of Lords in a complex judgment in *Johnson v Gore Wood & Co*[104] and has been the subject of further analysis by the Court of Appeal, particularly in *Giles v Rhind*[105] and *Gardner v Parker*.[106]

18-62   The result is that it is clear that no action lies at the suit of a shareholder suing to make good a diminution in value of his shareholding (including loss of dividends and all other payments which the shareholder might have obtained from the company had it not been deprived of its funds,[107] and whether those payments would have been received in the capacity of shareholder or otherwise[108]) where that claim merely reflects the loss suffered by the company, and that loss would have been made good if the company had enforced in full its rights against the defendant wrongdoer. No action by a shareholder lies even if the company acting through its constitutional organs declines or fails to make good that loss.[109] If the company has been disabled by the wrongdoer (as opposed to chooses not to sue or settles the claim

---

[100] [1982] 1 All ER 354.

[101] [1982] 1 All ER 354 at 366–7; see also *Stein v Blake* [1998] 1 All ER 724. It matters not whether the shareholder's claim is for breach of contract, in tort, or for breach of fiduciary duty: *Gardner v Parker* [2004] 2 BCLC 554; *Shaker v Al-Bedrawi* [2003] 1 BCLC 517. The *Prudential* principle does not apply where a duty is owed only to the shareholder so that the company has no claim or where there is a separate duty owed to the shareholder breach of which causes a loss distinct and separate from that suffered by the company (and which is not remedied therefore by recovery by the company): *Giles v Rhind* [2003] 1 BCLC 1 at 14; *Day v Cook* [2002] 1 BCLC 1 at 16, 25; *Johnson v Gore Wood & Co* [2001] 1 BCLC 313 at 338, per Lord Bingham; and see *Pearce v European Reinsurance Consultants* [2005] 2 BCLC 366 where the shareholder did have a distinct claim; also *Jafari-Fini v Skillglass Ltd* [2005] BCC 842 at 848.

[102] See *Gardner v Parker* [2004] 2 BCLC 554, CA; *Giles v Rhind* [2003] 1 BCLC 1, CA; *Shaker v Al-Bedrawi* [2003] 1 BCLC 517, CA.

[103] See *Johnson v Gore Wood & Co* [2001] 1 BCLC 313, HL; *Day v Cook* [2002] 1 BCLC 1.

[104] [2001] 1 BCLC 313, HL. See Ferran, 'Litigation by shareholders and reflective loss' (2001) CLJ 245; Watts, 'The Shareholder as Co-promisee' (2001) 117 LQR 388; Mitchell, 'Shareholders' Claims for Reflective Loss' (2004) 120 LQR 457; also Mukwari, 'The No Reflective Loss Principle' (2005) 26 Co Law 304; Lee Suet Lin, 'Barring Recovery for Diminution in Value of Shares on Reflective Loss Claims' (2007) CLJ 533.

[105] [2003] 1 BCLC 1.

[106] [2004] 2 BCLC 554, affirming the decision of Blackburne J, see [2004] 1 BCLC 417.

[107] See *Johnson v Gore Wood & Co* [2001] 1 BCLC 313 at 370, per Lord Millett.

[108] For example, as a creditor or employee of the company, see *Johnson v Gore Wood & Co* [2001] 1 BCLC 313 at 370, per Lord Millett; *Gardner v Parker* [2004] 2 BCLC 554 at 572, per Neuberger LJ.

[109] See *Johnson v Gore Wood & Co* [2001] 1 BCLC 313 at 337, per Lord Bingham.

disadvantageously[110]) from pursuing the loss, however, the shareholder can maintain a claim for what is reflective loss, a qualification established by *Giles v Rhind*.[111]

This rule against the recovery of reflective loss is not concerned with debarring causes   **18-63**
of action as such, but with barring recovery of certain types of loss.[112] The foundation
of the rule is the need to avoid double recovery.[113] As Lord Millett explained in *Johnson*:
'If the shareholder is allowed to recover in respect of such loss, then either there will
be double recovery at the expense of the defendant or the shareholder will recover at
the expense of the company and its creditors and other shareholders. Neither course
can be permitted.'[114] He went on: 'Justice to the defendant requires the exclusion of one
claim or the other; protection of the interests of the company's creditors requires that
it is the company which is allowed to recover to the exclusion of the shareholder.'[115] As
Arden LJ put it in *Day v Cook*,[116] 'the company's claim, if it exists, will always trump
that of the shareholder's', subject now to the 'disability' exception in *Giles v Rhind*.[117]
Given that foundation, a claim will be barred even where there is a breach of duty to
the company *and* the shareholder, and even if the claim is in another capacity, for
example as a creditor of the company. If the substance of the claim is the same, though
the cause of action is different, the rule applies.[118]

In *Gardner v Parker*[119] a company had suffered significant losses and gone into admin-   **18-64**
istrative receivership as a result of breaches of duty by the company's sole director. The
company's receivers had settled all claims against the director. A claim against the
director by the minority shareholder in the company for losses suffered in its capacity
as a shareholder in and creditor of the company (the shareholder had made a substantial loan to the company) was rejected for its losses would have been made good if the
company had enforced its rights against the defendant. The rule against recovery of
reflective loss therefore applied and the claim was dismissed.

---

[110] See *Gardner v Parker* [2004] 2 BCLC 554 at 570, per Neuberger LJ; *Johnson v Gore Wood & Co* [2001] 1 BCLC 313 at 369, per Lord Millett.

[111] [2003] 1 BCLC 1, noted Hirt [2003] JBL 420. As the Court of Appeal noted in this case, it was the defendant director's wrong (essentially he 'stole' the company's business reducing it to insolvency) that had disabled the company from pursuing any claim for damages against him which wrong he then compounded by an application for security for costs against the company when his own breach made it impossible for the company to provide such security (see [2003] 1 BCLC 1 at 25, 28). The Court of Appeal considered that *Johnson v Gore Wood & Co* [2001] 1 BCLC 313 had no application to that situation which had not been in the contemplation of the House of Lords. See also *Perry v Day* [2005] 2 BCLC 405.

[112] *Gardner v Parker* [2004] 2 BCLC 554 at 567, per Neuberger LJ.

[113] *Johnson v Gore Wood & Co* [2001] 1 BCLC 313; *Gardner v Parker* [2004] 2 BCLC 554.

[114] *Johnson v Gore Wood & Co* [2001] 1 BCLC 313 at 365.   [115] [2001] 1 BCLC 313 at 366.

[116] [2002] 1 BCLC 1 at 15.   [117] [2003] 1 BCLC 1.

[118] *Gardner v Parker* [2004] 2 BCLC 554 applying *Shaker v Al-Bedrawi* [2003] 1 BCLC 157. That is not to say, Neuberger J noted, that a creditor is without remedies. The creditor may sue the company for repayment if it is solvent (leaving the company to pursue the defendant director) and, if the company is insolvent, the creditor can either fund an action by the liquidator against the defendant or take an assignment of the com-pany's claim against the defendant, see [2004] 2 BCLC 554 at 573; also *Johnson v Gore Wood & Co* [2001] 1 BCLC 313 at 369.

[119] [2004] 2 BCLC 554.

18-65   The position now reached on the recovery of reflective loss is clear [120] and it is a position based on a combination of policy and practical considerations. The principle reflects the first limb of the rule in *Foss v Harbottle*.[121] It looks to company autonomy and ensures that the interests of the company are respected and that a party does not recover compensation for a loss suffered by another.[122] It protects the interests of the company's creditors and ensures they are not prejudiced by an action by an individual shareholder.[123] At a practical level, it prevents a multitude of cases being brought by shareholders with the courts being required to act as referee between the different claimants and with an eye to the need to protect the company's creditors. In the circumstances, it is procedurally efficient to exclude all claims other than those of the company, save where the company has been disabled by the wrongdoer from bringing its claim. It also facilitates settlements of claims for, in the absence of the prohibition of recovery of reflective loss, wrongdoers will be unwilling to compromise or settle claims with the company for fear of being met by a further claim by a shareholder.[124]

18-66   In future, there may be scope for a shareholder to get around the no reflective loss principle given the availability now of a statutory derivative claim. If the problem in many instances is that the company has not pursued its remedy against the wrongdoer director, the solution may lie in the shareholder pursuing the claim for the company via a derivative claim. Of course, it may be that the reason the company has not pursued the wrongdoer is that the company is in liquidation and the question then is whether a derivative claim can be brought when a company is in liquidation. The common law answer is no,[125] but it is unclear whether Part 11 should be regarded as a new start such that the courts should not be bound by that previous common law position.[126]

D Personal actions at common law

18-67   It may be that a shareholder wishes to remedy not a wrong done to the company but a wrong done to him personally. Such a personal action is unaffected by the rule in *Foss v Harbottle*.[127] A shareholder may bring a personal claim to obtain an injunction to

---

[120] Even if there is some criticism of the courts for not having adopted a more nuanced approach to these issues rather than the bright line approach of Lord Bingham and Lord Millett, see Mitchell (2004) 120 LQR 457 at 464–5.

[121] (1843) 2 Hare 461.

[122] See *Johnson v Gore Wood & Co* [2002] 1 BCLC 313 at 338, per Lord Bingham; at 365, per Lord Millett.

[123] See *Johnson v Gore Wood & Co* [2002] 1 BCLC 313 at 338, per Lord Bingham; at 366, per Lord Millett.

[124] See *Johnson v Gore Wood & Co* [2002] 1 BCLC 313 at 370, per Lord Millett; *Giles v Rhind* [2003] 1 BCLC 1 at 30, per Chadwick LJ.

[125] See *Fargro v Godfroy* [1986] BCLC 370.

[126] See Keay, 'Can Derivative Proceedings be Commenced when a Company is in Liquidation' (2008) 21 Insolv Int 49 who is cautiously optimistic that, given the new procedure, the courts will be willing to entertain applications by members when the company is in liquidation.

[127] (1843) 2 Hare 461.

restrain proposed illegal or ultra vires acts,[128] but this option is of limited significance since it is rare for shareholders to be aware of a proposed illegal or ultra vires act in time to seek an injunction.

Essentially when considering the possibility of a personal claim, the issues will revolve around the enforcement of the articles of association with a shareholder looking either to enforce what he perceives to be his rights under the articles or to prevent breaches by the majority of the articles, or even to prevent the articles from being altered. All these issues are considered in detail in Chapter 4 to which the reader is referred. Trying to enforce particular rights or to prevent the majority from acting in breach of particular provisions is not a straightforward matter with the courts generally taking a restrictive approach to these issues, precisely in order not to undermine the rule in *Foss v Harbottle,* see **4-68**.   **18-68**

In practice, a shareholder aggrieved at difficulties in enforcing his rights under the articles of association, or at non-compliance by the majority with the terms of the articles, is likely to petition for relief under CA 2006, s 994, alleging that the affairs of the company are being conducted in a manner which is unfairly prejudicial to his interests.   **18-69**

E Statutory remedies

As noted above, the preferred statutory remedy for shareholders with general grievances about the unfairly prejudicial manner in which the affairs of the company are being conducted is to bring a petition for relief under CA 2006, s 994 and that remedy is discussed in detail in Chapter 17. Additionally, the IA 1986, s 122(1)(g) provides a shareholder remedy in the form of a right to seek a winding-up order on the just and equitable ground and the CA 2006 provides for a number of specific statutory remedies and rights which shareholders may be able to invoke in an appropriate case.   **18-70**

Winding up on the just and equitable ground

A member may petition under IA 1986, s 122(1)(g) for a winding-up order on the just and equitable ground,[129] a provision which has traditionally provided the court with a wide discretionary jurisdiction.[130] In practice, this jurisdiction has been all but superseded now by the unfairly prejudicial jurisdiction (CA 2006, s 994).   **18-71**

---

[128] See *Simpson v Westminster Palace Hotel Co* (1860) 8 HL Cas 712; *Parke v Daily News* [1962] 2 All ER 929; *Smith v Croft (No 2)* [1987] BCLC 206. It had been thought that shareholders could bring a personal action with respect to losses arising from illegal or ultra vires acts, but in *Smith v Croft (No 2)* Knox J took the view that such actions are to recover corporate losses arising from the transaction and, as such, should be the subject of an action by the company, or by the shareholders on a derivative basis, but no personal action will lie.

[129] Various other parties (including the directors and creditors) may also petition for a winding up: see **24-27**. Here we deal only with petitioning shareholders.

[130] See *Re Yenidje Tobacco Co* [1916] 2 Ch 426; *Loch v John Blackwood Ltd* [1924] AC 783; *Ebrahimi v Westbourne Galleries Ltd* [1972] 2 All ER 492; *Re Zinotty Properties Ltd* [1984] 3 All ER 754; *Re A & BC Chewing Gum Ltd* [1975] 1 All ER 1017; *Re Guidezone Ltd* [2000] 2 BCLC 321.

Procedural matters

18-72   An application to the court for a winding-up order may be made by a contributory,[131] defined as every person liable to contribute to the assets of a company in the event of its being wound up.[132] For example, a partly paid-up shareholder (and it is rare now for shareholders to be partly paid) who remains liable to contribute the amount unpaid on his shares in the event of the company being wound up is a contributory. A fully paid-up member must establish that he has a tangible interest in the winding up, defined as a prima facie probability of surplus assets remaining after the creditors have been paid for distribution amongst the shareholders.[133] In other words, in an insolvent company, a fully paid-up member has no locus standi to seek a winding up.

18-73   A further condition is that a contributory is not entitled to present a winding-up petition unless the number of members is reduced below two; or the shares held by him, or some of them, either were originally allotted to him, or have been held by him and registered in his name for at least six months during the 18 months before the commencement of the winding up, or have devolved on him through the death of a former holder (IA 1986, s 124).

18-74   A petitioner seeking a winding-up order on the just and equitable ground must come with clean hands.[134] If the breakdown in the conduct of the company's affairs is a result of the petitioner's own misconduct,[135] or the petitioner has acquiesced in the conduct of which he now complains,[136] the court will refuse the application. However, if the petitioner can establish sufficient grounds for petitioning, the fact that he also has an ulterior, perhaps personal, motive for pursuing the matter does not render those grounds insufficient.[137]

18-75   The court has a discretion under IA 1986, s 125(2) to refuse to make a winding-up order where there is some alternative remedy available to the petitioner and he is acting unreasonably in seeking to have the company wound up instead of pursuing that other remedy. An obvious alternative remedy is the ability to petition for relief on the unfairly prejudicial ground under CA 2006, s 994. In *Re a company (No 001363 of 1988), ex p S-P*[138] the court accepted that the availability of relief, possibly wider relief, under the unfairly prejudicial remedy does not of itself make it plainly unreasonable

---

[131] IA 1986, s 124(1).

[132] IA 1986, s 79(1); and every present and past member is included in the definition: s 74(1); but, in the case of a company limited by shares, no contribution is required from any member exceeding the amount (if any) unpaid on the shares in respect of which he is a liable as a present or past member: s 74(2)(d).

[133] *Re Rica Gold Washing Co* (1879) 11 Ch D 36; *Re Expanded Plugs Ltd* [1966] 1 All ER 877; *Re Othery Construction Ltd* [1966] 1 WLR 69; *Re Bellador Silk Ltd* [1965] 1 All ER 667. See also *Re Chesterfield Catering Co Ltd* [1976] 3 All ER 294 at 299 where Oliver J suggested that 'tangible interest' is not limited to surplus assets but could cover where, as a member of the company, the shareholder will achieve some advantage or avoid or minimise some disadvantage which would accrue to him by virtue of his membership of the company.

[134] *Ebrahimi v Westbourne Galleries Ltd* [1972] 2 All ER 492 at 507, per Lord Cross.

[135] *Ebrahimi v Westbourne Galleries Ltd* [1972] 2 All ER 492 at 507, per Lord Cross.

[136] *Re Fildes Bros Ltd* [1970] 1 All ER 923.   [137] *Bryanston Finance Ltd v De Vries* [1976] 1 All ER 25.

[138] [1989] BCLC 579.

to seek a winding-up order so as to justify striking out the petition. However, it is clear that Parliament and the judiciary consider winding up to be a remedy of last resort[139] and, given the width of the jurisdiction under CA 2006, s 994, generally the courts would expect a petitioner to seek alternative relief under the unfairly prejudicial jurisdiction.[140]

Another option which may be open to the aggrieved shareholder is to exit from the company by selling his shares via a purchase mechanism provided by the articles of association or pursuant to an offer to acquire his shares made by the other shareholders. The courts initially took quite a strict line and regarded a refusal to use such mechanisms as unreasonable and ground for striking out the winding-up petition.[141] This approach was somewhat harsh, given that in many instances the mechanism in the articles or offer requires the petitioner to accept a valuation of his shares as determined by the company's auditor. Petitioners often feel that such valuations are arbitrary and biased in favour of the majority shareholder hence their preference for obtaining a winding-up order from the court.   **18-76**

The strict position altered with the decision in *Virdi v Abbey Leisure Ltd*[142] which established that there is no hard-and-fast rule that a petitioner who declines to utilise an exit mechanism in the articles or to accept an offer to acquire his shares is necessarily acting unreasonably in pursuing a winding-up order.[143] It depends on the fairness of the purchase mechanism and in *Virdi* the Court of Appeal found that the petitioner's refusal to use the mechanism was not unreasonable, given that the value of his shares might be discounted under that scheme though on the facts a discount was inappropriate.[144] But where a fair offer is available,[145] a petitioner will be acting unreasonably in seeking to have the company wound up rather than pursuing that alternative: he is not entitled to his day or month in court.[146]   **18-77**

Grounds for the petition

The courts have been reluctant to limit the just and equitable jurisdiction by categorising the grounds on which a petition might be brought but certain recognised (and overlapping) categories have developed over the years which centre on quasi-partnerships to a large degree and the breakdown in relations between the   **18-78**

---

[139] See *Re Guidezone Ltd* [2000] 2 BCLC 321 at 357; *Re a Company (No 004415 of 1996)* [1997] 1 BCLC 479.

[140] See, for example, *Re a Company (No 004415 of 1996)* [1997] 1 BCLC 479.

[141] See *Re a Company (No 002567 of 1982)* [1983] 2 All ER 854; *Re a Company (No 004377 of 1986)* [1987] BCLC 94 at 103; *Re a Company (No 003843 of 1986)* [1987] BCLC 562; *Re a Company (No 003096 of 1987)* (1988) 4 BCC 80; *Re a Company (No 005685 of 1988), ex p Schwarcz (No 2)* [1989] BCLC 427 at 452.

[142] [1990] BCLC 342, CA.

[143] See *Re a Company (No 00330 of 1991), ex p Holden* [1991] BCLC 597 at 604.

[144] [1990] BCLC 342 at 349. See also *Re a Company (No 001363 of 1988), ex p S-P* [1989] BCLC 579 where the petitioner's refusal to accept an offer for his shares under the articles was not unreasonable when there was a dispute as to the number of shares to which he was actually entitled.

[145] The guidance as to what is a fair offer provided in *O'Neill v Phillips* [1999] 2 BCLC 1 at 16–17 will be influential on this point.

[146] See *Fuller v Cyracuse Ltd* [2001] 1 BCLC 187 at 193.

parties and a lack of probity in the conduct of the company's affairs.[147] In *Re Yenidje Tobacco Co Ltd*[148] the relationship between the two shareholders (who were also the directors) had completely broken down. They refused to talk to one another and all communications were through a third party. The court found that the company was in essence a partnership and that there was such a state of animosity between the parties as to preclude all reasonable hope of reconciliation or friendly co-operation.[149] In such circumstances, it is just and equitable that the company be wound up. In *Loch v John Blackwood Ltd*[150] the directors failed to hold general meetings or submit accounts or recommend a dividend. Instead the majority shareholder treated the business as if it was his own business and ran it down with a view to forcing the minority shareholder to sell out at an undervalue. The lack of probity in the conduct of the company's affairs merited a winding-up order.[151]

18-79   It was also possible to get a winding-up order if it was or became impossible or illegal to achieve the main objectives for which a company was formed.[152] These loss of substratum cases, as they were known, are obsolete now as modern drafting techniques ensure that companies have many and varied objects such that loss of substratum is not an issue and, of course, companies formed under the CA 2006 have unrestricted objects unless the parties choose to restrict them (see s 31).

The modern jurisdiction

18-80   The landmark modern authority on the just and equitable jurisdiction is the decision of the House of Lords in *Ebrahimi v Westbourne Galleries Ltd*[153] which established that where a company has the characteristics of a quasi-partnership, as described by Lord Wilberforce below, the court may subject the exercise of legal rights to equitable considerations, i.e. considerations of a personal character arising between one individual and another which might make it unjust or inequitable to insist on strict legal rights or to exercise them in a particular way. It may therefore be just and equitable to wind up a company where the majority have acted in disregard of those equitable considerations.

18-81   In this instance, two shareholders (E and N) had formed a company which operated on a quasi-partnership basis including an understanding that both would be involved in the management of the company. N's son later joined the company. The majority shareholders (N and his son) were not entitled in those circumstances subsequently

---

[147] See Chesterman, 'The Just and Equitable Winding Up of Small Private Companies' (1973) 36 MLR 129; Prentice, 'Winding up on the Just and Equitable Ground' (1973) 89 LQR 107.

[148] [1916] 2 Ch 426. See *Symington v Symington Quarries Ltd* 1906 SC 121; *Re Davis and Collett Ltd* [1935] Ch 693; *Re Wondoflex Textiles Pty Ltd* [1951] VLR 458; also *Re Worldhams Park Golf Course Ltd, Whidbourne v Troth* [1998] 1 BCLC 554; *Jesner v Jarrad Properties Ltd* [1993] BCLC 1032.

[149] [1916] 2 Ch 426 at 430, per Cozens Hardy MR.   [150] [1924] AC 783.

[151] See also *Re Worldhams Park Golf Course Ltd, Whidbourne v Troth* [1998] 1 BCLC 554.

[152] The doctrine originated in *Re Suburban Hotel Co* (1867) 2 Ch App 737. See also *Re Haven Gold Mining Co* (1882) 20 Ch D 151; *Re German Date Coffee Co* (1882) 20 Ch D 169; *Re Red Rock Gold Mining Co Ltd* (1889) 61 LT 785; *Re Baku Consolidated Oilfields Ltd* [1944] 1 All ER 24; *Re Kitson & Co Ltd* [1946] 1 All ER 435.

[153] [1972] 2 All ER 492, HL.

to exercise their undoubted legal power to remove the minority shareholder (E) as a director and, having done so, the House of Lords concluded that the only just and equitable course was to dissolve the association and to grant E a winding-up order under IA 1986, s 122(1)(g).

The House of Lords found that, as a matter of law, the majority shareholders had acted completely within their rights, within the provisions of the articles, and the Companies Act in removing E as a director. But the just and equitable jurisdiction was not limited to proven cases of mala fides and the legal correctness of their conduct did not make it unassailable.   **18-82**

The words 'just and equitable' were: **18-83**

'…a recognition of the fact that a limited company is more than a mere judicial entity, with a personality in law of its own: that there is room in company law for recognition of the fact that behind it, or amongst it, there are individuals, with rights, expectations and obligations inter se which are not necessarily submerged in the company structure. That structure is defined by the Companies Act 1948 and by the articles of association by which shareholders agree to be bound. In most companies and in most contexts, this definition is sufficient and exhaustive, equally so whether the company is large or small. The "just and equitable" provision does not, as the respondents suggest, entitle one party to disregard the obligation he assumes by entering a company, nor the court to dispense him from it. It does, as equity always does, enable the court to subject the exercise of legal rights to equitable considerations; considerations, that is, of a personal character arising between one individual and another, which may make it unjust, or inequitable, to insist on legal rights, or to exercise them in a particular way.'[154]

As to when these equitable considerations will arise, Lord Wilberforce noted: **18-84**

'Certainly the fact that a company is a small one, or a private company, is not enough. There are very many of these where the association is a purely commercial one, of which it can safely be said that the basis of association is adequately and exhaustively laid down in the articles. The superimposition of equitable considerations requires something more, which typically may include one, or probably more, of the following elements: (i) an association formed or continued on the basis of a personal relationship, involving mutual confidence—this element will often be found where a pre-existing partnership has been converted into a limited company; (ii) an agreement, or understanding, that all, or some (for there may be "sleeping" members), of the shareholders shall participate in the conduct of the business; (iii) restriction on the transfer of the members' interest in the company—so that if confidence is lost, or one member is removed from management, he cannot take out his stake and go elsewhere. It is these, and analogous, factors which may bring into play the just and equitable clause, and they do so directly, through the force of the words themselves.'[155]

Lord Wilberforce went on to note that such companies are commonly called quasi-partnerships, though he cautioned against the use of that term.[156] The position then is   **18-85**

---

[154] [1972] 2 All ER 492 at 500.
[155] [1972] 2 All ER 492 at 500. See also *CVC/Opportunity Equity Partners Ltd v Demarco Almeida* [2002] 2 BCLC 108 at 117.   [156] [1972] 2 All ER 492 at 500.

that a winding-up order on the just and equitable ground may be sought where there has been a breach of the Companies Act or the company's constitution or where the majority shareholders have purported to exercise their legal powers in circumstances where equitable considerations have arisen which prevent them from exercising those powers. It can be seen that these grounds are precisely the grounds on which an unfairly prejudicial petition might be brought under CA 2006, s 994 and the question is whether, given the availability of relief under s 994, there is any role left to be played by the winding-up remedy.

Relationship with the unfairly prejudicial remedy

18-86   Whether any role remains for petitioning for winding up on the just and equitable ground depends on whether there are circumstances where relief under CA 2006, s 994 would not be available but relief would be available under IA 1986, s 122(1)(g). The point was considered by Jonathan Parker J in *Re Guidezone Ltd*[157] who warned against attempts to transfer business from the unfairly prejudicial jurisdiction to the winding-up jurisdiction.[158] He concluded that conduct which is not unfair within CA 2006, s 994 cannot found a petition for winding up, for that jurisdiction is, at the very least, no wider than CA 2006, s 994. In so far as *Re R A Noble & Sons (Clothing) Ltd*[159] suggested to the contrary, it was inconsistent, in his view,[160] with the decision of the House of Lords in *O'Neill v Phillips*[161] (see **17-39**).

18-87   The approach adopted by Jonathan Parker J in *Re Guidezone Ltd* has been criticised as a conflation of the two jurisdictions which is not required by anything said by Lord Hoffmann in *O'Neill v Phillips*.[162] It is also argued that the jurisdiction under IA 1986, s 122(1)(g) is wider than the unfairly prejudicial jurisdiction in that it will apply to those deadlock cases involving a breakdown in mutual trust (such as *Re Yenidje Ltd*,[163] discussed above at **18-78**) where winding up is warranted but where there is no objective unfairness to support a petition under CA 2006, s 994.[164] Jonathan Parker J in *Re Guidezone Ltd*,[165] relying on Lord Hoffmann in *O'Neill v Phillips*,[166] considered that such breakdown cases are cases of unfairness, the unfairness arising from the majority using its legal powers to maintain the association in circumstances to which the minority can reasonably say it did not agree, and therefore such cases are within CA 2006, s 994.[167] It is fair to say that, given the expansive jurisdiction under s 994,

---

[157] [2000] 2 BCLC 321.   [158] [2000] 2 BCLC 321 at 357.

[159] [1983] BCLC 273 (exclusion of petitioner from management of the company was not unfair when he had brought it upon himself, but the breakdown in relations between the parties justified the winding up of the company on the just and equitable ground). See also *Jesner v Jarrad Properties Ltd* [1993] BCLC 1032 to similar effect.

[160] [2000] 2 BCLC 321 at 357.   [161] [1999] 2 BCLC 1.

[162] See Boyle, *Minority Shareholders' Remedies* (2002), pp 96–100; Acton, 'Just and Equitable Winding up: the Strange Case of the Disappearing Jurisdiction' (2001) 22 Co Lawyer 134.   [163] [1916] 2 Ch 426.

[164] See Boyle, *Minority Shareholders' Remedies* (2002), pp 98–100; Acton, 'Just and Equitable Winding up: the Strange Case of the Disappearing Jurisdiction' (2001) 22 Co Lawyer 134.

[165] [2000] 2 BCLC 321 at 356.   [166] [1999] 2 BCLC 1 at 11.

[167] It might be noted that this point had not been reached in *O'Neill* where the parties were still able to work together (assisted by the fact that one of them worked in Germany and one in the UK) despite having

it is difficult to envisage cases where relief will not be available under that section but would and should be available under winding up. On the other hand, there may be some unforeseeable situation where that would be the case, in which case it is useful that the winding-up remedy remains on the books as a weapon of last resort. Leaving aside that slim possibility, all the other factors (the effect of IA 1986, s 125(2) (see **18-75**), the decision in *Guidezone*, and a Practice Direction restricting inappropriate use of winding-up petitions: see **17-103**) show clearly a Parliamentary and judicial predisposition to restrict the use of winding up as a shareholder remedy.

Statutory rights under the CA 2006

A number of provisions in the CA 2006 are designed to enhance shareholders' rights   **18-88**
of engagement (e.g. rights of access to information/participation in meetings/ability to circulate resolutions etc) and are particularly of interest in larger companies. In each case, the relevant section sets thresholds, such as the holders of not less than 5% of the total voting rights of all the members who have the right to vote, which need to be met to exercise the particular right and these vary from provision to provision. Of particular value are the following rights:

- the right to obtain copies of the company's constitutional documents: CA 2006, s 32;
- the right to inspect the register of members, subject to the company's right to go to court to refuse access: CA 2006, s 117, see **14-94**;
- the right to require the holding of a general meeting: CA 2006, s 303; and where the directors fail to call the meeting, the right of shareholders to call it themselves: CA 2006, s 305, see **15-46**;
- the right of members of a private company to require the circulation of a written resolution; CA 2006, s 292, see **15-28**; and, for public companies, the right to require the circulation of resolutions for annual general meetings: CA 2006, s 338, see **15-31**; and, for all companies, the right to require the circulation of statements with respect to proposed resolutions or business to be conducted at a general meeting: CA 2006, s 314, see **15-38**;
- the right of members of a quoted company (defined CA 2006, s 385: see s 361) to require an independent report on any poll taken, or to be taken, at a general meeting of the company: CA 2006, s 342, see **15-15**;
- the right of members to copies of the company's accounts and reports: CA 2006, ss 431 and 432, see **16-31**;
- the right of members of a quoted company to require the company to publish on a website a statement setting out audit concerns that the members propose to

---

fallen out with the result that the court was able to conclude that there had been no unfairly prejudicial conduct in that case. The petitioner was simply attempting to exercise a stark right of unilateral exit which does not exist: see [1999] 2 BCLC 1 at 13.

raise at the next accounts meeting (defined CA 2006, s 437(3)) of the company: CA 2006, s 527, see **16-50**.

18-89   Other provisions allow shareholders to object to a particular corporate act, such as the variation of class rights. Again, the statutory provision will set a minimum threshold for invoking the particular remedy (for example, the holders of not less than 15% of the class who have not agreed to the variation of the class rights: CA 2006, s 633) and possibly a time-limit within which the relief must be sought (for example, within 21 days of the consent to the variation). Examples of these provisions would be:

- the right to object to the re-registration of a public company as a private company: CA 2006, s 98;
- the right to challenge a variation of class rights: CA 2006, s 633, see **14-38**;
- the right to apply for rectification of the register of members: CA 2006, s 125, see **14-102**;
- the right to require the company to exercise its powers under CA 2006, s 793 requiring information about the holders of interests in shares: s 803;
- the right of a minority shareholder to be bought out by an offeror where there has been a takeover offer for all the shares in the company: CA 2006, s 983, see **26–95**.

18-90   Other statutory schemes do not provide a specific shareholder remedy as such, but the ability of the company to proceed with the scheme may be dependent on court confirmation, as in the case of a reduction of capital by special resolution confirmed by the court under CA 2006, ss 645–651, see **20-71** and a scheme of arrangement under CA 2006, s 899, see **26-117**, and the protection of the minority in such instances lies in the requirement for court sanction.

18-91   Finally, shareholders have the right to remove a director by an ordinary resolution under CA 2006, s 168, although exercise of this power may itself give rise to further problems, see **6-34**. Issues to bear in mind will be any entitlement to damages which may arise (see CA 2006, s 168(5)); the possibility that the director in question can command a sufficient majority of votes to prevent his removal and, most importantly, the possibility in quasi-partnerships that removal (without a fair offer for the dismissed director's shares) may trigger a petition for unfairly prejudicial conduct under CA 2006, s 994: see discussion at **17-66**.

PART IV

CORPORATE FINANCE— SHARE AND LOAN CAPITAL

19

Share capital—capital raising and payment

A Introduction

This chapter considers the statutory rules governing share capital requirements, especially those relating to the allotment of, and payment for, shares. The share capital rules, while statutory, frequently reflect long-established common law rules. **19-1**

The general approach is that the capital rules are stricter for public companies than for private companies.[1] This position is a reflection of the general policy that public companies with their greater exposure to investors and creditors should be subject to a more rigorous regime than private companies. More specifically, the stricter capital rules with respect to public companies reflect the requirements of the Second EC Company Law Directive (hereinafter the Second Directive) with regard to the establishment and maintenance of share capital in public companies.[2] The requirements of the Directive limited the extent to which amendments could be made in the CA 2006 to the capital rules as they apply to public companies, though the Directive was relaxed subsequently in some respects.[3] **19-2**

In 2007, the European Commission consulted on possible simplification (including repeal) of a broad sweep of company law, accounting and audit requirements including the Second Directive.[4] The overall response to the consultation, however, was that the focus should be on simplification rather than repeal of the Directives on the basis that they bring legal certainty and repealing them would involve additional costs[5] **19-3**

---

[1] As 99.5% of the companies on the register are private companies, the stricter rules have limited application. Of course, the stricter rules may have some partial influence on the choice of type of company and the preference for private companies is likely to be even more marked under the CA 2006 which significantly relaxes many of the more prescriptive elements of the statute for private companies.

[2] Directive 77/91/EEC, OJ L 26/1, 31.1.1977. See generally Edwards, *EC Company Law* (1999), Ch III.

[3] See Directive 2006/68/EC amending Directive 77/91/EEC, OJ L 264/32, 25.9.2006.

[4] See Communication from the Commission on a simplified business environment for companies in the areas of company law, accounting and auditing: COM (2007) 394, 10.7.2007.

[5] See 'Synthesis of the Reactions Received to the Commission Communication on a Simplified Business Environment' December 2007, see above n 4, available at http://ec.europa.eu/internal_market/company/docs/simplification/consultation_report_20071219_en.pdf; SEC (2008) 467, 17.4.2008; also UK Response to the Communication, available at http://circa.europa.eu/Public/irc/markt/markt_consultations/library?l=/company_law/simplifying_environment/department_regulatory/_EN_1.0_&a=d.

(though the UK's preference was for outright repeal of the Second Directive).[6] The Commission also launched an external assessment of the capital maintenance regime established by the Second Directive which was carried out by KPMG and published in early 2008.[7] These matters are discussed further in Chapter 20 (see **20-8**), but the main conclusion of the KPMG study was that, despite assertions to the contrary, the current regime established by the Second Directive does not seem to cause significant operational problems for companies. In the light of that, the Commission has announced that 'no follow-up measures or changes to the Second Company Law Directive are foreseen in the immediate future'.[8]

19-4   As far as private companies are concerned, their capital requirements are a domestic matter not subject to the Second Directive and there is room for a more laissez-faire approach. In fact, most companies on the register are rarely troubled by the statutory requirements as to share capital with 78% of all companies (1.9m companies) having an issued share capital of £100 or less and 91% having a share capital of £10,000 or less (all figures in this paragraph are for 2006–07).[9] For those companies with less than £100, many of these are £2 companies with an issued share capital of two £1 pound shares. In such companies no share capital is ever issued subsequent to the initial two shares on incorporation and for these companies the rules governing share capital are irrelevant. Even outside the £100 category, share capital is relatively insignificant with only 4.5% of the register having between £10,000 and £100,000 issued share capital and only 2.4% having between £100,000 and £1m. Only 1.4% of the register, some 35,500 companies, had an issued share capital in excess of £1m. That final statistic also cautions us against assuming that only public companies have significant share capital. There were only 11,500 public companies on the register in 2006/07 so the 35,500 companies with an issued share capital in excess of £1m must include a large number of private companies.[10] Given this overall position as to share capital, it is not surprising that the Company Law Review noted that: 'our

[6] See 'European Commission Consultation on the Simplification of EU Company Law and Accounting and Audit Regulation, Note and Request for Views by the Department for Business, Enterprise and Regulatory Reform', August 2007, para 11.

[7] KPMG, 'Feasibility study on an alternative to the capital maintenance regime established by the Second Company Law Directive 77/91/EEC of 13 December 1976 and an examination of the impact on profit distribution of the new EU accounting regime', January 2008, available on the Commission website at http:// ec.europa.eu/internal_market/company/capital/index_en.htm.

[8] Commission statement on the results of the external study on the feasibility of an alternative to the Capital Maintenance Regime of the Second Company Law Directive and the impact of the adoption of IFRS on profit distribution (undated), available on the Commission website at http://ec.europa.eu/ internal_market/company/capital/index_en.htm.

[9] Of the 2,457,400 companies on the register at 31 March 2007 with an issued share capital, 1,921,700 (or 78%) had an issued share capital of up to £100, while 91% had an issued share capital of less than £10,000: see Companies House, *Statistical Tables on Companies Register Activities 2006-2007*, Table A7. These statistical tables are available on the Companies House website: www.companieshouse.gov.uk. and this type of capital profile is repeated year on year in these statistics though Table A7 has been omitted from 2007–08 tables.

[10] Equally notable is that of 106 companies incorporated in 2006–07 with an issued share capital in excess of £50m, all but nine of them were private companies: see Companies House, *Statistical Tables 2006-07*, Table B3.

limited enquiries tend to indicate that creditors and potential creditors do not any longer regard the amount of a company's issued share capital as a significant matter when it comes to deciding whether or not to extend credit'.[11] This absence of significant equity (share) funding means that such companies must fund its activities in other ways, primarily, but not exclusively, through loan capital (typically term loans and bank overdrafts) which may mean that the company is subject to greater economic pressures than would be the case if it had more substantial equity funds. It may also mean, especially at the lowest end of the scale, that the directors/shareholders in these companies have to commit themselves to personal guarantees to secure bank lending so reducing the value to them of limited liability. Overall, the absence of significant equity funding acts as a brake on the development of these businesses though obviously many of the micro-businesses are content to remain at that level. For those with an interest in expanding their business, once they have exhausted their own personal resources, attracting equity funding to smaller companies can be a problem.[12] Equally, for many entrepreneurs, however, the risk of losing control of the company as their holdings are diluted by further issues of shares acts as a deterrent in any event to seeking further equity investment.

B Share capital requirements

Nominal value of shares

Shares must have a fixed nominal (or par) value (CA 2006, s 542(1)) and this figure is **19-5** settled on incorporation (it may change thereafter as and when new classes of shares are created or capital restructuring takes place). As discussed in Chapter 1, A and B may form a company with shares with a nominal value of £1, equally they may have shares with a nominal value of 1p. Typically, the figure is set quite low, for example, £1, 25p and 1p are quite common nominal values. The relevance of par value to the shareholder is that the company may not issue its shares for less than the par value, something which is discussed in greater detail below. Of course, once the company has been trading for a while and is prospering, A and B will not be willing to sell further shares at £1. They will want a higher figure to reflect the increased value of the company. For example, they might consider that £2 is more appropriate in which case C who buys at £2 is said to contribute £1 of share capital and £1 of share premium, premium being any sum which is obtained above the nominal or par value.

---

[11] Company Law Review, *Strategic Framework* (1999), para 5.4.3.

[12] See HM Treasury/Small Business Service, *Bridging the Finance Gap: Next steps in improving access to growth capital for small businesses* (December 2003) and the preceding consultation document of the same name issued in April 2003. The report notes (para E7) that there is an equity gap between the amount of money which individuals can raise and the stage at which venture capital becomes available which appears to be most acute for investments between £250,000 and £1m (though many would argue that the gap extends much higher than £1m).

19-6   Companies used to have shares of a high par value but today low par values are the norm as they are seen to increase the marketability of the shares and are preferred by investors. Many jurisdictions allow shares of no par value[13] and the issue was considered by the Company Law Review which noted that the requirement of a nominal value was an anachronism which was confusing for the layman. It initially favoured the mandatory introduction of no par shares for all companies while recognising that the requirements of the Second Directive precludes such a change for public companies.[14] On consultation, a variety of concerns emerged about these proposals, not least regarding the transitional difficulties which would arise given the many contracts and agreements already in place which make express reference to par values. The major obstacle, however, was that par values would have to be retained for public companies, so that there would be different requirements in this regard for public and private companies. This outcome would make transition from one classification to the other difficult which would be a serious drawback in practice. In the light of these concerns, the Company Law Review reluctantly concluded that the obligation for all companies to have shares with a nominal or par value should be retained,[15] hence CA 2006, s 542(1) requires shares to have a fixed nominal value.[16]

19-7   Nominal or par values may be denominated in any currency and different classes of shares may be denominated in different currencies (CA 2006, s 542(3)). The minimum authorised allotted share capital for a public company (discussed below) may be in sterling (£50,000) or euros (€65,600, the prescribed euro equivalent)[17] but it cannot be partially in sterling and partially in euros.[18]

19-8   On formation, a company with a share capital provides the registrar of companies with a statement of capital and initial holdings (CA 2006, s 9(4)(a)). That statement of capital contains the following information:

> (1) the total number of shares of the company to be taken on formation by the subscribers to the memorandum (see s 8(1));
>
> (2) the aggregate nominal value of those shares;
>
> (3) for each class of shares,[19] the number of shares of that class, their aggregate nominal value; and the prescribed particulars of the rights attached to those shares; and

---

[13] The Gedge Committee in 1954 (see Cmnd 9112) and the Jenkins Committee in 1962 (see Cmnd 1749) recommended that no par value shares be permitted in the UK but an attempt to introduce such reforms in the Companies Act 1967 failed.

[14] See Company Law Review, *Strategic Framework* (1999), paras 5.4.26–5.4.33; *Company Formation and Capital Maintenance* (1999), para 3.8; *Capital Maintenance: Other Issues* (2000), paras 8–23.

[15] Company Law Review, *Completing the Structure* (2000), paras 7.2–7.3; *Final Report*, vol I (2001), para 10.7.

[16] An allotment of a share that does not have a fixed nominal value is void: CA 2006, s 542(2); and the company and any officer in default commits an offence: s 542(4), (5).

[17] CA 2006, s 763 and The Companies (Authorised Minimum) Regulations 2008, SI 2008/729, reg 2.

[18] CA 2006, ss 763(1), 765(1).

[19] Most companies have only one type of share, ordinary shares, and a company with only one type of share does not have classes of shares and so this information is not required.

(4) the amount to be paid up[20] and the amount (if any) to be unpaid on each share[21] (s 10(2)).

Thereafter, every time the company makes a further allotment of shares, it must deliver to the registrar a return of allotment[22] and a statement of capital setting out the total capital position of the company[23] so ensuring that the public record always contains an up-to-date statement of the position.

Issued and allotted share capital

While the terms 'issued' and 'allotted' with respect to shares are often used inter-   **19-9** changeably, they refer to distinct processes.[24] For the purposes of the Companies Acts, shares are taken to be allotted when a person acquires the unconditional right to be included in the company's register of members in respect of those shares.[25] An allotment creates an enforceable contract for the issue of the shares and the shares are issued when an application to the company has been followed by allotment and notification to the purchaser and completed by entry on the company's register of members.[26]

Minimum capital requirements

Public companies

Public companies are required by the Second Directive[27] to have a minimum share   **19-10** capital, and the authorised minimum in relation to the nominal value of a public company's allotted share capital is £50,000 or €65,600 (the prescribed euro equivalent).[28]

A company registered as a public company on its original incorporation may not do   **19-11** business or exercise any borrowing powers unless the registrar of companies has certified under CA 2006, s 761, that he is satisfied that the nominal value of the company's allotted share capital is not less than the authorised minimum.[29] A trading certificate

---

[20] The amount to be paid up includes any share premium.

[21] Most shares are issued fully paid up so usually there will be no amount unpaid: see **19-16**.

[22] See CA 2006, s 555(2); also see The Companies (Shares and Share Capital) Regulations 2009, SI 2009/388 as to the prescribed contents of the return of allotment.

[23] CA 2006, s 555(3); and see s 555(4) as to the prescribed contents of the statement of capital.

[24] See *Clarke's Case* (1878) 8 Ch D 635 at 638, CA; also CA 2006, s 546(1). It would seem that the meaning of 'issue' depends on the context of the enactment in which the word occurs: *National Westminster Bank plc v Inland Revenue Commissioners* [1994] 3 All ER 1, HL.

[25] CA 2006, s 558; see also s 546. The company must maintain a register of its members: s 113.

[26] *National Westminster Bank plc v Inland Revenue Commissioners* [1994] 3 All ER 1, HL (tax relief to investors in shares was altered in respect of shares 'issued' after 16 March 1993: here shares had been allotted prior to that date but registration took place after the date: held (3–2 majority) shares were 'issued' after 16 March 1993). See also *Clarke's Case* (1878) 8 Ch D 635 at 638, CA.

[27] Second EC Company Law Directive, Council Directive (EEC) 77/91, [1977] OJ L 26/1, art 6.

[28] CA 2006, ss 763, 765. See The Companies (Authorised Minimum) Regulations 2008, SI 2008/729, reg 2.

[29] The application for a trading certificate must be accompanied by a statement of compliance that the company meets the requirements for a trading certificate and the registrar may accept that statement as sufficient evidence of the matters stated in it: CA 2006, s 762(2), (3).

to this effect is conclusive evidence that the company is entitled to do business and exercise any borrowing powers.[30] Once a public company has this trading certificate, it can redenominate the minimum capital into any currency, subject to any prohibition or restriction in the company's articles.[31]

19-12   If a company does business or exercises any borrowing powers without this trading certificate, the company and any officer in default is liable to a fine (CA 2006, s 767(1)), but the validity of any transaction entered into by the company is not affected (s 767(3)). If, however, a company enters into a transaction in contravention of this requirement and fails to comply with its obligations in that connection within 21 days of being called upon to do so, the directors of the company who were the directors at the time the company entered into the transaction are jointly and severally liable to indemnify the other party to the transaction in respect of any loss or damage suffered by him by reason of the company's failure to comply with those obligations.[32]

19-13   This requirement of a trading certificate is of limited practical significance as most companies are formed as private companies and subsequently re-register as public companies (see **1-47**), a process which requires them to have the minimum share capital[33] but does not require them to obtain a trading certificate.

19-14   In addition to requiring public companies to have a minimum allotted share capital, the Second Directive also provides that where a public company has suffered a serious loss of capital so that its net assets are half or less of its called-up share capital (see **19-16**), the directors must call an extraordinary general meeting to consider whether any, and if so what, steps should be taken to deal with the situation.[34]

Private companies

19-15   There is no minimum share capital required for private companies. As noted at **19-4**, one consequence of this is that approximately 78% of all private companies have an issued share capital of £100 or less.[35] A minimum share capital for private companies is common in continental systems[36] and this disparity in approach has had some impact on the choice of jurisdiction of incorporation with businesses in other Member States choosing to incorporate here because of the lack of a minimum capital as well as the speed and ease of incorporation. This practice caused some concerns for other Member States and raised issues as to freedom of establishment

---

[30] CA 2006, s 761(4). A public company registered as such on its original incorporation which has not obtained a trading certificate and more than a year has expired since it was registered as a public company may be wound up by the court: IA 1986, s 122(1)(b).   [31] CA 2006, ss 617(4), 622(1), (7).

[32] CA 2006, s 767(3), (4), although it would be difficult to establish such loss or damage.

[33] See CA 2006, ss 90(2)(b), 91(1)(a).

[34] Directive 77/91/EEC, OJ L 26/1, 31.1.1977, art 17, implemented by CA 2006, s 656.

[35] See above n 9.

[36] For example, looking at roughly equivalent limited company structures, in Germany, a GmbH requires a minimum capital of €25,000, half of which must be paid up; in Spain, an SL requires €3006 which must be fully paid up; in Italy, the SRL requires a minimum €10,000.

under arts 43 and 48 of the EC Treaty.[37] The European Court of Justice resolved the matter firmly in favour of freedom of establishment and corporate mobility in a number of notable cases, especially *Centros*,[38] *Uberseering*[39] and *Inspire Art*,[40] which are discussed at **2-38**.

Paid-up share capital

Shares may be fully or partly paid up. In the latter case, the company can make calls   **19-16** on the shareholder up to the amount of the share price which has not been paid. For example, a share may be issued at £3.50 of which only £1.50p is paid up on allotment leaving the company later to call up the remaining £2. It is uncommon today to find companies with partly-paid shares as they prefer to obtain from the outset the capital which they have raised and so avoid the administrative burden of making calls on shareholders.

Public companies must not allot a share except as paid up at least as to one-quarter   **19-17** of its nominal value and the whole of any premium, i.e. any amount in excess of the nominal value of the share (CA 2006, s 586(1)). In the event of a breach, the allotment is still valid, but the allottee is liable to pay the company the minimum amount which should have been received in respect of the shares less any consideration actually paid: s 586(3). Given the insignificance of the nominal value in respect of the market value of shares in most public companies, the effect in practice of this requirement that the whole of the premium be paid up is that shares in public companies are fully paid. As to the manner of payment, see the discussion below at **19-62**.

C Issuing shares at par, premium or a discount

A company may issue its shares: **19-18**

(1) at par, i.e. for the nominal or par value set by the company (nominal value is discussed at **19-5**); or

(2) at a premium, i.e. for a figure in excess of the nominal or par value; but

(3) it must not issue its shares at a discount, i.e. for a figure less than the nominal or par value.

---

[37] Article 43 provides for freedom of establishment and art 48 requires companies formed in a Member State to be treated in the same way as natural persons who are nationals of Member States.

[38] *Centros Ltd v Erhvervs-og Selskabsstyrelsen* Case C-212/97, [1999] ECR I-1459, [2000] 2 BCLC 68, ECJ.

[39] *Uberseering BV v Nordic Construction Co Baumanagement Gmbh (NCC)* Case C-208/00, [2002] ECR I-9919, [2005] 1 WLR 315, ECJ.

[40] *Kamer van Koophandel en Fabrieken voor Amsterdam v Inspire Art Ltd* Case C-167/01, [2003] ECR I-10155, [2005] 3 CMLR 34, ECJ.

Issue at a premium

19-19   While the initial subscribers to the memorandum may take their shares at the nominal or par value, it is common thereafter for shares to be issued at a premium, i.e. at more than par value. For example, a share with a par value of £1 may be issued for £1.30, £1.50 or any higher figure which the market will bear.

19-20   There is no requirement for companies to issue shares at a premium.[41] It depends on the circumstances of each case whether it is prudent or possible to do so and this is a matter for the directors to decide.[42] An example of a situation where the company may forgo some of the available premium is where the company makes a rights issue[43] to raise further capital from its shareholders and does so, as is normally the practice, at a price which is at a discount to the market price. In this instance, the company forgoes the maximum available premium, but the discount ensures (usually) that the shares are taken up and, in some cases, this may mean that the company saves on the expense of having the issue underwritten.[44] In some circumstances, however, directors may be in breach of their duties to the company in not obtaining the greatest financial return from an issue of shares.[45]

19-21   A premium may arise whether shares are issued for cash or for a non-cash consideration. Shares issued for a consideration other than cash are issued at a premium if the value of the assets in consideration of which they are issued is more than the nominal value of the shares. The point arose in *Henry Head & Co Ltd v Ropner Holdings Ltd*[46] where there was an amalgamation of two shipping companies through the formation of a new holding company. There was a one-for-one exchange of shares by the shareholders of the two companies for shares in the holding company. The assets of the companies were under-valued and were worth £5m more than the nominal value of the shares in the new holding company. The question was whether it was correct for the holding company to transfer £5m to a share premium account. The court found that it was necessary for a transfer to be made to the share premium account and this decision was followed in *Shearer (Inspector of Taxes) v Bercain Ltd*.[47]

19-22   When a company issues shares at a premium, whether for cash or otherwise, a sum equal to the aggregate amount or value of the premiums on those shares must be transferred to a share premium account (CA 2006, s 610). There are some exceptions to this requirement set out in ss 611–614 which identify certain circumstances when either a share premium account is not required or only a limited amount need be transferred

---

[41] *Hilder v Dexter* [1902] AC 474; *Lowry v Consolidated African Selection Trust Ltd* [1940] 2 All ER 545.

[42] *Hilder v Dexter* [1902] AC 474 at 480, per Lord Davey.

[43] Essentially, an offer of further shares to the company's existing shareholders, see the discussion below at **19-36**.

[44] Underwriting involves the use of professional intermediaries (such as investment banks and institutional investors) which undertake, in return for a fee, to subscribe or procure subscriptions for shares to the extent that the public or other persons do not subscribe for them.

[45] *Hilder v Dexter* [1902] AC 474 at 481, per Lord Davey, an allotment at par when a premium is available may be open to challenge as improvident or an abuse or in excess of the powers of management committed to the directors. See also *Lowry v Consolidated African Selection Trust Ltd* [1940] 2 All ER 545 at 565.

[46] [1951] 2 All ER 994.   [47] [1980] 3 All ER 295.

to such an account. These provisions were introduced in response to the decisions in *Henry Head & Co Ltd v Ropner Holdings Ltd*[48] and *Shearer (Inspector of Taxes) v Bercain Ltd*,[49] noted above, and the net effect is to allow certain group reconstructions and mergers to take place without a transfer (or only a limited transfer) to a share premium account so releasing certain assets which may be distributed to the members as a dividend.

Share premium is treated in most respects as share capital and its use is restricted to writing off any expenses incurred or commission paid on the issue of the shares in respect of which the premium has arisen and to paying up new shares to be allotted to members as fully paid bonus shares (discussed below at **19-59**).[50]   **19-23**

Prohibition on issue at a discount

A company's shares must not be allotted at a discount, i.e. for less than the nominal or par value (CA 2006, s 580(1)). If shares are allotted in contravention of this requirement, the allottee is liable to pay the company an amount equal to the amount of the discount, with interest at the appropriate rate.[51] The company and any officer in default is liable on conviction to a fine (s 590). This statutory rule reflects the long-established common law to this effect laid down in *Ooregum Gold Mining Co of India Ltd v Roper*.[52]   **19-24**

In this case, a company purported to issue £1 preference shares credited with 15 shillings paid up, leaving only five shillings to be paid on allotment. The House of Lords held that there was no power under the Companies Acts to do this and the allotment was ultra vires with the allottees liable to pay the full amount of £1 on each of their shares.[53] As Lord Macnaghten noted, in a limited liability company shareholders purchase immunity from liability beyond the amount due on their shares but they do so on the basis that they remain liable up to that limit.[54]   **19-25**

---

[48] [1951] 2 All ER 994.   [49] [1980] 3 All ER 295.

[50] CA 2006, s 610(2). The CA 2006 tightened the rules on use of share premium. It is no longer possible to use the share premium account to write off (1) the company's preliminary expenses on formation, or (2) the expenses incurred, commission paid or discount allowed on any issue of debentures or in providing for the premium payable on redemption of debentures of the company, as was the case under CA 1985, s 130.

[51] CA 2006, s 580(2). Directors who allot shares at a discount are guilty of a breach of duty to the company and are liable to pay the amount of the discount and interest to the company if that amount cannot be recovered from the allottee or holder of the shares, as where the shares have passed into the hands of a bona fide purchaser for value from the original allottee: *Hirsche v Sims* [1894] AC 654, PC.

[52] [1892] AC 125, HL. See also *Re Eddystone Marine Insurance Co* [1893] 3 Ch 9; *Welton v Saffery* [1897] AC 299. The rule cannot be evaded by issuing convertible debentures at a discount which are capable of being immediately converted to ordinary shares: *Mosely v Koffyfontein Mines Ltd* [1904] 2 Ch 108.

[53] Allowing the company to allot at a discount is unfair to shareholders who paid the full amount and misleading for creditors who rely on the stated par value as indicating the minimum price at which the company has issued and will issue its shares.

[54] [1892] AC 125 at 145. Equally, the company cannot thereafter increase the member's liability to contribute to the company's share capital without his consent: CA 2006, s 25(1)(b).

19-26 As a limited exception to the no-discount rule, companies are permitted to pay underwriting commissions, provided such payments are authorised by the articles and the amount involved does not exceed specified limits (CA 2006, ss 552–553). Underwriting involves the use of professional intermediaries (such as investment banks and institutional investors) which undertake, in return for a fee, to subscribe or procure subscriptions for shares to the extent that the public or other persons do not subscribe for them. This fee could be prohibited as a discount on the shares were it not for s 553 expressly permitting such payments.

19-27 Finally, it should be noted that, while a company may not allot shares at a discount to the nominal value, payment for shares may be in the form of money or money's worth (CA 2006, s 582(1)). Where money's worth is received and the company is a private company, the courts will not inquire into the adequacy of the consideration unless it is illusory or manifestly inadequate.[55] In such circumstances, it is possible that the issue of shares for a non-cash consideration disguises what is, in effect, an issue of shares at a discount. This problem is considered later in this chapter, see **19-66**.

D Alteration of share capital

19-28 A company needs flexibility in dealing with its share capital to enable it to react to changing business circumstances and so the statute allows a company to alter its share capital in the following ways, subject to any prohibition or restriction in the company's articles. Authorisation from the shareholders is also required, usually by an ordinary resolution of the shareholders, but a special resolution is required for a reduction of capital (CA 2006, s 641). A company may:

(1) increase its share capital by allotting new shares (discussed at **19-30**);

(2) reduce its share capital (discussed at **20-56**);

(3) sub-divide or consolidate all or any of its share capital into shares of smaller/larger amount than its existing shares. Sub-division involves dividing a share into a number of new shares and is usually done to increase the marketability of shares where companies feel their nominal value is too high. For example, £1 shares can be sub-divided in four 25p shares or ten 10p shares. Consolidation involves combining a number of shares into a new share of commensurate nominal value. For example, 10 £1 shares may be consolidated into one £10 share. This process is less common now as investors prefer shares of lower rather than higher nominal value but it is sometimes used when a capital reorganisation leaves the company with shares of an unwieldy nominal value, for example, 12.5p shares may be consolidated into 50p or £1 shares. This exercise has no financial impact on a shareholder who now holds fewer shares of greater nominal value but representing the same percentage interest in the company as the shareholder held previously;

[55] *Re Wragg Ltd* [1897] 1 Ch 796.

(4) reconvert any stock into paid-up shares of any denomination. It is rare for UK companies to have stock (which arises from a conversion of fully paid shares) but this power is retained to allow any company which still has stock to convert it back into shares (CA 2006, s 620). Companies are no longer able to convert shares into stock;

(5) redenominate all or any of its share capital into another currency. The ability to redenominate shares into another currency is a new power introduced by the CA 2006, ss 622–628. It is intended to facilitate companies in changing their capital structures without the need for more complex schemes involving a reduction or purchase of shares followed by the cancellation of those shares and a new allotment in a different currency. It is open to any company, public or private, to redenominate its shares into any currency or into multiple currencies.

Notice of any of the above alterations must be given to the registrar of companies typically within one month of the alteration (15 days if a reduction of capital).[56] In each case the notice must be accompanied by a statement of capital.[57] In the event of default in complying with any of these disclosure requirements, the company and any officer in default is liable to a fine.[58]   **19-29**

E Allotment of shares

Quite apart from the ability to raise money for the company, the authority granted to the directors to make an allotment of shares is important because an allotment will affect the balance of power within the company, given that shares typically carry one vote per share. An allotment may be used improperly to oppress minority shareholders by diluting their holdings, or to alter the voting position so as to ensure that the directors cannot be voted out of office or that opponents cannot be appointed to the board,[59] or to prevent a takeover of the company. Statutory controls are imposed therefore to restrain directors from acting improperly in this regard and these are discussed below.   **19-30**

The statutory framework also operates against a backdrop of other constraints which should prevent improper allotments. First, directors are under a fiduciary duty to exercise their powers for the purpose for which they are conferred (and a power to allot shares is primarily, but not exclusively, conferred in order that the company may raise capital). These issues are discussed in detail in Chapter 8. Secondly, the directors must also be mindful of their fiduciary duty to act to promote the success of the company   **19-31**

---

[56] CA 2006, s 555(2) (allotment of shares), s 619(1) (sub-division and consolidation), s 621(1) (redenomination). In the case of a reduction of capital, notice must be given within 15 days of the passing of the resolution for reduction: ss 627(1), 644(1).

[57] CA 2006, ss 555(3), 619(2), 621(2), 625(2), 627(2), 644(1).

[58] CA 2006, ss 557(1), 619(4), 621(4), 625(4), 627(7), 644(9).

[59] See *Re Looe Fish Ltd* [1993] BCLC 1160.

(CA 2006, s 172(1)) having regard (amongst other matters) to the need to act fairly as between the members (s 172(1)(f)). Section 172 is discussed in Chapter 9.

19-32   Thirdly, minority shareholders may petition for relief in an appropriate case under CA 2006, s 994, alleging that the allotment amounts to the conduct of the company's affairs in an unfairly prejudicial manner: see **17-53**.

Authorisation to allot

19-33   As a general rule, directors may exercise the power to allot shares only if authorised to do so by the articles or by an ordinary resolution (CA 2006, s 551(1)).[60] Authorisation may be general or particular, conditional or unconditional, and must specify the maximum number of shares and may be for a period of up to five years (s 551(2)–(3)). Public companies typically seek authority to allot at successive annual general meetings, but for relatively modest amounts, so if the company subsequently decides on the need to have a large share issue, a general meeting has to be called and approval sought.[61]

19-34   An important exception to the general rule is that in the case of a private company with only one class of shares (and most private companies fall into this category) the directors may allot shares of that class, without the need for any express authorisation, *unless* they are prohibited from doing so by the company's articles (CA 2006, s 550). This general permission to allot was introduced by the CA 2006 following a recommendation by the Company Law Review that the requirement for authorisation to allot shares should not apply to private companies.[62] In many private companies, the directors and the shareholders are the same people so the Review considered it an unnecessary complication to require A and B, as shareholders, to authorise A and B, as directors, to allot shares. In so far as there is potential for abuse of this power, it is constrained, as noted above, by the requirements of fiduciary duty and the potential

---

[60] Allotments must be notified to the registrar of companies within one month of the allotment: CA 2006, s 555; companies must register an allotment in the register of members within two months of the allotment: s 554. In the case of public companies, these requirements are derived from art 25(1) of the Second EC Company Law Directive (77/91/EEC) [1977] OJ L 26/1 which article can be invoked by an individual against the state: *Karella v Minister of Industry, Energy and Technology* [1994] 1 BCLC 774 (Greek administrative authorities purported to exercise the power to increase the share capital of a company which the authorities had taken over).

[61] The Association of British Insurers (ABI) Guidelines on allotment were revised in December 2008 to allow for greater flexibility, especially in the context of rights issues: see discussion at **19-58**. In future, ABI members will regard as routine requests for authorisation to allot up to one-third of a company's existing share capital. They will also regard as routine requests for authorisation to allot a further one-third of the company's existing share capital where the allotment in that case is to be on the basis of a rights issue only. If that rights issue exceeds one-third of the company's existing capital and the monetary proceeds realised exceed one-third of the pre-issue market capitalisation, the expectation is that all members of the board will stand for re-election at the next annual general meeting of the company: see ABI Guidelines on Directors' Powers to Allot Share Capital (December 2008) available at http://www.ivis.co.uk/ShareholdersPreemptionRight.aspx.

[62] Company Law Review, *Developing the Framework* (2000), paras 7.28–7.32; *Completing the Structure* (2000), para 2.16; *Final Report*, vol I (2001), para 4.5.

for minority relief under s 994. Furthermore, the requirement for authorisation remains if:

(1) the articles prohibit the exercise of the power to allot;

(2) the directors are to allot shares of a different class; or

(3) the private company has more than one class of shares.

A further constraint, as we shall see, is that, while the directors have a power to allot, the statutory framework dictates to whom the shares must be allotted. A rights issue (CA 2006, s 561), essentially an allotment to the existing shareholders, is required unless the shareholders choose to exclude or disapply that rights requirement.   **19-35**

Rights issues

A rights issue requires a company to offer a new issue of shares to existing sharehold-   **19-36**
ers in proportion to their existing shareholdings. Such pre-emption rights, if taken up, enable the existing shareholders to retain their proportionate shareholdings in the company and prevents the dilution of their holdings which would otherwise occur if a fresh issue of shares was offered to only some of the existing shareholders or to outside investors. As public companies usually offer a fresh issue of shares at a discount to the market price, the obligation to offer the shares on a rights basis to the existing share-holders means not only that they can protect their percentage holding in the company, but also that they, rather than outside investors, get the benefit of any discount to the market price.

The statutory scheme is set out in CA 2006, Part 17, Ch 3, ss 560 et seq and refer-   **19-37**
ence must be made to the precise wording of the somewhat complicated provisions which, as regards public companies, implement the requirements of the Second Company Law Directive.[63] The overall scheme is that a company (including a private company) proposing to make an allotment of shares must do so on a rights basis (i.e. to existing shareholders in proportion to their existing holdings) unless the case falls within one of the exceptions, exclusions or disapplications permitted by the statute.

A company proposing to allot equity securities[64] (essentially ordinary shares[65] but   **19-38**
including a sale of treasury shares held by the company[66]) must first make an offer to

---

[63] Directive 77/91/EEC, OJ L 26/1, 31.1.1977, art 29.

[64] See the definition of 'allotment of equity securities' in CA 2006, s 560(2).

[65] See CA 2006, s 560(1). 'Equity securities' means ordinary shares in the company or a right to subscribe for, or to convert securities into, ordinary shares in the company; and ordinary shares means shares other than shares that as respects dividends and capital carry a right to participate only up to a specified amount in a distribution.

[66] CA 2006, s 560(2)(b). The effect is that a sale of treasury shares held by a company must be on a rights basis unless that requirement is excluded or disapplied. Institutional shareholders insisted on this require-ment for fear that otherwise directors would use sales of treasury shares as an easy way of evading the pre-emption requirements. See CA 2006, s 724(5) as to when shares are treasury shares; also **20-38**.

each person who holds ordinary shares in the company to allot to him on the same or more favourable terms a proportion of those shares that is as nearly as practicable equal to the proportion in nominal value held by him of the ordinary share capital of the company (CA 2006, s 561(1)(a)).

19-39   The offer may be made in hard copy or electronic form and must state a period of not less than 21 days during which the offer may be accepted[67] and the offer must not be withdrawn before the end of that period.[68] The company cannot allot any of those shares to any person unless the period during which any such offer to the existing holders may be accepted has expired or the company has received notice of the acceptance or refusal of every offer so made (CA 2006, s 561(1)(b)).

19-40   In the event of a contravention of the requirement to make an allotment on a rights basis or of the provisions concerning the communication of pre-emption offers, the company, and every officer of it who knowingly authorised or permitted the contravention, are jointly and severally liable to compensate any person to whom an offer should have been made for any loss, damage, costs or expenses which the person has sustained or incurred by reason of the contravention.[69] A failure to comply with the pre-emption requirement may be grounds for a petition alleging unfairly prejudicial conduct.[70]

19-41   These requirements are subject to a variety of exceptions and exclusions and may be disapplied by the shareholders in certain circumstances. Again, reference should be made to the detailed wording of the provisions.

Exceptions

19-42   *Allotment of bonus shares*   The pre-emption requirement does not apply in relation to an allotment of bonus shares (CA 2006, s 564). Bonus shares are discussed at **19-59**.

19-43   *Allotments other than for cash*   The pre-emption requirement does not apply to a particular allotment if the shares are, or are to be, wholly or partly paid up otherwise than in cash

---

[67] The 21-day period may be reduced (but not to less than 14 days) or increased by regulations made under CA 2006, s 562(6); no regulations have been made to date but the period is expected to be reduced: see discussion at **19-58**.

[68] CA 2006, s 562(2), (4)–(5); in certain circumstances, a notice in the *Gazette* suffices: s 562(3).

[69] CA 2006, s 563(1), (2), subject to a two-year limitation period: s 563(3). No provision is made for allotments in breach of these requirements to be set aside, but see *Re Thundercrest Ltd* [1995] 1 BCLC 117 where the court did set aside an allotment by directors in their own favour which was made in breach of the statutory requirements.

[70] Under CA 2006, s 994 which is discussed in Chapter 17. See *Re a Company (No 005134 of 1986), ex p Harries* [1989] BCLC 383 at 396. An allotment on a pre-emption basis in accordance with the statutory provisions may be challenged if it is being proposed for a collateral purpose: see *Re a Company (No 002612 of 1984)* [1985] BCLC 80; *Re Regional Airports Ltd* [1999] 2 BCLC 30. Where there was a genuine desire to raise capital, a scheme proposed by the directors, although devised so as to avoid the need for a rights issue, was not conduct which was unfairly prejudicial to those shareholders thereby denied the possibility of taking up additional shares: see *CAS (Nominees) Ltd v Nottingham Forest FC plc* [2002] 1 BCLC 613.

(CA 2006, s 565). This exception is a common method of avoiding the requirement to have a rights issue.[71]

Allotments held under an employees' share scheme   The pre-emption requirement does not apply to an allotment that would (apart from any renunciation or assignment) be held under an employees' share scheme (CA 2006, s 566).   **19-44**

Exclusions

Exclusion by private companies   All or any of the requirements as to pre-emption (or the provisions governing communication of pre-emption offers to shareholders) may be excluded by a private company by a provision contained in the articles (CA 2006, s 567).[72] As noted above, the pre-emption requirements for public companies are mandatory as they are required by the Second Company Law Directive, art 29.   **19-45**

Allotments to a class   The pre-emption requirement does not apply where a company is required by its articles to make an allotment on a rights basis to a class of shares in pursuance of a class right to that effect (CA 2006, s 568(1)). If a member of the class (or anyone in whose favour he has renounced his right to the allotment) does not accept the shares offered to him, any subsequent offer of those shares is on a pre-emption basis to the rest of the shareholders rather than to the general public unless, in the case of a private company, the articles exclude the need for a rights issue in this situation[73] or the requirement for a rights issue is disapplied.[74]   **19-46**

Disapplication of pre-emption rights

Private company with only one class of shares   The directors of a private company that has only one class of shares may be given power by the articles, or by a special resolution of the company, to allot ordinary shares of that class as if the pre-emption requirement does not apply or applies with such modifications as the directors may determine (CA 2006, s 569(1)).   **19-47**

Disapplication by other companies   Any public or private company may disapply the statutory scheme of pre-emption, either by way of a general disapplication or by way of a limited disapplication done with regard to a specified allotment. These provisions are complicated and reference should be made to their precise wording. Their application is linked to the authority to allot shares granted to the directors under CA 2006, s 551 (see **19-33**).   **19-48**

A general disapplication   Where the directors of a company have a general authority to allot shares under CA 2006, s 551, they may be given power by the articles, or by a special resolution of the company, to allot ordinary shares pursuant to that authority as if the requirement for a rights issue does not apply, or as if it applies to the allotment with such modifications as the directors may determine (s 570(1)).   **19-49**

---

[71] See *Siemens AG v Nold: Case C-42/95* [1997] 1 BCLC 291. As to when a share is deemed paid up in cash or allotted for cash, see CA 2006, s 583.

[72] The pre-emption rights may be excluded generally or in relation to allotments of a particular description: CA 2006, s 567(2); and see s 567(3).

[73] CA 2006, s 568(2), (3).   [74] I.e. under CA 2006, ss 570, 571 or 573.

19-50   *A specific disapplication*   Where the directors of a company have an authority to allot shares under CA 2006, s 551 (whether generally or otherwise), the company may by special resolution resolve either that the rights requirement does not apply to a specified allotment of shares to be made pursuant to that authority, or that the rights requirement applies to the allotment with such modifications as may be specified in the resolution (s 571(1)). This special resolution must be recommended by the directors who must circulate to the shareholders a written statement setting out their reasons for making the recommendation, the amount to be paid to the company in respect of the shares to be allotted and the directors' justification of that amount.[75]

19-51   As the disapplication in each case is linked to the authority to allot shares granted to the directors under CA 2006, s 551, the disapplication ceases when that authority under s 551 is revoked or expires, but if the authority to allot is renewed, the disapplication can also be renewed by a special resolution.[76]

19-52   *Disapplication on sale of treasury shares*   As noted in **19-38**, the pre-emption requirement applies on a sale of treasury shares,[77] but this requirement can be the subject of a general or specific disapplication. The directors may be given power by the articles, or by a special resolution of the company, to sell treasury shares as if the requirement for a rights issue does not apply, or as if it applies to the sale with such modifications as the directors may determine (CA 2006, s 573(1)). Alternatively, the company may by special resolution resolve either that the rights requirement does not apply to a specified sale of treasury shares, or that that rights requirement applies to a specified sale with such modifications as may be specified in the resolution (s 573(4)).

Institutional investors and pre-emption rights

19-53   As noted at **19-36**, pre-emption rights are a protective device ensuring that existing shareholders cannot have their percentage holdings diluted without their having an opportunity to acquire additional shares. Pre-emption rights are also valuable commercially because existing shareholders get the benefit of any discount to market price so that the value of the company is transferred to them and not to outside investors. Pre-emption rights also ensure that long-term shareholders cannot suddenly find control of the company has passed to new investors. In the light of those factors, it is unsurprising that institutional investors (who are the most significant shareholders in listed public companies) see considerable value in the statutory requirement (reflecting the Second Directive) for rights issues.

19-54   Equally, the statute recognises that, on occasion, companies may wish to avoid the administrative burden of a rights issue (which can be cumbersome, costly and time-consuming to conduct) hence the provisions for exceptional cases and the ability to disapply the provisions on a more general basis.

---

[75] CA 2006, s 571(5)–(6); and see s 572 as to penalties for misleading, false or deceptive statements. Where the resolution is proposed as a written resolution, the statement must be supplied to every eligible member at or before the time at which the resolution is sent or submitted to him for signature; where the resolution is to be at a meeting, the statement must be circulated with the notice of meeting: s 571(7).

[76] CA 2006, ss 570(3), 571(3).   [77] CA 2006, s 560(2)(b).

In practice, the tension between the needs of the companies for flexibility and the   **19-55**
desire of the institutional shareholders to retain rights issues has been resolved
through voluntary guidelines on pre-emption drawn up in 1987 by the Pre-Emption
Group which is made up of representatives of listed companies, institutional investors
and intermediaries. The guidelines were reissued in 2006, and revised with minor
amendments in 2008, as a Statement of Principles. The Statement is intended to provide guidance on the factors to be taken into account by a company when considering
making a request to the shareholders for disapplying the pre-emption rights.[78]

The Statement of Principles relates to issues of equity securities for cash other than   **19-56**
on a pre-emptive basis by all UK companies which have a primary listing on the
Main Market of the London Stock Exchange.[79] The Statement reiterates that the
overarching principle remains that pre-emption rights are a cornerstone of company law and protect shareholders against inappropriate dilution of their investments
but it is also accepted that a degree of flexibility is appropriate in circumstances where
new issues of shares on a non-pre-emptive basis would be in the interests of companies and their owners.[80] Disapplication is considered a routine matter (and therefore shareholders would expect to agree) where the company seeks authority to issue
shares on a non-rights basis up to no more than 5% of the company's ordinary share
capital in any one year and no more than 7.5% of the company's ordinary capital in
any rolling three-year period. Any discount at which ordinary shares are issued for
cash other than to existing shareholders is of major concern so companies should
restrict the discount to a maximum of 5% of the immediately preceding market price.
Disapplication requests which exceed these percentage levels are not ruled out but
would be considered by shareholders in the light of the business case made by the company on a case-by-case basis.[81]

This re-consideration in 2006 of the original guidelines by the Pre-Emption Group   **19-57**
was a result of concerns that the insistence on pre-emption rights limits the flexibility
of smaller listed companies and makes it more complicated and expensive for such
companies to raise capital, particularly in developing sectors such as biotechnology.[82]
Against that background, the DTI commissioned a report from an advisory group
headed by Paul Myners to examine these issues.[83] The Myners Report generally called
for greater flexibility and dialogue between companies and shareholders on these
matters, but did not recommend wholesale changes to the operation of the statutory
scheme. Likewise, the Company Law Review did not recommend any significant

---

[78] See 'Disapplying Pre-emption Rights, A Statement of Principles', available at www.pre-emptiongroup.
org.uk. The Statement is supported by the Association of British Insurers, the National Association of
Pension Funds and the Investment Managers Association representing owners and investment managers.
The Pre-emption Group intends to report annually on how the Statement is being applied by companies.

[79] Companies on AIM (see **1-62**) are encouraged to apply the Statement of Principles but it is recognised
that greater flexibility is likely to be justified in such companies, see Statement of Principles, para 5.

[80] Statement of Principles, paras 1 and 2.   [81] Statement of Principles, paras 14–15.

[82] See HM Treasury, *Smaller Quoted Companies—a Report to the Paymaster General* (November 1998)
paras 46–7.

[83] DTI, *Pre-emption rights: Final Report* URN 05/679 (February 2005).

changes to the general scheme. In any event, for public companies, pre-emption is a requirement under the Second EC Directive, art 29, and, as discussed at **19-3**, the European Commission has no plans for reform of the Second Directive. Indeed, even though the UK advocated the repeal of the Second Directive, it acknowledged that the requirements on pre-emption are sufficiently important that they would have to be retained, even if relocated to another Directive such as the Shareholders Rights Directive.[84] Institutional investors, for their part, have indicated their determination that pre-emption rights should stay.[85]

19-58   The position on pre-emption rights came under domestic review in 2008 as companies, especially financial institutions, struggled to raise capital in the face of significant losses, the credit crunch and an economy in recession.[86] Criticism centred in part on the length of the process which can take anything from 39 days to two months or more.[87] The company needs to seek shareholder approval for an allotment, a general meeting must be called, extensive documentation produced and then the offer period must remain open for at least 21 days. In volatile markets, the period can see even a deeply discounted offer price come under pressure with the result that shareholders may shun the offer and the shares must be taken by underwriters and sub-underwriters which ultimately increases the cost of capital.[88] A joint Treasury and FSA review group was set up in response and it reported in November 2008.[89] The report identified various short-term measures which address the immediate concerns while also noting matters for ongoing consideration such as the possibility of adapting for UK purposes methods used to accelerate capital raising in other jurisdictions. The

---

[84] See UK Response to Commission Communication on a Simplified Business Environment, para 11, available on the Commission website at http://circa.europa.eu/Public/irc/markt/markt_consultations/library?l=/company_law/simplifying_environment/department_regulatory/_EN_1.0_&a=d. The Response describes pre-emption rights as a fundamental element of market confidence and as contributing to and enhancing shareholder engagement and good corporate governance (presumably because of the need for dialogue between investors and companies as stressed by the Pre-Emption Group Statement of Principles).

[85] See 'UK investors dig in over pre-emption rights' *Financial Times*, 22 October 2007; 'UK should advocate a hard line on pre-emption' *Financial Times*, 23 October 2007.

[86] The most notable example of the difficulties was the disastrous HBOS rights issue when only 8.3% of shareholders took up the shares leaving the rest with the underwriters: see 'HBOS shares fall after rights issue flop', *Financial Times*, 21 July 2008. Three months later HBOS was forced into a rescue merger with Lloyds TSB: see *Financial Times*, 18 September 2008.

[87] Wider concerns related to the role of hedge funds as underwriters, short selling of shares in companies undertaking rights issues, leaks to the market ahead of the announcement of a rights issue and other issues of market abuse. The FSA attempted to address some of the concerns by additional disclosure requirements in respect of significant short positions in companies undertaking rights issues: see the Code of Market Conduct, MAR 1.9.2A.

[88] Underwriting involves the use of professional intermediaries (such as investment banks and institutional investors) which undertake, in return for a fee, to subscribe or procure subscriptions for shares to the extent that the public or other persons do not subscribe for them.

[89] See HM Treasury, *A Report to the Chancellor of the Exchequer by the Rights Issue Review Group* (November 2008). This review was preceded by a discussion paper by the Association of British Insurers which reaffirmed the importance of pre-emption rights: see ABI, 'Rights Issues and Capital Raising—An ABI Discussion Paper' (July 2008). The Pre-Emption Group for its part had stressed that the difficulties companies have faced have raised issues of process rather than principle: see Press Release by the Pre-Emption Group, Press Notice 2, 7 July 2008.

immediate focus is on shortening the rights issue period and the FSA and BERR are to consult on reducing the rights issue subscription period from 21 to 14 days. The report also invited the Association of British Insurers (ABI) to review its guidance on allotments so as to allow companies greater flexibility and in particular to enable them to announce and launch a rights issue without having to call a general meeting to seek authority to allot and the ABI has already reissued its guidance in this respect.[90]

Bonus issues

A bonus issue of shares occurs where a company capitalises profits or revenue reserves or some other permissible fund[91] and applies the proceeds in paying up bonus shares which go to existing members in proportion to their entitlement to dividend, so providing the shareholders with additional fully paid shares in the company.[92] It is essentially an accounting exercise as the company's reserves are reduced but its share capital fund is increased. **19-59**

From the point of view of the shareholders, calling the issue a bonus issue is somewhat misleading for the company is still worth the same as before the bonus issue and the total value of their shareholding has not altered.[93] All that has happened is that each shareholder holds more shares but each share is worth less than before. **19-60**

One advantage so far as the company and shareholders are concerned is that a bonus issue is not a distribution[94] for the purposes of the distribution rules in CA 2006, Part 23 so funds which would not be available for distribution as dividends may be used for this purpose. Distributions are discussed in Chapter 20: see **20-75**. **19-61**

F Payment for shares

Having considered the requirements as to the issuing of shares, we turn now to the rules concerning payment for share capital and, by way of background, the reader is referred to the discussion of the doctrine of capital maintenance at the beginning of Chapter 20. **19-62**

---

[90] See above n 61, FSA, CP09/4; see also LR 9.5.6 reducing the rights issue period to 10 business days.

[91] The company may use its share premium account (CA 2006, s 610(3)), redenomination reserve (s 628(2)) or capital redemption reserve (s 733(5)) to finance a fully paid bonus issue. See *Re Cleveland Trust plc* [1991] BCLC 424 where a bonus issue was declared void on the ground of common mistake when the directors and shareholders were mistaken as to the availability of profits which could be capitalised; also *EIC Services Ltd v Phipps* [2004] 2 BCLC 589, CA (bonus issue in breach of articles void).

[92] As this appears to be a case of the company allotting shares without receiving money or money's worth, it would seem to fall foul of CA 2006, s 582(1) but s 582(2)(a) provides that this requirement does not prevent the company from allotting bonus shares.

[93] Of course, it is not strictly accurate to say that there is no difference in value before and after a bonus issue, for the market may respond favourably to a bonus issue so the shares may gain a little in value but essentially the shareholder's position does not alter.   [94] CA 2006, s 829(2)(a).

Payment for shares in money or money's worth

19-63   A company cannot make a gratuitous allotment of its shares nor an allotment at a discount.[95] The allottee must pay in full at least the nominal value of the shares and will possibly pay a premium as well. The sum due may be paid up in money or money's worth including goodwill and know-how (CA 2006, s 582).[96]

19-64   An extended definition of an allotment for cash is set out in CA 2006, s 583 which provides that a share in a company is deemed paid up (as to its nominal value or any premium on it) in cash or allotted for cash if the consideration received for the allotment or payment up is a cash consideration. A cash consideration for these purposes means (s 583(3)):

    (a) cash received by the company;

    (b) a cheque received by the company in good faith which the directors have no reason for suspecting will not be paid;

    (c) a release of a liability of the company for a liquidated sum;

    (d) an undertaking to pay cash to the company at a future date;[97] or

    (e) payment by any other means giving rise to a present or future entitlement (of the company or person acting on the company's behalf) to payment, or credit equivalent to payment, in cash.[98]

19-65   Category (c) requires a little explanation. This provision reflects the decision in *Re Harmony and Montague Tin and Copper Mining Co, Spargo's Case*[99] which illustrates how an allotment which appears to be on a non-cash basis may in fact be regarded as being for cash. It is necessary to regard the transaction as being in two stages: first, an individual sells assets to the company and the company becomes indebted to him for a stated amount (a liquidated sum); secondly, the company allots fully paid shares to him and in return the company is released from the liability to pay the liquidated sum. In *Spargo's Case*, Sir W M James LJ explained that it is not necessary that the formality should be gone through of the money being handed over and taken back again. If the two demands are set off against each other (the demand

---

[95] *Re Wragg Ltd* [1897] 1 Ch 796; *Ooregum Gold Mining Co of India Ltd v Roper* [1892] AC 125; *Re Eddystone Marine Insurance Co* [1893] 3 Ch 9; CA 2006, s 580.

[96] Details of any non-cash consideration is given in the return of allotment to the registrar of companies: CA 2006, s 555; and The Companies (Shares and Share Capital) Regulations 2009, SI 2009/388, reg 14(c). Shares taken by a subscriber to the memorandum of a public company in pursuance of an undertaking of his in the memorandum, and any premium on the shares, must be paid up in cash: CA 2006, s 584.

[97] An assignment of a debt is not an undertaking to pay cash at a future date for these purposes, see *System Control plc v Munro Corporate plc* [1990] BCLC 659.

[98] Category (e) is intended to clarify uncertainty which had existed as to whether payments within a computerised share settlement system, such as CREST, are a cash consideration. These automated systems provide for assured payment obligations which are to be treated as equivalent to cash: see Explanatory Notes, *Companies Act 2006*, para 880. The Secretary of State has power to expand category (5) by statutory instrument: CA 2006, s 583(4).

[99] (1873) 8 Ch App 407.

for payment for the shares and the liability for a liquidated sum), the shares have been paid up in cash.[100]

The possible inconsistency between prohibiting the allotment of shares at a discount **19-66** (CA 2006, s 580(1)), but allowing payment in money's worth (s 582(1)) which may disguise an allotment at a discount, was noted by Lindley LJ in *Re Wragg Ltd*[101] who accepted that the difference between issuing shares at a discount and issuing them at a price put upon property or services by the vendor and agreed to by the company may not always be very apparent in practice. In the court's opinion, however, the two transactions were essentially different and a company is entitled to issue fully paid-up shares in return for a non-cash consideration provided it does so honestly and not colourably, and provided that it has not been so imposed upon as to be entitled to be relieved from its bargain.[102]

The question whether the consideration is colourable is one of fact in each case[103] and, **19-67** as Lord Watson noted in *Ooregum Gold Mining Co of India Ltd v Roper*,[104] 'so long as the company honestly regards the consideration given as fairly representing the nominal value of the shares in cash, its estimate ought not to be critically examined'.

It is only where the consideration is illusory or it is manifest on the face of the instru- **19-68** ment that the shares are issued at a discount that the court will be prepared to consider the adequacy of the consideration.[105] This judicial attitude is in keeping with the courts' traditional reluctance to interfere in business matters.

Payment rules applicable to public companies

The common law approach to non-cash consideration noted above is rather lax and **19-69** applied to public companies issuing shares for a non-cash consideration would not be acceptable in view of the general policy to regulate such companies more strictly in the public interest[106] nor would it meet the requirements of the Second Company Law Directive,[107] art 10 of which requires an independent valuation of any non-cash consideration for the issue of shares by a public company, though these provisions have been relaxed to a limited extent (see **19-76**). Hence the need for further controls on the consideration which may be accepted by public companies as payment for their shares.

---

[100] (1873) 8 Ch App 407 at 412.   [101] [1897] 1 Ch 796.

[102] Lindley LJ cautioned against being misled by talking of value: 'The value paid to the company is measured by the price at which the company agrees to buy what it thinks it worth its while to acquire. Whilst the transaction is unimpeached, this is the only value to be considered': [1897] 1 Ch 796 at 831. The consideration in this case for the allotment of the shares was the transfer of a business comprising land, stock, and goodwill.

[103] *Re Innes & Co Ltd* [1903] 2 Ch 254 at 262.   [104] [1892] AC 125 at 137.

[105] See *Re White Star Line Ltd* [1938] 1 Ch 458 (certificates, essentially credit notes, equal in nominal amount to the sum due on the shares were accepted which, to the knowledge of all the parties, were always worth less than the nominal value).

[106] It has already been noted that public companies must have a minimum allotted capital (CA 2006, ss 761, 763) and must call a general meeting in the event of a serious loss of capital (s 656).

[107] Directive 77/91/EEC, OJ L 26/1, 31.1.1977.

Valuation of non-cash consideration

19-70   A public company must not allot shares as fully or partly paid up (as to their nominal value or any premium on them) otherwise than in cash[108] unless:

(1) the consideration for the allotment has been independently valued;[109]

(2) the valuer's report has been made to the company during the six months immediately preceding the allotment of the shares; and

(3) a copy of the report has been sent to the proposed allottee.[110]

19-71   If a company allots shares in contravention of these requirements and either the allottee has not received the valuer's report, or there has been some other contravention of the requirements as to the independent valuation and report which the allottee knew or ought to have known amounted to a contravention, the allottee is liable to pay the company an amount equal to the aggregate of the nominal value of the shares and the whole of any premium or, if the case so requires, so much of that aggregate as is treated as paid up by the consideration with interest at the appropriate rate.[111]

19-72   A copy of the valuation report must be filed by the company with the registrar of companies at the same time as it files the return of allotment of those shares by the company.[112]

19-73   The valuation of the non-cash consideration and the report required thereon must be made by an independent person ('the valuer'), that is to say a person eligible to be the statutory auditor of the company and who meets the independence criteria set out in CA 2006, s 1151.[113]

19-74   The valuer's report must state:

(1) the nominal value of the shares to be wholly or partly paid for by the consideration in question;

(2) the amount of any premium payable on the shares;

---

[108] See CA 2006, s 583(3) (set out at **19-64**) as to when a share in a company is deemed paid up in cash or allotted for cash.

[109] Detailed rules as to the independent valuation and report are in CA 2006, ss 1150–1153. Any person who knowingly or recklessly makes a statement which is misleading, false or deceptive in a material particular in connection with the preparation of such report commits an offence: s 1153(2).

[110] CA 2006, s 593(1); bonus issues are not caught by these provisions: s 593(2). These requirements for independent valuation do not apply to an allotment of shares in connection with: (1) a share exchange for all or some of the shares in another company or of a particular class of shares in another company; or (2) a proposed merger of the company with another: ss 594–595.

[111] CA 1985, s 593(3). The effect is to create an immediate liability as if the allottee had agreed to take up the shares for cash: *Re Bradford Investments Ltd* [1991] BCLC 224 at 233. These penalties can be onerous, see *Re Ossory Estates plc* [1988] BCLC 213; *Re Bradford Investments plc (No 2)* [1991] BCLC 688, but may be mitigated by the court's powers under CA 2006, s 606 to give relief: see below.

[112] CA 2006, s 597. A return of allotment is required within one month of the allotment: s 555.

[113] CA 2006, s 1150. To be independent, the person must not be an officer or employee of the company or of an associate or a partner or employee of such a person. The company's existing auditor is not included in the categories of excluded persons and so may act as the valuer for these purposes: s 1151. The valuer may also delegate the valuation to another person: s 1150(2).

(3) the description of the consideration, the method used to value it and the date of the valuation;

(4) the extent to which the nominal value of the shares and any premium are to be treated as paid up by the consideration or in cash (CA 2006, s 596(2)).

The report must also state that: **19-75**

(1) the method of valuation (and any delegation of responsibility) was reasonable in all the circumstances;

(2) it appears to the valuer that there has been no material change in the value of the consideration since the valuation; and

(3) on the basis of the valuation, the value of the consideration (together with any cash by which the nominal value of the shares or any premium payable on them is to be paid up) is not less than so much of the aggregate of the nominal value and the whole of any such premium as is treated as paid up by the consideration and any such cash (CA 2006, s 596(3)).

The Second Directive has been amended to allow public companies to allot shares   **19-76** for a non-cash consideration without the need to go through these formalities for independent valuation in cases where there is some other method of valuing the asset in question.[114] For example, where the assets are financial instruments traded on a regulated market, the valuation can be taken to be the average market valuation during the relevant period; or where an asset has already been the subject of a fair valuation by an independent expert in the previous six months; or the fair value can be determined from the statutory accounts, duly audited. In each case, shareholders holding at least 5% of the company's issued capital may demand a valuation by an independent expert. To date no steps have been taken by the UK to adopt these optional changes and it may be that the UK will not implement them.

Transfers to public company of non-cash assets

Further controls are imposed on agreements for: **19-77**

(1) any transfer of non-cash assets[115] to the company (or another) by a subscriber to the memorandum of association of a public company incorporated as such within two years from the date of the company being issued with a trading certificate[116] (CA 2006, s 598);

(2) any such transfers by a member of a private company within two years of the company re-registering as a public company (s 603);

(3) for a consideration equal in value to 10% or more of the company's issued share capital[117] at that time.

[114] Directive 2006/68/EC amending Directive 77/91/EEC, OJ L 264/32, 25.9.2006.

[115] 'Non-cash asset' is defined in CA 2006, s 1163 as meaning any property or interest in property other than cash; and see s 1163(2) as to the transfer of a non-cash asset.

[116] I.e. a certificate of entitlement to do business required by CA 2006, s 761: see discussion at **19-11**. In most cases, this will mean within two years of incorporation.

[117] See definition in CA 2006, s 546.

19-78   In practice, transactions within (1) are unusual and the statutory provisions apply mainly to transactions within (2). Not all agreements within these provisions (ss 598, 603) will involve an allotment of shares, but as many do, it is appropriate to consider these matters here.

19-79   The company must not enter into the agreements outlined above in **19-77** unless the following conditions are met:

(1) the consideration to be received by the company,[118] and any consideration other than cash to be given by the company, must be independently valued by a valuer in the same way[119] as outlined above with respect to CA 2006, s 596 (shares allotted for a non-cash consideration) and the valuer's report must be made to the company during the six months immediately preceding the date of the agreement;[120]

(2) the terms of the agreement must be approved by an ordinary resolution of the company;[121] and

(3) copies of the valuer's report must be circulated to the members, where a written resolution is used, at or before the time when the resolution was submitted to the members, and, if a meeting is held, the report must be circulated no later than the date on which notice of the meeting is given and the report must be circulated to the other party to the agreement if not then a member of the company.[122]

19-80   These requirements do not apply where it is part of the company's ordinary business to acquire such assets as are to be transferred and the agreement is entered into in the ordinary course of business of that company, a potentially wide category (CA 2006, 598(4)).[123]

19-81   In the event of contravention of these valuation requirements, the company is enitled to recover from the other party any consideration given by it under the agreement, or an amount equal to the value of the consideration at the time of the agreement; and the agreement, so far as not carried out, is void.[124]

19-82   There is clearly a degree of overlap between the requirement for a non-cash consideration to be valued before an allotment of shares (CA 2006, s 593), discussed at **19-70**, and these provisions governing the transfer to a public company of non-cash assets in the initial period (ss 598–603), but it is important to appreciate the different scope of the provisions.

19-83   Section 593 applies whenever a public company accepts a non-cash consideration from anyone as consideration for an allotment of shares. Section 598 applies to any

---

[118] See CA 2006, ss 599(2), 603.   [119] See CA 2006, ss 600, 603.

[120] CA 2006, ss 599(1)(b), 603. The contents of the report are set out in s 600 and are essentially the same as those required under s 596, outlined above at **19-74** et seq.   [121] CA 2006, ss 601, 603.

[122] CA 2006, ss 599(1), 601(3), 603. Copies of the valuer's report and the resolution must be delivered to the registrar of companies within 15 days of passing the resolution: ss 602, 603.

[123] Nor do they apply to agreements entered into as a result of a court order or under court control: CA 2006, s 598(5).   [124] CA 2006, s 604(1), (2).

transfer of a non-cash asset from a subscriber or member to the company whether the consideration for the transfer is an allotment of shares or something else. There are also different exceptions to each provision.

It is possible for the provisions to be applicable in the same instance since the provi-   **19-84**
sions are not mutually exclusive. Any allotment of shares for a non-cash consideration to a subscriber or member within the two-year period is potentially within CA 2006, s 593 and ss 598–603 which is not unduly burdensome as the requirements for an independent valuation and report are similar. The major difference is that ss 598–603 require the relevant agreements to be approved by an ordinary resolution. On the other hand, ss 598–603 do not apply where it is part of the company's ordinary business to acquire such assets as are to be transferred and the agreement is entered into in the ordinary course of that business.[125] The type of transaction which is within ss 598–603 but not within s 593 is where the transaction does not involve an allotment of shares but is simply a transfer of non-cash assets by a subscriber or member within the relevant time-frame to a public company or a company re-registered as a public company.

Undertakings to do work or perform services

A public company must not accept at any time, in payment up of its shares or any   **19-85**
premium on them, an undertaking given by any person that he or another should do work or perform services for the company or any other person (CA 2006, s 585(1)). If a public company accepts such an undertaking, the holder of the shares when they or the premium are treated as paid up (in whole or in part) by the undertaking is liable to pay the company in respect of those shares an amount equal to their nominal value, together with the whole of any premium or, if the case so requires, such proportion of that amount as is treated as paid up by the undertaking, together with interest (s 585(2)). In the event of a contravention, the company and any officer in default is liable on conviction to a fine (s 590). Despite any contravention, any undertaking given by any person to do work or perform services or to do any other thing remains enforceable by the company.[126]

Restriction on long-term undertakings

A public company must not allot shares as fully or partly paid (as to their nominal   **19-86**
value or any premium on them) otherwise than in cash if the consideration for the allotment is or includes an undertaking which is to be, or may be, performed more than five years after the date of the allotment.[127] In the event of breach, the allottee is liable to pay the company an amount equal to the aggregate of the nominal value and the whole of any premium due.[128]

---

[125] CA 2006, ss 598(4), 603.   [126] CA 2006, s 591, subject to s 589.
[127] CA 2006, s 587. The provision also applies to a contract which did not originally contravene this provision but is subsequently varied and results in a contravention. In such cases, the variation is void. Equally caught is the situation where an undertaking was to have been performed within five years but was not: s 587(3) and (4).   [128] CA 2006, s 587(2).

Consequences of breach of the payment rules

19-87   The consequences of breach of any of the statutory payment and valuation rules are relatively uniform.

19-88   As a general rule, the allottee remains liable to pay an amount equal to the nominal amount and any premium due together with interest.[129] Subsequent holders are jointly and severally liable unless they are purchasers for value and did not have actual notice of the contravention or they took from a holder who was not himself liable under these provisions.[130]

19-89   These penalties can be quite onerous. In *Re Ossory Estates plc*[131] property was sold to a company and the vendor received as part of the consideration 8m shares in the company. As this was an allotment of shares for a non-cash consideration, an independent valuation and report was required. No such report was ever made with the result that the allottee, despite having transferred his property to the company, was liable to pay the company £1.76m as the price of the shares. Not surprisingly, this was described by Harman J as a somewhat startling conclusion.[132]

19-90   It is possible for a person so liable to make an application to the court to be exempted in whole or in part from the liability (CA 2006, ss 589(1), 606(1)). If such liability arises in relation to payment in respect of any shares, the court may exempt the applicant from the liability only if and to the extent that it appears to the court just and equitable to do so having regard to the matters mentioned below (CA 2006, ss 589(3), 606(2)). The matters to be taken into account by the court are:

(1)   whether the applicant has paid, or is liable to pay, any amount in respect of any other liability arising in relation to those shares under any of the relevant provisions, or of any liability arising by virtue of any undertaking given in or in connection with payment for those shares;

(2)   whether any person other than the applicant has paid or is likely to pay (whether in pursuance of an order of the court or otherwise) any such amount; and

(3)   whether the applicant or any other person has performed, in whole or in part, or is likely so to perform any such undertaking, or has done or is likely to do any other thing in payment or part payment for the shares.[133]

19-91   In determining whether it should exempt the applicant in whole or in part from any liability, the court must have regard to the following overriding principle,[134] namely

---

[129] The effect is to create an immediate liability as if the allottee had agreed to take up the shares for cash: see *Re Bradford Instruments plc* [1991] BCLC 224 at 233.

[130] CA 2006, ss 588(1), (2), 605(3).   [131] [1988] BCLC 213.   [132] [1988] BCLC 213 at 214.

[133] CA 2006, s 589(3). See *Re Bradford Investments plc (No 2)* [1991] BCLC 688 at 693 where Hoffmann J thought that, in the light of what is now CA 2006, s 589(5) (see **19-91**), these matters are not intended to be an exhaustive statement of the matters to which the court should or may have regard.

[134] See *Re Bradford Investments plc (No 2)* [1991] BCLC 688 at 694 where Hoffmann J thought that the designation 'overriding principle' did not oblige the court to refuse relief unless the company had received at least the nominal value of the allotted shares and any premium: had that been the intention, the requirement would have been framed as a rule.

that a company which has allotted shares should receive money or money's worth at least equal in value to the aggregate of the nominal value of those shares and the whole of any premium or, if the case so requires, so much of that aggregate as is treated as paid up (CA 2006, ss 589(5), 606(4)).

In *Re Ossory Estates plc*,[135] noted at **19-89**, relief was granted as the company had sold some of the property transferred to it in consideration for the allotment at a substantial profit and had undoubtedly received at least money or money's worth equal in value, and probably exceeding, the aggregate of the nominal value of the shares and any premium. It was just and equitable that the allottee should be relieved from any further liability.   **19-92**

This outcome can be contrasted with that in *System Control plc v Munro Corporate plc*[136] where the court said there was no prospect of relief being granted when there was absolutely no evidence that the company had received the minimum amount; likewise in *Re Bradford Investments plc (No 2)*[137] where the applicants failed to discharge the burden of showing that the company had received value for its shares.   **19-93**

Where a person is liable under CA 2006, s 604(2) to a company as a result of the transfer to a public company of a non-cash asset in the initial period,[138] the court may, on application, exempt him in whole or in part from that liability if and to the extent that it appears to the court just and equitable to do so having regard to any benefit accruing to the company by virtue of anything done by him towards the carrying out of the agreement for transfer (CA 2006, s 606(6)).   **19-94**

In addition to the civil consequences, where there is a breach of these provisions, the company and officers in default are also guilty of an offence and liable to a fine.[139] Directors may also be in breach of duty, for example the duty to exercise their powers for a proper purpose (CA 2006, s 171(b)) and to promote the success of the company (s 172) and liable to make good any damage suffered by the company as a result of these contraventions.[140]   **19-95**

G Capital raising

Introduction

The basic function of companies is to provide a vehicle for entrepreneurial activity. Large-scale entrepreneurial activity may require amounts of capital which can only be provided by inviting outside investors to pool their resources and invest in an enterprise over which they may have relatively little control. To persuade such   **19-96**

---

[135] [1988] BCLC 213.   [136] [1990] BCLC 659.   [137] [1991] BCLC 688.
[138] The restrictions on such transfers were discussed at **19-77** and are contained in CA 2006, ss 598, 603.
[139] CA 2006, ss 590, 607.   [140] *Hirsche v Sims* [1894] AC 654.

investors to come forward two incentives are needed. One is limited liability and that is provided by the companies legislation.[141] The other is an active stock market to provide a means by which investors can realise their investment. Without such a market investors will require a higher return on their investment to compensate for the lack of liquidity. The existence of a market for shares thus not only makes it possible for companies to raise external funding but makes it cheaper for them to do so as well. A stock market meets these needs of the company and the investors by providing a primary market through which the company can offer its shares to the public and a secondary market where investors can trade in those shares. Admission to a market offers the company the ability to raise capital from investors and, for the existing owners, it is an opportunity to realise their investment in the business and to sell out to a new generation of owners. Once admitted to trading, the company may use the stock market to raise further capital in all manner of ways. It may make further public offers of its shares[142] from time to time and, with a broader shareholder base, it may find that a rights issue (i.e. the offer of new shares to existing shareholders in proportion to their existing holdings: see **19-36**) is an appropriate way of raising additional capital. As well as the ability to issue shares to investors to raise capital, traded companies commonly offer their shares as consideration for a takeover or in consideration for the acquisition of an asset where the shares are offered to the target company's shareholders or to the vendors of the asset (and in some instances immediately resold on their behalf). These offers are described as acquisition or merger issues or vendor consideration issues. This ability of companies to fund acquisitions and mergers by offering shares instead of cash is one of the main advantages of being a traded company and, as we discuss below, all of these advantages are applicable only to a public company, for a private company is prohibited from offering its shares to the public (CA 2006, s 755).

19-97   In terms of raising capital, the choice typically lies between a public offer (often referred to as an IPO, initial public offer) or a placing, with IPOs being restricted by cost to the larger companies looking to raise significant sums of money while placings are typically used to raise more modest sums. A placing allows the securities to be marketed to specified persons or clients of the sponsor or any securities house assisting in the placing.[143] Where the company itself offers to the public shares not yet in issue or allotted, this is known as an offer for subscription[144] and persons who acquire the shares directly from the company are known as subscribers. Where the offer of

---

[141] As to the importance of limited liability to investors, see Easterbrook and Fischel, *The Economic Structure of Corporate Law* (1991), Ch 2; Halpern, Trebilcock and Turnbull, 'An Economic Analysis of Limited Liability in Corporation Law' (1980) 30 Univ of Toronto Law Jo 117.

[142] It is also possible to issue debt securities, typically corporate bonds, to raise loan capital. For large companies, debt securities are a much more important source of funding than equity securities (shares). For example, for the year to December 2008, companies raised £54bn in equity issues, but £433bn in Eurobond issues: see London Stock Exchange, *Main Market, Market Statistics*, Market Summary Table (December 2008). These monthly statistics produced by the London Stock Exchange are available at www.londonstockexchange.com/en-gb/about/statistics/factsheets/mmfs.htm.

[143] Listing Rules, App 1.1. Relevant Definitions, see 'placing'.

[144] Listing Rules, App 1.1. Relevant Definitions, see 'offer for subscription'.

shares to the public is not by the company itself, but by a third party holding shares already in issue or allotted (such as an investment bank), it is called an offer for sale and persons who acquire the shares are known as purchasers.[145]

Private companies and public offers

A private company is prohibited from offering to the public any securities (i.e. shares or debentures) of the company (CA 2006, s 755(1), (5)).[146] A company proposing to contravene this prohibition can be restrained by court order (s 757)[147] and if the contravention has already occurred, on an application being made, the court must require the company to re-register as a public company, save where it is impracticable or undesirable to so order (s 758(2)).[148] If re-registration is not an option, the court may still make a remedial order[149] or a winding-up order or both (s 758(3)).[150] A breach of the prohibition does not affect the validity of any allotment or sale of any securities (s 760).

19-98

An offer is not to be regarded as an offer to the public if it can properly be regarded, in all the circumstances:

19-99

(1) as not being calculated to result, directly or indirectly, in the shares or debentures becoming available to persons other than those receiving the offer; or

(2) as being a private concern of the person receiving and making it (s 756(3)).

Furthermore, an offer is presumed to be of a private concern of the person making and receiving it if the company offers the shares to its existing members, employees and their families, or an existing debenture holder, or a trustee of a trust where the principal beneficiary of the trust is within these categories, or if the offer is an offer under an employees' share scheme;[151] and, if the offer is renounceable, it is renounceable only to these restricted groups (s 756(4), (5)). The intention with these exceptions is to ensure that a private company may still raise equity capital, but from a limited circle of people.

19-100

This prohibition on the offer of shares to the public is not always clearly understood by private companies and they may offer their shares to a wider audience than that

19-101

---

[145] Listing Rules, App 1.1. Relevant Definitions, see 'offer for sale'.

[146] The prohibition extends to allotments to third parties with a view to the securities being offered to the public, see CA 2006, s 755(2) and note the presumption that this is the case in certain circumstances.

[147] An application can be made by any member, creditor or the Secretary of State and note the unusual requirement that an order must be made by the court where, in unfairly prejudicial proceedings under CA 2006, Part 30 (see s 994), it appears to the court that the company is proposing to act in contravention of this prohibition on public offers by private companies: s 757(1).

[148] See CA 2006, s 758(4) for the categories of persons who can apply for an order in this case.

[149] Defined in CA 2006, s 759 as an order for the purpose of putting a person affected by the contravention in the position he would have been in had there not been the contravention.

[150] This power is discretionary because it may be that the prohibition has been breached but the company has not allotted the shares or the company has withdrawn the offer and undertaken not to make a further offer so a remedial order is unnecessary: see Explanatory Notes to the Companies Act 2006, para 1061.

[151] Defined CA 2006, s 1166.

specified above which has a number of consequences. First, it is a breach of the prohibition in CA 2006, s 755, as discussed above. Secondly, it is unlawful for a company to offer transferable securities to the public without first publishing an approved prospectus (Financial Services and Markets Act 2000 (FSMA 2000), s 85): see **19-109**. Depending on the circumstances, there may also be a breach of the rules governing financial promotion.[152] Each of these provisions apply to different categories of offers and different types of securities and compliance with one set of requirements does not necessarily mean compliance with the others, so private companies need to be alert to the various consequences if they make an offer to the public; but the starting point of their concerns should be compliance with CA 2006, s 755. This prohibition on public offers in s 755 restates the prohibition in CA 1985, s 81, but it removes the criminal sanction which the 1985 Act imposed.

19-102   The prohibition on public offers by private companies is not an arbitrary barrier, as the CA 2006 makes clear,[153] rather it is the precise point at which the public interest intrudes. Corporate self-interest in raising capital meets the public interest in the protection of investors. A company which wishes to offer shares to the public must submit to the greater regulation imposed on public companies in the interests of investors by the CA 2006 and by the Financial Services Authority (FSA) acting under the FSMA 2000. The mischief at which CA 2006, s 755 is aimed is companies making offers to the public without complying with the range of regulatory requirements (in respect of company accounts and disclosure, capital and corporate governance requirements) imposed on public companies in the interests of investor protection—hence the leeway allowed to private companies which are technically in breach of s 755 but which are in the process of re-registering and do so re-register (s 755(3)). The presumption in s 758 is therefore that private companies in breach of the prohibition on public offers should be made to re-register as public companies and so be subject to the appropriate level of regulation.

Publicly traded companies

19-103   Being a public company is not synonymous with being listed on a stock market nor are all markets for listed securities. As noted in Chapter 1, technology allows markets to operate in a much more segmented way than previously which gives rise to a somewhat more complex picture as exchanges attempt to meet the demands of investors and issuers (companies looking to raise equity or loan capital): see **1-62**. The result is that

---

[152] Financial promotion is governed by FSMA 2000, s 21 and The Financial Services and Markets Act 2000 (Financial Promotion) Order 2005, SI 2005/1529, as amended. Extensive guidance on the application of s 21 is found in the FSA *Perimeter Guidance Manual*, PERG 8, Financial Promotion. Essentially, it is a criminal offence for persons other than authorised persons, in the course of business, to communicate an invitation or inducement to engage in investment activity. See *Re UK-Euro Group plc* [2007] 1 BCLC 812 (compulsory winding up on public interest grounds when company raised its share capital in clear breach of FSMA 2000, s 21).

[153] The CA 2006, s 4(4) identifies two major differences between private and public companies, namely the requirement for a minimum share capital (s 761: see **19-10**) and this prohibition on public offers by a private company (s 755).

exchanges are no longer single-tier entities for listed companies but instead offer a variety of markets with differing requirements. This development is driven to some extent by regulatory pressures which have meant a greater focus on regulated markets rather than on listing as such.[154] A regulated market essentially means that UK companies traded on them are subject to all the requirements of the EU Directives on disclosure and transparency etc[155] as admission to trading on a regulated market is the standard threshold for application of the EU Directives.[156] To accommodate the desire of issuers to trade their securities in a less regulated environment, exchanges now often provide an exchange regulated market which allows for a lesser degree of regulation though still subject to the general oversight of the FSA.[157] The questions for public companies therefore are: (1) whether they wish to offer their shares to the public at all (they are not required to do so); (2) whether they wish also to be admitted to trading (which usually goes hand in hand with a desire to offer their shares to the public since the public will only be willing to buy the shares if they can then trade them); and (3) whether they wish to trade through a regulated market or an exchange regulated market. The regulatory requirements of these markets are beyond the scope of this work;[158] here it suffices to note briefly the main ways in which public companies use the markets. The common position is that larger established companies look for a listing on the Main Market (a regulated market) run by the London Stock Exchange (LSE) while newer, smaller, less established companies tend to look to be admitted to trading on the Alternative Investment Market (AIM, an exchange regulated market) also run by the LSE. Competition to the LSE is emerging; for example, Plus Markets plc gained regulated market status for its Plus-listed market in 2007, but for the moment the LSE maintains its dominant position.

Securities are listed when they are admitted to the Official List maintained by the **19-104** FSA which is the competent authority for these purposes and is known as the UK Listing Authority (UKLA) in this context (FSMA 2000, s 74(1)).[159] Securities admitted

[154] See FSA Discussion Paper 08/1, *A review of the Structure of the Listing Regime* (January 2008) for a valuable overview of the role of listing and FSA, CP08/21, feedback on DP 08/1.

[155] A special concern had been the impact of the Prospectus Directive (Directive 2003/71/EC on the prospectus to be published when securities are offered to the public or admitted to trading and amending Directive 2001/34/EC, OJ L 345, 31.12.2003, p 64); and the Transparency Directive (Directive 2004/109/EC on the harmonisation of transparency requirements in relation to information about issuers whose securities are admitted to trading on a regulated market: OJ L 390, 31.12.2004, p. 38).

[156] The FSA maintains the register of regulated markets required by the art 47 of the Markets in Financial Instruments Directive (2004/39/EC) (Mifid). The full list is available at http://www.fsa.gov.uk/register/exchanges.do. The most relevant regulated markets for our purposes are the London Stock Exchange and the PLUS-listed market run by PLUS Markets plc.

[157] An example of regulatory flight is the development of the Professional Securities Market which was set up in 2005 and is run by the London Stock Exchange as an exchange regulated market for listed debt securities. This market allows securities to be listed (so meeting the needs of investors who are restricted to investing in listed securities) but, as the market is not a regulated market, the issuers are not subject to the requirements of the Prospectus Directive or the Transparency Directive which are seen as burdensome for the type of debt securities listed on this market.

[158] See generally Hudson, *Securities Law* (2008); Ferran, *Principles of Corporate Finance Law* (2008).

[159] The requirements for admission to listing are set out in FSA, Listing Rules 2 and include that the securities must be admitted to trading on a recognised investment exchange and they must be freely transferable

to the Official List must also be admitted to trading on a recognised investment exchange for listed securities[160] which (at the time of writing) means on the Main Market of the London Stock Exchange or, since 2007, on the listed segment of the Plus Markets. As mentioned, these markets are regulated markets for the purposes of EU Directives and listed UK companies traded on them are subject, in addition to the CA 2006 and the FSMA 2000, to the Listing Rules drawn up by the FSA. The Listing Rules contain a number of continuing obligations which a listed company is required to observe[161] such as compliance with the disclosure and transparency rules imposed by the Transparency Directive and the Model Code on dealings in the company's securities by directors and other persons with managerial responsibilities.[162] In the event of any breach of any provision of the Listing Rules, UKLA can impose a penalty of such amount as it considers appropriate or it may publish a statement of censure with respect to the issuer and any director knowingly concerned in the contravention.[163]

19-105   It is also possible for a company to be unlisted (i.e. its securities are not admitted to the Official List maintained by UKLA) but to be admitted to trading on an exchange regulated market, as is the case with AIM. Companies trading on AIM are subject to a simpler regime and with more relaxed criteria for entry to the market. Companies are not required to have reached a certain size, or to have a defined percentage of shares in public hands, or to provide a lengthy trading history.[164] All companies must produce an admission document making certain disclosures about such matters as their directors' backgrounds, their promoters, and business activities.[165] Once admitted to AIM, a company has to accept certain ongoing requirements mainly imposing disclosure requirements with respect to financial matters and company transactions and changes in the business and the management structures.[166]

19-106   There were 10,500 public companies on the register of companies as at 31 March 2008.[167] There were 1,098 UK listed companies (as of September 2008) so approximately 10% of public companies are listed companies[168] while 90% are unlisted. There were

with an expected market value of at least £700,000. For a listing of equity securities, additional requirements are set out in LR 6 including a requirement of a three-year trading record with published audited accounts over that period; an independent auditor; a sufficient number (usually at least 25%) of the shares being listed must be distributed to the public; and the securities must be capable of electronic settlement.

[160] Listing Rules, 2.2.3.   [161] See Listing Rules, 9.1.1R.

[162] See Listing Rules, 9.2.5G; 9.2.7R; 9.2.8R. Listed companies with a primary listing of equity securities must also observe the Listing Principles set out in LR 7.2 which include, for example, a requirement for a listed company to take reasonable steps to enable its directors to understand their responsibilities and obligations as directors and that the company must act with integrity towards holders and potential holders of its listed equity securities.

[163] FSMA 2000, s 91.

[164] The company must be judged to be appropriate to join AIM by a nominated adviser (generally known as a nomad) who must be on a register of nomads maintained by the London Stock Exchange. The company must retain a nomad at all times and the nomad is responsible for guiding and helping the company to comply with the market rules: AIM Rules, r 1.

[165] AIM Rules, r 3 and Sch 1.   [166] AIM Rules, rr 10–36.

[167] See Companies House, *Statistical Tables on Companies Registration Activities 2007–08*, Table A2. These statistical tables are available on the Companies House website: www.companieshouse.gov.

[168] Monthly statistics on listed companies can be obtained from the London Stock Exchange website: see www.londonstockexchnage.com. Another term commonly used as synonymous with listed company is

1,608 UK companies trading on AIM (as of September 2008) so these are unlisted public companies trading on an exchange regulated market. The result is that more companies now trade on AIM than on the Main Market of the Stock Exchange (though of course the companies on the Main Market are much larger in terms of economic size), a result in part of the flight in recent years from regulation and from the high costs of listing. The statistics also show that more than 70% of public companies are not traded on any market. For those businesses, being a public company is about status and credibility with suppliers and customers rather than any need or desire to raise share or loan capital.

Public offers of securities

Much of the law relating to securities regulation generally and including public offers of shares derives from EU Directives which shape the domestic legislation on these matters.[169] The objectives with respect to EU securities regulation (as broadly reflected in the preambles to the various Directives) would include: **19-107**

- to establish an equivalent level of securities disclosure and investor protection throughout the EU;

- to contribute to the correct functioning and development of securities markets and to the maintenance of confidence in those markets;

- to facilitate cross-border listings and offers of shares in order to promote greater inter-penetration of national securities markets with a view to ensuring a genuine EU capital market;

- to prevent forum shopping by companies seeking jurisdictions within the EU with the lowest regulatory requirements.

The key Directive in the context of public offers is the Prospectus Directive[170] which was adopted in 2003 and came into force on 1 July 2005. It was implemented here by amendments to FSMA 2000, Part VI, discussed below, effected by the Prospectus Regulations 2005, SI 2005/1433, which allow for the core rules governing content and   **19-108**

'quoted company' but the term 'quoted company' has a precise meaning in the CA 2006 where it is used in the context of certain disclosure requirements, for example, with regard to website publication of poll results (CA 2006, s 341); the directors' remuneration report (s 420); website publication of accounts (s 430); and the right of members to require publication of audit concerns on the website (s 527). This category of 'quoted company' is broader than that of listed company and is defined in s 385 as encompassing a company whose equity share capital is officially listed in the UK or in an EEA State or is admitted to dealing either on the NYSE or Nasdaq (i.e. the main American stock exchanges).

[169] For an invaluable and comprehensive account of the role played at the European level, see Moloney, *EC Securities Regulation* (2nd edn, 2008). See also Edwards, *EC Company Law* (1999), Chs 10–15.

[170] Directive 2003/71/EC on the prospectus to be published when securities are offered to the public or admitted to trading and amending Directive 2001/34/EC, OJ L 345, 31.12.2003, p 64. There is an associated Prospectus Directive Regulation 2004/809/EC, OJ L 149, 30.4.2004, p 1, which provides the technical detail as to the content and format of prospectuses and see also the CESR Recommendations for the consistent implementation of the Regulation on Prospectuses (809/2004) published by the Committee of European Securities Regulators (CESR).

delivery of prospectuses to be drawn up by the FSA: hence the governing requirements are FSMA 2000, Part VI and the FSA Prospectus Rules, breach of which attracts
the penalties specified in FSMA 2000, s 91 (monetary penalties and public censure).

19-109   It is unlawful for transferable securities to be offered to the public in the UK unless an
approved prospectus is available to the public before the offer is made (FSMA 2000,
s 85(1)). Likewise, it is unlawful to request an admission to trading on a regulated market situated or operating in the UK unless an approved prospectus is publicly available
before the request is made (s 85(2)). The consequence of the dual prohibition is that
even though an offer may be exempt from the requirement for a prospectus, if the
securities are the subject of a request for admission to a regulated market, then an
approved prospectus is required.[171] A breach of either prohibition is a criminal offence
and attracts civil liability for breach of statutory duty (s 85(3), (4)).

19-110   The prospectus must be submitted to UKLA for approval and must be formally
approved before publication.[172] The UKLA must be satisfied that it is the home state
authority[173] in relation to the issuer; that the prospectus contains the necessary information (discussed below); and all other requirements relating to a prospectus have
been complied with (FSMA 2000, s 87A(1)). The UKLA merely satisfies itself that these
requirements are met by the issuer; it does not investigate or verify the accuracy of
the information in the prospectus. A key feature of EU requirements now is 'passporting' whereby a document approved in one Member State must be accepted by
other Member States without the imposition of any further substantive requirements.
UKLA has to accept incoming prospectuses approved in EEA States, provided they are
accompanied by a certificate of approval from the home competent authority and, if
requested, a translation of the summary of the prospectus (s 87H). UKLA also has to
provide a facility whereby UK companies can request that a prospectus be approved
by UKLA so that it may be used in another Member State even though there is to be
no public offer or request for admission to trading in the UK.[174] A prospectus must be
made available free of charge to the public as soon as possible after approval at various
locations including the offices of the relevant exchange or the issuer or any intermediary involved in selling the securities, or it must be published in a newspaper widely
circulated in the state where the offer is made, or made available on the issuer's website
or the exchange's website.[175]

---

[171] It was for this reason that the Alternative Investment Market (AIM) run by the London Stock Exchange
altered its status in October 2004 to an exchange regulated market ahead of the implementation of the
Prospectus Directive, see above n 170. Most companies using AIM could frame an offer in a way which is
an exempt offer, but a prospectus would still have been required to gain admission to AIM as long as AIM
remained a regulated market, hence the change in status.

[172] Prospectus Rules, 3.1.1R.   [173] See FSMA 2000, s 102C.

[174] See UKLA Factsheet No 4, *Passporting Factsheet* (October 2008) as to the process. The home authority
generally is the authority where the company has its registered office but there are some exceptions to that
general principle. CESR (see above n 170) now provides quarterly statistics on the use of passporting which
shows a significant and increasing level of 'passporting' which suggests that this new mechanism is working
well.

[175] Prospectus Rules, 3.2.4R. A person is guilty of an offence if he contravenes the provision requiring the
publication of a prospectus: FSMA 2000, s 85(1), (3).

There are detailed requirements with regard to the content and form of the prospectus[176] in keeping with its status as a critically important document intended to ensure that investors are in a position to make an informed decision as to the acquisition of any securities. A prospectus is only required, however, where transferable securities are offered to the public and offers of certain securities, such as government and public securities, are excluded.[177] There is also an important exclusion for transferable securities included in an offer where the total consideration of the offer is less than €2.5m which is important in practice as it allows companies to raise small but useful sums of money without the need for an approved prospectus.[178] As to what is an offer to the public, FSMA 2000, s 102B offers the widest possible definition. For these purposes, there is an offer of transferable securities to the public if there is a communication in any form or by any means to any person which presents sufficient information on the transferable securities to be offered and the terms on which they are offered to enable an investor to decide to buy or subscribe for the securities in question (s 102B(1), (3)).[179] Certain categories of exempt offers (where an approved prospectus is not required) are set out in s 86, namely offers to qualified investors,[180] to fewer than 100 members, or where the total consideration payable for the securities cannot exceed €100,000; the minimum consideration which may be paid by any person is at least €50,000; or the securities are denominated in amounts of at least €50,000. In these situations, the investor protection goals which drive the requirement for the publication of a prospectus are of less significance either because of the nature of the securities (low value) or the nature of the would-be purchaser (qualified) or the scale of the would-be purchase (high denomination securities). **19-111**

The necessary information which must be contained in a prospectus if it is to be approved by UKLA is the information necessary to enable an investor to make an informed assessment of the assets and liabilities, financial position, profits and losses, and prospects of the issuer of the securities and of any guarantor and the rights attaching to the securities.[181] In determining whether information is required to be included by virtue of this general duty of disclosure, regard is to be had to the particular nature of the securities and of the issuer (FSMA 2000, s 87A(4)). The information must also be presented in a form which is comprehensible and easy to analyse **19-112**

---

[176] See Prospectus Rules 2, but the key document as to contents and format is the Prospectus Directive Regulation (No 2004/809/EC): see above n 170.

[177] FSMA 2000, s 87(5)(a) and (b) exclude securities listed in Sch 11A and securities specified in the Prospectus Rules, 1.2.2R. 'Transferable securities' is defined in FSMA 2000, s 102A(3).

[178] FSMA 2000, s 85(5), Sch 11A, para 9.

[179] Furthermore, to the extent that an offer of transferable securities is made to a person in the UK it is an offer of transferable securities to the public in the UK: FSMA 2000, s 102B(2) which means it will fall within the requirement in s 85(1) for an approved prospectus.

[180] Qualified investors may be individuals or small or medium-sized firms and, assuming they meet the criteria laid down in the Prospectus Directive, above n 170, art 2(1)(e), (2), they must apply for entry on the register of qualified investors which is maintained by the FSA: see Prospectus Rules 5.4.

[181] FSMA 2000, s 87A(2). There are exceptions to the disclosure requirements, for example, on the grounds of public interest, serious detriment to the issuer and matters of minor importance: see s 87B(1). There is no longer any reference to the reasonable investor unlike in the previous law: see Hudson, *Securities Law* (2008), paras 12–56 et seq on this point.

(s 87A(3)). A supplementary prospectus is required where a significant new factor arises or a material mistake or inaccuracy arises in the prospectus (s 87G).

19-113   A prospectus may be made up of one document (including a summary) or several and where there are separate documents, the information must be divided between a registration document which concentrates on the issuer; a securities note which concentrates on the securities being offered or listed; and, save in certain circumstances, a summary note.[182] The summary must, briefly and in non-technical language, convey the essential characteristics of, and risks associated with, the issuer, any guarantor and the transferable securities to which the prospectus relates (FSMA 2000, s 87A(6)). Different formats of prospectus reflecting different types of securities, issuers and investors may be drawn up and it is possible to include information by reference to other previously published documents (such as the annual accounts or the company's constitution).[183] The prospectus must be in the language of the home Member State and, where it is to be used in other Member States, it must be in the language of that other state or in a language customarily used in international finance although the competent authority of the Member State may require the summary to be translated into its language.[184]

Responsibility and liability for a misleading prospectus

19-114   Compensation is payable by any person responsible for a prospectus when any person has acquired securities[185] and suffered loss in respect of them as a result of any untrue or misleading statements in, or the omission of any required information from, the prospectus (FSMA 2000, s 90).[186] The persons responsible for the prospectus where the offer is of equity securities are the issuer (and the offeror if different); each director;[187] any person who accepts responsibility for all or part of the prospectus and any person who authorised the contents of the particulars.[188] There are a number of defences set out in Sch 10; most crucially it is a defence if a person can satisfy the court (and the burden is on him) that he reasonably believed any statement for which he was responsible to be true and not misleading or that any information omitted was properly omitted.[189] Liability is imposed therefore for negligent or fraudulent false

---

[182] As to when a summary is not required, see FSMA 2000, s 87A(5); Prospectus Rules, 2.1.3R.

[183] See Prospectus Rules, 2.4.1R.   [184] See Prospectus Rules 4.1.

[185] Relief is not restricted to subscribers and purchasers in the market can claim compensation.

[186] The measure of compensation is the tort measure rather than the contract measure.

[187] Save in the unlikely situation where the prospectus is published without the director's knowledge or consent and on becoming aware of its publication, as soon as practicable, he gives reasonable public notice that it was published without his knowledge or consent: Prospectus Rules, 5.5.6R.

[188] Prospectus Rules, 5.5.3R. The 'persons responsible' for a prospectus are defined in PR 5.5.

[189] This defence applies not only to directors (who basically accept responsibility for the whole prospectus) but also to those experts who have contributed reports etc to the prospectus for which they must accept responsibility (but who are able to limit their potential liability in any event to the part for which they accept responsibility). In addition, any person who authorised the inclusion of an expert's statement is not liable for that statement if he reasonably believed that the expert was competent and had consented to the inclusion of the report: FSMA 2000, Sch 10, para 2(2).

statements. A person is also not liable if he satisfies the court that a timely correction was made of any false statements; that the false statement arose from the accurate and fair reproduction of an official statement or document; that the plaintiff was aware of the falsehood or the omitted information; or that he reasonably believed that a change in circumstances was not such as to warrant a supplementary listing particulars.[190] This statutory liability under s 90(1) does not preclude other remedies such as rescission of the contract by which shares were acquired, or claims for damages for deceit or damages for untrue or innocent misrepresentation under the Misrepresentation Act 1967. Proceeding under the statute is the most straightforward claim, however, especially as it imposes what Professor Davies has described as a strong version of liability, for it is for the defendant to prove that he was not negligent rather than for the claimant to prove that he was.[191]

This potential liability under FSMA 2000, s 90 can be contrasted with the current **19-115** tendency to provide a 'safe harbour' with respect to negligence by directors in directors' reports[192] or public statements required by the Transparency Directive,[193] leaving only liability for fraudulent misrepresentation (which is likely to be very difficult to establish). The safe harbour is to be extended to ad hoc and periodic disclosures by issuers by means of a recognised information service.[194] That this trend to restrict liability has not embraced prospectuses underlines the central role of this document in terms of investor protection.

---

[190] FSMA 2000, Sch 10, paras 3–7.

[191] See Davies Review of Issuer Liability, Liability for Misstatements To The Market: A Discussion Paper by Professor Paul Davies QC (HM Treasury, March 2007), para 28. Prof Davies also noted that it is accepted that the standard of accuracy in prospectuses is high and that this could be attributed in part to the imposition of a negligence standard (see at para 71).

[192] See CA 2006, s 463 (directors liable only to company and only in deceit with respect to untrue or misleading statements in the directors' report, the remuneration report or any summary financial statement derived therefrom).

[193] See FSMA 2000, s 90A inserted by CA 2006, s 1270; only the issuer can be liable to the person acquiring shares and only in deceit.

[194] The Government has indicated that it intends to implement provisions that substantially follow the Davies recommendations (see below), see HM Treasury Consultation Document, 'Extension of the statutory regime for issuer liability' (July 2008). The intention is to broaden the range of issuers and markets and announcements within the safe harbour provided by FSMA 2000, s 90A. This largesse is tempered by allowing sellers as well as buyers to claim for losses incurred through reliance on fraudulent misstatements and to permit recovery for losses resulting from dishonest delay of a disclosure (should it be possible to establish dishonesty in this context). See Davies, *Review of Issuer Liability, Final Report* (June 2007) preceded by a consultation paper of the same name (March 2007), published by HM Treasury.

20

The doctrine of capital maintenance

A An overview of the doctrine of capital maintenance

With the advent of limited liability in 1855, the courts' concern turned to the protection **20-1** of creditors. To that end there developed the doctrine of capital maintenance which essentially is a collection of rules designed to ensure, first, that a company obtains the capital which it has purported to raise (hence the rules governing payment for share capital which are discussed at **19-62**) and, secondly, that that capital is maintained, subject to the exigencies of the business, for the benefit and protection of the company's creditors and the discharge of its liabilities. In particular, the doctrine of capital maintenance precludes the return of capital, directly or indirectly, to the shareholders ahead of a winding up of the company.[1]

The landmark case on the doctrine of capital maintenance is the decision of the House **20-2** of Lords in *Trevor v Whitworth*[2] which established the fundamental principle that there can be no return of capital to the members other than on a proper reduction of capital duly sanctioned by the courts. At issue in the case was whether a company could purchase its own shares. The House of Lords rejected any such possibility, holding that a company had no such power under the Companies Acts, even if so authorised by its articles of association. Creditors had to be protected from a reduction of capital in this way without the company adhering to the statutory provisions on reduction of capital which required any reduction to be confirmed by the court.[3] Their Lordships noted that creditors took the risk of a company losing its capital in trading, but they also had

---

[1] For an interesting overview of this doctrine, see the judgment of Harman J in *Barclays Bank plc v British & Commonwealth Holdings plc* [1996] 1 BCLC 1 at 6–10, Ch D, aff'd on different grounds [1996] 1 BCLC 27, CA. See also *Aveling Barford Ltd v Perion Ltd* [1989] BCLC 626 at 630–3. Of course, on a winding up of the company, shareholders can retrieve their capital only if all the creditors have been paid.

[2] (1887) 12 App Cas 409. See also *Re Exchange Banking Co, Flitcroft's Case* (1882) 21 Ch D 519 at 533; *Ooregum Gold Mining Co of India Ltd v Roper* [1892] AC 125 at 133, per Lord Halsbury LC, HL. See generally Payne, 'Legal Capital in the UK following the CA 2006' in Armour & Payne, *Rationality in Company Law* (2009); Armour, 'Share capital and creditor protection: Efficient Rules for a Modern Company Law' (2000) 63 MLR 355; Ferran, 'Creditors' Interests and "Core" Company Law' (1999) 20 Co Law 314.

[3] See CA 2006, s 641(1). It is possible now for private companies to reduce capital without court approval: see ss 642–644.

a right to rely on the company not diminishing its capital by returning any part of it to its shareholders.[4] Lord Watson explained the position as follows:[5]

> 'Paid-up capital may be diminished or lost in the course of the company's trading; that is a result which no legislation can prevent; but persons who deal with, and give credit to a limited company, naturally rely upon the fact that the company is trading with a certain amount of capital already paid, as well as upon the responsibility of its members for the capital remaining at call; and they are entitled to assume that no part of the capital which has been paid into the coffers of the company has been subsequently paid out, except in the legitimate course of its business.'

20-3   Within the limits then of what the law can achieve, the courts set about developing a set of rules concerning the establishment and maintenance of capital, rules now reflected in the provisions of the CA 2006 governing payment for share capital, the purchase of a company's own shares including financial assistance for such purchases, the reduction of capital and, crucially, distributions to shareholders. Although in the earliest cases, such as *Trevor v Whitworth*,[6] the term 'return of capital' did mean an actual return of share capital subscribed, over the years the capital maintenance doctrine has broadened into a prohibition on any payment out of or transfer of company assets to a shareholder other than by way of a distribution (typically a dividend) lawfully made, an authorised reduction of capital, or other lawfully authorised procedure.[7]

20-4   Linked to the prohibition on the return of capital to the members is an equal prohibition on giving away the company's capital to non-members through a gratuitous disposition of the company's assets other than in furtherance of the company's objectives.[8] As Nourse LJ explained in *Brady v Brady*:[9]

> '...the principle is that a company cannot give away its assets. So stated, it is subject to the qualification that in the realm of theory a memorandum of association may authorise a company to give away all its assets to whomsoever it pleases, including its shareholders. But in the real world of trading companies, charitable or political donations, pensions to widows of ex-employees and the like apart, it is obvious that such a power would never be taken. The principle is only a facet of the wider rule, the corollary of limited liability, that the integrity of a company's assets, except to the extent allowed by its constitution, must be preserved for the benefit of all those who are interested in them, most pertinently its creditors.'

---

[4] See (1887) 12 App Cas 409 at 415, per Lord Herschell.   [5] (1887) 12 App Cas 409 at 423, 424.

[6] (1887) 12 App Cas 409.

[7] See Harman J on this point in *Barclays Bank plc v British & Commonwealth plc* [1996] 1 BCLC 1 at 14–15. See also Sealy & Worthington, *Cases and Materials* in *Company Law* (8th edn, 2007), p 422 who note that, for example, the 'capital' returned in *Re Halt Garage (1964) Ltd* [1982] 3 All ER 1016 was several thousand pounds whereas the shareholder had only contributed £1 (and retained that £1 after the 'return' of capital); and the recipient of 'capital' in *Aveling Barford Ltd v Perion Ltd* [1989] BCLC 626 was not a shareholder but a corporate vehicle used by a shareholder.

[8] *Ridge Securities Ltd v IRC* [1964] 1 All ER 275; and see Hannigan, 'Limitations on a Shareholder's Right to Vote—Effective Ratification Revisited' [2000] JBL 493 at 495–9.

[9] [1988] BCLC 20 at 38; reversed on other grounds [1988] BCLC 579, HL.

From *Trevor v Whitworth*[10] onwards, the approach of the courts has been consistently   **20-5**
to the effect that a company cannot, without the leave of the court or the adoption of a
special procedure, return its capital to its shareholders nor give away its capital in the
case of dispositions to non-shareholders. Such transactions or dispositions are ultra
vires and void and cannot be ratified, not even by the shareholders unanimously.[11]

Statutory reinforcement of the protection afforded to creditors by the CA 2006 and   **20-6**
the common law can be found in the IA 1986 which allows transactions which prove
injurious to creditors to be challenged, for example, on the ground that the transaction is at an undervalue (IA 1986, s 238: see **25-53**) or is a preference (IA 1986, s 239:
see **25-68**). Directors also run the risk of personal liability for wrongful trading under
IA 1986, s 214, see **25-17**, if they allow the company to continue trading past a point
when they know or ought reasonably to know that there is no reasonable prospect of
avoiding insolvent liquidation. The capital maintenance doctrine and the rules which
comprise it are broader in application than the provisions of the IA 1986 for there is no
requirement that the company actually be insolvent at the time of the transaction or
be rendered insolvent by the transaction.[12]

It would be fair to say that the doctrine of capital maintenance has its critics. Doubts   **20-7**
have been expressed, for example, as to whether the rules on distributions are too
restrictive and too costly to apply, whether the rules on financial assistance are part of
the doctrine of capital maintenance at all (though this issue is less significant now that
the prohibition on financial assistance applies only to public companies[13]), and, more
fundamentally, as to whether the rules achieve their aim of creditor protection.

There is little doubt that the doctrine of capital maintenance can appear complex,   **20-8**
not least because (and despite the statutory interventions) so much of the law has
developed from those early cases such as *Trevor v Whitworth*[14] which the courts continue to cite. The result has probably been to obscure (because of the reliance on the
language of pre-1900 cases) rather than clarify the modern doctrine. Initially, there
was a self-contained and relatively narrow doctrine about the inability of a company
to return share capital to its members intended to provide some protection for creditors dealing with companies with limited liability. More than a century later there
is a multi-faceted (and therefore untidy) doctrine, still concerned (in part) with the
protection of creditors, but also operating to constrain directors and to reinforce
their duty to exercise their powers for the purposes for which they are conferred and
to act to promote the success of the company (CA 2006, ss 171, 172). In this modern guise, these rules offer protection to creditors, but also to shareholders, against
improper conduct by the directors and the unauthorised dissipation of the company's
assets. The label 'capital maintenance' may have a dated ring to it, but the mischief at
which it is aimed, unauthorised depletion of the company's assets, remains. It is also

---

[10] (1887) 12 App Cas 409.   [11] See Hannigan, above n 8.
[12] See *Aveling Barford Ltd v Perion Ltd* [1989] BCLC 626 at 633 where Hoffmann J refutes any such limitation; also *Ridge Securities v IRC* [1964] 1 All ER 275.
[13] See CA 2006, s 678.   [14] (1887) 12 App Cas 409.

the case that when an independent review of the capital maintenance doctrine was undertaken for the European Commission (in the context of a review of the Second Company Law Directive which in effect applies the doctrine of capital maintenance to public companies) the result was a finding that the costs arising from the application of the doctrine are not excessive and the doctrine does not unduly hinder companies in the conduct of their affairs.[15] The same is probably true in the domestic context with the notable exception of the rules governing financial assistance which were complex and costly and time consuming to apply, but which have now been repealed in respect of private companies (99.5% of the register). It is possible that the perception of the costs and complexity of the capital maintenance regime does not quite match the business reality. It is also the case that a change to any new system also would involve costs and uncertainty[16] which may be a reason for continuing the existing settled position which is well understood by company advisers. The one area which remains controversial, perhaps, is with respect to distributions, a matter which is considered at the end of this chapter.

B Purchase and redemption of a company's own shares

Introduction

20-9   As noted at **20-2**, the landmark decision of the House of Lords in *Trevor v Whitworth*[17] established the fundamental principle that there can be no return of capital to the members other than one duly sanctioned by the courts. At issue in the case was whether a company could purchase its own shares. The House of Lords rejected any such possibility holding that a company had no such power under the Companies Acts, even if so authorised by its articles of association. Creditors had to be protected from a reduction of capital in this way without the company adhering to the statutory provisions on reduction of capital which required any reduction to be confirmed by the court. The capital maintenance principle established by this case remains a foundation stone of company law but modern business needs have persuaded Parliament that some aspects of the doctrine may be relaxed, in particular with respect to the issue in the case, namely the purchase by a company of its own shares. More recently, the

---

[15] KPMG, 'Feasibility Study on an alternative to the capital maintenance regime established by the Second Company Law Directive, etc (January 2008) available at http://ec.europa.eu/internal_market/company/docs/capital/feasbility/study_en.pdf.

[16] Payne, above n 2, suggests allowing contract law and the IA 1986 to fill any gap in creditor protection arising from abolishing the doctrine of capital maintenance, but that in itself would involve costs for creditors (so far as they would need to adopt new contractual tools or refine their existing ones) and while it would protect the large creditors in a position to use these mechanisms, smaller creditors typically find it difficult to exercise any contractual power. As for reliance on the IA 1986, the relevant creditor protection provisions are currently underused because of problems in their drafting and application and crucially the lack of funding for liquidators who have primary responsibility for pursuing these matters, see discussion in Chapter 25.   [17] (1887) 12 App Cas 409.

CA 2006 also relaxed the requirement for court confirmation of a reduction of capital: see discussion at **20-56**.

The relaxation of the prohibition on a company acquiring its own shares came initially   **20-10** in the Companies Act 1981 which permitted companies to issue redeemable shares (i.e. shares redeemable at the option of the company or the shareholder),[18] to purchase back their own shares and, in the case of private companies, to purchase back out of capital, so effecting the very reduction of capital which concerned the House of Lords in *Trevor v Whitworth*.[19]

This statutory change was just one of a series of measures (including tax and other   **20-11** incentives) introduced in the early 1980s designed to make it easier for small companies to raise equity (share) capital. The difficulties which small companies face in trying to raise equity investment are well documented.[20] Many small businesses are family concerns where the individuals concerned, much as they might welcome an injection of capital, are reluctant to raise it through an issue of shares for fear of losing control of the business to an outsider. Equally, outside investors are reluctant to contribute their capital to an enterprise when the shares are not easily marketable and where they risk being locked in. Any scheme to assist such companies has to be flexible enough to increase the marketability of the shares without necessarily depriving the existing owners of control and without jeopardising the position of the company's creditors.

Allowing a company to have complementary powers to issue redeemable shares and   **20-12** to purchase back its own shares was thought to meet these requirements and give companies the flexible equity capital structure they wanted.[21] A company may issue redeemable shares envisaging from the outset that the shareholder's commitment is to be a short-term one or at least for a definite period. The company has the use of the capital for this period while the investor knows that he is not locked in. The purchase powers, on the other hand, enable the company at some point in the future to buy back shares without having to anticipate that eventuality at the time of issue. As far as investors are concerned, the possibility that the company will purchase the shares reduces the chances of their being locked into the company.

It was thought that these new powers might accommodate family re-arrangements,   **20-13** for example by enabling founding shareholders to resign and realise their investment without the remaining family members being required personally to fund the purchase back of their shares. The provisions might offer a means of dealing with the

---

[18] The power to issue redeemable shares was not new in 1981 as companies had been able from 1929 to issue redeemable preference shares but the power was extended to any type of redeemable shares.

[19] (1887) 12 App Cas 409.

[20] See HM Treasury/Small Business Service, *Bridging the Finance Gap: Next steps in improving access to growth capital for small businesses* (December 2003) and the preceding consultation document of the same name issued in April 2003. The report notes (para E7) that there is an equity gap between the amount of money which individuals can raise and the stage at which venture capital becomes available which appears to be most acute for investments between £250,000 and £1m (though many would argue that the gap extends much higher than £1m).

[21] See DTI, *The Purchase by a Company of its Own Shares, A Consultative Document* (Cmnd 7944, 1980).

holdings of deceased members, or buying out discontented shareholders, or buying employee shareholdings when the employment is terminated.

20-14   All of these factors pointed towards these powers being of greatest use in private companies, but the powers are also available to public companies and commonly used by them. Indeed, it is standard practice for listed public companies to seek authority from their shareholders each year to purchase back their own shares. Obviously, the use of the powers by such companies is not driven by concerns about any lack of marketability of their shares, rather they see a variety of other advantages in having this flexibility.[22] For example, buy-backs, as purchase schemes are commonly called, may be a means of enhancing earnings per share when market conditions otherwise make this difficult. In addition, cash-rich companies may want to return capital to shareholders to enable the shareholders to make their individual investment decisions with regard to that capital rather than have the company use it in unsuitable and wasteful ways simply to reduce the company's cash holdings. Buy-backs can also prove attractive to institutional shareholders who because of the size of their holdings find it difficult to offload their holdings in the market in the normal way. On occasion, concerns have been voiced that listed companies might use these powers, for example as a defensive mechanism against takeover bids (by buying up shares in the market) or might in effect be insider dealing in their own shares. The general constraints on such conduct (the Takeover Code, the Listing Rules, the criminal law) are sufficient to address any such concerns, however, and there has been no evidence of any such abuses occurring.

20-15   A final point to remember is that the exercise of these powers may have tax consequences for both the company and the shareholders involved and that factor weighs heavily in any decision to use these provisions.

The statutory framework

20-16   Given the fundamental shift away from the prohibition on the purchase of a company's own shares as laid down in *Trevor v Whitworth*,[23] Parliament surrounds the exercise of these redemption and purchase powers with stringent procedural requirements designed to ensure that the powers can only be exercised in certain circumstances, using certain funds and in the full glare of publicity. The question is whether such requirements are effective to minimise the erosion of the doctrine of capital maintenance. A broader question, as noted above, is whether the doctrine itself is an effective way of protecting creditors.

20-17   The starting point is CA 2006, s 658(1) which, reflecting the rule in *Trevor v Whitworth*,[24] provides that a limited company may not acquire its own shares[25]

---

[22] See Pettet, 'Share Buy-Backs' in Rider (ed), *The Corporate Dimension* (1998).
[23] (1887) 12 App Cas 409.   [24] (1887) 12 App Cas 409.
[25] See also CA 2006, s 136 which generally prohibits a company from being a member of its holding company and ss 660–661 (shares held by company's nominee are treated as held by the nominee on his own

whether by purchase, subscription or otherwise[26] except in accordance with the statutory provisions of CA 2006, Part 18, i.e. redemption in accordance with ss 684–689 or purchase under ss 690–737. This prohibition on a company acquiring its own shares does not apply to:

(1) the acquisition of shares in a reduction of capital duly made (discussed below);

(2) the purchase of shares in pursuance of a court order under certain statutory provisions[27] (which rarely occurs); or

(3) the forfeiture of shares, or the acceptance of shares surrendered in lieu, in pursuance of the articles, for failure to pay any sum payable in respect of the shares (which rarely occurs) (s 659(2)).

The statutory provisions on redemption and purchase are complex and the procedures, while similar, are not identical. On issues of detail, therefore, the precise wording of the statutory provisions should be consulted.

20-18

Strict adherence to the statutory procedures is required[28] for it is only redemption or purchase in accordance with the statutory provisions which is permissible (CA 2006, s 658(1)). The courts may allow some dispensing with or waiver of some procedural requirements when agreed to informally but unanimously by the members,[29] but not if the provision in question is intended to protect a wider class of persons, in particular the company's creditors, rather than merely the current shareholders.[30] In the event of a contravention, the company is liable on conviction to a fine, every officer of the company who is in default is liable to imprisonment or a fine, and the purported acquisition is void.[31]

20-19

Redemption of own shares

A private limited company may issue shares that are to be redeemed or are liable to be redeemed, subject to any exclusion or restriction in the company's articles, while a public company may only issue redeemable shares if it is authorised to do so by its articles (CA 2006, s 684(1)–(3)). Redeemable shares cannot be issued unless the company has other shares in issue which are not redeemable (s 684(4)).

20-20

---

account). The prohibition on the acquisition of its own shares does not prevent a company (A) from acquiring the shares of another company (B) in circumstances where the sole asset of the acquired company (B) is shares in the acquiring company (A): *Acatos & Hutcheson plc v Watson* [1995] 1 BCLC 218.

[26] A company may acquire its fully paid shares other than for valuable consideration: CA 2006, s 659(1).

[27] I.e. under CA 2006, s 98 (objections to resolution for public company to be re-registered as private); s 721(6) (objection to redemption or purchase out of capital); s 759 (breach of prohibition of public offers by private company) or Part 30 (relief on the grounds of unfair prejudice to members): s 659(2).

[28] *Re R W Peak (Kings Lynn) Ltd* [1998] 1 BCLC 193.

[29] *Kinlan v Crimmin* [2007] 2 BCLC 67 at 81; *Dashfield v Davidson* [2008] BCC 222; *BDG Roof-Bond Ltd v Douglas* [2000] 1 BCLC 401 at 417; *Re Torvale Group Ltd* [1999] 2 BCLC 603.

[30] *Kinlan v Crimmin* [2007] 2 BCLC 67 at 81; *Dashfield v Davidson* [2008] BCC 222; *BDG Roof-Bond Ltd v Douglas* [2000] 1 BCLC 401 at 417; *Re Torvale Group Ltd* [1999] 2 BCLC 603.

[31] CA 2006, s 658(2), (3); *Trevor v Whitworth* (1887) 12 App Cas 409.

20-21   The directors may determine the terms, conditions and manner of redemption if they are authorised to do so by the articles or by an ordinary resolution of the company,[32] otherwise the terms, conditions and manner of redemption must be stated in the articles.[33] The directors, if so authorised, must determine those terms etc before the shares are allotted and details of the terms etc must be included in the statement of capital which must be provided to the registrar of companies when the shares are allotted.[34]

20-22   Shares to be redeemed must be fully paid up (otherwise the creditors would lose a valuable asset on liquidation, namely uncalled capital) and payment must be made at the time when the shares are redeemed unless the terms of redemption provide for deferred payment[35] by agreement between the company and the holder (CA 2006, s 686). It had been thought that 'payment' had to be in cash, but in *BDG Roof-Bond Ltd v Douglas*[36] the court considered that a non-cash consideration may be agreed—the CA 2006 does not clarify this point. The funds which may be used for payment are restricted to distributable profits and the proceeds of a fresh issue made for the purposes of the redemption (s 687(2)), save in the case of a private company which may redeem out of capital (s 687(1)): see **20-42**.

20-23   Shares acquired are cancelled on redemption so reducing the company's issued capital by the nominal value of the shares redeemed (CA 2006, s 688). Because of the requirement to establish a capital redemption reserve (s 733: see **20-35**), a reduction of capital does not occur save in the exceptional case where a private company redeems out of capital. Within one month of the redemption, notice must given to the registrar of companies specifying the shares redeemed together with a statement of capital (s 689(1), (2)).

20-24   If, having agreed to do so, a company fails to redeem shares, the company is not liable in damages in respect of any such failure.[37] Specific performance may still be available but not if the company shows that it is unable to meet the costs of redeeming the shares in question out of distributable profits.[38]

---

[32] CA 2006, s 685(1). Details of the earliest and latest dates on which the company has power to redeem the shares; whether the shares are redeemable in any event or liable to be redeemed at the option of the company or of the shareholder; and whether any (and if so, what) premium is payable on redemption must be included in the notes to the accounts: s 396(3); The Large and Medium-sized Companies and Groups (Accounts and Reports) Regulations 2008, SI 2008/410, Sch 1, Part 3, para 47(2).

[33] CA 2006, s 685(4); and see *Dashfield v Davidson* [2008] BCC 222 where the contract was contained in the articles.

[34] CA 2006, s 685(3); see also s 555(3)(b).

[35] Allowing for deferred payment is new in the CA 2006, previously deferred payment rendered the transaction void, see *Kinlan v Crimmin* [2007] 2 BCLC 67.

[36] [2000] 1 BCLC 401.

[37] CA 2006, s 735(2). The section is concerned with direct claims for damages as a result of a breach by the company of its obligation to redeem or purchase the shares. It does not preclude the recovery of damages claimed by a plaintiff against the company for breach of a financing agreement even though the measure of damages for that breach may well be the equivalent of damages for failure to redeem: *Barclays Bank plc v B & C Holdings plc* [1996] 1 BCLC 1, CA.

[38] CA 2006, s 735(3). As to the position where the company goes into winding up, see s 735(4)–(6).

Purchase of own shares

Any company (public or private) may purchase its own shares (including redeemable shares) in accordance with the statutory scheme, subject to any restrictions in the company's articles, and provided that the company is not left with only redeemable shares or shares held as treasury shares (see **20-38**).[39] Shares to be purchased must be fully paid up and (unlike redemption) payment must be made at the time when the shares are purchased (s 691). The general requirement of payment on purchase is to prevent companies from oppressing shareholders by purchasing their shares so depriving them of their status as members but without actually paying over the proceeds. This requirement also resolves difficulties of timing and valuation. It had been thought that 'payment' had to be in cash, but in *BDG Roof-Bond Ltd v Douglas*[40] the court considered that a non-cash consideration may be agreed—the CA 2006 does not clarify this point. Payment may be made from distributable profits or the proceeds of a fresh issue made for the purposes of financing the purchase (s 692(2)), and a private company may purchase its own shares out of capital (s 692(1)), see discussion at **20-42** below.

20-25

On purchase, (with the exception of treasury shares, discussed below), the shares are cancelled, so reducing the company's issued capital by the nominal value of the shares purchased (CA 2006, s 706). Cancellation reduces the impact which purchase schemes can have within the company, for example, by ensuring that directors cannot exercise any voting rights in respect of those shares. Cancellation should increase the earnings of the remaining shares although this depends on factors such as the market's perception of the wisdom of redemption or purchase, the price paid and whether there has been a fresh issue of shares. Because of the requirement to establish a capital redemption reserve (s 733: see **20-35**), a reduction of capital does not occur save in the exceptional case where a private company purchases out of capital. If, having agreed to do so, a company fails to purchase shares, the company is not liable in damages in respect of any such failure.[41] Specific performance may still be available but not if the company shows that it is unable to meet the costs of purchasing the shares in question out of distributable profits.[42]

20-26

Off-market and market purchases

The scheme of purchase differs depending on whether the share purchases are 'off-market' or 'market' purchases as defined in CA 2006, s 693. A lower level of regulation of market purchases is appropriate in recognition of the fact that the market authorities[43] impose additional regulatory requirements which, coupled with the higher degree of publicity attaching to such purchases, are sufficient to deter any abuses.

20-27

---

[39] CA 2006, s 690. A listed company which intends to purchase more than 15% of its shares must do so by way of a tender offer to all the shareholders: Listing Rules, r 12.4.1.

[40] [2000] 1 BCLC 401.   [41] CA 2006, s 735(2). See also above n 37.

[42] CA 2006, s 735(3). As to the position where the company goes into winding up, see s 735(4)–(6).

[43] I.e. the UK Listing Authority, which is part of the FSA, and market operators such as the London Stock Exchange.

20-28   A market purchase is made where the purchase is made on a recognised investment exchange (RIE) and subject to a marketing arrangement on the exchange,[44] i.e.
where the shares are listed[45] or are capable of being dealt with on the RIE without a
requirement for permission for individual transactions.[46] An off-market purchase is
where the purchase does not take place on an RIE or the purchase is on an RIE but the
company's shares are not listed or traded on the exchange.[47]

20-29   As a general rule, private companies and public companies which are not publicly
traded make off-market purchases while publicly traded companies normally make
market purchases, but in some instances may transact off-market purchases.

20-30   In relation to an off-market purchase, the terms of a specific contract of purchase must
be authorised in advance by the company by a special resolution.[48] In the case of a
public company, the resolution must specify a date on which the authority to purchase
is to expire and that date must not be later than 18 months after the date on which the
resolution is passed.[49]

20-31   Where the resolution is a written resolution, a member who holds shares to which the
resolution relates is not an eligible member, i.e. is not entitled to vote, so the resolution
must be carried without his support.[50] Where the resolution is to be passed at a meeting, the resolution is not effective if any member of the company holding shares to
which the resolution relates exercises the voting rights carried by any of those shares[51]
in voting on the resolution and the resolution would not have been passed if he had not
done so (CA 2006, s 695(3)). The special resolution is not validly passed, where a written
resolution is used, unless a copy of the contract (if it is in writing) or a memorandum
of its terms (if it is not) is circulated to the members at or before the time the resolution is sent or submitted to the members (s 696(2)(a)). The copy or memorandum must

---

[44] CA 2006, s 693(3). 'Recognised investment exchange' means a body (other than an overseas investment exchange) which is a recognised investment exchange for the purposes of the FSMA 2000, Part 18: CA
2006, s 693(5). There are seven RIEs of which the most important share dealing exchanges are the London
Stock Exchange, Plus Markets plc and SWX Europe Ltd: the full list is available on the FSA website: see www.
fsa.gov.uk/register/home.do.

[45] I.e. listed by the UKLA, the UK Listing Authority, which maintains the official list of securities, see
FSMA 2000, s 74; UKLA is part of the Financial Services Authority (FSA).

[46] CA 2006, s 693(3), (4). Purchases of shares in companies traded on AIM (the Alternative Investment
Market) (see **1-62**) are market purchases therefore.

[47] CA 2006, s 693(2).

[48] CA 2006, ss 693(1)(a), 694. The authority conferred by the resolution may be varied, revoked or from
time to time renewed by a further special resolution: s 694(4). See *Dashfield v Davidson* [2008] BCC 222.
Shareholder approval is sought because the funding of the purchase comes primarily from distributable
profits and these are funds which could otherwise be distributed to all the shareholders so their approval is
needed for a decision to use the funds for the benefit of some shareholders only. This potential disadvantage
to all shareholders explains why the Listing Rules require listed companies which wish to purchase 15%
or more of their shares to make a tender offer to all the shareholders so that they all have the opportunity
to participate.

[49] CA 2006, s 694(5).   [50] CA 2006, s 695(2).

[51] This is less restrictive than the position with respect to a written resolution where the member affected
is entirely disenfranchised, whereas on a resolution at a meeting, a member is only restricted from exercising
the votes attached to the shares to be acquired.

give the names of the members holding shares which are to be purchased.[52] Where a meeting is held, the copy or memorandum must be available for inspection by members of the company both at the company's registered office (for not less than 15 days prior to the meeting) and at the meeting itself (s 696(2)(b)).

A company may not make a market purchase unless the purchase has first been **20-32** authorised by an ordinary resolution (CA 2006, s 701(1)). The authority may be general or limited to the purchase of shares of any particular class or description and may be conditional or unconditional (s 701(1)). The authority must specify the maximum number of shares which may be acquired, determine both the maximum and minimum price which may be paid for the shares[53] and specify a date on which the authority is to expire which must in any event be not later than 18 months from the date when the resolution is passed (s 701(5)). Any resolution conferring, varying, revoking or renewing such an authority to purchase must be sent to the registrar of companies within 15 days after it is passed.[54] No question of disenfranchising any shares arises in this context since the authority is not specifically aimed at any particular shares but is a general authority.

Financing of redemption and purchase-back schemes

A crucial element in any redemption or purchase-back scheme is the source of the **20-33** funding to pay for it. The risk to creditors is that capital is returned to the shareholders leaving a shell with inadequate assets to pay off the company's creditors in full. The legislation attempts to prevent that happening by providing that, save in the case of private companies which may redeem or purchase out of capital, companies must fund redemption or purchase-back:

(1) out of distributable profits;[55] or the proceeds of a fresh issue of shares made for the purpose of redemption or financing the purchase; and

(2) any premium payable on redemption or purchase must be paid out of distributable profits of the company, subject to certain exceptions.[56]

Essentially, the company must use funds (distributable profits) which could have gone **20-34** to the shareholders anyway (usually in the form of dividends), or it must substitute

---

[52] CA 2006, s 696(3), (4).

[53] CA 2006, s 701(3). The price may be determined either by specifying a particular sum or providing a basis or formula for calculating the price in question without reference to any person's discretion or opinion: s 701(7). This is to ensure that the directors are not in a position to enter into transactions at varying prices depending on their relationship with the vendors.

[54] CA 2006, ss 701(8), 30(1). This is an exception to the general rule that ordinary resolutions do not have to be delivered to the registrar of companies.

[55] I.e. profits out of which the company could make a distribution within the meaning of CA 2006, s 830: s 736. The rules establishing what is a lawful distribution are set out in CA 2006, Part 23, discussed at **20-83**.

[56] CA 2006, ss 687(2), (3), 692(2); the exceptions are where the shares redeemed or purchased back were originally issued at a premium in which case the proceeds of a fresh issue may be used to pay the premium to a limited extent: see ss 687(4), 692(3).

new capital brought in by a fresh issue of shares for the capital which it is repaying. Neither has any impact on the company's creditors so there is no erosion of the capital maintenance doctrine. Furthermore, to ensure that this is in fact the case, the company must set up a capital redemption reserve fund which is one of the company's undistributable reserves (CA 2006, s 733(1)).

20-35   Where shares of a company are redeemed or purchased wholly out of the company's profits, the amount by which the company's issued share capital is diminished on cancellation of the shares redeemed or purchased must be transferred to the capital redemption reserve (s 733(2)).

20-36   If the shares are redeemed or purchased wholly or partly out of the proceeds of a fresh issue and the aggregate amount of those proceeds is less than the aggregate nominal value of the shares redeemed or purchased, the amount of the difference must be transferred to the capital redemption reserve; but this does not apply if the proceeds of the fresh issue are applied by the company in making a redemption or purchase of its own shares in addition to a payment out of capital.[57] Payments out of capital are discussed below.

20-37   The provisions of the Companies Act relating to the reduction of a company's share capital[58] apply as if the capital redemption reserve were paid-up share capital of the company, except that the reserve may be applied by the company in paying up shares to be allotted to members of the company as fully-paid bonus shares (CA 2006, s 733(5), (6)). Reduction of capital is discussed at **20-56** below.

Treasury shares

20-38   Where companies purchase 'qualifying shares' out of distributable profits, they may hold those shares 'in treasury' rather than cancel them (CA 2006, ss 724(3), 706). 'Qualifying shares' for these purposes are: listed shares, i.e. shares included on the official list maintained by the UKLA in accordance with the FSMA 2000, Part 6; shares traded on AIM, the Alternative Investment Market; shares listed in an EEA State; and shares traded on a regulated market.[59] The maximum number of shares which may be held in treasury in this way is 10% of the nominal value of the company's issued share capital.[60]

---

[57] CA 2006, s 733(3); in the latter case, it is accepted that there will be a reduction of capital.

[58] See CA 2006, ss 641–652.

[59] CA 2006, s 724(2). Regulated markets are markets so designated under the Markets in Financial Instruments Directive (2004/39/EC) (the Mifid Directive) and UKLA maintains the list of regulated markets for these purposes. There are seven regulated markets of which the most important share dealing exchanges are the London Stock Exchange, Plus Markets plc and SWX Europe Ltd. The full list is available on the FSA website: see www.fsa.gov.uk/register/home.do.

[60] CA 2006, s 725(1), reflecting the requirements of the Second EC Company Law Directive, 77/91/EEC, arts 19–22, OJ L 26, 31.1.1977, p 1. For the background to these provisions which were first introduced in 2003, see Morse, 'The Introduction of Treasury Shares into English Law and Practice' [2004] JBL 303. The Second Company Law Directive has been amended by Directive 2006/68/EC, OJ L 264/32, 25.9.2006 to allow Member States to remove this 10% cap. BERR intends to consult on the issue.

Once shares are held in treasury, the voting rights attached to such shares are sus-   **20-39**
pended and the company is prohibited from paying any dividend or making any other
distribution to itself as a result of it holding treasury shares (CA 2006, s 726). The holding of treasury shares by nominees is not permitted and the fact that the company is
holding the shares as treasury shares will be apparent because the company must be
entered in the register of members as the holder of the shares (s 724(4)).

Treasury shares may be sold for cash by the company, transferred for the purposes   **20-40**
of or pursuant to any employees' share scheme, or cancelled.[61] The ability to sell the
shares for cash gives the company flexibility to raise additional funds without the need
for further allotments of shares but, as noted at **19-38**, any sale of treasury shares is
subject to the pre-emption requirements. Details of any shares held as treasury shares
must be given in the notes to the company's accounts.[62] Contravention of any of these
provisions is an offence by the company and every officer in default (CA 2006, s 732).

Disclosure requirements

Within 28 days of any shares purchased being delivered to the company, a return must   **20-41**
be delivered to the registrar of companies distinguishing between treasury shares and
other shares and stating the number and nominal value of the shares and the date on
which they were delivered to the company (CA 2006, s 707(1)). In the case of a public
company, further details relating to the aggregate amount paid by the company for the
shares, and the maximum and minimum paid by the company for shares of each class
purchased must be included (s 707(4)). A copy of any contract of purchase, or a written
memorandum of its terms, must be kept at the company's registered office or other
specified place for 10 years from the date of purchase and must be available for inspection by any member of the company and, if it is a public company, by any other person
(s 702(2)–(6)). Details of any purchases must also be given in the directors' report.[63]

Private companies—redemption or purchase out of capital

Subject to any restrictions or prohibitions in its articles, a private company may   **20-42**
redeem or purchase its own shares otherwise than out of distributable profits or the
proceeds of a fresh issue of shares (CA 2006, s 709(1)). Permitting private companies in
certain circumstances to redeem or purchase shares out of capital is something which
potentially has a significant impact on creditors. It is unsurprising therefore that the
statutory provisions surround such purchases with even more stringent requirements
than those already noted.

---

[61] CA 2006, ss 727(1), 729(1).

[62] CA 2006, s 396; The Large and Medium-sized Companies and Groups (Accounts and Reports)
Regulations 2008, SI 2008/410, Sch 1, Part 3, para 47(1)(b).

[63] CA 2006, s 396; The Large and Medium-sized Companies and Groups (Accounts and Reports)
Regulations 2008, SI 2008/410, Sch 7, Part 2, para 9.

20-43   First, to minimise the amount which may be paid out of capital, the company must first use any available distributable profits[64] and the proceeds of any fresh issue made for the purpose of redemption or purchase before resorting to capital with the amount then needed being described as 'the permissible capital payment'.[65] On the other hand, there is no requirement to have any available distributable profits or to have a fresh issue of shares.

20-44   Secondly, a payment out of capital is not lawful (CA 2006, s 713(1)) unless the following requirements are met:

- a directors' statement and auditor's report is required;
- the payment must be approved by special resolution;
- there must be public notice of the proposed payment;
- the directors' statement and auditor's report must be available for inspection before approval.

20-45   The company's directors must make a statement[66] specifying the amount of the permissible capital payment for the shares in question and stating that, having made full inquiry into the affairs and prospects of the company, they have formed the opinion:

(1)   as regards its initial situation immediately following the date on which the payment out of capital is proposed to be made, that there will be no grounds on which the company could then be found unable to pay its debts;[67] and

(2)   as regards its prospects for the year immediately following that date that, having regard to:

(a)   their intentions with respect to the management of the company's business during that year; and

(b)   the amount and character of the company's financial resources that will in their view be available to the company during that year, the company will be able to continue to carry on business as a going concern (and will accordingly be able to pay its debts as they fall due) throughout that year (CA 2006, s 714(3)).

20-46   This emphasis on solvency reflects the overriding concern that creditors must be protected from injudicious use of redemption or purchase schemes. Any director who makes this statement without having reasonable grounds for the opinion expressed

---

[64] Whether there are available profits is determined in this instance in accordance with CA 2006, s 712 rather than Part 23 which applies generally: s 711(2).

[65] CA 2006, s 710. See s 734(2), (3) as to the necessary transfers to, or reduction of, the capital redemption reserve.

[66] The statement must be in the prescribed form: CA 2006, s 714(5). The requirements are asset out in The Companies (Shares and Share Capital) Regulations 2009, SI 2009/388, reg 14: the statement be in writing, indicate that it is the directors' statement, it must be signed by each director, and must state whether the company's business includes that of a banking or insurance company.

[67] CA 2006, s 714(3)(a). In forming their opinion for these purposes, the directors must take into account all of the company's liabilities (including contingent or prospective liabilities): s 714(4).

in it is liable to imprisonment or a fine or both (CA 2006, s 715). More significant, however, is the potential liability where a company is wound up and it has made a payment out of capital and its assets prove insufficient for the payment of its debts and liabilities and the expenses of winding up.[68] If the winding up commenced within one year of the date on which the relevant payment out of capital was made, then the person whose shares were redeemed or purchased and the directors who signed the statement are, so as to enable the insufficiency to be met, liable to contribute to the company's assets.[69]

The person whose shares were so redeemed or purchased is liable to contribute an amount not exceeding so much of the relevant payment as was made by the company in respect of his shares and the directors are jointly and severally liable with that person to contribute that amount.[70] A director will be excused liability if he shows that he had reasonable grounds for forming the opinion set out in the declaration.[71] Presumably he will claim that he was justified in relying on the auditors who, after all, agreed with his opinion because annexed to the directors' statement must be a report by the company's auditor stating that: **20-47**

(1) he has inquired into the company's state of affairs;[72]

(2) the amount specified in the statement as the permissible capital payment for the shares in question is in his view properly determined in accordance with CA 2006, ss 710–712; and

(3) he is not aware of anything to indicate that the opinion expressed by the directors in their statement as to any of the matters in s 714(3) (set out above) is unreasonable in all the circumstances (s 714(6)).

Any payment out of capital must be approved by a special resolution.[73] Where a written resolution is used, a member who holds shares to which the resolution relates is not an eligible member, i.e. is not entitled to vote (CA 2006, s 717(2)). Where the resolution is passed at a meeting, the resolution is not effective if any member of the company holding shares to which the resolution relates exercises the voting rights carried by any of those shares in voting on the resolution and the resolution would not have been passed if he had not done so (s 717(3)).   **20-48**

The resolution is also ineffective unless the required directors' statement and auditor's report (discussed above) are circulated with or before the written resolution is circulated to the members or the statement and report are available for inspection by   **20-49**

---

[68] See IA 1986, s 76(1).   [69] IA 1986, s 76(2).   [70] IA 1986, s 76(3).   [71] IA 1986, s 76(2)(b).

[72] A failure by an auditor to inquire to the extent that an auditor of reasonable competence would do means that the auditor is not in a position to say whether the directors' opinion is reasonable or not and, in consequence, the auditor cannot properly give an opinion for these purposes; if he does give an opinion in such circumstances, he is liable in negligence, see *Cook v Green* (unreported, 2 May 2008), Ch D District Registry (Manchester) which concerned the equivalent auditors' statement then required for the purposes of financial assistance by a private company.

[73] CA 2006, s 716. The resolution must be passed on or within the week immediately following the date of the directors' statement required by s 714. The actual payment out of capital must be made no more than five and not later than seven weeks after the date of the resolution: s 723(1).

members of the company at the meeting at which the resolution is passed (CA 2006, s 718(2), (3)).

20-50 Various disclosure requirements apply which are aimed at bringing the proposed payment to the attention of creditors who may wish to apply to the court for an order prohibiting payment (see discussion below). Within the week immediately following the date of the resolution for payment out of capital, the company must cause to be published in the *Gazette* a notice:

(1) stating that the company has approved a payment out of capital for the purpose of acquiring its own shares by redemption or purchase (as the case may be);

(2) specifying the amount of the permissible capital payment and the date of the resolution;

(3) stating that the directors' statement and the auditor's report are available for inspection; and

(4) stating that any creditor of the company may at any time within the five weeks immediately following the date of the resolution apply to the court for an order prohibiting payment (CA 2006, s 719(1)).

20-51 A similar notice must be published in a national newspaper or a notice in writing to that effect must be given to each creditor (s 719(2)). A copy of the directors' statement and the auditor's report must also be sent to the registrar of companies at the same time (s 719(4)).

20-52 In recognition of the potential for abuse when companies are permitted to redeem or purchase back out of capital, provision is made in CA 2006, s 721 for an application by an objecting creditor or member to the court for cancellation of the resolution authorising payment out of capital. No such procedure is available in respect of purchase or redemption in any other instance.

20-53 An application must be within five weeks of the date on which the resolution was passed and may be made by any member of the company (other than one who consented to or voted in favour of the resolution) or by any creditor of the company.[74] No minimum shareholding or debt is required but the more insignificant the amounts, the less weight is likely to be attached to the objections. The difficulty for those objecting, particularly if they are members, is to persuade the court to set aside something which has been approved by a special resolution and without the votes of any member who holds shares to which the resolution relates. The courts in such circumstances tend to refuse redress, stating that the members know best and that it is not for the court to interfere in what is essentially a difference as to business policy.[75]

---

[74] CA 2006, s 721(1), (2); notice of the application must also be given immediately to the registrar of companies: s 722(1).

[75] The position would not be dissimilar to that of shareholders trying to persuade the court not to confirm a reduction of capital sanctioned by special resolution. They have usually been unsuccessful. See **20-75** below.

The jurisdiction of the court on any application is open-ended. The court may   **20-54**
adjourn the proceedings in order that an arrangement can be made for the purchase
of the interests of dissentient members or for the protection of dissentient creditors, as
the case may be (CA 2006, s 721(3)). Without prejudice to such powers, the court must
make an order on such terms and conditions as it thinks fit either confirming or cancelling the resolution. The court's order may, in particular, provide for the purchase
by the company of the shares of any members and for the reduction of the company's
capital accordingly.[76]

Purchase out of capital/reduction of capital

The Company Law Review recommended the retention generally of the provisions   **20-55**
on redemption and purchase of own shares, subject to some technical improvements
and one substantive change.[77] The CLR recommended the introduction of a simplified
procedure for a reduction of capital on the basis of a special resolution and a declaration of solvency by the directors (see CA 2006, s 641), discussed below. The CLR
considered that such a procedure would mean that there was no need to retain the
procedure allowing for redemption or purchase out of capital.[78] The Government was
persuaded, however, that there are sufficient differences between the two regimes to
justify the retention of the power to purchase out of capital. The distinct elements of
a purchase out of capital include that the directors' statement has to be backed up by
an auditor's report, the requirement for publicity in the *Gazette* and a national newspaper, and the ability of a creditor to go to court to challenge the transaction. Those
elements may in some circumstances provide greater reassurance for creditors than a
reduction of capital on the basis of a solvency statement by the directors under s 641,
hence the need for both procedures.

C Reduction of capital

The statutory framework

At the beginning of this chapter, we noted that the House of Lords in *Trevor v*   **20-56**
Whitworth[79] had established the fundamental principle that there can be no return of
capital by a company to its members other than on a proper reduction of capital duly

---

[76] CA 2006, s 721(6). A copy of any order must be delivered to the registrar of companies: s 722(3).

[77] Company Law Review, *Final Report*, vol I (2001), para 10.6; *Completing the Structure* (2000), paras
7.16–7.19; *Company Formation and Capital Maintenance* (1999), paras 3.49–3.64 and Annex B.

[78] See *Modernising Company Law* (Cm 5553-I, 2002), para 6.5.

[79] (1887) 12 App Cas 409. The courts are alert to attempts to disguise what is in effect a return of capital to the shareholders, see *Aveling Barford Ltd v Perion Ltd* [1989] BCLC 626 a sale (at a gross undervalue) of an asset to a company controlled by a shareholder did not hide the true nature of the transaction
which was an unauthorised return of capital to that shareholder. See also Harman J in *Barclays Bank plc v
British & Commonwealth Holdings plc* [1996] 1 BCLC 1 at 10–11, Ch D, aff'd on different grounds [1996] 1
BCLC 27, CA.

sanctioned by the courts. The statute now allows for reduction in a number of ways, some of which we have already considered, such as a reduction of capital on a redemption or purchase of its own shares by a private company out of capital.[80] Creditors and members are protected in such cases by the extensive statutory provisions governing such schemes which were discussed in detail at **20-42** above. Reduction can also occur as a consequence of a court order for the purchase by the company of shares held by an objecting member under a variety of provisions[81] or as a result of forfeiture or surrender by members. For example, a public company may provide in its articles that shares may be forfeited for non-payment of calls in respect of sums remaining unpaid on the shares.[82]

20-57   In practice, the most important ways in which a limited company may reduce its share capital are set out in CA 2006, s 641(1), namely:

(1) in the case of a private company limited by shares, by special resolution supported by a solvency statement (ss 642–644);

(2) in any case, by special resolution confirmed by the court (ss 645–651).

20-58   The Company Law Review initially favoured the replacement of the procedure for reduction subject to court confirmation with the scheme based on a special resolution supported by a declaration of solvency.[83] Consultations showed that the finality which is given to disputes by a court confirmation is valued highly in practice, however, and so the Review concluded that the court-based procedure should be retained.[84]

20-59   These powers to reduce capital are subject to any restriction or prohibition contained in the company's articles[85] (CA 2006, s 641(6)) and, in the case of a private company, it cannot reduce capital under s 641(1)(a) if the effect would be to leave the company

---

[80] Reduction does not occur in the case of redemption or purchase otherwise than out of capital for, in those instances, an amount equivalent to the amount redeemed or purchased must be transferred to the capital redemption reserve which, for most purposes, is treated as if it were share capital): CA 2006, s 733(6).

[81] For example, under CA 2006, s 98 (proceedings objecting to resolution for public company to be re-registered as private); s 721(6) (objection to redemption or purchase out of capital; s 759 (remedial order in case of breach of prohibition of public offers by private company) or Part 30 (seeking relief on the grounds of unfair prejudice to members): s 659(2).

[82] See The Companies (Model Articles) Regulations 2008, SI 2008/3229, reg 4, Sch 3, arts 58–61 (public companies) and see CA 2006, ss 662–664. Forfeiture does not fall foul of the prohibition on a company acquiring its own shares: s 659(2)(c). Forfeiture provisions are penal provisions and must be construed strictly: *Johnson v Lyttle's Iron Agency* (1877) 5 Ch D 687, CA. A public company's articles also commonly provide for the surrender of shares in lieu of forfeiture: see SI 2008/3229, reg 4, Sch 3, paras 62. A surrender of shares in a public company is governed by the same rules as those applying to forfeiture: CA 2006, s 662(1).

[83] Company Law Review, *Strategic Framework* (1999), paras 5.4.4–5.4.13; *Company Formation and Capital Maintenance* (1999), paras 3.27–3.35 and Annex B.

[84] Company Law Review, *Completing the Structure* (2000), paras 7.9–7.10; *Final Report*, vol I (2001), para 10.6.

[85] In public companies, the articles typically state that the reduction must not have the effect of reducing the share capital below the authorised minimum, i.e. £50,000 or €65,600, the prescribed euro equivalent (see CA 2006, s 763). Such a provision does not rule out a reduction by a company which momentarily reduces the company's capital to nil before following it with an increase in capital to above that minimum: *Re MB Group plc* [1989] BCLC 672. When a reduction does result in the capital of a public company falling

without any member holding other than redeemable shares.[86] Subject to that limitation, a company may:

(1) extinguish or reduce the liability on any of its shares in respect of share capital not paid up; or

(2) either with or without extinguishing or reducing liability on any of its shares,

    (a) cancel any paid-up share capital that is lost or unrepresented by available assets; or

    (b) repay any paid-up share capital in excess of the company's wants (s 641(4)).

The courts have emphasised on many occasions that there is no question of limiting or controlling the power available to the company to reduce its capital in any way,[87] but the categories identified in s 641(4), above, remain the most common methods of reduction.   **20-60**

Extinction or reduction of liability on shares not paid up

Reduction in this instance appears to involve risk to creditors for it extinguishes a liability (namely the obligation on the part of the holders of partly-paid shares (see **19-16**) to pay the amount due on those shares) which would be a valuable asset to the creditors in the event of a winding up, assuming that those shareholders were in a position to meet their liability on those shares. This category is of limited significance, however, for it is unusual for shares to be issued as partly-paid so there is rarely any question of there being any unpaid share capital outstanding.   **20-61**

Cancellation of share capital lost or unrepresented by available assets

The cancellation of paid-up share capital which is lost or unrepresented by available assets appears to have an impact on creditors for it reduces the minimum level of assets which must be maintained by the company. However, reduction in this instance is usually a necessary exercise to restore reality to the company's accounts. If a company had at one time a paid-up share capital of £200,000 but, following trading losses, its net assets now amount only to £50,000, little is achieved by maintaining the figure of £200,000 in the accounts as the capital yardstick. A reduction of capital in such circumstances will also be crucial to the company's ability to make or resume dividend payments to its shareholders and it is important to appreciate the impact of the distribution rules in CA 2006, Part 23, discussed in detail below, in this context. The need under those distribution rules to have regard to accumulated profits and losses means that it will be necessary for the company to reduce its capital to take account of past losses so as to be in a position to resume the payment of dividends from current profits.   **20-62**

below the authorised minimum, see CA 2006, ss 650, 651 which allow for expedited re-registration in that case as a private company.

[86] CA 2006, s 641(2).

[87] See *British & American Trustee Corpn v Couper* [1894] AC 399 at 410; *Poole v National Bank of China* [1907] AC 229 at 237–8; *Re Thomas de la Rue & Co Ltd* [1911] 2 Ch 361 at 365; *Ex p Westburn Sugar Refineries Ltd* [1951] 1 All ER 881 at 884.

20-63 The court must be satisfied that the capital is lost and that that loss is permanent (so far as presently foreseeable) for, if it is not permanently lost, a cancellation of paid-up share capital may prejudice the interests of the creditors. In *Re Jupiter House Investments (Cambridge) Ltd*,[88] where the loss could not be proved to be permanent,[89] the court confirmed the reduction subject to an undertaking by the company which ensured that if the loss of capital was in fact recovered, it would not be distributed to the shareholders as dividends but would be placed to a capital reserve. On the other hand, in *Re Grosvenor Press plc*[90] the court was loath to require such an undertaking, noting that there are already statutory safeguards[91] to protect the interests of future creditors and shareholders and there is no need, except in special circumstances, for the court to require a reserve to be set aside indefinitely. It suffices if the reserve is made undistributable as long as any creditor at the time of the reduction remains unpaid.[92]

Repay share capital in excess of company's wants

20-64 The repayment of paid-up share capital in excess of the company's needs poses no risk to creditors[93] and may simply reflect a shrinking of the company's activities. It might be noted that it is only in this instance that capital is actually returned to the shareholders. In the other instances of reduction noted above, either the capital has never been received or the capital is lost.

20-65 It is not necessary that the shareholders who are being paid off should actually receive cash. Non-cash assets may be used instead[94] and in that case there need not be an exact correlation between the capital reduced and the value of the assets transferred.[95] This may appear to offer some opportunity for abuse but the courts have indicated that the important matter is not how much is returned to the shareholders but how much is retained for the protection of creditors.[96] If what is offered to the shareholder is illusory, however, the court will refuse to confirm the reduction.[97]

Reduction supported by solvency statement

20-66 This procedure is only available to private companies and is subject to any restriction or prohibition in the company's articles.[98] Some creditors may be uneasy about

---

[88] [1985] BCLC 222.

[89] The loss arose from defects in a substantial building which the company owned. The company had been advised that it had more than an even chance of recovering the loss by an action for damages against a third party.   [90] [1985] BCLC 286.

[91] Creditors and shareholders are protected by the publicity requirements surrounding a reduction of capital and the need for the company's accounts to give a true and fair view of the state of its affairs.

[92] [1985] BCLC 286 at 289.

[93] A reduction of capital by repayment is not a distribution for the purposes of CA 2006, Part 23: see s 829(2)(b)(ii).

[94] *Ex p Westburn Sugar Refineries Ltd* [1951] 1 All ER 881; *Re Thomas de la Rue & Co Ltd* [1911] 2 Ch 361.

[95] In *Ex p Westburn Sugar Refineries Ltd* [1951] 1 All ER 881 at 885, Lord Reid made the point that this must be the position because in many cases it is impossible to make any exact valuation of the non-cash assets.

[96] See, for example, *Ex p Westburn Sugar Refineries Ltd* [1951] 1 All ER 881 at 884, per Lord Normand.

[97] *Re Thomas de la Rue & Co Ltd* [1911] 2 Ch 361.

[98] The drawback for the creditors is that the articles can be changed by a special resolution under CA 2006, s 21 so the protection afforded by a prohibition in the articles is limited.

a company using a procedure based solely on a directors' solvency statement and so there may be pressure on companies to include restrictions or prohibitions in their articles. Equally, it may be that an attempt to exercise the power will be a default trigger under loan agreements so in effect preventing the company from using the procedure.[99] In the absence of any restrictions, all that is required is a special resolution and a solvency statement in the prescribed form.[100]

Where a written resolution is used, a copy of the solvency statement must be sent or submitted to every member at the time when the proposed resolution is sent. If the resolution is passed at a meeting, the solvency statement must be available for inspection by members throughout the meeting. In either case, a failure to comply with this requirement does not affect the validity of the resolution (presumably because of the difficulty of unravelling these transactions if the non-compliance does not come to light for some time), but non-compliance is a criminal offence.[101] **20-67**

The statement must be to the effect that each of the directors: **20-68**

(1) has formed the opinion,[102] as regards the company's situation at the date of the statement, that there is no ground on which the company could then be found unable to pay (or otherwise discharge) its debts; and

(2) has also formed the opinion:

(a) if it is intended to commence the winding up of the company within 12 months of that date, that the company will be able to pay (or otherwise discharge) its debts in full within 12 months of the commencement of the winding up; or

(b) in any other case, that the company will be able to pay (or otherwise discharge) its debts as they fall due during the year immediately following that date (CA 2006, s 643(1)).

This statement must be delivered to the registrar of companies within 15 days of the resolution being passed together with a copy of the resolution and a statement of **20-69**

---

[99] A prohibition or restriction on the exercise of the power by the company outside of the articles would not be effective: *Russell v Northern Bank Development Corp Ltd* [1992] BCLC 1016, but making an exercise a default event has the same practical effect.

[100] CA 2006, s 643(3). See The Companies (Reduction of Share Capital) Order 2008, SI 2008/1915, art 2. The solvency statement must be in writing, be signed by each director, and indicate that it is a solvency statement for the purposes of CA 2006, s 642. As to the requirement of 'each director', this includes de facto directors which may cause a problem, see *Re In a Flap Envelope Co Ltd* [2004] 1 BCLC 64 (in a different context, but still relevant).

[101] CA 2006, ss 642(2)–(4), 644(7).

[102] In forming their opinion for these purposes, the directors must take into account all of the company's liabilities (including contingent or prospective liabilities): CA 2006, s 643(2). There is no express requirement for the directors to make full inquiry into the affairs and prospects of the company, as is required by s 714(3) in the case of a purchase of own shares out of capital, but such a requirement is probably implicit in any case: see Hannigan and Prentice, *The Companies Act 2006, A Commentary* (2007), para 7.12; also *Re In a Flap Envelope Co Ltd* [2004] 1 BCLC 64. A director could not have reasonable grounds for his opinion unless he has made such inquiries as he ought to make to enable him to express such an opinion: *Cook v Green* (unreported, 2 May 2008), Ch D, Dist Reg Manchester, concerning an auditor's report on a financial assistance scheme, but relevant in this context also.

capital (CA 2006, s 644(1)) and the reduction does not take effect until those documents are registered (s 644(4)). It is an offence for a director to make a statement and deliver it to the registrar without having reasonable grounds for the opinions expressed in it (s 643(4)).

20-70 The notable features of this procedure are: the absence of any requirement for an auditor's report to back up the directors' solvency statement; the absence of any publicity to alert creditors either through notification in the *Gazette* or by an advertisement in a national newspaper; and the absence of any mechanism for objections by shareholders or creditors. For these reasons, creditors may want companies to place restrictions or prohibitions in their articles to curtail the directors' freedom of action. The risk for the creditors is the usual one, that directors will take advantage of the scheme to return capital to the shareholders before the company later collapses to the detriment of the creditors. On the other hand, directors may be wary of giving solvency statements, given the criminal sanction which attaches to the giving of a statement without reasonable grounds for the opinions expressed in it, and they may prefer to have a supporting auditor's opinion, even though it is not a legal requirement. Despite the apparent simplicity of these procedures, business practice may dictate that it is not used as much as currently anticipated. Equally, once settled practice emerges, reduction of capital in this way may become routine, just as buy-backs have become routine. A key practical issue which will encourage its use is that the reserve arising on a reduction whether on the basis of a solvency statement or a reduction confirmed by the court is to be treated as a realised profit and therefore distributable, subject in either case to any contrary provision in the court order, the resolution for reduction or the company's memorandum or articles of association.[103]

Reduction subject to court confirmation

20-71 The alternative procedure (and the only option for public companies) is to pass a special resolution (CA 2006, s 641(1)(b)) and seek court confirmation of the reduction (s 645(1)) which order the court may make on such terms and conditions as it thinks fit,[104] subject to the position of the company's creditors having been safeguarded (s 648(1), (2)).

20-72 Every creditor of the company whose claim would be admissible in a winding up *and* who shows that there is a real likelihood that the proposed reduction will put at risk the due discharge of the claim is entitled to object to the reduction of capital.[105]

---

[103] CA 2006, s 654(1) and The Companies (Reduction of Share Capital) Order 2008, SI 2008/1915, art 3(2)–(4).

[104] The court can confirm a resolution even if there is a factual error in it, provided that it is so insignificant that no one could be thought to be prejudiced by its correction: *Re Willaire Systems plc* [1987] BCLC 67. See also *Re European Home Products plc* [1988] BCLC 690 where a more significant error occurred but the court reluctantly confirmed the reduction as creditors were not affected and no shareholder regarded the mistake as being of such importance as to seek the court's refusal.

[105] CA 2006, ss 645(2), 646(1): these provisions have not yet been amended to the position as stated in the text but it is expected that they will be in due course: see explanation in n 106 below.

Where there are creditors so entitled to object, a list of creditors must be settled (CA 2006, s 646(3)) and the court has to be satisfied that any such creditor has either consented to the reduction, or his debt or claim has been discharged or has been determined, or has been secured, before it makes an order confirming the reduction (s 648(2)). This limitation of the right to object to creditors who can show (the onus is on the creditor) that the proposed reduction will put at risk the due discharge of the claim is a recent change brought about by amendments to the Second Company Law Directive.[106] Previously all creditors were entitled to object and it was standard practice for the court to dispense with the settling of the list of creditors as invariably the company would have reached an agreement with its creditors who would either have been paid off or have consented to the scheme subject to bank guarantees from the company covering the amounts due to them. In other words, the onus was on the company to reach an accommodation with its creditors. The new position puts the onus on the objecting creditor to show to the court how he is at risk from any reduction. There had been concerns that the previous procedures gave creditors a degree of excessive protection[107] and the amendments to the Second Company Law Directive are designed to re-balance the position between the company and its creditors.

It is not clear whether the change will make much difference in practice. If companies choose to rely on it strictly then creditors will have to establish that they are entitled to object and it is not entirely clear how a creditor will have sufficient knowledge of the company's financial position to show that he is at risk from the reduction of capital. Equally, companies may consider that the potential delay to the reduction caused by delay in settling the list of creditors may mean that it is more sensible to proceed as before by addressing the concerns of creditors through payment (though the debt is not yet due) or by means of agreements and guarantees.   **20-73**

Where the procedures are followed properly and the necessary special resolution passed, the court's role is little more than to endorse the company's plans. The consent of the creditors entitled to object will usually have been secured by the company and shareholders will have little interest in objecting other than in the context of a variation of class rights (see discussion at **20-80** below). There are no specific statutory provisions dealing with the shareholders' position; instead it is for objecting shareholders (objecting in effect to being expelled from the company) to persuade the court not to confirm the reduction.   **20-74**

---

[106] Directive 2006/68/EC amending Directive 77/91/EEC, OJ L 264/32, 25.9.2006, see art 9. For the moment only the CA 1985 has been amended to reflect the provisions of Directive 2006/68: see CA 1985, s 136(3) as substituted by The Companies (Reduction of Capital) (Creditor Protection) Regulations 2008, SI 2008/719, reg 2, with effect from 6 April 2008. But CA 1985, s 136 will be repealed as of 1 October 2009 when the CA 2006 comes fully into force and therefore to give effect to the Second Directive further regulations will make the same amendments to CA 2006, s 646. The relevant regulations, The Companies (Creditors' Protection and Treasury Shares) Regulations 2009, are not available at the time of writing.

[107] Company Law Review, *Strategic Framework* (1999), paras 5.4.10–5.4.12; *Company Formation and Capital Maintenance* (1999), para 3.31.

Role of the court

20-75   The court has a discretion whether or not to confirm a reduction[108] and the main question for the court is whether the proposed reduction is fair and equitable as between the different classes of shareholders,[109] given that the position of the creditors is protected by the procedures outlined above.

20-76   Speaking generally, a reduction of capital need not be spread equally or rateably over all the shares of the company.[110] If there is nothing unfair or inequitable in the transaction, the shares of one or more shareholders may be extinguished without affecting other shares of the same or a different class.[111] However, a reduction which does not provide for uniform treatment of shareholders whose rights are similar is narrowly scrutinised.[112]

20-77   It is rare for there to be any difficulty about securing court confirmation which is seen as a purely routine matter. The scheme in question is always supported by a large majority of the shareholders (necessarily so, for the statute requires a special resolution) and raises issues of internal management and business judgement which are for the company to decide upon and not the courts.[113]

20-78   The approach of the courts was explained by Harman J in *Re Ratners Group plc*[114] as follows:

> 'The court has over the years established...three principles on which the court will require to be satisfied. Those principles are, first, that all shareholders are treated

---

[108] *British & American Trustee Corpn v Couper* [1894] AC 399; *Re Thomas de la Rue Ltd* [1911] 2 Ch 361.

[109] *British & American Trustee Corpn v Couper* [1894] AC 399; *Re Thomas de la Rue Ltd* [1911] 2 Ch 361; *Poole v National Bank of China Ltd* [1907] AC 229; *Scottish Insurance Co Ltd v Wilsons & Clyde Coal Co Ltd* 1948 SC 360, aff'd [1949] AC 462, HL; *Ex p Westburn Sugar Refineries Ltd* [1951] 1 All ER 881. As long as creditors and shareholders are not prejudiced, wider public concerns do not influence the court and it is not concerned with any ulterior purpose for the reduction provided it is lawful. Thus reduction schemes for reasons of tax avoidance (as opposed to evasion) or to avoid some of the consequences of nationalisation have in the past been approved: *Ex p Westburn Sugar Refineries Ltd* [1951] 1 All ER 881.

[110] *Re Agricultural Hotel Co* [1891] 1 Ch 396; *Re Floating Dock Co of St Thomas Ltd* [1895] 1 Ch 691; *Re London and New York Investment Corpn* [1895] 2 Ch 860; *British and American Trustee and Finance Corpn v Couper* [1894] AC 399.

[111] *British and American Trustee and Finance Corpn v Couper* [1894] AC 399 at 406, 415, 417, HL; *Bannatyne v Direct Spanish Telegraph Co* (1886) 34 Ch D 287, CA; *Re Direct Spanish Telegraph Co* (1886) 34 Ch D 307; *Re Thomas de la Rue & Co Ltd and Reduced* [1911] 2 Ch 361.

[112] In *Re Robert Stephen Holdings Ltd* [1968] 1 WLR 522, it was stated that the better practice in cases where one part of a class is to be treated differently from another part of the same class (unless all the shareholders consent) is to proceed by way of a scheme of arrangement under what is now CA 2006, Part 26, as this affords better protection to a non-assenting minority. In this case the court did confirm the reduction despite its affecting shareholders of the same class in different ways but no shareholder appeared to oppose the confirmation.

[113] See *Poole v National Bank of China Ltd* [1907] AC 229 at 236, per Lord Loreburn '...it is no part of the business of a Court of justice to determine the wisdom of a course adopted by a company in the management of its own affairs'.

[114] [1988] BCLC 685 at 687. See also *Re Thorn EMI plc* [1989] BCLC 612. The other qualification on the court's discretion noted by Harman J in both of these cases was that the court must not be asked to confirm a reduction which is for no discernible purpose.

equitably in any reduction. That usually means that they are treated equally, but may mean that they are treated equally save as to some who have consented to their being treated unequally, so that counsel's word "equitably" is the correct word which I adopt and accept. The second principle to be applied is that the shareholders at the general meeting had the proposals properly explained to them so that they could exercise an informed judgment on them. And the third principle is that creditors of the company are safeguarded so that money cannot be applied in any way which would be detrimental to creditors.'

In most instances, the creditors, shareholders and the company are in complete agreement about the proposed reduction and the court's role is limited to endorsing their plans so even the presence of dissentient shareholders is unlikely to alter the court's willingness to approve a reduction scheme. **20-79**

What has troubled the courts to a slightly greater degree in some of the cases has been a claim by preference shareholders that the effect of a proposed reduction of capital[115] is to vary or abrogate their class rights and so requires their consent before the reduction can be confirmed by the court. That issue is discussed at **14-44**. It suffices to note here that where the proposed reduction is in accordance with the class rights as they would apply on a winding up of the company, the reduction does not amount to a variation of class rights and the consent of the class to the reduction is not required.[116] Preference shareholders can avoid the danger of a restrictive interpretation of what constitutes a variation of their class rights by the courts by identifying in the terms of issue those matters (such as a reduction of capital) which are deemed to be a variation or abrogation of the rights attached to that class and which therefore do require the consent of the class under CA 2006, s 630. If a scheme of reduction does vary or abrogate class rights, despite the generality of the court's power to confirm (and some suggestions to the contrary in older cases),[117] the court will not confirm a reduction without the appropriate class consent having been obtained.[118] **20-80**

Registration of court order

The registrar, on production of the court order confirming the reduction and the delivery of a copy of the order and of a statement of capital (approved by the court), registers the order and statement (CA 2006, s 649(1)) whereupon the resolution for the reduction of capital takes effect (s 649(3)(b), except in the case of a reduction of share capital that forms part of a compromise or arrangement sanctioned by the court under Part 26 (arrangements and reconstructions) in which case the reduction takes effect (1) on delivery of the order and statement of capital to the registrar, or (2) if the court so orders, on the registration of the order and statement of capital (s 649(3)(a)). The registrar certifies the registration of the order and statement of capital and this certificate of registration is conclusive evidence that all the requirements with respect to **20-81**

---

[115] Typically, a proposal for the reduction of capital by paying off the preference shares on the grounds of excessive capital.

[116] *Re Saltdean Estate Co Ltd* [1968] 3 All ER 829; *House of Fraser v ACGE Investments Ltd* [1987] AC 387, HL.   [117] See *Re William Jones & Sons Ltd* [1969] 1 All ER 913.

[118] See *Re Northern Engineering Industries plc* [1994] 2 BCLC 704 at 713, CA.

the reduction of share capital have been complied with and that the company's share capital is as stated in the statement of capital (s 649(5), (6)).

20-82   Where the court makes an order confirming a reduction of a public company's capital which has the effect of bringing the nominal value of its allotted share capital below the authorised minimum, the registrar of companies must not register the order unless the court so directs, or the company is first re-registered as a private company.[119]

D Distributions to the members

Introduction

20-83   The most common type of distribution is a dividend, expressed as so many pence per share, and paid to the shareholders according to the number of shares held by them. The statutory rules on distributions are wider in their application, however, applying to 'every description of distribution of a company's assets to its members, whether in cash or otherwise', subject to a limited number of statutory exceptions (CA 2006, s 829(1)).

20-84   The rules governing distributions are set out in CA 2006, Pt 23, ss 829–853 which essentially require the existence of available profits determined by accounts which have been properly prepared in accordance with the Companies Act.[120] Additional requirements are imposed on public companies[121] in keeping with the requirements of art 15 of the Second Company Law Directive (77/91/EEC).[122] The common law principle that dividends cannot be paid out of capital is also expressly retained by the statute (CA 2006, s 851).

20-85   The distribution rules, whether statutory or common law, are an important component of the capital maintenance regime. The rules address concerns that, if the directors and shareholders are able to collude in the distribution of the company's assets

---

[119] CA 2006, s 650. The authorised minimum is set at £50,000 or €65,600 the prescribed euro equivalent: s 763 and The Companies (Authorised Minimum) Regulations 2008, SI 2008/729, reg 2.

[120] See CA 2006, ss 830, 836. As discussed below, a company's accounts play a crucial role in determining whether a company has profits for distribution and key technical guidance on the accounting issues is provided by the Institute of Chartered Accountants for England and Wales (ICAEW): see ICAEW Tech 01/08 'Guidance on the Determination of Realised Profits and Losses in the Context of Distributions under the Companies Act 1985', hereinafter Tech 01/08. As noted in Tech 01/08, para 1.6, the CA 2006 has not made any significant changes to the law on distributions, but consequential amendments to Tech 01/08 are necessary to reflect the CA 2006. A draft 'Guidance on the Determination of Realised Profits and Losses in the Context of Distributions under the Companies Act 2006' has been issued for consultation, hereinafter Tech 07/08. Much of the guidance in Tech 07/08 is unchanged from that in Tech 01/08, except as necessary to take account of the CA 2006 (a comparison of the two documents is set out in Tech 08/08). It is expected that the Guidance on distributions under the CA 2006 will be finalised in summer 2009.

[121] See CA 2006, s 831. Further requirements are also imposed on investment companies, see ss 832–835.

[122] See OJ L 26, 31.1.1977, p 1.

to the members during the company's lifetime, the creditors will find the company stripped of its assets.[123] On liquidation, the creditors must be paid in full before any capital can be returned to the shareholders and an unlawful distribution of assets ahead of winding up defeats that priority.[124] Where a company wishes to return capital to its shareholders, it must do so via a purchase or redemption of shares or reduction of capital in accordance with the statutory schemes and not by way of an improper distribution of assets to the members.[125] Equally, the rules protect shareholders against dissipation of the company's assets by the directors for improper purposes in breach of duty.[126]

In addition to the legal issues, directors considering a dividend pay-out must have regard to broader commercial issues which will vary depending on the size and type of the company. Many private companies are small family concerns where all the shareholders also act as the directors and profits may be distributed by way of directors' remuneration instead of by formal declaration of dividends. On the other hand, there may be tax savings to be made, perhaps by paying dividends rather than paying national insurance contributions on salary, so the question of dividends or salary is determined in the light of the individual's positions. A further point of confusion in small private companies is that directors and shareholders often make withdrawals from the company without identifying clearly whether the payment is: (1) a dividend; (2) a loan from the company; or (3) remuneration.[127]   **20-86**

Other difficulties can arise in private companies where profits are distributed by way of remuneration but not all of the shareholders are directors. This can be a source of internal tension, particularly if the company has amassed considerable reserves and the directors' remuneration is generous. In such cases, a persistent failure to pay dividends when funds are available, coupled with high levels of directors' remuneration, may amount to unfairly prejudicial conduct meriting relief under CA 2006, s 994 (see at **17-71**).   **20-87**

Shareholders in public companies are much less likely to be directors and they expect dividend payments to be made to the shareholders when distributable profits are   **20-88**

---

[123] See *It's a Wrap (UK) Ltd v Gula* [2006] 2 BCLC 634 at 641, per Arden LJ, and at 645 where Sedley LJ comments that the ability to recover unlawful dividends from the recipients is 'designed to protect those who have a prior call on a company's funds from the appropriation of them by those who control the company'. A creditor does not have locus standi, however, to seek an injunction to prevent an unlawful dividend, only a shareholder can do that: *Mills v Northern Railways of Buenos Ayres Ltd* (1870) 5 Ch App 621.

[124] See *It's a Wrap (UK) Ltd v Gula* [2006] 2 BCLC 634 at 641 where Arden LJ notes that any leniency to shareholders in receipt of an improperly paid dividend detracts from the protection available to the creditors.

[125] See *Ridge Securities Ltd v IRC* [1964] 1 All ER 275 at 288; *Re Halt Garage (1964) Ltd* [1982] 3 All ER 1016.

[126] See *Bairstow v Queens Moat Houses plc* [2001] 2 BCLC 531 at 546, CA. See also Payne, 'Legal Capital in the UK following the CA 2006' in Armour & Payne, *Rationality in Company Law* (2009) who makes the point that the rules on distributions do not prevent assets being dissipated in other ways such as through excessive remuneration to directors, poor management decisions and fraud.

[127] See, for example, *Queensway Systems Ltd v Walker* [2007] 2 BCLC 577. Some of the problems are eased somewhat by the relaxation of the prohibitions on loans to directors by CA 2006, ss 197–214.

available. For listed public companies, a failure to maintain an appropriate level of dividend pay-out each year can have an adverse effect on the company's share price and may expose the company to potential takeover bids. It is also likely to be unpopular with the company's institutional investors.

20-89 Such market pressure for dividend payments is often criticised as contributing to the 'short-termism' problem in British companies. The argument is that it forces management to concentrate excessively on short-term strategies designed to give immediate shareholder returns and maintain the company's share price rather than on long-term planning which would be to the advantage of the company and the economy. Whether there is a short-termism problem as opposed to a perception problem and whether, if there is a problem, it should be attributed to shareholders' attitudes (institutional or otherwise) to dividends rather than managerial conduct (given the link between remuneration and short-term targets) has all been much debated, though firm conclusions have been elusive.[128] To some extent, the debate has moved on to a recognition of the need for a better dialogue between companies and their shareholders which, given their predominance, essentially means between companies and their institutional shareholders (on the role of the institutional investor: see **5-48**).

Statute, common law and directors' duties

20-90 The statutory distribution rules originated in the CA 1980 against a background of a common law principle which prohibits the payment of a dividend out of capital,[129] but the application of which was rather lax in some respects.[130] For example, the common law permitted dividends to be paid out of current trading profits without making good losses in fixed capital[131] or trading losses in previous years;[132] and allowed dividends to be paid out of an unrealised capital gain resulting from a bona fide revaluation of fixed assets;[133] and did not require companies to provide for depreciation.[134] Many of these legal rules were commercially unwise and contrary to good accounting practice, but the courts were reluctant to interfere with the directors' discretion as men of business.[135]

20-91 While the statutory provisions have modified many of the common law rules, the statute operates alongside the common law which is expressly retained by CA 2006,

---

[128] See Marsh, *Short-termism on Trial* (1990); Myners, *Developing a Winning Partnership: How companies and institutional investors are working together* (1996) pp 6–8.

[129] *Re Exchange Banking Co, Flitcroft's Case* (1882) 21 Ch D 519.

[130] For an interesting account of the historical development of the dividend rules, see Yamey, 'Aspects of the Law relating to Company Dividends' (1941) 4 MLR 273.

[131] *Lee v Neuchatel Asphalte Co* (1889) 41 Ch D 1; *Verner v General & Commercial Investment Trust* [1894] 2 Ch 239.

[132] *Ammonia Soda Co v Chamberlain* [1918] 1 Ch 266; *Re National Bank of Wales Ltd* [1899] 2 Ch 629.

[133] See *Dimbula Valley (Ceylon) Tea Co Ltd v Laurie* [1961] Ch 353 at 371–3.

[134] *Lee v Neuchatel Asphalte Co* (1889) 41 Ch D 1; *Bolton v̇ Natal Land & Colonization Co* [1892] 2 Ch 124.

[135] See *Lee v Neuchatel Asphalte Co* (1889) 41 Ch D 1 at 18, 21.

ss 851 and 852. These sections continue the application of any rule of law, any provision in the articles or in any other enactment 'restricting the sums out of which, or, the cases in which, a distribution may be made'. The result is the continued application of the common law principle that dividends cannot be paid out of capital[136] which has the important consequence that where a company has distributable profits for the purposes of CA 2006, Part 23, but those profits have been dissipated subsequent to the preparation of the accounts, the common law rule then applies to prevent a distribution out of capital.

20-92 The statutory provisions work also within the general framework of the law which imposes other constraints on directors. Directors must exercise their powers for the purposes for which they are conferred (CA 2006, s 171) and have a duty to act to promote the success of the company for the benefit of the members having regard to the factors set out in s 172. That duty is of particular importance in this context because it includes an obligation, in certain circumstances, to have regard to the interests of the company's creditors (s 172(3)), the circumstances being when the company is insolvent or of doubtful solvency (see **9-44**). The directors' duty to exercise care and skill (discussed in Chapter 10) is also relevant.[137] In that regard directors need to consider whether, whatever the position in terms of strict compliance with CA 2006, Part 23, it is prudent to declare a dividend, given the company's trading position and funding needs.[138] In a situation where the company's position is one of doubtful solvency, or the effect of the dividend would be to render the company insolvent or doubtfully solvent (given the duty to have regard to creditors' interests at that stage), a prudent director exercising care and skill would not recommend the payment of a dividend without ensuring that the company was in a position to meet the claims of its creditors as they fall due.[139]

20-93 The result is that directors considering distributions need to be alert to their fiduciary duties, the requirements of CA 2006, Part 23 and the common law principle precluding the payment of dividends out of capital. The retention of the common law alongside Part 23 means that various permutations can arise. A distribution may be valid at common law, but in breach of the statute, as where there are available profits but the accounts have not been properly prepared. Equally, a distribution may be valid under the statute but the available profits as determined by the last accounts have been exhausted by the time of the distribution so any distribution is out of capital and invalid at common law. Equally, there may be profits available for distribution but the directors are acting for an improper purpose in breach of their fiduciary duties and/or acting in breach of their duty of care and skill in making a distribution.

---

[136] *Re Exchange Banking Co, Flitcroft's Case* (1882) 21 Ch D 519. See also *Trevor v Whitworth* (1887) 12 App Cas 409. As to the application of the common law to distributions in kind, see CA 2006, ss 845, 851(2). In essence, the statute determines the quantum of a distribution in kind.

[137] See, for example, *Re Loquitur Ltd, IRC v Richmond* [2003] 2 BCLC 442 at 489–90.

[138] See Tech 01/08, above n 120, paras 2.4–2.5 (likewise Tech 07/08) which cautions prudence when considering a distribution from profits arising from changes in the value of financial instruments considered to be volatile, even if the profits are deemed by accounting principles to be realised profits for these purposes, a caution borne out by market events in 2008.

[139] See *Re Loquitur Ltd, IRC v Richmond* [2003] 2 BCLC 442 at 489–90.

20-94   Distributions in breach of the statutory requirements or requirements in the articles or of the common law principle that dividends cannot be paid out of capital are ultra vires and void and cannot be ratified by the company in general meeting.[140] Directors who authorise improper dividends in breach of their fiduciary duties are liable to make good the sums misapplied, given their responsibility as trustees of the company's assets, as discussed at **20-121**. The shareholders' liability as recipients of unlawful distributions is a statutory and common law matter (CA 2006, s 847(2), (3)), as discussed at **20-118**.

Distributions and distributable profits—CA 2006, Part 23

20-95   The basic rule is that a company may only make a distribution out of profits available for the purpose (CA 2006, s 830(1)).[141] A 'distribution' means every description of distribution of a company's assets to its members, whether in cash or otherwise, except distributions by way of:

(1) an issue of shares as fully or partly paid bonus shares;

(2) the reduction of share capital by extinguishing or reducing the liability of any of the members on any of the company's shares in respect of share capital not paid up, or by repaying paid-up share capital;

(3) the redemption or purchase of any of the company's own shares out of capital (including the proceeds of any fresh issue of shares) or out of unrealised profits in accordance with the statutory provisions; and

(4) a distribution of assets to members of the company on its winding up (s 829).

20-96   The label which the parties give to a transaction is not determinative of whether it is a 'distribution' for these purposes.[142] In *Re Halt Garage (1964) Ltd*[143] the court found that sums paid to a director, at a time when the company was insolvent (and therefore had no distributable profits) and in excess of what the director was entitled to under the articles for holding office as a director, were a disguised gift of capital or payment of dividends in recognition of her co-proprietorship of the business. As such, they were ultra vires and void. In *Aveling Barford Ltd v Perion Ltd*[144] a sale of property by a company (which had no distributable profits) at a considerable undervalue (sale was at £350,000, independent valuation valued it at £650,000) to another entity controlled by the company's sole beneficial shareholder was an unlawful distribution. As an unauthorised return of capital, it was ultra vires and void.

---

[140] *Re Exchange Banking Co, Flitcroft's Case* (1882) 21 Ch D 519; *Precision Dippings Ltd v Precision Dippings Marketing Ltd* [1985] BCLC 385; *Aveling Barford v Perion Ltd* [1989] BCLC 626; *Bairstow v Queens Moat Houses plc* [2001] 2 BCLC 531, CA.

[141] CA 2006, s 830(1), implementing Second Company Law Directive, (77/91) art 15, OJ L 26, 31.1.1977, p 1.

[142] See *Aveling Barford Ltd v Perion Ltd* [1989] BCLC 626 at 631; *Ridge Securities v IRC* [1964] 1 All ER 275.

[143] [1982] 3 All ER 1016.

[144] [1989] BCLC 626; see also *Ridge Securities Ltd v IRC* [1964] 1 All ER 275.

The profits available for distribution are defined as the company's accumulated real-   **20-97**
ised profits, so far as not previously utilised by distribution or capitalisation, less its
accumulated realised losses, so far as not previously written off in a reduction or
reorganisation of capital duly made (CA 2006, s 830(2)). Whether such sums exist
must be determined by reference, essentially, to the company's last annual accounts
and to specified items in those accounts,[145] the importance of which is discussed below.
Primarily the issue of whether there is a profit or realised profit or loss is a matter of
the application of accounting principles at the time the accounts are prepared.[146]

It is only *realised* profits or losses which enter the equation, a requirement designed   **20-98**
to prevent companies from relying on estimated or expected profits which might
never materialise. In accounting terms, profits are treated as realised for these purposes only when 'realised in the form of cash or other assets, the ultimate cash realisation of which can be assessed with reasonable certainty'.[147] On the other hand,
unrealised losses are not taken into account (save to the extent that they are reflected
in the accounts) unless the company is a public company and the losses mean that
the company's net assets are less than its called-up share capital and undistributable
reserves (see below). Equally important, the amount of *accumulated* realised losses
must be deducted before any distribution can be made which abrogates the common
law rule that losses made in previous accounting periods did not have to be made
good.[148] Accounting periods can no longer be regarded in isolation from one another,
hence the need in many cases to write off losses by way of a reduction of capital before
resuming the payment of dividends.

The decision in *Aveling Barford Ltd v Perion Ltd*,[149] noted above at **20-96**, caused   **20-99**
problems in practice for reconstructions involving intra-group transfers of assets
which were commonly done at book value rather than market value. Post-*Aveling
Barford* it was thought that such transactions were open to challenge as improper distributions unless the transferring company had distributable profits to cover the gap
between the book value and the market value. The issue is addressed by CA 2006, s 845
which deals with distributions consisting of or including, or treated as arising in consequence of, the sale, transfer or other disposition by the company of a non-cash asset.[150]

---

[145] CA 2006, s 836(1). In some circumstances, initial or interim accounts may be used instead: see
s 836(2).

[146] CA 2006, s 853(4), hence the importance of Tech 01/08 (and Tech 07/08): see above n 120. References
to profits and losses, except where the context otherwise requires, are to revenue or capital profits and losses
made at any time: s 853(2).

[147] Tech 01/08 (also Tech 07/08), above n 120, para 3.3. See too *In Re Oxford Benefit Building & Investment
Society* (1886) 35 Ch D 502 at 510: 'realised profits' must have its ordinary commercial meaning, which, if
not equivalent to 'reduced to actual cash in hand', must at least be 'rendered tangible for the purpose of division'. Tech 01/8 (also Tech 07/08), at para 3.1, notes that it is apparent that the concept of a realised profit is
intended to be dynamic, changing with the development of generally accepted accounting principles, bringing within the definition profits which might not in ordinary language be called realised.

[148] See *Ammonia Soda Co v Chamberlain* [1918] 1 Ch 266; *Re National Bank of Wales Ltd* [1899] 2
Ch 629.   [149] [1989] BCLC 626; see also *Ridge Securities Ltd v IRC* [1964] 1 All ER 275.

[150] Note that CA 2006, s 845 applies to distributions under the statute or distributions under the common
law: see s 851(2). On the application of s 845, see Tech 07/08, above n 120, para 2.9A.

For companies which have available profits, this provision determines the amount of the distribution (and therefore the amount which needs to be covered by those distributable profits). Where the amount of the consideration received by the company out of the transaction is not less than the book value of the asset, the amount of the distribution is zero (s 845(2)(a)). Where the amount of the consideration received by the company is less than the asset value, the company needs distributable profits equal to the difference between the consideration received and the book value (s 845(2)(b)).[151] Where the company has no distributable profits, the position remains as in *Aveling Barford Ltd v Perion Ltd.*[152]

20-100   In addition to having realised profits available for distribution (a requirement which precludes a payment out of capital), a public company must satisfy two further conditions before it makes a distribution. These additional requirements ensure that, not only does a public company not make a distribution out of capital, but a public company must also maintain a cushion of assets sufficient to cover the amount of its share capital and undistributable reserves.[153] CA 2006, s 831(1) provides therefore that a public company may only make a distribution:

(1) if the amount of its net assets is not less than the aggregate of its called-up share capital and undistributable reserves, and

(2) if, and to the extent that, the distribution does not reduce the amount of those assets to less than that aggregate.[154]

20-101   This requirement ensures that, even if a public company has trading profits, it cannot pay a dividend if it has a deficit on its reserves. A company's undistributable reserves under the CA 2006 are:

(1) its share premium account;

(2) its capital redemption reserve;

(3) the amount by which the company's accumulated unrealised profits (so far as not previously utilised by any capitalisation) exceed its accumulated unrealised losses (so far as not previously written off in a reduction or re-organisation of capital duly made); and

---

[151] To the extent that the book value represents an unrealised profit, it is treated as realised, for these purposes, see CA 2006, s 846.   [152] [1989] BCLC 626.

[153] These additional requirements reflect the Second Company Law Directive (77/91/EEC), art 15, OJ L 26, 31.1.1977, p 1. In response to criticisms that art 15 is unduly prescriptive, the Commission has pointed out that art 15 does not require non-distributable legal or statutory reserves, rather it recognises them if national law requires them. If there is no national law requirement, art 15 only requires that the net assets cover the amount of the called-up share capital and the Second Directive only requires a minimum share capital of €25,000 (art 6(1)), which the Commission notes is not a significant amount in this context. See DG Internal Market and Services, Position Paper on results of external study on the Feasibility of Alternative to the Capital Maintenance regime of the Second Company Law Directive, available at http://ec.europa.eu/internal_market/company/docs/capital/feasbility/markt-position_en.pdf.

[154] CA 2006, s 831(1), modified for investment companies, see ss 832, 835. For this purpose, 'net assets' means the aggregate of the company's assets less the aggregate of its liabilities: s 831(2); and 'called-up share capital' is widely defined to include capital called up but not yet paid and capital to be paid on a specified future date: s 547. The redenomination reserve is treated as if it is paid-up share capital: see s 628(3).

(4) any other reserve which the company is prohibited from distributing by any enactment or by its articles.[155]

Justification by reference to accounts

All of these matters as to distributable profits are determined in accordance with the company's last individual annual accounts[156] circulated to the members in accordance with CA 2006, s 423, properly prepared in accordance with the requirements of the Act[157] and accompanied by an auditor's report unless the company has claimed exemption from audit.[158] The amount of the distribution is to be determined by reference to specified items in the accounts (profits, losses, assets and liabilities, provisions, share capital and reserves).[159]   **20-102**

In some circumstances, initial or interim accounts may be used instead and these accounts generally must be sufficient to enable a reasonable judgment to be made as to whether there are available profits.[160] Where a public company wishes to rely on initial or interim accounts, there are specific requirements as to form and content and the accounts must be delivered to the registrar of companies.[161] Interim accounts are particularly useful when the company's position has improved significantly since the last accounts and it wishes to make a distribution larger than would be possible under those accounts. Contravention of the accounting requirements in CA 2006, ss 837–839 means that the distribution is in contravention of Part 23 (s 836(4)).   **20-103**

The central importance of these accounting requirements in determining whether a distribution is lawful was highlighted by the decision in *Bairstow v Queens Moat Houses plc*[162] where the Court of Appeal emphasised that the consequence of the accounts not being properly prepared or not giving a true and fair view as required is that the distribution is unlawful. In this case, the accounts gave the misleading impression of significant profits when the company did not have distributable profits. The defendant directors argued that, while the company did not have distributable profits, there were profits available in wholly-owned subsidiary companies which might have been paid up to the parent company and any breach with respect to the accounts of the parent company was purely technical.   **20-104**

This argument was emphatically rejected by the Court of Appeal which emphasised that the statutory requirements as to proper accounts are an important part of the   **20-105**

---

[155] CA 2006, s 831(4); see s 669(1) for an example of an undistributable reserve.

[156] CA 2006, s 836(1); group accounts are not relevant for this purpose.

[157] CA 2006, s 837(1), or have been properly prepared subject only to matters that are not material for determining (by reference to s 836(1)) whether the distribution would contravene Part 23: s 837(2). Accounts so prepared must only be approved by the directors if they give a true and fair account of the state of the company's affairs: s 393. Accounts properly prepared may be Companies Act accounts or IAS accounts: s 395.

[158] CA 2006, s 837(3). See also s 840 which deals with successive distributions on the basis of the same accounts and ensures that financial assistance and other payments from distributable profits are taken into account in determining whether there are sufficient profits for a further distribution.

[159] See CA 2006, s 836(1).   [160] CA 2006, ss 838(1), 839(1).

[161] See CA 2006, ss 836(2), (3), 838(6), 839(7). For an example of interim accounts being used, see *Re Loquitur Ltd, IRC v Richmond* [2003] 2 BCLC 442.   [162] [2001] 2 BCLC 531, CA.

protection provided by the Act and are not be regarded as a mere procedural formality. As the accounts in this case had been drawn up in breach of the statutory requirements, any distribution based upon them was an unlawful distribution and the directors were not entitled to go behind the accounts to argue that the company did have the required distributable profits.[163] The court held that the dividend was an unlawful distribution regardless of whether the company might have had distributable profits had the accounts been properly prepared. The point is clearly made in CA 2006, s 836(4) which provides that if the accounting requirements are not complied with, 'the accounts may not be relied on for the purposes of this Part and *the* [emphasis added] distribution is accordingly treated as contravening this Part'.

20-106   Likewise in *Allied Carpets Group plc v Nethercott*[164] where the court found that the company had declared a dividend on the strength of accounts which did not give a true and fair view. The figures in the accounts for turnover and sales were inflated by a practice known as pre-despatching whereby sales were treated as realised once customers placed an order for carpet although the company's policy was that sales should only be booked to the accounts when the carpet had actually been fitted. Whether the company would have had distributable profits had the accounts been properly prepared was irrelevant and the company was entitled to summary judgment for £227,491 with respect to unlawful dividends received by a director who knew of the pre-despatching practice and knew therefore that the accounts were false.

20-107   The possibility that the distribution might have been made lawfully (if the accounts had been properly prepared) may influence the court, however, in terms of the remedy which it is willing to grant, for example by allowing relief for the directors under CA 2006, s 1157 (acted honestly and reasonably and ought fairly to be excused)[165] or by tailoring the remedy which the court is prepared to grant, as in *Re Loquitur Ltd*.

20-108   In *Re Loquitur Ltd, IRC v Richmond*[166] a company failed to make appropriate provision in its accounts for a possible tax liability, though the company knew that the tax relief which the company was seeking was likely to be rejected by the Inland Revenue. A dividend of £5.9m was paid on the strength of those accounts to the company's parent company. On the company going into liquidation, the Inland Revenue successfully challenged the payment of the dividend under IA 1986, s 212 (misfeasance by directors). The court found that the failure to make provision for the possible tax liability meant that the accounts were improperly prepared and therefore the dividend was paid in contravention of the statutory requirements. The directors had acted in breach of their duties to have regard to the interests of their creditors and had failed to exercise appropriate care and skill in failing to retain sufficient assets to cover reasonably anticipated liabilities.[167] On that basis, the court did not think that

---

[163] [2001] 2 BCLC 531 at 544–5; *Inn Spirit Ltd v Burns* [2002] 2 BCLC 780 at 786.
[164] [2001] BCC 81.
[165] See *Bairstow v Queens Moat Houses plc* [2001] 2 BCLC 531 at 545; *Inn Spirit Ltd v Burns* [2002] 2 BCLC 780 at 786.
[166] [2003] 2 BCLC 442.   [167] See [2003] 2 BCLC 442 at 489–90.

the defendants as directors had acted honestly and reasonably in authorising and procuring payment of the dividend and they could not be granted relief under what is now CA 2006, s 1157.

The court declined to order repayment of the entire amount of the dividend, however, **20-109** and limited the order to the amount of the outstanding tax liability (exercising its jurisdiction under IA 1986, s 213(3) to make such order for the purposes of s 212 as the court thinks fit).[168] The court limited recovery in this way on the basis that, had the accounts been properly drawn up, it is likely that a substantial dividend could have been paid. Crucially, the court also considered that the subsequent insolvency of the company was not caused by the accounting failures, but by a disastrous fire at the company's premises.[169]

Another scenario is where profits are available and the accounts are properly pre- **20-110** pared but the company makes an excessive distribution, for example the company has £100,000 available profits for distribution but makes a distribution of £180,000. The question then is whether the distribution is unlawful as to the entire amount or only to the amount in excess of the available profits. In *Re Marini Ltd, Liquidator of Marini Ltd v Dickenson*[170] the court concluded that the prohibition is on making a distribution other than out of profits available for distribution (CA 2006, s 830(1)). To the extent therefore that a distribution is out of such profits, it cannot be unlawful, a conclusion supported by s 847(1) which envisages a shareholder being required to return part of a distribution.

Unless the company has taken advantage of the audit exemption available to small **20-111** companies, the auditor must have made his report on the accounts (CA 2006, s 837(3)). If the auditor has qualified his report, he must state in writing (either at the time of his report or subsequently) whether, in his opinion, the substance of the qualification is material for determining whether the proposed dividend would contravene Part 23, and a copy of that statement must have been circulated to the members of a private company and, in the case of a public company, laid before the company in general meeting before the distribution was made (CA 2006, s 837(4)).

The significance of this statement by the auditor was considered by the Court of **20-112** Appeal in *Precision Dippings Ltd v Precision Dippings Marketing Ltd*.[171] In this case, no auditor's statement had been made although the accounts had been qualified. A dividend of £60,000 was paid by Dippings to its parent company, Marketing. Dippings later went into liquidation. The auditors at that stage (i.e. post-distribution) issued a written declaration to the effect that the qualification in their report did not affect the validity of the dividend payment. The liquidator of Dippings successfully sued to recover the amount of the dividend from Marketing.

---

[168] See also *Re Paycheck Services 3 Ltd, Revenue and Customs Commissioners v Holland* [2008] 2 BCLC 613 (failure to make provision for corporation tax when director knew or ought reasonably to have known that it was required meant distribution was unlawful). Relief under what is now CA 2006, s 1157 was not granted, but the liability was limited to the amount of corporation tax due.
[169] See [2003] 2 BCLC 442 at 490–1.   [170] [2004] BCC 172.   [171] [1985] BCLC 385.

20-113 The court found that the accounting requirements, of which the auditor's statement forms part, are not mere procedural requirement but an important part of the scheme provided by the statutory provisions as a major protection for creditors.[172] The wording of the provision (now CA 2006, s 837(4)(a), 'must have stated') showed that the auditor's statement had to be available to the shareholders before the distribution was made. As it had not been so available, the statutory provisions had been contravened and the payment of the dividend was ultra vires and void.

Declaration and payment of dividends

20-114 Assuming that a company does have available profits as determined in accordance with the statutory provisions, the next question is whether this automatically entitles the shareholders to a dividend. The position is that it does so only if the articles expressly provide for the payment of a fixed dividend where the company has distributable profits.[173] More commonly, the articles will allow for the declaration of a dividend by ordinary resolution following a recommendation by the directors.[174]

20-115 Only when a dividend has been declared does it become payable and due to the members.[175] As a rule a dividend must be paid in cash, but the articles may allow for a non-cash distribution to be made[176] (e.g. in the form of additional shares). A dividend paid in the form of additional shares is known as a scrip dividend.

Consequences of unlawful distributions

20-116 An unlawful distribution, whether unlawful because not out of available profits (CA 2006, s 830(1)), or because in breach of the accounting requirements (s 836(4)), or in breach of the common law principle that dividends must not be paid out of capital, or in breach of directors' fiduciary duties is ultra vires and void and cannot be ratified by the company in general meeting;[177] likewise where a dividend is paid in breach of a restriction in the articles[178] or contrary to some other enactment.

---

[172] [1985] BCLC 385 at 389.   [173] See *Evling v Israel & Oppenheimer Ltd* [1918] 1 Ch 101.

[174] See The Companies (Model Articles) Regulations 2008, SI 2008/3229, Sch 1 art 30 (private companies), Sch 3, art 70 (public companies); the resolution may decrease but not increase the amount to be distributed. Informal unanimous assent will suffice, but only if the shareholders know what they are assenting to, see *Queensway Systems Ltd v Walker* [2007] 2 BCLC 577.

[175] The declaration of the dividend creates an immediate debt: *Re Severn and Wye and Severn Bridge Ry Co* [1896] 1 Ch 559, unless it is expressed as payable at a future date, in which case a shareholder has no right to enforce payment until the due date for payment arrives: *Re Kidner, Kidner v Kidner* [1929] 2 Ch 121. In the case of an interim dividend which the board has resolved to pay, it is open to the board at any time before payment to review its decision and resolve not to pay the dividend: *Lagunas Nitrate Co Ltd v Schroeder & Co and SchmidtI* (1901) 85 Law Times 22.

[176] See The Companies (Model Articles) Regulations 2008, SI 2008/3229, Sch 1 art 35 (private companies), Sch 3, art 76 (public companies); also *Wood v Odessa Waterworks Co* (1889) 42 Ch D 636.

[177] *Re Exchange Banking Co, Flitcroft's Case* (1882) 21 Ch D 519; *Precision Dippings Ltd v Precision Dippings Marketing Ltd* [1985] BCLC 385; *Aveling Barford v Perion Ltd* [1989] BCLC 626; *Bairstow v Queens Moat Houses plc* [2001] 2 BCLC 531, CA.

[178] *Guinness plc v Saunders* [1990] BCLC 402, HL.

Where an unlawful distribution has been made, the company may seek to recover **20-117** the amount distributed under the statute or at common law and the latter option offers the greatest range of possibilities. There are two main targets for any action by the company: (1) the recipient of the unlawful distribution; and (2) the directors who authorised the unlawful distribution.[179] As the shareholder recipients, especially in larger public companies, are frequently unaware of the circumstances surrounding a distribution in the form of a dividend and rely on the directors to act properly, there is little likelihood of successfully pursuing the shareholders (other than shareholders who are also directors) to recover unlawful dividends. It is more likely, though still comparatively rare, for the company (usually because a liquidator or new board of directors is in place) to pursue recovery from the directors who authorised the improper payments. Another possibility is that a creditor, such as the Inland Revenue, may bring a claim for misfeasance under IA 1986, s 212 against directors who authorise improper dividends.[180] Disqualification is also a possibility.[181]

Liability of recipients

Where a distribution, or part of a distribution,[182] is made in contravention of the **20-118** requirements of CA 2006, Part 23, any member who, at the time of the distribution, knows or has reasonable grounds for believing that it is so made is liable to repay the distribution (or part of it, as the case may be) to the company.[183] This statutory liability is without prejudice to any obligation imposed apart from the statutory provisions on a member to repay a distribution unlawfully made to him,[184] i.e. as a knowing recipient of trust funds.[185] An illustration of liability based on 'knowing receipt' can be found in *Precision Dippings Ltd v Precision Dippings Marketing Ltd*[186] where a dividend was paid by a company (Dippings) to its parent company (Marketing) and the directors

---

[179] Where the accounts have not been prepared properly and do not give a true and fair view as required, the company may also bring an action for negligence against its auditors.

[180] See *Re Loquitar Ltd, IRC v Richmond* [2003] 2 BCLC 444; *Re Paycheck Services 3 Ltd, Revenue and Customs Commissioners v Holland* [2008] 2 BCLC 613.

[181] See *Re AG (Manchester) Ltd, Official Receiver v Watson* [2008] 1 BCLC 321 where a director who was the wife of the controlling shareholder was disqualified. Though a director, she had left all financial and strategic decisions to an inner group of directors (including her husband) and was content to take substantial dividends from the company regardless of how and whether they could be paid. The court found her abdication of responsibility in failing to act independently and in the interests of the company justified her disqualification for four years.

[182] If the company has available profits and properly prepared accounts, but pays a dividend in excess of that amount, it is only the part in excess of the available profits that is in contravention of the Act and must be repaid to the company: see *Re Marini Ltd, Liquidator of Marini Ltd v Dickenson* [2004] BCC 172.

[183] CA 2006, s 847(1), (2)(a), implementing Second Company Law Directive (77/91/EEC), art 16, OJ L 26, 31.1.1977, p 1. Where the distribution is made otherwise than in cash, the statutory liability is to pay to the company a sum equal to the value of the distribution at the time of the distribution: s 847(2)(b), but at common law a proprietary claim may lie against the recipient.

[184] CA 2006, s 847(3).

[185] See *Bank of Credit and Commerce International (Oversea) Ltd v Akindele* [2000] 4 All ER 221, CA and the discussion at **13-37** as to liability on a 'knowing receipt' basis. See also *Rolled Steel Products (Holdings) Ltd v British Steel Corpn* [1986] Ch 246 at 297–8; *Belmont Finance Corpn Ltd v Williams Furniture Ltd (No 2)* [1980] 1 All ER 393 at 405; *Russell v Wakefield Waterworks Co* (1875) LR 20 Eq 474.

[186] [1985] BCLC 385, CA.

of Dippings were the only directors and shareholders of Marketing. The Court of Appeal held that the payment of the dividend in breach of the statutory provisions was an ultra vires act of the company. Marketing, when it received the money, had notice of the facts and held the £60,000 dividend on constructive trust for the company which was entitled to repayment.[187]

20-119   The flexibility to proceed either under the statutory provision or the common law is necessary since, as discussed above, it is possible for a distribution to a member to be valid under CA 2006, Part 23 (there are profits and the accounting requirements are met), so no statutory liability arises, but the payment is in breach of the common law, the company's constitution and/or the directors' fiduciary duty.[188] Also the test of liability as a recipient is different under the statute and at common law.[189] Statutory liability arises where the shareholder knows the facts which constitute the contravention of the Act.[190] Liability as a constructive trustee arises where the shareholder knows or ought to know that the distribution is unlawful.[191] Therefore, depending on the facts, one or other route may offer the best chance of recovery.

20-120   The statutory liability was considered by the Court of Appeal in *It's a Wrap (UK) Ltd v Gula*[192] where the focus was on the meaning of the requirement that the member 'knows or has reasonable grounds for believing' that the distribution is in contravention of the Act (now CA 2006, s 847(2)). The company had two members, a husband and wife, who were also the directors. The company made no profits during its brief (4 years) existence but the directors each took dividends of £14,000 per annum as a tax-efficient alternative to receiving a salary from the company. On the company going into insolvent liquidation, the liquidator sought to recover £56,000 in total from them, but they were found not liable at first instance on the basis that the section required knowledge of the legal position. The Court of Appeal swiftly overruled the decision and confirmed that it is not necessary to show that the shareholders know the statutory provisions. All that must be established is that the shareholders know the facts of the distribution which constitute the contravention. The defendants knew the company had no profits, therefore they knew of the contravention for the purpose of the statutory liability and they had to repay the sums which they had received.

Liability of directors

20-121   The statute deals with the position of the liability of the recipient of an unlawful dividend, but does not address the liability of the directors for authorising or procuring

---

[187] See [1985] BCLC 385 at 390, per Dillon LJ, applying *Rolled Steel Products (Holdings) Ltd v British Steel Corpn* [1986] Ch 246, [1985] 3 All ER 52.

[188] See *It's a Wrap (UK) Ltd v Gula* [2006] 2 BCLC 634 at 638–9 where Arden LJ comments on the distinction between the statutory and common law liability.

[189] See Arden LJ in *It's a Wrap (UK) Ltd v Gula* [2006] 2 BCLC 634 at 639 who comments that the statutory remedy is more absolute and stringent than that at common law.

[190] *It's a Wrap (UK) Ltd v Gula* [2006] 2 BCLC 634, CA.

[191] *Moxham v Grant* [1900] 1 QB 88; see also *Precision Dippings Ltd* v *Precision Dippings Marketing Ltd* [1985] BCLC 385; *Re Cleveland Trust plc* [1991] BCLC 424; *Allied Carpets Group plc v Nethercott* [2001] BCC 81.   [192] [2006] 2 BCLC 634, CA.

the payment of the dividend which remains a matter for the common law. The position is clear. Directors are trustees of the company's assets and as such are jointly and severally liable for the full amount of any unlawful distribution of the company's assets to the shareholders, whether the company is solvent or insolvent and whether or not profits could have been available.[193] The potential extent of this liability can be seen in *Bairstow v Queens Moat Houses plc*[194] where the company obtained a judgment for £78m against its former directors who, the court found, had deliberately (and dishonestly in certain cases) made unlawful dividend payments over a period of years. In this instance, the company sought to recover from the directors the entire amount paid to the shareholders.[195] To the extent that a distribution is made in excess of available profits as determined by properly prepared accounts, the liability extends only to the repayment of that part which is unlawful.[196]

The classic authority is *Re Exchange Banking Co, Flitcroft's Case*[197] where the directors had been in the habit of including among the company's assets a number of debts which they knew to be bad. The effect was to give the appearance of profits when in fact there were none. The directors recommended and the general meeting approved the payment of dividends over a period of several years on the strength of those accounts. On the company going into insolvent liquidation, the court ordered the directors jointly and severally to repay the moneys improperly expended in this way.   **20-122**

This liability to make repayment arises where the unlawful dividend payment is made with knowledge by the directors that the funds of the company are being misappropriated or with knowledge of the facts which establish the misappropriation.[198] In *Kingston Cotton Mill (No 2)*[199] the court was prepared to relieve directors from liability where they acted under an honest and reasonable belief that the payments were lawful, but higher standards of care and skill are expected of directors now and even in cases where the individual director is not directly implicated in the payment of an improper dividend, it is likely that the 'innocent' director has failed to exercise sufficient care and skill in allowing it to be declared.[200] For example, the innocent director may have   **20-123**

---

[193] *Re Exchange Banking Co, Flitcroft's Case* (1882) 21 Ch D 519; *Re Oxford Benefit Building & Investment Society* (1886) 35 Ch D 502; *Bairstow v Queens Moat Houses plc* [2001] 2 BCLC 531, CA; and see the discussion of directors' liabilities in Chapter 13. Directors who are liable for the entire amount of the distribution may seek an indemnity from the shareholders who received it: *Moxham v Grant* [1900] 1 QB 88.

[194] [2001] 2 BCLC 531, CA; *Re Denham & Co* [1884] LR 25 Ch D 752.

[195] As to whether the directors might have sought contribution from any shareholder recipients who had knowledge of the unlawful nature of the payments, see [2001] 2 BCLC 531 at 547–8; also *Moxham v Grant* [1900] 1 QB 88.

[196] *Re Marini Ltd, Liquidator of Marini Ltd v Dickenson* [2004] BCC 172 at 193. The distinguishing feature from *Bairstow v Queens Moat Houses plc* [2001] 2 BCLC 531 at 546, CA is that profits were available in *Marini* whereas in *Bairstow* there were no profits in the company and, even if there might have been elsewhere in the group, they had not been paid up into the company.   [197] (1882) 21 Ch D 519.

[198] *Re Exchange Banking Co, Flitcroft's Case* (1882) 21 Ch D 519; *Re Kingston Cotton Mill Co (No 2)* [1896] 1 Ch 331 at 347; *Precision Dippings Ltd v Precision Dippings Marketing Ltd* [1985] BCLC 385 at 390; *Bairstow v Queens Moat Houses plc* [2000] 1 BCLC 549 at 559, Ch D.   [199] [1896] 1 Ch 331 at 348.

[200] See *Bairstow v Queens Moat Houses plc* [2000] 1 BCLC 549 at 559–60, Ch D which contains a useful summation by Nelson J of the circumstances in which a director will be liable. The case was appealed on other grounds, see [2001] 2 BCLC 531, CA.

relied unduly on others in breach of his duty to exercise residual supervision of the management of the company's affairs and a failure to apply his mind to whether the distribution is proper is a breach of his duty of care and skill.[201]

20-124   It is also the case that the courts are reluctant to grant relief under CA 2006, s 1157 (power to give relief when officers have acted honestly and reasonably and ought fairly to be excused) to directors liable for improperly declared dividends when to do so would in effect allow the directors to retain benefits at the expense of the creditors.[202]

Alternative frameworks—solvency statements

20-125   The Company Law Review favoured only technical amendments to the statutory provisions on distribution rather than wholesale revision.[203] A more fundamental debate subsequently emerged at the European level (though influenced by developments here[204]) as to whether it is time to shift away from a statutory framework on distributions closely tied to the company's accounts and the determination of the existence of available profits under those accounts to a scheme based on directors' declarations of solvency (whereby if the directors certify that the company will remain solvent following a distribution, that should suffice). This approach, or variations thereof, is relied upon in other jurisdictions and the accounting profession seems keen on such reform.[205] The issue is part of a broader debate mentioned at **20-7** as to whether the capital maintenance doctrine is obsolete and serves no practical purpose.

20-126   Against that backdrop, the European Commission launched an external assessment of the capital maintenance regime established by the Second Directive which was carried out by KPMG and published in early 2008.[206] KPMG were asked to consider in particular the impact of International Financial Reporting Standards (IFRS, which must be used for consolidated accounts and may be used for individual accounts) on distributions and whether an alternative regime would be better. On the distribution

---

[201] See *Re AG (Manchester) Ltd, Official Receiver v Watson* [2008] 1 BCLC 321; *Queensway Systems Ltd v Walker* [2007] 2 BCLC 577; *Neville v Krikorian* [2007] 1 BCLC 1, CA. The liability arises either from a breach of care and skill or in effect from implicitly authorising the improper payment.

[202] See *Inn Spirit Ltd v Burns* [2002] 2 BCLC 780 at 787–8; *Re Loquitur Ltd, IRC v Richmond* [2003] 2 BCLC 442; *Re Marini Ltd, Liquidator of Marini Ltd v Dickenson* [2004] BCC 172 at 193; *Queensway Systems Ltd v Walker* [2007] 2 BCLC 577.

[203] See Company Law Review, *Final Report*, vol I (2001), para 10.6; *Completing the Structure* (2000), paras 7.20–7.23; *Company Formation and Capital Maintenance* (1999), paras 3.65–3.76 and Annex B; also *Capital Maintenance: Other Issues* (2000).

[204] See Rickford (ed), Reforming Capital: Report of the Interdisciplinary Group on Capital Maintenance' (2004) EBLR 919.

[205] See FEE Discussion Paper on Alternatives to Capital Maintenance Regimes, September 2007. FEE is an umbrella group for accountants in Europe representing 43 member bodies in 32 countries. For the views of a leading British proponent of a move to a solvency regime, see Rickford, 'Legal Approaches to Restricting Distributions to Shareholders: Balance Sheet Tests and Solvency Tests' (2006) 7 EBOR 135.

[206] KPMG, 'Feasibility study on an alternative to the capital maintenance regime established by the Second Company Law Directive 77/91/EEC of 13 December 1976 and an examination of the impact on profit distribution of the new EU accounting regime', January 2008, available on the Commission website at http://ec.europa.eu/internal_market/company/capital/index_en.htm.

issues, the KPMG study concluded that the requirements of the Second Directive were modest in relation to the cushion required before a distribution might be made, the use of IFRS as such did not cause companies problems in terms of distributions, and that those jurisdictions which do rely on solvency statements, frequently also impose a balance sheet test.[207] In the light of those findings, the Commission announced that 'no follow-up measures or changes to the Second Company Law Directive are foreseen in the immediate future'.[208] The result of the KPMG findings, even before the Commission's announcement, has been that the momentum for changes to the rules governing distribution has dissipated somewhat. Certainly, the European Commission is unlikely to support any wholesale change from the current system in the absence of identifiable benefits from doing so. Such future changes as may arise are likely to come from the development of accounting standards and possible changes to the Accounting Directives rather than change to the Second Company Law Directive. But, to some extent, these issues have been overtaken by market developments and the catastrophic banking failures of 2008 are likely to lead for demands for tighter regulation of business and even tighter accounting standards to prevent optimistic valuations and inappropriate distributions. There is likely to be little support in the coming months for measures which are perceived (even if that perception is errone-ous) to reduce protection for creditors.

E Financial assistance by a company for the acquisition of its own shares

The problem with financial assistance

Financial assistance given by a company for the purchase of its own shares can arise   **20-127**
in many circumstances but the classic abuse relates to the acquisition of a company by a bidder who borrows to fund the acquisition and then uses the company's assets once control has been secured to repay the funding. There are legitimate ways of car-rying out this manoeuvre, as we shall see, but the concern is that, once the bidder has gained control, an element of asset stripping may occur to the detriment of the creditors.[209] Shareholders who have not had or taken the opportunity to exit from the company may also suffer as a consequence, though the primary concern here is credi-tor protection which is why these rules are linked to the capital maintenance rules

---

[207] See Schon, 'Balance Sheet Tests or Solvency Tests—or Both?' (2006) EBOR 181 who argues for the dual approach.

[208] Commission statement on the results of the external study on the feasibility of an alternative to the Capital Maintenance Regime of the Second Company Law Directive and the impact of the adop-tion of IFRS on profit distribution (undated), available on Commission website at http://ec.europa.eu/internal_market/company/capital/index_en.htm.

[209] See Report of the Company Law Committee (the Jenkins Committee) (Cmnd 1749, 1962), para 176; see *Re VGM Holdings Ltd* [1942] 1 All ER 224 at 225.

discussed in this chapter. Concerns about the giving of financial assistance by a company for the purchase of its own shares date back to the 1920s. Though the statutory provisions have been restated on a number of occasions since their introduction in the Companies Act 1928, Arden LJ noted in *Chaston v SWP Group plc*[210] that:

> 'The general mischief, however, remains the same,[211] namely that the resources of the target company and its subsidiaries should not be used directly or indirectly to assist the purchaser or financially to make the acquisition. This may prejudice the interests of the creditors of the target or its group and the interests of any shareholders who do not accept the offer to acquire the shares or to whom the offer is not made.'

20-128   The mischief can arise in the context of significant companies with substantial assets, but it may also arise in smaller companies where typically the existing shareholders/directors wish to exit the business but cannot find a purchaser with funds to acquire their shares. The temptation or solution, depending on your viewpoint, is to use the company's assets to assist a possible purchaser. The risk is that the shareholders'/directors' personal determination to exit leaves them indifferent or reckless to the consequences of using the company's assets to assist an impecunious purchaser.[212] An example can be seen in *Re In A Flap Envelope Co Ltd*[213] where the directors of a company in financial difficulties sold their shareholding in the company to L. Some months later, when L had still not paid for the shares, it was agreed that the company would lend money to L to enable it to pay for the shares. L then paid the shareholders £355,000 approximately. Twelve months later the company collapsed owing £3.2m.

The legislative response

20-129   As noted, financial assistance was first made a criminal offence by the CA 1929. The current prohibition on the giving of financial assistance by companies for the purchase of their own shares is set out in CA 2006, ss 677–683[214] (previously CA 1985, ss 151–158[215]).

20-130   The provisions on financial assistance are wide-ranging and practitioners frequently complain of the additional expense and complexity involved in ensuring that innocuous transactions linked to the acquisition of companies do not fall foul of the prohibition, particularly given that it is a criminal offence.[216] A further problem is that, while the potential for abuse in funding acquisitions in this way is clear, it is

---

[210] [2003] 1 BCLC 675 at 686.

[211] For criticisms of the view that this mischief requires rules on financial assistance, see Ferran, 'Corporate Transactions and Financial Assistance: Shifting Policy Perceptions but Static Law' (2004) CLJ 225, esp at 239–41.

[212] The assistance may equally be given to the vendor or indeed to third parties, since the prohibitions apply to assistance given directly or indirectly, see CA 2006, s 678(1), (3), s 679(1).

[213] [2004] 1 BCLC 64.   [214] See generally Ferran, *Principles of Corporate Finance Law* (2008), Ch 10.

[215] For a comprehensive account of the 1985 provisions, see Roberts, *Financial Assistance for the Acquisition of Shares* (2005).

[216] The Company Law Review noted that the financial assistance provisions are ones on which legal advice is sought very frequently and it has been estimated that the cost to companies of the provisions concerned is some £20m per annum: see Company Law Review, *Strategic Framework* (1999), para 5.4.22.

also clear that if this type of funding is not possible, then many perfectly acceptable acquisitions will not occur, giving rise to economic loss and stagnation. Recognising these difficulties, the Companies Act 1981 introduced a 'whitewash' procedure for private companies which enabled such companies to give financial assistance provided certain conditions were met (CA 1985, ss 155–158). The whitewash procedure was complicated and costly to execute in that it required a special resolution by the shareholders, a directors' statement (essentially as to the solvency of the company at the time of giving the assistance and for a year thereafter) backed up by an auditors' statement and objecting shareholders could apply to the court to block the assistance. Crucially, the financial assistance could only be given if the company had net assets which were not thereby reduced or, to the extent that they were reduced, the assistance was provided out of distributable profits (CA 1985, s 155(2)).

On a variety of occasions in the early 1990s, the Department of Trade and Industry consulted as to possible reform of the statutory provisions but no progress was made, in part because the position with respect to public companies is constrained by the Second EC Company Law Directive which provides that such a company may not advance funds, nor make loans, nor provide security, with a view to the acquisition of its shares by a third party (art 23(1)).[217] The Company Law Review duly considered the issue and was highly critical of the statutory provisions (CA 1985, ss 151–158) noting that:[218]   **20-131**

> 'These provisions are among the most difficult of the Act, and in many cases it is all but impossible for a company to assess whether a proposed course of action is lawful or not. The provisions are arbitrary in their effect on private companies, and innocuous transactions may be rendered unlawful by criminal law requirements that are often unenforceable and by civil sanctions of wide and damaging effect. There are alternative remedies designed to deal with threats to creditors which are likely in most circumstances to be more effective. This unnecessary burden should be lifted from private companies.'

The Review recommended that the provisions on financial assistance should not apply to private companies (so dispensing with the need for the whitewash procedure) and that such abuses as prompted the legislation (asset stripping essentially) should be addressed through directors' duties and the insolvency legislation.[219] Public companies would remain subject to the prohibitions in the light of the Second Company Law Directive. These recommendations were adopted in the CA 2006, ss 677–683.   **20-132**

Repealing the prohibition on financial assistance by private companies is seen by the Government as one of the key de-regulatory measures of the CA 2006. That said, the remaining provisions are still complex and wide-ranging and do apply to some extent to private companies (where they are part of a group with public companies)   **20-133**

---

[217] Second Council Directive (77/91/EEC) [1977] OJ L 26/1.

[218] Company Law Review, *Final Report*, vol I (2001), para 2.30.

[219] See Company Law Review, *Final Report*, vol I (2001), para 10.6; *Completing the Structure* (2000), paras 7.12–7.15; *Company Formation and Capital Maintenance* (1999), paras 3.41–3.48 and Annex B; *Strategic Framework* (1999), paras 5.4.20–5.4.25.

so the position still needs careful consideration. It must also be appreciated that while the prohibition on the giving of financial assistance by private companies has been repealed, the broader protective rules discussed in this chapter, on distributions and reduction of capital, still apply as does the common law principle (*Trevor v Whitworth*[220]) prohibiting a return of capital to shareholders.[221] Any transaction which involves giving financial assistance needs to be looked at carefully to ensure it does not fall foul of those other rules or principles, for example where it gives rise to a reduction in net assets which cannot be covered by distributable reserves. The possibility that a transaction might be challenged subsequently as a transaction at an undervalue under IA 1986, s 238 also needs to be borne in mind. Directors' fiduciary duties also come into play when the company is giving financial assistance and the directors need to consider carefully (and probably minute carefully) whether they are exercising their powers for a proper purpose (CA 2006, s 171) and to promote the success of the company (s 172). The duty of care and skill is also relevant (s 174) and possibly even the duty to avoid a conflict of interest (under s 175 or even s 177). Removing the prohibition may not therefore have opened up the way for freewheeling financial assistance of the type which perhaps some of the proponents of abolition envisaged. Mindful of their duties and concerned about any infringement of the rules on distributions and reduction of capital and the risk of subsequent challenge, it is possible that directors of private companies may continue to seek the protection of shareholder approval and even an auditor's report before giving financial assistance. The result may be to reinstate voluntarily the very elements of the 'whitewash' procedure which were criticised as time-consuming and expensive. At this early stage, this risk must not be overstated and it remains to be seen whether practice will develop so as to minimise the need for such measures other than with respect to particularly risky or unusual transactions.

20-134   The position with respect to public companies is unchanged by the CA 2006. As noted, the position is governed by the Second Company Law Directive, art 23 which limited the scope for change in the CA 2006. The Second Directive was amended by Directive 2006/68/EC to allow Member States to permit public companies to grant financial assistance up to the limit of the company's distributable reserves.[222] The relaxation is surrounded by onerous procedural requirements, however (including prior shareholder approval based on a detailed report to be presented to the general meeting

---

[220] (1887) 12 App Cas 409, HL.

[221] In an attempt to allay concerns as to the extent to which the common law may still be relevant, an obscurely worded saving provision was included in The Companies Act 2006 (Commencement No. 5, Transitional Provisions and Savings) Order 2007, SI 2007/3495, art 9, Sch 4, para 52. The intention, apparently, is to ensure that private companies which are now released from the statutory prohibitions on financial assistance should not be subject to any residual common law restriction on financial assistance. The difficulty is that the common law restriction is a broader prohibition on a return of capital so the saving may prove pointless if it was intended to close off challenges on the basis of an improper return of capital. It does close off challenges on the grounds of improper financial assistance, but as the Department of Trade pointed out, that was the consequence of the repeal of the prohibition so far as it applied to private companies in any event. See the Explanatory Memorandum to the Fifth Commencement Order, para 7, available at www.opsi. gov.uk/si/si2007/em/uksiem_20073495_en.pdf.

[222] OJ L 264, 25.9.2006, pp 32–6.

and the creation of an undistributable reserve equal to the amount of the financial assistance) so the UK has decided not to implement this option.[223]

Public companies can take comfort, however, from evidence of a more pragmatic approach by the courts to financial assistance issues in recent years which respects genuine commercial transactions and seeks to constrain the prohibition to the mischief identified by Parliament, namely the risk to creditors of asset depletion from financial assistance. For example, the courts have been alert to attempts by parties to evade their commercial obligations on the basis of spurious claims of illegal financial assistance, as in *Dyment v Boyden*[224] and *Anglo Petroleum Ltd v TFB (Mortgages) Ltd*.[225] In *Dyment v Boyden*[226] a tenant tried to have an onerous lease declared void for illegal financial assistance when the reality was that she had made a bad bargain and was paying an extortionate rent. In *Anglo Petroleum Ltd v TFB (Mortgages) Ltd*[227] a borrower essentially tried to renege on a £15m loan and related guarantee by alleging illegal financial assistance when the reality was that its financial position had worsened and it was finding it difficult to make repayments. The courts have emphasised the importance of looking at the overall commercial realities of a situation instead of allowing a narrow focus on whether technically a transaction may be classified as financial assistance; see the discussion at **20-136** below. Further, the courts are minded to limit the scope of the resulting illegality. In *Anglo Petroleum Ltd v TFB (Mortgages) Ltd*,[228] for example, the Court of Appeal noted obiter that, even if it had found illegal financial assistance in respect of the use of funds borrowed by the company, the loan agreement and associated charges and guarantees would not have been illegal. Those agreements did not necessitate any breach of the law, Toulson LJ said, and no reason of public policy required those perfectly ordinary commercial transactions to be struck down.[229] All of these elements show a concern to keep the prohibition within appropriate boundaries.

20-135

The prohibition on financial assistance

There are three prohibitions in all. First, where a person is acquiring or is proposing to acquire any shares in a public company, it is not lawful for the company or a company that is a subsidiary of that company[230] to give financial assistance directly or indirectly for the purpose of that acquisition before or at the same time as the acquisition takes place (CA 2006, s 678(1)). The first scenario then is the acquisition of shares in a public company where the financial assistance is given by that (public) company or by a subsidiary company (which may be a private or public company).

20-136

---

[223] See criticism of the proposal for this Directive by Ferran 'Simplification of European Company law on Financial Assistance' (2005) 6 EBOR 93.

[224] [2005] 1 BCLC 163, CA.   [225] [2008] 1 BCLC 185, CA.   [226] [2005] 1 BCLC 163, CA.

[227] [2008] 1 BCLC 185, CA.   [228] [2008] 1 BCLC 185, CA.

[229] [2008] 1 BCLC 185 at 202–3, CA.

[230] The prohibition applies only to subsidiaries registered in this jurisdiction and a foreign subsidiary of an English parent company can give financial assistance for the acquisition of the latter's shares: *Arab Bank plc v Merchantile Holdings Ltd* [1994] 1 BCLC 330, but see also at 335; *AMG Global Nominees (Private) Ltd v SMM Holdings Ltd* [2008] 1 BCLC 447.

20-137   Secondly, where a person has acquired shares in a company and a liability has been incurred (by that or any other person) for the purpose of the acquisition, it is not lawful for that company or a company that is a subsidiary of that company[231] to give financial assistance directly or indirectly for the purpose of reducing or discharging the liability[232] if, at the time the assistance is given, the company in which the shares were acquired is a public company (CA 2006, s 678(3)). The second scenario covers the situation where shares have been acquired whether in a public or private company provided that at the time the assistance is given (again whether by a public or private company) to reduce or discharge the liability incurred on that purchase the company in which the shares are acquired is a public company.

20-138   Finally, where a person is acquiring or is proposing to acquire shares in a private company, it is not lawful for a public company that is a subsidiary of that company[233] to give financial assistance directly or indirectly for the purpose of that acquisition before or at the same time as the acquisition takes place (CA 2006, s 679(1)) or to give financial assistance directly or indirectly for the purpose of reducing or discharging a liability incurred for the purpose of the acquisition (s 679(3)).[234]

20-139   There is no requirement that the assistance be given to the vendor or the purchaser of the shares, it could be given to a subsidiary or associated company or other person nominated by one of the parties, provided it is for the purpose of the acquisition.[235]

20-140   A breach of these provisions is a criminal offence and the company is liable to a fine and every officer in default is liable to imprisonment or a fine or both (CA 2006, s 680). The civil consequences are not dealt with in the statute and remain a matter for the common law: see the discussion at **20-157**.

20-141   To establish liability, it is necessary to show that financial assistance was given and that it was given for the purpose of the acquisition or the reduction/discharge of a liability, as the case may be.[236]

The meaning of financial assistance

20-142   The legislation is broadly drafted to catch a wide variety of types of financial assistance, for example financial assistance given by way of gift, guarantee, security or indemnity, release or waiver or a loan, etc, all of which are listed in CA 2006, s 677(1). The requirement is that the transaction be of the type mentioned (and the terms

---

[231] See above n 230.

[232] A reference to a company giving financial assistance for the purpose of reducing or discharging a liability incurred by a person for the purpose of the acquisition of shares includes its giving such assistance for the purpose of wholly or partially restoring his financial position to what it was before the acquisition took place: CA 2006, s 683(2)(b).

[233] See above n 230.   [234] See above n 232.

[235] *Chaston v SWP Group plc* [2003] 1 BCLC 675 at 689, CA. But see criticisms by Ferran, above n 211, p 237 who argues that there is no need to extend the prohibition beyond assistance of benefit to purchasers, since that is the mischief at which the prohibition is aimed; also Look Chan Ho, 'Financial Assistance after Chaston and MT Realisations' (2003) JIBLR 424.

[236] *Charterhouse Investment Trust Ltd v Tempest Diesels Ltd* [1986] BCLC 1 at 10, per Hoffmann J.

used, indemnity etc, must be given their normal legal meaning) and also amount to financial assistance.[237] As Arden LJ pointed out in *Chaston v SWP Group plc*,[238] there is no requirement of detriment with regard to these elements, for example financial assistance via a loan could be on terms which are beneficial to the company.[239] Detriment is only essential under CA 2006, s 677(1)(d) which includes 'any other financial assistance given by a company where the net assets[240] of the company are reduced to a material extent[241] by the giving of the assistance, or the company has no net assets'. As Ward LJ noted in *Chaston v SWP Group plc*,[242] these words are 'as wide as can be' and so have the potential to catch the unwary as a transaction which does not appear to be financial assistance in any of the more obvious ways (loans, guarantees etc) may fall foul of this element. On the other hand, CA 2006, s 677(1)(d) is necessary precisely to catch transactions which do not fall into the more obvious categories of financial assistance listed in the section, such as where a company purchases an asset at an overvalue for the purpose of putting the vendor of the asset in funds with which to acquire the company's shares.[243]

20-143 Drawing lines can be difficult, however, as noted above. For example, the payment of a debt owed by the company cannot be financial assistance for that is a mere discharge of a debt.[244] Likewise the grant of security in respect of a debt cannot amount to financial assistance,[245] but the payment off of a parent company's debt by a subsidiary in order to facilitate an acquisition of the parent company's shares may constitute such assistance.[246] In *Chaston v SWP Group plc*[247] a subsidiary company agreed to pay certain adviser fees with respect to a report on the affairs of its parent company which report was carried out for the purpose of a proposed acquisition of the parent company's shares by another party and that was held by the Court of Appeal to be financial assistance for the purpose of the acquisition of the parent company shares.

20-144 The potential scope of the prohibition is wide, then, but the courts, starting with Hoffmann J in *Charterhouse Investment Trust Ltd v Tempest Diesels Ltd*,[248] have emphasised that, when deciding whether a transaction can properly be described as the giving of financial assistance by the company, the commercial realities of the transaction as a whole must be considered, bearing in mind that the section is a penal provision and should not be strained to cover transactions which are not fairly within

---

[237] *Barclays Bank plc v British & Commonwealth Holdings plc* [1996] 1 BCLC 1 at 38, CA.

[238] [2003] 1 BCLC 675 at 689.

[239] See Ferran, above n 211 at 231 who agrees with Arden LJ as a matter of statutory interpretation, but see Look Chan Ho, above n 235, who is more critical of this interpretation.

[240] 'Net assets' is defined as the aggregate of the company's assets less the aggregate of its liabilities: CA 2006, s 677(2).

[241] There is no definition of material extent, but in practice a reduction of 1% would be considered material.   [242] [2003] 1 BCLC 675 at 694.

[243] See *Belmont Finance Corpn Ltd v Williams Furniture Ltd* [1980] 1 All ER 393, CA.

[244] *Armour Hick Northern Ltd v Armour Trust Ltd* [1980] 3 All ER 833.

[245] *Anglo Petroleum Ltd v TFB (Mortgages) Ltd* [2008] 1 BCLC 185, CA.

[246] *Armour Hick Northern Ltd v Armour Trust Ltd* [1980] 3 All ER 833.

[247] [2003] 1 BCLC 675, CA.   [248] [1986] BCLC 1 at 10.

it. That view has been endorsed by the Court of Appeal,[249] most recently in *Anglo Petroleum Ltd v TFB Mortgages*,[250] where Toulson LJ crisply summed up the correct approach as follows: 'In cases where its application [the prohibition on financial assistance] is doubtful, it is important to remember its central purpose, to examine the commercial realities and to bear in mind that it is a penal statute.'

20-145 In *MT Realisations Ltd v Digital Equipment Co Ltd*,[251] a subsidiary company paid sums due under a secured loan to its parent company and those sums were used to pay off the liability incurred by the parent company in acquiring the shares in the subsidiary. In fact, for convenience, the sums were paid directly by the subsidiary to the vendor of the shares so it appeared that the subsidiary's funds were being used to pay liabilities arising on the acquisition of shares in the subsidiary. An allegation arose that this was illegal financial assistance. The Court of Appeal found that the commercial reality of this transaction was that (1) the subsidiary was not giving the parent company anything, (2) the parent company was exercising its entitlement as a secured creditor to require certain sums to be paid to it, and (3) as a matter of commercial convenience those sums were paid direct to the vendor rather than from the subsidiary to the parent to the vendor. As a matter of commercial reality and legal principle, the Court of Appeal held, such an agreement did not involve the subsidiary in giving financial assistance for the acquisition of its own shares.

20-146 A similarly robust approach is evident in *Anglo Petroleum Ltd v TFB (Mortgages) Ltd*.[252] In this case a company in financial difficulties (it owed £30m, unsecured, to its parent company) negotiated a reduction in that debt to £15m and gave a charge over its assets to secure the repayment of the £15m. At the same time, the parent company sold its entire shareholding in the company to K for £1 and K guaranteed to ensure that the company would repay the outstanding indebtedness. The court rejected a claim that the charge given to secure the repayment of the £15m was financial assistance for the acquisition of the shares by K. The court noted that it is well established that the repayment of a debt which is properly due from a company does not constitute financial assistance. If it is lawful for a company to repay its own indebtedness; the court held, it must also equally be lawful for the company to assist that repayment by providing security. In this case, the commercial reality was a restructuring of debt with a significant reduction in amount achieved in return for security. K subsequently borrowed £15m from TFB to pay off the outstanding £15m to the original parent company and that TFB borrowing was secured on the company's assets. It was then alleged that this TFB borrowing and charge too was financial assistance since it was done to reduce or discharge liability incurred in the acquisition of the shares. The Court of Appeal did not accept that this could be financial assistance. The issue is not where the money comes from,[253] but the use the company makes of it. The loan and related security is ordinary commercial lending, even where, as here, the bank knows the purpose

---

[249] *MT Realisations Ltd v Digital Equipment Co Ltd* [2003] 2 BCLC 117, CA; and *Chaston v SWP Group plc* [2003] 1 BCLC 675, CA.

[250] [2008] 1 BCLC 185 at 191.   [251] [2003] 2 BCLC 117.

[252] [2008] 1 BCLC 185, CA.   [253] [2008] 1 BCLC 185 at 195.

is to repay the original parent company. A bank cannot be expected to investigate whether that repayment might infringe rules of financial assistance. As noted above, the Court of Appeal did not believe that public policy required those perfectly ordinary commercial transactions be struck down,[254] a pragmatic position which must give considerable comfort to bankers. This approach is also consistent with the principle that where an agreement is capable of being performed in alternative ways, one lawful and one in breach of the provisions on financial assistance, it is to be presumed that the parties intend to carry out the agreement in a lawful and not an unlawful manner.[255] The bank is entitled to expect the company to use the funds it borrows in a legal and not illegal manner.

The purpose of the transaction

In addition to the assistance being financial assistance, the assistance must be given for the purpose of the acquisition or to reduce or discharge a liability incurred for the purpose of the acquisition.[256] In *Dyment v Boyden*[257] three individuals had been involved in running a nursing home together. As part of a deal to separate their various interests, A acquired all of the shares of B and C. This acquisition gave A total control of the company which ran the nursing home, but the freehold of the property from which the business was operated was controlled by B and C. They granted the company a lease of the premises at a very high rental. In subsequent proceedings, A tried to argue that the rental payments were linked to her acquisition of B and C's shares in the company and as such amounted to financial assistance given directly or indirectly for the purpose of that acquisition. The Court of Appeal found that the reason why the company entered into the lease was because the company needed the premises from which to conduct its business. The entry into the lease, the court said, could not be linked to A's acquisition of the shares.

20-147

In *Chaston v SWP Group plc*,[258] as noted at **20-143**, a subsidiary company paid fees with respect to a report drawn up about its parent company. The purpose of the arrangement was to facilitate the negotiations by a possible purchaser and to enable it to determine whether it wished to acquire the shares. As such, the court held, it was financial assistance given for the purpose of the acquisition of the shares.

20-148

Even if the assistance is given for the purpose of the acquisition etc, the prohibition does not apply if the company's principal purpose in giving that assistance is not to give it for the purpose of any such acquisition, or the giving of the assistance for that purpose is but an incidental part of some larger purpose of the company, and the assistance is given in good faith in the interests of the company (CA 2006, s 678(2)).

20-149

---

[254] [2008] 1 BCLC 185 at 202–3, CA. To the extent that *Re Hill & Tyler Ltd* [2005] 1 BCLC 41 supports striking down a loan and security in these circumstances, it must be considered now to be of doubtful authority.

[255] *Neilson v Stewart* [1991] BCC 713. See also *Brady v Brady* [1988] 2 All ER 617, HL; *Parlett v Guppys (Bridport) Ltd* [1996] 2 BCLC 34.

[256] See *Charterhouse Investment Trust Ltd v Tempest Diesels Ltd* [1986] BCLC 1 at 10, per Hoffmann J.

[257] [2005] 1 BCLC 163.

[258] [2003] 1 BCLC 675. See also *Corporate Development Partners LLC v E-Relationship Marketing Ltd* [2007] EWHC 436, [2007] All ER (D) 162 (Mar).

A similar exemption applies where the financial assistance is for the purpose of reducing or discharging a liability incurred in the acquisition of shares (CA 2006, s 678(2)). The scope of this 'principal purpose' etc exception was construed in an unhelpfully narrow way, however, by the House of Lords in *Brady v Brady*.[259] In this case, assistance was given by a company to reduce or discharge a liability incurred for the acquisition of shares in the company in prima facie breach of the statutory prohibition. The transaction arose as part of an elaborate scheme for the division of a family business between two brothers. It was argued that this division of the business was the larger purpose, as required by the statute, and the financial assistance was only incidental to it.

20-150   The House of Lords adopted a restrictive interpretation of the provision, distinguishing between a *purpose* and the *reason* why a purpose is formed. The fact that a company in giving financial assistance has some more important reason for the transaction than the giving of financial assistance, Lord Oliver said, is not the same thing as the company having a 'larger purpose' as envisaged by this provision.[260] The *purpose* of the transaction in *Brady* was to assist in the financing of the acquisition of the shares although the *reason* for the transaction was to facilitate a break-up of the business.[261] The financial assistance in *Brady* was not incidental to a larger purpose, therefore, and was provided in breach of the statute.

20-151   The approach adopted by the House of Lords in *Brady* was driven by a concern that companies always have a variety of motivations and reasons for transactions and if financial assistance can be justified as being part of wider corporate schemes, the section could be effectively nullified. The effect of this interpretation, however, has been to nullify this exception.

Exceptions to the prohibition on financial assistance

20-152   There are two categories of excepted transactions: (1) unconditional exceptions, and (2) conditional exceptions.

Unconditional exceptions

20-153   The prohibitions on the giving of financial assistance do not apply (CA 2006, s 681) to:

(1) a distribution of a company's assets by way of dividend lawfully made or a distribution in the course of the company's winding up;

(2) the allotment of bonus shares;

(3) a reduction of capital duly made in accordance with the statutory schemes;

(4) a redemption or purchase of shares made in accordance with the statutory provisions;

(5) anything done in pursuance of an order of the court under CA 2006, Pt 26 dealing with compromises and arrangements with creditors and members;

---

[259] [1988] 2 All ER 617, HL. See also *Plaut v Steiner* (1988) 5 BCC 352.
[260] [1988] 2 All ER 617 at 633, HL.   [261] [1988] 2 All ER 617 at 633, HL.

(6) anything done under an arrangement made in pursuance of the statutory provisions enabling liquidators in winding up to accept shares as consideration for the sale of property; or

(7) anything done under an arrangement made between a company and its creditors which is binding on the creditors by virtue of the statutory provisions relating to such arrangements when made by a company about to be or in the course of being wound up.

As noted, the prohibition of financial assistance is essentially based on the need to protect creditors from the improper depletion of the company's assets.[262] All of the transactions and schemes mentioned above are subject to statutory requirements designed to ensure the protection of creditors and prevent the misuse of assets and in a number of cases the schemes require the confirmation of the court. There is no need therefore to subject such transactions to the prohibition on financial assistance.   **20-154**

Conditional exceptions

This category provides exemptions for those companies where the lending of money is part of the ordinary business of the company[263] and exemptions designed to facilitate employees' share schemes.[264] A public company may rely on the exemptions in this category only if the company has net assets that are not thereby reduced by the giving of the assistance, or to the extent that those assets are so reduced, the financial assistance is provided out of distributable profits.[265]   **20-155**

Consequences of breach of the financial assistance provisions

Contravention of the provisions on financial assistance is a criminal offence (CA 2006, s 680) but the statute does not deal with the civil consequences which remain a matter for the common law.   **20-156**

The status of any agreement

An agreement to provide unlawful financial assistance is unenforceable by either party to it.[266] In *Heald v O'Connor*,[267] for example, where the financial assistance consisted of security given by the company for money lent to enable a person to purchase shares in the company, the court held that that security was unenforceable.[268] The court noted that such a result best furthers the policy of the legislation in that it deters potential lenders from lending money on security which might be held to contravene the statute.   **20-157**

---

[262] *Wallersteiner v Moir* [1974] 3 All ER 217 at 239, per Denning LJ.

[263] CA 2006, s 682(2)(a); see *Steen v Law* [1963] 3 All ER 770.

[264] CA 2006, s 682(b), (c), (d). For the definition of 'employees' share scheme', see s 1166.

[265] CA 2006, s 682(1)(b), (3)–(4).

[266] *Brady v Brady* [1988] 2 All ER 617, HL; *Plaut v Steiner* (1989) 5 BCC 352.

[267] [1971] 2 All ER 1105.

[268] *Victor Battery Co Ltd v Curry's Ltd* [1946] Ch 242 to the contrary effect is generally accepted to be wrongly decided: see *Selangor United Rubber Estates Ltd v Cradock (No 3)* [1968] 2 All ER 1073.

20-158   If the illegal element of the transaction can be severed from the agreement, the court will do so.[269] In *Carney v Herbert*,[270] the Privy Council took the view that the nature of the illegality in cases of financial assistance is not such as to preclude severance on the grounds of public policy and severance can take place provided that the financial assistance is ancillary to the overall transaction and its elimination would leave unchanged the subject-matter of the transaction.[271] In this case, the illegal financial assistance (in the form of mortgages) was severed from an agreement for the sale of shares which could then be enforced between the parties in the ordinary way.

20-159   It is important in this context to return to *Anglo Petroleum Ltd v TFB (Mortgages) Ltd*,[272] see **20-146**, where the Court of Appeal said, obiter, that, even if it had found illegal financial assistance in respect of the use of funds borrowed by the company, the loan agreement and associated charges and guarantees would not have been illegal. Those agreements did not necessitate any breach of the law, Toulson LJ said, and no reason of public policy required those perfectly ordinary commercial transactions to be struck down.[273] This is an important approach which narrows the range of transactions which can be struck down as illegal. The loan and the security is treated as ordinary commercial lending. The use which the company makes of the funds it borrows may amount to financial assistance, but that is a separate matter.

Breach of fiduciary duty

20-160   A director who authorises the giving of financial assistance in breach of the statutory provisions is in breach of his duties to the company.[274] As a trustee of the company's assets, the misapplication by a director of those assets is a breach of trust and the director is obliged to account for the full amount of the improper financial assistance.[275] A shareholder may seek an injunction to restrain the giving of financial assistance in breach of the statutory provisions or he may seek permission to bring a derivative action on behalf of the company to recover the sums expended.[276]

20-161   The involvement of third parties such as bankers is often crucial to the carrying out of an illegal financial assistance scheme and they may be liable either on the basis of 'dishonest assistance' in the breach of fiduciary duty or 'knowing receipt' of company funds. These matters are discussed in Chapter 13.

---

[269] *Herbert Spink (Bournemouth) Ltd v Spink* [1936] 1 All ER 597; *South Western Mineral Water Co Ltd v Ashmore* [1967] 2 All ER 953; *Carney v Herbert* [1985] 1 All ER 438, PC; *Neilson v Stewart* [1991] BCC 713, HL.

[270] [1985] 1 All ER 438, PC.   [271] [1985] 1 All ER 438 at 446, PC.

[272] [2008] 1 BCLC 185, CA.   [273] [2008] 1 BCLC 185 at 202–3, CA.

[274] See, for example, *Re In a Flap Envelope Co Ltd* [2004] 1 BCLC 64.

[275] See discussion in Chapter 13 of the liability of directors for beach of trust and see *JJ Harrison (Properties) Ltd v Harrison* [2002] 1 BCLC 162; *Rolled Steel Products (Holdings) Ltd v British Steel Corpn* [1985] 3 All ER 52; *Re Lands Allotment Co* [1894] 1 Ch 616.

[276] See *Smith v Croft* [1987] 3 All ER 909; the derivative action is discussed in detail in Chapter 18.

21

Loan capital—secured creditors and company charges

A Introduction to company charges

The majority of companies on the register of companies are private companies with **21-1** very limited amounts of share capital.[1] It follows that if those companies are carrying on business to any significant level, it must be on the basis of other forms of funding and there are many other methods of financing to which companies may resort.[2] For example, they may obtain goods under hire-purchase agreements[3] or conditional sale agreements.[4] They may use factoring[5] and invoice discounting[6] to realise sums due to them by users of their goods or services. For many companies, though, the starting point is usually loan capital, typically in the form of straightforward commercial borrowing from high street banks and financial institutions.[7]

---

[1] Of the 2,457,400 companies on the register at 31 March 2007 with an issued share capital, 1,921,700 (or 78%) had an issued share capital of up to £100 while 91% had an issued share capital of less than £10,000: see Companies House, *Statistical Tables on Companies Register Activities 2006–2007*, Table A7. Unfortunately, Table A7 has been omitted from the Tables for 2007–08. These statistical tables are available on the Companies House website: www.companieshouse.gov.uk.

[2] See Law Commission, *Registration of Security Interests: Company Charges and Property other than Land* (Consultation Paper No 164), 2002, Ch 6 where there is a very useful account of these other forms of financing which the Commission describes as involving a type of quasi-security.

[3] A hire-purchase agreement is an agreement for the hire of goods under which the hirer is given the option to purchase the goods at a certain point when a certain number of payments have been made.

[4] A conditional sale agreement is an agreement for the sale of goods under which the property in the goods remains with the seller until payment of the price is completed.

[5] Factoring involves a factor taking over responsibility for collection of the debts due by customers to a company. The factor pays between 80–85% of the value of those invoices up front to the company, so assisting its cash flow, and pays the balance when the customer pays, in return for a fee set as a percentage (typically 1–2.5%) of the debts together with service charges. Many of the high street banks operate specialist subsidiaries offering factoring services.

[6] Invoice discounting is very similar to factoring except that the discounter does not take over collection of the company's debts, but provides funds up front (again between 80–85% of the amount) for the company in respect of approved invoices in return for a fee set either as a monthly flat fee or as a percentage of the debts and a service charge. Many of the high street banks operate specialist subsidiaries providing this service.

[7] The collapse of financial institutions and general market turmoil in 2008 and the consequent difficulties in securing bank loans has resulted in some evidence of increased reliance on factoring and invoice discounting: see Asset Based Finance Association, *Economic Report* (September 2008).

21-2   Of course, when lending to a limited liability company, the lender is conscious of the need for security to cover the amount lent, knowing he cannot have recourse to the members to meet any deficiency on insolvency. On occasion, a lender may obtain personal guarantees from the directors, but personal guarantees are a poor substitute for security over tangible assets as the guarantor may not be good for the money when the lender needs to enforce the personal guarantee. The lender/creditor prefers therefore to look to security to protect its position in the event of the insolvency of the company. By security is meant that, in addition to the ability to sue the company for the discharge of the debt, the creditor is able to look to some property in which the company has an interest in order to enforce the discharge of the company's obligation to the creditor. At the same time as the lender seeks security, the company wants to be able to borrow without having to give such security to the lender that its ability to trade is affected by the constraints imposed by the security.[8] The company therefore wants freedom to trade, the lender wants security for its lending and the law needs to facilitate both the company and the lender.

Taking security

21-3   Central to the question of security is the issue of priority on insolvency. Obviously, if the company never becomes insolvent, no problem arises and the precise nature of the security obtained never becomes important. It is because the company may become insolvent that security must be sought and the type of security which is sought is dictated by the order of distribution of assets on insolvency. A creditor does not want a form of security which leaves the creditor in the queue behind several other creditors on insolvency. Therefore a creditor requires not just security but a form of security which gives sufficient prior claim to the assets on insolvency so that the creditor has some prospect of recovering the debt.

21-4   The order of distribution and winding up is discussed in detail in Chapter 24 and a broad overview suffices for our purposes here. On liquidation, the assets of the company fall into two categories, those secured to creditors, and the free assets. Those free assets form a common fund which, subject to the expenses of winding up and the rights of the preferential creditors (discussed below), are held on a statutory trust for the benefit of the unsecured creditors.[9] The secured creditors who, as we shall see, generally have fixed and floating charges over the company's assets, have rights in rem and they look to the secured assets for payment of their debts. They do not need to look to the common fund for repayment of their claims. However, the precise degree of priority depends on the nature of the security obtained and Parliament has intruded to establish a statutory priority for the payment of the expenses of winding

---

[8] As Nourse LJ noted in *Re New Bullas Trading Ltd* [1994] 1 BCLC 485 at 487: 'He who lends money to a trading company neither wishes nor expects it to become insolvent.... But against an evil day he wants the best security the company can give him consistently with its ability to trade meanwhile.'

[9] See *Ayerst (Inspector of Taxes) v C & K (Construction) Ltd* [1975] 2 All ER 537; *Webb v Whiffin* (1872) LR 5 HL 711 at 721, 724.

up (and administration) and the preferential debts which has the effect, as we shall see, of eroding the quality of floating charges held by creditors where the free assets of the company are insufficient to meet these prior claims (as they almost invariably are).[10] The two categories of assets overlap in that a deficiency in the 'free' assets must be met by the realisations held by the floating chargeholder to the extent dictated by Parliament. The fixed chargeholder is unaffected by this statutory interference.

The standard devices used by a lender to obtain security are legal mortgages, fixed **21-5** charges and floating charges. A mortgage needs no detailed description; it involves the transfer of legal ownership to the lender subject to the mortgagee's equity of redemption. In practice, since the Law of Property Act 1925, the form of legal mortgage of an estate in fee simple has been by a charge by deed expressed to be by way of legal mortgage. For various reasons, the charge by deed has become the standard form of mortgage so that the terms 'mortgage' and 'charge' have become interchangeable.[11] With that statutory exception of a legal charge, all charges, whether fixed or floating, are equitable.

Usually it is clear that the parties have created a charge (though whether it is a fixed **21-6** or a floating charge may be more problematic) but, in cases of doubt, it is a matter of construction whether the transaction gives rise to a charge. For example, if a contract gives a contracting party the right (on default by the other party) to sell machinery belonging to the other contracting party and to apply the proceeds of sale in discharge of the debts of the other party due under the contract, this provision creates a security interest, a charge, allowing one party to look to a particular asset or class of assets for the discharge of a debt.[12] The essence of an equitable charge, as Millett J explained, is that:[13]

> '... without any conveyance or assignment to the chargee, specific property of the chargor is expressly or constructively appropriated to or make answerable for the payment of a debt, and the chargee is given the right to resort to the property for the purpose of having it realised and applied in or towards payment of the debt.'

On the other hand, a contractual provision which merely allows one contracting **21-7** party to use a machine belonging to that other party in order to complete works required by the contract does not confer any security interest and is not a charge at all.[14]

---

[10] As Armour notes, one consequence of carving out a preference for certain claimants on insolvency is that the history of the floating charge (which is subject to these prior claims) is largely the story of the litigation ensuing from attempts by floating chargeholders to draft (at considerable cost) their charges in a way that defeats that statutory priority: see Armour, 'Should We Redistribute in Insolvency?' in Getzler & Payne, *Company Charges, Spectrum and Beyond* (2005).

[11] CA 2006, s 861(5) defines 'charge' for the purpose of Part 25 (Company Charges) as including 'mortgage'.

[12] See *Re Cosslett (Contractors) Ltd* [1999] 1 BCLC 205 at 216, CA; and sub nom, *Smith (Administrator of Cosslett (Contractors) Ltd) v Bridgend County Borough Council* [2002] 1 BCLC 77 at 88–9, 91, HL.

[13] *Re Charge Card Services Ltd* [1987] BCLC 17 at 40, per Millett J; see also *Re Cosslett (Contractors) Ltd* [1999] 1 BCLC 205 at 215.

[14] See *Re Cosslett (Contractors) Ltd* [1999] 1 BCLC 205 at 215.

21-8   As to whether the charge created is a fixed or floating charge, the distinction between them was explained by Lord Macnaghten in *Illingworth v Houldsworth*[15] as follows:

> 'A specific charge...is one that without more fastens on ascertained and definite property or property capable of being ascertained or defined. A floating charge, on the other hand, is ambulatory and shifting in its nature, hovering over and so to speak floating with the property which it is intended to affect until some event occurs or some act is done which causes it to settle and fasten on the subject of the charge within its reach and grasp.'

21-9   A fixed (or specific) charge is typically taken over identified assets not commonly used or dealt with in the day-to-day business of the company. A fixed charge gives the holder of the charge an immediate proprietary interest in the assets subject to the charge which means that a fixed charge is inappropriate for assets which the company needs to deal with in the ordinary course of business.[16]

21-10   A floating charge is an equitable invention, first recognised by the Court of Appeal in *Re Panama, New Zealand & Australian Royal Mail Co.*[17] The classic description of the characteristics of a floating charge is that of Romer LJ in *Re Yorkshire Woolcombers Association*,[18] where he stated that a floating charge is:

(1)   a charge on a class of assets of a company, present and future;

(2)   that class is one which, in the ordinary course of the business of the company, would be changing from time to time; and

(3)   by the charge it is contemplated that, until some future step is taken by or on behalf of those interested in the charge, the company may carry on its business in the ordinary way.

21-11   A floating charge is typically taken over the entire undertaking of the company,[19] meaning all of the company's assets, both present and future, including assets such as removable plant and equipment, tools, intellectual property rights, stock-in-trade, work in progress and book debts (i.e. sums due to the company by its debtors). These are circulating assets used in the normal course of business and they are constantly changing so they are not amenable to a fixed charge.[20] The hallmark of the floating charge is the freedom of the company to deal with the assets in the ordinary course of business without the need to obtain the consent of the chargee. The assets in this

---

[15] [1904] AC 355 at 358.

[16] See *Agnew v IRC (Re Brumark)* [2001] 2 BCLC 188 at 192, PC, per Lord Millett.

[17] (1878) LR 5 Ch App 318; and see *Re Florence Land & Public Works Co, ex p Moor* (1878) 10 Ch D 530. See generally the valuable collection of essays in Getzler & Payne, *Company Charges, Spectrum and Beyond* (2005) (hereinafter Getzler & Payne), also Gough, *Company Charges* (2nd edn, 1996).

[18] [1903] 2 Ch 284 at 295, although Romer LJ did not say that all three elements must be present in order for the charge to be a floating charge.

[19] As Lord Millett explained in *Agnew v IRC (Re Brumark)* [2001] 2 BCLC 188 at 191, a charge on the 'undertaking' is taken to mean a charge on all the assets of the company, both present and future, including its circulating assets, i.e. assets that are regularly turned over in the course of trade.

[20] See *Re Spectrum Plus Ltd* [2005] 2 BCLC 269 at 304, per Lord Scott.

instance remain under the control of the chargor, not the chargee, so avoiding the 'restricting (and in some cases, paralysing) effect on the use of the assets of the company resulting from a fixed charge'.[21] The charge floats or hovers over the assets until some event occurs causing it to crystallise which can occur in a variety of ways.[22] As a matter of law, a floating charge crystallises on the appointment of a receiver or administrator, or when the company goes into liquidation (on a resolution being passed or a compulsory winding up ordered) or there is otherwise a cessation of business on the part of the company, for the effect of these circumstances is to bring to an end the company's freedom to carry on business in the ordinary way.[23] Equally, the charge document may prescribe situations where the charge crystallises which may or may not require the intervention of the chargee. For example, the charge may crystallise on the appointment by the chargee of an administrator under the charge, or on the company exceeding defined financial thresholds, or on the company making a disposition of its assets other than by way of sale in the ordinary course of business, or on the service of a notice by the chargee (a method approved in *Re Brightlife Ltd*).[24] Once the charge has crystallised, the chargor's freedom to deal with the assets comprised in the charge comes to an end and the charge becomes a fixed charge attached to the assets within the scope of the charge. Despite the charge becoming a fixed charge at this point, its priority vis-à-vis other claimants on insolvency is determined by the fact that, *as created*, it was a floating charge.[25]

The freedom of the chargor to deal with the assets in the ordinary course of business includes a freedom to create further fixed charges ranking in priority to the floating charge,[26] though the courts have restricted the ability to create subsequent floating charges. A second floating charge over all of the property comprised in the first charge and ranking pari passu with or in priority to that charge is incompatible with the first charge and ranks subject to it.[27] A subsequent floating charge can rank pari passu with or in priority to the first floating charge, however, where the first floating charge

21-12

---

[21] *Re Keenan Bros Ltd* [1986] BCLC 242 at 245, per Walsh J (Irish S Ct).

[22] The nature of the chargee's interest ahead of crystallisation has been the subject of much debate (possibilities range from no interest, some form of present proprietary interest, which is probably the most generally accepted view, a modified defeasible fixed charge or a present equitable interest which may be overreached), see Goode, *Legal Problems of Credit and Security* (3rd edn, 2003), Ch 4; Turner, 'Floating Charges—A No Theory Theory' [2004] LMCLQ 319; Nolan, 'Property in a Fund' (2004) 120 LQR 108; also Worthington, 'Floating Charges: The Use and Abuse of Doctrinal Analysis' in Getzler & Payne, above n 17, esp at pp 37–44 who admits that the question is of limited practical significant—her view is that it is a modified defeasible form of fixed charge. See too Ferran, *Principles of Corporate Finance Law* (2008), p 373 who admits that the lack of certainty on this issue does not appear to cause major practical problems.

[23] *Evans v Rival Granite Quarries* Ltd [1910] 2 KB 979; *Re Woodroffes (Musical Instruments) Ltd* [1985] BCLC 227. See also *National Westminster Bank plc v Jones* [2002] 1 BCLC 55, CA.

[24] [1986] BCLC 418.

[25] See IA 1986, s 251. See *Re Beam Tube Products Ltd, Fanshawe v Amav Industries Ltd* [2007] 2 BCLC 732 (floating charge as created was not converted by subsequent conduct of the parties into a fixed charge). The solution is to create a new charge.

[26] *Wheatley v Silkstone Haigh Moor Coal Co* (1885) 29 Ch D 715.

[27] *Re Benjamin Cope & Sons Ltd* [1914] 1 Ch 800.

permits of such a charge and the second charge is over part only of the assets comprised in the original charge.[28]

21-13 The possibility that the chargor might grant subsequent charges over the assets within the reach of the floating charge (and so diminish its value) has resulted in the practice of including clauses in the charge document (the debenture), usually described as negative pledges, prohibiting the chargor from creating further fixed or floating charges ranking pari passu with or in priority to the current charge, but these clauses cannot bind a subsequent chargee for value without notice. Details of these clauses are often included by chargees in the particulars delivered to the registrar although they are not amongst the prescribed particulars and third parties cannot be affected by constructive notice of such extra-statutory material,[29] but they are affected by actual notice of the restriction if they search the register of charges. All chargees have constructive notice of prior registered charges.[30]

21-14 Where a high street bank provides funds to a company, therefore, the typical security package which the bank takes is: (1) a legal mortgage over the company's land or buildings; (2) a fixed charge over such of the company's plant, equipment, furniture and fittings as are not required in the day-to-day conduct of its business (and much ingenuity is expended on drafting charges which fall into this category since, as we shall see, it is the most effective type of charge; and (3) a floating charge over the entire undertaking of the company, meaning all the assets of the company not otherwise charged. In effect, the floating charge is often used as a catch-all final charge over anything else of value not yet encompassed by another charge. It will be appreciated that once a bank has secured this level of security, there is little security that the company can provide for subsequent creditors since, one way or another, every asset of any value has been appropriated to the payment of the bank borrowings.

21-15 In terms of enforcement, if the secured creditor has taken a legal mortgage of the company's property, land or buildings, the mortgagee is able to sell the property to recover the debts.[31] If the creditor has taken a fixed charge over the company's plant, equipment etc, the creditor has rights in rem with respect to those assets which are appropriated to the payment of that creditor's debts and do not fall into the pool of assets for the unsecured creditors. The chargee may take such steps to realise those assets are as permitted by the debenture which invariably provides for their sale to allow the chargee to be repaid. A floating charge, as noted, hovers over the assets within it and only subsequently attaches to those assets when the charge crystallises. Once the charge has crystallised, it becomes a fixed charge and the bank is entitled to realise the assets as provided for by the debenture which will usually provide for the appointment of an administrator: see **21-82** below.

---

[28] *Re Automatic Bottle Makers Ltd* [1926] Ch 412.

[29] See *Siebe Gorman & Co Ltd v Barclays Bank Ltd* [1979] 2 Lloyd's Rep 142 at 159–60, overruled on other grounds, *Re Spectrum Plus Ltd* [2005] 2 BCLC 269, HL.

[30] *Wilson v Kelland* [1910] 2 Ch 306; see *Siebe Gorman & Co Ltd v Barclays Bank Ltd* [1979] 2 Lloyd's Rep 142 at 160, overruled on other grounds, *Re Spectrum Plus Ltd* [2005] 2 BCLC 269, HL. See generally Gough, *Company Charges* (2nd edn, 1996), Ch 23.

[31] Either under the express terms of the mortgage deed or under the Law of Property Act 1925, s 101.

Finally, it should be noted that the document setting out the charge taken by a lender is   **21-16**
called a debenture, though 'debenture' has many other meanings also. For these purposes, however, it is a document acknowledging an indebtedness which may be (and
in this context is) secured by a charge or charges.[32] Hence a lender is often referred to
as a debenture holder.

B   Fixed and floating charges

The attraction of a floating charge for lenders, especially banks, was explained as fol-   **21-17**
lows by Lord Millett in *Agnew v IRC* (*Re Brumark*):[33]

> 'The floating charge is capable of affording the creditor, by a single instrument, an
> effective and comprehensive security upon the entire undertaking of the debtor com-
> pany and its assets from time to time, while at the same time leaving the company free
> to deal with its assets and pay its trade creditors in the ordinary course of business
> without reference to the holder of the charge.'

It would seem then that the floating charge meets the two key objectives which we   **21-18**
noted above: security for the lender, the chargee; and flexibility for the company, the
chargor. However, the value of a charge lies in the ability of the chargee on insolvency
to realise the assets charged to secure repayment of the debt without regard to the
insolvency rules governing the distribution of the common fund of unsecured assets.
The problem, noted at **21-4**, is that a floating charge is subject to the insolvency rules
(priority is given to other claims) in a way that affects the possible recoveries by a floating chargeholder. This is one of the most important distinctions between fixed and
floating charges.

A floating charge (but not a fixed charge) is subject to the prior claims of preferential   **21-19**
debts (debts accorded statutory priority, though the categories accorded such priority have been much reduced: see **24-90**)[34] and is subject to the 'prescribed part' provision in IA 1986, s 176A, which ring-fences certain funds in favour of unsecured

---

[32] See *Levy v Abercorris Slate & Slab Co* (1887) 37 Ch 260 at 264, per Chitty J.

[33] [2001] 2 BCLC 188 at 192. While the floating charge has played an important role in corporate financing
for many decades, the prevailing academic view (with some support from practitioners) is that the time has
come to abolish it and create a modern secured finance regime suitable for domestic purposes and for the
role that English law plays in international commerce. See Goode, 'The Case for the Abolition of the Floating
Charge' in Getzler & Payne, above n 17; also Worthington, above n 22, pp 45–9; Wood, 'A Review of *Brumark*
and *Spectrum*' in an International Setting' in Getzler & Payne, above n 17, pp 149–50.

[34] See IA 1986, ss 40, 175, Sch B1, para 65(2); CA 2006, s 754. The priority accorded to preferential debts
is not as important an issue as it once was as the preferential status accorded to certain categories of debts
(for example, debts to Inland Revenue, Customs and Excise and social security contributions) was abolished
by the Enterprise Act 2002, s 251 with effect from 15 September 2003 and the categories of preferential debt
are now much reduced, see IA 1986, Sch 6. See Worthington, above n 22, at p 46 who points out that there is
little by way of defensible justification for discriminating between fixed and floating chargeholders in this
way. Gullifer & Payne, 'The Characterization of Fixed and Floating Charges' in Getzler & Payne above n 17,
suggest the justification lies in the all-embracing nature of a floating charge and the fact that the floating
charge enables the company to continue to trade and incur fresh debt: see pp 79–81.

creditors: see **24-91**. The effect of the latter should be neutral for the chargeholder as the formula used to determine the 'prescribed part' (which must go to the unsecured creditors) is meant to equate to the gain to the floating charge holder from the reduction of the categories of preferential debts.[35] The application of the prescribed part therefore is not necessarily to the disadvantage of the floating chargeholder, but the floating charge's subordination to the prior claims of the preferential debts is a disadvantage when compared to a fixed charge.

21-20   More significantly, a floating charge, but not a fixed charge, is subject, if the company is in liquidation, to the prior claims of the expenses of liquidation[36] (see **24-81**) and, if the company is in administration, to the prior claims of the expenses of administration[37] (see **23-109**). In so far as these claims cannot be met from the unencumbered assets of the company, the deficiency must be made up out of the proceeds of the floating charge.[38] The creditor with a floating charge has security, therefore, in that assets are appropriated to the charge once it crystallises (as discussed at **21-11**), but it is a form of security which is not as comprehensive as a fixed charge because it is subject to these other (usually substantial) claims being met.

21-21   One of the major advantages of having a floating charge was that, on crystallisation, the chargeholder could appoint an administrative receiver to realise the assets and pay off the debt. This was an entirely contractual process within the control of the chargeholder and with limited regard being paid to the interests of other creditors. The right to appoint administrative receivers in this way was abolished for the most part (there are some exceptional cases[39]) by the Enterprise Act 2002 (EA 2002) with respect to floating charges created on or after 15 September 2003.[40] For qualifying floating charges (as defined in IA 1986, Sch B1, para 14(2)) created subsequently, the appropriate enforcement mechanism is the appointment of an administrator whose role and functions are statutory and not contractual: see **21-87**. An administrator is an officer of the court (IA 1986, Sch B1, para 5) and has a duty to perform his functions in the interests of the creditors as a whole (IA 1986, Sch B1, para 3(2)). An administrator can also dispose of property subject to a floating charge without the consent of the chargee whereas, if the charge is fixed, the consent of the court is required (IA 1986, Sch B1, paras 70, 71).

[35] The Insolvency Service has attempted to evaluate the impact of various reforms introduced by the Enterprise Act 2002. The initial conclusion is that the prescribed part has been set at an appropriate level, but the Insolvency Service admits that the sample which forms the basis for this conclusion is too small to draw any firm conclusions at this stage: see Insolvency Service, *Enterprise Act 2002—Corporate Insolvency Provisions: Evaluation Report* (January 2008), pp 136–8.

[36] To the extent provided for by IA 1986, s 176ZA, inserted by CA 2006, s 1282, reversing the decision of the House of Lords in *Re Leyland Daf Ltd, Buchler v Talbot* [2004] 1 BCLC 218 which had itself reversed decades of established law and had decided that the floating charge realisations were not subject to the expenses of winding up: see **24-81**.

[37] To the extent provided for by IA 1986, Sch B1, para 99. A floating charge, unlike a fixed charge, is also open to challenge by an administrator or liquidator under IA 1986, s 245 (avoidance of certain floating charges) see discussion at **25-83**.

[38] See IA 1986, ss 40, 175; Sch B1, para 65(2); CA 2006, s 754.   [39] See IA 1986, ss 72B–72GA.

[40] See IA 1986, s 72A.

It is clear that the fixed charge is the superior charge but there are reasons why it is still   **21-22**
worthwhile having a floating charge including:

(1) a qualifying floating charge is required if the lender is to secure valuable rights
with respect to the appointment of an administrator and in terms of the choice
of administrator.[41] This is very much a prime motivation for obtaining a floating charge. Administration is discussed in Chapter 23.

(2) a floating charge, when coupled with fixed charges, allows one chargee to have
comprehensive security over all of the company's assets;

(3) a floating charge gives the chargee a measure of control over the company's business because, while the charge is in existence and especially when coupled with
fixed charges, the chargor typically is expected to provide up-to-date accounts
to the lender so the lender is well placed to monitor its security;

(4) even if the floating charge is subject to the prior claims of preferential debts and
the expenses of winding up/administration, the charge still has priority over
the claims of the unsecured creditors (as noted at **21-19**, the position as between
the floating chargeholder and the unsecured creditors should be essentially
unchanged by the requirements of the prescribed part) and so the lender might
as well take a charge for that purpose.

Notwithstanding these advantages, it is still the case that a fixed charge offers   **21-23**
greater security than a floating charge and so much of the litigation in this area
involves disputes between creditors as to their respective places in the queue to claim
the company's assets on insolvency. For example, if Bank A can establish that it has
a fixed charge over Asset X, it is able to appropriate that asset to the payment of its
debt. On the other hand, if a liquidator or administrator can establish that the charge
is a floating charge subject to the expenses of winding up or administration, then the
bank's claim is subject to those expenses in the event that the unencumbered assets are
otherwise insufficient to meet those expenses. Likewise, if the preferential creditors
can establish that a charge is a floating charge, the preferential creditors have a prior
claim to the floating charge realisations if the company's assets are otherwise insufficient to meet the preferential claims.

The distinction between fixed and floating charges also affects registration under CA   **21-24**
2006, s 860. All floating charges must be registered (s 860(7)(g)) but fixed charges
need only be registered if they are over one of the specified classes of assets in s 860(7).
Admittedly, s 860(7) encompasses most classes of charges but there are some significant exceptions, such as fixed charges over shares which are not registrable. As a failure to register a registrable charge renders the charge void (s 874), a creditor may need
to argue that a charge is fixed and not within the registration requirements in the hope
of escaping that invalidity.[42] Equally, liquidators have an interest in establishing that
a particular arrangement is a registrable charge which is void for lack of registration

---

[41] See IA 1986, Sch B1, paras 14, 35–7.
[42] See, for example, *Arthur D Little Ltd v Ableco Finance LLC* [2002] 2 BCLC 799 at 812.

so forcing a creditor to claim as an unsecured creditor. For a variety of reasons then the nature of a charge is of real significance and, unsurprisingly, most of the litigation focuses on this issue.

C The approach to categorisation

21-25   In determining the character of a charge, neither the intentions of the parties nor the terms which they use to describe the transaction are necessarily determinative. If the parties describe a charge as fixed when it is in fact floating then, as Millett LJ noted, 'their ill-chosen language must yield to the substance'.[43] Deciding whether a charge is a fixed charge or a floating charge is a two-stage process, as was established by the Privy Council in *Agnew v IRC*[44] (better known as *Re Brumark*). First, the court must construe the instrument of charge and seek to gather the intention of the parties from the language used in order to ascertain the nature of the rights and obligations which the parties intended to grant each other in respect of the charged asset. Once that has been determined, the second stage of the process is one of legal categorisation and it is a matter of law for the courts to determine whether the charge, as created, is fixed or floating. This approach was swiftly endorsed by the House of Lords in *Smith (Administrator of Cosslett (Contractors) Ltd) v Bridgend County Borough Council*[45] (hereinafter *Re Cosslett*). Lord Hoffmann noted that the intentions of the parties are relevant only to establish their mutual rights and obligations: whether such rights and obligations are characterised as a floating charge is a question of law.[46]

21-26   In *Re Cosslett* a contractor abandoned a contract for some works with a local council. In accordance with a standard condition contained in the contract, the council then entered the site, seized the contractor's equipment and obtained another contractor to complete the contract using that equipment. The contract conditions also permitted the council, on a default by the contractor, to sell the contractor's plant and apply the proceeds in discharge of the contractor's debts to the council. The equipment was ultimately sold by the second contractor with the consent of the council.

21-27   An initial issue was whether the clause entitling the council to sell the plant and apply the proceeds was a charge. At first instance, the court concluded that the charge was a fixed charge, for there was a further term in the contract which precluded the removal of the equipment from the site until such time as the contract was completed.

---

[43] *Orion Finance Ltd v Crown Financial Management Ltd* [1996] 2 BCLC 78 at 84. See, for example, *Russell–Cooke Trust Co Ltd v Elliott* [2007] 2 BCLC 637 where the charge was described, oddly, as a floating deed, then as a floating charge, and then the document contained restrictions incompatible with a floating charge so leaving it to the court to determine the nature of the charge. In the light of the restrictions, the court decided it was a fixed charge.   [44] [2001] 2 BCLC 188.

[45] [2002] 1 BCLC 77 at 89 (per Lord Hoffmann), at 91–2 (per Lord Scott), HL.

[46] [2002] 1 BCLC 77 at 89; and Lord Scott of Foscote at 91–2. See also *Arthur D Little Ltd v Ableco Finance LLC* [2002] 2 BCLC 799 at 812; *Queens Moat Houses plc v Capita IRG Trustees Ltd* [2005] 2 BCLC 199 at 208; *Re Beam Tube Products Ltd, Fanshawe v Amav Industries Ltd* [2007] 2 BCLC 732.

Jonathan Parker J thought this restriction on the freedom of the chargor was inconsistent with the charge being a floating charge.[47] The Court of Appeal disagreed[48] and pointed out, first, that an unfettered freedom to carry on business is not essential to the existence of a floating charge. After all, floating charges commonly restrict the ability of the company to create further charges (see **21-13**). Secondly, the restriction on removal in this case had nothing to do with the security interest of the council, but was imposed to secure performance of the contract, and therefore did not affect the status of the charge as a floating charge, given that the equipment was not under the control of the chargee. That the charge was a floating charge was confirmed by the House of Lords where the case is reported as *Smith (Administrator of Cosslett (Contractors) Ltd) v Bridgend County Borough Council*,[49] Lord Hoffmann noting:[50]

> 'I do not see how a right to sell an asset belonging to a debtor and appropriate the proceeds to payment of the debt can be anything other than a charge. And because the property…(constructional plant, temporary works, goods and materials on the site) was a fluctuating body of assets which could be consumed or (subject to the approval of the engineer) removed from the site in the ordinary course of the contractor's business, it was a floating charge.'

In *Arthur D Little Ltd v Ableco Finance LLC*[51] the court had to determine the nature of **21-28** a charge created by a company over its shareholding in a subsidiary company where the charge was described as a first fixed charge but the chargor company retained the right to receive dividends and to exercise voting rights with respect to the shares. The chargee asserted that the charge was fixed. The company's administrator argued that it was a floating charge. The court, looking at categorisation as a matter of law, concluded that the charge was fixed. The class of asset involved was not a body of fluctuating assets changing in the ordinary course of business: it was simply the company's shareholding in its subsidiary. There were no dealings in that asset by the chargor company in the ordinary course of business and the shares could not be disposed of, dealt with or substituted by the chargor company. It followed that the asset was under the control of the chargee not the chargor. The charge was a fixed charge and the ability of the company to receive dividends and exercise voting rights did not alter that characteristic.

Once the court has determined by a process of construction the contractual rights **21-29** created between the parties, it is then for the law to determine the nature of the security arising. The focus, in particular, is on the third element of the description given by Romer LJ in *Re Yorkshire Woolcombers*,[52] set out at **21-10**, as to whether the chargor has continued freedom to deal with the assets charged in the ordinary course of business. This key issue of the control of the charged assets was central to a series of cases, all concerning book debts, which culminated in the landmark decisions of the Privy Council in *Agnew v IRC (Re Brumark)*,[53] and the House of Lords decision in *Re Spectrum Plus Ltd, National Westminster Bank plc v Spectrum Plus Ltd*.[54] These two

---

[47] See [1996] 1 BCLC 407, Ch D.   [48] [1999] 1 BCLC 205, CA.   [49] [2002] 1 BCLC 77, HL.
[50] [2002] 1 BCLC 77 at 88–9, HL.   [51] [2002] 2 BCLC 799.   [52] [1903] 2 Ch 284 at 295.
[53] [2001] 2 BCLC 188, PC.   [54] [2005] 2 BCLC 269, HL.

cases provide the authoritative statement of the law as to the correct approach to categorisation and the essential characteristics of a floating charge and, more specifically,
as to the nature of charges on book debts, an issue which had been the centre of much
of the litigation in recent years.

Re Brumark

21-30   Book debts or, to use the modern term, receivables (i.e. sums due to the company and
arising from goods or services supplied by the company in the course of its business),
are a valuable asset, assuming they are not bad debts, for they represent an income
stream for the company and therefore creditors are anxious to obtain security over
them.[55] Equally, book debts are precisely the sort of assets where the company is anxious to preserve its freedom to control the assets to the greatest extent possible, given
that book debts provide part of the company's cashflow. It is unsurprising therefore
that considerable efforts have been expended on drafting charges over book debts in
an attempt to meet these conflicting concerns.

21-31   In *Agnew v IRC, Re Brumark Investments Ltd*[56] (hereinafter *Re Brumark*) a company
created in favour of its bank a fixed charge over all book debts of the company arising
in its ordinary course of business. The proceeds of the book debts received by the company were excluded from the fixed charge unless the bank ordered (which it did not
do) payment into an account which the company could not operate freely whereupon
the proceeds would be treated as being subject to the fixed charge. If the bank did not
order the payment of proceeds into such an account, the proceeds were subject to a
floating charge in favour of the bank.

21-32   A dispute arose as between receivers appointed to the company and the preferential
creditors as to the nature of the charge on the book debts which were uncollected at
the time of the appointment of the receivers.[57] The New Zealand Court of Appeal
held that the charge was a floating charge and so subject to the claims of the preferential creditors.[58] The court considered that where the chargor was free to collect the

---

[55] It is now accepted that a bank may take a charge over a credit balance in an account maintained by a
customer with the bank: *Re BCCI (No 8)* [1998] 1 BCLC 68, so resolving the uncertainty which had arisen
on this matter as a result of Millett J's conclusion to the contrary in *Re Charge Card Services Ltd (No 2)*
[1987] BCLC 17 which had been affirmed by the Court of Appeal, see [1988] 3 All ER 702, but see Goode
(1998) 114 LQR 178. Such a charge is not a charge on book debts: *Northern Bank Ltd v Ross* [1991] BCLC
504; *Re Brightlife Ltd* [1986] BCLC 418; *Re Buildhead (No 2) Ltd* [2006] 1 BCLC 9 at 31–2. See also *Re SSSL
Realisations (2002) Ltd* [2005] 1 BCLC 1 at 19, a charge over a sum of money once it has been paid to a person
is not a charge over the debt or other right by reason of which the sum of money has come to be paid.

[56] [2001] 2 BCLC 188, PC. See Oditah, 'Fixed Charges over Book Debts after Brumark' (2001) Insolv Int 49;
Rumley & Jeffries, 'Brumark: Where are we now' (2003) Insolv Int 19; Pennington, 'The Interchangeability of
Fixed and Floating Charges' (2003) Co Law 60; Tamlyn & Fennessy, 'Fixed and Floating Charges: Brumark'
[2002] Insolv Law 56; Berg, 'Recharacterisation after Enron' [2003] JBL 205.

[57] The dispute arose subsequent to the decision of the English Court of Appeal in *Re New Bullas Trading
Ltd* [1994] 1 BCLC 485, CA which had held that it was possible to draft a charge so as to create a floating
charge over the proceeds of book debts once collected while retaining a fixed charge over the uncollected
proceeds. The debenture in this case was modelled on that in *New Bullas*.

[58] See [2000] 1 BCLC 353.

book debts, thus extinguishing them, and was free to deal with the proceeds in the normal course of its business, the charged book debts were not sufficiently under the control of the chargee to make the charge a fixed charge. The Court of Appeal also noted that '…we cannot see how the debate on whether book debts and their collected proceeds constitute separate security interests offers any new aid in determining whether a particular charge is fixed or floating'.[59] The matter was appealed to the Privy Council.

Giving the judgment of the Privy Council, Lord Millett outlined the two-stage process noted above at **21-25**. The first step is the ascertainment of the rights which the parties intended to grant each other in respect of the charged assets. Then the court can embark on the categorisation of the charge which is a matter of law and not a matter determined by the description attached to a charge by the parties. If the rights granted are inconsistent with the nature of a fixed charge, the charge cannot be a fixed charge, however the parties choose to describe it. The question, Lord Millett said, is whether the intention is that the company should be free to deal with the charged assets and withdraw them from the security without the consent of the holder of the charge or, to put it another way, whether the charged assets are intended to be under the control of the company or of the charge holder.[60] The fact that the company may be prohibited from assigning, factoring or charging the asset to anyone else is not sufficient to make a charge a fixed charge if the company retains the freedom to collect the asset in the ordinary course of business for its own benefit.[61] **21-33**

As for the fact that different charges were assigned to the debts and the proceeds, Lord Millett stated, and this passage is central to the issues surrounding charges on book debts so it is useful to quote his exact words:[62] **21-34**

> 'While a debt and its proceeds are two separate assets, however, the latter are merely the traceable proceeds of the former and represent its entire value. A debt is a receivable; it is merely a right to receive payment from the debtor. Such a right cannot be enjoyed in specie; its value can be exploited only by exercising the right or by assigning it for value to a third party. An assignment or charge of a receivable which does not carry with it the right to the receipt has no value. It is worthless as a security. Any attempt in the present context to separate the ownership of the debts from the ownership of their proceeds (even if conceptually possible) makes no commercial sense.'

The issue in the case of a charge on a debt then is who has control of the proceeds and the answer to that question determines the nature of the charge.[63] On the facts in *Re Brumark*,[64] the company's freedom to collect and use the proceeds of the book debts for its own benefit was inconsistent with the nature of a fixed charge. The decision of the New Zealand Court of Appeal that the charge was a floating charge was confirmed.[65] **21-35**

---

[59] See [2000] 1 BCLC 353 at 364.   [60] [2001] 2 BCLC 188 at 200.
[61] [2001] 2 BCLC 188 at 201.   [62] [2001] 2 BCLC 188 at 204.
[63] See also *Re Beam Tube Products Ltd, Fanshawe v Amav Industries Ltd* [2007] 2 BCLC 732 at 742.
[64] [2001] 2 BCLC 188, PC.   [65] [2001] 2 BCLC 188 at 205.

21-36   The Privy Council did not deny that a fixed charge might be created over book debts. This might be done where the chargee prohibits the company from realising the debts itself, whether by assignment or collection.[66] Moreover, it is not inconsistent with the fixed nature of a charge on book debts for the holder of the charge to appoint the company as its agent to collect the debts for its account and on its behalf. The Privy Council noted that a fixed charge had been created in *Re Keenan Bros Ltd*[67] by means of a requirement that funds collected by the company be paid into a blocked account with the charge holder. The prior written consent of the bank was required for each withdrawal from that account. As the debts are not available to the company as a source of its cashflow, such an arrangement is inconsistent with the charge being a floating charge.[68] The Privy Council emphasised, however, that the account must be operated in practice as a blocked account.[69]

21-37   A decision of the Privy Council while highly persuasive is not binding on the English courts. The banks therefore took what in effect was a test case to the House of Lords in order to secure a definitive statement of the English position which shows how important these issues are to everyday banking arrangements with companies.

Re Spectrum Plus

21-38   In *Re Spectrum Plus Ltd, National Westminster Bank plc v Spectrum Plus Ltd*,[70] (hereinafter *Re Spectrum Plus*) the charge in question stated that:

> 'With reference to the book debts and other debts hereby specifically charged the company shall pay into the company's account with the bank all moneys which it may receive in respect of such debts and shall not without the prior consent of the bank sell factor discount or otherwise charge or assign the same in favour of any other person or purport to do so and the company shall if called upon to do so by the bank from time to time execute legal assignments of such book debts and other debts to the bank.'

21-39   Provided the overdraft limit was not exceeded, the company was free to draw on the account, a current account, for its business purposes. The company duly collected its book debts, paid them into the account and drew on the account as it wished. The company went into voluntary liquidation and the liquidators declined to hand over the collected book debts to the bank. The bank sought a declaration that the proceeds

---

[66] [2001] 2 BCLC 188 at 204.   [67] [1986] BCLC 242 (Irish S Ct).   [68] [2001] 2 BCLC 188 at 204.

[69] [2001] 2 BCLC 188 at 204. This comment has attracted considerable controversy as to the extent to which post-charge conduct affects the determination of the nature of the charge, see Atherton & Mokal, 'Charges over chattels: issues in the fixed/floating jurisprudence' (2005) 26 Co Law 10; Oditah, 'Fixed Charges and the Recycling of Proceeds of Receivables' [2004] 120 LQR 533; also Berg, 'The Cuckoo in the Nest of Corporate Insolvency: Some Aspects of the *Spectrum* Case' [2006] JBL 22 at 33–44. The pragmatic position seems to be that the courts do not have regard to post-agreement conduct when construing the debenture to identify the rights that the parties have agreed to confer on one another, but that the court does look at it in determining the categorisation issue.

[70] [2005] 2 BCLC 269, HL. There are numerous commentaries on the case, see in particular Baird & Sidle, 'Spectrum Plus: House Of Lords Decision—A Cloud With A Silver Lining?' (2005) 18 Insolv Int 113; Hare, 'Charges over Book Debts: The End of an Era' [2005] LMCLQ 440; Berg, above n 69.

were the subject of a fixed charge in its favour. The issue is different here from in *Re Brumark* (which concerned the existence of two charges, one fixed and one floating) but the court is concerned with the same essential issue, the nature of a charge over the proceeds of a book debt.

At first instance, the court held that the charge was a floating rather than a fixed **21-40** charge over book debts, and that *Siebe Gorman & Co Ltd v Barclays Bank Ltd*[71] (where 25 years earlier Slade J held an identically worded charge to be a fixed charge and which wording was adopted by the banks thereafter) had been wrongly decided.[72] The Court of Appeal disagreed and held the charge to be a fixed charge. Lord Phillips considered that there were sufficient restrictions to put the bank in control of the proceeds and therefore the charge was fixed.[73] He also expressed a concern not to upset banking arrangements which have been in place for 25 years and which companies, banks and individual guarantors of company debts had relied upon.[74]

Allowing an appeal, their Lordships held[75] that the debenture, although expressed to **21-41** grant the bank a fixed charge over the company's book debts, in law granted only a floating charge.[76]

As far as book debts are concerned,[77] the main speech is by Lord Scott who agreed **21-42** with Lord Millett in *Brumark* that it is the third characteristic identified by Romer LJ in *Re Yorkshire Woolcombers Association*[78] (set out at **21-10**) that is the hallmark of the floating charge.[79] The essential characteristic of a floating charge, the characteristic

---

[71] [1979] 2 Lloyd's Rep 142. The restrictions imposed in *Siebe* were a requirement that the chargor pay all monies received in respect of such book debts into a designated bank account and a prohibition on the charging or assigning of those sums without the prior consent of the chargee. Additionally, and as a matter of construction of the debenture, Slade J considered that, while there was no express prohibition on the use by the company of the proceeds once collected, the debenture did restrict the company's access to those funds without the consent of the bank, see [1979] 2 Lloyd's Rep 142 at 159–60. These restrictions were such that, in Slade J's opinion, the charge was a fixed charge.

[72] See [2004] 1 BCLC 335, Ch D.

[73] [2005] 2 BCLC 30 at 58–9, CA, and see above n 71, as to the restrictions.

[74] [2005] 2 BCLC 30 at 59–60, CA.

[75] [2005] 2 BCLC 269, HL. As noted, n 77 below, the case was heard unusually by seven Law Lords, but on the book debts issues, only Lords Hope, Scott and Walker expressed a view. Lord Scott's judgment contains a particularly useful account of the development of the floating charge.

[76] The fact that banking practice had relied on it being a fixed charge for a lengthy period was not relevant for, like any first instance decision, *Siebe Gorman* was always open to correction by the higher courts, see [2005] 2 BCLC 269 at 294, HL.

[77] A further issue in the case was whether the House of Lords has power to deliver prospective rulings, applicable only to the future and whether, if so, the power should be exercised in the instant case. The significance of this issue resulted in the case being heard, unusually, by a panel of seven law lords. As for prospective overruling, their Lordships held that in a wholly exceptional case the interests of justice might require the House of Lords to declare that its decision was to operate only with prospective effect but the instant case did not fall into such an exceptional category.

[78] [1903] 2 Ch 284 at 295: the third characteristic was that by the charge it is contemplated that, until some future step is taken by or on behalf of those interested in the charge, the company may carry on its business in the ordinary way.

[79] [2005] 2 BCLC 269 at 308–9; also at 318, per Lord Walker.

that distinguishes it from a fixed charge, is that the asset subject to the charge is not finally appropriated as a security for the payment of the debt until the occurrence of some future event.[80] In the meantime the chargor is left free to use the charged asset and to remove it from the security. In any case where the chargor is free to remove the charged assets from the security, Lord Scott said, the charge should in principle be categorised as a floating charge for the assets would have the circulating, ambulatory, character distinctive of a floating charge.[81] Lord Walker too agreed that the crucial question is whether the chargor is free to deal with the book debts and withdraw them from the security without the consent of the bank.[82] This approach is entirely consistent with that in *Brumark* as to the issue of categorisation—the issue is whether the chargor has control of the asset such that it can be removed from the security without the consent of the chargee.

21-43   In this case, the company was free to draw on the account pending notice by the bank terminating the overdraft facility, requiring immediate repayment of the indebtedness and turning the account into a blocked account. Their Lordships were agreed that the restrictions imposed in this case were not sufficient as the chargor remained free to draw on the proceeds of the book debts in the ordinary course of business. So long as the chargor could draw on the account, and whether the account was in credit or debit, the money was available to the chargor and the charge was a floating charge,[83] an outcome entirely consistent with *Brumark*. The decision in *Siebe Gorman & Co Ltd v Barclays Bank Ltd*[84] which had determined commercial practice in this area since 1979 was wrong and overruled.

Charges on book debts

21-44   The decisions in *Re Brumark* and *Re Spectrum Plus Ltd* end the long-running saga as to the precise nature of charges on book debts. A book debt and its proceeds are indistinguishable, as the only value lies in the receipt and the nature of the charge is to be determined therefore by the control of the receipt. As it is practically impossible in most cases to give control to the chargee, charges on book debts will almost invariably be floating charges. The House of Lords did not deny that it is possible to create a fixed charge over book debts,[85] and it is open to the banks to alter their documentation to do so, but essentially to be a fixed charge the proceeds must be placed in a blocked account under the control of the chargee.[86] It will be appreciated that it is difficult to impose the level of control over the proceeds necessary for the charge to be classified as a fixed charge without paralysing the company's

---

[80] See [2005] 2 BCLC 269 at 310.   [81] See [2005] 2 BCLC 269 at 304.
[82] See [2005] 2 BCLC 269 at 323–4.   [83] See [2005] 2 BCLC 269 at 312.
[84] [1979] 2 Lloyd's Rep 142.

[85] See Lord Hope on possible methods of creating a fixed charge on book debts, [2005] 2 BCLC 269 at 291.

[86] See *Re Beam Tube Products Ltd, Fanshawe v Amav Industries Ltd* [2007] 2 BCLC 732 (charge on book debts was a floating charge as proceeds were available to company and the fact that the parties did eventually set up a blocked account into which the proceeds were paid did not alter that categorisation).

activities.[87] In *Re Keenan Bros Ltd*,[88] it will be recalled, the book debts were segregated in a designated account and were unusable by the chargor save with the prior written consent of the chargee.[89] Even where the chargee is a clearing bank, the degree of control required over the company's account is commercially impractical and unacceptable for most businesses. As Sir Roy Goode has said, 'for most practical purposes, the fixed charge on book debts is dead'.[90]

At one level, the decision was something of a blow for the banks since they had **21-45** depended for more than 20 years on obtaining a fixed charge, so defeating the prior claims of the preferential creditors who are the beneficiaries of the *Spectrum Plus* decision.[91] On the other hand, the outcome cannot have been surprising since the lower courts had been signalling for some time that inadequate constraints on the freedom of the chargor would mean that the charge was floating. For example, in *Re Brightlife Ltd*,[92] although there were some restrictions on the debtor company, it retained the freedom to collect in the debts and pay the proceeds into its bank account and to use them in the ordinary course of business and so the charge was a floating charge. In *Royal Trust Bank v National Westminster Bank plc*[93] there was a failure to require and control a designated account and so the charge was a floating charge. In *Re Double S Printers Ltd*[94] the chargee had no control over the debts or the proceeds and so the charge was a floating charge.

In any event, changed circumstances mean that the fixed charge issue is not as **21-46** significant as it once was. The desire of the banks to have fixed rather than floating charges over book debts was fuelled mainly by a desire to defeat the statutory priority afforded to the preferential debts which were frequently substantial in size (especially the sums due to the Inland Revenue and Customs and Excise). The Enterprise Act

---

[87] Although it is not impossible, see *William Gaskell Group Ltd v Highley* [1994] 1 BCLC 197.

[88] [1986] BCLC 242, (Irish S Ct).

[89] See Berg, above n 69, at 44–6 who cautions that there is more to *Re Keenan* than their Lordships seem to have appreciated and therefore merely drafting a charge in the manner of *Re Keenan* will not necessarily guarantee that the charge is a fixed charge.

[90] See Goode, above n 33. See *Re Beam Tube Products Ltd, Fanshawe v Amav Industries Ltd* [2007] 2 BCLC 732 (fixed charge over uncollected and floating charge over proceeds categorised as floating charge over proceed).

[91] Indeed the Crown Departments (Inland Revenue, HM Customs and Excise and the Redundancy Payments Service) were quick to issue a statement reserving the right to challenge any distributions made or proposed to be made to chargeholders after the Privy Council decision based on charges which purport to be fixed charges but which in reality are floating charges. See 'Statement on behalf of HM Revenue & Customs and the DTI Insolvency Service (The Crown Departments) in light of the HL judgment in the case of National Westminster Bank Plc v Spectrum Plus Limited' (2005) 18 Insolv Int 159.

[92] [1986] BCLC 418; also *Re Pearl Maintenance Services Ltd* [1995] 1 BCLC 449 (no restrictions on the freedom of the chargor to realise the book debts and to use the proceeds in the ordinary course of business: the charge was a floating charge although described as fixed).

[93] [1996] 2 BCLC 682, CA.

[94] [1999] 1 BCLC 220. See *Re ASRS Establishment Ltd* [2000] 2 BCLC 631 (charge on escrow account fell within charge on 'debts and other claims' which was designated as a fixed charge but chargor was free to use the proceeds of the escrow account in the ordinary course of business: the charge was a floating charge); also *Re Chalk v Kahn* [2000] 2 BCLC 361.

2002 abolished the main categories of preferential debts (including with respect to sums due to HMRC) leaving more limited preferential claims with respect to employees and some other claims: see **24-90**.[95] The result is that whether the charge is fixed or floating with respect to book debts is not as crucial an issue as it was previously.

21-47   While the claims of the preferential creditors have been significantly reduced, a floating charge is subject, however, to the prior claims of the expenses of winding up or administration. In view of that priority, a lender's preference would still be for a fixed charge. On the other hand, the holder of a qualifying floating charge has certain valuable rights and privileges with respect to appointing an administrator so there are some advantages in having a charge over book debts even it if is only a floating charge.

21-48   In any event, banks and other lenders do not rely on one type of security and so, while these decisions effectively prevent lenders from taking fixed charges on book debts, lenders will simply look to increase their protection in other ways, such as by taking fixed charges on other types of assets, or persuading companies to make increased use of factoring and/or invoice discounting which do not involve the creation of charges over the debts,[96] and perhaps, with regard to smaller companies, a greater insistence on personal guarantees from directors in respect of the company's borrowings.

Charges on other income-generating assets

21-49   The focus of *Re Brumark* and *Re Spectrum Plus* is clearly book debts so the issue then arises as to the implications, if any, for charges on other income-generating assets.[97] This issue centres to some extent on the decision of the Court of Appeal in *Re New Bullas Trading Ltd*[98] which had held that it was possible to create a floating charge over the proceeds of book debts once collected while retaining a fixed charge over the uncollected proceeds. The decision in *New Bullas* was much criticised on this 'two charges' point[99] and the Privy Council in *Brumark* had no doubt that *New Bullas* was wrongly decided.[100] Lords Scott and Walker in *Re Spectrum Plus* were also in agreement that it was wrongly decided.[101] Applying those decisions (*Brumark* and *Spectrum*) to the facts in *New Bullas*, there was no fixed charge in *New Bullas,* merely a floating charge over the proceeds of the debts. This does not mean that there cannot

---

[95] See IA 1986, Sch 6.

[96] As to factoring and invoice discounting, see nn 5 and 6 above. There is some evidence of an increase in invoice discounting in particular post-*Brumark*, see Armour, above n 10. The collapse of a number of financial institutions in 2008 may also result in a marked increase in invoice discounting as bank lending becomes more difficult to access, see Asset Based Finance Association, *Economic Report* (September 2008).

[97] See Frome & Gibbons, 'Spectrum—An End To The Conflict Or The Signal For A New Campaign?' in Getzler & Payne, above n 17, at pp 111–16 on this issue.

[98] [1994] 1 BCLC 485, CA.

[99] Most of the commentary was hostile, see Goode, 'Charges Over Book Debts: A Missed Opportunity' [1994] 110 LQR 592; Worthington, 'Fixed Charges Over Book Debts and Other Receivables' [1997] 113 LQR 562; Moss, 'Fixed Charges on Book Debts: Puzzles and Perils' (1995) Insolv Int 25; but not all: see Berg, 'Charges Over Book Debts: A Reply' [1995] JBL 433.

[100] [2001] 2 BCLC 188 at 205, PC.

[101] [2005] 2 BCLC 269 at 310 (Lord Scott), 322 (Lord Walker), HL.

be fixed charges on income-generating assets. The problem in respect of book debts, as *Re Brumark* and *Re Spectrum Plus* now show and as the dictum from Lord Millett in *Brumark*, noted above at **21-30** makes clear, is that while there are theoretically two assets (debts and proceeds), the debt is worthless as security without the proceeds so in effect the two assets are one asset—the receipt of the money due. Where there are distinct assets (Lord Millett gave the example in *Brumark*[102] of land generating rental income and which would also apply to other assets such as equipment and intellectual property rights which also generate income), then there can be distinct charges secured on the asset and on the income stream derived from the asset. The nature of those charges will be determined by the application of the two-step process already noted (see at **21-21**). There is no legal obstacle to having a fixed charge on the income stream, assuming the requisite control is in place though, as noted, that will often be impracticable and so the charge will be floating, but if the circumstances allow for control by the chargee, the charge can be fixed. In other words, *Re Brumark* and *Re Spectrum Plus*, in dictating that there is only one charge, are limited to charges on book debts and equivalent income streams where the asset and the proceeds of the asset are one and the same thing.[103]

Categorisation of charges

There is no doubt that there has been a concerted judicial effort to bring some clarity to   **21-50**
this area which is of such practical importance to companies and their banks and other lenders. The law is now clearly articulated in *Agnew v IRC (Re Brumark)*, PC[104] and *Re Spectrum Plus Ltd, National Westminster Bank plc v Spectrum Plus Ltd*, HL,[105] which convey a single consistent message. The categorisation of a charge involves a two-step process—determining the parties' rights and categorising those rights as a matter of law. Whether a charge is a fixed or a floating charge depends on whether the intention is that the company should be free to deal with the charged assets and withdraw them from the security without the consent of the holder of the charge or, to put it another way, whether the charged assets are intended to be under the control of the company or of the charge holder.[106] For most commercial lending to companies, that test can be

---

[102] [2001] 2 BCLC 188 at 203, PC.

[103] See Worthington, above n 22, at pp 37–44; and Wood, above n 33, at p 147 who makes the point that the decision in *Brumark* (and now *Spectrum*) must be limited to book debts and does not apply to a broad range of income-generating assets since the House of Lords cannot have intended that in all cases charges over such assets should be floating charges. The decisions in *Re Atlantic Computer Systems plc* [1991] BCLC 606, CA and *Re Atlantic Medical Ltd* [1993] BCLC 386, Ch D (charges over the income from equipment subleases where the chargor was allowed continued use of the income were fixed charges) are further undermined. They have always been the subject of criticism, see Goode, above n 99; Oditah, above n 56, 53: 'odd decisions of questionable application'; Moss (1995) 8 Insolv Int 25, unless it is possible to regard the charges over the leases as involving rights greater than merely rights to the income stream, see Frome & Gibbons, above n 97, at pp 113–15; *Arthur D Little Ltd v Ableco Finance LLC* [2002] 2 BCLC 799.

[104] [2001] 2 BCLC 188, PC.   [105] [2005] 2 BCLC 269, HL.

[106] [2001] 2 BCLC 188 at 200. The decision in *Queens Moat Houses plc v Capita IRG Trustees Ltd* [2005] 2 BCLC 199 appears difficult in this regard. The court held that it was not inconsistent with a fixed charge for the chargor to have a contractual right to withdraw property from the charge and distinguished that right

applied and can provide a clear answer. Of course, there is still uncertainty as to the precise degree of control which makes a charge fixed rather than floating, for example the extent to which 'sweeping' arrangements from a blocked account to an account to which the chargor has access is compatible with a fixed charge[107] and uncertainty as to the precise application of *Brumark* and *Spectrum Plus* to complex securitisations.[108] Nevertheless, these issues do not appear to have given rise to practical difficulties and the position post-*Spectrum* (at least in so far as it can be gauged from the dearth of litigation on these issues) would suggest that these decisions have brought certainty to a large swathe of the market and have not resulted in the sort of upheaval in lending practices nor the uncertainty in complex transactions such as securitisation which had been predicted.

D Registration of charges

The obligation to register

21-51   Particulars of charges of the type specified in CA 2006, s 860(7) created by a company registered in England and Wales must be delivered to the registrar of companies within 21 days of creation[109] and an unregistered charge is void to the extent prescribed by s 874 which is discussed below.[110]

21-52   The object of registration is not to provide a comprehensive account of all of a company's charges but to warn unsuspecting creditors that the debtor company has

from the chargor's freedom to deal with the charged assets in the ordinary course of business which would make a charge a floating charge. But if the feature of the fixed charge, to quote Lord Walker in *Spectrum Plus* [2005] 2 BCLC 269 at 318, is that the asset is permanently appropriated to the payment of the sum charged and that assets can be released from the charge only with the active concurrence of the chargee, then it is difficult to see how the charge here can be a fixed charge if the property subject to it can be altered by the chargor unilaterally.

[107] A better arrangement may be a sweep from an open access account to a blocked account so the charge is floating on the proceeds paid into the open account but the chargor is required to sweep a certain percentage amount to a blocked account over which the chargee has a fixed charge. Of course, evidence that the chargee sweeps funds back from the blocked account to the open account would raise issues as to whether the accounts were all part of the same arrangement and subject to a single floating charge, but clearly there are permutations here for banks and companies to consider: see Oditah [2004] 120 LQR 533 at 540–1.The uncertainties and practicalities combined may mean that it is cheaper all round to settle for a floating charge.

[108] See Calnan, *Taking Security, Law and Practice* (2006), pp 135–6; see too Frome & Gibbons, above n 97, at p 129 who conclude that the constraints on the SPV (special purpose vehicle) used for securitisation transactions are such that a court would consider the charge is fixed even though the chargor has some rights to use the income stream. See also Ferran, *Principles of Corporate Finance Law* (2008), pp 385–6.

[109] As the charge must be created by the company, security interests arising by law, such as liens and pledges, are excluded from the registration requirements.

[110] For a comprehensive account of registration, see McCormack, *Registration of Company Charges* (2nd edn, 2005).

charged its assets.[111] The register of charges is publicly available (CA 2006, s 885(6)) so enabling creditors taking security to appreciate to what extent the assets are already encumbered. The register also assists unsecured creditors because it allows them to appreciate the extent to which the assets are earmarked for other creditors in the event of insolvency.

Only charges included in CA 2006, s 860(7) (set out below) must be registered but those listed include practically all the forms of charges commonly given by companies, covering charges on land, goods (encompassed by the obscurely worded s 860(7)(b)), book debts, goodwill, intellectual property and floating charges over the undertaking.[112] The full list is: **21-53**

(1) a charge on land (wherever situated) or any interest in it, but not including a charge for any rent or other periodical sum issuing out of the land;

(2) a charge created or evidenced by an instrument which, if executed by an individual, would require registration as a bill of sale;

(3) a charge for the purpose of securing any issue of debentures;

(4) a charge on uncalled share capital of the company;

(5) a charge on calls made but not paid;

(6) a charge on book debts of the company;

(7) a floating charge on the company's undertaking or property;

(8) a charge on a ship or aircraft, or any share in a ship;

(9) a charge on goodwill, or on any intellectual property (CA 2006, s 860(7)).

A significant omission is charges on shares, particularly shares in subsidiary companies, which can be a valuable source of security.[113] Registration is required even if the property charged is situated abroad (CA 2006, s 866) and charges existing on property acquired by the company must also be registered.[114]   **21-54**

The prescribed particulars and the instrument of charge must be delivered to the registrar of companies within 21 calendar days after the date of creation, i.e. the date of the execution of the charge.[115] The problem which this period creates is that anyone   **21-55**

---

[111] See *Re Welsh Irish Ferries Ltd* [1985] BCLC 327 at 332.

[112] There is an overlap between a number of the categories so, for example, a charge could be registrable because it falls within CA 2006, s 860(7)(f) or (g), i.e. as a charge on book debts and as a floating charge. Equally, notwithstanding the scope of the provision, some charges are not registrable, such as a fixed charge on a credit balance at a bank; or a fixed charge on shares; or a fixed charge on an insurance policy (see *Paul & Frank Ltd v Discount Bank (Overseas) Ltd* [1966] 2 All ER 922).

[113] For an example, see *Arthur D Little Ltd v Ableco Finance LLC* [2002] 2 BCLC 799.

[114] CA 2006, s 862, assuming the charge is of a kind which, if it had been created by the company after the acquisition of the property, would require registration under s 860. A failure to register as required by this provision does not attract the statutory invalidity of s 874, but merely a fine: s 862(5).

[115] CA 2006, ss 860(1), 870(1); and see The Companies (Particulars of Company Charges) Regulations 2008, SI 2008/2996. If because of errors in the particulars provided, the registrar is required to return the forms to the presenter for correction, re-submission must occur within the 21-day limit. If the registrar improperly rejects a form, for example, because of doubts as to whether the charge is within s 860(7), the charge is not

searching the register of charges with respect to the company and finding no charges cannot be sure that there are not charges which have been created but have not yet been registered. Searchers of the register must not rely therefore on the absence of charges and must ask the company to confirm that no other charges have been created which have yet to be registered.

21-56   It is the company's duty to deliver the particulars and the original charge instrument to the registrar of companies.[116] In practice, because of the consequences of non-delivery, the majority of registrations are undertaken by the chargee (CA 2006, s 860(2)).

21-57   There is no mechanism whereby subsequent variations in the terms of the charge, for example an increase in the secured moneys or a variation of priorities as between chargees, can be registered. In effect, the parties must register the variation under CA 2006, s 860, as if an entirely new charge has been created. While a little confusing, the practice at least has the merit that the variation appears on the company's public record.

21-58   Following delivery of the prescribed particulars and the original instrument of charge, the registrar checks the accuracy of the particulars against the charge instrument. It is important that the particulars reflect the full extent of the charge so as to ensure that any person searching the public register is not misled as to the extent of the security, but it can be difficult for the registrar's staff to ensure that this is the case, given the nature of the documentation submitted by chargees. Indeed it is often difficult to deduce from the instrument delivered either the nature of the charge which the parties have purported to create or the assets which are the subject of the charge. It is the opaqueness of these documents which leads to so much litigation on these matters later and it is clear that few commercial lenders regularly review their standard documentation to ensure its continued appropriateness, both generally in terms of creating security, and specifically in the context of the company in question. For example, many lenders continue to claim fixed charges on book debts when it is clear post-*Re Spectrum Plus Ltd*[117] that the charges they have created are floating charges (though this may be as much through commercial inertia as any real expectation that such charges are fixed).

21-59   Once checked against the particulars, the original instrument is returned to the presenter together with a certificate of registration and an entry is made on the register of charges (CA 2006, s 869). The certificate is conclusive as to compliance with the registration requirements even if it is inaccurate.[118]

---

invalidated as delivery will have occurred within the 21-day period. The 21-day period is extended where the charge is created outside of the UK over property situated outside of the UK: see s 870(2).

[116] CA 2006, s 860(1). A registration fee of £13 is payable: The Companies (Fees) Regulations 2004, SI 2004/2621, Sch 4.   [117] [2005] 2 BCLC 269, HL.

[118] CA 2006, s 869(6)(b) and see *Re Mechanisations (Eaglescliffe) Ltd* [1966] Ch 20 (amount secured wrongly stated). The certificate is conclusive even if it shows the wrong date of creation of the charge, so that the charge may not have been delivered within the 21-day period: *Re C L Nye Ltd* [1970] 3 All ER 1061.

A copy of the instrument of charge must be available at the company's registered **21-60** office or other specified location for inspection by any creditor or member (CA 2006, s 875). The company must maintain a register of all charges (whether or not registrable under s 860) at the registered office or other specified place and that register is available for inspection by any person (s 877).

There is no statutory requirement to notify the registrar of companies of the satis- **21-61** faction or release of any charge. Companies which want to clear debts of their public record can make a statement under CA 2006, s 872, however, to the effect either that the debt for which the charge was given has been paid or satisfied in whole or in part, or that part of the property or undertaking charged has been released from the charge or has ceased to form part of the company's property or undertaking. On receipt of that statement, the registrar may enter on the register a memorandum of satisfaction to this effect.

Statutory invalidity for non-registration

The consequence of a failure to deliver the prescribed particulars within the **21-62** required period means that the charge is void against the liquidator or administrator and any creditor of the company (CA 2006, s 874(1)), but it is a limited invalidity. The statute 'makes void a security; not the debt, not the cause of action, but the security, and not as against everybody, not as against the company grantor, but against the liquidator, [and now an administrator] and against any creditor'.[119]

The invalidity of the security is without prejudice to the obligation for repayment of **21-63** the money secured by the charge and the money secured immediately becomes payable (CA 2006, s 874(3)). This liability to immediate repayment allows a creditor to insist on recovering his money once he has lost his security as a result of the failure to deliver the particulars within 21 days.

The nature of the statutory invalidity imposed by CA 2006, s 874(1) was considered by **21-64** the House of Lords in *Smith (Administrator of Cosslett (Contractors) Ltd) v Bridgend County Borough Council*,[120] which was noted at **21-26**.

As discussed above, a council had contracted with a company (the contractor) to **21-65** carry out coal washing on a particular site for the council. The terms of the contract allowed the council, in the event of default by the contractor, to enter the site, use the machinery of the contractor to complete the job and to sell the machinery and apply the proceeds to the liabilities of the contractor under the contract. When the company defaulted on the contract, the council duly entered the site, seized the contractor's machinery and obtained another contractor to complete the contract using that machinery. The council then permitted the second contractor to remove and sell the machinery. A variety of legal proceedings ensued, part of which concluded, as

---

[119] *Re Monolithic Building Company* [1915] 1 Ch 643 at 667, per Phillimore LJ; and see *Re Cosslett Ltd* [2002] 1 BCLC 77 at 84: it is not void against the company when it is a going concern, but it is void when the company is in liquidation or administration.   [120] [2002] 1 BCLC 77.

discussed at **21-27**, that the council's right to sell the machinery and apply the proceeds to the debt due by the contractor to the council amounted to a floating charge which charge was void for non-registration under what is now CA 2006, s 874.

21-66   The administrator then brought successful proceedings claiming damages from the council for conversion of the machinery by allowing the second contractor to remove it from the site. The Court of Appeal allowed an appeal by the council against that liability for conversion, finding that the contractual conditions as to the use and sale of the machinery etc (despite being an unregistered floating charge void as against the administrator for non-registration under what is now CA 2006, s 874) remained valid as against the company. The council's power of sale under the contractual condition remained valid against the company and was the answer, the Court of Appeal said, to the conversion claim.[121]

21-67   On appeal to the House of Lords, their Lordships rejected this finding by the Court of Appeal as a narrow and arbitrary construction of what is now CA 2006, s 874(1) and reversed the decision. The statutory provision does not invalidate a charge against a company while it is a going concern but makes an unregistered but registrable charge void against a company acting by its liquidator or administrator, that is to say void against a company in liquidation or in administration.[122] The council could not therefore rely on its terms against the company or the administrator of the company. As the council's charge was void for non-registration, the council had no proprietary interest in the machinery and therefore allowing the second contractor to remove the equipment was a violation of the first contractor's right of possession. That was sufficient to amount to a conversion in respect of which the administrator could seek damages. The council's claim for damages for breach of contract by the contractor would have to be pursued in the liquidation of the company.[123]

21-68   This attempt by the Court of Appeal to ascribe a type of partial invalidity to the unregistered charge was, Lord Hoffmann said, 'a startling and unorthodox approach' to what is now CA 2006, s 874(1). He noted that the Court of Appeal may have been influenced in adopting that approach by its perception of the merits of the case. The local council found itself in a position where it had no security for the debts owed to it (which included a large amount advanced by the council to the contractor to enable the contractor to acquire the machinery in the first place) as its floating charge was void for non-registration and it was liable in conversion to the administrator.

Remedial measures in cases of non-registration

21-69   Where the required particulars have not been delivered to the registrar of companies and the 21-day period has elapsed so attracting the statutory invalidity, there are a

---

[121] See [2000] 1 BCLC 775, CA.   [122] See [2002] 1 BCLC 77 at 84, per Lord Hoffmann.

[123] Counsel for the council attempted to secure some redress by claiming the benefit of some equitable set-off so as to set off the council's breach of contract claim against the administrator's claim for conversion. The House of Lords was robust in rejecting this possibility, Lord Scott noting that, given that the council's security was invalid because of a failure to comply with the statutory provisions as to registration, it was no part of equity to provide, via equitable set-off, an alternative security: see [2002] 1 BCLC 77 at 97.

number of options open to the company and the chargee. The main option is an application by either party to the court for registration out of time under CA 2006, s 873 and this step should be taken without delay once the failure to register is discovered.

Section 873 allows the court to extend the time for registration if satisfied that the **21-70** omission to register a charge within the time required was accidental, or due to inadvertence or to some other sufficient cause, or is not of a nature to prejudice the position of creditors or shareholders of the company, or that on other grounds it is just and equitable to grant relief.[124] Even if the court's discretion does arise, the court may decide not to exercise it as where the application is made only after long delay.[125] But in general, the practice of the court is to exercise the power to extend the period for registration, subject to the proviso that registration is without prejudice to any rights acquired between the date of creation of the charge and the date of its actual registration,[126] so as to ensure that intervening creditors are not adversely affected.[127]

As an alternative to applying to the court, the chargee may attempt to remedy the situ- **21-71** ation by getting another charge executed by the company and registered before any third party intervenes.[128] This approach is a risky strategy for, if it fails, the court may look unfavourably on an application under CA 2006, s 873.[129] A further risk with executing a new charge is that if the company goes into insolvent liquidation or administration shortly thereafter, the new charge may be open to challenge as a vulnerable transaction under IA 1986, ss 239, 245 (discussed in Chapter 25).

Another possibility is that the chargee can seek immediate repayment of the sum **21-72** secured (see CA 2006, s 874(3)) and this ability to demand immediate repayment of the entire amount may assist him in obtaining a new charge from the company. If the unregistered chargee succeeds in securing repayment before liquidation or administration, the charge is spent and there is nothing for the statutory invalidity to bite on.[130]

---

[124] The final 'just and equitable' category allows for any reason, whether specified in the section or not, to be put forward: *Re Braemar Investments Ltd* [1988] BCLC 556 at 561. See also *Confinance Ltd v Timespan Images Ltd* [2005] 2 BCLC 693.

[125] See *Re Telomatic Ltd* [1994] 1 BCLC 90; *Victoria Housing Estates Ltd v Ashpurton Estates Ltd* [1982] 3 All ER 665.

[126] *Re Joplin Brewery Co Ltd* [1902] 1 Ch 79 (as modified following the decision in *Watson v Duff Morgan & Vermont (Holdings) Ltd* [1974] 1 All ER 794); and see *Victoria Housing Estates Ltd v Ashpurton Estates Ltd* [1982] 3 All ER 665 at 670 for the history of this proviso; and see *Barclays Bank plc v Stuart Landon Ltd* [2001] 2 BCLC 316.

[127] The extension may also be subject to the proviso in *Re L H Charles & Co Ltd* [1935] WN 15 allowing the company, through any liquidator subsequently appointed, to apply within a specified period (for example, 42 days) after the commencement of the winding up to discharge the order granting an extension of time and containing an undertaking by the applicant for late registration to abide by any order which the court may make.

[128] A process which may be fraught with difficulties: see *Re Telomatic Ltd* [1994] 1 BCLC 90.

[129] See *Victoria Housing Estates Ltd v Ashpurton Estates Ltd* [1982] 3 All ER 665 at 677 (the court should look askance at a chargee who deliberately defers his application in order to see which way the wind is going to blow).

[130] *Mercantile Bank of India Ltd v Chartered Bank of India, Australia and China* [1937] 1 All ER 231; *Re Row Dal Construction Pty Ltd* [1966] VR 249 at 258; *NV Slavenburg's Bank NV v Intercontinental Natural Resources Ltd* [1980] 1 All ER 955.

Priority as between charges

21-73 The registration of a charge as required by CA 2006, s 860 does not determine priorities as between successive chargees, save to the extent of the statutory invalidity affecting any unregistered charge.

21-74 Priority issues are determined at common law with the basic rules being that legal interests prevail over equitable, fixed charges over floating charges, and where the equities are equal, the first in time prevails. The position is then complicated by issues of notice and, in particular, the application of the doctrine of constructive notice. Anyone dealing with a company is deemed under the doctrine of constructive notice to have notice of its public documents including the articles of association which doctrine was extended, obiter, by *Wilson v Kelland*[131] to the register of charges but only to the extent that there is constructive notice of the existence of a registered charge and not of any special provisions contained in the charge.[132] It means, however, that successive chargees have notice of the preceding charges (assuming they are registered). The position with respect to the creation of further charges post the granting of a floating charge was discussed above at **21-12**.

Reform of registration requirements

21-75 The Company Law Review (CLR) initially consulted on the option of retaining the core of the registration requirements while updating and amending them to incorporate certain improvements.[133] By the time of its final report, the CLR had opted for a much more radical proposal, namely that the current scheme of registration as outlined above should be replaced by a system of 'notice filing'.[134] Given it had not been possible to consult on that more radical proposal, the CLR recommended that the DTI refer the issue of registration to the Law Commission which was duly done. The Commission's terms of reference excluded any intrusion into insolvency law, however, a somewhat significant restriction when security issues by their very nature are most acute in the context of insolvency.

21-76 The Law Commission duly noted a variety of weaknesses in the current registration requirements such as: the statutory list of charges which require registration (now in CA 2006, s 860(7)) is outdated; the information provided to the registrar of companies is not always reliable or completely accurate with prudent searchers looking to the chargor company for further information; dual registration at Companies House and specialist registries is required in a number of cases such as for charges on land, aircraft and ships; and while a failure to register a registrable charge has

---

[131] [1910] 2 Ch 306.

[132] See *Siebe Gorman & Co Ltd v Barclays Bank Ltd* [1979] 2 Lloyd's Rep 142 at 160, overruled on other grounds, *Re Spectrum Plus Ltd* [2005] 2 BCLC 269. See generally Gough, *Company Charges* (2nd edn, 1996), Ch 23.

[133] See CLR, *Modern Company Law for a Competitive Economy, Registration of Company Charges* (October 2000).

[134] See CLR, *Modern Company Law for a Competitive Economy, Final Report*, vol 1 (July 2001), Ch 12.

consequences as against an administrator, liquidator or other creditors, registration itself is not a priority point and does not determine priorities.

The Law Commission published a Consultation Paper[135] on registration of security **21-77** interests in July 2002 followed by a Consultative Report[136] in 2004 advocating radical reform of personal property security law including the abolition of the floating charge, but its final Report[137] in 2005 contained more modest proposals.[138]

Responding at the consultative stage, the influential Law Society Committee on **21-78** Company Law broadly welcomed the proposal for introducing a system of notice filing, but noted that the proposals were potentially very major reforms going well beyond the confines of company law and that it would be inappropriate to make such major changes to security law and transfer of title law in a Companies Act or by way of secondary legislation pursuant to a Companies Act. The Law Society Committee also commented that:[139]

'...it is fair to say that the present system has not come in for extensive criticism from those who use it. It works relatively well in practice although its interrelationship with the specialist title registries is somewhat unsatisfactory. In short, it is not an obstacle to the obtaining of credit and we doubt whether business would suffer if the present system (subject possibly to some limited amendment) were allowed to continue.'

As noted, the Commission's Final Report backed away from its earlier prefer- **21-79** ence for radical reform and concentrated on recommending the introduction of an electronic notice-filing system, akin to the systems in operation in the US and many Commonwealth countries, to replace the current system of registration. The Commission proposed that the filing of a security interest should be done electronic-ally; there would no longer be any need to register in specialist registries; the scheme could apply to all charges unless expressly excluded; priority would generally be deter-mined by the date of filing. The effect of a failure to register would be invalidity against an administrator or liquidator and a loss of priority against a subsequent secured cred-itor who filed. There would be no 21-day period for registration for it would be in the creditor's interest to file as soon as possible.

The Government consulted further on whether to implement the Law Commission's **21-80** recommendations,[140] specifically in terms of the economic benefits of so doing, but

[135] See Law Commission, *Registration of Security Interests: Company Charges and Property other than Land* (Consultation Paper No 164), July 2002; also McCormack, 'The Floating Charge and The Law Commission's Consultation Paper on Registration of Security Interests' [2003] Insol Law 2.

[136] See Law Commission, *Company Security Interests* (Consultation Paper No 176), 2004.

[137] Law Commission, *Company Security Interests* (Law Comm No 296, Cm 6654).

[138] For a detailed account of the process and the proposals by the Law Commissioner with responsibil-ity for the project, see Beale, 'Reform of The Law Of Security Interests Over Personal Property' in Lowry & Mistelis (eds), *Commercial Law: Perspectives and Practice* (2006); also Goode on how the proposals came to move from radical reform to something of a damp squib: see Goode, above n 33, 16–20.

[139] See Law Society Company Law Committee, *The Registration of Security Interests: Company Charges and Property other than Land* (October 2002), Memo No 448, para 12.2.

[140] See DTI, *Registration of Companies Security Interests (Company Charges)* (July 2005).

there was little or no support.[141] In the end, really through pressure of time, it was not possible to carry the matter forward in any way to the CA 2006. The most the Government was able to do was to secure a power to amend CA 2006, Part 25 dealing with company charges by regulations (s 894) so reform is possible in the future without the need for primary legislation. The Secretary of State also has power to make regulations under s 893 dealing with the problem of overlapping registration requirements between Companies House and other registries such as the Land Registry.

21-81   There is much academic respect for the groundwork done by the Law Commission[142] (though not everyone would support the idea of notice filing[143]) and support for the view that the time has come to abolish the floating charge[144] and to look to a fundamental restatement and reform of personal property security law[145] coupled with electronic filing of security documents. But there is little sense of any Government interest in pursuing such fundamental change.

E Enforcement of a floating charge

Receivers, administrative receivers and administrators

21-82   The appointment of a receiver by the Court of Chancery was an ancient equitable remedy available to creditors whether secured or unsecured,[146] but, in the modern business context, receiverships are associated particularly with a default by a corporate borrower on a secured loan.[147]

21-83   During the nineteenth century conveyancers realised the advantages in terms of costs and speed of providing for the appointment of a receiver as a contractual remedy under a debenture without the necessity of going to court. A *receiver*, strictly speaking, is appointed just to receive the rent or other income from property.[148] Over time, appointments of receivers for this purpose became the accepted practice, so much so that the power to appoint a receiver of income is now implied into mortgages by deed unless the parties provided otherwise and such receivers are known as LPA

---

[141] See McCormack, *Registration of Company Charges* (2nd edn, 2005), pp 53–75 for a comprehensive account of the difficulties with the Law Commission's proposals and why they are unlikely to be adopted; also McCormack (2005) 68 MLR 286.

[142] See Goode, above n 33, 17 '...the intermediate consultative report was a superb document'.

[143] See McCormack, *Registration of Company Charges* (2nd edn, 2005), pp 66–8.

[144] For varying reasons, see Goode, above n 33; Mokal, *Corporate Insolvency Law* (2005), pp 219–23.

[145] See Worthington, above n 22; Wood, above n 33.

[146] The power to appoint a receiver is vested in the High Court, see the Supreme Court Act 1981, s 37. For an outline of the development of receivers, see Rigby LJ in *Gaskell v Gosling* [1896] 1 QB 669 at 691–3.

[147] See generally, Finch, *Corporate Insolvency Law: perspectives and principles* (2002), Ch 8.

[148] The powers conferred by the LPA 1925 are limited in this way but they may be varied or extended by the mortgage deed: s 101(3) and they are typically extended to include powers to sell and to manage the mortgaged property.

receivers.[149] If it is desirable for the receiver to manage the property or to carry on the debtor's business, the receiver must also be appointed under the terms of the debenture as a manager with appropriate powers and such a person is often referred to as a receiver and manager.[150] Again such powers are commonplace. The result is that the debenture commonly provides for the appointment of receivers with wide power to receive income, to manage the business and to sell the assets secured for the benefit of the chargee. In addition to receivers, and receivers and managers, the IA 1986, s 29(2) provides for a further category, administrative receivers, defined essentially as receivers appointed under a floating charge over all or substantially all of the company's property. Most appointments of receivers in recent years were appointment of administrative receivers, reflecting the prevalence of floating charges over all or substantially all the company's assets. The IA 1986 as amended by the EA 2002 now prohibits the appointment of administrative receivers, however, where the floating charge is created on or after 15 September 2003 (IA 1986, s 72A). To understand why this prohibition was imposed, it is necessary to understand how administrative receiverships operated prior to the EA 2002.

Essentially, administrative receivership worked in the following way. A secured creditor (typically a clearing bank with fixed and floating charges over the company and its undertaking) would appoint a receiver following a default by the corporate borrower. Appointment was purely a contractual issue requiring no assistance from the courts and the receiver's primary function was to realise sufficient of the company's assets comprised in the security to discharge the debt due to the secured creditor. The receiver had to decide quite quickly whether to continue the business in order to sell it as a going concern or to sell off the company's assets piecemeal. In theory, once the receiver completed his task of realising sufficient funds to satisfy his appointor, the company could continue trading. In practice, the receiver would commonly not realise sufficient even to pay his appointor in full and the company would go into liquidation. Moreover, as the appointment of a receiver did not impose a moratorium on other creditors enforcing their rights, his appointment usually galvanised other creditors into asserting their rights and remedies. For example, creditors might petition the court for a compulsory winding up order or the members might resolve to put the company into voluntary liquidation.

21-84

There were obvious advantages to administrative receiverships, particularly for the appointor, most notably the ease and speed with which an appointment might be

21-85

---

[149] See Law of Property Act 1925, s 101(1)(iii). The use of LPA receivers can be quite effective where the borrower has properties which are generating rental income which the lender would like to secure to repay the mortgage interest, at least, especially when it may be difficult to sell the property to recover the capital. The powers of an LPA receiver are usually increased by the terms of the deed and an LPA receiver need not be a qualified insolvency practitioner.

[150] As to the distinction, see *Re Manchester and Milford Rly Co* (1880) 14 Ch D 645 at 653 where Jessel MR noted that: 'A "receiver" is a term which was well known...as meaning a person who receives rents or other income paying ascertained outgoings, but who does not...manage the property in the sense of buying or selling or anything of that kind.... If it was desired to continue the trade at all, it was necessary to appoint a manager, or a receiver and manager as it was generally called.'

made once the borrower was in default and the focus on realising sufficient assets to satisfy the debt due to the debenture holder. But receiverships were frequently criticised precisely because of this focus on one secured creditor to the exclusion of other interests, in particular, the interests of unsecured creditors: see **23-3**. As a matter of policy, the Government decided their use should not be continued and its preference was for a collective process for the benefit of the creditors as a whole—administration.

21-86   The holder of a qualifying floating charge is prohibited then from appointing an administrative receiver of the company where the charge was created on or after the 15 September 2003.[151] It is still possible to appoint an administrative receiver under charges created prior to that date but creditors prefer now to appoint an administrator even where they have power to appoint an administrative receiver.[152] The right to appoint an administrative receiver is retained by IA 1986, ss 72B–72GA for specialist areas such as public–private partnership projects, utility projects and urban regeneration projects[153] but those specialist cases are beyond the scope of this work.

21-87   For a floating charge holder outside of those specialist contexts, the means of enforcement is through the appointment of an administrator under the IA 1986, Sch B1, and it is possible to do so out of court in a manner very similar (in terms of speed and efficiency) to the appointment of an administrative receiver: see **23-42**. Administration is discussed in detail in Chapter 23 and it will be seen that an administrator is able to realise the assets quickly (see **23-80**) and to make distributions to secured creditors (see **23-86**) in a manner which can look very like administrative receivership. The process of enforcement may have changed, but the outcome may be very similar: see **23-114**.

---

[151] IA 1986, s 72A; SI 2003/2095.

[152] Figures for Great Britain show that the number of receiverships halved between 2003–04 (1,284) and 2007–08 (634), see *Statistical Tables on Companies Registration Activities 2007–08*, Table C2, available on Companies House website at www.companieshouse.gov.uk/about/companiesRegActivities.shtml.

[153] IA 1986, s 72A.

PART V

CORPORATE RESCUE AND RESTRUCTURING

22

Company voluntary arrangements

A Introduction

One of the most important options for those managing a company in financial difficulty **22-1** is the ability to make binding compromises or arrangements with the creditors of the company. For any compromise or arrangement to work effectively, it is necessary for all the creditors to be bound by it. This can be achieved either by ensuring that the creditors unanimously agree to the plan (which is usually impractical) or by making use of statutory provisions which enable a specified majority to bind the minority.

One option might be to use the provisions governing schemes of arrangement (con- **22-2** tained in CA 2006, Part 26) but these complex provisions are time-consuming and expensive to operate especially with respect to identifying distinct classes of creditors who are entitled to separate meetings, see **26-104**. Schemes of arrangement are discussed in Chapter 26 and, though they are of value in a variety of situations, they are an inappropriate rescue mechanism for companies in financial difficulty other than in complex cases.[1]

The option usually chosen is a company voluntary arrangement, invariably known **22-3** as a CVA. There are two types of CVA: a CVA under IA 1986, Part 1 or a CVA with a moratorium governed by IA 1986, Sch A1. This chapter concentrates on the former with only a brief account of CVAs with a moratorium. The latter CVA was an innovation introduced by the Insolvency Act 2000 but it has proved unpopular (it is administratively burdensome and therefore expensive). Most CVAs therefore remain CVAs under IA 1986, Part 1 which suffer from the disadvantage of not having a moratorium but that is overcome commonly by preparing proposals for a voluntary arrangement in conjunction with the appointment of an administrator. There is a close link between administration and CVAs since if a company in administration is to be rescued as a going concern (see **23-8**) this frequently means entering into a CVA with the company's creditors and most CVAs are entered into in the context of administrations.[2] A particular attraction of a CVA (outside of administration) for the directors is

---

[1] For an example, see the T & N litigation, the background to which is set out at [2006] 2 BCLC 374 at 379–82.

[2] See Frisby, *Report on Insolvency Outcomes*, presented to the Insolvency Service (2006), p 63, who notes that of those surveyed for this report, the general view was that 'the only genuine insolvency rescue mechanism is the CVA within the protection of administration.'

that they retain control over the choice of nominee/supervisor who will conduct the CVA, they remain in post and, crucially, a nominee/supervisor under a CVA is not required to make reports as to the directors' conduct under the Company Directors Disqualification Act 1986. Even so, CVAs remain one of the least used insolvency procedures[3] perhaps not least because they have a high failure rate.[4]

B Company voluntary arrangements—IA 1986, Pt I

Proposing an arrangement

22-4 A voluntary arrangement, defined as a composition in satisfaction of the company's debts, or a scheme of arrangement of its affairs, may be proposed:

(1) by the directors of the company (where the company is neither in administration nor in winding up); or

(2) by an administrator where the company is in administration; or

(3) by a liquidator where the company is being wound up (IA 1986, s 1(1), (3)).

22-5 In practice, a proposal from a liquidator would be exceptional and CVAs are really a matter for the directors or an administrator. Neither creditors nor members may initiate a voluntary arrangement. There is no requirement that the company is unable to pay its debts, but obviously the company must be in financial difficulty or anticipating financial difficulties for the directors to consider a voluntary arrangement.

22-6 The proposal must provide for a nominee to act either as trustee or otherwise for the purpose of supervising the implementation of the voluntary arrangement and the nominee must be a qualified insolvency practitioner or authorised to act as nominee in relation to the voluntary arrangement.[5]

22-7 Where the proposal is made by the directors, they draw up and submit to the nominee a document setting out the terms of the proposed voluntary arrangement and a statement of the company's affairs and, in practice, they usually do this with the assistance of the nominee whom they will have approached already about the company's difficulties (IA 1986, s 2(3)). Having assisted them with drawing up their proposals and agreed to be the nominee, within 28 days of being given notice of the proposals[6] the nominee submits a report to the court stating whether, in his opinion, the

---

[3] In 2007–08, for example, 466 companies (518 in 2006–07) went into a CVA compared with 2,733 (3,536) companies in administration and 15,281 (15,241) insolvent liquidations: see *Statistical Tables on Companies Registration Activities 2007–08*, Table C2, available on Companies House website at www.companieshouse.gov.uk/about/companiesRegActivities.shtml.

[4] See Frisby, *Report on Insolvency Outcomes*, presented to the Insolvency Service (2006), p 63.

[5] IA 1986, s 1(2); persons who are not qualified insolvency practitioners may be recognised by the Secretary of State as authorised to act as nominees and supervisors of CVAs (and IVAs): ss 389, 389A.

[6] The court can allow a longer period: IA 1986, s 2(2).

proposed voluntary arrangement has a reasonable prospect of being approved and implemented,[7] whether meetings of the company and its creditors should be summoned to consider the proposal and stating the date, time and place where such meetings will be held (s 2(2)). His report is merely filed with the court and, unless there is an objection, there is no court hearing. The nominee proceeds to summon the required meetings and, with respect to creditors, the summons will extend to all creditors of whose claim and address the nominee is aware.[8]

Where the proposal for the CVA is put forward by an administrator and he is to act as the nominee, he proceeds to summon the necessary meetings of the members and the creditors at such time, date and place as he thinks fit without any need to notify the court (IA 1986, s 3(2)).   **22-8**

Approving an arrangement

The purpose of the meetings is to decide whether to approve the proposed voluntary arrangement, with or without modifications (IA 1986, s 4(1)). No proposal or modification can be approved which affects the right of a secured creditor of the company to enforce his security without the concurrence of the creditor concerned.[9] No proposal or modification can be approved under which any preferential debt of the company is to be paid otherwise than in priority to non-preferential debts, or other than on a pro rata basis to other preferential debts, again without the concurrence of the preferential creditor concerned.[10] However, this requirement of priority for preferential debts does not preclude the payment of non-preferential creditors by third parties from their own funds.[11] The significance of preferential debts is much reduced in any event: see **24-89**. The agreement of the secured creditors, on the other hand, is crucial to the viability of any CVA, not least because the secured creditor is likely to be a bank which will need to provide funding to support the company during the CVA.   **22-9**

Apart from those limitations with respect to secured and preferential creditors, any proposal can be presented for approval, provided it meets the general requirement that it is a voluntary arrangement as defined, namely a composition in satisfaction of the company's debts or a scheme of arrangement of its affairs.[12] In *Commissioners of Inland Revenue v Adam & Partners Ltd*,[13] the Revenue Commissioners sought a   **22-10**

---

[7] There are some concerns as to the basis on which the nominee might reach this opinion, given that he will be unable to sound out the creditors as to whether they will approve the CVA for fear of sparking precipitate action by them.

[8] IA 1986, s 3(1), (3). The meetings must take place not less than 14 days from and not more than 28 days from the filing of the nominee's report with the court: IR 1986, r 1.9(1).

[9] IA 1986, s 4(3); as to the definition of 'secured creditor', see s 248.

[10] IA 1986, s 4(4); see s 386 and Sch 6.

[11] See *IRC v Wimbledon Football Club Ltd* [2005] 1 BCLC 66. If a third party chooses to pay certain non-preferential creditors out of his own funds, that is not a breach of IA 1986, s 4(4) conferring priority on preferential creditors. The creditors in this case were paid off by the buyer of the company's assets under a sale agreement and not under the CVA.

[12] IA 1986, s 1(1).   [13] [2001] 1 BCLC 222.

declaration that a proposal purportedly approved by the creditors was not a CVA within the meaning of the Insolvency Act. The scheme envisaged that preferential and unsecured creditors would receive no payments while the company's main secured creditor (its bank) would receive a better return than would otherwise be the case under any other procedure. The Court of Appeal agreed that the proposal did not amount to a composition of the company's debts which is an agreement between the compounding debtor and all or some of the creditors by which the compounding creditors agree with the debtor to accept from the debtor payment of less than the amount due to them in full satisfaction of the whole of their claims.[14] The court did accept, however, that the proposal was for a scheme of arrangement which is different from a composition and involves something less than the release or discharge of creditors' debts.[15] On its proper construction, the scheme involved a moratorium on the prosecution of claims by creditors, which moratorium did not prevent the Inland Revenue and other unsecured creditors from subsequently asserting their contractual rights as creditors of the company after the moratorium ended. The scheme had the requisite element of give and take as between the creditors to qualify as a 'scheme of arrangement'.

22-11   Typically, the agreement includes express terms precluding the commencement of proceedings by the CVA creditors against the company and/or the enforcement of their debts during the continuance of the agreement, provided the company is complying with the CVA. In the absence of an express term, the court may imply such a term in order to give business efficacy to the agreement.[16] The proposal must also state how it is proposed to deal with the claims of unknown creditors (discussed below).[17] Neither the supervisor (as the nominee becomes once the proposal is approved) nor the courts have any power to amend a CVA and so it is important that the arrangement contains an express power for its terms to be varied or altered.[18]

22-12   In *Prudential Assurance Co Ltd v PRG Powerhouse Ltd*[19] the court accepted that a CVA could operate to release third parties from obligations to the company. In this case, the claimant landlords were creditors of the insolvent company and the beneficiaries of guarantees (of rental payments due to them) given by the parent company of the insolvent company. The CVA allowed for the release of the company from its liabilities on the payment of 28p in the £1 to the creditors. The terms of the agreement required the claimants to treat the guarantees too as having been released and, the court said, the company (but not the parent) was entitled to enforce that obligation

---

[14] See [2001] 1 BCLC 222 at 231.

[15] [2001] 1 BCLC 222 at 231, relying on Lightman J in *March Estates Ltd v Gunmark Ltd* [1996] 2 BCLC 1.

[16] See *Johnson v Davies* [1998] 2 BCLC 252 (term implied that creditors would take no enforcement steps); *Sea Voyager Maritime Inc v Bielecki* [1999] 1 BCLC 133 at 149–51 (court considered that term might be implied to preclude commencement of proceedings); *Alman v Approach Housing Ltd* [2001] 1 BCLC 530 (strong grounds would be needed to imply term precluding commencement of proceedings).

[17] IR 1986, r 1.3(2)(fa).

[18] See *Re Alpha Lighting Ltd* [1997] BPIR 341, CA, noted Jones (1997) 10 Insolv Int 60; also *Raja v Rubin* [1999] 1 BCLC 621, CA; *Re Broome, Thompson v Broome* [1999] 1 BCLC 356.

[19] [2008] 1 BCLC 289; and see Swain, 'Power Surge for Landlords' (2007) 20 Insolv Int 123.

against the landlords. The court went on to find the agreement was unfairly prejudicial to the landlord creditors, a point which is discussed below, but that does not detract from the court's acceptance that a CVA may release third parties from their obligations provided the agreement is not otherwise unfairly prejudicial.

The voting rules

A significant advantage of a CVA is that there is no requirement for separate class meetings though, as can be seen from *Prudential Assurance Co Ltd v PRG Powerhouse Ltd*,[20] this can work to the disadvantage of a class of creditors who find themselves outvoted by other creditors with different interests.[21] There is just one meeting for creditors and one for members, with the meetings held on the same or different days, in either case with the creditors' meeting taking place first and the meetings must be held within seven days of each other.[22]

22-13

At the members' meeting, a majority of more than half in value of the ordinary shareholders is required in favour of the resolution and members vote according to the rights attached to their shares by the articles.[23] At the creditors' meeting, the proposal must be approved by a majority in excess of 75% in value of the creditors present (in person or by proxy) and voting on the resolution.[24] On other matters, a majority in excess of half in value is required.[25]

22-14

Each creditor who has notice of the creditors' meeting is entitled to vote and his vote is calculated according to the amount of his debt.[26] Secured creditors may not vote other than with respect to any element which is unsecured.[27] A creditor may vote in respect of a debt for an unliquidated amount and any debt where the value of the debt is unascertained and, for the purpose of voting only, the debt must be valued at £1 unless the chairman of the meeting agrees to put a higher value on it.[28] The result is that the creditor in respect of an unliquidated or unascertained debt becomes a creditor entitled to vote. A contingent creditor is also a 'creditor' for these purposes.[29]

22-15

---

[20] [2008] 1 BCLC 289.

[21] A concern which may be met by making the consent of a class of creditors a term of the CVA, see Baird and Look Chan Ho, 'CVA—The Restructuring Trends' (2007) 20 Insolv Int 124.

[22] IR 1986, r 1.13(3), (4).   [23] See IR 1986, rr 1.18; 1.20.

[24] IR 1986, r 1.19(1); a majority in number of creditors is not required. 'Creditor' for these purposes includes a person entitled to a future or contingently payable debt, such as future payments of rent under an existing lease: *Re Cancol Ltd* [1996] 1 BCLC 100. If half in value of the creditors who are unconnected with the company vote against the resolution, the resolution is invalid, see IR 1986, r 1.19(4).

[25] IR 1986, r 1.19(2); and see the important constraint in r 1.19(4) noted above.

[26] IR 1986, r 1.17(1), (2). The chairman determines the entitlement to vote and if he is in doubt as to whether to admit a claim, he must mark it as being objected to and allow the votes to be cast, subject to their being ruled invalid subsequently: see r 1.17A.

[27] IR 1986, r 1.19(3)(b).

[28] IR 1986, r 1.17(3). In *Doorbar v Alltime Securities Ltd* [1996] 1 BCLC 487 the Court of Appeal concluded that 'agrees' in this context does not require an agreement between the creditor and the chairman as to the estimated value, it simply means that the chairman must agree to place a value on the debt. See also *Re Newlands (Seaford) Educational Trust, Chittenden v Pepper* [2007] BCC 195.

[29] *Re T & N Ltd* [2006] 2 BCLC 374.

22-16 This issue of entitlement to vote is crucial because a CVA which is approved binds every person entitled to vote at the creditors' meeting (whether or not he was present or represented at it) as if he were a party to the voluntary arrangement (IA 1986, s 5(2)). It is of crucial importance to the efficacy of the agreement that it should bind all the creditors as far as possible and it would be too easy for creditors to defeat a CVA merely by staying away from the meeting.[30]

22-17 A creditor is also bound even if for some reason he did not receive notice of the meeting and he is bound even if he is a creditor of whom the nominee was unaware and therefore was not someone to whom any notice was sent (IA 1986, s 5(2)). This latter point is an important change effected by the IA 2000 which is intended to make the binding effect of a CVA more extensive so that unknown creditors cannot undermine the agreement by appearing subsequently and pursuing their individual claims. Redress for the creditor who is bound but who was unaware of the CVA lies in his ability to go to court to challenge the approval of the CVA under IA 1986, s 6, discussed at **22-33** below.

22-18 The only creditors who are not bound are those who are not 'entitled to vote' and as entitlement to vote has been expanded, as noted above, to include those with unliquidated debts and debts for unascertained amounts, the result is that only secured creditors are excluded and not bound by the CVA.[31] In practice, while not bound by it, the secured creditors must have indicated their support for the CVA, otherwise it is unlikely that the proposals would have come before a meeting of the creditors.

22-19 The chairman of the meetings must report the result of the meetings to the court within four days[32] (though it is merely a report and there is no need to seek court approval) and he must send the report to every person who was sent notice of the meetings.[33] Once appointed, the supervisor (the title now given to the nominee) must forthwith send a copy of the chairman's report to the registrar of companies.[34]

22-20 Finally, it is an offence for an officer of the company for the purpose of obtaining the approval of the members or creditors to a proposal for a voluntary arrangement to make any false representations or fraudulently do or omit to do anything, even if the proposal is not approved (IA 1986, s 6A).

22-21 A decision to approve a CVA has effect if it is taken by the meeting of the company and the creditors or if it is taken by the creditors' meeting (IA 1986, s 4A(2)). In other words, the CVA has effect as long as the creditors approve it, even if the members reject it. If that happens, a member may apply to the court which may order the members' decision to have effect instead of a decision of the creditors or it may make such order as it thinks fit (s 4A(3)–(6)). It is unlikely that the court would overrule the decision of the creditors' meeting given that, without their commitment to the company and

---

[30] See *Doorbar v Alltime Securities Ltd* [1996] 1 BCLC 487 at 497 on this point.

[31] See IA 1986, s 4(3).   [32] IA 1986, s 4(6); also IR 1986, r 1.24(3).

[33] IR 1986, r 1.24(4). Typically, the chairman is the nominee but he may need to nominate another, see IR 1986, r 1.14.   [34] IR 1986, r 1.24(5).

the proposed arrangement, it would be very difficult to make a CVA work effectively. In the light of this ability of the creditors to overrule the members' meeting, it might be asked whether there is any point in holding the members' meeting. The reason why it is still appropriate to hold a members' meeting is that the company is not necessarily insolvent and the members retain a residual interest in its assets. It is appropriate therefore that they should be able to express their views at a meeting, even if the creditors' interests prevail.

If the CVA is approved by the appropriate meetings, the voluntary arrangement **22-22** takes effect as if made at the creditors' meeting. It binds every person entitled to vote at that meeting (whether or not he was present or represented at it) or who would have been so entitled if he had had notice of it, as if he were a party to the voluntary arrangement (IA 1986, s 5(2)). As noted above, this outcome explains the importance of establishing a creditor's entitlement to vote.

Challenging the approval

Anyone entitled to vote at the members' meeting or the creditors' meeting (or who **22-23** would have been entitled to vote at the creditors' meeting if he had had notice of it), or the nominee, or the liquidator or administrator (if the company is being wound up or is in administration) may apply to the court under IA 1986, s 6 on one or both of the following grounds:[35]

(1) that a voluntary arrangement which has taken effect[36] unfairly prejudices the interests of a creditor, member or contributory of the company;

(2) that there has been some material irregularity at or in relation to either of those meetings.

If the court is satisfied as to either of these grounds, it may revoke or suspend any deci- **22-24** sion giving effect to the CVA or any decision taken by a meeting where there has been a material irregularity and it may give directions to any person for the summoning of further meetings (IA 1986, s 6(4)–(6)).

The unfair prejudice must be to the interests of creditors as creditors and not in any **22-25** other capacity.[37] The requirement is some prejudice arising from the terms of the arrangement itself, in particular prejudice resulting from the discriminatory treatment of a creditor or class of creditors, though differential treatment of itself does not prove unfair prejudice.[38] If an administrator or liquidator puts forward a proposal

---

[35] Note the important time-limits within which this application must be made, essentially within 28 days of the report of the meetings being filed with the court, but with greater flexibility for a creditor who was unaware of, but who is bound by, the CVA: IA 1986, s 6(3); also s 6(7).

[36] I.e. has effect under IA 1986, s 4A which provides that the approval of the CVA takes effect either on the approval of both meetings or the approval of the creditors' meeting.

[37] *Doorbar v Alltime Securities Ltd* [1996] 1 BCLC 487; *Sea Voyager Maritime Inc v Bielecki* [1999] 1 BCLC 133; *Sisu Capital Fund Ltd v Tucker* [2006] BCC 463.

[38] See *Re a debtor (No 101 of 1999)* [2001] 1 BCLC 54; *Re a debtor (No 87 of 1993) (No 2)* [1996] 1 BCLC 63 at 86, per Rimer J; *Re a debtor (No 259 of 1990)* [1992] 1 All ER 641 at 643, per Hoffmann J. Equally, the

which he considers to be fair then, unless it is established that he acted other than in good faith or that he was partisan to the interests of some only of the creditors, the court should not speculate about what other proposals might have gained acceptance and been capable of implementation.[39]

22-26   The authorities on unfair prejudice for these purposes were reviewed by Lightman J in *IRC v Wimbledon*[40] where he considered the following points established: (1) to constitute a good ground of challenge the unfair prejudice complained of must be caused by the terms of the arrangement itself; (2) the existence of unequal or differential treatment of creditors of the same class will not of itself constitute unfairness, but may give cause to inquire and require an explanation; (3) in determining whether or not there is unfairness, it is necessary to consider all the circumstances including, as alternatives to the arrangement proposed, not only liquidation but the possibility of a different fairer scheme; (4) depending on the circumstances, differential treatment may be necessary to ensure fairness; and (5) differential treatment may be necessary to secure the continuation of the company's business which underlies the arrangement.

22-27   In *Prudential Assurance Co Ltd v PRG Powerhouse Ltd*,[41] noted at **22-12** above, without the CVA, the landlords were in a position to rely on a guarantee of the rent due to them which had been given by the parent company of the insolvent company; within the CVA, they were obliged to treat the guarantees as having been released and could expect a dividend of 28p in the £1. The court noted that there is no single or universal test for judging the fairness of a CVA for the purposes of IA 1986, s 6. The court looks at all the circumstances including the alternatives available and the practical consequences of a decision to confirm or reject an arrangement. Unfairness may be assessed from a number of different angles including comparison with the position on winding up and, in some cases, comparison with the position if, instead of a CVA, there had been a formal scheme of arrangement, while acknowledging that these are different processes. Differential treatment of creditors is a relevant factor for the court to consider but it does not necessarily mean unfair prejudice. Under this CVA, all the creditors, other than the landlords, were to be paid in full. In substance, the court said, the landlords' claims were to be discharged at a fraction of their value in order that other creditors were paid in full. While the authorities clearly show that there may be circumstances in which a CVA may properly provide for one set of creditors to be paid in full while others receive only a fraction of the sums due to them, the unusual feature of this case, the court said, was that on a winding up the landlords would still have had the benefit of the valuable guarantees of the parent company, whereas the other unsecured creditors would receive nothing. In other words, the court said, the landlords were the class of creditors that would suffer least in the event of an

---

prejudice may arise from failing to distinguish between creditors, as where creditors with interests under the Third Party (Rights Against Insurers) Act 1930 are not treated differently from other creditors: see *Sea Voyager Maritime Inc v Bielecki* [1999] 1 BCLC 133.

[39] *Sisu Capital Fund Ltd v Tucker* [2006] BCC 463.
[40] [2005] 1 BCLC 66. See also *Sisu Capital Fund Ltd v Tucker* [2006] BCC 463.
[41] [2008] 1 BCLC 289.

insolvent liquidation of the company, but they were the group most prejudiced by the CVA. In effect, the votes of those unsecured creditors who stood to lose nothing from the CVA and had everything to gain from it swamped the votes of the landlords who were significantly disadvantaged by it. The court was satisfied that the CVA unfairly prejudiced the interests of the claimants as creditors of the company and the approval of the proposal was set aside.

Implementing the arrangement

On approval of the scheme, the nominee becomes the supervisor (IA 1986, s 7(2)) and **22-28** he sets about the implementation of the CVA. Typically he holds any funds in his possession on trust for the CVA creditors pursuant to the terms of the voluntary arrangement.[42] He may apply to the court for directions if necessary (s 7(4)). Any creditor or any other person dissatisfied by the conduct of the supervisor may apply to the court which may confirm, reverse or modify any act or decision or give the supervisor directions or make such other order as it thinks fit (s 7(3)).

Terminating the arrangement

A CVA may be completed either at the end of a specified period or earlier if all the **22-29** payments required by the CVA have been made. Equally, it may not prove possible to proceed with the CVA and it may be necessary to terminate the agreement, typically because the company has failed to maintain the level of payments to creditors required by the CVA. In that case, the supervisor can petition for winding up or for an administration order.[43] Indeed while the CVA is continuing, it is possible that the members will resolve to place the company into voluntary liquidation, even if that has the effect of breaching the arrangement; likewise a non-CVA creditor may petition the court for the compulsory winding up of the company.[44]

Following completion (or termination) of the CVA, the supervisor must send notice to **22-30** this effect within 28 days to all the creditors and members bound by the CVA together with a copy of a report drawn up by him and summarising all receipts and payments by him.[45] Notice must also be given within the 28-day period to the registrar of companies and to the court (IR 1986, r 1.29).

The effect on the CVA if the CVA is terminated by the company going into liquid- **22-31** ation was the subject of a number of conflicting first instance decisions[46] which

---

[42] *Re Leisure Study Group Ltd* [1994] 2 BCLC 65; *Re NT Gallagher & Son Ltd* [2002] 3 All ER 474; see also *Welburn v Dibb Lupton Broomhead* [2003] BPIR 768, CA.

[43] IA 1986, s 7(4); and the supervisor may then be appointed as the liquidator: s 140(2). Typically, a CVA provides that the supervisor must petition for the compulsory winding up of the company if the company is not complying with the CVA.

[44] See *Re Arthur Rathbone Kitchens Ltd* [1997] 2 BCLC 280; *Re Excalibur Airways Ltd* [1998] 1 BCLC 436.

[45] IR 1986, r 1.29. In the case of termination, the report must explain why the CVA has been terminated.

[46] The authorities are considered in *Re NT Gallagher & Son Ltd* [2002] 2 BCLC 133 at 143–6.

differed as to whether the trust in favour of the CVA creditors continued or whether the supervisor had to hand over any assets of the company in his control to the liquidator which assets were then freed from any trust for the creditors under the CVA and became subject to the statutory trusts arising on compulsory liquidation.

22-32　The matter was resolved by the Court of Appeal in *Re NT Gallagher & Son Ltd*.[47] The company in this case entered into a CVA in 1995 before going into a creditors' voluntary winding up in October 1997. The company's assets were a claim against a principal customer (for £2.3m); a claim against another company for £350,000; and realisable assets of £98,000. Its total liabilities were just over £5m of which £2.5m were post-CVA liabilities. The liquidators sought a direction as to whether sums retained by the supervisors of the CVA (some £570,000), the benefit of the cause of action against the principal customer and the other assets, were held on trust for the sole benefit of the CVA creditors or were available for distribution to all the creditors of the company in accordance with the statutory scheme applicable on winding up. The Court of Appeal reached the following conclusions.

22-33　Where a CVA provides for monies or other assets to be paid to or transferred or held for the benefit of the CVA creditors, this creates a trust of those monies or assets for those creditors, but which assets are the subject of the trust depends on the terms of the arrangement. On the facts in this case, the sums retained by the supervisors and the claim against the principal customer were the subject of the CVA trust but the other realisable assets were not.

22-34　The effect of the liquidation of the company on the trust created by the CVA depends on the provisions of the CVA which can, and should, provide for what is to happen to the assets on the termination of the CVA.

22-35　If the CVA provides what is to happen on liquidation, effect must be given thereto. If the CVA does not so provide, the trust continues notwithstanding the liquidation and must take effect according to its terms. The court thought that to conclude otherwise would run counter to the general law which left trusts of assets not held for a company unaffected by its liquidation. Furthermore, as a matter of policy, in the absence of any provision in the CVA as to what should happen to trust assets on liquidation of the company, the applicable default rule should be one that furthered rather than hindered what might be taken to be the statutory purpose of IA 1986, Pt I.

22-36　The Court of Appeal acknowledged the possibility that there may be post-CVA creditors who are unaware of the CVA and its terms,[48] but it thought that in practice there is likely to be a considerable overlap between CVA and post-CVA creditors and, in any event, no one is forced to become a creditor of a company without making such inquiries as are thought appropriate to ascertain the financial position of the company. The court considered that Parliament plainly intended to encourage companies

---

[47] [2002] 2 BCLC 133, CA.

[48] Despite the existence of the CVA being reported to the registrar of companies by the supervisor: see IR 1986, r 1.24(5).

and creditors to enter into CVAs so as to provide creditors with a means of recovering what they were owed without recourse to the more expensive means provided by winding up or administration while giving companies the opportunity to continue to trade. If the trust was terminated, trust assets under the CVA which happened not to have been distributed before the liquidation would become available to the post-CVA creditors as well as CVA creditors which would be a disincentive to creditors to agree to a CVA and to keep it in operation.

Furthermore, since the liquidation of the company brought the CVA to an end, though not the trust created thereunder, it was only just that the CVA creditors should be able to prove in the liquidation for so much of their debt as remained after payment of what had been or would be recovered under the trust.   **22-37**

This ruling by the Court of Appeal acts as an incentive for creditors to enter into CVAs, given this ring-fencing of the CVA assets in the hands of the supervisor on liquidation. Equally, however, it may make it difficult to ensure continued support by post-CVA creditors and may therefore make continued trading while in a CVA more difficult.   **22-38**

C Company voluntary arrangement with a moratorium

As noted the IA 1986 was amended by the IA 2000 to allow directors wishing to propose a CVA to obtain a moratorium from actions against the company by creditors so making it easier to negotiate a CVA.[49] Where the directors wish to proceed in this way, the CVA is governed by IA 1986, Sch A1. In practice the scheme has proved unpopular. The advantage of the moratorium is outweighed by the relative complexity (and resulting costs) of the scheme. The necessary publicity attached to the moratorium also renders the process unsuitable for companies where publicity given to financial difficulties will drive their customers away and render future trading impossible. The onerous obligations and possible liabilities which attach to the supervisor also make it unattractive. Finally, the scheme was overtaken by the reforms to administration effected by the EA 2002 which allows in particular for the speedy appointment out of court of administrators (see **23-13**) and companies in administration benefit from a moratorium.   **22-39**

The first limitation on use of the CVA with a moratorium is that many classes of companies are excluded or ineligible[50] leaving as eligible companies essentially small private companies which meet two out of the three criteria for 'small' in CA 2006, s 382. The requirements are that the company has a turnover of not more than £6.5m; a balance sheet total of not more than £3.26m; and the number of employees must   **22-40**

---

[49] IA 1986, s 1A.   [50] See IA 1986, Sch A1, paras 2–4.

not exceed 50. Additionally, the company must not be a holding company of a group of companies which does not qualify as a small group or a medium-sized group in respect of the last financial year of the company before the date of filing of the required documents.[51] The company must not be in administration, or being wound up; there must not be an administrative receiver or a provisional liquidator in place or a voluntary arrangement in effect in relation to the company; and there must not have been an administrator appointed or a failed CVA in the previous 12 months.[52]

Obtaining a moratorium

22-41   Where the directors of a company wish to obtain a moratorium, they must submit to the nominee a document setting out the terms of the proposed voluntary arrangement and a statement of the company's affairs and any other information requested by the nominee.[53] It is an offence for an officer of the company for the purpose of obtaining a moratorium or an extension of a moratorium to make any false representations or fraudulently do or omit to do anything.[54] The nominee in turn must submit to the directors a statement indicating whether in his opinion:[55]

(1) the proposed voluntary arrangement has a reasonable prospect of being approved and implemented;

(2) the company is likely to have sufficient funds available to it during the proposed moratorium to enable it to carry on its business; and

(3) meetings of the company and its creditors should be summoned to consider the proposed voluntary arrangement.

22-42   If the nominee supports the proposed voluntary arrangement, the directors must file with the court:

(1) a document setting out the terms of the proposed voluntary arrangement;

(2) a statement of the company's affairs;

(3) a statement that the company is eligible for a moratorium;

(4) a statement from the nominee that he has given his consent to act; and

(5) a statement from the nominee that, in his opinion the proposed voluntary arrangement has a reasonable prospect of being approved and implemented, and the company is likely to have sufficient funds available to it during the

---

[51] IA 1986, Sch A1, para 3(4). A group qualifies as small or medium-sized if it qualifies as such under CA 2006, s 383(2)–(7) (small) or s 466(2)–(7) (medium): para 3(5).

[52] See IA 1986, Sch A1, para 4(1).

[53] IA 1986, Sch A1, para 6(1). The nominee must be a qualified insolvency practitioner or someone authorised to act as nominee in relation to the voluntary arrangement: s 1(2). The statement of affairs must contain such particulars of the company's creditors and of its debts and other liabilities and of its assets as is prescribed by IR 1986, r 1.37.

[54] IA 1986, Sch A1, para 42.

[55] IA 1986, Sch A1, para 6(2). In forming his opinion, the nominee is entitled to rely on the information submitted to him by the directors unless he has reason to doubt its accuracy: para 6(3).

proposed moratorium to enable it to carry on its business, and that meetings of the company and its creditors should be summoned to consider the proposed voluntary arrangement (Sch A1, para 7(1)).

The moratorium comes into force when these documents are filed by the directors   **22-43** with the court.[56] When a moratorium comes into force, the directors must notify the nominee[57] and the nominee must advertise that fact,[58] and notify the registrar of companies, the company and any petitioning creditor of the company of whose claim he is aware, of that fact.[59] Every invoice, order for goods or services, business letter or order form which is issued by or on behalf of the company and all the company's websites must contain the nominee's name and a statement that the moratorium is in force for the company.[60]

Duration and effect of the moratorium

The moratorium ends at the end of the last day on which the meetings of the com-   **22-44** pany and its creditors (summoned by the nominee) are first held,[61] and the nominee has 28 days from the date of filing of the documents securing the moratorium to call those meetings. The moratorium may last 28 days therefore, but it may be shorter as where, for example, the meetings are held much earlier in the 28-day period and decide to approve a voluntary arrangement[62] or reject the agreement.[63] The meetings summoned may resolve that the moratorium be extended but the moratorium may not be extended for more than two months from the date of the meeting.[64] The moratorium comes to an end if the nominee withdraws his consent to act or the court so orders.[65] When a moratorium comes to an end, the nominee must advertise that fact forthwith and notify the court, the registrar of companies, the company and any creditor of the company of whose claim he is aware, of that fact.[66]

The restrictions arising under the moratorium are very similar to those which   **22-45** apply on a company going into administration (see the detailed discussion at **23-56**). The standard restrictions apply: no petition (other than public interest petitions) may be presented for the winding up of the company;[67] no administration application may be made in respect of the company: and no administrator may be appointed out of

---

[56] IA 1986, Sch A1, para 8(1).   [57] IA 1986, Sch A1, para 9(1).

[58] I.e. in the *London Gazette* and a newspaper: see IR 1986, r 1.40(2).

[59] IA 1986, Sch A1, para 10(1); and see IR 1986, r 1.40(3). A 'petitioning creditor' means a creditor by whom a winding-up petition has been presented before the beginning of the moratorium, as long as the petition has not been dismissed or withdrawn; see IA 1986, Sch A1, para 10(2).

[60] IA 1986, Sch A1, para 16(1).   [61] IA 1986, Sch A1, para 8(2).

[62] IA 1986, Sch A1, para 8(7).   [63] IA 1986, Sch A1, para 8(6)(c).

[64] IA 1986, Sch A1, para 32(2) and if the meetings are held on separate dates, the extension is from the date when the last meeting is held. The nominee must set out the expected costs of the extension and the meetings must approve those expected costs otherwise the moratorium comes to an end: see para 32(4), (5). If a decision is taken to extend the moratorium by either the company and the creditors or by the creditors, the extension takes effect and the nominee must notify the registrar of companies and the court: para 34(1).

[65] See IA 1986, Sch A1, paras 8(6)(b), 25(4).

[66] IA 1986, Sch A1, para 11; and see IR 1986, r 1.42.   [67] IA 1986, Sch A1, para 12(4), (5).

court (IA 1986, Sch A1, para 12(1)). No other steps may be taken to enforce any security over the company's property, or to repossess goods in the company's possession under any hire-purchase agreement, except with the leave of the court and subject to such terms as the court may impose; and no other proceedings and no execution or other legal process may be commenced or continued, and no distress may be levied, against the company or its property except with the leave of the court and subject to such terms as the court may impose.[68]

22-46 Various restrictions are imposed on the company's activities during the period of the moratorium, such as a restriction on the ability to raise credit and limitations on the power to dispose of any company property other than in the ordinary course of business.[69] Transactions entered into in breach of these restrictions remain valid,[70] but the company is liable to a fine and any officer of the company who authorises or permits the contravention, without reasonable excuse, is liable to imprisonment or a fine, or both.[71]

Role of the nominee during the moratorium

22-47 During a moratorium, the nominee must monitor the company's affairs[72] and he must withdraw his consent to act if, at any time during a moratorium, he forms the opinion that:

(1) the proposed voluntary arrangement no longer has a reasonable prospect of being approved or implemented; or

(2) the company will not have sufficient funds available to it during the remainder of the moratorium to enable it to continue to carry on its business; or

(3) he becomes aware that, on the date of filing of the documents with the court, the company was not eligible for a moratorium; or

(4) the directors fail to provide him with the necessary information to carry out his monitoring obligations (IA 1986, Sch A1, para 25(2)).

22-48 If the nominee withdraws his consent to act, the moratorium comes to an end and he must notify the court, the registrar of companies, the company and any creditor of the company of whose claim he is aware, of his withdrawal and the reason for it.[73]

22-49 Any creditor, director or member of the company, or any other person affected by a moratorium, who is dissatisfied by the conduct of the nominee during the moratorium, may apply to the court either during the moratorium or after it has

---

[68] IA 1986, Sch A1, para 12(1); and see the limitation on enforcement in para 13(5).

[69] IA 1986, Sch A1, paras 17(1), 18(1), (2), 19(1).   [70] IA 1986, Sch A1, para 15(2).

[71] See IA 1986, Sch A1, paras 17(3), 18(3), 19(3).

[72] IA 1986, Sch A1, para 24(1). The directors must submit to the nominee any information necessary to enable him to comply with this monitoring obligation which he requests from them: para 24(2). In forming his opinion, the nominee is entitled to rely on the information submitted to him by the directors unless he has reason to doubt its accuracy: para 24(3).

[73] IA 1986, Sch A1, para 25(4), (5); see also IR 1986, r 1.44.

ended.[74] Additionally, where there are reasonable grounds for believing that as a result of any act etc of the nominee during the moratorium, the company has suffered loss, but the company does not intend to pursue any claim it may have against the nominee, any creditor may apply to the court during the moratorium or after it has ended.[75] The court may order the company to pursue any claim against the nominee, authorise any creditor to pursue such a claim in the name of the company, or make such other order as it thinks fit, unless the court is satisfied that the act etc of the nominee was in all the circumstances reasonable.[76] The combination of the obligation to monitor with the risk of potential challenge and liability under these provisions is a significant deterrent to use of this form of CVA.

Role of the directors during the moratorium

The onerous obligations imposed on supervisors arise in part out of concerns that   **22-50**
unscrupulous directors might use the 28-day moratorium, given that they remain in control of the company, to deal with the assets in an unacceptable way—hence the requirement that the nominee has an ongoing responsibility for monitoring the conduct of the company's affairs during the moratorium and his obligation to withdraw his consent to act in certain cases, so bringing the moratorium to an end.[77] Additionally, provision is made for creditors and members to challenge the conduct of the directors in court and the civil remedies are bolstered by a number of criminal offences.[78]

A creditor or member of the company may apply to the court during or after the   **22-51**
moratorium for an order on the ground that the company's affairs are being or have been managed by the directors in a manner which is unfairly prejudicial to the interests of its creditors or members generally, or of some part of its creditors or members (including at least the petitioner), or that any actual or proposed act or omission of the directors is or would be so prejudicial.[79] The court has wide powers on any such application to make any appropriate order.[80]

Approving an arrangement

Where a moratorium is in force, the nominee must summon meetings of the com-   **22-52**
pany and its creditors (i.e. every creditor of whose claim the nominee is aware) as he

---

[74] IA 1986, Sch A1, para 26(1), (2).   [75] IA 1986, Sch A1, para 27(1), (2).
[76] IA 1986, Sch A1, para 27(3).   [77] See IA 1986, Sch A1, paras 24, 25(2), (4).
[78] See IA 1986, Sch A1, para 41, also IA 1986, s 7A which makes further provision for the prosecution of these offences and in particular imposes an obligation on the nominee or supervisor where it appears a criminal offence may have been committed to report that matter to the appropriate authority (the Secretary of State).
[79] IA 1986, Sch A1, para 40(2), (3).
[80] Including an order regulating the management by the directors during the remainder of the moratorium; requiring them to do or refrain from doing any act; summoning a meeting of the creditors or members or bringing the moratorium to an end, see IA 1986, Sch A1, para 40(4), (5).

thinks fit and not later than 28 days after the date on which the moratorium came into force.[81] The meetings must decide whether to approve the proposed voluntary arrangement (with or without modifications).[82] As with CVAs without a moratorium, no proposal or modification may affect the rights of secured or preferential creditors without their consent.[83] The voting requirements are similar in most respects also to those discussed above at **22-13**. After the conclusion of either meeting, the chairman of the meeting must report the result of the meeting to the court within four days[84] and, immediately after reporting to the court, must give notice of the result of the meeting to every person who has sent notice of the meeting.[85]

22-53   A decision to approve the CVA or an extension to the moratorium or a decision to bring the moratorium to an end has effect if it has been taken by the meeting of the company and the creditors or if it has been taken by the creditors' meeting.[86] Where a decision approving a voluntary arrangement has effect,[87] the CVA takes effect as if made at the creditors' meeting and binds every person who was entitled to vote at that meeting (whether or not he was present or represented at it), or would have been so entitled if he had had notice of it, as if he were a party to the voluntary arrangement.[88] Following approval, any petition for the winding up of the company (other than a public interest petition) presented before the beginning of the moratorium, must be dismissed by the court.[89] If, when the moratorium comes to an end, no CVA has been approved, one or more creditors may present a petition for winding up the company on that ground,[90] i.e. without establishing that the company is unable to pay its debts.

22-54   As is the case with a CVA without a moratorium, it is possible to challenge the approval of a CVA by applying to the court on the grounds that the CVA unfairly prejudices the interests of a creditor, member or contributory of the company, and/or that there has been some material irregularity at or in relation to the meetings:[91] see the discussion at **22-23**.

Implementing the arrangement

22-55   Where a voluntary arrangement approved by one or both of the meetings has taken effect, the implementation of the CVA is as discussed at **22-28**. The nominee is known as the supervisor of the voluntary arrangement;[92] and on approval of the CVA, he must send a copy of the chairman's report of the result of the meetings to the registrar

---

[81] IA 1986, Sch A1, para 29(1), (2); IR 1986, r 1.48.   [82] IA 1986, Sch A1, para 31(1).

[83] IA 1986, Sch A1, para 31(4), (5).   [84] IR 1986, r 1.54(2) applying r 1.24(3)–(5).

[85] IA 1986, Sch A1, para 30(3); see IR 1986, r 1.24(4) which applies: r 1.54(3)(b).

[86] IA 1986, Sch A1, para 36(2).

[87] I.e. the CVA is agreed at a meeting of the company and of the creditors or a meeting of the creditors: IA 1986, Sch A1, para 36(2).

[88] IA 1986, Sch A1, para 37(1), (2).   [89] IA 1986, Sch A1, para 37(4), and subject to para 37(5).

[90] IA 1986, ss 122(1)(fa), 124(3A).

[91] IA 1986, Sch A1, para 38(1), (2); and see the time-limits within which this application must be made: para 38(3).

[92] IA 1986, Sch A1, para 39(1), (2).

of companies.[93] Once in post, the supervisor sets about the implementation of the CVA and he holds any funds in his possession on trust for the CVA creditors pursuant to the terms of the voluntary arrangement.[94]

Terminating the arrangement

The CVA may come to an end through completion or termination, as discussed above, **22-56** and the supervisor must send notice to this effect within 28 days to all the creditors and members bound by the CVA, together with a copy of a report drawn up by the supervisor and summarising all receipts and payments by him.[95] Notice must also be given to the registrar of companies and to the court.[96] Where the company goes into liquidation, the effect on the CVA creditors and assets held by the supervisor is as discussed above at **21-31** et seq.

---

[93] IR 1986, r 1.54(2) applying r 1.24(5).   [94] *Re NT Gallagher & Son Ltd* [2002] 2 BCLC 133, CA.

[95] IR 1986, r 1.29. In the case of termination, the report must explain why the CVA has been terminated.

[96] IR 1986, r 1.29.

23

Corporate rescue—administration

A Introduction

Background—rescue and the Cork Committee

The origins of administration lie in the recommendation of the Cork Committee on **23-1** Insolvency Law that provision should be made to enable a person called an administrator to be appointed to an insolvent but potentially viable company with all the powers normally conferred upon a receiver and manager under a floating charge, including power to carry on the business of the company and to borrow for that purpose.[1] The intention was to provide a breathing-space, free from the pressure of creditors' claims, which would enable the administrator to consider whether the business could be rescued and/or to negotiate with creditors regarding any possible arrangement or compromise of the company's debts.

Administration was introduced by the Insolvency Act 1985 and consolidated in the **23-2** Insolvency Act 1986, Pt 11, before being entirely recast and reformed by the Enterprise Act 2002 as a result of a decade of consultation as to the role, purpose and structure of administration.[2] By 2001 the Government had concluded that administrative receivership (discussed at **21-84**) should cease to be a major insolvency procedure and there should be wholesale reform of the administration regime.[3]

Essentially, the Government's concerns with respect to the appointment of adminis- **23-3** trative receivers related to issues such as the extent to which that procedure provided adequate incentives to maximise economic value; whether there was an adequate level of transparency and accountability to a range of stakeholders; unease with the fact that the administrative receiver's principal obligations were towards his appointor even

---

[1] The Cork Committee Report, para 497, see **2-3**. The Cork Committee envisaged administration as being a secondary procedure to administrative receivership and of use primarily where, for whatever reason, an administrative receiver could not be appointed: see para 503. As discussed in this chapter, administration has evolved in a very different way to that envisaged by Cork.

[2] See Insolvency Service, *The Insolvency Act 1986, Company Voluntary Arrangements and Administration Orders, A Consultative Document* (October 1993); *A Review of Company Rescue and Business Reconstruction Mechanisms* (September 1999); *A Review of Company Rescue and Business Reconstruction Mechanisms, Report by the Review Group* (May 2000).

[3] DTI, 'Productivity and Enterprise—Insolvency: A Second Chance' (Cm 5234, 2001) (hereinafter 'Productivity and Enterprise').

though receivership impacted substantially on the interests of the unsecured creditors; and the fact that administrative receiverships fitted badly into international law which generally emphasises collective procedures.[4] The Government's view was that on the grounds of both equity and efficiency the time had come to:[5]

'tip the balance firmly in favour of collective insolvency procedures—proceedings in which all creditors participate, under which a duty is owed to all creditors and in which all creditors may look to an office-holder for an account of his dealings with the company's assets'.

23-4   It therefore concluded that administrative receivership should cease to be a major insolvency procedure and there should be a statutory restriction on the right to appoint an administrative receiver (other than with respect to certain transactions in the capital markets).[6] Instead, a floating charge holder would be able to petition for an administration order and, in some cases, to petition without notice and, given this shift to administration as the main rescue procedure, that procedure would be reformed to ensure it was operating in a fully effective way.[7] Overall, the Government believed that the result would be a procedure which would be as flexible and cost-effective as administrative receivership, but with an administrator owing a duty to act in the interests of all creditors, with unsecured creditors having an opportunity for input and participation and the process being subject to the oversight and direction of the court in a public and transparent way.[8] The Government subsequently updated its proposals to make provision for out-of-court routes into administration.[9]

23-5   The reforms were effected by the Enterprise Act 2002 which left the statutory position as follows:

- The IA 1986, Part II (the original provisions on administration) applies to special situations, namely water companies, railway companies, air traffic services companies, public–private partnership companies and building societies.

- The administration provisions of general application are set out in IA 1986, Sch B1 (which was inserted by the EA 2002). This chapter looks only to these provisions and all references to paragraphs (paras) are to paragraphs in that Schedule.

B The purpose of administration

23-6   The 'purpose of administration' is a term of art spelt out in IA 1986, Sch B1, para 3(1) as follows:

'The administrator of a company must perform his functions with the objective of—

(a) rescuing the company as a going concern, or

---

[4] See *Productivity and Enterprise*, paras 2.2–2.3.   [5] *Productivity and Enterprise*, para 2.5.
[6] *Productivity and Enterprise*, para 2.5.   [7] *Productivity and Enterprise*, paras 2.8, 2.10.
[8] *Productivity and Enterprise*, para 2.12.
[9] See Insolvency Service, *An Update on the Corporate Insolvency Proposals* (14 January 2002).

(b) achieving a better result for the company's creditors as a whole than would be likely if the company were wound up (without first being in administration), or

(c) realising property in order to make a distribution to one or more secured or preferential creditors.'

In order to address concerns that administrators appointed by banks would have little regard to paras 3(1)(a) and (b) and would merely proceed under para 3(1)(c) to make distributions to the secured and preferential creditors in a manner little different from the appointment of an administrative receiver, the statute lays down a hierarchy as between these objectives. The administrator must perform his functions with the objective specified in para 3(1)(a) unless he thinks either: (1) that it is not reasonably practicable to achieve that objective; or (2) that the objective specified in para 3(1)(b) would achieve a better result for the company's creditors as a whole (para 3(3)). The administrator may perform his functions with the objective specified in para 3(1)(c) only if (1) he thinks that it is not reasonably practicable to achieve either of the objectives in paras 3(1)(a) or (b), and (2) he does not unnecessarily harm the interests of the creditors of the company as a whole (para 3(4)). There is some flexibility as between paras 3(1)(a) and 3(1)(b) and it is a commercial decision for the administrator (who must be a qualified insolvency practitioner, para 6) as to how to proceed. In practice, administrators always seek to achieve one or more of these purposes and the most common purpose given is para 3(1)(b). Throughout the administrator must perform his functions as quickly and efficiently as is reasonably practicable (para 4)[10] and he must perform his functions in the interests of the creditors of the company as a whole (para 3(2)). The intention is to create an appropriate balance between the need for the administrator to have flexibility to act to maximise economic value and the Government's view that collective procedures in the interests of all the creditors is the right approach.   **23-7**

Rescuing the company as a going concern

This option envisages the company continuing as a going concern with all or a significant part of its business. This option is likely to involve the creditors agreeing to the company entering a CVA (discussed in Chapter 22) or a scheme of arrangement (discussed in Chapter 26).[11] This use of administration as a 'wrapper' for a CVA can   **23-8**

---

[10] This provision was added at a late stage to the legislation. The Government intention had been that administration would be a quick procedure with rapid decision-making as to whether it was possible to rescue the company and if not a speedy move on a conclusion. For example, the Government had intended that proposals should be put to creditors by the administrator within 28 days of his appointment, but this period was lengthened during the Parliamentary debates to 10 weeks. Likewise, the Government had intended that an administration should be completed within three months, but this period was lengthened during debate to 12 months. Imposing a duty on the administrator to act quickly and efficiently is an attempt to counterbalance these time-limits and prevent administration becoming a rather slow process.

[11] The Explanatory Notes to the Enterprise Act 2002, paras 647, 649 indicate that a proposal that would result in a 'shell' company remaining after all the assets have been sold would not be considered a rescue for these purpose. Seeking administration merely to sell the company's assets at a better price (possibly) than may be achieved by a receiver under the Law of Property Act 1925 is not a 'rescue as a going concern' for these purposes so as to justify an administration order: *Doltable Ltd v Lexi Holding plc* [2006] 1 BCLC 384.

be a useful option on occasion for companies in difficulties, though the number of companies entering CVAs remains small.[12]

Achieving a better result than on a winding up

23-9   On occasion, there are circumstances where continued trading for a short period is advantageous, for example to complete an order so ensuring a higher return to the creditors. The Explanatory Notes to the Enterprise Act 2002 suggest that this option would be relevant where there is no financing available and so the administrator can quickly reach the conclusion that rescue is not possible or where the time-scale for rescue is too long in terms of realising economic value.[13] The idea here is that the administrator has the flexibility to sell all or some of the business as a going concern or concerns while accepting that this is not possible with all of the business. The aim is to maximise the economic value of the assets.[14]

Realising property for preferential and secured creditors

23-10   Clearly, the other options have to be exhausted before the administrator considers this possibility and even then this option must be exercised in a way which does not unnecessarily harm the interests of the creditors of the company as a whole (Sch B1, para 3(4)). In these cases, the business is not viable and it is just a case of selling the assets that are available and seeing how many creditors can get paid.[15] Issues such as the timing of the realisation of assets, the manner of sale and the identity of the purchasers will be important, given the requirement not to unnecessarily harm the interests of the creditors of the company as a whole.

23-11   Administrators are anxious to be seen to be acting in accordance with the statutory purposes and to explain (as they are required to do) to the creditors the options which they have taken (Sch B1, para 49). In considering the various possibilities, the administrators have to keep in mind their obligation to perform their functions in the interests of the creditors as a whole and as quickly and efficiently as reasonably practicable.[16] Administrators are also mindful of the fact that creditors are able to apply to the court for relief on the ground that the administrator has acted or is proposing to act in a way which is unfairly harmful to their interests or that the administrator has not acted as quickly and as efficiently as he ought (Sch B1, para 74) and that actions

---

[12] See Baird & Chan Ho, 'CVAs—The Restructuring Trend' (2007) Insolv Int 124. In 2003–04, 756 companies went into a CVA compared with 466 in 2007–08: see *Statistical Tables on Companies Registration Activities 2007–08*, Table C2, available on Companies House website at www.companieshouse.gov.uk/about/companiesRegActivities.shtml.

[13] See Explanatory Notes to the Enterprise Act 2002, paras 648, 650.

[14] For example, in *Re Logitext UK Ltd* [2005] 1 BCLC 326, administration would give a better return possibly than liquidation when funding was available in an administration but not in a liquidation for the investigation of whether company assets had been improperly transferred away and might be recovered.

[15] See Explanatory Notes to the Enterprise Act 2002, paras 651–2.

[16] IA 1986, Sch B1, paras 3(2), 4. Administrators were already expected, as officers of the court, to reach decisions speedily: see *Re Atlantic Computer Systems plc* [1992] 1 All ER 476 at 490.

for misfeasance may be brought (Sch B1, para 75) and for their removal from office (Sch B1, para 88). In *Coyne v DRC Distribution Ltd*[17] the Court of Appeal was highly critical of administrators when, as the court put it, the administration took a wrong turn early on from which the process never recovered. Prior to the administration, the director (who appointed the administrators) transferred most of the business and assets away from the company for no consideration to another company set up by him. At first instance, the trial judge found that the administrators had not acted expeditiously or robustly enough in trying to unravel those dubious transactions before offering the company for sale. A creditor's application for removal of the administrators fell away when the administrators successfully made an application for the compulsory winding up of the company. The court nevertheless ordered that the administrators personally and the director jointly and severally pay the creditor's costs. On appeal, the Court of Appeal confirmed the order. The court noted that the administrators' conduct of the administration had the potential for disaster written all over it. They had failed to take the elementary steps which ought to have been taken in an attempt to make the administration a successful one. They had not acted expeditiously or with the necessary robustness of purpose and it was right that they be penalised in costs.

At the same time, the courts are anxious not to second-guess the administrator, given that administrative and commercial decisions by the administrator are not matters for the courts, as they have indicated in earlier decisions.[18] Equally, the courts are anxious that the Parliamentary intention to make administration quicker and more flexible is not defeated by litigious creditors attempting to straitjacket an administrator and, of course, vexatious applications can be penalised in costs.   **23-12**

C The appointment of an administrator

There are three routes into administration. An administrator may be appointed (Sch B1, para 2):[19]   **23-13**

(1) by administration order of the court under para 10;

(2) by the holder of a floating charge under para 14;

(3) by the company or its directors under para 22.

---

[17] [2008] BCC 612, CA.

[18] See *Re T & D Industries plc* [2000] 1 BCLC 471; *Re CE King Ltd* [2000] 2 BCLC 297.

[19] In practice the majority of appointments are out of court. The Insolvency Service, *Evaluation Report on the Enterprise Act 2002—Corporate Insolvency Provisions* (January 2008), hereinafter *Insolvency Service Evaluation Report* (2008), noted that of the sample of administrations reviewed for the purposes of the evaluation, 30% were by court order and 70% were out-of-court appointments of which 70% were made by the directors and only 18% by floating charge holders (see para 3.3), though the report also notes that many of the appointments by directors may well be instigated by charge holders who prefer not to make the appointment directly so as to avoid any adverse publicity: see para 3.10.

23-14   There are certain general restrictions on the appointment of an administrator (for example, with respect to certain banking and insurance companies: Sch B1, para 9). More broadly, no administrator may be appointed:

- where the company is already in administration (Sch B1, para 7);
- where the company is in liquidation by virtue of a resolution for voluntary winding up, except on an application to the court by the liquidator;[20]
- where the company is in compulsory liquidation by virtue of a court order, except on an application to the court by the holder of a qualifying floating charge or the liquidator.[21]

23-15   An administrator, however appointed, is an officer of the court[22] and must be a qualified insolvency practitioner (Sch B1, para 6). In the absence of special circumstances, the administrator owes his duties to the company and not to the creditors, individually or collectively.[23]

The interim moratorium

23-16   In certain circumstances prior to the formal appointment of an administrator, an interim moratorium precluding actions against the company by creditors and others applies (Sch B1, para 44). The moratorium ensures that the status quo is preserved regarding the company's assets pending the granting or dismissal of the administration application or the appointment or otherwise of an administrator. If there is an administrative receiver of the company when the administration application is made, the interim moratorium does not begin to apply until the person by or on behalf of whom the receiver was appointed consents to the making of the administration order (Sch B1, para 44(6)). This ability to secure a moratorium which continues once the company enters administration is one of the most important features of administration.

23-17   An interim moratorium applies where:

(1)   an application for an administration order has been made to the court;

(2)   a qualifying floating charge holder has filed with the court a copy of a notice of intention to appoint an administrator;[24]

(3)   the company or the directors have filed with the court a copy of a notice of intention to appoint an administrator.[25]

---

[20] IA 1986, Sch B1, paras 8(1)(a), 38.   [21] IA 1986, Sch B1, paras 8(1)(b), 37, 38.

[22] IA 1986, Sch B1, para 5; and therefore subject to the rule in *Ex p James* (1874) 9 Ch App 609 as to the high standards of conduct expected of officers of the court; see *Re Collins & Aikman Europe Ltd* [2007] 1 BCLC 182 (administrators should honour undertakings given to foreign creditors); also *Re British American Racing (Holdings) Ltd* [2005] 2 BCLC 234; but the rule in *Ex p James* cannot be used to justify distributions of the company's assets in a way that is incompatible with the company's interests and the interests of any preferential creditor: *Re Farepak Food & Gifts Ltd* [2007] 2 BCLC 1.

[23] *Kyrris v Oldham* [2004] 1 BCLC 305, CA.

[24] In many cases, the qualifying floating charge holder, as discussed below, will be able to appoint without the need for an interim moratorium and therefore will not file a notice of intention to appoint an administrator.   [25] IA 1986, Sch B1, para 44(1)–(4).

The extent of the moratorium is set out in Sch B1, paras 42 and 43 and once the **23-18** company is in administration, the moratorium continues: see the discussion below at **23-55**. Essentially the moratorium means that the company cannot be placed in winding up (save on a public interest petition, see below), security cannot be enforced, goods cannot be repossessed, leases forfeited or legal processes instituted without the permission of the court (Sch B1, para 44(5)).

The interim moratorium does not prevent and the permission of the court is not **23-19** required for:

(1) the presentation of a petition on public interest grounds;[26]

(2) the appointment of an administrator by a qualifying floating charge holder;

(3) the appointment of an administrative receiver; or

(4) the carrying out by an administrative receiver (whenever appointed) of his functions (Sch B1, para 44(7)).

Obviously, categories (3) and (4) become increasingly obsolete with the passage of **23-20** time since administrative receivers can only be appointed under floating charges created before 15 September 2003 (IA 1986, s 72A) and, as noted at **21-86**, even when such a charge exists, it is unusual now for an administrative receiver to be appointed. The important provision is (2) which allows a qualifying floating charge to 'trump' a proposed appointment by making their own appointment of an administrator: see discussion below at **23-42**.

The duration of this interim moratorium depends on the route into administration **23-21** which is being pursued. If the administrator is to be appointed by the court, the interim moratorium applies where an administration application has been made and the application has not yet been granted or dismissed or the application has been granted but the administration order has not yet taken effect.[27]

If the administrator is to be appointed by a qualifying floating charge holder, the **23-22** interim moratorium applies from the time when a copy of the notice of intention to appoint is filed with the court until the appointment of the administrator takes effect[28] or the period of five business days beginning with the date of filing expires without an administrator being appointed (Sch B1, para 44(2), (3)).

If the administrator is to be appointed by the company or the directors, the interim **23-23** moratorium applies from the time when a copy of the notice of intention to appoint is filed with the court until the appointment of the administrator takes effect[29] or

---

[26] I.e. petitions for winding up on public interest grounds under IA 1986, ss 124A, 124B, by the Secretary of State or under FSMA 2000, s 367 by the Financial Services Authority: IA 1986, Sch B1, para 42(2), (3).

[27] IA 1986, Sch B1, para 44(1). An administration order takes effect in accordance with para 13(2), either at the time appointed by the order or, if no time is appointed, when the order is made. If the time appointed by the order is at some point in the future, this provision ensures that the interim moratorium continues until that time.

[28] An appointment in this case takes effect in accordance with IA 1986, Sch B1, para 19.

[29] An appointment in this case takes effect in accordance with IA 1986, Sch B1, para 31.

the period of 10 business days beginning with the date of filing expires without an administrator being appointed (Sch B1, para 44(4)).

Appointment of an administrator by the court

23-24   An application to the court for an administration order (described as an administration application) may be made by:

(1) the company;

(2) the directors of the company;[30]

(3) one or more creditors of the company (see also **23-36**);[31]

(4) the designated officer for a magistrates' court;[32]

(5) a combination of persons listed in (1)–(4).[33]

23-25   The members have no right to apply for an administration order other than by a resolution of the company. The directors are given the right to apply because of their potential liability for wrongful trading under IA 1986, s 214, see **25-17**.[34] While the holders of qualifying floating charges are able to appoint an administrator out of court, for all other creditors, the only method of appointing an administrator is through an application to the court.

23-26   In practice, few creditors who are not holders of qualifying floating charges are likely to have any interest in seeking to put the company into administration, but an unusual example can be found in *Hammonds v Pro-Fit USA Ltd*.[35] In this case, a firm of solicitors was owed a significant sum for advisory work for a company. While negotiations were underway as to payment of the debt, certain intellectual property rights were transferred by the company to an associated company. The negotiations collapsed and the firm applied to the court for an administration order. The company disputed the debt and cross-claimed alleging negligent advice. Among the issues for the court was whether the firm could be a 'creditor', given any damages that might be awarded on the cross-claim. The court held that a person may be a 'creditor' for these purposes even if the debt is bona fide disputed or there is a cross-claim. Crucially, the court considered that there is no need to follow the practice which applies in relation to winding-up petitions which normally means that a winding-up petition would be dismissed in such circumstances. That practice arose, the court said, because of the very

---

[30] Either by all the directors unanimously or by a majority of the directors: IA 1986, Sch B1, para 105 which resolves previous uncertainty on this issue.

[31] Defined IA 1986, Sch B1, para 12(4) to include contingent and prospective creditors.

[32] See IA 1986, Sch B1, para 12(1)(d)—an application in this case is made in exercise of the power conferred by the Magistrates' Courts Act 1980, s 87A (fine imposed on company).

[33] IA 1986, Sch B1, para 12(1); an application cannot be withdrawn without the permission of the court: para 12(3).

[34] An important defence to that liability is for the directors to show that they took every step to minimise potential loss to creditors: IA 1986, s 214(3). Such a step might be applying for the appointment of an administrator.

[35] [2008] 2 BCLC 159.

serious consequence of bringing a company's life to an end by winding up whereas the consequences of an administration order are not so drastic. On the evidence, the company was or was likely to become unable to pay its debts, for even if the company was able to pay its debts as they fell due, it was likely (in the sense of more probable than not) that it would be unable to do so in the foreseeable future. Though the court did not think this was a compelling case for an administration order, an administration would enable the administrator to investigate the circumstances of the transfer of the intellectual property rights and whether the transaction was at an undervalue and therefore the court would exercise its discretion to make an administration order subject to the respondent being given the opportunity to obtain a surrender of the rights which had been transferred.

In addition to the categories of applicant noted above, a liquidator may apply for an administration order (Sch B1, para 38). This power is included in order to give maximum flexibility to rescue a company should that appear possible, even if a liquidation of the company has been initiated. Previously there was no method of reversing out of a liquidation, but if a liquidator considers now that it is possible that administration is a more appropriate process, he may apply to the court for an administration order. A supervisor of a company voluntary arrangement may also apply for an administrator to be appointed,[36] as may the Financial Services Authority in certain circumstances.[37]   **23-27**

Conditions which must be met for court to order administration

For an administration order to be made, the court must be satisfied that the company is or is likely to become unable to pay its debts (Sch B1, para 11(a)),[38] and that the administration order is reasonably likely to achieve the purpose of administration (Sch B1, para 11(b)).[39] The court's jurisdiction to make such an order is also subject to the EC Regulation on Insolvency Proceedings (see **24-8**) which limits the court's power to open main proceedings to cases where the debtor's centre of main interests is in the UK.[40]   **23-28**

These thresholds were considered by Lewison J in *Re AA Mutual International Insurance Co Ltd*[41] where he concluded that it is necessary for the company to show both that it is more probable than not that it is or will become unable to pay its debts,   **23-29**

---

[36] IA 1986, s 7(4)(b); Sch A1, para 39(5).   [37] See FSMA 2000, s 359.

[38] Whether a company is unable to pay its debts is determined in accordance with IA 1986, s 123, i.e. it must be proved to the satisfaction of the court that the company is either cash-flow insolvent (unable to pay its debts as they fall due) or balance sheet insolvent (after taking into account its contingent and prospective liabilities, the value of its assets is less than the amount of its liabilities): Sch B1, para 111(1); see *Hammonds v Pro-Fit USA Ltd* [2008] 2 BCLC 159.

[39] The application to the court must include the matters referred to in IR 1986, rr 2.2–2.4 including details of the company's financial position. Note the distinction between 'likely' in Sch B1, para 11(a) and 'reasonably likely' in para 11(b) and see Lewison J in *Re AA Mutual International Insurance Co Ltd* [2005] 2 BCLC 8 at 13.

[40] See EC Regulation, art 3. See, for example, *Re Collins & Aikman Europe Ltd* [2007] 1 BCLC 182 where administration orders were made in England in respect of companies in Spain, Sweden, Germany, Belgium, Italy and the Netherlands.

[41] [2005] 2 BCLC 8.

and that there is a real prospect that an administration order would achieve the purpose of a better result for the company's creditors as a whole than was likely if the company were wound up. In this instance, as the company (an insurance company) had no income coming in because it no longer wrote any new business, the court thought it was more probable than not that the company's liabilities would exceed its assets within a short space of time. The company had also established to the court's satisfaction that there was a real prospect of achieving a better result for the creditors through an administration than a winding up, because administration would save the ongoing costs of run-off and the prospective costs of dealing with threatened arbitration proceedings, it would provide a moratorium against other claims, it would facilitate the preparation of a scheme of arrangement, and it would possibly enable the company to enter into a commercial arrangement with the Financial Services Compensation Scheme on more advantageous terms. For those reasons, the court made an administration order.

23-30   While it is a precondition for making an administration order that there is a real prospect that an administration order would achieve one of the objectives in Sch B1, para 3 outlined at **23-6** above, it is not strictly necessary for an applicant or prospective administrator to identify in advance with certainty which of those objectives it is intended to be attained, merely that the prospective administrator considers that one of those objectives would be achieved if the prior objective or objectives proves not to be possible.[42] In practice, it is common for more than one of the options to be put forward so as to give the administrator maximum flexibility in approaching his task.

23-31   Once satisfied that the required thresholds are met, it is still for the court in the exercise of its discretion to make an order, see **23-40**.[43] For example, an administration order was made in *Re DKLL Solicitors*[44] (involving an insolvent partnership) in the face of opposition from the Inland Revenue because the court was entitled in the exercise of its discretion to take into account not merely the interests of the partnership's creditors, but the fact that the proposed sale of the partnership (which was to be the purpose of the administration) was likely to save the jobs of partnership employees and would result in minimum disruption to the affairs of the partnership's clients. Likewise in *Hammonds v Pro-Fit USA Ltd*,[45] discussed at **23-26** above, while the court did not think the case for an administration order was too compelling, the court did decide in favour of an order because it would allow a transfer of assets by the company to be investigated. On the other hand, in *Doltable Ltd v Lexi Holdings plc*[46] the court did not think it appropriate to make an order where the substance of the matter was a dispute between the company and a secured creditor over the terms on which the creditor was proposing to sell the company's only asset.

---

[42] *Hammonds v Pro-Fit USA Ltd* [2008] 2 BCLC 159.

[43] *Re Harris Simons Construction Ltd* [1989] BCLC 202; also *Re Imperial Motors (UK) Ltd* [1990] BCLC 29 (order refused because on balance it was not a suitable case: petitioning creditor was fully secured); see also *Re Arrows Ltd (No 3)* [1992] BCLC 555. In approaching this issue, the interests of secured creditors carries less weight than those of other creditors: *Re Consumer & Industrial Press Ltd* [1988] BCLC 177.

[44] [2008] 1 BCLC 112.   [45] [2008] 2 BCLC 159.   [46] [2006] 1 BCLC 384.

Position with respect to administrative receiverships

As soon as is reasonably practicable after the making of an administration applica-   **23-32**
tion, the applicant must notify: (1) any person who has appointed an administrative
receiver or who is or may be entitled to appoint an administrative receiver; and (2) any
holder of a qualifying floating charge who is or may be entitled to appoint an administrator out of court.[47]

If the company is already in administrative receivership, the court must dismiss an   **23-33**
administration application in respect of the company unless the person by or on
behalf of whom the receiver was appointed consents to the making of an administration order, or the security under which the receiver is appointed would be liable to
be released or discharged or avoided under various provisions[48] (Sch B1, para 39). If
the company is not yet in administrative receivership, anyone entitled to do so may
proceed to appoint an administrative receiver following the making of the administration application for, as noted at **23-19** above, the interim moratorium which arises
on the making of an administration application does not prevent the appointment of
an administrative receiver.[49] If an appointment is made by the time of the court hearing, the administration application must be dismissed. As noted, these rights are of
diminishing significance as it is not possible now to appoint an administrative receiver
under a floating charge created on or after 15 September 2003 (IA 1986, s 72A).

Once an administration order is made, no administrative receiver may then be   **23-34**
appointed (Sch B1, para 41(1)). These are mutually exclusive procedures and a company can be in administrative receivership or administration but it cannot be in both
at the same time.[50]

Special rights of floating charge holders on application to the court

Various special rights are conferred on floating charge holders to balance the loss of   **23-35**
the right to appoint an administrative receiver under a floating charge created on or
after 15 September 2003.

First, a qualifying floating charge holder who has the option of appointing out of   **23-36**
court may prefer the security of a court order and therefore provision is made for an
administration application to court by the floating charge holder (Sch B1, para 35).[51]
In this instance, the court may make an administration order whether or not satisfied
that the company is or is likely to become unable to pay its debts, provided the floating charge holder satisfies the court that an appointment could be made out of court
(Sch B1, para 35(2)).

---

[47] IA 1986, Sch B1, para 12(2); and see also IR 1986, r 2.7.

[48] I.e. under IA 1986, ss 238–240, 245—transaction at an undervalue, preferences and avoidance of certain
floating charges.

[49] IA 1986, Sch B1, para 44(1), (5), (7).   [50] See also IA 1986, Sch B1, paras 17(b), 25(c).

[51] A court-based appointment may be preferable and necessary where there is an international element to
the insolvency, though out-of-court administration appointments are recognised as insolvency proceedings
for the purposes of the EC Insolvency Regulation 2000/1346.

23-37 Secondly, where the administration application is made by someone other than a qualifying floating charge holder, the charge holder can intervene and apply to the court for the appointment of his choice of administrator and not the person chosen by the applicant (Sch B1, para 36(1)). In that case, the court must grant that application by the floating charge holder unless the court thinks it right to refuse because of the particular circumstances of the case (Sch B1, para 36(2)).

23-38 This provision was controversial because this presumption in favour of the floating charge holder's nominee is seen as enabling banks via administration to remain much in the same position as before—the appointment of their nominee to recover their money—despite the restriction on the appointment of administrative receivers.[52] There are a variety of mechanisms in the legislation designed to ensure that these concerns are misplaced:

   (1) the administrator is an officer of the court and must be a qualified insolvency practitioner (Sch B1, paras 5, 6); as such he is subject to high standards of conduct;

   (2) the administrator is constrained in his conduct of the administration by the specified purpose of administration as expressed in Sch B1, para 3, see **23-6**;

   (3) the administrator must explain his conduct to the creditors and in particular he must explain why he has not pursued the objective of rescuing the company as a going concern or achieving a better result for the creditors as a whole than would have been likely on a winding up (Sch B1, para 49(2));

   (4) the administrator must perform his functions in the interests of the creditors as a whole (Sch B1, para 3(2));

   (5) an administrator is open to challenge by creditors who feel their interests have been unfairly harmed by his conduct and to actions for misfeasance (Sch B1, paras 74, 75) and to removal from office (Sch B1, para 88).

23-39 Thirdly, a qualifying floating charge holder may apply to the court for an administration order where the company has gone into compulsory winding up (Sch B1, para 37), despite the general restriction on appointing an administrator in such circumstances (Sch B1, para 8(1)(b)). If the court makes an administration order, it will make such consequential provision dealing with the winding up as is necessary, including the discharge of the winding-up order (Sch B1, para 37(3)).

Powers of court

23-40 The court's powers on an application, see **23-24**, are to make an administration order or to dismiss the application, to adjourn it, or to make an interim order or any other order which the court thinks appropriate (Sch B1, para 13(1)). The court may also treat the application as a winding-up petition and make any order which it could make on such a petition.[53] Where an administration order is made, the court appoints the administrator and, as noted above at **23-37**, a qualifying floating charge holder can

---

[52] See IA 1986, s 72A.
[53] I.e. such order as might be made under IA 1986, s 125: Sch B1, para 13(1)(e).

intervene to secure his choice of administrator unless the court thinks it right to refuse because of the particular circumstances of the case (Sch B1, para 36).

Any petition for the winding up of a company must be dismissed on the making **23-41** of the administration order unless the petition is a public interest petition.[54] Any administrative receiver must vacate office and any receiver of part of the company's property must vacate on being asked to do so by the administrator.[55]

Appointment of administrator by holder of floating charge

The holder of a qualifying floating charge in respect of a company's property may **23-42** appoint an administrator out of court (Sch B1, para 14(1)), but not if the company is already in administration;[56] or is in liquidation;[57] or if a provisional liquidator has been appointed,[58] or if an administrative receiver is in office.[59] There is no requirement in this instance that the company is or is likely to become unable to pay its debts. The important concepts of a 'qualifying floating charge' and the 'holder of a qualifying floating charge' are defined in detail in IA 1986, Sch B1, paras 14(2) and (3).

A 'qualifying floating charge' is a charge created by an instrument which: **23-43**

   (1) states that Sch B1, para 14(2) applies to a floating charge; or

   (2) purports to empower the holder of the floating charge to appoint an administrator of the company; or

   (3) purports to empower the holder of the floating charge to make an appointment which would be the appointment of an administrative receiver (Sch B1, para 14(2)).

A person is a 'holder of a qualifying floating charge' if he holds one or more debentures **23-44** of the company secured:

   (1) by a qualifying floating charge which relates to the whole or substantially the whole of the company's property;[60]

   (2) by a number of qualifying floating charges which together relate to the whole or substantially the whole of the company's property; or

   (3) by charges or other forms of security which together relate to the whole or substantially the whole of the company's property and at least one of which is a qualifying floating charge (Sch B1, para 14(3)).

---

[54] IA 1986, Sch B1, para 40(1), (2). As to public interest petitions: see above n 26.

[55] IA 1986, Sch B1, para 41. Of course, the court could only have made an administration order in this situation if the person entitled to appoint the administrative receiver consented to the order or if the charge under which the receiver was appointed was open to challenge: see para 39.

[56] IA 1986, Sch B1, para 7.

[57] IA 1986, Sch B1, para 8. If the company is in compulsory liquidation, the holder of a qualifying floating charge can still make an application to the court for an administration order under para 37: para 8(1)(b), (3).

[58] IA 1986, Sch B1, para 17(a).   [59] IA 1986, Sch B1, para 17(b).

[60] If a charge holder has a charge which relates only to part of the company's assets, as a creditor he may apply to the court for an administration order under IA 1986, Sch B1, para 22: see **23-24** above.

23-45   In order to exercise this power to appoint, the floating charge on which the appointment relies must be enforceable (Sch B1, para 16) in the sense that some default or
other event must have occurred which, under the terms of the charge, allows for its
enforcement. The holder must give at least two business days' written notice to the
holder of any prior qualifying floating charge of his intention to appoint an administrator or the holder of a prior qualifying floating charge must consent in writing to
the making of the appointment (Sch B1, para 15(1)).[61] There is no requirement to give
advance notice of the appointment to the company. This ensures that floating charge
holders are able to act with the same degree of speed which was a feature of appointments of administrative receivers.[62]

23-46   A person who appoints an administrator under this procedure must file with a court
a notice of appointment[63] which must include a statutory declaration by or on behalf
of the person making the appointment that the person is the holder of a qualifying
floating charge; that each floating charge relied on in making the appointment is or
was enforceable at the date of appointment and that the appointment is in accordance
with Sch B1.[64] The appointment takes effect when the person appointing has filed these
documents with the court.[65] Any outstanding winding-up petition (other than a public interest petition) is suspended following the appointment of an administrator out
of court by a qualifying floating charge holder.[66]

23-47   The notice of appointment must identify the administrator and be accompanied by
a statement by him that he consents to the appointment; that in his opinion the purpose of administration (as defined in Sch B1, para 3: see **23-6**) is reasonably likely to
be achieved; and the statement must give details of any prior professional relationship
which the administrator has had with the company.[67]

23-48   There is some potential for disputes surrounding the process since the time of
appointment is of some importance and, as the notice of appointment and other

---

[61] A prior floating charge is one within IA 1986, Sch B1, para 15(2), namely, one created first or one
treated as having priority because of an agreement to which the holder of each floating charge was party.
A junior floating charge holder can secure an interim moratorium by filing a notice of intention to appoint:
see para 44(2), (3) which allows some breathing space for the chargeholders to consult together as to how to
proceed.

[62] In the event of an invalid appointment, the appointor may be ordered by the court to indemnify the
administrator against loss, Sch B1, para 21, but the administrator is likely to require an indemnity in any
event as a term of this appointment.

[63] IA 1986, Sch B1, para 18(1). The notice and any accompanying documents must be as prescribed by
IR 1986, r 2.16(2) and the statutory declaration must be made no more than five business days before filing:
IR 1986, r 2.16(3); IA 1986, Sch B1, para 18(5), (6). As to penalties for false statements in a statutory declaration, see para 18(7). A failure to serve a copy of the notice of intention to appoint in the prescribed form
prevents the interim moratorium coming into effect: see IA 1986, Sch B1, para 44(2), (3).

[64] IA 1986, Sch B1, para 18(2).

[65] IA 1986, Sch B1, para 19. Given the importance of filing the notice of appointment, it is possible to file
notice of the appointment by fax outside of court opening hours, see IR 1986, r 2.19.

[66] IA 1986, Sch B1, para 40(1)(b), (2).

[67] IA 1986, Sch B1, para 18(3); IR 1986, r 2.3(5); to prevent undue investigation and therefore expense, the
administrator in making his statement is entitled to rely on information provided by the directors unless he
has reason to doubt its accuracy: Sch B1, para 18(4).

documents must meet certain requirements, there may be challenges as to their effectiveness and as to whether the appointment has taken effect. In order to minimise confusion on this issue, the floating charge holder appointing an administrator out of court is required to notify the administrator as soon as it is reasonably practicable that the notice of appointment etc has been filed with the court and a copy of the notice of appointment must be sent to any person who has made an administration application to court and to the court to which the application has been made.[68]

Appointment of administrator by company or directors

The company by an ordinary resolution or the directors[69] may appoint an administrator out of court under IA 1986, Sch B1, para 22, but not if the company is already in administration or is in liquidation,[70] or essentially if in the past 12 months the company was previously put into administration by the company or the directors or during that period the company has unsuccessfully pursued a CVA.[71] The intention is to prevent the directors switching between these procedures to the detriment of creditors who constantly find that some form of moratorium is in place affecting their rights. While an appointment out of court cannot take place, an application to the court for an administration order under Sch B1, para 12 is still possible: see **23-24**. Also, the company or the directors may not look to appoint an administrator out of court under Sch B1, para 22 if a petition for winding up has been presented and not yet disposed of;[72] an administration application has been made to the court and is not yet disposed of; or an administrative receiver is in office (Sch B1, para 25).   **23-49**

A person who proposes to make an appointment under Sch B1, para 22 must give at least five business days' written notice to any floating charge holder who is or may be entitled to appoint an administrative receiver or to appoint an administrator out of court.[73] No appointment may be made unless this required notice has been given and the period specified has expired or the recipient of the notice has consented in writing to the appointment (Sch B1, para 28(1)). In practice, the company will have consulted the floating charge holder about the appointment in advance.   **23-50**

A person who gives notice of intention to appoint must file a copy of the notice with the court as soon as is reasonably practicable.[74] That filing sets running a period of 10   **23-51**

---

[68] See IA 1986, Sch B1, para 20; IR 1986, r 2.18.

[69] Either the directors acting unanimously or by a majority: see IA 1986, Sch B1, para 105.

[70] IA 1986, Sch B1, paras 7 and 8.   [71] IA 1986, Sch B1, paras 23, 34.

[72] The presentation of a winding-up petition takes place when the petition is delivered to the court for filing notwithstanding that that date might be well in advance of the date when the petition is sealed and issued by the court for service which makes it difficult for those considering making an appointment to know whether there is a pending petition: see *Re Blights Builders Ltd* [2008] 1 BCLC 245 (administrators' appointment invalid as a winding-up petition had been presented and had not been disposed of).

[73] IA 1986, Sch B1, para 26(1); and notice of the intention to appoint must be given to those persons prescribed by IR 1986, r 2.20(2). The notice must be in the prescribed form and identify the proposed administrator: IA 1986, Sch B1, para 26(3). In the event that there are no persons to whom notice must be given under this provision: see para 30.

[74] IA 1986, Sch B1, para 27(1); IR 1986, r 2.22.

business days beginning with the date on which the notice of intention to appoint is filed within which an appointment of an administrator by the company or directors must take place (Sch B1, para 28(2)). Once the notice of intention to appoint is filed with the court, the interim moratorium applies (Sch B1, para 44(4)).

23-52   Once the appointment is made, the appointor must file with the court a notice of appointment including a statutory declaration made not more than five business days before the filing by or on behalf of the person making the appointment that the company/directors are entitled to make an appointment under these provisions; that the appointment is in accordance with IA 1986, Sch B1, and that, as far as the person is reasonably able to ascertain, the statements made and information given in the statutory declaration filed with the notice of intention to appoint remain accurate.[75]

23-53   The notice of appointment must identify the administrator and be accompanied by a statement by him that he consents to the appointment; that in his opinion the purpose of administration (as defined in Sch B1, para 3: see **23-6**) is reasonably likely to be achieved and the statement must give details of any prior professional relationship which the administrator has had with the company.[76]

23-54   The appointment of an administrator under these powers takes effect when the requirements as to the filing with the court of the notice of appointment (and accompanying documents) are satisfied (Sch B1, para 31). In order to minimise confusion on this issue, the person appointing is required to notify the administrator as soon as it is reasonably practicable that the notice of appointment etc has been filed with the court.[77] If before the requirements as to the filing of the notice of appointment are satisfied, the company enters into administration by virtue of a court order or an appointment out of court by a qualifying floating charge holder, the appointment by the company/directors under Sch B1, para 22 does not take effect (Sch B1, para 33).

D The company in administration

23-55   As noted above, one of the key elements of administration is the moratorium on the enforcement of creditors' rights and other processes. It is essential to the continuation of business by the administrator that he should have the right to use the property of the company free from interference by creditors and others.[78] In particular, the intention is to prevent a litigation free-for-all by creditors with administrators feeling obliged

---

[75] IA 1986, Sch B1, para 29(1), (2), (5); IR 1986, rr 2.23–2.24. For the criminal penalties for a false statement in a statutory declaration, see Sch B1, para 29(7).

[76] IA 1986, Sch B1, para 29(3); IR 1986, r 2.3(5); to avoid unnecessary investigation and expense, the administrator may rely on information provided by the directors unless he has reason to doubt its accuracy: Sch B1, para 29(4).

[77] See IA 1986, Sch B1, para 32; IR 1986, r 2.26(2); it is an offence to fail to comply without reasonable excuse.

[78] See *Bristol Airport plc v Powdrill* [1990] BCLC 585 at 594.

to compromise on weak claims because the cost of defending them to a conclusion would be difficult to justify.[79] The effect of the moratorium is that owners of property, and charges over property, are disabled from exercising their proprietary rights unless the administrator consents or the court gives permission.[80] A moratorium is just that, however, a moratorium on the enforcement of the creditor's right and it does not affect the substantive rights of the creditor.[81]

Once the company is in administration, the extent of the moratorium is governed by   **23-56**
IA 1986, Sch B1, paras 42 and 43 which provide that:

(1) no resolution may be passed or order made for the winding up of the company, other than on public interest petitions;[82]

(2) no step may be taken to enforce security over the company's property;[83]

(3) no step may be taken to repossess goods in the company's possession[84] under any hire-purchase agreement;[85]

(4) a landlord may not exercise a right of forfeiture by peaceable re-entry in relation to premises let to the company;[86]

(5) no legal process (including legal proceedings, execution, distress and diligence) may be instituted or continued against the company or property of the company;[87]

---

[79] See Laddie J in *Holdenhurst Securities plc v Cohen* [2001] 1 BCLC 460 at 463–4.

[80] *Re Atlantic Computer Systems plc* [1992] 1 All ER 476 at 488, CA, per Nicholls LJ.

[81] *Barclays Mercantile Business Finance Ltd v Sibec Developments* [1992] 2 All ER 195.

[82] IA 1986, Sch B1, para 42; as to public interest petitions, see above n 26.

[83] IA 1986, Sch B1, para 43(2). 'Security' is defined as 'any mortgage, charge, lien or other security': s 248(b) (ii). In *Bristol Airport plc v Powdrill* [1990] 2 All ER 493, CA, 'security' was held to include the exercise of a statutory lien, in this case the right of an airport to detain aircraft for unpaid airport charges under the Civil Aviation Act 1982; see also *Re Sabre International Products Ltd* [1991] BCLC 470 (enforcement of a lien). 'Property' is defined in IA 1986, s 436 as including money, goods, things in action, land and every description of property wherever situated and also obligations and every description of interest, whether present or future or vested or contingent, arising out of, or incidental to, property.

[84] In *David Meek Plant Ltd, Re David Meek Access Ltd* [1994] 1 BCLC 680, the court found goods to be 'in the company's possession under a hire-purchase agreement' although the hire-purchase agreement had terminated: it was sufficient that the possession was attributable to or derived from a hire-purchase agreement at some time, not necessarily one still subsisting; see also *Re Atlantic Computer Systems plc* [1992] 1 All ER 476, CA: equipment held by a company on hire-purchase was in the company's possession for these purposes whether the equipment remained on the company's premises, was entrusted to others for repair, or was sub-let by the company as part of its trade with others. See also *Fashoff (UK) Ltd v Linton* [2008] 2 BCLC 362 as to whether goods obtained subject to a retention of title clause had remained in the constructive possession of the company in administration.

[85] IA 1986, Sch B1, para 43(3). A hire-purchase agreement is defined as including a conditional sale, a chattel lease and a retention of title agreement: para 111(1): see *Re City Logistics Ltd* [2002] 2 BCLC 103.

[86] IA 1986, Sch B1, para 43(4). Earlier litigation had established that such a right of a landlord did not amount to the enforcing of security over the company's property within (2) above in the text and therefore the permission of the court was not required by the landlord: see *Re Lomax Leisure Ltd* [1999] 2 BCLC 126. That position has now been reversed.

[87] IA 1986, Sch B1, para 43(6). See *Re Olympia & York Canary Wharf Ltd* [1994] BCLC 453 (legal process means a process which requires the assistance of the court and does not extend to the service of a contractual notice which renders time of the essence or terminates a contract by reason of the company's anticipatory

except in cases (2)–(5) with the permission of the court or the consent of the administrator.[88]

23-57   Two issues related to the moratorium have particularly concerned the courts: (1) the scope of the prohibition on instituting or continuing a 'legal process'; and (2) the nature of the court's discretion to grant permission to persons to act against the company despite the moratorium.

Restriction on legal process

23-58   The restriction on any 'legal process' extends to any legal or quasi-legal proceedings, such as arbitration proceedings,[89] tribunal proceedings[90] or adjudication procedures.[91] It is not limited to proceedings by creditors.[92] It can include proceedings brought by a competitor[93] and it applies to criminal proceedings against the company.[94] In all these cases, the permission of the court or the administrator is required.

23-59   On the other hand, a direction by a rail regulator against a rail company is not a legal process or proceeding for these purposes for the regulator performs a broader role than that required of a judicial or quasi-judicial decision-maker and does not act as a result of a legal process against the company.[95] If the regulator subsequently needs the court's assistance to enforce his direction, this would be a legal process requiring the consent of the court or the administrator. Equally, an application for the late registration of a charge is not within the mischief aimed at although such applications are subject to the court's discretion in any case.[96]

Setting aside the moratorium—the permission of the court

23-60   In *Royal Trust Bank v Buchler*[97] the court noted that its discretion to grant leave under IA 1986 s 11(3) (now a requirement for the permission of the court under IA 1986, Sch B1, para 42) is a general discretion which requires the court to have regard to all the relevant circumstances. Having regard to those circumstances, it could be appropriate for a secured creditor to be given leave to enforce its security even if no

---

breach). Despite the prohibition on the institution of legal processes, an administration does not stop time running for limitation purposes: *Re Maxwell Fleet and Facilities (Management) Ltd* [2000] 1 All ER 464.

[88] IA 1986, Sch B1, para 43; the court's permission may be conditional, see para 43(7).

[89] *Bristol Airport plc v Powdrill* [1990] BCLC 585 at 600.

[90] Such as an industrial tribunal: see *Carr v British International Helicopters Ltd* [1994] 2 BCLC 474.

[91] Such as those brought under the Housing Grants Construction and Regeneration Act 1986: see *A Straume (UK) Ltd v Bradlor Developments Ltd* [2000] BCC 333.

[92] In so far as *Air Ecosse v Civil Aviation Authority* (1987) 3 BCC 492 took the contrary view, it has not been followed by the English courts: see *Environment Agency v Clark (Re Rhondda Waste Disposal Ltd)* [2000] BCC 653 at 678.

[93] See *Biosource Technologies Inc v Axis Genetics plc* [2000] 1 BCLC 286 (competitor company precluded from taking proceedings against company in administration for the revocation of a patent held by that company without consent of administrator or permission of the court).

[94] *Environment Agency v Clark (Re Rhondda Waste Disposal Ltd)* [2001] Ch 57.

[95] *Re Railtrack plc, Winsor v Bloom* [2002] 4 All ER 435, CA.

[96] *Re Barrow Borough Transport Ltd* [1989] BCLC 653.   [97] [1989] BCLC 130.

criticism could be made of the administrator. In this case, the property at the centre of the dispute between the secured creditor and the administrator was an office block. After months of fruitless efforts by the administrator to find tenants for the property, the creditor wanted to appoint a receiver to sell the property, with or without tenants, before the value of the property (and therefore its security) deteriorated further. As the property would realise more money if sold as fully let, the administrator wanted more time to find tenants.

Weighing up the conflicting interests, the court decided that appointing a receiver would result in additional costs and further reduce the net proceeds available to the creditors. On the other hand, the administration in this case had gone on for a long time and it was therefore reasonable to require the administrator to return to court in two months if he had not by then achieved a binding contract of sale when a further application by the creditor could be considered. **23-61**

Many of the main issues with regard to the release of a security holder from the constraints of the moratorium were considered at length by the Court of Appeal in *Re Atlantic Computer Systems plc*[98] and the guidance provided therein has proved very influential. In this case, the company in administration supplied computers on sublease to end-users. The company in turn obtained the computers either on hire-purchase or on lease from finance companies ('the funders'). Throughout the period of administration the end-users had continued to pay the rentals due under the subleases, but the administrators had not paid any sums due to the funders under the leases. The funders wishes to ascertain, inter alia, whether the equipment could be repossessed by the funders and whether, if the court's leave was required to do so, it would be granted. **23-62**

In addressing these issues, the Court of Appeal used the opportunity to set out the following general observations regarding cases where leave is sought to exercise existing proprietary rights, including security rights, against a company in administration:[99] **23-63**

- '• It is for the person seeking permission to make out his case.
- • Leave should normally be given to a lessor of land or the hirer of goods (a 'lessor') to exercise his proprietary rights and repossess his land or goods where that is unlikely to impede the achievement of the purpose for which the administration order was made (now to be read in the light of the statutory purpose of administration, set out at **23-6**).[100]
- • In other cases, the court has to carry out a balancing exercise, balancing the legitimate interests of the lessor and the legitimate interests of the other creditors of the company.[101]

---

[98] [1992] 1 All ER 476, CA.   [99] [1992] 1 All ER 476 at 500–2, CA.

[100] Undue delay in seeking leave is itself sufficient to justify a refusal of permission since delay is contrary to the objectives of the legislation and a delay may also mean that an order of the court at a late stage is likely to impede the purpose of the administration: *Fashoff (UK) Ltd v Linton* [2008] 2 BCLC 362.

[101] See also *Royal Bank Trust v Buchler* [1989] BCLC 130. The conduct of the parties may also be relevant to the issue of whether leave should be granted: *Bristol Airport plc v Powdrill* [1990] 2 All ER 493, CA.

- In carrying out the balancing exercise, great weight is normally to be given to the proprietary interests of the lessor and an administration for the benefit of unsecured creditors should not be conducted at the expense of those seeking to exercise their proprietary rights, save to the extent that this is unavoidable and even then this will usually be acceptable only to a strictly limited extent.

- Therefore, leave will normally be granted if significant loss would be caused to the lessor by a refusal; but if substantially greater loss would be caused to others by the grant of leave, or loss which is out of all proportion to the benefit which leave would confer on the lessor, that may outweigh the loss to the lessor caused by a refusal.

- In assessing these respective losses, the court will have regard to matters such as: the financial position of the company, its ability to pay the rental arrears and the continuing rentals, the administrator's proposals, the period for which the administration order has already been in force and is expected to remain in force, the effect on the administration if leave were given, the effect on the applicant if leave were refused, the end result sought to be achieved by the administration, the prospects of that result being achieved, and the history of the administration so far.

- If leave is refused, it may commonly be on terms, for example, that the administrator pay the current rent which should be possible, since if the administration order has been rightly made the business should generally be sufficiently viable to hold down current outgoings.

- The comments were mainly directed to the situation where a lessor of land or the owner of goods seeks to repossess his land or goods because of non-payment of rentals but a broadly similar approach would be applicable on many applications to enforce a security. On such applications, an important consideration will often be whether the applicant is fully secured. If he is, delay in enforcement is likely to be of less prejudice than in cases where his security is insufficient.'

23-64   Returning to the facts in *Re Atlantic Computer Systems plc*,[102] the court found that the administrators wanted to remain in possession of the computers partly in order to renegotiate the arrangements between the company and the funders which negotiations would be conducted in circumstances where the funders were not in a position to rely on their full rights. The court concluded that it was never intended that administration should strengthen the administrator's hands in negotiations with property owners who could not assert their full rights because of the moratorium and accordingly the court would grant leave to the funders to enforce their rights.[103]

23-65   In *Re David Meek Plant Ltd, Re David Meek Access Ltd*[104] leave to repossess goods on hire-purchase to a company in administration was refused, the court having balanced the interests of those leasing creditors against the legitimate interests of the other creditors. To have allowed repossession would have ensured that

---

[102] [1992] 1 All ER 476, CA.   [103] [1992] 1 All ER 476 at 498–9, CA.   [104] [1994] 1 BCLC 680.

the administration would be abortive and that would deprive the creditors of the opportunity of considering proposals designed to achieve a more advantageous real-isation of the assets than would have been the case in a winding up. In *AES Barry Ltd v TXU Europe Energy Trading Ltd*[105] the court held that only in very exceptional cir-cumstances would the court allow a creditor whose claim was simply a monetary one a right to take proceedings.

In a different context, in *Environment Agency v Clark (Re Rhondda Waste Disposal Ltd)*[106] the Court of Appeal overruled a refusal by the trial judge to grant permis-sion to the Environment Agency to bring a criminal prosecution against a company in administration. The Court of Appeal concluded that the trial judge had given too much weight to the interests of the company's creditors and insufficient interest to the wider public interest in the prosecution, including the Agency's concerns that any criminal liability should not be evaded by a company going into administration. In the event of a conviction, the court was obliged to fix any fine taking into account the financial circumstances of the company.   **23-66**

E The role and powers of the administrator

As soon as is reasonably practicable after his appointment (by whatever route),[107] the administrator must send a notice of his appointment to the company and publish a notice of his appointment.[108] He must obtain a list of the company's creditors;[109] send a notice of his appointment to the registrar of companies within seven days;[110] call on officers or employees of the company for a statement of the affairs of the company;[111] and take custody or control of all the property of the company (Sch B1, para 67). While the company is in administration, every business document issued by or on behalf of the company or the administrator and all the company's websites must state the name of the administrator and that the affairs, business and property of the company are being managed by him.[112]   **23-67**

The administrator effectively replaces the directors in the management of the business, given that all power to manage the business is vested in him (Sch B1,

---

[105] [2005] 2 BCLC 22.   [106] [2001] Ch 57, CA.

[107] His appointment takes effect according to the manner in which it is made: see IA 1986, Sch B1, paras 13(2), 19, 31.

[108] His appointment must be published in accordance with the requirements of IR 1986, r 2.27, essen-tially in the *Gazette* and in one appropriate newspaper: IA 1986, Sch B1, para 46(2).

[109] He is required to send a notice of his appointment to each creditor of whose claim and address he is aware: IA 1986, Sch B1, para 46(3), but the court may direct that this requirement does not apply: para 46(7)(a).

[110] IA 1986, Sch B1, para 46(4); and to those persons prescribed by IR 1986 r 2.27(2). This notice to the registrar must be sent before the end of seven days beginning with the date of the order appointing him or the date of his receiving notice of his appointment: para 46(6).

[111] IA 1986, Sch B1, para 47; IR 1986, r 2.28(2).

[112] IA 1986, Sch B1, para 45(1). 'Business document' is defined in para 45(3).

para 59(1)).[113] The directors do not vacate office and remain subject to their usual range of duties, including their statutory obligations to file documents with the registrar of companies.[114] A company in administration or an officer of a company in administration may not exercise a management power, however, without the consent of the administrator, which consent may be general or specific.[115]

Proposals to creditors

23-69   Once appointed, the administrator must make a statement setting out proposals for achieving the purpose of administration and also indicating how it is proposed that the administration will end (a requirement which means that from the outset the administrator needs to be focused on an expeditious process[116] with a definite end in prospect).[117] A copy of this statement must be sent to the registrar of companies and to every creditor of whose claim and address the administrator is aware and to every member of the company of whose address he is aware as soon as reasonably practicable after the company enters administration,[118] but in any event not later than the end of eight weeks commencing with the company entering administration.[119]

23-70   The proposals have to take into account the purpose of administration as set out in IA 1986, Sch B1, para 3 and therefore they need to be directed to: (1) rescuing the company as a going concern, or (2) achieving a better result for the creditors as a whole than would have been achieved if the company has been wound up, or (3) if neither of the above is reasonably practicable, the realisation of the company's property in order to make distributions to one or more secured or preferential creditors.

23-71   For example, if the administrator considers that the rescue of the company is achievable, the proposals will probably relate to a CVA or a scheme of arrangement; if he considers that rescue is not possible but it is possible to secure a better result than on a winding up, the proposals will probably relate to ways in which the business might be sold as a going concern, either entirely or in separate lots; and if it is not reasonably practicable to achieve either of the objectives, the proposal will be for the realisation of

---

[113] As a consequence, the administrator owes his duties to the company, in the manner that the directors do: see *Kyrris v Oldham* [2004] 1 BCLC 305, CA.

[114] The administrator also has power to remove any director of the company and to appoint any person to be a director of it, whether to fill a vacancy or otherwise: IA 1986, Sch B1, para 59(1).

[115] IA 1986, Sch B1, para 64(1). A management power is defined as a power which could be exercised so as to interfere with the exercise of the administrator's powers: para 64(2).

[116] An administration terminates automatically after one year unless the period is extended by consent of the creditors or order of the court: IA 1986, Sch B1, para 76.

[117] IA 1986, Sch B1, para 49(1), (3). The contents of the statement are prescribed by IR 1986, r 2.33. The rules anticipate that the purpose of the administration may be achieved before the proposals are sent to the creditors: see r 2.33(6).

[118] As to when a 'company enters into administration', see IA 1986, Sch B1, para 1(2)(b).

[119] IA 1986, Sch B1, para 49(4), (5). The time period may be varied and extended by the court or administrator in accordance with Sch B1, paras 107, 108. It suffices for these purposes if the administrator publishes a notice undertaking to send a copy of his proposals to any member who applies in writing: see para 49(6).

property in order to make a distribution to one or more secured or preferential creditors. In this case, the proposal must explain why the administrator thinks that the other objectives cannot be achieved.[120]

Most importantly, the proposals may not include any proposal which affects the   **23-72**
rights of a secured creditor without his consent; likewise, no proposal may provide
for the payment of preferential debts other than in priority to non-preferential debts
or other than on a pro rata basis to other preferential debts without the consent of the
preferential creditor.[121]

Initial creditors' meeting

This statement by the administrator of his proposals must be accompanied by an invi-   **23-73**
tation to an initial creditors' meeting (Sch B1, para 51(1)). An initial creditors' meeting
need not be held where the administrator thinks (Sch B1, para 52(1)) that:

(1) the company has sufficient property to enable each creditor to be paid in full;

(2) the company has insufficient property to enable a distribution to be made to
     unsecured creditors other than in accordance with the rules governing the pre-
     scribed part under IA 1986, s 176A(2): see **24-91**); or

(3) neither of the objectives specified in IA 1986, Sch B1, para 3(1)(a) (rescue) and
     (b) (better realisation than on a winding up) can be achieved.

If an initial creditors' meeting is to be held, it must be held as soon as is reasonably   **23-74**
practicable after the company enters administration but not later than the end of 10
weeks beginning with the company entering administration (Sch B1, para 51(2)).[122]

The administrator must present a copy of his proposals to the meeting which may   **23-75**
approve or reject the proposals[123] but approval with modifications is only permissible
if the administrator consents to each modification.[124] For the proposals to be accepted,
they must be accepted by a majority in value of the creditors present and voting, in
person or by proxy.[125] Any resolution is invalid if those voting against it include more
than half in value of the creditors to whom notice of the meeting was sent and who are
not, to the best of the chairman's belief, persons connected with the company.[126]

---

[120] IA 1986, Sch B1, para 49(2)(b).

[121] IA 1986, Sch B1, para 73, unless the proposal is for a CVA or scheme of arrangement which would require the consent of the secured or preferential creditors in any event.

[122] The time period can be varied or extended by the court or the administrator under IA 1986, Sch B1, paras 107, 108.

[123] If a creditors' meeting is not held, approval of the proposals is assumed under IR 1986, r 2.33.

[124] IA 1986, Sch B1, paras 51(3), 53(1).

[125] IR 1986, r 2.28(1). Votes are calculated according to the amount of the creditor's debt as at the date of administration, deducting any amounts paid in respect of the debt after that date: r 2.22(4). A secured creditor is entitled to vote only in respect of the balance of his debt after deducting the value of his security as estimated by him: r 2.24.

[126] IR 1986, r 2.28(1A).

23-76   After the meeting, the administrator must as soon as is reasonably practicable report any decision taken to the court and to the registrar of companies and to the prescribed persons[127] but there is no hearing and, in particular, no requirement for the court to approve the proposals. The remedy of any creditor or member who feels aggrieved by the approval of the proposals is to apply to the court to challenge the administrator's conduct (see the discussion at **23-93**).

23-77   If the administrator subsequently wishes to revise his proposals and he thinks that the proposed revision is substantial, he is required to go through this process again and to present the revised proposals to the creditors and have them approved and then to report the matter to the court.[128]

23-78   If the report is that the creditors have failed to approve the proposals or the revised proposals, as the case may be, the court may provide that the appointment of the administrator shall cease, or may adjourn the hearing, or may make an interim order, or may make an order on any winding-up petition which had been suspended once the company had gone into administration;[129] or it may make any other order that it thinks appropriate (Sch B1, para 55(2)).[130]

23-79   Apart from the initial creditors' meeting, the administrator may call a meeting of creditors at any time (Sch B1, para 62) and must call a meeting of creditors if requested by creditors whose debts amount to at least 10% of the total debts of the company (Sch B1, para 52(2))[131] or if directed to hold a creditors' meeting by the court (Sch B1, para 56).[132] The creditors may also decide to set up a creditors' committee and the committee may require the administrator to attend before it and to provide it with information as to the exercise of his functions (Sch B1, para 57).

Disposals ahead of the initial creditors' meeting

23-80   Although the initial creditors' meeting is supposed to approve the administrator's proposals, it may happen that the administrator must decide at short notice whether to accept an offer for the company's business. Whether he could do so ahead of the

---

[127] IA 1986, Sch B1, para 53(2); IR 1986, r 2.46.

[128] IA 1986, Sch B1, para 54. See the suggestion by Neuberger J in *Re Dana (UK) Ltd* [1999] 2 BCLC 239 that the original proposals should include a streamlined mechanism to get around the potentially cumbersome need for more meetings. Matters are made easier now by the ability to use correspondence (including electronic communication) in place of meetings, see IA 1986, Sch B1, paras 58, 111.

[129] I.e. under IA 1986, Sch B1, para 40(1)(b).

[130] The court may authorise the implementation of the proposals even in the face of the opposition of the majority creditor, see *Re Structures & Computers Ltd* [1998] 2 BCLC 292; also *Re DKLL Solicitors* [2008] 1 BCLC 112 at 119.

[131] See IR 1986, r 2.37. The creditors must act quickly and a request to hold a meeting must be made within 12 days of the administrator's proposals being sent out. The creditors are liable for the costs (and must give security for the costs) unless the meeting resolves otherwise.

[132] Equally, any matter which might be dealt with at a creditors' meeting may be dealt with by correspondence (including electronic communication) and a requirement to hold a meeting (including the requirement to hold the initial creditors' meeting) may be satisfied by correspondence instead of by an actual meeting: IA 1986, Sch B1, paras 58, 111; also IR 1986, r 2.48.

initial meeting was the subject of much debate until Neuberger J in *Re T & D Industries plc*[133] took a robust line concluding that the administrator could dispose of assets without the leave of the court, unless the administration order provided otherwise. In his view, this power was necessary in order to avoid unnecessary delay and expense. To preclude sales would be inconsistent with the policy of administration which is meant to provide a more flexible, cheaper and comparatively informal alternative to liquidation.[134] That position was confirmed by Lawrence Collins J in *Re Transbus International Ltd*[135] and the matter is now settled. An administrator (however appointed) has a power of sale ahead of a creditors' meeting and neither the sanction of the creditors nor a direction from the court is required. This position is consistent with the underlying policies of expeditious administration with minimum court involvement. It is also essential to the use of pre-pack administration as is discussed at **23-114**. While a sale is permissible, this does not mean that the conduct of the administrator is not open to challenge, for example as unfairly harming the creditors (IA 1986, Sch B1, para 74) or misfeasance (Sch B1 para 75): see at **23-93**.[136]

Managing the business

An administrator may do anything necessary or expedient for the management of the affairs, business and property of the company (Sch B1, para 59(1));[137] and a person who deals with the administrator in good faith and for value need not inquire whether the administrator is acting within his powers (Sch B1, para 59(3)). In exercising his functions, the administrator acts as the company's agent which is bound by and liable for his acts (Sch B1, para 69).   **23-81**

The administrator has the powers set out in IA 1986, Sch 1 (Sch B1, para 60) which are derived from the wide powers commonly provided by debenture for administrative receivers and include inter alia and without prejudice to the generality of his powers to manage the company's affairs: **23-82**

- the power to take possession of, collect and get in the property of the company (Sch 1, para 1);

- the power to sell or otherwise dispose of the property of the company (Sch 1, para 2);

- the power to raise or borrow money and grant security (Sch 1, para 3);

- the power to bring and defend any action or other legal proceedings (Sch 1, para 5);

---

[133] [2000] 1 BCLC 471.   [134] See [2000] 1 BCLC 471 at 477, 483–4.   [135] [2004] 2 BCLC 550.

[136] See Statement of Insolvency Practice 16, 'Pre-Packaged Sales in Administration,' para 3 (effective 1 January 2009); and discussion at **23-116**.

[137] The power to manage the company's affairs extends to the company's pension scheme since such a scheme is integrally connected with the management of the staff of the company: *Denny v Yeldon* [1995] 1 BCLC 560.

- the power to make any payment which is necessary or incidental to the performance of his functions (Sch 1, para 13);
- the power to carry on the business of the company (Sch 1, para 14).

23-83 An administrator may call a meeting of the members of the company at any time (Sch B1, para 62). An administrator has the same powers as a liquidator to challenge transactions at an undervalue or preferences,[138] extortionate credit transactions and certain floating charges,[139] all of which powers are discussed in Chapter 25. The administrator has no power to seek contributions to the company's assets with respect to fraudulent or wrongful trading,[140] however, but he does have to report on whether the directors' conduct may merit their disqualification.[141]

23-84 In carrying out his functions, it has to be borne in mind that an administrator, however appointed, is an officer of the court (Sch B1, para 5). Moreover, in managing the company's affairs etc, the administrator must act in accordance with any proposals or revised proposals approved by the creditors (Sch B1, para 68(1)). An administrator may apply to the court for directions in connection with his functions and he must comply with any directions given.[142] The court may only give directions if: no proposals have been approved by the creditors;[143] the directions are consistent with any proposals which have been approved; the court thinks the directions are required by changed circumstances; or the court thinks the directions are desirable because of a misunderstanding about proposals or revised proposals (Sch B1, para 68(3)). The courts are anxious to stop administrators making unnecessary use of the power to seek directions in order to ensure that their decisions are free from legal challenge.[144] Seeking directions adds to the costs of the administration and may unnecessarily delay matters.

23-85 An administrator is not personally liable on any contracts entered into during the administration as he acts as the company's agent (Sch B1, para 69), but priority is accorded to debts or liabilities arising out of any contract entered into by an administrator: see **23-110**. The appointment of an administrator in itself has no effect on existing contracts of the company and, subject to the need to obtain the consent of the court or administrator for proceedings, any right to specific performance, lien, set-off, rescission or injunction available against the company before administration continues to be available against the company in administration.[145] In practice, contracts often provide for termination on one of the parties going into administration. Likewise the appointment of an administrator as such has no effect on contracts of employment, but administrators will frequently need to reduce the workforce and so dismissals may follow. For contracts of employment adopted by the administrators, priority is also accorded to certain sums arising with respect to such contracts, as is discussed at **23-111**.

---

[138] IA 1986, ss 238, 239.   [139] IA 1986, ss 244, 245.   [140] I.e. under IA 1986, ss 213, 214.
[141] Company Directors Disqualification Act 1986, s 7(3)(c).   [142] IA 1986, Sch B1, paras 63, 68(2).
[143] I.e. because the initial creditors' meeting has not been held.
[144] See comments by Neuberger J in *Re T and D Industries plc* [2000] 1 BCLC 471 at 478.
[145] *Astor Chemicals Ltd v Synthetic Technology Ltd* [1990] BCLC 1. See also *Re P & C and R & T (Stockport) Ltd* [1991] BCLC 366

Distributions to creditors

A particular problem for administrators prior to the reforms effected by the EA 2002 **23-86** was that there was no general power to make distributions to creditors and creative schemes had to be devised which allowed for payments to be sanctioned as ancillary matters to the discharge of the administration.[146] The legislation now specifically provides that an administrator may make a distribution to a creditor of the company, subject to the application of IA 1986, s 175 (preferential debts) as it applies on a winding up,[147] and where the creditor is neither secured nor preferential, the permission of the court is required (Sch B1, para 65).[148] This provision has proved invaluable in the light of the way in which administration has developed with it now being common for the administrator to seek permission to make a distribution to unsecured creditors (where funds are available for that purpose) and then to have the company dissolved expeditiously by notice to the registrar in accordance with Sch B1, para 84, discussed at **23-106**.[149] The breadth of the jurisdiction to make distributions under Sch B1, para 65 can be seen from decisions such as *Re HPJ UK Ltd*[150] where the court accepted that the power is wide enough to allow a distribution to a specified creditor (HMRC in this case) in full satisfaction of all claims even though this was not a rateable distribution. The crucial considerations were that the creditors unanimously approved of the distribution and the court considered the distribution to be important in attaining the objectives of the administration in the interests of the creditors as a whole. In *Re MG Rover Belux SA*[151] the court was willing to authorise a distribution (to Belgian creditors) otherwise than in accordance with the priorities which would apply under English law, again because the court considered the payments would help in the attainment of the purpose of the administration.

In addition, an administrator may make a payment to any creditor if he thinks it is **23-87** likely to assist achievement of the purpose of administration (Sch B1, para 66).[152] In *Re Collins & Aikman Europe SA*,[153] following the opening of main insolvency proceedings in England, the administrators were anxious to preclude the opening of secondary proceedings in other countries which would have impeded the achievement of the purpose of the administration. The administrators therefore gave undertakings to creditors in those other jurisdictions that, if they desisted from opening secondary proceedings, their respective financial positions as creditors under local law would

---

[146] See *Re Lune Metal Products Ltd* [2007] 2 BCLC 746, an 'old' case which reviews the mechanisms which were used to get around these problems.

[147] The relevant date for determining the amount of preferential debts is the date when the company entered administration: IA 1986, s 387. The preferential debts are those debts set out in IA 1986, Sch 6.

[148] Once permission has been granted, the administrator must adhere to the detailed rules governing distributions laid down in IR 1986, rr 2.68–2.105 which include (in r 2.85) rules on set-off broadly similar to those applicable in liquidation (see **24-76**), the difference being that the set-off rule only applies if the administrator makes a distribution to unsecured creditors.

[149] See for example *Re Ballast plc* [2005] 1 BCLC 446.

[150] [2007] BCC 284.   [151] [2007] BCC 446.

[152] There is an uncertain overlap between this provision and IA 1986, Sch 1, para 13 (power to make any payment which is necessary or incidental to the performance of the administrator's functions).

[153] [2007] 1 BCLC 182.

be respected, so far as possible, in the English administration. On seeking directions to this effect, the court considered that the payments could be regarded as being
properly made if the administrators reasonably thought them to be 'likely to assist
achievement of the purpose of administration' within Sch B1, para 66. On the facts,
the administrator did so consider and the court could direct that they should honour
their undertakings.

Selling the business

23-88   In selling the business, the administrator owes a duty to the company to take reasonable care, judged by the standard of the ordinary skilled insolvency practitioner, to
obtain the best price that the circumstances permit, including a duty to take reasonable care in choosing the time at which to sell the property.[154]

Dealing with charged property

23-89   A matter of concern for secured creditors or creditors with proprietary rights is the
power of an administrator to deal with certain assets as if the company has an unencumbered title to them. This power is thought necessary particularly if the administrator wishes to sell the business as a going concern. There are two categories of
powers, depending on whether the administrator needs the consent of the court.

23-90   With an order of the court, an administrator may dispose of assets subject to a security other than a floating charge as if the property were not subject to the security or he
may dispose of goods in the possession of the company under a hire-purchase agreement (which includes under a retention of title agreement)[155] as if the rights of the
owner were vested in the company; in each case, the court must think that the disposal
would be likely to promote the purpose of administration in respect of the company.[156]
The court's order will be conditional on the application of the net proceeds of the disposal (or market value, if higher) towards discharging the sums secured by the security or payable under the hire-purchase agreement.[157]

23-91   In considering whether or not to consent to the disposal of charged property, the
court's approach is similar to that considered at **23-60** above in relation to the granting of permission for actions otherwise restrained by the moratorium. The court will
balance the prejudice felt by a secured creditor if an order is made against the prejudice that would otherwise be felt by those interested in the promotion of the purpose
of administration.[158]

23-92   An administrator may dispose of or take action relating to property which is subject to
a floating charge as if the property were not subject to the charge.[159] Where such prop-

---

[154] *Re Charnley Davies Ltd (No 2)* [1990] BCLC 760.   [155] Defined IA 1986, Sch B1, para 111(1).
[156] IA 1986, Sch B1, paras 71(2), 72(2). A copy of any order made by the court under these provisions
must, within 14 days starting with the date of the order, be sent by the administrator to the registrar of companies: paras 71(5), 72(4).
[157] IA 1986, Sch B1, paras 71(3), 72(3).   [158] See *Re ARV Aviation Ltd* [1989] BCLC 664.
[159] IA 1986, Sch B1, para 70(1). As to whether a charge is fixed or floating, see the discussion in Chapter
21; in cases of uncertainty, there has been something of a tendency to find charges to be floating rather than

erty is disposed of, the charge holder has the same priority in respect of property which directly or indirectly represents the property disposed of as he had in respect of that property.[160] There is no need to obtain the consent of the creditor or the court in this instance. Of course, since the proceeds of the property disposed of may be used by the administrator to meet the expenses of administration, there may be no property to which the interest of the floating charge holder can transfer. The existence of this power is one reason why the debenture holder needs to consider carefully whether he wants to prevent the appointment by others of an administrator and instead appoint an administrative receiver, if that option is available to him, or perhaps to appoint an administrator out of court. A creditor who objects to a disposal by an administrator can challenge the conduct of the administrator.

Challenging the administrator's conduct

Unfairly harm

Any creditor or member of a company in administration may apply to the court claim-   **23-93**
ing that:

(1) the administrator is acting or has acted so as unfairly to harm the interests of the applicant (whether alone or in common with some or all other members or creditors); or

(2) the administrator proposes to act in a way which would unfairly harm the interests of the applicant (whether alone or in common with some or all other members or creditors) (Sch B1, para 74(1)).

The wording of this provision (unfairly harm) was altered from 'unfairly prejudicial'   **23-94**
in the 'old' provision which latter term is well established in the context of shareholder remedies and the CA 2006, s 994 (see Chapter 17). This welcome distancing of this quite distinct provision from that remedy may also suggest a lowering of the threshold. The harm required is harm to the interests of the creditor or member arising from the actions of the administrator and it must be unfair to the creditor.[161] An order can be made under this provision whether or not the action complained of is within the administrator's powers under Sch B1 or was taken in reliance on a court order allowing for the disposal of property of a creditor (Sch B1, para 74(5)). The court's powers on any application are noted below.

---

fixed which is to the advantage of the administrator since the property within the change then falls within his powers of disposal.

[160] IA 1986, Sch B1, para 70(2), (3).

[161] See *Re Lehman Bros, Four Private Investment Funds v Lomas* [2008] EWHC 2869, [2008] All ER (D) 237 (Nov) (where administrators were acting in accordance with their obligations under IA 1986, Sch B1, the court thought it was difficult to see how an unwillingness on the administrators' part to devote more time and resources than they had already done to answering questions put to them by a particular group of creditors, directed to eliciting information about assets in which the creditors claimed an interest, could be said to be unfair, even if the refusal to provide the information sought was potentially harmful).

Inefficient

23-95   It will be recalled that an administrator is under an obligation to perform his functions as quickly and efficiently as is reasonably practicable (Sch B1, para 4), see **23-7**. To provide an incentive to adhere to that obligation, a creditor or member of a company in administration may apply to the court claiming that the administrator is in breach of this requirement (Sch B1, para 74(2)).

23-96   The court may take a variety of steps on an application on either of the grounds above including granting relief, dismissing the application, adjourning the hearing, making an interim order or any other order it thinks appropriate; but an order must not impede or prevent the implementation of a voluntary arrangement or a scheme of arrangement or any proposals approved by the creditors.[162] The range of possible orders includes requiring an administrator to do or not to do a specified thing or requiring a creditors' meeting to be held for a specified purpose (Sch B1, para 74(4)).

Misfeasance

23-97   The court on the application of the Official Receiver, an administrator or liquidator of the company, or a creditor or contributory of the company may examine the conduct of an administrator (Sch B1, para 75(1), (2)). The grounds for such an investigation are allegations that the administrator has misapplied or retained or become accountable for money or other property of the company, or has breached a fiduciary or other duty in relation to the company, or has been guilty of misfeasance (Sch B1, para 75(3)). The court may order the administrator to repay or account for money to the company, to pay interest, and to contribute a sum to the company's property by way of compensation for breach of duty or misfeasance (Sch B1, para 75(4)). This provision is an improvement on the previous position which required the company to go into liquidation before a misfeasance action could be brought against an administrator.

F   Ending administration—exit routes

23-98   The appointment of an administrator ceases at the end of the period of one year beginning with the date on which it takes effect, but the period may be extended by the court for a specified period on the application of the administrator.[163] The creditors may extend the administrator's term of office (once) for a specified period not exceeding six months by consent, which is defined as the consent of each secured creditor and more than 50% of the unsecured creditors who respond to the request to

---

[162] IA 1986, Sch B1, para 74(3), (4), and (6).

[163] IA 1986, Sch B1, para 76(1), (2); and the court may do so even if the period has already been extended by order or consent: para 77(1). The *Insolvency Service Evaluation Report* (2008), above n 19, found that 80% of administrations within the sample reviewed were completed within one year and the remainder within 18 months and so these findings would suggest that the time parameters set by the Act are suitable: see *Evaluation Report*, para 3.5.

give consent.[164] An extension by consent cannot be given after an extension has been ordered by the court.

Termination of administration

An administrator must apply to the court to bring the administration to an end if he **23-99** thinks the purpose of administration cannot be achieved; or that the company should not have entered administration; or if required to do so by a creditors' meeting (Sch B1, para 79(2)). The administrator must also apply to the court to bring an administration to an end where he has been appointed by the court and he has achieved the purpose of administration.[165]

Additionally, a creditor can apply to the court to have an administration stopped if **23-100** he or she considers that the appointment was made for an improper motive (Sch B1, para 81). The court may also order that the appointment of an administrator is to cease where a winding-up order is made on a public interest petition.[166]

Where the administrator has been appointed out of court, i.e. by a qualifying floating **23-101** charge holder or by the company or directors, and he considers that the purpose of administration has been sufficiently achieved, he may file a notice with the court and the registrar of companies and his appointment ceases on that filing.[167]

Administration to voluntary winding up

An administrator can end the administration and convert to a voluntary winding **23-102** up where the administrator thinks that the secured creditors have received all that they are likely to receive (remember the administrator can make distributions to secured and preferential creditors) and there is money available for the unsecured creditors (Sch B1, para 83).[168] The Insolvency Service found that this ability to convert from administration to a creditors' voluntary liquidation was one of the most marked consequences of the reforms effected by the EA 2002 and the result is that the lines between the two processes have become somewhat blurred.[169] Indeed, the use of this

---

[164] IA 1986, Sch B1, paras 76(2)(b), 78(1). It may be that only the consent of preferential and secured creditors is required: see para 78(2).

[165] IA 1986, Sch B1, para 79(3). On the hearing of the application, the court may adjourn the hearing, dismiss the application, make any interim order, or make any order it thinks appropriate: para 79(4).

[166] IA 1986, Sch B1, para 82; equally, the court may order that the administrator remain in post, see para 82(3). As to a public interest petition, see above n 26.

[167] IA 1986, Sch B1, para 80(1)–(3). The administrator must send a copy of this notice to every creditor of whom he is aware: para 80(4), (5).

[168] Indeed, even if this mechanism is not available (because the administrator does not think he can make a distribution to unsecured creditors), an administrator can seek an order under IA 1986, Sch B1, para 79 that the administration end at a specified time, that time being the passing of a resolution for the company to go into a creditors' voluntary liquidation, so allowing a seamless passage from administration to a CVL in this way: see *Re T M Kingdom Ltd* [2007] BCC 480.

[169] See *Insolvency Service Evaluation Report* (2008), above n 19, paras 3.6 and 3.8, which also notes that this means that administration is often a terminal event with few companies emerging from the process as 'active' companies, see para 3.7.

process has raised queries as to whether there remains a need for the creditors' voluntary liquidation procedure or whether the normal gateway for a CVL should be via administration.[170]

23-103   This conversion option is available even to an administrator appointed by court order, and it is not necessary in that case first to obtain a court order terminating the administration.[171] Whether it is appropriate to convert the administration to voluntary winding up (i.e. whether the circumstances exist for the use of the procedure) is a matter for the administrator[172] and the administrator is not subject to any objective test when so deciding.[173]

23-104   The administrator must send the appropriate notice to the registrar of companies and a copy of this notice is filed with the court and sent to each of the company's creditors of whom he is aware (Sch B1, para 83(5)). Once the notice is registered by the registrar of companies, the administrator's appointment ends and the company moves into a creditors' voluntary winding up as if a resolution for winding up had been passed on the date of registration of the notice (Sch B1, para 83(6)).[174] The administrator becomes the liquidator unless the creditors choose to appoint someone else (Sch B1, para 83(7)). It is the registration of the notice from the administrator which causes the appointment of the administrator to cease to have effect and the operative date is the date of registration and the Parliamentary intention is that the company passes from administration to winding up without any hiatus.[175]

23-105   A particular problem under the old law related to the position of the preferential creditors who were disadvantaged if the company went from administration into voluntary rather than compulsory liquidation for reasons to do with the date at which the preferential debts were calculated. Various contorted schemes were devised to address this difficulty,[176] but the issue has been resolved, for the date for determining the relevant preferential debts, even if the company subsequently goes into liquidation, is now the date on which the company enters administration (IA 1986, s 387).

Administration to dissolution

23-106   If the administrator thinks that the company has no property or no remaining property which might permit a distribution to its creditors, he must send a notice to that effect to the registrar of companies (Sch B1, para 84) and this requirement

---

[170] See Frisby, *Report on Insolvency Outcomes—presented to the Insolvency Service* (2006), p 81.

[171] *Re Ballast plc* [2005] 1 BCLC 446.   [172] *Re Ballast plc* [2005] 1 BCLC 446.

[173] *Unidare plc v Cohen* [2006] 2 BCLC 140.

[174] A notice sent but not registered before the administration automatically ended (one year having elapsed, Sch B1, para 76) is still effective for these purposes for the crucial requirement is that it is sent by an administrator before his appointment ceases to have effect: *Re E Squared Ltd* [2006] 2 BCLC 277.

[175] *Re E Squared Ltd* [2006] 2 BCLC 277. See Todd, 'Administration Post-Enterprise Act—What are the Options for Exits' (2006) 19 Insolv Int 17 who comments that this mechanism makes 'for a very slick exit indeed' with no need to advertise the liquidator's appointment or to hold a creditors' meeting and with the administrator becoming liquidator (though he can later be replaced).

[176] See, for example, *Re Mark One (Oxford St) plc* [2000] 1 BCLC 462.

applies to administrators appointed by the court and out of court.[177] On receipt of this notice, the registrar must register it and three months after the filing, the company is deemed dissolved. As under Sch B1, para 83, this option is entirely a matter for the administrator, even an administrator appointed by court order, and it is not necessary to obtain a court order terminating the administration.[178]

The nature of the obligation imposed on the administrator by Sch B1, para 84 was   **23-107** considered in *Re GHE Realisations Ltd*[179] where the court held that once the administrator 'thinks' that the company has no further assets (regardless of whether the company had assets which had previously been distributed) he is under a duty to serve a notice under Sch B1, para 84(1), subject always to the option of making an application under para 84(2) for the court to disapply para 84(1). In other words, para 84 is not limited to the scenario where the company never had any assets for distribution.

Vacation of office

An administrator can resign his office by giving the required notice (Sch B1, para 87),   **23-108** he can be removed from office by the court (Sch B1, para 88), and he must vacate his office if he ceases to be qualified to act as an insolvency practitioner (Sch B1, para 89).

G Administration expenses and liabilities

Where a person ceases to be an administrator,[180] his remuneration and any expenses   **23-109** are charged on and payable out of property of which he had custody or control immediately before he ceased to be the company's administrator and are payable in priority to any security which, as created, was a floating charge (Sch B1, para 99(1)–(3)).[181] This provision gives the administrator's claim for remuneration and expenses priority over the claims of the holder of a floating charge.[182]

---

[177] *Re Ballast plc* [2005] 1 BCLC 446.   [178] *Re Ballast plc* [2005] 1 BCLC 446.
[179] [2006] 1 All ER 357.

[180] Although strictly speaking the Insolvency Act envisages these payments being made when the administration ceases, in fact the administrator will pay these expenses as they arise in the course of the administration: see *Powdrill v Watson* [1994] 2 BCLC 118 at 142.

[181] The detailed rules as to administration expenses is set out at IR 1986, r 2.67 which mimics r 4.218 in respect of liquidation expenses. For an account of the problems which arise from the adoption of the 'liquidation expenses' approach in administration, see Moss, 'Rescue Culture Speared by Trident' (2007) 20 Insolv Int 72 which also addresses specifically the problems arising from the ruling in *Re Trident Fashions Ltd, Exeter City Co v Bairstow* [2007] 2 BCLC 455 (business rates payable in respect of occupied property were 'necessary disbursements' falling within IR 1986, r 2.67(1)(f) and therefore administration expenses; likewise with respect to unoccupied premises).The specific issue of rates for unoccupied premises which Moss and others had argued would make administration for retail companies with large numbers of properties unworkable (because of the costs involved) has been resolved by SI 2008/386 which exempts companies in administration from rates on unoccupied premises as is the case for companies in liquidation.

[182] A floating charge holder is also subject to the application of the prescribed part under IA 1986, s 176A which applies in administration as in liquidation: see **24-91**.

23-110   Priority over both the administrator's remuneration and expenses and the claim of a floating charge holder is given in respect of any sum payable in respect of debts or liabilities arising out of a contract entered into by the former administrator before he ceased to be the administrator (Sch B1, para 99(4)).[183] This provision creates a statutory charge in favour of these claimants which attaches to any property of which the administrator had custody or control immediately before he ceased to be the administrator and, if that property is insufficient to meet all of those claims, the claimants must be paid pari passu.[184]

23-111   This super-priority, as it is often called, for contractual liabilities extends to any liability arising out of a contract of employment adopted by the former administrator before he ceased to be the company's administrator.[185] For this purpose, the administrator is not to be taken to have adopted a contract of employment by reason of anything done within 14 days of his appointment; and no account is taken of any liabilities by reference to anything done before the adoption of the contract and no account is taken of a liability to make a payment other than wages or salary.[186] 'Salary' for these purposes does include an employer's liability to pay PAYE and National Insurance Contributions to the Revenue since these payments are part of a salary and liability for them can only arise when a salary payment is made to an employee. Therefore such sums have priority over the payment of the administrator's remuneration and expenses of administration.[187] But payments in lieu of notice and protective awards,[188] redundancy and unfair dismissal payments[189] and wrongful dismissal awards[190] are not wages or salary for these purposes and therefore do not benefit from

---

[183] This 'super-priority' does not extend to expenses incurred under contracts entered into by the company prior to administration: *Centre Reinsurance International Co v Freakley* [2007] 1 BCLC 85 (expenses incurred by a company's insurers in administering and handling claims by employees under an insurance policy were not recoverable as such expenses did not represent a debt payable or a liability incurred under a contract entered into by the administrators in carrying out their functions for these purposes).

[184] *Re Spread Betting Media Ltd* [2008] 2 BCLC 89; and in these circumstances the court, in the exercise of its inherent jurisdiction may order that the administrators be paid a reasonable sum out of the available funds.

[185] IA 1986, Sch B1, para 99(5). These provisions originated in the IA 1994: see *Re a company (No 005174 of 1999)* [2001] 1 BCLC 593 at 597–8.

[186] IA 1986, Sch B1, para 99(5); and 'wages or salary' are defined in para 99(6) to include contributions to an occupational pension scheme. See *Powdrill v Watson* [1995] 2 All ER 65, HL.

[187] *Inland Revenue Commissioners v Lawrence* [2001] 1 BCLC 204, CA.

[188] *Re Huddersfield Fine Worsteds Ltd* [2006] 2 BCLC 160. Payments of protective awards and most payments in lieu of notice in respect of employees whose contracts of employment are adopted do not have priority to the expenses of the administration. The only exception is with respect to one limited category of payments in lieu of notice. The exception is where an employer, having given notice to an employee, decides not to require the employee to work his notice and pays the wages attributable to the notice period in a lump sum (so-called 'garden leave'). Such payments are 'wages' since they are payments in lieu of the wages which would have been payable had the notice been worked and, as such, are entitled to super-priority over the expenses of the administration.

[189] *Re Allders Department Stores Ltd* [2006] 2 BCLC 1.

[190] *Re Leeds United AFC Ltd* [2008] BCC 11. If a payment is not referable to an obligation of an employee under a subsisting contract of employment to render his services, it does not fall within the ordinary meaning of the word 'wages'. Any payment on account of an employee's claim for damages for breach of contract is not a payment of 'wages' in the ordinary meaning of that word.

the statutory super-priority on insolvency. The courts are anxious not to take such a wide construction of 'wages or salary' as to undermine the rescue culture by making administration more expensive.[191]

The result is that in the context of administration, claims are to be ranked as fol- **23-112**
lows: (1) secured creditors with fixed charges in relation to their security; (2) debts and liabilities arising from contracts entered into by the administrator including liabilities for 'wages or salary' arising under contracts of employment adopted by the administrator; (3) expenses of administration including the administrator's remuneration; (4) claims under a floating charge (subject to the application of the prescribed part under IA 1986, s 176A: see **24-91**); and (5) unsecured creditors.[192]

H Concluding issues—trends in administration

With 'new' administration (see **23-2**) now well established and the number of appoint- **23-113**
ments of administrators steadily rising,[193] certain key issues have emerged as to the administration regime and, no doubt, managing the credit crunch will throw up further concerns in due course.[194]

Pre-pack administrations

A particular issue is the development of pre-pack administrations (pre-packs) by **23-114**
which is meant the process whereby a company in difficulty consults an insolvency practitioner for assistance and a plan emerges (in consultation typically with a major bank creditor) for the sale of the business often to the existing management,[195] but perhaps to an outside purchaser. All aspects of the pre-pack deal are determined ahead of the company being put into administration, typically by an out-of-court appointment by the bank or the directors. On going into administration, the business

---

[191] *Re Huddersfield Fine Worsteds Ltd* [2006] 2 BCLC 160 at 190–1, CA; *Re Allders Department Stores Ltd* [2006] 2 BCLC 1.

[192] See *Re a company (No 005174 of 1999)* [2001] 1 BCLC 593 at 597–8.

[193] In 2004–05 there were 1,786 appointments of administrators, in 2007–08 the figure had risen to 2,733: see *Statistical Tables on Companies Registration Activities 2007–08*, Table C2, available on Companies House website at www.companieshouse.gov.uk/about/companiesRegActivities.shtml.

[194] See generally Finch, 'Corporate Rescue in a World of Debt' [2008] JBL 756 who questions whether new rescue mechanisms are going to be needed to deal with the emergence of debt as a commodity which has been traded and dealt with in a way far removed from the banker–lender role as envisaged by many insolvency processes. Much valuable work on the evaluation of the EA 2002 reforms has been conducted for the Insolvency Service by insolvency expert Dr Sandra Frisby: see Frisby, 'The Pre-Pack Progression: Latest Empirical Findings' (2008) 21 Insolv Int 154; Frisby, *Report on Insolvency Outcomes—presented to the Insolvency Service* (2006); also Frisby, *Interim Report to the Insolvency Service on Returns to Creditors from Pre- and Post-Enterprise Insolvency Procedures* (2007) which have been the basis, with other studies, for the Insolvency Service's own *Evaluation Report* (2008), above n 19.

[195] Sales to the directors when the company is in administration do not require shareholder approval under CA 2006, s 190: see s 193(1).

is instantly sold without any creditors' meeting being called or any proposals being approved (as the administrator is entitled to do, as discussed at **23-80**). The proceeds of sale are distributed by the administrator and, where there are no funds for distribution to the unsecured creditors, the administrator files notice with the registrar and the company is dissolved under Sch B1, para 84, as discussed at **23-106**. One of the interesting aspects of this development is the mismatch between the legislation 'on the books' and how administration has developed in practice since, as one commentator put it, pre-packs are invisible in the insolvency legislation.[196]

23-115   Pre-packs have attracted a great deal of comment, much of it critical.[197] There are concerns about various matters including:

(1) it is unclear to what extent, given the speed involved, the administrator can be said to be acting in accordance with the priorities laid down in Sch B1, para 3 (see **23-6**);[198]

(2) there are concerns about the sidelining of the unsecured creditors given one of the aims of administration was to allow them to have a greater say (or at least involvement) in the process;

(3) the general lack of transparency about the deal raises issues (especially when the business is sold to the existing management) as to whether true market value was secured and whether other purchasers might have been willing to offer a higher price, and this concern persists even though independent valuations are standard;[199]

(4) the role of the administrator and whether he has fettered his discretion and has a conflict of interest between his pre-administration role in advising the company on its difficulties and his post-appointment role which requires him to act in the interests of the creditors as a whole. There are also issues as to the ability of the administrator to recover his pre-appointment costs and the manner in which such costs are funded.[200] The courts have been reluctant

---

[196] See Davies, 'Pre-pack—he who pays the piper calls the tune' Recovery (Summer 2006) p 16; also Walton, 'Pre-Packaged Administration—Trick or Treat' (2006) 19 Insolv Int 113.

[197] See generally Frisby, *Report to the Association of Business Recovery Professionals, A Preliminary Analysis of pre-packaged administrations* (August 2007); Walton, 'Pre-appointment administration fees— papering over the cracks in pre-packs?' (2008) 21 Insolv Int 72; Kastrinou, 'An analysis of the pre-pack technique and recent developments in the area' (2008) 29 Co Law 259; Qi, 'The Rise of Pre-Packaged Corporate Rescue on Both Sides of the Atlantic' (2007) 20 Insolv Int 129; Finch, 'Pre-packaged administrations: bargains in the shadow of insolvency or shadowy bargains?' [2006] JBL 568.

[198] On this point, see SIP 16, n 202 below, para 7 which reminds administrators to bear these purposes in mind and that they should be able to demonstrate that they have acted in the interests of the creditors as a whole and in making a distribution to secured or preferential creditors have avoided unnecessarily harming the interests of the creditors as a whole.

[199] Though independent valuations are used, a perception of a 'stitch-up' can remain: see Frisby, *Report on Insolvency Outcomes—presented to the Insolvency Service* (2006), p 70.

[200] See Walton, 'Pre-Appointment Administration Fees—Papering Over the Cracks in Pre-Packs' (2008) 21 Insolv Int 72 who is sharply critical of Insolvency Service proposals to modify the Insolvency Rules to facilitate the recovery of pre-appointment fees in a way which may further sideline the unsecured creditors; see also Bacon, 'Administration Costs: Some Welcome News' (2007) 20 Insolv Int 1. The intention is

to express any disapproval of pre-packs as such and the Insolvency Service, with its proposals to allow for the recovery of pre-appointment costs, seems equally untroubled by the rise of the pre-pack though in favour of greater transparency.[201]

This need for greater transparency is highlighted in guidance on pre-packs issued   **23-116**
to insolvency practitioners which came into effect on 1 January 2009. A Statement of Insolvency Practice (SIP 16) sets out very detailed requirements as to the extensive information which must be disclosed to creditors in all cases where there is a pre-packed sale.[202] The information to be disclosed includes the extent of the administrator's involvement with the company prior to his appointment as administrator; any alternative courses of action that were considered; an explanation of why it was not appropriate to continue trading and sell the business as a going concern; details of the assets involved, the identity of the purchaser and any connection between the purchaser and the directors, shareholders or secured creditors of the company.[203] The Statement notes that this information should be provided in all cases unless there are exceptional circumstances and that, if the sale is to a connected party, it is unlikely that considerations of commercial confidentiality would outweigh the need for creditors to be provided with this information.[204] The Statement also stresses the need for practitioners to bear in mind the nature and extent of their role in the pre-appointment period when regard needs to be had to the interests of the company and any duties which may be owed to creditors while the directors should be encouraged to take independent advice.[205] It will be interesting to see whether compliance with this guidance (which is required of practitioners) will reduce the concerns raised about the use of pre-packs.

The arguments in favour of pre-packaged administration are that it offers precisely   **23-117**
the sort of rapid, solution-driven, process which is required when a company is in financial difficulties and does so without the business being visibly in an insolvency process, so maximising value. The focus is on 'rescuing' those elements of the business which can be salvaged, preserving brands and employment and the expedition enables costs to be reduced.[206] The reality in many instances is that there are no funds for unsecured creditors and no willing purchasers other than the existing management for whom a pre-pack is an opportunity to salvage something from

that the administrators will be required to explain their actions in selling companies through a pre-pack to the full body of creditors as a precondition for getting the creditors to authorise the payment of any pre-appointment expenses. While welcoming the requirement for an explanation, the Insolvency Practices Council has noted that the ability to recover pre-appointment expenses may provide a perverse incentive to ignore the conflict of interest involved in acting pre-appointment and post-appointment: see Insolvency Practices Council, *Annual Report 2007*, p 11.

[201] See above n 200.

[202] Statement of Insolvency Practice (SIP) 16, 'Pre-Packaged Sales in Administration,' effective 1 January 2009, hereafter SIP 16.

[203] SIP 16, para 9.   [204] SIP 16, para 10.   [205] SIP 16, paras 5–7.

[206] Initial research suggest that pre-packs perform better than business sales in preserving employment, see Frisby, *Preliminary Analysis*, above n 197, p 71.

the situation.[207] Also aggrieved creditors are not without mechanism for redress, as noted above at **23-93**.

The role of liquidation

23-118   As noted above, it is becoming increasingly common for administrators either to convert an administration into a creditors' voluntary liquidation or to make a distribution to unsecured creditors and then file notice for dissolution under Sch B1, para 84.[208] In other words, the process either becomes a liquidation or is conducted as a liquidation followed by dissolution and the issue is whether there is some abuse of process involved in this development.[209] On the one hand, it is difficult to see a risk of abuse—the administrator is a licensed insolvency practitioner, as is a liquidator; the administrator has power to challenge vulnerable transactions and must report on whether the directors are unfit and should be disqualified, as does a liquidator. The expenses of administration as set out in IR 1986, r 2.67 mirror those set out for liquidation in IR 1986, r 4.218.[210] The requirement to set aside a prescribed part for unsecured creditors applies in administration and liquidation. In other words, in some ways the processes are very similar so it may not matter very much which route is used. On the other hand, there are concerns that administrators are using the process as a way of increasing their fees by having the company go into administration first and then into liquidation when objectively it might have been evident that the purpose of administration cannot be achieved and the company should have gone straight into liquidation with lower costs to creditors.[211] An abuse may lie in the speed of the pre-pack where the entire matter is completed very quickly with little engagement with the unsecured creditors in particular. In a liquidation a liquidator has a duty to investigate the causes of collapse (though the extent to which this happens in a voluntary liquidation is debatable) and the directors' conduct may be open to greater scrutiny. For

---

[207] See Frisby, *Preliminary Analysis*, above n 197, p 46 who found a demonstrable trend towards pre-pack sales to connected persons.

[208] In 2004–05, 361 administrations were converted into a creditors' voluntary liquidation, by 2007–08 the figure was 1,101; see *Statistical Tables on Companies Registration Activities 2007–08*, Table C2, available on Companies House website at www.companieshouse.gov.uk/about/companiesRegActivities.shtml.

[209] See Keay, 'What future for liquidation in light of the Enterprise Act Reforms?' [2005] JBL 143; Frieze, 'The Company in Financial Difficulties: The Alternatives' (2008) 21 Insolv Int 124 at 126.

[210] The temporary advantage of administration over liquidation in terms of the ability to have resort to floating charge realisations to pay the expenses of administration including the administrator's remuneration (Sch B1, para 99(3)(b)), created by the decision in *Re Leyland Daf, Buchler v Talbot* [2004] 1 BCLC 281, no longer applies following the reversal of that decision by the CA 2006: see now IA 1986, s 176ZA.

[211] See Mumford & Katz, 'Study of Administration Cases' (2007) 20 Insolv Int 97 at 102 who found that while the majority of cases studied by them were situations where the company had been properly put into administration, they found that in 29% of the cases studied, there were greater doubts about why the company was in administration rather than liquidation, but those 29% of cases involved smaller companies which amounted to only 3% by asset value of the companies surveyed. The Insolvency Service view is that, if there are concerns about the appropriateness of some administrations, that is a matter for the regulatory body of the relevant administrator to consider: see *Insolvency Service Evaluation Report* (2008), above n 19, para 3.8.

example, a liquidator, but not an administrator, can bring a claim for wrongful trading or fraudulent trading under IA 1986, ss 213, 214, see **25-6**. A director also has to face a creditors' meeting in a creditors' voluntary liquidation (IA 1986, s 99(1)) but can avoid this process in an administration.

The demise of administrative receivership

As predicted, even when creditors are able to appoint administrative receivers, because they have a qualifying floating charge created before 15 September 2003, the trend is to appoint an administrator rather than an administrative receiver.[212]   **23-119**

The position of the unsecured creditor

As mentioned above, one of the aims of administration is that it is to be a collective procedure conducted in the interests of the creditors as a whole and the intention was to move away from the days when an administrative receiver could conduct a receivership with little or no regard to the interests of other creditors. As mentioned, the rise of the pre-pack and the ability, even when there is no pre-pack, for an administrator to sell assets without the need for the consent of the creditors or a direction of the court (see **23-80**) has meant that the unsecured creditors are in many ways as sidelined under this process as they were under administrative receiverships.[213] That situation might be tolerable if it could be shown that returns to the unsecured creditors have improved, but the picture on shareholder returns is mixed.[214] Essentially, secured and preferential creditors have maintained, if not improved, their levels of returns on administration compared to administrative receiverships, but ordinary unsecured creditors have yet to see much improvement in returns to them from administration[215] (though their position may improve because of the prescribed part: see **24-91**).[216]   **23-120**

---

[212] Figures for Great Britain show that the number of receiverships halved between 2003–04 (1,284) and 2007–08 (634): see *Statistical Tables on Companies Registration Activities 2007–08*, Table C2, available on Companies House website at www.companieshouse.gov.uk/about/companiesRegActivities.shtml.

[213] See Walton, 'Pre-Appointment Administration Fees—Papering Over the Cracks in Pre-Packs' (2008) 21 Insolv Int 72.

[214] See Mumford & Katz, 'Study of Administration Cases' (2007) 20 Insolv Int 97 at 102 who believe that administration is likely to produce a result at least equal to that achievable in a creditors' voluntary liquidation.

[215] See Frisby, *Preliminary Analysis*, above n 197, who found that the average return to secured creditors in pre-packs was 42% and in business sales the average return was 28%; the equivalent figures for preferential creditors were 13% and 38%; and for unsecured creditors were 1% and 3%: see pp 53–7.

[216] See *Insolvency Service Evaluation Report* (2008), above n 19, para 3.10; Frisby, *Report on Insolvency Outcomes—presented to the Insolvency Service* (2006), p 73; Frisby, *Interim Report to the Insolvency Service on Returns to Creditors from Pre- and Post-Enterprise Insolvency Procedures* (2007). Also note that while realisations may have increased in administration compared to receiverships, there is clear evidence of higher costs as well: see Armour, Hsu and Walters, 'The Impact of the Enterprise Act 2002 on Realisations and Costs in Corporate Rescue Proceedings, A Report Prepared for the Insolvency Service' (2006), paras 3.4–3.5.

A rescue culture

23-121   As to whether administration has resulted in more businesses being rescued, the jury is still out and a longer period of evaluation is required. No doubt, the current recession will produce a suitable database for review, say in five years' time when the legislation is 10 years old. The Insolvency Service evaluation to date has noted that the proportion of actual rescue is very low, which raises the question in their view as to whether any formal insolvency process is almost bound to be terminal.[217] The standard outcome of administration in many cases is an asset sale via a pre-pack, as discussed above, so the outcome is not dissimilar to receivership.[218]

[217] See *Insolvency Service Evaluation Report* (2008), para 3.7.
[218] See Frisby, *Report on Insolvency Outcomes—presented to the Insolvency Service* (2006), p 59.

24

Liquidation and dissolution—
winding up the insolvent company

A Introduction

Winding up is a term commonly associated with the ending of a company's existence.   **24-1**
In fact, winding up or liquidation (the terms are synonymous) is the process by which
the assets of the company are collected in and realised, its liabilities discharged and
the net surplus, if there is one, distributed to the persons entitled to it.[1] Only when
this has been done is the company's existence finally terminated by a process known
as dissolution. Companies cannot be made bankrupt: bankruptcy is the legal process
by which the assets of an insolvent individual or partnership are realised and the proceeds distributed to the creditors.[2]

A company being wound up may be solvent or insolvent. A solvent company may   **24-2**
be wound up because the business opportunity which the company was formed to
exploit has come to an end, or because the members of a family business may wish to
retire, or because of internal disputes. Winding up on the just and equitable ground
under IA 1986, s 122(1)(g) in cases where the relationship between the members has
completely broken down is one of the shareholder remedies discussed in Chapter 18:
see **18-71**. This chapter concentrates on the winding up of insolvent companies.

Insolvent winding up occurs essentially when companies are unable to pay their debts   **24-3**
in full. When a company cannot pay its debts in full, difficult problems arise as to how
the assets that are available should be distributed. In theory, as we shall see, the law
tries to maintain an equality between creditors so that assets are pooled and distributed pari passu, i.e. rateably according to the size of each creditor's claim. In fact, as
the level of distribution to creditors claiming against the pooled assets is likely to be
very small, much effort is expended by creditors and their advisers in devising ways
of ensuring that they do not have to claim against the pooled assets on the company's
insolvency. This they do in various ways such as by taking security with respect to the
debt due to them. All these issues are discussed below.

A further distinction is that winding up may be either compulsory or voluntary (IA   **24-4**
1986, s 73(1)). A compulsory winding up is where a court orders that the company be

---

[1] See IA 1986, ss 107, 143(1).   [2] The bankruptcy rules are set out in IA 1986, ss 264–385.

wound up; a voluntary winding up is where the members of the company resolve that the company be wound up. Each is considered below.

24-5   As discussed in Chapter 23, the lines between administration and liquidation have been blurred: see **23-118**. In many administrations, the outcome is an asset sale followed by a distribution to the creditors (including to unsecured creditors with the consent of the court) and the company is then dissolved by notice to the registrar under IA 1986, Sch B1, para 84. Alternatively, many administrations are converted to creditors' voluntary liquidations under Sch B1, para 83 with the administrator becoming the liquidator, a process which short-circuits many of the provisions discussed below. It may be that matters will evolve such that administration becomes the gateway for all creditors' voluntary liquidations: see discussion at **23-118**. It is also the case that where a receiver or administrative receiver has been appointed, the unsecured creditors may decide to put the company into liquidation so receivership may be, although it need not be, a forerunner to liquidation. It is then the case that a company may go directly into liquidation or it may be that winding up is preceded by some other form of insolvency proceedings.

The legislative framework

24-6   The core insolvency legislation is the Insolvency Act 1986 which must be read together with Insolvency Rules 1986 which contain the procedural rules and requirements (new consolidated Insolvency Rules 2009 are planned for October 2009). As discussed at **23-2**, the Insolvency Act 1986 has been amended on a number of occasions, in particular, by the Enterprise Act 2002 which restricted the right to appoint administrative receivers and provided for a new regime for administration. That Act also significantly reduced the categories of preferential or Crown debts and made provision for the 'prescribed part' (a sum to be set aside from floating charge realisations for the benefit of unsecured creditors), all of which are discussed below.

24-7   One of the most important insolvency developments in recent years has been the recognition that the nature of corporate business and structures (in particular the widespread use of corporate groups) is such that many insolvencies of any size now involve a cross-border element. This factor raises many issues, the most basic being the need to decide which jurisdiction should govern any insolvency process. The choice is essentially between territorialism (each jurisdiction acts with regard to assets within its jurisdiction), universalism (one jurisdiction assumes responsibility for all the assets and liabilities wherever located) or, more pragmatically, a modified universalism which involves identifying the jurisdiction best placed to deal with the insolvent entities while recognising the sovereign right of other jurisdictions to manage aspects of the insolvency process within their territories in respect of assets and liabilities located there.[3]

---

[3] See the discussion in *Re HIH Casualty and General Insurance Ltd; McMahon v McGrath* [2008] 3 All ER 869, HL.

The European framework reflecting these issues is the EC Regulation on Insolvency **24-8** Proceedings (Council Regulation (EC) No 1346/2000)[4] which came into effect on 31 May 2002 throughout the EU (with the exception of Denmark) and which applies to relevant insolvency proceedings (see **24-9**) opened on or after that date. As a Regulation, it has direct effect and it is now an integral element of our insolvency law. Implementing legislation was not required but consequential amendments were made to the Insolvency Act 1986 and the Insolvency Rules 1986 to ensure the effective operation of the Regulation.[5] The aim of the Regulation is to improve the efficiency and effectiveness of insolvency proceedings having cross-border effect, but it does not attempt to harmonise insolvency procedures throughout the EU and generally the applicable law is the national law of the state in which proceedings are opened. The Regulation applies only when the debtor has his centre of main interests within the EU (other than Denmark) and it deals only with procedures, assets and creditors within the EU.[6]

The insolvency proceedings within the UK which are affected by the Regulation **24-9** (and which therefore can only be opened in accordance with the rules laid down by the Regulation) and which enjoy automatic recognition and enforcement under the Regulation are:

(1) compulsory winding up[7] and creditors' voluntary winding up with confirmation of the court[8] (winding-up procedures are discussed below); and

(2) voluntary arrangements and administration (which are discussed in Chapters 22 and 23, respectively).

The Regulation does not apply to receiverships, winding up on the just and equitable ground (a shareholder remedy) or members' voluntary winding up (company is not insolvent).

The main advantage of the Regulation is that it establishes a clear structure for the **24-10** commencement and recognition of insolvency proceedings where there is a cross-border element involving business in more than one Member State. Essentially, the

---

[4] OJ L 160/1, 30 June 2000; see generally Fletcher, *The Law of Insolvency* (4th edn, 2009), Ch 31; Moss, Fletcher and Isaacs, *The EC Regulation on Insolvency Proceedings: A Commentary and Annotated Guide* (2nd edn, 2009); also Omar, 'Addressing the Reform of the Insolvency Regulation: Wishlists or Fancies' (2007) 20 Insolv Int 7.

[5] See, in particular, The Insolvency Act 1986 (Amendment) Regulations 2002, SI 2002/1037; The Insolvency Act 1986 (Amendment) (No 2) Regulations 2002, SI 2002/1240; and The Insolvency (Amendment) Rules 2002, SI 2002/1307.

[6] The Regulation also confers jurisdiction on the courts of a Member State to open insolvency proceedings in relation to a company incorporated outside the Community, if the centre of the company's main interests is in that Member State: *Re BRAC Rent-a-Car International Inc* [2003] 1 BCLC 470.

[7] In *Re Marann Brooks CSV Ltd* [2003] BPIR 1159 Patten J thought, obiter, that the Regulation has no application to winding-up petitions brought by the Secretary of State on public interest grounds under IA 1986, s 124A.

[8] A creditors' voluntary winding up does not require confirmation by the court but a liquidator in such a winding up may apply to the court for a confirmation order for the purposes of the EC Regulation: see IR 1986, r 7.62.

Regulation provides for main proceedings, territorial proceedings and secondary proceedings (see art 3).

24-11 Main proceedings may be opened in the Member State where the debtor had his 'centre of main interests' which is presumed, in the case of a company, to be the place of the registered office.[9] Territorial proceedings may be opened in any Member State where the debtor has an establishment,[10] but such proceedings are restricted to the assets situated in that Member State. Where the territorial proceedings are commenced after the opening of main proceedings, the proceedings are described as secondary proceedings and they must be winding up rather than rescue proceedings. Territorial proceedings may be opened prior to the opening of main proceedings only in the circumstances set out in art 3(4), namely where main proceedings cannot be opened because of some jurisdictional difficulty in the Member State where the centre of the debtor's main interests is situated; or the creditor requesting the territorial proceedings has his domicile, habitual residence or registered office in the same territory in which the establishment of the debtor is situated or whose claim arises from the operation of that establishment. Where main proceedings are opened in the UK (which can only be if the debtor's centre of main interests is in the UK) and there are no secondary proceedings elsewhere in the EU, the liquidator may deal with all the assets wherever situated in the EU. If secondary proceedings are opened elsewhere in the EU, the liquidator in the main proceedings cannot deal with assets in those Member States (art 18).

24-12 Main proceedings are effective in all Member States as long as no territorial proceedings have been opened (art 17) and the liquidator appointed in the main proceedings is able immediately to exercise his powers in other Member States in accordance with the general law of that Member State (art 18) and is required to furnish only a certified copy of his appointment in order so to act (art 19). To ensure that all concurrent proceedings are properly co-ordinated, the liquidators in the main proceedings and in the secondary proceedings have a duty to co-operate and communicate with each other (art 31).

24-13 More recently the UK has given effect to the UNCITRAL Model Law on Cross-Border Insolvency Proceedings by the Cross-Border Insolvency Regulations 2006.[11] This Model Law (in the manner of the EU Regulation) does not seek to unify the

---

[9] An extensive jurisprudence is building up on the location of the centre of main interests ('COMI') since that determines which Member State has jurisdiction for main proceedings; the issue is especially important with regard to the 'comi' of corporate groups: see *Re Eurofood IFSC Ltd* (C-341/04) [2007] 2 BCLC 151; *Re BRAC Rent-A-Car International Inc* [2003] 1 BCLC 470; *Re Daisytek-ISA Ltd* [2004] BPIR 30. Also Moss and Haravon, 'Building Europe—The French Case Law on COMI' (2007) 20 Insolv Int 20; Mevorach, 'The "home country" of a multinational enterprise group facing insolvency' (2008) ICLQ 427.

[10] Defined in the EC Regulation as 'any place of operations where the debtor carries out a non-transitory economic activity with human means and goods': EC Regulation 1346/2000, art 2(h), OJ L 160, 30.06.2000, p 1.

[11] SI 2006/1030. See generally Fletcher, 'The UNCITRAL Model Law in the United Kingdom' (2007) 20 Insolv Int 138; Fletcher, ' "Better Late Than Never": The UNCITRAL Model Law enters into force in Great Britain' (2006) 19 Insolv Int 86.

substantive and procedural law on insolvency of the enacting States. It simply seeks to ease the access of foreign representatives and creditors to the courts and insolvency procedures of Great Britain and it is thought to be particularly valuable in the context of UK/US insolvencies. The Model Law entitles a foreign representative to apply directly to the courts to commence insolvency proceedings and to participate in such a proceeding once commenced. The Model Law also addresses specific issues such as the recognition of foreign proceedings, co-ordination of proceedings concerning the same debtor, rights of foreign creditors, the rights and duties of foreign representatives, and co-operation between national authorities. In the event of a conflict between the application of the Model Law and the EC Regulation, the Regulation prevails.

B Voluntary winding up

Resolution of the company

In practice, voluntary winding up is the most common form of winding up.[12] The advantage of proceeding in this way is that there is no court involvement so costs and time-scales may be reduced and the nomination of the liquidator is a matter for the members and/or the creditors. The official receiver (an official in the Insolvency Service who is appointed as the liquidator in a compulsory winding up) has no involvement in a voluntary winding up.   **24-14**

A voluntary winding up begins with a resolution passed by the members. An ordinary resolution is sufficient in the unusual case where the articles specify that the company is to be dissolved after the expiration of a fixed period of time or on the happening of a particular event, and that time has passed or event occurred (IA 1986, s 84(1)(a)). Alternatively, a special resolution that the company be wound up voluntarily may be passed (s 84(1)(b)). Five business days' notice of the intention to pass a resolution for voluntary winding up must be given to a floating charge holder which gives the charge holder an opportunity to appoint an administrator instead (s 84(2A)): see **23-42**.   **24-15**

A copy of the resolution for winding up must be forwarded to the registrar of companies within 15 days of being passed (IA 1986, s 84(3); and the company must give notice of the resolution by advertisement in the *Gazette* (s 85(1)). A voluntary winding up, whether a members' voluntary or a creditors' voluntary, is deemed to commence at the time of the passing of the resolution for voluntary winding up (s 86). From that commencement, the company ceases to carry on its business, except so far as may be required for its beneficial winding up (s 87(1)).   **24-16**

---

[12] In 2007–08, out of 15,281 insolvencies, 7,773 were creditors' voluntary liquidations (CVLs) and 1,101 administrations converted to CVLs; there were 6,407 compulsory liquidations and 4,914 members' voluntary liquidations: see *Statistical Tables on Companies Registration Activities 2007–08*, Table C2, available on Companies House website at www.companieshouse.gov.uk/about/companiesRegActivities.shtml.

Declaration of solvency—members' voluntary winding up

24-17 If in the five weeks immediately preceding the date of the resolution to wind up the company, or on the date of the resolution but before it is passed, the directors or a majority of the directors make a statutory declaration of solvency, the winding up is a members' voluntary winding up (IA 1986, ss 89, 90).

24-18 The statutory declaration must be to the effect that the directors have made a full enquiry into the affairs of the company and have formed the opinion that the company will be able to pay its debts in full (together with interest at the official rate) within such period, not exceeding 12 months from the date of the commencement of the winding up (i.e. the date of the passing of the resolution for winding up)[13] as may be specified in the declaration.[14]

24-19 The advantage to the directors in making such a declaration is that it enables the appointment of the liquidator by the members. The risk in doing so is that if the declaration is made by a director without reasonable grounds, he commits a criminal offence and, if the debts are not paid in full within the specified time, that raises a rebuttable presumption that the director did not have reasonable grounds for making the declaration.[15]

24-20 If it turns out that the declaration is erroneous and the liquidator appointed by the members is of opinion that the company will be unable to pay its debts in full within the 12-month period, he must summon a meeting of creditors within 28 days (IA 1986, s 95(1), (2)). As from the day of that meeting, the situation is treated as if no declaration of solvency was made and the winding up becomes from that date onwards a creditors' voluntary winding up.[16]

No declaration of solvency—creditors' voluntary winding up

24-21 If the directors do not make a statutory declaration of solvency, the winding up is a creditors' voluntary winding up (IA 1986, s 90). In this case, in addition to the meeting of members called to pass a resolution for the company to go into liquidation, as outlined above, a meeting of creditors must be summoned to take place not more than 14 days after the members' meeting (s 98(1)(a)).[17] The directors must lay before that meeting a statement as to the company's affairs showing, in particular, the company's assets, debts and liabilities and one of the directors must preside at the creditors' meeting (s 99(1)).[18]

---

[13] IA 1986, s 86.

[14] IA 1986, s 89(1). The statutory declaration must be delivered to the registrar of companies within 15 days after the resolution for winding up is passed: s 89(3). Failure to do so gives rise to criminal penalties.

[15] IA 1986, s 89(4), (5). As for the obligations of the directors in making this declaration, see Simmons, 'The Statutory Declaration of Solvency—Voluntary Winding Up of Companies—Members or Creditors' (1996) 9 Insolv Int 33.

[16] IA 1986, s 96. The general meeting already held and the creditors' meeting under s 95 are treated as if they were the meetings required under s 98 in the case of a creditors' voluntary winding up: s 96(b).

[17] IA 1986, s 98(1)(a).

[18] It is the duty of the director so appointed to attend and preside at the meeting and it is a criminal offence to fail to do so: IA 1986, s 99(1), (3).

Appointing a liquidator

Having passed a resolution for voluntary winding up, the members or the creditors proceed to appoint a liquidator. In a members' voluntary winding up, the members at their meeting to pass the resolution for winding up must appoint a liquidator (IA 1986, s 91(1)). In a creditors' voluntary winding up, the creditors may appoint a liquidator[19] and, if desired, a liquidation committee.[20] A liquidation committee essentially oversees the conduct of the liquidation and consists of creditors' (and possibly members') representatives.[21]

24-22

It is clear that a significant difference between a members' and a creditors' voluntary winding up is with respect to the choice of liquidator which rests with the members in a members' voluntary winding up and with the creditors in a creditors' voluntary winding up. In the past, members (who are often also the directors) were thought to be prone to appointing liquidators who were unlikely to probe too deeply into the conduct of the directors. Since the IA 1986, these concerns have been alleviated somewhat by a requirement in all liquidations (compulsory or voluntary) that a liquidator, apart from the official receiver, must be a qualified insolvency practitioner.[22] This means, among other things, that he or she must be an individual in respect of whom appropriate financial security is in force, who is authorised either as a member of a recognised professional body or as an individual by the Secretary of State and who is independent of the company concerned.[23] This regulation of insolvency practitioners is designed to bring greater independence and professionalism to the role of liquidator.

24-23

Where there is no liquidator appointed for whatever reason, the court may appoint (IA 1986, s 108). In that situation, the directors' powers to deal with the company's assets pending the appointment of a liquidator are essentially restricted to the preservation of the assets.[24] Likewise, in a creditors' voluntary winding up, if the members' meeting has nominated a liquidator prior to the creditors' meeting being held, the liquidator has power only to protect and preserve the company's property or to dispose of perishable items and he otherwise requires the consent of the court to act.[25]

24-24

Once appointed, the liquidator must publish in the *Gazette* and deliver to the registrar of companies a notice of his appointment (IA 1986, s 109). The company ceases to carry on business and all the directors' powers cease[26] although, in a voluntary winding up, they are not automatically removed from office.[27]

24-25

---

[19] IA 1986, s 100(1); the members' meeting may already have nominated a liquidator but, in the event of a conflict, the creditors' choice prevails: s 100(2). Objectors may apply to the court for an appointment in place of the creditors' choice: s 100(3).   [20] IA 1986, s 101.

[21] IA 1986, ss 141 and 101. Detailed rules governing the operation of a liquidation committee are contained in IR 1986, rr 4.151–4.172A.   [22] IA 1986, ss 230(1)–(5); 389, 390.

[23] IA 1986, ss 390–393; the Insolvency Practitioners Regulations 2005, SI 2005/524.

[24] IA 1986, s 114; and see *Re a company (No 006341 of 1992), ex p B Ltd* [1994] 1 BCLC 225.

[25] IA 1986, s 166 (2), (3).

[26] See IA 1986, s 91(2) (members' voluntary winding up), except so far as the company or the liquidator sanctions their continuance; s 103 (creditors' voluntary winding up), except so far as the liquidation committee or the creditors sanction their continuance.

[27] *Madrid Bank Ltd v Bayley* (1866) LR 2 QB 37.

C Compulsory winding up

24-26   A compulsory winding up requires a court order and the court's jurisdiction to make such an order is subject to the EC Regulation on Insolvency Proceedings which limits the court's power to open main proceedings to cases where the debtor's centre of main interests is in the UK and territorial proceedings to cases where the debtor possesses an establishment within the UK (see discussion at **24-11**).[28]

Petitioners for a winding-up order

24-27   The vast majority of petitions for winding up are presented by creditors,[29] but a petition can be presented by, amongst others, the company, its directors and contributories (essentially members).[30] Equally, provision is made for public interest petitions, for example by the official receiver where there are concerns as to the conduct of a voluntary winding up;[31] by the Secretary of State on public interest grounds;[32] and also by the Financial Services Authority.[33] It is also possible that the company has been the subject of some other insolvency process and it may be appropriate for the company to proceed to compulsory winding up. Hence provision is made for petitions for a winding-up order by a supervisor of a company voluntary arrangement (CVA)[34] and by an administrator,[35] and by a liquidator appointed in main proceedings in another Member State under the EC Insolvency Regulation.[36]

24-28   A contributory (essentially a member) is not entitled to present a winding-up petition unless either the number of members is reduced below two (except where the company is a single member company);[37] or the shares held by him were originally allotted to him or have been held by him for at least six months during the 18 months before the commencement of the winding up, or have devolved to him through the death of a former holder.[38] This provision is designed to prevent individuals from purchasing shares with a view to winding up a company, although a six-month period seems inadequate for this purpose. In fact, winding-up petitions by members are rare,

---

[28] See IA 1986, s 117(7); EC Regulation, art 3.

[29] A creditor may petition even though the company is in voluntary winding up: IA 1986, s 116.

[30] IA 1986, s 124(1). A petition by the directors may be presented by all the directors or pursuant to a majority decision of the board, see *Re Equiticorp International plc* [1989] BCLC 397; and see *Re Minrealm Ltd* [2008] 2 BCLC 141 where a majority of the directors petitioned for a winding-up order and the minority of the directors then opposed the petition. 'Contributory' encompasses members of the company as well as others not registered as members but who are liable to contribute to the assets of the company: see IA 1986, s 79.

[31] See IA 1986, s 124(5).   [32] I.e. under IA 1986, ss 122 (1)(b), (c) or 124A.

[33] See Financial Services and Markets Act 2000, s 367.   [34] IA 1986, s 7(4)(b); Sch A1, para 39(5)(b).

[35] IA 1986, Sch 1, para 21; Sch B1, para 60.   [36] IA 1986, s 124(1).   [37] IA 1986, s 124(2)(a).

[38] IA 1986, s 124(2)(b). Where the locus standi of a contributory to petition is disputed, the court will consider all the circumstances, including the likelihood of damage to the company if the petition is not dismissed, in deciding whether first to require the petitioner to seek the determination of his status outside of the winding-up petition: *Alipour v Ary, Re a company (No 002180 of 1996)* [1997] 1 BCLC 557, CA; and see *Alipour v UOC Corp* [2002] 2 BCLC 770.

other than, occasionally, petitions to have the company wound up on the just and equitable ground under IA 1986, s 122(1)(g). Even those petitions are unusual now, given the availability of more appropriate relief under CA 2006, s 994 (the unfairly prejudicial remedy), as discussed at **18-86**.

In addition to the criteria noted above, a contributory must establish an interest in the winding up. For example, a partly paid-up shareholder who remains liable to contribute the amount unpaid on his shares in the event of the company being wound up has an interest. For a fully paid-up member to establish that he has a tangible interest in the winding up, he must show a prima facie probability of surplus assets remaining after the creditors have been paid for distribution among the shareholders.[39] **24-29**

Grounds for compulsory winding up

The process of obtaining a winding-up order begins with a petition based on one of the grounds set out in the IA 1986, s 122(1). Some of these grounds are relevant to solvent companies, for example where a petition is brought for winding up on the just and equitable ground which is essentially a shareholder remedy.[40] For insolvent companies, the ground relied on is that the company is unable to pay its debts (s 122(1)(f)) and, in such cases, the petition is invariably brought by a creditor.[41] **24-30**

Company is unable to pay its debts

The circumstances in which a company is deemed to be unable to pay its debts are defined in IA 1986, s 123 which provides a cashflow or commercial test of insolvency (s 123(1)(e)) and a balance sheet test of insolvency (s 123(2)). **24-31**

'(1) A company is deemed unable to pay its debts—

    (a) if a creditor...to whom the company is indebted in a sum exceeding £750 then due has served on the company, by leaving it at the company's registered office, a written demand (in the prescribed form) requiring the company to pay the sum so due and the company has for 3 weeks thereafter neglected to pay the sum or to secure or compound for it to the reasonable satisfaction of the creditor,[42] or

---

[39] *Re Rica Gold Washing Co* (1879) 11 Ch D 36; *Re Expanded Plugs Ltd* [1966] 1 All ER 877; *Re Othery Construction Ltd* [1966] 1 All ER 145; *Re Bellador Silk Ltd* [1965] 1 All ER 667. See *Re Greenhaven Motors Ltd* [1997] 2 BCLC 739.

[40] I.e. under IA 1986, s 122(1)(g): see **18-71**. Other grounds include that the company has resolved by a special resolution to be wound up by the court; that the company is a public company and has not been issued with a trading certificate under CA 2006, s 761; that the company has not commenced business within one year of incorporation or has suspended its business for a whole year: IA 1986, s 122(1)(a), (b), (d).

[41] Additionally, a creditor (only) may petition for winding up where a CVA with a moratorium comes to an end without a voluntary arrangement being approved: IA 1986, ss 122(1)(fa); 124(3A); the advantage of using this option is that the creditor does not have to establish that the company is unable to pay its debts.

[42] The intention is to raise this figure to £1,500 from 1 October 2009. As to the detailed requirements concerning this statutory demand, see IR 1986, rr 4.4–4.6. The demand must be for a liquidated amount. A demand must be for a debt 'then due' and a contingent debt when the contingency has not happened has not fallen due: *JSF Finance & Currency Exchange Co Ltd v Akma Solutions Inc* [2001] 2 BCLC 307.

(b) if, in England and Wales, execution or other process issued on a judgment, decree or order of any court in favour of a creditor of the company is returned unsatisfied in whole or in part, or

(c) if, in Scotland,... or

(d) if, in Northern Ireland,... or

(e) if it is proved to the satisfaction of the court that the company is unable to pay its debts as they fall due.

(2) A company is also deemed unable to pay its debts if it is proved to the satisfaction of the court that the value of a company's assets is less than the amount of its liabilities, taking into account its contingent and prospective liabilities.'

24-32   Section 123(1)(a) is the easiest way to establish insolvency since it merely requires the facts about the statutory demand to be established. Most difficulties concern the application of s 123(1)(e) which enables a creditor, without serving a statutory demand or attempting to enforce a judgment, to satisfy the court by suitable evidence of the company's inability to pay,[43] but it can be difficult to establish that this is the case to the satisfaction of the court. A company is not entitled to have the petition struck out, or prevent it being issued, merely because it is in fact solvent.[44] Failure to pay an undisputed debt, despite repeated requests, must prima facie mean an inability to pay and a winding-up order may be sought by a creditor.[45]

24-33   If the debt is due and is undisputed, the petition proceeds to hearing and adjudication in the normal way, but it is an abuse of process to present a winding-up petition under IA 1986, s 123(1)(e) if the debt is bona fide disputed and the petition is being used as a means of pressurising the company.[46] In such a case the petition will be dismissed or the creditor can be restrained by injunction from presenting a petition.[47] A petition may also be dismissed if the company has a genuine and serious cross-claim for an amount which exceeds the petitioner's debt and which the company has been unable to litigate, subject to the court's residual discretion to consider whether there are any special circumstances which might make it inappropriate to dismiss the petition.[48]

---

[43] *Taylors Industrial Flooring Ltd v M & H Plant Hire (Manchester) Ltd* [1990] BCLC 216, CA.

[44] *Cornhill Insurance plc v Improvement Services Ltd* [1986] BCLC 26.

[45] *Taylors Industrial Flooring Ltd v M & H Plant Hire (Manchester) Ltd* [1990] BCLC 216, CA; *Cornhill Insurance plc v Improvement Services Ltd* [1986] BCLC 26. The courts will not allow a winding-up petition to enforce what is essentially a small debt and so in effect they impose a minimum debt of the amount required for a statutory demand: see Fletcher, *The Law of Insolvency* (3rd edn, 2002), para 21–006.

[46] See *Re MCI WorldCom Ltd* [2003] 1 BCLC 330; *Re Ringinfo Ltd* [2002] 1 BCLC 210; *Re a company (No 006685 of 1996)* [1997] 1 BCLC 639; *Re a company (No 0010656 of 1990)* [1991] BCLC 464; but the court will look for evidence that there is a bona fide dispute founded on substantial grounds and not just a debtor trying to have the petition dismissed on spurious grounds: see *Re Ringinfo Ltd* [2002] 1 BCLC 210; *Re a company (No 006685 of 1996)* [1997] 1 BCLC 639.

[47] *Re a company* [1984] 3 All ER 78. If the debt is disputed, the petitioner may not actually be 'a creditor' and therefore lacks locus standi to bring a petition: see *Re Bayoil SA* [1999] 1 BCLC 62 at 66, CA.

[48] *Re Bayoil SA* [1999] 1 BCLC 62, CA; see also *Re Latreefers Inc* [1999] 1 BCLC 271; *Re Ringinfo Ltd* [2002] 1 BCLC 210; *Orion Media Marketing Ltd v Media Brook Ltd* [2002] 1 BCLC 184; *Montgomery v Wanda Modes Ltd* [2002] 1 BCLC 289; *Re V P Developments Ltd* [2005] 2 BCLC 607. The significance of the 'inability to litigate' requirement was doubted in *Montgomery v Wanda Modes Ltd* as not forming part of the ratio of

This long-established approach of dismissing the petition where the debt is bona fide   **24-34**
disputed is a rule of practice only, however, and it must give way to circumstances which
make it desirable that the petitioner should proceed.[49] A petition will not be dismissed
if the petitioning creditor has a good arguable case that he is a creditor and the effect
of the dismissal would be to deprive the petitioner of a remedy or otherwise injustice
would result or for some other sufficient reason the petition should proceed.[50]

The three methods of establishing an inability to pay debts noted above (statutory   **24-35**
demand, unsatisfied judgment and inability to pay debts as they fall due) are based
on petitioning creditors who have debts that are immediately due and payable. But
petitions may also be brought by contingent or prospective creditors.[51] It might be the
case that a creditor has lent money to a company which is not due to be repaid until
some date in the future but the creditor is concerned that the present financial position
of the company suggests it will not be able to repay the debt when payment is due. Such
a creditor may rely on IA 1986, s 123(1)(e) by showing that the company is now unable
to pay its debts as they fall due or it may rely on the balance sheet test in s 123(2) if it
can be proved to the satisfaction of the court that the value of the company's assets is
less than the amount of its liabilities, taking into account its contingent and prospective liabilities.

The nature of the cashflow and balance sheet insolvency tests was considered in detail   **24-36**
in *Re Cheyne Finance plc*,[52] the facts of which are irrelevant for our purposes but which
concerned the terms of a commercial agreement. The court drew attention to the fact
that in IA 1986, s 123 the cashflow and balance sheet tests are separate (under the CA
1985, they had been combined) and IA 1986, s 123(2) imposes a mandatory requirement to consider contingent and prospective liabilities only in the context of balance
sheet insolvency. The question for the court was whether, as a consequence of s 123(2),
future debts could not be taken into account when relying on cashflow insolvency. The
answer lay, the court thought, in the key phrase in s 123(1)(e), 'debts as they fall due'.
These words add a key element of futurity and 'fall due' is synonymous with 'become
due'. The effect of the alterations to the insolvency test found in IA 1986, s 123(1)(e)
is to replace one futurity requirement, namely the CA 1985 requirement to include
contingent and prospective liabilities in the cashflow insolvency test, with another

Bayoil. Park J noted that there is nothing objectionable in a company which has refrained from pursuing
a claim which it believed it has against another party, later deciding to pursue that cross-claim if the other
party threatens it with winding-up proceedings; he thought it would be undesirable for companies to be
penalised for refraining from litigating a claim or if parties were to be encouraged to litigate possible claims
sooner rather than later; see also *Re a debtor (No 87 of 1999)* [2000] BPIR 589 to the same effect and on which
Park J relied.

[49] *Parmalat Capital Finance Ltd v Food Holdings Ltd* [2008] BCC 371, PC; *Brinds Ltd v Offshore Oil NL*
(1986) 2 BCC 98, 916.

[50] *Alipour v Ary, Re a company (No 002180 of 1996)* [1997] 1 BCLC 557, CA; see also *Re Claybridge Shipping
Co SA* [1997] 1 BCLC 572, (CA, 1981).

[51] IA 1986, s 124(1); IR 1986, r 13.12(3).

[52] [2008] 1 BCLC 741; see Baird & Sidle, 'Cash Flow Insolvency' (2008) 21 Insolv Int 40 for a critical look
at this decision.

more flexible and fact-sensitive requirement encapsulated in the new phrase 'as they fall due'. Future debts are then relevant to the question of cashflow insolvency even if the inclusion of contingent and prospective liabilities is limited by IA 1986, s 123(2) to balance sheet insolvency. Briggs J commented in this case that, quite apart from other considerations, it is a common-sense requirement not to ignore the relevant future. Liquidity therefore needs to be considered in the context of a period longer than 'now', but how much in the future it is necessary to look is unclear.

The court's discretion to make a winding-up order

24-37   Having grounds for the presentation of a petition does not necessarily entitle the creditor to a winding-up order, though if the creditor has standing and the court is satisfied that the company is unable to pay its debts, a winding-up order should follow unless there is some special reason why it should not.[53] Winding up is a collective or class remedy, however, and an order may be refused if the petitioner is merely seeking to obtain some private advantage,[54] but if the purpose of the petition is legitimate, it does not matter that the motive of the petitioner is malicious.[55]

24-38   There may well be differences of opinion among the creditors as to whether a compulsory winding up is appropriate in which case the court can direct meetings to be held to ascertain the creditors' wishes (IA 1986, s 195). A particular aspect of this clash of opinions is where a company is already in voluntary winding up and the court is asked to substitute a compulsory winding-up order for that voluntary process. Again, the court takes account of the wishes of the majority of the creditors and where the majority oppose the making of a compulsory winding-up order, the onus is on those seeking the order to show good reason why it should be granted.[56] The court looks carefully at the quality of the creditors on either side as well as the quantity and where some of the creditors are also shareholders or directors of the company or their associates, their views may be given less weight or disregarded altogether.[57] Principles of fairness and commercial morality are taken into account and may require that the creditors secure the independent scrutiny of the company's affairs which is a consequence of a compulsory winding-up order.[58]

---

[53] See *Re Demaglass Holdings Ltd* [2001] 2 BCLC 633; *Re Lummus Agricultural Services Ltd* [2001] BCLC 137. But see *Re Minrealm Ltd* [2008] 2 BCLC 141 where the court adjourned the petition to await the resolution of unfairly prejudicial proceedings.

[54] *Re a Company (No 001573 of 1983)* [1983] BCLC 492.

[55] *Bryanston Finance Ltd v De Vries (No 2)* [1976] 1 All ER 25, CA; *Re a Company (No 001573 of 1983)* [1983] BCLC 492.

[56] *Re JD Swain Ltd* [1965] 2 All ER 761; *Re Magnus Consultants Ltd* [1995] 1 BCLC 203; *Re Gordon and Breach Science Publishers Ltd* [1995] 2 BCLC 189. It may be more appropriate in some cases simply to apply under IA 1986, s 171 for the appointment of a different liquidator: see *Re Inside Sport Ltd* [2000] 1 BCLC 302.

[57] *Re Demaglass Holdings Ltd* [2001] 2 BCLC 633; *Re Lummus Agricultural Services Ltd* [2001] BCLC 137; *Re Gordon and Breach Science Publishers Ltd* [1995] 2 BCLC 189; *Re Falcon (R J) Developments Ltd* [1987] BCLC 437.

[58] *Re Lowerstoft Traffic Services Ltd* [1986] BCLC 81; *Re Palmer Marine Surveys Ltd* [1986] BCLC 106; *Re Gordon and Breach Science Publishers Ltd* [1995] 2 BCLC 189.

On the making of the winding-up order and by virtue of his office, the official   **24-39**
receiver becomes the liquidator.[59] If the official receiver considers it worthwhile, or
if 25% in value of creditors request it, the official receiver calls separate meetings of
creditors and of members for the purpose of choosing a person to be the liquidator of
the company in his place.[60] Each meeting may nominate a liquidator and, in the event
of different nominations, the creditors' nominee is appointed.[61] If no meetings are
held or no nominations made, the official receiver remains as liquidator.[62] Three copies
of the winding-up order are sent to the official receiver; one copy is served by him on
the company at its registered office and one copy is sent to the registrar of companies.[63]
The order is notified in the *Gazette* and advertised in a local paper.[64]

Consequences of winding up

In the case of a compulsory winding up, the winding up is deemed to commence at   **24-40**
the time of the presentation of the petition, unless the company passes a resolution
for voluntary winding up prior to the presentation of the petition, in which case the
winding up is deemed to commence at the date of the passing of the resolution.[65] In a
compulsory winding up, the directors are automatically dismissed from office on the
making of the order[66] and the liquidator takes the company's property into his custody
and control (IA 1986, s 144).

Dispositions of the company's property

A compulsory winding up commences with the presentation of the petition but   **24-41**
there is a risk that property which should be available to the creditors may be disposed of in the period (which may be quite lengthy) between the presentation of the
petition and the making of the winding-up order. To preserve such property for the
creditors, any disposition of the company's property, and any transfers of shares, or
alteration in the status of the company's members, after the commencement of a compulsory winding up is void, unless the court otherwise orders (IA 1986, s 127).[67] The
value of this provision is that it enables liquidators to challenge certain dispositions
with a view to recovering assets for the benefit of the creditors generally. Equally, the
court's discretion to validate transactions offers some relief for those dealing with
the company in this situation. The application of s 127 is therefore of considerable
practical importance.

---

[59] IA 1986, s 136(1), (2). The court also has power to appoint a provisional liquidator prior to the making of the winding-up order: see s 135.

[60] IA 1986, s 136(4), (5).   [61] IA 1986, s 139(2), (3).

[62] The Secretary of State may appoint a replacement liquidator on the application of the official receiver
or following the failure of the meetings to appoint: IA 1986, s 137(1)–(3).

[63] IR 1986, r 4.21(1)–(3); IA 1986, s 130(1).   [64] IR 1986, r 4.21(4).

[65] IA 1986, s 129. Presentation of the petition takes place when the petition is delivered to the court for
issue, not when it is issued: *Re Blights Builders Ltd* [2008] 1 BCLC 245.

[66] *Measures v Measures* [1910] 2 Ch 248.

[67] See IA 1986, s 88 (which applies in a voluntary winding up) to similar effect, but it is limited in
application to transfers of shares and alterations in the status of the company's members.

24-42 In exercising this discretion to validate dispositions, the court looks to see if the disposition was made bona fide to assist the company,[68] such as the repayment of or the grant of security for loans made to the company after the commencement of winding up.[69] But the court generally refuses to validate payments which have the effect of preferring pre-insolvency creditors[70] unless the payment confers a benefit on creditors generally.[71] It is open to the company or any creditor to apply to the court to validate a transaction in advance of it taking place and this is particularly useful where the company carries on business in the period between the presentation of a winding-up petition and the making of a winding-up order. In such circumstances, the court adopts the same general approach and takes into account the benefit to the creditors generally of keeping a business going with a view to selling it as a going concern.

24-43 The application of IA 1986, s 127 is limited to where there is 'a disposition of the company's property' and a particular issue in that regard concerns payments into and out of the company's bank account. This issue was comprehensively addressed by the Court of Appeal in *Hollicourt (Contracts) Ltd v Bank of Ireland.*[72] In this case, after the presentation of a petition for the winding up of the company, the bank continued to operate the company's bank account for a period of three months, having overlooked the advertisement of the petition. The bank debited the company's account, which was in credit throughout, with payments in favour of third parties totalling £156,200. The account was not frozen until the bank became aware of the petition. The liquidator commenced proceedings against the bank seeking repayment by the bank of the monies paid out on the basis that the payments were 'dispositions' of the company's property within IA 1986, s 127 and void.

24-44 At first instance, Blackburne J decided that all the post-presentation payments made out of the account were void and required the bank to reconstitute the account.[73] A contrary approach to these issues was taken by Lightman J a fortnight later in *Coutts & Co v Stock,*[74] leaving the matter ripe for resolution by the Court of Appeal. It duly upheld the approach of Lightman J in *Coutts* and rejected the approach of Blackburne J.[75]

24-45 In *Hollicourt,* the Court of Appeal concluded that IA 1986, s 127 only invalidates dispositions by the company of its property to the payees of the cheques. It enabled the company to recover the amounts disposed of, but only from the payees. It did not enable the company to recover the amounts from the bank which had only acted

---

[68] *Re J Leslie Engineering Co Ltd* [1976] 2 All ER 85.

[69] *Re Steane's (Bournemouth) Ltd* [1950] 1 All ER 21; *Re Clifton Place Garage Ltd* [1970] 1 All ER 353, CA.

[70] *Re Civil Service and General Store Ltd* (1887) 57 LJ Ch 119.

[71] *Re A I Levy (Holdings) Ltd* [1963] 2 All ER 556.

[72] [2001] 1 BCLC 233, CA; see Hare, 'Banker's Liability for Post-Petition Dispositions' (2001) CLJ 468.

[73] [2000] 1 BCLC 171.   [74] [2000] 1 BCLC 183.

[75] In reaching its conclusions, the Court of Appeal was very doubtful of the value of dicta on broader issues of bank payments in *Re Gray's Inn Construction Co Ltd* [1980] 1 All ER 814, a case which was much cited on the matter over the years, but whose ratio is confined to payments made into an overdrawn account.

in accordance with the company's instructions as the company's agent to make payments to the payees out of the company's bank account. Even if the company's bank account had been in overdraft, the legal effect of s 127 would have been the same. The purpose of s 127 is to prevent the directors of a company, when liquidation is imminent, from disposing of the company's assets to the prejudice of its creditors and to preserve those assets for the benefit of the general body of creditors. The policy promoted by s 127 is not aimed at imposing on a bank restitutionary liability to a company in respect of payments made by cheques in favour of the creditors in addition to the unquestioned liability of the payees of the cheques. The section impinged on the end result of the process of payment initiated by the company, i.e. the point of ultimate receipt of the company's property in consequence of a disposition by the company. The statutory purpose is accomplished without any need for the section to impinge on the legal validity of intermediate steps, such as banking transactions, which are merely part of the process by which dispositions of the company's property are made.[76]

Though not necessary to its decision (the account in *Hollicourt* was in credit throughout), the Court of Appeal made the point that, even if the payments had been made out of an overdrawn account (as in *Coutts v Stock*[77]), the outcome would have been the same in respect of a claim for recovery against the bank. The court thought that this result has the very real practical advantage of not requiring what could be a complex analysis of whether payments were made out of an account which was in debit or in credit.[78]   **24-46**

The outcome in *Hollicourt* is logically coherent and pragmatic and provides very considerable comfort for the banking community which need not be concerned that restitutionary liability will fall on a bank which, through error, fails to freeze an account on a petition for winding up being presented. It avoids the situation where the banks are the deep pockets pursued by liquidators rather than the payees in respect of whom the liquidators have an undoubted claim.   **24-47**

These cases concerned payments *out* of a company's bank account. Payments by a company *into* an overdrawn account with its bank with the resulting reduction in its indebtedness to the bank is a disposition requiring consent[79] while a payment into an account which is in credit simply results in an adjustment of the records between the company and its bank and is not a disposition of the company's property for these purposes.[80] Where a bank seeks a validation order with respect to payments into an overdrawn account, the essential question is whether the payments into the account are in the ordinary course of business and whether they are likely to be for the benefit of the creditors generally, but where there is no real benefit to the creditors generally, merely a reduction in the amount owed to the bank, a validation order will not be made.[81]   **24-48**

---

[76] [2001] 1 BCLC 233 at 239.   [77] [2000] 1 BCLC 183.   [78] [2001] 1 BCLC 233 at 242.

[79] *Re Gray's Inn Construction Co Ltd* [1980] 1 All ER 814, CA; although this case was much criticised in *Hollicourt (Contracts) Ltd v Bank of Ireland* [2001] 1 BCLC 233, CA, on this point it remains valid; see also *Re Tain Construction Ltd* [2003] 2 BCLC 374.

[80] *Re Barn Crown Ltd* [1994] 4 All ER 42.   [81] *Re Tain Construction Ltd* [2003] 2 BCLC 374.

To do so would breach the pari passu principle and result in the bank's pre-liquidation debt being repaid to the detriment of the other creditors.[82]

Control of legal proceedings and enforcement of remedies

24-49 When a winding-up order is made, all pending proceedings are automatically halted and no new proceedings may be commenced, except by the leave of the court under IA 1986, s 130(2).[83] In practice, the court allows the enforcement of rights by secured creditors[84] (since such proceedings cannot adversely affect the position of unsecured creditors), but in relation to other matters the court must decide whether there is any sensible point in allowing the proceedings to continue and what is right and fair in the circumstances of the particular case.[85] Once a winding-up order has been made, IA 1986, s 128(1) appears to render void any enforcement of a remedy (attachment, sequestration, distress or execution) after the commencement of the winding up.[86] It is invariably treated, however, as also subject to the court's discretion under s 130(2) to allow the enforcement to continue.[87] The court has a broad and unfettered discretion to do what is right and fair in the circumstances of the particular case, but it must not allow the individual creditor the benefit of enforcing the judgment if this will

---

[82] *Re Tain Construction Ltd* [2003] 2 BCLC 374.

[83] The court also has power to stay any legal proceedings against the company at any time between the presentation of the winding-up petition and before the winding-up order is made: IA 1986, s 126(1). Distress (essentially taking possession of goods in satisfaction of a debt) is an 'action or proceeding' within s 130(2) and requires court consent: *Re Memco Engineering Ltd* [1985] BCLC 424; *Herbert Berry Associates Ltd v IRC* [1978] 1 All ER 161, HL. Distress includes use of the procedure in the Tribunals, Courts and Enforcement Act 2007, Sch 12: IA 1986, s 463.

[84] *Re David Lloyd & Co, Lloyd v David Lloyd & Co* (1877) 6 Ch D 339, CA and *Re Aro Co Ltd* [1980] 1 All ER 1067, CA (secured creditors enforcing security); *Re Coregrange Ltd* [1984] BCLC 453 (creditor suing for specific performance). A freezing order over assets, without more, does not constitute a security for these purposes, for it does not impose an obligation to satisfy any judgment debt out of those frozen assets: *Flightline Ltd v Edwards* [2003] 1 BCLC 427, CA.

[85] *New Cap Reinsurance Corp Ltd v HIH Casualty & General Insurance* Ltd [2002] 2 BCLC 228, CA. Leave will not be given if the issues can conveniently be decided in the winding up: *Craven v Blackpool Greyhound Stadium and Racecourse Ltd* [1936] 3 All ER 513, CA; *Re Exchange Securities and Commodities Ltd* [1983] BCLC 186; but will be given if the issues are better decided by an action: *Currie v Consolidated Kent Collieries Corpn Ltd* [1906] 1 KB 134, CA.

[86] This provision is limited to compulsory winding up and there is no directly equivalent provision with respect to voluntary winding up, but the liquidator would apply to the court for directions under IA 1986, s 112 with a view to the court exercising its discretion as to whether to permit execution following the commencement of the winding up. If proceedings have already resulted in a judgment against the company, but enforcement of that judgment has not been completed prior to the commencement of the winding up, the proceeds of an execution etc cannot be retained by the creditor against the liquidator unless the court orders otherwise, see IA 1986, s 183, which applies to compulsory and voluntary winding up.

[87] *Re Lancashire Cotton Spinning Co, ex p Carnelly* (1887) 35 Ch D 656, CA. If distress is in progress at the commencement of the winding up but not completed, the courts will allow it to continue unless there is something inequitable in allowing the distraining party to have the fruits of the distress. See *Re Memco Engineering Ltd* [1985] BCLC 424; *Herbert Berry Associates Ltd v IRC* [1978] 1 All ER 161, HL; *Re Bellaglade Ltd* [1977] 1 All ER 319. The Tribunals, Courts and Enforcement Act 2007 abolishes the common law right to distrain for arrears of rent, instead there is a limited right for the recovery of rent arrears due under a lease of commercial premises only: see ss 71 and 72.

prejudice the equal treatment of creditors generally.[88] On the other hand, the court has allowed an individual creditor to succeed where the debtor forced,[89] tricked[90] or persuaded[91] the creditor to abstain from enforcing a judgment sometime before the winding up commenced.

D The role and powers of a liquidator

In a compulsory liquidation, the liquidator is an officer of the court. A liquidator, though not strictly speaking a trustee, is in a fiduciary relationship with the company and must not place himself in a position of a conflict of interests.[92] A liquidator must not make any unauthorised profit from his position and any purchase by him of the company's property is liable to be set side.[93] A liquidator may also be liable for negligence in realising the company's property.[94] Duties owed by liquidators are owed to the company and not to individual contributories or creditors.[95] Thus in *Knowles v Scott*[96] a liquidator was not liable for loss caused by delay in making a distribution to a contributory, nor was the liquidator liable in *Lomax Leisure Ltd v Miller*[97] when he cancelled a dividend declared in error.

24-50

Title to the company's assets is not automatically vested in the liquidator but remains vested in the company unless, exceptionally, the court so orders (IA 1986, s 145). When carrying out his functions, the liquidator acts as an agent of the company. Any contracts entered into by him are entered into by the company and the liquidator incurs no personal liability unless the terms of the contract show that he is undertaking a personal liability.[98]

24-51

The basic duty of the liquidator in all types of liquidation is to wind up the company's affairs, to collect in and realise the company's assets and to make distributions to the creditors in accordance with the statutory scheme, with any surplus being returned to the shareholders.[99] To assist in these tasks, an extensive array of powers

24-52

---

[88] *New Cap Reinsurance Corp Ltd v HIH Casualty & General Insurance* Ltd [2002] 2 BCLC 228, CA; *Re Aro Co Ltd* [1980] 1 All ER 1067, CA; *Roberts Petroleum Ltd v Bernard Kenny Ltd* [1983] 1 All ER 564, HL; *Re Grosvenor Metal Co Ltd* [1950] Ch 63.

[89] *Re London Cotton Co* (1866) LR 2 Eq 53.

[90] *Armorduct Manufacturing Co Ltd v General Incandescent Co Ltd* [1911] 2 KB 143, CA.

[91] *Re Grosvenor Metal Co Ltd* [1950] Ch 63; *Re Suidair International Airways Ltd* [1950] 2 All ER 920; *Re Redman (Builders) Ltd* [1964] 1 All ER 851.

[92] *Re Corbenstoke Ltd (No 2)* [1990] BCLC 60 at 62, per Harman J.

[93] *Silkstone and Haigh Moor Coal Co v Edey* [1900] 1 Ch 167. See also IR 1986, r 4.149.

[94] *Re Windsor Steam Coal Co (1901) Ltd* [1928] Ch 609; *Re Home and Colonial Insurance Co Ltd* [1920] 1 Ch 102.

[95] See *Lomax Leisure Ltd v Miller* [2008] 1 BCLC 262; IR 1986, r 4.182(3).

[96] [1891] 1 Ch 717.   [97] [2008] 1 BCLC 262.

[98] *Stewart v Engel* [2000] 2 BCLC 528; *Re Anglo-Moravian Hungarian Junction Rly Co, ex p Watkin* (1875) 1 Ch D 130, CA; *Stead, Hazel & Co v Cooper* [1933] 1 KB 840.

[99] IA 1986, ss 91(1), 100(1), 107 (voluntary winding up); s 143(1) (compulsory winding up).

are conferred on a liquidator by IA 1986, Sch 4. Some of these powers can be exercised by a liquidator of his own volition, others need the appropriate approval or sanction. In a compulsory or creditors' voluntary winding up, the sanction needed is that of the court or the liquidation committee if one has been appointed.[100] Additionally, in the case of a creditors' voluntary winding up, a power may be exercised with the sanction of a meeting of the company's creditors where there is no liquidation committee.[101] In a members' voluntary winding up, the sanction required is a special resolution of the company.[102]

Powers exercisable with sanction in a compulsory winding up or voluntary winding up—Sch 4, Part I

(1) to pay any class of creditors in full;

(2) to make any compromise or arrangement with any creditors or claimants against the company;

(3) to compromise all calls and liabilities to calls against contributories etc; and all questions in any way relating to or affecting the assets or the winding up of the company;

(4) power to bring legal proceedings under IA 1986, ss 213, 214, 238, 239, 242, 243, or 423 (these are provisions allowing actions to be brought to recover assets or seek contributions to the company's assets) and see **24-87**.

Additional powers exercisable without sanction in a voluntary winding up and with sanction in a compulsory winding up—Sch 4, Part II

(1) to bring or defend any legal proceedings in the name and on behalf of the company;

(2) to carry on the business of the company so far as may be necessary for the beneficial winding up of the company.[103]

Powers exercisable without sanction in either a compulsory or a voluntary winding up—Sch 4, Part III

(1) to sell any of the company's property;

---

[100] IA 1986, s 167(1). Consent should be sought first from the liquidation committee and application to the court made if consent is refused or given subject to conditions that the liquidator will not accept. The liquidator should tell the committee of his application to the court so that their views may be heard as well: *Re Consolidated Diesel Engine Manufacturers Ltd* [1915] 1 Ch 192. A creditor or contributory of the company is entitled to be heard on an application by a liquidator for the sanction of the court: *Re Greenhaven Motors Ltd* [1999] 1 BCLC 635, CA.

[101] IA 1986, s 165(2)(b).   [102] IA 1986, s 165(2)(a).

[103] Note the limitation 'so far as may be necessary for the beneficial winding up of the business', i.e. if the continuation may be expected to produce a better return for the creditors, but not if the object is to seek to continue or resuscitate the business for the benefit of the members: *Re Wreck Recovery and Salvage Co* (1880) 15 Ch D 353, CA; see also *Re Great Eastern Electric Co Ltd* [1941] 1 All ER 409. A liquidator who thinks the business can be rescued may apply to the court for an administration order under IA 1986, Sch B1, para 38.

(2) to do all acts and to execute, in the name and on behalf of the company, all deeds, receipts and other documents;

(3) to prove, rank and claim in the bankruptcy, insolvency or sequestration of any contributory for any balance against his estate;

(4) to draw, accept, make and indorse any bill of exchange or promissory note in the name and on behalf of the company;

(5) to raise any requisite money on the security of the assets of the company;

(6) to take out in his official name letters of administration to any deceased contributory, and to do in his official name any other act necessary to obtain payment of any money due from a contributory or his estate;

(7) to appoint an agent to do any business which the liquidator is unable to do himself;

(8) to do all such other things as may be necessary for winding up the company's affairs and distributing its assets.

When deciding whether to sanction the exercise of a power within Part I or Part II above, the decision for the court or the liquidation committee is not whether the liquidator is acting bona fide and reasonably, but whether the interests of those creditors or contributories who have a real interest in the assets of the company in liquidation are likely to be best served by permitting the company to enter into the proposed transaction.[104] A liquidator can assign a cause of action available to the company as it forms part of the company's 'property' which can be sold.[105] This entitlement to assign in this way is an exemption from the rules of champerty, which exemption is conferred because the statutory powers of liquidators place them in a privileged position.[106]

24-53

To assist liquidators get a complete picture of the company's affairs, liquidators have extensive powers to inquire into the company's dealings and to seek the court's assistance by summoning persons to appear before it, or requiring persons to submit affidavits or produce books, documents or other records relating to the company.[107] In a compulsory winding up, the liquidator may summon general meetings of the creditors or contributories for the purpose of ascertaining their wishes; and in some

24-54

---

[104] *Re Barings plc (No 7)* [2002] 1 BCLC 401; *Re Greenhaven Motors Ltd* [1999] 1 BCLC 635, CA.

[105] *Guy v Churchill* (1889) 40 Ch D 481 at 485, per Chitty J; see also *Norglen Ltd v Reeds Rains Prudential Ltd* [1998] 1 BCLC 176 at 182–3, HL. But the 'property' must be property of the company at the commencement of the litigation and it does not include property which only arises after the liquidation and is recoverable by the liquidator pursuant to his statutory powers, such as the fruits of a wrongful trading action under IA 1986, s 214: *Re Oasis Merchandising Services Ltd, Ward v Aitken* [1997] 1 BCLC 689, CA.

[106] See *Norglen Ltd v Reeds Rains Prudential Ltd* [1998] 1 BCLC 176 at 182; *ANC Ltd v Clark Goldring & Page Ltd* [2001] BCC 479.

[107] IA 1986, ss 235, 236. An extensive case-law exists on the scope of s 236, see especially *Re Daltek Europe Ltd* [2005] 1 BCLC 594; *Re RBG Resources plc, Shierson v Rastogi* [2002] BCC 1005, CA; *British and Commonwealth Holdings plc v Spicer and Oppenheim* [1992] 4 All ER 876, HL; *Cloverbay Ltd v Bank of Credit and Commerce International SA* [1991] 1 All ER 894. Provision for public examination of the officers of a company in compulsory winding up is made by IA 1986, s 133; and see *Re Richbell Strategic Holdings Ltd (No 2)* [2000] 2 BCLC 794.

circumstances he can be compelled to call such meetings.[108] He may also apply to the court for directions in relation to any particular matter arising in the winding up.[109]

24-55   A particularly useful power which a liquidator has is the power of disclaimer. Disclaimer is a means by which a liquidator can terminate certain future obligations of the company or disclaim ownership of unsaleable assets and he can exercise the power to disclaim onerous property notwithstanding that he has taken possession of the property, endeavoured to sell it, or otherwise exercised rights of ownership in relation to it (IA 1986, s 178(2)). 'Onerous property' is defined as: (1) any unprofitable contract; and (2) any other property of the company which is unsaleable or not readily saleable or is such that it may give rise to a liability to pay money or perform any other onerous act (s 178(3)).[110] Any person sustaining loss or damage as a consequence of the operation of a disclaimer has a statutory right to compensation (s 178(6)).[111]

24-56   A contract is not an 'unprofitable contract' in this context merely because it is financially disadvantageous or merely because the company could have made a better bargain.[112] In the context of disclaimer, it is a necessary feature of an 'unprofitable contract' that it imposes future obligations (i.e. obligations yet to be performed), the performance of which might be detrimental to creditors by prejudicing the liquidator's obligation to realise the company's property and pay a dividend to the creditors within a reasonable time.[113] One purpose behind the power to disclaim is to enable the winding up to be completed without undue delay or, in some cases, to be completed at all. But disclaimer also enables the liquidator unilaterally to terminate onerous contracts so that, for example, the other party to a contract cannot insist on performing the contract, adding unnecessarily to the debts of the company, but can be compelled to sue for damages as an unsecured creditor. The position was explained by Morritt LJ in *Re Celtic Extraction Ltd*[114] as follows:

> '...An important aspect of the implementation of that policy [that the property of insolvents should be divided equally amongst their unsecured creditors] is the ability to disclaim onerous property; otherwise the available assets are, in practice, appropriated to the future or prospective creditor who holds the right corresponding to the onerous property...'

---

[108] IA 1986, s 168(1), (2). But see *Re Barings plc, Hamilton v Law Debenture Trustee Ltd* [2001] 2 BCLC 159: court can order the liquidator not to comply with a requisition by creditors to convene a meeting.

[109] IA 1986, s 168(3) (compulsory winding up); s 112 (voluntary winding up).

[110] 'Property' is defined in IA 1986, 436 and extends to a waste disposal licence under the Environmental Protection Act 1990 which may be disclaimed by a liquidator: *Re Celtic Extraction Ltd* [1999] 2 BCLC 555, CA.

[111] See *Re Park Air Services plc* [1999] 1 BCLC 155, HL: lease disclaimed, landlord was entitled to compensation for loss of his right to future rent, but not the rent itself, to which he no longer had any claim because the disclaimer brought to an end both the tenant's liability to pay rent and the landlord's right to receive it. In assessing the quantum of loss, the matter should be approached in the same way as a claim for damages for breach of a contract which has been wrongfully terminated.

[112] *Re SSSL Realisations (2002) Ltd* [2007] 1 BCLC 29, CA.

[113] *Re SSSL Realisations (2002) Ltd* [2007] 1 BCLC 29, CA.   [114] [1999] 2 BCLC 555 at 568, CA.

Disclaimer is effected by the liquidator serving a notice[115] and the effect of a dis-   **24-57**
claimer is to terminate, as from the date of the disclaimer, the rights and liabilities of
the company in the property disclaimed (IA 1986, s 178(4)(a)). But, it does not, except
so far as is necessary for the purposes of releasing the company from any liability, affect
the rights or liabilities of any other person.[116] There is no time-limit within which the
liquidator must decide whether to disclaim property, but any person with an interest
in the property can serve a notice on the liquidator requiring the liquidator to disclaim
within 28 days or lose the right to do so (s 178(5)). The court can interfere with a disclaimer only if it is exercised in bad faith or the liquidator's decision is perverse.[117]

Challenging the exercise of the liquidator's powers

In a compulsory liquidation, individual contributories or creditors may apply to   **24-58**
the court to control the exercise or proposed exercise of any of the liquidator's
powers.[118] There is no equivalent provision with respect to voluntary liquidation, but
an application to the court may be made under IA 1986, s 112(1) by any contributory
or any creditor to determine any question arising in the winding up. Furthermore, in
a compulsory winding up, any person aggrieved by an act or decision of the liquidator
may apply to the court under s 168(5) which may confirm, reverse or modify the act
or decision complained of and may make such order as it thinks fit.[119] The court will
not interfere with the business decisions of a liquidator, however, and it is necessary
to establish that the liquidator has acted mala fide or in a way in which no reasonable
liquidator would have acted.[120]

Individual contributories or creditors may use the summary misfeasance procedure   **24-59**
under IA 1986, s 212 to ask the court to compel the liquidator to restore property to the
company or compensate it for breach of duty. The power to make such an application
continues after the winding up is completed and notwithstanding the release of the
liquidator from all liability connected with the liquidation,[121] but any application in
these circumstances requires the court's consent (s 212(4)).

---

[115] For the rules as to the proper service of the notice and the persons on whom it must be served, see
IR 1986, rr 4.187–4.194.

[116] IA 1986, s 178(4)(b); and see *Hindcastle Ltd v Barbara Attenborough Associates Ltd* [1996] 2 BCLC 234,
HL; *Capital Prime Properties plc v Worthgate Ltd* [2000] 1 BCLC 647; *Groveholt Ltd v Hughes* [2005] 2 BCLC
421, CA.

[117] *Re Hans Place Ltd* [1993] BCLC 768.

[118] IA 1986, s 167(3). A contributory has locus standi for these purposes only if he can show a tangible
interest in the liquidation: *Re Rica Gold Washing Ltd* (1879) 11 Ch D 36; *Re Greenhaven Motors* Ltd [1997] 1
BCLC 739; *Re Barings plc (No 7)* [2002] 1 BCLC 401.

[119] Applications under IA 1986, s 168(5) may be brought by creditors or contributories or persons directly
affected by the exercise of a power given specifically to a liquidator and who otherwise would not be able to
challenge the exercise of that power: *Mahomed v Morris* [2000] 2 BCLC 526, CA.

[120] See *Re Greenhaven Motors* Ltd [1997] 1 BCLC 739; *Re Edennote Ltd, Tottenham Hotspur plc v Ryman*
[1996] 2 BCLC 389, CA; *Leon v York-O-Matic Ltd* [1966] 3 All ER 277; *Harold M Pitman & Co v Top Business
Systems (Nottingham) Ltd* [1984] BCLC 593.

[121] IA 1986, ss 173(4), 174(6).

E The distribution of the company's assets

Overview

24-60 On liquidation all the assets of the company form a common fund which, subject to the expenses of the winding up and the rights of the preferential creditors, are subject to a statutory trust for the benefit of all the unsecured creditors.[122] The secured creditors look not to the statutory trust but to their security for payment of the sums due to them,[123] though the holder of a floating charge, while a secured creditor, is subject to the prior claims of the expenses of winding up, the preferential creditors and the 'prescribed part', all of which are discussed below.

24-61 The unsecured creditors must be paid in accordance with the principle of pari passu distribution which requires that all creditors participate in the pooled assets in proportion to the size of their claim, and where the assets are insufficient to meet all the claims, they abate proportionately.[124] Payment on a pari passu basis means, for example, that if there are three unsecured creditors who are owed £100,000 (A), £200,000 (B) and £300,000 (C) and £240,000 remains available for distribution by the liquidator, A gets £40,000, B gets £80,000 and C £120,000.

24-62 In theory, the pari passu principle is the fundamental basis for the distribution of the assets on insolvency but, as we shall see below, many creditors take steps to avoid being subject to its application and, with few funds available for distribution to unsecured creditors in any event, its practical application is limited. This disparity between the theory of pari passu distribution and the reality on winding up has led a number of commentators to question whether realistically we can go on asserting that the governing principle in insolvency is pari passu distribution since it has, in effect, become the exception rather than the rule.[125] Despite the undoubted truth of that position, the courts at the highest levels continually reassert the primacy of the rule of pari passu distribution.[126]

24-63 The result of these elements is that secured creditors look to realise their security outside of the liquidation while the fund available for distribution in the liquidation is disbursed in the following order: (1) the expenses of liquidation; (2) the preferential debts; (3) the claims of the floating charge holder from which must be deducted the prescribed part if the charge was created on or after 15 September 2003; (4) the

---

[122] See *Ayerst (Inspector of Taxes) v C & K (Construction) Ltd* [1975] 2 All ER 537; *Webb v Whiffin* (1872) LR 5 HL 711 at 721, 724.

[123] As noted in *Hague v Nam Tai Electronics Inc* [2007] 2 BCLC 194 at 200, PC, a secured creditor is not concerned to enforce its rights against the assets available for distribution in a liquidation and the amount which it can recover out of its security is therefore unaffected by the liquidation.

[124] IA 1986, s 107; IR 1986, r 4.181.

[125] See Mokal, *Corporate Insolvency Law* (2005) Ch 4; Finch, *Corporate Insolvency Law: Perspectives and Principles* (2002), Chs 13, 14; Goode, *Principles of Corporate Insolvency Law* (3rd edn, 2005), Ch 7.

[126] For example, see *Hague v Nam Tai Electronics Inc* [2007] 2 BCLC 194 at 198, PC; *Re HIH Casualty and General Insurance Ltd*; *McMahon v McGrath* [2008] 3 All ER 869, HL.

unsecured creditors on a pari passu basis. The extent to which these claims can be satisfied depends, obviously, on the size of the fund and therefore there are some rules affecting that fund which need to be borne in mind.

Establishing the estate—the no-deprivation principle

Clearly it is important that an insolvent company should not be able to remove assets **24-64**
from its estate at the point of insolvency so leaving the creditors to claim against a smaller estate. From the earliest days the courts adopted a rule, known as 'the rule in *Ex p Mackay*'[127] which provides that any contractual provision designed to defeat the insolvency distribution rules, i.e. the pari passu distribution of the insolvent's assets on insolvency, and in effect to prefer one unsecured creditor ahead of the others is void:[128]

> '...a man is not allowed by stipulation with a creditor, to provide for a different distribution of his effects in the event of bankruptcy [insolvency for our purposes] from that which the law provides.'

This principle was described in *Money Markets International Stockbrokers Ltd v* **24-65**
London Stock Exchange Ltd[129] by Neuberger J as the no-deprivation principle. A person cannot arrange his affairs so that what is his property is taken away in the event of insolvency and does not fall within the insolvent estate. Any contractual provision to that effect is void on the grounds of public policy, regardless of whether the intention is to disadvantage the creditors of the insolvent company, applying *British Eagle International Airlines Ltd v Cie Nationale Air France*.[130]

The result of the no-deprivation principle and its invalidation of any removal of **24-66**
assets from the pool on insolvency is that creditors go to great lengths to ensure that, *prior* to insolvency occurring, assets are available *outside* of the pool to meet their claims. Indeed, in many cases, these devices ensure that there are no unencumbered assets available to the unsecured creditors. The mechanism involved include, for example, taking security over the assets (even if a floating charge is subject to some prior claims) or retaining title to the goods so that those assets never become part of the company's assets on liquidation and are not swept by the rule in *ex p Mackay* into the pool for pari passu distribution. A clause in a sale of goods contract preventing property in the goods passing to the purchaser until payment of debts due to the supplier ensures that such goods remain in the ownership of the supplier pending payment and do not form part of the assets of the company available to any unsecured creditors in a winding up.[131]

---

[127] *Ex p Mackay, ex p Brown, re Jeavons* (1873) 8 Ch App 643 (a bankruptcy case but the doctrine applies in corporate insolvency as well).
[128] (1873) 8 Ch App 643 at 647, per Sir W M James LJ.   [129] [2001] 2 BCLC 347.
[130] [1975] 2 All ER 390, HL.
[131] See *Aluminium Industries Vaassen v Romalpa Ltd* [1976] 2 All ER 552; *Clough Mill Ltd v Martin* [1985] BCLC 64. On retention of title clauses generally, see *Benjamin Sale of Goods* (6th edn, 2002), paras 5-144–5-170.

24-67   Unsecured creditors may escape from the pool if they are in a position to benefit from the doctrine of set-off which is discussed below. Another useful mechanism for some creditors is a trust. It is only property to which the company is beneficially entitled that is available to its creditors so, if the company holds property on trust for others, that property is not available to the company's creditors.[132] This has led to the use of the trust as a means of protecting unsecured creditors by making them benefici-aries under a trust, especially in the situation where suppliers are providing goods and customers are making advance payments to a company when the company is already in some financial difficulty.[133] An example can be seen in *Re Kayford Ltd*[134] where a mail order company in financial difficulties in November 1972 opened a separate bank account into which it paid money sent in advance for goods by customers. When the company went into liquidation in December 1972, it was held that the £11,000 in the account was held on trust for those customers whose money had been deposited there and was not available for the general creditors. The use of such trusts is relatively com-monplace now and the disputes then centre on whether the three certainties, of inten-tion, subject matter and objects, required of any trust, are present.[135] As these trusts are often hastily constructed as financial problems mount, it is not unusual for there to be issues as to whether they have been correctly constituted.

Establishing the liabilities—proof of debts and set-off

24-68   Contrary to what might be supposed, the administration of an insolvent debtor's estate does not involve the payment and discharge of all the debts owing by the debtor. Instead, it is only those debts which are provable in the insolvency and which are proved which will receive any payment.

Submission of proofs

24-69   The rules specifying which debts are provable and the procedure to be followed in establishing a claim are contained in the Insolvency Rules 1986.[136] All claims by cred-itors are provable as debts against the company whether they are present or future, certain or contingent, ascertained or sounding only in damages (IR 1986, r 12.3(1)). The debt may be a debt to which the company is subject at the date on which the com-pany goes into liquidation;[137] or it may be a debt which arises after the company goes

---

[132] See *Barclays Bank Ltd v Quistclose Investments Ltd* [1968] 3 All ER 651, HL; also *Carreras Rothmans Ltd v Freeman Matthew's Treasure Ltd* [1985] 1 All ER 155.

[133] For a valuable account of the advantages and disadvantages of using trusts in this way, see Ellis & Verrill, 'Twilight Trusts' (2007) 20 Insolv Int 151.

[134] [1975] 1 All ER 604.

[135] See *Re Lewis's of Leicester Ltd* [1995] 1 BCLC 428; *Re Holiday Promotions (Europe) Ltd* [1996] 2 BCLC 618; *Re Fleet Disposal Services Ltd, Spratt v AT & T Automotive Services Ltd* [1995] 1 BCLC 345; *Re Sendo International Ltd* [2007] 1 BCLC 141; *Re Farepak Food & Gifts Ltd* [2007] 2 BCLC 1.

[136] IR 1986, rr 4.73–4.94.

[137] IR 1986, r 13.12(1)(a). A company goes into liquidation if it passes a resolution for voluntary winding up or an order for its winding up is made by the court at a time when it has not already gone into liquidation by passing such a resolution: IA 1986, s 247(2).

into liquidation provided that it is in respect of an obligation incurred before that date.[138] Thus a contractual promise, entered into before going into liquidation, to pay a sum of money at a date occurring after the company has gone into liquidation gives rise to a provable debt. Any liability in tort is a debt provable in the winding up, if either (1) the cause of action has accrued at the date on which the company goes into liquidation; or (2) all the elements necessary to establish the cause of action exist at that date except for actionable damage.[139] The liquidator is given power to estimate the value of contingent liabilities or debts of an uncertain amount.[140]

In a compulsory winding up, creditors are required to submit a written claim and the document by which a creditor seeks to establish his claim is known as his 'proof'.[141] In a voluntary winding up, it is for the liquidator to decide whether he requires written proofs[142] and in practice he will require the submission of proofs. The liquidator examines the proof and may admit all or part of the debt or may reject it.[143] Parties aggrieved by his decision may apply to the court.[144] The liquidator has four months from the last date for proving to declare a dividend which he must do, provided he has sufficient funds (IR 1986, r 4.180), unless he has cause to postpone or cancel the dividend (r 11.5). But the liquidator is not personally liable in respect of a dividend and there is no relationship of debtor and creditor between the liquidator and any creditor.[145] If a liquidator fails to pay a declared dividend, an aggrieved creditor can apply to the court for an order directing payment.[146]   **24-70**

In the case of secured creditors, if they are content to rely solely on their security they do not submit a proof of debt at all. Alternatively, they realise their security and prove for any unsecured balance, or surrender their security and prove for the whole amount.[147]   **24-71**

Set-off

A further restriction on the amount for which creditors may prove arises from the application of the set-off rule in IR 1986, r 4.90 where, before the company goes into liquidation, there have been mutual credits, mutual debts or other mutual dealings (subject to certain exclusions, r 4.90(2)) between the company and any creditor of the company proving or claiming to prove for a debt in the liquidation.[148] In that   **24-72**

---

[138] IR 1986, r 13.12(1)(b).

[139] IR 1986, r 13.12(2). This rule is new and was substituted by SI 2006/1272 to redress the problems created by the decision in *Re T & N Ltd* [2005] EWHC 2870, [2006] 2 BCLC 374 where the court held that future asbestos claims were not provable debts for the purposes of winding up because the cause of action had not accrued by the liquidation date. See Toube, 'Future Contingent Claims' (2008) 21 Insolv Int 12 for the background to the change.

[140] IR 1986, r 4.86. In cases of difficulty, application may be made to the court for assistance: IA 1986, s 168(3), (5).

[141] IR 1986, r 4.73(1), (3).   [142] IR 1986, r 4.73(2).   [143] IR 1986, r 4.82.

[144] IR 1986, r 4.83.   [145] *Lomax Leisure v Miller* [2008] 1 BCLC 262.

[146] See *Lomax Leisure v Miller* [2008] 1 BCLC 262.

[147] IR 1986, r 4.88(1), (2). As to the liquidator's right to redeem the security at the creditor's valuation, see r 4.97.

[148] IR 1986, r 4.90 was restated by the Insolvency (Amendment) Rules 2005, SI 2005/527.

case, an account must be taken of what is due from each party to the other in respect of the mutual dealings and the sums due from one party must be set off against the sums due from the other.[149]

24-73   The effect of this rule is that if creditors of a company also owe money to the company they must set off the debts against each other and can only prove for the balance.[150] In practice, set-off benefits creditors, for instead of having to prove with other creditors for the whole of their debt (i.e. having to claim against the pooled assets and possibly risk not being paid at all) creditors can set off debts which they owe to the company and prove or pay only the balance.[151]

24-74   Creditors will therefore seek to acquire rights of set-off, but there must be mutual credits, mutual debts or other mutual dealings giving rise to set-off which must have occurred before the company went into liquidation (IR 1986, r 4.90(1)). 'Mutual debts' does not in itself require anything more than commensurable cross-obligations between the same people in the same capacity and the origin of the debt (whether contract, statute, tort, voluntarily or by compulsion) is immaterial.[152] 'Mutual dealings' merely requires that there should be 'dealings' (in an extended sense which includes the commission of a tort or the imposition of a statutory obligation) giving rise to commensurable cross-claims.[153] There are limits, however, to the claims which may be set off. In *Manson v Smith*[154] the Court of Appeal refused to allow a director to set off his claim against the insolvent company for sums which he had lent to the company (£109,000) and the company's claim against him with respect to sums which he had misappropriated from the company (£27,000). The court concluded that a misappropriation of assets is not a 'dealing' with the company for these purposes[155] and his liability to repay the sums misappropriated only arose as a result of misfeasance proceedings brought after the winding up. Accordingly, the director's liability to repay money could not be set off against sums owed to him by the company. Equally, there can be no set-off where the creditors, at the time the sums became due to them from the company, have notice of the summoning of a creditors' meeting (creditors' voluntary winding up) or that a petition for the winding up of the company is pending (compulsory winding up) (IR 1986, r 4.90(2)(a)).

---

[149] IR 1986, r 4.90(3) and see r 4.90(4) as to when a sum is regarded as due to or from the company.

[150] A creditor who is owed both secured and unsecured debts by the company is entitled to exercise the right of set-off against the unsecured part of the total debt since it is only in respect of that amount that the creditor will submit a proof: *Re Norman Holding Co Ltd* [1990] 3 All ER 757.

[151] See *Stein v Blake* [1995] 2 All ER 961, HL. This is a bankruptcy case, but the principles are essentially common to winding up and bankruptcy.

[152] *Re West End Networks Ltd, Secretary of State for Trade and Industry v Frid* [2004] 2 BCLC 1, HL.

[153] *Re West End Networks Ltd, Secretary of State for Trade and Industry v Frid* [2004] 2 BCLC 1, HL (there was mutuality and therefore set-off was permissible when a company had a claim against Customs & Excise for a VAT credit and there was a claim against the company by the Secretary of State with respect to redundancy payments).

[154] [1997] 2 BCLC 161, CA. See also *Re a company (No 1641 of 2003)* [2004] 1 BCLC 210.

[155] In *Smith (Administrator of Cosslett Contractors Ltd) v Bridgend County BC* [2002] 1 BCLC 77, HL, the court refused to allow a county council to set off a claim which it had (in respect of money lent by the council to a company) against a claim which the company had against the council for damages for conversion (the council had sold equipment belonging to the company) since conversion of a company's property could not amount to a 'dealing' for these purposes: see at p 87.

Set-off is mandatory and creditors are not allowed to contract out of their right of   **24-75**
set-off.[156] As Hoffmann LJ explained: 'If there have been mutual dealings before the
winding-up order which have given rise to cross claims, nether party can prove or
sue for his full claim. An account must be taken and he must prove or sue (as the case
may be) for the balance.'[157] Set-off is automatic and self-executing as at the date of
the winding-up order[158] with the original claims extinguished and only a net balance
remaining.[159]

Set-off is strictly limited to mutual claims existing at the time of liquidation[160] and   **24-76**
there

> '…can be no set-off of claims by third parties, even with their consent. To do so would
> be to allow the parties by agreement to subvert the fundamental principle of pari passu
> distribution of the insolvent company's assets.'[161]

The *BCCI* case, involving the collapse with massive debts of the Bank of Credit and   **24-77**
Commerce International, was a rich source of litigation on the right of set-off, presenting as it did a situation where individuals both saved with the bank and borrowed
from the bank and so were in the capacity of both creditors and debtors. Set-off was
critical to minimising their losses. An absence of set-off would mean that such individuals might lose their savings (being unsecured creditors) while being liable to the
liquidators for their borrowings.

In many instances, the Bank had lent money to companies on the security of depos-   **24-78**
its made with the Bank. In such straightforward cases, the amount of the loan outstanding at the time of liquidation would be set off against the company's deposit at the
bank leaving a balance, one way or the other. In some cases, however, the deposits used
as security for the company's loan were deposits in the name of the company's directors or third parties. The issue arose as to whether there was a sufficient element of
mutuality to allow a loan from the Bank to the company to be set off against a deposit
in the name of a director or third party. If there was no set-off, the companies (often
owned by the directors or third parties) would still be liable to repay all their borrowings, and the directors and third parties would be left to prove in the liquidation for
their deposits.[162] Set-off was therefore critical to their attempts to salvage something
from the collapse of the bank.

---

[156] *National Westminster Bank Ltd v Halesowen Presswork and Assemblies Ltd* [1972] 1 All ER 641, HL;
Stein v Blake [1995] 2 All ER 961, HL, noted Berg [1997] LMCLQ 49; *MS Fashions Ltd v Bank of Credit and
Commerce International SA (No 2)* [1993] 3 All ER 769, Ch D, CA.

[157] *MS Fashions Ltd v Bank of Credit and Commerce International SA (No 2)* [1993] 3 All ER 769 at 775.

[158] *MS Fashions Ltd v Bank of Credit and Commerce International SA (No 2)* [1993] 3 All ER 769 at 775.

[159] *Re Bank of Credit and Commerce International SA (No 8)* [1997] 4 All ER 568, HL, aff'g [1996] 2 All
ER 121, CA; *Stein v Blake* [1995] 2 All ER 961, HL. Any balance can be assigned by the party entitled to it:
Stein v Blake, above. The mutual debts must have existed before the company went into liquidation and the
company cannot seek to create a set-off after that date: see *Hague v Nam Tai Electronics Inc* [2007] 2 BCLC
194 at 198, PC.

[160] The time of liquidation is defined in IA 1986, s 247(2), see above n 137.

[161] *Re Bank of Credit and Commerce International SA (No 8)* [1997] 4 All ER 568 at 573, HL, per Lord
Hoffmann.

[162] As Lord Hoffmann noted, the sense of injustice felt by the depositors in this situation arose not so
much from the operation of the rules of set-off but from the principle that a company is a person separate

24-79   In *MS Fashions Ltd v Bank of Credit and Commerce International SA (No 2)*[163] the bank advanced money to a company and repayment was guaranteed by a director who had a deposit account with the bank. As between himself and the bank, the director was expressed to be a principal debtor. It was held that the company director, as a principal debtor, could rely on the right of set-off to reduce or extinguish the debt owed to the bank by him and his company by the amount standing to his credit in his own deposit account with the bank. The key point, however, was that under the terms of this particular loan, the director was deemed to be the principal debtor.

24-80   In *Re Bank of Credit and Commerce International SA (No 8)*[164] the House of Lords confronted this issue of whether third party deposits[165] which secured loans of borrowers (companies) should be set off against the company's debt or whether the liquidators were entitled to claim the entire debt from the companies leaving the depositors to prove in liquidation for their deposits. The House of Lords held that set-off was limited to mutual claims existing at the date of the winding-up order and there could be no set off of claims by third parties, even with their consent, as to do so would be to allow parties by agreement to subvert the fundamental principle of pari passu distribution of an insolvent company's assets.[166] There was no mutuality between the depositor and the bank which would permit the sum owed by the bank to the depositor (i.e. the amount of the deposit and interest) to be set off against the amount owed by the depositor to the bank under the security document as the depositor did not owe anything to the bank (not having taken on any personal liability for the borrower's debt), but had simply created an effective charge over the deposit in favour of the bank.[167] *MS Fashions Ltd v Bank of Credit and Commerce International SA (No 2)* was distinguishable on the basis of the very unusual security documents executed by the depositor in that case which resulted in the depositor being personally liable to the bank and so the bank's liability to the depositor and the depositor's liability to the bank constituted mutual dealings falling to be set off under IR 1986, r 4.90.[168]

The order of distribution

The expenses of winding up

24-81   Section 115 of the IA 1986 provides that all expenses properly claimed in the winding up, including the remuneration of the liquidator, are payable out of the company's assets in priority to all other claims. The company's assets for this purpose include the proceeds of any legal action taken by a liquidator in his own name or on behalf of the company or arising from any arbitration or other dispute resolution

---

from its controlling shareholders; see *Re Bank of Credit and Commerce International SA (No 8)* [1997] 4 All ER 568 at 573, HL.

[163] [1993] 3 All ER 769.

[164] [1997] 4 All ER 568, HL; aff'g [1996] 2 All ER 121, CA. See also *Tam Wing Chuen v Bank of Credit and Commerce Hong Kong Ltd* [1996] 2 BCLC 69, PC.

[165] The third parties were the beneficial owners of the companies.

[166] [1997] 4 All ER 568 at 573.   [167] [1997] 4 All ER 568 at 574, 576, 577.

[168] See [1997] 4 All ER 568 at 574; see Calnan (1998) 114 LQR 174; Goode (1998) 114 LQR 178.

procedure.[169] The assets for this purpose until the decision in *Re Leyland Daf*[170] included property subject to a charge which as created is a floating charge.[171] This long-established priority was overruled by the House of Lords in *Re Leyland Daf, Buchler v Talbot*[172] which ruled that the expenses of a winding up were not payable out of the assets comprised in a crystallised floating charge in priority to the claims of the charge holder. In their Lordships' view, there were two distinct funds, one the assets subject to the floating charge and the other the 'free assets' of the company. Each fund must bear its own costs of administration; neither was required to bear the costs of administering the other; and in particular the assets comprised in the floating charge were not required to bear the costs and expenses of the winding up as well as those of the receivership. This outcome was very favourable to the floating charge holder, leaving floating charge realisations subject only to the expenses of realisation, preferential debts (a priority imposed by IA 1986, s 175(2) but much reduced by the EA 2002: see **24-89**) and the 'prescribed part' requirements imposed by IA 1986, s 176A (discussed at **24-91**) in favour of the unsecured creditors. But the decision raised major concerns as to the payment of the expenses of liquidation, given that in a typical case, it is very unlikely that the company's free assets will be adequate to meet the costs of winding up. For that reason primarily, the result in *Re Leyland Daf* proved unworkable in practice and the CA 2006, s 1282 reversed the decision. The position is now governed by IA 1986, s 176ZA[173] and related amendments to IR 1986, r 4.218.

Section 176ZA provides that the expenses of winding up have priority over any **24-82** claims to property comprised in or subject to any floating charge and must be paid out of such property to the extent that the assets of the company available for payment of general creditors (excluding any sum set aside under the prescribed part provisions: see **24-91**) is insufficient to meet the expenses of winding up.[174] As discussed below, the preferential creditors also have priority over the claims to property of a floating charge holder and are entitled be paid out of such property to the extent that the assets of the company available for payment of general creditors are insufficient to meet the preferential debts (s 175(2)).[175] The result is that the expenses of winding up and the preferential debts must be paid in priority to the claims of the floating charge holder and to the extent that the assets available to the general creditors are inadequate for this purposes, these prior claims must be met out of property subject to the floating charge.

Obviously, given the priority accorded to expenses of the winding up, if extensive **24-83** costs can be recovered as expenses, then less is available to pay the general unsecured creditors. Creditors have an interest therefore in what is an expense of the winding up, both in terms of whether they can bring their claim within that category and secure priority and, vice versa, whether they can prevent undue depletion of such funds as

---

[169] IA 1986, r 4.218(2)(a).   [170] [2004] 1 BCLC 281, HL.
[171] *Re Barleycorn Enterprises Ltd* [1970] 2 All ER 155, CA; *Re Portbase Clothing Ltd* [1993] 3 All ER 829.
[172] [2004] 1 BCLC 281, HL, overruling *Re Barleycorn Enterprises Ltd* [1970] 2 All ER 155, CA.
[173] Inserted by CA 2006, s 1282 and applicable to liquidations post-6 April 2008, subject to certain transitional provisions; see Fletcher, 'CA 2006, Reversal of *Leyland Daf*' (2007) 20 Insolv Int 30.
[174] IA 1986, s 176ZA(1), (2)(a).   [175] A point reinforced by IA 1986, s 176ZA(2)(b)(ii).

are available by challenging whether a particular cost is indeed an expense of the winding up.

24-84   The issue of what amounts to an 'expense of the winding up' was for many years a hotly disputed matter, both as to what constituted an 'expense' and as to the order of priority to be accorded inter se. The position was clarified initially by the decision of the House of Lords in *Re Toshoku Finance UK plc*[176] and by subsequent changes to the key provision which is IR 1986, r 4.218 which identifies 18 classes of debts as expenses of the winding up and sets out the order of priority in which they are to be paid.

24-85   In *Re Toshoku Finance UK plc*[177] the House of Lords reviewed the operation of IR 1986, r 4.218 and concluded that the rule is a definitive statement of what counts as an expense of the liquidation. It is a complete statement of liquidation expenses, subject only to the qualifications contained in the rules themselves and subject to the principle, which Lord Hoffmann described as the principle in the *Lundy Granite* case,[178] which allows liabilities incurred before the liquidation in respect of property afterwards retained by the liquidator for the benefit of the insolvent estate to be treated as expenses in the winding up (such as liabilities arising under a pre-existing lease). To that limited extent, benefit of the estate is a relevant issue, but it is irrelevant to the payment of an item expressly provided for by IR 1986, r 4.218.[179] The only power reserved to the court is that conferred by IA 1986, s 156 which gives the court in a compulsory winding up a discretion to rearrange the priorities of the listed expenses inter se.[180]

24-86   The result is that IA 1986, s 115 determines the priority of expenses of winding up as against other claims and IR 1986, r 4.218 determines both what is an expense and the order of priority of expenses inter se.[181] Turning to r 4.218, two of the most important categories of debts identified therein are

- expenses properly chargeable or incurred by the official receiver or the liquidator in preserving, realising or getting in any of the assets of the company or otherwise in the preparation or conduct of any legal proceedings, arbitration or other dispute resolution procedures which he has power to bring or defend whether in his own name or the name of the company or relating to the settlement or compromise of any action or dispute to which the proceedings or procedures relate (r 4.218(3)(a)(ii)); and

- any necessary disbursements by the liquidator in the course of his administration (r. 4.218(3)(m)).

24-87   In relation to IR 1986, r 4.218(3)(a)(ii) the issue of legal costs had been controversial with creditors concerned that such realisations as the liquidator might have in hand

---

[176] [2002] 1 BCLC 598, HL.   [177] [2002] 1 BCLC 598, HL.
[178] *Re Lundy Granite Co, ex p Heaven* (1871) 6 Ch App 462.
[179] In reaching this conclusion the House of Lords rejected the so-called liquidation expenses principles as expressed in *Re Atlantic Computers plc* [1992] Ch 505 at 519–23 to the effect that all expenses incurred post-liquidation were payable provided they were incurred for the benefit of the insolvent estate.
[180] See also IR 1986, r 4.220(1).   [181] *Re Toshoku Finance UK plc* [2002] 1 BCLC 598.

should not be 'wasted' on litigation by the liquidator against the former directors on grounds such as wrongful trading (IA 1986, s 214: see at **25-17**) or transactions at an undervalue or preferences (IA 1986, ss 238, 239: see at **25-53, 25-68**). Liquidators for their part were anxious to pursue possible claims, but not if the costs were not permissible as an expense in the winding up, as the courts in fact confirmed.[182] The issue is resolved by IR 1986, r 4.218(3)(a)(ii) which expressly allows litigation costs to be recoverable as an expense in the winding up. Creditor concerns about 'wasteful' litigation are met by the requirement imposed by IA 1986, Sch 4, Part 1 that a liquidator who wishes to exercise his power to bring proceedings under IA 1986, ss 213, 214, 238, 239, 242, 243, or 423 (all provisions allowing actions to be brought to recover assets or seek contributions to the company's assets) requires the sanction of the court or liquidation committee or creditors (depending on the type of winding up: see at **24-52**). In other words, a balance has been struck. A liquidator cannot go off on a frolic of his own running up litigation expenses without consent, but where proceedings are duly sanctioned, the expenses are an expense in the winding up within IR 1986, r 4.218 and recoverable as such in priority to other claims. A further limitation is that litigation expenses which exceed £5,000 are only recoverable out of floating charge realisations where approval or authorisation of such litigation expenses has been granted in accordance with IR 1986, rr 4.218A to 4.218E (i.e. by the preferential creditor or charge holder with a claim to the realisations or by the court).[183]

As for necessary disbursements under IR 1986, r 4.218(3)(m), which was the actual   **24-88** issue in *Re Toshoku Finance UK plc*,[184] specifically the company's liability to corporation tax, the liquidators argued that payment was not required, for the liquidation expenses principle meant that a liability need only be met if it arose as a result of a step taken with a view to, or for the purpose of, obtaining a benefit for the insolvent estate. Applying the analysis set out at **24-85**, the House of Lords rejected this argument. As this tax liability is expressly made an expense in the winding up by r 4.218, issues of benefit to the estate are irrelevant and the court has no discretion to decide other than that the tax liability is a post-liquidation liability which the liquidators are bound to discharge. The rule on this issue has been modified and while any necessary disbursements by the liquidator in the course of his administration are allowed as an expense in the winding up, this does not include any payment of corporation tax on chargeable gains accruing on the realisation of any asset of the company (IR 1986, r 4.218(3)(m), (3)(p)).

Preferential debts

Preferential debts are debts (sometimes described as Crown debts) which Parliament   **24-89** has decided should be paid in priority to all other debts, other than the expenses of

---

[182] See *Re Floor Fourteen Ltd, Lewis v IRC* [2001] 2 BCLC 392, CA; *Re R S & M Engineering Ltd, Mond v Suddards* [1999] 2 BCLC 485; *Re M C Bacon Ltd (No 2)* [1999] 2 BCLC 485.

[183] IR 1986, r 4.218(2)(b) inserted by SI 2008/737; see IR 1986, rr 4.218A–4.128E as to the procedure for obtaining that approval or authorisation.

[184] [2002] 1 BCLC 598, HL.

winding up (IA 1986, s 175). The categories of debts which qualify as preferential debts are set out in IA 1986, Sch 6. Preferential debts rank equally amongst themselves and must be paid in full unless the assets are insufficient to meet them, in which case they abate in equal proportions.[185] In so far as the assets available for payment of general creditors are insufficient for the payment of the preferential debts, the preferential debts have priority over the claims of holders of debentures under a floating charge.[186]

24-90   The categories of preferential debts are now much reduced[187] and preferential status is accorded only to contributions due by employers to certain occupational and state pension schemes and certain limited amounts due as remuneration of employees.[188] Employees are entitled to claim as a preferential debt wages or salary for services rendered in the four months before winding up but up to a maximum amount of £800 per employee.[189] In addition, all accrued holiday remuneration has priority and is not counted towards the £800 limit.[190] In practice, payments to employees of insolvent companies are guaranteed by the state for the employee of an insolvent employer is entitled to make a claim to the National Insurance Fund for certain payments in accordance with the Employment Rights Act 1996, Pt XII. The payments, which must not exceed £350 per employee per week, include arrears of wages or salaries for up to eight weeks and up to six weeks' holiday pay to which the employee may have become entitled in the 12 months before winding up.[191] Once a payment is made out of the fund to an employee, the Secretary of State stands in the shoes of the employee in respect of the debt, including with regard to any preferential status. Any sums recovered by the Secretary of State in the exercise of these subrogated rights are paid into the National Insurance Fund.[192]

The floating charge holder—the prescribed part

24-91   The floating charge holder is entitled to be paid once the liabilities in respect of the expenses of winding up and the preferential debts have been met. As noted above, the categories of preferential debts were much reduced by the Enterprise Act 2002. This reduction in Crown preference was one of the steps (coupled with the abolition

---

[185] A creditor owed preferential and non-preferential debts must exercise any right of set-off proportionately against each class of debt: *Re Unit 2 Windows Ltd* [1985] 3 All ER 647.

[186] See IA 1986, s 175(2)(b), see also s 176ZA(2)(b). 'Floating charge' is defined in s 251. Note also that in a compulsory winding up where distress is levied in the three months before a winding-up order, the preferential debts constitute a first charge on the proceeds of the distress: s 176(2),(3). This does not apply in a voluntary winding up: *Herbert Berry Associates Ltd v IRC* [1978] 1 All ER 161, HL.

[187] The Enterprise Act 2002, s 251 removed the preference afforded to categories of claims payable to the Inland Revenue, Customs and Excise and certain social security contributions.

[188] Also retained, but of limited practical relevance, are certain levies on coal and steel production: IA 1986, Sch 6, para 15A.

[189] IA 1986, Sch 6, paras 9–12; The Insolvency Proceedings (Monetary Limits) Order 1986, SI 1986/1996, art 4.

[190] IA 1986, Sch 6, para 10.   [191] Employment Rights Act 1996, s 186.

[192] Employment Rights Act 1996, s 189.

of administrative receiverships and the reform of administration) intended to foster a rescue culture, see **23-4**. The intention was to release funds from the Crown in a way which would benefit unsecured creditors and so hopefully save such creditors from insolvency themselves. To ensure this outcome, it was necessary to provide a mechanism whereby the sums released from Crown preference did not merely increase the returns to the floating charge holder but would percolate down to the unsecured creditor. The mechanism used is the 'prescribed part' imposed by IA 1986, s 176A. The prescribed part is that part of the estate of a company which must be set aside for unsecured creditors out of sums which would otherwise be available to the holders of a floating charge.[193] The percentage share of the company's assets which must be set aside in this way for unsecured creditors is:[194]

(1) where the company's net property does not exceed £10,000 in value, 50% of that property;

(2) where the company's net property exceeds £10,000 in value, 50% of the first £10,000 in value; and 20% of that part of the company's net property which exceeds £10,000 in value, subject to a maximum of £600,000.

The prescribed part only applies to floating charges created on or after 15 September 2003 (IA 1986, s 176A(9)). It is possible to disapply the requirement to set aside the prescribed part if the net property amounts to less than £10,000 and the office-holder thinks that the cost of making a distribution to the unsecured creditors would be disproportionate to the benefits (s 176A(3)). It is also possible for the prescribed part to be disapplied as part of a company voluntary arrangement or a scheme of arrangement (s 176A(4)) or by court order (s 176A(5)) where costs are disproportionate to the benefits.[195] **24-92**

A fixed or floating charge holder with a shortfall in their security cannot be classed as unsecured creditors so as to participate in the prescribed part which is held for the benefit of unsecured creditors alone. In *Re Airbase (UK Ltd), Thorniley v Revenue and Customs Comrs*[196] and in *Re Permacell Finesse Ltd*, the courts rejected such claims concluding that, as a matter of construction of IA 1986, s 176A and, as a matter of policy, secured creditors are precluded from participation in the prescribed part. **24-93**

Unsecured creditors—the pari passu principle

On liquidation, the assets of the company form a common fund which, subject to the discharging of the expenses of the winding up and the rights of the preferential **24-94**

---

[193] The prescribed part is not subject to the expenses of winding up: see IA 1986, s 176ZA(2)(a).

[194] See The IA 1986 (Prescribed Part) Order 2003, SI 2003/ 2097, art 3.

[195] The power to disapply the prescribed part is a power to disapply it in its entirety or not at all: *Re Courts plc* [2008] BCC 917 (court refused to disapply the prescribed part in a way which would have allowed the 37 largest creditors (with claims in excess of £28,000) to take the prescribed part in its entirety while leaving the remaining 260 creditors (claims below that amount) to receive nothing. See also *Re Hydroserve Ltd* [2008] BCC 175.

[196] [2008] 1 BCLC 437 (also reported as *Re Airbase (UK) Ltd*).

creditors, are subject to a statutory trust for the benefit of all the creditors,[197] other than the secured creditors who look to their security for payment of their debts. The assets must be used to pay the unsecured creditors in accordance with the principle of pari passu distribution that all creditors participate in the pooled assets in proportion to the size of their claim and, where the assets are insufficient to meet all the claims, then they abate proportionately.[198]

24-95   As noted, the widespread use of various mechanisms (i.e. security, trusts and retention of title clauses) means that the pooled assets will usually be insubstantial and quite inadequate to meet the claims of the unsecured creditors. For such creditors who through a lack of foresight or limited contractual or financial power have not taken steps to obtain some protection prior to insolvency, the pari passu rule designed to ensure equal treatment applies. In fact, as Professor Milman noted, the application of the rule may simply secure an equality of misery[199] and the Cork Committee's comments in 1982 remain valid today:

> 'The principle of pari passu distribution has been greatly eroded during the last century or so until to-day it remains as a theoretical doctrine only, with scarcely any application in real life. In a great number of cases, insolvency results in the distribution of the assets among the preferential creditors…and the holders of floating charges…with little if anything for the ordinary unsecured creditors.'[200]

24-96   The position is alleviated somewhat by the prescribed part, as discussed above. Also, a liquidator may be able to swell the assets available to the unsecured creditors by challenging transactions entered into in by the company prior to winding up on the grounds, for example, that they were transactions at an undervalue or preferences. Equally, it may be possible to bring an action against the company's directors for misfeasance or wrongful trading which can result in a contribution by them to the company's assets: all these issues are discussed in Chapter 25. As noted at **24-52**, a liquidator needs the sanction of the court or the creditors to bring litigation under these provisions so as to ensure that the company's assets are not further depleted by the pursuit of what turn out to be pointless claims.

24-97   There is nothing to prevent an unsecured creditor with a claim against the pooled assets from agreeing as a matter of contract to subordinate his claim until such time as all other unsecured creditors are paid,[201] for such an agreement does not have the effect of shrinking the pool of assets available to the creditors. In *Re SSSL*

---

[197] See *Ayerst (Inspector of Taxes) v C & K (Construction) Ltd* [1975] 2 All ER 537; *Webb v Whiffin* (1872) LR 5 HL 711 at 720, 724.

[198] IA 1986, s 107; IR 1986, r 4.181.

[199] See Milman, 'Priority Rights on Corporate Insolvency' in Clarke (ed), *Current Issues in Insolvency Law* (1991), p 77.

[200] The Cork Committee Report (Cmnd 8558), para 233.

[201] See *Re Maxwell Communications Corp plc (No 2)* [1994] 1 BCLC 1; Nolan, 'Less Equal than Others: *Maxwell* and Subordinated Unsecured Obligations' [1995] JBL 485; also *Re British & Commonwealth Holdings (No 3) plc* [1992] BCLC 322.

Realisations (2002) Ltd[202] the Court of Appeal concluded that if a group of companies enters into a subordination agreement (that no group company will prove for an inter-company debt in the liquidation of any group company until a principal creditor was paid in full), it is commercially important that the group companies be held to that agreement when the very circumstances which it addressed (insolvent group companies) arise.[203]

Deferred debts

Certain debts are deferred by statute until all the other debts of the company have been paid. Thus interest on all proved debts, whether or not the debt was an interest-bearing debt, from the company going into liquidation until the date of actual payment, is deferred until the payment of all debts, but any surplus then remaining must be applied in paying interest before being applied for any other purpose.[204]   **24-98**

Another deferred debt is where a company has contracted to redeem or purchase some of its own shares and the company has not completed the transaction by the time of the commencement of the winding up; purchase and redemption of a company's shares are discussed in Chapter 20. The company may be compelled to complete the bargain but only after all other debts and liabilities of the company (other than any due to members in their character as such) have been paid, see **20-24**.[205]   **24-99**

A further deferred payment is any debt or liability due to a member in his character of a member whether by way of dividends, profits or otherwise (IA 1986, s 74(2)(f)). The scope of this provision was considered by the House of Lords in *Soden v British and Commonwealth Holdings plc*[206] where a member of a company brought an action against the company for damages for an alleged misrepresentation which was said to have induced the member to acquire the share capital of the company. That action had not been determined but, the company being insolvent, a preliminary issue arose as to whether damages due under that claim were sums due to a member in his character as a member and so subordinate to the claims of the other creditors of the company.[207]   **24-100**

The House of Lords held that the damages sought by the member did not arise under the statutory contract between a company and its members (i.e. under CA 1985, s 14, now CA 2006, s 33) and therefore were not sums due to a member in his character as such and were not to be subordinated to the claims of other creditors.   **24-101**

---

[202] [2007] 1 BCLC 29, CA.   [203] [2007] 1 BCLC 29 at 59, CA.

[204] IA 1986, s 189(1), (2); for the purposes of interest under this provision, all debts rank pari passu and it makes no difference, for example, whether the debt was preferential: s 189(3).

[205] CA 2006, s 735(4)–(6).   [206] [1997] 2 BCLC 501, HL.

[207] Although the issue was hypothetical, given the size of the potential damages (in the region of £500m), the House of Lords thought it proper to decide this preliminary issue.

24-102   A distinction has to be drawn between sums due to a member in his character of a member by way of dividends, profits or otherwise and sums due to a member of a company otherwise than in his character as a member. A sum is due to a member of a company 'in his character of a member' if the right to receive it is based on a cause of action founded on the statutory contract between the members and the company imposed by CA 1985, s 14 (now CA 2006, s 33) and such other provisions of the Act as conferred rights or imposed liabilities on members. The rationale of IA 1986, s 74(2)(f), Lord Browne-Wilkinson noted, is to ensure that the rights of members *as such* do not compete with the rights of the general body of creditors.[208] A member having a cause of action independent of the statutory contract is in no worse a position than any other creditor.

24-103   Debts due to members in other capacities such as trade creditors or lenders rank, therefore, alongside similar debts due to non-members. This can be a source of abuse. A company may be incorporated with a share capital of, say, two £1 shares and the shareholders then lend the company money for the business. Moreover, since they control the company it is a simple matter for them to secure their loan on the assets of the company. So when the crunch comes, the shareholders, in their capacity as secured creditors, are the first to be paid. The Cork Committee considered this question and recommended that 'on the winding up of a company those of its liabilities, whether secured or unsecured, which are owed to connected persons or companies, and which appear to the court to represent all or part of the long-term capital structure of the company, shall be deferred to the claims of other creditors and be paid only after all such claims have been met in full'.[209] The Committee's recommendation was not enacted in the form they proposed. The courts do have a power, however, to defer payment of debts due from the company to persons found liable for fraudulent or wrongful trading in relation to it until all other debts owed by the company (and interest) have been paid.[210]

Shareholders

24-104   It is only on a solvent winding up that there can be any return of capital or surplus to the shareholders and the priorities as amongst the shareholders and classes of shareholders are discussed in Chapter 14, see **14-21**. On an insolvent liquidation, there will be insufficient funds to pay the creditors in full and therefore there will be no funds remaining for the shareholders who lose their capital, but whose losses are limited to that amount and who bear no responsibility for payments to creditors (assuming they have not given personal guarantees to any creditor).

---

[208] [1997] 2 BCLC 501 at 506.

[209] For the background, see the Cork Committee Report, para 1963.

[210] IA 1986, s 215(4). This provision is of limited practical significance, see the discussion of wrongful and fraudulent trading in Chapter 25.

F Dissolution of the company

Dissolution after winding up

After completion of the winding-up process, the company is removed from the **24-105** register of companies, a process known as dissolution, and it ceases to exist. In both compulsory and voluntary liquidation, dissolution occurs automatically three months after the registration by the registrar of companies of the liquidator's final return at Companies House.[211] An official receiver acting as the liquidator in a compulsory liquidation may apply to the registrar for early dissolution of the company where the realisable assets are insufficient to cover the expenses of winding up and the affairs of the company do not warrant further investigation. In that case, the company is dissolved three months after the application for early dissolution.[212] On being dissolved, any property of the company is deemed to be bona vacantia and vests in the Crown (CA 2006, s 1012).

Striking companies off the register of companies

In practice, the majority of companies that are dissolved in England and Wales each **24-106** year are not formally wound up at all. Instead, they cease to exist when the registrar of companies strikes them off the register as defunct. The registrar has power to do this where the registrar has reasonable cause to believe that a company is not carrying on business or is not in operation (CA 2006, s 1000(1)).[213] Many of the companies targeted will have failed to file annual returns and accounts which may suggest that the company has ceased trading. If the company is still trading, the threat of being struck off the register concentrates the minds of those running the company on the need to fulfil their filing obligations.

The procedure is for the registrar initially to send two letters to the company, enquir- **24-107** ing about the company's activities; subsequently notice is given in the *Gazette* and to the company warning of striking off in three months unless cause is shown to the contrary (CA 2006, s 1000(1)–(3)).[214] At the expiry of the three-month period, unless cause is shown, the registrar may strike off the company's name and must publish notice to this effect in the *Gazette*; on publication of this notice in the *Gazette*, the company is dissolved (s 1000(4)–(6)).

---

[211] IA 1986, s 201(1), (2) (voluntary winding up); s 205(1), (2) (compulsory winding up).

[212] IA 1986, s 202(2), (5).

[213] The registrar may also strike off a company under this procedure where the company has gone into liquidation but no liquidator is acting or the final returns have not been delivered: see CA 2006, s 1001.

[214] CA 2006, s 1000(3). See *Statistical Tables on Companies Registration Activities 2007–08*, Table C1 which shows that 216,000 companies were struck off in 2007–08 (206,800 in the previous year) while 17,900 companies went through either voluntary or compulsory liquidation (18,700 in the previous year). These statistical tables are available on the Companies House website at hwww.companieshouse.gov.uk/about/companiesRegActivities.shtml.

24-108   Alternatively, any company may apply to be struck off the register on payment of the appropriate fee (currently £10). This procedure is governed by CA 2006, s 1003–1011 and is designed to enable companies quickly and inexpensively to be dissolved and removed from the register. The application for striking off must be made by the company's directors or a majority of them (s 1003(2)). Elaborate provision is made for notifying members, creditors and interested parties (via the *Gazette* and otherwise) of the application to be struck off (ss 1003(3), 1006).

Restoration to the register by court order

24-109   The CA 1985 provided for two methods (ss 651 and 653 respectively) by which companies could be restored to the register following their removal. The Company Law Review found these two methods were overlapping and confusing[215] and recommended that there should be only one court route for restoring companies to the register, a recommendation now reflected in CA 2006, s 1029.

24-110   An application may be made to the court for an order restoring a company to the register where the company has been dissolved or deemed dissolved on liquidation or administration or has been struck off either by the registrar of companies or following an application for striking off (CA 2006, s 1029(1), (2)). In other words, the power of the court to restore a company to the register applies regardless of the route by which the removal occurred.

24-111   The application may be made by a wide variety of persons including by the Secretary of State, a former director, any person with a potential legal claim against the company, any former member, creditor or liquidator (for example, where additional assets of the company have come to light), or by any other person appearing to the court to have an interest in the matter.

24-112   Any application for restoration must be made within six years of the date of the dissolution (CA 2006, s 1030(4)). There is no time-limit in the case of an application for the purposes of bringing proceedings against the company for damages for personal injuries, but an order will not be made if it appears to the court that the proceedings would in any case be statute-barred (s 1030(2)), subject to the court's power to order that the period between the date of striking off and any order for restoration should not count for limitation purposes (s 1030(3)).[216]

24-113   The court may make a restoration order: if, where the company was struck off as defunct, the company was at the time of the striking off carrying on business or in operation; if the company was struck off following an application for striking off and any procedural requirement for such applications was not complied with;

---

[215] Company Law Review, *Final Report*, vol 1 (2001), paras 11.17–11.20; also *Completing the Structure* (2000), paras 8.31–8.35; *Developing the Framework* (2000), paras 10.90–10.135.

[216] The circumstances in which it would be appropriate for the court to make such a limitation declaration are addressed by the Court of Appeal in *Smith v White Knight Laundry Ltd* [2001] 2 BCLC 206; and see generally Keay, 'The Pursuit of Legal Proceedings against Dissolved Companies' [2000] JBL 405.

or if in any other case, the court considers it just that the company be restored to the register.[217]

The position under the CA 1985 (which is unchanged, presumably, under the CA 2006) **24-114** was that exercising the court's discretion against restoration should be the exception, not the rule.[218] The restoration takes effect when a copy of the court's order is delivered to the registrar (CA 2006, s 1031(2)). The effect of the restoration under the CA 1985 was to restore, to the fullest extent possible, the 'as you were' position of the company as if the company had never been removed from the register[219] and that position is retained by CA 2006, s 1032.[220]

When a company is restored to the register, property which had vested in the Crown **24-115** as bona vacantia re-vests in the company, unless it has already been disposed of, in which case the Crown must account for any consideration received (CA 2006, s 1034(1), (2)), subject to the Crown's ability to recoup any expenses incurred in connection with the disposition (s 1034(3)).

Administrative restoration to the register

The CLR recommended the introduction of a procedure of administrative restora- **24-116** tion whereby the registrar of companies is able to restore companies to the register when they have been struck off as defunct by the registrar.[221] That procedure is now contained in CA 2006, ss 1024–1028. The application must be made within 6 years of the date of dissolution and can be made only by a former director or former member of the company (s 1024(3), (4)).

The company must be restored to the register if, and only if, the following conditions **24-117** for restoration are met:

(i) the company was carrying on business or in operation at the time of its striking off;

(ii) the Crown's representative has given any consent that may be necessary (because any property of the company has vested in the Crown as *bona vacantia*);

(iii) the applicant has delivered any documents necessary to bring the public record up to date (typically annual accounts and appointments of directors) and has paid any penalties (for late filing of accounts) due at the date of dissolution or striking off (CA 2006, s 1025).

---

[217] CA 2006, s 1031(1). As to the nature of this jurisdiction, see *Re Priceland Ltd, Waltham Forest LBC v Registrar of Companies* [1997] 1 BCLC 467; also *Steans Fashions Ltd v Legal and General Assurance Society Ltd* [1995] 1 BCLC 332, CA; *Re Blenheim Leisure (Restaurants) Ltd* [2000] BCC 554; *Re Blenheim Leisure (Restaurants) Ltd (No 2)* [2000] BCC 821.

[218] *Re Priceland Ltd, Waltham Forest LBC v Registrar of Companies* [1997] 1 BCLC 467; and see *Re Blue Note Enterprises Ltd* [2001] 2 BCLC 427.

[219] See *Top Creative Ltd v St Albans DC* [2000] 2 BCLC 379, CA.

[220] Detailed provision is made as to the name of the company on restoration: see CA 2006, s 1033.

[221] Company Law Review, *Final Report*, vol 1 (2001), para 11.19.

24-118   The application must be accompanied by a statement of compliance with the requirements as to the standing of the applicant and with the conditions for restoration (CA 2006, s 1026). If satisfied, the registrar gives notice to the applicant of the decision to restore the company and restoration takes effect from the date that notice is sent (s 1027). As with court restoration, the effect of restoration is that the company is deemed to have continued in existence as if it had not been struck off (s 1028(1)).[222]

---

[222] Detailed provision is made as to the name of the company on restoration, see CA 2006, s 1033. If need be, an application can be made to the court for such directions and provisions as may be necessary to place the company and other persons in the position they would have been in had the company not been struck off: s 1028(3), (4).

25

Directors' liabilities and vulnerable transactions on insolvency

A Introduction

In addition to the formal processes of dealing with the insolvent company (liquidation, administration etc), the collapse of the company is also the time when the conduct of the directors of the company is reviewed.[1] Generally, the emphasis is on civil remedies and recoveries for creditors. There are a small number of provisions (essentially IA 1986, ss 206–211) which create criminal offences, as does CA 2006, s 993 (fraudulent trading) although the number of prosecutions under these provisions is low. The offences under the IA 1986 relate mainly to offences committed by officers of the company in the course of or just prior to winding up and they range from fraudulently removing the company's property, to destroying or falsifying entries in the company's books, to failing to co-operate and assist the liquidator in a winding up. **25-1**

On the civil side, redress for breach of duty by directors is available through the summary action for misfeasance (IA 1986, s 212) while particular types of trading are targeted for civil recoveries, namely fraudulent trading (s 213) and wrongful trading (s 214). A liquidator or administrator may also seek to challenge certain transactions which took place in the run-up to liquidation or administration, either on the basis that they were transactions at an undervalue or intended to prefer a particular creditor (see below). Criminal and civil provision is made to deal with what is called the phoenix syndrome, i.e. continuing to trade using the name by which the insolvent company was known or a name which is so similar as to suggest an association with that company (ss 216–218). More broadly, the overall conduct of the directors is reviewed in order to determine whether disqualification is an appropriate response. Disqualification is considered in detail in Chapter 6. It suffices to note here that the most common ground for disqualification is that, following a company going into insolvent liquidation or administration, the conduct of a director is found to have **25-2**

---

[1] A number of the provisions, e.g. IA 1986, ss 206–211, apply to 'officers' which includes a director, manager or secretary (see CA 2006, s 1173, applied by IA 1986, s 251), but our discussion focuses primarily on directors. See generally Fletcher, *The Law of Insolvency* (4th edn, 2009); Goode, *Principles of Corporate Insolvency* Law (3rd edn, 2005), Chs 11, 12; Finch, *Corporate Insolvency Law* (2001), Ch 15.

fallen below the standards of probity and competence appropriate to a director of a limited liability company.[2]

25-3   With the exception of disqualification proceedings, few of the other provisions are used to any significant extent, in part because of the investigative difficulties which liquidators face in trying to bring cases against directors, but especially because of a lack of funding to pursue these matters and the need therefore to obtain the sanction of the court or the creditors (which may not be forthcoming) before proceeding: see 24-87. When claims are brought, they are often brought on multiple grounds so it is not uncommon to find allegations of misfeasance, wrongful trading, transactions at an undervalue and preferences all in the one case.[3] While claims are limited by the funding difficulties mentioned above, the provisions are thought to have some deterrent value and provide liquidators with some negotiating weapons when dealing with a director whose company has collapsed.

B Misfeasance procedure—IA 1986, s 212

25-4   The misfeasance provision is a procedural mechanism whereby actions may be brought, typically by liquidators (though the section is wider than that) typically against directors (again the section is wider than that), with a view to holding them liable for a breach of duty to the company.[4] The section provides 'a summary procedure in a liquidation for obtaining a remedy against delinquent directors without the need for an action in the name of the company. It does not create new rights and obligations'.[5]

25-5   The section enables the court, on the application of the official receiver, the liquidator, or any creditor, or a contributory with the leave of the court,[6] to examine the conduct of any officer of the company, to see if they have misapplied or retained or become accountable for money or other property of the company or been guilty of any misfeasance or breach of fiduciary or other breach of duty to the company (so negligence is included).[7] The court can order the person to repay, restore or account for the money or property or to make contribution to the assets of the company (payment is to the company and not to the applicant) as the court thinks just, but the court's power

---

[2] See CDDA 1986, s 6 and discussion at **6-71**.

[3] See, for example, *Re MDA Investment Management Ltd, Whalley v Doney* [2004] 1 BCLC 217.

[4] In a compulsory winding up, a liquidator can only bring a misfeasance claim with the sanction of the court or the creditors: IA 1986, Sch 4, Part II, para 4.

[5] *Cohen v Selby* [2001] 1 BCLC 176 at 183, per Chadwick LJ; see also *Re DKG Contractors Ltd* [1990] BCC 903; and generally Doyle, 'Misfeasance Proceedings: Chasing the Delinquents' (1994) 7 Insolv Int 25, 35; Oditah, 'Misfeasance Proceedings against Company Directors' [1992] LMCLQ 207.

[6] IA 1986, s 212(5).

[7] See *Re Barton Manufacturing Co Ltd* [1998] 1 BCLC 740; *Re D'Jan of London Ltd, Copp v D'Jan* [1994] 1 BCLC 561; also *Re Welfab Engineers Ltd* [1990] BCLC 833.

is discretionary.[8] Any recoveries on the grounds of misfeasance are in respect of pre-existing rights of the company and are therefore capable of being charged or assigned by the liquidator.[9] Such recoveries (as an asset of the company) are subject to the claims of a floating charge holder (i.e. where the charge is over the whole of the undertaking as is commonly the case, the recoveries fall within the grasp of the charge) but equally are subject to the prior payment of the expenses of winding up (IA 1986, s 115) and the preferential debts (s 175).[10]

C Fraudulent and wrongful trading

Fraudulent trading

Liability for fraudulent trading is imposed on persons knowingly a party to the carry-ing on of any business of a company with intent to defraud creditors of the company, or creditors of any other person, or for any fraudulent purpose.[11]   **25-6**

There are two aspects to fraudulent trading:[12]   **25-7**

- a civil liability in IA 1986, s 213 which applies when the company is in the course of winding up when a liquidator (only) may apply for a declaration that any per-sons knowingly parties to the carrying on of the business in the manner stated are to be liable to make such contribution to the company's assets as the court thinks proper;[13]

- a criminal offence contained in CA 2006, s 993 which applies regardless of whether the company is in winding up.

Civil liability

The civil liability is less important now in the light of the provision on wrongful trading in IA 1986, s 214 (based on negligence), see **25-17** and any liquidator inter-ested in seeking civil recoveries is likely to look to that provision so avoiding the dif-ficult task of establishing an intent to defraud. On occasion, recourse to s 213 is useful,   **25-8**

---

[8] See, for example, *Kinlan v Crimmin* [2007] 2 BCLC 67 where, despite breaches of the statutory require-ments regarding a purchase of shares, the court declined to order a director to make repayment to a liquid-ator given his good faith change of position in the belief that the purchase agreement was valid and binding. See also *Manson v Smith* [1997] 2 BCLC 161, CA: no set off is available between a debt due from the company to a director and his liability to repay money under misfeasance proceedings because a misappropriation of assets is not a mutual dealing as required for the purposes of set off: see **24-74**.

[9] *Re Oasis Merchandising Services Ltd* [1997] 1 BCLC 689.

[10] See discussion at **24-81** and IR 1986, r 4.218 as to the expenses of winding up.

[11] The word 'creditor'…in its ordinary meaning, denotes one to whom money is owed; whether that debt can presently be sued for is immaterial: *R v Smith (Wallace Duncan)* [1996] 2 BCLC 109, CA.

[12] See generally Keay, *Company Directors' Responsibilities to Creditors* (2007), Chs 3–6.

[13] In a creditors' voluntary liquidation or a compulsory winding up, a liquidator can only bring a claim under this section with sanction of the court or the creditors: IA 1986, Sch 4, Part I, para 3: see **24-52**.

however, because it applies to a wider category of respondents ('any persons') whereas s 214 applies only to directors or shadow directors. The point can be illustrated by *Re BCCI (No 15), Morris v Bank of India*[14] where the liquidators of BCCI used the provision against the defendant bank which the liquidators alleged knowingly participated in the fraudulent trading of BCCI. As discussed in Chapter 3, the court attributed to the bank the knowledge of an employee who was the general manager of the London branch of the bank (see **3-98** on attribution). This employee had a senior position in the bank, he brought the transactions at issue to the bank, the board relied on him in relation to them, he was given a free hand to negotiate them and they were plainly suspicious.[15] Given the purpose of the provision, it was necessary in the court's view to attribute his knowledge to the bank which was therefore liable under IA 1986, s 213 as a person knowingly party to the carrying on of the business of BCCI with intent to defraud.[16] The bank was ordered to pay $82m to the liquidators of BCCI. The Court of Appeal justified attributing the knowledge of this employee to the bank by reference to the purpose of IA 1986, s 213. The paramount purpose of the provision, the court said, is compensation for those who suffer loss as a result of fraudulent trading and that purpose is emasculated if liability is limited to those cases in which the board of directors is directly privy to the fraud, see **3-109**.[17]

25-9   A distinction must be drawn between an individual creditor who is defrauded in the course of the carrying on of the business of the company—he has his individual remedy under the general law—and fraudulent trading.[18] Fraudulent trading requires that the business of the company has been carried on with intent to defraud creditors of the company. If that is the position, liability arises, even if only one creditor is shown to have been defrauded.[19] These points were clarified by the Court of Appeal in *Morphitis v Bernasconi*.[20] In this case, a company got into financial difficulties particularly because it was subject to onerous obligations under a lease. A scheme was devised (with legal advice) to restructure the business by transferring it to a new company and paying off the company's trade creditors other than the landlord.[21] For the scheme to work, it was necessary to avoid action by the landlord for a period of time while the scheme was put in place so rent continued to be paid, though only after numerous requests by the landlord. Eventually, a payment of rent was promised for the following month which it was not intended to pay and which was not paid. On the company going into winding up, the liquidator brought a fraudulent trading action against the directors, essentially alleging that the directors intended to deceive the landlord when the directors knew that no further payments of rent would be made. The Court of Appeal reversed a finding that the directors were liable for fraudulent

---

[14] [2005] 2 BCLC 328.   [15] [2005] 2 BCLC 328 at 360–1.   [16] [2005] 2 BCLC 328 at 360–1.
[17] [2005] 2 BCLC 328 at 356, per Mummery LJ.   [18] *Morphitis v Bernasconi* [2003] 2 BCLC 53, CA.
[19] *Re Gerald Cooper Chemicals Ltd* [1978] 2 All ER 49; *Morphitis v Bernasconi* [2003] 2 BCLC 53, CA.
[20] [2003] 2 BCLC 53, CA.
[21] Due regard was had to the need to transfer the assets at market value, to avoid preferring any creditors and to the prohibitions on the new company trading under a prohibited name in breach of IA 1986, s 216.

trading for it had not been established that the business of the company had been carried on with an intent to defraud.[22]

Although obiter in the light of the finding as to liability, the Court of Appeal in *Morphitis v Bernasconi*[23] offered some valuable insight into the nature of civil liability under s 213. The power to order a contribution is compensatory and not penal[24] as the penal position is preserved in CA 2006, s 993, and Parliament could not have intended that the civil power would be used to punish a wrongdoer.[25] The principle on which the contribution power should be exercised is that the contribution to the assets in which the company's creditors will share in the liquidation should reflect (and compensate for) the loss which has been caused to those creditors by the carrying on of the business with an intent to defraud.[26]   **25-10**

Any sums recovered by the liquidator are impressed with a statutory trust in favour of the unsecured creditors (rather than the creditor defrauded).[27] Recoveries do not form part of the assets of the company so as to be within the grasp of any floating charge,[28] but they are subject to the prior claims of the expenses of the winding up and any preferential debts, see **24-89**.[29]   **25-11**

Criminal offence

As noted fraudulent trading is also a criminal offence under CA 2006, s 993 and prosecutors find it useful because of the wide variety of company frauds which may fall within its scope, assuming of course that it is possible to establish an intent to defraud to the criminal burden of proof. On the other hand, it may prove of diminishing importance as the Fraud Act 2006 offers prosecutors a greater range of open-ended fraud provisions which may be more suitable in a given case.   **25-12**

The section applies not just to the carrying on of the business of the company with an intent to defraud creditors, but to the carrying on of business for any fraudulent purpose.[30] Provided the business has been carried on with an intent to defraud, it suffices even though only one creditor has been defrauded,[31] although most cases would involve a pattern of fraudulent trading by the defendants.   **25-13**

---

[22] Not everyone agrees with the result in this case: see Keay, above n 12, p 43.

[23] [2003] 2 BCLC 53, CA.

[24] *Re BCCI (No 15), Morris v Bank of India* [2005] 2 BCLC 328 at 356, CA; *Morphitis v Bernasconi* [2003] 2 BCLC 53, CA.

[25] *Morphitis v Bernasconi* [2003] 2 BCLC 53, CA.

[26] *Morphitis v Bernasconi* [2003] 2 BCLC 53, CA.

[27] *Re Esal (Commodities) Ltd* [1997] 1 BCLC 705, CA.

[28] *Re Oasis Merchandising Services Ltd, Ward v Aitken* [1997] 1 BCLC 689, CA.

[29] See discussion at **24-81** and IR 1986, r 4.218 as to the expenses of winding up.

[30] See *R v Kemp* [1988] QB 645, CA (victims here were not creditors but customers of the company who were induced to accept worthless goods which they were duped into buying); see also *Re Sarflax Ltd* [1979] 1 All ER 529 (distributing the proceeds of the realisation of assets could constitute carrying on business); also *Re Augustus Barnett & Son Ltd* [1986] BCLC 170.

[31] *Morphitis v Bernasconi* [2003] 2 BCLC 53, CA; *Re Gerald Cooper Chemicals Ltd* [1978] 2 All ER 49.

25-14   The type of conduct commonly involved includes the obtaining of credit from suppliers with no intention of paying for those goods; persuading customers to place large deposits with no intention of supplying the goods; obtaining credit from banks and factors by false invoices or accounts; falsifying accounts to show inflated profits; and trading to defraud the Inland Revenue. But the mere granting of a preference to a creditor is not, without more, fraudulent trading.[32]

25-15   The essence of fraudulent trading is dishonesty[33] and it is not enough to show that the company has continued to trade while insolvent (although such conduct may give rise to liability for wrongful trading: discussed below). Instead the conduct must 'involve actual dishonesty, involving, according to current notions of fair trading among commercial men, real moral blame.'[34] Although this is a strict standard, it will clearly be satisfied where directors allow a company to incur credit when they have no reason to think the creditors will ever be paid.[35] It will also be established, as the Court of Appeal made clear in *R v Grantham*,[36] where credit is incurred at a time when the directors have no good reason to think funds will become available to pay the creditors when their debts become due or shortly thereafter.

25-16   Liability extends beyond directors to any persons 'knowingly parties to the carrying on of the business' with intent to defraud which will include those exercising at least some positive role in the management of the business;[37] and see the discussion at **25-8**. Creditors can be party to fraudulent trading if they accept money knowing it has been procured by carrying on business with intent to defraud creditors and for the very purpose of paying their debts.[38] Third parties who are involved in and who assist and benefit from the offending business, or the business carried on in an offending way, and do so knowingly and therefore dishonestly do fall, or at least can fall, within the provision.[39] A company secretary who merely carries out the administrative functions of such an office, however, is not concerned in the management of the company or in carrying on its business.[40]

Wrongful trading

25-17   The difficulties in establishing the intent to defraud necessary to give rise to liability for fraudulent trading led the Cork Committee to recommend the introduction of a provision for wrongful trading under which civil liability could arise without proof of fraud or dishonesty and without requiring the criminal standard of proof.[41]

---

[32] *R v Sarflax* [1979] 1 All ER 529.

[33] The ordinary criminal law test of dishonesty as laid down in *R v Ghosh* [1982] 2 All ER 689 applies.

[34] *Re Patrick and Lyon Ltd* [1933] Ch 786 at 790, per Maugham J. See *R v Cox, R v Hedges* [1983] BCLC 169.

[35] *Re William C Leitch Bros Ltd* [1932] 2 Ch 71.   [36] [1984] 3 All ER 166, CA.

[37] Someone who orchestrates, organises or can seize control of the business concerned is within the provision: *Re BCCI, Banque Arabe v Morris* [2001] 1 BCLC 263.

[38] *Re Gerald Cooper Chemicals Ltd* [1978] 2 All ER 49.

[39] *Re BCCI, Banque Arabe v Morris* [2001] 1 BCLC 263.

[40] *Re Maidstone Building Provisions Ltd* [1971] 3 All ER 363.

[41] See the Cork Committee Report (Cmnd 8558), Ch 44, see **2-3**.

IA 1986, s 214 allows a liquidator (only[42]) of a company in the course of winding up   **25-18**
to apply where certain conditions are met for an order that a director (including a
shadow director) make such contribution[43] to the company's assets as the court thinks
proper.[44] The conditions are that:

- the company has gone into insolvent liquidation;[45] and

- at some time before the commencement of the winding up, the director knew or
  ought to have concluded that there was no reasonable prospect that the company
  would avoid going into insolvent liquidation (s 214(2)).

Section 214(4) provides that the facts which a director of a company ought to know
or ascertain, the conclusions which he ought to reach and the steps which he ought to
take are those which would be known or ascertained, or reached or taken, by a reasonably diligent person having both:

(1) the general knowledge, skill and experience that may reasonably be expected of
    a person carrying out the same functions as are carried out by that director in
    relation to the company, and

(2) the general knowledge, skill and experience that that director has.

As discussed in Chapter 10, IA 1986, s 214(4) was taken to set the standard of care and   **25-19**
skill for directors in all contexts and not just in relation to wrongful trading, hence it
is replicated now in CA 2006, s 174 as one of the general duties of directors. As noted
there, the standard imposed by IA 1986, s 214(4) is as an objective minimum standard,
that of a reasonably diligent person who has accepted the office of director, set in the
context of the functions undertaken, with that objective minimum standard capable
of being raised in the light of the particular attributes of the director in question.[46] See
the detailed discussion in Chapter 10 as to the content of this duty and the standard
expected of directors.

The 'twilight' zone

The most difficult issue in applying IA 1986, s 214 is identifying the point in time   **25-20**
when directors acting to the standard required by s 214(4) knew or ought to have

---

[42] Strangely an administrator has no power in this regard, a position which will become increasingly
anomalous as administration becomes the insolvency process of choice, as discussed at **23-118**; see also
Keay, above n 12, p 125.

[43] The declaration by the court is for the recovery of a sum of money, although there is nothing to preclude
the liquidator from accepting property to satisfy that liability: see *Re Farmezier Products Ltd* [1997] BCC
655, CA, aff'g [1995] 2 BCLC 462.

[44] IA 1986, s 214(1), (7). Once found liable, the court can also make a disqualification order under CDDA
1986, s 10. As to wrongful trading generally, see Keay, above n 12, Chs 7–10; Mokal, *Corporate Insolvency
Law, Theory and Application* (2005), Ch 8; Simmons, 'Wrongful Trading' [2001] 14 Insolv Intell 12. For a
broader perspective on the difficulty in balancing directors' duties to shareholders and to creditors in the
vicinity of insolvency, see Davies, 'Directors' Creditor—Regarding Duties in Respect of Wrongful Trading
Decisions in the Vicinity of Insolvency' (2006) 7 EBOR 301.

[45] Defined IA 1986, s 214(6): a company goes into insolvent liquidation for these purposes if it goes into
liquidation at a time when its assets are insufficient for the payment of its debts and other liabilities and the
expenses of the winding up.

[46] See *Re Brian D Pierson (Contractors) Ltd* [2001] 1 BCLC 275 at 302.

concluded there was no reasonable prospect of avoiding insolvent liquidation. Of course, there is something of an overlap between the director's duty to have regard (under CA 2006, s 172(3)) to creditors' interests in cases of insolvency or doubtful solvency, discussed at **9-42**, and IA 1986, s 214.[47] As discussed in the context of CA 2006, s 172(3), directors are subject to a variety of obligations in terms of maintaining financial records and preparing accounts which should help them appreciate at any given time the company's financial position. Proper regard to their duties of care and skill should also ensure that they are well informed about the company's financial position: see the discussion at **9-52**. The purpose of IA 1986, s 214 is in effect to force them to act on that knowledge or risk a personal liability under this provision, but often whether out of optimism or 'head in the sand' blindness, directors fail to act until too late, with disastrous consequences for the company's creditors.

25-21   In *Re Cubelock Ltd*[48] the question was whether the directors were liable for wrongful trading from the beginning of trading as the company was balance sheet insolvent (assets insufficient to meet its liabilities) from the outset. The court rejected the claim, noting that it is common for companies to trade in this manner in the initial months of business. The issue for the purpose of IA 1986, s 214 is whether the directors continued trading after a point in time when they either knew or on any realistic view ought to have known that there was no reasonable prospect of avoiding insolvent liquidation. In *Official Receiver v Doshi*,[49] for example, a director who knew that his company could only continue to trade as a result of fraudulent invoicing ought to have concluded that there was no reasonable prospect that the company would avoid going into insolvent liquidation.

25-22   A more specific issue regarding the level of knowledge required was canvassed in *Re Continental Assurance Co of London plc*[50] which involved the collapse of a small insurance company in 1992. Large and unexpected losses had arisen which came to the board's attention in June 1991. The liquidators sought contributions to the company's assets from the directors on the grounds of wrongful trading and/or misfeasance. In particular, it was alleged that the company applied inappropriate accounting policies which showed the company to be solvent when, had an appropriate accounting policy been adopted by the company, the directors would and should have appreciated that the company was insolvent and they should have taken steps to stop trading.[51]

25-23   The court found that for the directors to have reached these conclusions would have required of them knowledge of accounting concepts of a particularly sophisticated nature. Park J rejected any idea that IA 1986, s 214(4) imposes such an unrealistically high standard of skill. He commented:[52]

---

[47] See Davies, above n 44, at 329 who notes that the duty plays a useful supplementary role to IA 1986, s 214.

[48] [2001] BCC 523.   [49] [2001] 2 BCLC 235.   [50] [2007] 2 BCLC 287.

[51] In fact, the court concluded that, even if an alternative accounting approach had been taken, the company was solvent in June 1991: see [2007] 2 BCLC 287 at 399.

[52] *Re Continental Assurance Co of London plc* [2007] 2 BCLC 287 at 402–3.

'...In my view, [the directors] would have been expected to be intelligent laymen. They would need to have a knowledge of what the basic accounting principles for an insurance company were.... They would be expected to be able to look at the company's accounts and, with the guidance which they could reasonably expect to be available from the finance director and the auditors, to understand them. They would be expected to be able to participate in a discussion of the accounts, and to ask intelligent questions of the finance director and the auditors. What I do not accept is that they could have been expected to show the sort of intricate appreciation of recondite accounting details possessed by a specialist in the field...'

On the facts, he found that the directors had taken a wholly responsible and   **25-24** conscientious attitude both to the company's position and to their own responsibilities as directors at all times from and after the first crisis board meeting in 1991 when major and unexpected losses were reported to them. The directors did not ignore the question of whether the company could properly continue to trade; on the contrary, the court found that they considered it directly, closely and frequently.[53] They were entitled, the court said, to have regard to the accounts before them and to the opinion of the finance director and the auditors that the company was solvent. They did not just accept in an unquestioning way the figures which were put before them, but questioned the executive directors closely and at length on them and were satisfied with the explanations given.[54] Overall, the court considered that the way in which the directors reacted to the financial crisis which blew up in the middle of 1991 was entirely appropriate. There was no liability either on the ground of wrongful trading or on the ground of misfeasance.[55]

In *Re The Rod Gunner Organisation Ltd, Rubin v Gunner*[56] the company had been   **25-25** trading at a loss for some time when, in March 1998, S was appointed as a director and chief executive officer. During the months following his appointment, S contributed in excess of £275,000 to the company but these funds were never on a scale large enough to meet the company's needs. From July 1998 he continually gave the other two directors assurances that he would raise further funds for the company through a variety of different arrangements, but none of the funds ever materialised. In June 1999, the company went into insolvent liquidation. The liquidator successfully brought a wrongful trading action against the other two directors, S having become bankrupt.

---

[53] *Re Continental Assurance Co of London plc* [2007] 2 BCLC 287 at 360.

[54] *Re Continental Assurance Co of London plc* [2007] 2 BCLC 287 at 404.

[55] See Keay, above n 12, p 98 who criticises the emphasis placed by Park J on the need for some blameworthy behaviour by the directors when the section does not require the establishment of any wrongdoing. The issue, Keay says, is merely whether the directors should have concluded that there was no reasonable prospect of avoiding insolvent liquidation. While that is undoubtedly true on a reading of the section, it is clear that the judiciary are unwilling to take that literal approach and it can be argued that the court is not so much looking to establish blameworthiness but merely using that measure as a device to determine the question Keay asks, namely whether the directors should have concluded there was no reasonable prospect of avoiding insolvent liquidation.

[56] [2004] 2 BCLC 110.

25-26   The court considered that from his appointment in March 1998 to the end of
September 1998, the respondents had been entitled to rely on S's assurances that further much more significant sums would be forthcoming, given he did provide some
funding to the company. However, by October 1998 none of the proposed arrangements had yielded any further capital contributions from S who repeatedly failed to
make good on his promises and the company was under intense financial pressure.
In the circumstances, the court said, no reasonably diligent director faced with such
overwhelming losses and substantial accrued debts would have believed that S would
provide the necessary funding. The respondents should not have continued to give S
the benefit of the doubt and should have known that there was no reasonable prospect that the company would avoid going into insolvent liquidation. They were liable
accordingly and an inquiry was ordered to determine the appropriate contribution
to be made by them.

25-27   In deciding when the point in time is reached—when the directors knew or ought to
have known that there was no reasonable prospect of avoiding insolvent liquidation—
the courts are torn between ensuring that the statutory provision does impose an
element of pressure on directors, as Parliament intended, so that they do not continue
to display inappropriate optimism in the face of mounting losses of the creditors. On
the other hand, the courts are anxious not to judge commercial situations with hindsight and take such a strict approach that cautious directors, for fear of wrongful trading, rush too soon to put their companies into administration or liquidation.

25-28   Even if it is established that a director knew or ought to have concluded that insolvent liquidation could not be avoided, the director has a defence if he can satisfy the
court that, after that point in time was reached, he took every step with a view to
minimising the potential loss to the company's creditors as he ought to have taken
(IA 1986, s 214(3)).[57] Having said that, the threshold set is high ('every step').[58] In *Re
Brian D Pierson Ltd*,[59] the court noted that it is not sufficient for these purposes for
a director to claim that he continued to trade with the intention of trying to make a
profit. The provision is intended to apply, the court said, to cases 'where, for example,
directors take specific steps with a view to preserving or realising assets or claims for
the benefit of creditors, even if they fail to achieve that result, and it does not cover
the very act of wrongful trading itself'.[60] Equally, it is difficult to know what practical
steps would convince the court that the director took 'every step', but presumably steps
such as attempting to secure additional financing, reaching agreements with creditors, taking professional advice, and working closely with the company's bank would
all be steps which the court would accept as steps designed to protect the creditors'
interests. Cautious and risk-adverse directors may consider that the only appropriate
step is to put the company into administration, liquidation etc, but that is not what the

---

[57] Relief is not available under CA 2006, s 1157: see **13-55**; *Re Produce Marketing Consortium Ltd* [1989]
3 All ER 1.
[58] As Goode points out, this may mean no more than 'every reasonable step' when read with 'reasonably
diligent person', see Goode, *Principles of Corporate Insolvency Law* (2005), para 12–37.
[59] [2001] 1 BCLC 275.   [60] [2001] 1 BCLC 275 at 308.

legislation necessarily demands though, obviously, it may be the only practical step in many instances.

Extent of any liability

Once liability is established, the extent of any contribution to the company's assets is a matter for the court's discretion and the aim here is primarily compensatory rather than penal to ensure that any depletion of the assets attributable to the period of wrongful trading is made good.[61] On the issue of the quantum of liability for wrongful trading, the section offers no guidance and to that extent imposes no limits, but there is much of interest in the obiter comments of Park J in *Re Continental Assurance Co of London plc*[62] discussed at **25-22**. Although Park J concluded that the directors had acted perfectly properly in that case in continuing to trade, having heard argument on the issue of quantum, he thought it proper to deal with the issue in some detail. In his view, the quantum of liability can be summed up as one of an increase in net deficiency reflecting the loss to the company of the continued trading between the date when the company should have been put into liquidation and the date of actual liquidation.[63] But even then there must be a connection between that increase and the conduct of the directors which resulted in the wrongful trading. Park J was anxious not to describe this as an issue of causation,[64] nevertheless he thought that there must be some nexus between the wrongfulness of the directors' conduct and the losses which the liquidator seeks to recover. For example, the company might incur losses during the period of wrongful trading as a result of bad weather which had nothing to do with the directors' conduct.[65] He considered that the proper principle would be that liability should be limited to those consequences which are attributable to that which made the act wrongful. Furthermore, in his view, the starting point for liability under IA 1986, s 214 is that it is a several liability (i.e. a personal liability of the director) and not a joint and several liability, for it is plain that the focus of the section is on the individual director and his conduct and not on the joint conduct of the board as a whole.[66] Of course, the court in the exercise of its discretion could still order that the liability be joint and several.[67]

25-29

Park J's position was endorsed in *Re Marini Ltd*[68] where the court agreed that, before any question of invoking the powers of the court could arise, it has to be shown that the company at the date of actual liquidation was in a worse position than it would have been in if trading had ceased at the time it is contended it should have done. The

25-30

---

[61] *Re Produce Marketing Consortium Ltd (No 2)* [1989] BCLC 520 at 553–4; see also *Re Purpoint Ltd* [1991] BCLC 49. The court has the power to defer debts owing from the company to any person found liable for wrongful trading: IA 1986, s 215(4).

[62] [2007] 2 BCLC 287. [63] [2007] 2 BCLC 287 at 294, 296, 413.

[64] Park J noted that Chadwick LJ had been content in *Cohen v Selby* [2001] 1 BCLC 176 at 183–4 to assume that it may not be necessary to establish a causal link between the wrongful trading and any particular loss.

[65] Citing *Re Brian D Pierson (Contractors) Ltd* [2001] 1 BCLC 275, see in particular at 310.

[66] But see Prentice, 'Corporate Personality, Limited Liability and the Protection of Creditors' in Grantham & Rickett (eds), *Corporate Personality in the 20th Century* (1998) at pp 122–3.

[67] See *Re Brian D Pierson (Contractors) Ltd* [2001] 1 BCLC 275 at 311.

[68] [2004] BCC 172 at 197–8; see also note on the case by Spence (2004) 17 Insolv Int 11.

appropriate comparison, the court said, was between the net deficiency in the assets of the company as at the date at which it was contended that trading should have ceased and the day on which trading did in fact cease. The appropriate test was not whether new debt had been incurred after the first date, or whether cash had been paid out after that date; the only proper question was whether, on a net basis, it was shown that the company was worse off as a result of the continuation of trading.[69]

25-31   Any recoveries obtained under this provision, not being property of the company, but property which arises only after the liquidation of the company, and which is recoverable only by the liquidator pursuant to his statutory powers, is held by him on a statutory trust for distribution to the company's unsecured creditors.[70] These sums are not subject therefore to the claims of a floating charge holder over all the undertaking of the company. The contribution recovered goes to meet the claims of all the unsecured creditors rather than specifically the claims of creditors whose debt arose in the period of wrongful trading. The recoveries are subject, however, to the prior claim of the expenses of winding up which include litigation costs incurred by the liquidator, see **24-87**, and preferential debts, see **24-89**.[71] Though the floating charge holder does not benefit directly from the recoveries, the charge holder benefits indirectly in that the floating charge realisations are subject to the prior claims of the expenses of winding up to the extent that the general assets of the company are insufficient (IA 1986, s 176ZA). So if the recoveries swell the general assets, there is less need to have resort to the floating charge realisations, so to that extent the floating charge holder benefits. But as litigation costs can be considerable, two further constraints are imposed. First, a liquidator can only bring s 214 proceedings with the sanction of the court or the creditors, depending on the type of liquidation:[72] see **24-52**. Secondly, litigation costs in excess of £5,000 can only be treated as expenses of the winding up with the prior approval of the floating charge or preferential creditors, as the case may be: see **24-87**. Clearly, therefore, a liquidator is in effect prevented from bringing proceedings without securing the consent of the floating charge holder. These complications as to consent, as well as the difficulty of actually obtaining funding and the risk of adverse costs orders should the case be lost, mean that there has been limited use of s 214 and it is clear, as Professor Keay puts it, that the section has not lived up to its early promise.[73]

Effectiveness of the provision

25-32   It is clear from the small number of reported cases that, for the reasons noted at **25-3**, there is limited use of s 214.[74] Liquidators lack the resources to bring claims and creditors are reluctant to fund litigation given the uncertain scope of the provision. There is

---

[69] On the facts in *Re Marini*, there was little evidence to support that allegation and the wrongful trading claim was dismissed.

[70] *Re Oasis Merchandising Services Ltd, Ward v Aitken* [1997] 1 BCLC 689, CA; see Keay, above n 12, pp 104–6.

[71] IA 1986, s 115; IR 1986, r 4.218(2)(a)(i).   [72] See IA 1986, Sch 4, para 3A.

[73] See Keay, above n 12, Ch 10 who summarises the many defects of the provision and points out that it needs to be redrafted and refocused if it is to prove useful.

[74] Admittedly, as Davies, above n 44, 325, points out, the link between the impact of any law and the level of reported cases is complex, but it is an initial indicator of the use of the provision.

clearly some reluctance on the part of the judiciary to hold directors liable, recognising what Park J called the real and unenviable dilemma of directors in deciding whether to close down or try to turn the company around.[75] On the other hand, there is some anecdotal evidence that the section is effective in terms of dictating how directors behave when their companies face financial difficulties. If it is effective in influencing how directors actually act (and that is necessarily difficult to quantify), it may be quite useful that there is some uncertainty as to the point in time at which the provision is triggered and the extent of the potential liability under the provision.

Certainly advisers in large companies often advise on the potential liability for **25-33** wrongful trading and directors in such companies appear alert to the risks of wrongful trading, despite the fact that claims for wrongful trading in such contexts are rare (and unlikely to succeed where the directors have behaved responsibly: see *Re Continental Assurance*[76] and **25-22**). While concerned about the potential (unquantifiable) civil liability, though they have insurance cover, such directors are concerned particularly about the reputational damage involved if they are sued for wrongful trading. For smaller companies,[77] the issues are different but equally pressing in that a personal liability would wipe out the advantages of having incorporated with limited liability in the first place. Given that the directors are likely also to be shareholders and employees, a significant personal liability as directors on top of the loss of whatever capital they have contributed (which admittedly may be small) and the loss of their employment is a matter of some concern to them (and they are very unlikely to have insurance cover). For that reason, such companies also show some awareness of this potential liability.

D Prohibition on the re-use of company names

When a company has gone into insolvent liquidation, its directors may be tempted to **25-34** set up another company immediately under the same or a similar name or may already have several other companies incorporated, all with similar names. The business then continues much as before, a practice often referred to as the phoenix syndrome. The second company frequently operates from the same premises, commonly using the same assets acquired in a fire sale from the liquidator and exploiting what remains of the former company's goodwill. Not surprisingly, existing creditors are aggrieved by these practices and the public concerned about the ability of such 'rogue' directors to operate in this fashion. The problem has been reduced since the IA 1986 required liquidators to be licensed insolvency practitioners so collusive deals to pass over assets

---

[75] See *Re Continental Assurance Co of London plc* [2007] 2 BCLC 287 at 409, also 360, 443. See too Spence (2004) 17 Insolv Int 11; Keay, above n 12, pp 96–9.

[76] *Re Continental Assurance Co of London plc* [2007] 2 BCLC 287.

[77] Keay, above n 12, makes the point that the reported cases where liability has been imposed have been exclusively small closely held companies.

are much less likely, though the Company Law Review took the view that the phoenix problem remains significant.[78]

25-35 The phoenix syndrome is governed by IA 1986, s 216 which renders the re-use of the name of a company which has been wound up insolvent a criminal offence in certain circumstances.[79] Any directors concerned (and others) may incur personal liability under s 217 for debts incurred during the period of the offence, though proceedings are unusual. There is some limited evidence recently of increased use of this provision, perhaps as creditors explore every avenue of recovery,[80] perhaps encouraged by the views of the Court of Appeal in *Ricketts v Ad Valorem Factors Ltd*[81] where Simon Brown LJ noted the 'surprisingly long reach' of the legislation.[82] In the same case, Mummery LJ wondered that more use is not made of the provision by creditors to fasten directors with personal liability given it is a departure from the general principle of corporate law that creditors do not have a right of recourse to the assets of the directors or members for payment of the company's debts.[83]

The prohibition

25-36 Where a company has gone into insolvent liquidation,[84] it is an offence (except with the leave of the court or in such exceptional circumstances as laid down in the Insolvency Rules 1986, rr 4.226–4.230) for a director or shadow director of the company who was in post any time in the 12 months preceding the liquidation:

(1) to be a director of, or in any way directly or indirectly be concerned or take part in the promotion, formation or management of, any other company known under a prohibited name; or

(2) in any way, directly or indirectly, be concerned or take part in the carrying on of a business carried on (otherwise than by a company) under a prohibited name (IA 1986, s 216(1), (3)).

25-37 A prohibited name is a name by which the company was known[85] in the 12 months preceding liquidation or a name which is so similar to it as to suggest an association with that company (IA 1986, s 216(1), (3)). The prohibition on the use of the name lasts for five years (s 216(3)). The penalty for contravention is imprisonment or a fine

---

[78] See Company Law Review, *Final Report* (July 2001), paras 15.55–15.77; also Milman, 'The Phoenix Syndrome' [2001] Insol L 199. See generally Carter, 'The Phoenix Syndrome—The Personal Liability of Directors' (2006) 19 Insolv Int 38.

[79] It is an offence of strict liability: *R v Cole, Lees, Birch* [1998] 2 BCLC 235. Any misuse of the name is a factor to be taken into account in disqualification proceedings: *Re Migration Services International Ltd* [2000] 1 BCLC 666.

[80] See claims by factors in *First Independent Factors Ltd v Mountford* [2008] 2 BCLC 297; *First Independent Factors Ltd v Churchill* [2007] 1 BCLC 293.

[81] [2004] 1 BCLC 1, CA.   [82] [2004] 1 BCLC 1 at 8, CA.   [83] [2004] 1 BCLC 1 at 3, CA.

[84] For these purposes, a company goes into insolvent liquidation if it goes into liquidation at a time when its assets are insufficient for the payment of its debts and other liabilities and the expenses of the winding up: IA 1986, s 216(7).

[85] I.e. including business names as well as the company's registered name.

(s 216(4)) but, as noted, it is the civil penalty under s 217 which most concerns directors (and others). Section 217 imposes a personal liability for all the debts and other liabilities incurred by the company when a person, in contravention of s 216, is involved in the management of a company or when a person acts or is willing to act on the instructions of a person whom he knows to be acting in contravention of s 216. Liability therefore extends beyond the director or shadow director acting in breach of s 216 to persons who act on their instructions. Liability is joint and several with the company for the relevant debts (s 217(4), (5)). An assignee of a debt may bring proceedings and it makes no difference to the legitimacy of the debt which is the basis of a s 217 claim whether the debt was acquired before or after the defunct company went into liquidation.[86] A claim may be brought by any creditor or assignee of the debt for a declaration that the directors are personally liable for the relevant debt or debts and recovery is by the applicant for the debt owed to him.

The emphasis in the provision is on the use of the name. The prohibition is on the re-use **25-38** of the name or a similar name by a director or shadow director. It does not prevent those directors from being directors of another company as long as that company does not use a prohibited name, nor does it stop another company from using the name as long as the directors and shadow directors have no connection with that company. The intention is to prevent any exploitation by the directors of any remaining goodwill in the insolvent company, but these sections do not address concerns about the ability of individuals to set up again in business following an earlier insolvency. That problem is addressed through disqualification, which is discussed in Chapter 6.

If a name is a prohibited name within the meaning of IA 1986, s 216(2), the restric- **25-39** tions apply even if the privileges of limited liability had not been exploited.[87] In *Ricketts v Ad Valorem Factors Ltd*[88] a director had been found liable for acting in breach of IA 1986, s 216. He was a director of a company (Air Component Co Ltd) which traded in air compressors and which went into insolvent liquidation in February 1998. In March 1998 the appellant became a director of another company (Air Equipment Co Ltd), the successor company, which also traded in air compressors and covered the same geographical region as the first company. In October 1999 the successor company too went into insolvent liquidation. Having been found liable for a breach of IA 1986, s 216, the appellant appealed, contending that the application of the section should be restricted to those cases in which the privileges of limited liability are exploited. On the facts, there had been no transfer of assets by the first company to the second company at an undervalue, the companies had not been used to run up debts or to avoid their payment and no creditors of the second company or anyone else had been misled by the similarity of the two companies' names or by the fact that the appellant was a director of both of them. The Court of Appeal dismissed the appeal. In the instant case, making the necessary comparison of the names of the two companies in the context of all the circumstances in which they were actually used or likely to

---

[86] *First Independent Factors Ltd v Mountford* [2008] 2 BCLC 297; *Ricketts v Ad Valorem Factors Ltd* [2004] 1 BCLC 1, CA.

[87] *Ricketts v Ad Valorem Factors Ltd* [2004] 1 BCLC 1, CA.   [88] [2004] 1 BCLC 1, CA.

be used,[89] the name of Air Equipment Co Ltd suggested an association with The Air Component Co Ltd. Having reached that conclusion, the court had no discretion in the matter of the personal liability of the appellant. The case fell within IA 1986, ss 216, 217 even in the absence of proof that there had been any express misrepresentation or that anyone had actually been deceived or confused into thinking that there was an association.

25-40   This case confirms that the key question is whether the name is a prohibited name. If it is, liability arises under the statutory provision regardless of whether there is any abuse, unless the director has sought to protect his position by leave of the court or he can rely on the exceptions provided by the Insolvency Rules 1986 (IR 1986) (discussed below).

25-41   As to whether a name suggests an association with another company, the question to be asked, according to Lewison J in *First Independent Factors Ltd v Mountford*,[90] is whether the similarity between the two names is such as to give rise to a probability that members of the public, comparing the names in the relevant context, would associate the two companies with each other, whether as successor companies or as part of the same group. In assessing the degree of similarity between names, it is necessary to make a comparison of the names of the two companies in the context of all the circumstances in which they are actually used or likely to be used, looking at the situation through the eyes of someone who might deal with the company or business.

25-42   In this case, the defendant director traded through a company 'Classic Roofs Ltd' which went into insolvent liquidation whereupon another company owned by the defendant, 'Classic Conservatories & Windows Ltd', bought most of the assets from the liquidator and continued to trade before also going into liquidation a year later. A claim against the director was brought by a creditor. Having reviewed the facts, the court thought that, in the context in which the two names had been used, the company's name (Classic Conservatories & Windows Ltd) had suggested an association with 'Classic Roofs Ltd'. The second company's name was then a prohibited name and the defendant director did not fall within any of the exemptions provided by the IR 1986, rr 4.228–4.230 (see below). Accordingly, he was personally liable for the debts of Classic Conservatories & Windows Ltd incurred during the period of contravention of IA 1986, s 216.

The exceptions

25-43   As noted, the prohibitions apply save where re-use of the name is permitted with the leave of the court or in such circumstances as are prescribed in the IR 1986 which provides for three exceptional cases.

---

[89] I.e. looking at: the types of product dealt in, the location of the business, the types of customers dealing with the companies and those involved in the operation of the two companies.
[90] [2008] 2 BCLC 297.

Case 1

The first excepted case is set out in IR 1986, r 4.228 which was amended following **25-44** the decision of the Court of Appeal in *First Independent Factors and Finance Ltd v Churchill.*[91] Essentially this first exemption is intended to allow directors to continue to act when a successor company acquires the whole or substantially the whole of the business from the liquidator and notice is given to the creditors that the director will be acting in that capacity in the successor company. The Court of Appeal interpreted the wording of 'old' r 4.228 in a way that limited its operation to where directors of the company in liquidation were not directors of, or involved in the management of, the successor company at the date when the notice was given. Notice had to be given to creditors before the director started to involve himself in the management of the successor company, the court said, so that such creditors could make an informed assessment of the risk of extending credit to the new company. In *Churchill*, the director was a director of the successor company ahead of its purchase of the insolvent company's business and therefore he was not within the exemption provided by the rule and was liable personally.

As this scenario (successor company owned and managed by some of those associ- **25-45** ated with the insolvent company) quite commonly arises, not least because the existing owners and directors may be the only people interested in purchasing the business of the insolvent company, it was thought that this interpretation of IR 1986, r 4.228 was unduly restrictive. The provision has therefore been amended and new r 4.228 requires that in certain circumstances prior notice of the director's intention to act *or continue to act* in any of the prohibited ways must be published in the *Gazette* and given to all creditors known to the director or whose names and addresses could be ascertained by him by making reasonable enquiries. The rule clarifies in particular that notice may be given:

(1) prior to the insolvent company entering liquidation, where a director intends to act in any of the prohibited ways and where the business is (or is to be) acquired by another company from the liquidator or other officeholder and whether or not at the time of giving notice the director is a director of the acquiring company; and

(2) where a director intends to act in any of the prohibited ways and he is already a director of another company which has acquired (or is to acquire) the whole or substantially the whole of the business of the insolvent company from a liquidator and where the acquiring company intends, following the giving of the notice by the director, to adopt a prohibited name.

Case 2

The second excepted case is set out in IR 1986, r 4.229. The court which winds up **25-46** the insolvent company may give a director leave to use a prohibited name. A director who applies for leave (within seven days of his company going into liquidation) may

---

[91] [2007] 1 BCLC 293.

continue to act without being in breach of IA 1986, s 216 for a period for six weeks from the date on which the company goes into liquidation or for a shorter period if the court disposes of the application earlier. The proper approach to the exercise of this jurisdiction was considered in *Penrose v Official Receiver*[92] where Chadwick J thought the court should exercise its discretion to grant leave with regard only to the purposes for which IA 1986, s 216 was enacted and not on the more general basis that the public requires some protection from the applicant's activities as a company director. The (limited) question is whether future creditors of the new company would be misled by the fact that it will be trading under the control of the applicants with a name similar to the name of the old company.

Case 3

25-47   The third excepted case is set out in IR 1986, r 4.230. A former director can continue to act in the affairs of an established company even though it is known by a prohibited name, provided that that company has been using that name for at least a year before the insolvent company went into liquidation and the company was not a dormant company (i.e. inactive) during that time.[93] This exception addresses the situation, noted at **25-34**, where a director may have numerous companies all with quite similar names and, when one becomes insolvent, he wishes to continue his business activities as a director of or be involved in the management of the others. As the other companies are known by prohibited names, were it not for this exemption, he would be caught by the prohibition. There is a certain element of overlap between r 4.228 and this exception.

E Avoidance of transactions prior to winding up

Introduction

25-48   One of the main concerns of the Cork Committee (see **2-3**) was that there should be adequate powers to unravel dubious transactions entered into prior to the company going into insolvent liquidation.[94]

25-49   A typical scenario would be that before Company A goes into liquidation, the directors transfer some or all of its remaining assets to Company B, or to certain individuals connected with the directors, so that the directors are in a position to recommence

---

[92] [1996] 1 BCLC 389; followed in *Re Lightning Electrical Contractors Ltd* [1996] 2 BCLC 302. The court rejected the stricter approach adopted in *Re Bonus Breaks Ltd* [1991] BCC 546 where the court had reviewed the director's responsibility for the first company's insolvency and the structure and financing of the second company in a manner akin to a judge exercising the discretion to grant a disqualified director leave to act under the CDDA 1986, s 17.

[93] It is sufficient for the purpose of IR 1986, r 4.230 that either the registered name or a trading name of the established company is a prohibited name. In either circumstance, if the company is 'known by' a prohibited name during the relevant period, a director is entitled to rely on r 4.230: *ESS Production Ltd v Sully* [2005] 2 BCLC 547, CA.

[94] See the Cork Committee Report, Ch 28, see **2-3**.

business after the insolvency of Company A, leaving the creditors of Company A to look to the shell of that company for payment of their debts. Those associated with Company A would then be found running a profitable Company B having left their creditors behind at Company A 'to whistle for their money'.[95] The transactions involved might include the sale of assets held by Company A to Company B or even directly to Company A's own directors or shareholders (often the same people) at an undervalue. Directors' loans to Company A may be repaid ahead of payments due to other creditors so as to ensure that the directors do not find themselves as creditors of Company A on insolvency. Essentially, every effort is made to strip anything of value out of the company so as to facilitate the directors/shareholders in any new venture that they might undertake.

It is important therefore that there are adequate statutory powers to challenge such **25-50** transactions so as to ensure that the assets of Company A transferred out of it in dubious circumstances just prior to winding up are recovered for the benefit of the whole body of creditors of Company A. As discussed in Chapter 24, any measures which will swell the assets available to the unsecured creditors is to be welcomed: see **24-95**. Additionally, many of the transactions would suggest misconduct and breach of duty by the directors who have not reached the standards of probity and competence appropriate for directors of a limited company and these transactions are commonly relied on therefore as grounds for disqualification of directors.

The general approach taken in the Insolvency Act 1986 is that specific transactions **25-51** are open to challenge by liquidators (and administrators) with the emphasis on civil actions seeking contributions to the assets of the company for the benefit of creditors. In this chapter we examine, in turn, transactions at an undervalue, preferences, extortionate credit transactions and the avoidance of certain floating charges.[96]

Before considering the scope of the statutory provisions, it must be borne in mind **25-52** that enforcement of the provisions is somewhat problematic, given that the liquidator or administrator may not be able to secure the funding necessary to pursue a civil action against the directors and others. A liquidator or administrator requires the sanction of the court or liquidation committee or creditors (depending on the circumstance) to bring proceedings under IA 1986, ss 213, 214, 238, 239, 242, 243, or 423 (all provisions allowing actions to be brought to recover assets or seek contributions to the company's assets), see **24-52**. If duly sanctioned to bring proceedings, the expenses or costs are liquidation expenses within IR 1986, r 4.218 and payable in priority therefore from the assets of the company, but subject to a requirement that the secured or preferential creditors must consent to litigation expenses in excess of £5,000: see **24-87**. Any sums recovered by the liquidator are impressed with a statutory trust in favour of the

---

[95] See *Re Paramount Airways Ltd* [1992] 3 All ER 1 at 3, per Sir Donald Nicholls V-C.

[96] A liquidator will often seek to challenge a transaction under more than one of these grounds: see *Re Brian D Pierson* [2001] 1 BCLC 275; *Re Fairway Magazines Ltd, Fairbairn v Hartigan* [1993] 1 BCLC 643; *Re DKG Contractors Ltd* [1990] BCC 903. See generally, Goode, *Principles of Corporate Insolvency Law* (2005), Ch 11; Armour and Bennett (eds), *Vulnerable Transactions in Corporate Insolvency* (2003); Parry, *Transaction Avoidance in Insolvencies* (2001).

unsecured creditors.[97] Recoveries do not form part of the assets of the company so as to be within the grasp of any floating charge,[98] which may mean that secured creditors may be reluctant to sanction proceedings, but recoveries are subject to the prior claims of the expenses of the winding up,[99] which may give a floating charge holder a reason to sanction proceedings since to the extent that the assets are insufficient to meet the expenses of winding up, the expenses must be met out of the floating charge realisations, see **24-81**.[100] Whether to sanction proceedings therefore becomes a tactical issue for a floating charge holder.

Transactions at an undervalue—IA 1986, s 238

25-53   Section 238 essentially allows a liquidator or administrator to challenge a transaction previously entered into by the company as being at an undervalue and the court is able to make such order as it thinks fit for restoring the position to what it would have been if the company had not entered into the transaction. There is considerable similarity between IA 1986, s 238 and IA 1986, s 423 (transactions defrauding creditors), and therefore a certain cross-over between the authorities on these provisions, hence the authorities from each provision are relied on below. There are a number of differences to note, however, between the provisions.[101] Essentially, IA 1986, s 423 is applicable in a broader range of circumstances; it is not dependent on the company being in liquidation or administration and there is no time period limiting the review of the transaction, unlike the two-year limit in s 238. Secondly, applications under s 423 can be by the liquidator or the administrator but also, with the leave of the court, by any victim of the transaction.[102] Thirdly, it must be shown under s 423(3) that the company's intention was to put assets beyond the reach of the claimant or otherwise prejudice a claimant.

25-54   The key questions under IA 1986, s 238 are:

- has the company gone into administration or liquidation?
- did the company enter into a transaction at an undervalue with any person[103] within the period of two years ending with the onset of insolvency?[104] and
- was this transaction at a time when the company was unable to pay its debts[105] or did it become unable to pay its debts in consequence of the transaction?[106] This

---

[97] *Re Esal (Commodities) Ltd* [1997] 1 BCLC 705, CA.

[98] *Re Oasis Merchandising Services Ltd, Ward v Aitken* [1997] 1 BCLC 689, CA.

[99] IA 1986, s 115; IR 1986, r 4.218(2)(a)(i) and subject to any preferential debts, see **24-89**.

[100] IA 1986, s 176ZA.

[101] See generally Stubbs, 'Section 423 of the Insolvency Act in Practice' (2008) 21 Insolv Int 17.

[102] IA 1986, s 424(1)(a); see *National Bank of Kuwait v Menzies* [1994] 2 BCLC 306, CA.

[103] The provision applies to any person wherever resident and an application may be made against a person resident abroad with no place of business in the UK and who does not carry on business within the jurisdiction, provided that the defendant has a sufficient connection with England for it to be just and proper to make an order against him, despite the foreign element: *Re Paramount Airways Ltd* [1992] 3 All ER 1, CA.

[104] The expression 'the onset of insolvency' is defined in detail in IA 1986, s 240(3).

[105] Within the meaning of IA 1986, s 123.

[106] IA 1986, s 240(2).

requirement is presumed when the transaction is entered into by the company with a connected person.[107]

- An undervalue arises if

  (a) the company makes a gift to that person or otherwise enters into a transaction with that person on terms that provide for the company to receive no consideration; or

  (b) the company enters into a transaction with that person for a consideration the value of which, in money or money's worth, is significantly less than the value, in money or money's worth, of the consideration provided by the company.[108]

Where these elements can be established, a liquidator or an administrator may apply to the court which may make such order as it thinks fit for restoring the position to what it would have been if the company had not entered into that transaction.[109]   **25-55**

The court will not make an order if it is satisfied that the company entered into the transaction in good faith and for the purpose of carrying on its business, and at the time it did so there were reasonable grounds for believing that the transaction would benefit the company (IA 1986, s 238(5)).   **25-56**

In determining whether there is a transaction at an undervalue, the court starts by identifying the relevant transaction and the consideration for that transaction.[110] The issue is whether the consideration provided by the transferee is 'significantly less' than the value provided by the transferor company.[111] On this point, a comparison must be made between the value obtained by the company and the value of the consideration provided by the company,[112] though it may be difficult to assess the relative weight of the consideration provided when the transaction may already be several years old by the time the liquidator has an opportunity to review it. Both the consideration provided and received must be measurable in money or moneys' worth; both must be considered from the company's point of view and a comparison must be made between two figures representing the actual value of the consideration.[113]   **25-57**

---

[107] IA 1986, s 240(2). The precise definition of persons connected with the company is complex: see IA 1986, ss 249 and 435 but broadly it includes any directors or shadow directors of the company: ss 249(a), 251; and their families, partners, and associated companies: s 435(2), (3), (6), (8).

[108] IA 1986, s 238(4). See *Re Taylor Sinclair (Capital) Ltd* [2001] 2 BCLC 176 where the court considered that, with the exception of gifts which are expressly included, a transaction must have an element of dealing between the parties.

[109] IA 1986, s 238(3). Despite the word 'shall' in the statute, the power vested in the court is discretionary: *Re Paramount Airways Ltd* [1992] 3 All ER 1, CA.

[110] *National Westminster Bank plc v Jones* [2002] 1 BCLC 55, CA (a s 423 case).

[111] *National Westminster Bank plc v Jones* [2002] 1 BCLC 55, CA.

[112] *Re MC Bacon Ltd* [1990] BCLC 324.

[113] *Re MC Bacon Ltd* [1990] BCLC 324. See the difficulties in valuing the consideration received by the company in *Lord v Sinai Securities Ltd* [2005] 1 BCLC 295.

25-58   The issue of the transaction and the nature of the consideration to be valued was considered by the House of Lords in *Phillips v Brewin Dolphin Bell Lawrie Ltd.*[114] The company carried on business as stockbrokers and its assets included computer equipment which it held on lease. A purchaser wished to acquire part of the company's business for £1.25m. For commercial and tax reasons, the transaction was structured into two elements, one the sale of the business via a wholly owned subsidiary of the company, with the purchaser buying the shares in the subsidiary for a nominal £1 and taking on the costs of certain redundancy payments. Another company associated with the purchaser leased the computer equipment from the company on an annual rent. The company was wound up and the liquidator contended, as against the purchaser and the associated company, that the share sale agreement was a transaction at an undervalue within the meaning of IA 1986, s 238.

25-59   The trial judge held that the equipment lease was not part of the consideration which was limited to the £1 and the redundancy payments (worth approximately £325,000) and, since the prima facie value of the business sold was £1.05m, the transaction was at an undervalue, a decision affirmed by the Court of Appeal.[115] An appeal was dismissed, but the House of Lords disagreed with the lower courts as to the nature of the transaction. In the view of Lord Scott, the transaction was clear—the sale of shares in return for agreements by the company and the associated company. It was plain that, apart from the consideration under the share sale agreement, the sub-lease agreement also formed part of the consideration. The key issue was the value of that consideration. On the facts, the sub-lease provided no value since the company was not entitled to sub-lease the equipment in this way and it had been repossessed shortly after the agreement had been entered into. Therefore, while the lease was part of the consideration, it added nothing of value to the agreement. It followed that the company had entered into a transaction, namely the share sale agreement, at an undervalue and that the amount of the undervalue was £725,000, i.e. £1,050,000 (the value of the asset sold) less £325,000 (the value received and which had been paid in respect of redundancies).[116]

25-60   The value of the asset sold by the company, i.e. the value of the shares in the subsidiary, Lord Scott noted, is prima facie not less than what a reasonably well-informed purchaser is prepared to pay in an arm's length negotiation.[117] As for the value of the consideration received, where the value of any consideration is speculative, as in the case of the lease agreement, it is for the party who relies on that consideration to establish its value.

---

[114] [2001] 1 BCLC 145; noted by Parry [2001] Insolv Law 58; Moss [2001] 14 Insolv Int 29; see also Mokal and Ho, 'Consideration, Characterisation, Evaluation: Transactions at an Undervalue after *Phillips v Brewin Dolphin*' (2001) JCLS 359.

[115] See [1999] 1 BCLC 714, CA.

[116] [2001] 1 BCLC 145 at 157.

[117] [2001] 1 BCLC 145 at 156.

This willingness of the House of Lords to treat the lease agreement and the share sale **25-61** agreement as one transaction is of practical importance since there may be, as here, good business and taxation reasons for dividing the consideration into a number of separate, though linked, transactions, not all of them necessarily with the company. By treating the combined elements as the transaction, this approach maximises the consideration provided and lessens the possibility of there being an undervalue unless, as here, some element of the consideration is of doubtful value. At the same time, the policy of the legislation is upheld by the finding that those who provide speculative consideration must establish its value and, where they cannot, the result will be recovery by the liquidator.

A debatable point is whether the creation by a company of a charge over its assets in **25-62** favour of a creditor is a transaction at an undervalue. In *Re MC Bacon Ltd*[118] Millett J ruled against such a conclusion. In his view the creation of a charge could not amount to an undervalue as it does not deplete the company's assets and neither the granting of the debenture nor the consideration received by the company in granting the charge can be measured in money or money's worth.[119] Arden LJ makes the point in *Hill v Spread Trustee Co Ltd*[120] that the grant of a charge could be for no consideration (and therefore would be within IA 1986, s 238(4)(a) even if the application of s 238(4) (b) is ruled out, see **25-54**) as where a charge is granted to a creditor who is not in fact pressing for repayment so there is no forbearance as consideration (as there was in *Re MC Bacon Ltd*).[121] Equally, Arden LJ queried why the value of the creditor's right to recourse to the security and to take priority over the other creditors should be left out of account.[122] Professor Goode makes the point that a charge in these circumstances should be challenged as a preference and not as an undervalue, since the creditor benefits from being able to look to the assets secured to his claim rather than being left to claim as an unsecured creditor.[123] As Millett J noted, the creation of the security adversely affects the rights of other creditors in the event of insolvency.[124]

The order of the court

Section 241 lists a wide variety of orders which the court may make in the context **25-63** of restoring the company to the position it would have been in had the company not entered into the transaction at an undervalue, including orders requiring property to be vested back in the company and requiring any person to make payments to the administrator or liquidator in respect of benefits received by him from the company.[125]

---

[118] [1990] BCLC 324.   [119] [1990] BCLC 324 at 341; *Re Mistral Finance Ltd* [2001] BCC 27.
[120] [2007] 1 BCLC 450 at 473, 485.
[121] The bank exercised forbearance in that case by not calling in its overdraft and honouring cheques and it provided fresh advances to the company: see [1990] BCLC 324 at 340.
[122] See [2007] 1 BCLC 450 at 485.
[123] See Goode, *Principles of Corporate Insolvency* Law (3rd edn, 2005), para 11–37.
[124] [1990] BCLC 324 at 340.
[125] See *Re Paramount Airways Ltd* [1992] 3 All ER 1 at 7, CA. The good faith, or lack of knowledge of the relevant circumstances, of the other party to the transaction are irrelevant but sub-transferees acquiring

The power is very wide and extends to recovery from any person who has received a benefit from the company unless that person can show (and the onus is on him) that he acted in good faith and for value.[126] In *Phillips v Brewin Dolphin Bell Lawrie Ltd*,[127] discussed at **25-58**, as the transaction could not be reversed, the court ordered the purchaser of the shares to pay the amount of the undervalue to the liquidator. In *National Westminster Bank plc v Jones*[128] the court ordered that a suspect transfer of assets be reversed so as to place assets back in the ownership of an individual who was subject to various outstanding mortgages.

25-64   The court's discretion extends to not making any order, as happened in *Re MDA Investment Management Ltd*,[129] even though there was a clear transaction at an undervalue. The company's business had been sold for £2.41m, but the company had only received £1m since the rest of the consideration had been diverted by a director, in breach of duty, to a partnership of which he was a partner. The company was in insolvent liquidation and therefore an order to restore the company to the position prior to the transactions would have been positively detrimental to the company, since the company would have been in an even worse position if it had not entered into the transaction at all (at least it had received £1m).

25-65   The court is less concerned with protecting the position of the other party to the transaction. In *Lord v Sinai Securities*[130] Hart J noted that it is arguable that the court's primary and possibly only concern is the restoration of the company's position. The position of the counterparty needs to be considered by the court as a general matter of discretion, but the court is not obliged to ensure that his position is restored in every particular to the status quo before the transaction. There will be many cases where that is simply impossible.

25-66   The court will not make an order if it is satisfied that the company entered into the transaction in good faith and for the purpose of carrying on its business, and at the time it did so there were reasonable grounds for believing that the transaction would benefit the company (IA 1986, s 238(5)). For example, a sale of an asset at what appears, with hindsight, to be an undervalue may be explicable as having been the best option available to the company at that time when it was undergoing serious cashflow difficulties which could only be solved by an expeditious sale. The onus of proof in this regard is on those opposing the court's order.[131]

25-67   Any recoveries obtained under this provision, not being property of the company, but property which arises only after the liquidation of the company, and which is recoverable only by the liquidator pursuant to his statutory powers is held by him on a

interests or benefits in good faith and for value are protected: IA 1986, s 241(2); and there is a presumption of the interest being acquired or the benefit received other than in good faith in the circumstances outlined in s 241(2A), (3)–(3C).

[126] See IA 1986, s 241(2); also *Re Sonatacus Ltd* [2007] 2 BCLC 627.   [127] [2001] 1 All ER 673, HL.
[128] [2002] 1 BCLC 55, CA.   [129] [2004] 1 BCLC 217.   [130] [2005] 1 BCLC 295.
[131] *Re Barton Manufacturing Co Ltd* [1999] 1 BCLC 740 (a considerable volume of evidence will be needed to convince the court of the bona fides of a gift made by the company in these circumstances).

statutory trust for distribution to the company's unsecured creditors,[132] but subject to the expenses of winding up,[133] see **25-31** and any preferential debts, see **24-89**.

Preferences—IA 1986, s 239

One of the main objectives in the winding up of an insolvent company (see **24-60**) is to ensure the equal treatment of creditors. To help achieve this the court is given a power to set aside, on the application of a liquidator or administrator, transactions or arrangements entered into by the company which have the effect of preferring a creditor or creditors ahead of other creditors.   **25-68**

A preference can arise, for example, where an unsecured creditor is paid by the company in circumstances where this is done to ensure that on insolvency he is not left to claim against the pooled assets with the risk of non-payment which that entails; or where the company at the eleventh hour gives security to an unsecured creditor, again to ensure that he is not left to claim against the pool; or where the directors ensure that the company pays those creditors whose debts are personally guaranteed by the directors.[134] The rules on preferences do not stop companies from paying their creditors as insolvency looms, but the company has to show that the transaction was as a result of pressure from the creditor or other commercial considerations.   **25-69**

Section 239 sets out in some detail what constitutes a preference and there are a variety of conditions which must be satisfied: **25-70**

- the company must have gone into administration or liquidation;[135]
- the company must have given a preference to a person;
- the preference must have been given within the period of six months ending with the onset of insolvency[136] or, in the case of a connected person, within the period of two years ending with the onset of insolvency;[137]
- at the time of giving the preference, the company must have been unable to pay its debts[138] or it must have become unable to pay its debts in consequence of the preference;

---

[132] *Re Oasis Merchandising Services Ltd, Ward v Aitken* [1997] 1 BCLC 689, CA.

[133] IA 1986, s 115; IR 1986, r 4.218(2)(a)(i).

[134] Such conduct may also merit disqualification on the grounds of unfitness, see *Re Sykes (Butchers) Ltd, Secretary of State for Trade and Industry v Richardson* [1998] 1 BCLC 110 (director caused the company to reduce its bank overdraft which he had personally guaranteed instead of settling the claims of the company's trade creditors).   [135] IA 1986, ss 239(1), 238(1).

[136] The expression 'the onset of insolvency' is defined in detail in IA 1986, s 239(3).

[137] IA 1986, s 240(1). 'Connected person' is defined expansively in IA 1986, s 249; and see also s 435. See *Re Thirty-Eight Building Ltd* [1999] 1 BCLC 416 as to connected persons—trustees of a pension scheme which was the recipient of large sums of company money in circumstances which would otherwise amount to a preference but which had been received more than six months prior to the insolvency were not connected persons due to the exception in IA 1986, s 435(5)(b) despite the fact that four of the five trustees were beneficiaries of the trust and were connected persons—the presence of a fifth independent trustee and the fact that they acted collectively meant they were not connected persons; and see also [2000] 1 BCLC 201.

[138] Within the meaning of IA 1986, s 123. There is no presumption with respect to this element of this provision, unlike under IA 1986, s 238, see s 240(2).

- there must have been a desire on the company's part to prefer that person; and there is a presumption of a desire to prefer in the case of a connected person.[139]

25-71 A company gives a preference to a person if:

- that person is one of the company's creditors or a surety or guarantor for any of the company's debts or other liabilities; and

- the company does anything or suffers anything to be done which (in either case) has the effect of putting that person into a position which, in the event of the company going into insolvent liquidation, will be better than the position he would have been in if that thing had not been done (IA 1986, s 239(4)).

25-72 A key element in establishing the existence of a preference is that there is a desire to prefer that creditor on an insolvent liquidation (IA 1986, s 239(5)). Whether there was such a desire must be considered by reference to the date on which the company gave the preference,[140] but where the preference is in favour of a connected person, there is a presumption of a desire to prefer, unless the contrary is shown.[141]

25-73 The requirement of a desire to prefer was considered in *Re MC Bacon Ltd*[142] where a liquidator applied to the court to set aside, as a preference, a debenture granted by the company to its bank. The company had gone into insolvent liquidation in August 1987 (the onset of insolvency) with an estimated deficiency as regards unsecured creditors of £329,435. At that date, the company's overdraft at the bank stood at £235,530. This overdraft was secured by a debenture granted by the company in May 1987 (i.e. within the six months prior to the onset of insolvency at a time when the company was unable to pay its debts). The court emphasised that a key element in the test of what is a preference is that the company did what it did out of a positive wish to improve the creditor's position in the event of its own insolvent liquidation. There is no need for there to be direct evidence of the requisite desire; its existence may be inferred from the circumstances of the case. The mere presence of the requisite desire is not sufficient by itself; however, it must have influenced the decision of the company to enter into the transaction. But it is sufficient if it is one of the factors which operated on the minds of those who made the decision and it need not have been the only factor or even the decisive one.[143] Here the company did not positively wish to improve the bank's position, its only concern was that the bank should not call in the overdraft and force the company to stop trading. When the company gave the security to the bank, it did so out of a desire to continue trading. The debenture was not therefore void as a preference.

---

[139] IA 1986, s 239(6); save where the person is connected by reason only of being an employee of the company.

[140] *Wills v Corfe Joinery Ltd* [1997] BCC 511. A desire to prefer is insufficient if, on the facts, no actual preference occurred, see *Lewis v Hyde* [1997] BCC 976, PC (on the equivalent New Zealand provision).

[141] IA 1986, s 239(6); save where the person is connected by reason only of being an employee of the company.

[142] [1990] BCLC 324, Ch D. See Fletcher [1991] JBL 71.

[143] [1990] BCLC 324 at 335–6, Ch D; see also *Re Living Images Ltd* [1996] 1 BCLC 348.

Given the need to establish a desire to prefer in this way, it is not surprising that the   **25-74**
preference provisions operate most effectively with respect to connected persons
where the liquidator is assisted by the statutory presumption of a desire to prefer.[144]
Where the preference is not in favour of a connected person, but rather with an arm's
length creditor pressing for payment, commercial considerations of the kind present
in *Re MC Bacon Ltd*[145] are usually the motivating force rather than any desire to prefer
the creditor.

Certainly, preferences given to connected persons just prior to the collapse of the com-   **25-75**
pany are the precise types of transaction which the Cork Committee thought should
be challenged.[146] A typical example can be seen in *Re Exchange Travel (Holdings) Ltd*[147]
where in July 1990 the company repaid loans made by the directors to the company of
£200,000 (approximately) before going into administration in September 1990 with a
deficiency running into millions of pounds. In that situation, the directors are anxious
obviously to recover their money before the company goes into insolvency. The courts
have little difficulty in finding such repayments to be preferences and the transactions
will be reversed leaving the directors to claim as unsecured creditors in the liquidation
with no real prospect of recovering the sums due to them.

Similarly, in *Wills v Corfe Joinery Ltd*[148] repayment of directors' loans by the company   **25-76**
(on 2 February 1995) just prior to ceasing to trade (on 6 February 1995) constituted
a preference. The payments were made at a time when other creditors were pressing,
employees were being made redundant and so, the court asked, why did the directors
choose to pay these creditors? 'In the absence of evidence to show that it was purely for
commercial reasons, there is nothing to rebut the statutory presumption [of a desire to
prefer] and, indeed, everything to support that statutory presumption.'[149]

Another common scenario is where a director ensures that a particular creditor gets   **25-77**
paid because the director has personally guaranteed that debt. In *Re Agriplant Services
Ltd*,[150] S was a director of A Ltd which hired equipment from C Ltd and S personally
guaranteed any indebtedness arising from that equipment hire. S ensured that A Ltd
paid £20,000 to C Ltd two weeks before A Ltd was placed in voluntary liquidation.

The court held that the £20,000 payment constituted a preference given to the credi-   **25-78**
tor and to the director since it had the effect of improving the position of the creditor
and the director, as a contingent creditor under his guarantee,[151] in the event of the
insolvent liquidation of the company. The director tried to persuade the court that
the payment was motivated by the commercial needs of A Ltd, namely the need to

---

[144] IA 1986, s 239(6). 'Connected person' is defined in IA 1986, s 249 and s 435. The statutory presumption may be rebutted, see for example *Re Brian D Pierson* [2001] 1 BCLC 275 at 298; *Re Fairway Magazines
Ltd, Fairbairn v Hartigan* [1993] 1 BCLC 643 at 649–50.

[145] [1990] BCLC 324.   [146] See the Cork Committee Report, paras 1257–8, see **2-3**.
[147] [1996] 2 BCLC 524.   [148] [1997] BCC 511.
[149] [1997] BCC 511 at 517, per Lloyd J. See also *Re DKG Contractors Ltd* [1990] BCC 903 (payments of
£417,763 to one of the directors in the 10 months before liquidation).
[150] [1997] 2 BCLC 598.   [151] See IA 1986, s 239(4) at **25-71** above.

keep machinery on site so that A Ltd could continue in operation. The court found, however, that his main motivation was his own personal guarantee of that indebtedness. The director clearly had a desire to prefer himself, Jonathan Parker J noted, but it was only by improving the position of the creditor on an insolvent liquidation of the company that his own position under the guarantee could itself be improved. The payment was therefore a preference in relation to the creditor and the director. The court ordered the creditor to repay the £20,000 to the company with interest and ordered the director to pay the creditor £20,000 pursuant to his guarantee so that the position was restored to what it would have been on insolvency—i.e. the director would have had to meet the creditor's claim under his guarantee.

25-79   In *Re Sonatacus Ltd*[152] the company made a payment of £50,000 to C Ltd at a time when it was insolvent or it became insolvent as a consequence of the payment. The payment arose because C Ltd had lent £65,000 to a director of the company who had then lent the money on to the company. The company therefore owed its director £65,000 and he owed C Ltd. The Court of Appeal held that the payment to C Ltd constituted a preference to the director (the director was the creditor) since the company was in effect repaying to him a loan from him to the company. C Ltd in turn had received a benefit from the preference given by the company to its director and an order could be made against it for recovery of the benefit under IA 1986, s 241(1)(d). It could only retain the benefit therefore if the benefit had been received in good faith (s 214(2)). In the instant case, the evidence fell short of establishing that C Ltd had received the money in good faith and the onus was on C Ltd to establish its good faith. The controller of C Ltd knew of the financial difficulties of the company which is why he had been reluctant to lend directly to the company. He must have known, the court found, that it was likely that the repayment had been by the company at a time when it was insolvent, or at the least he must have shut his eyes to that possibility. Accordingly, C Ltd was liable to repay the £50,000 to the liquidator.

25-80   Where the court is satisfied that a preference has been given, the court may make such order as it thinks fit for restoring the position to what it would have been if the company had not given that preference.[153] Typically the court orders the repayment by the creditor of the amount received. For example, the directors in *Re Exchange Travel (Holdings) Ltd*[154] were ordered to pay the amounts received by them back to the liquidator leaving them to claim as unsecured creditors for the amounts of directors' loans outstanding and due to them from the company, see **25-75**.

25-81   Any recoveries obtained under this provision, not being property of the company, but property which arises only after the liquidation of the company, and which is recoverable only by the liquidator pursuant to his statutory powers is held by him on a

---

[152] [2007] 2 BCLC 627.
[153] IA 1986, s 239(3). The range of orders the court can make is the same as in relation to a transaction at an undervalue: s 241(1), discussed above at **25-63**. The court may make an order against only some of the parties involved: see *Re Agriplant Services Ltd* [1997] 2 BCLC 598 at 610.
[154] [1996] 2 BCLC 524.

statutory trust for distribution to the company's unsecured creditors,[155] but subject to the expenses of winding up,[156] see **25-31**, and any preferential debts, see **24-89**.

Extortionate credit transactions—IA 1986, s 244

Liquidators and administrators may challenge under IA 1986, s 244, any extortionate credit transaction (i.e. where the company is a party to a transaction for, or involving, the provision of credit to the company) entered into by the company in the three years before the company went into administration or liquidation (IA 1986, s 244(1), (2)). The test of whether a transaction is extortionate is whether, having regard to the risk accepted by the person providing the credit, the terms of it require grossly exorbitant payments in respect of the provision of the credit, or it otherwise grossly contravenes ordinary principles of fair dealing (s 244(3)). It is presumed, unless the contrary is proved, that a transaction with respect to which an application is made under this provision is or was extortionate (s 244(4)). It is for those who seek to uphold the transaction to show that it is or was not an extortionate credit transaction. If the office holder's challenge is successful, the court's powers extend to setting aside the whole or part of any obligations created by the transaction, varying any of its terms, or requiring the creditor to repay any sums to the liquidator.[157]   **25-82**

Avoidance of floating charges—IA 1986, s 245

Section 245 is designed to invalidate floating charges given close to insolvency which simply secure past indebtedness and provide no new benefits to the company.[158] The effect of the invalidity is to deprive the creditor of the security which he thought he had obtained and to prevent the substitution of a secured debt for an unsecured debt. Only the charge is rendered void, the underlying debt remains valid and, if the debt is repaid before winding up, the fact that the charge would have been void in the winding up does not affect the repayment.[159] In appropriate circumstances, it may be possible to challenge the repayment as a preference.   **25-83**

A floating charge is invalid and open to challenge by a liquidator or administrator under IA 1986, s 245 if the charge was created within the 12 months ending with the onset of insolvency[160] and at the time, or as a result of the transaction, the company   **25-84**

---

[155] *Re Oasis Merchandising Services Ltd, Ward v Aitken* [1997] 1 All ER 1009, CA. See McCormack, 'Swelling Corporate Assets: Changing what is on the menu' (2006) JCLS 39 at 55–8.

[156] IA 1986, s 115; IR 1986, r 4.218(2)(a)(i).

[157] IA 1986, s 244(4). One of the functions of this section is to prevent companies in effect preferring a creditor by agreeing artificially high rates of interest on the creditor's debt. If arrears of interest are allowed to build up, the creditor's proof of debt is artificially increased. See the Cork Committee Report, paras 1379–81, see **2-3**.

[158] For the background to this provision, see the Cork Committee Report, paras 1551–6, see **2-3**.

[159] *Mace Builders (Glasgow) Ltd v LuAnn* [1987] Ch 191, CA.

[160] The 'onset of insolvency' is defined in detail in IA 1986, s 245(5).

was unable to pay its debts.[161] Where the charge was created in favour of a person connected with the company, the relevant period is extended to two years before the onset of insolvency and it is irrelevant whether or not the company was unable to pay its debts at the time.[162] Even if the above conditions are satisfied, the floating charge is nevertheless valid to the extent that money is paid or goods or services are supplied to the company, or any debt of the company is reduced or discharged at the same time as, or after, the creation of the charge.[163]

25-85 In *Power v Sharp Investments Ltd*,[164] the board of a company (Shoe Lace Ltd) resolved in March 1990 to grant a debenture to its parent company, Sharp. The debenture granting a fixed and floating charge was duly executed on 24 July 1990 in respect of sums of money which had been advanced by Sharp in April, May, June and finally on 16 July 1990. A petition for winding up was presented on 4 September and the company was compulsorily wound up on 20 November. The liquidator challenged the validity of the charge in the light of IA 1986, s 245.

25-86 The Court of Appeal found that there was insufficient contemporaneity between the prior payments made by the debenture holder and the execution of the charge so as to bring it within the section which required the consideration to be paid at the same time as, or after, the creation of the charge. The words were clearly included by the legislature, the court said, for the purpose of excluding from the exemption the amount of moneys paid to the company before the creation of the charge, even though they were paid in consideration for the charge. On any other construction, these words would have been mere surplusage.[165] Sir Christopher Slade concluded that:[166]

> '...no moneys paid before the execution of a debenture will qualify for the exemption under the subsection [i.e. under s 245(2)(a)] unless the interval between payment and execution is so short that it can be regarded as minimal and payment and execution can be regarded as contemporaneous.'

25-87 As the court noted, 'it is always open to the lender not to lend until the charge has actually been executed; that must be the prudent course'.[167] This situation is distinguishable, the court said, from the case where the promise to execute a debenture creates a present equitable security and moneys are advanced in reliance upon it. In that case, the delay between the advances and the execution of the formal instrument of charge are immaterial as the charge has already been created and is immediately registrable, so that other creditors have the opportunity of learning of its existence.[168]

---

[161] IA 1986, s 245(2), (3)(b), (4).   [162] IA 1986, s 245(2), (3)(a).
[163] IA 1986, s 245(2).   [164] [1994] 1 BCLC 111, CA.
[165] [1994] 1 BCLC 111 at 122, CA.   [166] [1994] 1 BCLC 111 at 123, CA.
[167] [1994] 1 BCLC 111 at 123, CA, quoting Hoffmann J at first instance, see [1992] BCLC 636, Ch D.
[168] [1994] 1 BCLC 111 at 122, CA.

The fresh sums received must be received by the company and it is insufficient if sums **25-88** are advanced by the third party to the company's bank to reduce the company's overdraft which the third party has guaranteed. The money paid direct to the bank never becomes freely available to the company and thus is not paid 'to it' within the meaning of the section.[169]

[169] *Re Fairway Magazines Ltd, Fairbairn v Hartigan* [1993] 1 BCLC 643; see Prentice (1993) 109 LQR 371; also *Re Orleans Motor Co Ltd* [1911] 2 Ch 41.

26

Corporate takeovers and reconstruction

A Introduction

In this chapter we examine aspects of the regulation of takeovers and mergers. The **26-1** conventional meaning of 'takeover' is the acquisition by one company (the bidder) of sufficient shares in another company (the target) to give the bidder control of the target company. In the Takeover Code, the bidder company is described as the offeror company and the target company is described as the offeree company. 'Merger' means the uniting of two companies, but as this is possibly done through an acquisition by one company of a controlling holding of shares in another, it is not surprising that the terms 'takeover' and 'merger' have become almost synonymous. 'Merger' is often used to describe a recommended takeover bid rather than a hostile one, i.e. one opposed by the board of the offeree company. Essentially takeovers involve bids for publicly traded companies. In the case of private companies and public companies which are not publicly traded a sale of the company is normally a matter for private negotiation rather than a formal takeover bid.

An offer for shares

A takeover bid in the form of an offer for shares is an offer made by the offeror com- **26-2** pany to the offeree company's shareholders to acquire their shares. The offeror may offer cash for those shares, or shares in the offeror company, or a combination of cash and shares.

A scheme of arrangement

The other standard mechanism (and one which is increasingly used) to effect a takeo- **26-3** ver/merger/reconstruction is a scheme of arrangement under court supervision. The Takeover Panel's Annual Report for 2007–08 noted that for the year 2001–02 about 10% of takeover offers were effected through schemes while the figure for 2007–08 was 41%.[1] In recognition of this fact, and rather than continuing to proceed on a

---

[1] See Takeover Panel *Annual Report for 2007–08*, p 13.

case-by-case basis, the Takeover Code now specifically addresses (in Appendix 7) how the Code applies to a takeover effected by a scheme. Essentially the aim is that the Code should apply in the usual way with necessary modifications to accommodate the court-based schemes. The decision as to whether to proceed with a contractual offer or a scheme of arrangement depends on a variety of factors such as whether the approach is hostile or friendly (a hostile approach normally cannot proceed under a scheme, for the assistance of the offeree board is required to convene the various meetings required by a scheme) and the time-scale envisaged (a scheme may prove quicker in some circumstances than a bid). There may well be taxation issues (stamp duty is usually less on a scheme) and even political considerations (particularly if there are cross-border elements) where jurisdictions may have a preference as to the manner in which control changes hands. The major attraction of using a scheme is that the 75% approval required for a scheme binds all the members (or the creditors in a reconstruction), as the case may be (CA 2006, s 899(3)). The disadvantages of schemes relate to the complexity of the class meetings required—if the classes are constituted improperly, the court will refuse to sanction the scheme (see **26-97** et seq where schemes are discussed)—and the costs involved, given the court involvement. Schemes of arrangements are also commonly used to restructure insolvent companies where they are typically devised within an administration or following the appointment of a provisional liquidator. It is also possible to effect a reconstruction via a voluntary winding up under IA 1986, s 110, discussed below.

26-4   Takeovers are the means by which business expansion occurs. Companies may seek vertical integration (i.e. takeovers of companies at different stages in the production process) or horizontal integration (takeovers of companies at the same stage of the production process) or seek to diversify, as in the case of conglomerates. Takeovers tend to be associated in the public mind with aggressive or predatory management. In practice, a management that wishes to expand a company's business may have a choice of doing so via organic growth or through an acquisition or merger and may choose the latter simply because of the advantage it offers in terms of shorter time-scales.

26-5   As with any major investment decision, there may be a variety of motives for a company making a takeover bid for another company.[2] For example, a company may be concerned about its access to raw materials or vital components and thus seek a merger with one of its suppliers. It may be concerned to safeguard outlets for its products and so seek to merge with or take over one of its distributors or dealers. A company may want to diversify its activities by taking over a company in a completely different field. Equally, companies may be motivated less by economic considerations and more by financial or fiscal ones of improving the appearance of their balance sheet or reducing their liability to tax. Directors too may be motivated in part by personal 'empire-building' rather than any grand corporate strategy.

---

[2] For a readable account of the issues from a business perspective, see Moeller & Brady, *Intelligent M&A* (2007).

More broadly, for many years, there has been a debate (mainly conducted by econo-   **26-6**
mists) about whether takeovers and mergers are generally beneficial or harmful to the
overall economy.[3] The economic argument in favour of takeovers essentially is that the
business synergies arising from the deal result in efficiency gains and lower costs as
the new management extracts higher value from the company's assets. Takeovers thus
enable less productive or less efficient management to be replaced by more efficient
management and it is in this way that takeovers are said to form part of the market
for control of corporate assets.[4] Even an unsuccessful takeover bid, or the mere threat
that a takeover bid could be made, acts as a discipline and a spur to efficiency by ensuring that management make the most productive use of resources under their control.
Finally, takeovers offer shareholders the opportunity to recover a premium on their
investment.

On the other hand, it is argued that there is little evidence that hostile bids perform   **26-7**
a disciplining function and, even when there is a disciplining effect, it is argued that
a takeover is a costly way of dealing with an underperforming incumbent management, occurring in only a random and opportunistic way, and requiring significant
fees to advisers who may in fact be instrumental in initiating many takeovers.[5] The
critics of takeovers would argue that improved corporate governance mechanisms
(such as better board monitoring, better informed non-executive directors and more
active investors) are able to address the issue of removing ineffective managers in a less
expensive and disruptive way.[6] Fears have also been expressed that takeovers, or the
threat of takeovers, far from leading to productive use of assets, compel managements
to concentrate too much on short-term profitability to boost the share price and ward
off a takeover while avoiding long-term investment and innovation. There is also controversy as to the cost of the bid to the offeror company's shareholders (much of the
evidence suggests that these shareholders may be the losers in any takeover bid) and
the motivation of the offeror company's management in pursuing a bid.[7]

[3] See generally Romano, 'A Guide to Takeovers: Theory, Evidence and Regulation' in Hopt & Wymeersch
(eds), *European Takeovers—Law and Practice* (1992); also Cranston, 'The Rise and Rise of the Hostile
Takeover' in the same volume; Fairburn & Kay (eds), *Mergers and Merger Policy* (1989); Chiplin & Wright,
The Logic of Mergers (1987).

[4] See Bradley, 'Corporate Control: Markets and Rules' (1990) 53 MLR 170; Fairburn & Kay (eds), *Mergers
and Merger Policy* (1989), Introduction; Jensen and Ruback, 'The Market for Corporate Control' (1983) 11 J
of Fin Econ 5; Manne, 'Mergers and the Market for Corporate Control' (1965) 73 J of Pol Econ 110.

[5] Franks & Mayer, 'Hostile Takeovers and the Correction of Management Failure' (1996) 40 J of Fin
Econ 163; also Franks, Mayer and Renneborg, 'Managerial Disciplining and the Market for (partial)
Corporate Control in the UK' in McCahery et al (eds), *Corporate Governance Regimes: Convergence and
Diversity* (2002). See Hughes, 'The Impact of Merger: A Survey of Empirical Evidence for the UK' in Fairburn
& Kay (eds), *Mergers and Merger Policy* (1989). Having reviewed the empirical evidence, Hughes concluded
(at p 96) that 'Takeover or the threat of it, as a disciplinary stock market device, leaves a lot to be desired.'

[6] See Moerland, 'Alternative Disciplinary Mechanisms in Different Corporate Systems' (1995) 26 J of
Econ Behaviour & Organization 17; Coffee, 'Institutional Investors as Corporate Monitors: Are Takeovers
Obsolete' in Farrar (ed), *Takeovers, Institutional Investors and the Modernization of Corporate Laws* (1993);
Baums, 'Takeovers versus Institutions in Corporate Governance in Germany' in Prentice & Holland (eds),
Contemporary Issues in Corporate Governance (1993); Marsh, *Short-termism on trial* (1990).

[7] See Moerland, 'Alternative Disciplinary Mechanisms in Different Corporate Systems' (1995) 26 J of
Econ Behaviour & Organization 17 at 29, 30.

B The regulatory framework

26-8   The regulatory framework is found in the Takeover Code administered by the Takeover Panel and the Companies Act 2006, Parts 26 and 28, which together reflect the pre-existing domestic position and also the requirements of the 13th EC Directive on Company Law Concerning Takeover Bids (Directive 2004/25/EC).[8] The Takeover Directive applies to takeover bids for securities of a company governed by the law of a Member State where all or some of the securities are admitted to trading on a regulated market in the EU (art 1). The Directive lays down a minimum framework of principles as well as detailed rules as to the conduct of the bid, disclosure requirements etc. The impact of the Directive is reduced by a variety of Member State opt-outs which were necessary to secure the adoption of the Directive. Of course, as a minimum standard Directives Member States may choose to go further than the requirements of the Directive, as is the case with the Takeover Code, reflecting its long-established role in the UK. Nevertheless, given the history to the Directive, it was an achievement merely to have secured a framework for the conduct of takeovers throughout the EU.

The Takeover Directive

26-9   The Takeover Directive was under negotiation from 1989 (albeit intermittently) before being adopted in 2004 and coming into force on 20 May 2006.[9] The European Commission considered it important to secure a Takeover Directive because of its belief that shareholders of listed companies, especially minority shareholders, throughout the internal market should enjoy equivalent safeguards in the event of a change of control. To that end, the Commission thought that there should be minimum guidelines for, and transparency in, the conduct of takeover bids and there should be an appropriate supervisory authority, particularly for bids with a cross-border element. The Takeover Directive was seen as a key element in the integration of financial markets and specifically included in the Financial Services Action Plan which aimed to ensure a single financial market.

26-10   Initially there was considerable opposition to the proposed Directive from a variety of bodies, such as the then Department of Trade and Industry (now BERR) and the Takeover Panel. In particular, there were concerns about the effect which the Takeover Directive would have on the position of the Takeover Panel and uncertainty as to the impact which a Takeover Directive (given its legally binding status) would have on the Panel's decision-making and rule-making powers. One of the often identified strengths of the Takeover Code is the flexibility inherent in the requirement to adhere to the spirit of the Code rather than rigid adherence to rules

---

[8] Directive 2004/25/EC on takeover bids, OJ L 142, 30.4.2004, p 12 (hereinafter Takeover Directive).

[9] The first proposal for a Takeover Directive was put forward by the European Commission in 1989: see OJ C 64/8 14.3.1989. It was revised in 1990: see OJ C 240/7, 6.9.1990; in 1996: see COM (95) 655, 07.02.1996; in 1997, see OJ C 378, 13.12.97; followed by a new proposal in 2002, see OJ C 45 E, 25.02.2003, p 1.

and the ability to change the Code quickly to meet changing market practices and it was not clear that that flexibility could be retained under the Directive. There were also concerns about the potential loss of speed of decision-making by the Takeover Panel and any limits which might be imposed on the flexible application of the rules within the framework of the General Principles as set out in the Takeover Code. A particular concern was that implementation of the Takeover Directive and the consequential change in the Panel's and the Code's status would open up the regulation of takeovers to greater legal challenge in the form of nuisance or tactical litigation.[10] More broadly, the argument was made that the true obstacles to takeovers within the internal market lay not in the regulations governing the conduct of a takeover bid, but in structural and cultural barriers to takeovers in various Member States. These barriers in turn are reinforced by mechanisms within Member States' company laws which permit structures such as unequal voting rights, cross-holdings, restrictive proxy voting arrangements and the use of defensive measures by management to prevent hostile takeovers.[11]

The first proposal for a draft Takeover Directive on takeovers was put forward by the European Commission in 1989.[12] Various revisions then followed[13] and, after much further negotiation, a common position was agreed in June 2000[14] only for the proposed Takeover Directive to be rejected, in July 2001, on a tied vote in Parliament.[15] The European Parliament was concerned, in particular, about the inadequate protection of employee interests and of minority shareholders and about restrictions on the rights of boards to take defensive measures once a bid is announced. Some Member

26-11

---

[10] According to the Explanatory Memorandum to SI 2006/1183 (interim regulations implementing the Takeover Directive, see n 27 below) such litigation is undesirable because it impedes the fluidity of the takeover market, undermines the certainty with which a bidder can launch a bid and adds to the costs: see para 45.

[11] See, for example, DTI, *EC Proposal for a 13th Company Law Directive Concerning Takeovers, A Consultative Document* (August 1989); DTI, *Proposal for a 13th Company Law Directive Concerning Takeovers, A Consultative Document* (April 1996); HL Select Committee on the European Communities, Session 1995–96, 13th Report, *Takeover Bids* (1996, HL Paper 100); and further report, Session 2002–03, 28th Report, HL Paper 128. See DTI, *Barriers to Takeovers in the European Community, A Consultative Document* (January 1990) which identified barriers to takeovers on the Continent such as the prevalence of bank finance, the lack of listed companies, the concentration of shareholdings in the hands of management and the widespread use of bearer shares; see also Hopt, 'European Takeover Regulation: Barriers to and Problems of Harmonizing Takeover Laws in the European Communities' in Hopt & Wymeersch (eds), *European Takeovers—Law and Practice* (1992).

[12] See OJ C 64/8, 14.3.1989 and explanatory memorandum Bull. EC Supplement 3/89; also DTI, *EC Proposal for a 13th Company Law Directive Concerning Takeovers, A Consultative Document* (August 1989).

[13] Revised proposals were put forward in 1990, see OJ C 240/7, 6.9.1990, COM (90) 416 final; and in 1996, see COM (96) 655 final, 07.02.1996; DTI, *Consultative Document: Proposal for a Thirteenth Directive on Company Law Concerning Takeover Bids* (April 1996); HL Select Committee on the European Communities, Session 1995–96, 13th Report, *Takeover Bids* (1996, HL Paper 100); and in 1997, see Amended proposal for a 13th European Parliament and Council Directive on company law concerning takeover bids, COM (97) 565 final, OJ C 378, 13.12.97.

[14] See OJ C 23, 24.1.2001.

[15] See Alcock, 'The Regulation of Takeovers' (2001) 3 J Int'l Fin Mkt 163 on the reasons why the Parliament rejected the proposals.

States, in particular Germany, were concerned that, given there was no level playing field across Europe for takeovers,[16] imposing restrictions on the ability of management to 'defend' their companies against hostile takeover bids would mean, in the context of their particular Member State, that their businesses would be open to 'foreign' take-over while businesses in other Member States (because of different structural devices) would not be subject to the same possibilities.[17] More broadly, there was a concern that the boards of US companies are able under US law to adopt defensive strategies to render themselves bid-proof against European takeovers (although this is an over-simplification of the US position),[18] but the Takeover Directive would mean that US bidders would not encounter such defensive measures when bidding for European companies.

26-12   The European Commission responded to the concerns of the European Parliament in September 2001 by asking a High Level Group of Company Law Experts to assist the Commission in preparing a new proposal. The High Level Group reported in January 2002[19] and its recommendations were reflected in a new proposal for a Takeover Directive[20] brought forward by the Commission in October 2002. Both the High Level Group and the Commission reiterated the fundamental principle that the ultimate decision as to control of a company must be for the shareholders and not the incumbent management who have a clear conflict of interest in a bid situation. After further tortuous negotiations, the Takeover Directive was finally adopted on 21 April 2004 and came into force on 20 May 2006.[21]

26-13   This lengthy process necessarily impacted on the final version of the Directive which reflects the various compromises necessary to secure its adoption. In particular, Member States are allowed to opt out of two important provisions, art 9 on frustrating action by company boards and art 11, the breakthrough provision (the detail of these provisions is discussed below).[22] By the time of the adoption of the Directive, many of

---

[16] A lack of a level playing field is shorthand for the fact that across the EU there are different rules providing different levels of protection for shareholders, differing levels of entrenchment for incumbent management and differing prospects of success for would-be bidders.

[17] As to these concerns, see Fox, 'Not so European' (2001) 12 ICCLR 175.

[18] As many commentators have noted, while it is the case that the boards of US companies are often entitled under the law of the state of incorporation to adopt defensive measures, in practice the directors of such companies are subject to significant shareholder control, not least through easier shareholder access to class actions against management, and many boards relinquish their defensive measures when it is clear that their shareholders wish the offer to proceed. In reality, therefore, such companies are not immune from hostile bids; see Mennicke, 'A New Takeover Regime for Germany: The Act on the Acquisition of Securities and Takeovers' (2003) 24 Co Law 26.

[19] See *Report of the High Level Group of Company Law Experts on Issues Related to Takeover Bids* (10 January 2002, Brussels).

[20] See the Proposed Takeover Directive on Takeover Bids, COM (2002) 534 final, 2.10.2002 and Explanatory Memorandum; also Commission Press Release IP/02/1402, 2.10.2002; and speech by European Commissioner Bolkestein to the Committee on Legal Affairs and the Internal Market, European Parliament, 2.10.2002.

[21] OJ L 142, 30.4.2004, p 12. The operation of the Directive will be reviewed in 2011: see art 20.

[22] See Clarke, 'Articles 9 and 11 of the Takeover Directive and the Market for Corporate Control' [2006] JBL 355.

the concerns of the UK and some other Member States had been overtaken by market developments as takeover activity increased throughout the Continental Member States. A number of countries such as Belgium, The Netherlands, France, Spain, Italy and Germany had introduced their own takeover codes, modelled mainly on the UK Code.[23] Furthermore, the final version of the Takeover Directive was framed in terms sufficiently close to the terms of the Takeover Code to mean that the UK had relatively few concerns as to its implementation. The real merit of the Takeover Directive may lie therefore in providing those Member States with little experience of takeovers with a framework for their domestic regulation rather than requiring them to devise a regulatory system for themselves.

The Companies Act 2006

The regulatory framework for takeovers is provided by CA 2006, Parts 26–28:   **26-14**

- Part 26, ss 895–901 deals with schemes of arrangement which, as noted, is one of the main methods of effecting a takeover. Schemes of arrangement are discussed below at **26-97**.

- Part 27 deals with mergers and divisions of public companies. This Part implements the Third and the Sixth Company Law Directives which are concerned with mergers and divisions of public companies within a single Member State.[24] They are of limited significance in this jurisdiction since they apply to mergers by way of the transfer of assets and liabilities from one company to another, whereas acquisitions by the purchase of the shares in the entity rather than the underlying assets is the mechanism commonly used here. The package is completed by the Tenth Company Law Directive[25] which facilitates mergers of companies from different Member States and was implemented by the Cross-Border Mergers Regulations 2007,[26] though for the same reasons it is unlikely that much use will be made by UK companies of these mechanisms. These matters are not considered further in this chapter.

- Part 28 implements the Takeover Directive and, for the first time, places the Takeover Panel on a statutory footing.[27] The Panel is given power to make rules, to require the disclosure of information and documents, to apply to court for

---

[23] For a lucid account of the dramatic change in German regulation of takeovers in recent years, see Mennicke, 'A New Takeover Regime for Germany: The Act on the Acquisition of Securities and Takeovers' (2003) 24 Co Law 26.

[24] Third Company Law Directive 78/855/EEC concerning mergers of public limited liability companies, OJ L 295, 20.10.1978, p 36; Sixth Company Law Directive 82/891/EEC concerning the division of public limited liability companies, OJ L 378, 31.12.1982, p 47.

[25] Directive 2005/56/EC on cross-border mergers of limited liability companies, OJ L 310, 25.11.2005, p 1.

[26] See The Companies (Cross-Border Mergers) Regulations 2007, SI 2007/2974.

[27] Initial implementation was via Interim Regulations (SI 2006/1183) because the Companies Bill was still progressing through Parliament. These Regulations were revoked when CA 2006, Part 28 came into force on 6 April 2007.

enforcement orders and to impose sanctions for contravention of the Takeover Code. The Government's concern in implementing the Takeover Directive was to preserve the strengths of the Panel such as its flexibility, speed and certainty in decision-making as well as its independence and regulatory autonomy, professional expertise and consensual approach to regulation among those involved in the markets.[28] The Government was therefore anxious in CA 2006, Part 28 to provide the necessary statutory underpinning of the regulatory activities of the Panel while leaving the Panel to operate as before. In this it appears to have been successful and the Panel has reported that the overall picture, post-implementation of the Directive, is one of business as usual.[29]

Other regulatory issues

26-15   Quite apart from company law issues, takeovers provide the context in which issues of market abuse or manipulation may arise, for example through improper financial assistance (contrary to CA 2006, s 678: see **20-127**) given to effect a share support scheme to boost the offeror company's share price. The price of the offeror's shares can be crucial if the consideration being offered to the offeree company's shareholders includes shares in the offeror.[30] Many of these price-support schemes and other manipulations of the markets ahead of or during a bid fall within the market abuse provisions of the Financial Services and Markets Act 2000 which is policed by the Financial Services Authority (FSA).[31] The Panel and the FSA work closely together[32] and regard is had by the FSA to the extent to which the behaviour under scrutiny complies with the Takeover Code although it is not determinative as to whether it amounts to market abuse. The FSA will not take action against a person over behaviour which (1) complies with the Takeover Code and (2) falls within the safe harbours provided by the FSA Code of Market Conduct which states that behaviour so conforming does not amount to market abuse.[33] In any case where the FSA is of the opinion that any potential exercise of its enforcement powers[34] may affect the timetable or the outcome of a

---

[28] For the background to implementation, see the very useful Explanatory Memorandum to SI 2006/1183 (above n 27), esp paras 11–12; see also DTI, *Implementation of the European Directive on Takeover Bids, A Consultative Document* (2005), URN 05/511.

[29] See Takeover Panel, *Annual Report for 2006–07*, p 9. The report notes that there are no signs that the independence of the Panel, its constitution or its efficacy has been adversely affected by implementation.

[30] A share support scheme on a massive scale was at the heart of the Guinness takeover of Distillers: see **26-36**; see DTI, *Guinness plc, Investigation under ss 432(2) and 442 of the Companies Act 1985* (1997).

[31] See *FSA Handbook, Market Conduct Rules*.

[32] For example, the FSA will not normally make public the fact that it is or is not investigating a particular matter, or any of the findings or conclusions of an investigation, but it may do so where the matter in question has occurred in the context of a takeover bid, and the FSA has not appointed, and does not propose to appoint, investigators and considers (following discussion with the Takeover Panel) that such an announcement is appropriate in the interests of preventing or eliminating public uncertainty, speculation or rumour: *FSA Handbook, Enforcement Guide*, para 6.

[33] See FSMA 2000, s 120; as to the safe harbours with respect to the Takeover Code, see *FSA Handbook*, MAR 1.10.3G–1.10.6(C).

[34] I.e. under FSMA 2000, s 380 (injunctions and restitution), s 381 (injunctions in cases of market abuse).

takeover bid, the FSA consults the Takeover Panel before taking any steps to exercise its powers and the FSA is required to give due weight to the Panel's views.[35] Where the Takeover Panel is in a position to require appropriate redress, the FSA will not generally exercise its own powers to seek restitution.[36] Likewise the Panel stresses that it is a priority for the Panel to ensure that the FSA is fully informed and supported by the Panel Executive in those areas of bid activity where the FSA also has responsibilities for enforcement.[37]

Takeovers also present the ideal occasion for insider dealing, as information before and during a bid is highly price-sensitive inside information which can have a dramatic effect on the share prices of the companies involved, especially the offeree company. Individuals who have inside information from an inside source are subject to prohibitions on dealing in price-affected securities, encouraging another person to deal, and communicating the inside information to another person, all of which are offences in the circumstances set out in Part V of the Criminal Justice Act 1993. These broader dimensions to the regulation of takeovers therefore also need to be borne in mind.   **26-16**

Finally, any takeover or merger may raise competition issues, either nationally or at the EU level. Competition issues are beyond the scope of the work and readers are referred to the specialist works on competition law.   **26-17**

C The Takeover Panel

Composition and role

Set up in 1968, the Takeover Panel is an independent body which issues and administers the City Code on Takeovers and Mergers,[38] hereinafter the Takeover Code. As the Introduction notes, the Takeover Code is not concerned with the financial or commercial advantages or disadvantages of a takeover, nor with matters such as competition policy.[39] The Code is designed principally to ensure shareholders are treated fairly and are not denied an opportunity to decide on the merits of a takeover and that shareholders of the same class are afforded equivalent treatment by an offeror. The Code provides an orderly framework within which takeovers are conducted[40] and it is   **26-18**

---

[35] *FSA Handbook, Enforcement Guide*, para 10.3(11).

[36] *FSA Handbook, Enforcement Guide*, para 11.3(6).

[37] See Takeover Panel, *Annual Report for 2004–05*, p 9.

[38] At the time of writing, the current edition is the 8th edition of the Takeover Code published in 2006, hereinafter the Takeover Code. The Takeover Code is available on the Panel's website: www.thetakeover-panel.org.uk. See generally, Weinberg & Blank, *Takeovers and Mergers* (5th edn, 1989) (a looseleaf work); also Morse, 'Controlling Takeovers—the self-regulation option in the United Kingdom' [1998] JBL 58; Morse, 'The City Takeover Code on Takeovers and Mergers—Self Regulation or Self Protection' [1991] JBL 509. The Takeover Code developed out of the Notes for Amalgamations of British Businesses issued in 1959 by the Issuing Houses Association. For the historical background, see Johnston, *The City Takeover Code* (1980).

[39] Takeover Code, Introduction, para 2(a).   [40] Takeover Code, Introduction, para 2(a).

also designed to promote, in conjunction with other regulatory regimes, the integrity of the financial markets. The Code is said to represent the collective opinion of those professionally involved in the field of takeovers as to appropriate business standards and as to how fairness to shareholders and an orderly framework for takeovers can be achieved.[41]

26-19   The Panel is the designated supervisory authority for the purposes of the Takeover Directive and it is obliged to make rules as required by the Directive. Though the requirement to implement the Takeover Directive has meant putting the Panel on a statutory footing, the Panel remains an unincorporated body and it is not a statutory body constituted by the statute (CA 2006, s 942).[42] This approach to implementation of the Takeover Directive is designed to give effect to the Directive without unduly impinging on the manner in which the Panel operates: see **26-14**. The Panel has up to 33 members, up to 22 of whom are appointed by the Panel.[43] The remaining 11 members are nominated by major financial and business institutions.[44]

26-20   The Panel has overall responsibility for the policy, financing and administration of the Panel's functions and for the functioning and operation of the Code.[45] The Panel has a number of committees, one of which is the Code Committee with responsibility for rule-making and for keeping the Code under review and for consulting on, making and issuing amendments to the Code.[46]

26-21   The day-to-day work of takeover supervision and regulation is carried out by the Panel Executive which operates independently of the Panel.[47] Headed by a Director General, it is staffed by a mixture of secondees (from City institutions, banks, accountancy and law firms) and permanent appointments. The Panel Executive is available for consultation and may give guidance and rulings on the interpretation, application or effect of the Code.[48] Any person in doubt as to whether a proposed course of conduct is in accordance with the Takeover Code must consult the Executive in advance.[49] Legal or other professional advice on the interpretation or application of the Code is not

---

[41] Takeover Code, Introduction, para 2(a). The courts may on occasion look to the Takeover Code to identify what is good practice on a particular matter: see *Fiske Nominees Ltd v Dwyka Diamond Ltd* [2002] 2 BCLC 108.

[42] See *Explanatory Notes to the Companies Act 2006*, paras 1180–1.

[43] The House of Lords Delegated Powers and Regulatory Reform Committee expressed concerns and sought assurances that the Panel would continue to be an appropriate body and that no changes are possible to its constitution which would change its suitability to be a rule-making authority: see 9th Report, Session 2005–06, HL Paper 86, para 16. The Government gave such an assurance in the Parliamentary debates: see 680 HL Debs, GC 285–7, 28 March 2006.

[44] The bodies represented include: the Association of British Insurers; the Association of Investment Companies; the Association of Private Client Investment Managers and Stockbrokers; the British Bankers' Association; the Confederation of British Industry; the Institute of Chartered Accountants in England and Wales; the Investment Management Association; the London Investment Banking Association (three representatives); and the National Association of Pension Funds.

[45] Takeover Code, Introduction, para 4(a). The Panel must publish an annual report: CA 2006, s 963.

[46] Takeover Code, Introduction, para 4(b).

[47] CA 2006, s 942(3); Takeover Code, Introduction, para 5.

[48] Takeover Code, Introduction, para 5. The Executive issues Practice Statements from time to time.

[49] Takeover Code, Introduction, para 6(b).

an appropriate alternative to obtaining a ruling from the Executive.[50] The Executive or the Panel may take active steps to regulate the conduct of the bid while it is in progress, for example by requiring announcements or clarifications from the parties.

Rulings of the Executive are subject to review by the Hearings Committee which is a committee of the Panel (CA 2006, s 951(1)). The Hearings Committee can also be convened where the Executive wishes to refer a matter to the Committee without itself giving any ruling where it considers that there is a particularly unusual, important or difficult point at issue. Disciplinary proceedings may be instituted by the Executive before the Hearings Committee where it considers that there has been a breach of the Code or of a ruling of the Executive or of the Panel.[51]   **26-22**

The Takeover Appeal Board is an independent body which hears appeals against rulings of the Hearings Committee (CA 2006, s 951(3)). The chairman and deputy chairman of the Appeal Board must usually have held high judicial office and are appointed by the Master of the Rolls. The Appeal Board may confirm, vary, set aside, annul or replace a contested ruling.   **26-23**

The Panel's rule-making powers

The Panel is the designated supervisory authority for the purpose of the Takeover Directive with power to make rules and it must make rules giving effect to the Directive.[52] But the Panel's powers are wider than that and it has power to make rules for or in connection with the regulation of takeover bids, merger transactions, and other transactions which have or may have, directly or indirectly, an effect on the ownership or control of companies.[53] Takeovers not within the Takeover Directive but which could be the subject of the Code would include takeovers of public companies which are not traded on a regulated market. In other words, the Panel has power to make rules as necessary for the Takeover Directive and also to regulate domestic takeovers in the manner in which it has always done. It was a deliberate policy choice that all of the Panel's regulatory functions should fall within the new legal framework and the Government did not want a two-tier regulatory regime, one part dealing with takeovers within the Takeover Directive and another regime for takeovers outside the Directive.[54] The Panel has retained its traditional flexibility in that it may permit   **26-24**

---

[50] Takeover Code, Introduction, para 6(b).   [51] Takeover Code, Introduction, para 11(a).

[52] CA 2006, s 943. See the *Explanatory Notes to the Companies Act 2006*, paras 1180–8: the specified articles of the Takeover Directive in respect of which rules must be made are the general principles (art 3.1), jurisdictional rules (art 4.2), matters relating to protection of minority shareholders, mandatory bid and equitable price (art 5), contents of the bid documentation (art 6.1–6.3), time allowed for acceptance of the bids and publication of the bid (arts 7 and 8), obligations of the management of the target company (art 9) and other rules applicable to the conduct of bids (art 13). The Government decided that the Panel would not make rules with regard to art 11 (barriers to takeover), arts 15 and 16 (squeeze-out and sell-out provisions) and art 10 (information to be published by companies in the annual reports), it being preferable to deal with these matters in the CA 2006.

[53] CA 2006, ss 942(2), 943(2). This general power to make rules is expressed very broadly in s 943(2). In particular, rules may be made with regard to any matter similar to a matter provided for by the Panel as it operated prior to the passing of the CA 2006: s 943(3).

[54] 680 HL Debs, GC289, 28 March 2006, see also HC, session 2005-06, Standing Committee D, col 781, 15 June 2006.

derogations from the rules in particular cases and with regard to any circumstances (CA 2006, s 944(1)(d)), subject to the Panel giving reasons for any derogation or modification of a rule and provided, in the case of a transaction and rule subject to the requirements of the Directive, that the General Principles (see **26-41**) are respected.[55]

26-25   In addition to making rules, the Panel may give rulings on the interpretation, application and effect of the rules (CA 2006, s 945(1)) and, for the first time, the rulings of the Panel have binding effect (s 945(2)). The rules may confer power on the Panel to give directions to restrain a person from acting or continuing to act in breach of the rules or to restrain a person from doing or continuing to do a particular thing, pending determination of whether that conduct is or would be a breach of the rules; and otherwise to secure compliance with the rules (s 946). As discussed at **26-35**, failure to comply with the rules or with a direction of the Panel may attract sanctions under s 952.

Access to information

26-26   The Panel has significant new powers to require by notice in writing the production of such documents and information as it may reasonably require in connection with the exercise of its functions (CA 2006, s 947), subject to an exception regarding documents or information covered by legal professional privilege (s 947(10)) and subject to the privilege against self-incrimination (s 962). There are restrictions on the onward disclosure of information obtained by the Panel (other than with the consent of the person or business in question) backed up by criminal sanctions (ss 948–949).

26-27   Disclosure is permitted for the purpose of facilitating the carrying out by the Panel of any of its functions (CA 2006, s 948(3)). This provision allows disclosure, for example, to the Takeover Appeal Board or to the court in any application for an enforcement order under s 955. Disclosure is also permitted via the gateways set out in CA 2006, Sch 2. Part 1 of the Schedule identifies specified persons to whom disclosure may be made; Part 2 identifies 70 specific types of disclosure which are permissible; and Part 3 deals with disclosure to overseas bodies. In other words, the gateways in Sch 2 are extensive and familiar now from other legislation.[56] These gateways permit disclosure to all the usual regulatory and supervisory bodies such as BERR, the Bank of England, the Treasury, the Financial Services Authority, the Insolvency Service and also the Revenue and the police. In fact, the Panel has always co-operated with other regulatory authorities and the statute merely formalises the existing co-operation

---

[55] Takeover Code, Introduction, para 2(c).

[56] The precedent is FSMA 2000, ss 348, 349 and related regulations, see FSMA (Disclosure of Confidential Information) Regulations 2001, SI 2001/2188. There was some Parliamentary concern that whereas in the past parties were content to deal with the Panel in an open, candid way, they might be less willing in future in view of these disclosure provisions (see 680 HL Debs, GC 293–4, 28 March 2006). The Government justified the disclosure requirements in part on the fact that art 4(3) of the Takeover Directive treats information obtained by the Panel as confidential with the result that it cannot be disclosed unless gateways are provided (see 680 HL Debs, GC 294–6, 28 March 2006), but that explanation does not explain why the gateways are so extensive.

and makes provision for co-operation with overseas authorities as required by the Takeover Directive. The Panel is in any event a designated body under FSMA 2000 and under CA 1985, s 449 (a provision which remains in force), so it can receive restricted information obtained as a result of investigations under those statutes.[57]

The general prohibition on disclosure other than through the approved gateways (CA 2006, s 948(2)) does not apply to the onward disclosure of information given by the Panel to the FSA; or to any designated supervisory authority under the Takeover Directive (every Member State is required to designate a supervisory authority); or to any overseas authority exercising functions of the public nature within the EEA, which functions are similar to those of the Panel or the FSA (s 948(6), (7)). Onward disclosure is permitted because such bodies in turn are subject to restrictions on disclosure which ensures that information that originates from the Panel is protected from improper further disclosure.[58] Linked to this possibility of onward transmission, the Panel is required (under s 950) to co-operate with the FSA, other supervisory authorities designated as such for the purposes of the Directive, and any other person or body exercising functions of a public nature in any country outside the UK that appear to the Panel to be similar to its own functions or those of the FSA.[59] The relationship between these provisions is that s 948 allows for the disclosure of information, while s 950 provides for co-operation which can be co-operation, in ways other than the sharing of information.

26-28

Challenging the Panel

One of the concerns with regard to the implementation of the Takeover Directive and the designation of the Takeover Panel as the supervisory authority was that this might expose the Panel to greater legal challenge. In order to reduce the possibilities of tactical or nuisance litigation, the Takeover Directive makes it clear in art 4(6) that it is for the Member States to designate judicial or other authorities responsible for dealing with disputes and to regulate whether and under which circumstances parties to bids are entitled to bring administrative or judicial proceedings. The position in the UK is that judicial review is possible, but only once a bid is completed and only with a view to a declaration as to how future bids might be conducted. This approach was laid down in *R v Panel on Take-overs and Mergers, ex p Datafin plc*[60] (though the emphasis there on the Panel's lack of legal authority has been overtaken by the CA 2006).

26-29

---

[57] See FSMA 2000, ss 348, 349; Financial Services and Markets Act 2000 (Disclosure of Confidential Information) Regulations 2001, SI 2001/2188, regs 9, 10 and 12, Sch 1; and with respect to CA 1985, s 449, see Sch 15C and 15D.

[58] See the *Explanatory Notes to the Companies Act 2006*, para 1197.

[59] CA 2006, s 950(1). In particular the Panel can be required to assist an overseas regulatory authority in the service of documents on persons within this jurisdiction. This duty to co-operate applies to similar bodies operating in any country outside the UK and is not restricted to countries within the EEA, unlike s 948 (6), (7).

[60] [1987] 1 All ER 564, CA; noted Hilliard (1987) 50 MLR 372; (1987) 103 LQR 323; see also Lord Alexander, 'Judicial Review and City Regulators' (1989) 52 MLR 640.

26-30   In that case, two companies had been rival bidders for a third target company. The defeated bidder alleged that the successful bidder had had the assistance of a concert party.[61] The Panel upheld a ruling by the Executive that there was no concert party. The defeated bidder appealed to the courts for judicial review of the Panel's decision. Giving judgment, Sir John Donaldson MR noted that the Panel was a remarkable self-regulating body which involved a group of people using their collective power to force themselves and others to comply with a code of conduct of their own devising.[62] He went on:[63]

> 'Lacking any authority de jure, it [the Panel] exercises immense power de facto by devising, promulgating, amending and interpreting the City Code on Takeovers and Mergers, by waiving or modifying the application of the code in particular circumstances, by investigating and reporting on alleged breaches of the code and by the application or threat of sanctions. These sanctions are no less effective because they are applied indirectly and lack a legally enforceable base.'

26-31   Notwithstanding its unusual status, the court thought that the Panel should be subject to judicial review for three main reasons. First, the Secretary of State for Trade and Industry had indicated a willingness to limit legislation in the field of takeovers and mergers and instead to use the Panel to regulate this area; secondly, those subject to the Panel's jurisdiction could be subject to a range of contractual or statutory sanctions by other bodies if they transgressed the Takeover Code; thirdly, as the rights of citizens (some of whom will not have consented) can be affected by the Panel's decisions, the Panel in carrying out its responsibilities was performing a public duty and was amenable to judicial review.[64] No one would dispute that the Panel's functions then and especially now mean that it is amenable to judicial review, but crucially Sir John went on to say:[65]

> '…I wish to make it clear beyond a peradventure that in the light of the special nature of the Panel, its functions, the market in which it is operating, the time scales which are inherent in that market and the need to safeguard the position of third parties, who may be numbered in thousands, all of whom are entitled to continue to trade on an assumption of the validity of the Panel's rules and decisions, unless and until they are quashed by the court, I should expect the relationship between the Panel and the court to be historic rather than contemporaneous.'

26-32   Decisions of the Panel stand and the court will only intervene in retrospect by way of a declaration to enable the Panel not to repeat any error or to relieve individuals of any disciplinary consequences of an erroneous decision.[66] This approach was wel-

---

[61] Persons acting in concert are defined in the Takeover Code as 'persons who, pursuant to an agreement or understanding (whether formal or informal) co-operate to obtain or consolidate control of a company or to frustrate the successful outcome of an offer for a company': see Takeover Code, Definitions section.

[62] [1987] 1 All ER 564 at 567, CA.   [63] [1987] 1 All ER 564 at 567, CA.

[64] [1987] 1 All ER 564 at 577, CA.   [65] [1987] 1 All ER 564 at 579, CA.

[66] [1987] 1 All ER 564 at 579, CA. See also *R v Panel on Takeovers and Mergers, ex p Guinness plc* [1989] 1 All ER 509, CA: the test is whether something has gone wrong with the Panel's procedure so as to cause real injustice and require the intervention of the court. (Panel's decision not to adjourn a hearing of a concert party allegation could be criticised but overall the conduct of the Panel had been fair and had not caused

comed in the City as a pragmatic response, allowing for judicial review but doing so in a way designed to prevent parties indulging in tactical litigation as a defensive mechanism.[67]

A similarly pragmatic approach was taken by David Richards J in *Re Expro Inter-* **26-33** *national Group plc*[68] which concerned a takeover effected through a scheme of arrangement which, as noted at **26-98**, is subject to the Code which is applied to a scheme in the manner set out in Appendix 7 to the Code. Interestingly, the court considered that in relation to takeovers effected via a scheme, there is what might be described as a dual jurisdiction of the courts and the Panel. The court refused to delay court sanction of a scheme to see whether another bid might emerge for the company. The shareholder meetings had approved the scheme and had done so in the knowledge of the possibility of a further bid being made by a particular cut-off date. That date, having passed, it was not appropriate for the court on the applica- tion of certain shareholders to permit a further adjournment. The court noted that in reaching this conclusion on an adjournment, it did so on its merits and in accord- ance with the established principles applicable to the consideration of schemes of arrangement. But Richards J went on to say that he was concerned that there should, if possible, be a common approach to the conduct of bids, whether they are struc- tured as an offer or as a scheme. He did not think it desirable that the court proced- ure involved in a scheme should allow in an undesirable level of uncertainty which the provisions of the Code have successfully reduced or eliminated in the case of ordinary offers. Under the Code rules, as discussed below, the prospective bidder had been asked by the Panel to 'put up or shut up' (see **26-46**) and having failed to put up in accordance with that schedule established by the Code, the court was not willing to open up the whole situation again by adjourning the application for sanc- tion. The Panel subsequently noted that 'on this evidence it does not appear that there is any current likelihood of the courts playing a more active role in determin- ing the outcome of offers'.[69]

In implementing the Takeover Directive, the Government also included a number of **26-34** measures intended to limit the scope for tactical litigation as follows:[70]

    (1) by providing initially for appeals from decisions of the Executive to go to the Hearings Committee and from there to the Takeover Appeal Board chaired by a former member of the judiciary before there is recourse to the courts, as noted at **26-22**;

---

injustice.) See also *R v Panel on Takeovers and Mergers, ex p Fayed* [1992] BCLC 938; noted Morse, 'Panel disciplinary hearings and judicial review' [1992] JBL 596.

   [67] For a more critical view: see 'New vistas of judicial review' (1987) 103 LQR 323; also Hilliard, 'The Take- over Panel and the courts' (1987) 50 MLR 372 at 377: '…a Panel subject to review the scope of which is so hedged about with qualification that any notion of substantive supervision is illusory.'

   [68] [2008] EWHC 1543, 26 June 2008.   [69] See Takeover Panel, *Annual Report for 2007–08*, p 14.

   [70] See the Explanatory Memorandum to SI 2006/1183 (above n 27), para 47. See generally Mukwiri, 'The Myth of Tactical Litigation in UK Takeovers' (2008) JCLS 373; Ogowewo, 'Tactical Litigation in Takeover Contests' [2007] JBL 589.

(2) by excluding any new right of action for breach of statutory duty for a breach of the Panel's rules (CA 2006, s 956);

(3) by protecting concluded transactions from challenge for breach of the Panel's rules (CA 2006, s 956(2) provides that any contravention of a rule-based requirement does not make any transaction void or unenforceable or affect the validity of any other thing);

(4) by exempting the Panel and its individual members, officers and staff, from liability in damages for things done in the discharge of the regulatory functions of the Panel, save in the case of bad faith (CA 2006, s 961).

Sanctions for breach of the Takeover Code

26-35   The rule-making powers of the Takeover Panel extend to rules conferring power on the Panel to impose sanctions on a person who has acted in breach of the rules or failed to comply with a direction given by the Panel (CA 2006, s 952).

Compensation

26-36   The rules may confer a power on the Panel to order a person to pay such compensation as it thinks just and reasonable, but it is not a general power to order compensation, but a deliberately limited power to order compensation only where the rule which has been breached required the payment of money (s 954).[71] The Panel states that its practice with respect to breaches of the Code is to focus on the specific consequences of the breach with the aim of providing appropriate remedial or compensatory action in a timely manner.[72] An important example of the exercise of the Panel's powers in this regard came in the Guinness case where the Panel was able to compel (even if somewhat belatedly) the offeror company (Guinness) to provide significant financial redress (an additional £75m approximately) for offeree shareholders (in Distillers) where there had been serious breaches of the Code resulting in a false market in the offeror's shares.[73] Despite the sanction element apparent in this ruling, the Panel stated that this exercise was restricted to compensating the offeree shareholders and was specifically not of a disciplinary nature.[74] The Panel believes that this requirement to pay is an effective step for it focuses on the consequences for shareholders of breaches of the rules rather than simply on disciplinary action in respect of the breach. The fact remains that Guinness successfully took over Distillers using a massive share support scheme hidden from the market in breach of the Takeover Code.[75] As the DTI

---

[71] Takeover Code, Introduction, para 10(c).   [72] Takeover Code, Introduction, para 10.

[73] See Takeover Panel, *Annual Report for 1988–89*; Panel Press Summary 1989/13; also *Panel Report on the various hearings and appeal by Guinness: Takeover Panel, Guinness plc/The Distillers Company plc* (1989). For the background to the payment, see [1989] JBL 520.

[74] See Panel Statement 1992/6, 14 February 1992.

[75] The inspectors' report found that 78m Guinness shares, some 25% of the issued share capital at that time, were purchased by supporters of the Guinness cause at a total cost of £257m: see DTI, *Guinness plc, Investigation under ss 432(2) and 442 of the Companies Act 1985* (1997), para 5.3.

inspectors who investigated the affair noted, an extra £75m might seem to some a reasonable additional expense to secure the prize of Distillers.[76]

Other sanctions

In addition to acting to provide redress for shareholders, the Panel may also consider disciplinary action as appropriate.[77] If the Hearings Committee finds a breach of the Code or of a ruling of the Panel, it may issue a private letter of criticism or a public statement of censure;[78] or suspend or withdraw any exemption, approval or other special status which the Panel has granted; or report the offender to a UK or overseas regulatory authority or professional body (most notably the FSA) so that authority or body can consider whether to take disciplinary or enforcement action.[79] Also, the Hearings Committee may publish a Panel Statement indicating that the offender is someone who, in the Hearings Committee's opinion, is not likely to comply with the Code. The rules of the FSA and certain professional bodies oblige their members not to act for that person in a transaction subject to the Takeover Code (so-called 'cold-shouldering').[80] It is a feature of the Code that it applies to a wide variety of professionals involved in bids including company advisers, especially financial advisers, and directors of companies subject to the Code, all of whom are expected to be aware of and to comply with the Code.[81] It is the professionals who must operate in

26-37

---

[76] See DTI, *Guinness plc, Investigation under ss 432(2) and 442 of the Companies Act 1985* (1997), para 12.11. The inspectors' report provides a fascinating account of this controversial takeover by Guinness of Distillers which took place in January–April 1986; the inspectors' report was delayed by the various court proceedings arising from the takeover.

[77] Takeover Code, Introduction, paras 10, 11(b). The available sanctions are all sanctions which the Panel was able to impose prior to the commencement of CA 2006, Part 28. If the Panel wishes to adopt any new sanctions, it can only do so in accordance with the procedure set out in s 952(3): s 952(2). These limitations on the power to devise new sanctions were added to the legislation to meet concerns expressed by the House of Lords Delegated Powers and Regulatory Reform Committee, see 9th Report, Session 2005–06, HL Paper 86, para 15; 680 HL Debs, GC307, 28 March 2006.

[78] For examples of public criticism, see Takeover Panel Statement 2007/29, *iSoft Group plc* and 2007/06, *Plusnet plc* available at www.thetakeoverpanel.org.uk, although as Morse notes: 'the whole concept of "public" criticism in this context is a highly specialised one': see Morse, 'Assessing the impact of the Takeover Panel's Takeover Code Committee—Takeover Code reform institutionalised?' [2003] JBL 314 at 325; Morse also questions the effectiveness of public censure as a sanction: see [1998] JBL 58 at 71. These powers are used rarely in any event. In 2007–08, the Panel issued four private letters of criticism and issued one public statement of censure, the preceding year the corresponding figures were nine and one: see Takeover Panel, *Annual Report for 2007–08*, p 17.

[79] The FSA enforcement powers are extensive and include public censure, fines, prosecutions, the removal of authorisation, the imposition of injunctions and orders for restitution: see *FSA Handbook, Enforcement Guide*.

[80] See *FSA Handbook* MAR 4.3.3–4.3.5. On the question of sanctions by the Panel, see Morse, 'Assessing the impact of the Takeover Panel's Takeover Code Committee—Takeover Code reform institutionalised?' [2003] JBL 314 at 326–7; also [1992] JBL 428–33 where he criticises the Panel for being rather more willing to criticise outsiders than City practitioners caught in breach of the Takeover Code, also [1992] JBL 106; Morse, 'The City Takeover Code on Takeovers and Mergers—Self Regulation or Self Protection' [1991] JBL 509.

[81] Takeover Code, Introduction, para 3(f).

the London marketplace who are most susceptible to the Panel's disciplinary powers and who would be most concerned about any possible cold-shouldering.[82]

Court orders

26-38   The Panel alone may apply to the court for a court order to secure compliance with any rule-based requirement[83] or any disclosure requirement[84] (CA 2006, s 955). The court will only make an order if it is satisfied that there is a reasonable likelihood that a person will contravene a rule-based requirement or has contravened a rule-based requirement or a disclosure requirement.

D The conduct of takeovers under the Takeover Code

Application of the Code

26-39   The Takeover Directive applies to takeover bids for securities of a company governed by the law of a Member State where all or some of the securities are admitted to trading on a regulated market in the EU (art 1).[85] A key issue when the Takeover Directive was being negotiated was which supervisory authority would have control of the bid in circumstances where a company might have its registered office in one Member State while admitted to trading on a regulated market in another Member State. The compromise reached is to allow for shared jurisdiction in certain circumstances. A further jurisdictional issue was whether it was appropriate for what might be described as company law issues to be determined by any state other than the state of incorporation. On this issue the complicated solution devised by the Takeover Directive is to draw a distinction between bid issues to do with consideration and procedures[86] and employee and company law issues to do with information, voting control and frustrating action by directors, with the latter issues, in keeping with the core rule of private international law, remaining subject to the law of the state of incorporation (art 4(2)(e)). Consideration and procedural matters are subject to the rules of the Member State of the competent authority supervising the bid. Employee and company law issues are matters for the Member State in which the offeree company has its registered office. This distinction drawn between 'consideration and procedural

---

[82] Although Morse [1992] JBL 106, 428, suggests that the Panel is often more lenient with professionals who are in breach of the Takeover Code than with other parties such as directors.

[83] This strange wording of CA 2006, s 955 was criticised in the Parliamentary debates, but the Government stated that it was 'perfectly functional' and that it was clear that this requirement includes any decisions or rulings of the Panel made pursuant to the rules: 680 HL Debs, GC313, 28 March 2006.

[84] A disclosure requirement is defined as any requirement to disclose documents or information under CA 2006, s 947, discussed above at **26-26**.

[85] A regulated market is a market within the meaning of the Markets in Financial Investments Directive, Directive 2004/39/EC, (Mifid), art 47, OJ L 145, 30.4.2004, p1.

[86] Bid issues are matters relating to the consideration offered in the case of a bid, in particular the price, and matters relating to the bid procedure, in particular the information on the offeror's decision to make a bid, the contents of the offer document and the disclosure of the bid.

issues' and 'employee and company law' matters is not very clear and may lead to difficulties in complex cases.

These elaborate jurisdictional requirements are reflected in the Takeover Code **26-40** which also has to allow for the traditional jurisdiction of the Panel which extends beyond bids for publicly traded companies.[87] The need to accommodate these domestic and Takeover Directive issues is reflected in the complex provisions governing the application of the Code which essentially applies to:[88]

(1) all offers (not falling within paragraph (3) below) for companies which have their registered offices in the UK, the Channel Islands or the Isle of Man if any of their securities are admitted to trading on a regulated market in the UK or on any stock exchange in the Channel Islands or the Isle of Man;

(2) all offers (not falling within paragraph (1) above or paragraph (3) below) for public and private companies[89] which have their registered offices in the UK, the Channel Islands or the Isle of Man and which are considered by the Panel to be resident in one of those jurisdictions.

In either of these cases, the Code is concerned with regulating takeover bids and merger transactions of the relevant companies, however effected, including by means of statutory merger or Court-approved scheme of arrangement.[90]

(3) Shared jurisdiction—UK and other EEA registered and traded companies. The Code also applies to offers for the following companies:[91]

(a) a company which has its registered office in the UK whose securities are admitted to trading on a regulated market in one or more Member States of the European Economic Area (EEA) but not on a regulated market in the UK.

In cases within this category, the Code applies in respect of 'employee information and company law matters'; 'consideration and procedural matters' are governed by the rules of the Member State supervising the bid.

---

[87] Member States may extend the scope of the Takeover Directive so the Takeover Code can continue to apply to all unlisted public companies and to some private companies: see n 89 below.

[88] See Takeover Code, Introduction, para 3.

[89] The Takeover Code applies to private companies essentially only if their securities have been listed/traded/marketed or been the subject of a public offer during the 10 years prior to the date on which an announcement is made of a proposed or possible offer for the company: see Takeover Code, Introduction, para 3(a)(ii).

[90] The Takeover Code is also concerned with regulating other transactions (including offers by a parent company for shares in its subsidiary, dual holding company transactions, new share issues, share capital reorganisations and offers to minority shareholders) which have as their objective or potential effect (directly or indirectly) obtaining or consolidating control of the relevant companies, as well as partial offers (including tender offers) to shareholders for securities in the relevant companies: Takeover Code, Introduction, para 3(b).

[91] 'Offers' in this context means any public offer (other than by the company itself) made to the holders of the company's securities to acquire those securities (whether mandatory or voluntary) which follows or has as its objective the acquisition of control of the offeree company: Takeover Directive, art 2; Takeover Code, Introduction, para 3(b). 'Control' is a matter to be defined by each Member State and is defined in the Takeover Code as 'an interest, or interests, in shares carrying in aggregate 30% or more of the voting rights of a company, irrespective of whether such interest or interests give de facto control'.

(b) a company which has its registered office in another Member State of the EEA whose securities are admitted to trading only on a regulated market in the UK.

In this case, the Code applies in respect of 'consideration and procedural matters' and 'employee information and company law matters' are governed by the rules of the Member State where the offeree company has its registered office.

General Principles

26-41   The Takeover Code is based upon a number of General Principles which are set out in art 3 of the Directive (though their origin was the Takeover Code which has long been based on a series of General Principles). The General Principles are expressed in broad terms and they are essentially statements of standards of commercial behaviour which are applied by the Panel in accordance with their spirit to achieve their underlying purpose.[92] In addition to the General Principles, the Code contains a series of rules (currently 38) with extensive accompanying notes. The rules must be interpreted in order to achieve their underlying purpose and the spirit as well as the letter of a rule must be observed.[93] The General Principles in the Takeover Code (identical to the Directive requirements) are as follows:

(1) All holders of the securities of an offeree company of the same class must be afforded equivalent treatment; moreover, if a person acquires control of a company, the other holders of securities must be protected.

(2) The holders of the securities of an offeree company must have sufficient time and information to enable them to reach a properly informed decision on the bid; where it advises the holders of securities, the board of the offeree company must give its views on the effects of implementation of the bid on employment, conditions of employment and the locations of the company's places of business.

(3) The board of an offeree company must act in the interests of the company as a whole and must not deny the holders of securities the opportunity to decide on the merits of the bid.

(4) False markets must not be created in the securities of the offeree company, of the offeror company or of any other company concerned by the bid in such a way that the rise or fall of the prices of the securities becomes artificial and the normal functioning of the markets is distorted.

(5) An offeror must announce a bid only after ensuring that he/she can fulfil in full any cash consideration, if such is offered, and after taking all reasonable measures to secure the implementation of any other type of consideration.

(6) An offeree company must not be hindered in the conduct of its affairs for longer than is reasonable by a bid for its securities

---

[92] Takeover Code, Introduction, para 2(b).   [93] Takeover Code, Introduction, para 2(b).

These principles can be expressed as the following broad propositions: treat all share-   **26-42**
holders of the offeree company in an equivalent way; give the shareholders time to
reach an informed judgment; directors must remember that it is for the shareholders
to decide on the bid; there must be no market abuse, no offers if the offeror cannot
afford the deal and no laying siege to the offeree company.

The rules governing takeover bids

As noted at **26-2**, a takeover offer is a contractual offer to acquire the shares of the   **26-43**
offeree company, but a takeover bid can also be effected through a scheme of arrangement. The provisions of the Code apply to an offer effected by means of a scheme of
arrangement in the same way as they apply to an offer effected by means of a contractual offer, as modified by Code Appendix 7 which sets out how the Code applies in the
context of a scheme. Appendix 7 was introduced in 2007 in the light of the increasing
use of schemes to effect a takeover.

Announcements

There must be absolute secrecy before an announcement of a bid[94] for information   **26-44**
regarding a pending takeover bid is highly price-sensitive and provides significant
opportunities for insider dealing. Any offer must be put first to the board of the offeree
company or to its advisers and the board of the offeree must make an immediate
announcement when a firm intention to make an offer is notified to the board from a
serious source.[95] To avoid any distortion of the market or the misleading of the shareholders, an offeror should only announce an offer after the most careful and responsible consideration and only when the offeror has every reason to believe that it can and
will continue to be able to implement the offer; responsibility in this connection also
rests on the financial adviser to the offeror.[96]

Before any approach has been made to the offeree company, an announcement of a   **26-45**
possible offer may be required of the offeror where there are rumours about a bid or
untoward movement in the offeree's share price and there is reason for concluding that
it is the potential offeror's actions which have led to this situation.[97] These 'possible
offer announcements' (sometimes described as virtual takeover offers) are usually subject to certain conditions being met, such as regulatory consents being forthcoming.
Equally, there may be an announcement by the offeror of a firm intention to make an
offer but subject to pre-conditions.[98] During this period of rumour and speculation,
the shareholders of the offeree company may be confused as to whether or not an offer
will be forthcoming and the management of the target company may be distracted

---

[94] See Takeover Code, Rule 2.1.
[95] See Takeover Code, Rule 1(a); Rules 2.2–2.3. Responsibility for an announcement may lie either with
the offeror or the offeree as dictated by Rule 2.3.
[96] Takeover Code, General Principle 5; Rule 2.5(a).
[97] Takeover Code, Rule 2.2(d); and see Rule 2.4 on the announcement of a possible offer.
[98] See Takeover Code, Rule 2.5.

from the management of the company by the threat of a possible bid. The markets may also be uncertain as to the offeree company's prospects.

26-46   The Panel's response to a virtual takeover offer is generally not to intervene so long as the management of the offeree company is content with the situation, but the management may ask (and usually does ask) the Panel to require the offeror to 'put up or shut up', as it is described.[99] The Panel may impose a time-limit for the potential offeror to clarify its intentions, at the end of which the potential offeror must announce either a firm intention to make an offer or that it does not intend to make an offer.[100] If the potential offeror states that it has no intention to bid, normally it is bound by that statement for a period of six months.[101]

26-47   Once an offer has been announced, the offer cannot be withdrawn without the consent of the Panel, unless the offer was subject to pre-conditions which have not been met.[102] This restriction on the right to withdraw is imposed in order to prevent offerors making opportunistic bids based on particular market conditions or attempting to manipulate the market with no intention of carrying through a bid. The Panel will not normally give consent to the withdrawal of a bid merely because market conditions have altered and the offer is now at an unrealistically high price. Parties can make an offer subject to conditions, including a material adverse change clause which allows the offer to be withdrawn in certain circumstances.

26-48   The issue of material adverse change (MAC) clauses was reviewed by the Panel in the context of an offer by WPP Group Plc for Tempus Group plc when the Panel rejected an attempt by WPP Group plc to rely on the terrorist attacks on the US on 11 September 2001 as triggering a MAC clause.[103] The Panel's view is that what is required to invoke such a clause is an adverse change of very considerable significance striking at the heart of the transaction in question, analogous to something that would justify frustration of a contract. A change which undermines, from the offeror's perspective, the rationale for having made the bid is not sufficient. Commentators have been critical of this interpretation which means that it will be difficult to rely on a MAC clause, for it will be rare for the circumstances to amount in effect to legal frustration of a contract.

The price to be paid

26-49   General Principle 5 stresses that an offeror must announce a bid only after ensuring that he/she can fulfil in full any cash consideration, if such is offered, and after taking all reasonable measures to secure the implementation of any other type of consideration. This principle is reinforced by Rule 2.5 which provides that announcement of a bid should be made only when an offeror has every reason to believe that it can and will continue to be able to implement the offer. Responsibility in this connection also

---

[99] The Panel's annual report each year lists the 'put up or shut up' statements made in the period, see *Annual Report 2007–08* which lists 20 such statement in that period: see p 25.
[100] Takeover Code, Rule 2.4(b).   [101] See Takeover Code, Rule 2.8.
[102] Takeover Code, Rule 2.7.
[103] See the Panel Statement 2001/15, 'Offer by WPP Group Plc for Tempus Group plc', 6 November 2001.

rests on the financial adviser to the offeror. If, in the three months prior to the offer, the offeror purchases shares in the offeree company, the offer to shareholders of the same class must be on no less favourable terms, unless the Panel otherwise agrees.[104] Likewise, if, during the offer, the offeror buys shares at above the offer price, the offer price for all must be correspondingly increased.[105]

Publicity and information to shareholders and employees

A variety of provisions in the Takeover Directive focus on information and, in par-   **26-50** ticular, provide for the communication of information to the supervisory authority, to the shareholders, to employee representatives of the offeree and offeror company and to the market.[106]

The decision to make a bid must be made public without delay and the Panel informed.[107]   **26-51** As soon as a bid is made public, the boards of the offeree company and of the offeror must inform the employee representatives (Rule 2.6(b)). An offeror must draw up and make public an offer document (the minimum contents of which are prescribed)[108] which must be sent to the supervisory authority and, once it is made public, communicated to the employee representatives.[109]

The board of the offeree company must provide the shareholders and the   **26-52** employee representatives with a document setting out its opinion on the bid (the response document or circular), including its views on the effects of implementation of the bid on all of the company's interests and specifically employment.[110] This document is crucially important if the directors of the offeree company are to dissuade the shareholders from accepting the offer. If the board of the offeree company receives in good time an opinion from the employee representatives on the effects of the bid on employment, that opinion must be appended to the board's document. It will be recalled that the European Parliament was instrumental in making sure that the Directive imposed obligations with respect to information for employees: see **26-11**. The board of the offeree company must obtain competent independent advice on any offer and the substance of such advice must be made known to its shareholders (Rule 3.1).[111]

In the case of a takeover bid for a company that has securities carrying voting rights   **26-53** admitted to trading on a regulated market in the UK, criminal sanctions apply where

---

[104] Takeover Code, Rule 6.1.   [105] Takeover Code, Rule 6.2.

[106] See Takeover Directive, above n 8, art 6; Takeover Code, Rule 2.6(b).

[107] Takeover Directive, above n 8, art 6(1)).   [108] Takeover Directive, above n 8, art 6(3).

[109] Takeover Directive, above n 8, art 6(2); the information to the employee representatives need only be conveyed once the bid is public to avoid the risk of insider dealing which might arise if there was wide circulation of unpublished price sensitive information of this nature.

[110] Takeover Directive, above n 8, art 9(5).

[111] Rule 3.3. is quite detailed as to who is independent for these purposes since advisers may have conflicting interests and reasons of their own for promoting a particular offeror, but the Executive has indicated that it believes that relationships between financial advisers and their clients are, in many cases, now less exclusive than was previously the case and it has therefore concluded that it should be more flexible in its approach to determining the independence of an adviser: Practice Statement No 21, March 2008.

there are failures to comply with the rules governing either the offer document or the response document. In the case of a non-compliant offer document, an offence is committed by the bidder and by any director or officer who knew that the offer document did not comply (or was reckless as to whether it did so) and failed to take reasonable steps to ensure that it did comply with the requirements of the rules (CA 2006, s 953(1)–(3)). In the case of a non-compliant response document, an offence may be committed by the directors or officers of the target company who knew that the response document did not comply (or was reckless as to whether it did so) and failed to take reasonable steps to ensure that it did comply with the requirements of the rules (s 953(4)).

26-54   The criminal sanction is deliberately limited to these two documents and applies only with respect to takeover bids as defined in CA 2006, s 953(1), i.e. takeovers within the Directive. The imposition of criminal sanctions in these circumstances was the subject of much debate in Parliament, but the Government's view was that these provisions were necessary in order to implement art 17 of the Takeover Directive which requires Member States to put in place sanctions which are effective, proportionate and dissuasive.[112] In the Government's view, the sanctions available to the Panel (discussed at **26-35** and the Panel does not propose to use its rule-making powers to extend its sanctions beyond those already available to it)[113] are inadequate for this purpose. In particular, there was a concern that there might be serious or deliberate misstatements in the documentation that might only come to light some time after the bid had been completed and in respect of which sanctions of the Panel would be inadequate.[114] Imposing a criminal liability is an appropriate way of closing that loophole, the Government said, especially given that the documentation is not only of direct concern to shareholders, but also to employees and others affected by the bid. In the Government's view, this is a carefully targeted offence aimed specifically at those who fail to comply with the bid documentation rules and it provides them with an incentive to take the task of drawing up these documents seriously.[115]

26-55   The Takeover Code imposes extensive disclosure requirements beyond that required by the Directive and the offeror documents must give comprehensive details of the financial position of the offeror and the manner in which it intends to fund the bid (Rule 24) and, in the case of offeree documents, there must be disclosure of particulars of all service contracts of any director or proposed director of the offeree company with the company or any of its subsidiaries (Rule 25).

The timetable

26-56   General Principle 2 provides that the shareholders of an offeree company must have sufficient time and information to enable them to reach a properly informed decision on the bid. There are two guiding principles as far as the timetable of an offer

---

[112] See 680 HL Debs, GC 304–5, 28 March 2006.   [113] See 680 HL Debs, GC 304, 28 March 2006.
[114] See 680 HL Debs, GC 305, 28 March 2006.   [115] See 680 HL Debs, GC 305, 28 March 2006.

is concerned: first that the duration of a bid should be limited; secondly, that the shareholders should have time to consider the bid. The object is to avoid the process being so hurried that there is inadequate time for advice and information to be obtained and considered. At the same time, the process must not be so drawn out that uncertainty is created in the market and the management of the offeree company is distracted from the management of the business (sometimes described as the siege principle—the offeree company must not remain under siege for an indefinite period). Once an offer is referred to the Competition Commission or action is taken by the competition authorities of the European Commission, the offer period ends and a new offer period only begins when the competition process has ended.[116] The Takeover Directive requires that a bid must be open for acceptances for not less than two weeks and not more than 10 weeks[117] but the timetable may be extended by a Member State, subject to the 'siege principle', as expressed in General Principle 6.[118]

26-57 The timetable under the Takeover Code runs from the posting of the offer document known as Day 1, which normally must be within 28 days of the announcement of a firm intention to make an offer.[119] The board of the offeree company must give advice (the response or defence document or circular) to their shareholders by the end of Day 14, i.e. within 14 days of the publication of the offer document.[120] To ensure shareholders in the offeree company have time to consider the offer and are not rushed into acceptance, an offer must remain open for at least 21 days, so Day 21 is the first possible closing date for the offer.[121]

26-58 After Day 39 there must be no further announcements by the board of the offeree company of any material new information (including trading results, profit or dividend forecasts, assets valuations or proposals for dividend payments or for any material acquisitions or disposals) without the consent of the Panel[122] and Day 46 is the last date for revision of the offer by the offeror.[123] Day 60 is the last possible closing date and no offer may be left open for more than 60 days without the consent of the Panel which may be granted, for example, if a competing offer is announced.[124]

26-59 At the end of Day 60, the offeror announces whether it has received sufficient acceptances. The offeror must secure acceptances for at least 50% of the voting rights to secure control and, if it is a voluntary bid, it may have stipulated (and usually does stipulate) that it requires 90% acceptances. If the offeror has secured the requisite level of acceptances, the offer goes unconditional as to acceptances and must be left open

---

[116] Takeover Code, Rule 12.2.   [117] Takeover Directive, above n 8, art 7.
[118] See Takeover Directive, above n 8, art 7(1).   [119] Takeover Code, Rule 30.1.
[120] Takeover Code, Rule 30.2.   [121] Takeover Code, Rule 31.1.   [122] Takeover Code, Rule 31.9.
[123] Takeover Code, Rule 32.1. Problems can arise where there are still competing bids at this stage, see Rule 32.5 which provides that if a competitive situation continues to exist in the later stages of the offer period, the Panel will normally require revised offers to be published in accordance with an auction procedure, the terms of which will be determined by the Panel.
[124] Takeover Code, Rule 31.6. An acceptor is entitled to withdraw his acceptance from the date which is 21 days after the first closing date of the initial offer (normally 42 days from the offer being made), if the offer has not by such date become or been declared unconditional as to acceptances, to the date when the offer is declared unconditional as to acceptances: Takeover Code, Rule 34.

for a further 14 days.[125] Except with the consent of the Panel, the consideration for the offer must be posted within 14 days of the offer becoming unconditional.[126]

26-60   Where an offer has not become unconditional by Day 60 and has therefore lapsed, the offeror may not make another offer for the offeree company during the next 12 months nor acquire any shares which would oblige it to make a mandatory offer, except with the consent of the Panel.[127] This restriction can be of crucial importance to a company which has successfully resisted an unwelcome bid as it secures for it a breathing space before the offeror can return. The Panel will normally grant a dispensation from this restriction where, for example, the new offer is recommended by the board of the offeree company or the previous offer lapsed on a reference to the Competition Commission or action by the European Commission.[128]

Board neutrality

26-61   As noted at **26-11**, one of the controversial issues before the European Parliament was the extent to which board neutrality should be imposed. In a bid situation there is a clear conflict of interest between the board and the shareholders of the offeree company. The shareholders have an economic interest in receiving any available offers for their shares but, given they commonly lose their positions following a successful takeover, the directors have an interest in warding off takeovers or in favouring takeovers from bidders who may have links to the directors or who make promises to them with respect to their positions. The directors may hinder other bidders who might be willing to offer a higher price for the shares. It is important therefore to limit the scope for directors to erect defences against takeovers save where they have the consent of the shareholders to do so.[129]

26-62   Article 9(2) of the Takeover Directive provides that from the time when the board of the offeree company receives information that a bid is to be made until the result of the bid is made public or the bid lapses, the board of the offeree company must obtain the prior authorisation of the general meeting of shareholders before taking any action (other than seeking alternative bids) which may result in the frustration of the bid. In particular, the specific authorisation of the shareholders is required before the board issues any shares which may result in a lasting impediment to the offeror in acquiring control over the offeree company. This article is designed to ensure that if a company is to be insulated from takeover bids, it is as a consequence of decisions taken by the shareholders and not by the directors. Further, as regards decisions taken before the board receives information that a bid is to be made, but not fully implemented, shareholder approval is also required where the matter in question does not form part of the normal course of the company's business and its implementation may result in the frustration of the bid.[130] To facilitate the seeking of shareholder approval, a Member

---

[125] Takeover Code, Rule 31.4.   [126] Takeover Code, Rule 31.8.
[127] Takeover Code, Rule 35(1)(a).   [128] Takeover Code, Notes on rules 35.1, 35.2.
[129] See generally Clarke, 'Articles 9 and 11 of the Takeover Directive and the Market for Corporate Control' [2006] JBL 355.
[130] See Takeover Directive, above n 8, art 9(3).

State may adopt provisions for the calling of meetings on short notice, but no shorter than two weeks.[131] The crucial importance of the board's role is underlined by General Principle 3 which provides that the board of an offeree company must act in the interests of the company as a whole and must not deny the holders of securities the opportunity to decide on the merits of the bid.

Unfortunately, as noted at **26-8**, art 9(2) is one of the optional articles under art 12 **26-63** and a number of Member States have chosen to opt out of this provision.[132] The UK has opted into art 9 since it is consistent with the long-established position on frustrating action established by the Code,[133] Rule 21 of which expands on this requirement. Rule 21 provides that during the course of an offer, or even before the date of the offer if the board of the offeree company has reason to believe that a bona fide offer might be imminent, the board must not without the approval of the shareholders in general meeting:

'(a) take any action which may result in any offer or bona fide possible offer being frustrated or in shareholders being denied the opportunity to decide on its merits; or

(b)

    (i)   issue any authorised but unissued shares or transfer or sell, or agree to transfer or sell, any shares out of treasury;[134]

    (ii) issue or grant options in respect of any unissued shares;

    (iii) create or issue, or permit the creation or issue of, any securities carrying rights of conversion into or subscription for shares;

    (iv) sell, dispose of or acquire, or agree to sell, dispose of or acquire, assets of a material amount;[135] or

    (v) enter into contracts otherwise than in the ordinary course of business.'[136]

These restrictions on the actions which may be taken by the board without shareholder **26-64** approval are imposed in order to prevent the board of an offeree company making the

---

[131] See Takeover Directive, above n 8, art 9(4).

[132] See generally Clarke, 'Articles 9 and 11 of the Takeover Directive and the Market for Corporate Control' [2006] JBL 355; also Gatti, 'Optionality Arrangements and Reciprocity in the European Takeover Directive' (2005) 6 EBOR 553.

[133] The European Commission's initial review of the implementation of the Takeover Directive found that 18 Member States had imposed or were expected to impose the board neutrality rule, but that for only one of these States was this a new requirement. Further, five of these Member States had introduced the reciprocity requirement so implementation had increased the management's powers to take frustrating action: see SEC (2007) 268, 21.02.2007, para 2.1.3(b).

[134] Directors are subject to various constraints in any event on their powers to allot shares including the proper purpose duty imposed by CA 2006, s 171(b): see **8-44** and see *Howard Smith Ltd v Ampol Petroleum Ltd* [1974] 1 All ER 1126, PC. Statutory constraints on allotments are discussed at **19-30**.

[135] For these purposes, the Panel normally considers a material amount to be 10% or more of the assets, but the amount could be less if the asset is of particular significance to the company: see Takeover Code, Notes on Rule 21.1.

[136] Amendments to directors' service contracts are not regarded as contracts in the ordinary course of business where the new or amended contracts constitute an abnormal increase in the emoluments or a significant improvement in the terms of service: Takeover Code, Note on Rule 21.1, para 6.

company unattractive to the offeror by disposing of the assets which the offeror most wishes to acquire or by increasing significantly the costs involved in dispensing with the incumbent management should the bid be successful. Directors are not prevented from seeking alternative bidders, so-called 'white knights', nor do these constraints prevent companies putting defensive measures in place before any bid is under contemplation. Increasingly companies have an in-built defence mechanism in the form of an unfunded pension deficit which makes a takeover prohibitively expensive for a bidder who may be required to make good that deficiency.

26-65   In the US, more exotic variations of these frustrating devices are described as 'poison pills'[137] and the courts here had a rare opportunity to consider the validity of so-called 'poison pill' arrangements in *Criterion Properties plc v Stratford UK Properties LLC*.[138] In this case, a managing director had his company enter into an agreement with a substantial shareholder (Oaktree) which amounted to a 'poison pill', i.e. a device designed to ensure that any would-be bidder for the company would be deterred from proceeding.[139] The effect of the agreement was to require the company to buy out Oaktree at a very high price in the event of any change of control of the company or certain changes in board personnel, including the removal from the board of the managing director who drew up and executed the agreement on behalf of the company. The managing director was sacked subsequently and the issue arose as to whether the agreement could be enforced against the company. In the Court of Appeal, Carnwath LJ commented briefly on the extent to which a 'poison pill' arrangement is permissible in English law. He agreed with counsel that it may be legitimate, depending on the circumstances, for the board to exercise its power to issue shares in order to deter a takeover which would cause serious economic harm to the company.[140] He also noted, however, that the gratuitous disposition of the company's assets for this purpose had never been upheld by any reported authority, whether in the US or the Commonwealth. Without having to determine the extent to which 'poison pills' limited to seeing off a particular predator might be permissible in English Law, the agreement in this case, he thought, went far beyond anything which could be justified for the purpose of deterring an unwelcome predator and could not be a reasonable exercise of the board's powers in the interests of the company.

26-66   On appeal to the House of Lords, their Lordships decided that the lower courts had wrongly focused on the role and knowledge of Oaktree and the case was remitted for trial on the issue identified by their Lordships as crucial, namely whether the directors who signed the agreement had authority, actual or apparent, to do so. It was not necessary therefore for their Lordships to consider the validity of a poison pill, but it is clear from Lord Scott's judgment that he was very doubtful that it could be permissible.

---

[137] See Herzel & Shepro, *Bidders and Targets, Mergers and Acquisitions in the US* (1990), Ch 8.

[138] [2006] 1 BCLC 729, HL overruling [2003] 2 BCLC 129, CA. See Clarke, 'Regulating Poison Pill Devices' (2004) JCLS 51.

[139] As the agreement was entered into at a time when there was neither an offer nor a potential offer for the company, the provisions of the Takeover Code requiring shareholder approval did not come into play.

[140] See [2003] 2 BCLC 129 at 139.

First, he noted that whether it is open to a board of directors of a public company to authorise the signing on the company's behalf of a 'poison pill' agreement intended to deter outsiders from making offers to shareholders to purchase their shares is an issue of considerable public importance. Secondly, when considering whether the directors might have had apparent authority to enter into the agreement, he asked:

> 'Is it open to a board to authorise the signing of a "poison pill" agreement where, as here, the deterrence consists of a contingent divesting of company assets? The issue of the apparent authority of the [directors] must also take into account the features of the [agreement] that went beyond simply including provisions to deter an unwanted predator but would have deterred also the most desirable of predators, would have entrenched the chairman's and the managing director's continuance in their then current offices, and would have put them in a position in which their voluntary decision to relinquish office would potentially attract a heavy financial penalty for their company. Could it be said that they, or any of them, had apparent authority to conclude such an agreement?'[141]

Clearly, Lord Scott was very doubtful that such agreements, or at least such far reaching agreements could be valid. That view is impliedly accepted by all concerned in takeovers and it is very unusual for companies here to adopt poison pill agreements. They would in any event be contrary to the spirit of General Principle 3 that the board must not deny the shareholders the opportunity to decide on the merits of the bid.

26-67 The Code draws attention to the responsibility of the board as a whole to monitor the conduct of a bid.[142] Directors of an offeror and the offeree company must always, in advising their shareholders, act only in their capacity as directors and not have regard to their personal or family shareholdings or to their personal relationships with the companies. It is the shareholders' interests taken as a whole, together with those of employees and creditors, which should be considered when the directors are giving advice to shareholders.

26-68 In a number of cases concerning takeover bids, the courts have had to consider the relationship between the directors and their shareholders in this context. Where a takeover bid has been made, the directors must give sufficient information to the shareholders and refrain from misleading them.[143] In the case of competing bids, the directors must do nothing to prevent the shareholders from choosing to take the best price,[144] but the courts do not accept that the board must inevitably be under a positive duty to recommend and take all steps within its power to facilitate whichever is the highest offer.[145]

26-69 A particular issue in the takeover context is whether directors can agree with an offeror to recommend that particular bid and not to solicit other bids and not to co-operate with any other offeror that might emerge. While there was some initial uncertainty

---

[141] [2006] 1 BCLC 729 at 740, HL; see also **8-59**.   [142] See Takeover Code, Appendix 3.

[143] *Re a Company* [1986] BCLC 382; *Gething v Kilner* [1972] 1 All ER 1166; *Dawson International plc v Coats Paton plc* [1989] BCLC 233.

[144] *Heron International Ltd v Lord Grade* [1983] BCLC 244.   [145] *Re a Company* [1986] BCLC 382.

as to the position, its resolution appears from the decision of the Court of Appeal in *Fulham Football Club Ltd v Cabra Estates plc*[146] (a non-takeover case). The court distinguished between directors fettering their discretion, which is prohibited,[147] and directors exercising their discretion in a way which restricts their future conduct, which is permissible, assuming that the exercise of that discretion can be justified as being in the interests of the company.[148] It is therefore possible to enter into a lock-out agreement, but the directors must be able to justify that decision as being (in the language of CA 2006, s 172) to promote the success of the company. This is unlikely given that the interests of the company for these purposes are the interests of the current shareholders in the company which lie in the company being on the market for any bidder. It is not their interests as sellers of their shares but their interests as members in an open market for corporate control which, of course, impacts on the value of their shares as any competing offer will necessarily be for a higher price. A lock-out agreement is therefore possible in theory, but any attempt to enforce it is likely to result in considerable debate as to whether the directors acted to promote the success of the company in entering into it and they will only do so if they leave open the possibility of recommending an alternative offer. Bidders have turned therefore to break or inducement fees as a method of ensuring the support of the offeree board or at least the payment of financial compensation for the withdrawal of that support.

26-70   A break or inducement fee is a contractual agreement whereby the offeree company agrees to pay the offeror a fee in the event of certain circumstances arising which result in the failure of the offeror's bid, such as the endorsement by the offeree board of a competing bid.[149] The board of the offeree company can justify such agreements as being in the interests of the company on a number of grounds: (1) break fee arrangements are typically mutual arrangements—the offeror also typically agrees to pay the offeree a fee in the event that the offeror decides not to proceed; (2) the break fee is a means of ensuring that the offeror (who may in fact be the only offeror available) will proceed to make an offer to the shareholders; and (3) the amount payable is reasonable.[150] As to the amount payable, the Takeover Code restricts such inducements to not more than 1% of the value of the offeree company calculated by

---

[146] [1994] 1 BCLC 363, CA; noted Griffiths (1993) JBL 576.

[147] *Motherwell v Schoof* (1949) 4 DLR 812 (Alta SC); *Selangor United Rubber Estates Ltd v Cradock (a bankrupt) (No 3)* [1968] 2 All ER 1073.

[148] See discussion of this case at **10-50**.

[149] For example, in the case of the P&O Princess / Royal Caribbean / Carnival takeover (which ultimately resulted in Carnival taking over P & O Princess), P & O Princess paid £62.5m as a break fee to Royal Caribbean for breaking an agreement to recommend a joint venture with Royal Caribbean. The Carnival offer proved economically more valuable for the shareholders and therefore the board of P & O Princess withdrew their support for the Royal Caribbean venture: see 'Carnival set to capture P & O Princess' *Financial Times*, 26 October 2002.

[150] The range of arrangement covered by Takeover Code Rule 21 is wide including arrangements for cash payments and any other favourable arrangements with an offeror or potential offeror which have a similar or comparable financial or economic effect, even if such arrangements do not actually involve any cash payment, see notes to rule 21. Care must be taken to ensure that the arrangement does not fall foul of the provisions governing financial assistance, now CA 2006, s 678: see Charnley & Breslin, 'Break Fees: Financial Assistance and Directors' Duties' (2000) 21 Co Law 269; financial assistance is discussed at **20-127**.

reference to the offer price (Rule 21.2). The courts would be guided by that formula in determining whether a particular arrangement was one which a board might enter into in the interests of the company. A break fee arrangement necessarily diminishes the assets secured by the successful offeror (in the event that a significant sum has to be paid to a failed bidder) and in effect transfers the risk of a failed bid from the (ultimately unsuccessful) offeror to the offeree company, hence the importance of limiting the amount of the company's assets which may be committed in this way; hence too the requirement that there be full disclosure of any such arrangements (Rule 21.2). In addition, the board of the offeree company and its financial adviser must confirm to the Panel in writing that they believe the fee to be in the best interests of the shareholders.

As to 'public interest' defensive measures, such as the use by governments of golden **26-71** shares to retain control over companies (see **14-25**, n 31) that matter has been left by the European Commission to the European Court of Justice which has essentially concluded that such measures are contrary to the free movement of capital, but may in some circumstances be permissible in the protection of the public interest, provided the measures adopted are proportionate, objective and non-discriminatory.[151]

Breakthrough provisions

It will be recalled that some members of the European Parliament were concerned that **26-72** imposing a requirement of board neutrality (Takeover Directive, art 9(2): see **26-62**) would mean that companies in their Member States would be exposed to hostile take-overs while companies in other Member States with protective mechanisms (such as restrictions on the transfer of shares and on the exercise of voting rights) which are equally protective of incumbent management are not so exposed: see **26-11**.

The High Level Group of Company Law Experts, see **26-12** considered that the solu- **26-73** tion to this lack of a level playing field lay in the introduction of break-through pro-visions, i.e. provisions which break through structural defensive mechanisms and prevent them from operating to defeat an offeror.[152] A break-through provision is con-tained in art 11 of the Takeover Directive, the effect of which is that:

- any restrictions on the transfer of securities, whether in the articles of association or in a shareholders' agreement entered into on or after 21 April 2004—the date of adoption of the Takeover Directive—do not apply vis-à-vis the offeror during the period of the bid (so the offeror is able to acquire those securities);
- any restrictions on voting rights, whether in the articles of association or in a shareholders' agreement entered into on or after 21 April 2004—the date of adop-tion of the Directive—do not have effect at any general meeting called to decide

---

[151] See *Commission v Portugal* (Case C-367/98), *Commission v France* (Case C-483/99), *Commission v Belgium* (Case C-503/99) [2003] QB 233; and see Commission Press release, 'Free Movement of Capital: Commission calls on Germany to apply Court ruling on its Volkswagen Law' IP/08/873, 5 June 2008; also *Commission v Federal Republic of Germany* (Case C-112/05) OJ C 315, 22.12.2007, p 5.

[152] See *Report of the High Level Group of Company Law Experts on Issues Related to Takeover Bids* (10 January 2002, Brussels), Ch 1.

whether to authorise defensive measures after a bid has been announced (so all shareholders get to vote on these matters);

- multiple vote securities carry only one vote each at any general meeting of shareholders which decides on any defensive measures (so ensuring that existing controllers cannot carry the vote);

- once the offeror holds 75% of the voting shares,[153] no restrictions on the transfer of securities or on voting rights, nor any extraordinary rights of shareholders concerning the appointment or removal of board members apply (so ensuring that the offeror now holding 75% is not affected by these limitations). Multiple vote securities carry only one vote each at the first general meeting following closure of the bid (so remaining multiple vote holders cannot use the meeting to outvote the offeror holding 75% at the meeting). The effect of the break-through provision is that the offeror is able to exercise the voting rights attached to the 75% holding which he has secured to alter the composition of the board and the company's constitution, regardless of restrictions on these matters in the articles or a shareholders' agreement. In this way, the offeror breaks through the defensive structures and secures control.

26-74   This break-through provision in art 11 was always controversial[154] with the result that by the time the Takeover Directive was approved, it had been reduced to a voluntary element which Member States can opt out of. Article 12 provides that where a Member State opts out of art 11, it must still give companies in that Member State the option of making use of such breakthrough provisions. A further refinement is that companies given that option may also be given an option (having opted into art 11) to opt out again (in other words, they can rely on defensive measures otherwise restricted by art 11) if they are the subject of a bid by an offeror company which has not also opted in to art 11 (the so-called reciprocity rule: see art 12(3)). An initial report of the European Commission on the Implementation of the Takeover Directive on Takeover Bids found that, as at January 2007, only three Member States (Estonia, Latvia and Lithuania) had opted into art 11 and imposed on their companies a requirement to adhere to the break-through provision.[155] The rest of the Member States have opted out of art 11 and simply acted in accordance with art 12, i.e. they have made provision to allow their companies to opt into art 11 if they wish, as is the case in the UK. Here companies may opt in (and subsequently opt out) of art 11, the break-through provision, by way of a special resolution (CA 2006, ss 966–972), but the UK did not take up the reciprocity option in art 12(3), so a company which opts in is not able to opt out when

---

[153] The bidder must reach 75% of the nominal value of the company's voting shares: see 680 HL Debs, GC318, 28 March 2006.

[154] Though art 11 is much less radical and extensive than the breakthrough provision proposed by the High Level Group, see *Report of the High Level Group of Company Law Experts on Issues Related to Takeover Bids* (10 January 2002, Brussels), Ch 1, para 4.2, see **26-12**.

[155] See *Report on the Implementation of the Directive on Takeover Bids*, SEC (2007) 268, 21.02.2007, para 2.1.4.

faced by an offeror who has not opted into art 11. It is not expected that UK companies will opt into art 11.[156]

The opt-in, opt-out provisions apply only to companies with voting shares admitted to trading on a regulated market and only to such companies which do not have shares conferring special rights on a Minister, i.e. 'golden shares' (see **26-71**) (CA 2006, s 966(4)). A company may pass a special resolution to opt into the break-through provisions in ss 966–973 provided the articles meet the following conditions. The company's articles of association must not contain any of the restrictions on voting rights, share transfers etc mentioned in art 11 (and identified at **26-73**) or, if they do, the provisions must not apply on a bid being made, and the articles must not otherwise contain provisions which are incompatible with art 11. The special resolution must specify the date from which it is to have effect (CA 2006, s 967(1)).[157] As noted above, the effect of opting into the provision would be that none of these restrictions would apply to a bidder. In addition, the bidder has the right to require the directors of the company to call a general meeting of the company once he has acquired 75% in value of all the voting shares (s 969). The calling of the meeting is crucial to enable him to alter the constitution to remove the restrictions on voting rights or on the transfer of shares and to appoint a new board. If the company opts into the provision and any person suffers loss as a result of any act or omission that would (but for these provisions) be a breach of an agreement between the parties (for example, as to restrictions on transfers or voting) that person is entitled to compensation of such amount as the court considers just and equitable from any person[158] who would (but for these provisions) be liable for committing or inducing the breach (s 968(6)).[159] Having opted into the break-through provision, a company can opt out again by way of a special resolution (s 966(5)), but it cannot opt out for a period of one year (s 967(6)).[160]   **26-75**

Transparency requirements

As part of the effort to restrict the use of defensive measures by boards and companies, or at least to alert the market to the existence of defensive measures, art 10 of the Takeover Directive imposes extensive disclosure requirements on companies   **26-76**

---

[156] The only conceivable advantage (and it is a remote possibility) is that a company would opt in so that if it is a bidder for a company which has also opted in, that offeree company cannot then put up takeover barriers since the reciprocity requirement is met in this scenario, but it is very unlikely.

[157] A company which opts in (or opts out) must notify the Takeover Panel (and possibly other supervisory authorities) within 15 days of passing the resolution: CA 2006, s 970(1); criminal penalties attach to non-compliance: s 970(3).

[158] The *Explanatory Notes to the Companies Act 2006* suggest that the bidder in the first instance should be the person to pay compensation, but that is not indicated in the section, see para 1240.

[159] All of which is quite problematic, but anticipating that UK companies would not be interesting in opting in, the Government did not think it necessary to make further provision in this regard.

[160] It is not entirely clear why this time-limit was imposed; the Government said it was to provide certainty and also to ensure that companies thinking of opting in would focus on the consequence of so doing: see 680 HL Debs, GC317, 28 March 2006.

which must be met in the directors' report which must also contain any necessary explanatory material with regard to the information disclosed.[161] While much of the required disclosure is available in any event in a company's public documents, this requirement means that the information must be set out in one place. The hope is that these disclosures in the annual report will enable the market to identify clearly those companies with closed structures and will price their shares accordingly. In turn, such market pressures should result in companies voluntarily giving up these restrictive structures.[162]

26-77   The disclosure focuses in particular on disclosure of the capital structures and mechanisms that could hinder an offeror in securing control of the company, such as restrictions on share transfer and on voting rights and the existence of cross-holdings. It also requires identification of the holders of any shares with special control rights and the disclosure of any agreements between shareholders that can affect voting or transfer rights that are known to the company (though the company is frequently unaware of these agreements). Disclosure is also required of any agreements between the company and its directors or employees providing for compensation for loss of office or employment (whether through resignation, purported redundancy or otherwise) that occurs because of a takeover bid.[163] The company must disclose any rules that the company has about appointment and replacement of directors, or amendment of the company's articles of association and the powers of the company's directors, including in particular any powers in relation to the issuing or buying back by the company of its shares.[164] The company must disclose any significant agreements to which the company is a party that take effect, alter or terminate upon a change of control of the company following a takeover bid, and the effects of any such agreements (there is an exemption if disclosure of the agreement would be seriously prejudicial to the company).[165] In other words, disclosure must be made of poison pill-type agreements (discussed at **26-65**) so that a potential offeror can see whether there are arrangements in place which would make it prohibitively expensive or difficult to take over the company.

26-78   These disclosure requirements are designed to bring greater transparency to the market and accordingly apply to all companies registered in the UK which have voting shares admitted to trading on a regulated market at the end of the relevant financial year.[166] These disclosure requirements apply annually regardless of whether or not the company is subject to a takeover bid.

---

[161] CA 2006, s 416(4); SI 2008/410, reg 10, Sch 7, Part 6, paras 13, 14.

[162] See speech by European Commissioner Bolkestein to the Committee on Legal Affairs and the Internal Market, European Parliament, 2.10.2002.

[163] See SI 2008/410, reg 10, Sch 7, Part 6, para 13(2)(k).

[164] See SI 2008/410, reg 10, Sch 7, Part 6, para 13(2)(h), (2)(i).

[165] See Takeover Directive, above n 8, art 10(1)(j); SI 2008/410, reg 10, Sch 7, Part 6, para 13(2)(k).

[166] See SI 2008/410, reg 10, Sch 7, Part 6, para 13(1).

E Protection of minority shareholders

Mandatory bids

As part of the insistence on equivalent treatment of shareholders, it has always been **26-79** a fundamental principle underlying the Takeover Code that a shareholder should have a right to exit from the company by selling his shares on a change of control of the company.[167] Accordingly, in some circumstances there is a mandatory bid requirement (i.e. a requirement for a general offer for all the remaining shares of the company) governed by Rule 9, although provision is made for some dispensations from this general requirement.[168] If an offeror acquires or enhances a controlling stake in a company, a similar offer must be extended to all shareholders. The price paid for control is thus extended to all shareholders and control is effectively treated as an asset of the company, reflected in the value of each share, rather than as an asset of the controlling shareholder. All the shareholders share in the premium paid by the offeror and can exit from the company on a change of control.

The Takeover Directive also includes a requirement for a mandatory bid for all hold- **26-80** ings, so allowing the minority shareholders to exit the company at an 'equitable price' on a change of control. The threshold at which the mandatory bid is triggered by the acquisition of voting rights by a person and those acting in concert with him is a matter for the Member State in which the offeree company has its registered office.[169] The 'equitable price' which must be paid is defined by the Takeover Directive (art 5(4)): it must be the highest price paid for the same securities by the offeror, or by persons acting in concert with him, over a period of between six and 12 months (as the Member State decides) prior to the bid, with the possibility of an adjustment to that price by the supervisory authority in exceptional circumstances.[170] As noted, it is for Member States to set the level at which a mandatory bid is required and while a number of Member States have set it at 30%, a number have set substantially higher figures.[171]

---

[167] See generally Jennings, 'Mandatory Bids Revisited' (2005) JCLS 37.

[168] See Takeover Code, Notes on Dispensations from Rule 9. For example, a mandatory bid is not required where there is an independent vote at a shareholders' meeting approving an issue of new shares as consideration for an acquisition or cash subscription which would otherwise trigger a mandatory bid, or where a 30% holding is acquired in the context of a rescue operation, or on the enforcement by a creditor of security for a loan, or through inadvertent mistake.

[169] See Takeover Directive, above n 8, art 5(1), (3). See Wymeersch, 'The Mandatory Bid: A Critical View' in Hopt & Wymeersch (eds), *European Takeovers—Law and Practice* (1992).

[170] Consideration payable may be securities (provided they are admitted to trading on a regulated market which ensures they are liquid securities) or a Member State may require cash, at least as an alternative and, in some circumstances, a cash alternative must be provided: see Takeover Directive, above n 8, art 5(5).

[171] See *Report on the Implementation of the Directive on Takeover Bids*, SEC (2007) 268, 21.02.2007, Annex 2 which lists the Member State thresholds and shows about 12 Member States setting 30–33% as the trigger requirements with some States on 40%, some on 50% and Poland on 66%.

26-81   A mandatory bid is required by Takeover Code Rule 9:[172]

(1) where any person acquires an interest in shares which (taken together with shares in which persons acting in concert with him are interested) carry 30% or more of the voting rights of a company; or

(2) any person, together with persons acting in concert with him, is interested in shares which carry not less than 30% of the voting rights of a company but not more than 50% of such voting rights and such person, or any person acting in concert with him, acquires an interest in any other shares which increases the percentage of shares carrying voting rights in which he is interested.[173]

26-82   Mandatory offers must be for cash or with a cash alternative at not less than the highest price paid by the offeror or persons acting in concert with it for shares of that class in the preceding 12 months.[174] Mandatory bids may not include any conditions other than a requirement for acceptances in respect of shares carrying more than 50% of the voting rights of the company and a provision that the bid will lapse automatically on reference to the competition authorities.[175] These restrictions as to the conditions which may be attached to a mandatory bid are designed to prevent the offeror defeating the purpose of Rule 9 by attaching conditions to the offer which would make acceptance unattractive to the shareholders. These limitations also make a mandatory bid unattractive to the bidder as he cannot insist on 90% acceptances, which is important if statutory powers to acquire minority holdings (discussed below) are to be used. In fact, few mandatory bids are made, as offerors take care to ensure that they do not find themselves in a position where a mandatory bid is required. The vast majority of bids are voluntary bids where the offeror has greater flexibility as to the conditions which may be attached.[176] For example, the offeror may make the bid conditional on the approval of 90% of the offeree's shareholders; or the approval of its own shareholders; or subject to regulatory consents; or subject to material changes in circumstances.

Squeeze-out and sell-out rights

26-83   Where a company makes an offer for the shares in another company, it may be content simply to acquire sufficient shares to give it control of the offeree company. But, in

---

[172] Takeover Code, Rule 9.1(a). Partial bids, i.e. bids for shares carrying over 30% but less than 100% of the voting rights of a company, are discouraged and cannot be made without the Panel's consent: see Rule 36.

[173] If a person already owns over 50%, he may continue to acquire shares without making a general offer since strengthening a controlling stake which is already over 50% is not regarded as affecting the minority shareholder to the same extent.

[174] Takeover Code, Rule 9.5.   [175] Takeover Code, Rule 9.3, 9.4.

[176] The Annual Reports of the Takeover Panel consistently show only a very small number (typically below a dozen in any year) of mandatory bids. For example, in 2007–08, 130 formal offer documents were sent to shareholders of which only nine involved mandatory bids; in 2006–07, 143 offer documents were sent of which only five involved mandatory bids; in 2005–06, 147 offer documents were sent out of which only 11 involved mandatory bids.

many circumstances, the offeror will want to acquire 100% of the shares in the offeree company. Since 1929, there has been a specific statutory procedure, now contained in CA 2006, ss 974–991, whereby an offeror, whose offer has been accepted by holders of 90% or more of the shares to which the offer relates, can compulsorily acquire the remaining shares (squeeze-out), unless the court upholds an objection by a dissenting shareholder and, vice versa, a minority shareholder can demand to be bought out (sell-out). The purpose of these provisions is to facilitate the acquisition by an offeror of 100% of the shares in a target company, so enabling the offeror to operate the subsidiary as a wholly-owned subsidiary without regard to minority shareholders. Equally, the provisions facilitate the exit of minority shareholders from a target company so enabling such shareholders to avoid the problems arising from being locked into a company under new control. The Takeover Directive in arts 15 and 16 makes provision for squeeze-out and sell-out rights which allow:

- an offeror to require the remaining shareholders to sell their holdings to him at a fair price[177] when he has secured a set level of acceptances (to be determined by each Member State[178] and to be on the acquisition of between 90% and 95% of the capital);[179] and

- a minority shareholder to require an offeror to acquire his shares at a fair price when the offeror has secured 90–95% of the capital, again the threshold to be determined by each Member State.[180]

The statutory procedures in the CA 2006 have been amended to reflect the require-   **26-84**
ments of the Takeover Directive and recommendations made by the Company Law Review, which focused on technical changes to make the provisions operate more effectively.[181]

---

[177] A Member State must ensure a fair price and the same form of consideration as offered in the bid: Takeover Directive, art 15(5).

[178] See *Report on the Implementation of the Directive on Takeover Bids*, SEC (2007) 268, 21.02.2007, Annex 4 which shows the thresholds chosen by the Member States, the majority of whom have opted for a 90% threshold.

[179] The High Level Group favoured compulsory powers to acquire minority shareholders on a variety of grounds noting that minority shareholders can impose disproportionately high costs on bidders, for example, by preventing full integration of the bidder and target companies, by 'free-riding' on the success of the new owners and by demanding extortionate prices for their shares, see *Report of the High Level Group of Company Law Experts on Issues Related to Takeover Bids*, 10 January 2002, Brussels, para 3.1, see **26-12**.

[180] The High Level Group favoured sell-out powers for minority shareholders on a variety of grounds noting that after a takeover bid, the majority shareholder may be tempted to abuse his dominant position, also post-takeover, minority shareholders cannot obtain appropriate compensation by simply selling their shares in the market; the sell-out right is an appropriate mechanism to counter the pressure on shareholders to tender in the takeover bid; and the sell-out right is a fair counterpart for the squeeze-out right conferred on the majority shareholders: see *Report of the High Level Group of Company Law Experts on Issues Related to Takeover Bids* (10 January 2002, Brussels), para 3.2 see **26-12**.

[181] See *Explanatory Notes to the Companies Act 2006*, para 1248. Also Company Law Review, *Final Report* (2001), Ch 13; *Completing the Structure* (2000), Ch 11.

F Compulsory acquisition of minority shareholdings

Application of compulsory acquisition powers

26-85 The statutory scheme for compulsory acquisition applies where an offeror has made a takeover offer to acquire all the shares,[182] or where there is more than one class of shares, all of the shares of one or more classes of shares, in a company (other than those already held at the date of the offer by the offeror or its associates);[183] and the offer must be on the same terms for all the shares of the same class.[184] Two important time-limits are imposed:

(1) the offeror must, by virtue of acceptances of the offer, have acquired or unconditionally contracted to acquire not less than 90% in value of the shares to which the offer relates (and for this purpose the offeror need only bring into the calculation shares which are actually in issue (i.e. allotted) at the relevant time),[185] and, where the shares are voting shares, not less than 90% of the voting rights carried by those shares (CA 2006, s 979(2));[186]

(2) once the offeror has secured such acceptances, he has three months from the date when he reached the 90% threshold to notify dissentient shareholders that he wishes to exercise his statutory powers to acquire their shares;[187] or in the case of a takeover which is not subject to the Takeover Directive, within a period of six months of the date of the offer if this is earlier than the period ending three months after the end of the offer (see s 980(2), (3)).

26-86 Assuming no application is made to the court by dissenting shareholders within six weeks of receiving the notice of acquisition (see CA 2006, s 986, and discussion

---

[182] The bidder must make an offer and not merely an invitation to treat: see *Re Chez Nico (Restaurants) Ltd* [1992] BCLC 192. An offer can be for all the shares in a company although it is not communicated to, or is impossible or difficult to accept by some shareholders by reasons of the laws of another jurisdiction, provided the conditions set out in CA 2006, s 978 are met; and see *Winpar Holdings Ltd v Joseph Holt Group Plc* [2001] 2 BCLC 604.

[183] CA 2006, ss 975, 977. In ascertaining the offeror's position at the start of the bid, shares which he has conditionally or unconditionally contracted to acquire are treated as shares already held by the offeror: s 975(1), but shares which are the subject of irrevocable undertakings do count towards the 90% calculation: s 975(2).

[184] CA 2006, s 974(1), (3); and see s 976(2) an offer can be treated as being on the same terms even if the offeror agrees to pay more depending on dividend rights or pays different but equivalent consideration to shareholders in countries outside the UK.

[185] CA 2006, s 979(5).

[186] The second element, 90% of the voting rights carried by those shares, was introduced to implement the Takeover Directive, art 15. In practice, this makes little difference in this jurisdiction where most shares carry voting rights so anyone holding 90% of the shares will have 90% of the voting rights, but in other Member States it is common to have varied votes rights so it is possible to acquire 90% of the shares without acquiring 90% of the voting rights.

[187] CA 2006, s 980(2). The notice given must also be sent to the company accompanied by a statutory declaration by the offeror stating that the conditions for giving notice have been satisfied: s 980(4). See *Re Chez Nico (Restaurants) Ltd* [1992] BCLC 192 (lateness in complying with requirement re statutory declaration does not nullify the whole procedure).

below), the offeror is entitled and bound to acquire the shares at the end of six weeks from the date of the notice on the terms of the offer.[188] The offeror sends a copy of the notice to the target company and pays to it the consideration for the shares to which the notice relates (s 988(6)). That consideration is held on trust for payment to the former shareholders who have now been compulsorily acquired by the offeror. At this point, the company removes the names of those former members from the share register and enters the name of the offeror on the register as the holder of those shares.[189]

Obviously it is essential to many offerors to get to the necessary 90% acceptances **26-87** (which is why it is a common condition in a takeover bid) but various matters need to be borne in mind when considering whether an offeror has crossed that threshold and the statute has a variety of provision which help with the calculations. The first problem is where the offeror continues to buy shares in the offeree company in the market during the period of the offer. The difficulty here is that shareholders who sell during the bid are people who might otherwise have accepted the offer, thus making it harder to obtain a 90% acceptance of the actual offer as a result. This problem is resolved by providing that shares acquired during the offer by the offeror or its associates can be treated as acceptances of the offer provided that the consideration does not exceed the offer price or, if it does, that the offer price is correspondingly increased.[190] Another issue is whether raising the offer amounts to a new offer and so acceptances have to be counted of the new offer only. The answer is that a revised offer is not a fresh offer as long as the original offer allowed for revision and for acceptance of previous terms to be treated as acceptance of revised terms.[191] Another problem in the calculation is that some of the shareholders to whom the offer has been made will prove to be untraceable and those people may make all the difference in determining whether the offeror has 90% acceptance of the bid. This issue can be dealt with by the court which, provided certain conditions are met, may make an order authorising compulsory notices to be given.[192]

Objecting shareholders

A shareholder who receives a notice from an offeror of the intention to acquire the **26-88** holder's shares under the procedure outlined above has six weeks in which to apply to the court asking it to disallow the acquisition or to specify terms different from those in the offer.[193] The court may not reduce the consideration payable to below the consideration offered in the bid, but a shareholder may apply to the court for consideration higher than that offered in the bid in exceptional circumstances (CA 2006, s 986(4)). A shareholder who decides to apply to the court must promptly notify the offeror and in turn the offeror is required, at the earliest opportunity, to notify other shareholders who are not a party to the application that proceedings have been initiated. Once an

---

[188] CA 2006, s 981(2).   [189] CA 2006, s 981(7), (8).   [190] CA 2006, s 978(8), (10).
[191] CA 2006, s 974(7); and see *Re Chez Nico (Restaurants) Ltd* [1992] BCLC 192.
[192] CA 2006, s 986(9), (10).   [193] CA 2006, s 986.

application is made, the offeror cannot proceed to enforce the compulsory acquisition notices already given until the application is resolved (s 986(2)).

26-89   The courts are unsympathetic generally when faced with challenges to the procedure by minority shareholders and are much swayed by the fact that 90% of the shareholders think the offer is acceptable. The onus, therefore, is on the dissenters to convince the court that the offer for their shares is unfair.[194] The test is whether the offer is fair to the shareholders as a body without reference to the particular circumstances of the applicant to the court, so it will not be relevant that the dissenting shareholders will be forced to sell at a loss,[195] nor is it sufficient to show that the scheme was open to criticism or capable of improvement.[196]

26-90   Although normally the onus of proof is on the dissenting shareholders to show that the offer is unfair, the position is reversed if those accepting are in effect the offerors. In *Re Bugle Press Ltd*[197] the 90% acceptances in the offeree company came from two persons who owned all the shares in the offeror company and it was held that the onus of proof was on them to show positively that the offer was fair rather than on the dissenter to show the offer was unfair. Since they produced no evidence at all, the court refused to allow the compulsory acquisition of the dissenter. This shift in the onus of proof where the bidder is an insider in the offeree company was endorsed in *Re Chez Nico (Restaurants) Ltd*.[198]

26-91   In *Fiske Nominees Ltd v Dwyka Diamonds Ltd*[199] also the court agreed that, while the onus is on those objecting to the compulsory acquisition notice to establish affirmatively that the offer to acquire their shares is unfair, the court will look at factors such as the relationship between the bidder and those accepting the offer. In any event, the court has a discretion as to the order which may be made. It may order that the shares should not be acquired, or permit acquisition but on different terms, or dismiss the application so that the compulsory notice stands and the shares may be acquired on the terms of the offer.

26-92   In *Fiske*, the transaction was not subject to the Takeover Code, but the court looked to the Code as evidence of good practice. For an offer to be fair, it must be made in sufficient detail to enable the offeree to make an informed decision. By the standards

---

[194] *Re Grierson, Oldham and Adams Ltd* [1967] 1 All ER 192; *Re Sussex Brick Co Ltd* [1960] 1 All ER 772n; *Re Press Caps Ltd* [1949] 1 All ER 1013; *Re Hoare & Co Ltd* (1933) 150 LT 374. It will be helpful to their cause if the dissenters can show substantial non-compliance with the Takeover Code: see *Re Chez Nico (Restaurants) Ltd* [1992] BCLC 192. See Morse [1992] JBL 316.

[195] *Re Grierson, Oldham and Adams Ltd* [1967] 1 All ER 192; where the shares are quoted on the Stock Exchange and the offer price is above the market price, that raises a presumption that the price is fair. See also *Re Press Caps Ltd* [1949] 1 All ER 1013.

[196] *Re Grierson, Oldham and Adams Ltd* [1967] 1 All ER 192; *Re Sussex Brick Co Ltd* [1960] 1 All ER 772n.

[197] [1960] 3 All ER 791, CA.

[198] [1992] BCLC 192; on the facts, the case did not fall within the compulsory acquisition scheme in any event, as the court found that the offeror had not made a 'takeover bid' within the meaning of the statutory provisions.

[199] [2002] 2 BCLC 123.

of the Code, insufficient information had been provided to the shareholders as to the value of the consideration which would be provided for the shares and the offer was not fair. Furthermore, given that there was a connection between the accepting shareholders and the offeror, the fact that 90% had accepted the offer could not be given any real weight, still less decisive weight. The defendants were not entitled to acquire the objectors' shares on the terms of the offer, but the court did order that the defendants purchase the shares on different terms, in this case at a price to be determined by an independent valuer.

Another interesting case on these compulsory acquisition powers is *Re Greythorn Ltd*[200] where a minority shareholder opposed a compulsory acquisition notice which the offeror then purported to withdraw. The shareholder wished to continue her application to the court arguing that, while she did not accept compulsory acquisition on the terms of the offer, she did wish her shares to be acquired on terms to be determined by the court.[201] The court concluded that not only has the court the discretion to set different terms for the purchase of the shares, it also has the power to require the offeror to implement such terms; otherwise the applicant and the court are engaged in a fruitless exercise. The court further considered that an offeror has no right to withdraw a compulsory acquisition notice once served, but having given notice is entitled and bound to acquire the shares.[202] The court noted that, had Parliament intended to confer such a right of withdrawal, it would have done so expressly. **26-93**

Of course, if a compulsory acquisition notice cannot be withdrawn once served, but the shareholder who is the subject of the notice may persuade the court to order that the shares be acquired on terms other than those offered by the offeror, the result may not be to the liking of the offeror. In *Fiske Nominees Ltd v Dwyka Diamonds Ltd*,[203] noted above, instead of being able to insist on a share-for-share offer, the offeror was required to acquire the minority's shares for cash at a price determined by an independent valuer. There are therefore tactical issues to be considered by an offeror before deciding to activate the compulsory acquisition mechanism; equally, a minority shareholder must decide whether to accept the terms on offer or whether to apply to the court in the hope of securing different terms. Of course, a minority shareholder may find that the offeror takes no steps to utilise these compulsory acquisition powers, in which case the minority may choose to activate the process under CA 2006, s 983. **26-94**

Right of minority to be bought out

Those shareholders who do not accept the takeover bid may well have rejected it because they thought some other plan for the company's future preferable. When it **26-95**

---

[200] [2002] 1 BCLC 437.

[201] Note that the Takeover Code Rule 35.3. prohibits an offeror who holds more than 50% of the voting rights from offering more favourable terms than those available under the offer to a shareholder for a period of six months.

[202] CA 2006, s 981(2).   [203] [2002] 2 BCLC 123.

turns out that the takeover bid has been overwhelmingly successful, they may not wish to remain as minority shareholders in the company given its new controllers. The statute therefore allows them to insist on being bought out by the offeror at the price paid to the other shareholders or on such other terms as may be agreed or the court may fix.[204]

26-96 This right to be bought out by the offeror arises where the offeror has made a takeover offer for all the shares (or all the shares of a class) in a company and, before the offer expires, the offeror and its associates own at least 90% in value of those shares (or the shares of that class) and 90% of the voting rights carried by those shares or by that class of shares.[205] In these circumstances, any shareholder who has not accepted the offer may require the offeror to acquire his shares. To ensure that the minority are aware of this option, within one month of the above conditions being satisfied, the offeror must give those shareholders notice of their right to sell, specifying a closing date not less than three months after the expiry of the offer.[206] This right to sell out may be exercised either within the period of three months from the end of the offer or, if later, three months from the notice given to the shareholder of his right to exercise sell-out rights.

G Schemes of arrangement—CA 2006, Part 26

Introduction

26-97 As noted at **26-3**, it is now quite common to effect an agreed takeover by way of a scheme of arrangement and there are various advantages noted there to using a scheme rather than a takeover bid. Schemes of arrangements are also commonly used to restructure insolvent companies where a scheme may be used in conjunction with the appointment of an administrator or where a provisional liquidator is in place.[207] The major attraction of using a scheme is that the 75% approval required for a scheme binds all the members or the creditors, as the case may be (CA 2006, s 899(3)). This ability to reach a binding settlement in this way is invaluable, especially in complex situations. Much use is made of schemes in the context of insolvent insurance companies, for example where there may be a wide range of claimants and reinsurers involved and multiple group companies, some solvent and some insolvent.[208] Schemes have also been used extensively in respect of mass tort claims especially asbestos claims which have involved an indeterminate number of claimants (actual and contingent) against

---

[204] CA 2006, ss 983, 985; and see s 986(3) where an application may be made to the court by either the shareholder or the offeror to determine the terms on which the offeror must acquire the shares.

[205] CA 2006, s 983(2)–(4). This 90% threshold is not limited to 90% arising from acceptances of the bid.

[206] CA 2006, s 984(3).

[207] See Finch, *Corporate Insolvency Law* (2002), Ch 10, esp pp 324–31.

[208] See for example *Re Sovereign Marine & General Insurance Co Ltd* [2007] 1 BCLC 228.

large groups with activities in many jurisdictions. These asbestos scheme have been before the courts frequently in recent years.[209]

The decision as to whether to proceed with a straight bid or a scheme of arrange-   **26-98**
ment depends on a variety of factors as noted at **26-3**, but the choice of a scheme or a bid is dictated normally by whether the approach is hostile or friendly. It is only possible to proceed by way of a scheme if the offeror has the approval of the board of the offeree company because the board's co-operation is needed in calling the various meetings required under a scheme. Any offer for a company effected through a scheme of arrangement is still within and subject to the Takeover Code which expressly applies to takeovers and mergers effected by means of a scheme and which is modified to accommodate schemes as set out in Appendix 7 to the Code.[210]

A typical scheme of arrangement effecting a transfer of control provides for the can-   **26-99**
cellation of the shares in the target company and the capitalisation of the reserve arising on the cancellation of those shares to pay up new shares in the target to be allotted, credited as fully paid, to the bidder. In consideration of the allotment of the target company's shares to the bidder, the bidder allots fully paid shares in the bidder company to the shareholders of the target company. The result is that the target company becomes a subsidiary of the bidder company and the target company's shareholders become shareholders in the bidder company.[211] Equally, a scheme may be used to merge two companies into a new third company.

Where a compromise or arrangement is proposed between a company and its cred-   **26-100**
itors, or any class of them, or between the company and its members, or any class of them, the court may on the application of the company or any creditor or member (or a liquidator or administrator as the case may be) order a meeting of the creditors or class of creditors, or of the members of the company or class of members, to be summoned in such manner as the court directs (CA 2006, ss 895, 896).[212]

A scheme must be between the company (either through its board or by a majority of   **26-101**
the members in general meeting) and the members or creditors.[213] Though binding the members or creditors to the same extent as if they had made a contract, a scheme is not a contract, but a statutory procedure subject to court approval.[214] 'Arrangement' is interpreted widely by the courts which are anxious not to restrict a provision which Parliament has not limited.[215] An 'arrangement' involves some element of give and

---

[209] See in particular the Turner & Newall asbestos claims, see *Re T & N Ltd (No 2)* [2006] 2 BCLC 374; *Re T & N Ltd (No 3)* [2007] 1 BCLC 563. See also *Re Cape plc* [2007] 2 BCLC 546 (also asbestos claims).

[210] Takeover Code, Introduction, para 3(b).   [211] See, for example, *Re BTR plc* [1999] 2 BCLC 675.

[212] It is possible for a scheme to apply to only some of a company's creditors: *Re PT Garuda Indonesia* [2001] All ER (D) 53 (Oct), Ch D.

[213] *Re Savoy Hotel Ltd* [1981] 3 All ER 646; *Re Cape plc* [2007] 2 BCLC 546 at 570; *Re T & N Ltd (No 3)* [2007] 1 BCLC 563 at 582.

[214] *Re Cape plc* [2007] 2 BCLC 546 at 571 (a scheme is not subject therefore to the Unfair Contract Terms Act 1977).

[215] See *Re T & N Ltd (No 3)* [2007] 1 BCLC 563 at 585.

take, some element of accommodation on each side[216] and, although an arrangement often alters rights between the company and the creditors or members, it need not alter the rights provided that overall the scheme constitutes an arrangement.[217] A compromise and an arrangement are separate concepts and an arrangement need not involve a compromise or be confined to a case of dispute or difficulty.[218] As David Richards J noted in *Re T & N Ltd (No 3)*[219] a scheme used to effect a takeover bid (as described at **26-99**) is not a compromise, but it is an arrangement between the company and its members because it involves a change in the membership of the company. 'Creditor' for these purposes is to be construed widely in keeping with the purpose of the statutory provisions which is to encourage arrangements which avoid liquidation and facilitate the financial rehabilitation of the company and it therefore includes contingent creditors such as future tort claimants[220] and actual or potential claimants for contribution with an accrued right to claim contribution under the Civil Liability (Contribution) Act 1978.[221]

26-102   Each class affected by the proposed scheme must approve the scheme by a majority in number representing 75% in value of those present and voting either in person or by proxy (CA 2006, s 899(1)). Once sanctioned by the court, the scheme becomes binding on all the creditors or class of creditors, or members or class of members, as the case may be (s 899(3));[222] and it becomes effective upon a copy of the court order being delivered to the registrar of companies (s 899(4)). It is this capacity to bind dissenting or apathetic members which makes s 899 such a formidable section. The protection for dissenters lies in the majority both in number and value that is required and in the need for the court's sanction of the scheme. Once the classes summoned to the meetings have approved the scheme, the proposers of the scheme must return to the court for it to be sanctioned.

26-103   There are then three distinct stages to a scheme of arrangement:

(1) the application to the court for an order convening the necessary meeting or meetings of members or creditors, as the case may be (the convening hearing, CA 2006, s 896);

(2) the holding of the meetings for approval by the requisite majority (i.e. 75%); and

(3) the application to the court for the sanctioning of the scheme under s 899 (the sanction hearing).

---

[216] *Re Savoy Hotel Ltd* [1981] 3 All ER 646; *Re NFU Development Trust Ltd* [1973] 1 All ER 135. See also CA 2006, s 895(2).

[217] *Re T & N Ltd (No 3)* [2007] 1 BCLC 563.

[218] *Re Guardian Assurance Co* [1917] 1 Ch 431; *Re T & N Ltd (No 3)* [2007] 1 BCLC 563 at 583.

[219] [2007] 1 BCLC 563 at 583.   [220] *Re T & N Ltd (No 2)* [2006] 2 BCLC 374.

[221] *Re T & N Ltd (No 3)* [2007] 1 BCLC 563.

[222] Any agreement entered into pursuant to the court's order is binding even though it might otherwise be ultra vires and void, unless steps are taken to have the order set aside: *British and Commonwealth Holdings plc v Barclays Bank plc* [1996] 1 All ER 381, CA. While a scheme requires the approval of the court, it does not as a consequence become an order of the court and therefore the court has no jurisdiction to make a material alteration to the scheme: *Kemp v Ambassador Insurance Co* [1998] 1 BCLC 234, PC.

Identifying the classes

It is obvious from a consideration of the three stages of the procedure that the **26-104** identification of the classes in respect of which separate meetings must be held and approval obtained is crucial. If the class meetings are improperly constituted, the court will refuse to sanction the scheme.[223] It is often the case that objectors to a scheme will hope to prevent it proceeding by alleging that the class meetings were incorrectly composed. Equally, the courts are aware of the importance of schemes of arrangement to the resolution of very real practical difficulties in many cases of insolvency and reorganisation and they are anxious that objectors should not be able to rely on unrealistic distinctions so as to thwart the approval of the scheme. These issues have been before the courts on numerous occasions. The position is governed now by the restatement of the correct test by the Court of Appeal in *Re Hawk Insurance plc*[224] clarifying the application of the classic definition of a class for these purposes by Bowen LJ in *Sovereign Life Assurance Co v Dodd*[225] to the effect that a class consists of 'those persons whose rights are not so dissimilar as to make it impossible for them to consult together with a view to their common interest'.

In *Re BTR plc*[226] the court was asked by an objecting shareholder not to sanction a **26-105** scheme to effect a merger between two companies on the basis that more than one meeting of members should have been held, given that the members considering the scheme had differing interests. For example, some of the shareholders already held shares in the bidder company and their interests might therefore be different from other shareholders. The court held that whether or not a separate class meeting needs to be held depends on whether the shares have different rights attached to them as opposed to whether the shareholders have different interests.[227] A requirement to hold different meetings for those with different interests would render the statutory scheme unworkable. In reaching this conclusion, Jonathan Parker J relied on dicta by Nazareth J in the High Court of Hong Kong in *Re Industrial Equity (Pacific) Ltd* where he said:[228]

'Is every different interest to constitute a different class? Clearly not, but where then is the line to be drawn? The difficulties in identifying shareholders with such interests...could raise in terms of practicality virtually insuperable difficulties. It is determination by reference to rights of shareholders that meets such difficulties, while leaving any conflict of interest which may result in a minority being overborne or coerced to be dealt with by the courts when their sanction is sought.'

[223] See, for example, *Re British Aviation Insurance Co Ltd* [2006] 1 BCLC 665.

[224] [2001] 2 BCLC 480, CA.

[225] [1892] 2 QB 573 at 583, CA (holders of matured insurance policies constituted a different class from holders of unmatured policies); see also *Re United Provident Assurance Co Ltd* [1910] 2 Ch 477 (partly-paid shares and fully-paid shares are different classes requiring separate meetings).

[226] [1999] 2 BCLC 675.

[227] [1999] 2 BCLC 675 at 682, per Jonathan Parker J, with whom the Court of Appeal agreed: see [2000] 1 BCLC 740. In so far as *Re Hellenic & General Trust Ltd* [1975] 3 All ER 38 might be seen as suggesting a broader approach, it should be seen as limited to its facts (see [1999] 2 BCLC 675 at 682).

[228] [1991] 2 HKLR 614 at 625.

26-106   As Nazareth J emphasised, the issue of conflicting interests should be considered by the court at the sanction stage and not at the stage of determining the composition of the classes. Indeed, in *Re BTR plc*[229] even the objecting shareholder could not identify easily the number of classes with different interests in respect of which meetings might have to be held. In *Re Anglo American Insurance Co Ltd*[230] Neuberger J agreed that, unless a practical approach is adopted, there is a danger that 'one could end up with virtually as many classes as there are members of a particular group'.

26-107   This emphasis on differing rights as the determining factor was endorsed by the Court of Appeal in *Re Hawk Insurance Co Ltd*[231] which concerned a scheme to deal with an insolvent insurance company. The scheme had been approved unanimously at a single meeting of the scheme creditors, but the court at first instance declined to sanction the scheme as it was not satisfied that the scheme creditors constituted a single class, though no creditor appeared to oppose the scheme. On appeal, the Court of Appeal held that it is settled law that in determining whether creditors fall into separate classes, the test to be applied is that of Bowen LJ in *Sovereign Life Assurance Co v Dodd*[232] to the effect that a class consists of 'those persons whose rights are not so dissimilar as to make it impossible for them to consult together with a view to their common interest'. But Chadwick LJ stressed that:[233]

> 'When applying Bowen LJ's test to the question "are the rights of those who are to be affected by the scheme proposed such that the scheme can be seen as a single arrangement; or ought it to be regarded, on a true analysis, as a number of linked arrangements?" it is necessary to ensure not only that those whose rights really are so dissimilar that they cannot consult together with a view to a common interest should be treated as parties to distinct arrangements—so that they should have their own separate meetings—but also that those whose rights are sufficiently similar to the rights of others that they can properly consult together should be required to do so; lest by ordering separate meetings the court gives a veto to a minority group.'

26-108   On the facts, the judge had fallen into error in concluding that the creditors fell into more than one class. Neither the rights released or varied nor the new rights given under the proposed scheme were so dissimilar as to make it impossible for the creditors to consult together with a view to their common interest. That common interest lay in a simple, inexpensive and expeditious winding up of the company's affairs without the need for a formal liquidation. The scheme would be sanctioned.

26-109   As noted above, Chadwick LJ stressed that it is important that Bowen LJ's test should not be applied in such a way that it becomes an instrument of oppression by a minority and the protection for any shareholder who feels aggrieved at the composition of the meeting lies in the requirement that the court must sanction a scheme.[234] As had been, noted earlier in *Re BTR plc*,[235] 'Parliament has recognised that it is for the court...to

---

[229] See [1999] 2 BCLC 675 at 683; and see [2000] 1 BCLC 740 at 747.   [230] [2001] 1 BCLC 755.

[231] [2001] 2 BCLC 480. See Moss, 'Hawk Triumphant: A vindication of the modern approach to classes in s 425 schemes' [2003] 40 Insolv Int 41.

[232] [1892] 2 QB 573 at 583, CA.   [233] [2001] 2 BCLC 480 at 519.

[234] [2001] 2 BCLC 480 at 519.   [235] [2000] 1 BCLC 740 at 748.

hold the ring between different interests; and to decline to sanction a scheme if satisfied that members having one interest have sought to take advantage over those having another'.

The net effect is that the onus is still on the company to ensure that the meetings are properly constituted according to the rights of the members or creditors, as the case may be, and the court will not sanction a scheme where separate meetings have not been held for those with different substantive rights. But a class is not wrongly composed simply because it contains within it persons with differing interests. The significance of those differing interests is a matter for the court in deciding whether to sanction the scheme.[236] There remains a risk, of course, that the company may not correctly identify the classes for which separate meetings are required and so, at the later stage, it will find that the court will not sanction the scheme. But that risk has been reduced by a change of practice on these matters following the decision in *Re Hawk Insurance Co Ltd*.[237]

26-110

In *Re Hawk Insurance Co Ltd*[238] Chadwick LJ had commented on the need to re-examine the (then) established practice of the court not to decide on the composition of the classes but to leave it to the company (or liquidator etc) to determine which meetings need to be called, with the risk that an erroneous decision as to the composition of the meetings would result in the court subsequently refusing to sanction the scheme with all the delay and expense which that would entail.[239] This message was duly noted by the lower courts which when asked to sanction the calling of scheme meetings began to consider the issue of the composition of the meetings to a greater degree than previously while still leaving it to those promoting a scheme to satisfy themselves that the correct meetings are convened. An example of the change in approach in the lower courts can be seen in *Re Equitable Life Assurance Society*[240] where Lloyd J agreed that it was appropriate for the court to attempt to formulate a prima facie view as to whether the class or classes put forward by the company were appropriate while emphasising that this could only be a provisional conclusion, and was subject to contrary submissions when the court was asked subsequently to sanction the scheme.[241]

26-111

The effect is to require the company (and its advisers) at a preliminary stage to focus its efforts on identifying the classes correctly in order to satisfy the court that it should order the convening of meetings. The greater the focus at that stage, the more likely it is that the company will have identified the classes correctly. These changes were reflected in a 2002 Practice Statement (*Companies: schemes of arrangement*) which clarifies the approach taken by the courts on scheme applications so as to enable issues concerning the composition of classes of creditor and the summoning of meetings to be identified and if appropriate resolved early in the proceedings.[242] Essentially,

26-112

---

[236] See *Re Cape plc* [2007] 2 BCLC 546 at 562; *Re T & N Ltd (No 3)* [2007] 1 BCLC 563 at 599.
[237] [2001] 2 BCLC 480.   [238] [2001] 2 BCLC 480.   [239] [2001] 2 BCLC 480 at 513.
[240] [2002] BCC 319.   [241] See also *Re Telewest Communications plc (No 1)* [2005] 1 BCLC 752.
[242] The full text of the Practice Statement is set out at [2002] 3 All ER 96.

the responsibility for the composition of the classes remains with the applicant who must draw the attention of the court to any issue as to composition which may arise. Indeed, any issue which goes to the jurisdiction of the court to sanction a scheme or which would otherwise lead the court to refuse to sanction the scheme should be raised at this stage.[243] The applicant must take all steps reasonably open to it to notify any person affected by the scheme which gives parties an opportunity to make representations as to the composition of the meetings.[244] While creditors who consider that they have been unfairly treated are still able to appear and raise objections at the hearing to sanction the scheme, the court will expect them to show good reason why they did not raise a creditor issue at an earlier stage. In other words, the company must expend greater effort in determining the composition of the classes and objectors must make their case earlier, while not excluding the possibility of a challenge to the scheme at the subsequent sanction hearing. The courts are anxious to eliminate as much as possible the risk of a successful challenge at the sanction stage when the company has already been put to a great deal of expense in advancing the scheme. In practice, once the court has formed a prima facie view as to the correct composition of the class meetings, it may prove difficult to challenge that conclusion at the sanction stage save in cases of significant substantive error. The result is greater commercial certainty with some concerns (probably overstated) that this certainty has been achieved at the expense of minority protection.

26-113   The application of the test as laid down in *Re Hawk Insurance Co Ltd*[245] was lucidly explained by David Richards J in *Re T & N Ltd (No 3)*[246] as follows:

> 'The application of this test requires a consideration of (a) the rights of creditors in the absence of the scheme and (b) any new rights to which the creditors become entitled under the scheme. If there is a material difference between the rights of different groups of creditors under (a) or (b), they may constitute different classes for the purposes of [CA 2006, s 899]. Whether they do so will depend on a judgment as to whether such differences make it impossible for the different groups to consult together with a view to their common interest (see *Re Anglo American Insurance Ltd* [2001] 1 BCLC 755, *Re Hawk Insurance Co Ltd*, and *Re Telewest Communications plc (No 1)*, *Re Telewest Finance (Jersey) Ltd (No 1)* [2004] EWHC 924 (Ch), [2005] 1 BCLC 752).
>
>   In considering the rights of creditors which are to be affected by the scheme, it is essential to identify the correct comparator. In the case of rights against an insolvent company, where the scheme is proposed as an alternative to an insolvent liquidation, it is their rights as creditors in an insolvent liquidation of the company (see *Re Hawk Insurance Co Ltd*). Those rights may be very different from the creditors' rights against a company which is solvent and will continue in business. In the latter case the creditors' rights against the company as a continuing entity are the appropriate comparator (see *Re British Aviation Insurance Co Ltd* [2005] EWHC 1621 (Ch), [2006] 1 BCLC 665).'

---

[243] See *Re T & N Ltd (No 3)* [2007] 1 BCLC 563 at 574, per David Richards J.

[244] See *Re British Aviation Insurance Co Ltd* [2006] 1 BCLC 665 (requirements as to notification are not absolute and do not apply if there are good reasons, such as time and expense, why they should not apply).

[245] [2001] 2 BCLC 480.   [246] [2007] 1 BCLC 563 at 596.

The importance of the comparator was also emphasised by the same judge in *Re*   **26-114**
Cape plc.[247] For example, if the alternative to a scheme is insolvent liquidation, then
the effect of the scheme on the rights of creditors is to be compared with their rights
in an insolvent liquidation, as happened in *Re Hawk Insurance Co Ltd*.[248] If the alternative, as in *Re British Aviation Insurance Co Ltd*,[249] was that the insurance company
would continue in solvent run-off, then the effect of the scheme has to be compared
with rights against the company as a continuing entity.[250]

The meetings of the class

The notice calling the meeting must be accompanied by a statement explaining   **26-115**
the scheme,[251] disclosing any material interests of the directors and whether the
arrangement affects them differently from others with a similar interest (CA 2006,
s 897(1), (2)). If there is any material alteration to the circumstances after the notice
is sent, a further communication is required, otherwise there is a risk that the court
may not approve the scheme, for those voting must be informed as to the issues before
them.[252] Save where a class consists of only one member, a meeting must be attended
(whether in person or by the use of technology) by more than one person and the court
has no jurisdiction to sanction a scheme which provides for a class meeting of creditors to be constituted by the attendance of one creditor.[253] It is possible for a person to
fall into two classes and properly attend each meeting.[254]

Each class affected by the proposed scheme must approve the scheme by a majority in   **26-116**
number representing 75% in value of those present and voting either in person or by
proxy (CA 2006, s 899(1)).

The sanction of the court

Once the meetings have been held, a further application is made to the court for the   **26-117**
court to sanction the scheme. The court considers whether the statutory scheme
has been adhered to, whether the meetings have been properly held and, applying the test of Maugham J in *Re Dorman, Long & Co Ltd, South Durham Steel and*

---

[247] [2007] 2 BCLC 546 at 558. See also *Re British Aviation Insurance Co Ltd* [2006] 1 BCLC 665.

[248] [2001] 2 BCLC 480.   [249] [2006] 1 BCLC 665.

[250] See *Re T & N Ltd (No 3)* [2007] 1 BCLC 563 at 596.

[251] The statement must explain how the scheme affects the creditors or shareholders commercially
and the extent of the information required depends on the facts of the particular case: see *Re Heron
International NV* [1994] 1 BCLC 667; *Re Allied Domecq plc* [2000] 1 BCLC 134.

[252] *Re Jessel Trust Ltd* [1985] BCLC 119; *Re Minster Assets plc* [1985] BCLC 200: the role of the court is to
be satisfied that no reasonable shareholder would have changed his decision as to how to act on the scheme
if the information had been disclosed: *Re Heron International NV* [1994] 1 BCLC 667; *Re Allied Domecq plc*
[2000] 1 BCLC 134.

[253] *Re Altitude Scaffolding Ltd; Re T&N Ltd* [2007] 1 BCLC 199.

[254] *Re Alabama, New Orleans, Texas and Pacific Junction Rly Co* [1891] 1 Ch 213, CA; *Re Cape plc* [2007]
2 BCLC 546 at 555.

Iron Co Ltd,[255] whether the proposal is such that an intelligent and honest man, a member of the class concerned and acting in respect of his interest, might reasonably approve.

26-118   Generally the courts have been content to endorse the following statement in *Buckley on the Companies Acts* which explains the role of the court in these terms:[256]

> 'In exercising its power of sanction the court will see, first, that the provisions of the statute have been complied with, second, that the class was fairly represented by those who attended the meeting and that the statutory majority are acting bona fide and are not coercing the minority in order to promote interests adverse to those of the class whom they purport to represent, and thirdly, that the arrangement is such as an intelligent and honest man, a member of the class concerned and acting in respect of his interest, might reasonably approve. The court does not sit merely to see that the majority are acting bona fide and thereupon to register the decision of the meeting, but, at the same time, the court will be slow to differ from the meeting, unless either the class has not been properly consulted, or the meeting has not considered the matter with a view to the interests of the class which it is empowered to bind, or some blot is found in the scheme.' ((14th edn, 1981), vol 1, at pp 473–4)

26-119   In practice, the courts are reluctant to interfere if a proper majority has approved the scheme, and typically the scheme is approved by a majority considerably in excess of the required 75%, so it would be unusual for a scheme to be refused sanction at this stage.[257] In *Re Equitable Life Assurance Society*,[258] for example, having agreed that the correct classes of creditors (policyholders of the company) had been identified, Lloyd J turned to consider whether the court should exercise its discretion to sanction the scheme. He noted that there had been a very wide range of objections to the sanctioning of the scheme, but in essence many came down to a view that the scheme was unfair because it did not adequately compensate the policyholders for the claims which they were giving up. In each vote of the classes less than 2% in value of the policyholders had voted against the scheme while 98% had voted in favour. In the absence of any evidence that those voting in favour had been misled or that they had acted on inadequate information, the court concluded that the scheme was one which

---

[255] [1934] Ch 635 at 657. See also *Re Alabama, New Orleans, Texas and Pacific Junction Rly Co* [1891] 1 Ch 213, CA. The court can approve a scheme which is to be binding after liquidation; and can approve a scheme, exceptionally, which involves a departure from the rules as to mutual credit and set-off in insolvency: *Re Anglo American Insurance Co Ltd* [2001] 1 BCLC 755. The court's approval may be subject to undertakings; as to the types of undertakings which might be required, see *Re Osiris Insurance Ltd* [1999] 1 BCLC 182; *Re Allied Domecq plc* [2000] 1 BCLC 134.

[256] This statement was approved by Plowman J in *Re National Bank Ltd* [1966] 1 All ER 1006 at 1012, and has subsequently been cited and applied by the courts on numerous occasions, see *Re Allied Domecq plc* [2000] 1 BCLC 134 at 142; *Re RAC Motoring Services Ltd* [2000] 1 BCLC 307 at 321; *Re BTR plc* [1999] 2 BCLC 675 at 680; *Re Osiris Insurance Ltd* [1999] 1 BCLC 182 at 188.

[257] Which is why the rejection of the scheme at first instance in *Re Hawk Insurance Co Ltd* [2001] 2 BCLC 480 when it had been unanimously approved by the creditors, was so exceptional. For a rare example of a case where the court did refuse to sanction a scheme although it had been approved by the requisite majority, see *Re NFU Development Trust* [1973] 1 All ER 135 (the court concluded that the scheme properly examined was a scheme which no member voting in the interests of the members as a whole could reasonably approve).

[258] [2002] 2 BCLC 510.

an intelligent and honest man, a member of the class concerned and acting in respect of his interest, might reasonably approve and which the court might sanction. On the other hand, in *Re British Aviation Insurance Co Ltd*[259] the court did refuse to sanction a scheme because the class meetings had not been correctly constituted, but also because, in any event, the court did not think the scheme was fair to creditors, though beneficial to the company and its shareholders.

In *Re Cape plc*[260] David Richards J held that the court has jurisdiction to sanction **26-120** a scheme of arrangement which contains provision for future amendment either of the scheme itself or of agreements and other documents to be made pursuant to the scheme, but that there are strong reasons why in most cases the court is unlikely to sanction a scheme with provisions for future amendments. The reasons for not sanctioning would include the need for creditors and the court to know with clarity and certainty the terms of the arrangement and how they will affect creditors. Creditors may be content with the arrangement in its original form but not as it is subsequently amended. On the other hand, in some unusual contexts, such as in this case where the scheme was to deal with asbestos-related claims which are likely to continue for 40 to 50 years, there is a clear case for some flexibility. He therefore ordered meetings to be convened to consider the scheme without pre-empting a consideration of the fairness of the scheme at the subsequent sanction hearing.

In *Re National Bank Ltd*[261] the question arose as to whether, if a scheme of arrange-   **26-121** ment involves the compulsory elimination of minority shareholders, the court should impose a 90% acceptance level (which would apply if compulsory acquisition powers were to be used following a takeover bid, see at **26-85**) as a condition for approving the scheme. Plowman J rejected the argument stating that these statutory schemes are quite distinct.[262] Jonathan Parker J in *Re BTR plc*[263] agreed with this approach noting that Parliament had clearly intended that a scheme of arrangement should be available as a means of effecting a binding compromise between a company and its members and that it should be available as an alternate to the use of compulsory acquisition following a takeover offer.[264]

When the scheme being sanctioned is for the purposes of, or in connection with, a   **26-122** reconstruction or amalgamation and the transfer of the whole or part of one or more companies' businesses to another company, the court has extensive powers under CA 2006, s 900 to make such ancillary orders as are necessary.[265] The court can by

---

[259] [2006] 1 BCLC 665.   [260] [2007] 2 BCLC 546.

[261] [1966] 1 All ER 1006; see also *Singer Manufacturing Co v Robinow* 1971 SC 11 in which the offeror company, which already owned 92% of the shares in the offeree company, used a scheme of arrangement with its lower acceptance level requirement to compulsorily acquire the remaining 8% of shares, rather than comply with the conditions for compulsory acquisition discussed at **26-85** above.

[262] [1966] 1 All ER 1006 at 1013.   [263] [1999] 2 BCLC 675 at 684.

[264] [2000] 1 BCLC 740 at 747, per Chadwick LJ. In so far as Templeman J suggested to the contrary in *Re Hellenic and General Trust Ltd* [1975] 3 All ER 382, that case must be regarded as of doubtful validity on this point.

[265] In *Re Mytravel Group plc* [2005] 2 BCLC 123, Mann J held that the essence of a reconstruction is that substantially the same shareholders should be involved in both the old and the new companies. On the facts

order transfer not only the whole or any part of a company's undertaking or property but also its liabilities (s 900(2)(a)). Creditors could agree to be transferred and, if appropriate meetings of creditors were held, a majority in number representing 75% in value could bind them all. But in cases where the company is solvent and there is no risk to creditors, the courts will not require meetings of creditors to be held but will transfer the liabilities by court order. It has been held that property rights which are not assignable by law cannot be transferred[266] nor can functions which are personal to the company concerned.[267] But the former rule, that contracts of employment could not be transferred[268] is now reversed, for they are automatically transferred when the undertaking or part thereof is transferred whether the transfer is effected by sale or by some other disposition or by operation of law.[269]

H Reconstruction in the course of voluntary liquidation

26-123   A reconstruction may also be effected under IA 1986, s 110, whereby a liquidator may be authorised (in a members' voluntary winding up, by special resolution; and in the case of a creditors' voluntary winding up, by a special resolution of the members and with the sanction of the court of the liquidation committee[270]) to sell the whole or part of the company's business or property to another company in return for shares (or other consideration[271]) in that other company which are then distributed among the members of the company in liquidation.[272]

26-124   In its simplest form, where one company transfers its business to a new company, this is called reconstruction. Historically, this was usually done either because the new company had wider or different objects than the old company, or to change the rights of different classes of shareholders by giving them shares with altered rights in a new company. But this provision can be used to effect a merger by putting one company into liquidation and transferring its business to the other in return for shares in that other, or by putting two companies into liquidation and transferring their businesses to a third company, which issues shares to the two liquidators for distribution to the shareholders in the two companies now in liquidation. Equally, businesses may use

in this case where 4% by value of the shareholding in the new company was held by 100% of the shareholders in the old, the case was not one in which there was a substantial identity between the two bodies of shareholders of the shares in the new company and therefore the scheme did not fall within what is now CA 2006, s 900 (then CA 1985, s 427). The case was appealed to the Court of Appeal but there was no appeal on this point.

[266] *Re L Hotel Co Ltd and Langham Hotel Co Ltd* [1946] 1 All ER 319.

[267] See *Re Skinner* [1958] 3 All ER 273.

[268] *Nokes v Doncaster Amalgamated Collieries Ltd* [1940] 3 All ER 549, HL.

[269] Transfer of Undertakings (Protection of Employment) Regulations 2006, SI 2006/246.

[270] IA 1986, s 110(3)(b).   [271] See IA 1986, s 110(2), (4).   [272] IA 1986, s 110 (1), (2), (3)(a).

this type of scheme where they are demerging, i.e. splitting off their businesses into more discrete units.[273]

The sale or arrangement is binding on all the members of the company[274] subject to the right of any members who did not vote for the resolution, to give notice in writing to the liquidator, within seven days after the passing of the resolution, requiring the liquidator either to abstain from carrying out the resolution or to purchase their interest at a price to be determined by agreement or arbitration.[275] Effectively, therefore, the dissenters have to be paid off under this scheme or, more commonly, agreement will already have been reached with them as to the manner of their exit. This does not, however, mean that shareholders who neither assent nor give formal notice of dissent are bound to take the shares in the transferor company. They may instead forfeit their interest in the company altogether[276] or the scheme may provide for the shares of such shareholders to be sold and the proceeds paid to them.[277]   **26-125**

The consideration received by the liquidator must be distributed among the shareholders entitled to it strictly in accordance with their respective rights as shareholders.[278] In other words, although their rights as shareholders in the new company may be very different from their rights in the old company, the shares in the new company must somehow be distributed in a way that exactly reflects the rights of shareholders in the old company.   **26-126**

The sale or arrangement agreed to by the special resolution is also binding on the creditors of the old company.[279] They are not transferred with the business to the new company but remain creditors of the old company and they must look to the liquidator of the old company to retain sufficient assets or to realise sufficient of the consideration received from the transferee company to be able to pay them.[280] If they doubt whether the liquidator will be able to pay them, their remedy is to petition for the compulsory liquidation of the company. If an order for winding up is made within a year of the special resolution being passed, the resolution is not valid unless sanctioned by the court (IA 1986, s 110(6)). Liquidators will therefore usually make adequate provision for creditors since they will not want to run the risk of the whole transaction being invalidated, as would be the case if the special resolution were invalidated.   **26-127**

It will be apparent that any transaction that could come within the IA 1986, s 110 could in principle come within a scheme of arrangement as well. The courts have held,   **26-128**

---

[273] As to the use of IA 1986, s 110 schemes for demergers, see Dwyer, 'Section 110 Reconstructions in Private Equity Transactions' [2002] 13 ICCLR 295.

[274] IA 1986, s 110(5).

[275] IA 1986, s 111(1), (2). A shareholder may also be able to halt the transaction by obtaining a winding-up order: s 110(6); see *Re Consolidated South Rand Mines Deep Ltd* [1909] 1 Ch 491 (where scheme is eminently unfair).

[276] *Re Bank of Hindustan, China and Japan Ltd, Higgs's Case* (1865) 2 Hem & M 657; *Burdett-Coutts v True Blue (Hannan's) Gold Mine* [1899] 2 Ch 616, CA.

[277] *Fuller v White Feather Reward Ltd* [1906] 1 Ch 823.   [278] *Griffith v Paget* (1877) 6 Ch D 511.

[279] *Re City and County Investment Co* (1879) 13 Ch D 475, CA.

[280] *Pulsford v Devenish* [1903] 2 Ch 625.

however, that the special protection afforded to dissenting shareholders (of compelling the liquidator to buy them out or drop the transaction) must be made available to dissenting shareholders if a similar scheme is effected under a scheme of arrangement.[281] Where the company is transferring only part of its undertaking or assets and is continuing in existence with the remaining assets rather than going into liquidation so that IA 1986, s 110 would not apply, there is no necessity for dissenting shareholders to be given a cash option.[282]

[281] *Re Anglo-Continental Supply Co Ltd* [1922] 2 Ch 723.
[282] *Watt v London & Northern Assets Corpn* [1898] 2 Ch 469, CA.

Appendix 1

CA 2006, Part 10

Chapter 2
General Duties of Directors

Introductory

170 Scope and nature of general duties

(1) The general duties specified in sections 171 to 177 are owed by a director of a company to the company.

(2) A person who ceases to be a director continues to be subject—

    (a) to the duty in section 175 (duty to avoid conflicts of interest) as regards the exploitation of any property, information or opportunity of which he became aware at a time when he was a director, and

    (b) to the duty in section 176 (duty not to accept benefits from third parties) as regards things done or omitted by him before he ceased to be a director.

To that extent those duties apply to a former director as to a director, subject to any necessary adaptations.

(3) The general duties are based on certain common law rules and equitable principles as they apply in relation to directors and have effect in place of those rules and principles as regards the duties owed to a company by a director.

(4) The general duties shall be interpreted and applied in the same way as common law rules or equitable principles, and regard shall be had to the corresponding common law rules and equitable principles in interpreting and applying the general duties.

(5) The general duties apply to shadow directors where, and to the extent that, the corresponding common law rules or equitable principles so apply.

171 Duty to act within powers

A director of a company must—

    (a) act in accordance with the company's constitution, and

    (b) only exercise powers for the purposes for which they are conferred.

172 Duty to promote the success of the company

(1) A director of a company must act in the way he considers, in good faith, would be most likely to promote the success of the company for the benefit of its members as a whole, and in doing so have regard (amongst other matters) to—

  (a) the likely consequences of any decision in the long term,

  (b) the interests of the company's employees,

  (c) the need to foster the company's business relationships with suppliers, customers and others,

  (d) the impact of the company's operations on the community and the environment,

  (e) the desirability of the company maintaining a reputation for high standards of business conduct, and

  (f) the need to act fairly as between members of the company.

(2) Where or to the extent that the purposes of the company consist of or include purposes other than the benefit of its members, subsection (1) has effect as if the reference to promoting the success of the company for the benefit of its members were to achieving those purposes.

(3) The duty imposed by this section has effect subject to any enactment or rule of law requiring directors, in certain circumstances, to consider or act in the interests of creditors of the company.

173 Duty to exercise independent judgment

(1) A director of a company must exercise independent judgment.

(2) This duty is not infringed by his acting—

  (a) in accordance with an agreement duly entered into by the company that restricts the future exercise of discretion by its directors, or

  (b) in a way authorised by the company's constitution.

174 Duty to exercise reasonable care, skill and diligence

(1) A director of a company must exercise reasonable care, skill and diligence.

(2) This means the care, skill and diligence that would be exercised by a reasonably diligent person with—

  (a) the general knowledge, skill and experience that may reasonably be expected of a person carrying out the functions carried out by the director in relation to the company, and

  (b) the general knowledge, skill and experience that the director has.

175 Duty to avoid conflicts of interest

(1) A director of a company must avoid a situation in which he has, or can have, a direct or indirect interest that conflicts, or possibly may conflict, with the interests of the company.

(2) This applies in particular to the exploitation of any property, information or opportunity (and it is immaterial whether the company could take advantage of the property, information or opportunity).

(3) This duty does not apply to a conflict of interest arising in relation to a transaction or arrangement with the company.

(4) This duty is not infringed—

    (a) if the situation cannot reasonably be regarded as likely to give rise to a conflict of interest; or

    (b) if the matter has been authorised by the directors.

(5) Authorisation may be given by the directors—

    (a) where the company is a private company and nothing in the company's constitution invalidates such authorisation, by the matter being proposed to and authorised by the directors; or

    (b) where the company is a public company and its constitution includes provision enabling the directors to authorise the matter, by the matter being proposed to and authorised by them in accordance with the constitution.

(6) The authorisation is effective only if—

    (a) any requirement as to the quorum at the meeting at which the matter is considered is met without counting the director in question or any other interested director, and

    (b) the matter was agreed to without their voting or would have been agreed to if their votes had not been counted.

(7) Any reference in this section to a conflict of interest includes a conflict of interest and duty and a conflict of duties.

176 Duty not to accept benefits from third parties

(1) A director of a company must not accept a benefit from a third party conferred by reason of—

    (a) his being a director, or

    (b) his doing (or not doing) anything as director.

(2) A 'third party' means a person other than the company, an associated body corporate or a person acting on behalf of the company or an associated body corporate.

(3) Benefits received by a director from a person by whom his services (as a director or otherwise) are provided to the company are not regarded as conferred by a third party.

(4) This duty is not infringed if the acceptance of the benefit cannot reasonably be regarded as likely to give rise to a conflict of interest.

(5) Any reference in this section to a conflict of interest includes a conflict of interest and duty and a conflict of duties.

177 Duty to declare interest in proposed transaction or arrangement

(1) If a director of a company is in any way, directly or indirectly, interested in a proposed transaction or arrangement with the company, he must declare the nature and extent of that interest to the other directors.

(2) The declaration may (but need not) be made—

    (a) at a meeting of the directors, or

    (b) by notice to the directors in accordance with—

        (i) section 184 (notice in writing), or

        (ii) section 185 (general notice).

(3) If a declaration of interest under this section proves to be, or becomes, inaccurate or incomplete, a further declaration must be made.

(4) Any declaration required by this section must be made before the company enters into the transaction or arrangement.

(5) This section does not require a declaration of an interest of which the director is not aware or where the director is not aware of the transaction or arrangement in question.

For this purpose a director is treated as being aware of matters of which he ought reasonably to be aware.

(6) A director need not declare an interest—

    (a) if it cannot reasonably be regarded as likely to give rise to a conflict of interest;

    (b) if, or to the extent that, the other directors are already aware of it (and for this purpose the other directors are treated as aware of anything of which they ought reasonably to be aware); or

    (c) if, or to the extent that, it concerns terms of his service contract that have been or are to be considered—

        (i) by a meeting of the directors, or

        (ii) by a committee of the directors appointed for the purpose under the company's constitution.

Supplementary provisions

178 Civil consequences of breach of general duties

(1) The consequences of breach (or threatened breach) of sections 171 to 177 are the same as would apply if the corresponding common law rule or equitable principle applied.

(2) The duties in those sections (with the exception of section 174 (duty to exercise reasonable care, skill and diligence)) are, accordingly, enforceable in the same way as any other fiduciary duty owed to a company by its directors.

179 Cases within more than one of the general duties

Except as otherwise provided, more than one of the general duties may apply in any given case.

180 Consent, approval or authorisation by members

(1) In a case where—

    (a) section 175 (duty to avoid conflicts of interest) is complied with by authorisation by the directors, or

    (b) section 177 (duty to declare interest in proposed transaction or arrangement) is complied with, the transaction or arrangement is not liable to be set aside by virtue of any common law rule or equitable principle requiring the consent or approval of the members of the company.

This is without prejudice to any enactment, or provision of the company's constitution, requiring such consent or approval.

(2) The application of the general duties is not affected by the fact that the case also falls within Chapter 4 (transactions requiring approval of members), except that where that Chapter applies and—

    (a) approval is given under that Chapter, or

    (b) the matter is one as to which it is provided that approval is not needed, it is not necessary also to comply with section 175 (duty to avoid conflicts of interest) or section 176 (duty not to accept benefits from third parties).

(3) Compliance with the general duties does not remove the need for approval under any applicable provision of Chapter 4 (transactions requiring approval of members).

(4) The general duties—

    (a) have effect subject to any rule of law enabling the company to give authority, specifically or generally, for anything to be done (or omitted) by the directors, or any of them, that would otherwise be a breach of duty, and

    (b) where the company's articles contain provisions for dealing with conflicts of interest, are not infringed by anything done (or omitted) by the directors, or any of them, in accordance with those provisions.

(5) Otherwise, the general duties have effect (except as otherwise provided or the context otherwise requires) notwithstanding any enactment or rule of law.

181 Modification of provisions in relation to charitable companies

(1) In their application to a company that is a charity, the provisions of this Chapter have effect subject to this section.

(2) Section 175 (duty to avoid conflicts of interest) has effect as if—

    (a) for subsection (3) (which disapplies the duty to avoid conflicts of interest in the case of a transaction or arrangement with the company) there were substituted—

    '(3) This duty does not apply to a conflict of interest arising in relation to a transaction or arrangement with the company if or to the extent that the company's articles allow that duty to be so disapplied, which they may do only in relation to descriptions of transaction or arrangement specified in the company's articles.';

    (b) for subsection (5) (which specifies how directors of a company may give authority under that section for a transaction or arrangement) there were substituted—

    '(5) Authorisation may be given by the directors where the company's constitution includes provision enabling them to authorise the matter, by the matter being proposed to and authorised by them in accordance with the constitution.'.

(3) Section 180(2)(b) (which disapplies certain duties under this Chapter in relation to cases excepted from requirement to obtain approval by members under Chapter 4) applies only if or to the extent that the company's articles allow those duties to be so disapplied, which they may do only in relation to descriptions of transaction or arrangement specified in the company's articles.

(4) After section 26(5) of the Charities Act 1993 (c. 10) (power of Charity Commission to authorise dealings with charity property etc) insert—

'(5A) In the case of a charity that is a company, an order under this section may authorise an act notwithstanding that it involves the breach of a duty imposed on a director of the company under Chapter 2 of Part 10 of the Companies Act 2006 (general duties of directors).'.

(5) This section does not extend to Scotland.

Chapter 3
Declaration of Interest in Existing Transaction or Arrangement

182 Declaration of interest in existing transaction or arrangement

(1) Where a director of a company is in any way, directly or indirectly, interested in a transaction or arrangement that has been entered into by the company, he must declare the nature and extent of the interest to the other directors in accordance with this section. This section does not apply if or to the extent that the interest has been declared under section 177 (duty to declare interest in proposed transaction or arrangement).

(2) The declaration must be made—

    (a) at a meeting of the directors, or

    (b) by notice in writing (see section 184), or

    (c) by general notice (see section 185).

(3) If a declaration of interest under this section proves to be, or becomes, inaccurate or incomplete, a further declaration must be made.

(4) Any declaration required by this section must be made as soon as is reasonably practicable.

    Failure to comply with this requirement does not affect the underlying duty to make the declaration.

(5) This section does not require a declaration of an interest of which the director is not aware or where the director is not aware of the transaction or arrangement in question.

    For this purpose a director is treated as being aware of matters of which he ought reasonably to be aware.

(6) A director need not declare an interest under this section—

    (a) if it cannot reasonably be regarded as likely to give rise to a conflict of interest;

    (b) if, or to the extent that, the other directors are already aware of it (and for this purpose the other directors are treated as aware of anything of which they ought reasonably to be aware); or

    (c) if, or to the extent that, it concerns terms of his service contract that have been or are to be considered—

        (i) by a meeting of the directors, or

        (ii) by a committee of the directors appointed for the purpose under the company's constitution.

183 Offence of failure to declare interest

(1) A director who fails to comply with the requirements of section 182 (declaration of interest in existing transaction or arrangement) commits an offence.

(2) A person guilty of an offence under this section is liable—

    (a) on conviction on indictment, to a fine;

    (b) on summary conviction, to a fine not exceeding the statutory maximum.

184 Declaration made by notice in writing

(1) This section applies to a declaration of interest made by notice in writing.

(2) The director must send the notice to the other directors.

(3) The notice may be sent in hard copy form or, if the recipient has agreed to receive it in electronic form, in an agreed electronic form.

(4) The notice may be sent—

    (a) by hand or by post, or

    (b) if the recipient has agreed to receive it by electronic means, by agreed electronic means.

(5) Where a director declares an interest by notice in writing in accordance with this section—

    (a) the making of the declaration is deemed to form part of the proceedings at the next meeting of the directors after the notice is given, and

    (b) the provisions of section 248 (minutes of meetings of directors) apply as if the declaration had been made at that meeting.

185 General notice treated as sufficient declaration

(1) General notice in accordance with this section is a sufficient declaration of interest in relation to the matters to which it relates.

(2) General notice is notice given to the directors of a company to the effect that the director—

    (a) has an interest (as member, officer, employee or otherwise) in a specified body corporate or firm and is to be regarded as interested in any transaction or arrangement that may, after the date of the notice, be made with that body corporate or firm, or

    (b) is connected with a specified person (other than a body corporate or firm) and is to be regarded as interested in any transaction or arrangement that may, after the date of the notice, be made with that person.

(3) The notice must state the nature and extent of the director's interest in the body corporate or firm or, as the case may be, the nature of his connection with the person.

(4) General notice is not effective unless—

    (a) it is given at a meeting of the directors, or

    (b) the director takes reasonable steps to secure that it is brought up and read at the next meeting of the directors after it is given.

186 Declaration of interest in case of company with sole director

(1) Where a declaration of interest under section 182 (duty to declare interest in existing transaction or arrangement) is required of a sole director of a company that is required to have more than one director—

    (a) the declaration must be recorded in writing,

    (b) the making of the declaration is deemed to form part of the proceedings at the next meeting of the directors after the notice is given, and

    (c) the provisions of section 248 (minutes of meetings of directors) apply as if the declaration had been made at that meeting.

(2) Nothing in this section affects the operation of section 231 (contract with sole member who is also a director: terms to be set out in writing or recorded in minutes).

187 Declaration of interest in existing transaction by shadow director

(1) The provisions of this Chapter relating to the duty under section 182 (duty to declare interest in existing transaction or arrangement) apply to a shadow director as to a director, but with the following adaptations.

(2) Subsection (2)(a) of that section (declaration at meeting of directors) does not apply.

(3) In section 185 (general notice treated as sufficient declaration), subsection (4) (notice to be given at or brought up and read at meeting of directors) does not apply.

(4) General notice by a shadow director is not effective unless given by notice in writing in accordance with section 184.

Index